D0463179

Praise for the *Sun Certified Programmer & Developer for Java 2 Study Guide*

"Kathy Sierra is one of the few people in the world who can make complicated things seem damn simple. And as if that isn't enough, she can make boring things seem interesting. I always look forward to reading whatever Kathy writes—she's one of my favorite authors."
—*Paul Wheaton, Trail Boss JavaRanch.com*

"Who better to write a Java study guide than Kathy Sierra, the reigning queen of Java instruction? Kathy Sierra has done it again—here is a study guide that almost guarantees you a certification!"
—*James Cubeta, Systems Engineer, SGI*

"The thing I appreciate most about Kathy is her quest to make us all remember that we are teaching people and not just lecturing about Java. Her passion and desire for the highest quality education that meets the needs of the individual student is positively unparalleled at SunEd. Undoubtedly there are hundreds of students who have benefited from taking Kathy's classes."
—*Victor Peters, founder Next Step Education & Software Sun Certified Java Instructor*

"I want to thank Kathy for the EXCELLENT Study Guide. The book is well written, every concept is clearly explained using a real life example, and the book states what you specifically need to know for the exam. The way it's written, you feel that you're in a classroom and someone is actually teaching you the difficult concepts, but not in a dry, formal manner. The questions at the end of the chapters are also REALLY good, and I am sure they will help candidates pass the test. Watch out for this Wickedly Smart book."
—*Alfred Raouf, Web Solution Developer*

"The Sun Certification exam was certainly no walk in the park, but Kathy's material allowed me to not only pass the exam, but Ace it!"
—*Mary Whetsel, Sr. Technology Specialist,*
Application Strategy and Integration, The St. Paul Companies

"Bert has an uncanny and proven ability to synthesize complexity into simplicity offering a guided tour into learning what's needed for the certification exam."
—*Thomas Bender, President, Gold Hill Software Design, Inc.*

SCJP Sun® Certified Programmer for Java™ 6 Study Guide

(Exam 310-065)

SCJP Sun® Certified Programmer for Java™ 6 Study Guide

Exam (310-065)

Kathy Sierra
Bert Bates

New York Chicago San Francisco Lisbon London Madrid
Mexico City Milan New Delhi San Juan Seoul Singapore Sydney Toronto

The McGraw-Hill Companies

Cataloging-in-Publication Data is on file with the Library of Congress

McGraw-Hill books are available at special quantity discounts to use as premiums and sales promotions, or for use in corporate training programs. To contact a special sales representative, please visit the Contact Us page at www.mhprofessional.com.

SCJP Sun® Certified Programmer for Java™ 6 Study Guide (Exam 310-065)

4567890   DOC DOC   019

ISBN: Book p/n 978-0-07-159108-9 and CD p/n 978-0-07-159109-6
of set 978-0-07-159106-5

MHID: Book p/n 0-07-159108-7 and CD p/n 0-07-159109-5
of set 0-07-159106-0

Sponsoring Editor
Timothy Green

Editorial Supervisor
Jody McKenzie

Project Manager
Madhu Bhardwaj,
International
Typesetting
and Composition

Acquisitions Coordinator
Jennifer Housh

Copy Editor
Lisa Theobald

Proofreader
Anju Panthari

Indexer
Kevin Broccoli

Production Supervisor
Jim Kussow

Composition
International
Typesetting
and Composition

Illustration
International
Typesetting
and Composition

Art Director, Cover
Jeff Weeks

About the Authors

Kathy Sierra was a lead developer for the SCJP exam for Java 5 and Java 6. Sierra worked as a Sun "master trainer," and in 1997, founded JavaRanch.com, the world's largest Java community website. Her bestselling Java books have won multiple Software Development Magazine awards, and she is a founding member of Sun's Java Champions program.

Bert Bates was a lead developer for many of Sun's Java certification exams including the SCJP for Java 5 and Java 6. He is also a forum moderator on JavaRanch.com, and has been developing software for more than 20 years. Bert is the co-author of several bestselling Java books, and he's a founding member of Sun's Java Champions program.

About the Technical Review Team

Johannes de Jong has been the leader of our technical review teams for ever and ever. (He has more patience than any three people we know.) For this book, he led our biggest team ever. Our sincere thanks go out to the following volunteers who were knowledgeable, diligent, patient, and picky, picky, picky!

Rob Ross, Nicholas Cheung, Jane Griscti, Ilja Preuss, Vincent Brabant, Kudret Serin, Bill Seipel, Jing Yi, Ginu Jacob George, Radiya, LuAnn Mazza, Anshu Mishra, Anandhi Navaneethakrishnan, Didier Varon, Mary McCartney, Harsha Pherwani, Abhishek Misra, and Suman Das.

About LearnKey

LearnKey provides self-paced learning content and multimedia delivery solutions to enhance personal skills and business productivity. LearnKey claims the largest library of rich streaming-media training content that engages learners in dynamic media-rich instruction complete with video clips, audio, full motion graphics, and animated illustrations. LearnKey can be found on the Web at www.LearnKey.com.

Technical Review Superstars

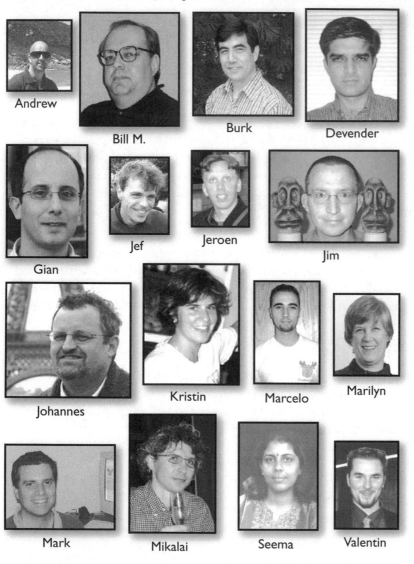

Andrew
Bill M.
Burk
Devender
Gian
Jef
Jeroen
Jim
Johannes
Kristin
Marcelo
Marilyn
Mark
Mikalai
Seema
Valentin

We don't know who burned the most midnight oil, but we can (and did) count everybody's edits—so in order of most edits made, we proudly present our Superstars.

Our top honors go to **Kristin Stromberg**—every time you see a semicolon used correctly, tip your hat to Kristin. Next up is **Burk Hufnagel** who fixed more code than we care to admit. **Bill Mietelski** and **Gian Franco Casula** caught every kind of error we threw at them—awesome job, guys! **Devender Thareja** made sure we didn't use too much slang, and **Mark Spritzler** kept the humor coming. **Mikalai Zaikin** and **Seema Manivannan** made great catches every step of the way, and **Marilyn de Queiroz** and **Valentin Crettaz** both put in another stellar performance (saving our butts yet again).

Marcelo Ortega, **Jef Cumps** (another veteran), **Andrew Monkhouse**, and **Jeroen Sterken** rounded out our crew of superstars—thanks to you all. **Jim Yingst** was a member of the Sun exam creation team, and he helped us write and review some of the twistier questions in the book (bwa-ha-ha-ha).

As always, every time you read a clean page, thank our reviewers, and if you do catch an error, it's most certainly because your authors messed up. And oh, one last thanks to **Johannes**. You rule dude!

The Java 6 Elite Review Team

Fred

Marc P.

Marc W.

Mikalai

Christophe

Since the upgrade to the Java 6 exam was a like a small, surgical strike we decided that the technical review team for this update to the book needed to be similarly fashioned. To that end we hand-picked an elite crew of JavaRanch's top gurus to perform the review for the Java 6 exam.

Our endless gratitude goes to **Mikalai Zaikin**. Mikalai played a huge role in the Java 5 book, and he returned to help us out again for this Java 6 edition. We need to thank Volha, Anastasia, and Daria for letting us borrow Mikalai. His comments and edits helped us make huge improvements to the book. Thanks, Mikalai!

Marc Peabody gets special kudos for helping us out on a double header! In addition to helping us with Sun's new SCWCD exam, Marc pitched in with a great set of edits for this book—you saved our bacon this winter Marc! (BTW, we didn't learn until late in the game that Marc, Bryan Basham, and Bert all share a passion for ultimate Frisbee!)

Like several of our reviewers, not only does **Fred Rosenberger** volunteer copious amounts of his time moderating at JavaRanch, he also found time to help us out with this book. Stacey and Olivia, you have our thanks for loaning us Fred for a while.

Marc Weber moderates at some of JavaRanch's busiest forums. Marc knows his stuff, and uncovered some really sneaky problems that were buried in the book. While we really appreciate Marc's help, we need to warn you all to watch out—he's got a Phaser!

Finally, we send our thanks to **Christophe Verre**—if we can find him. It appears that Christophe performs his JavaRanch moderation duties from various locations around the globe, including France, Wales, and most recently Tokyo. On more than one occasion Christophe protected us from our own lack of organization. Thanks for your patience, Christophe!

It's important to know that these guys all donated their reviewer honorariums to JavaRanch! The JavaRanch community is in your debt.

To the Java Community

CONTENTS AT A GLANCE

CONTENTS

ACKNOWLEDGMENTS

Kathy and Bert would like to thank the following people:

- All the incredibly hard-working folks at McGraw-Hill: Tim Green, Jim Kussow, Jody McKenzie, Madhu Bhardwaj, and Jennifer Housh for all their help, and for being so responsive and patient—well, okay, not all that patient—but so professional and the nicest group of people you could hope to work with.

- To our saviors Solveig Haugland and Midori Batten, for coming to our rescue when we were really in a bind!

- Some of the software professionals and friends who helped us in the early days: Tom Bender, Peter Loerincs, Craig Matthews, Dave Gustafson, Leonard Coyne, Morgan Porter, and Mike Kavenaugh.

- The wonderful and talented Certification team at Sun Educational Services, primarily the most persistent get-it-done person we know, Evelyn Cartagena.

- Our great friends and gurus, Bryan Basham, Kathy Collina, and Simon Roberts.

- To Eden and Skyler, for being horrified that adults—out of school— would study this hard for an exam.

- To the JavaRanch Trail Boss Paul Wheaton, for running the best Java community site on the Web, and to all the generous and patient JavaRanch moderators.

- To all the past and present Sun Ed Java instructors for helping to make learning Java a fun experience including (to name only a few): Alan Petersen, Jean Tordella, Georgianna Meagher, Anthony Orapallo, Jacqueline Jones, James Cubeta, Teri Cubeta, Rob Weingruber, John Nyquist, Asok Perumainar, Steve Stelting, Kimberly Bobrow, Keith Ratliff, and the most caring and inspiring Java guy on the planet, Jari Paukku.

- To Darren and Mary, thanks for keeping us sane and for helping us with our new furry friends Andi, Kara, Birta, Sola, Draumur, and Tjara.

- Finally, to Eric and Beth Freeman for your continued inspiration.

This book's primary objective is to help you prepare for and pass Sun Microsystem's SCJP certification for Java 6 or Java 5. The Java 6 and Java 5 exams are almost identical in scope, and they are both much broader than their predecessor, the Java 1.4 exam. For the remainder of this book we'll typically reference the Java 6 exam, but remember that other than the addition of the System.Console class and Navigable collections, the Java 5 and Java 6 exams are identical in scope. We recommend that you take the Java 6 exam and not the Java 5 exam, but if you do decide to take the Java 5 exam, this book is still appropriate. The new exam's objectives touch on many of the more commonly used of Java's APIs. The key word here is "touch." The exam's creators intended that passing the exam will demonstrate that the candidate understands the *basics* of APIs such as those for file I/O and regular expressions. This book follows closely both the breadth and the depth of the real exam. For instance, after reading this book, you probably won't emerge as a regex guru, but if you study the material, and do well on the self tests, you'll have a basic understanding of regex, and you'll do well on the exam. After completing this book, you should feel confident that you have thoroughly reviewed all of the objectives that Sun has established for the exam.

In This Book

This book is organized to optimize your learning of the topics covered by the SCJP Java 6 exam. Whenever possible, we've organized the chapters to parallel the Sun objectives, but sometimes we'll mix up objectives or partially repeat them in order to present topics in an order better suited to learning the material.

In addition to fully covering the SCJP Java 6 exam, we have also included on the CD eight chapters that cover important aspects of Sun's SCJD exam.

In Every Chapter

We've created a set of chapter components that call your attention to important items, reinforce important points, and provide helpful exam-taking hints. Take a look at what you'll find in every chapter:

- Every chapter begins with the **Certification Objectives**—what you need to know in order to pass the section on the exam dealing with the chapter topic.

xxi

The Certification Objective headings identify the objectives within the chapter, so you'll always know an objective when you see it!

■ **Exam Watch** notes call attention to information about, and potential pitfalls in, the exam. Since we were on the team that created the exam, we know what you're about to go through!

■ **On the Job** callouts discuss practical aspects of certification topics that might not occur on the exam, but that will be useful in the real world.

■ **Exercises** are interspersed throughout the chapters. They help you master skills that are likely to be an area of focus on the exam. Don't just read through the exercises; they are hands-on practice that you should be comfortable completing. Learning by doing is an effective way to increase your competency with a product.

■ **From the Classroom** sidebars describe the issues that come up most often in the training classroom setting. These sidebars give you a valuable perspective into certification- and product-related topics. They point out common mistakes and address questions that have arisen from classroom discussions.

■ The **Certification Summary** is a succinct review of the chapter and a restatement of salient points regarding the exam.

✓ ■ The **Two-Minute Drill** at the end of every chapter is a checklist of the main points of the chapter. It can be used for last-minute review.

Q&A ■ The **Self Test** offers questions similar to those found on the certification exam, including multiple choice, and pseudo drag-and-drop questions. The answers to these questions, as well as explanations of the answers, can be found at the end of every chapter. By taking the Self Test after completing each chapter, you'll reinforce what you've learned from that chapter, while becoming familiar with the structure of the exam questions.

INTRODUCTION

Organization

This book is organized in such a way as to serve as an in-depth review for the Sun Certified Programmer for both the Java 6 and Java 5 exams, for experienced Java professionals and those in the early stages of experience with Java technologies. Each chapter covers at least one major aspect of the exam, with an emphasis on the "why" as well as the "how to" of programming in the Java language. The CD included with the book also includes an in-depth review of the essential ingredients for a successful assessment of a project submitted for the Sun Certified Java Developer exam.

What This Book Is Not

You will not find a beginner's guide to learning Java in this book. All 800 pages of this book are dedicated solely to helping you pass the exams. If you are brand new to Java, we suggest you spend a little time learning the basics. You shouldn't start with this book until you know how to write, compile, and run simple Java programs. We do not, however, assume any level of prior knowledge of the individual topics covered. In other words, for any given topic (driven exclusively by the actual exam objectives), we start with the assumption that you are new to that topic. So we assume you're new to the individual topics, but we assume that you are not new to Java.

We also do not pretend to be both preparing you for the exam and simultaneously making you a complete Java being. This is a certification exam study guide, and it's very clear about its mission. That's not to say that preparing for the exam won't help you become a better Java programmer! On the contrary, even the most experienced Java developers often claim that having to prepare for the certification exam made them far more knowledgeable and well-rounded programmers than they would have been without the exam-driven studying.

On the CD

For more information on the CD-ROM, please see Appendix A.

xxiii

Some Pointers

Once you've finished reading this book, set aside some time to do a thorough review. You might want to return to the book several times and make use of all the methods it offers for reviewing the material:

1. Re-read all the Two-Minute Drills, or have someone quiz you. You also can use the drills as a way to do a quick cram before the exam. You might want to make some flash cards out of 3 × 5 index cards that have the Two-Minute Drill material on them.

2. Re-read all the Exam Watch notes. Remember that these notes are written by authors who helped create the exam. They know what you should expect— and what you should be on the lookout for.

3. Re-take the Self Tests. Taking the tests right after you've read the chapter is a good idea, because the questions help reinforce what you've just learned. However, it's an even better idea to go back later and do all the questions in the book in one sitting. Pretend that you're taking the live exam. (Whenever you take the self tests mark your answers on a separate piece of paper. That way, you can run through the questions as many times as you need to until you feel comfortable with the material.)

4. Complete the Exercises. The exercises are designed to cover exam topics, and there's no better way to get to know this material than by practicing. Be sure you understand why you are performing each step in each exercise. If there is something you are not clear on, re-read that section in the chapter.

5. Write lots of Java code. We'll repeat this advice several times. When we wrote this book, we wrote hundreds of small Java programs to help us do our research. We have heard from hundreds of candidates who have passed the exam, and in almost every case the candidates who scored extremely well on the exam wrote lots of code during their studies. Experiment with the code samples in the book, create horrendous lists of compiler errors—put away your IDE, crank up the command line, and write code!

Introduction to the Material in the Book

The Sun Certified Java Programmer (SCJP) exam is considered one of the hardest in the IT industry, and we can tell you from experience that a large chunk of exam candidates go in to the test unprepared. As programmers, we tend to learn only what we need to complete our current project, given the insane deadlines we're usually under.

But this exam attempts to prove your complete understanding of the Java language, not just the parts of it you've become familiar with in your work.

Experience alone will rarely get you through this exam with a passing mark, because even the things you think you know might work just a little different than you imagined. It isn't enough to be able to get your code to work correctly; you must understand the core fundamentals in a deep way, and with enough breadth to cover virtually anything that could crop up in the course of using the language.

The Sun Certified Developer Exam (covered in chapters that are contained on the CD) is unique to the IT certification realm, because it actually evaluates your skill as a developer rather than simply your knowledge of the language or tools. Becoming a Certified Java Developer is, by definition, a development experience.

Who Cares About Certification?

Employers do. Headhunters do. Programmers do. Sun's programmer exam has been considered the fastest-growing certification in the IT world, and the number of candidates taking the exam continues to grow each year. Passing this exam proves three important things to a current or prospective employer: you're smart; you know how to study and prepare for a challenging test; and, most of all, you know the Java language. If an employer has a choice between a candidate who has passed the exam and one who hasn't, the employer knows that the certified programmer does not have to take time to learn the Java language.

But does it mean that you can actually develop software in Java? Not necessarily, but it's a good head start. To really demonstrate your ability to develop (as opposed to just your knowledge of the language), you should consider pursuing the Developer Exam, where you're given an assignment to build a program, start to finish, and submit it for an assessor to evaluate and score.

Sun's Certification Program

Currently there are eight Java certification exams (although several of them might have more than one live version). The Associate exam, the Programmer exam, and the Developer exam are all associated with the Java Standard Edition. The Web Component exam, the Business Component exam, the Web Services exam, and the Enterprise Architect exam are all associated with the Java Enterprise Edition. The Mobile Application exam is associated with the Java Micro Edition.

The Associate, Programmer, Web Component, Business Component, Web Services, and Mobile Application exams are exclusively multiple-choice and drag-and-drop exams taken at a testing center, while the Developer and Architect exams also involve submitting a project.

The Associate Exam (CX-310-019)

Sun Certified Java Associate (SCJA)

The Associate exam is for candidates just entering an application development or a software project management career using Java technologies. This exam tests basic knowledge of object-oriented concepts, the basics of UML, the basics of the Java programming language, and general knowledge of Java Platforms and Technologies. This exam has no prerequisites.

The Programmer Exams (CX-310-065)

Sun Certified Java Programmer (SCJP) for Java 6

The Programmer exam is designed to test your knowledge of the Java programming language itself. It requires detailed knowledge of language syntax, core concepts, and a number of common application programming interfaces (APIs). This exam also tests intermediate knowledge of object-oriented design concepts. It does not test any issues related to architecture, and it does not ask why one approach is better than another, but rather it asks whether the given approach works in a particular situation. This exam has no prerequisites. As of May, 2008, two older versions of this exam are still available, the 1.4 and the 5.0.

The Developer Exam (CX-310-252A, CX-310-027)

Sun Certified Java Developer (SCJD)

The Developer exam picks up where the Programmer exam leaves off. Passing the Programmer exam is required before you can start the Developer exam. The Developer exam requires you to develop an actual program and then defend your design decisions. It is designed to test your understanding of why certain approaches are better than others in certain circumstances, and to prove your ability to follow a specification and implement a correct, functioning, and user-friendly program.

The Developer exam consists of two pieces: a project assignment and a follow-up essay exam. Candidates have an unlimited amount of time to complete the project, but once the project is submitted, the candidate then must go to a testing center and complete a short follow-up essay exam, designed primarily to validate and verify that it was you who designed and built the project.

The Web Component Developer Exam (CX-310-083)

Sun Certified Web Component Developer for Java EE Platform (SCWCD)
The web developer exam is for those who are using Java servlet and JSP (Java Server Pages) technologies to build Web applications. It's based on the Servlet and JSP specifications defined in the Java Enterprise Edition (Java EE). This exam requires that the candidate is a Sun Certified Java Programmer.

The Business Component Developer Exam (CX-310-091)

Sun Certified Business Component Developer for Java EE Platform (SCBCD)
The business component developer exam is for those candidates who are using Java EJB technology to build business-tier applications. The exam is based on the EJB specification defined in the Java Enterprise Edition (Java EE). This exam requires that the candidate is a Sun Certified Java Programmer.

The Web Services Developer Exam (CX-310-220)

Sun Certified Developer for Web Services for Java EE Platform (SCDJWS)
The web services exam is for those candidates who are building applications using Java EE and Java Web Services Developer Pack technologies. This exam requires that the candidate is a Sun Certified Java Programmer.

The Architect Exam (CX-310-052, CX-310-301A, CX-310-062)

Sun Certified Enterprise Architect for J2EE Technology (SCEA)
This certification is for enterprise architects, and thus does not require that the candidate pass the Programmer exam. The Architect exam is in three pieces: a knowledge-based multiple-choice exam, an architectural design assignment, and a follow-up essay exam. You must successfully pass the multiple-choice exam before registering and receiving the design assignment.

The Mobile Exam (CX-310-110)

Sun Certified Mobile Application Developer for Java ME (SCMAD)
The mobile application developer exam is for candidates creating applications for cell phones or other Java enabled devices. The exam covers the Java Technology for Wireless Industry (JTWI) specification, the Wireless Messaging API, and Mobile Media APIs. This exam requires that the candidate is an SCJP.

Taking the Programmer's Exam

In a perfect world, you would be assessed for your true knowledge of a subject, not simply how you respond to a series of test questions. But life isn't perfect, and it just isn't practical to evaluate everyone's knowledge on a one-to-one basis.

For the majority of its certifications, Sun evaluates candidates using a computer-based testing service operated by Sylvan Prometric. This service is quite popular in the industry, and it is used for a number of vendor certification programs, including Novell's CNE and Microsoft's MCSE. Thanks to Sylvan Prometric's large number of facilities, exams can be administered worldwide, generally in the same town as a prospective candidate.

For the most part, Sylvan Prometric exams work similarly from vendor to vendor. However, there is an important fact to know about Sun's exams: they use the traditional Sylvan Prometric test format, not the newer adaptive format. This gives the candidate an advantage, since the traditional format allows answers to be reviewed and revised during the test.

Many experienced test takers do not go back and change answers unless they have a good reason to do so. Only change an answer when you feel you may have misread or misinterpreted the question the first time. Nervousness may make you second-guess every answer and talk yourself out of a correct one.

To discourage simple memorization, Sun exams present a potentially different set of questions to different candidates. In the development of the exam, hundreds of questions are compiled and refined using beta testers. From this large collection, questions are pulled together from each objective and assembled into many different versions of the exam.

Each Sun exam has a specific number of questions (the Programmer's exam contains 72 questions) and test duration (210 minutes for the Programmer's exam) is designed to be generous. The time remaining is always displayed in the corner of the testing screen, along with the number of remaining questions. If time expires during an exam, the test terminates, and incomplete answers are counted as incorrect.

At the end of the exam, your test is immediately graded, and the results are displayed on the screen. Scores for each subject area are also provided, but the system will not indicate which specific questions were missed. A report is automatically printed at the proctor's desk for your files. The test score is electronically transmitted back to Sun.

exam
ⓦatch

When you find yourself stumped answering multiple-choice questions, use your scratch paper to write down the two or three answers you consider the strongest, then underline the answer you feel is most likely correct. Here is an example of what your scratch paper might look like when you've gone through the test once:

21. B or C
33. A or C

This is extremely helpful when you mark the question and continue on. You can then return to the question and immediately pick up your thought process where you left off. Use this technique to avoid having to re-read and re-think questions. You will also need to use your scratch paper during complex, text-based scenario questions to create visual images to better understand the question. This technique is especially helpful if you are a visual learner.

Question Format

Sun's Java exams pose questions in either multiple-choice or drag-and-drop formats.

Multiple Choice Questions

In earlier versions of the exam, when you encountered a multiple-choice question you were not told how many answers were correct, but with each version of the exam, the questions have become more difficult, so today each multiple-choice question tells you how many answers to choose. The Self Test questions at the end of each chapter are closely matched to the format, wording, and difficulty of the real exam questions, with two exceptions:

■ Whenever we can, our questions will NOT tell you how many correct answers exist (we will say "Choose all that apply"). We do this to help you master the material. Some savvy test-takers can eliminate wrong answers when the number of correct answers is known. It's also possible, if you know how many answers are correct, to choose the most plausible answers. Our job is to toughen you up for the real exam!

■ The real exam typically numbers lines of code in a question. Sometimes we do not number lines of code—mostly so that we have the space to add comments at key places. On the real exam, when a code listing starts with line 1, it means that you're looking at an entire source file. If a code listing starts at a line number greater than 1, that means you're looking at a partial source file. When looking at a partial source file, assume that the code you can't see is correct. (For instance, unless explicitly stated, you can assume that a partial source file will have the correct import and package statements.)

Drag-and-Drop Questions

Although many of the other Sun Java certification exams have been using drag-and-drop questions for several years, this is the first version of the SCJP exam that includes drag-and-drop questions. As we discussed earlier, the exam questions you receive are randomized, but you should expect that about 20–25% of the questions you encounter will be drag-and-drop style.

Drag-and-drop questions typically consist of three components:

■ **A scenario**   A short description of the task you are meant to complete.

■ **A partially completed task**   A code listing, a table, or a directory tree. The partially completed task will contain empty slots, which are indicated with (typically yellow) boxes. These boxes need to be filled to complete the task.

■ **A set of possible "fragment" answers**   You will click on fragments (typically blue boxes) and drag-and-drop them into the correct empty slots. The question's scenario will tell you whether you can reuse fragments.

Most drag-and-drop questions will have anywhere from 4 to 10 empty slots to fill, and typically a few more fragments than are needed (usually some fragments are left unused). Drag-and-drop questions are often the most complex on the exam, and the number of possible answer combinations makes them almost impossible to guess.

exam

watch

In regards to drag-and-drop questions, there is a huge problem with the testing software at many of the Prometric centers world-wide. In general, the testing software allows you to review questions you've already answered as often as you'd like.

In the case of drag-and-drop questions, however, many candidates have reported that if they choose to review a question, the software will erase their previous answer! BE CAREFUL! Until this problem is corrected, we recommend that you keep a list of which questions are drag and drop, so that you won't review one unintentionally. Another good idea is to write down your drag-and-drop answers so that if one gets erased it will be less painful to recreate the answer.

This brings us to another issue that some candidates have reported. The testing center is supposed to provide you with sufficient writing implements so that you can work problems out "on paper." In some cases, the centers have provided inadequate markers and dry-erase boards which are too small and cumbersome to use effectively. We recommend that you call ahead and verify that you will be supplied with actual pencils and at least several sheets of blank paper.

Tips on Taking the Exam

There are 72 questions on the 310-065 (Java 6) exam. You will need to get at least 47 of them correct to pass—around 65%. You are given over three hours to complete the exam. This information is subject to change. Always check with Sun before taking the exam, at www.suned.sun.com.

You are allowed to answer questions in any order, and you can go back and check your answers after you've gone through the test. There are no penalties for wrong answers, so it's better to at least attempt an answer than to not give one at all.

A good strategy for taking the exam is to go through once and answer all the questions that come to you quickly. You can then go back and do the others. Answering one question might jog your memory for how to answer a previous one.

Be very careful on the code examples. Check for syntax errors first: count curly braces, semicolons, and parenthesis and then make sure there are as many left ones as right ones. Look for capitalization errors and other such syntax problems before trying to figure out what the code does.

Many of the questions on the exam will hinge on subtleties of syntax. You will need to have a thorough knowledge of the Java language in order to succeed.

Tips on Studying for the Exam

First and foremost, give yourself plenty of time to study. Java is a complex programming language, and you can't expect to cram what you need to know into a single study session. It is a field best learned over time, by studying a subject and then applying your knowledge. Build yourself a study schedule and stick to it, but be reasonable about the pressure you put on yourself, especially if you're studying in addition to your regular duties at work.

One easy technique to use in studying for certification exams is the 15-minutes-per-day effort. Simply study for a minimum of 15 minutes every day. It is a small but significant commitment. If you have a day where you just can't focus, then give up at 15 minutes. If you have a day where it flows completely for you, study longer. As long as you have more of the "flow days," your chances of succeeding are excellent.

We strongly recommend you use flash cards when preparing for the Programmer's exam. A flash card is simply a 3 x 5 or 4 x 6 index card with a question on the front, and the answer on the back. You construct these cards yourself as you go through a chapter, capturing any topic you think might need more memorization or practice time. You can drill yourself with them by reading the question, thinking through the answer, and then turning the card over to see if you're correct. Or you can get another person to help you by holding up the card with the question facing you, and then verifying your answer. Most of our students have found these to be tremendously helpful, especially because they're so portable that while you're in study mode, you can take them everywhere. Best not to use them while driving, though, except at red lights. We've taken ours everywhere—the doctor's office, restaurants, theaters, you name it.

Certification study groups are another excellent resource, and you won't find a larger or more willing community than on the JavaRanch.com Big Moose Saloon certification forums. If you have a question from this book, or any other mock exam question you may have stumbled upon, posting a question in a certification forum will get you an answer, in nearly all cases, within a day—usually, within a few hours. You'll find us (the authors) there several times a week, helping those just starting out on their exam preparation journey. (You won't actually think of it as anything as pleasant-sounding as a "journey" by the time you're ready to take the exam.)

Finally, we recommend that you write a lot of little Java programs! During the course of writing this book we wrote hundreds of small programs, and if you listen to what the most successful candidates say (you know, those guys who got 98%), they almost always report that they wrote a lot of code.

Scheduling Your Exam

The Sun exams are purchased directly from Sun, but are scheduled through Sylvan Prometric. For locations outside the United States, your local number can be found on Sylvan's Web site at http://www.2test.com. Sylvan representatives can schedule your exam, but they don't have information about the certification programs. Questions about certifications should be directed to Sun's Worldwide Training department. These representatives are familiar enough with the exams to find them by name, but it's best if you have the exam number handy when you call. You wouldn't want to be scheduled and charged for the wrong exam.

Exams can be scheduled up to a year in advance, although it's really not necessary. Generally, scheduling a week or two ahead is sufficient to reserve the day and time you prefer. When scheduling, operators will search for testing centers in your area. For convenience, they can also tell which testing centers you've used before.

When registering for the exam, you will be asked for your ID number. This number is used to track your exam results back to Sun. It's important that you use the same ID number each time you register, so that Sun can follow your progress. Address information provided when you first register is also used by Sun to ship certificates and other related material. In the United States, your Social Security Number is commonly used as your ID number. However, Sylvan can assign you a unique ID number if you prefer not to use your Social Security Number.

Arriving at the Exam

As with any test, you'll be tempted to cram the night before. Resist that temptation. You should know the material by this point, and if you're groggy in the morning, you won't remember what you studied anyway. Get a good night's sleep.

Arrive early for your exam; it gives you time to relax and review key facts. Take the opportunity to review your notes. If you get burned out on studying, you can usually start your exam a few minutes early. We don't recommend arriving late. Your test could be cancelled, or you might not have enough time to complete the exam.

When you arrive at the testing center, you'll need to sign in with the exam administrator. In order to sign in, you need to provide two forms of identification. Acceptable forms include government-issued IDs (for example, passport or driver's license), credit cards, and company ID badges. One form of ID must include a photograph. They just want to be sure that you don't send your brilliant Java guru next-door-neighbor-who-you've-paid to take the exam for you.

Aside from a brain full of facts, you don't need to bring anything else to the exam room. In fact, your brain is about all you're allowed to take into the exam!

All the tests are closed-book, meaning you don't get to bring any reference materials with you. You're also not allowed to take any notes out of the exam room. The test administrator will provide you with paper and a pencil. Some testing centers may provide a small marker board instead (we recommend that you don't settle for a whiteboard). We do recommend that you bring a water bottle. Three hours is a long time to keep your brain active, and it functions much better when well hydrated.

Leave your pager and telephone in the car, or turn them off. They only add stress to the situation, since they are not allowed in the exam room, and can sometimes still be heard if they ring outside of the room. Purses, books, and other materials must be left with the administrator before entering the exam.

Once in the testing room, the exam administrator logs onto your exam, and you have to verify that your ID number and the exam number are correct. If this is the first time you've taken a Sun test, you can select a brief tutorial of the exam software. Before the test begins, you will be provided with facts about the exam, including the duration, the number of questions, and the score required for passing. The odds are good that you will be asked to fill out a brief survey before the exam actually begins. This survey will ask you about your level of Java experience. The time you spend on the survey is NOT deducted from your actual test time—nor do you get more time if you fill out the survey quickly. Also remember that the questions you get on the exam will NOT change depending on how you answer the survey questions. Once you're done with the survey, the real clock starts ticking and the fun begins.

The testing software is Windows-based, but you won't have access to the main desktop or any of the accessories. The exam is presented in full screen, with a single question per screen. Navigation buttons allow you to move forward and backward between questions. In the upper-right corner of the screen, counters show the number of questions and time remaining. Most important, there is a Mark check box in the upper-left corner of the screen—this will prove to be a critical tool, as explained in the next section.

Test-Taking Techniques

Without a plan of attack, candidates can become overwhelmed by the exam or become side-tracked and run out of time. For the most part, if you are comfortable with the material, the allotted time is more than enough to complete the exam. The trick is to keep the time from slipping away during any one particular problem.

Your obvious goal is to answer the questions correctly and quickly, but other factors can distract you. Here are some tips for taking the exam more efficiently.

Size Up the Challenge

First, take a quick pass through all the questions in the exam. "Cherry-pick" the easy questions, answering them on the spot. Briefly read each question, noticing the type of question and the subject. As a guideline, try to spend less than 25 percent of your testing time in this pass.

This step lets you assess the scope and complexity of the exam, and it helps you determine how to pace your time. It also gives you an idea of where to find potential answers to some of the questions. Sometimes the wording of one question might lend clues or jog your thoughts for another question.

If you're not entirely confident in your answer to a question, answer it anyway, but check the Mark box to flag it for later review. In the event that you run out of time, at least you've provided a "first guess" answer, rather than leaving it blank.

Second, go back through the entire test, using the insight you gained from the first go-through. For example, if the entire test looks difficult, you'll know better than to spend more than a minute or two on each question. Create a pacing with small milestones—for example, "I need to answer 10 questions every 25 minutes."

At this stage, it's probably a good idea to skip past the time-consuming questions, marking them for the next pass. Try to finish this phase before you're 50–60 percent through the testing time.

Third, go back through all the questions you marked for review, using the Review Marked button in the question review screen. This step includes taking a second look at all the questions you were unsure of in previous passes, as well as tackling the time-consuming ones you deferred until now. Chisel away at this group of questions until you've answered them all.

If you're more comfortable with a previously marked question, unmark the Review Marked button now. Otherwise, leave it marked. Work your way through the time-consuming questions now, especially those requiring manual calculations. Unmark them when you're satisfied with the answer.

By the end of this step, you've answered every question in the test, despite having reservations about some of your answers. If you run out of time in the next step, at least you won't lose points for lack of an answer. You're in great shape if you still have 10–20 percent of your time remaining.

Review Your Answers

Now you're cruising! You've answered all the questions, and you're ready to do a quality check. Take yet another pass (yes, one more) through the entire test (although you'll probably want to skip a review of the drag-and-drop questions!), briefly re-reading each question and your answer.

Carefully look over the questions again to check for "trick" questions. Be particularly wary of those that include a choice of "Does not compile." Be alert for last-minute clues. You're pretty familiar with nearly every question at this point, and you may find a few clues that you missed before.

The Grand Finale

When you're confident with all your answers, finish the exam by submitting it for grading. After what will seem like the longest 10 seconds of your life, the testing software will respond with your score. This is usually displayed as a bar graph, showing the minimum passing score, your score, and a PASS/FAIL indicator.

If you're curious, you can review the statistics of your score at this time. Answers to specific questions are not presented; rather, questions are lumped into categories, and results are tallied for each category. This detail is also on a report that has been automatically printed at the exam administrator's desk.

As you leave, you'll need to leave your scratch paper behind or return it to the administrator. (Some testing centers track the number of sheets you've been given, so be sure to return them all.) In exchange, you'll receive a copy of the test report.

This report will be embossed with the testing center's seal, and you should keep it in a safe place. Normally, the results are automatically transmitted to Sun, but occasionally you might need the paper report to prove that you passed the exam.

In a few weeks, Sun will send you a package in the mail containing a nice paper certificate, a lapel pin, and a letter. You may also be sent instructions for how to obtain artwork for a logo that you can use on personal business cards.

Re-Testing

If you don't pass the exam, don't be discouraged. Try to have a good attitude about the experience, and get ready to try again. Consider yourself a little more educated. You know the format of the test a little better, and the report shows which areas you need to strengthen.

If you bounce back quickly, you'll probably remember several of the questions you might have missed. This will help you focus your study efforts in the right area.

Ultimately, remember that Sun certifications are valuable because they're hard to get. After all, if anyone could get one, what value would it have? In the end, it takes a good attitude and a lot of studying, but you can do it!

1
Declarations and Access Control

- Declare Classes & Interfaces

- Develop Interfaces & Abstract Classes

- Use Primitives, Arrays, Enums, & Legal Identifiers

- Use Static Methods, JavaBeans Naming, & Var-Args

✓ Two-Minute Drill

Q&A Self Test

W e assume that because you're planning on becoming certified, you already know the basics of Java. If you're completely new to the language, this chapter—and the rest of the book—will be confusing; so be sure you know at least the basics of the language before diving into this book. That said, we're starting with a brief, high-level refresher to put you back in the Java mood, in case you've been away for awhile.

Java Refresher

A Java program is mostly a collection of *objects* talking to other objects by invoking each other's *methods*. Every object is of a certain *type*, and that type is defined by a *class* or an *interface*. Most Java programs use a collection of objects of many different types.

■ **Class**   A template that describes the kinds of state and behavior that objects of its type support.

■ **Object**   At runtime, when the Java Virtual Machine (JVM) encounters the new keyword, it will use the appropriate class to make an object which is an instance of that class. That object will have its own state, and access to all of the behaviors defined by its class.

■ **State (instance variables)**   Each object (instance of a class) will have its own unique set of instance variables as defined in the class. Collectively, the values assigned to an object's instance variables make up the object's state.

■ **Behavior (methods)**   When a programmer creates a class, she creates methods for that class. Methods are where the class' logic is stored. Methods are where the real work gets done. They are where algorithms get executed, and data gets manipulated.

Identifiers and Keywords

All the Java components we just talked about—classes, variables, and methods—need names. In Java these names are called *identifiers*, and, as you might expect, there are rules for what constitutes a legal Java identifier. Beyond what's *legal*, though, Java programmers (and Sun) have created *conventions* for naming methods, variables, and classes.

Like all programming languages, Java has a set of built-in *keywords*. These keywords must *not* be used as identifiers. Later in this chapter we'll review the details of these naming rules, conventions, and the Java keywords.

Inheritance

Central to Java and other object-oriented (OO) languages is the concept of *inheritance*, which allows code defined in one class to be reused in other classes. In Java, you can define a general (more abstract) superclass, and then extend it with more specific subclasses. The superclass knows nothing of the classes that inherit from it, but all of the subclasses that inherit from the superclass must explicitly declare the inheritance relationship. A subclass that inherits from a superclass is automatically given accessible instance variables and methods defined by the superclass, but is also free to override superclass methods to define more specific behavior.

For example, a Car *super*class class could define general methods common to all automobiles, but a Ferrari *sub*class could override the `accelerate()` method.

Interfaces

A powerful companion to inheritance is the use of interfaces. Interfaces are like a 100-percent abstract superclass that defines the methods a subclass must support, but not *how* they must be supported. In other words, an `Animal` interface might declare that all `Animal` implementation classes have an `eat()` method, but the `Animal` interface doesn't supply any logic for the `eat()` method. That means it's up to the classes that implement the Animal interface to define the actual code for how that particular Animal type behaves when its `eat()` method is invoked.

Finding Other Classes

As we'll see later in the book, it's a good idea to make your classes *cohesive*. That means that every class should have a focused set of responsibilities. For instance, if you were creating a zoo simulation program, you'd want to represent aardvarks with one class, and zoo visitors with a different class. In addition, you might have a Zookeeper class, and a Popcorn vendor class. The point is that you don't want a class that has both Aardvark *and* Popcorn behaviors (more on that in Chapter 2).

Even a simple Java program uses objects from many different classes: some that *you* created, and some built by others (such as Sun's Java API classes). Java organizes classes into *packages*, and uses *import* statements to give programmers a consistent way to manage naming of, and access to, classes they need. The exam covers a *lot* of concepts related to packages and class access; we'll explore the details in this—and later—chapters.

CERTIFICATION OBJECTIVE

Identifiers & JavaBeans (Objectives 1.3 and 1.4)

1.3   Develop code that declares, initializes, and uses primitives, arrays, enums, and objects as static, instance, and local variables. Also, use legal identifiers for variable names.

1.4   Develop code that declares both static and non-static methods, and—if appropriate—use method names that adhere to the JavaBeans naming standards. Also develop code that declares and uses a variable-length argument list.

Remember that when we list one or more Certification Objectives in the book, as we just did, it means that the following section covers at least some part of that objective. Some objectives will be covered in several different chapters, so you'll see the same objective in more than one place in the book. For example, this section covers declarations, identifiers, and JavaBeans naming, but *using* the things you declare is covered primarily in later chapters.

So, we'll start with Java identifiers. The three aspects of Java identifiers that we cover here are

- **Legal Identifiers**   The rules the compiler uses to determine whether a name is legal.
- **Sun's Java Code Conventions**   Sun's recommendations for naming classes, variables, and methods. We typically adhere to these standards throughout the book, except when we're trying to show you how a tricky exam question might be coded. You won't be asked questions about the Java Code Conventions, but we strongly recommend that programmers use them.
- **JavaBeans Naming Standards**   The naming requirements of the JavaBeans specification. You don't need to study the JavaBeans spec for the exam, but you do need to know a few basic JavaBeans naming rules we cover in this chapter.

Legal Identifiers

Technically, legal identifiers must be composed of only Unicode characters, numbers, currency symbols, and connecting characters (like underscores). The exam doesn't dive into the details of which ranges of the Unicode character set are considered to qualify as letters and digits. So, for example, you won't need to know that Tibetan digits range from \u0420 to \u0f29. Here are the rules you *do* need to know:

- Identifiers must start with a letter, a currency character ($), or a connecting character such as the underscore (_). Identifiers cannot start with a number!
- After the first character, identifiers can contain any combination of letters, currency characters, connecting characters, or numbers.
- In practice, there is no limit to the number of characters an identifier can contain.
- You can't use a Java keyword as an identifier. Table 1-1 lists all of the Java keywords including one new one for 5.0, enum.
- Identifiers in Java are case-sensitive; foo and FOO are two different identifiers.

Examples of legal and illegal identifiers follow, first some legal identifiers:

```
int _a;
int $c;
int _____ 2_w;
int _$;
int this_is_a_very_detailed_name_for_an_identifier;
```

The following are illegal (it's your job to recognize why):

```
int :b;
int -d;
int e#;
int .f;
int 7g;
```

TABLE 1-1		Complete List of Java Keywords (assert added in 1.4, enum added in 1.5)			
abstract	boolean	break	byte	case	catch
char	class	const	continue	default	do
double	else	extends	final	finally	float
for	goto	if	implements	import	instanceof
int	interface	long	native	new	package
private	protected	public	return	short	static
strictfp	super	switch	synchronized	this	throw
throws	transient	try	void	volatile	while
assert	enum				

Sun's Java Code Conventions

Sun estimates that over the lifetime of a standard piece of code, 20 percent of the effort will go into the original creation and testing of the code, and 80 percent of the effort will go into the subsequent maintenance and enhancement of the code. Agreeing on, and coding to, a set of code standards helps to reduce the effort involved in testing, maintaining, and enhancing any piece of code. Sun has created a set of coding standards for Java, and published those standards in a document cleverly titled "Java Code Conventions," which you can find at java.sun.com. It's a great document, short and easy to read and we recommend it highly.

That said, you'll find that many of the questions in the exam don't follow the code conventions, because of the limitations in the test engine that is used to deliver the exam internationally. One of the great things about the Sun certifications is that the exams are administered uniformly throughout the world. In order to achieve that, the code listings that you'll see in the real exam are often quite cramped, and do not follow Sun's code standards. In order to toughen you up for the exam, we'll often present code listings that have a similarly cramped look and feel, often indenting our code only two spaces as opposed to the Sun standard of four.

We'll also jam our curly braces together unnaturally, and sometimes put several statements on the same line...ouch! For example:

```
1. class Wombat implements Runnable {
2.   private int i;
3.   public synchronized void run() {
4.     if (i%5 != 0) { i++; }
5.     for(int x=0; x<5; x++, i++)
```

```
 6.        { if (x > 1) Thread.yield(); }
 7.      System.out.print(i + " ");
 8.    }
 9.    public static void main(String[] args) {
10.      Wombat n = new Wombat();
11.      for(int x=100; x>0; --x) { new Thread(n).start(); }
12.  } }
```

Consider yourself forewarned—you'll see lots of code listings, mock questions, and real exam questions that are this sick and twisted. Nobody wants you to write your code like this. Not your employer, not your coworkers, not us, not Sun, and not the exam creation team! Code like this was created only so that complex concepts could be tested within a universal testing tool. The one standard that *is* followed as much as possible in the real exam are the naming standards. Here are the naming standards that Sun recommends, and that we use in the exam and in most of the book:

■ **Classes and interfaces**   The first letter should be capitalized, and if several words are linked together to form the name, the first letter of the inner words should be uppercase (a format that's sometimes called "camelCase"). For classes, the names should typically be nouns. For example:

```
Dog
Account
PrintWriter
```

For interfaces, the names should typically be adjectives like

```
Runnable
Serializable
```

■ **Methods**   The first letter should be lowercase, and then normal camelCase rules should be used. In addition, the names should typically be verb-noun pairs. For example:

```
getBalance
doCalculation
setCustomerName
```

■ **Variables** Like methods, the camelCase format should be used, starting with a lowercase letter. Sun recommends short, meaningful names, which sounds good to us. Some examples:

```
buttonWidth
accountBalance
myString
```

■ **Constants** Java constants are created by marking variables `static` and `final`. They should be named using uppercase letters with underscore characters as separators:

```
MIN_HEIGHT
```

JavaBeans Standards

The JavaBeans spec is intended to help Java developers create Java components that can be easily used by other Java developers in a visual Integrated Development Environment (IDE) tool (like Eclipse or NetBeans). As a Java programmer, you want to be able to use components from the Java API, but it would be great if you could also buy the Java component you want from "Beans 'R Us," that software company down the street. And once you've found the components, you'd like to be able to access them through a development tool in such a way that you don't have to write all your code from scratch. By using naming rules, the JavaBeans spec helps guarantee that tools can recognize and use components built by different developers. The JavaBeans API is quite involved, but you'll need to study only a few basics for the exam.

First, JavaBeans are Java classes that have *properties*. For our purposes, think of properties as `private` instance variables. Since they're `private`, the only way they can be accessed from outside of their class is through *methods* in the class. The methods that change a property's value are called *setter* methods, and the methods that retrieve a property's value are called *getter* methods. The JavaBean naming rules that you'll need to know for the exam are the following:

JavaBean Property Naming Rules

■ If the property is not a boolean, the getter method's prefix must be *get*. For example, `getSize()` is a valid JavaBeans getter name for a property named "size." Keep in mind that you do not need to have a variable named *size* (although some IDEs expect it). The name of the property is *inferred* from the getters and setters, not through any variables in your class. What you return from `getSize()` is up to you.

- If the property is a boolean, the getter method's prefix is either `get` or `is`. For example, `getStopped()` or `isStopped()` are both valid JavaBeans names for a boolean property.

- The setter method's prefix must be *set*. For example, `setSize()` is the valid JavaBean name for a property named *size*.

- To complete the name of a getter or setter method, change the first letter of the property name to uppercase, and then append it to the appropriate prefix (`get`, `is`, or `set`).

- Setter method signatures must be marked `public`, with a `void` return type and an argument that represents the property type.

- Getter method signatures must be marked `public`, take no arguments, and have a return type that matches the argument type of the setter method for that property.

Second, the JavaBean spec supports *events*, which allow components to notify each other when something happens. The event model is often used in GUI applications when an event like a mouse click is multicast to many other objects that may have things to do when the mouse click occurs. The objects that receive the information that an event occurred are called *listeners*. For the exam, you need to know that the methods that are used to add or remove listeners from an event must also follow JavaBean naming standards:

JavaBean Listener Naming Rules

- Listener method names used to "register" a listener with an event source must use the prefix `add`, followed by the listener type. For example, `addActionListener()` is a valid name for a method that an event source will have to allow others to register for Action events.

- Listener method names used to remove ("unregister") a listener must use the prefix `remove`, followed by the listener type (using the same rules as the registration add method).

- The type of listener to be added or removed must be passed as the argument to the method.

- Listener method names must end with the word "Listener".

Examples of valid JavaBean method signatures are

```
public void setMyValue(int v)
public int getMyValue()
public boolean isMyStatus()
public void addMyListener(MyListener m)
public void removeMyListener(MyListener m)
```

Examples of *invalid* JavaBean method signatures are

```
void setCustomerName(String s)            // must be public
public void modifyMyValue(int v)          // can't use 'modify'
public void addXListener(MyListener m)   // listener type mismatch
```

e x a m
w a t c h

The objective says you have to know legal identifiers only for variable names, but the rules are the same for ALL Java components. So remember that a legal identifier for a variable is also a legal identifier for a method or a class. However, you need to distinguish between legal identifiers and naming conventions, such as the JavaBeans standards, that indicate how a Java component should be named. In other words, you must be able to recognize that an identifier is legal even if it doesn't conform to naming standards. If the exam question is asking about naming conventions—not just whether an identifier will compile—JavaBeans will be mentioned explicitly.

CERTIFICATION OBJECTIVE

Declare Classes (Exam Objective 1.1)

1.1   Develop code that declares classes (including abstract and all forms of nested classes), interfaces, and enums, and includes the appropriate use of package and import statements (including static imports).

When you write code in Java, you're writing classes or interfaces. Within those classes, as you know, are variables and methods (plus a few other things). How you declare your classes, methods, and variables dramatically affects your code's behavior. For example, a `public` method can be accessed from code running anywhere in your application. Mark that method `private`, though, and it vanishes from everyone's radar (except the class in which it was declared). For this objective, we'll study the ways in which you can declare and modify (or not) a class. You'll find that we cover modifiers in an extreme level of detail, and though we know you're already familiar with them, we're starting from the very beginning. Most Java programmers think they know how all the modifiers work, but on closer study often find out that they don't (at least not to the degree needed for the exam). Subtle distinctions are everywhere, so you need to be absolutely certain you're completely solid on everything in this section's objectives before taking the exam.

Source File Declaration Rules

Before we dig into class declarations, let's do a quick review of the rules associated with declaring classes, `import` statements, and `package` statements in a source file:

- There can be only one `public` class per source code file.
- Comments can appear at the beginning or end of any line in the source code file; they are independent of any of the positioning rules discussed here.
- If there *is* a `public` class in a file, the name of the file must match the name of the `public` class. For example, a class declared as `public class Dog { }` must be in a source code file named `Dog.java`.
- If the class is part of a package, the `package` statement must be the first line in the source code file, before any `import` statements that may be present.
- If there are `import` statements, they must go *between* the `package` statement (if there is one) and the class declaration. If there isn't a `package` statement, then the `import` statement(s) must be the first line(s) in the source code file. If there are no `package` or `import` statements, the class declaration must be the first line in the source code file.
- `import` and `package` statements apply to *all* classes within a source code file. In other words, there's no way to declare multiple classes in a file and have them in different packages, or use different imports.
- A file can have more than one nonpublic class.

■   Files with no public classes can have a name that does not match any of the classes in the file.

In Chapter 10 we'll go into a lot more detail about the rules involved with declaring and using imports, packages, and a feature new to Java 5, static imports.

Class Declarations and Modifiers

Although nested (often called inner) classes are on the exam, we'll save nested class declarations for Chapter 8. You're going to love that chapter. No, really. Seriously. The following code is a bare-bones class declaration:

```
class MyClass { }
```

This code compiles just fine, but you can also add modifiers before the class declaration. Modifiers fall into two categories:

■   Access modifiers: `public`, `protected`, `private`.
■   Non-access modifiers (including `strictfp`, `final`, and `abstract`).

We'll look at access modifiers first, so you'll learn how to restrict or allow access to a class you create. Access control in Java is a little tricky because there are four access *controls* (levels of access) but only three access *modifiers*. The fourth access control level (called *default* or *package* access) is what you get when you don't use any of the three access modifiers. In other words, *every* class, method, and instance variable you declare has an access *control*, whether you explicitly type one or not. Although all four access *controls* (which means all three *modifiers*) work for most method and variable declarations, a class can be declared with only `public` or *default* access; the other two access control levels don't make sense for a class, as you'll see.

on the
job

Java is a package-centric language; the developers assumed that for good organization and name scoping, you would put all your classes into packages. They were right, and you should. Imagine this nightmare: Three different programmers, in the same company but working on different parts of a project, write a class named `Utilities`. *If those three* `Utilities` *classes have not been declared in any explicit package, and are in the classpath, you won't have any way to tell the compiler or JVM which of the three you're trying to reference. Sun recommends that developers use reverse domain names, appended with division and/or project names. For example, if your domain name is* `geeksanonymous.com`, *and you're working on the client code for the TwelvePointOSteps program, you would name your package something like* `com.geeksanonymous.steps.client`. *That would essentially change the name of your class to* `com.geeksanonymous.steps.client.Utilities`. *You might still have name collisions within your company, if you don't come up with your own naming schemes, but you're guaranteed not to collide with classes developed outside your company (assuming they follow Sun's naming convention, and if they don't, well, Really Bad Things could happen).*

Class Access

What does it mean to access a class? When we say code from one class (class A) has access to another class (class B), it means class A can do one of three things:

- Create an *instance* of class B.
- *Extend* class B (in other words, become a subclass of class B).
- *Access* certain methods and variables within class B, depending on the access control of those methods and variables.

In effect, access means *visibility*. If class A can't *see* class B, the access level of the methods and variables within class B won't matter; class A won't have any way to access those methods and variables.

Default Access   A class with default access has *no* modifier preceding it in the declaration! It's the access control you get when you don't type a modifier in the class declaration. Think of *default* access as *package*-level access, because a class with default access can be seen only by classes within the same package. For example, if class A and class B are in different packages, and class A has default access, class B won't be able to create an instance of class A, or even declare a variable or return type of class A. In fact, class B has to pretend that class A doesn't even exist, or the compiler will complain. Look at the following source file:

```
package cert;
class Beverage { }
```

Now look at the second source file:

```
package exam.stuff;
import cert.Beverage;
class Tea extends Beverage { }
```

As you can see, the superclass (Beverage) is in a different package from the subclass (Tea). The `import` statement at the top of the Tea file is trying (fingers crossed) to import the Beverage class. The Beverage file compiles fine, but when we try to compile the Tea file we get something like:

```
Can't access class cert.Beverage. Class or interface must be
public, in same package, or an accessible member class.
import cert.Beverage;
```

Tea won't compile because its superclass, Beverage, has default access and is in a different package. You can do one of two things to make this work. You could put both classes in the same package, or you could declare Beverage as `public`, as the next section describes.

When you see a question with complex logic, be sure to look at the access modifiers first. That way, if you spot an access violation (for example, a class in package A trying to access a default class in package B), you'll know the code won't compile so you don't have to bother working through the logic. It's not as if you don't have anything better to do with your time while taking the exam. Just choose the "Compilation fails" answer and zoom on to the next question.

Public Access A class declaration with the `public` keyword gives all classes from all packages access to the `public` class. In other words, *all* classes in the Java Universe (JU) have access to a `public` class. Don't forget, though, that if a `public` class you're trying to use is in a different package from the class you're writing, you'll still need to import the `public` class.

In the example from the preceding section, we may not want to place the subclass in the same package as the superclass. To make the code work, we need to add the keyword `public` in front of the superclass (Beverage) declaration, as follows:

```
package cert;
public class Beverage { }
```

This changes the Beverage class so it will be visible to all classes in all packages. The class can now be instantiated from all other classes, and any class is now free to subclass (extend from) it—unless, that is, the class is also marked with the nonaccess modifier `final`. Read on.

Other (Nonaccess) Class Modifiers

You can modify a class declaration using the keyword `final`, `abstract`, or `strictfp`. These modifiers are in addition to whatever access control is on the class, so you could, for example, declare a class as both `public` and `final`. But you can't always mix nonaccess modifiers. You're free to use `strictfp` in combination with `final`, for example, but you must never, ever, ever mark a class as both `final` *and* `abstract`. You'll see why in the next two sections.

You won't need to know how `strictfp` works, so we're focusing only on modifying a class as `final` or `abstract`. For the exam, you need to know only that `strictfp` is a keyword and can be used to modify a class or a method, but never a variable. Marking a class as `strictfp` means that any method code in the class will conform to the IEEE 754 standard rules for floating points. Without that modifier, floating points used in the methods might behave in a platform-dependent way. If you don't declare a class as `strictfp`, you can still get `strictfp` behavior on a method-by-method basis, by declaring a method as `strictfp`. If you don't know the IEEE 754 standard, now's not the time to learn it. You have, as we say, bigger fish to fry.

Final Classes   When used in a class declaration, the `final` keyword means the class can't be subclassed. In other words, no other class can ever extend (inherit from) a `final` class, and any attempts to do so will give you a compiler error.

So why would you ever mark a class `final`? After all, doesn't that violate the whole object-oriented (OO) notion of inheritance? You should make a `final` class only if you need an absolute guarantee that none of the methods in that class will ever be overridden. If you're deeply dependent on the implementations of certain methods, then using `final` gives you the security that nobody can change the implementation out from under you.

You'll notice many classes in the Java core libraries are `final`. For example, the `String` class cannot be subclassed. Imagine the havoc if you couldn't guarantee how a `String` object would work on any given system your application is running on! If programmers were free to extend the String class (and thus substitute their new String subclass instances where java.lang.String instances are expected), civilization—as we know it—could collapse. So use final for safety, but only when you're certain that your final class has indeed said all that ever needs to be said in its methods. Marking a class final means, in essence, your class can't ever be improved upon, or even specialized, by another programmer.

A benefit of having nonfinal classes is this scenario: Imagine you find a problem with a method in a class you're using, but you don't have the source code. So you can't modify the source to improve the method, but you can extend the class and override the method in your new subclass, and substitute the subclass everywhere the original superclass is expected. If the class is final, though, then you're stuck.

Let's modify our Beverage example by placing the keyword final in the declaration:

```
package cert;
public final class Beverage {
  public void importantMethod() { }
}
```

Now, if we try to compile the Tea subclass:

```
package exam.stuff;
import cert.Beverage;
class Tea extends Beverage { }
```

We get an error something like

```
Can't subclass final classes: class
cert.Beverage class Tea extends Beverage{
1 error
```

In practice, you'll almost never make a final class. A final class obliterates a key benefit of OO—extensibility. So unless you have a serious safety or security issue, assume that some day another programmer will need to extend your class. If you don't, the next programmer forced to maintain your code will hunt you down and <insert really scary thing>.

Abstract Classes   An abstract class can never be instantiated. Its sole purpose, mission in life, raison d'être, is to be extended (subclassed). (Note, however, that you can compile and execute an abstract class, as long as you don't try to make an instance of it.) Why make a class if you can't make objects out of it? Because the class might be just too, well, *abstract*. For example, imagine you have a class Car that has generic methods common to all vehicles. But you don't want anyone actually creating a generic, abstract Car object. How would they initialize its state? What color would it be? How many seats? Horsepower? All-wheel drive? Or more importantly, how would it behave? In other words, how would the methods be implemented?

No, you need programmers to instantiate actual car types such as BMWBoxster and SubaruOutback. We'll bet the Boxster owner will tell you his car does things the Subaru can do "only in its dreams." Take a look at the following abstract class:

```
abstract class Car {
    private double price;
    private String model;
    private String year;
    public abstract void goFast();
    public abstract void goUpHill();
    public abstract void impressNeighbors();
    // Additional, important, and serious code goes here
}
```

The preceding code will compile fine. However, if you try to instantiate a Car in another body of code, you'll get a compiler error something like this:

```
AnotherClass.java:7: class Car is an abstract
class. It can't be instantiated.
      Car x = new Car();
1 error
```

Notice that the methods marked abstract **end in a semicolon rather than curly braces.**

Look for questions with a method declaration that ends with a semicolon, rather than curly braces. If the method is in a class—as opposed to an interface—then both the method and the class must be marked abstract. You might get a question that asks how you could fix a code sample that includes a method ending in a semicolon, but without an abstract modifier on the class or method. In that case, you could either mark the method and class abstract, or change the semicolon to code (like a curly brace pair). Remember, if you change a method from abstract to nonabstract, don't forget to change the semicolon at the end of the method declaration into a curly brace pair!

We'll look at abstract methods in more detail later in this objective, but always remember that if even a single method is `abstract`, the whole class must be declared `abstract`. One abstract method spoils the whole bunch. You can, however, put nonabstract methods in an `abstract` class. For example, you might have methods with implementations that shouldn't change from Car type to Car type, such as `getColor()` or `setPrice()`. By putting nonabstract methods in an abstract class, you give all concrete subclasses (concrete just means not abstract) inherited method implementations. The good news there is that concrete subclasses get to inherit functionality, and need to implement only the methods that define subclass-specific behavior.

(By the way, if you think we misused *raison d'être* earlier, don't send an e-mail. We'd like to see *you* work it into a programmer certification book.)

Coding with abstract class types (including interfaces, discussed later in this chapter) lets you take advantage of polymorphism, and gives you the greatest degree of flexibility and extensibility. You'll learn more about polymorphism in Chapter 2.

You can't mark a class as both `abstract` and `final`. They have nearly opposite meanings. An `abstract` class must be subclassed, whereas a `final` class must not be subclassed. If you see this combination of `abstract` and `final` modifiers, used for a class or method declaration, the code will not compile.

EXERCISE 1-1

Creating an Abstract Superclass and Concrete Subclass

The following exercise will test your knowledge of `public`, default, `final`, and abstract classes. Create an `abstract` superclass named `Fruit` and a concrete subclass named `Apple`. The superclass should belong to a package called `food` and the subclass can belong to the default package (meaning it isn't put into a package explicitly). Make the superclass `public` and give the subclass default access.

1. Create the superclass as follows:

```
package food;
public abstract class Fruit{ /* any code you want */}
```

2. Create the subclass in a separate file as follows:

```
import food.Fruit;
class Apple extends Fruit{ /* any code you want */}
```

3. Create a directory called `food` off the directory in your class path setting.

4. Attempt to compile the two files. If you want to use the `Apple` class, make sure you place the `Fruit.class` file in the `food` subdirectory.

CERTIFICATION OBJECTIVE

Declare Interfaces (Exam Objectives 1.1 and 1.2)

1.1 Develop code that declares classes (including abstract and all forms of nested classes), interfaces, and enums, and includes the appropriate use of package and import statements (including static imports).

1.2 Develop code that declares an interface. Develop code that implements or extends one or more interfaces. Develop code that declares an abstract class. Develop code that extends an abstract class.

Declaring an Interface

When you create an interface, you're defining a contract for *what* a class can do, without saying anything about *how* the class will do it. An interface is a contract. You could write an interface `Bounceable`, for example, that says in effect, "This is the `Bounceable` interface. Any class type that implements this interface must agree to write the code for the `bounce()` and `setBounceFactor()` methods."

By defining an interface for Bounceable, any class that wants to be treated as a Bounceable thing can simply implement the `Bounceable` interface and provide code for the interface's two methods.

Interfaces can be implemented by any class, from any inheritance tree. This lets you take radically different classes and give them a common characteristic. For example, you might want both a Ball and a Tire to have bounce behavior, but Ball and Tire don't share any inheritance relationship; Ball extends Toy while Tire extends only `java.lang.Object`. But by making both Ball and Tire implement Bounceable, you're saying that Ball and Tire can be treated as, "Things that can bounce," which in Java translates to "Things on which you can invoke the `bounce()` and `setBounceFactor()` methods." Figure 1-1 illustrates the relationship between interfaces and classes.

FIGURE 1-1

The Relationship between interfaces and classes

```
interface Bounceable

void bounce ( );
void setBounceFactor(int bf);
```

What you declare.

```
interface Bounceable

public abstract void bounce ( );
public abstract void setBounceFactor(int bf);
```

What the compiler sees.

```
Class Tire implements Bounceable
public void bounce ( ){...}
public void setBounceFactor(int bf){ }
```

What the implementing class must do.

(All interface methods must be implemented, and must be marked public.)

Think of an interface as a 100-percent `abstract` class. Like an `abstract` class, an interface defines abstract methods that take the following form:

```
abstract void bounce();   // Ends with a semicolon rather than
                          // curly braces
```

But while an `abstract` class can define both `abstract` and non-abstract methods, an interface can have only `abstract` methods. Another way interfaces differ from `abstract` classes is that interfaces have very little flexibility in how the methods and variables defined in the interface are declared. These rules are strict:

■ All interface methods are implicitly `public` and `abstract`. In other words, you do not need to actually type the `public` or `abstract` modifiers in the method declaration, but the method is still always `public` and `abstract`.

■ All variables defined in an interface must be `public`, `static`, and `final`— in other words, interfaces can declare only constants, not instance variables.

- Interface methods must not be `static`.
- Because interface methods are abstract, they cannot be marked `final`, `strictfp`, or `native`. (More on these modifiers later.)
- An interface can *extend* one or more other interfaces.
- An interface cannot extend anything but another interface.
- An interface cannot implement another interface or class.
- An interface must be declared with the keyword `interface`.
- Interface types can be used polymorphically (see Chapter 2 for more details).

The following is a legal interface declaration:

```
public abstract interface Rollable { }
```

Typing in the `abstract` modifier is considered redundant; interfaces are implicitly abstract whether you type `abstract` or not. You just need to know that both of these declarations are legal, and functionally identical:

```
public abstract interface Rollable { }
public interface Rollable { }
```

The `public` modifier is required if you want the interface to have public rather than default access.

We've looked at the interface declaration but now we'll look closely at the methods within an interface:

```
public interface Bounceable {
    public abstract void bounce();
    public abstract void setBounceFactor(int bf);
}
```

Typing in the `public` and `abstract` modifiers on the methods is redundant, though, since all interface methods are implicitly `public` and `abstract`. Given that rule, you can see that the following code is exactly equivalent to the preceding interface:

```
public interface Bounceable {
    void bounce();                  // No modifiers
    void setBounceFactor(int bf);   // No modifiers
}
```

You must remember that all interface methods are public and abstract regardless of what you see in the interface definition.

Look for interface methods declared with any combination of `public`, `abstract`, or no modifiers. For example, the following five method declarations, if declared within their own interfaces, are legal and identical!

```
void bounce();
public void bounce();
abstract void bounce();
public abstract void bounce();
abstract public void bounce();
```

The following interface method declarations won't compile:

```
final void bounce();       // final and abstract can never be used
                           // together, and abstract is implied
static void bounce();      // interfaces define instance methods
private void bounce();     // interface methods are always public
protected void bounce();    // (same as above)
```

Declaring Interface Constants

You're allowed to put constants in an interface. By doing so, you guarantee that any class implementing the interface will have access to the same constant.

By placing the constants right in the interface, any class that implements the interface has direct access to the constants, just as if the class had inherited them.

You need to remember one key rule for interface constants. They must always be

```
public static final
```

So that sounds simple, right? After all, interface constants are no different from any other publicly accessible constants, so they obviously must be declared `public`, `static`, and `final`. But before you breeze past the rest of this discussion, think about the implications: **Because interface constants are defined in an interface, they don't have to be *declared* as `public`, `static`, or `final`. They must be public, static, and final, but you don't have to actually declare them that way.** Just as interface methods are always public and abstract whether you say so in the code or not, any variable defined in an interface must be—and implicitly is—a public constant. See if you can spot the problem with the following code (assume two separate files):

```
interface Foo {
  int BAR = 42;
  void go();
}

class Zap implements Foo {
  public void go() {
     BAR = 27;
  }
}
```

You can't change the value of a constant! Once the value has been assigned, the value can never be modified. The assignment happens in the interface itself (where the constant is declared), so the implementing class can access it and use it, but as a read-only value. So the BAR = 27 assignment will not compile.

e x a m

ⓦatch   *Look for interface definitions that define constants, but without explicitly using the required modifiers. For example, the following are all identical:*

```
public int x = 1;          // Looks non-static and non-final,
                           // but isn't!
int x = 1;                 // Looks default, non-final,
                           // non-static, but isn't!
static int x = 1;          // Doesn't show final or public
final int x = 1;           // Doesn't show static or public
public static int x = 1;      // Doesn't show final
public final int x = 1;       // Doesn't show static
static final int x = 1        // Doesn't show public
public static final int x = 1;  // what you get implicitly
```

Any combination of the required (but implicit) modifiers is legal, as is using no modifiers at all! On the exam, you can expect to see questions you won't be able to answer correctly unless you know, for example, that an interface variable is final *and can never be given a value by the implementing (or any other) class.*

CERTIFICATION OBJECTIVE

Declare Class Members (Objectives 1.3 and 1.4)

1.3 Develop code that declares, initializes, and uses primitives, arrays, enums, and objects as static, instance, and local variables. Also, use legal identifiers for variable names.

1.4 Develop code that declares both static and non-static methods, and—if appropriate—use method names that adhere to the JavaBeans naming standards. Also develop code that declares and uses a variable-length argument list.

We've looked at what it means to use a modifier in a class declaration, and now we'll look at what it means to modify a method or variable declaration.

Methods and instance (nonlocal) variables are collectively known as members. You can modify a member with both access and nonaccess modifiers, and you have more modifiers to choose from (and combine) than when you're declaring a class.

Access Modifiers

Because method and variable members are usually given access control in exactly the same way, we'll cover both in this section.

Whereas a *class* can use just two of the four access control levels (default or `public`), *members* can use all four:

- `public`
- `protected`
- default
- `private`

Default protection is what you get when you don't type an access modifier in the member declaration. The default and `protected` access control types have almost identical behavior, except for one difference that will be mentioned later.

It's crucial that you know access control inside and out for the exam. There will be quite a few questions with access control playing a role. Some questions test several concepts of access control at the same time, so not knowing one small part of access control could blow an entire question.

What does it mean for code in one class to have access to a member of another class? For now, ignore any differences between methods and variables. If class A has access to a member of class B, it means that class B's member is visible to class A. When a class does not have access to another member, the compiler will slap you for trying to access something that you're not even supposed to know exists!

You need to understand two different access issues:

- Whether method code in one class can *access* a member of another class
- Whether a subclass can *inherit* a member of its superclass

The first type of access is when a method in one class tries to access a method or a variable of another class, using the dot operator (.) to invoke a method or retrieve a variable. For example:

```
class Zoo {
  public String coolMethod() {
    return "Wow  baby";
  }
}
class Moo {
  public void useAZoo() {
    Zoo z = new Zoo();
    // If the preceding line compiles Moo has access
    // to the Zoo class
    // But... does it have access to the coolMethod()?
    System.out.println("A Zoo says, " + z.coolMethod());
    // The preceding line works because Moo can access the
    // public method
  }
}
```

The second type of access revolves around which, if any, members of a superclass a subclass can access through inheritance. We're not looking at whether the subclass can, say, invoke a method on an instance of the superclass (which would just be an example of the first type of access). Instead, we're looking at whether the subclass *inherits* a member of its superclass. Remember, if a subclass *inherits* a member, it's exactly as if the subclass actually declared the member itself. In other words, if a subclass *inherits* a member, the subclass *has* the member.

```
class Zoo {
  public String coolMethod() {
    return "Wow  baby";
  }
}
class Moo extends Zoo {
  public void useMyCoolMethod() {
    // Does an instance of Moo inherit the coolMethod()?
    System.out.println("Moo says, " + this.coolMethod());
    // The preceding line works because Moo can inherit the
    // public method
    // Can an instance of Moo invoke coolMethod() on an
    // instance of Zoo?
    Zoo z = new Zoo();
    System.out.println("Zoo says, " + z.coolMethod());
    // coolMethod() is public, so Moo can invoke it on a Zoo
    //reference
  }
}
```

Figure 1-2 compares a class inheriting a member of another class, and accessing a member of another class using a reference of an instance of that class.

Much of access control (both types) centers on whether the two classes involved are in the same or different packages. Don't forget, though, if class A *itself* can't be accessed by class B, then no members within class A can be accessed by class B.

You need to know the effect of different combinations of class and member access (such as a default class with a public variable). To figure this out, first look at the access level of the class. If the class itself will not be visible to another class, then none of the members will be either, even if the member is declared public. Once you've confirmed that the class is visible, then it makes sense to look at access levels on individual members.

Public Members

When a method or variable member is declared public, it means all other classes, regardless of the package they belong to, can access the member (assuming the class itself is visible).

FIGURE 1-2   Comparison of inheritance vs. dot operator for member access.

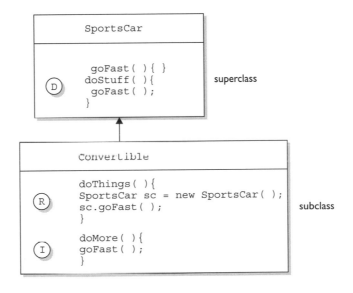

Three ways to access a method:

(D) Invoking a method declared in the same class

(R) Invoking a method using a reference of the class

(I) Invoking an inherited method

Look at the following source file:

```
package book;
import cert.*;  // Import all classes in the cert package
class Goo {
  public static void main(String[] args) {
    Sludge o = new Sludge();
    o.testIt();
  }
}
```

Now look at the second file:

```
package cert;
public class Sludge {
  public void testIt() { System.out.println("sludge"); }
}
```

As you can see, Goo and Sludge are in different packages. However, Goo can invoke the method in Sludge without problems because both the Sludge class and its testIt() method are marked public.

For a subclass, if a member of its superclass is declared public, the subclass inherits that member regardless of whether both classes are in the same package:

```
package cert;
public class Roo {
  public String doRooThings() {
    // imagine the fun code that goes here
    return "fun";
  }
}
```

The Roo class declares the doRooThings() member as public. So if we make a subclass of Roo, any code in that Roo subclass can call its own inherited doRooThings() method.

```
package notcert;    //Not the package Roo is in
import cert.Roo;
class Cloo extends Roo {
  public void testCloo() {
    System.out.println(doRooThings());
  }
}
```

Notice in the preceding code that the doRooThings() method is invoked without having to preface it with a reference. Remember, if you see a method invoked (or a variable accessed) without the dot operator (.), it means the method or variable belongs to the class where you see that code. It also means that the method or variable is implicitly being accessed using the this reference. So in the preceding code, the call to doRooThings() in the Cloo class could also have been written as this.doRooThings(). The reference this always refers to the currently executing object—in other words, the object running the code where you see the this reference. Because the this reference is implicit, you don't need to preface your member access code with it, but it won't hurt. Some programmers include it to make the code easier to read for new (or non) Java programmers.

Besides being able to invoke the doRooThings() method on itself, code from some other class can call doRooThings() on a Cloo instance, as in the following:

```
class Toon {
  public static void main(String[] args) {
    Cloo c = new Cloo();
    System.out.println(c.doRooThings()); //No problem; method
                                         // is public
  }
}
```

Private Members

Members marked private can't be accessed by code in any class other than the class in which the private member was declared. Let's make a small change to the Roo class from an earlier example.

```
package cert;
public class Roo {
  private String doRooThings() {
    // imagine the fun code that goes here, but only the Roo
    // class knows
    return "fun";
  }
}
```

The doRooThings() method is now private, so no other class can use it. If we try to invoke the method from any other class, we'll run into trouble:

```
package notcert;
import cert.Roo;
class  UseARoo {
  public void testIt() {
    Roo r = new Roo(); //So far so good; class Roo is public
    System.out.println(r.doRooThings()); //Compiler error!
  }
}
```

If we try to compile UseARoo, we get a compiler error something like this:

```
cannot find symbol
symbol  : method doRooThings()
```

It's as if the method doRooThings() doesn't exist, and as far as any code outside of the Roo class is concerned, it's true. A private member is invisible to any code outside the member's own class.

What about a subclass that tries to inherit a private member of its superclass? When a member is declared private, a subclass can't inherit it. For the exam, you need to recognize that a subclass can't see, use, or even think about the private members of its superclass. You can, however, declare a matching method in the subclass. But regardless of how it looks, *it is not an overriding method!* It is simply a method that happens to have the same name as a private method (which you're not supposed to know about) in the superclass. The rules of overriding do not apply, so you can make this newly-declared-but-just-happens-to-match method declare new exceptions, or change the return type, or anything else you want to do with it.

```
package cert;
public class Roo {
   private String doRooThings() {
     // imagine the fun code that goes here, but no other class
     // will know
     return "fun";
   }
}
```

The doRooThings() method is now off limits to all subclasses, even those in the same package as the superclass:

```
package cert;              //Cloo and Roo are in the same package
class  Cloo extends Roo {  //Still OK, superclass Roo is public
  public void testCloo() {
    System.out.println(doRooThings()); //Compiler error!
  }
}
```

If we try to compile the subclass Cloo, the compiler is delighted to spit out an error something like this:

```
%javac Cloo.java
Cloo.java:4: Undefined method: doRooThings()
     System.out.println(doRooThings());
1 error
```

Although you're allowed to mark instance variables as `public`, *in practice it's nearly always best to keep all variables* `private` *or* `protected`. *If variables need to be changed, set, or read, programmers should use public accessor methods, so that code in any other class has to ask to get or set a variable (by going through a method), rather than access it directly. JavaBean-compliant accessor methods take the form get<propertyName> or, for booleans, is<propertyName> and set<propertyName>, and provide a place to check and/or validate before returning or modifying a value.*

Without this protection, the weight variable of a Cat object, for example, could be set to a negative number if the offending code goes straight to the public variable as in `someCat.weight = 20`. *But an accessor method,* `setWeight(int wt)`, *could check for an inappropriate number. (OK, wild speculation, but we're guessing a negative weight might be inappropriate for a cat. Or not.) Chapter 2 will discuss this data protection (encapsulation) in more detail.*

Can a `private` method be overridden by a subclass? That's an interesting question, but the answer is technically no. Since the subclass, as we've seen, cannot inherit a `private` method, it therefore cannot override the method—overriding depends on inheritance. We'll cover the implications of this in more detail a little later in this section as well as in Chapter 2, but for now just remember that a method marked `private` cannot be overridden. Figure 1-3 illustrates the effects of the `public` and `private` modifiers on classes from the same or different packages.

FIGURE 1-3

The effect of private access control

Effects of public and
private access

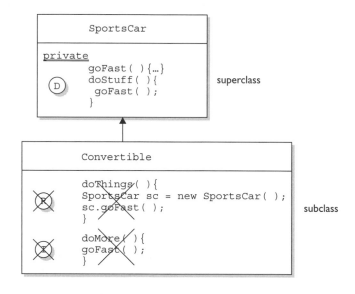

Three ways to access a method:

(D) Invoking a method declared in the same class

(R) Invoking a method using a reference of the class

(I) Invoking an inherited method

Protected and Default Members

The protected and default access control levels are almost identical, but with one
critical difference. A *default* member may be accessed only if the class accessing the
member belongs to the same package, whereas a *protected* member can be accessed
(through inheritance) by a subclass *even if the subclass is in a different package.*

Take a look at the following two classes:

```
package certification;
public class OtherClass {
  void testIt() {    // No modifier means method has default
                     // access
    System.out.println("OtherClass");
  }
}
```

In another source code file you have the following:

```
package somethingElse;
import certification.OtherClass;
class AccessClass {
  static public void main(String[] args) {
    OtherClass o = new OtherClass();
    o.testIt();
  }
}
```

As you can see, the testIt() method in the first file has *default* (think: *package-level*) access. Notice also that class OtherClass is in a different package from the AccessClass. Will AccessClass be able to use the method testIt()? Will it cause a compiler error? Will Daniel ever marry Francesca? Stay tuned.

```
No method matching testIt() found in class
certification.OtherClass.   o.testIt();
```

From the preceding results, you can see that AccessClass can't use the OtherClass method testIt() because testIt() has default access, and AccessClass is not in the same package as OtherClass. So AccessClass can't see it, the compiler complains, and we have no idea who Daniel and Francesca are.

Default and *protected* behavior differ only when we talk about subclasses. If the protected keyword is used to define a member, any subclass of the class declaring the member can access it *through inheritance*. It doesn't matter if the superclass and subclass are in different packages, the protected superclass member is still visible to the subclass (although visible only in a very specific way as we'll see a little later). This is in contrast to the default behavior, which doesn't allow a subclass to access a superclass member unless the subclass is in the same package as the superclass.

Whereas default access doesn't extend any special consideration to subclasses (you're either in the package or you're not), the protected modifier respects the parent-child relationship, even when the child class moves away (and joins a new package). So, when you think of *default* access, think *package* restriction. No exceptions. But when you think *protected*, think *package + kids*. A class with a protected member is marking that member as having package-level access for all classes, but with a special exception for subclasses outside the package.

But what does it mean for a subclass-outside-the-package to have access to a superclass (parent) member? It means the subclass inherits the member. It does not, however, mean the subclass-outside-the-package can access the member using a reference to an instance of the superclass. In other words, protected = inheritance. Protected does not mean that the subclass can treat the protected superclass member as though it were public. So if the subclass-outside-the-package gets a reference to the superclass (by, for example, creating an instance of the superclass somewhere in the subclass' code), the subclass cannot use the dot operator on the superclass reference to access the protected member. To a subclass-outside-the-package, a protected member might as well be default (or even private), when the subclass is using a reference to the superclass. **The subclass can see the** `protected` **member only through inheritance.**

Are you confused? So are we. Hang in there and it will all become clear with the next batch of code examples. (And don't worry; we're not actually confused. We're just trying to make you feel better if you are. You know, like it's OK for you to feel as though nothing makes sense, and that it isn't your fault. Or is it? <insert evil laugh>)

Protected Details

Let's take a look at a `protected` instance variable (remember, an instance variable is a member) of a superclass.

```
package certification;
public class Parent {
    protected int x = 9; // protected access
}
```

The preceding code declares the variable x as `protected`. This makes the variable *accessible* to all other classes *inside* the certification package, as well as *inheritable* by any subclasses *outside* the package. Now let's create a subclass in a different package, and attempt to use the variable x (that the subclass inherits):

```
package other; // Different package
import certification.Parent;
class Child extends Parent {
    public void testIt() {
        System.out.println("x is " + x); // No problem; Child
                                         // inherits x
    }
}
```

The preceding code compiles fine. Notice, though, that the Child class is accessing the protected variable through inheritance. Remember, any time we talk about a subclass having access to a superclass member, we could be talking about the subclass inheriting the member, not simply accessing the member through a reference to an instance of the superclass (the way any other nonsubclass would access it). Watch what happens if the subclass Child (outside the superclass' package) tries to access a protected variable using a Parent class reference.

```
package other;
import certification.Parent;
class Child extends Parent {
    public void testIt() {
        System.out.println("x is " + x); // No problem; Child
                                         // inherits x
        Parent p = new Parent(); // Can we access x using the
                                 // p reference?
        System.out.println("X in parent is " + p.x); // Compiler
                                                      // error!
    }
}
```

The compiler is more than happy to show us the problem:

```
%javac -d . other/Child.java
other/Child.java:9: x has protected access in certification.Par-
ent
System.out.println("X in parent is " + p.x);
                                          ^

1 error
```

So far we've established that a protected member has essentially package-level or default access to all classes except for subclasses. We've seen that subclasses outside the package can inherit a protected member. Finally, we've seen that subclasses outside the package can't use a superclass reference to access a protected member. *For a subclass outside the package, the protected member can be accessed only through inheritance.*

But there's still one more issue we haven't looked at...what does a protected member look like to other classes trying to use the subclass-outside-the-package to get to the subclass' inherited protected superclass member? For example, using our previous Parent/Child classes, what happens if some other class—Neighbor, say—in the same package as the Child (subclass), has a reference to a Child instance and wants to access the member variable x ? In other words, how does that protected member behave once the subclass has inherited it? Does it maintain its protected status, such that classes in the Child's package can see it?

No! Once the subclass-outside-the-package inherits the protected member, that member (as inherited by the subclass) becomes private to any code outside the subclass, with the exception of subclasses of the subclass. So if class Neighbor instantiates a Child object, then even if class Neighbor is in the same package as class Child, class Neighbor won't have access to the Child's inherited (but protected) variable x. Figure 1-4 illustrates the effect of protected access on classes and subclasses in the same or different packages.

Whew! That wraps up protected, the most misunderstood modifier in Java. Again, it's used only in very special cases, but you can count on it showing up on the exam. Now that we've covered the protected modifier, we'll switch to default member access, a piece of cake compared to protected.

Default Details

Let's start with the default behavior of a member in a superclass. We'll modify the Parent's member x to make it default.

```
package certification;
public class Parent {
  int x = 9; // No access modifier, means default
             // (package) access
}
```

Notice we didn't place an access modifier in front of the variable x. Remember that if you don't type an access modifier before a class or member declaration, the access control is default, which means package level. We'll now attempt to access the default member from the Child class that we saw earlier.

FIGURE 1-4

Effects of
protected
access

When we compile the child file, we get an error something like this:

```
Child.java:4: Undefined variable: x
      System.out.println("Variable x is " + x);
1 error
```

The compiler gives the same error as when a member is declared as `private`. The subclass Child (in a different package from the superclass Parent) can't see or use the default superclass member x ! Now, what about default access for two classes in the same package?

```
package certification;
public class Parent{
  int x = 9; // default access
}
```

And in the second class you have the following:

```
package certification;
class Child extends Parent{
  static public void main(String[] args) {
    Child sc = new Child();
    sc.testIt();
  }
  public void testIt() {
    System.out.println("Variable x is " + x); // No problem;
  }
}
```

The preceding source file compiles fine, and the class Child runs and displays the value of x. Just remember that default members are visible to subclasses only if those subclasses are in the same package as the superclass.

Local Variables and Access Modifiers

Can access modifiers be applied to local variables? NO!

There is never a case where an access modifier can be applied to a local variable, so watch out for code like the following:

```
class Foo {
  void doStuff() {
    private int x = 7;
    this.doMore(x);
  }
}
```

You can be certain that any local variable declared with an access modifier will not compile. In fact, there is only one modifier that can ever be applied to local variables—`final`.

That about does it for our discussion on member access modifiers. Table 1-2 shows all the combinations of access and visibility; you really should spend some time with it. Next, we're going to dig into the other (nonaccess) modifiers that you can apply to member declarations.

TABLE 1-2   Determining Access to Class Members

Visibility	Public	Protected	*Default*	Private
From the same class	Yes	Yes	Yes	Yes
From any class in the same package	Yes	Yes	Yes	No
From a subclass in the same package	Yes	Yes	Yes	No
From a subclass outside the same package	Yes	Yes, *through inheritance*	No	No
From any non-subclass class outside the package	Yes	No	No	No

Nonaccess Member Modifiers

We've discussed member access, which refers to whether code from one class can invoke a method (or access an instance variable) from another class. That still leaves a boatload of other modifiers you can use on member declarations. Two you're already familiar with—`final` and `abstract`—because we applied them to class declarations earlier in this chapter. But we still have to take a quick look at `transient`, `synchronized`, `native`, `strictfp`, and then a long look at the Big One—`static`.

We'll look first at modifiers applied to methods, followed by a look at modifiers applied to instance variables. We'll wrap up this section with a look at how `static` works when applied to variables and methods.

Final Methods

The final keyword prevents a method from being overridden in a subclass, and is often used to enforce the API functionality of a method. For example, the Thread class has a method called isAlive() that checks whether a thread is still active. If you extend the Thread class, though, there is really no way that you can correctly implement this method yourself (it uses native code, for one thing), so the designers have made it final. Just as you can't subclass the String class (because we need to be able to trust in the behavior of a String object), you can't override many of the methods in the core class libraries. This can't-be-overridden restriction provides for safety and security, but you should use it with great caution. Preventing a subclass from overriding a method stifles many of the benefits of OO including extensibility through polymorphism. A typical final method declaration looks like this:

```
class SuperClass{
  public final void showSample() {
    System.out.println("One thing.");
  }
}
```

It's legal to extend SuperClass, since the *class* isn't marked final, but we can't override the final *method* showSample(), as the following code attempts to do:

```
class SubClass extends SuperClass{
  public void showSample() { // Try to override the final
                             // superclass method
    System.out.println("Another thing.");
  }
}
```

Attempting to compile the preceding code gives us something like this:

```
%javac FinalTest.java
FinalTest.java:5: The method void showSample() declared in class
SubClass cannot override the final method of the same signature
declared in class SuperClass.
Final methods cannot be overridden.
    public void showSample() { }
1 error
```

Final Arguments

Method arguments are the variable declarations that appear in between the parentheses in a method declaration. A typical method declaration with multiple arguments looks like this:

```
public Record getRecord(int fileNumber, int recNumber) {}
```

Method arguments are essentially the same as local variables. In the preceding example, the variables `fileNumber` and `recNumber` will both follow all the rules applied to local variables. This means they can also have the modifier `final`:

```
public Record getRecord(int fileNumber, final int recordNumber) {}
```

In this example, the variable `recNumber` is declared as `final`, which of course means it can't be modified within the method. In this case, "modified" means reassigning a new value to the variable. In other words, a `final` argument must keep the same value that the parameter had when it was passed into the method.

Abstract Methods

An abstract method is a method that's been *declared* (as `abstract`) but not *implemented*. In other words, the method contains no functional code. And if you recall from the earlier section "Abstract Classes," an abstract method declaration doesn't even have curly braces for where the implementation code goes, but instead closes with a semicolon. In other words, *it has no method body*. You mark a method `abstract` when you want to force subclasses to provide the implementation. For example, if you write an abstract class Car with a method goUpHill(), you might want to force each subtype of Car to define its own goUpHill() behavior, specific to that particular type of car.

```
public abstract void showSample();
```

Notice that the abstract method ends with a semicolon instead of curly braces. **It is illegal to have even a single abstract method in a class that is not explicitly declared `abstract`!** Look at the following illegal class:

```
public class IllegalClass{
  public abstract void doIt();
}
```

The preceding class will produce the following error if you try to compile it:

```
IllegalClass.java:1: class IllegalClass must be declared
abstract.
It does not define void doIt() from class IllegalClass.
public class IllegalClass{
1 error
```

You can, however, have an abstract class with no abstract methods. The following example will compile fine:

```
public abstract class LegalClass{
   void goodMethod() {
      // lots of real implementation code here
   }
}
```

In the preceding example, `goodMethod()` is not `abstract`. Three different clues tell you it's not an `abstract` method:

- The method is not marked `abstract`.
- The method declaration includes curly braces, as opposed to ending in a semicolon. In other words, the method has a method body.
- The method provides actual implementation code.

Any class that extends an `abstract` class must implement all `abstract` methods of the superclass, unless the subclass is *also* `abstract`. The rule is this:

The first concrete subclass of an abstract class must implement *all* abstract methods of the superclass.

Concrete just means nonabstract, so if you have an abstract class extending another abstract class, the abstract subclass doesn't need to provide implementations for the inherited abstract methods. Sooner or later, though, somebody's going to make a nonabstract subclass (in other words, a class that can be instantiated), and that subclass will have to implement all the abstract methods from up the inheritance tree. The following example demonstrates an inheritance tree with two abstract classes and one concrete class:

```
public abstract class Vehicle {
  private String type;
  public abstract void goUpHill();   // Abstract method
  public String getType() {          // Non-abstract method
    return type;
  }
}

public abstract class Car extends Vehicle {
  public abstract void goUpHill();   // Still abstract
  public void doCarThings() {
    // special car code goes here
  }
}

public class Mini extends Car {
  public void goUpHill() {
    // Mini-specific going uphill code
  }
}
```

So how many methods does class Mini have? Three. It inherits both the
getType() and doCarThings() methods, because they're public and concrete
(nonabstract). But because goUpHill() is abstract in the superclass Vehicle,
and is never implemented in the Car class (so it remains abstract), it means
class Mini—as the first concrete class below Vehicle   must implement the
goUpHill() method. In other words, class Mini can't pass the buck (of abstract
method implementation) to the next class down the inheritance tree, but class Car
can, since Car, like Vehicle, is abstract. Figure 1-5 illustrates the effects of the
abstract modifier on concrete and abstract subclasses.

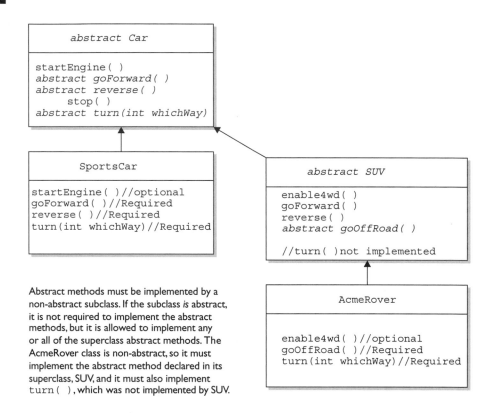

FIGURE 1-5 The effects of the `abstract` modifier on concrete and `abstract` subclasses

Look for concrete classes that don't provide method implementations for abstract methods of the superclass. The following code won't compile:

```
public abstract class A {
  abstract void foo();
}
class B extends A {
  void foo(int I) { }
}
```

Class B won't compile because it doesn't implement the inherited `abstract` method `foo()`. Although the `foo(int I)` method in class B might appear to be an implementation of the superclass' abstract method, it is simply an overloaded method (a method using the same identifier, but different arguments), so it doesn't fulfill the requirements for implementing the superclass' abstract method. We'll look at the differences between overloading and overriding in detail in Chapter 2.

A method can never, ever, ever be marked as both abstract and final, or both abstract and private. Think about it—abstract methods must be implemented (which essentially means overridden by a subclass) whereas final and private methods cannot ever be overridden by a subclass. Or to phrase it another way, an abstract designation means the superclass doesn't know anything about how the subclasses should behave in that method, whereas a final designation means the superclass knows everything about how all subclasses (however far down the inheritance tree they may be) should behave in that method. The abstract and final modifiers are virtually opposites. Because private methods cannot even be seen by a subclass (let alone inherited), they too cannot be overridden, so they too cannot be marked abstract.

Finally, you need to know that the abstract modifier can never be combined with the static modifier. We'll cover static methods later in this objective, but for now just remember that the following would be illegal:

```
abstract static void doStuff();
```

And it would give you an error that should be familiar by now:

```
MyClass.java:2· illegal combination of modifiers: abstract and
static
  abstract static void doStuff();
```

Synchronized Methods

The synchronized keyword indicates that a method can be accessed by only one thread at a time. We'll discuss this nearly to death in Chapter 9, but for now all we're concerned with is knowing that the synchronized modifier can be applied only to methods—not variables, not classes, just methods. A typical synchronized declaration looks like this:

```
public synchronized Record retrieveUserInfo(int id) { }
```

You should also know that the synchronized modifier can be matched with any of the four access control levels (which means it can be paired with any of the three access modifier keywords).

Native Methods

The native modifier indicates that a method is implemented in platform-dependent code, often in C. You don't need to know how to use native methods for the exam, other than knowing that native is a modifier (thus a reserved keyword) and that native can be applied only to *methods*—not classes, not variables, just methods. Note that a native method's body must be a semicolon (;) (like abstract methods), indicating that the implementation is omitted.

Strictfp Methods

We looked earlier at using strictfp as a class modifier, but even if you don't declare a class as strictfp, you can still declare an individual method as strictfp. Remember, strictfp forces floating points (and any floating-point operations) to adhere to the IEEE 754 standard. With strictfp, you can predict how your floating points will behave regardless of the underlying platform the JVM is running on. The downside is that if the underlying platform is capable of supporting greater precision, a strictfp method won't be able to take advantage of it.

You'll want to study the IEEE 754 if you need something to help you fall asleep. For the exam, however, you don't need to know anything about strictfp other than what it's used for, that it can modify a class or method declaration, and that a variable can never be declared strictfp.

Methods with Variable Argument Lists (var-args)

As of 5.0, Java allows you to create methods that can take a variable number of arguments. Depending on where you look, you might hear this capability referred to as "variable-length argument lists," "variable arguments," "var-args," "varargs," or our personal favorite (from the department of obfuscation), "variable arity parameter." They're all the same thing, and we'll use the term "var-args" from here on out.

As a bit of background, we'd like to clarify how we're going to use the terms "argument" and "parameter" throughout this book.

- **arguments** The things you specify between the parentheses when you're *invoking* a method:

```
doStuff("a", 2);  // invoking doStuff, so a & 2 are arguments
```

- **parameters** The things in the *method's signature* that indicate what the method must receive when it's invoked:

```
void doStuff(String s, int a) { } // we're expecting two
                                  // parameters: String and int
```

We'll cover using var-arg methods more in the next few chapters, for now let's review the declaration rules for var-args:

- **Var-arg type** When you declare a var-arg parameter, you must specify the type of the argument(s) this parameter of your method can receive. (This can be a primitive type or an object type.)
- **Basic syntax** To declare a method using a var-arg parameter, you follow the type with an ellipsis (...), a space, and then the name of the array that will hold the parameters received.
- **Other parameters** It's legal to have other parameters in a method that uses a var-arg.
- **Var-args limits** The var-arg must be the last parameter in the method's signature, and you can have only one var-arg in a method.

Let's look at some legal and illegal var-arg declarations:

Legal:

```
void doStuff(int... x) { }  // expects from 0 to many ints
                            // as parameters
void doStuff2(char c, int... x)  { }  // expects first a char,
                                      // then 0 to many ints
void doStuff3(Animal... animal) { }    // 0 to many Animals
```

Illegal:

```
void doStuff4(int x...) { }              // bad syntax
void doStuff5(int... x, char... y) { }  // too many var-args
void doStuff6(String... s, byte b) { }  // var-arg must be last
```

Constructor Declarations

In Java, objects are constructed. Every time you make a new object, at least one constructor is invoked. Every class has a constructor, although if you don't create one explicitly, the compiler will build one for you. There are tons of rules concerning constructors, and we're saving our detailed discussion for Chapter 2. For now, let's focus on the basic declaration rules. Here's a simple example:

```
class Foo {
   protected Foo() { }          // this is Foo's constructor

   protected void Foo() { }     // this is a badly named,
                                // but legal, method
}
```

The first thing to notice is that constructors look an awful lot like methods. A key difference is that a constructor can't ever, ever, ever, have a return type...ever! Constructor declarations can however have all of the normal access modifiers, and they can take arguments (including var-args), just like methods. The other BIG RULE, to understand about constructors is that they must have the same name as the class in which they are declared. Constructors can't be marked static (they are after all associated with object instantiation), they can't be marked final or abstract (because they can't be overridden). Here are some legal and illegal constructor declarations:

```
class Foo2 {

   // legal constructors

   Foo2() { }
   private Foo2(byte b) { }
   Foo2(int x) { }
   Foo2(int x, int... y) { }

   // illegal constructors

   void Foo2() { }              // it's a method, not a constructor
   Foo() { }                    // not a method or a constructor
   Foo2(short s);               // looks like an abstract method
   static Foo2(float f) { }     // can't be static
   final Foo2(long x) { }       // can't be final
   abstract Foo2(char c) { }    // can't be abstract
   Foo2(int... x, int t) { }    // bad var-arg syntax
}
```

Variable Declarations

There are two types of variables in Java:

- **Primitives**   A primitive can be one of eight types: `char`, `boolean`, `byte`, `short`, `int`, `long`, `double`, or `float`. Once a primitive has been declared, its primitive type can never change, although in most cases its value can change.

- **Reference variables**   A reference variable is used to refer to (or access) an object. A reference variable is declared to be of a specific type and that type can never be changed. A reference variable can be used to refer to any object of the declared type, or of a *subtype* of the declared type (a compatible type). We'll talk a lot more about using a reference variable to refer to a subtype in Chapter 2, when we discuss polymorphism.

Declaring Primitives and Primitive Ranges

Primitive variables can be declared as class variables (statics), instance variables, method parameters, or local variables. You can declare one or more primitives, of the same primitive type, in a single line. In Chapter 3 we will discuss the various ways in which they can be initialized, but for now we'll leave you with a few examples of primitive variable declarations:

```
byte b;
boolean myBooleanPrimitive;
int x, y, z;                        // declare three int primitives
```

On previous versions of the exam you needed to know how to calculate ranges for all the Java primitives. For the current exam, you can skip some of that detail, but it's still important to understand that for the integer types the sequence from small to big is `byte`, `short`, `int`, `long`, and that `doubles` are bigger than `floats`.

You will also need to know that the number types (both integer and floating-point types) are all signed, and how that affects their ranges. First, let's review the concepts.

All six number types in Java are made up of a certain number of 8-bit bytes, and are *signed*, meaning they can be negative or positive. The leftmost bit (the most significant digit) is used to represent the sign, where a 1 means negative and 0 means positive, as shown in Figure 1-6. The rest of the bits represent the value, using two's complement notation.

FIGURE 1-6 The Sign bit for a byte

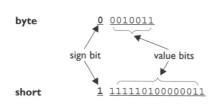

byte

    0 0010011

sign bit   value bits

short

    1 111110100000011

sign bit: 0 = positive
      1 = negative

value bits:

byte: 7 bits can represent 2^7 or 128 different values: 0 thru 127 -or- −128 thru −1

short: 15 bits can represent 2^{15} or 32768 values: 0 thru 32767 -or- −32768 thru −1

Table 1-3 shows the primitive types with their sizes and ranges. Figure 1-6 shows that with a byte, for example, there are 256 possible numbers (or 2^8). Half of these are negative, and half -1 are positive. The positive range is one less than the negative range because the number zero is stored as a positive binary number. We use the formula $-2^{(bits-1)}$ to calculate the negative range, and we use $2^{(bits-1)}-1$ for the positive range. Again, if you know the first two columns of this table, you'll be in good shape for the exam.

TABLE 1-3 Ranges of Numeric Primitives

Type	Bits	Bytes	Minimum Range	Maximum Range
byte	8	1	-2^7	2^7-1
short	16	2	-2^{15}	$2^{15}-1$
int	32	4	-2^{31}	$2^{31}-1$
long	64	8	-2^{63}	$2^{63}-1$
float	32	4	n/a	n/a
double	64	8	n/a	n/a

The range for floating-point numbers is complicated to determine, but luckily you don't need to know these for the exam (although you are expected to know that a double holds 64 bits and a float 32).

For `boolean` types there is not a range; a `boolean` can be only `true` or `false`. If someone asks you for the bit depth of a `boolean`, look them straight in the eye and say, "That's virtual-machine dependent." They'll be impressed.

The `char` type (a character) contains a single, 16-bit Unicode character. Although the extended ASCII set known as ISO Latin-1 needs only 8 bits (256 different characters), a larger range is needed to represent characters found in languages other than English. Unicode characters are actually represented by unsigned 16-bit integers, which means 2^{16} possible values, ranging from 0 to 65535 (2^{16}) 1. You'll learn in Chapter 3 that because a `char` is really an integer type, it can be assigned to any number type large enough to hold 65535 (which means anything larger than a `short`. Although both `char`s and `short`s are 16-bit types, remember that a `short` uses 1 bit to represent the sign, so fewer positive numbers are acceptable in a short).

Declaring Reference Variables

Reference variables can be declared as static variables, instance variables, method parameters, or local variables. You can declare one or more reference variables, of the same type, in a single line. In Chapter 3 we will discuss the various ways in which they can be initialized, but for now we'll leave you with a few examples of reference variable declarations:

```
Object o;
Dog myNewDogReferenceVariable;
String s1, s2, s3;                    // declare three String vars.
```

Instance Variables

Instance variables are defined inside the class, but outside of any method, and are only initialized when the class is instantiated. Instance variables are the fields that belong to each unique object. For example, the following code defines fields (instance variables) for the name, title, and manager for employee objects:

```
class Employee {
   // define fields (instance variables) for employee instances
   private String name;
   private String title,
```

```
        private String manager;
        // other code goes here including access methods for private
        // fields
}
```

The preceding Employee class says that each employee instance will know its own name, title, and manager. In other words, each instance can have its own unique values for those three fields. If you see the term "field," "instance variable," "property," or "attribute," they mean virtually the same thing. (There actually are subtle but occasionally important distinctions between the terms, but those distinctions aren't used on the exam.)

For the exam, you need to know that instance variables

- Can use any of the four access *levels* (which means they can be marked with any of the three access *modifiers*)
- Can be marked `final`
- Can be marked `transient`
- Cannot be marked `abstract`
- Cannot be marked `synchronized`
- Cannot be marked `strictfp`
- Cannot be marked `native`
- Cannot be marked `static`, because then they'd become class variables.

We've already covered the effects of applying access control to instance variables (it works the same way as it does for member methods). A little later in this chapter we'll look at what it means to apply the `final` or `transient` modifier to an instance variable. First, though, we'll take a quick look at the difference between instance and local variables. Figure 1-7 compares the way in which modifiers can be applied to methods vs. variables.

FIGURE 1-7 Comparison of modifiers on variables vs. methods

	Local Variables	Variables (non-local)	Methods
	final	final public protected private static transient volatile	final public protected private static abstract synchronized strictfp native

Local (Automatic/Stack/Method) Variables

Local variables are variables declared within a method. That means the variable is not just initialized within the method, but also declared within the method. Just as the local variable starts its life inside the method, it's also destroyed when the method has completed. Local variables are always on the stack, not the heap. (We'll talk more about the stack and the heap in Chapter 3). Although the value of the variable might be passed into, say, another method that then stores the value in an instance variable, the variable itself lives only within the scope of the method.

Just don't forget that while the local variable is on the stack, if the variable is an object reference, the object itself will still be created on the heap. There is no such thing as a stack object, only a stack variable. You'll often hear programmers use the phrase, "local object," but what they really mean is, "locally declared reference variable." So if you hear a programmer use that expression, you'll know that he's just too lazy to phrase it in a technically precise way. You can tell him we said that—unless he knows where we live.

Local variable declarations can't use most of the modifiers that can be applied to instance variables, such as `public` (or the other access modifiers), `transient`, `volatile`, `abstract`, or `static`, but as we saw earlier, local variables can be marked `final`. And as you'll learn in Chapter 3 (but here's a preview), before a local variable can be *used*, it must be *initialized* with a value. For instance:

```
class TestServer {
  public void logIn() {
    int count = 10;
  }
}
```

Typically, you'll initialize a local variable in the same line in which you declare it, although you might still need to reinitialize it later in the method. The key is to remember that a local variable must be initialized before you try to use it. The compiler will reject any code that tries to use a local variable that hasn't been assigned a value, because—unlike instance variables—local variables don't get default values.

A local variable can't be referenced in any code outside the method in which it's declared. In the preceding code example, it would be impossible to refer to the variable count anywhere else in the class except within the scope of the method logIn(). Again, that's not to say that the value of count can't be passed out of the method to take on a new life. But the variable holding that value, count, can't be accessed once the method is complete, as the following illegal code demonstrates:

```
class TestServer {
  public void logIn() {
    int count = 10;
  }
  public void doSomething(int i) {
    count = i;  // Won't compile! Can't access count outside
                // method logIn()
  }
}
```

It is possible to declare a local variable with the same name as an instance variable. It's known as *shadowing*, as the following code demonstrates:

```
class TestServer {
   int count = 9;  // Declare an instance variable named count
   public void logIn() {
      int count = 10;  // Declare a local variable named count
      System.out.println("local variable count is " + count);
   }
   public void count() {
      System.out.println("instance variable count is " + count);
   }
   public static void main(String[] args) {
```

```
        new TestServer().logIn();
        new TestServer().count();
    }
}
```

The preceding code produces the following output:

```
local variable count is 10
instance variable count is 9
```

Why on earth (or the planet of your choice) would you want to do that? Normally, you won't. But one of the more common reasons is to name a parameter with the same name as the instance variable to which the parameter will be assigned.

The following (wrong) code is trying to set an instance variable's value using a parameter:

```
class Foo {
    int size = 27;
    public void setSize(int size) {
        size = size;  // ??? which size equals which size???
    }
}
```

So you've decided that—for overall readability—you want to give the parameter the same name as the instance variable its value is destined for, but how do you resolve the naming collision? Use the keyword this. The keyword this always, always, always refers to the object currently running. The following code shows this in action:

```
class Foo {
 int size = 27;
 public void setSize(int size) {
    this.size = size;  // this.size means the current object's
                       // instance variable, size. The size
                       // on the right is the parameter

    }
}
```

Array Declarations

In Java, arrays are objects that store multiple variables of the same type, or variables that are all subclasses of the same type. Arrays can hold either primitives or object references, but the array itself will always be an object on the heap, even if the array is declared to hold primitive elements. In other words, there is no such thing as a primitive array, but you can make an array of primitives.

For the exam, you need to know three things:

- How to make an array reference variable (declare)
- How to make an array object (construct)
- How to populate the array with elements (initialize)

For this objective, you only need to know how to declare an array, we'll cover constructing and initializing arrays in Chapter 3.

Arrays are efficient, but many times you'll want to use one of the Collection types from java.util (including HashMap, ArrayList, and TreeSet). Collection classes offer more flexible ways to access an object (for insertion, deletion, reading, and so on) and unlike arrays, can expand or contract dynamically as you add or remove elements. There's a Collection type for a wide range of needs. Do you need a fast sort? A group of objects with no duplicates? A way to access a name-value pair? Chapter 7 covers them in more detail.

Arrays are declared by stating the type of elements the array will hold (an object or a primitive), followed by square brackets to either side of the identifier.

Declaring an Array of Primitives

```
int[] key;  // Square brackets before name (recommended)
int key []; // Square brackets after name (legal but less
            // readable)
```

Declaring an Array of Object References

```
Thread[] threads;  // Recommended
Thread threads []; // Legal but less readable
```

When declaring an array reference, you should always put the array brackets immediately after the declared type, rather than after the identifier (variable name). That way, anyone reading the code can easily tell that, for example, key *is a reference to an* int *array object, and not an* int *primitive.*

We can also declare multidimensional arrays, which are in fact arrays of arrays. This can be done in the following manner:

```
String[][][] occupantName;
String[] managerName [];
```

The first example is a three-dimensional array (an array of arrays of arrays) and the second is a two-dimensional array. Notice in the second example we have one square bracket before the variable name and one after. This is perfectly legal to the compiler, proving once again that just because it's legal doesn't mean it's right.

exam
ⓦatch

It is never legal to include the size of the array in your declaration. Yes, we know you can do that in some other languages, which is why you might see a question or two that include code similar to the following:

```
int[5] scores;
```

The preceding code won't compile. Remember, the JVM doesn't allocate space until you actually instantiate the array object. That's when size matters.

In Chapter 3, we'll spend a lot of time discussing arrays, how to initialize and use them, and how to deal with multi-dimensional arrays...stay tuned!

Final Variables

Declaring a variable with the `final` keyword makes it impossible to reinitialize that variable once it has been initialized with an explicit value (notice we said explicit rather than default). For primitives, this means that once the variable is assigned a value, the value can't be altered. For example, if you assign 10 to the `int` variable x, then x is going to stay 10, forever. So that's straightforward for primitives, but what does it mean to have a `final` object reference variable? A reference variable marked `final` can't ever be reassigned to refer to a different object. The data within the object can be modified, but the reference variable cannot be changed. In other words, a `final` reference still allows you to modify the state of the object it refers to, but you can't modify the reference variable to make it refer to a different object. Burn this in: there are no `final` objects, only `final` references. We'll explain this in more detail in Chapter 3.

We've now covered how the `final` modifier can be applied to classes, methods, and variables. Figure 1-8 highlights the key points and differences of the various applications of `final`.

FIGURE 1-8   Effect of `final` on variables, methods, and classes

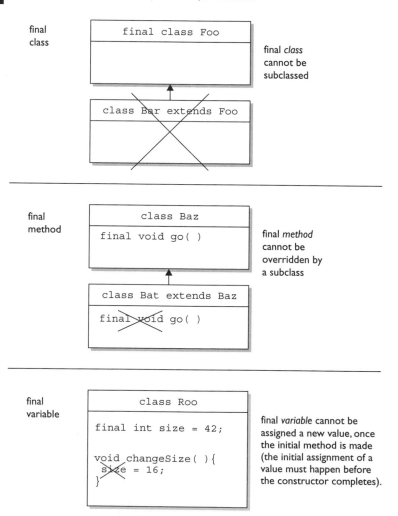

Transient Variables

If you mark an instance variable as `transient`, you're telling the JVM to skip (ignore) this variable when you attempt to serialize the object containing it. Serialization is one of the coolest features of Java; it lets you save (sometimes called "flatten") an object by writing its state (in other words, the value of its instance variables) to a special type of I/O stream. With serialization you can save an object to a file, or even ship it over a wire for reinflating (deserializing) at the other end, in another JVM. Serialization has been added to the exam as of Java 5, and we'll cover it in great detail in Chapter 6.

Volatile Variables

The `volatile` modifier tells the JVM that a thread accessing the variable must always reconcile its own private copy of the variable with the master copy in memory. Say what? Don't worry about it. For the exam, all you need to know about `volatile` is that, as with `transient`, it can be applied only to instance variables. Make no mistake, the idea of multiple threads accessing an instance variable is scary stuff, and very important for any Java programmer to understand. But as you'll see in Chapter 9, you'll probably use synchronization, rather than the `volatile` modifier, to make your data thread-safe.

The `volatile` *modifier may also be applied to project managers :)*

Static Variables and Methods

The `static` modifier is used to create variables and methods that will exist independently of any instances created for the class. All `static` members exist before you ever make a new instance of a class, and there will be only one copy of a `static` member regardless of the number of instances of that class. In other words, all instances of a given class share the same value for any given `static` variable. We'll cover `static` members in great detail in the next chapter.

Things you can mark as `static`:

- Methods
- Variables
- A class nested within another class, but not within a method (more on this in Chapter 8).
- Initialization blocks

Things you can't mark as `static`:

- Constructors (makes no sense; a constructor is used only to create instances)
- Classes (unless they are nested)
- Interfaces
- Method local inner classes (we'll explore this in Chapter 8)
- Inner class methods and instance variables
- Local variables

Declaring Enums

As of 5.0, Java lets you restrict a variable to having one of only a few pre-defined values—in other words, one value from an enumerated list. (The items in the enumerated list are called, surprisingly, `enums`.)

Using enums can help reduce the bugs in your code. For instance, in your coffee shop application you might want to restrict your size selections to BIG, HUGE, and OVERWHELMING. If you let an order for a LARGE or a GRANDE slip in, it might cause an error. Enums to the rescue. With the following simple declaration, you can guarantee that the compiler will stop you from assigning anything to a `CoffeeSize` except BIG, HUGE, or OVERWHELMING:

```
enum CoffeeSize { BIG, HUGE, OVERWHELMING };
```

From then on, the only way to get a `CoffeeSize` will be with a statement something like this:

```
CoffeeSize cs = CoffeeSize.BIG;
```

It's not required that `enum` constants be in all caps, but borrowing from the Sun code convention that constants are named in caps, it's a good idea.

The basic components of an `enum` are its constants (i.e., BIG, HUGE, and OVERWHELMING), although in a minute you'll see that there can be a lot more to an enum. Enums can be declared as their own separate class, or as a class member, however they must not be declared within a method!

Declaring an enum *outside* a class:

```
enum CoffeeSize { BIG, HUGE, OVERWHELMING }  // this cannot be
                                             // private or protected

class Coffee {
   CoffeeSize size;
}

public class CoffeeTest1 {
   public static void main(String[] args) {
      Coffee drink = new Coffee();
      drink.size = CoffeeSize.BIG;         // enum outside class
   }
}
```

The preceding code can be part of a single file. (Remember, the file must be named CoffeeTest1.java because that's the name of the public class in the file.) The key point to remember is that an enum that isn't enclosed in a class can be declared with only the public or default modifier, just like a non-inner class. Here's an example of declaring an enum *inside* a class:

```
class Coffee2 {
  enum CoffeeSize {BIG, HUGE, OVERWHELMING }

  CoffeeSize size;
}

public class CoffeeTest2 {
  public static void main(String[] args) {
    Coffee2 drink = new Coffee2();
    drink.size = Coffee2.CoffeeSize.BIG;   // enclosing class
                                           // name required
  }
}
```

The key points to take away from these examples are that enums can be declared as their own class, or enclosed in another class, and that the syntax for accessing an enum's members depends on where the enum was declared.

The following is NOT legal:

```
public class CoffeeTest1 {
  public static void main(String[] args) {
    enum CoffeeSize { BIG, HUGE, OVERWHELMING } // WRONG! Cannot
                                                 // declare enums
                                                 // in methods

    Coffee drink = new Coffee();
    drink.size = CoffeeSize.BIG;
  }
}
```

To make it more confusing for you, the Java language designers made it optional to put a semicolon at the end of the enum declaration (when no other declarations for this enum follow):

```
public class CoffeeTest1 {

  enum CoffeeSize { BIG, HUGE, OVERWHELMING }; // <--semicolon
                                               // is optional here
  public static void main(String[] args) {
    Coffee drink = new Coffee();
    drink.size = CoffeeSize.BIG;
  }
}
```

So what gets created when you make an enum? The most important thing to remember is that enums are not Strings or ints! Each of the enumerated CoffeeSize types are actually instances of CoffeeSize. In other words, BIG is of type CoffeeSize. Think of an enum as a kind of class, that looks something (but not exactly) like this:

```
// conceptual example of how you can think
// about enums

class CoffeeSize {
    public static final CoffeeSize BIG =
                            new CoffeeSize("BIG", 0);
    public static final CoffeeSize HUGE =
                            new CoffeeSize("HUGE", 1);
    public static final CoffeeSize OVERWHELMING =
                            new CoffeeSize("OVERWHELMING", 2);
```

```
public CoffeeSize(String enumName, int index) {
    // stuff here
  }
  public static void main(String[] args) {
    System.out.println(CoffeeSize.BIG);
  }
}
```

Notice how each of the enumerated values, BIG, HUGE, and OVERWHELMING, are instances of type CoffeeSize. They're represented as `static` and `final`, which in the Java world, is thought of as a constant. Also notice that each enum value knows its index or position...in other words, the order in which enum values are declared matters. You can think of the CoffeeSize enums as existing in an array of type CoffeeSize, and as you'll see in a later chapter, you can iterate through the values of an enum by invoking the `values()` method on any enum type. (Don't worry about that in this chapter.)

Declaring Constructors, Methods, and Variables in an enum

Because an enum really is a special kind of class, you can do more than just list the enumerated constant values. You can add constructors, instance variables, methods, and something really strange known as a *constant specific class body*. To understand why you might need more in your enum, think about this scenario: imagine you want to know the actual size, in ounces, that map to each of the three CoffeeSize constants. For example, you want to know that BIG is 8 ounces, HUGE is 10 ounces, and OVERWHELMING is a whopping 16 ounces.

You could make some kind of a lookup table, using some other data structure, but that would be a poor design and hard to maintain. The simplest way is to treat your enum values (BIG, HUGE, and OVERWHELMING), as objects that can each have their own instance variables. Then you can assign those values at the time the enums are initialized, by passing a value to the enum constructor. This takes a little explaining, but first look at the following code:

```
enum CoffeeSize {
    // 8, 10 & 16 are passed to the constructor
    BIG(8), HUGE(10), OVERWHELMING(16);
    CoffeeSize(int ounces) { // constructor
      this.ounces = ounces;
    }

    private int ounces;      // an instance variable
    public int getOunces() {
```

```
        return ounces;
      }
  }

class Coffee {
    CoffeeSize size;      // each instance of Coffee has an enum

    public static void main(String[] args) {
       Coffee drink1 = new Coffee();
       drink1.size = CoffeeSize.BIG;

       Coffee drink2 = new Coffee();
       drink2.size = CoffeeSize.OVERWHELMING;

       System.out.println(drink1.size.getOunces()); // prints 8
       for(CoffeeSize cs: CoffeeSize.values())
          System.out.println(cs + " " + cs.getOunces());
    }
}
```

Which produces:

```
8
BIG 8
HUGE 10
OVERWHELMING 16
```

Note: Every enum has a static method, values(), that returns an array of the enum's values in the order they're declared.

The key points to remember about enum constructors are

- You can NEVER invoke an enum constructor directly. The enum constructor is invoked automatically, with the arguments you define after the constant value. For example, BIG(8) invokes the CoffeeSize constructor that takes an int, passing the int literal 8 to the constructor. (Behind the scenes, of course, you can imagine that BIG is also passed to the constructor, but we don't have to know—or care—about the details.)

- You can define more than one argument to the constructor, and you can overload the enum constructors, just as you can overload a normal class constructor. We discuss constructors in much more detail in Chapter 2. To initialize a CoffeeType with both the number of ounces and, say, a lid type, you'd pass two arguments to the constructor as BIG(8, "A"), which means you have a constructor in CoffeeSize that takes both an int and a String.

And finally, you can define something really strange in an enum that looks like an anonymous inner class (which we talk about in Chapter 8). It's known as a constant specific class body, and you use it when you need a particular constant to override a method defined in the enum.

Imagine this scenario: you want enums to have two methods—one for ounces and one for lid code (a String). Now imagine that most coffee sizes use the same lid code, "B", but the OVERWHELMING size uses type "A". You can define a getLidCode() method in the CoffeeSize enum that returns "B", but then you need a way to override it for OVERWHELMING. You don't want to do some hard-to-maintain if/then code in the getLidCode() method, so the best approach might be to somehow have the OVERWHELMING constant override the getLidCode() method.

This looks strange, but you need to understand the basic declaration rules:

```
enum CoffeeSize {
    BIG(8),
    HUGE(10),
    OVERWHELMING(16) {      // start a code block that defines
                            // the "body" for this constant

      public String getLidCode() {    // override the method
                                       // defined in CoffeeSize

        return "A";
      }
    };    // the semicolon is REQUIRED when more code follows

    CoffeeSize(int ounces) {
      this.ounces = ounces;
    }

  private int ounces;

  public int getOunces() {
    return ounces;
  }
  public String getLidCode() {  // this method is overridden
                                // by the OVERWHELMING constant

    return "B";    // the default value we want to return for
                   // CoffeeSize constants

  }
}
```

CERTIFICATION SUMMARY

After absorbing the material in this chapter, you should be familiar with some of the nuances of the Java language. You may also be experiencing confusion around why you ever wanted to take this exam in the first place. That's normal at this point. If you hear yourself saying, "What was I thinking?" just lie down until it passes. We would like to tell you that it gets easier...that this was the toughest chapter and it's all downhill from here...

Let's briefly review what you'll need to know for the exam.

There will be many questions dealing with keywords indirectly, so be sure you can identify which are keywords and which aren't.

Although naming conventions like the use of camelCase won't be on the exam directly, you will need to understand the basics of JavaBeans naming, which uses camelCase.

You need to understand the rules associated with creating legal identifiers, and the rules associated with source code declarations, including the use of `package` and `import` statements.

You now have a good understanding of access control as it relates to classes, methods, and variables. You've looked at how access modifiers (`public`, `protected`, and `private`) define the access control of a class or member.

You learned that `abstract` classes can contain both `abstract` and nonabstract methods, but that if even a single method is marked `abstract`, the class must be marked `abstract`. Don't forget that a concrete (nonabstract) subclass of an `abstract` class must provide implementations for all the `abstract` methods of the superclass, but that an `abstract` class does not have to implement the `abstract` methods from its superclass. An `abstract` subclass can "pass the buck" to the first concrete subclass.

We covered interface implementation. Remember that interfaces can extend another interface (even multiple interfaces), and that any class that implements an interface must implement all methods from all the interfaces in the inheritance tree of the interface the class is implementing.

You've also looked at the other modifiers including `static`, `final`, `abstract`, `synchronized`, and so on. You've learned how some modifiers can never be combined in a declaration, such as mixing `abstract` with either `final` or `private`.

Keep in mind that there are no `final` objects in Java. A reference variable marked `final` can never be changed, but the object it refers to can be modified.

You've seen that `final` applied to methods means a subclass can't override them, and when applied to a class, the final class can't be subclassed.

Remember that as of Java 5, methods can be declared with a var-arg parameter (which can take from zero to many arguments of the declared type), but that you can have only one var-arg per method, and it must be the method's last parameter.

Make sure you're familiar with the relative sizes of the numeric primitives. Remember that while the values of non-final variables can change, a reference variable's type can never change.

You also learned that arrays are objects that contain many variables of the same type. Arrays can also contain other arrays.

Remember what you've learned about `static` variables and methods, especially that `static` members are per-class as opposed to per-instance. Don't forget that a `static` method can't directly access an instance variable from the class it's in, because it doesn't have an explicit reference to any particular instance of the class.

Finally, we covered a feature new to Java 5, enums. An `enum` is a much safer and more flexible way to implement constants than was possible in earlier versions of Java. Because they are a special kind of class, enums can be declared very simply, or they can be quite complex—including such attributes as methods, variables, constructors, and a special type of inner class called a constant specific class body.

Before you hurl yourself at the practice test, spend some time with the following optimistically named "Two-Minute Drill." Come back to this particular drill often, as you work through this book and especially when you're doing that last-minute cramming. Because—and here's the advice you wished your mother had given you before you left for college—it's not what you know, it's when you know it.

For the exam, knowing what you can't do with the Java language is just as important as knowing what you can do. Give the sample questions a try! They're very similar to the difficulty and structure of the real exam questions, and should be an eye opener for how difficult the exam can be. Don't worry if you get a lot of them wrong. If you find a topic that you are weak in, spend more time reviewing and studying. Many programmers need two or three serious passes through a chapter (or an individual objective) before they can answer the questions confidently.

TWO-MINUTE DRILL

Remember that in this chapter, when we talk about classes, we're referring to non-inner classes, or *top-level* classes. We'll devote all of Chapter 8 to inner classes.

Identifiers (Objective 1.3)

❑ Identifiers can begin with a letter, an underscore, or a currency character.

❑ After the first character, identifiers can also include digits.

❑ Identifiers can be of any length.

❑ JavaBeans methods must be named using camelCase, and depending on the method's purpose, must start with `set`, `get`, `is`, `add`, or `remove`.

Declaration Rules (Objective 1.1)

❑ A source code file can have only one `public` class.

❑ If the source file contains a `public` class, the filename must match the `public` class name.

❑ A file can have only one `package` statement, but multiple `imports`.

❑ The `package` statement (if any) must be the first (non-comment) line in a source file.

❑ The `import` statements (if any) must come after the `package` and before the class declaration.

❑ If there is no `package` statement, `import` statements must be the first (non-comment) statements in the source file.

❑ `package` and `import` statements apply to all classes in the file.

❑ A file can have more than one nonpublic class.

❑ Files with no `public` classes have no naming restrictions.

Class Access Modifiers (Objective 1.1)

❑ There are three access modifiers: `public`, `protected`, and `private`.

❑ There are four access levels: public, protected, default, and private.

❑ Classes can have only `public` or default access.

❑ A class with default access can be seen only by classes within the same package.

❑ A class with `public` access can be seen by all classes from all packages.

❑ Class visibility revolves around whether code in one class can
  ❑ Create an instance of another class
  ❑ Extend (or subclass), another class
  ❑ Access methods and variables of another class

Class Modifiers (Nonaccess) (Objective 1.2)

❑ Classes can also be modified with `final`, `abstract`, or `strictfp`.
❑ A class cannot be both `final` and `abstract`.
❑ A `final` class cannot be subclassed.
❑ An `abstract` class cannot be instantiated.
❑ A single `abstract` method in a class means the whole class must be abstract.
❑ An `abstract` class can have both `abstract` and nonabstract methods.
❑ The first concrete class to extend an `abstract` class must implement all of its `abstract` methods.

Interface Implementation (Objective 1.2)

❑ Interfaces are contracts for what a class can do, but they say nothing about the way in which the class must do it.
❑ Interfaces can be implemented by any class, from any inheritance tree.
❑ An interface is like a 100-percent `abstract` class, and is implicitly abstract whether you type the `abstract` modifier in the declaration or not.
❑ An interface can have only abstract methods, no concrete methods allowed.
❑ Interface methods are by default `public` and `abstract`—explicit declaration of these modifiers is optional.
❑ Interfaces can have constants, which are always implicitly `public`, `static`, and `final`.
❑ Interface constant declarations of `public`, `static`, and `final` are optional in any combination.
❑ A legal nonabstract implementing class has the following properties:
  ❑ It provides concrete implementations for the interface's methods.
  ❑ It must follow all legal override rules for the methods it implements.
  ❑ It must not declare any new checked exceptions for an implementation method.

❑ It must not declare any checked exceptions that are broader than the exceptions declared in the interface method.

❑ It may declare runtime exceptions on any interface method implementation regardless of the interface declaration.

❑ It must maintain the exact signature (allowing for covariant returns) and return type of the methods it implements (but does not have to declare the exceptions of the interface).

❑ A class implementing an interface can itself be `abstract`.

❑ An `abstract` implementing class does not have to implement the interface methods (but the first concrete subclass must).

❑ A class can extend only one class (no multiple inheritance), but it can implement many interfaces.

❑ Interfaces can extend one or more other interfaces.

❑ Interfaces cannot extend a class, or implement a class or interface.

❑ When taking the exam, verify that interface and class declarations are legal before verifying other code logic.

Member Access Modifiers (Objectives 1.3 and 1.4)

❑ Methods and instance (nonlocal) variables are known as "members."

❑ Members can use all four access levels: public, protected, default, private.

❑ Member access comes in two forms:

   ❑ Code in one class can access a member of another class.

   ❑ A subclass can inherit a member of its superclass.

❑ If a class cannot be accessed, its members cannot be accessed.

❑ Determine class visibility before determining member visibility.

❑ `public` members can be accessed by all other classes, even in other packages.

❑ If a superclass member is public, the subclass inherits it—regardless of package.

❑ Members accessed without the dot operator (.) must belong to the same class.

❑ `this.` always refers to the currently executing object.

❑ `this.aMethod()` is the same as just invoking `aMethod()`.

❑ `private` members can be accessed only by code in the same class.

❑ `private` members are not visible to subclasses, so private members cannot be inherited.

❑ Default and `protected` members differ only when subclasses are involved:

    ❑ Default members can be accessed only by classes in the same package.

    ❑ `protected` members can be accessed by other classes in the same package, plus subclasses regardless of package.

    ❑ `protected` = package plus kids (kids meaning subclasses).

    ❑ For subclasses outside the package, the `protected` member can be accessed only through inheritance; a subclass outside the package cannot access a `protected` member by using a reference to a superclass instance (in other words, inheritance is the only mechanism for a subclass outside the package to access a `protected` member of its superclass).

    ❑ A `protected` member inherited by a subclass from another package is not accessible to any other class in the subclass package, except for the subclass' own subclasses.

Local Variables (Objective 1.3)

❑ Local (method, automatic, or stack) variable declarations cannot have access modifiers.

❑ `final` is the only modifier available to local variables.

❑ Local variables don't get default values, so they must be initialized before use.

Other Modifiers—Members (Objective 1.3)

❑ `final` methods cannot be overridden in a subclass.

❑ `abstract` methods are declared, with a signature, a return type, and an optional throws clause, but are not implemented.

❑ `abstract` methods end in a semicolon—no curly braces.

❑ Three ways to spot a non-abstract method:

    ❑ The method is not marked `abstract`.

    ❑ The method has curly braces.

    ❑ The method has code between the curly braces.

❑ The first nonabstract (concrete) class to extend an `abstract` class must implement all of the `abstract` class' `abstract` methods.

❑ The `synchronized` modifier applies only to methods and code blocks.

❑ `synchronized` methods can have any access control and can also be marked `final`.

❑ `abstract` methods must be implemented by a subclass, so they must be inheritable. For that reason:

  ❑ `abstract` methods cannot be `private`.

  ❑ `abstract` methods cannot be `final`.

❑ The `native` modifier applies only to methods.

❑ The `strictfp` modifier applies only to classes and methods.

Methods with var-args (Objective 1.4)

❑ As of Java 5, methods can declare a parameter that accepts from zero to many arguments, a so-called var-arg method.

❑ A var-arg parameter is declared with the syntax `type... name`; for instance: `doStuff(int... x) { }`

❑ A var-arg method can have only one var-arg parameter.

❑ In methods with normal parameters and a var-arg, the var-arg must come last.

Variable Declarations (Objective 1.3)

❑ Instance variables can

  ❑ Have any access control

  ❑ Be marked `final` or `transient`

❑ Instance variables can't be `abstract`, `synchronized`, `native`, or `strictfp`.

❑ It is legal to declare a local variable with the same name as an instance variable; this is called "shadowing."

❑ `final` variables have the following properties:

  ❑ `final` variables cannot be reinitialized once assigned a value.

  ❑ `final` reference variables cannot refer to a different object once the object has been assigned to the `final` variable.

  ❑ `final` reference variables must be initialized before the constructor completes.

❑ There is no such thing as a `final` object. An object reference marked `final` does not mean the object itself is immutable.

❑ The `transient` modifier applies only to instance variables.

❑ The `volatile` modifier applies only to instance variables.

Array Declarations (Objective 1.3)

❑ Arrays can hold primitives or objects, but the array itself is always an object.

❑ When you declare an array, the brackets can be to the left or right of the variable name.

❑ It is never legal to include the size of an array in the declaration.

❑ An array of objects can hold any object that passes the IS-A (or instanceof) test for the declared type of the array. For example, if Horse extends Animal, then a Horse object can go into an Animal array.

Static Variables and Methods (Objective 1.4)

❑ They are not tied to any particular instance of a class.

❑ No classes instances are needed in order to use `static` members of the class.

❑ There is only one copy of a `static` variable / class and all instances share it.

❑ `static` methods do not have direct access to non-static members.

Enums (Objective 1.3)

❑ An `enum` specifies a list of constant values assigned to a type.

❑ An `enum` is NOT a String or an int; an enum constant's type is the enum type. For example, SUMMER and FALL are of the enum type Season.

❑ An `enum` can be declared outside or inside a class, but NOT in a method.

❑ An `enum` declared outside a class must NOT be marked `static`, `final`, `abstract`, `protected`, or `private`.

❑ Enums can contain constructors, methods, variables, and constant class bodies.

❑ `enum` constants can send arguments to the enum constructor, using the syntax BIG(8), where the int literal 8 is passed to the enum constructor.

❑ `enum` constructors can have arguments, and can be overloaded.

❑ `enum` constructors can NEVER be invoked directly in code. They are always called automatically when an `enum` is initialized.

❑ The semicolon at the end of an `enum` declaration is optional. These are legal:

```
enum Foo { ONE, TWO, THREE}
enum Foo { ONE, TWO, THREE};
```

❑ `MyEnum.values()` returns an array of `MyEnum`'s values.

SELF TEST

The following questions will help you measure your understanding of the material presented in this chapter. Read all of the choices carefully, as there may be more than one correct answer. Choose all correct answers for each question. Stay focused.

If you have a rough time with these at first, don't beat yourself up. Be positive. Repeat nice affirmations to yourself like, "I am smart enough to understand enums" and "OK, so that other guy knows enums better than I do, but I bet he can't <insert something you *are* good at> like me."

1. Which is true? (Choose all that apply.)

    A. "X extends Y" is correct if and only if X is a class and Y is an interface

    B. "X extends Y" is correct if and only if X is an interface and Y is a class

    C. "X extends Y" is correct if X and Y are either both classes or both interfaces

    D. "X extends Y" is correct for all combinations of X and Y being classes and/or interfaces

2. Which method names follow the JavaBeans standard? (Choose all that apply.)

    A. `addSize`

    B. `getCust`

    C. `deleteRep`

    D. `isColorado`

    E. `putDimensions`

3. Given:

```
1. class Voop {
2.   public static void main(String [] args) {
3.     doStuff(1);
4.     doStuff(1,2);
5.   }
6.   // insert code here
7. }
```

Which, inserted independently at line 6, will compile? (Choose all that apply.)

    A. `static void doStuff(int... doArgs) { }`

    B. `static void doStuff(int[] doArgs) { }`

    C. `static void doStuff(int doArgs...) { }`

    D. `static void doStuff(int... doArgs, int y) { }`

    E. `static void doStuff(int x, int... doArgs) { }`

4. Given:

```
1. enum Animals {
2.    DOG("woof"), CAT("meow"), FISH("burble");
3.    String sound;
4.    Animals(String s) { sound = s; }
5. }
6. class TestEnum {
7.    static Animals a;
8.    public static void main(String[] args) {
9.       System.out.println(a.DOG.sound + " " + a.FISH.sound);
10.   }
11. }
```

What is the result?

A. `woof burble`

B. Multiple compilation errors

C. Compilation fails due to an error on line 2

D. Compilation fails due to an error on line 3

E. Compilation fails due to an error on line 4

F. Compilation fails due to an error on line 9

5. Given two files:

```
1. package pkgA;
2. public class Foo {
3.    int a = 5;
4.    protected int b = 6;
5.    public int c = 7;
6. }
```

```
3. package pkgB;
4. import pkgA.*;
5. public class Baz {
6.    public static void main(String[] args) {
7.       Foo f = new Foo();
8.       System.out.print(" " + f.a);
9.       System.out.print(" " + f.b);
10.      System.out.println(" " + f.c);
11.   }
12. }
```

What is the result? (Choose all that apply.)

A. 5 6 7

B. 5 followed by an exception

C. Compilation fails with an error on line 7

D. Compilation fails with an error on line 8

E. Compilation fails with an error on line 9

F. Compilation fails with an error on line 10

6. Given:

```
1. public class Electronic implements Device
        { public void doIt() { } }
2.
3. abstract class Phone1 extends Electronic { }
4.
5. abstract class Phone2 extends Electronic
      { public void doIt(int x) { } }
6.
7. class Phone3 extends Electronic implements Device
        { public void doStuff() { } }
8.
9. interface Device { public void doIt(); }
```

What is the result? (Choose all that apply.)

A. Compilation succeeds

B. Compilation fails with an error on line 1

C. Compilation fails with an error on line 3

D. Compilation fails with an error on line 5

E. Compilation fails with an error on line 7

F. Compilation fails with an error on line 9

7. Given:

```
4. class Announce {
5.   public static void main(String[] args) {
6.     for(int __x = 0; __x < 3; __x++) ;
7.       int #1b = 7;
```

```
8.      long [] x [5];
9.      Boolean []ba[];
10.     enum Traffic { RED, YELLOW, GREEN };
11.   }
12. }
```

What is the result? (Choose all that apply.)

A. Compilation succeeds

B. Compilation fails with an error on line 6

C. Compilation fails with an error on line 7

D. Compilation fails with an error on line 8

E. Compilation fails with an error on line 9

F. Compilation fails with an error on line 10

8. Given:

```
3. public class TestDays {
4.    public enum Days { MON, TUE, WED };
5.    public static void main(String[] args) {
6.      for(Days d : Days.values() )
7.          ;
8.      Days [] d2 = Days.values();
9.      System.out.println(d2[2]);
10.   }
11. }
```

What is the result? (Choose all that apply.)

A. TUE

B. WED

C. The output is unpredictable

D. Compilation fails due to an error on line 4

E. Compilation fails due to an error on line 6

F. Compilation fails due to an error on line 8

G. Compilation fails due to an error on line 9

9. Given:

```
4. public class Frodo extends Hobbit {
5.    public static void main(String[] args) {
6.       Short myGold = 7;
7.       System.out.println(countGold(myGold, 6));
8.    }
9. }
10. class Hobbit {
11.    int countGold(int x, int y) { return x + y; }
12. }
```

What is the result?

A. 13

B. Compilation fails due to multiple errors

C. Compilation fails due to an error on line 6

D. Compilation fails due to an error on line 7

E. Compilation fails due to an error on line 11

SELF TEST ANSWERS

1. Which is true? (Choose all that apply.)
    A. "X extends Y" is correct if and only if X is a class and Y is an interface
    B. "X extends Y" is correct if and only if X is an interface and Y is a class
    C. "X extends Y" is correct if X and Y are either both classes or both interfaces
    D. "X extends Y" is correct for all combinations of X and Y being classes and/or interfaces

Answer:

☑ **C** is correct.

☒ **A** is incorrect because classes implement interfaces, they don't extend them. **B** is incorrect because interfaces only "inherit from" other interfaces. **D** is incorrect based on the preceding rules. (Objective 1.2)

2. Which method names follow the JavaBeans standard? (Choose all that apply.)
    A. `addSize`
    B. `getCust`
    C. `deleteRep`
    D. `isColorado`
    E. `putDimensions`

Answer:

☑ **B** and **D** use the valid prefixes `'get'` and `'is'`.

☒ **A** is incorrect because `'add'` can be used only with Listener methods. **C** and **E** are incorrect because `'delete'` and `'put'` are not standard JavaBeans name prefixes. (Objective 1.4)

3. Given:
```
1. class Voop {
2.   public static void main(String[] args) {
3.     doStuff(1);
4.     doStuff(1,2);
5.   }
6.   // insert code here
7. }
```

Which, inserted independently at line 6, will compile? (Choose all that apply.)

A. `static void doStuff(int... doArgs) { }`

B. `static void doStuff(int[] doArgs) { }`

C. `static void doStuff(int doArgs...) { }`

D. `static void doStuff(int... doArgs, int y) { }`

E. `static void doStuff(int x, int... doArgs) { }`

Answer:

☑ **A** and **E** use valid var-args syntax.

☒ **B** and **C** are invalid var-arg syntax, and **D** is invalid because the var-arg must be the last of a method's arguments. (Objective 1.4)

4. Given:

```
1. enum Animals {
2.    DOG("woof"), CAT("meow"), FISH("burble");
3.    String sound;
4.    Animals(String s) { sound = s; }
5. }
6. class TestEnum {
7.    static Animals a;
8.    public static void main(String [] args) {
9.       System.out.println(a.DOG.sound + " " + a.FISH.sound);
10.   }
11. }
```

What is the result?

A. `woof burble`

B. Multiple compilation errors

C. Compilation fails due to an error on line 2

D. Compilation fails due to an error on line 3

E. Compilation fails due to an error on line 4

F. Compilation fails due to an error on line 9

Answer:

☑ **A** is correct; enums can have constructors and variables.

☒ **B, C, D, E,** and **F** are incorrect; these lines all use correct syntax. (Objective 1.3)

5. Given two files:
```
1. package pkgA;
2. public class Foo {
3.    int a = 5;
4.    protected int b = 6;
5.    public int c = 7;
6. }
```

```
3. package pkgB;
4. import pkgA.*;
5. public class Baz {
6.    public static void main(String[] args) {
7.       Foo f = new Foo();
8.       System.out.print(" " + f.a);
9.       System.out.print(" " + f.b);
10.      System.out.print(" " + f.c);
11.   }
12. }
```

What is the result? (Choose all that apply.)

A. 5 6 7

B. 5 followed by an exception

C. Compilation fails with an error on line 7

D. Compilation fails with an error on line 8

E. Compilation fails with an error on line 9

F. Compilation fails with an error on line 10

Answer:

☑ **D** and **E** are correct. Variable a has default access, so it cannot be accessed from outside the package. Variable b has protected access in pkgA.

☒ **A, B, C,** and **F** are incorrect based on the above information. (Objective 1.1)

6. Given:
```
1. public class Electronic implements Device
         { public void doIt() { } }
2.
3. abstract class Phone1 extends Electronic { }
4.
5. abstract class Phone2 extends Electronic
       { public void doIt(int x) { } }
6.
```

```
7. class Phone3 extends Electronic implements Device
     { public void doStuff() { } }
8.
9. interface Device { public void doIt(); }
```

What is the result? (Choose all that apply.)

A. Compilation succeeds

B. Compilation fails with an error on line 1

C. Compilation fails with an error on line 3

D. Compilation fails with an error on line 5

E. Compilation fails with an error on line 7

F. Compilation fails with an error on line 9

Answer:

☑ **A** is correct; all of these are legal declarations.

☒ **B, C, D, E,** and **F** are incorrect based on the above information. (Objective 1.2)

7. Given:

```
4. class Announce {
5.    public static void main(String[] args) {
6.      for(int __x = 0; __x < 3; __x++) ;
7.      int #lb = 7;
8.      long [] x [5];
9.      Boolean []ba[];
10.     enum Traffic { RED, YELLOW, GREEN };
11.   }
12. }
```

What is the result? (Choose all that apply.)

A. Compilation succeeds

B. Compilation fails with an error on line 6

C. Compilation fails with an error on line 7

D. Compilation fails with an error on line 8

E. Compilation fails with an error on line 9

F. Compilation fails with an error on line 10

Answer:

☑ **C, D,** and **F** are correct. Variable names cannot begin with a #, an array declaration can't include a size without an instantiation, and enums can't be declared within a method.

☒ **A, B,** and **E** are incorrect based on the above information. (Objective 1.3)

8. Given:

```
3. public class TestDays {
4.    public enum Days { MON, TUE, WED };
5.    public static void main(String[] args) {
6.      for(Days d : Days.values() )
7.        ;
8.      Days [] d2 = Days.values();
9.      System.out.println(d2[2]);
10.   }
11. }
```

What is the result? (Choose all that apply.)

A. TUE

B. WED

C. The output is unpredictable

D. Compilation fails due to an error on line 4

E. Compilation fails due to an error on line 6

F. Compilation fails due to an error on line 8

G. Compilation fails due to an error on line 9

Answer:

☑ **B** is correct. Every enum comes with a static `values()` method that returns an array of the enum's values, in the order in which they are declared in the enum.

☒ **A, C, D, E, F,** and **G** are incorrect based on the above information. (Objective 1.3)

9. Given:

```
4. public class Frodo extends Hobbit {
5.    public static void main(String[] args) {
6.      Short myGold = 7;
7.      System.out.println(countGold(myGold, 6));
8.    }
9. }
10. class Hobbit {
11.   int countGold(int x, int y) { return x + y; }
12. }
```

What is the result?

A. 13

B. Compilation fails due to multiple errors

C. Compilation fails due to an error on line 6

D. Compilation fails due to an error on line 7

E. Compilation fails due to an error on line 11

Answer:

☑ **D** is correct. The `Short myGold` is autoboxed correctly, but the `countGold()` method cannot be invoked from a static context.

☒ **A, B, C,** and **E** are incorrect based on the above information. (Objective 1.4)

2

Object Orientation

Being an SCJP 6 means you must be at one with the object-oriented aspects of Java. You must dream of inheritance hierarchies, the power of polymorphism must flow through you, cohesion and loose coupling must become second nature to you, and composition must be your bread and butter. This chapter will prepare you for all of the object-oriented objectives and questions you'll encounter on the exam. We have heard of many experienced Java programmers who haven't really become fluent with the object-oriented tools that Java provides, so we'll start at the beginning.

Encapsulation (Exam Objective 5.1)

5.1   Develop code that implements tight encapsulation, loose coupling, and high cohesion in classes, and describe the benefits.

Imagine you wrote the code for a class, and another dozen programmers from your company all wrote programs that used your class. Now imagine that later on, you didn't like the way the class behaved, because some of its instance variables were being set (by the other programmers from within their code) to values you hadn't anticipated. *Their* code brought out errors in *your* code. (Relax, this is just hypothetical.) Well, it is a Java program, so you should be able just to ship out a newer version of the class, which they could replace in their programs without changing any of their own code.

This scenario highlights two of the promises/benefits of Object Orientation (OO): flexibility and maintainability. But those benefits don't come automatically. You have to do something. You have to write your classes and code in a way that supports flexibility and maintainability. So what if Java supports OO? It can't design your code for you. For example, imagine if you made your class with `public` instance variables, and those other programmers were setting the instance variables directly, as the following code demonstrates:

```
public class BadOO {
    public int size;
```

```
    public int weight;
    ...
}
public class ExploitBadOO {
    public static void main (String [] args) {
        BadOO b = new BadOO();
        b.size = -5; // Legal but bad!!
    }
}
```

And now you're in trouble. How are you going to change the class in a way that lets you handle the issues that come up when somebody changes the size variable to a value that causes problems? Your only choice is to go back in and write method code for adjusting size (a setSize(int a) method, for example), and then protect the size variable with, say, a private access modifier. But as soon as you make that change to your code, you break everyone else's!

The ability to make changes in your implementation code without breaking the code of others who use your code is a key benefit of encapsulation. You want to hide implementation details behind a public programming interface. By interface, we mean the set of accessible methods your code makes available for other code to call—in other words, your code's API. By hiding implementation details, you can rework your method code (perhaps also altering the way variables are used by your class) without forcing a change in the code that calls your changed method.

If you want maintainability, flexibility, and extensibility (and of course, you do), your design must include encapsulation. How do you do that?

- Keep instance variables protected (with an access modifier, often `private`).
- Make `public` accessor methods, and force calling code to use those methods rather than directly accessing the instance variable.
- For the methods, use the JavaBeans naming convention of `set<someProperty>` and `get<someProperty>`.

Figure 2-1 illustrates the idea that encapsulation forces callers of our code to go through methods rather than accessing variables directly.

FIGURE 2-1

The nature of
encapsulation

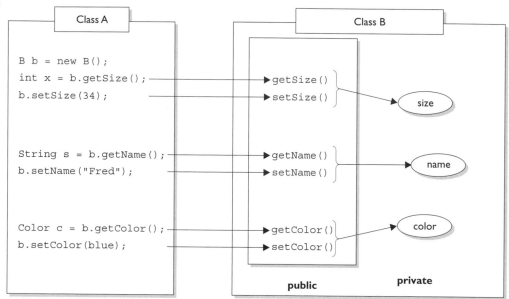

Class A cannot access Class B instance variable data
without going through getter and setter methods. Data is
marked private; only the accessor methods are public.

We call the access methods getters and setters although some prefer the fancier
terms accessors and mutators. (Personally, we don't like the word "mutate".)
Regardless of what you call them, they're methods that other programmers must go
through in order to access your instance variables. They look simple, and you've
probably been using them forever:

```
public class Box {
    // protect the instance variable; only an instance
    // of Box can access it
    private int size;
    // Provide public getters and setters
    public int getSize() {
        return size;
```

```
    }
    public void setSize(int newSize) {
        size = newSize;
    }
}
```

Wait a minute...how useful is the previous code? It doesn't even do any validation or processing. What benefit can there be from having getters and setters that add no additional functionality? The point is, you can change your mind later, and add more code to your methods without breaking your API. Even if today you don't think you really need validation or processing of the data, good OO design dictates that you plan for the future. To be safe, force calling code to go through your methods rather than going directly to instance variables. *Always*. Then you're free to rework your method implementations later, without risking the wrath of those dozen programmers who know where you live.

exam
ⓦatch

Look out for code that appears to be asking about the behavior of a method, when the problem is actually a lack of encapsulation. Look at the following example, and see if you can figure out what's going on:

```
class Foo {
    public int left = 9;
    public int right = 3;
    public void setLeft(int leftNum) {
        left = leftNum;
        right = leftNum/3;
    }
    // lots of complex test code here
}
```

Now consider this question: Is the value of right always going to be one-third the value of left? It looks like it will, until you realize that users of the Foo *class don't need to use the* setLeft() *method! They can simply go straight to the instance variables and change them to any arbitrary* int *value.*

CERTIFICATION OBJECTIVE

Inheritance, Is-A, Has-A (Exam Objective 5.5)

5.5 Develop code that implements "is-a" and/or "has-a" relationships.

Inheritance is everywhere in Java. It's safe to say that it's almost (almost?) impossible to write even the tiniest Java program without using inheritance. In order to explore this topic we're going to use the instanceof operator, which we'll discuss in more detail in Chapter 4. For now, just remember that instanceof returns true if the reference variable being tested is of the type being compared to. This code:

```
class Test {
  public static void main(String [] args) {
    Test t1 = new Test();
    Test t2 = new Test();
    if (!t1.equals(t2))
      System.out.println("they're not equal");
    if (t1 instanceof Object)
      System.out.println("t1's an Object");
  }
}
```

Produces the output:

```
they're not equal
t1's an Object
```

Where did that equals method come from? The reference variable t1 is of type Test, and there's no equals method in the Test class. Or is there? The second if test asks whether t1 is an instance of class Object, and because it *is* (more on that soon), the if test succeeds.

Hold on...how can t1 be an instance of type Object, we just said it was of type Test? I'm sure you're way ahead of us here, but it turns out that every class in Java is a subclass of class Object, (except of course class Object itself). In other words, every class you'll ever use or ever write will inherit from class Object. You'll always have an equals method, a clone method, notify, wait, and others, available to use. Whenever you create a class, you automatically inherit all of class Object's methods.

Why? Let's look at that `equals` method for instance. Java's creators correctly assumed that it would be very common for Java programmers to want to compare instances of their classes to check for equality. If class Object didn't have an `equals` method, you'd have to write one yourself; you and every other Java programmer. That one `equals` method has been inherited billions of times. (To be fair, `equals` has also been *overridden* billions of times, but we're getting ahead of ourselves.)

For the exam you'll need to know that you can create inheritance relationships in Java by *extending* a class. It's also important to understand that the two most common reasons to use inheritance are

- To promote code reuse
- To use polymorphism

Let's start with reuse. A common design approach is to create a fairly generic version of a class with the intention of creating more specialized subclasses that inherit from it. For example:

```
class GameShape {
   public void displayShape() {
     System.out.println("displaying shape");
   }
   // more code
}

class PlayerPiece extends GameShape {
   public void movePiece() {
     System.out.println("moving game piece");
   }
   // more code
}


public class TestShapes {
   public static void main (String[] args) {
      PlayerPiece shape = new PlayerPiece();
      shape.displayShape();
      shape.movePiece();
   }
}
```

Outputs:

```
displaying shape
moving game piece
```

Notice that the PlayingPiece class inherits the generic display() method from the less-specialized class GameShape, and also adds its own method, movePiece(). Code reuse through inheritance means that methods with generic functionality (like display())—that could apply to a wide range of different kinds of shapes in a game—don't have to be reimplemented. That means all specialized subclasses of GameShape are guaranteed to have the capabilities of the more generic superclass. You don't want to have to rewrite the display() code in each of your specialized components of an online game.

But you knew that. You've experienced the pain of duplicate code when you make a change in one place and have to track down all the other places where that same (or very similar) code exists.

The second (and related) use of inheritance is to allow your classes to be accessed polymorphically—a capability provided by interfaces as well, but we'll get to that in a minute. Let's say that you have a GameLauncher class that wants to loop through a list of different kinds of GameShape objects, and invoke display() on each of them. At the time you write this class, you don't know every possible kind of GameShape subclass that anyone else will ever write. And you don't want to have to redo *your* code just because somebody decided to build a Dice shape six months later.

The beautiful thing about polymorphism ("many forms") is that you can treat any *subclass* of GameShape as a GameShape. In other words, you can write code in your GameLauncher class that says, "I don't care what kind of object you are as long as you inherit from (extend) GameShape. And as far as I'm concerned, if you extend GameShape then you've definitely got a display() method, so I know I can call it."

Imagine we now have two specialized subclasses that extend the more generic GameShape class, PlayerPiece and TilePiece:

```java
class GameShape {
   public void displayShape() {
     System.out.println("displaying shape");
   }
   // more code
}
```

```
class PlayerPiece extends GameShape {
   public void movePiece() {
     System.out.println("moving game piece");
   }
   // more code
}

class TilePiece extends GameShape {
    public void getAdjacent() {
      System.out.println("getting adjacent tiles");
    }
    // more code
}
```

Now imagine a test class has a method with a declared argument type of GameShape, that means it can take any kind of GameShape. In other words, any subclass of GameShape can be passed to a method with an argument of type GameShape. This code

```
public class TestShapes {
    public static void main (String[] args) {
        PlayerPiece player = new PlayerPiece();
        TilePiece tile = new TilePiece();
        doShapes(player);
        doShapes(tile);
    }

    public static void doShapes(GameShape shape) {
      shape.displayShape();
    }
}
```

Outputs:

```
displaying shape
displaying shape
```

The key point is that the doShapes() method is declared with a GameShape argument but can be passed any subtype (in this example, a subclass) of GameShape. The method can then invoke any method of GameShape, without any concern for the actual runtime class type of the object passed to the method. There are implications, though. The doShapes() method knows only that the objects are a type of GameShape, since that's how the parameter is declared. And using a reference variable declared as type GameShape—regardless of whether the variable is a method parameter, local variable, or instance variable—means that *only* the methods of GameShape can be invoked on it. The methods you can call on a reference are totally dependent on the *declared* type of the variable, no matter what the actual object is, that the reference is referring to. That means you can't use a GameShape variable to call, say, the getAdjacent() method even if the object passed in *is* of type TilePiece. (We'll see this again when we look at interfaces.)

IS-A and HAS-A Relationships

For the exam you need to be able to look at code and determine whether the code demonstrates an IS-A or HAS-A relationship. The rules are simple, so this should be one of the few areas where answering the questions correctly is almost a no-brainer.

IS-A

In OO, the concept of IS-A is based on class inheritance or interface implementation. IS-A is a way of saying, "this thing is a type of that thing." For example, a Mustang is a type of horse, so in OO terms we can say, "Mustang IS-A Horse." Subaru IS-A Car. Broccoli IS-A Vegetable (not a very fun one, but it still counts). You express the IS-A relationship in Java through the keywords extends (for *class* inheritance) and implements (for *interface* implementation).

```
public class Car {
  // Cool Car code goes here
}

public class Subaru extends Car {
   // Important Subaru-specific stuff goes here
   // Don't forget Subaru inherits accessible Car members which
   // can include both methods and variables.
}
```

A Car is a type of Vehicle, so the inheritance tree might start from the Vehicle class as follows:

```
public class Vehicle { ... }
public class Car extends Vehicle { ... }
public class Subaru extends Car { ... }
```

In OO terms, you can say the following:

Vehicle is the superclass of Car.
Car is the subclass of Vehicle.
Car is the superclass of Subaru.
Subaru is the subclass of Vehicle.
Car inherits from Vehicle.
Subaru inherits from both Vehicle and Car.
Subaru is derived from Car.
Car is derived from Vehicle.
Subaru is derived from Vehicle.
Subaru is a subtype of both Vehicle and Car.

Returning to our IS-A relationship, the following statements are true:

"Car extends Vehicle" means "Car IS-A Vehicle."
"Subaru extends Car" means "Subaru IS-A Car."

And we can also say:

"Subaru IS-A Vehicle" because a class is said to be "a type of" anything further up in its inheritance tree. If the expression (`Foo instanceof Bar`) is `true`, then class `Foo` IS-A `Bar`, even if `Foo` doesn't directly extend `Bar`, but instead extends some other class that is a subclass of `Bar`. Figure 2-2 illustrates the inheritance tree for `Vehicle`, `Car`, and `Subaru`. The arrows move from the subclass to the superclass. In other words, a class' arrow points toward the class from which it extends.

FIGURE 2-2

Inheritance tree
for Vehicle, Car,
Subaru

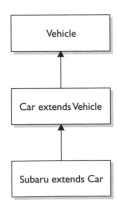

HAS-A

HAS-A relationships are based on usage, rather than inheritance. In other words, class A HAS-A B if code in class A has a reference to an instance of class B. For example, you can say the following,

A Horse IS-A Animal. A Horse HAS-A Halter.
The code might look like this:

```
public class Animal { }
public class Horse extends Animal {
    private Halter myHalter;
}
```

In the preceding code, the Horse class has an instance variable of type Halter, so you can say that "Horse HAS-A Halter." In other words, Horse has a reference to a Halter. Horse code can use that Halter reference to invoke methods on the Halter, and get Halter behavior without having Halter-related code (methods) in the Horse class itself. Figure 2-3 illustrates the HAS-A relationship between Horse and Halter.

FIGURE 2-3

HAS-A
relationship
between Horse
and Halter

Horse class has a Halter, because Horse
declares an instance variable of type Halter.
When code invokes tie() on a Horse instance,
the Horse invokes tie() on the Horse
object's Halter instance variable.

HAS-A relationships allow you to design classes that follow good OO practices by not having monolithic classes that do a gazillion different things. Classes (and their resulting objects) should be specialists. As our friend Andrew says, "specialized classes can actually help reduce bugs." The more specialized the class, the more likely it is that you can reuse the class in other applications. If you put all the Halter-related code directly into the Horse class, you'll end up duplicating code in the Cow class, UnpaidIntern class, and any other class that might need Halter behavior. By keeping the Halter code in a separate, specialized Halter class, you have the chance to reuse the Halter class in multiple applications.

FROM THE CLASSROOM

Object-Oriented Design

IS-A and HAS-A relationships and encapsulation are just the tip of the iceberg when it comes to object-oriented design. Many books and graduate theses have been dedicated to this topic. The reason for the emphasis on proper design is simple: money. The cost to deliver a software application has been estimated to be as much as ten times more expensive for poorly designed programs. Having seen the ramifications of poor designs, I can assure you that this estimate is not far-fetched.

Even the best object-oriented designers make mistakes. It is difficult to visualize the relationships between hundreds, or even thousands, of classes. When mistakes are discovered during the implementation (code writing) phase of a project, the amount of code that has to be rewritten can sometimes cause programming teams to start over from scratch.

The software industry has evolved to aid the designer. Visual object modeling languages, like the Unified Modeling Language (UML), allow designers to design and easily modify classes without having to write code first,

because object-oriented components are represented graphically. This allows the designer to create a map of the class relationships and helps them recognize errors before coding begins. Another innovation in object-oriented design is design patterns. Designers noticed that many object-oriented designs apply consistently from project to project, and that it was useful to apply the same designs because it reduced the potential to introduce new design errors. Object-oriented designers then started to share these designs with each other. Now, there are many catalogs of these design patterns both on the Internet and in book form.

Although passing the Java certification exam does not require you to understand object-oriented design this thoroughly, hopefully this background information will help you better appreciate why the test writers chose to include encapsulation, and IS-A, and HAS-A relationships on the exam.

—Jonathan Meeks, Sun Certified Java Programmer

Users of the `Horse` class (that is, code that calls methods on a `Horse` instance), think that the `Horse` class has `Halter` behavior. The `Horse` class might have a `tie(LeadRope rope)` method, for example. Users of the `Horse` class should never have to know that when they invoke the `tie()` method, the `Horse` object turns around and delegates the call to its `Halter` class by invoking `myHalter.tie(rope)`. The scenario just described might look like this:

```
public class Horse extends Animal {
   private Halter myHalter = new Halter();
   public void tie(LeadRope rope) {
      myHalter.tie(rope);   // Delegate tie behavior to the
                            // Halter object
   }
}
public class Halter {
   public void tie(LeadRope aRope) {
      // Do the actual tie work here
   }
}
```

In OO, we don't want callers to worry about which class or which object is actually doing the real work. To make that happen, the `Horse` class hides implementation details from `Horse` users. `Horse` users ask the `Horse` object to do things (in this case, tie itself up), and the `Horse` will either do it or, as in this example, ask something else to do it. To the caller, though, it always appears that the `Horse` object takes care of itself. Users of a `Horse` should not even need to know that there is such a thing as a `Halter` class.

CERTIFICATION OBJECTIVE

Polymorphism (Exam Objective 5.2)

5.2   Given a scenario, develop code that demonstrates the use of polymorphism. Further, determine when casting will be necessary and recognize compiler vs. runtime errors related to object reference casting.

Remember, any Java object that can pass more than one IS-A test can be considered polymorphic. Other than objects of type Object, *all* Java objects are polymorphic in that they pass the IS-A test for their own type and for class Object.

Remember that the only way to access an object is through a reference variable, and there are a few key things to remember about references:

- A reference variable can be of only one type, and once declared, that type can never be changed (although the object it references can change).

- A reference is a variable, so it can be reassigned to other objects, (unless the reference is declared final).

- A reference variable's type determines the methods that can be invoked on the object the variable is referencing.

- A reference variable can refer to any object of the same type as the declared reference, or—this is the big one—**it can refer to any** *subtype* **of the declared type!**

- A reference variable can be declared as a class type or an interface type. If the variable is declared as an interface type, it can reference any object of any class that *implements* the interface.

Earlier we created a GameShape class that was extended by two other classes, PlayerPiece and TilePiece. Now imagine you want to animate some of the shapes on the game board. But not *all* shapes can be animatable, so what do you do with class inheritance?

Could we create a class with an animate() method, and have only *some* of the GameShape subclasses inherit from that class? If we can, then we could have PlayerPiece, for example, extend *both* the GameShape class and Animatable class, while the TilePiece would extend only GameShape. But no, this won't work! Java supports only single inheritance! That means a class can have only one immediate superclass. In other words, if PlayerPiece is a class, there is no way to say something like this:

```
class PlayerPiece extends GameShape, Animatable { // NO!
  // more code
}
```

A *class* cannot *extend* more than one class. That means one parent per class. A class *can* have multiple ancestors, however, since class B could extend class A, and class C could extend class B, and so on. So any given class might have multiple classes up its inheritance tree, but that's not the same as saying a class directly extends two classes.

on the **job**

Some languages (like C++) allow a class to extend more than one other class. This capability is known as "multiple inheritance." The reason that Java's creators chose not to allow multiple inheritance is that it can become quite messy. In a nutshell, the problem is that if a class extended two other classes, and both superclasses had, say, a doStuff() method, which version of doStuff() would the subclass inherit? This issue can lead to a scenario known as the "Deadly Diamond of Death," because of the shape of the class diagram that can be created in a multiple inheritance design. The diamond is formed when classes B and C both extend A, and both B and C inherit a method from A. If class D extends both B and C, and both B and C have overridden the method in A, class D has, in theory, inherited two different implementations of the same method. Drawn as a class diagram, the shape of the four classes looks like a diamond.

So if that doesn't work, what else could you do? You could simply put the `animate()` code in `GameShape`, and then disable the method in classes that can't be animated. But that's a bad design choice for many reasons, including it's more error-prone, it makes the `GameShape` class less cohesive (more on cohesion in a minute), and it means the `GameShape` API "advertises" that all shapes can be animated, when in fact that's not true since only some of the `GameShape` subclasses will be able to successfully run the `animate()` method.

So what *else* could you do? You already know the answer—create an `Animatable` *interface*, and have only the `GameShape` subclasses that can be animated implement that interface. Here's the interface:

```
public interface Animatable {
    public void animate();
}
```

And here's the modified `PlayerPiece` class that implements the interface:

```
class PlayerPiece extends GameShape implements Animatable {
   public void movePiece() {
     System.out.println("moving game piece");
   }
   public void animate() {
     System.out.println("animating...");
   }
   // more code
}
```

So now we have a `PlayerPiece` that passes the IS-A test for both the `GameShape` class and the `Animatable` interface. That means a `PlayerPiece` can be treated polymorphically as one of four things at any given time, depending on the declared type of the reference variable:

- An `Object` (since any object inherits from `Object`)
- A `GameShape` (since `PlayerPiece` extends `GameShape`)
- A `PlayerPiece` (since that's what it really is)
- An `Animatable` (since `PlayerPiece` implements `Animatable`)

The following are all legal declarations. Look closely:

```
PlayerPiece player = new PlayerPiece();
Object o = player;
GameShape shape = player;
Animatable mover = player;
```

There's only one object here—an instance of type `PlayerPiece`—but there are four different types of reference variables, all referring to that one object on the heap. Pop quiz: which of the preceding reference variables can invoke the `displayShape()` method? Hint: only two of the four declarations can be used to invoke the `displayShape()` method.

Remember that method invocations allowed by the compiler are based solely on the declared type of the reference, regardless of the object type. So looking at the four reference types again—`Object`, `GameShape`, `PlayerPiece`, and `Animatable`—which of these four types know about the `displayShape()` method?

You guessed it—both the `GameShape` class and the `PlayerPiece` class are known (by the compiler) to have a `displayShape()` method, so either of those reference types can be used to invoke `displayShape()`. Remember that to the compiler, a `PlayerPiece` IS-A `GameShape`, so the compiler says, "I see that the declared type is `PlayerPiece`, and since `PlayerPiece` extends `GameShape`, that means `PlayerPiece` inherited the `displayShape()` method. Therefore, `PlayerPiece` can be used to invoke the `displayShape()` method."

Which methods can be invoked when the `PlayerPiece` object is being referred to using a reference declared as type `Animatable`? Only the `animate()` method. Of course the cool thing here is that any class from any inheritance tree can also implement `Animatable`, so that means if you have a method with an argument declared as type `Animatable`, you can pass in `PlayerPiece` objects, `SpinningLogo` objects, and anything else that's an instance of a class that implements `Animatable`. And you can use that parameter (of type `Animatable`) to invoke the `animate()` method, but not the `displayShape()` method (which it might not even have), or anything other than what is known to the compiler based on the reference type. The compiler always knows, though, that you can invoke the methods of class `Object` on any object, so those are safe to call regardless of the reference—class or interface—used to refer to the object.

We've left out one big part of all this, which is that even though the compiler only knows about the declared reference type, the Java Virtual Machine (JVM) at runtime knows what the object really is. And that means that even if the `PlayerPiece` object's `displayShape()` method is called using a `GameShape` reference variable, if the `PlayerPiece` overrides the `displayShape()` method, the JVM will invoke the `PlayerPiece` version! The JVM looks at the real object at the other end of the reference, "sees" that it has overridden the method of the declared reference variable type, and invokes the method of the object's actual class. But one other thing to keep in mind:

> **Polymorphic method invocations apply only to *instance methods*. You can always refer to an object with a more general reference variable type (a superclass or interface), but at runtime, the ONLY things that are dynamically selected based on the actual *object* (rather than the *reference* type) are instance methods. Not *static* methods. Not *variables*. Only overridden instance methods are dynamically invoked based on the real object's type.**

Since this definition depends on a clear understanding of overriding, and the distinction between static methods and instance methods, we'll cover those next.

Overriding / Overloading (Exam Objectives 1.5 and 5.4)

1.5   Given a code example, determine if a method is correctly overriding or overloading another method, and identify legal return values (including covariant returns), for the method.

5.4   Given a scenario, develop code that declares and/or invokes overridden or overloaded methods and code that declares and/or invokes superclass, overridden, or overloaded constructors.

Overridden Methods

Any time you have a class that inherits a method from a superclass, you have the opportunity to override the method (unless, as you learned earlier, the method is marked `final`). The key benefit of overriding is the ability to define behavior that's specific to a particular subclass type. The following example demonstrates a Horse subclass of Animal overriding the Animal version of the eat() method:

```
public class Animal {
    public void eat() {
        System.out.println("Generic Animal Eating Generically");
    }
}
class Horse extends Animal {
    public void eat() {
        System.out.println("Horse eating hay, oats, "
                           + "and horse treats");
    }
}
```

For abstract methods you inherit from a superclass, you have no choice. You *must* implement the method in the subclass **unless the subclass is also abstract.** Abstract methods must be *implemented* by the concrete subclass, but this is a lot like saying that the concrete subclass *overrides* the abstract methods of the superclass. So you could think of abstract methods as methods you're forced to override.

The Animal class creator might have decided that for the purposes of polymorphism, all Animal subtypes should have an eat() method defined in a unique, specific way. Polymorphically, when someone has an Animal reference that refers not to an Animal instance, but to an Animal subclass instance, the caller should be able to invoke eat() on the Animal reference, but the actual runtime object (say, a Horse instance) will run its own specific eat() method. Marking the eat() method abstract is the Animal programmer's way of saying to all subclass developers, "It doesn't make any sense for your new subtype to use a generic eat() method, so you have to come up with your *own* eat() method implementation!" A (non-abstract), example of using polymorphism looks like this:

```
public class TestAnimals {
  public static void main (String [] args) {
    Animal a = new Animal();
    Animal b = new Horse();   //Animal ref, but a Horse object
    a.eat(); // Runs the Animal version of eat()
    b.eat(); // Runs the Horse version of eat()
  }
}
class Animal {
  public void eat() {
    System.out.println("Generic Animal Eating Generically");
  }
}
class Horse extends Animal {
  public void eat() {
    System.out.println("Horse eating hay, oats, "
                       + "and horse treats");
  }
  public void buck() { }
}
```

In the preceding code, the test class uses an Animal reference to invoke a method on a Horse object. Remember, the compiler will allow only methods in class Animal to be invoked when using a reference to an Animal. The following would not be legal given the preceding code:

```
Animal c = new Horse();
c.buck();  // Can't invoke buck();
           // Animal class doesn't have that method
```

To reiterate, the compiler looks only at the reference type, not the instance type. Polymorphism lets you use a more abstract supertype (including an interface) reference to refer to one of its subtypes (including interface implementers).

The overriding method cannot have a more restrictive access modifier than the method being overridden (for example, you can't override a method marked `public` and make it `protected`). Think about it: if the Animal class advertises a `public` eat() method and someone has an Animal reference (in other words, a reference declared as type Animal), that someone will assume it's safe to call eat() on the Animal reference regardless of the actual instance that the Animal reference is referring to. If a subclass were allowed to sneak in and change the access modifier on the overriding method, then suddenly at runtime—when the JVM invokes the true object's (Horse) version of the method rather than the reference type's (Animal) version—the program would die a horrible death. (Not to mention the emotional distress for the one who was betrayed by the rogue subclass.) Let's modify the polymorphic example we saw earlier in this section:

```
public class TestAnimals {
  public static void main (String [] args) {
    Animal a = new Animal();
    Animal b = new Horse();  //Animal ref, but a Horse object
    a.eat(); // Runs the Animal version of eat()
    b.eat(); // Runs the Horse version of eat()
  }
}
class Animal {
  public void eat() {
    System.out.println("Generic Animal Eating Generically");
  }
}
class Horse extends Animal {
  private void eat() {  // whoa! - it's private!
    System.out.println("Horse eating hay, oats, "
                     + "and horse treats");
  }
}
```

If this code compiled (which it doesn't), the following would fail at runtime:

```
Animal b = new Horse();  // Animal ref, but a Horse
                         // object , so far so good
b.eat();                 // Meltdown at runtime!
```

The variable b is of type `Animal`, which has a `public eat()` method. But remember that at runtime, Java uses virtual method invocation to dynamically select the actual version of the method that will run, based on the actual instance. An Animal reference can always refer to a Horse instance, because Horse IS-A(n) Animal. What makes that superclass reference to a subclass instance possible is that the subclass is guaranteed to be able to do everything the superclass can do. Whether the Horse instance overrides the inherited methods of Animal or simply inherits them, anyone with an Animal reference to a Horse instance is free to call all accessible Animal methods. For that reason, an overriding method must fulfill the contract of the superclass.

The rules for overriding a method are as follows:

- The argument list must exactly match that of the overridden method. If they don't match, you can end up with an overloaded method you didn't intend.
- The return type must be the same as, or a subtype of, the return type declared in the original overridden method in the superclass. (More on this in a few pages when we discuss covariant returns.)
- The access level can't be more restrictive than the overridden method's.
- The access level CAN be less restrictive than that of the overridden method.
- Instance methods can be overridden only if they are inherited by the subclass. A subclass within the same package as the instance's superclass can override any superclass method that is not marked `private` or `final`. A subclass in a different package can override only those non-`final` methods marked `public` or `protected` (since `protected` methods are inherited by the subclass).
- The overriding method CAN throw any unchecked (runtime) exception, regardless of whether the overridden method declares the exception. (More in Chapter 5.)
- The overriding method must NOT throw checked exceptions that are new or broader than those declared by the overridden method. For example, a method that declares a FileNotFoundException cannot be overridden by a method that declares a SQLException, Exception, or any other non-runtime exception unless it's a subclass of FileNotFoundException.
- The overriding method can throw narrower or fewer exceptions. Just because an overridden method "takes risks" doesn't mean that the overriding subclass' exception takes the same risks. Bottom line: an overriding method doesn't

have to declare any exceptions that it will never throw, regardless of what the overridden method declares.

■ You cannot override a method marked `final`.

■ You cannot override a method marked `static`. We'll look at an example in a few pages when we discuss `static` methods in more detail.

■ If a method can't be inherited, you cannot override it. Remember that overriding implies that you're reimplementing a method you inherited! For example, the following code is not legal, and even if you added an `eat()` method to Horse, it wouldn't be an override of Animal's `eat()` method.

```
public class TestAnimals {
    public static void main (String [] args) {
        Horse h =  new Horse();
        h.eat(); // Not legal because Horse didn't inherit eat()
    }
}
class Animal {
    private void eat() {
        System.out.println("Generic Animal Eating Generically");
    }
}
class Horse extends Animal { }
```

Invoking a Superclass Version of an Overridden Method

Often, you'll want to take advantage of some of the code in the superclass version of a method, yet still override it to provide some additional specific behavior. It's like saying, "Run the superclass version of the method, then come back down here and finish with my subclass additional method code." (Note that there's no requirement that the superclass version run before the subclass code.) It's easy to do in code using the keyword super as follows:

```
public class Animal {
    public void eat() { }
    public void printYourself() {
        // Useful printing code goes here
    }
}
class Horse extends Animal {
    public void printYourself() {
        // Take advantage of Animal code, then add some more
```

```
            super.printYourself();   // Invoke the superclass
                                     // (Animal) code
                                     // Then do Horse-specific
                                     // print work here
        }
    }
```

Note: Using super to invoke an overridden method only applies to instance methods. (Remember, static methods can't be overridden.)

e x a m
ⓦ a t c h
If a method is overridden but you use a polymorphic (supertype) reference to refer to the subtype object with the overriding method, the compiler assumes you're calling the supertype version of the method. If the supertype version declares a checked exception, but the overriding subtype method does not, the compiler still thinks you are calling a method that declares an exception (more in Chapter 5). Let's take a look at an example:

```
class Animal {
  public void eat() throws Exception {
    // throws an Exception
  }
}
class Dog2 extends Animal {
  public void eat() { /* no Exceptions */}
  public static void main(String [] args) {
    Animal a = new Dog2();
    Dog2 d = new Dog2();
    d.eat();            // ok
    a.eat();            // compiler error -
                        // unreported exception
  }
}
```

This code will not compile because of the Exception declared on the Animal eat() method. This happens even though, at runtime, the eat() method used would be the Dog version, which does not declare the exception.

Examples of Legal and Illegal Method Overrides

Let's take a look at overriding the eat() method of Animal:

```
public class Animal {
    public void eat() { }
}
```

Table 2-1 lists examples of illegal overrides of the Animal eat() method, given the preceding version of the Animal class.

TABLE 2-1   Examples of Illegal Overrides

Illegal Override Code	Problem with the Code
`private void eat() { }`	Access modifier is more restrictive
`public void eat() throws IOException { }`	Declares a checked exception not defined by superclass version
`public void eat(String food) { }`	A legal overload, not an override, because the argument list changed
`public String eat() { }`	Not an override because of the return type, not an overload either because there's no change in the argument list

Overloaded Methods

You're wondering what overloaded methods are doing in an OO chapter, but we've included them here since one of the things newer Java developers are most confused about are all of the subtle differences between over*loaded* and over*ridden* methods.

Over*loaded* methods let you reuse the same method name in a class, but with different arguments (and optionally, a different return type). Overloading a method often means you're being a little nicer to those who call your methods, because your code takes on the burden of coping with different argument types rather than forcing the caller to do conversions prior to invoking your method. The rules are simple:

- Overloaded methods MUST change the argument list.
- Overloaded methods CAN change the return type.
- Overloaded methods CAN change the access modifier.
- Overloaded methods CAN declare new or broader checked exceptions.

■ A method can be overloaded in the *same* class or in a *subclass*. In other words, if class A defines a doStuff(int i) method, the subclass B could define a doStuff(String s) method without overriding the superclass version that takes an int. So two methods with the same name but in different classes can still be considered overloaded, if the subclass inherits one version of the method and then declares another overloaded version in its class definition.

e x a m
ⓦatch
Be careful to recognize when a method is overloaded rather than overridden. You might see a method that appears to be violating a rule for overriding, but that is actually a legal overload, as follows:

```
public class Foo {
    public void doStuff(int y, String s) { }
    public void moreThings(int x) { }
}
class Bar extends Foo {
    public void doStuff(int y, long s) throws IOException { }
}
```

It's tempting to see the IOException as the problem, because the overridden doStuff() method doesn't declare an exception, and IOException is checked by the compiler. But the doStuff() method is not overridden! Subclass Bar overloads the doStuff() method, by varying the argument list, so the IOException is fine.

Legal Overloads

Let's look at a method we want to overload:

```
public void changeSize(int size, String name, float pattern) { }
```

The following methods are legal overloads of the changeSize() method:

```
public void changeSize(int size, String name) { }
public int changeSize(int size, float pattern) { }
public void changeSize(float pattern, String name)
                       throws IOException { }
```

Invoking Overloaded Methods

Note that there's a lot more to this discussion on how the compiler knows which method to invoke, but the rest is covered in Chapter 3 when we look at boxing and var-args—both of which have a huge impact on overloading. (You still have to pay attention to the part covered here, though.)

When a method is invoked, more than one method of the same name might exist for the object type you're invoking a method on. For example, the Horse class might have three methods with the same name but with different argument lists, which means the method is overloaded.

Deciding which of the matching methods to invoke is based on the arguments. If you invoke the method with a String argument, the overloaded version that takes a String is called. If you invoke a method of the same name but pass it a `float`, the overloaded version that takes a `float` will run. If you invoke the method of the same name but pass it a Foo object, and there isn't an overloaded version that takes a Foo, then the compiler will complain that it can't find a match. The following are examples of invoking overloaded methods:

```
class Adder {
  public int addThem(int x, int y) {
    return x + y;
  }

  // Overload the addThem method to add doubles instead of ints
  public double addThem(double x, double y) {
    return x + y;
  }
}
// From another class, invoke the addThem() method
public class TestAdder {
  public static void main (String [] args) {
    Adder a = new Adder();
    int b = 27;
    int c = 3;
    int result = a.addThem(b,c); // Which addThem is invoked?
    double doubleResult = a.addThem(22.5,9.3); // Which addThem?
  }
}
```

In the preceding TestAdder code, the first call to a.addThem(b,c) passes two ints to the method, so the first version of addThem()—the overloaded version that takes two int arguments—is called. The second call to a.addThem(22.5, 9.3) passes two doubles to the method, so the second version of addThem()—the overloaded version that takes two double arguments—is called.

Invoking overloaded methods that take object references rather than primitives is a little more interesting. Say you have an overloaded method such that one version takes an Animal and one takes a Horse (subclass of Animal). If you pass a Horse object in the method invocation, you'll invoke the overloaded version that takes a Horse. Or so it looks at first glance:

```
class Animal { }
class Horse extends Animal { }
class UseAnimals {
   public void doStuff(Animal a) {
      System.out.println("In the Animal version");
   }
   public void doStuff(Horse h) {
      System.out.println("In the Horse version");
   }
   public static void main (String [] args) {
      UseAnimals ua = new UseAnimals();
      Animal animalObj = new Animal();
      Horse horseObj = new Horse();
      ua.doStuff(animalObj);
      ua.doStuff(horseObj);
   }
}
```

The output is what you expect:

```
in the Animal version
in the Horse version
```

But what if you use an Animal reference to a Horse object?

```
Animal animalRefToHorse = new Horse();
ua.doStuff(animalRefToHorse);
```

Which of the overloaded versions is invoked? You might want to say, "The one that takes a Horse, since it's a Horse object at runtime that's being passed to the method." But that's not how it works. The preceding code would actually print:

```
in the Animal version
```

Even though the actual object at runtime is a Horse and not an Animal, the choice of which overloaded method to call (in other words, the signature of the method) is NOT dynamically decided at runtime. Just remember, the *reference* type (not the object type) determines which overloaded method is invoked! To summarize, which over*ridden* version of the method to call (in other words, from which class in the inheritance tree) is decided at *runtime* based on *object* type, but which over*loaded* version of the method to call is based on the *reference* type of the argument passed at *compile* time. If you invoke a method passing it an Animal reference to a Horse object, the compiler knows only about the Animal, so it chooses the overloaded version of the method that takes an Animal. It does not matter that at runtime there's actually a Horse being passed.

Polymorphism in Overloaded and Overridden Methods

How does polymorphism work with overloaded methods? From what we just looked at, it doesn't appear that polymorphism matters when a method is overloaded. If you pass an Animal reference, the overloaded method that takes an Animal will be invoked, even if the actual object passed is a Horse. Once the Horse masquerading as Animal gets in to the method, however, the Horse object is still a Horse despite being passed into a method expecting an Animal. So it's true that polymorphism doesn't determine which overloaded version is called; polymorphism does come into play when the decision is about which overridden version of a method is called. But sometimes, a method is both overloaded and overridden. Imagine the Animal and Horse classes look like this:

```
public class Animal {
   public void eat() {
      System.out.println("Generic Animal Eating Generically");
   }
}
public class Horse extends Animal {
   public void eat() {
      System.out.println("Horse eating hay ");
   }
   public void eat(String s) {
      System.out.println("Horse eating " + s);
   }
}
```

Notice that the Horse class has both overloaded and overridden the eat() method. Table 2-2 shows which version of the three eat() methods will run depending on how they are invoked.

TABLE 2-2	Examples of Illegal Overrides	

Method Invocation Code	Result
`Animal a = new Animal();` `a.eat();`	`Generic Animal Eating Generically`
`Horse h = new Horse();` `h.eat();`	`Horse eating hay`
`Animal ah = new Horse();` `ah.eat();`	`Horse eating hay` Polymorphism works—the actual object type (Horse), not the reference type (Animal), is used to determine which eat() is called.
`Horse he = new Horse();` `he.eat("Apples");`	`Horse eating Apples` The overloaded eat(String s) method is invoked.
`Animal a2 = new Animal();` `a2.eat("treats");`	Compiler error! Compiler sees that Animal class doesn't have an eat() method that takes a String.
`Animal ah2 = new Horse();` `ah2.eat("Carrots");`	Compiler error! Compiler *still* looks only at the reference, and sees that Animal doesn't have an eat() method that takes a String. Compiler doesn't care that the actual object might be a Horse at runtime.

e x a m

ⓦ a t c h

Don't be fooled by a method that's overloaded but not overridden by a subclass. It's perfectly legal to do the following:

```
public class Foo {
    void doStuff() { }
}
class Bar extends Foo {
    void doStuff(String s) { }
}
```

The Bar class has two `doStuff()` *methods: the no-arg version it inherits from Foo (and does not override), and the overloaded* `doStuff(String s)` *defined in the Bar class. Code with a reference to a Foo can invoke only the no-arg version, but code with a reference to a Bar can invoke either of the overloaded versions.*

Table 2-3 summarizes the difference between overloaded and overridden methods.

TABLE 2-3	Differences Between Overloaded and Overridden Methods	
	Overloaded Method	**Overridden Method**
Argument(s)	Must change.	Must not change.
Return type	Can change.	Can't change except for covariant returns.
Exceptions	Can change.	Can reduce or eliminate. Must not throw new or broader checked exceptions.
Access	Can change.	Must not make more restrictive (can be less restrictive).
Invocation	*Reference* type determines which overloaded version (based on declared argument types) is selected. Happens at *compile* time. The actual *method* that's invoked is still a virtual method invocation that happens at runtime, but the compiler will already know the *signature* of the method to be invoked. So at runtime, the argument match will already have been nailed down, just not the *class* in which the method lives.	*Object* type (in other words, *the type of the actual instance on the heap*) determines which method is selected. Happens at *runtime*.

The current objective (5.4) covers both method and constructor overloading, but we'll cover constructor overloading in the next section, where we'll also cover the other constructor-related topics that are on the exam. Figure 2-4 illustrates the way overloaded and overridden methods appear in class relationships.

FIGURE 2-4
Overloaded and overridden methods in class relationships

Overriding

Tree
showLeaves()

Oak
showLeaves()

Overloading

Tree
setFeatures(String name)

Oak
setFeatures(String name, int leafSize) setFeatures(int leafSize)

Reference Variable Casting (Objective 5.2)

5.2 Given a scenario, develop code that demonstrates the use of polymorphism. Further, determine when casting will be necessary and recognize compiler vs. runtime errors related to object reference casting.

We've seen how it's both possible and common to use generic reference variable types to refer to more specific object types. It's at the heart of polymorphism. For example, this line of code should be second nature by now:

```
Animal animal = new Dog();
```

But what happens when you want to use that `animal` reference variable to invoke a method that only class `Dog` has? You know it's referring to a `Dog`, and you want to do a `Dog`-specific thing? In the following code, we've got an array of `Animals`, and whenever we find a `Dog` in the array, we want to do a special `Dog` thing. Let's agree for now that all of this code is OK, except that we're not sure about the line of code that invokes the `playDead` method.

```
class Animal {
  void makeNoise() {System.out.println("generic noise"); }
}
class Dog extends Animal {
  void makeNoise() {System.out.println("bark"); }
  void playDead() { System.out.println("roll over"); }
}

class CastTest2 {
  public static void main(String [] args) {
    Animal [] a = {new Animal(), new Dog(), new Animal() };
    for(Animal animal : a) {
      animal.makeNoise();
      if(animal instanceof Dog) {
        animal.playDead();          // try to do a Dog behavior ?
      }
    }
  }
}
```

When we try to compile this code, the compiler says something like this:

```
cannot find symbol
```

The compiler is saying, "Hey, class Animal doesn't have a `playDead()` method". Let's modify the `if` code block:

```
if(animal instanceof Dog) {
    Dog d = (Dog) animal;      // casting the ref. var.
    d.playDead();
}
```

The new and improved code block contains a cast, which in this case is sometimes called a *downcast*, because we're casting down the inheritance tree to a more specific class. Now, the compiler is happy. Before we try to invoke `playDead`, we cast the animal variable to type `Dog`. What we're saying to the compiler is, "We know it's really referring to a `Dog` object, so it's okay to make a new `Dog` reference variable to refer to that object." In this case we're safe because before we ever try the cast, we do an `instanceof` test to make sure.

It's important to know that the compiler is forced to trust us when we do a downcast, even when we screw up:

```
class Animal { }
class Dog extends Animal { }
class DogTest {
  public static void main(String [] args) {
    Animal animal = new Animal();
    Dog d = (Dog) animal;            // compiles but fails later
  }
}
```

It can be maddening! This code compiles! When we try to run it, we'll get an exception something like this:

```
java.lang.ClassCastException
```

Why can't we trust the compiler to help us out here? Can't it see that `animal` is of type `Animal`? All the compiler can do is verify that the two types are in the same inheritance tree, so that depending on whatever code might have come before the downcast, it's possible that `animal` is of type `Dog`. The compiler must allow things that might possibly work at runtime. However, if the compiler knows with certainty that the cast could not possibly work, compilation will fail. The following replacement code block will NOT compile:

```
Animal animal = new Animal();
Dog d = (Dog) animal;
String s = (String) animal;  // animal can't EVER be a String
```

In this case, you'll get an error something like this:

```
inconvertible types
```

Unlike downcasting, upcasting (casting *up* the inheritance tree to a more general type) works implicitly (i.e., you don't have to type in the cast) because when you upcast you're implicitly restricting the number of methods you can invoke, as opposed to *down*casting, which implies that later on, you might want to invoke a more *specific* method. For instance:

```
class Animal { }
class Dog extends Animal { }

class DogTest {
  public static void main(String [] args) {
    Dog d = new Dog();
    Animal a1 = d;           // upcast ok with no explicit cast
    Animal a2 = (Animal) d;  // upcast ok with an explicit cast
  }
}
```

Both of the previous upcasts will compile and run without exception, because a Dog IS-A Animal, which means that anything an Animal can do, a Dog can do. A Dog can do more, of course, but the point is—anyone with an Animal reference can safely call Animal methods on a Dog instance. The Animal methods may have been overridden in the Dog class, but all we care about now is that a Dog can always do at least everything an Animal can do. The compiler and JVM know it too, so the implicit upcast is always legal for assigning an object of a subtype to a reference of one of its supertype classes (or interfaces). If Dog implements Pet, and Pet defines beFriendly(), then a Dog can be implicitly cast to a Pet, but the only Dog method you can invoke then is beFriendly(), which Dog was forced to implement because Dog implements the Pet interface.

One more thing…if `Dog implements Pet`, then if `Beagle extends Dog`, but Beagle does not *declare* that it implements Pet, Beagle is still a Pet! Beagle is a Pet simply because it extends Dog, and Dog's already taken care of the Pet parts of itself, and all its children. The Beagle class can always override any methods it inherits from Dog, including methods that Dog implemented to fulfill its interface contract.

And just one more thing…if Beagle does declare it implements Pet, just so that others looking at the Beagle class API can easily see that Beagle IS-A Pet, without having to look at Beagle's superclasses, Beagle still doesn't need to implement the beFriendly() method if the Dog class (Beagle's superclass) has already taken care of that. In other words, if Beagle IS-A Dog, and Dog IS-A Pet, then Beagle IS-A Pet, and has already met its Pet obligations for implementing the `beFriendly()` method since it inherits the `beFriendly()` method. The compiler is smart enough to say, "I know Beagle already IS a Dog, but it's OK to make it more obvious."

So don't be fooled by code that shows a concrete class that declares that it implements an interface, but doesn't implement the *methods* of the interface. Before you can tell whether the code is legal, you must know what the superclasses of this implementing class have declared. If any superclass in its inheritance tree has already provided concrete (i.e., non-abstract) method implementations, then, regardless of whether the superclass declares that it implements the interface, the subclass is under no obligation to re-implement (override) those methods.

e x a m

ⓦ a t c h **The exam creators will tell you that they're forced to jam tons of code into little spaces "because of the exam engine." While that's partially true, they ALSO like to obfuscate. The following code:**

```
Animal a = new Dog();
Dog d = (Dog) a;
d.doDogStuff();
```

Can be replaced with this easy-to-read bit of fun:

```
Animal a = new Dog();
((Dog)a).doDogStuff();
```

In this case the compiler needs all of those parentheses, otherwise it thinks it's been handed an incomplete statement.

CERTIFICATION OBJECTIVE

Implementing an Interface (Exam Objective 1.2)

1.2   Develop code that declares an interface...

When you implement an interface, you're agreeing to adhere to the contract defined in the interface. That means you're agreeing to provide legal implementations for every method defined in the interface, and that anyone who knows what the interface methods look like (not how they're implemented, but how they can be called and what they return) can rest assured that they can invoke those methods on an instance of your implementing class.

For example, if you create a class that implements the Runnable interface (so that your code can be executed by a specific thread), you must provide the `public void run()` method. Otherwise, the poor thread could be told to go execute your Runnable object's code and—surprise surprise—the thread then discovers the object has no `run()` method! (At which point, the thread would blow up and the JVM would crash in a spectacular yet horrible explosion.) Thankfully, Java prevents this meltdown from occurring by running a compiler check on any class that claims to implement an interface. If the class says it's implementing an interface, it darn well better have an implementation for each method in the interface (with a few exceptions we'll look at in a moment).

Assuming an interface, Bounceable, with two methods: `bounce()`, and `setBounceFactor()`, the following class will compile:

```
public class Ball implements Bounceable {  // Keyword
                                           // 'implements'
    public void bounce() { }
    public void setBounceFactor(int bf) { }
}
```

OK, we know what you're thinking: "This has got to be the worst implementation class in the history of implementation classes." It compiles, though. And runs. The interface contract guarantees that a class will have the method (in other words, others can call the method subject to access control), but it never guaranteed a good implementation—or even any actual implementation code in the body of the method. The compiler will never say to you, "Um, excuse me, but did you really mean to put nothing between those curly braces? HELLO. This is a method after all, so shouldn't it do something?"

Implementation classes must adhere to the same rules for method implementation as a class extending an `abstract` class. In order to be a legal implementation class, a nonabstract implementation class must do the following:

- Provide concrete (nonabstract) implementations for all methods from the declared interface.
- Follow all the rules for legal overrides.
- Declare no checked exceptions on implementation methods other than those declared by the interface method, or subclasses of those declared by the interface method.
- Maintain the signature of the interface method, and maintain the same return type (or a subtype). (But it does not have to declare the exceptions declared in the interface method declaration.)

But wait, there's more! An implementation class can itself be `abstract`! For example, the following is legal for a class Ball implementing Bounceable:

```
abstract class Ball implements Bounceable { }
```

Notice anything missing? We never provided the implementation methods. And that's OK. If the implementation class is `abstract`, it can simply pass the buck to its first concrete subclass. For example, if class BeachBall extends Ball, and BeachBall is not `abstract`, then BeachBall will have to provide all the methods from Bounceable:

```
class BeachBall extends Ball {
   // Even though we don't say it in the class declaration above,
   // BeachBall implements Bounceable, since BeachBall's abstract
   // superclass (Ball) implements Bounceable

   public void bounce() {
      // interesting BeachBall-specific bounce code
   }
   public void setBounceFactor(int bf) {
      // clever BeachBall-specific code for setting
      // a bounce factor
   }
```

```
    // if class Ball defined any abstract methods,
    // they'll have to be
    // implemented here as well.
}
```

Look for classes that claim to implement an interface but don't provide the correct method implementations. Unless the implementing class is abstract, the implementing class must provide implementations for all methods defined in the interface.

Two more rules you need to know and then we can put this topic to sleep (or put you to sleep; we always get those two confused):

1. A class can implement more than one interface. It's perfectly legal to say, for example, the following:

```
public class Ball implements Bounceable, Serializable, Runnable
{ ... }
```

You can extend only one class, but implement many interfaces. But remember that subclassing defines who and what you are, whereas implementing defines a role you can play or a hat you can wear, despite how different you might be from some other class implementing the same interface (but from a different inheritance tree). For example, a Person extends HumanBeing (although for some, that's debatable). But a Person may also implement Programmer, Snowboarder, Employee, Parent, or PersonCrazyEnoughToTakeThisExam.

2. An interface can itself extend another interface, but never implement anything. The following code is perfectly legal:

```
public interface Bounceable extends Moveable { }    // ok!
```

What does that mean? The first concrete (nonabstract) implementation class of Bounceable must implement all the methods of Bounceable, plus all the methods of Moveable! The subinterface, as we call it, simply adds more requirements to the contract of the superinterface. You'll see this concept applied in many areas of Java, especially J2EE where you'll often have to build your own interface that extends one of the J2EE interfaces.

Hold on though, because here's where it gets strange. An interface can extend more than one interface! Think about that for a moment. You know that when we're talking about classes, the following is illegal:

```
public class Programmer extends Employee, Geek { } // Illegal!
```

As we mentioned earlier, a class is not allowed to extend multiple classes in Java. An interface, however, is free to extend multiple interfaces.

```
interface Bounceable extends Moveable, Spherical {    // ok!
    void bounce();
    void setBounceFactor(int bf);
}
interface Moveable {
    void moveIt();
}
interface Spherical {
    void doSphericalThing();
}
```

In the next example, Ball is required to implement Bounceable, plus all methods from the interfaces that Bounceable extends (including any interfaces those interfaces extend, and so on until you reach the top of the stack—or is it the bottom of the stack?). So Ball would need to look like the following:

```
class Ball implements Bounceable {

    public void bounce() { }   // Implement Bounceable's methods
    public void setBounceFactor(int bf) { }

    public void moveIt() { }    // Implement Moveable's method

    public void doSphericalThing() { }   // Implement Spherical
}
```

If class Ball fails to implement any of the methods from Bounceable, Moveable, or Spherical, the compiler will jump up and down wildly, red in the face, until it does. Unless, that is, class Ball is marked `abstract`. In that case, Ball could choose to implement any, all, or none of the methods from any of the interfaces, thus leaving the rest of the implementations to a concrete subclass of Ball, as follows:

```
abstract class Ball implements Bounceable {
   public void bounce() { ... }  // Define bounce behavior
   public void setBounceFactor(int bf) { ... }
   // Don't implement the rest; leave it for a subclass
}
class SoccerBall extends Ball {  // class SoccerBall must
            // implement the interface methods that Ball didn't
   public void moveIt() { ... }
   public void doSphericalThing() { ... }
   // SoccerBall can choose to override the Bounceable methods
   // implemented by Ball
   public void bounce() { ... }
}
```

Figure 2-5 compares concrete and abstract examples of extends and implements, for both classes and interfaces.

FIGURE 2-5   Comparing concrete and abstract examples of extends and implements

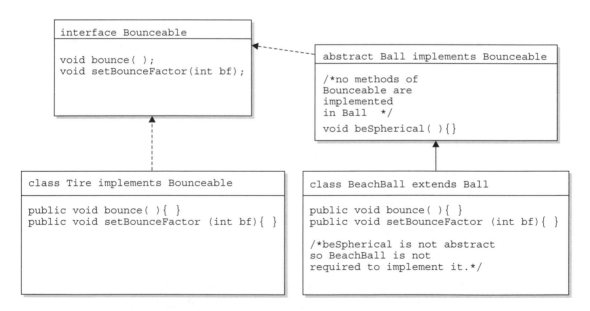

Because BeachBall is the first concrete class to implement Bounceable, it must provide implementations for all methods of Bounceable, except those defined in the abstract class Ball. Because Ball did not provide implementations of Bounceable methods, BeachBall was required to implement all of them.

exam
watch *Look for illegal uses of extends and implements. The following shows examples of legal and illegal class and interface declarations:*

```
class Foo { }                         // OK
class Bar implements Foo { }          // No! Can't implement a class
interface Baz { }                     // OK
interface Fi { }                      // OK
interface Fee implements Baz { }      // No! Interface can't
                                      // implement an interface
interface Zee implements Foo { }      // No! Interface can't
                                      // implement a class
interface Zoo extends Foo { }         // No! Interface can't
                                      // extend a class
interface Boo extends Fi { }          // OK. Interface can extend
                                      // an interface
class Toon extends Foo, Button { }    // No! Class can't extend
                                      // multiple classes
class Zoom implements Fi, Baz { }     // OK. class can implement
                                      // multiple interfaces
interface Vroom extends Fi, Baz { }   // OK. interface can extend
                                      // multiple interfaces
class Yow extends Foo implements Fi { } // OK. Class can do both
                                        // (extends must be 1st)
```

Burn these in, and watch for abuses in the questions you get on the exam. Regardless of what the question appears to be testing, the real problem might be the class or interface declaration. Before you get caught up in, say, tracing a complex threading flow, check to see if the code will even compile. (Just that tip alone may be worth your putting us in your will!) (You'll be impressed by the effort the exam developers put into distracting you from the real problem.) (How did people manage to write anything before parentheses were invented?)

Legal Return Types (Exam Objective 1.5)

1.5   Given a code example, determine if a method is correctly overriding or overloading another method, and identify legal return values (including covariant returns), for the method.

This objective covers two aspects of return types: what you can declare as a return type, and what you can actually return as a value. What you can and cannot declare is pretty straightforward, but it all depends on whether you're overriding an inherited method or simply declaring a new method (which includes overloaded methods). We'll take just a quick look at the difference between return type rules for overloaded and overriding methods, because we've already covered that in this chapter. We'll cover a small bit of new ground, though, when we look at polymorphic return types and the rules for what is and is not legal to actually return.

Return Type Declarations

This section looks at what you're allowed to declare as a return type, which depends primarily on whether you are overriding, overloading, or declaring a new method.

Return Types on Overloaded Methods

Remember that method overloading is not much more than name reuse. The overloaded method is a completely different method from any other method of the same name. So if you inherit a method but overload it in a subclass, you're not subject to the restrictions of overriding, which means you can declare any return type you like. What you can't do is change *only* the return type. To overload a method, remember, you must change the argument list. The following code shows an overloaded method:

```
public class Foo{
    void go() { }
}
public class Bar extends Foo {
    String go(int x) {
```

```
        return null;
    }
}
```

Notice that the Bar version of the method uses a different return type. That's perfectly fine. As long as you've changed the argument list, you're overloading the method, so the return type doesn't have to match that of the superclass version. What you're NOT allowed to do is this:

```
public class Foo{
    void go() { }
}
public class Bar extends Foo {
    String go() { // Not legal! Can't change only the return type
        return null;
    }
}
```

Overriding and Return Types, and Covariant Returns

When a subclass wants to change the method implementation of an inherited method (an override), the subclass must define a method that matches the inherited version exactly. Or, as of Java 5, you're allowed to change the return type in the overriding method as long as the new return type is a *subtype* of the declared return type of the overridden (superclass) method.

Let's look at a covariant return in action:

```
class Alpha {
  Alpha doStuff(char c) {
    return new Alpha();
  }
}

class Beta extends Alpha {
  Beta doStuff(char c) {      // legal override in Java 1.5
    return new Beta();
  }
}
```

As of Java 5, this code will compile. If you were to attempt to compile this code with a 1.4 compiler or with the source flag as follows:

```
javac -source 1.4 Beta.java
```

you would get a compiler error something like this:

```
attempting to use incompatible return type
```

(We'll talk more about compiler flags in Chapter 10.)

Other rules apply to overriding, including those for access modifiers and declared exceptions, but those rules aren't relevant to the return type discussion.

For the exam, be sure you know that overloaded methods can change the return type, but overriding methods can do so only within the bounds of covariant returns. Just that knowledge alone will help you through a wide range of exam questions.

Returning a Value

You have to remember only six rules for returning a value:

1. You can return `null` in a method with an object reference return type.

   ```
   public Button doStuff() {
     return null;
   }
   ```

2. An array is a perfectly legal return type.

   ```
   public String[] go() {
     return new String[] {"Fred", "Barney", "Wilma"};
   }
   ```

3. In a method with a primitive return type, you can return any value or variable that can be implicitly converted to the declared return type.

   ```
   public int foo() {
     char c = 'c';
     return c;  // char is compatible with int
   }
   ```

4. In a method with a primitive return type, you can return any value or variable that can be explicitly cast to the declared return type.

```
public int foo () {
   float f = 32.5f;
   return (int) f;
}
```

5. You must *not* return anything from a method with a void return type.

```
public void bar() {
   return "this is it";   // Not legal!!
}
```

6. In a method with an object reference return type, you can return any object type that can be implicitly cast to the declared return type.

```
public Animal getAnimal() {
   return new Horse();   // Assume Horse extends Animal
}

public Object getObject() {
   int[] nums = {1,2,3};
   return nums;   // Return an int array,
                  // which is still an object
}

public interface Chewable { }
public class Gum implements Chewable { }

public class TestChewable {
    // Method with an interface return type
   public Chewable getChewable() {
      return new Gum();   // Return interface implementer
   }
}
```

e x a m

ⓦ a t c h   *Watch for methods that declare an abstract class or interface return type, and know that any object that passes the IS-A test (in other words, would test true using the instanceof operator) can be returned from that method— for example:*

```
public abstract class Animal { }
public class Bear extends Animal { }
public class Test {
    public Animal go() {
        return new Bear();   // OK, Bear "is-a" Animal
    }
}
```

This code will compile, the return value is a subtype.

CERTIFICATION OBJECTIVE

Constructors and Instantiation (Exam Objectives 1.6, 5.3, and 5.4)

1.6   Given a set of classes and superclasses, develop constructors for one or more of the classes. Given a class declaration, determine if a default constructor will be created, and if so, determine the behavior of that constructor. Given a nested or nonnested class listing, write code to instantiate the class.

5.3   Explain the effect of modifiers on inheritance with respect to constructors, instance or static variables, and instance or static methods.

5.4   Given a scenario, develop code that declares and/or invokes overridden or overloaded methods and code that declares and/or invokes superclass, overridden, or overloaded constructors.

Objects are constructed. You can't make a new object without invoking a constructor. In fact, you can't make a new object without invoking not just the constructor of the object's actual class type, but also the constructor of each of its superclasses! Constructors are the code that runs whenever you use the keyword new. OK, to be a bit more accurate, there can also be initialization blocks that run when you say new, but we're going to cover them (init blocks), and their static initialization counterparts, in the next chapter. We've got plenty to talk about here—we'll look at how constructors are coded, who codes them, and how they work at runtime. So grab your hardhat and a hammer, and let's do some object building.

Constructor Basics

Every class, *including abstract classes*, MUST have a constructor. Burn that into your brain. But just because a class must have one, doesn't mean the programmer has to type it. A constructor looks like this:

```
class Foo {
    Foo() { } // The constructor for the Foo class
}
```

Notice what's missing? There's no return type! Two key points to remember about constructors are that they have no return type and their names must exactly match the class name. Typically, constructors are used to initialize instance variable state, as follows:

```
class Foo {
    int size;
    String name;
    Foo(String name, int size) {
        this.name = name;
        this.size = size;
    }
}
```

In the preceding code example, the Foo class does not have a no-arg constructor. That means the following will fail to compile:

```
Foo f = new Foo();   // Won't compile, no matching constructor
```

but the following will compile:

```
Foo f = new Foo("Fred", 43);   // No problem. Arguments match
                               // the Foo constructor.
```

So it's very common (and desirable) for a class to have a no-arg constructor, regardless of how many other overloaded constructors are in the class (yes, constructors can be overloaded). You can't always make that work for your classes; occasionally you have a class where it makes no sense to create an instance without supplying information to the constructor. A `java.awt.Color` object, for example, can't be created by calling a no-arg constructor, because that would be like saying to the JVM, "Make me a new Color object, and I really don't care what color it is...you pick." Do you seriously want the JVM making your style decisions?

Constructor Chaining

We know that constructors are invoked at runtime when you say new on some class type as follows:

```
Horse h = new Horse();
```

But what *really* happens when you say new Horse() ?
(Assume Horse extends Animal and Animal extends Object.)

1. Horse constructor is invoked. Every constructor invokes the constructor of its superclass with an (implicit) call to super(), unless the constructor invokes an overloaded constructor of the same class (more on that in a minute).

2. Animal constructor is invoked (Animal is the superclass of Horse).

3. Object constructor is invoked (Object is the ultimate superclass of all classes, so class Animal extends Object even though you don't actually type "extends Object" into the Animal class declaration. It's implicit.) At this point we're on the top of the stack.

4. Object instance variables are given their explicit values. By *explicit* values, we mean values that are assigned at the time the variables are declared, like "int x = 27", where "27" is the explicit value (as opposed to the default value) of the instance variable.

5. Object constructor completes.

6. Animal instance variables are given their explicit values (if any).

7. Animal constructor completes.

8. Horse instance variables are given their explicit values (if any).
9. Horse constructor completes.

Figure 2-6 shows how constructors work on the call stack.

FIGURE 2-6

Constructors on
the call stack

| 4. Object() |
| 3. Animal() calls super() |
| 2. Horse() calls super() |
| 1. main() calls new Horse() |

Rules for Constructors

The following list summarizes the rules you'll need to know for the exam (and to understand the rest of this section). You MUST remember these, so be sure to study them more than once.

- Constructors can use any access modifier, including private. (A private constructor means only code within the class itself can instantiate an object of that type, so if the private constructor class wants to allow an instance of the class to be used, the class must provide a static method or variable that allows access to an instance created from within the class.)
- The constructor name must match the name of the class.
- Constructors must not have a return type.
- It's legal (but stupid) to have a method with the same name as the class, but that doesn't make it a constructor. If you see a return type, it's a method rather than a constructor. In fact, you could have both a method and a constructor with the same name—the name of the class—in the same class, and that's not a problem for Java. Be careful not to mistake a method for a constructor—be sure to look for a return type.
- If you don't type a constructor into your class code, a default constructor will be automatically generated by the compiler.
- The default constructor is ALWAYS a no-arg constructor.
- If you want a no-arg constructor and you've typed any other constructor(s) into your class code, the compiler won't provide the no-arg constructor (or

any other constructor) for you. In other words, if you've typed in a constructor with arguments, you won't have a no-arg constructor unless you type it in yourself!

■ Every constructor has, as its first statement, either a call to an overloaded constructor (this()) or a call to the superclass constructor (super()), although remember that this call can be inserted by the compiler.

■ If you do type in a constructor (as opposed to relying on the compiler-generated default constructor), and you do not type in the call to super() or a call to this(), the compiler will insert a no-arg call to super() for you, as the very first statement in the constructor.

■ A call to super() can be either a no-arg call or can include arguments passed to the super constructor.

■ A no-arg constructor is not necessarily the default (i.e., compiler-supplied) constructor, although the default constructor is always a no-arg constructor. The default constructor is the one the compiler provides! While the default constructor is always a no-arg constructor, you're free to put in your own no-arg constructor.

■ You cannot make a call to an instance method, or access an instance variable, until after the super constructor runs.

■ Only static variables and methods can be accessed as part of the call to super() or this(). (Example: super(Animal.NAME) is OK, because NAME is declared as a static variable.)

■ Abstract classes have constructors, and those constructors are always called when a concrete subclass is instantiated.

■ Interfaces do not have constructors. Interfaces are not part of an object's inheritance tree.

■ The only way a constructor can be invoked is from within another constructor. In other words, you can't write code that actually calls a constructor as follows:

```
class Horse {
  Horse() { } // constructor
  void doStuff() {
    Horse();  // calling the constructor - illegal!
  }
}
```

Determine Whether a Default Constructor Will Be Created

The following example shows a Horse class with two constructors:

```
class Horse {
   Horse() { }
   Horse(String name) { }
 }
```

Will the compiler put in a default constructor for the class above? No!
How about for the following variation of the class?

```
class Horse {
   Horse(String name) { }
 }
```

Now will the compiler insert a default constructor? No!
What about this class?

```
class Horse { }
```

Now we're talking. The compiler will generate a default constructor for the preceding class, because the class doesn't have any constructors defined.
OK, what about this class?

```
class Horse {
   void Horse() { }
 }
```

It might look like the compiler won't create one, since there already is a constructor in the Horse class. Or is there? Take another look at the preceding Horse class.
What's wrong with the Horse() constructor? It isn't a constructor at all! It's simply a method that happens to have the same name as the class. Remember, the return type is a dead giveaway that we're looking at a method, and not a constructor.

How do you know for sure whether a default constructor will be created?
Because you didn't write any constructors in your class.

How do you know what the default constructor will look like?
Because...

■ The default constructor has the same access modifier as the class.

■ The default constructor has no arguments.

■ The default constructor includes a no-arg call to the super constructor (`super()`).

Table 2-4 shows what the compiler will (or won't) generate for your class.

What happens if the super constructor has arguments?
Constructors can have arguments just as methods can, and if you try to invoke a method that takes, say, an int, but you don't pass anything to the method, the compiler will complain as follows:

```
class Bar {
    void takeInt (int x) { }
}

class UseBar {
   public static void main (String [] args) {
     Bar b = new Bar();
     b.takeInt();  // Try to invoke a no-arg takeInt() method
   }
}
```

The compiler will complain that you can't invoke takeInt() without passing an int. Of course, the compiler enjoys the occasional riddle, so the message it spits out on some versions of the JVM (your mileage may vary) is less than obvious:

```
UseBar.java:7: takeInt(int) in Bar cannot be applied to ()
    b.takeInt();
      ^
```

But you get the idea. The bottom line is that there must be a match for the method. And by match, we mean that the argument types must be able to accept the values or variables you're passing, and in the order you're passing them. Which brings us back to constructors (and here you were thinking we'd never get there), which work exactly the same way.

| **TABLE 2-4** | Compiler-Generated Constructor Code |

Class Code (What You Type)	Compiler Generated Constructor Code (in Bold)

`class Foo { }`	`class Foo {`
	  `Foo() {`
	    `super();`
	  `}`
	`}`

`class Foo {`
  `Foo() { }`
`}`
	`class Foo {`
	  `Foo() {`
	    `super();`
	  `}`
	`}`

`public class Foo { }`	`public class Foo {`
	  `public Foo() {`
	    `super();`
	  `}`
	`}`

`class Foo {`
  `Foo(String s) { }`
`}`
	`class Foo {`
	  `Foo(String s) {`
	    `super();`
	  `}`
	`}`

`class Foo {`
  `Foo(String s) {`
    `super();`
  `}`
`}`
	Nothing, compiler doesn't need to insert anything.

`class Foo {`
  `void Foo() { }`
`}`
	`class Foo {`
	  `void Foo() { }`
	  `Foo() {`
	    `super();`
	  `}`
	`}`
	`(void Foo()` *is a method, not a constructor.)*

So if your super constructor (that is, the constructor of your immediate superclass/parent) has arguments, you must type in the call to super(), supplying the appropriate arguments. Crucial point: if your superclass does not have a no-arg constructor, you must type a constructor in your class (the subclass) because you need a place to put in the call to super with the appropriate arguments.

The following is an example of the problem:

```
class Animal {
    Animal(String name) { }
}

class Horse extends Animal {
    Horse() {
        super();   // Problem!
    }
}
```

And once again the compiler treats us with the stunningly lucid:

```
Horse.java:7: cannot resolve symbol
symbol  : constructor Animal   ()
location: class Animal
        super();  // Problem!
        ^
```

If you're lucky (and it's a full moon), *your* compiler might be a little more explicit. But again, the problem is that there just isn't a match for what we're trying to invoke with super()—an Animal constructor with no arguments.

Another way to put this is that if your superclass does *not* have a no-arg constructor, then in your subclass you will not be able to use the default constructor supplied by the compiler. It's that simple. Because the compiler can *only* put in a call to a no-arg super(), you won't even be able to compile something like this:

```
class Clothing {
    Clothing(String s) { }
}
class TShirt extends Clothing { }
```

Trying to compile this code gives us exactly the same error we got when we put a constructor in the subclass with a call to the no-arg version of super():

```
Clothing.java:4: cannot resolve symbol
symbol  : constructor Clothing   ()
location: class Clothing
```

```
class TShirt extends Clothing { }
      ^
```

In fact, the preceding Clothing and TShirt code is implicitly the same as the following code, where we've supplied a constructor for TShirt that's identical to the default constructor supplied by the compiler:

```
class Clothing {
   Clothing(String s) { }
}
class TShirt extends Clothing {
                   // Constructor identical to compiler-supplied
                   // default constructor
   TShirt() {
      super(); // Won't work!
   }           // Invokes a no-arg Clothing() constructor,
}              // but there isn't one!
```

One last point on the whole default constructor thing (and it's probably very obvious, but we have to say it or we'll feel guilty for years), *constructors are never inherited.* They aren't methods. They can't be overridden (because they aren't methods and only instance methods can be overridden). So the type of constructor(s) your superclass has in no way determines the type of default constructor you'll get. Some folks mistakenly believe that the default constructor somehow matches the super constructor, either by the arguments the default constructor will have (remember, the default constructor is always a no-arg), or by the arguments used in the compiler-supplied call to super().

So, although constructors can't be overridden, you've already seen that they can be overloaded, and typically are.

Overloaded Constructors

Overloading a constructor means typing in multiple versions of the constructor, each having a different argument list, like the following examples:

```
class Foo {
   Foo() { }
   Foo(String s) { }
}
```

The preceding Foo class has two overloaded constructors, one that takes a string, and one with no arguments. Because there's no code in the no-arg version, it's actually identical to the default constructor the compiler supplies, but remember— since there's already a constructor in this class (the one that takes a string), the compiler won't supply a default constructor. If you want a no-arg constructor to overload the with-args version you already have, you're going to have to type it yourself, just as in the Foo example.

Overloading a constructor is typically used to provide alternate ways for clients to instantiate objects of your class. For example, if a client knows the animal name, they can pass that to an Animal constructor that takes a string. But if they don't know the name, the client can call the no-arg constructor and that constructor can supply a default name. Here's what it looks like:

```
1. public class Animal {
2.    String name;
3.    Animal(String name) {
4.       this.name = name;
5.    }
6.
7.    Animal() {
8.       this(makeRandomName());
9.    }
10.
11.   static String makeRandomName() {
12.      int x = (int) (Math.random() * 5);
13.      String name = new String[] {"Fluffy", "Fido",
                                     "Rover", "Spike",
                                     "Gigi"}[x];
14.      return name;
15.   }
16.
17.   public static void main (String [] args) {
18.      Animal a = new Animal();
19.      System.out.println(a.name);
20.      Animal b = new Animal("Zeus");
21.      System.out.println(b.name);
22.   }
23. }
```

Running the code four times produces this output:

```
% java Animal
Gigi
Zeus

% java Animal
Fluffy
Zeus

% java Animal
Rover
Zeus

% java Animal
Fluffy
Zeus
```

There's a lot going on in the preceding code. Figure 2-7 shows the call stack for constructor invocations when a constructor is overloaded. Take a look at the call stack, and then let's walk through the code straight from the top.

<table>
<tr><td>**FIGURE 2-7**</td><td>4. Object()</td></tr>
<tr><td rowspan="3">Overloaded constructors on the call stack</td><td>3. Animal(String s) calls super()</td></tr>
<tr><td>2. Animal() calls this(randomlyChosenNameString)</td></tr>
<tr><td>1. main() calls new Animal()</td></tr>
</table>

- **Line 2**   Declare a String instance variable name.
- **Lines 3–5**   Constructor that takes a String, and assigns it to instance variable name.
- **Line 7**   Here's where it gets fun. Assume every animal needs a name, but the client (calling code) might not always know what the name should be, so you'll assign a random name. The no-arg constructor generates a name by invoking the makeRandomName() method.
- **Line 8**   The no-arg constructor invokes its own overloaded constructor that takes a String, in effect calling it the same way it would be called if

client code were doing a `new` to instantiate an object, passing it a String for the name. The overloaded invocation uses the keyword `this`, but uses it as though it were a method name, `this()`. So line 8 is simply calling the constructor on line 3, passing it a randomly selected String rather than a client-code chosen name.

- **Line 11** Notice that the `makeRandomName()` method is marked `static`! That's because you cannot invoke an instance (in other words, nonstatic) method (or access an instance variable) until after the super constructor has run. And since the super constructor will be invoked from the constructor on line 3, rather than from the one on line 7, line 8 can use only a static method to generate the name. If we wanted all animals not specifically named by the caller to have the same default name, say, "Fred," then line 8 could have read `this("Fred");` rather than calling a method that returns a string with the randomly chosen name.

- **Line 12** This doesn't have anything to do with constructors, but since we're all here to learn...it generates a random integer between 0 and 4.

- **Line 13** Weird syntax, we know. We're creating a new String object (just a single String instance), but we want the string to be selected randomly from a list. Except we don't have the list, so we need to make it. So in that one line of code we

  1. Declare a String variable, name.
  2. Create a String array (anonymously—we don't assign the array itself to anything).
  3. Retrieve the string at index [x] (x being the random number generated on line 12) of the newly created String array.
  4. Assign the string retrieved from the array to the declared instance variable name. We could have made it much easier to read if we'd just written

```
String[] nameList = {"Fluffy", "Fido", "Rover", "Spike",
                     "Gigi"};
String name = nameList[x];
```

But where's the fun in that? Throwing in unusual syntax (especially for code wholly unrelated to the real question) is in the spirit of the exam. Don't be startled! (OK, be startled, but then just say to yourself, "Whoa" and get on with it.)

- **Line 18**   We're invoking the no-arg version of the constructor (causing a random name from the list to be passed to the other constructor).

- **Line 20**   We're invoking the overloaded constructor that takes a string representing the name.

The key point to get from this code example is in line 8. Rather than calling super(), we're calling this(), and this() always means a call to another constructor in the same class. OK, fine, but what happens after the call to this()? Sooner or later the super() constructor gets called, right? Yes indeed. A call to this() just means you're delaying the inevitable. Some constructor, somewhere, must make the call to super().

Key Rule: The first line in a constructor must be a call to super() or a call to this().

No exceptions. If you have neither of those calls in your constructor, the compiler will insert the no-arg call to super(). In other words, if constructor A() has a call to this(), the compiler knows that constructor A() will not be the one to invoke super().

The preceding rule means a constructor can never have both a call to super() and a call to this(). Because each of those calls must be the first statement in a constructor, you can't legally use both in the same constructor. That also means the compiler will not put a call to super() in any constructor that has a call to this().

Thought question: What do you think will happen if you try to compile the following code?

```
class A {
    A() {
        this("foo");
    }
    A(String s) {
        this();
    }
}
```

Your compiler may not actually catch the problem (it varies depending on your compiler, but most won't catch the problem). It assumes you know what you're doing. Can you spot the flaw? Given that a super constructor must always be called, where would the call to super() go? Remember, the compiler won't put in a default constructor if you've already got one or more constructors in your class. And when the compiler doesn't put in a default constructor, it still inserts a call to super() in any constructor that doesn't explicitly have a call to the super constructor—unless, that is, the constructor already has a call to this(). So in the preceding code, where can super() go? The only two constructors in the class both have calls to this(), and in fact you'll get exactly what you'd get if you typed the following method code:

```
public void go() {
    doStuff();
}

public void doStuff() {
    go();
}
```

Now can you see the problem? Of course you can. The stack explodes! It gets higher and higher and higher until it just bursts open and method code goes spilling out, oozing out of the JVM right onto the floor. Two overloaded constructors both calling this() are two constructors calling each other. Over and over and over, resulting in

```
% java A
Exception in thread "main" java.lang.StackOverflowError
```

The benefit of having overloaded constructors is that you offer flexible ways to instantiate objects from your class. The benefit of having one constructor invoke another overloaded constructor is to avoid code duplication. In the Animal example, there wasn't any code other than setting the name, but imagine if after line 4 there was still more work to be done in the constructor. By putting all the other constructor work in just one constructor, and then having the other constructors invoke it, you don't have to write and maintain multiple versions of that other important constructor code. Basically, each of the other not-the-real-one overloaded constructors will call another overloaded constructor, passing it whatever data it needs (data the client code didn't supply).

Constructors and instantiation become even more exciting (just when you thought it was safe), when you get to inner classes, but we know you can stand to have only so much fun in one chapter, so we're holding the rest of the discussion on instantiating inner classes until Chapter 8.

Statics (Exam Objective 1.3)

1.3 Develop code that declares, initializes, and uses primitives, arrays, enums, and objects as static, instance, and local variables. Also, use legal identifiers for variable names.

Static Variables and Methods

The static modifier has such a profound impact on the behavior of a method or variable that we're treating it as a concept entirely separate from the other modifiers. To understand the way a static member works, we'll look first at a reason for using one. Imagine you've got a utility class with a method that always runs the same way; its sole function is to return, say, a random number. It wouldn't matter which instance of the class performed the method—it would always behave exactly the same way. In other words, the method's behavior has no dependency on the state (instance variable values) of an object. So why, then, do you need an object when the method will never be instance-specific? Why not just ask the class itself to run the method?

Let's imagine another scenario: Suppose you want to keep a running count of all instances instantiated from a particular class. Where do you actually keep that variable? It won't work to keep it as an instance variable within the class whose instances you're tracking, because the count will just be initialized back to a default value with each new instance. The answer to both the utility-method-always-runs-the-same scenario and the keep-a-running-total-of-instances scenario is to use the static modifier. Variables and methods marked static belong to the class, rather than to any particular instance. In fact, you can use a static method or variable without having any instances of that class at all. You need only have the class available to be able to invoke a static method or access a static variable. static variables, too, can be accessed without having an instance of a class. But if there are instances, a static variable of a class will be shared by all instances of that class; there is only one copy.

The following code declares and uses a static counter variable:

```
class Frog {
   static int frogCount = 0;  // Declare and initialize
                              // static variable
   public Frog() {
      frogCount += 1;  // Modify the value in the constructor
   }
   public static void main (String [] args) {
      new Frog();
      new Frog();
      new Frog();
      System.out.println("Frog count is now " + frogCount);
   }
}
```

In the preceding code, the static frogCount variable is set to zero when the Frog class is first loaded by the JVM, before any Frog instances are created! (By the way, you don't actually need to initialize a static variable to zero; static variables get the same default values instance variables get.) Whenever a Frog instance is created, the Frog constructor runs and increments the static frogCount variable. When this code executes, three Frog instances are created in main(), and the result is

```
Frog count is now 3
```

Now imagine what would happen if frogCount were an instance variable (in other words, nonstatic):

```
class Frog {
   int frogCount = 0;  // Declare and initialize
                       // instance variable
   public Frog() {
      frogCount += 1;  // Modify the value in the constructor
   }
   public static void main (String [] args) {
      new Frog();
      new Frog();
      new Frog();
      System.out.println("Frog count is now " + frogCount);
   }
}
```

When this code executes, it should still create three Frog instances in main(), but the result is...a compiler error! We can't get this code to compile, let alone run.

```
Frog.java:11: nonstatic variable frogCount cannot be referenced
from a static context
    System.out.println("Frog count is " + frogCount);
                                           ^
```

```
1 error
```

The JVM doesn't know which Frog object's frogCount you're trying to access. The problem is that `main()` is itself a `static` method, and thus isn't running against any particular instance of the class, rather just on the class itself. A `static` method can't access a nonstatic (instance) variable, because there is no instance! That's not to say there aren't instances of the class alive on the heap, but rather that even if there are, the `static` method doesn't know anything about them. The same applies to instance methods; a `static` method can't directly invoke a nonstatic method. Think static = class, nonstatic = instance. Making the method called by the JVM (`main()`) a `static` method means the JVM doesn't have to create an instance of your class just to start running code.

exam

w a t c h *One of the mistakes most often made by new Java programmers is attempting to access an instance variable (which means nonstatic variable) from the static* `main()` *method (which doesn't know anything about any instances, so it can't access the variable). The following code is an example of illegal access of a nonstatic variable from a static method:*

```
class Foo {
    int x = 3;
    public static void main (String [] args) {
        System.out.println("x is " + x);
    }
}
```

Understand that this code will never compile, because you can't access a nonstatic (instance) variable from a static method. Just think of the compiler saying, "Hey, I have no idea which Foo object's x variable you're trying to print!" Remember, it's the class running the `main()` *method, not an instance of the class.*

(continued) Of course, the tricky part for the exam is that the question won't look as obvious as the preceding code. The problem you're being tested for— accessing a nonstatic variable from a static method—will be buried in code that might appear to be testing something else. For example, the preceding code would be more likely to appear as

```
class Foo {
    int x = 3;
    float y = 4.3f;
    public static void main (String [] args) {
        for (int z = x; z < ++x; z--, y = y + z)
            // complicated looping and branching code
    }
}
```

So while you're trying to follow the logic, the real issue is that x and y can't be used within `main()`, *because x and y are instance, not static, variables! The same applies for accessing nonstatic methods from a static method. The rule is, a static method of a class can't access a nonstatic (instance) method or variable of its own class.*

Accessing Static Methods and Variables

Since you don't need to have an instance in order to invoke a static method or access a static variable, then how do you invoke or use a static member? What's the syntax? We know that with a regular old instance method, you use the dot operator on a reference to an instance:

```
class Frog {
    int frogSize = 0;
    public int getFrogSize() {
        return frogSize;
    }
    public Frog(int s) {
        frogSize = s;
    }
    public static void main (String [] args) {
```

```
        Frog f = new Frog(25);
        System.out.println(f.getFrogSize()); // Access instance
                                             // method using f
    }
}
```

In the preceding code, we instantiate a Frog, assign it to the reference variable f, and then use that f reference to invoke a method on the Frog instance we just created. In other words, the getFrogSize() method is being invoked on a specific Frog object on the heap.

But this approach (using a reference to an object) isn't appropriate for accessing a static method, because there might not be any instances of the class at all! So, the way we access a static method (or static variable) is to use the dot operator on the class name, as opposed to using it on a reference to an instance, as follows:

```
class Frog {
    static int frogCount = 0;  // Declare and initialize
                               // static variable
    public Frog() {
        frogCount += 1;  // Modify the value in the constructor
    }
}

class TestFrog {
    public static void main (String [] args) {
        new Frog();
        new Frog();
        new Frog();
        System.out.print("frogCount:"+Frog.frogCount); //Access
                                                        // static variable
    }
}
```

But just to make it really confusing, the Java language also allows you to use an object reference variable to access a static member:

```
Frog f = new Frog();
int frogs = f.frogCount; // Access static variable
                         // FrogCount using f
```

In the preceding code, we instantiate a Frog, assign the new Frog object to the reference variable f, and then use the f reference to invoke a `static` method! But even though we are using a specific Frog instance to access the `static` method, the rules haven't changed. This is merely a syntax trick to let you use an object reference variable (but not the object it refers to) to get to a `static` method or variable, but the `static` member is still unaware of the particular instance used to invoke the `static` member. In the Frog example, the compiler knows that the reference variable f is of type Frog, and so the Frog class `static` method is run with no awareness or concern for the Frog instance at the other end of the f reference. In other words, the compiler cares only that reference variable f is declared as type Frog. Figure 2-8 illustrates the effects of the static modifier on methods and variables.

FIGURE 2-8

The effects of static on methods and variables

```
                class Foo

  int size = 42;
  static void doMore ( ){
      int x = size;
  }
```
static method cannot access an instance (non-static) variable

```
                class Bar

  void go ( );
  static void doMore ( ){
      go ( );
  }
```
static method cannot access a non-static method

```
                class Baz

  static int count;
  static void woo ( ){ }
  static void doMore ( ){
      woo ( );
      int x = count;
  }
```
static method *can* access a static method or variable

Finally, remember that *static methods can't be overridden!* This doesn't mean they can't be redefined in a subclass, but redefining and overriding aren't the same thing. Let's take a look at an example of a redefined (remember, not overridden), `static` method:

```
class Animal {
  static void doStuff() {
    System.out.print("a ");
  }
}
class Dog extends Animal {
  static void doStuff() {              // it's a redefinition,
                                       // not an override
    System.out.print("d ");
  }
  public static void main(String [] args) {
    Animal [] a = {new Animal(), new Dog(), new Animal()};
    for(int x = 0; x < a.length; x++)
      a[x].doStuff();                  // invoke the static method
  }
}
```

Running this code produces the output:

```
a a a
```

Remember, the syntax `a[x].doStuff()` is just a shortcut (the syntax trick)...the compiler is going to substitute something like `Animal.doStuff()` instead. Notice that we didn't use the Java 1.5 *enhanced* `for` *loop* here (covered in Chapter 5), even though we could have. Expect to see a mix of both Java 1.4 and Java 5 coding styles and practices on the exam.

CERTIFICATION OBJECTIVE

Coupling and Cohesion (Exam Objective 5.1)

5.1   Develop code that implements tight encapsulation, loose coupling, and high cohesion in classes, and describe the benefits.

We're going to admit it up front. The Sun exam's definitions for cohesion and coupling are somewhat subjective, so what we discuss in this chapter is from the perspective of the exam, and by no means The One True Word on these two OO design principles. It may not be exactly the way that you've learned it, but it's what you need to understand to answer the questions. You'll have very few questions about coupling and cohesion on the real exam.

These two topics, coupling and cohesion, have to do with the quality of an OO design. In general, good OO design calls for *loose coupling* and shuns tight coupling, and good OO design calls for *high cohesion*, and shuns low cohesion. As with most OO design discussions, the goals for an application are

- Ease of creation
- Ease of maintenance
- Ease of enhancement

Coupling

Let's start by making an attempt at a definition of coupling. Coupling is the degree to which one class knows about another class. If the only knowledge that class A has about class B, is what class B has exposed through its interface, then class A and class B are said to be loosely coupled…that's a good thing. If, on the other hand, class A relies on parts of class B that are not part of class B's interface, then the coupling between the classes is tighter…*not* a good thing. In other words, if A knows more than it should about the way in which B was implemented, then A and B are tightly coupled.

Using this second scenario, imagine what happens when class B is enhanced. It's quite possible that the developer enhancing class B has no knowledge of class A, why would she? Class B's developer ought to feel that any enhancements that don't break the class's interface should be safe, so she might change some noninterface part of the class, which then causes class A to break.

At the far end of the coupling spectrum is the horrible situation in which class A knows non-API stuff about class B, and class B knows non-API stuff about class A… this is REALLY BAD. If either class is ever changed, there's a chance that the other class will break. Let's look at an obvious example of tight coupling, which has been enabled by poor encapsulation:

```
class DoTaxes {
  float rate;
```

```
   float doColorado() {
     SalesTaxRates str = new SalesTaxRates();
     rate = str.salesRate;        // ouch
                                  // this should be a method call:
                                  // rate = str.getSalesRate("CO");

     // do stuff with rate
   }
}

class SalesTaxRates {
  public float salesRate;           // should be private
  public float adjustedSalesRate;   // should be private

  public float getSalesRate(String region) {
    salesRate = new DoTaxes().doColorado();    // ouch again!
    // do region-based calculations
    return adjustedSalesRate;
  }
}
```

All nontrivial OO applications are a mix of many classes and interfaces working together. Ideally, all interactions between objects in an OO system should use the APIs, in other words, the contracts, of the objects' respective classes. Theoretically, if all of the classes in an application have well-designed APIs, then it should be possible for all interclass interactions to use those APIs exclusively. As we discussed earlier in this chapter, an aspect of good class and API design is that classes should be well encapsulated.

The bottom line is that coupling is a somewhat subjective concept. Because of this, the exam will test you on really obvious examples of tight coupling; you won't be asked to make subtle judgment calls.

Cohesion

While coupling has to do with how classes interact with each other, cohesion is all about how a single class is designed. The term *cohesion* is used to indicate the degree to which a class has a single, well-focused purpose. Keep in mind that cohesion is a subjective concept. The more focused a class is, the higher its cohesiveness—a good thing. The key benefit of high cohesion is that such classes are typically much easier to maintain (and less frequently changed) than classes with low cohesion. Another benefit of high cohesion is that classes with a well-focused purpose tend to be more reusable than other classes. Let's take a look at a pseudo-code example:

```
class BudgetReport {
  void connectToRDBMS(){ }
  void generateBudgetReport() { }
  void saveToFile() { }
  void print() { }
}
```

Now imagine your manager comes along and says, "Hey you know that accounting application we're working on? The clients just decided that they're also going to want to generate a revenue projection report, oh and they want to do some inventory reporting also. They do like our reporting features however, so make sure that all of these reports will let them choose a database, choose a printer, and save generated reports to data files..." Ouch!

Rather than putting all the printing code into one report class, we probably would have been better off with the following design right from the start:

```
class BudgetReport {
  Options getReportingOptions() { }
  void generateBudgetReport(Options o) { }
}

class ConnectToRDBMS {
  DBconnection getRDBMS() { }
}

class PrintStuff {
  PrintOptions getPrintOptions() { }
}

class FileSaver {
  SaveOptions getFileSaveOptions() { }
}
```

This design is much more cohesive. Instead of one class that does everything, we've broken the system into four main classes, each with a very specific, or *cohesive*, role. Because we've built these specialized, reusable classes, it'll be much easier to write a new report, since we've already got the database connection class, the printing class, and the file saver class, and that means they can be reused by other classes that might want to print a report.

CERTIFICATION SUMMARY

We started the chapter by discussing the importance of encapsulation in good OO design, and then we talked about how good encapsulation is implemented: with private instance variables and public getters and setters.

Next, we covered the importance of inheritance; so that you can grasp overriding, overloading, polymorphism, reference casting, return types, and constructors.

We covered IS-A and HAS-A. IS-A is implemented using inheritance, and HAS-A is implemented by using instance variables that refer to other objects.

Polymorphism was next. Although a reference variable's type can't be changed, it can be used to refer to an object whose type is a subtype of its own. We learned how to determine what methods are invocable for a given reference variable.

We looked at the difference between overridden and overloaded methods, learning that an overridden method occurs when a subclass inherits a method from a superclass, and then reimplements the method to add more specialized behavior. We learned that, at runtime, the JVM will invoke the subclass version on an instance of a subclass, and the superclass version on an instance of the superclass. Abstract methods must be "overridden" (technically, abstract methods must be implemented, as opposed to overridden, since there really isn't anything to override).

We saw that overriding methods must declare the same argument list and return type (or, as of Java 5, they can return a subtype of the declared return type of the superclass overridden method), and that the access modifier can't be more restrictive. The overriding method also can't throw any new or broader checked exceptions that weren't declared in the overridden method. You also learned that the overridden method can be invoked using the syntax `super.doSomething();`.

Overloaded methods let you reuse the same method name in a class, but with different arguments (and, optionally, a different return type). Whereas overriding methods must not change the argument list, overloaded methods must. But unlike overriding methods, overloaded methods are free to vary the return type, access modifier, and declared exceptions any way they like.

We learned the mechanics of casting (mostly downcasting), reference variables, when it's necessary, and how to use the `instanceof` operator.

Implementing interfaces came next. An interface describes a *contract* that the implementing class must follow. The rules for implementing an interface are similar to those for extending an abstract class. Also remember that a class can implement more than one interface, and that interfaces can extend another interface.

We also looked at method return types, and saw that you can declare any return type you like (assuming you have access to a class for an object reference return type), unless you're overriding a method. Barring a covariant return, an overriding method must have the same return type as the overridden method of the superclass. We saw that while overriding methods must not change the return type, overloaded methods can (as long as they also change the argument list).

Finally, you learned that it is legal to return any value or variable that can be implicitly converted to the declared return type. So, for example, a short can be returned when the return type is declared as an int. And (assuming Horse extends Animal), a Horse reference can be returned when the return type is declared an Animal.

We covered constructors in detail, learning that if you don't provide a constructor for your class, the compiler will insert one. The compiler-generated constructor is called the default constructor, and it is always a no-arg constructor with a no-arg call to super(). The default constructor will never be generated if there is even a single constructor in your class (regardless of the arguments of that constructor), so if you need more than one constructor in your class and you want a no-arg constructor, you'll have to write it yourself. We also saw that constructors are not inherited, and that you can be confused by a method that has the same name as the class (which is legal). The return type is the giveaway that a method is not a constructor, since constructors do not have return types.

We saw how all of the constructors in an object's inheritance tree will always be invoked when the object is instantiated using new. We also saw that constructors can be overloaded, which means defining constructors with different argument lists. A constructor can invoke another constructor of the same class using the keyword this(), as though the constructor were a method named this(). We saw that every constructor must have either this() or super() as the first statement (although the compiler can insert it for you).

We looked at static methods and variables. Static members are tied to the class, not an instance, so there is only one copy of any static member. A common mistake is to attempt to reference an instance variable from a static method. Use the class name with the dot operator to access static members.

We discussed the OO concepts of coupling and cohesion. Loose coupling is the desirable state of two or more classes that interact with each other only through their respective API's. Tight coupling is the undesirable state of two or more classes that know inside details about another class, details not revealed in the class's API. High cohesion is the desirable state of a single class whose purpose and responsibilities are limited and well-focused.

And once again, you learned that the exam includes tricky questions designed largely to test your ability to recognize just how tricky the questions can be.

✓ TWO-MINUTE DRILL

Here are some of the key points from each certification objective in this chapter.

Encapsulation, IS-A, HAS-A (Objective 5.1)

❑ Encapsulation helps hide implementation behind an interface (or API).

❑ Encapsulated code has two features:

  ❑ Instance variables are kept protected (usually with the private modifier).

  ❑ Getter and setter methods provide access to instance variables.

❑ IS-A refers to inheritance or implementation.

❑ IS-A is expressed with the keyword extends.

❑ IS-A, "inherits from," and "is a subtype of" are all equivalent expressions.

❑ HAS-A means an instance of one class "has a" reference to an instance of another class or another instance of the same class.

Inheritance (Objective 5.5)

❑ Inheritance allows a class to be a subclass of a superclass, and thereby inherit public and protected variables and methods of the superclass.

❑ Inheritance is a key concept that underlies IS-A, polymorphism, overriding, overloading, and casting.

❑ All classes (except class Object), are subclasses of type Object, and therefore they inherit Object's methods.

Polymorphism (Objective 5.2)

❑ Polymorphism means "many forms."

❑ A reference variable is always of a single, unchangeable type, but it can refer to a subtype object.

❑ A single object can be referred to by reference variables of many different types—as long as they are the same type or a supertype of the object.

❑ The reference variable's type (not the object's type), determines which methods can be called!

❑ Polymorphic method invocations apply only to overridden *instance* methods.

Overriding and Overloading (Objectives 1.5 and 5.4)

❑ Methods can be overridden or overloaded; constructors can be overloaded but not overridden.

❑ Abstract methods must be overridden by the first concrete (non-abstract) subclass.

❑ With respect to the method it overrides, the overriding method

    ❑ Must have the same argument list.

    ❑ Must have the same return type, except that as of Java 5, the return type can be a subclass—this is known as a covariant return.

    ❑ Must not have a more restrictive access modifier.

    ❑ May have a less restrictive access modifier.

    ❑ Must not throw new or broader checked exceptions.

    ❑ May throw fewer or narrower checked exceptions, or any unchecked exception.

❑ `final` methods cannot be overridden.

❑ Only inherited methods may be overridden, and remember that private methods are not inherited.

❑ A subclass uses `super.overriddenMethodName()` to call the superclass version of an overridden method.

❑ Overloading means reusing a method name, but with different arguments.

❑ Overloaded methods

    ❑ Must have different argument lists

    ❑ May have different return types, if argument lists are also different

    ❑ May have different access modifiers

    ❑ May throw different exceptions

❑ Methods from a superclass can be overloaded in a subclass.

❑ Polymorphism applies to overriding, not to overloading.

❑ Object type (not the reference variable's type), determines which overridden method is used at runtime.

❑ Reference type determines which overloaded method will be used at compile time.

Reference Variable Casting (Objective 5.2)

❑ There are two types of reference variable casting: downcasting and upcasting.

❑ Downcasting: If you have a reference variable that refers to a subtype object, you can assign it to a reference variable of the subtype. You must make an explicit cast to do this, and the result is that you can access the subtype's members with this new reference variable.

❑ Upcasting: You can assign a reference variable to a supertype reference variable explicitly or implicitly. This is an inherently safe operation because the assignment restricts the access capabilities of the new variable.

Implementing an Interface (Objective 1.2)

❑ When you implement an interface, you are fulfilling its contract.

❑ You implement an interface by properly and concretely overriding all of the methods defined by the interface.

❑ A single class can implement many interfaces.

Return Types (Objective 1.5)

❑ Overloaded methods can change return types; overridden methods cannot, except in the case of covariant returns.

❑ Object reference return types can accept `null` as a return value.

❑ An array is a legal return type, both to declare and return as a value.

❑ For methods with primitive return types, any value that can be implicitly converted to the return type can be returned.

❑ Nothing can be returned from a void, but you can return nothing. You're allowed to simply say `return`, in any method with a `void` return type, to bust out of a method early. But you can't return nothing from a method with a non-void return type.

❑ Methods with an object reference return type, can return a subtype.

❑ Methods with an interface return type, can return any implementer.

Constructors and Instantiation (Objectives 1.6 and 5.4)

❑ A constructor is always invoked when a new object is created.

- ❏ Each superclass in an object's inheritance tree will have a constructor called.
- ❏ Every class, even an abstract class, has at least one constructor.
- ❏ Constructors must have the same name as the class.
- ❏ Constructors don't have a return type. If you see code with a return type, it's a method with the same name as the class, it's not a constructor.
- ❏ Typical constructor execution occurs as follows:
  - ❏ The constructor calls its superclass constructor, which calls its superclass constructor, and so on all the way up to the Object constructor.
  - ❏ The Object constructor executes and then returns to the calling constructor, which runs to completion and then returns to its calling constructor, and so on back down to the completion of the constructor of the actual instance being created.
- ❏ Constructors can use any access modifier (even `private`!).
- ❏ The compiler will create a default constructor if you don't create any constructors in your class.
- ❏ The default constructor is a no-arg constructor with a no-arg call to `super()`.
- ❏ The first statement of every constructor must be a call to either `this()` (an overloaded constructor) or `super()`.
- ❏ The compiler will add a call to `super()` unless you have already put in a call to `this()` or `super()`.
- ❏ Instance members are accessible only after the super constructor runs.
- ❏ Abstract classes have constructors that are called when a concrete subclass is instantiated.
- ❏ Interfaces do not have constructors.
- ❏ If your superclass does not have a no-arg constructor, you must create a constructor and insert a call to `super()` with arguments matching those of the superclass constructor.
- ❏ Constructors are never inherited, thus they cannot be overridden.
- ❏ A constructor can be directly invoked only by another constructor (using a call to `super()` or `this()`).
- ❏ Issues with calls to `this()`
  - ❏ May appear only as the first statement in a constructor.
  - ❏ The argument list determines which overloaded constructor is called.

❑ Constructors can call constructors can call constructors, and so on, but sooner or later one of them better call super() or the stack will explode.

❑ Calls to this() and super() cannot be in the same constructor. You can have one or the other, but never both.

Statics (Objective 1.3)

❑ Use static methods to implement behaviors that are not affected by the state of any instances.

❑ Use static variables to hold data that is class specific as opposed to instance specific—there will be only one copy of a static variable.

❑ All static members belong to the class, not to any instance.

❑ A static method can't access an instance variable directly.

❑ Use the dot operator to access static members, but remember that using a reference variable with the dot operator is really a syntax trick, and the compiler will substitute the class name for the reference variable, for instance:

```
d.doStuff();
```

becomes:

```
Dog.doStuff();
```

❑ static methods can't be overridden, but they can be redefined.

Coupling and Cohesion (Objective 5.1)

❑ Coupling refers to the degree to which one class knows about or uses members of another class.

❑ Loose coupling is the desirable state of having classes that are well encapsulated, minimize references to each other, and limit the breadth of API usage.

❑ Tight coupling is the undesirable state of having classes that break the rules of loose coupling.

❑ Cohesion refers to the degree in which a class has a single, well-defined role or responsibility.

❑ High cohesion is the desirable state of a class whose members support a single, well-focused role or responsibility.

❑ Low cohesion is the undesirable state of a class whose members support multiple, unfocused roles or responsibilities.

SELF TEST

1. Given:

   ```
   public abstract interface Frobnicate { public void twiddle(String s); }
   ```

   Which is a correct class? (Choose all that apply.)

   A. ```
      public abstract class Frob implements Frobnicate {
          public abstract void twiddle(String s) { }
      }
      ```

   B. `public abstract class Frob implements Frobnicate { }`

   C. ```
      public class Frob extends Frobnicate {
          public void twiddle(Integer i) { }
      }
      ```

   D. ```
      public class Frob implements Frobnicate {
          public void twiddle(Integer i) { }
      }
      ```

   E. ```
      public class Frob implements Frobnicate {
          public void twiddle(String i) { }
          public void twiddle(Integer s) { }
      }
      ```

2. Given:

   ```
   class Top {
     public Top(String s) { System.out.print("B"); }
   }
   public class Bottom2 extends Top {
     public Bottom2(String s) { System.out.print("D"); }
     public static void main(String [] args) {
       new Bottom2("C");
       System.out.println(" ");
     }
   }
   ```

   What is the result?

   A. BD

   B. DB

   C. BDC

   D. DBC

   E. Compilation fails

3. Given:

```
class Clidder {
  private final void flipper() { System.out.println("Clidder"); }
}

public class Clidlet extends Clidder {
  public final void flipper() { System.out.println("Clidlet"); }
  public static void main(String [] args) {
    new Clidlet().flipper();
  }
}
```

What is the result?

A. `Clidlet`

B. `Clidder`

C. `Clidder`
   `Clidlet`

D. `Clidlet`
   `Clidder`

E. Compilation fails

4. Using the **fragments** below, complete the following **code** so it compiles.
Note, you may not have to fill all of the slots.

Code:

```
class AgedP {

  _____  _____  _____  _____  _____

  public AgedP(int x) {

    _____  _____  _____  _____  _____

  }
}
public class Kinder extends AgedP {

  _____  _____  _____  _____  _____

  public Kinder(int x) {

    _____  _____  _____  _____  _____ ();

  }
}
```

Fragments: Use the following fragments zero or more times:

AgedP	super	this	
(	)	{	}
;			

5. Which statement(s) are true? (Choose all that apply.)

   A. Cohesion is the OO principle most closely associated with hiding implementation details

   B. Cohesion is the OO principle most closely associated with making sure that classes know about other classes only through their APIs

   C. Cohesion is the OO principle most closely associated with making sure that a class is designed with a single, well-focused purpose

   D. Cohesion is the OO principle most closely associated with allowing a single object to be seen as having many types

6. Given the following,

```
 1. class X { void do1() { } }
 2. class Y extends X { void do2() { } }
 3.
 4. class Chrome {
 5.    public static void main(String [] args) {
 6.       X x1 = new X();
 7.       X x2 = new Y();
 8.       Y y1 = new Y();
 9.       // insert code here
10. } }
```

Which, inserted at line 9, will compile? (Choose all that apply.)

   A. x2.do2();

   B. (Y)x2.do2();

   C. ((Y)x2).do2();

   D. None of the above statements will compile

7. Given:

    1. ClassA has a ClassD
    2. Methods in ClassA use public methods in ClassB
    3. Methods in ClassC use public methods in ClassA
    4. Methods in ClassA use public variables in ClassB

    Which is most likely true? (Choose the most likely.)

    A. ClassD has low cohesion
    B. ClassA has weak encapsulation
    C. ClassB has weak encapsulation
    D. ClassB has strong encapsulation
    E. ClassC is tightly coupled to ClassA

8. Given:

```
3. class Dog {
4.   public void bark() { System.out.print("woof "); }
5. }
6. class Hound extends Dog {
7.   public void sniff() { System.out.print("sniff "); }
8.   public void bark() { System.out.print("howl "); }
9. }
10. public class DogShow {
11.   public static void main(String[] args) { new DogShow().go(); }
12.   void go() {
13.     new Hound().bark();
14.     ((Dog) new Hound()).bark();
15.     ((Dog) new Hound()).sniff();
16.   }
17. }
```

What is the result? (Choose all that apply.)

A. `howl howl sniff`
B. `howl woof sniff`
C. `howl howl` followed by an exception
D. `howl woof` followed by an exception
E. Compilation fails with an error at line 14
F. Compilation fails with an error at line 15

9. Given:

```
3. public class Redwood extends Tree {
4.    public static void main(String[] args) {
5.      new Redwood().go();
6.    }
7.    void go() {
8.      go2(new Tree(), new Redwood());
9.      go2((Redwood) new Tree(), new Redwood());
10.   }
11.   void go2(Tree t1, Redwood r1) {
12.       Redwood r2 = (Redwood)t1;
13.       Tree t2 = (Tree)r1;
14.   }
15. }
16. class Tree { }
```

What is the result? (Choose all that apply.)

A. An exception is thrown at runtime

B. The code compiles and runs with no output

C. Compilation fails with an error at line 8

D. Compilation fails with an error at line 9

E. Compilation fails with an error at line 12

F. Compilation fails with an error at line 13

10. Given:

```
3. public class Tenor extends Singer {
4.    public static String sing() { return "fa"; }
5.    public static void main(String[] args) {
6.      Tenor t = new Tenor();
7.      Singer s = new Tenor();
8.      System.out.println(t.sing() + " " + s.sing());
9.    }
10. }
11. class Singer { public static String sing() { return "la"; } }
```

What is the result?

A. fa fa

B. fa la

C. la la

D. Compilation fails

E. An exception is thrown at runtime

11. Given:

```
3. class Alpha {
4.   static String s = " ";
5.   protected Alpha() { s += "alpha "; }
6. }
7. class SubAlpha extends Alpha {
8.   private SubAlpha() { s += "sub "; }
9. }
10. public class SubSubAlpha extends Alpha {
11.   private SubSubAlpha() { s += "subsub "; }
12.   public static void main(String[] args) {
13.     new SubSubAlpha();
14.     System.out.println(s);
15.   }
16. }
```

What is the result?

A. subsub

B. sub subsub

C. alpha subsub

D. alpha sub subsub

E. Compilation fails

F. An exception is thrown at runtime

12. Given:

```
3. class Building {
4.   Building() {  System.out.print("b ");  }
5.   Building(String name) {
6.     this();   System.out.print("bn " + name);
7.   }
8. }
9. public class House extends Building {
10.   House() {  System.out.print("h ");  }
11.   House(String name) {
12.     this();   System.out.print("hn " + name);
13.   }
14.   public static void main(String[] args) { new House("x "); }
15. }
```

What is the result?

A. h hn x

B. hn x h

C. b h hn x

D. b hn x h

E. bn x h hn x

F. b bn x h hn x

G. bn x b h hn x

H. Compilation fails

13. Given:

```
3. class Mammal {
4.    String name = "furry ";
5.    String makeNoise() { return "generic noise"; }
6. }
7. class Zebra extends Mammal {
8.    String name = "stripes ";
9.    String makeNoise() { return "bray"; }
10. }
11. public class ZooKeeper {
12.    public static void main(String[] args) { new ZooKeeper().go(); }
13.    void go() {
14.       Mammal m = new Zebra();
15.       System.out.println(m.name + m.makeNoise());
16.    }
17. }
```

What is the result?

A. furry bray

B. stripes bray

C. furry generic noise

D. stripes generic noise

E. Compilation fails

F. An exception is thrown at runtime

14. You're designing a new online board game in which Floozels are a type of Jammers, Jammers can have Quizels, Quizels are a type of Klakker, and Floozels can have several Floozets. Which of the following fragments represent this design? (Choose all that apply.)

A.
```
import java.util.*;
interface Klakker { }
class Jammer { Set<Quizel> q; }
class Quizel implements Klakker { }
public class Floozel extends Jammer { List<Floozet> f; }
interface Floozet { }
```

B.
```
import java.util.*;
class Klakker { Set<Quizel> q; }
class Quizel extends Klakker { }
class Jammer { List<Floozel> f; }
class Floozet extends Floozel { }
public class Floozel { Sct<Klakker> k; }
```

C.
```
import java.util.*;
class Floozet { }
class Quizel implements Klakker { }
class Jammer { List<Quizel> q; }
interface Klakker { }
class Floozel extends Jammer { List<Floozet> f; }
```

D.
```
import java.util.*;
interface Jammer extends Quizel { }
interface Klakker { }
interface Quizel extends Klakker { }
interface Floozel extends Jammer, Floozet { }
interface Floozet { }
```

15. Given:

```
3. class A { }
4. class B extends A { }
5. public class ComingThru {
6.    static String s = "-";
7.    public static void main(String[] args) {
8.       A[] aa = new A[2];
9.       B[] ba = new B[2];
10.      sifter(aa);
11.      sifter(ba);
12.      sifter(7);
13.      System.out.println(s);
14.   }
```

```
15.    static void sifter(A[]... a2)      { s += "1"; }
16.    static void sifter(B[]... b1)      { s += "2"; }
17.    static void sifter(B[] b1)         { s += "3"; }
18.    static void sifter(Object o)       { s += "4"; }
19. }
```

What is the result?

A. -124

B. -134

C. -424

D. -434

E. -444

F. Compilation fails

SELF TEST ANSWERS

1. Given:

```
public abstract interface Frobnicate { public void twiddle(String s); }
```

Which is a correct class? (Choose all that apply.)

A. ```
   public abstract class Frob implements Frobnicate {
        public abstract void twiddle(String s) { }
   }
   ```
B. ```
   public abstract class Frob implements Frobnicate { }
   ```
C. ```
   public class Frob extends Frobnicate {
        public void twiddle(Integer i) { }
   }
   ```
D. ```
   public class Frob implements Frobnicate {
        public void twiddle(Integer i) { }
   }
   ```
E. ```
   public class Frob implements Frobnicate {
        public void twiddle(String i) { }
        public void twiddle(Integer s) { }
   }
   ```

Answer:

☑ **B** is correct, an abstract class need not implement any or all of an interface's methods. **E** is correct, the class implements the interface method and additionally overloads the `twiddle()` method.

☒ **A** is incorrect because abstract methods have no body. **C** is incorrect because classes implement interfaces they don't extend them. **D** is incorrect because overloading a method is not implementing it.
(Objective 5.4)

2. Given:

```
class Top {
  public Top(String s) { System.out.print("B"); }
}
public class Bottom2 extends Top {
  public Bottom2(String s) { System.out.print("D"); }
  public static void main(String [] args) {
    new Bottom2("C");
    System.out.println(" ");
} }
```
```

What is the result?

A. BD

B. DB

C. BDC

D. DBC

E. Compilation fails

Answer:

☑ **E** is correct. The implied `super()` call in Bottom2's constructor cannot be satisfied because there isn't a no-arg constructor in Top. A default, no-arg constructor is generated by the compiler only if the class has no constructor defined explicitly.

☒ **A, B, C,** and **D** are incorrect based on the above.
(Objective 1.6)

3. Given:

```
class Clidder {
  private final void flipper() { System.out.println("Clidder"); }
}

public class Clidlet extends Clidder {
  public final void flipper() { System.out.println("Clidlet");  }
  public static void main(String [] args) {
    new Clidlet().flipper();
} }
```

What is the result?

A. `Clidlet`

B. `Clidder`

C. `Clidder`
   `Clidlet`

D. `Clidlet`
   `Clidder`

E. Compilation fails

Answer:

☑ **A** is correct. Although a final method cannot be overridden, in this case, the method is private, and therefore hidden. The effect is that a new, accessible, method flipper is created. Therefore, no polymorphism occurs in this example, the method invoked is simply that of the child class, and no error occurs.

☒ **B, C, D,** and **E** are incorrect based on the preceding.
(Objective 5.3)

4. Using the **fragments** below, complete the following **code** so it compiles.
Note, you may not have to fill all of the slots.

Code:

```
class AgedP {

_____  _____    _____  _____

  public AgedP(int x) {

    _____  _____   _____  _____  _____

  }
}
public class Kinder extends AgedP {

_____  _____   _____  _____  _____  _____

  public Kinder(int x) {

    _____  _____   _____  _____  _____  ();

  }
}
```

Fragments: Use the following fragments zero or more times:

AgedP	super	this	
(	)	{	}
;			

Answer:

```
class AgedP {
  AgedP() {}
  public AgedP(int x) {
  }
}
public class Kinder extends AgedP {
  public Kinder(int x) {
    super();
  }
}
```

As there is no droppable tile for the variable x and the parentheses (in the Kinder constructor), are already in place and empty, there is no way to construct a call to the superclass constructor

that takes an argument. Therefore, the only remaining possibility is to create a call to the no-argument superclass constructor. This is done as: `super();`. The line cannot be left blank, as the parentheses are already in place. Further, since the superclass constructor called is the no-argument version, this constructor must be created. It will not be created by the compiler because there is another constructor already present.
(Objective 5.4)

5 Which statement(s) are true? (Choose all that apply.)

A. Cohesion is the OO principle most closely associated with hiding implementation details

B. Cohesion is the OO principle most closely associated with making sure that classes know about other classes only through their APIs

C. Cohesion is the OO principle most closely associated with making sure that a class is designed with a single, well-focused purpose

D. Cohesion is the OO principle most closely associated with allowing a single object to be seen as having many types

Answer:

☑ Answer **C** is correct.

☒ **A** refers to encapsulation, **B** refers to coupling, and **D** refers to polymorphism.
(Objective 5.1)

6. Given the following,

```
 1. class X { void do1() { } }
 2. class Y extends X { void do2() { } }
 3.
 4. class Chrome {
 5.   public static void main(String [] args) {
 6.     X x1 = new X();
 7.     X x2 = new Y();
 8.     Y y1 = new Y();
 9.     // insert code here
10.   }
11. }
```

Which, inserted at line 9, will compile? (Choose all that apply.)

A. `x2.do2();`

B. `(Y)x2.do2();`

C. `((Y)x2).do2();`

D. None of the above statements will compile

Answer:

☑ **C** is correct. Before you can invoke Y's `do2` method you have to cast `x2` to be of type `Y`. Statement **B** looks like a proper cast but without the second set of parentheses, the compiler thinks it's an incomplete statement.

☒ **A, B** and **D** are incorrect based on the preceding.
(Objective 5.2)

7. Given:

1. ClassA has a ClassD

2. Methods in ClassA use public methods in ClassB

3. Methods in ClassC use public methods in ClassA

4. Methods in ClassA use public variables in ClassB

Which is most likely true? (Choose the most likely.)

A. ClassD has low cohesion

B. ClassA has weak encapsulation

C. ClassB has weak encapsulation

D. ClassB has strong encapsulation

E. ClassC is tightly coupled to ClassA

Answer:

☑ **C** is correct. Generally speaking, public variables are a sign of weak encapsulation.

☒ **A, B, D,** and **E** are incorrect, because based on the information given, none of these statements can be supported.
(Objective 5.1)

8. Given:

```
3. class Dog {
4.   public void bark() { System.out.print("woof "); }
5. }
6. class Hound extends Dog {
7.   public void sniff() { System.out.print("sniff "); }
```

```
 8.    public void bark() { System.out.print("howl "); }
 9. }
10. public class DogShow {
11.    public static void main(String[] args) { new DogShow().go(); }
12.    void go() {
13.      new Hound().bark();
14.      ((Dog) new Hound()).bark();
15.      ((Dog) new Hound()).sniff();
16.    }
17. }
```

What is the result? (Choose all that apply.)

A. `howl howl sniff`

B. `howl woof sniff`

C. `howl howl` followed by an exception

D. `howl woof` followed by an exception

E. Compilation fails with an error at line 14

F. Compilation fails with an error at line 15

Answer:

☑ **F** is correct. Class `Dog` doesn't have a `sniff` method.

☒ **A, B, C, D,** and **E** are incorrect based on the above information.
(Objective 5.2)

9. Given:

```
 3. public class Redwood extends Tree {
 4.    public static void main(String[] args) {
 5.      new Redwood().go();
 6.    }
 7.    void go() {
 8.      go2(new Tree(), new Redwood());
 9.      go2((Redwood) new Tree(), new Redwood());
10.    }
11.    void go2(Tree t1, Redwood r1) {
12.       Redwood r2 = (Redwood)t1;
13.       Tree t2 = (Tree)r1;
14.    }
15. }
16. class Tree { }
```

What is the result? (Choose all that apply.)

A. An exception is thrown at runtime

B. The code compiles and runs with no output

C. Compilation fails with an error at line 8

D. Compilation fails with an error at line 9

E. Compilation fails with an error at line 12

F. Compilation fails with an error at line 13

Answer:

☑ **A** is correct, a ClassCastException will be thrown when the code attempts to downcast a Tree to a Redwood.

☒ **B, C, D, E,** and **F** are incorrect based on the above information. (Objective 5.2)

10. Given:

```
3. public class Tenor extends Singer {
4.    public static String sing() { return "fa"; }
5.    public static void main(String[] args) {
6.       Tenor t = new Tenor();
7.       Singer s = new Tenor();
8.       System.out.println(t.sing() + " " + s.sing());
9.    }
10. }
11. class Singer { public static String sing() { return "la"; } }
```

What is the result?

A. `fa fa`

B. `fa la`

C. `la la`

D. Compilation fails

E. An exception is thrown at runtime

Answer:

☑ **B** is correct. The code is correct, but polymorphism doesn't apply to static methods.

☒ **A, C, D,** and **E** are incorrect based on the above information. (Objective 5.2)

11. Given:

```
3. class Alpha {
4.   static String s = " ";
5.   protected Alpha() { s += "alpha "; }
6. }
7. class SubAlpha extends Alpha {
8.   private SubAlpha() { s += "sub "; }
9. }
10. public class SubSubAlpha extends Alpha {
11.   private SubSubAlpha() { s += "subsub "; }
12.   public static void main(String[] args) {
13.     new SubSubAlpha();
14.     System.out.println(s);
15.   }
16. }
```

What is the result?

A. subsub

B. sub subsub

C. alpha subsub

D. alpha sub subsub

E. Compilation fails

F. An exception is thrown at runtime

Answer:

☑ **C** is correct. Watch out, SubSubAlpha extends Alpha! Since the code doesn't attempt to make a SubAlpha, the private constructor in SubAlpha is okay.

☒ **A, B, D, E,** and **F** are incorrect based on the above information. (Objective 5.3)

12. Given:

```
3. class Building {
4.   Building() {  System.out.print("b ");  }
5.   Building(String name) {
6.     this();   System.out.print("bn " + name);
7.   }
8. }
9. public class House extends Building {
```

```
10.    House() {  System.out.print("h ");  }
11.    House(String name) {
12.      this();   System.out.print("hn " + name);
13.    }
14.    public static void main(String[] args) { new House("x "); }
15. }
```

What is the result?

A. h hn x

B. hn x h

C. b h hn x

D. b hn x h

E. bn x h hn x

F. b bn x h hn x

G. bn x b h hn x

H. Compilation fails

Answer:

☑ **C** is correct. Remember that constructors call their superclass constructors, which execute first, and that constructors can be overloaded.

☒ **A, B, D, E, F, G,** and **H** are incorrect based on the above information. (Objectives 1.6, 5.4)

13. Given:

```
3. class Mammal {
4.    String name = "furry ";
5.    String makeNoise() { return "generic noise"; }
6. }
7. class Zebra extends Mammal {
8.    String name = "stripes ";
9.    String makeNoise() { return "bray"; }
10. }
11. public class ZooKeeper {
12.    public static void main(String[] args) { new ZooKeeper().go(); }
13.    void go() {
14.      Mammal m = new Zebra();
15.      System.out.println(m.name + m.makeNoise());
16.    }
17. }
```

What is the result?

A. `furry bray`

B. `stripes bray`

C. `furry generic noise`

D. `stripes generic noise`

E. Compilation fails

F. An exception is thrown at runtime

Answer:

☑ **A** is correct. Polymorphism is only for instance methods.

☒ **B, C, D, E,** and **F** are incorrect based on the above information. (Objectives 1.5, 5.4)

14. You're designing a new online board game in which Floozels are a type of Jammers, Jammers can have Quizels, Quizels are a type of Klakker, and Floozels can have several Floozets. Which of the following fragments represent this design? (Choose all that apply.)

A.
```
import java.util.*;
interface Klakker { }
class Jammer { Set<Quizel> q; }
class Quizel implements Klakker { }
public class Floozel extends Jammer { List<Floozet> f; }
interface Floozet { }
```

B.
```
import java.util.*;
class Klakker { Set<Quizel> q; }
class Quizel extends Klakker { }
class Jammer { List<Floozel> f; }
class Floozet extends Floozel { }
public class Floozel { Set<Klakker> k; }
```

C.
```
import java.util.*;
class Floozet { }
class Quizel implements Klakker { }
class Jammer { List<Quizel> q; }
interface Klakker { }
class Floozel extends Jammer { List<Floozet> f; }
```

D.
```
import java.util.*;
interface Jammer extends Quizel { }
interface Klakker { }
interface Quizel extends Klakker { }
interface Floozel extends Jammer, Floozet { }
interface Floozet { }
```

Answer:

☑ **A** and **C** are correct. The phrase "type of" indicates an "is-a" relationship (extends or implements), and the phrase "have" is of course a "has-a" relationship (usually instance variables).

☒ **B** and **D** are incorrect based on the above information.
(Objective 5.5)

15. Given:

```
3. class A { }
4. class B extends A { }
5. public class ComingThru {
6.    static String s = "-";
7.    public static void main(String[] args) {
8.       A[] aa = new A[2];
9.       B[] ba = new B[2];
10.      sifter(aa);
11.      sifter(ba);
12.      sifter(7);
13.      System.out.println(s);
14.   }
15.   static void sifter(A[]... a2)   { s += "1"; }
16.   static void sifter(B[]... b1)   { s += "2"; }
17.   static void sifter(B[] b1)      { s += "3"; }
18.   static void sifter(Object o)    { s += "4"; }
19. }
```

What is the result?

A. -124

B. -134

C. -424

D. -434

E. -444

F. Compilation fails

Answer:

☑ **D** is correct. In general, overloaded var-args methods are chosen last. Remember that arrays are objects. Finally, an int can be boxed to an Integer and then "widened" to an Object.

☒ **A, B, C, E,** and **F** are incorrect based on the above information.
(Objective 1.5)

3

Assignments

Stack and Heap—Quick Review

For most people, understanding the basics of the stack and the heap makes it far easier to understand topics like argument passing, polymorphism, threads, exceptions, and garbage collection. In this section, we'll stick to an overview, but we'll expand these topics several more times throughout the book.

For the most part, the various pieces (methods, variables, and objects) of Java programs live in one of two places in memory: the stack or the heap. For now, we're going to worry about only three types of things: instance variables, local variables, and objects:

- Instance variables and objects live on the heap.

- Local variables live on the stack.

Let's take a look at a Java program, and how its various pieces are created and map into the stack and the heap:

```
1. class Collar { }
2.
3. class Dog {
4.    Collar c;          // instance variable
5.    String name;       // instance variable
6.
7.    public static void main(String [] args) {
8.
9.      Dog d;                            // local variable: d
10.     d = new Dog();
11.     d.go(d);
12.    }
13.    void go(Dog dog) {                 // local variable: dog
14.      c = new Collar();
15.      dog.setName("Aiko");
16.    }
17.    void setName(String dogName) {    // local var: dogName
18.      name = dogName;
19.      // do more stuff
20.    }
21. }
```

Figure 3-1 shows the state of the stack and the heap once the program reaches line 19. Following are some key points:

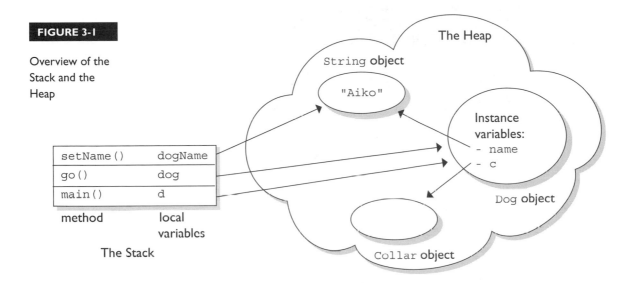

FIGURE 3-1

Overview of the
Stack and the
Heap

- Line 7—`main()` is placed on the stack.
- Line 9—reference variable `d` is created on the stack, but there's no `Dog` object yet.
- Line 10—a new `Dog` object is created and is assigned to the `d` reference variable.
- Line 11—a copy of the reference variable `d` is passed to the `go()` method.
- Line 13—the `go()` method is placed on the stack, with the `dog` parameter as a local variable.
- Line 14—a new `Collar` object is created on the heap, and assigned to `Dog`'s instance variable.
- Line 17—`setName()` is added to the stack, with the `dogName` parameter as its local variable.
- Line 18—the `name` instance variable now also refers to the String object.
- Notice that two *different* local variables refer to the same `Dog` object.
- Notice that one local variable and one instance variable both refer to the same String `Aiko`.
- After Line 19 completes, `setName()` completes and is removed from the stack. At this point the local variable `dogName` disappears too, although the String object it referred to is still on the heap.

Literals, Assignments, and Variables (Exam Objectives 1.3 and 7.6)

1.3   Develop code that declares, initializes, and uses primitives, arrays, enums, and objects as static, instance, and local variables. Also, use legal identifiers for variable names.

7.6   Write code that correctly applies the appropriate operators including assignment operators (limited to: =, +=, -=)...

Literal Values for All Primitive Types

A primitive literal is merely a source code representation of the primitive data types—in other words, an integer, floating-point number, boolean, or character that you type in while writing code. The following are examples of primitive literals:

```
'b'            // char literal
42             // int literal
false          // boolean literal
2546789.343    // double literal
```

Integer Literals

There are three ways to represent integer numbers in the Java language: decimal (base 10), octal (base 8), and hexadecimal (base 16). Most exam questions with integer literals use decimal representations, but the few that use octal or hexadecimal are worth studying for. Even though the odds that you'll ever actually use octal in the real world are astronomically tiny, they were included in the exam just for fun.

Decimal Literals   Decimal integers need no explanation; you've been using them since grade one or earlier. Chances are you don't keep your checkbook in hex. (If you do, there's a Geeks Anonymous [GA] group ready to help.) In the Java language, they are represented as is, with no prefix of any kind, as follows:

```
int length = 343;
```

Octal Literals   Octal integers use only the digits 0 to 7. In Java, you represent an integer in octal form by placing a zero in front of the number, as follows:

```
class Octal {
  public static void main(String [] args) {
    int six = 06;      // Equal to decimal 6
    int seven = 07;    // Equal to decimal 7
    int eight = 010;   // Equal to decimal 8
    int nine = 011;    // Equal to decimal 9
    System.out.println("Octal 010 = " + eight);
  }
}
```

Notice that when we get past seven and are out of digits to use (we are allowed only the digits 0 through 7 for octal numbers), we revert back to zero, and one is added to the beginning of the number. You can have up to 21 digits in an octal number, not including the leading zero. If we run the preceding program, it displays the following:

```
Octal 010 = 8
```

Hexadecimal Literals   Hexadecimal (hex for short) numbers are constructed using 16 distinct symbols. Because we never invented single digit symbols for the numbers 10 through 15, we use alphabetic characters to represent these digits. Counting from 0 through 15 in hex looks like this:

```
0 1 2 3 4 5 6 7 8 9 a b c d e f
```

Java will accept capital or lowercase letters for the extra digits (one of the few places Java is not case-sensitive!). You are allowed up to 16 digits in a hexadecimal number, not including the prefix 0x or the optional suffix extension L, which will be explained later. All of the following hexadecimal assignments are legal:

```
class HexTest {
  public static void main (String [] args) {
    int x = 0X0001;
    int y = 0x7fffffff;
    int z = 0xDeadCafe;
    System.out.println("x = " + x + " y = " + y + " z = " + z);
  }
}
```

Running HexTest produces the following output:

```
x = 1 y = 2147483647 z = -559035650
```

Don't be misled by changes in case for a hexadecimal digit or the 'x' preceding it. 0XCAFE and 0xcafe are both legal *and have the same value*.

All three integer literals (octal, decimal, and hexadecimal) are defined as int by default, but they may also be specified as long by placing a suffix of L or l after the number:

```
long jo = 110599L;
long so = 0xFFFFl;  // Note the lowercase 'l'
```

Floating-Point Literals

Floating-point numbers are defined as a number, a decimal symbol, and more numbers representing the fraction.

```
double d = 11301874.9881024;
```

In the preceding example, the number 11301874.9881024 is the literal value. Floating-point literals are defined as double (64 bits) by default, so if you want to assign a floating-point literal to a variable of type float (32 bits), you must attach the suffix F or f to the number. If you don't, the compiler will complain about a possible loss of precision, because you're trying to fit a number into a (potentially) less precise "container." The F suffix gives you a way to tell the compiler, "Hey, I know what I'm doing, and I'll take the risk, thank you very much."

```
float f = 23.467890;         // Compiler error, possible loss
                             // of precision
float g = 49837849.029847F;  // OK; has the suffix "F"
```

You may also optionally attach a D or d to double literals, but it is not necessary because this is the default behavior.

```
double d = 110599.995011D; // Optional, not required
double  g = 987.897;       // No 'D' suffix, but OK because the
                           // literal is a double by default
```

Look for numeric literals that include a comma, for example,

```
int x = 25,343;  // Won't compile because of the comma
```

Boolean Literals

Boolean literals are the source code representation for boolean values. A boolean value can only be defined as `true` or `false`. Although in C (and some other languages) it is common to use numbers to represent `true` or `false`, this will not work in Java. Again, repeat after me, "Java is not C++."

```
boolean t = true;  // Legal
boolean  f = 0;     // Compiler error!
```

Be on the lookout for questions that use numbers where booleans are required. You might see an `if` test that uses a number, as in the following:

```
int x = 1;  if (x) {  } // Compiler error!
```

Character Literals

A char literal is represented by a single character in single quotes.

```
char a = 'a';
char b = '@';
```

You can also type in the Unicode value of the character, using the Unicode notation of prefixing the value with \u as follows:

```
char letterN = '\u004E'; // The letter 'N'
```

Remember, characters are just 16-bit unsigned integers under the hood. That means you can assign a number literal, assuming it will fit into the unsigned 16-bit range (65535 or less). For example, the following are all legal:

```
char a = 0x892;        // hexadecimal literal
char b = 982;          // int literal
char c = (char)70000;  // The cast is required; 70000 is
                       // out of char range
```

```
char d = (char) -98;    // Ridiculous, but legal
```

And the following are not legal and produce compiler errors:

```
char e = -29;    // Possible loss of precision; needs a cast
char f = 70000   // Possible loss of precision; needs a cast
```

You can also use an escape code if you want to represent a character that can't be typed in as a literal, including the characters for linefeed, newline, horizontal tab, backspace, and single quotes.

```
char c = '\"';    // A double quote
char d = '\n';    // A newline
```

Literal Values for Strings

A string literal is a source code representation of a value of a String object. For example, the following is an example of two ways to represent a string literal:

```
String s = "Bill Joy";
System.out.println("Bill" + " Joy");
```

Although strings are not primitives, they're included in this section because they can be represented as literals—in other words, typed directly into code. The only other nonprimitive type that has a literal representation is an array, which we'll look at later in the chapter.

```
Thread t = ???  // what literal value could possibly go here?
```

Assignment Operators

Assigning a value to a variable seems straightforward enough; you simply assign the stuff on the right side of the = to the variable on the left. Well, sure, but don't expect to be tested on something like this:

```
x = 6;
```

No, you won't be tested on the no-brainer (technical term) assignments. You will, however, be tested on the trickier assignments involving complex expressions and casting. We'll look at both primitive and reference variable assignments. But before we begin, let's back up and peek inside a variable. What is a variable? How are the variable and its value related?

Variables are just bit holders, with a designated type. You can have an `int` holder, a `double` holder, a Button holder, and even a String[] holder. Within that holder is a bunch of bits representing the value. For primitives, the bits represent a numeric value (although we don't know what that bit pattern looks like for `boolean`, luckily, we don't care). A `byte` with a value of 6, for example, means that the bit pattern in the variable (the `byte` holder) is 00000110, representing the 8 bits.

So the value of a primitive variable is clear, but what's inside an object holder? If you say,

```
Button b = new Button();
```

what's inside the Button holder b? Is it the Button object? No! A variable referring to an object is just that—a *reference* variable. A reference variable bit holder contains bits representing a *way to get to the object*. We don't know what the format is. The way in which object references are stored is virtual-machine specific (it's a pointer to something, we just don't know what that something really is). All we can say for sure is that the variable's value is *not* the object, but rather a value representing a specific object on the heap. Or null. If the reference variable has not been assigned a value, or has been explicitly assigned a value of `null`, the variable holds bits representing—you guessed it—`null`. You can read

```
Button b = null;
```

as "The Button variable b is not referring to any object."

So now that we know a variable is just a little box o' bits, we can get on with the work of changing those bits. We'll look first at assigning values to primitives, and finish with assignments to reference variables.

Primitive Assignments

The equal (=) sign is used for assigning a value to a variable, and it's cleverly named the assignment operator. There are actually 12 assignment operators, but only the five most commonly used are on the exam, and they are covered in Chapter 4.

You can assign a primitive variable using a literal or the result of an expression.

Take a look at the following:

```
int x = 7;     // literal assignment
int y = x + 2; // assignment with an expression
               // (including a literal)
int z = x * y; // assignment with an expression
```

The most important point to remember is that a literal integer (such as 7) is always implicitly an `int`. Thinking back to Chapter 1, you'll recall that an `int` is a 32-bit value. No big deal if you're assigning a value to an `int` or a `long` variable, but what if you're assigning to a `byte` variable? After all, a `byte`-sized holder can't hold as many bits as an `int`-sized holder. Here's where it gets weird. The following is legal,

```
byte b = 27;
```

but only because the compiler automatically narrows the literal value to a `byte`. In other words, the compiler puts in the *cast*. The preceding code is identical to the following:

```
byte b = (byte) 27; // Explicitly cast the int literal to a byte
```

It looks as though the compiler gives you a break, and lets you take a shortcut with assignments to integer variables smaller than an `int`. (Everything we're saying about `byte` applies equally to `char` and `short`, both of which are smaller than an `int`.) We're not actually at the weird part yet, by the way.

We know that a literal integer is always an `int`, but more importantly, the result of an expression involving anything `int`-sized or smaller is always an `int`. In other words, add two `bytes` together and you'll get an `int`—even if those two bytes are tiny. Multiply an `int` and a `short` and you'll get an `int`. Divide a `short` by a `byte` and you'll get...an `int`. OK, now we're at the weird part. Check this out:

```
byte a = 3;     // No problem, 3 fits in a byte
byte b = 8;     // No problem, 8 fits in a byte
byte c = b + c; // Should be no problem, sum of the two bytes
                // fits in a byte
```

The last line won't compile! You'll get an error something like this:

```
TestBytes.java:5: possible loss of precision
found    : int
required: byte
     byte c = a + b;
                ^
```

We tried to assign the sum of two bytes to a `byte` variable, the result of which (11) was definitely small enough to fit into a `byte`, but the compiler didn't care. It knew the rule about `int`-or-smaller expressions always resulting in an `int`. It would have compiled if we'd done the *explicit* cast:

```
byte c = (byte) (a + b);
```

Primitive Casting

Casting lets you convert primitive values from one type to another. We mentioned primitive casting in the previous section, but now we're going to take a deeper look. (Object casting was covered in Chapter 2.)

Casts can be implicit or explicit. An implicit cast means you don't have to write code for the cast; the conversion happens automatically. Typically, an implicit cast happens when you're doing a widening conversion. In other words, putting a smaller thing (say, a `byte`) into a bigger container (like an `int`). Remember those `"possible loss of precision"` compiler errors we saw in the assignments section? Those happened when we tried to put a larger thing (say, a `long`) into a smaller container (like a `short`). The large-value-into-small-container conversion is referred to as *narrowing* and requires an explicit cast, where you tell the compiler that you're aware of the danger and accept full responsibility. First we'll look at an implicit cast:

```
int a = 100;
long b = a; // Implicit cast, an int value always fits in a long
```

An explicit casts looks like this:

```
float a = 100.001f;
int b = (int)a; // Explicit cast, the float could lose info
```

Integer values may be assigned to a `double` variable without explicit casting, because any integer value can fit in a 64-bit `double`. The following line demonstrates this:

```
double d = 100L; // Implicit cast
```

In the preceding statement, a `double` is initialized with a `long` value (as denoted by the `L` after the numeric value). No cast is needed in this case because a `double` can hold every piece of information that a `long` can store. If, however, we want to assign a `double` value to an integer type, we're attempting a narrowing conversion and the compiler knows it:

```
class Casting {
  public static void main(String [] args) {
    int x = 3957.229; // illegal
  }
}
```

If we try to compile the preceding code, we get an error something like:

```
%javac Casting.java
Casting.java:3: Incompatible type for declaration. Explicit cast
needed to convert double to int.
      int x = 3957.229; // illegal
1 error
```

In the preceding code, a floating-point value is being assigned to an integer variable. Because an integer is not capable of storing decimal places, an error occurs. To make this work, we'll cast the floating-point number into an `int`:

```
class Casting {
  public static void main(String [] args) {
    int x = (int)3957.229; // legal cast
    System.out.println("int x = " + x);
  }
}
```

When you cast a floating-point number to an integer type, the value loses all the digits after the decimal. The preceding code will produce the following output:

```
int x = 3957
```

We can also cast a larger number type, such as a `long`, into a smaller number type, such as a `byte`. Look at the following:

```
class Casting {
  public static void main(String [] args) {
    long l = 56L;
    byte b = (byte)l;
    System.out.println("The byte is " + b);
  }
}
```

The preceding code will compile and run fine. But what happens if the `long` value is larger than 127 (the largest number a `byte` can store)? Let's modify the code:

```
class Casting {
  public static void main(String [] args) {
    long l = 130L;
    byte b = (byte)l;
    System.out.println("The byte is " + b);
  }
}
```

The code compiles fine, and when we run it we get the following:

```
%java Casting
The byte is -126
```

You don't get a runtime error, even when the value being narrowed is too large for the type. The bits to the left of the lower 8 just...go away. If the leftmost bit (the sign bit) in the `byte` (or any integer primitive) now happens to be a 1, the primitive will have a negative value.

EXERCISE 3-1

Casting Primitives

Create a `float` number type of any value, and assign it to a `short` using casting.

1. Declare a `float` variable: `float f = 234.56F;`
2. Assign the `float` to a short: `short s = (short)f;`

Assigning Floating-Point Numbers   Floating-point numbers have slightly different assignment behavior than integer types. First, you must know that every floating-point literal is implicitly a `double` (64 bits), not a `float`. So the literal `32.3`, for example, is considered a `double`. If you try to assign a `double` to a `float`, the compiler knows you don't have enough room in a 32-bit `float` container to hold the precision of a 64-bit `double`, and it lets you know. The following code looks good, but won't compile:

```
float f = 32.3;
```

You can see that `32.3` should fit just fine into a float-sized variable, but the compiler won't allow it. In order to assign a floating-point literal to a `float` variable, you must either cast the value or append an `f` to the end of the literal. The following assignments will compile:

```
float f = (float) 32.3;
float g = 32.3f;
float h = 32.3F;
```

Assigning a Literal That Is Too Large for the Variable   We'll also get a compiler error if we try to assign a literal value that the compiler knows is too big to fit into the variable.

```
byte a = 128; // byte can only hold up to 127
```

The preceding code gives us an error something like

```
TestBytes.java:5: possible loss of precision
found   : int
required: byte
byte a = 128;
```

We can fix it with a cast:

```
byte a = (byte) 128;
```

But then what's the result? When you narrow a primitive, Java simply truncates the higher-order bits that won't fit. In other words, it loses all the bits to the left of the bits you're narrowing to.

Let's take a look at what happens in the preceding code. There, 128 is the bit pattern 10000000. It takes a full 8 bits to represent 128. But because the literal 128 is an int, we actually get 32 bits, with the 128 living in the right-most (lower-order) 8 bits. So a literal 128 is actually

00000000000000000000000010000000

Take our word for it; there are 32 bits there.

To narrow the 32 bits representing 128, Java simply lops off the leftmost (higher-order) 24 bits. We're left with just the 10000000. But remember that a byte is signed, with the leftmost bit representing the sign (and not part of the value of the variable). So we end up with a negative number (the 1 that used to represent 128 now represents the negative sign bit). Remember, to find out the value of a negative number using two's complement notation, you flip all of the bits and then add 1. Flipping the 8 bits gives us 01111111, and adding 1 to that gives us 10000000, or back to 128! And when we apply the sign bit, we end up with –128.

You must use an explicit cast to assign 128 to a byte, and the assignment leaves you with the value –128. A cast is nothing more than your way of saying to the compiler, "Trust me. I'm a professional. I take full responsibility for anything weird that happens when those top bits are chopped off."

That brings us to the compound assignment operators. The following will compile,

```
byte b = 3;
b += 7;          // No problem - adds 7 to b (result is 10)
```

and is equivalent to

```
byte b = 3;
b = (byte) (b + 7);  // Won't compile without the
                     // cast, since b + 7 results in an int
```

The compound assignment operator += lets you add to the value of b, without putting in an explicit cast. In fact, +=, -=, *=, and /= will all put in an implicit cast.

Assigning One Primitive Variable to Another Primitive Variable

When you assign one primitive variable to another, the contents of the right-hand variable are copied. For example,

```
int a = 6;
int b = a;
```

This code can be read as, "Assign the bit pattern for the number 6 to the int variable a. Then copy the bit pattern in a, and place the copy into variable b."

So, both variables now hold a bit pattern for 6, but the two variables have no other relationship. We used the variable a *only* to copy its contents. At this point, a and b have identical contents (in other words, identical values), but if we change the contents of *either* a or b, the other variable won't be affected.

Take a look at the following example:

```
class ValueTest {
    public static void main (String [] args) {
        int a = 10;  // Assign a value to a
        System.out.println("a = " + a);
        int b = a;
        b = 30;
        System.out.println("a = " + a + " after change to b");
    }
}
```

The output from this program is

```
%java ValueTest
a = 10
a = 10 after change to b
```

Notice the value of a stayed at 10. The key point to remember is that even after you assign a to b, a and b are not referring to the same place in memory. The a and b variables do not share a single value; they have identical copies.

Reference Variable Assignments

You can assign a newly created object to an object reference variable as follows:

```
Button b = new Button();
```

The preceding line does three key things:

- Makes a reference variable named b, of type `Button`
- Creates a new `Button` object on the heap
- Assigns the newly created `Button` object to the reference variable b

You can also assign `null` to an object reference variable, which simply means the variable is not referring to any object:

```
Button c = null;
```

The preceding line creates space for the Button reference variable (the bit holder for a reference value), but doesn't create an actual Button object.

As we discussed in the last chapter, you can also use a reference variable to refer to any object that is a subclass of the declared reference variable type, as follows:

```
public class Foo {
    public void doFooStuff() { }
}
public class Bar extends Foo {
    public void doBarStuff() { }
}
class Test {
    public static void main (String [] args) {
        Foo reallyABar = new Bar();   // Legal because Bar is a
                                      // subclass of Foo
        Bar reallyAFoo = new Foo();   // Illegal! Foo is not a
                                      // subclass of Bar

    }
}
```

The rule is that you can assign a subclass of the declared type, but not a superclass of the declared type. Remember, a Bar object is guaranteed to be able to do anything a Foo can do, so anyone with a Foo reference can invoke Foo methods even though the object is actually a Bar.

In the preceding code, we see that Foo has a method doFooStuff() that someone with a Foo reference might try to invoke. If the object referenced by the Foo variable is really a Foo, no problem. But it's also no problem if the object is a Bar, since Bar inherited the doFooStuff() method. You can't make it work

in reverse, however. If somebody has a Bar reference, they're going to invoke
`doBarStuff()`, but if the object is a Foo, it won't know how to respond.

Variable Scope

Once you've declared and initialized a variable, a natural question is "How long will
this variable be around?" This is a question regarding the scope of variables. And not
only is scope an important thing to understand in general, it also plays a big part in
the exam. Let's start by looking at a class file:

```
class Layout {                          // class

    static int s = 343;                 // static variable

    int x;                              // instance variable

    { x = 7; int x2 = 5; }              // initialization block

    Layout() { x += 8; int x3 = 6;}     // constructor

    void doStuff() {                    // method

        int y = 0;                      // local variable

        for(int z = 0; z < 4; z++) {    // 'for' code block
            y += z + x;
        }
    }
}
```

As with variables in all Java programs, the variables in this program (s, x, x2, x3,
y, and z) all have a scope:

- ■ s is a static variable.
- ■ x is an instance variable.
- ■ y is a local variable (sometimes called a "method local" variable).
- ■ z is a block variable.
- ■ x2 is an init block variable, a flavor of local variable.
- ■ x3 is a constructor variable, a flavor of local variable.

For the purposes of discussing the scope of variables, we can say that there are four
basic scopes:

- Static variables have the longest scope; they are created when the class is loaded, and they survive as long as the class stays loaded in the Java Virtual Machine (JVM).

- Instance variables are the next most long-lived; they are created when a new instance is created, and they live until the instance is removed.

- Local variables are next; they live as long as their method remains on the stack. As we'll soon see, however, local variables can be alive, and still be "out of scope".

- Block variables live only as long as the code block is executing.

Scoping errors come in many sizes and shapes. One common mistake happens when a variable is *shadowed* and two scopes overlap. We'll take a detailed look at shadowing in a few pages. The most common reason for scoping errors is when you attempt to access a variable that is not in scope. Let's look at three common examples of this type of error:

- Attempting to access an instance variable from a static context (typically from main()).

```
class ScopeErrors {
  int x = 5;
  public static void main(String[] args) {
    x++;   // won't compile, x is an 'instance' variable
  }
}
```

- Attempting to access a local variable from a nested method.

  When a method, say go(), invokes another method, say go2(), go2() won't have access to go()'s local variables. While go2() is executing, go()'s local variables are still *alive*, but they are *out of scope*. When go2() completes, it is removed from the stack, and go() resumes execution. At this point, all of go()'s previously declared variables are back in scope. For example:

```
class ScopeErrors {
  public static void main(String [] args) {
    ScopeErrors s = new ScopeErrors();
    s.go();
  }
  void go() {
    int y = 5;
```

```
        go2();
        y++;              // once go2() completes, y is back in scope
    }
    void go2() {
        y++;              // won't compile, y is local to go()
    }
}
```

■ Attempting to use a block variable after the code block has completed.

It's very common to declare and use a variable within a code block, but be careful not to try to use the variable once the block has completed:

```
void go3() {
    for(int z = 0; z < 5; z++) {
        boolean test = false;
        if(z == 3) {
            test = true;
            break;
        }
    }
    System.out.print(test);   // 'test' is an ex-variable,
                              // it has ceased to be...
}
```

In the last two examples, the compiler will say something like this:

```
cannot find symbol
```

This is the compiler's way of saying, "That variable you just tried to use? Well, it might have been valid in the distant past (like one line of code ago), but this is Internet time baby, I have no memory of such a variable."

Pay extra attention to code block scoping errors. You might see them in switches, try-catches, for, do, and while loops.

Using a Variable or Array Element That Is Uninitialized and Unassigned

Java gives us the option of initializing a declared variable or leaving it uninitialized. When we attempt to use the uninitialized variable, we can get different behavior depending on what type of variable or array we are dealing with (primitives or objects). The behavior also depends on the level (scope) at which we are declaring our variable. An instance variable is declared within the class but outside any method or constructor, whereas a local variable is declared within a method (or in the argument list of the method).

Local variables are sometimes called stack, temporary, automatic, or method variables, but the rules for these variables are the same regardless of what you call them. Although you can leave a local variable uninitialized, the compiler complains if you try to use a local variable before initializing it with a value, as we shall see.

Primitive and Object Type Instance Variables

Instance variables (also called *member* variables) are variables defined at the class level. That means the variable declaration is not made within a method, constructor, or any other initializer block. Instance variables are initialized to a default value each time a new instance is created, although they may be given an explicit value after the object's super-constructors have completed. Table 3-1 lists the default values for primitive and object types.

TABLE 3-1   Default Values for Primitives and Reference Types

Variable Type	Default Value
Object reference	null (not referencing any object)
byte, short, int, long	0
float, double	0.0
boolean	false
char	'\u0000'

Primitive Instance Variables

In the following example, the integer year is defined as a class member because it is within the initial curly braces of the class and not within a method's curly braces:

```
public class BirthDate {
  int year;                                      // Instance variable
  public static void main(String [] args) {
    BirthDate bd = new BirthDate();
    bd.showYear();
  }
  public void showYear() {
    System.out.println("The year is " + year);
  }
}
```

When the program is started, it gives the variable year a value of zero, the default value for primitive number instance variables.

on the
job

It's a good idea to initialize all your variables, even if you're assigning them with the default value. Your code will be easier to read; programmers who have to maintain your code (after you win the lottery and move to Tahiti) will be grateful.

Object Reference Instance Variables

When compared with uninitialized primitive variables, object references that aren't initialized are a completely different story. Let's look at the following code:

```
public class Book {
  private String title;              // instance reference variable
  public String getTitle() {
    return title;
  }
  public static void main(String [] args) {
    Book b = new Book();
    System.out.println("The title is " + b.getTitle());
  }
}
```

This code will compile fine. When we run it, the output is

```
The title is null
```

The title variable has not been explicitly initialized with a String assignment, so the instance variable value is null. Remember that null is not the same as an empty String (""). A null value means the reference variable is not referring to any object on the heap. The following modification to the Book code runs into trouble:

```
public class Book {
  private String title;           // instance reference variable
  public String getTitle() {
    return title;
  }
  public static void main(String [] args) {
    Book b = new Book();
    String s = b.getTitle();      // Compiles and runs
    String t = s.toLowerCase();   // Runtime Exception!
  }
}
```

When we try to run the Book class, the JVM will produce something like this:

```
Exception in thread "main" java.lang.NullPointerException
    at Book.main(Book.java.9)
```

We get this error because the reference variable title does not point (refer) to an object. We can check to see whether an object has been instantiated by using the keyword null, as the following revised code shows:

```
public class Book {
  private String title;               // instance reference variable
  public String getTitle() {
    return title;
  }
  public static void main(String [] args) {
    Book b = new Book();
    String s = b.getTitle(); // Compiles and runs
    if (s != null) {
      String t = s.toLowerCase();
    }
```

```
      }
   }
```

The preceding code checks to make sure the object referenced by the variable s is not null before trying to use it. Watch out for scenarios on the exam where you might have to trace back through the code to find out whether an object reference will have a value of null. In the preceding code, for example, you look at the instance variable declaration for title, see that there's no explicit initialization, recognize that the title variable will be given the default value of null, and then realize that the variable s will also have a value of null. Remember, the value of s is a copy of the value of title (as returned by the getTitle() method), so if title is a null reference, s will be too.

Array Instance Variables

Later in this chapter we'll be taking a very detailed look at declaring, constructing, and initializing arrays and multidimensional arrays. For now, we're just going to look at the rule for an array element's default values.

An array is an object; thus, an array instance variable that's declared but not explicitly initialized will have a value of null, just as any other object reference instance variable. But...if the array is initialized, what happens to the elements contained *in* the array? All array elements are given their default values—the same default values that elements of that type get when they're instance variables. *The bottom line: Array elements are always, always, always given default values, regardless of where the array itself is declared or instantiated.*

If we initialize an array, object reference elements will equal null if they are not initialized individually with values. If primitives are contained in an array, they will be given their respective default values. For example, in the following code, the array year will contain 100 integers that all equal zero by default:

```
public class BirthDays {
   static int [] year = new int[100];
   public static void main(String [] args) {
      for(int i=0;i<100;i++)
         System.out.println("year[" + i + "] = " + year[i]);
   }
}
```

When the preceding code runs, the output indicates that all 100 integers in the array equal zero.

Local (Stack, Automatic) Primitives and Objects

Local variables are defined within a method, and they include a method's parameters.

Local Primitives

In the following time travel simulator, the integer year is defined as an automatic variable because it is within the curly braces of a method.

```
public class TimeTravel {
  public static void main(String [] args) {
    int year = 2050;
    System.out.println("The year is " + year);
  }
}
```

Local variables, including primitives, always, always, always must be initialized *before* you attempt to use them (though not necessarily on the same line of code). Java does not give local variables a default value; you must explicitly initialize them with a value, as in the preceding example. If you try to use an uninitialized primitive in your code, you'll get a compiler error:

```
public class TimeTravel {
  public static void main(String [] args) {
    int year; // Local variable (declared but not initialized)
    System.out.println("The year is " + year); // Compiler error
  }
}
```

Compiling produces output something like this:

```
%javac TimeTravel.java
TimeTravel.java:4: Variable year may not have been initialized.
          System.out.println("The year is " + year);
1 error
```

To correct our code, we must give the integer year a value. In this updated example, we declare it on a separate line, which is perfectly valid:

```
public class TimeTravel {
  public static void main(String [] args) {
    int year;       // Declared but not initialized
    int day;        // Declared but not initialized
    System.out.println("You step into the portal.");
    year = 2050;    // Initialize (assign an explicit value)
    System.out.println("Welcome to the year " + year);
  }
}
```

Notice in the preceding example we declared an integer called day that never gets initialized, yet the code compiles and runs fine. Legally, you can declare a local variable without initializing it as long as you don't use the variable, but let's face it, if you declared it, you probably had a reason (although we have heard of programmers declaring random local variables just for sport, to see if they can figure out how and why they're being used).

on the **Job**

The compiler can't always tell whether a local variable has been initialized before use. For example, if you initialize within a logically conditional block (in other words, a code block that may not run, such as an if *block or* for *loop without a literal value of* true *or* false *in the test), the compiler knows that the initialization might not happen, and can produce an error. The following code upsets the compiler:*

```
public class TestLocal {
  public static void main(String [] args) {
    int x;
    if (args[0] != null) { // assume you know this will
                           // always be true
```

```
    x = 7;                  // compiler can't tell that this
                            // statement will run
  }
  int y = x;                // the compiler will choke here
 }
}
```

The compiler will produce an error something like this:

```
TestLocal.java:9: variable x might not have been initialized
```

Because of the compiler-can't-tell-for-certain problem, you will sometimes need to initialize your variable outside the conditional block, just to make the compiler happy. You know why that's important if you've seen the bumper sticker, "When the compiler's not happy, ain't nobody happy."

Local Object References

Objects references, too, behave differently when declared within a method rather than as instance variables. With instance variable object references, you can get away with leaving an object reference uninitialized, as long as the code checks to make sure the reference isn't null before using it. Remember, to the compiler, null is a value. You can't use the dot operator on a null reference, because *there is no object at the other end of it,* but a null reference is not the same as an *uninitialized* reference. Locally declared references can't get away with checking for null before use, unless you explicitly initialize the local variable to null. The compiler will complain about the following code:

```
import java.util.Date;
public class TimeTravel {
  public static void main(String [] args) {
    Date date;
    if (date == null)
      System.out.println("date is null");
  }
}
```

Compiling the code results in an error similar to the following:

```
%javac TimeTravel.java
TimeTravel.java:5: Variable date may not have been initialized.
          if (date == null)
1 error
```

Instance variable references are always given a default value of null, until explicitly initialized to something else. But local references are not given a default value; in other words, *they aren't null*. If you don't initialize a local reference variable, then by default, its value is...well that's the whole point—it doesn't have any value at all! So we'll make this simple: Just set the darn thing to `null` explicitly, until you're ready to initialize it to something else. The following local variable will compile properly:

```
Date date = null; // Explicitly set the local reference
                  // variable to null
```

Local Arrays

Just like any other object reference, array references declared within a method must be assigned a value before use. That just means you must declare and construct the array. You do not, however, need to explicitly initialize the elements of an array. We've said it before, but it's important enough to repeat: array elements are given their default values (0, `false`, `null`, `'\u0000'`, etc.) regardless of whether the array is declared as an instance or local variable. The array object itself, however, will not be initialized if it's declared locally. In other words, you must explicitly initialize an array reference if it's declared and used within a method, but at the moment you construct an array object, all of its elements are assigned their default values.

Assigning One Reference Variable to Another

With primitive variables, an assignment of one variable to another means the contents (bit pattern) of one variable are *copied* into another. Object reference variables work exactly the same way. The contents of a reference variable are a bit pattern, so if you assign reference variable a to reference variable b, the bit pattern in a is *copied* and the new *copy* is placed into b. (Some people have created a game around counting how many times we use the word *copy* in this chapter...this copy concept is a biggie!) If we assign an existing instance of an object to a new reference variable, then two reference variables will hold the same bit pattern—a bit pattern referring to a specific object on the heap. Look at the following code:

```
import java.awt.Dimension;
class ReferenceTest {
  public static void main (String [] args) {
    Dimension a = new Dimension(5,10);
    System.out.println("a.height = " + a.height);
    Dimension b = a;
    b.height = 30;
    System.out.println("a.height = " + a.height +
                        " after change to b");
  }
}
```

In the preceding example, a Dimension object a is declared and initialized with a width of 5 and a height of 10. Next, Dimension b is declared, and assigned the value of a. At this point, both variables (a and b) hold identical values, because the contents of a were copied into b. There is still only one Dimension object—the one that both a and b refer to. Finally, the height property is changed using the b reference. Now think for a minute: is this going to change the height property of a as well? Let's see what the output will be:

```
%java ReferenceTest
a.height = 10
a.height = 30 after change to b
```

From this output, we can conclude that both variables refer to the same instance of the Dimension object. When we made a change to b, the height property was also changed for a.

One exception to the way object references are assigned is String. In Java, String objects are given special treatment. For one thing, String objects are immutable; you can't change the value of a String object (lots more on this concept in Chapter 6). But it sure looks as though you can. Examine the following code:

```
class StringTest {
  public static void main(String [] args) {
    String x = "Java";   // Assign a value to x
    String y = x;        // Now y and x refer to the same
                         // String object

    System.out.println("y string = " + y);
    x = x + " Bean";     // Now modify the object using
                         // the x reference
```

```
         System.out.println("y string = " + y);
     }
 }
```

You might think String `y` will contain the characters `Java Bean` after the variable `x` is changed, because Strings are objects. Let's see what the output is:

```
%java StringTest
y string = Java
y string = Java
```

As you can see, even though `y` is a reference variable to the same object that `x` refers to, when we change `x`, it doesn't change `y`! For any other object type, where two references refer to the same object, if either reference is used to modify the object, both references will see the change because there is still only a single object. *But any time we make any changes at all to a String, the VM will update the reference variable to refer to a different object.* The different object might be a new object, or it might not, but it will definitely be a different object. The reason we can't say for sure whether a new object is created is because of the String constant pool, which we'll cover in Chapter 6.

You need to understand what happens when you use a String reference variable to modify a string:

■ A new string is created (or a matching String is found in the String pool), leaving the original String object untouched.

■ The reference used to modify the String (or rather, make a new String by modifying a copy of the original) is then assigned the brand new String object.

So when you say

```
1. String s = "Fred";
2. String t = s;        // Now t and s refer to the same
                        // String object
3. t.toUpperCase();     // Invoke a String method that changes
                        // the String
```

you haven't changed the original String object created on line 1. When line 2 completes, both `t` and `s` reference the same String object. But when line 3 runs, rather than modifying the object referred to by `t` (which is the one and only String object up to this point), a brand new String object is created. And then abandoned. Because the new String isn't assigned to a String variable, the newly created String (which holds the string "FRED") is toast. So while two String objects were created in the preceding code, only one is actually referenced, and both t and s refer to it. The behavior of Strings is extremely important in the exam, so we'll cover it in much more detail in Chapter 6.

CERTIFICATION OBJECTIVE

Passing Variables into Methods (Objective 7.3)

7.3   Determine the effect upon object references and primitive values when they are passed into methods that perform assignments or other modifying operations on the parameters.

Methods can be declared to take primitives and/or object references. You need to know how (or if) the caller's variable can be affected by the called method. The difference between object reference and primitive variables, when passed into methods, is huge and important. To understand this section, you'll need to be comfortable with the assignments section covered in the first part of this chapter.

Passing Object Reference Variables

When you pass an object variable into a method, you must keep in mind that you're passing the object *reference*, and not the actual object itself. Remember that a reference variable holds bits that represent (to the underlying VM) a way to get to a specific object in memory (on the heap). More importantly, you must remember that you aren't even passing the actual reference variable, but rather a *copy* of the reference variable. A copy of a variable means you get a copy of the bits in that variable, so when you pass a reference variable, you're passing a copy of the bits representing how to get to a specific object. In other words, both the caller and the called method will now have identical copies of the reference, and thus both will refer to the same exact (*not* a copy) object on the heap.

For this example, we'll use the Dimension class from the java.awt package:

```
1.  import java.awt.Dimension;
2.  class ReferenceTest {
```

```
3.    public static void main (String [] args) {
4.       Dimension d = new Dimension(5,10);
5.       ReferenceTest rt = new ReferenceTest();
6.       System.out.println("Before modify() d.height = "
                                 + d.height);
7.       rt.modify(d);
8.       System.out.println("After modify() d.height = "
                                 + d.height);
9.    }
10.   void modify(Dimension dim) {
11.      dim.height = dim.height + 1;
12.      System.out.println("dim = " + dim.height);
13.   }
14. }
```

When we run this class, we can see that the modify() method was indeed able to modify the original (and only) Dimension object created on line 4.

```
C:\Java Projects\Reference>java ReferenceTest
Before modify() d.height = 10
dim = 11
After modify() d.height = 11
```

Notice when the Dimension object on line 4 is passed to the modify() method, any changes to the object that occur inside the method are being made to the object whose reference was passed. In the preceding example, reference variables d and dim both point to the same object.

Does Java Use Pass-By-Value Semantics?

If Java passes objects by passing the reference variable instead, does that mean Java uses pass-by-reference for objects? Not exactly, although you'll often hear and read that it does. Java is actually pass-by-value for all variables running within a single VM. Pass-by-value means pass-by-variable-value. And that means, pass-by-copy-of-the-variable! (There's that word *copy* again!)

It makes no difference if you're passing primitive or reference variables, you are always passing a copy of the bits in the variable. So for a primitive variable, you're passing a copy of the bits representing the value. For example, if you pass an int variable with the value of 3, you're passing a copy of the bits representing 3. The called method then gets its own copy of the value, to do with it what it likes.

And if you're passing an object reference variable, you're passing a copy of the bits representing the reference to an object. The called method then gets its own copy of the reference variable, to do with it what it likes. But because two identical reference variables refer to the exact same object, if the called method modifies the object (by invoking setter methods, for example), the caller will see that the object the caller's original variable refers to has also been changed. In the next section, we'll look at how the picture changes when we're talking about primitives.

The bottom line on pass-by-value: the called method can't change the caller's variable, although for object reference variables, the called method can change the object the variable referred to. What's the difference between changing the variable and changing the object? For object references, it means the called method can't reassign the caller's original reference variable and make it refer to a different object, or null. For example, in the following code fragment,

```
void bar() {
    Foo f = new Foo();
    doStuff(f);
}
void doStuff(Foo g) {
    g.setName("Boo");
    g = new Foo();
}
```

reassigning g does not reassign f! At the end of the bar() method, two Foo objects have been created, one referenced by the local variable f and one referenced by the local (argument) variable g. Because the doStuff() method has a copy of the reference variable, it has a way to get to the original Foo object, for instance to call the setName() method. But, the doStuff() method does *not* have a way to get to the f reference variable. So doStuff() can change values within the object f refers to, but doStuff() can't change the actual contents (bit pattern) of f. In other words, doStuff() can change the state of the object that f refers to, but it can't make f refer to a different object!

Passing Primitive Variables

Let's look at what happens when a primitive variable is passed to a method:

```
class ReferenceTest {
  public static void main (String [] args) {
```

```
        int a = 1;
        ReferenceTest rt = new ReferenceTest();
        System.out.println("Before modify() a = " + a);
        rt.modify(a);
        System.out.println("After modify() a = " + a);
    }
  void modify(int number) {
    number = number + 1;
    System.out.println("number = " + number);
    }
}
```

In this simple program, the variable a is passed to a method called modify(), which increments the variable by 1. The resulting output looks like this:

```
Before modify() a = 1
number = 2
After modify() a = 1
```

Notice that a did not change after it was passed to the method. Remember, it was a copy of a that was passed to the method. When a primitive variable is passed to a method, it is passed by value, which means pass-by-copy-of-the-bits-in-the-variable.

FROM THE CLASSROOM

The Shadowy World of Variables

Just when you think you've got it all figured out, you see a piece of code with variables not behaving the way you think they should. You might have stumbled into code with a shadowed variable. You can shadow a variable in several ways. We'll look at the one most likely to trip you up: hiding an instance variable by shadowing it with a local variable. Shadowing involves redeclaring a variable that's already been declared somewhere else.

The effect of shadowing is to hide the previously declared variable in such a way that it may look as though you're using the hidden variable, but you're actually using the shadowing variable. You might find reasons to shadow a variable intentionally, but typically it happens by accident and causes hard-to-find bugs. On the exam, you can expect to see questions where shadowing plays a role.

FROM THE CLASSROOM

You can shadow an instance variable by declaring a local variable of the same name, either directly or as part of an argument:

```
class Foo {
  static int size = 7;
  static void changeIt(int size) {
    size = size + 200;
    System.out.println("size in changeIt is " + size);
  }
  public static void main (String [] args) {
    Foo f = new Foo();
    System.out.println("size = " + size);
    changeIt(size);
    System.out.println("size after changeIt is " + size);
  }
}
```

The preceding code appears to change the size instance variable in the changeIt() method, but because changeIt() has a parameter named size, the local size variable is modified while the instance variable size is untouched. Running class Foo prints

```
%java Foo
size = 7
size in changeIt is 207
size after changeIt is 7
```

Things become more interesting when the shadowed variable is an object reference, rather than a primitive:

```
class Bar {
  int barNum = 28;
}
```

FROM THE CLASSROOM

```
class Foo {
  Bar myBar = new Bar();
  void changeIt(Bar myBar) {
    myBar.barNum = 99;
    System.out.println("myBar.barNum in changeIt is " + myBar.barNum);
    myBar = new Bar();
    myBar.barNum = 420;
    System.out.println("myBar.barNum in changeIt is now " + myBar.barNum);
  }
  public static void main (String [] args) {
    Foo f = new Foo();
    System.out.println("f.myBar.barNum is " + f.myBar.barNum);
    f.changeIt(f.myBar);
    System.out.println("f.myBar.barNum after changeIt is "
                       + f.myBar.barNum);
  }
}
```

The preceding code prints out this:

```
f.myBar.barNum is 28
myBar.barNum in changeIt is 99
myBar.barNum in changeIt is now 420
f.myBar.barNum after changeIt is 99
```

You can see that the shadowing variable (the local parameter myBar in changeIt()) can still affect the myBar instance variable, because the myBar parameter receives a reference to the same Bar object. But when the local myBar is reassigned a new Bar object, which we then modify by changing its barNum value, Foo's original myBar instance variable is untouched.

CERTIFICATION OBJECTIVE

Array Declaration, Construction, and Initialization (Exam Objective 1.3)

1.3   Develop code that declares, initializes, and uses primitives, arrays, enums, and objects as static, instance, and local variables. Also, use legal identifiers for variable names.

Arrays are objects in Java that store multiple variables of the same type. Arrays can hold either primitives or object references, but the array itself will always be an object on the heap, even if the array is declared to hold primitive elements. In other words, there is no such thing as a primitive array, but you can make an array of primitives. For this objective, you need to know three things:

- How to make an array reference variable (declare)
- How to make an array object (construct)
- How to populate the array with elements (initialize)

There are several different ways to do each of those, and you need to know about all of them for the exam.

on the
ⓙob

Arrays are efficient, but most of the time you'll want to use one of the Collection types from java.util (including HashMap, ArrayList, TreeSet). Collection classes offer more flexible ways to access an object (for insertion, deletion, and so on) and unlike arrays, can expand or contract dynamically as you add or remove elements (they're really managed arrays, since they use arrays behind the scenes). There's a Collection type for a wide range of needs. Do you need a fast sort? A group of objects with no duplicates? A way to access a name/value pair? A linked list? Chapter 7 covers them in more detail.

Declaring an Array

Arrays are declared by stating the type of element the array will hold, which can be an object or a primitive, followed by square brackets to the left or right of the identifier.

Declaring an array of primitives:

```
int[] key;  // brackets before name (recommended)
int key [];  // brackets after name (legal but less readable)
            // spaces between the name and [] legal, but bad
```

Declaring an array of object references:

```
Thread[] threads;   // Recommended
Thread threads[];   // Legal but less readable
```

When declaring an array reference, you should always put the array brackets immediately after the declared type, rather than after the identifier (variable name). That way, anyone reading the code can easily tell that, for example, key is a reference to an int array object, and not an int primitive.

We can also declare multidimensional arrays, which are in fact arrays of arrays. This can be done in the following manner:

```
String[][][] occupantName;   // recommended
String[] ManagerName [];      // yucky, but legal
```

The first example is a three-dimensional array (an array of arrays of arrays) and the second is a two-dimensional array. Notice in the second example we have one square bracket before the variable name and one after. This is perfectly legal to the compiler, proving once again that just because it's legal doesn't mean it's right.

It is never legal to include the size of the array in your declaration. Yes, we know you can do that in some other languages, which is why you might see a question or two that include code similar to the following:

```
int[5] scores;
```

The preceding code won't make it past the compiler. Remember, the JVM doesn't allocate space until you actually instantiate the array object. That's when size matters.

Constructing an Array

Constructing an array means creating the array object on the *heap* (where all objects live)—i.e., doing a new on the array type. To create an array object, Java must know how much space to allocate on the heap, so you must specify the size of the array at creation time. The size of the array is the number of elements the array will hold.

Constructing One-Dimensional Arrays

The most straightforward way to construct an array is to use the keyword new followed by the array type, with a bracket specifying how many elements of that type the array will hold. The following is an example of constructing an array of type int:

```
int[] testScores;        // Declares the array of ints
testScores = new int[4]; // constructs an array and assigns it
                         // to the testScores variable
```

The preceding code puts one new object on the heap—an array object holding four elements—with each element containing an int with a default value of 0. Think of this code as saying to the compiler, "Create an array object that will hold four ints, and assign it to the reference variable named testScores. Also, go ahead and set each int element to zero. Thanks." (The compiler appreciates good manners.) Figure 3-2 shows the testScores array on the heap, after construction.

FIGURE 3-2

A one-dimensional array on the Heap

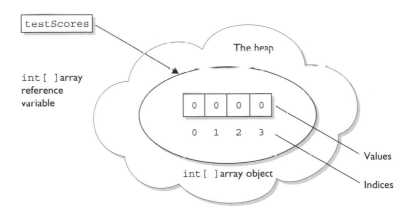

You can also declare and construct an array in one statement as follows:

```
int[] testScores = new int[4];
```

This single statement produces the same result as the two previous statements. Arrays of object types can be constructed in the same way:

```
Thread[] threads = new Thread[5];
```

Remember that—despite how the code appears—the Thread constructor is not being invoked. We're not creating a Thread instance, but rather a single Thread array object. After the preceding statement, there are still no actual Thread objects!

exam
ⓦatch
Think carefully about how many objects are on the heap after a code statement or block executes. The exam will expect you to know, for example, that the preceding code produces just one object (the array assigned to the reference variable named threads). The single object referenced by threads holds five Thread reference variables, but no Thread objects have been created or assigned to those references.

Remember, arrays must always be given a size at the time they are constructed. The JVM needs the size to allocate the appropriate space on the heap for the new array object. It is never legal, for example, to do the following:

```
int[] carList = new int[]; // Will not compile; needs a size
```

So don't do it, and if you see it on the test, run screaming toward the nearest answer marked "Compilation fails."

exam
ⓦatch
You may see the words "construct", "create", and "instantiate" used interchangeably. They all mean, "An object is built on the heap." This also implies that the object's constructor runs, as a result of the construct/create/instantiate code. You can say with certainty, for example, that any code that uses the keyword new, *will (if it runs successfully) cause the class constructor and all superclass constructors to run.*

In addition to being constructed with new, arrays can also be created using a kind of syntax shorthand that creates the array while simultaneously initializing the array elements to values supplied in code (as opposed to default values). We'll look at that in the next section. For now, understand that because of these syntax shortcuts, objects can still be created even without you ever using or seeing the keyword new.

Constructing Multidimensional Arrays

Multidimensional arrays, remember, are simply arrays of arrays. So a two-dimensional array of type int is really an object of type int array (int []), with each element in that array holding a reference to another int array. The second dimension holds the actual int primitives. The following code declares and constructs a two-dimensional array of type int:

```
int [] [] myArray = new int [3] [] ;
```

Notice that only the first brackets are given a size. That's acceptable in Java, since the JVM needs to know only the size of the object assigned to the variable myArray.

Figure 3-3 shows how a two-dimensional int array works on the heap.

FIGURE 3-3

A two-dimensional array on the Heap

Picture demonstrates the result of the following code:

```
int [ ] [ ] myArray = new int [3] [ ];
myArray[0]  = new int [2];
myArray[0] [0]  = 6;
myArray[0] [1]  = 7;
myArray[1]  = new int [3];
myArray[1] [0]  = 9;
myArray[1] [1]  = 8;
myArray[1] [2]  = 5;
```

Initializing an Array

Initializing an array means putting things into it. The "things" in the array are the array's elements, and they're either primitive values (2, x, `false`, and so on), or objects referred to by the reference variables in the array. If you have an array of objects (as opposed to primitives), the array doesn't actually hold the objects, just as any other nonprimitive variable never actually holds the object, but instead holds a *reference* to the object. But we talk about arrays as, for example, "an array of five strings," even though what we really mean is, "an array of five references to String objects." Then the big question becomes whether or not those references are actually pointing (oops, this is Java, we mean referring) to real String objects, or are simply `null`. Remember, a reference that has not had an object assigned to it is a `null` reference. And if you try to actually use that `null` reference by, say, applying the dot operator to invoke a method on it, you'll get the infamous NullPointerException.

The individual elements in the array can be accessed with an index number. The index number always begins with zero, so for an array of ten objects the index numbers will run from 0 through 9. Suppose we create an array of three Animals as follows:

```
Animal [] pets = new Animal[3];
```

We have one array object on the heap, with three `null` references of type Animal, but we don't have any Animal objects. The next step is to create some Animal objects and assign them to index positions in the array referenced by `pets`:

```
pets[0] = new Animal();
pets[1] = new Animal();
pets[2] = new Animal();
```

This code puts three new Animal objects on the heap and assigns them to the three index positions (elements) in the `pets` array.

```
int[] x = new int[5];
x[4] = 2;  // OK, the last element is at index 4
x[5] = 3;  // Runtime  exception. There is no element at index
5!

int[] z = new int[2];
int y = -3;
z[y] = 4; // Runtime exception. y is a negative number
```

These can be hard to spot in a complex loop, but that's where you're most likely to see array index problems in exam questions.

A two-dimensional array (an array of arrays) can be initialized as follows:

```
int[][] scores = new int[3][];
// Declare and create an array holding three references
// to int arrays

scores[0] = new int[4];
// the first element in the scores array is an int array
// of four int elements

scores[1] = new int[6];
// the second element in the scores array is an int array
// of six int elements

scores[2] = new int[1];
// the third element in the scores array is an int array
// of one int element
```

Initializing Elements in a Loop

Array objects have a single public variable, length that gives you the number of elements in the array. The last index value, then, is always one less than the length. For example, if the length of an array is 4, the index values are from 0 through 3. Often, you'll see array elements initialized in a loop as follows:

```
Dog[] myDogs = new Dog[6]; // creates an array of 6
                           // Dog references
for(int x = 0; x < myDogs.length; x++) {
    myDogs[x] = new Dog(); // assign a new Dog to the
                           // index position x
}
```

The `length` variable tells us how many elements the array holds, but it does not tell us whether those elements have been initialized.

Declaring, Constructing, and Initializing on One Line

You can use two different array-specific syntax shortcuts to both initialize (put explicit values into an array's elements) and construct (instantiate the array object itself) in a single statement. The first is used to declare, create, and initialize in one statement as follows:

```
1.  int x = 9;
2.  int[] dots = {6,x,8};
```

Line 2 in the preceding code does four things:

- Declares an `int` array reference variable named `dots`.
- Creates an `int` array with a length of three (three elements).
- Populates the array's elements with the values 6, 9, and 8.
- Assigns the new array object to the reference variable `dots`.

The size (length of the array) is determined by the number of comma-separated items between the curly braces. The code is functionally equivalent to the following longer code:

```
int[] dots;
dots = new int[3];
int x = 9;
dots[0] = 6;
dots[1] = x;
dots[2] = 8;
```

This begs the question, "Why would anyone use the longer way?" One reason come to mind. You might not know—at the time you create the array—the values that will be assigned to the array's elements. This array shortcut alone (combined with the stimulating prose) is worth the price of this book.

With object references rather than primitives, it works exactly the same way:

```
Dog puppy = new Dog("Frodo");
Dog[] myDogs = {puppy, new Dog("Clover"), new Dog("Aiko")};
```

The preceding code creates one Dog array, referenced by the variable myDogs, with a length of three elements. It assigns a previously created Dog object (assigned to the reference variable puppy) to the first element in the array. It also creates two new Dog objects (Clover and Aiko), and adds them to the last two Dog reference variable elements in the myDogs array. Figure 3-4 shows the result.

FIGURE 3-4

Declaring, constructing, and initializing an array of objects

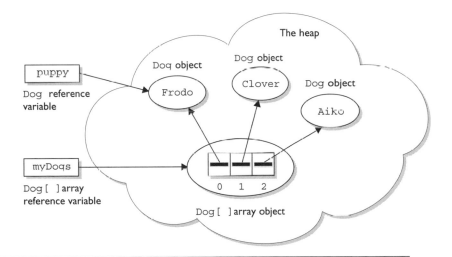

Picture demonstrates the result of the following code:
```
Dog puppy = new Dog ("Frodo");
Dog[ ] myDogs = {puppy, new Dog("Clover"), new Dog("Aiko")};
```

Four objects are created:
1 Dog object referenced by puppy and by myDogs[0]
1 Dog[ ] array referenced by myDogs
2 Dog object referenced by myDogs[1] and myDogs[2]

You can also use the shortcut syntax with multidimensional arrays, as follows:

```
int[][] scores = {{5,2,4,7}, {9,2}, {3,4}};
```

The preceding code creates a total of four objects on the heap. First, an array of int arrays is constructed (the object that will be assigned to the scores reference variable). The scores array has a length of three, derived from the number of items (comma-separated) between the outer curly braces. Each of the three elements in the scores array is a reference variable to an int array, so the three int arrays are constructed and assigned to the three elements in the scores array.

The size of each of the three int arrays is derived from the number of items within the corresponding inner curly braces. For example, the first array has a length of four, the second array has a length of two, and the third array has a length of two. So far, we have four objects: one array of int arrays (each element is a reference to an int array), and three int arrays (each element in the three int arrays is an int value). Finally, the three int arrays are initialized with the actual int values within the inner curly braces. Thus, the first int array contains the values 5, 2, 4, and 7. The following code shows the values of some of the elements in this two-dimensional array:

```
scores[0]    // an array of four ints
scores[1]    // an array of 2 ints
scores[2]    // an array of 2 ints
scores[0][1] // the int value 2
scores[2][1] // the int value 4
```

Figure 3-5 shows the result of declaring, constructing, and initializing a two-dimensional array in one statement.

Constructing and Initializing an Anonymous Array

The second shortcut is called "anonymous array creation" and can be used to construct and initialize an array, and then assign the array to a previously declared array reference variable:

```
int[] testScores;
testScores = new int[] {4,7,2};
```

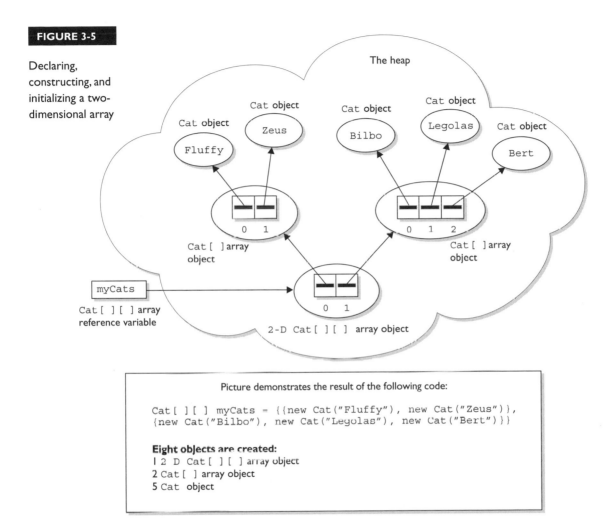

FIGURE 3-5

Declaring, constructing, and initializing a two-dimensional array

> Picture demonstrates the result of the following code:
>
> ```
> Cat [ ] [ ] myCats = {{new Cat("Fluffy"), new Cat("Zeus")},
> {new Cat("Bilbo"), new Cat("Legolas"), new Cat("Bert")}}
> ```
>
> **Eight objects are created:**
> 1 2 D Cat [ ] [ ] array object
> 2 Cat [ ] array object
> 5 Cat object

The preceding code creates a new int array with three elements, initializes the three elements with the values 4, 7, and 2, and then assigns the new array to the previously declared int array reference variable testScores. We call this anonymous array creation because with this syntax you don't even need to assign the new array to anything. Maybe you're wondering, "What good is an array if you don't assign it to a reference variable?" You can use it to create a just-in-time array to use, for example, as an argument to a method that takes an array parameter. The following code demonstrates a just-in-time array argument:

```
public class Foof {
  void takesAnArray(int []  someArray) {
    // use the array parameter
  }
  public static void main (String [] args) {
    Foof f = new Foof();
    f.takesAnArray(new int[] {7,7,8,2,5}); // we need an array
                                           // argument
  }
}
```

e x a m
ⓦatch
Remember that you do not specify a size when using anonymous array creation syntax. The size is derived from the number of items (comma-separated) between the curly braces. Pay very close attention to the array syntax used in exam questions (and there will be a lot of them). You might see syntax such as

```
new Object[3] {null, new Object(), new Object()};
    // not legal;size must not be specified
```

Legal Array Element Assignments

What can you put in a particular array? For the exam, you need to know that arrays can have only one declared type (int [], Dog[], String [], and so on), but that doesn't necessarily mean that only objects or primitives of the declared type can be assigned to the array elements. And what about the array reference itself? What kind of array object can be assigned to a particular array reference? For the exam, you'll need to know the answers to all of these questions. And, as if by magic, we're actually covering those very same topics in the following sections. Pay attention.

Arrays of Primitives

Primitive arrays can accept any value that can be promoted implicitly to the declared type of the array. For example, an int array can hold any value that can fit into a 32-bit int variable. Thus, the following code is legal:

```
int[] weightList = new int[5];
byte b = 4;
char c = 'c';
short s = 7;
weightList[0] = b;   // OK, byte is smaller than int
weightList[1] = c;   // OK, char is smaller than int
weightList[2] = s;   // OK, short is smaller than int
```

Arrays of Object References

If the declared array type is a class, you can put objects of any subclass of the declared type into the array. For example, if Subaru is a subclass of Car, you can put both Subaru objects and Car objects into an array of type Car as follows:

```
class Car {}
class Subaru extends Car {}
class Ferrari extends Car {}
...
Car [] myCars = {new Subaru(), new Car(), new Ferrari()};
```

It helps to remember that the elements in a Car array are nothing more than Car reference variables. So anything that can be assigned to a Car reference variable can be legally assigned to a Car array element.

If the array is declared as an interface type, the array elements can refer to any instance of any class that implements the declared interface. The following code demonstrates the use of an interface as an array type:

```
interface Sporty {
  void beSporty();
}

class Ferrari extends Car implements Sporty {
  public void beSporty() {
    // implement cool sporty method in a Ferrari-specific way
  }
}
class RacingFlats extends AthleticShoe implements Sporty {
  public void beSporty() {
    // implement cool sporty method in a RacingShoe-specific way
  }
```

```
    }
    class GolfClub { }
    class TestSportyThings {
      public static void main (String [] args) {
        Sporty[] sportyThings = new Sporty [3];
        sportyThings[0] = new Ferrari();       // OK, Ferrari
                                               // implements Sporty
        sportyThings[1] = new RacingFlats();   // OK, RacingFlats
                                               // implements Sporty
        sportyThings[2] = new GolfClub();

           // Not OK; GolfClub does not implement Sporty
           // I don't care what anyone says
      }
    }
```

The bottom line is this: any object that passes the "IS-A" test for the declared array type can be assigned to an element of that array.

Array Reference Assignments for One-Dimensional Arrays

For the exam, you need to recognize legal and illegal assignments for array reference variables. We're not talking about references in the array (in other words, array elements), but rather references to the array object. For example, if you declare an int array, the reference variable you declared can be reassigned to any int array (of any size), but cannot be reassigned to anything that is not an int array, including an int value. Remember, all arrays are objects, so an int array reference cannot refer to an int primitive. The following code demonstrates legal and illegal assignments for primitive arrays:

```
int[] splats;
int[] dats = new int[4];
char[] letters = new char[5];
splats = dats; // OK, dats refers to an int array
splats = letters; // NOT OK, letters refers to a char array
```

It's tempting to assume that because a variable of type byte, short, or char can be explicitly promoted and assigned to an int, an array of any of those types could be assigned to an int array. You can't do that in Java, but it would be just like those cruel, heartless (but otherwise attractive) exam developers to put tricky array assignment questions in the exam.

Arrays that hold object references, as opposed to primitives, aren't as restrictive. Just as you can put a Honda object in a Car array (because Honda extends Car), you can assign an array of type Honda to a Car array reference variable as follows:

```
Car[] cars;
Honda[] cuteCars = new Honda[5];
cars = cuteCars; // OK because Honda is a type of Car
Beer[] beers = new Beer [99];
cars = beers; // NOT OK, Beer is not a type of Car
```

Apply the IS-A test to help sort the legal from the illegal. Honda IS-A Car, so a Honda array can be assigned to a Car array. Beer IS-A Car is not true; Beer does not extend Car (plus it doesn't make sense, unless you've already had too much of it).

The rules for array assignment apply to interfaces as well as classes. An array declared as an interface type can reference an array of any type that implements the interface. Remember, any object from a class implementing a particular interface will pass the IS-A (instanceof) test for that interface. For example, if Box implements Foldable, the following is legal:

```
Foldable[] foldingThings;
Box[] boxThings = new Box[3];
foldingThings = boxThings;
// OK, Box implements Foldable, so Box IS-A Foldable
```

Array Reference Assignments for Multidimensional Arrays

When you assign an array to a previously declared array reference, the array you're assigning must be the same dimension as the reference you're assigning it to. For example, a two-dimensional array of int arrays cannot be assigned to a regular int array reference, as follows:

```
int[] blots;
int[][] squeegees = new int[3][];
blots = squeegees;          // NOT OK, squeegees is a
                            // two-d array of int arrays
int[] blocks = new int[6];
blots = blocks;             // OK, blocks is an int array
```

Pay particular attention to array assignments using different dimensions. You might, for example, be asked if it's legal to assign an int array to the first element in an array of int arrays, as follows:

```
int[][]  books = new int[3][];
int[] numbers = new int[6];
int aNumber = 7;
books[0] = aNumber;     // NO, expecting an int array not an int
books[0] = numbers;     // OK, numbers is an int array
```

Figure 3-6 shows an example of legal and illegal assignments for references to an array.

Initialization Blocks

We've talked about two places in a class where you can put code that performs operations: methods and constructors. Initialization blocks are the third place in a Java program where operations can be performed. Initialization blocks run when the class is first loaded (a static initialization block) or when an instance is created (an instance initialization block). Let's look at an example:

```
class SmallInit {
  static int x;
  int y;

  static { x = 7 ; }      // static init block
  { y = 8; }              // instance init block
}
```

FIGURE 3-6 Legal and illegal array assignments

Illegal Array Reference Assignments	KEY
A `myCats = myCats[0];` `// Can't assign a 1-D array to a 2-D array reference`	
B `myCats = myCats[0][0];` `// Can't assign a nonarray object to a 2-D array reference`	Legal
C `myCats[1] = myCats[1][2];` `// Can't assign a nonarray object to a 1-D array reference`	Illegal

D `myCats[0][1] = moreCats;`
`// Can't assign an array object to a nonarray reference`
`//myCats[0][1] can only refer to a Cat object`	

As you can see, the syntax for initialization blocks is pretty terse. They don't have names, they can't take arguments, and they don't return anything. A *static* initialization block runs *once*, when the class is first loaded. An *instance* initialization block runs once *every time a new instance is created*. Remember when we talked about the order in which constructor code executed? Instance init block code runs right after the call to `super()` in a constructor, in other words, after all super-constructors have run.

You can have many initialization blocks in a class. It is important to note that unlike methods or constructors, *the order in which initialization blocks appear in a class matters*. When it's time for initialization blocks to run, if a class has more than one, they will run in the order in which they appear in the class file...in other words, from the top down. Based on the rules we just discussed, can you determine the output of the following program?

```
class Init {
  Init(int x) { System.out.println("1-arg const"); }
  Init() { System.out.println("no-arg const"); }
  static { System.out.println("1st static init"); }
  { System.out.println("1st instance init"); }
  { System.out.println("2nd instance init"); }
  static { System.out.println("2nd static init"); }

  public static void main(String [] args) {
    new Init();
    new Init(7);
  }
}
```

To figure this out, remember these rules:

- Init blocks execute in the order they appear.
- Static init blocks run once, when the class is first loaded.
- Instance init blocks run every time a class instance is created.
- Instance init blocks run after the constructor's call to `super()`.

With those rules in mind, the following output should make sense:

```
1st static init
2nd static init
1st instance init
2nd instance init
no-arg const
1st instance init
2nd instance init
1-arg const
```

As you can see, the instance init blocks each ran twice. Instance init blocks are often used as a place to put code that all the constructors in a class should share. That way, the code doesn't have to be duplicated across constructors.

Finally, if you make a mistake in your static init block, the JVM can throw an `ExceptionInInitializationError`. Let's look at an example,

```
class InitError {
  static int [] x = new int[4];
  static { x[4] = 5; }            // bad array index!
  public static void main(String [] args) { }
}
```

which produces something like:

```
Exception in thread "main" java.lang.ExceptionInInitializerError
Caused by: java.lang.ArrayIndexOutOfBoundsException: 4
        at InitError.<clinit>(InitError.java:3)
```

exam
ⓦatch

By convention, init blocks usually appear near the top of the class file, somewhere around the constructors. However, this is the SCJP exam we're talking about. Don't be surprised if you find an init block tucked in between a couple of methods, looking for all the world like a compiler error waiting to happen!

CERTIFICATION OBJECTIVE

Using Wrapper Classes and Boxing (Exam Objective 3.1)

3.1   Develop code that uses the primitive wrapper classes (such as Boolean, Character, Double, Integer, etc.), and/or autoboxing & unboxing. Discuss the differences between the String, StringBuilder, and StringBuffer classes.

The wrapper classes in the Java API serve two primary purposes:

■ To provide a mechanism to "wrap" primitive values in an object so that the primitives can be included in activities reserved for objects, like being added to Collections, or returned from a method with an object return value. Note: With Java 5's addition of autoboxing (and unboxing), which we'll get to in a few pages, many of the wrapping operations that programmers used to do manually are now handled automatically.

■ To provide an assortment of utility functions for primitives. Most of these functions are related to various conversions: converting primitives to and from String objects, and converting primitives and String objects to and from different bases (or radix), such as binary, octal, and hexadecimal.

An Overview of the Wrapper Classes

There is a wrapper class for every primitive in Java. For instance, the wrapper class for int is Integer, the class for float is Float, and so on. Remember that the primitive name is simply the lowercase name of the wrapper except for char, which maps to Character, and int, which maps to Integer. Table 3-2 lists the wrapper classes in the Java API.

TABLE 3-2	Wrapper Classes and Their Constructor Arguments	
Primitive	**Wrapper Class**	**Constructor Arguments**
boolean	Boolean	boolean or String
byte	Byte	byte or String
char	Character	char
double	Double	double or String
float	Float	float, double, or String
int	Integer	int or String
long	Long	long or String
short	Short	short or String

Creating Wrapper Objects

For the exam you need to understand the three most common approaches for creating wrapper objects. Some approaches take a String representation of a primitive as an argument. Those that take a String throw NumberFormatException if the String provided cannot be parsed into the appropriate primitive. For example "two" can't be parsed into "2". *Wrapper objects are immutable.* Once they have been given a value, that value cannot be changed. We'll talk more about wrapper immutability when we discuss boxing in a few pages.

The Wrapper Constructors

All of the wrapper classes except Character provide two constructors: one that takes a primitive of the type being constructed, and one that takes a String representation of the type being constructed—for example,

```
Integer i1 = new Integer(42);
Integer i2 = new Integer("42");
```

or

```
Float f1 = new Float(3.14f);
Float f2 = new Float("3.14f");
```

The Character class provides only one constructor, which takes a char as an argument—for example,

```
Character c1 = new Character('c');
```

The constructors for the Boolean wrapper take either a boolean value true or false, or a String. If the String's case-insensitive value is "true" the Boolean will be true—any other value will equate to false. Until Java 5, a Boolean object couldn't be used as an expression in a boolean test—for instance,

```
Boolean b = new Boolean("false");
if (b)      // won't compile, using Java 1.4 or earlier
```

As of Java 5, a Boolean object *can* be used in a boolean test, because the compiler will automatically "unbox" the Boolean to a boolean. We'll be focusing on Java 5's autoboxing capabilities in the very next section—so stay tuned!

The valueOf() Methods

The two (well, usually two) static `valueOf()` methods provided in most of the wrapper classes give you another approach to creating wrapper objects. Both methods take a String representation of the appropriate type of primitive as their first argument, the second method (when provided) takes an additional argument, `int radix`, which indicates in what base (for example binary, octal, or hexadecimal) the first argument is represented—for example,

```
Integer i2 = Integer.valueOf("101011", 2);   // converts 101011
                                              // to 43 and
                                              // assigns the value
                                              // 43 to the
                                              // Integer object i2
```

or

```
Float f2 = Float.valueOf("3.14f");    // assigns 3.14 to the
                                      // Float object f2
```

Using Wrapper Conversion Utilities

As we said earlier, a wrapper's second big function is converting stuff. The following methods are the most commonly used, and are the ones you're most likely to see on the test.

xxxValue()

When you need to convert the value of a wrapped numeric to a primitive, use one of the many `xxxValue()` methods. All of the methods in this family are no-arg methods. As you can see by referring to Table 3-3, there are 36 `xxxValue()` methods. Each of the six numeric wrapper classes has six methods, so that any numeric wrapper can be converted to any primitive numeric type—for example,

```
Integer i2 = new Integer(42);   //  make a new wrapper object
byte b = i2.byteValue();        //  convert i2's value to a byte
                                //  primitive
short s = i2.shortValue();      //  another of Integer's xxxValue
                                //  methods
double d = i2.doubleValue();    //  yet another of Integer's
                                //  xxxValue methods
```

or

```
Float f2 = new Float(3.14f);    // make a new wrapper object
short s = f2.shortValue();      // convert f2's value to a short
                                // primitive
System.out.println(s);          // result is 3  (truncated, not
                                // rounded)
```

parseXxx() and valueOf()

The six parseXxx() methods (one for each numeric wrapper type) are closely related to the valueOf() method that exists in all of the numeric wrapper classes. Both parseXxx() and valueOf() take a String as an argument, throw a NumberFormatException (a.k.a. NFE) if the String argument is not properly formed, and can convert String objects from different bases (radix), when the underlying primitive type is any of the four integer types. (See Table 3-3.) The difference between the two methods is

■ parseXxx() returns the named primitive.

■ valueOf() returns a newly created wrapped object of the type that invoked the method.

Here are some examples of these methods in action:

```
double d4 = Double.parseDouble("3.14");    // convert a String
                                           // to a primitive
System.out.println("d4 = " + d4);          // result is d4 = 3.14

Double d5 = Double.valueOf("3.14");        // create a Double obj
System.out.println(d5 instanceof Double); // result is "true"
```

The next examples involve using the radix argument (in this case binary):

```
long L2 = Long.parseLong("101010", 2);    // binary String to a
                                          // primitive
System.out.println("L2 = " + L2);         // result is: L2 = 42

Long L3 = Long.valueOf("101010", 2);      // binary String to
                                          // Long object
System.out.println("L3 value = " + L3);   // result is:
                                          // L3 value = 42
```

toString()

Class Object, the alpha class, has a `toString()` method. Since we know that all other Java classes inherit from class Object, we also know that all other Java classes have a `toString()` method. The idea of the `toString()` method is to allow you to get some meaningful representation of a given object. For instance, if you have a Collection of various types of objects, you can loop through the Collection and print out some sort of meaningful representation of each object using the `toString()` method, which is guaranteed to be in every class. We'll talk more about `toString()` in the Collections chapter, but for now let's focus on how `toString()` relates to the wrapper classes which, as we know, are marked `final`. All of the wrapper classes have a no-arg, nonstatic, instance version of `toString()`. This method returns a String with the value of the primitive wrapped in the object—for instance,

```
Double d = new Double("3.14");
System.out.println("d = "+ d.toString() ); // result is d = 3.14
```

All of the numeric wrapper classes provide an overloaded, `static toString()` method that takes a primitive numeric of the appropriate type (`Double. toString()` takes a `double`, `Long.toString()` takes a `long`, and so on) and, of course, returns a String:

```
String d = Double.toString(3.14);       // d = "3.14"
```

Finally, Integer and Long provide a third toString() method. It's static, its first argument is the primitive, and its second argument is a radix. The radix tells the method to take the first argument, which is radix 10 (base 10) by default, and convert it to the radix provided, then return the result as a String—for instance,

```
String s = "hex = "+ Long.toString(254,16); // s = "hex = fe"
```

toXxxString() (Binary, Hexadecimal, Octal)

The Integer and Long wrapper classes let you convert numbers in base 10 to other bases. These conversion methods, `toXxxString()`, take an `int` or `long`, and return a String representation of the converted number, for example,

```
String s3 = Integer.toHexString(254);  // convert 254 to hex
System.out.println("254 is " + s3);    // result: "254 is fe"

String s4 = Long.toOctalString(254); // convert 254 to octal
System.out.print("254(oct) ="+ s4);   // result: "254(oct) =376"
```

Studying Table 3-3 is the single best way to prepare for this section of the test. If you can keep the differences between xxxValue(), parseXxx(), and valueOf() straight, you should do well on this part of the exam.

| TABLE 3-3 | Common Wrapper Conversion Methods |

Method s = static n = NFE exception	Boolean	Byte	Character	Double	Float	Integer	Long	Short
byteValue		x		x	x	x	x	x
doubleValue		x		x	x	x	x	x
floatValue		x		x	x	x	x	x
intValue		x		x	x	x	x	x
longValue		x		x	x	x	x	x
shortValue		x		x	x	x	x	x
parseXxx s,n		x		x	x	x	x	x
parseXxx s,n (with radix)		x				x	x	x
valueOf s,n	s	x		x	x	x	x	x
valueOf s,n (with radix)		x				x	x	x
toString	x	x	x	x	x	x	x	x
toString s (primitive)	x	x	x	x	x	x	x	x
toString s (primitive, radix)						x	x	

In summary, the essential method signatures for Wrapper conversion methods are

    primitive xxxValue()   – to convert a Wrapper to a primitive

    primitive parseXxx(String)   – to convert a String to a primitive

    Wrapper valueOf(String)   – to convert a String to a Wrapper

Autoboxing

New to Java 5 is a feature known variously as: autoboxing, auto-unboxing, boxing, and unboxing. We'll stick with the terms boxing and unboxing. Boxing and unboxing make using wrapper classes more convenient. In the old, pre–Java 5 days, if you wanted to make a wrapper, unwrap it, use it, and then rewrap it, you might do something like this:

```
Integer y = new Integer(567);    // make it
int x = y.intValue();            // unwrap it
x++;                             // use it
y = new Integer(x);              // re-wrap it
System.out.println("y = " + y);  // print it
```

Now, with new and improved Java 5 you can say

```
Integer y = new Integer(567);    // make it
y++;                             // unwrap it, increment it,
                                 // rewrap it
System.out.println("y = " + y);  // print it
```

Both examples produce the output:

```
y = 568
```

And yes, you read that correctly. The code appears to be using the postincrement operator on an object reference variable! But it's simply a convenience. Behind the scenes, the compiler does the unboxing and reassignment for you. Earlier we mentioned that wrapper objects are immutable... this example appears to contradict that statement. It sure looks like y's value changed from 567 to 568. What actually happened, is that a second wrapper object was created and its value was set to 568. If only we could access that first wrapper object, we could prove it...

Let's try this:

```
Integer y = 567;                      // make a wrapper
Integer x = y;                        // assign a second ref
                                      // var to THE wrapper

System.out.println(y==x);             // verify that they refer
                                      // to the same object
```

```
y++;                              // unwrap, use, "rewrap"
System.out.println(x + " " + y);  // print values

System.out.println(y==x);         // verify that they refer
                                  // to different objects
```

Which produces the output:

```
true
567 568
false
```

So, under the covers, when the compiler got to the line y++; it had to substitute something like this:

```
int x2 = y.intValue();   // unwrap it
x2++;                     // use it
y = new Integer(x2);      // re-wrap it
```

Just as we suspected, there's gotta be a call to new in there somewhere.

Boxing, ==, and equals()

We just used == to do a little exploration of wrappers. Let's take a more thorough look at how wrappers work with ==, !=, and equals(). We'll talk a lot more about the equals() method in later chapters. For now all we have to know is that the intention of the equals() method is to determine whether two instances of a given class are "meaningfully equivalent." This definition is intentionally subjective; it's up to the creator of the class to determine what "equivalent" means for objects of the class in question. The API developers decided that for all the wrapper classes, two objects are equal if they are of the same type and have the same value. It shouldn't be surprising that

```
Integer i1 = 1000;
Integer i2 = 1000;
if(i1 != i2) System.out.println("different objects");
if(i1.equals(i2)) System.out.println("meaningfully equal");
```

Produces the output:

```
different objects
meaningfully equal
```

It's just two wrapper objects that happen to have the same value. Because they have the same `int` value, the `equals()` method considers them to be "meaningfully equivalent", and therefore returns `true`. How about this one:

```
Integer i3 = 10;
Integer i4 = 10;
if(i3 == i4) System.out.println("same object");
if(i3.equals(i4)) System.out.println("meaningfully equal");
```

This example produces the output:

```
same object
meaningfully equal
```

Yikes! The `equals()` method seems to be working, but what happened with `==` and `!=` ? Why is `!=` telling us that `i1` and `i2` are different objects, when `==` is saying that `i3` and `i4` are the same object? In order to save memory, two instances of the following wrapper objects (created through boxing), will always be `==` when their primitive values are the same:

- `Boolean`
- `Byte`
- `Character` from `\u0000` to `\u007f`   (7f is 127 in decimal)
- `Short` and `Integer` from -128 to 127

Note: When `==` is used to compare a primitive to a wrapper, the wrapper will be unwrapped and the comparison will be primitive to primitive.

Where Boxing Can Be Used

As we discussed earlier, it's very common to use wrappers in conjunction with collections. Any time you want your collection to hold objects and primitives, you'll want to use wrappers to make those primitives collection-compatible. The general rule is that boxing and unboxing work wherever you can normally use a primitive or a wrapped object. The following code demonstrates some legal ways to use boxing:

```
class UseBoxing {
  public static void main(String [] args) {
    UseBoxing u = new UseBoxing();
    u.go(5);
  }
  boolean go(Integer i) {        // boxes the int it was passed
    Boolean ifSo = true;         // boxes the literal
    Short s = 300;               // boxes the primitive
```

```
                    if(ifSo) {                    // unboxing
                        System.out.println(++s);  // unboxes, increments, reboxes
                    }
                    return !ifSo;                 // unboxes, returns the inverse
                }
            }
```

exam
ⓦatch

Remember, wrapper reference variables can be null. That means that you have to watch out for code that appears to be doing safe primitive operations, but that could throw a NullPointerException:

```
class Boxing2 {
    static Integer x;
    public static void main(String [] args) {
        doStuff(x);
    }
    static void doStuff(int z) {
        int z2 = 5;
        System.out.println(z2 + z);
} }
```

This code compiles fine, but the JVM throws a NullPointerException *when it attempts to invoke* doStuff(x), *because* x *doesn't refer to an* Integer *object, so there's no value to unbox.*

CERTIFICATION OBJECTIVE

Overloading (Exam Objectives 1.5 and 5.4)

1.5   Given a code example, determine if a method is correctly overriding or overloading another method, and identify legal return values (including covariant returns), for the method.

5.4   Given a scenario, develop code that declares and/or invokes overridden or overloaded methods...

Overloading Made Hard—Method Matching

Although we covered some rules for overloading methods in Chapter 2, in this chapter we've added some new tools to our Java toolkit. In this section we're going to take a look at three factors that can make overloading a little tricky:

- Widening
- Autoboxing
- Var-args

When a class has overloaded methods, one of the compiler's jobs is to determine which method to use whenever it finds an invocation for the overloaded method. Let's look at an example that doesn't use any new Java 5 features:

```
class EasyOver {
  static void go(int x) { System.out.print("int "); }
  static void go(long x) { System.out.print("long "); }
  static void go(double x) { System.out.print("double "); }

  public static void main(String [] args) {
    byte b = 5;
    short s = 5;
    long l = 5;
    float f = 5.0f;

    go(b);
    go(s);
    go(l);
    go(f);
  }
}
```

Which produces the output:

```
int int long double
```

This probably isn't much of a surprise; the calls that use byte and the short arguments are implicitly widened to match the version of the go() method that takes an int. Of course, the call with the long uses the long version of go(), and finally, the call that uses a float is matched to the method that takes a double.

In every case, when an exact match isn't found, the JVM uses the method with the smallest argument that is wider than the parameter.

You can verify for yourself that if there is only one version of the go() method, and it takes a double, it will be used to match all four invocations of go().

Overloading with Boxing and Var-args

Now let's take our last example, and add *boxing* into the mix:

```
class AddBoxing {
  static void go(Integer x) { System.out.println("Integer"); }
  static void go(long x) { System.out.println("long"); }

  public static void main(String [] args) {
    int i = 5;
    go(i);              // which go() will be invoked?
  }
}
```

As we've seen earlier, if the only version of the go() method was one that took an Integer, then Java 5's boxing capability would allow the invocation of go() to succeed. Likewise, if only the long version existed, the compiler would use it to handle the go() invocation. The question is, given that both methods exist, which one will be used? In other words, does the compiler think that widening a primitive parameter is more desirable than performing an autoboxing operation? The answer is that the compiler will choose widening over boxing, so the output will be

```
long
```

Java 5's designers decided that the most important rule should be that preexisting code should function the way it used to, so since widening capability already existed, a method that is invoked via widening shouldn't lose out to a newly created method that relies on boxing. Based on that rule, try to predict the output of the following:

```
class AddVarargs {
  static void go(int x, int y) { System.out.println("int,int");}
  static void go(byte... x) { System.out.println("byte... "); }
  public static void main(String[] args) {
    byte b = 5;
    go(b,b);              // which go() will be invoked?
  }
}
```

As you probably guessed, the output is

```
int,int
```

Because, once again, even though each invocation will require some sort of conversion, the compiler will choose the older style before it chooses the newer style, keeping existing code more robust. So far we've seen that

- Widening beats boxing
- Widening beats var-args

At this point, inquiring minds want to know, does boxing beat var-args?

```
class BoxOrVararg {
  static void go(Byte x, Byte y)
                { System.out.println("Byte, Byte"); }
  static void go(byte... x) { System.out.println("byte... "); }

  public static void main(String [] args) {
    byte b = 5;
    go(b,b);            // which go() will be invoked?
  }
}
```

As it turns out, the output is

```
Byte, Byte
```

A good way to remember this rule is to notice that the var-args method is "looser" than the other method, in that it could handle invocations with any number of `byte` parameters. A var-args method is more like a catch-all method, in terms of what invocations it can handle, and as we'll see in Chapter 5, it makes most sense for catch-all capabilities to be used as a *last resort*.

Widening Reference Variables

We've seen that it's legal to widen a primitive. Can you widen a reference variable, and if so, what would it mean? Let's think back to our favorite polymorphic assignment:

```
Animal a = new Dog();
```

Along the same lines, an invocation might be:

```
class Animal {static void eat() { } }

class Dog3 extends Animal {
  public static void main(String[] args) {
    Dog3 d = new Dog3();
    d.go(d);                  // is this legal ?
  }
  void go(Animal a) { }
}
```

No problem! The `go()` method needs an Animal, and `Dog3` IS-A Animal. (Remember, the `go()` method thinks it's getting an Animal object, so it will only ask it to do Animal things, which of course anything that inherits from Animal can do.) So, in this case, the compiler widens the `Dog3` reference to an Animal, and the invocation succeeds. The key point here is that reference widening depends on inheritance, in other words the IS-A test. Because of this, it's not legal to widen from one wrapper class to another, because the wrapper classes are peers to one another. For instance, it's NOT valid to say that Short IS-A Integer.

Overloading When Combining Widening and Boxing

We've looked at the rules that apply when the compiler can match an invocation to a method by performing a single conversion. Now let's take a look at what happens when more than one conversion is required. In this case the compiler will have to widen and then autobox the parameter for a match to be made:

```
class WidenAndBox {
  static void go(Long x) { System.out.println("Long"); }

  public static void main(String [] args) {
    byte b = 5;
    go(b);                  // must widen then box - illegal
  }
}
```

This is just too much for the compiler:

```
WidenAndBox.java:6: go(java.lang.Long) in WidenAndBox cannot be
applied to (byte)
```

Strangely enough, it IS possible for the compiler to perform a boxing operation followed by a widening operation in order to match an invocation to a method. This one might blow your mind:

```
class BoxAndWiden {
  static void go(Object o) {
    Byte b2 = (Byte) o;         // ok - it's a Byte object
    System.out.println(b2);
  }

  public static void main(String [] args) {
    byte b = 5;
    go(b);          // can this byte turn into an Object ?
  }
}
```

This compiles (!), and produces the output:

5

Wow! Here's what happened under the covers when the compiler, then the JVM, got to the line that invokes the go() method:

1. The byte b was boxed to a Byte.

2. The Byte reference was widened to an Object (since Byte extends Object).

3. The go() method got an Object reference that actually refers to a Byte object.

4. The go() method cast the Object reference back to a Byte reference (re member, there was never an object of type Object in this scenario, only an object of type Byte!).

5. The go() method printed the Byte's value.

Why didn't the compiler try to use the box-then-widen logic when it tried to deal with the WidenAndBox class? Think about it...if it tried to box first, the byte would have been converted to a Byte. Now we're back to trying to widen a Byte to a Long, and of course, the IS-A test fails.

Overloading in Combination with Var-args

What happens when we attempt to combine var-args with either widening or boxing in a method-matching scenario? Let's take a look:

```
class Vararg {
  static void wide_vararg(long... x)
              { System.out.println("long..."); }
  static void box_vararg(Integer... x)
              { System.out.println("Integer..."); }
  public static void main(String [] args) {
    int i = 5;
    wide_vararg(i,i);     // needs to widen and use var-args
    box_vararg(i,i);      // needs to box and use var-args
  }
}
```

This compiles and produces:

```
long...
Integer...
```

As we can see, you can successfully combine var-args with either widening or boxing. Here's a review of the rules for overloading methods using widening, boxing, and var-args:

- Primitive widening uses the "smallest" method argument possible.
- Used individually, boxing and var-args are compatible with overloading.
- You CANNOT widen from one wrapper type to another. (IS-A fails.)
- You CANNOT widen and then box. (An int can't become a Long.)
- You can box and then widen. (An int can become an Object, via Integer.)
- You can combine var-args with either widening or boxing.

There are more tricky aspects to overloading, but other than a few rules concerning generics (which we'll cover in Chapter 7), this is all you'll need to know for the exam. Phew!

Garbage Collection (Exam Objective 7.4)

7.4 Given a code example, recognize the point at which an object becomes eligible for garbage collection, and determine what is and is not guaranteed by the garbage collection system, and recognize the behaviors of the Object finalize() method.

Overview of Memory Management and Garbage Collection

This is the section you've been waiting for! It's finally time to dig into the wonderful world of memory management and garbage collection.

Memory management is a crucial element in many types of applications. Consider a program that reads in large amounts of data, say from somewhere else on a network, and then writes that data into a database on a hard drive. A typical design would be to read the data into some sort of collection in memory, perform some operations on the data, and then write the data into the database. After the data is written into the database, the collection that stored the data temporarily must be emptied of old data or deleted and recreated before processing the next batch. This operation might be performed thousands of times, and in languages like C or C++ that do not offer automatic garbage collection, a small flaw in the logic that manually empties or deletes the collection data structures can allow small amounts of memory to be improperly reclaimed or lost. Forever. These small losses are called memory leaks, and over many thousands of iterations they can make enough memory inaccessible that programs will eventually crash. Creating code that performs manual memory management cleanly and thoroughly is a nontrivial and complex task, and while estimates vary, it is arguable that manual memory management can double the development effort for a complex program.

Java's garbage collector provides an automatic solution to memory management. In most cases it frees you from having to add any memory management logic to your application. The downside to automatic garbage collection is that you can't completely control when it runs and when it doesn't.

Overview of Java's Garbage Collector

Let's look at what we mean when we talk about garbage collection in the land of Java. From the 30,000 ft. level, garbage collection is the phrase used to describe automatic memory management in Java. Whenever a software program executes (in Java, C, C++, Lisp, Ruby, and so on), it uses memory in several different ways. We're not going to get into Computer Science 101 here, but it's typical for memory to be used to create a stack, a heap, in Java's case constant pools, and method areas. The heap is that part of memory where Java objects live, and it's the one and only part of memory that is in any way involved in the garbage collection process.

A heap is a heap is a heap. For the exam it's important to know that you can call it the heap, you can call it the garbage collectible heap, or you can call it Johnson, but there is one and only one heap.

So, all of garbage collection revolves around making sure that the heap has as much free space as possible. For the purpose of the exam, what this boils down to is deleting any objects that are no longer reachable by the Java program running. We'll talk more about what reachable means, but let's drill this point in. When the garbage collector runs, its purpose is to find and delete objects that cannot be reached. If you think of a Java program as being in a constant cycle of creating the objects it needs (which occupy space on the heap), and then discarding them when they're no longer needed, creating new objects, discarding them, and so on, the missing piece of the puzzle is the garbage collector. When it runs, it looks for those discarded objects and deletes them from memory so that the cycle of using memory and releasing it can continue. Ah, the great circle of life.

When Does the Garbage Collector Run?

The garbage collector is under the control of the JVM. The JVM decides when to run the garbage collector. From within your Java program you can ask the JVM to run the garbage collector, but there are no guarantees, under any circumstances, that the JVM will comply. Left to its own devices, the JVM will typically run the garbage collector when it senses that memory is running low. Experience indicates that when your Java program makes a request for garbage collection, the JVM will usually grant your request in short order, but there are no guarantees. Just when you think you can count on it, the JVM will decide to ignore your request.

How Does the Garbage Collector Work?

You just can't be sure. You might hear that the garbage collector uses a mark and sweep algorithm, and for any given Java implementation that might be true, but the Java specification doesn't guarantee any particular implementation. You might hear that the garbage collector uses reference counting; once again maybe yes maybe no. The important concept to understand for the exam is when does an object become eligible for garbage collection? To answer this question fully, we have to jump ahead a little bit and talk about threads. (See Chapter 9 for the real scoop on threads.) In a nutshell, every Java program has from one to many threads. Each thread has its own little execution stack. Normally, you (the programmer) cause at least one thread to run in a Java program, the one with the main() method at the bottom of the stack. However, as you'll learn in excruciating detail in Chapter 9, there are many really cool reasons to launch additional threads from your initial thread. In addition to having its own little execution stack, each thread has its own lifecycle. For now, all we need to know is that threads can be alive or dead. With this background information, we can now say with stunning clarity and resolve that *an object is eligible for garbage collection when no live thread can access it.* (Note: Due to the vagaries of the String constant pool, the exam focuses its garbage collection questions on non-String objects, and so our garbage collection discussions apply to only non-String objects too.)

Based on that definition, the garbage collector does some magical, unknown operations, and when it discovers an object that can't be reached by any live thread, it will consider that object as eligible for deletion, and it might even delete it at some point. (You guessed it; it also might not ever delete it.) When we talk about reaching an object, we're really talking about having a reachable reference variable that refers to the object in question. If our Java program has a reference variable that refers to an object, and that reference variable is available to a live thread, then that object is considered reachable. We'll talk more about how objects can become unreachable in the following section.

Can a Java application run out of memory? Yes. The garbage collection system attempts to remove objects from memory when they are not used. However, if you maintain too many live objects (objects referenced from other live objects), the system can run out of memory. Garbage collection cannot ensure that there is enough memory, only that the memory that is available will be managed as efficiently as possible.

Writing Code That Explicitly Makes Objects Eligible for Collection

In the preceding section, we learned the theories behind Java garbage collection. In this section, we show how to make objects eligible for garbage collection using actual code. We also discuss how to attempt to force garbage collection if it is necessary, and how you can perform additional cleanup on objects before they are removed from memory.

Nulling a Reference

As we discussed earlier, an object becomes eligible for garbage collection when there are no more reachable references to it. Obviously, if there are no reachable references, it doesn't matter what happens to the object. For our purposes it is just floating in space, unused, inaccessible, and no longer needed.

The first way to remove a reference to an object is to set the reference variable that refers to the object to null. Examine the following code:

```
1. public class GarbageTruck {
2.    public static void main(String [] args) {
3.       StringBuffer sb = new StringBuffer("hello");
4.       System.out.println(sb);
5.       // The StringBuffer object is not eligible for collection
6.       sb = null;
7.       // Now the StringBuffer object is eligible for collection
8.    }
9. }
```

The StringBuffer object with the value hello is assigned to the reference variable sb in the third line. To make the object eligible (for GC), we set the reference variable sb to null, which removes the single reference that existed to the

StringBuffer object. Once line 6 has run, our happy little `hello` StringBuffer object is doomed, eligible for garbage collection.

Reassigning a Reference Variable

We can also decouple a reference variable from an object by setting the reference variable to refer to another object. Examine the following code:

```
class GarbageTruck {
    public static void main(String [] args) {
        StringBuffer s1 = new StringBuffer("hello");
        StringBuffer s2 = new StringBuffer("goodbye");
        System.out.println(s1);
        // At this point the StringBuffer "hello" is not eligible
        s1 = s2; // Redirects s1 to refer to the "goodbye" object
        // Now the StringBuffer "hello" is eligible for collection
    }
}
```

Objects that are created in a method also need to be considered. When a method is invoked, any local variables created exist only for the duration of the method. Once the method has returned, the objects created in the method are eligible for garbage collection. There is an obvious exception, however. If an object is returned from the method, its reference might be assigned to a reference variable in the method that called it; hence, it will not be eligible for collection. Examine the following code:

```
import java.util.Date;
public class GarbageFactory {
    public static void main(String [] args) {
        Date d = getDate();
        doComplicatedStuff();
        System.out.println("d = " + d);
    }

    public static Date getDate() {
        Date d2 = new Date();
        StringBuffer now = new StringBuffer(d2.toString());
        System.out.println(now);
        return d2;
    }
}
```

In the preceding example, we created a method called getDate() that returns a Date object. This method creates two objects: a Date and a StringBuffer containing the date information. Since the method returns the Date object, it will not be eligible for collection even after the method has completed. The StringBuffer object, though, will be eligible, even though we didn't explicitly set the now variable to null.

Isolating a Reference

There is another way in which objects can become eligible for garbage collection, even if they still have valid references! We call this scenario "islands of isolation."

A simple example is a class that has an instance variable that is a reference variable to another instance of the same class. Now imagine that two such instances exist and that they refer to each other. If all other references to these two objects are removed, then even though each object still has a valid reference, there will be no way for any live thread to access either object. When the garbage collector runs, it can *usually* discover any such islands of objects and remove them. As you can imagine, such islands can become quite large, theoretically containing hundreds of objects. Examine the following code:

```
public class Island {
  Island i;
  public static void main(String [] args) {

    Island i2 = new Island();
    Island i3 = new Island();
    Island i4 = new Island();

    i2.i = i3;    // i2 refers to i3
    i3.i = i4;    // i3 refers to i4
    i4.i = i2;    // i4 refers to i2

    i2 = null;
    i3 = null;
    i4 = null;

    // do complicated, memory intensive stuff
  }
}
```

When the code reaches // do complicated, the three Island objects (previously known as i2, i3, and i4) have instance variables so that they refer to each other, but their links to the outside world (i2, i3, and i4) have been nulled. These three objects are eligible for garbage collection.

This covers everything you will need to know about making objects eligible for garbage collection. Study Figure 3-7 to reinforce the concepts of objects without references and islands of isolation.

Forcing Garbage Collection

The first thing that should be mentioned here is that, contrary to this section's title, garbage collection cannot be forced. However, Java provides some methods that allow you to request that the JVM perform garbage collection.

Note: As of the Java 6 exam, the topic of using System.gc() has been removed from the exam. The garbage collector has evolved to such an advanced state that it's recommended that you never invoke System.gc() in your code - leave it to the JVM. We are leaving this section in the book in case you're studying for a version of the exam prior to SCJP 6.

FIGURE 3-7   "Island" objects eligible for garbage collection

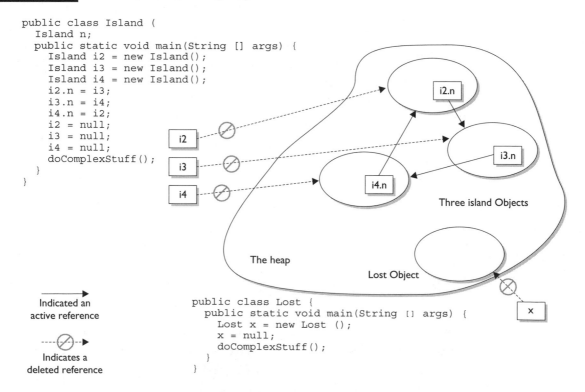

In reality, it is possible only to suggest to the JVM that it perform garbage collection. However, there are no guarantees the JVM will actually remove all of the unused objects from memory (even if garbage collection is run). It is essential that you understand this concept for the exam.

The garbage collection routines that Java provides are members of the Runtime class. The Runtime class is a special class that has a single object (a Singleton) for each main program. The Runtime object provides a mechanism for communicating directly with the virtual machine. To get the Runtime instance, you can use the method Runtime.getRuntime(), which returns the Singleton. Once you have the Singleton you can invoke the garbage collector using the gc() method. Alternatively, you can call the same method on the System class, which has static methods that can do the work of obtaining the Singleton for you. The simplest way to ask for garbage collection (remember—just a request) is

```
System.gc();
```

Theoretically, after calling System.gc(), you will have as much free memory as possible. We say theoretically because this routine does not always work that way. First, your JVM may not have implemented this routine; the language specification allows this routine to do nothing at all. Second, another thread (again, see the Chapter 9) might grab lots of memory right after you run the garbage collector.

This is not to say that System.gc() is a useless method—it's much better than nothing. You just can't rely on System.gc() to free up enough memory so that you don't have to worry about running out of memory. The Certification Exam is interested in guaranteed behavior, not probable behavior.

Now that we are somewhat familiar with how this works, let's do a little experiment to see if we can see the effects of garbage collection. The following program lets us know how much total memory the JVM has available to it and how much free memory it has. It then creates 10,000 Date objects. After this, it tells us how much memory is left and then calls the garbage collector (which, if it decides to run, should halt the program until all unused objects are removed). The final free memory result should indicate whether it has run. Let's look at the program:

```
1.   import java.util.Date;
2.   public class CheckGC {
3.      public static void main(String [] args) {
4.         Runtime rt = Runtime.getRuntime();
5.         System.out.println("Total JVM memory: "
                              + rt.totalMemory());
```

```
6.            System.out.println("Before Memory = "
                              + rt.freeMemory());
7.         Date d = null;
8.         for(int i = 0;i<10000;i++) {
9.            d = new Date();
10.           d = null;
11.        }
12.        System.out.println("After Memory = "
                              + rt.freeMemory());
13.        rt.gc();   // an alternate to System.gc()
14.        System.out.println("After GC Memory = "
                              + rt.freeMemory());
15.     }
16.  }
```

Now, let's run the program and check the results:

```
Total JVM memory: 1048568
Before Memory = 703008
After Memory = 458048
After GC Memory = 818272
```

As we can see, the JVM actually did decide to garbage collect (i.e., delete) the eligible objects. In the preceding example, we suggested to the JVM to perform garbage collection with 458,048 bytes of memory remaining, and it honored our request. This program has only one user thread running, so there was nothing else going on when we called `rt.gc()`. Keep in mind that the behavior when `gc()` is called may be different for different JVMs, so there is no guarantee that the unused objects will be removed from memory. About the only thing you can guarantee is that if you are running very low on memory, the garbage collector will run before it throws an OutOfMemoryException.

EXERCISE 3-2

Garbage Collection Experiment

Try changing the CheckGC program by putting lines 13 and 14 inside a loop. You might see that not all memory is released on any given run of the GC.

Cleaning Up Before Garbage Collection—the finalize() Method

Java provides you a mechanism to run some code just before your object is deleted by the garbage collector. This code is located in a method named `finalize()` that all classes inherit from class Object. On the surface this sounds like a great idea; maybe your object opened up some resources, and you'd like to close them before your object is deleted. The problem is that, as you may have gathered by now, you can't count on the garbage collector to ever delete an object. So, any code that you put into your class's overridden `finalize()` method is not guaranteed to run. The `finalize()` method for any given object might run, but you can't count on it, so don't put any essential code into your `finalize()` method. In fact, we recommend that in general you don't override `finalize()` at all.

Tricky Little finalize() Gotcha's

There are a couple of concepts concerning `finalize()` that you need to remember.

- For any given object, `finalize()` will be called only once (at most) by the garbage collector.
- Calling `finalize()` can actually result in saving an object from deletion.

Let's look into these statements a little further. First of all, remember that any code that you can put into a normal method you can put into `finalize()`. For example, in the `finalize()` method you could write code that passes a reference to the object in question back to another object, effectively *uneligiblizing* the object for garbage collection. If at some point later on this same object becomes eligible for garbage collection again, the garbage collector can still process this object and delete it. The garbage collector, however, will remember that, for this object, `finalize()` already ran, and it will not run `finalize()` again.

CERTIFICATION SUMMARY

This was a monster chapter! Don't worry if you find that you have to review some of these topics as you get into later chapters. This chapter has a lot of foundation stuff that will come into play later.

We started the chapter by reviewing the stack and the heap; remember local variables live on the stack, and instance variables live with their objects on the heap.

We reviewed legal literals for primitives and Strings, then we discussed the basics of assigning values to primitives and reference variables, and the rules for casting primitives.

Next we discussed the concept of scope, or "How long will this variable live?" Remember the four basic scopes, in order of lessening life span: static, instance, local, block.

We covered the implications of using uninitialized variables, and the importance of the fact that local variables MUST be assigned a value explicitly. We talked about some of the tricky aspects of assigning one reference variable to another, and some of the finer points of passing variables into methods, including a discussion of "shadowing."

The next topic was creating arrays, where we talked about declaring, constructing, and initializing one-, and multi-dimensional arrays. We talked about anonymous arrays, and arrays of references.

Next we reviewed static and instance initialization blocks, what they look like, and when they are called.

Phew!

We continued the chapter with a discussion of the wrapper classes; used to create immutable objects that hold a primitive, and also used to provide conversion capabilities for primitives: remember valueOf(), xxxValue(), and parseXxx().

Closely related to wrappers, we talked about a big new feature in Java 5, autoboxing. Boxing is a way to automate the use of wrappers, and we covered some of its trickier aspects such as how wrappers work with == and the equals() method.

Having added boxing to our toolbox, it was time to take a closer look at method overloading and how boxing and var-args, in conjunction with widening conversions, make overloading more complicated.

Finally, we dove into garbage collection, Java's automatic memory management feature. We learned that the heap is where objects live and where all the cool garbage collection activity takes place. We learned that in the end, the JVM will perform garbage collection whenever it wants to. You (the programmer) can request a garbage collection run, but you can't force it. We talked about garbage collection only applying to objects that are eligible, and that eligible means "inaccessible from any live thread." Finally, we discussed the rarely useful finalize() method, and what you'll have to know about it for the exam. All in all, one fascinating chapter.

✓ # TWO-MINUTE DRILL

Here are some of the key points from this chapter.

Stack and Heap

❑ Local variables (method variables) live on the stack.

❑ Objects and their instance variables live on the heap.

Literals and Primitive Casting (Objective 1.3)

❑ Integer literals can be decimal, octal (e.g. `013`), or hexadecimal (e.g. `0x3d`).

❑ Literals for `long`s end in `L` or `l`.

❑ Float literals end in `F` or `f`, `double` literals end in a digit or `D` or `d`.

❑ The `boolean` literals are `true` and `false`.

❑ Literals for `char`s are a single character inside single quotes: `'d'`.

Scope (Objectives 1.3 and 7.6)

❑ Scope refers to the lifetime of a variable.

❑ There are four basic scopes:

   ❑ Static variables live basically as long as their class lives.

   ❑ Instance variables live as long as their object lives.

   ❑ Local variables live as long as their method is on the stack; however, if their method invokes another method, they are temporarily unavailable.

   ❑ Block variables (e.g., in a `for` or an `if`) live until the block completes.

Basic Assignments (Objectives 1.3 and 7.6)

❑ Literal integers are implicitly ints.

❑ Integer expressions always result in an `int`-sized result, never smaller.

❑ Floating-point numbers are implicitly doubles (64 bits).

❑ Narrowing a primitive truncates the *high order* bits.

❑ Compound assignments (e.g. `+=`), perform an automatic cast.

❑ A reference variable holds the bits that are used to refer to an object.

❑ Reference variables can refer to subclasses of the declared type but not to superclasses.

❑ When creating a new object, e.g., `Button b = new Button();`, three things happen:
   ❑ Make a reference variable named `b`, of type Button
   ❑ Create a new Button object
   ❑ Assign the Button object to the reference variable `b`

Using a Variable or Array Element That Is Uninitialized and Unassigned (Objectives 1.3 and 7.6)

❑ When an array of objects is instantiated, objects within the array are not instantiated automatically, but all the references get the default value of null.

❑ When an array of primitives is instantiated, elements get default values.

❑ Instance variables are always initialized with a default value.

❑ Local/automatic/method variables are never given a default value. If you attempt to use one before initializing it, you'll get a compiler error.

Passing Variables into Methods (Objective 7.3)

❑ Methods can take primitives and/or object references as arguments.

❑ Method arguments are always copies.

❑ Method arguments are never actual objects (they can be references to objects).

❑ A primitive argument is an unattached copy of the original primitive.

❑ A reference argument is another copy of a reference to the original object.

❑ Shadowing occurs when two variables with different scopes share the same name. This leads to hard-to-find bugs, and hard-to-answer exam questions.

Array Declaration, Construction, and Initialization (Obj. 1.3)

❑ Arrays can hold primitives or objects, but the array itself is always an object.

❑ When you declare an array, the brackets can be left or right of the name.

❑ It is never legal to include the size of an array in the declaration.

❑ You must include the size of an array when you construct it (using `new`) unless you are creating an anonymous array.

❑ Elements in an array of objects are not automatically created, although primitive array elements are given default values.

❑ You'll get a NullPointerException if you try to use an array element in an object array, if that element does not refer to a real object.

❑ Arrays are indexed beginning with zero.

❑ An ArrayIndexOutOfBoundsException occurs if you use a bad index value.

❑ Arrays have a `length` variable whose value is the number of array elements.

❑ The last index you can access is always one less than the length of the array.

❑ Multidimensional arrays are just arrays of arrays.

❑ The dimensions in a multidimensional array can have different lengths.

❑ An array of primitives can accept any value that can be promoted implicitly to the array's declared type;. e.g., a `byte` variable can go in an `int` array.

❑ An array of objects can hold any object that passes the IS-A (or instanceof) test for the declared type of the array. For example, if Horse extends Animal, then a Horse object can go into an Animal array.

❑ If you assign an array to a previously declared array reference, the array you're assigning must be the same dimension as the reference you're assigning it to.

❑ You can assign an array of one type to a previously declared array reference of one of its supertypes. For example, a Honda array can be assigned to an array declared as type Car (assuming Honda extends Car).

Initialization Blocks (Objectives 1.3 and 7.6)

❑ Static initialization blocks run once, when the class is first loaded.

❑ Instance initialization blocks run every time a new instance is created. They run after all super-constructors and before the constructor's code has run.

❑ If multiple init blocks exist in a class, they follow the rules stated above, AND they run in the order in which they appear in the source file.

Using Wrappers (Objective 3.1)

❑ The wrapper classes correlate to the primitive types.

❑ Wrappers have two main functions:

  ❑ To wrap primitives so that they can be handled like objects

  ❑ To provide utility methods for primitives (usually conversions)

❑ The three most important method families are

  ❑ `xxxValue()`   Takes no arguments, returns a primitive

  ❑ `parseXxx()`   Takes a String, returns a primitive, throws NFE

  ❑ `valueOf()`   Takes a String, returns a wrapped object, throws NFE

❑ Wrapper constructors can take a String or a primitive, except for Character, which can only take a `char`.

❑ Radix refers to bases (typically) other than 10; octal is radix = 8, hex = 16.

Boxing (Objective 3.1)

❑ As of Java 5, boxing allows you to convert primitives to wrappers or to convert wrappers to primitives automatically.

❑ Using == with wrappers created through boxing is tricky; those with the same small values (typically lower than 127), will be ==, larger values will not be ==.

Advanced Overloading (Objectives 1.5 and 5.4)

❑ Primitive widening uses the "smallest" method argument possible.

❑ Used individually, boxing and var-args are compatible with overloading.

❑ You CANNOT widen from one wrapper type to another. (IS-A fails.)

❑ You CANNOT widen and then box. (An `int` can't become a Long.)

❑ You can box and then widen. (An `int` can become an Object, via an Integer.)

❑ You can combine var-args with either widening or boxing.

Garbage Collection (Objective 7.4)

❑ In Java, garbage collection (GC) provides automated memory management.

❑ The purpose of GC is to delete objects that can't be reached.

❑ Only the JVM decides when to run the GC, you can only suggest it.

❑ You can't know the GC algorithm for sure.

❑ Objects must be considered eligible before they can be garbage collected.

❑ An object is eligible when no live thread can reach it.

❑ To reach an object, you must have a live, reachable reference to that object.

❑ Java applications can run out of memory.

❑ Islands of objects can be GCed, even though they refer to each other.

❑ Request garbage collection with `System.gc();` (only before the SCJP 6).

❑ Class Object has a `finalize()` method.

❑ The `finalize()` method is guaranteed to run once and only once before the garbage collector deletes an object.

❑ The garbage collector makes no guarantees, `finalize()` may never run.

❑ You can uneligibilize an object for GC from within `finalize()`.

SELF TEST

1. Given:

```
class CardBoard {
  Short story = 200;
  CardBoard go(CardBoard cb) {
    cb = null;
    return cb;
  }
  public static void main(String[] args) {
    CardBoard c1 = new CardBoard();
    CardBoard c2 = new CardBoard();
    CardBoard c3 = c1.go(c2);
    c1 = null;
    // do Stuff
} }
```

When `// doStuff` is reached, how many objects are eligible for GC?

A. 0

B. 1

C. 2

D. Compilation fails

E. It is not possible to know

F. An exception is thrown at runtime

2. Given:

```
class Alien {
  String invade(short ships) { return "a few"; }
  String invade(short... ships) { return "many"; }
}
class Defender {
  public static void main(String [] args) {
    System.out.println(new Alien().invade(7));
  }
}
```

What is the result?

A. `many`

B. `a few`

C. Compilation fails

D. The output is not predictable

E. An exception is thrown at runtime

3. Given:

```
1. class Dims {
2.   public static void main(String[] args) {
3.     int[][] a = {{1,2,}, {3,4}};
4.     int[] b = (int[]) a[1];
5.     Object o1 = a;
6.     int[][] a2 = (int[][]) o1;
7.     int[] b2 = (int[]) o1;
8.     System.out.println(b[1]);
9. } }
```

What is the result?

A. 2

B. 4

C. An exception is thrown at runtime

D. Compilation fails due to an error on line 4

E. Compilation fails due to an error on line 5

F. Compilation fails due to an error on line 6

G. Compilation fails due to an error on line 7

4. Given:

```
class Mixer {
  Mixer() { }
  Mixer(Mixer m) { m1 = m; }
  Mixer m1;
  public static void main(String[] args) {
    Mixer m2 = new Mixer();
    Mixer m3 = new Mixer(m2);   m3.go();
    Mixer m4 = m3.m1;           m4.go();
    Mixer m5 = m2.m1;           m5.go();
  }
  void go() { System.out.print("hi "); }
}
```

What is the result?

A. `hi`

B. `hi hi`

C. `hi hi hi`

D. Compilation fails

E. `hi`, followed by an exception

F. `hi hi`, followed by an exception

5. Given:

```
class Fizz {
  int x = 5;
  public static void main(String[] args) {
    final Fizz f1 = new Fizz();
    Fizz f2 = new Fizz();
    Fizz f3 = FizzSwitch(f1,f2);
    System.out.println((f1 == f3) + " " + (f1.x == f3.x));
  }
  static Fizz FizzSwitch(Fizz x, Fizz y) {
    final Fizz z = x;
    z.x = 6;
    return z;
  } }
```

What is the result?

A. `true true`

B. `false true`

C. `true false`

D. `false false`

E. Compilation fails

F. An exception is thrown at runtime

6. Given:

```
class Bird {
  { System.out.print("b1 "); }
  public Bird() { System.out.print("b2 "); }
}
class Raptor extends Bird {
  static { System.out.print("r1 "); }
  public Raptor() { System.out.print("r2 "); }
  { System.out.print("r3 "); }
  static { System.out.print("r4 "); }
}
class Hawk extends Raptor {
  public static void main(String[] args) {
    System.out.print("pre ");
    new Hawk();
    System.out.println("hawk ");
  }
}
```

What is the result?

A. pre b1 b2 r3 r2 hawk

B. pre b2 b1 r2 r3 hawk

C. pre b2 b1 r2 r3 hawk r1 r4

D. r1 r4 pre b1 b2 r3 r2 hawk

E. r1 r4 pre b2 b1 r2 r3 hawk

F. pre r1 r4 b1 b2 r3 r2 hawk

G. pre r1 r4 b2 b1 r2 r3 hawk

H. The order of output cannot be predicted

I. Compilation fails

7. Given:

```
3. public class Bridge {
4.    public enum Suits {
5.       CLUBS(20), DIAMONDS(20), HEARTS(30), SPADES(30),
6.       NOTRUMP(40) { public int getValue(int bid) {
                          return ((bid-1)*30)+40; } };
7.       Suits(int points) {  this.points = points;  }
8.       private int points;
9.       public int getValue(int bid) { return points * bid; }
10.    }
11.    public static void main(String[] args) {
12.       System.out.println(Suits.NOTRUMP.getValue(3));
13.       System.out.println(Suits.SPADES + " " + Suits.SPADES.points);
14.       System.out.println(Suits.values());
15.    }
16. }
```

Which are true? (Choose all that apply.)

A. The output could contain 30

B. The output could contain @bf73fa

C. The output could contain DIAMONDS

D. Compilation fails due to an error on line 6

E. Compilation fails due to an error on line 7

F. Compilation fails due to an error on line 8

G. Compilation fails due to an error on line 9

H. Compilation fails due to an error within lines 12 to 14

8. Given:

```
3. public class Ouch {
4.    static int ouch = 7;
5.    public static void main(String[] args) {
6.       new Ouch().go(ouch);
7.       System.out.print(" " + ouch);
8.    }
9.    void go(int ouch) {
10.      ouch++;
11.      for(int ouch = 3; ouch < 6; ouch++)
12.         ;
13.      System.out.print(" " + ouch);
14.   }
15. }
```

What is the result?

A. 5 7

B. 5 8

C. 8 7

D. 8 8

E. Compilation fails

F. An exception is thrown at runtime

9. Given:

```
3. public class Bertha {
4.    static String s = "";
5.    public static void main(String[] args) {
6.       int x = 4; Boolean y = true; short[] sa = {1,2,3};
7.       doStuff(x, y);
8.       doStuff(x);
9.       doStuff(sa, sa);
10.      System.out.println(s);
11.   }
12.   static void doStuff(Object o)        { s += "1"; }
13.   static void doStuff(Object... o)     { s += "2"; }
14.   static void doStuff(Integer... i)    { s += "3"; }
15.   static void doStuff(Long L)          { s += "4"; }
16. }
```

What is the result?

A. 212

B. 232

C. 234

D. 312

E. 332

F. 334

G. Compilation fails

10. Given:

```
3. class Dozens {
4.    int[] dz = {1,2,3,4,5,6,7,8,9,10,11,12};
5. }
6. public class Eggs {
7.    public static void main(String[] args) {
8.        Dozens [] da = new Dozens[3];
9.        da[0] = new Dozens();
10.       Dozens d = new Dozens();
11.       da[1] = d;
12.       d = null;
13.       da[1] = null;
14.       // do stuff
15.    }
16. }
```

Which two are true about the objects created within main(), and eligible for garbage collection when line 14 is reached?

A. Three objects were created

B. Four objects were created

C. Five objects were created

D. Zero objects are eligible for GC

E. One object is eligible for GC

F. Two objects are eligible for GC

G. Three objects are eligible for GC

11. Given:

```
3. class Beta { }
4. class Alpha {
5.   static Beta b1;
6.   Beta b2;
7. }
8. public class Tester {
9.   public static void main(String[] args) {
10.     Beta b1 = new Beta();    Beta b2 = new Beta();
11.     Alpha a1 = new Alpha();  Alpha a2 = new Alpha();
12.     a1.b1 = b1;
13.     a1.b2 = b1;
14.     a2.b2 = b2;
15.     a1 = null;  b1 = null;  b2 = null;
16.     // do stuff
17.   }
18. }
```

When line 16 is reached, how many objects will be eligible for garbage collection?

A. 0

B. 1

C. 2

D. 3

E. 4

F. 5

12. Given:

```
3. class Box {
4.   int size;
5.   Box(int s) { size = s; }
6. }
7. public class Laser {
8.   public static void main(String[] args) {
9.     Box b1 = new Box(5);
10.     Box[] ba = go(b1, new Box(6));
11.     ba[0] = b1;
12.     for(Box b : ba) System.out.print(b.size + " ");
13.   }
14.   static Box[] go(Box b1, Box b2) {
15.     b1.size = 4;
16.     Box[] ma = {b2, b1};
17.     return ma;
18.   }
19. }
```

What is the result?

A. 4 4

B. 5 4

C. 6 4

D. 4 5

E. 5 5

F. Compilation fails

13. Given:

```
3. public class Dark {
4.    int x = 3;
5.    public static void main(String[] args) {
6.      new Dark().go1();
7.    }
8.    void go1() {
9.      int x;
10.     go2(++x);
11.   }
12.   void go2(int y) {
13.     int x = ++y;
14.     System.out.println(x);
15.   }
16. }
```

What is the result?

A. 2

B. 3

C. 4

D. 5

E. Compilation fails

F. An exception is thrown at runtime

SELF TEST ANSWERS

1. Given:

```
class CardBoard {
  Short story = 200;
  CardBoard go(CardBoard cb) {
    cb = null;
    return cb;
  }
  public static void main(String[] args) {
    CardBoard c1 = new CardBoard();
    CardBoard c2 = new CardBoard();
    CardBoard c3 = c1.go(c2);
    c1 = null;
    // do Stuff
} }
```

When `// doStuff` is reached, how many objects are eligible for GC?

A. 0

B. 1

C. 2

D. Compilation fails

E. It is not possible to know

F. An exception is thrown at runtime

Answer:

☑ **C** is correct. Only one `CardBoard object (c1)` is eligible, but it has an associated Short wrapper object that is also eligible.

☒ **A, B, D, E,** and **F** are incorrect based on the above. (Objective 7.4)

2. Given:

```
class Alien {
  String invade(short ships) { return "a few"; }
  String invade(short... ships) { return "many"; }
}
class Defender {
  public static void main(String [] args) {
    System.out.println(new Alien().invade(7));
} }
```

What is the result?

A. many

B. a few

C. Compilation fails

D. The output is not predictable

E. An exception is thrown at runtime

Answer:

☑ **C** is correct, compilation fails. The var-args declaration is fine, but `invade` takes a `short`, so the argument 7 needs to be cast to a `short`. With the cast, the answer is **B**, `'a few'`.

☒ **A, B, D,** and **E** are incorrect based on the above. (Objective 1.3)

3. Given:

```
1. class Dims {
2.    public static void main(String[] args) {
3.        int[][] a = {{1,2,}, {3,4}};
4.        int[] b = (int[]) a[1];
5.        Object o1 = a;
6.        int[][] a2 = (int[][]) o1;
7.        int[] b2 = (int[]) o1;
8.        System.out.println(b[1]);
9. } }
```

What is the result?

A. 2

B. 4

C. An exception is thrown at runtime

D. Compilation fails due to an error on line 4

E. Compilation fails due to an error on line 5

F. Compilation fails due to an error on line 6

G. Compilation fails due to an error on line 7

Answer:

☑ **C** is correct. A `ClassCastException` is thrown at line 7 because o1 refers to an `int[][]` not an `int[]`. If line 7 was removed, the output would be 4.

☒ **A, B, D, E, F,** and **G** are incorrect based on the above. (Objective 1.3)

4. Given:

```
class Mixer {
  Mixer() { }
  Mixer(Mixer m) { m1 = m; }
  Mixer m1;
  public static void main(String[] args) {
    Mixer m2 = new Mixer();
    Mixer m3 = new Mixer(m2);  m3.go();
    Mixer m4 = m3.m1;          m4.go();
    Mixer m5 = m2.m1;          m5.go();
  }
  void go() { System.out.print("hi "); }
}
```

What is the result?

A. hi

B. hi hi

C. hi hi hi

D. Compilation fails

E. hi, followed by an exception

F. hi hi, followed by an exception

Answer:

☑ **F** is correct. The m2 object's m1 instance variable is never initialized, so when m5 tries to use it a NullPointerException is thrown.

☒ **A, B, C, D,** and **E** are incorrect based on the above. (Objective 7.3)

5. Given:

```
class Fizz {
  int x = 5;
  public static void main(String[] args) {
    final Fizz f1 = new Fizz();
    Fizz f2 = new Fizz();
    Fizz f3 = FizzSwitch(f1,f2);
    System.out.println((f1 == f3) + " " + (f1.x == f3.x));
  }
  static Fizz FizzSwitch(Fizz x, Fizz y) {
    final Fizz z = x;
    z.x = 6;
    return z;
  } }
```

What is the result?

A. `true true`

B. `false true`

C. `true false`

D. `false false`

E. Compilation fails

F. An exception is thrown at runtime

Answer:

☑ **A** is correct. The references `f1`, `z`, and `f3` all refer to the same instance of `Fizz`. The `final` modifier assures that a reference variable cannot be referred to a different object, but `final` doesn't keep the object's state from changing.

☒ **B, C, D, E,** and **F** are incorrect based on the above. (Objective 7.3)

---

6. Given:

```
class Bird {
    { System.out.print("b1 "); }
    public Bird() { System.out.print("b2 "); }
}
class Raptor extends Bird {
    static { System.out.print("r1 "); }
    public Raptor() { System.out.print("r2 "); }
    { System.out.print("r3 "); }
    static { System.out.print("r4 "); }
}
class Hawk extends Raptor {
    public static void main(String[] args) {
        System.out.print("pre ");
        new Hawk();
        System.out.println("hawk ");
    }
}
```

What is the result?

A. `pre b1 b2 r3 r2 hawk`

B. `pre b2 b1 r2 r3 hawk`

C. `pre b2 b1 r2 r3 hawk r1 r4`

D. `r1 r4 pre b1 b2 r3 r2 hawk`

E. `r1 r4 pre b2 b1 r2 r3 hawk`

F. `pre r1 r4 b1 b2 r3 r2 hawk`

G. `pre r1 r4 b2 b1 r2 r3 hawk`

H. The order of output cannot be predicted

I. Compilation fails

> Answer:
>
> ☑ **D** is correct. Static init blocks are executed at class loading time, instance init blocks run right after the call to `super()` in a constructor. When multiple init blocks of a single type occur in a class, they run in order, from the top down.
>
> ☒ **A, B, C, E, F, G, H,** and **I** are incorrect based on the above. Note: you'll probably never see this many choices on the real exam! (Objective 1.3)

7. Given:

```
3. public class Bridge {
4.    public enum Suits {
5.       CLUBS(20), DIAMONDS(20), HEARTS(30), SPADES(30),
6.       NOTRUMP(40) { public int getValue(int bid) {
                       return ((bid-1)*30)+40; } };
7.       Suits(int points) { this.points = points;   }
8.       private int points;
9.       public int getValue(int bid) { return points * bid; }
10.   }
11.   public static void main(String[] args) {
12.      System.out.println(Suits.NOTRUMP.getBidValue(3));
13.      System.out.println(Suits.SPADES + " " + Suits.SPADES.points);
14.      System.out.println(Suits.values());
15.   }
16. }
```

Which are true? (Choose all that apply.)

A. The output could contain `30`

B. The output could contain `@bf73fa`

C. The output could contain `DIAMONDS`

D. Compilation fails due to an error on line 6

E. Compilation fails due to an error on line 7

F. Compilation fails due to an error on line 8

G. Compilation fails due to an error on line 9

H. Compilation fails due to an error within lines 12 to 14

Answer:

☑ **A** and **B** are correct. The code compiles and runs without exception. The `values()` method returns an array reference, not the contents of the enum, so DIAMONDS is never printed.

☒ **C, D, E, F, G,** and **H** are incorrect based on the above. (Objective 1.3)

---

8. Given:

```
3. public class Ouch {
4.    static int ouch = 7;
5.    public static void main(String[] args) {
6.       new Ouch().go(ouch);
7.       System.out.print(" " + ouch);
8.    }
9.    void go(int ouch) {
10.      ouch++;
11.      for(int ouch = 3; ouch < 6; ouch++)
12.         ;
13.      System.out.print(" " + ouch);
14.   }
15. }
```

What is the result?

A. 5 7

B. 5 8

C. 8 7

D. 8 8

E. Compilation fails

F. An exception is thrown at runtime

Answer:

☑ **E** is correct. The parameter declared on line 9 is valid (although ugly), but the variable name ouch cannot be declared again on line 11 in the same scope as the declaration on line 9.

☒ **A, B, C, D,** and **F** are incorrect based on the above. (Objective 1.3)

9. Given:

```
3. public class Bertha {
4.    static String s = "";
5.    public static void main(String[] args) {
6.      int x = 4; Boolean y = true; short[] sa = {1,2,3};
7.      doStuff(x, y);
8.      doStuff(x);
9.      doStuff(sa, sa);
10.     System.out.println(s);
11.   }
12.   static void doStuff(Object o)        { s += "1"; }
13.   static void doStuff(Object... o)     { s += "2"; }
14.   static void doStuff(Integer... i)    { s +- "3"; }
15.   static void doStuff(Long L)          { s += "4"; }
16. }
```

What is the result?

A. 212

B. 232

C. 234

D. 312

E. 332

F. 334

G. Compilation fails

Answer:

☑ **A** is correct. It's legal to autobox and then widen. The first call to doStuff() boxes the int to an Integer then passes two objects. The second call cannot widen and then box (making the Long method unusable), so it boxes the int to an Integer. As always, a var-args method will be chosen only if no non-var-arg method is possible. The third call is passing two objects—they are of type 'short array.'

☒ **B, C, D, E, F,** and **G** are incorrect based on the above. (Objective 3.1)

10. Given:

```
3. class Dozens {
4.    int[] dz = {1,2,3,4,5,6,7,8,9,10,11,12};
5. }
6. public class Eggs {
7.    public static void main(String[] args) {
```

```
 8.      Dozens [] da = new Dozens[3];
 9.      da[0] = new Dozens();
10.      Dozens d = new Dozens();
11.      da[1] = d;
12.      d = null;
13.      da[1] = null;
14.      // do stuff
15.    }
16.  }
```

Which two are true about the objects created within `main()`, and eligible for garbage collection when line 14 is reached?

A.   Three objects were created

B.   Four objects were created

C.   Five objects were created

D.   Zero objects are eligible for GC

E.   One object is eligible for GC

F.   Two objects are eligible for GC

G.   Three objects are eligible for GC

Answer:

☑   **C** and **F** are correct. `da` refers to an object of type "Dozens array," and each Dozens object that is created comes with its own "int array" object. When line 14 is reached, only the second Dozens object (and its "int array" object) are not reachable.

☒   **A, B, D, E,** and **G** are incorrect based on the above. (Objective 7.4)

11. Given:

```
 3. class Beta { }
 4. class Alpha {
 5.   static Beta b1;
 6.   Beta b2;
 7. }
 8. public class Tester {
 9.   public static void main(String[] args) {
10.     Beta b1 = new Beta();      Beta b2 = new Beta();
11.     Alpha a1 = new Alpha();    Alpha a2 = new Alpha();
12.     a1.b1 = b1;
13.     a1.b2 = b1;
14.     a2.b2 = b2;
15.     a1 = null;  b1 = null;  b2 = null;
```

```
16.     // do stuff
17.   }
18. }
```

When line 16 is reached, how many objects will be eligible for garbage collection?

A. 0

B. 1

C. 2

D. 3

E. 4

F. 5

Answer:

☑ **B** is correct. It should be clear that there is still a reference to the object referred to by a2, and that there is still a reference to the object referred to by a2.b2. What might be less clear is that you can still access the other Beta object through the static variable a2.b1—because it's static.

☒ **A, C, D, E,** and **F** are incorrect based on the above. (Objective 7.4)

12. Given:

```
3. class Box {
4.   int size;
5.   Box(int s) { size = s; }
6. }
7. public class Laser {
8.   public static void main(String[] args) {
9.     Box b1 = new Box(5);
10.     Box[] ba = go(b1, new Box(6));
11.     ba[0] = b1;
12.     for(Box b : ba) System.out.print(b.size + " ");
13.   }
14.   static Box[] go(Box b1, Box b2) {
15.      b1.size = 4;
16.      Box[] ma = {b2, b1};
17.      return ma;
18.   }
19. }
```

What is the result?

A. 4 4

B. 5 4

C. 6 4

D. 4 5

E. 5 5

F. Compilation fails

> Answer:
>
> ☑ **A** is correct. Although `main()`'s `b1` is a different reference variable than `go()`'s `b1`, they refer to the same Box object.
>
> ☒ **B, C, D, E,** and **F** are incorrect based on the above. (Objective 7.3)

13. Given:

```
3. public class Dark {
4.    int x = 3;
5.    public static void main(String[] args) {
6.       new Dark().go1();
7.    }
8.    void go1() {
9.       int x;
10.      go2(++x);
11.   }
12.   void go2(int y) {
13.      int x = ++y;
14.      System.out.println(x);
15.   }
16. }
```

What is the result?

A. 2

B. 3

C. 4

D. 5

E. Compilation fails

F. An exception is thrown at runtime

> Answer:
>
> ☑ **E** is correct. In `go1()` the local variable `x` is not initialized.
>
> ☒ **A, B, C, D,** and **F** are incorrect based on the above. (Objective 1.3)

4

Operators

I f you've got variables, you're going to modify them. You'll increment them, add them together, and compare one to another (in about a dozen different ways). In this chapter, you'll learn how to do all that in Java. For an added bonus, you'll learn how to do things that you'll probably never use in the real world, but that will almost certainly be on the exam.

CERTIFICATION OBJECTIVE

Java Operators (Exam Objective 7.6)

7.6   Write code that correctly applies the appropriate operators including assignment operators (limited to: =, +=, -=), arithmetic operators (limited to: +, -, *, /, %, ++, --), relational operators (limited to: <, <=, >, >=, ==, !=), the instanceof operator, logical operators (limited to: &, |, ^, !, &&, ||), and the conditional operator (? :), to produce a desired result. Write code that determines the equality of two objects or two primitives.

Java operators produce new values from one or more operands (just so we're all clear, remember the operands are the things on the right or left side of the operator). The result of most operations is either a `boolean` or numeric value. Because you know by now that Java is not C++, you won't be surprised that Java operators aren't typically overloaded. There are, however, a few exceptional operators that come overloaded:

- The + operator can be used to add two numeric primitives together, or to perform a concatenation operation if either operand is a String.
- The &, |, and ^ operators can all be used in two different ways, although as of this version of the exam, their bit-twiddling capabilities won't be tested.

Stay awake. Operators are often the section of the exam where candidates see their lowest scores. Additionally, operators and assignments are a part of many questions in other topics…it would be a shame to nail a really tricky threads question, only to blow it on a pre-increment statement.

Assignment Operators

We covered most of the functionality of the assignment operator, "=", in Chapter 3. To summarize:

- When assigning a value to a primitive, *size* matters. Be sure you know when implicit casting will occur, when explicit casting is necessary, and when truncation might occur.

- Remember that a reference variable isn't an object; it's a way to *get* to an object. (We know all you C++ programmers are just dying for us to say "it's a pointer", but we're not going to.)

- When assigning a value to a reference variable, *type* matters. Remember the rules for supertypes, subtypes, and arrays.

Next we'll cover a few more details about the assignment operators that are on the exam, and when we get to Chapter 7, we'll take a look at how the assignment operator "=" works with Strings (which are immutable).

exam
watch

Don't spend time preparing for topics that are no longer on the exam! In a nutshell, the Java 5 exam differs from the 1.4 exam by moving away from bits, and towards the API. Many 1.4 topics related to operators have been removed from the exam, so in this chapter you WON'T see

- bit shifting operators
- bitwise operators
- two's complement
- divide by zero stuff

It's not that these aren't important topics, it's just that they're not on the exam anymore, and we're really focused on the exam.

Compound Assignment Operators

There are actually 11 or so compound assignment operators, but only the four most commonly used (+=, -=, *=, and /=), are on the exam (despite what the objectives say). The compound assignment operators let lazy typists shave a few keystrokes off their workload. Here are several example assignments, first without using a compound operator,

```
y = y - 6;
x = x + 2 * 5;
```

Now, with compound operators:

```
y -= 6;
x += 2 * 5;
```

The last two assignments give the same result as the first two.

e x a m

ⓌＷ a t c h

Earlier versions of the exam put big emphasis on operator precedence (like: What's the result of: $x = y++ + ++x/z;$ *). Other than a very basic knowledge of precedence (such as:* ***** *and* **/** *are higher precedence than* **+** *and* **-***), you won't need to study operator precedence, except that when using a compound operator, the expression on the right side of the* **=** *will always be evaluated first. For example, you might expect*

```
x *= 2 + 5;
```

to be evaluated like this:

```
x = (x * 2) + 5;   // incorrect precedence
```

since multiplication has higher precedence than addition. But instead, the expression on the right is always placed inside parentheses. it is evaluated like this:

```
x = x * (2 + 5);
```

Relational Operators

The exam covers six relational operators (<, <=, >, >=, ==, and !=). Relational operators always result in a boolean (`true` or `false`) value. This `boolean` value is most often used in an `if` test, as follows,

```
int x = 8;
if (x < 9) {
  // do something
}
```

but the resulting value can also be assigned directly to a `boolean` primitive:

```
class CompareTest {
  public static void main(String [] args) {
    boolean b = 100 > 99;
    System.out.println("The value of b is " + b);
  }
}
```

Java has four relational operators that can be used to compare any combination of integers, floating-point numbers, or characters:

- `>`   greater than
- `>=` greater than or equal to
- `<`   less than
- `<=` less than or equal to

Let's look at some legal comparisons:

```
class CucssAnimal {
  public static void main(String[] args) {
    String animal = "unknown";
    int weight = 700;
    char sex = 'm';
    double colorWaveLength = 1.630;
    if (weight >= 500) { animal = "elephant"; }
    if (colorWaveLength > 1.621) { animal = "gray " + animal; }
    if (sex <= 'f') { animal = "female " + animal; }
    System.out.println("The animal is a " + animal);
  }
}
```

In the preceding code, we are using a comparison between characters. It's also legal to compare a character primitive with any number (though it isn't great programming style). Running the preceding class will output the following:

```
The animal is a gray elephant
```

We mentioned that characters can be used in comparison operators. When comparing a character with a character, or a character with a number, Java will use the Unicode value of the character as the numerical value, for comparison.

"Equality" Operators

Java also has two relational operators (sometimes called "equality operators") that compare two similar "things" and return a `boolean` the represents what's true about the two "things" being equal. These operators are

- == equals (also known as "equal to")
- != not equals (also known as "not equal to")

Each individual comparison can involve two numbers (including `char`), two `boolean` values, or two object reference variables. You can't compare incompatible types, however. What would it mean to ask if a `boolean` is equal to a `char`? Or if a `Button` is equal to a `String` array? (Exactly, nonsense, which is why you can't do it.) There are four different types of things that can be tested:

- numbers
- characters
- boolean primitives
- Object reference variables

So what does == look at? The value in the variable—in other words, the bit pattern.

Equality for Primitives

Most programmers are familiar with comparing primitive values. The following code shows some equality tests on primitive variables:

```
class ComparePrimitives {
  public static void main(String[] args) {
    System.out.println("char 'a' == 'a'? " + ('a' == 'a'));
    System.out.println("char 'a' == 'b'? " + ('a' == 'b'));
    System.out.println("5 != 6? " + (5 != 6));
    System.out.println("5.0 == 5L? " + (5.0 == 5L));
    System.out.println("true == false? " + (true == false));
  }
}
```

This program produces the following output:

```
char 'a' == 'a'? true
char 'a' == 'b'? false
5 != 6? true
5.0 == 5L? true
true == false? false
```

As we can see, usually if a floating-point number is compared with an integer and the values are the same, the == operator returns true as expected.

Equality for Reference Variables

As we saw earlier, two reference variables can refer to the same object, as the following code snippet demonstrates:

```
JButton a = new JButton("Exit");
JButton b = a;
```

After running this code, both variable a and variable b will refer to the same object (a JButton with the label Exit). Reference variables can be tested to see if they refer to the same object by using the == operator. Remember, the == operator is looking at the bits in the variable, so for reference variables this means that if the

watch

Don't mistake **=** *for* **==** *in a boolean expression. The following is legal:*

```
11. boolean b = false;
12. if (b = true) { System.out.println("b is true");
13. } else { System.out.println("b is false");   }
```

Look carefully! You might be tempted to think the output is b is false *but look at the boolean test in line 12. The boolean variable* b *is not being compared to* true, *it's being set to* true, *so the* println *executes and we get* b is true *. The result of any assignment expression is the value of the variable following the assignment. This substitution of = for == works only with boolean variables, since the* if *test can be done only on boolean expressions. Thus, this does not compile:*

```
7. int x = 1;
8. if (x = 0) { }
```

Because x *is an integer (and not a* boolean*), the result of* (x = 0) *is* **0** *(the result of the assignment). Primitive* ints *cannot be used where a boolean value is expected, so the code in line 8 won't work unless changed from an assignment (=) to an equality test (==) as follows:*

```
8. if (x == 0) { }
```

bits in both reference variables are identical, then both refer to the same object.
Look at the following code:

```
import javax.swing.JButton;
class CompareReference {
  public static void main(String[] args) {
    JButton a = new JButton("Exit");
    JButton b = new JButton("Exit");
    JButton c = a;
    System.out.println("Is reference a == b? " + (a == b));
    System.out.println("Is reference a == c? " + (a == c));
  }
}
```

This code creates three reference variables. The first two, a and b, are separate
JButton objects that happen to have the same label. The third reference variable, c,
is initialized to refer to the same object that a refers to. When this program runs, the
following output is produced:

```
Is reference a == b? false
Is reference a == c? true
```

This shows us that a and c reference the same instance of a JButton. The ==
operator will not test whether two objects are "meaningfully equivalent," a concept
we'll cover in much more detail in Chapter 7, when we look at the equals() *method*
(as opposed to the equals *operator* we're looking at here).

Equality for Enums

Once you've declared an enum, it's not expandable. At runtime, there's no way to
make additional enum constants. Of course, you can have as many variables as you'd
like refer to a given enum constant, so it's important to be able to compare two
enum reference variables to see if they're "equal", i.e. do they refer to the same enum
constant. You can use either the == operator or the equals() method to determine
if two variables are referring to the same enum constant:

```
class EnumEqual {
  enum Color {RED, BLUE}                    // ; is optional
  public static void main(String[] args) {
    Color c1 = Color.RED;  Color c2 = Color.RED;
    if(c1 == c2) { System.out.println("=="); }
    if(c1.equals(c2)) { System.out.println("dot equals"); }
} }
```

(We know } } is ugly, we're prepping you). This produces the output:

```
==
dot equals
```

instanceof Comparison

The `instanceof` operator is used for object reference variables only, and you can use it to check whether an object is of a particular type. By type, we mean class or interface type—in other words, if the object referred to by the variable on the left side of the operator passes the IS-A test for the class or interface type on the right side (Chapter 2 covered IS-A relationships in detail). The following simple example

```java
public static void main(String[] args) {
  String s = new String("foo");
  if (s instanceof String) {
    System.out.print("s is a String");
  }
}
```

prints this: `s is a String`

Even if the object being tested is not an actual instantiation of the class type on the right side of the operator, `instanceof` will still return `true` if the object being compared is *assignment compatible* with the type on the right.

The following example demonstrates a common use for `instanceof`: testing an object to see if it's an instance of one of its subtypes, before attempting a "downcast":

```java
class A { }
class B extends A {
  public static void main (String [] args) {
    A myA = new B();
    m2(myA);
  }
  public static void m2(A a) {
    if (a instanceof B)
      ((B)a).doBstuff();        // downcasting an A reference
                                // to a B reference
  }
  public static void doBstuff() {
    System.out.println("'a' refers to a B");
  }
}
```

The preceding code compiles and produces the output:

```
'a' refers to a B
```

In examples like this, the use of the `instanceof` operator protects the program from attempting an illegal downcast.

You can test an object reference against its own class type, or any of its superclasses. This means that *any* object reference will evaluate to `true` if you use the `instanceof` operator against type `Object`, as follows,

```
B b = new B();
if (b instanceof Object) {
    System.out.print("b is definitely an Object");
}
```

which prints this: `b is definitely an Object`

---

exam
ⓦatch

Look for instanceof questions that test whether an object is an instance of an interface, when the object's class implements the interface indirectly. An indirect implementation occurs when one of an object's superclasses implements an interface, but the actual class of the instance does not—for example,

```
interface Foo { }
class A implements Foo { }
class B extends A { }
...
A a = new A();
B b = new B();
```

the following are true:

```
a instanceof Foo
b instanceof A
b instanceof Foo  // implemented indirectly
```

An object is said to be of a particular interface type (meaning it will pass the `instanceof` **test) if any of the object's superclasses implement the interface.**

In addition, it is legal to test whether the `null` reference is an instance of a class. This will always result in `false`, of course. For example:

```
class InstanceTest {
   public static void main(String [] args) {
      String a = null;
      boolean b = null instanceof String;
      boolean c = a instanceof String;
      System.out.println(b + " " + c);
   }
}
```

prints this: `false false`

instanceof Compiler Error

You can't use the `instanceof` operator to test across two different class hierarchies. For instance, the following will NOT compile:

```
class Cat { }
class Dog {
  public static void main(String [] args) {
    Dog d = new Dog();
    System.out.println(d instanceof Cat);
  }
}
```

Compilation fails—there's no way d could ever refer to a Cat or a subtype of Cat.

---

exam
watch

Remember that arrays are objects, even if the array is an array of primitives. Watch for questions that look something like this:

```
int [] nums = new int[3];
if (nums instanceof Object) { } // result is true
```

An array is always an instance of Object. Any array.

Table 4-1 summarizes the use of the `instanceof` operator given the following:

```
interface Face { }
class Bar implements Face{ }
class Foo extends Bar { }
```

TABLE 4-1   Operands and Results Using *instanceof* Operator.

First Operand (Reference Being Tested)	instanceof Operand (Type We're Comparing the Reference Against)	Result
null	Any class or interface type	false
Foo instance	Foo, Bar, Face, Object	true
Bar instance	Bar, Face, Object	true
Bar instance	Foo	false
Foo []	Foo, Bar, Face	false
Foo []	Object	true
Foo [1]	Foo, Bar, Face, Object	true

Arithmetic Operators

We're sure you're familiar with the basic arithmetic operators.

- + addition
- – subtraction
- * multiplication
- / division

These can be used in the standard way:

```
int x = 5 * 3;
int y = x - 4;
System.out.println("x - 4 is " + y);  // Prints 11
```

The Remainder (%) Operator

One operator you might not be as familiar with is the remainder operator, %. The remainder operator divides the left operand by the right operand, and the result is the remainder, as the following code demonstrates:

```
class MathTest {
  public static void main (String [] args) {
    int x = 15;
    int y = x % 4;
    System.out.println("The result of 15 % 4 is the "
      + "remainder of 15 divided by 4. The remainder is " + y);
  }
}
```

Running class MathTest prints the following:

```
The result of 15 % 4 is the remainder of 15 divided by 4. The
remainder is 3
```

(Remember: Expressions are evaluated from left to right by default. You can change this sequence, or *precedence*, by adding parentheses. Also remember that the *, /, and % operators have a higher precedence than the + and operators.)

String Concatenation Operator

The plus sign can also be used to concatenate two strings together, as we saw earlier (and as we'll definitely see again):

```
String animal = "Grey " + "elephant";
```

String concatenation gets interesting when you combine numbers with Strings. Check out the following:

```
String a = "String";
int b = 3;
int c = 7;
System.out.println(a + b + c);
```

Will the + operator act as a plus sign when adding the int variables b + c? Or will the + operator treat 3 and 7 as characters, and concatenate them individually? Will the result be String10 or String37? OK, you've had long enough to think about it. The int values were simply treated as characters and glued on to the right side of the String, giving the result:

```
String37
```

So we could read the previous code as

> "Start with `String a`, `String`, and add the character `3` (the value of `b`) to it, to produce a new string `String3`, and then add the character `7` (the value of `c`) to that, to produce a new string `String37`, then print it out."

However, if you put parentheses around the two `int` variables, as follows,

```
System.out.println(a + (b + c));
```

you'll get this: `String10`

Using parentheses causes the `(b + c)` to evaluate first, so the rightmost + operator functions as the addition operator, given that both operands are `int` values. The key point here is that within the parentheses, the left-hand operand is not a `String`. If it were, then the + operator would perform `String` concatenation. The previous code can be read as

> "Add the values of `b + c` together, then take the sum and convert it to a `String` and concatenate it with the `String` from variable a."

The rule to remember is this:

> *If either operand is a* String, *the + operator becomes a* String *concatenation operator. If both operands are numbers, the + operator is the addition operator.*

You'll find that sometimes you might have trouble deciding whether, say, the left-hand operator is a `String` or not. On the exam, don't expect it to always be obvious. (Actually, now that we think about it, don't expect it ever to be obvious.) Look at the following code:

```
System.out.println(x.foo() + 7);
```

You can't know how the + operator is being used until you find out what the `foo()` method returns! If `foo()` returns a `String`, then 7 is concatenated to the returned

String. But if `foo()` returns a number, then the + operator is used to add 7 to the return value of `foo()`.

Finally, you need to know that it's legal to mush together the compound additive operator (+=) and Strings, like so:

```
String s = "123";
s += "45";
s += 67;
System.out.println(s);
```

Since both times the += operator was used and the left operand was a String, both operations were concatenations, resulting in

```
1234567
```

exam

ⓦatch   *If you don't understand how String concatenation works, especially within a* `print` *statement, you could actually fail the exam even if you know the rest of the answer to the questions! Because so many questions ask, "What is the result?", you need to know not only the result of the code running, but also how that result is printed. Although there will be at least a few questions directly testing your String knowledge, String concatenation shows up in other questions on virtually every objective. Experiment! For example, you might see a line such as*

```
int b = 2;
System.out.println("" + b + 3);
```

which prints   23

but if the print statement changes to

```
System.out.println(b + 3);
```

then the result becomes   5

Increment and Decrement Operators

Java has two operators that will increment or decrement a variable by exactly one. These operators are composed of either two plus signs (++) or two minus signs (--):

- ++ increment (prefix and postfix)
- -- decrement (prefix and postfix)

The operator is placed either before (prefix) or after (postfix) a variable to change its value. Whether the operator comes before or after the operand can change the outcome of an expression. Examine the following:

```
1. class MathTest {
2.    static int players = 0;
3.      public static void main (String [] args) {
4.        System.out.println("players online: " + players++);
5.        System.out.println("The value of players is "
                                    + players);
6.        System.out.println("The value of players is now "
                                    + ++players);
7.    }
8. }
```

Notice that in the fourth line of the program the increment operator is *after* the variable players. That means we're using the postfix increment operator, which causes players to be incremented by one but only *after* the value of players is used in the expression. When we run this program, it outputs the following:

```
%java MathTest
players online: 0
The value of players is 1
The value of players is now 2
```

Notice that when the variable is written to the screen, at first it says the value is 0. Because we used the postfix increment operator, the increment doesn't happen until after the players variable is used in the print statement. Get it? The "post" in postfix means *after*. Line 5 doesn't increment players; it just outputs its value to the screen, so the newly incremented value displayed is 1. Line 6 applies the prefix increment operator to players, which means the increment happens *before* the value of the variable is used, so the output is 2.

Expect to see questions mixing the increment and decrement operators with other operators, as in the following example:

```
int x = 2;  int y = 3;
if ((y == x++) | (x < ++y)) {
  System.out.println("x = " + x + " y = " + y);
 }
```

The preceding code prints: x = 3 y = 4

You can read the code as follows: "If 3 is equal to 2 OR 3 < 4"

The first expression compares x and y, and the result is false, because the increment on x doesn't happen until *after* the == test is made. Next, we increment x, so now x is 3. Then we check to see if x is less than y, but we increment y *before* comparing it with x! So the second logical test is (3 < 4). The result is true, so the print statement runs.

As with String concatenation, the increment and decrement operators are used throughout the exam, even on questions that aren't trying to test your knowledge of how those operators work. You might see them in questions on for loops, exceptions, even threads. Be ready.

Conditional Operator

The conditional operator is a *ternary* operator (it has *three* operands) and is used to evaluate boolean expressions, much like an if statement except instead of executing a block of code if the test is true, a conditional operator will assign a value to a variable. In other words, the goal of the conditional operator is to decide which of two values to assign to a variable. This operator is constructed using a ? (question mark) and a : (colon). The parentheses are optional. Its structure is:

```
x = (boolean expression) ? value to assign if true : value to assign if false
```

Let's take a look at a conditional operator in code:

```
class Salary {
  public static void main(String [] args) {
    int numOfPets = 3;
    String status = (numOfPets<4) ? "Pet limit not exceeded"
                        : "too many pets";
    System.out.println("This pet status is " + status);
  }
}
```

You can read the preceding code as

Set numOfPets equal to 3. Next we're going to assign a String to the status variable. If numOfPets is less than 4, assign "Pet limit not exceeded" to the status variable; otherwise, assign "too many pets" to the status variable.

A conditional operator starts with a boolean operation, followed by two possible values for the variable to the left of the assignment (=) operator. The first value (the one to the left of the colon) is assigned if the conditional (boolean) test is true, and the second value is assigned if the conditional test is false. You can even nest conditional operators into one statement:

```
class AssignmentOps {
  public static void main(String [] args) {
    int sizeOfYard = 10;
    int numOfPets = 3;
    String status = (numOfPets<4)?"Pet count OK"
        :(sizeOfYard > 8)? "Pet limit on the edge"
          :"too many pets";
    System.out.println("Pet status is " + status);
```

```
        }
}
```

Don't expect many questions using conditional operators, but remember that conditional operators are sometimes confused with assertion statements, so be certain you can tell the difference. Chapter 5 covers assertions in detail.

Logical Operators

The exam objectives specify six "logical" operators (&, |, ^, !, &&, and ||). Some Sun documentation uses other terminology for these operators, but for our purposes the "logical operators" are the six listed above, and in the exam objectives.

Bitwise Operators (Not on the Exam!)

Okay, this is going to be confusing. Of the six logical operators listed above, three of them (&, |, and ^) can also be used as "bitwise" operators. Bitwise operators were included in previous versions of the exam, but they're not on the Java 5 exam. Here are several legal statements that use bitwise operators:

```
byte b1 = 6 & 8;
byte b2 = 7 | 9;
byte b3 = 5 ^ 4;
System.out.println(b1 + " " + b2 + " " + b3);
```

Bitwise operators compare two variables bit by bit, and return a variable whose bits have been set based on whether the two variables being compared had respective bits that were either both "on" (&), one or the other "on" (|), or exactly one "on" (^). By the way, when we run the preceding code, we get

```
0 15 1
```

Having said all this about bitwise operators, the key thing to remember is this:

BITWISE OPERATORS ARE NOT ON THE EXAM!

So why did we bring them up? If you get hold of an old exam preparation book, or if you find some mock exams that haven't been properly updated, you're bound to find questions that perform bitwise operations. Unless you're a glutton for punishment, you can skip this kind of mock question.

Short-Circuit Logical Operators

There are five logical operators on the exam that are used to evaluate statements that contain more than one `boolean` expression. The most commonly used of the five are the two *short-circuit* logical operators. They are

- `&&`   short-circuit AND
- || short-circuit OR

They are used to link little `boolean` expressions together to form bigger `boolean` expressions. The `&&` and || operators evaluate only `boolean` values. For an AND (`&&`) expression to be `true`, both operands must be `true`—for example,

```
if ((2 < 3) && (3 < 4)) { }
```

The preceding expression evaluates to `true` because *both* operand one (2 < 3) and operand two (3 < 4) evaluate to `true`.

The short-circuit feature of the && operator is so named because it doesn't waste its time on pointless evaluations. A short-circuit `&&` evaluates the left side of the operation first (operand one), and if it resolves to `false`, the `&&` operator doesn't bother looking at the right side of the expression (operand two) since the `&&` operator already *knows* that the complete expression can't possibly be `true`.

```
class Logical {
  public static void main(String [] args) {
    boolean b = true && false;
    System.out.println("boolean b = " + b);
  }
}
```

When we run the preceding code, we get

```
%java Logical
boolean b = false
```

The || operator is similar to the `&&` operator, except that it evaluates to `true` if EITHER of the operands is true. If the first operand in an OR operation is `true`, the result will be true, so the short-circuit || doesn't waste time looking at the right side of the equation. If the first operand is `false`, however, the short-circuit || has to evaluate the second operand to see if the result of the OR operation will be true or false. Pay close attention to the following example; you'll see quite a few questions like this on the exam:

```
1.  class TestOR {
2.    public static void main(String[] args) {
3.      if ((isItSmall(3)) || (isItSmall(7))) {
4.        System.out.println("Result is true");
5.      }
6.      if ((isItSmall(6)) || (isItSmall(9))) {
7.        System.out.println("Result is true");
8.      }
9.    }
10.
11.    public static boolean isItSmall(int i) {
12.      if (i < 5) {
13.        System.out.println("i < 5");
14.        return true;
15.      } else {
16.        System.out.println("i >= 5");
17.        return false;
18.      }
19.    }
20.  }
```

What is the result?

```
% java TestOR
i < 5
Result is true
i >= 5
i >= 5
```

Here's what happened when the main() method ran:

1. When we hit line 3, the first operand in the || expression (in other words, the *left* side of the || operation) is evaluated.

2. The isItSmall(3) method is invoked, prints "i < 5", and returns true.

3. Because the *first* operand in the || expression on line 3 is true, the || operator doesn't bother evaluating the second operand. So we never see the "i >= 5" that would have printed had the *second* operand been evaluated (which would have invoked isItSmall(7)).

4. Line 6 is evaluated, beginning with the *first* operand in the | | expression.

5. The isItSmall(6) method is called, prints "i >= 5", and returns false.

6. Because the *first* operand in the | | expression on line 6 is false, the | | operator can't skip the *second* operand; there's still a chance the expression can be true, if the *second* operand evaluates to true.

7. The isItSmall(9) method is invoked and prints "i >= 5".

8. The isItSmall(9) method returns false, so the expression on line 6 is false, and thus line 7 never executes.

e x a m

ⓦatch

The || and && operators work only with boolean operands. The exam may try to fool you by using integers with these operators:

```
if (5 && 6) { }
```

It looks as though we're trying to do a bitwise AND on the bits representing the integers 5 and 6, but the code won't even compile.

Logical Operators (Not Short-Circuit)

There are two *non-short-circuit* logical operators.

- **&**   non-short-circuit AND
- **|**   non-short-circuit OR

These operators are used in logical expressions just like the && and | | operators are used, but because they aren't the short-circuit operators, they evaluate both sides of the expression, always! They're inefficient. For example, even if the *first* operand (left side) in an & expression is false, the *second* operand will still be evaluated—even though it's now impossible for the result to be true! And the | is just as inefficient: if the *first* operand is true, the Java Virtual Machine (JVM) still plows ahead and evaluates the *second* operand even when it knows the expression will be true regardless.

You'll find a lot of questions on the exam that use both the short-circuit and non-short-circuit logical operators. You'll have to know exactly which operands are evaluated and which are not, since the result will vary depending on whether the second operand in the expression is evaluated:

```
int z = 5;
if(++z > 5 || ++z > 6) z++;    // z = 7 after this code
```

versus:

```
int z = 5;
if(++z > 5 | ++z > 6) z++;    // z = 8 after this code
```

Logical Operators ^ and !

The last two logical operators on the exam are

- ^   exclusive-OR (XOR)
- !   boolean invert

The ^ (exclusive-OR) operator evaluates only `boolean` values. The ^ operator is related to the non-short-circuit operators we just reviewed, in that it always evaluates *both* the left and right operands in an expression. For an exclusive-OR (^) expression to be `true`, EXACTLY one operand must be `true`—for example,

```
System.out.println("xor " + ((2<3) ^ (4>3)));
```

produces the output: `xor false`

The preceding expression evaluates to **false** because BOTH operand one (2 < 3) and operand two (4 > 3) evaluate to `true`.

The ! (boolean invert) operator returns the opposite of a boolean's current value:

```
if(!(7 == 5)) { System.out.println("not equal"); }
```

can be read "if it's not true that 7 == 5," and the statement produces this output:

```
not equal
```

Here's another example using booleans:

```
boolean t = true;
boolean f = false;
System.out.println("! " + (t & !f) + " " + f);
```

produces the output:

```
! true false
```

In the preceding example, notice that the & test succeeded (printing `true`), and that the value of the `boolean` variable `f` did not change, so it printed `false`.

CERTIFICATION SUMMARY

If you've studied this chapter diligently, you should have a firm grasp on Java operators, and you should understand what equality means when tested with the `==` operator. Let's review the highlights of what you've learned in this chapter.

The logical operators (`&&` , `| |`, `&`, `|`, and `^`) can be used only to evaluate two `boolean` expressions. The difference between `&&` and `&` is that the `&&` operator won't bother testing the right operand if the left evaluates to `false`, because the result of the `&&` expression can never be `true`. The difference between `| |` and `|` is that the `| |` operator won't bother testing the right operand if the left evaluates to `true`, because the result is already known to be `true` at that point.

The `==` operator can be used to compare values of primitives, but it can also be used to determine whether two reference variables refer to the same object.

The `instanceof` operator is used to determine if the object referred to by a reference variable passes the IS-A test for a specified type.

The `+` operator is overloaded to perform `String` concatenation tasks, and can also concatenate `Strings` and primitives, but be careful—concatenation can be tricky.

The conditional operator (a.k.a. the "ternary operator") has an unusual, three-operand syntax—don't mistake it for a complex assert statement.

The `++` and `--` operators will be used throughout the exam, and you must pay attention to whether they are prefixed or postfixed to the variable being updated.

Be prepared for a lot of exam questions involving the topics from this chapter. Even within questions testing your knowledge of another objective, the code will frequently use operators, assignments, object and primitive passing, and so on.

TWO-MINUTE DRILL

Here are some of the key points from each section in this chapter.

Relational Operators (Objective 7.6)

❑ Relational operators always result in a boolean value (true or false).

❑ There are six relational operators: >, >=, <, <=, ==, and !=. The last two (== and !=) are sometimes referred to as *equality operators*.

❑ When comparing characters, Java uses the Unicode value of the character as the numerical value.

❑ Equality operators

  ❑ There are two equality operators: == and !=.

  ❑ Four types of things can be tested: numbers, characters, booleans, and reference variables.

❑ When comparing reference variables, == returns true only if both references refer to the same object.

instanceof Operator (Objective 7.6)

❑ instanceof is for reference variables only, and checks for whether the object is of a particular type.

❑ The instanceof operator can be used only to test objects (or null) against class types that are in the same class hierarchy.

❑ For interfaces, an object passes the instanceof test if any of its superclasses implement the interface on the right side of the instanceof operator.

Arithmetic Operators (Objective 7.6)

❑ There are four primary math operators: add, subtract, multiply, and divide.

❑ The remainder operator (%), returns the remainder of a division.

❑ Expressions are evaluated from left to right, unless you add parentheses, or unless some operators in the expression have higher precedence than others.

❑ The *, /, and % operators have higher precedence than + and -.

String Concatenation Operator (Objective 7.6)

❑ If either operand is a `string`, the + operator concatenates the operands.

❑ If both operands are numeric, the + operator adds the operands.

Increment/Decrement Operators (Objective 7.6)

❑ Prefix operators (++ and --) run before the value is used in the expression.

❑ Postfix operators (++ and --) run after the value is used in the expression.

❑ In any expression, both operands are fully evaluated *before* the operator is applied.

❑ Variables marked `final` cannot be incremented or decremented.

Ternary (Conditional Operator) (Objective 7.6)

❑ Returns one of two values based on whether a `boolean` expression is `true` or `false`.

   ❑ Returns the value after the ? if the expression is `true`.

   ❑ Returns the value after the : if the expression is `false`.

Logical Operators (Objective 7.6)

❑ The exam covers six "logical" operators: &, |, ^, !, &&, and | |.

❑ Logical operators work with two expressions (except for !) that must resolve to `boolean` values.

❑ The && and & operators return `true` only if both operands are `true`.

❑ The | | and | operators return `true` if either or both operands are `true`.

❑ The && and | | operators are known as short-circuit operators.

❑ The && operator does not evaluate the right operand if the left operand is `false`.

❑ The | | does not evaluate the right operand if the left operand is `true`.

❑ The & and | operators always evaluate both operands.

❑ The ^ operator (called the "logical XOR"), returns `true` if exactly one operand is `true`.

❑ The ! operator (called the "inversion" operator), returns the opposite value of the `boolean` operand it precedes.

SELF TEST

1. Given:

```
class Hexy {
  public static void main(String[] args) {
    Integer i = 42;
    String s = (i<40)?"life":(i>50)?"universe":"everything";
    System.out.println(s);
  }
}
```

What is the result?

A. null

B. life

C. universe

D. everything

E. Compilation fails

F. An exception is thrown at runtime

2. Given:

```
1. class Comp2 {
2.   public static void main(String[] args) {
3.     float f1 = 2.3f;
4.     float[][] f2 = {{42.0f}, {1.7f, 2.3f}, {2.6f, 2.7f}};
5.     float[] f3 = {2.7f};
6.     Long x = 42L;
7.     // insert code here
8.       System.out.println("true");
9.   }
10. }
```

And the following five code fragments:

```
F1.  if(f1 == f2)
F2.  if(f1 == f2[2][1])
F3.  if(x == f2[0][0])
F4.  if(f1 == f2[1,1])
F5.  if(f3 == f2[2])
```

What is true?

A. One of them will compile, only one will be `true`
B. Two of them will compile, only one will be `true`
C. Two of them will compile, two will be `true`
D. Three of them will compile, only one will be `true`
E. Three of them will compile, exactly two will be `true`
F. Three of them will compile, exactly three will be `true`

3. Given:

```
class Fork {
  public static void main(String[] args) {
    if(args.length == 1 | args[1].equals("test")) {
      System.out.println("test case");
    } else {
      System.out.println("production " + args[0]);
    }
  }
}
```

And the command-line invocation:

```
java Fork live2
```

What is the result?

A. `test case`
B. `production live2`
C. `test case live2`
D. Compilation fails
E. An exception is thrown at runtime

4. Given:

```
class Feline {
  public static void main(String[] args) {
    Long x = 42L;
    Long y = 44L;
    System.out.print(" " + 7 + 2 + " ");
    System.out.print(foo() + x + 5 + " ");
    System.out.println(x + y + foo());
  }
  static String foo() { return "foo"; }
}
```

What is the result?

A. 9 foo47 86foo

B. 9 foo47 4244foo

C. 9 foo425 86foo

D. 9 foo425 4244foo

E. 72 foo47 86foo

F. 72 foo47 4244foo

G. 72 foo425 86foo

H. 72 foo425 4244foo

I. Compilation fails

5. Place the fragments into the code to produce the output 33. Note, you must use each fragment exactly once.

CODE:
```
class Incr {
  public static void main(String[] args) {
    Integer x = 7;
    int y = 2;

    x    ___ ___;
    ___ ___ ___;
    ___ ___ ___;
    ___ ___ ___;

    System.out.println(x);
  }
}
```

FRAGMENTS:

y	y	y	y
y	x	x	
-=	*=	*=	*=

6. Given:

```
3. public class Twisty {
4.   { index = 1; }
5.   int index;
6.   public static void main(String[] args) {
7.     new Twisty().go();
8.   }
9.   void go() {
10.     int [][] dd = {{9,8,7}, {6,5,4}, {3,2,1,0}};
11.     System.out.println(dd[index++][index++]);
12.   }
13. }
```

What is the result? (Choose all that apply.)

A. 1

B. 2

C. 4

D. 6

E. 8

F. Compilation fails

G. An exception is thrown at runtime

7. Given:

```
3. public class McGee {
4.   public static void main(String[] args) {
5.     Days d1 = Days.TH;
6.     Days d2 = Days.M;
7.     for(Days d: Days.values()) {
8.       if(d.equals(Days.F)) break;
9.       d2 = d;
10.     }
11.     System.out.println((d1 == d2)?"same old" : "newly new");
12.   }
13.   enum Days {M, T, W, TH, F, SA, SU};
14. }
```

What is the result?

A. same old

B. newly new

C. Compilation fails due to multiple errors

D. Compilation fails due only to an error on line 7

E. Compilation fails due only to an error on line 8

F. Compilation fails due only to an error on line 11

G. Compilation fails due only to an error on line 13

8. Given:

```
4. public class SpecialOps {
5.    public static void main(String[] args) {
6.       String s = "";
7.       Boolean b1 = true;
8.       boolean b2 = false;
9.       if((b2 = false) | (21%5) > 2) s += "x";
10.       if(b1 || (b2 == true))        s += "y";
11.       if(b2 == true)                s += "z";
12.       System.out.println(s);
13.    }
14. }
```

Which are true? (Choose all that apply.)

A. Compilation fails

B. x will be included in the output

C. y will be included in the output

D. z will be included in the output

E. An exception is thrown at runtime

9. Given:

```
3. public class Spock {
4.    public static void main(String[] args) {
5.       int mask = 0;
6.       int count = 0;
7.       if( ((5<7) || (++count < 10)) | mask++ < 10 )   mask = mask + 1;
8.       if(   (6 > 8) ^ false)                           mask = mask + 10;
9.       if( !(mask > 1) && ++count > 1)                  mask = mask + 100;
10.       System.out.println(mask + " " + count);
11.    }
12. }
```

Which two are true about the value of mask and the value of count at line 10? (Choose two.)

A. mask is 0

B. mask is 1

C. mask is 2

D. mask is 10

E. mask is greater than 10

F. count is 0

G. count is greater than 0

10. Given:

```
3. interface Vessel { }
4. interface Toy { }
5. class Boat implements Vessel { }
6. class Speedboat extends Boat implements Toy { }
7. public class Tree {
8.    public static void main(String[] args) {
9.       String s = "0";
10.      Boat b = new Boat();
11.      Boat b2 = new Speedboat();
12.      Speedboat s2 = new Speedboat();
13.      if((b instanceof Vessel) && (b2 instanceof Toy))  s += "1";
14.      if((s2 instanceof Vessel) && (s2 instanceof Toy)) s += "2";
15.      System.out.println(s);
16.   }
17. }
```

What is the result?

A. 0

B. 01

C. 02

D. 012

E. Compilation fails

F. An exception is thrown at runtime

SELF TEST ANSWERS

1. Given:

```
class Hexy {
  public static void main(String[] args) {
    Integer i = 42;
    String s = (i<40)?"life":(i>50)?"universe":"everything";
    System.out.println(s);
  }
}
```

What is the result?

A. null

B. life

C. universe

D. everything

E. Compilation fails

F. An exception is thrown at runtime

Answer:

☑ **D** is correct. This is a ternary nested in a ternary with a little unboxing thrown in. Both of the ternary expressions are `false`.

☒ **A, B, C, E,** and **F** are incorrect based on the above.
(Objective 7.6)

2. Given:

```
1. class Comp2 {
2.   public static void main(String[] args) {
3.     float f1 = 2.3f;
4.     float[][] f2 = {{42.0f}, {1.7f, 2.3f}, {2.6f, 2.7f}};
5.     float[] f3 = {2.7f};
6.     Long x = 42L;
7.     // insert code here
8.        System.out.println("true");
9.   }
10. }
```

320 Chapter 4: Operators

And the following five code fragments:

```
F1.  if(f1 == f2)
F2.  if(f1 == f2[2][1])
F3.  if(x == f2[0][0])
F4.  if(f1 == f2[1,1])
F5.  if(f3 == f2[2])
```

What is true?

A. One of them will compile, only one will be true
B. Two of them will compile, only one will be true
C. Two of them will compile, two will be true
D. Three of them will compile, only one will be true
E. Three of them will compile, exactly two will be true
F. Three of them will compile, exactly three will be true

Answer:

☑ **D** is correct. Fragments F2, F3, and F5 will compile, and only F3 is true.

☒ **A, B, C, E,** and **F** are incorrect. F1 is incorrect because you can't compare a primitive to an array. F4 is incorrect syntax to access an element of a two-dimensional array. (Objective 7.6)

3. Given:

```
class Fork {
  public static void main(String[] args) {
    if(args.length == 1 | args[1].equals("test")) {
      System.out.println("test case");
    } else {
      System.out.println("production " + args[0]);
    }
  }
}
```

And the command-line invocation:

```
java Fork live2
```

What is the result?

A. test case
B. production live2

C. `test case live2`

D. Compilation fails

E. An exception is thrown at runtime

Answer:

☑ **E** is correct. Because the short circuit (`||`) is not used, both operands are evaluated. Since `args[1]` is past the args array bounds, an `ArrayIndexOutOfBoundsException` is thrown.

☒ **A, B, C,** and **D** are incorrect based on the above. (Objective 7.6)

4. Given:

```
class Feline {
  public static void main(String[] args) {
    Long x = 42L;
    Long y = 44L;
    System.out.print(" " + 7 + 2 + " ");
    System.out.print(foo() + x + 5 + " ");
    System.out.println(x + y + foo());
  }
  static String foo() { return "foo"; }
}
```

What is the result?

A. `9 foo47 86foo`

B. `9 foo47 4244foo`

C. `9 foo425 86foo`

D. `9 foo425 4244foo`

E. `72 foo47 86foo`

F. `72 foo47 4244foo`

G. `72 foo425 86foo`

H. `72 foo425 4244foo`

I. Compilation fails

Answer:

☑ **G** is correct. Concatenation runs from left to right, and if either operand is a `String`, the operands are concatenated. If both operands are numbers they are added together. Unboxing works in conjunction with concatenation.

☒ **A, B, C, D, E, F, H,** and **I** are incorrect based on the above. (Objective 7.6)

5. Place the fragments into the code to produce the output 33. Note, you must use each fragment exactly once.

CODE:

```
class Incr {
  public static void main(String[] args) {
    Integer x = 7;
    int y = 2;

    x    ___ ___;
    ___ ___ ___;
    ___ ___ ___;
    ___ ___ ___;

    System.out.println(x);
  }
}
```

FRAGMENTS:

y	y	y	y
y	x	x	
-=	*=	*=	*=

Answer:

```
class Incr {
  public static void main(String[] args) {
    Integer x = 7;
    int y = 2;

    x *= x;
    y *= y;
    y *= y;
    x -= y;

    System.out.println(x);
  }
}
```

Yeah, we know it's kind of puzzle-y, but you might encounter something like it on the real exam. (Objective 7.6)

6. Given:

```
3. public class Twisty {
4.    { index = 1; }
5.    int index;
6.    public static void main(String[] args) {
7.      new Twisty().go();
8.    }
9.    void go() {
10.     int [][] dd = {{9,8,7}, {6,5,4}, {3,2,1,0}};
11.     System.out.println(dd[index++][index++]);
12.   }
13. }
```

What is the result? (Choose all that apply.)

A. 1

B. 2

C. 4

D. 6

E. 8

F. Compilation fails

G. An exception is thrown at runtime

Answer:

☑ **C** is correct. Multidimensional arrays' dimensions can be inconsistent, the code uses an initialization block, and the increment operators are both post-increment operators.

☒ **A, B, D, E, F,** and **G** are incorrect based on the above. (Objective 1.3)

7. Given:

```
3. public class McGee {
4.    public static void main(String[] args) {
5.      Days d1 = Days.TH;
6.      Days d2 = Days.M;
7.      for(Days d: Days.values()) {
8.        if(d.equals(Days.F)) break;
9.        d2 = d;
10.     }
11.     System.out.println((d1 == d2)?"same old" : "newly new");
```

```
12.   }
13.   enum Days {M, T, W, TH, F, SA, SU};
14. }
```

What is the result?

A. `same old`

B. `newly new`

C. Compilation fails due to multiple errors

D. Compilation fails due only to an error on line 7

E. Compilation fails due only to an error on line 8

F. Compilation fails due only to an error on line 11

G. Compilation fails due only to an error on line 13

Answer:

☑ **A** is correct. All of this syntax is correct. The for-each iterates through the enum using the `values()` method to return an array. Enums can be compared using either `equals()` or `==`. Enums can be used in a ternary operator's Boolean test.

☒ **B, C, D, E, F,** and **G** are incorrect based on the above. (Objective 7.6)

8. Given:

```
4. public class SpecialOps {
5.   public static void main(String[] args) {
6.     String s = "";
7.     Boolean b1 = true;
8.     Boolean b2 = false;
9.     if((b2 = false) | (21%5) > 2) s += "x";
10.    if(b1 || (b2 = true))       s += "y";
11.    if(b2 == true)              s += "z";
12.    System.out.println(s);
13.   }
14. }
```

Which are true? (Choose all that apply.)

A. Compilation fails

B. x will be included in the output

C. y will be included in the output

D. z will be included in the output

E. An exception is thrown at runtime

Answer:

☑ **C** is correct. First of all, boxing takes care of the Boolean. Line 9 uses the modulus operator, which returns the remainder of the division, which in this case is 1. Also, line 9 sets b2 to false, and it doesn't test b2's value. Line 10 sets b2 to true, and it doesn't test its value; however, the short circuit operator keeps the expression b2 = true from being executed.

☒ **A, B, D,** and **E** are incorrect based on the above. (Objective 7.6)

9. Given:

```
3.  public class Spock {
4.    public static void main(String[] args) {
5.      int mask = 0;
6.      int count = 0;
7.      if( ((5<7) || (++count < 10)) | mask++ < 10 )    mask = mask + 1;
8.      if(   (6 > 8) ^ false)                           mask = mask + 10;
9.      if( !(mask > 1) && ++count > 1)                  mask = mask + 100;
10.     System.out.println(mask + " " + count);
11.   }
12. }
```

Which two answers are true about the value of mask and the value of count at line 10? (Choose two.)

A. mask is 0

B. mask is 1

C. mask is 2

D. mask is 10

E. mask is greater than 10

F. count is 0

G. count is greater than 0

Answer:

☑ **C** and **F** are correct. At line 7 the || keeps count from being incremented, but the | allows mask to be incremented. At line 8 the ^ returns true only if exactly one operand is true. At line 9 mask is 2 and the && keeps count from being incremented.

☒ **A, B, D, E,** and **G** are incorrect based on the above. (Objective 7.6)

10. Given:

```
3. interface Vessel { }
4. interface Toy { }
5. class Boat implements Vessel { }
6. class Speedboat extends Boat implements Toy { }
7. public class Tree {
8.   public static void main(String[] args) {
9.     String s = "0";
10.    Boat b = new Boat();
11.    Boat b2 = new Speedboat();
12.    Speedboat s2 = new Speedboat();
13.    if((b instanceof Vessel) && (b2 instanceof Toy))  s += "1";
14.    if((s2 instanceof Vessel) && (s2 instanceof Toy)) s += "2";
15.    System.out.println(s);
16.  }
17. }
```

What is the result?

A. 0

B. 01

C. 02

D. 012

E. Compilation fails

F. An exception is thrown at runtime

Answer:

☑ **D** is correct. First, remember that instanceof can look up through multiple levels of an inheritance tree. Also remember that instanceof is commonly used before attempting a downcast, so in this case, after line 15, it would be possible to say Speedboat s3 = (Speedboat)b2;.

☒ **A, B, C, E,** and **F** are incorrect based on the above. (Objective 7.6)

5

Flow Control, Exceptions, and Assertions

C an you imagine trying to write code using a language that didn't give you a way to execute statements conditionally? Flow control is a key part of most any useful programming language, and Java offers several ways to do it. Some, like if statements and for loops, are common to most languages. But Java also throws in a couple of flow control features you might not have used before—exceptions and assertions.

The if statement and the switch statement are types of conditional/decision controls that allow your program to behave differently at a "fork in the road," depending on the result of a logical test. Java also provides three different looping constructs—for, while, and do—so you can execute the same code over and over again depending on some condition being true. Exceptions give you a clean, simple way to organize code that deals with problems that might crop up at runtime. Finally, the assertion mechanism, added to the language with version 1.4, gives you a way to do testing and debugging checks on conditions you expect to smoke out while developing, when you don't necessarily need or want the runtime overhead associated with exception handling.

With these tools, you can build a robust program that can handle any logical situation with grace. Expect to see a wide range of questions on the exam that include flow control as part of the question code, even on questions that aren't testing your knowledge of flow control.

CERTIFICATION OBJECTIVE

if and switch Statements (Exam Objective 2.1)

2.1   Develop code that implements an if or switch statement; and identify legal argument types for these statements.

The if and switch statements are commonly referred to as decision statements. When you use decision statements in your program, you're asking the program to evaluate a given expression to determine which course of action to take. We'll look at the if statement first.

if-else Branching

The basic format of an `if` statement is as follows:

```
if (booleanExpression) {
  System.out.println("Inside if statement");
}
```

The expression in parentheses must evaluate to (a boolean) `true` or `false`.
Typically you're testing something to see if it's true, and then running a code block
(one or more statements) if it is true, and (optionally) another block of code if it
isn't. The following code demonstrates a legal `if-else` statement:

```
if (x > 3) {
  System.out.println("x is greater than 3");
} else {
  System.out.println("x is not greater than 3");
}
```

The `else` block is optional, so you can also use the following:

```
if (x > 3) {
  y = 2;
}
z += 8;
a = y + x;
```

The preceding code will assign 2 to y if the test succeeds (meaning x really is greater
than 3), but the other two lines will execute regardless. Even the curly braces
are optional if you have only one statement to execute within the body of the
conditional block. The following code example is legal (although not recommended
for readability):

```
if (x > 3)      // bad practice, but seen on the exam
  y = 2;
z += 8;
a = y + x;
```

Sun considers it good practice to enclose blocks within curly braces, even if
there's only one statement in the block. Be careful with code like the above, because
you might think it should read as,

"If x is greater than 3, then set y to 2, z to z + 8, and a to y + x."

But the last two lines are going to execute no matter what! They aren't part of the conditional flow. You might find it even more misleading if the code were indented as follows:

```
if (x > 3)
   y = 2;
   z += 8;
   a = y + x;
```

You might have a need to nest `if-else` statements (although, again, it's not recommended for readability, so nested `if` tests should be kept to a minimum). You can set up an `if-else` statement to test for multiple conditions. The following example uses two conditions so that if the first test fails, we want to perform a second test before deciding what to do:

```
if (price < 300) {
   buyProduct();
} else {
   if (price < 400) {
      getApproval();
   }
   else {
      dontBuyProduct();
   }
}
```

This brings up the other if-else construct, the `if, else if, else`. The preceding code could (and should) be rewritten:

```
if (price < 300) {
   buyProduct();
} else if (price < 400) {
   getApproval();
} else {
   dontBuyProduct();
}
```

There are a couple of rules for using `else` and `else if`:

- You can have zero or one else for a given if, and it must come after any else ifs.

- You can have zero to many else ifs for a given if and they must come before the (optional) else.

- Once an else if succeeds, none of the remaining else ifs or elses will be tested.

The following example shows code that is horribly formatted for the real world. As you've probably guessed, it's fairly likely that you'll encounter formatting like this on the exam. In any case, the code demonstrates the use of multiple else ifs:

```
int x = 1;
if ( x == 3 ) { }
else if (x < 4) {System.out.println("<4"); }
else if (x < 2) {System.out.println("<2"); }
else { System.out.println("else"); }
```

It produces the output:

```
<4
```

(Notice that even though the second else if is true, it is never reached.) Sometimes you can have a problem figuring out which if your else should pair with, as follows:

```
if (exam.done())
if (exam.getScore() < 0.61)
System.out.println("Try again.");
// Which if does this belong to?
else System.out.println("Java master!");
```

We intentionally left out the indenting in this piece of code so it doesn't give clues as to which if statement the else belongs to. Did you figure it out? Java law decrees that an else clause belongs to the innermost if statement to which it might possibly belong (in other words, the closest preceding if that doesn't have an else). In the case of the preceding example, the else belongs to the second if statement in the listing. With proper indenting, it would look like this:

```
if (exam.done())
  if (exam.getScore() < 0.61)
    System.out.println("Try again.");
  // Which if does this belong to?
  else
    System.out.println("Java master!");
```

Following our coding conventions by using curly braces, it would be even easier to read:

```
if (exam.done()) {
  if (exam.getScore() < 0.61) {
    System.out.println("Try again.");
  // Which if does this belong to?
  } else {
    System.out.println("Java master!");
  }
}
```

Don't get your hopes up about the exam questions being all nice and indented properly. Some exam takers even have a slogan for the way questions are presented on the exam: anything that can be made more confusing, will be.

Be prepared for questions that not only fail to indent nicely, but intentionally indent in a misleading way: Pay close attention for misdirection like the following:

```
if (exam.done())
  if (exam.getScore() < 0.61)
    System.out.println("Try again.");
else
  System.out.println("Java master!"); // Hmmmmm... now where does
                                      // it belong?
```

Of course, the preceding code is exactly the same as the previous two examples, except for the way it looks.

Legal Expressions for if Statements

The expression in an `if` statement must be a `boolean` expression. Any expression that resolves to a `boolean` is fine, and some of the expressions can be complex. Assume `doStuff()` returns `true`,

```
int y = 5;
int x = 2;
```

```
if (((x > 3) && (y < 2)) | doStuff()) {
   System.out.println("true");
}
```

which prints

```
true
```

You can read the preceding code as, "If both (x > 3) and (y < 2) are true, or if the result of doStuff() is true, then print true." So basically, if just doStuff() alone is true, we'll still get true. If doStuff() is false, though, then both (x > 3) and (y < 2) will have to be true in order to print true. The preceding code is even more complex if you leave off one set of parentheses as follows,

```
int y = 5;
int x = 2;
if ((x > 3) && (y < 2) | doStuff()) {
   System.out.println("true");
}
```

which now prints...nothing! Because the preceding code (with one less set of parentheses) evaluates as though you were saying, "If (x > 3) is true, and either (y < 2) or the result of doStuff() is true, then print true." So if (x > 3) is not true, no point in looking at the rest of the expression." Because of the short-circuit &&, the expression is evaluated as though there were parentheses around (y < 2) | doStuff(). In other words, it is evaluated as a single expression before the && and a single expression after the &&.

 Remember that the only legal expression in an if test is a boolean. In some languages, 0 == false, and 1 == true. Not so in Java! The following code shows if statements that might look tempting, but are illegal, followed by legal substitutions:

```
int trueInt = 1;
int falseInt = 0;
if (trueInt)              // illegal
if (trueInt == true)      // illegal
if (1)                    // illegal
if (falseInt == false)    // illegal
if (trueInt == 1)         // legal
if (falseInt == 0)        // legal
```

e x a m

w a t c h

One common mistake programmers make (and that can be difficult to spot), is assigning a boolean variable when you meant to test a boolean variable. Look out for code like the following:

```
boolean boo = false;
if (boo = true) { }
```

You might think one of three things:

1. *The code compiles and runs fine, and the* if *test fails because boo is* false.
2. *The code won't compile because you're using an assignment (=) rather than an equality test (==).*
3. *The code compiles and runs fine and the* if *test succeeds because boo is SET to* true *(rather than TESTED for* true*) in the* if *argument!*

*Well, number 3 is correct. Pointless, but correct. Given that the result of any assignment is the value of the variable after the assignment, the expression (*boo = true*) has a result of* true*. Hence, the* if *test succeeds. But the only variables that can be assigned (rather than tested against something else) are a* boolean *or a* Boolean; *all other assignments will result in something non-boolean, so they're not legal, as in the following:*

```
int x = 3;
if (x = 5) { }  // Won't compile because x is not a boolean!
```

Because if *tests require boolean expressions, you need to be really solid on both logical operators and* if *test syntax and semantics.*

switch Statements

A way to simulate the use of multiple if statements is with the switch statement. Take a look at the following if-else code, and notice how confusing it can be to have nested if tests, even just a few levels deep:

```
int x = 3;
if(x == 1) {
```

```
        System.out.println("x equals 1");
  }
  else if(x == 2) {
        System.out.println("x equals 2");
      }
    else if(x == 3) {
          System.out.println("x equals 3");
        }
        else {
          System.out.println("No idea what x is");
        }
```

Now let's see the same functionality represented in a switch construct:

```
int x - 3;
switch (x) {
   case 1:
       System.out.println("x is equal to 1");
       break;
   case 2:
       System.out.println("x is equal to 2");
       break;
   case 3:
       System.out.println("x is equal to 3");
       break;
   default:
       System.out.println("Still no idea what x is");
}
```

Note: The reason this switch statement emulates the nested ifs listed earlier is because of the break statements that were placed inside of the switch. In general, break statements are optional, and as we will see in a few pages, their inclusion or exclusion causes huge changes in how a switch statement will execute.

Legal Expressions for switch and case

The general form of the switch statement is:

```
switch (expression) {
  case constant1: code block
  case constant2: code block
  default: code block
}
```

A switch's expression must evaluate to a char, byte, short, int, or, as of Java 6, an enum. That means if you're not using an enum, only variables and values that can be automatically promoted (in other words, implicitly cast) to an int are acceptable. You won't be able to compile if you use anything else, including the remaining numeric types of long, float, and double.

A case constant must evaluate to the same type as the switch expression can use, with one additional—and big—constraint: the case constant must be a compile time constant! Since the case argument has to be resolved at compile time, that means you can use only a constant or final variable that is assigned a literal value. It is not enough to be final, it must be a compile time *constant*. For example:

```
final int a = 1;
final int b;
b = 2;
int x = 0;
switch (x) {
  case a:     // ok
  case b:     // compiler error
```

Also, the switch can only check for equality. This means that the other relational operators such as greater than are rendered unusable in a case. The following is an example of a valid expression using a method invocation in a switch statement. Note that for this code to be legal, the method being invoked on the object reference must return a value compatible with an int.

```
String s = "xyz";
switch (s.length()) {
  case 1:
    System.out.println("length is one");
    break;
  case 2:
    System.out.println("length is two");
    break;
  case 3:
    System.out.println("length is three");
    break;
  default:
    System.out.println("no match");
}
```

One other rule you might not expect involves the question, "What happens if I `switch` on a variable smaller than an `int`?" Look at the following `switch`:

```
byte g = 2;
switch(g) {
  case 23:
  case 128:
}
```

This code won't compile. Although the `switch` argument is legal—a byte is implicitly cast to an `int`—the second `case` argument (128) is too large for a `byte`, and the compiler knows it! Attempting to compile the preceding example gives you an error something like

```
Test.java:6: possible loss of precision
found    : int
required: byte
     case 128:
          ^
```

It's also illegal to have more than one `case` label using the same value. For example, the following block of code won't compile because it uses two cases with the same value of 80:

```
int temp = 90;
switch(temp) {
  case 80 :  System.out.println("80");
  case 80 :  System.out.println("80");   // won't compile!
  case 90 :  System.out.println("90");
  default :  System.out.println("default");
}
```

It *is* legal to leverage the power of boxing in a `switch` expression. For instance, the following is legal:

```
switch(new Integer(4)) {
  case 4: System.out.println("boxing is OK");
}
```

Look for any violation of the rules for switch *and* case *arguments.*
For example, you might find illegal examples like the following snippets:

```
switch(x) {
  case 0 {
    y = 7;
  }
}

switch(x) {
  0: { }
  1: { }
}
```

In the first example, the case *uses a curly brace and omits the colon.*
The second example omits the keyword case.

Break and Fall-Through in switch Blocks

We're finally ready to discuss the break statement, and more details about flow control within a switch statement. The most important thing to remember about the flow of execution through a switch statement is this:

> case **constants are evaluated from the top down, and the first** case **constant that matches the** switch's **expression is the execution** *entry point.*

In other words, once a case constant is matched, the JVM will execute the associated code block, and ALL subsequent code blocks (barring a break statement) too! The following example uses an enum in a case statement.

```
enum Color {red, green, blue}
class SwitchEnum {
  public static void main(String [] args) {
    Color c = Color.green;
    switch(c) {
```

```
      case red: System.out.print ("red ");
      case green: System.out.print ("green ");
      case blue: System.out.print ("blue ");
      default: System.out.println ("done");
    }
  }
}
```

In this example `case green:` matched, so the JVM executed that code block and all subsequent code blocks to produce the output:

```
green blue done
```

Again, when the program encounters the keyword `break` during the execution of a `switch` statement, execution will immediately move out of the `switch` block to the next statement after the `switch`. If `break` is omitted, the program just keeps executing the remaining `case` blocks until either a `break` is found or the `switch` statement ends. Examine the following code:

```
int x = 1;
switch(x) {
  case 1:  System.out.println("x is one");
  case 2:  System.out.println("x is two");
  case 3:  System.out.println("x is three");
}
System.out.println("out of the switch");
```

The code will print the following:

```
x is one
x is two
x is three
out of the switch
```

This combination occurs because the code didn't hit a `break` statement; execution just kept dropping down through each `case` until the end. This dropping down is actually called "fall-through," because of the way execution falls from one `case` to the next. Remember, the matching `case` is simply your entry point into the `switch` block! In other words, you must *not* think of it as, "Find the matching `case`, execute just that code, and get out." That's *not* how it works. If you do want that "just the matching code" behavior, you'll insert a `break` into each `case` as follows:

```
int x = 1;
switch(x) {
  case 1:  {
    System.out.println("x is one");  break;
  }
  case 2:  {
    System.out.println("x is two");  break;
  }
  case 3:  {
    System.out.println("x is two");  break;
  }
}
System.out.println("out of the switch");
```

Running the preceding code, now that we've added the break statements, will print

```
x is one
out of the switch
```

and that's it. We entered into the switch block at case 1. Because it matched the switch() argument, we got the println statement, then hit the break and jumped to the end of the switch.

An interesting example of this fall-through logic is shown in the following code:

```
int x = someNumberBetweenOneAndTen;

switch (x) {
  case 2:
  case 4:
  case 6:
  case 8:
  case 10: {
    System.out.println("x is an even number");  break;
  }
}
```

This switch statement will print x is an even number or nothing, depending on whether the number is between one and ten and is odd or even. For example, if x is 4, execution will begin at case 4, but then fall down through 6, 8, and 10, where it prints and then breaks. The break at case 10, by the way, is not needed; we're already at the end of the switch anyway.

Note: Because fall-through is less than intuitive, Sun recommends that you add a comment like: // fall through when you use fall-through logic.

The Default Case

What if, using the preceding code, you wanted to print "x is an odd number" if none of the cases (the even numbers) matched? You couldn't put it after the switch statement, or even as the last case in the switch, because in both of those situations it would always print x is an odd number. To get this behavior, you'll use the default keyword. (By the way, if you've wondered why there is a default keyword even though we don't use a modifier for default access control, now you'll see that the default keyword is used for a completely different purpose.) The only change we need to make is to add the default case to the preceding code:

```
int x = someNumberBetweenOneAndTen;

switch (x) {
  case 2:
  case 4:
  case 6:
  case 8:
  case 10: {
    System.out.println("x is an even number");
    break;
  }
  default: System.out.println("x is an odd number");
}
```

e x a m

ᗯatch

The default **case doesn't have to come at the end of the** switch. **Look for it in strange places such as the following:**

```
int x = 2;
switch (x) {
  case 2:  System.out.println("2");
  default: System.out.println("default");
  case 3: System.out.println("3");
  case 4: System.out.println("4");
}
```

exam
watch

Running the preceding code prints

```
2
default
3
4
```

And if we modify it so that the only match is the default case:

```
int x = 7;
switch (x) {
  case 2:  System.out.println("2");
  default: System.out.println("default");
  case 3: System.out.println("3");
  case 4: System.out.println("4");
}
```

Running the preceding code prints

```
default
3
4
```

The rule to remember is that default **works just like any other** case **for fall-through!**

EXERCISE 5-1

Creating a switch-case Statement

Try creating a switch statement using a char value as the case. Include a default behavior if none of the char values match.

- Make sure a char variable is declared before the switch statement.
- Each case statement should be followed by a break.
- The default case can be located at the end, middle, or top.

CERTIFICATION OBJECTIVE

Loops and Iterators (Exam Objective 2.2)

2.2   Develop code that implements all forms of loops and iterators, including the use of for, the enhanced for loop (for-each), do, while, labels, break, and continue; and explain the values taken by loop counter variables during and after loop execution.

Java loops come in three flavors: while, do, and for (and as of Java 6, the for loop has two variations). All three let you repeat a block of code as long as some condition is true, or for a specific number of iterations. You're probably familiar with loops from other languages, so even if you're somewhat new to Java, these won't be a problem to learn.

Using while Loops

The while loop is good for scenarios where you don't know how many times a block or statement should repeat, but you want to continue looping as long as some condition is true. A while statement looks like this:

```
while (expression) {
  // do stuff
}
    or

int x = 2;
while(x == 2) {
  System.out.println(x);
  ++x;
}
```

In this case, as in all loops, the expression (test) must evaluate to a boolean result. The body of the while loop will only execute if the expression (sometimes called the "condition") results in a value of true. Once inside the loop, the loop body will repeat until the condition is no longer met because it evaluates to false. In the previous example, program control will enter the loop body because x is equal to 2. However, x is incremented in the loop, so when the condition is checked again it will evaluate to false and exit the loop.

Any variables used in the expression of a `while` loop must be declared before the expression is evaluated. In other words, you can't say

```
while (int x = 2) { }   // not legal
```

Then again, why would you? Instead of testing the variable, you'd be declaring and initializing it, so it would always have the exact same value. Not much of a test condition!

The key point to remember about a `while` loop is that it might not ever run. If the test expression is `false` the first time the `while` expression is checked, the loop body will be skipped and the program will begin executing at the first statement *after* the `while` loop. Look at the following example:

```
int x = 8;
while (x > 8) {
  System.out.println("in the loop");
  x = 10;
}
System.out.println("past the loop");
```

Running this code produces

```
past the loop
```

Because the expression `(x > 8)` evaluates to `false`, none of the code within the `while` loop ever executes.

Using do Loops

The `do` loop is similar to the `while` loop, except that the expression is not evaluated until after the `do` loop's code is executed. Therefore the code in a `do` loop is guaranteed to execute at least once. The following shows a `do` loop in action:

```
do {
   System.out.println("Inside loop");
} while(false);
```

The `System.out.println()` statement will print once, even though the expression evaluates to `false`. Remember, the `do` loop will always run the code in the loop body at least once. Be sure to note the use of the semicolon at the end of the `while` expression.

Using for Loops

As of Java 6, the `for` loop took on a second structure. We'll call the old style of `for` loop the "basic `for` loop", and we'll call the new style of `for` loop the "enhanced `for` loop" (even though the Sun objective 2.2 refers to it as the `for-each`). Depending on what documentation you use (Sun's included), you'll see both terms, along with `for-in`. The terms `for-in`, `for each`, and "enhanced `for`" all refer to the same Java construct.

The basic `for` loop is more flexible than the enhanced `for` loop, but the enhanced `for` loop was designed to make iterating through arrays and collections easier to code.

The Basic for Loop

The `for` loop is especially useful for flow control when you already know how many times you need to execute the statements in the loop's block. The `for` loop declaration has three main parts, besides the body of the loop:

- Declaration and initialization of variables
- The `boolean` expression (conditional test)
- The iteration expression

The three `for` declaration parts are separated by semicolons. The following two examples demonstrate the `for` loop. The first example shows the parts of a `for` loop in a pseudocode form, and the second shows a typical example of a `for` loop.

```
for (/*Initialization*/ ; /*Condition*/ ;  /* Iteration */) {
  /* loop body */
}

for (int i = 0; i<10; i++) {
  System.out.println("i is " + i);
}
```

The Basic for Loop: Declaration and Initialization

The first part of the `for` statement lets you declare and initialize zero, one, or multiple variables of the same type inside the parentheses after the `for` keyword. If you declare more than one variable of the same type, then you'll need to separate them with commas as follows:

```
for (int x = 10, y = 3; y > 3; y++) { }
```

The declaration and initialization happens before anything else in a `for` loop. And whereas the other two parts—the boolean test and the iteration expression—will run with each iteration of the loop, the declaration and initialization happens just once, at the very beginning. You also must know that the scope of variables declared in the `for` loop ends with the `for` loop! The following demonstrates this:

```
for (int x = 1; x < 2; x++) {
  System.out.println(x);  // Legal
}
System.out.println(x);  // Not Legal! x is now out of scope
                        // and can't be accessed.
```

If you try to compile this, you'll get something like this:

```
Test.java:19: cannot resolve symbol
symbol  : variable x
location: class Test
  System.out.println(x);
                     ^
```

Basic for Loop: Conditional (boolean) Expression

The next section that executes is the conditional expression, which (like all other conditional tests) must evaluate to a `boolean` value. You can have only one logical expression, but it can be very complex. Look out for code that uses logical expressions like this:

```
for (int x = 0; ((((x < 10) && (y-- > 2)) | x == 3)); x++) { }
```

The preceding code is legal, but the following is not:

```
for (int x = 0; (x > 5), (y < 2); x++) { } // too many
                                           //expressions
```

The compiler will let you know the problem:

```
TestLong.java:20: ';' expected
for (int x = 0; (x > 5), (y < 2); x++) { }
                       ^
```

The rule to remember is this: *You can have only one test expression.*

In other words, you can't use multiple tests separated by commas, even though the other two parts of a for statement can have multiple parts.

Basic for Loop: Iteration Expression

After each execution of the body of the for loop, the iteration expression is executed. This is where you get to say what you want to happen with each iteration of the loop. Remember that it always happens after the loop body runs! Look at the following:

```
for (int x = 0; x < 1; x++) {
   // body code that doesn't change the value of x
}
```

The preceding loop executes just once. The first time into the loop x is set to 0, then x is tested to see if it's less than 1 (which it is), and then the body of the loop executes. After the body of the loop runs, the iteration expression runs, incrementing x by 1. Next, the conditional test is checked, and since the result is now false, execution jumps to below the for loop and continues on.

Keep in mind that barring a forced exit, evaluating the iteration expression and then evaluating the conditional expression are always the last two things that happen in a for loop!

Examples of forced exits include a `break`, a `return`, a `System.exit()`, or an exception, which will all cause a loop to terminate abruptly, without running the iteration expression. Look at the following code:

```
static boolean doStuff() {
  for (int x = 0; x < 3; x++) {
    System.out.println("in for loop");
    return true;
  }
  return true;
}
```

Running this code produces

```
in for loop
```

The statement only prints once, because a return causes execution to leave not just the current iteration of a loop, but the entire method. So the iteration expression never runs in that case. Table 5-1 lists the causes and results of abrupt loop termination.

TABLE 5-1	Causes of Early Loop Termination

Code in Loop	What Happens
break	Execution jumps immediately to the 1st statement after the `for` loop.
return	Execution jumps immediately back to the calling method.
System.exit()	All program execution stops; the VM shuts down.

Basic for Loop: for Loop Issues

None of the three sections of the `for` declaration are required! The following example is perfectly legal (although not necessarily good practice):

```
for( ; ; ) {
  System.out.println("Inside an endless loop");
}
```

In the preceding example, all the declaration parts are left out so the `for` loop will act like an endless loop. For the exam, it's important to know that with the absence of the initialization and increment sections, the loop will act like a `while` loop. The following example demonstrates how this is accomplished:

```
int i = 0;

for (;i<10;) {
  i++;
  //do some other work
}
```

The next example demonstrates a `for` loop with multiple variables in play. A comma separates the variables, and they must be of the same type. Remember that the variables declared in the `for` statement are all local to the `for` loop, and can't be used outside the scope of the loop.

```
for (int i = 0,j = 0; (i<10) && (j<10); i++, j++) {
  System.out.println("i is " + i + " j is " +j);
}
```

e x a m
ⓦatch

Variable scope plays a large role in the exam. You need to know that a variable declared in the `for` *loop can't be used beyond the* `for` *loop. But a variable only initialized in the* `for` *statement (but declared earlier) can be used beyond the loop. For example, the following is legal,*

```
int x = 3;
for (x = 12; x < 20; x++) { }
System.out.println(x);
```

while this is not

```
for (int x = 3; x < 20; x++) { } System.out.println(x);
```

The last thing to note is that all three sections of the `for` loop are independent of each other. The three expressions in the `for` statement don't need to operate on the same variables, although they typically do. But even the iterator expression, which many mistakenly call the "increment expression," doesn't need to increment or set anything; you can put in virtually any arbitrary code statements that you want to happen with each iteration of the loop. Look at the following:

```
int b = 3;
for (int a = 1;  b != 1; System.out.println("iterate")) {
  b = b - a;
}
```

The preceding code prints

```
iterate
iterate
```

e**x**a m

ⓦ a t c h   *Many questions in the new (Java 6) exam list "Compilation fails" and "An exception occurs at runtime" as possible answers. This makes it more difficult because you can't simply work through the behavior of the code. You must first make sure the code isn't violating any fundamental rules that will lead to compiler error, and then look for possible exceptions. Only after you've satisfied those two, should you dig into the logic and flow of the code in the question.*

The Enhanced for Loop (for Arrays)

The enhanced `for` loop, new to Java 6, is a specialized `for` loop that simplifies looping through an array or a collection. In this chapter we're going to focus on using the enhanced `for` to loop through arrays. In Chapter 7 we'll revisit the enhanced `for` as we discuss collections—where the enhanced `for` really comes into its own.

Instead of having *three* components, the enhanced `for` has *two*. Let's loop through an array the basic (old) way, and then using the enhanced `for`:

```
int [] a = {1,2,3,4};
for(int x = 0; x < a.length; x++)     // basic for loop
  System.out.print(a[x]);
for(int n : a)                        // enhanced for loop
  System.out.print(n);
```

Which produces this output:

```
12341234
```

More formally, let's describe the enhanced `for` as follows:

```
for(declaration : expression)
```

The two pieces of the `for` statement are

- **declaration**   The *newly declared* block variable, of a type compatible with the elements of the array you are accessing. This variable will be available within the `for` block, and its value will be the same as the current array element.
- **expression**   This must evaluate to the array you want to loop through. This could be an array variable or a method call that returns an array. The array can be any type: primitives, objects, even arrays of arrays.

Using the above definitions, let's look at some legal and illegal enhanced `for` declarations:

```
int x;
long x2;
Long [] La = {4L, 5L, 6L};
long [] la = {7L, 8L, 9L};
int [] [] twoDee = {{1,2,3}, {4,5,6}, {7,8,9}};
String [] sNums = {"one", "two", "three"};
Animal [] animals = {new Dog(), new Cat()};

// legal 'for' declarations
for(long y : la ) ;         // loop thru an array of longs
for(long lp : La) ;         // autoboxing the Long objects
                            // into longs
for(int[] n : twoDee) ;     // loop thru the array of arrays
for(int n2 : twoDee[2]) ;   // loop thru the 3rd sub-array
for(String s : sNums) ;     // loop thru the array of Strings
for(Object o : sNums) ;     // set an Object reference to
                            // each String
for(Animal a : animals) ;   // set an Animal reference to each
                            // element
```

```
// ILLEGAL 'for' declarations
for(x2 : la) ;            // x2 is already declared
for(int x2 : twoDee) ;    // can't stuff an array into an int
for(int x3 : la) ;        // can't stuff a long into an int
for(Dog d : animals) ;    // you might get a Cat!
```

The enhanced `for` loop assumes that, barring an early exit from the loop, you'll always loop through every element of the array. The following discussions of `break` and `continue` apply to both the basic and enhanced `for` loops.

Using break and continue

The `break` and `continue` keywords are used to stop either the entire loop (`break`) or just the current iteration (`continue`). Typically if you're using `break` or `continue`, you'll do an `if` test within the loop, and if some condition becomes `true` (or `false` depending on the program), you want to get out immediately. The difference between them is whether or not you continue with a new iteration or jump to the first statement below the loop and continue from there.

The `break` statement causes the program to stop execution of the innermost loop and start processing the next line of code after the block.

The `continue` statement causes only the current iteration of the innermost loop to cease and the next iteration of the same loop to start if the condition of the loop is met. When using a `continue` statement with a `for` loop, you need to consider the effects that `continue` has on the loop iteration. Examine the following code:

```
for (int i = 0; i < 10; i++) {
  System.out.println("Inside loop");
  continue;
}
```

The question is, is this an endless loop? The answer is no. When the `continue` statement is hit, the iteration expression still runs! It runs just as though the current iteration ended "in the natural way." So in the preceding example, i will still increment before the condition (i < 10) is checked again. Most of the time, a continue is used within an if test as follows:

```
for (int i = 0; i < 10; i++) {
  System.out.println("Inside loop");
  if (foo.doStuff() == 5) {
    continue;
  }
  // more loop code, that won't be reached when the above if
  // test is true
}
```

Unlabeled Statements

Both the break statement and the continue statement can be unlabeled or labeled. Although it's far more common to use break and continue unlabeled, the exam expects you to know how labeled break and continue statements work. As stated before, a break statement (unlabeled) will exit out of the innermost looping construct and proceed with the next line of code beyond the loop block. The following example demonstrates a break statement:

```
boolean problem = true;
while (true) {
  if (problem) {
    System.out.println("There was a problem");
    break;
  }
}
// next line of code
```

In the previous example, the break statement is unlabeled. The following is an example of an unlabeled continue statement:

```
while (!EOF) {
  //read a field from a file
  if (wrongField) {
    continue;    // move to the next field in the file
  }
  // otherwise do other stuff with the field
}
```

In this example, a file is being read one field at a time. When an error is encountered, the program moves to the next field in the file and uses the `continue` statement to go back into the loop (if it is not at the end of the file) and keeps reading the various fields. If the `break` command were used instead, the code would stop reading the file once the error occurred and move on to the next line of code after the loop. The `continue` statement gives you a way to say, "This particular iteration of the loop needs to stop, but not the whole loop itself. I just don't want the rest of the code in this iteration to finish, so do the iteration expression and then start over with the test, and don't worry about what was below the `continue` statement."

Labeled Statements

Although many statements in a Java program can be labeled, it's most common to use labels with loop statements like `for` or `while`, in conjunction with `break` and `continue` statements. A label statement must be placed just before the statement being labeled, and it consists of a valid identifier that ends with a colon (:).

You need to understand the difference between labeled and unlabeled `break` and `continue`. The labeled varieties are needed only in situations where you have a nested loop, and need to indicate which of the nested loops you want to break from, or from which of the nested loops you want to continue with the next iteration. A `break` statement will exit out of the labeled loop, as opposed to the innermost loop, if the `break` keyword is combined with a label. An example of what a label looks like is in the following code:

```
foo:
  for (int x = 3; x < 20; x++) {
    while(y > 7) {
      y--;
    }
  }
```

The label must adhere to the rules for a valid variable name and should adhere to the Java naming convention. The syntax for the use of a label name in conjunction with a `break` statement is the `break` keyword, then the label name, followed by a semicolon. A more complete example of the use of a labeled `break` statement is as follows:

```
boolean isTrue = true;
outer:
  for(int i=0; i<5; i++) {
    while (isTrue) {
```

```
      System.out.println("Hello");
      break outer;
   } // end of inner while loop
   System.out.println("Outer loop."); // Won't print
 } // end of outer for loop
System.out.println("Good-Bye");
```

Running this code produces

```
Hello
Good-Bye
```

In this example the word Hello will be printed one time. Then, the labeled break statement will be executed, and the flow will exit out of the loop labeled outer. The next line of code will then print out Good-Bye. Let's see what will happen if the continue statement is used instead of the break statement. The following code example is similar to the preceding one, with the exception of substituting continue for break:

```
outer:
  for (int i=0; i<5; i++) {
    for (int j=0; j<5; j++) {
      System.out.println("Hello");
      continue outer;
    } // end of inner loop
    System.out.println("outer"); // Never prints
  }
System.out.println("Good-Bye");
```

Running this code produces

```
Hello
Hello
Hello
Hello
Hello
Good-Bye
```

In this example, Hello will be printed five times. After the continue statement is executed, the flow continues with the next iteration of the loop identified with the label. Finally, when the condition in the outer loop evaluates to false, this loop will finish and Good-Bye will be printed.

EXERCISE 5-2

Creating a Labeled while Loop

Try creating a labeled while loop. Make the label outer and provide a condition to check whether a variable age is less than or equal to 21. Within the loop, increment age by one. Every time the program goes through the loop, check whether age is 16. If it is, print the message "get your driver's license" and continue to the outer loop. If not, print "Another year."

■ The outer label should appear just before the while loop begins.

■ Make sure age is declared outside of the while loop.

watch

Labeled continue *and* break *statements must be inside the loop that has the same label name; otherwise, the code will not compile.*

CERTIFICATION OBJECTIVE

Handling Exceptions (Exam Objectives 2.4 and 2.5)

2.4   Develop code that makes use of exceptions and exception handling clauses (try, catch, finally), and declares methods and overriding methods that throw exceptions.

2.5   Recognize the effect of an exception arising at a specific point in a code fragment. Note that the exception may be a runtime exception, a checked exception, or an error.

An old maxim in software development says that 80 percent of the work is used 20 percent of the time. The 80 percent refers to the effort required to check and handle errors. In many languages, writing program code that checks for and deals with errors is tedious and bloats the application source into confusing spaghetti.

Still, error detection and handling may be the most important ingredient of any robust application. Java arms developers with an elegant mechanism for handling errors that produces efficient and organized error-handling code: exception handling.

Exception handling allows developers to detect errors easily without writing special code to test return values. Even better, it lets us keep exception-*handling* code cleanly separated from the exception-*generating* code. It also lets us use the same exception-handling code to deal with a range of possible exceptions.

The exam has three objectives covering exception handling. We'll cover the first two in this section, and in the next section we'll cover those aspects of exception handling that are new to the exam as of Java 6.

Catching an Exception Using try and catch

Before we begin, let's introduce some terminology. The term "exception" means "exceptional condition" and is an occurrence that alters the normal program flow. A bunch of things can lead to exceptions, including hardware failures, resource exhaustion, and good old bugs. When an exceptional event occurs in Java, an exception is said to be "thrown." The code that's responsible for doing something about the exception is called an "exception handler," and it "catches" the thrown exception.

Exception handling works by transferring the execution of a program to an appropriate exception handler when an exception occurs. For example, if you call a method that opens a file but the file cannot be opened, execution of that method will stop, and code that you wrote to deal with this situation will be run. Therefore, we need a way to tell the JVM what code to execute when a certain exception happens. To do this, we use the `try` and `catch` keywords. The `try` is used to define a block of code in which exceptions may occur. This block of code is called a guarded region (which really means "risky code goes here"). One or more `catch` clauses match a specific exception (or group of exceptions—more on that later) to a block of code that handles it. Here's how it looks in pseudocode:

```
1. try {
2.    // This is the first line of the "guarded region"
3.    // that is governed by the try keyword.
4.    // Put code here that might cause some kind of exception.
5.    // We may have many code lines here or just one.
6. }
7. catch(MyFirstException) {
8.    // Put code here that handles this exception.
```

```
9.    // This is the next line of the exception handler.
10.   // This is the last line of the exception handler.
11. }
12. catch(MySecondException) {
13.   // Put code here that handles this exception
14. }
15.
16. // Some other unguarded (normal, non-risky) code begins here
```

In this pseudocode example, lines 2 through 5 constitute the guarded region that is governed by the `try` clause. Line 7 is an exception handler for an exception of type MyFirstException. Line 12 is an exception handler for an exception of type MySecondException. Notice that the `catch` blocks immediately follow the `try` block. This is a requirement; if you have one or more `catch` blocks, they must immediately follow the `try` block. Additionally, the `catch` blocks must all follow each other, without any other statements or blocks in between. Also, the order in which the `catch` blocks appear matters, as we'll see a little later.

Execution of the guarded region starts at line 2. If the program executes all the way past line 5 with no exceptions being thrown, execution will transfer to line 15 and continue downward. However, if at any time in lines 2 through 5 (the `try` block) an exception is thrown of type MyFirstException, execution will immediately transfer to line 7. Lines 8 through 10 will then be executed so that the entire `catch` block runs, and then execution will transfer to line 15 and continue.

Note that if an exception occurred on, say, line 3 of the `try` block, the rest of the lines in the `try` block (4 and 5) would never be executed. Once control jumps to the `catch` block, it never returns to complete the balance of the `try` block. This is exactly what you want, though. Imagine your code looks something like this pseudocode:

```
try {
  getTheFileFromOverNetwork
  readFromTheFileAndPopulateTable
}
catch(CantGetFileFromNetwork) {
  displayNetworkErrorMessage
}
```

The preceding pseudocode demonstrates how you typically work with exceptions. Code that's dependent on a risky operation (as populating a table with file data is dependent on getting the file from the network) is grouped into a `try` block in such a way that if, say, the first operation fails, you won't continue trying to run other code that's also guaranteed to fail. In the pseudocode example, you won't be able to read from the file if you can't get the file off the network in the first place.

One of the benefits of using exception handling is that code to handle any particular exception that may occur in the governed region needs to be written only once. Returning to our earlier code example, there may be three different places in our try block that can generate a MyFirstException, but wherever it occurs it will be handled by the same catch block (on line 7). We'll discuss more benefits of exception handling near the end of this chapter.

Using finally

Although try and catch provide a terrific mechanism for trapping and handling exceptions, we are left with the problem of how to clean up after ourselves if an exception occurs. Because execution transfers out of the try block as soon as an exception is thrown, we can't put our cleanup code at the bottom of the try block and expect it to be executed if an exception occurs. Almost as bad an idea would be placing our cleanup code in each of the catch blocks—let's see why.

Exception handlers are a poor place to clean up after the code in the try block because each handler then requires its own copy of the cleanup code. If, for example, you allocated a network socket or opened a file somewhere in the guarded region, each exception handler would have to close the file or release the socket. That would make it too easy to forget to do cleanup, and also lead to a lot of redundant code. To address this problem, Java offers the finally block.

A finally block encloses code that is always executed at some point after the try block, whether an exception was thrown or not. Even if there is a return statement in the try block, the finally block executes right after the return statement is encountered, and before the return executes!

This is the right place to close your files, release your network sockets, and perform any other cleanup your code requires. If the try block executes with no exceptions, the finally block is executed immediately after the try block completes. If there was an exception thrown, the finally block executes immediately after the proper catch block completes. Let's look at another pseudocode example:

```
1: try {
2:    // This is the first line of the "guarded region".
3: }
4: catch(MyFirstException) {
```

```
 5:    // Put code here that handles this exception
 6: }
 7: catch(MySecondException) {
 8:    // Put code here that handles this exception
 9: }
10: finally {
11:    // Put code here to release any resource we
12:    // allocated in the try clause.
13: }
14:
15: // More code here
```

As before, execution starts at the first line of the `try` block, line 2. If there are no exceptions thrown in the `try` block, execution transfers to line 11, the first line of the `finally` block. On the other hand, if a `MySecondException` is thrown while the code in the `try` block is executing, execution transfers to the first line of that exception handler, line 8 in the `catch` clause. After all the code in the `catch` clause is executed, the program moves to line 11, the first line of the `finally` clause. Repeat after me: `finally` always runs! OK, we'll have to refine that a little, but for now, start burning in the idea that `finally` always runs. If an exception is thrown, `finally` runs. If an exception is not thrown, `finally` runs. If the exception is caught, `finally` runs. If the exception is not caught, `finally` runs. Later we'll look at the few scenarios in which `finally` might not run or complete.

Remember, `finally` clauses are not required. If you don't write one, your code will compile and run just fine. In fact, if you have no resources to clean up after your `try` block completes, you probably don't need a `finally` clause. Also, because the compiler doesn't even require `catch` clauses, sometimes you'll run across code that has a `try` block immediately followed by a `finally` block. Such code is useful when the exception is going to be passed back to the calling method, as explained in the next section. Using a `finally` block allows the cleanup code to execute even when there isn't a `catch` clause.

The following legal code demonstrates a `try` with a `finally` but no `catch`:

```
try {
  // do stuff
} finally {
  //clean up
}
```

The following legal code demonstrates a try, catch, and finally:

```
try {
  // do stuff
} catch (SomeException ex) {
  // do exception handling
} finally {
  // clean up
}
```

The following ILLEGAL code demonstrates a try without a catch or finally:

```
try {
  // do stuff
}
// need a catch or finally here
System.out.println("out of try block");
```

The following ILLEGAL code demonstrates a misplaced catch block:

```
try {
  // do stuff
}
// can't have code between try/catch
System.out.println("out of try block");
catch(Exception ex) { }
```

e x a m
ⓦ a t c h

You can't sneak any code in between the try, catch, *or* finally *blocks.*
The following won't compile:

```
try {
  // do stuff
}
System.out.print("below the try");   //Illegal!
catch(Exception ex) { }
```

Propagating Uncaught Exceptions

Why aren't catch clauses required? What happens to an exception that's thrown in a try block when there is no catch clause waiting for it? Actually, there's no requirement that you code a catch clause for every possible exception that could be thrown from the corresponding try block. In fact, it's doubtful that you could accomplish such a feat! If a method doesn't provide a catch clause for a particular exception, that method is said to be "ducking" the exception (or "passing the buck").

So what happens to a ducked exception? Before we discuss that, we need to briefly review the concept of the call stack. Most languages have the concept of a method stack or a call stack. Simply put, the call stack is the chain of methods that your program executes to get to the current method. If your program starts in method main() and main() calls method a(), which calls method b(), which in turn calls method c(), the call stack consists of the following:

```
c
b
a
main
```

We will represent the stack as growing upward (although it can also be visualized as growing downward). As you can see, the last method called is at the top of the stack, while the first calling method is at the bottom. The method at the very top of the stack trace would be the method you were currently executing. If we move back down the call stack, we're moving from the current method to the previously called method. Figure 5-1 illustrates a way to think about how the call stack in Java works.

FIGURE 5-1

The Java method
call stack

1) The call stack while method3() is running.

4	method3()	method2 invokes method3
3	method2()	method1 invokes method2
2	method1()	main invokes method1
1	main()	main begins

The order in which methods are put on the call stack

2) The call stack after method3() completes
Execution returns to method2()

1	method2()	method2() will complete
2	method1()	method1() will complete
3	main()	main() will complete and the JVM will exit

The order in which methods complete

Now let's examine what happens to ducked exceptions. Imagine a building, say, five stories high, and at each floor there is a deck or balcony. Now imagine that on each deck, one person is standing holding a baseball mitt. Exceptions are like balls dropped from person to person, starting from the roof. An exception is first thrown from the top of the stack (in other words, the person on the roof), and if it isn't caught by the same person who threw it (the person on the roof), it drops down the call stack to the previous method, which is the person standing on the deck one floor down. If not caught there, by the person one floor down, the exception/ball again drops down to the previous method (person on the next floor down), and so on until it is caught or until it reaches the very bottom of the call stack. This is called exception propagation.

If an exception reaches the bottom of the call stack, it's like reaching the bottom of a very long drop; the ball explodes, and so does your program. An exception that's never caught will cause your application to stop running. A description (if one is available) of the exception will be displayed, and the call stack will be "dumped." This helps you debug your application by telling you what exception was thrown, from what method it was thrown, and what the stack looked like at the time.

exam
ⓦatch

You can keep throwing an exception down through the methods on the stack. But what about when you get to the main() *method at the bottom? You can throw the exception out of* main() *as well. This results in the Java Virtual Machine (JVM) halting, and the stack trace will be printed to the output.*

The following code throws an exception,

```
class TestEx {
  public static void main (String [] args) {
    doStuff();
  }
  static void doStuff() {
    doMoreStuff();
  }
  static void doMoreStuff() {
    int x = 5/0;   // Can't divide by zero!
                   // ArithmeticException is thrown here
  }
}
```

which prints out a stack trace something like,

```
%java TestEx
Exception in thread "main" java.lang.ArithmeticException: /
by zero
at TestEx.doMoreStuff(TestEx.java:10)
at TestEx.doStuff(TestEx.java:7)
at TestEx.main(TestEx.java:3)
```

EXERCISE 5-3

Propagating and Catching an Exception

In this exercise you're going to create two methods that deal with exceptions. One of the methods is the main() method, which will call another method. If an exception is thrown in the other method, main() must deal with it. A finally statement will be included to indicate that the program has completed. The method that main()

will call will be named `reverse`, and it will reverse the order of the characters in a String. If the String contains no characters, `reverse` will propagate an exception up to the `main()` method.

- Create a class called `Propagate` and a `main()` method, which will remain empty for now.
- Create a method called `reverse`. It takes an argument of a `String` and returns a `String`.
- In `reverse`, check if the `String` has a length of 0 by using the `String.length()` method. If the length is 0, the `reverse` method will throw an exception.
- Now include the code to reverse the order of the `String`. Because this isn't the main topic of this chapter, the reversal code has been provided, but feel free to try it on your own.

```
String reverseStr = "";
for(int i=s.length()-1;i>=0;--i) {
  reverseStr += s.charAt(i);
}
return reverseStr;
```

- Now in the `main()` method you will attempt to call this method and deal with any potential exceptions. Additionally, you will include a `finally` statement that displays when `main()` has finished.

Defining Exceptions

We have been discussing exceptions as a concept. We know that they are thrown when a problem of some type happens, and we know what effect they have on the flow of our program. In this section we will develop the concepts further and use exceptions in functional Java code. Earlier we said that an exception is an occurrence that alters the normal program flow. But because this is Java, anything that's not a primitive must be...an object. Exceptions are no, well, exception to this rule. Every exception is an instance of a class that has class `Exception` in its inheritance hierarchy. In other words, exceptions are always some subclass of `java.lang.Exception`.

When an exception is thrown, an object of a particular Exception subtype is instantiated and handed to the exception handler as an argument to the catch clause. An actual catch clause looks like this:

```
try {
    // some code here
}
catch (ArrayIndexOutOfBoundsException e) {
    e.printStackTrace();
}
```

In this example, e is an instance of the ArrayIndexOutOfBoundsException class. As with any other object, you can call its methods.

Exception Hierarchy

All exception classes are subtypes of class Exception. This class derives from the class Throwable (which derives from the class Object). Figure 5-2 shows the hierarchy for the exception classes.

Exception class
hierarchy

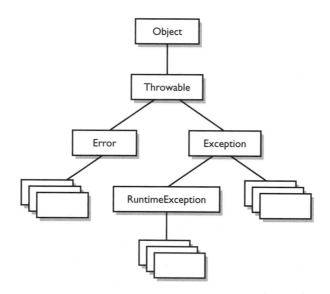

As you can see, there are two subclasses that derive from Throwable: Exception and Error. Classes that derive from Error represent unusual situations that are not caused by program errors, and indicate things that would not normally happen during program execution, such as the JVM running out of memory. Generally, your application won't be able to recover from an `Error`, so you're not required to handle them. If your code does not handle them (and it usually won't), it will still compile with no trouble. Although often thought of as exceptional conditions, Errors are technically not exceptions because they do not derive from class `Exception`.

In general, an exception represents something that happens not as a result of a programming error, but rather because some resource is not available or some other condition required for correct execution is not present. For example, if your application is supposed to communicate with another application or computer that is not answering, this is an exception that is not caused by a bug. Figure 5-2 also shows a subtype of `Exception` called `RuntimeException`. These exceptions are a special case because they sometimes do indicate program errors. They can also represent rare, difficult-to-handle exceptional conditions. Runtime exceptions are discussed in greater detail later in this chapter.

Java provides many exception classes, most of which have quite descriptive names. There are two ways to get information about an exception. The first is from the type of the exception itself. The next is from information that you can get from the exception object. Class `Throwable` (at the top of the inheritance tree for exceptions) provides its descendants with some methods that are useful in exception handlers. One of these is `printStackTrace()`. As expected, if you call an exception object's `printStackTrace()` method, as in the earlier example, a stack trace from where the exception occurred will be printed.

We discussed that a call stack builds upward with the most recently called method at the top. You will notice that the `printStackTrace()` method prints the most recently entered method first and continues down, printing the name of each method as it works its way down the call stack (this is called unwinding the stack) from the top.

Handling an Entire Class Hierarchy of Exceptions

We've discussed that the catch keyword allows you to specify a particular type of exception to catch. You can actually catch more than one type of exception in a single catch clause. If the exception class that you specify in the catch clause has no subclasses, then only the specified class of exception will be caught. However, if the class specified in the catch clause does have subclasses, any exception object that subclasses the specified class will be caught as well.

For example, class IndexOutOfBoundsException has two subclasses, ArrayIndexOutOfBoundsException and StringIndexOutOfBoundsException. You may want to write one exception handler that deals with exceptions produced by either type of boundary error, but you might not be concerned with which exception you actually have. In this case, you could write a catch clause like the following:

```
try {
  // Some code here that can throw a boundary exception
}
catch (IndexOutOfBoundsException e) {
  e.printStackTrace();
}
```

If any code in the try block throws ArrayIndexOutOfBoundsException or StringIndexOutOfBoundsException, the exception will be caught and handled. This can be convenient, but it should be used sparingly. By specifying an exception class's superclass in your catch clause, you're discarding valuable information about the exception. You can, of course, find out exactly what exception class you have, but if you're going to do that, you're better off writing a separate catch clause for each exception type of interest.

on the Job

Resist the temptation to write a single catchall exception handler such as the following:

```
try {
  // some code
}
catch (Exception e) {
  e.printStackTrace();
}
```

This code will catch every exception generated. Of course, no single exception handler can properly handle every exception, and programming in this way defeats the design objective. Exception handlers that trap many errors at once will probably reduce the reliability of your program because it's likely that an exception will be caught that the handler does not know how to handle.

Exception Matching

If you have an exception hierarchy composed of a superclass exception and a number of subtypes, and you're interested in handling one of the subtypes in a special way but want to handle all the rest together, you need write only two catch clauses.

When an exception is thrown, Java will try to find (by looking at the available catch clauses from the top down) a catch clause for the exception type. If it doesn't find one, it will search for a handler for a supertype of the exception. If it does not find a catch clause that matches a supertype for the exception, then the exception is propagated down the call stack. This process is called exception matching. Let's look at an example:

```
1:  import java.io.*;
2:  public class ReadData {
3:    public static void main(String args[]) {
4:      try {
5:        RandomAccessFile raf =
6:          new RandomAccessFile("myfile.txt", "r");
7:        byte b[] = new byte[1000];
8:        raf.readFully(b, 0, 1000);
9:      }
10:     catch(FileNotFoundException e) {
11:       System.err.println("File not found");
12:       System.err.println(e.getMessage());
13:       e.printStackTrace();
14:     }
15:     catch(IOException e) {
16:       System.err.println("IO Error");
17:       System.err.println(e.toString());
18:       e.printStackTrace();
19:     }
20:   }
21: }
```

This short program attempts to open a file and to read some data from it. Opening and reading files can generate many exceptions, most of which are some type of IOException. Imagine that in this program we're interested in knowing only whether the exact exception is a FileNotFoundException. Otherwise, we don't care exactly what the problem is.

FileNotFoundException is a subclass of IOException. Therefore, we could handle it in the catch clause that catches all subtypes of IOException, but then we would have to test the exception to determine whether it was a FileNotFoundException. Instead, we coded a special exception handler for the FileNotFoundException and a separate exception handler for all other IOException subtypes.

If this code generates a FileNotFoundException, it will be handled by the catch clause that begins at line 10. If it generates another IOException—perhaps EOFException, which is a subclass of IOException—it will be handled by the catch clause that begins at line 15. If some other exception is generated, such as a runtime exception of some type, neither catch clause will be executed and the exception will be propagated down the call stack.

Notice that the catch clause for the FileNotFoundException was placed above the handler for the IOException. This is really important! If we do it the opposite way, the program will not compile. The handlers for the most specific exceptions must always be placed above those for more general exceptions. The following will not compile:

```
try {
  // do risky IO things
} catch (IOException e) {
  // handle general IOExceptions
} catch (FileNotFoundException ex) {
  // handle just FileNotFoundException
}
```

You'll get a compiler error something like this:

```
TestEx.java:15: exception java.io.FileNotFoundException has
 already been caught
} catch (FileNotFoundException ex) {
  ^
```

If you think back to the people with baseball mitts (in the section "Propagating Uncaught Exceptions"), imagine that the most general mitts are the largest, and can thus catch many different kinds of balls. An IOException mitt is large enough and flexible enough to catch any type of IOException. So if the person on the fifth floor (say, Fred) has a big 'ol IOException mitt, he can't help but catch a FileNotFoundException ball with it. And if the guy (say, Jimmy) on the second floor is holding a FileNotFoundException mitt, that FileNotFoundException ball will never get to him, since it will always be stopped by Fred on the fifth floor, standing there with his big-enough-for-any-IOException mitt.

So what do you do with exceptions that are siblings in the class hierarchy? If one Exception class is not a subtype or supertype of the other, then the order in which the catch clauses are placed doesn't matter.

Exception Declaration and the Public Interface

So, how do we know that some method throws an exception that we have to catch? Just as a method must specify what type and how many arguments it accepts and what is returned, the exceptions that a method can throw must be *declared* (unless the exceptions are subclasses of RuntimeException). The list of thrown exceptions is part of a method's public interface. The throws keyword is used as follows to list the exceptions that a method can throw:

```
void myFunction() throws MyException1, MyException2 {
  // code for the method here
}
```

This method has a void return type, accepts no arguments, and declares that it can throw one of two types of exceptions: either type MyException1 or type MyException2. (Just because the method declares that it throws an exception doesn't mean it always will. It just tells the world that it might.)

Suppose your method doesn't directly throw an exception, but calls a method that does. You can choose not to handle the exception yourself and instead just declare it, as though it were your method that actually throws the exception. If you do declare the exception that your method might get from another method, and you don't provide a try/catch for it, then the method will propagate back to the method that called your method, and either be caught there or continue on to be handled by a method further down the stack.

Any method that might throw an exception (unless it's a subclass of RuntimeException) must declare the exception. That includes methods that aren't actually throwing it directly, but are "ducking" and letting the exception pass down to the next method in the stack. If you "duck" an exception, it is just as if you were the one actually throwing the exception. RuntimeException subclasses are exempt, so the compiler won't check to see if you've declared them. But all non-`RuntimeExceptions` are considered "checked" exceptions, because the compiler checks to be certain you've acknowledged that "bad things could happen here." Remember this:

Each method must either handle all checked exceptions by supplying a `catch` *clause or list each unhandled checked exception as a thrown exception.*

This rule is referred to as Java's "handle or declare" requirement. (Sometimes called "catch or declare.")

exam
watch

Look for code that invokes a method declaring an exception, where the calling method doesn't handle or declare the checked exception. The following code (which uses the `throw` keyword to throw an exception manually—more on this next) has two big problems that the compiler will prevent:

```
void doStuff() {
  doMore();
}
void doMore() {
  throw new IOException();
}
```

First, the `doMore()` method throws a checked exception, but does not declare it! But suppose we fix the `doMore()` method as follows:

```
void doMore() throws IOException { ... }
```

The `doStuff()` method is still in trouble because it, too, must declare the `IOException`, unless it handles it by providing a `try/catch`, with a `catch` clause that can take an `IOException`.

Again, some exceptions are exempt from this rule. An object of type RuntimeException may be thrown from any method without being specified as part of the method's public interface (and a handler need not be present). And even if a method does declare a RuntimeException, the calling method is under no obligation to handle or declare it. RuntimeException, Error, and all of their subtypes are unchecked exceptions and unchecked exceptions do not have to be specified or handled. Here is an example:

```
import java.io.*;
class Test {
  public int myMethod1() throws EOFException {
    return myMethod2();
  }
  public int myMethod2() throws EOFException {
    // code that actually could throw the exception goes here
    return 1;
  }
}
```

Let's look at myMethod1(). Because EOFException subclasses IOException and IOException subclasses Exception, it is a checked exception and must be declared as an exception that may be thrown by this method. But where will the exception actually come from? The public interface for method myMethod2() called here declares that an exception of this type can be thrown. Whether that method actually throws the exception itself or calls another method that throws it is unimportant to us; we simply know that we have to either catch the exception or declare that we throw it. The method myMethod1() does not catch the exception, so it declares that it throws it. Now let's look at another legal example, myMethod3().

```
public void myMethod3() {
  // code that could throw a NullPointerException goes here
}
```

According to the comment, this method can throw a NullPointerException. Because RuntimeException is the superclass of NullPointerException, it is an unchecked exception and need not be declared. We can see that myMethod3() does not declare any exceptions.

Runtime exceptions are referred to as *unchecked* exceptions. All other exceptions are *checked* exceptions, and they don't derive from java.lang.RuntimeException. A checked exception must be caught somewhere in your code. If you invoke a method that throws a checked exception but you don't catch the checked exception somewhere, your code will not compile. That's why they're called checked exceptions; the compiler checks to make sure that they're handled or declared. A number of the methods in the Java 2 Standard Edition libraries throw checked exceptions, so you will often write exception handlers to cope with exceptions generated by methods you didn't write.

You can also throw an exception yourself, and that exception can be either an existing exception from the Java API or one of your own. To create your own exception, you simply subclass `Exception` (or one of its subclasses) as follows:

```
class MyException extends Exception { }
```

And if you throw the exception, the compiler will guarantee that you declare it as follows:

```
class TestEx {
  void doStuff() {
    throw new MyException();  // Throw a checked exception
  }
}
```

The preceding code upsets the compiler:

```
TestEx.java:6: unreported exception MyException; must be caught
or
declared to be thrown
  throw new MyException();
  ^
```

e x a m
ⓦatch

```
        void doStuff() throws MyException {
          try {
            throw new MyException();
          }
          catch(MyException me) {
            throw me;
          }
        }
      }
```

You need to recognize that this code won't compile. If you try, you'll get

```
MyException.java:3: unreported exception MyException; must
be caught or declared to be thrown
doStuff();
     ^
```

Notice that someMethod() *fails to either handle or declare the exception
that can be thrown by* doStuff().

You need to know how an Error compares with checked and unchecked
exceptions. Objects of type Error are not Exception objects, although they do
represent exceptional conditions. Both Exception and Error share a common
superclass, Throwable, thus both can be thrown using the throw keyword. When an
Error or a subclass of Error is thrown, it's unchecked. You are not required to catch
Error objects or Error subtypes. You can also throw an Error yourself (although
other than AssertionError you probably won't ever want to), and you can catch
one, but again, you probably won't. What, for example, would you actually do if you
got an OutOfMemoryError? It's not like you can tell the garbage collector to run;
you can bet the JVM fought desperately to save itself (and reclaimed all the memory
it could) by the time you got the error. In other words, don't expect the JVM at that
point to say, "Run the garbage collector? Oh, thanks so much for telling me. That
just never occurred to me. Sure, I'll get right on it." Even better, what would you do
if a VirtualMachineError arose? Your program is toast by the time you'd catch the
Error, so there's really no point in trying to catch one of these babies. Just remember,
though, that you can! The following compiles just fine:

```
class TestEx {
  public static void main (String [] args) {
    badMethod();
  }
  static void badMethod() {  // No need to declare an Error
    doStuff();
  }
  static void doStuff() {  //No need to declare an Error
    try {
      throw new Error();
    }
    catch(Error me) {
      throw me; // We catch it, but then rethrow it
    }
  }
}
```

If we were throwing a checked exception rather than `Error`, then the `doStuff()` method would need to declare the exception. But remember, since `Error` is not a subtype of `Exception`, it doesn't need to be declared. You're free to declare it if you like, but the compiler just doesn't care one way or another when or how the `Error` is thrown, or by whom.

Because Java has checked exceptions, it's commonly said that Java forces developers to handle exceptions. Yes, Java forces us to write exception handlers for each exception that can occur during normal operation, but it's up to us to make the exception handlers actually do something useful. We know software managers who melt down when they see a programmer write:

```
try {
  callBadMethod();
} catch (Exception ex) { }
```

Notice anything missing? Don't "eat" the exception by catching it without actually handling it. You won't even be able to tell that the exception occurred, because you'll never see the stack trace.

Rethrowing the Same Exception

Just as you can throw a new exception from a `catch` clause, you can also throw the same exception you just caught. Here's a `catch` clause that does this:

```
catch(IOException e) {
  // Do things, then if you decide you can't handle it…
  throw e;
}
```

All other `catch` clauses associated with the same `try` are ignored, if a `finally` block exists, it runs, and the exception is thrown back to the calling method (the next method down the call stack). If you throw a checked exception from a `catch` clause, you must also declare that exception! In other words, you must handle *and* declare, as opposed to handle *or* declare. The following example is illegal:

```
public void doStuff() {
  try {
    // risky IO things
  } catch(IOException ex) {
    // can't handle it
    throw ex;  // Can't throw it unless you declare it
  }
}
```

In the preceding code, the doStuff() method is clearly able to throw a checked exception—in this case an IOException—so the compiler says, "Well, that's just peachy that you have a try/catch in there, but it's not good enough. If you might rethrow the IOException you catch, then you must declare it!"

EXERCISE 5-4

Creating an Exception

In this exercise we attempt to create a custom exception. We won't put in any new methods (it will have only those inherited from Exception), and because it extends Exception, the compiler considers it a checked exception. The goal of the program is to determine whether a command-line argument, representing a particular food (as a string), is considered bad or OK.

- Let's first create our exception. We will call it BadFoodException. This exception will be thrown when a bad food is encountered.
- Create an enclosing class called MyException and a main() method, which will remain empty for now.

- Create a method called `checkFood()`. It takes a `String` argument and throws our exception if it doesn't like the food it was given. Otherwise, it tells us it likes the food. You can add any foods you aren't particularly fond of to the list.

- Now in the `main()` method, you'll get the command-line argument out of the `String` array, and then pass that `String` on to the `checkFood()` method. Because it's a checked exception, the `checkFood()` method must declare it, and the `main()` method must handle it (using a `try/catch`). Do not have `main()` declare the exception, because if `main()` ducks the exception, who else is back there to catch it?

- As nifty as exception handling is, it's still up to the developer to make proper use of it. Exception handling makes organizing our code and signaling problems easy, but the exception handlers still have to be written. You'll find that even the most complex situations can be handled, and your code will be reusable, readable, and maintainable.

CERTIFICATION OBJECTIVE

Common Exceptions and Errors (Exam Objective 2.6)

2.6   *Recognize situations that will result in any of the following being thrown: ArrayIndexOutOfBoundsException, ClassCastException, IllegalArgumentException, IllegalStateException, NullPointerException, NumberFormatException, AssertionError, ExceptionInInitializerError, StackOverflowError, or NoClassDefFoundError. Understand which of these are thrown by the virtual machine and recognize situations in which others should be thrown programmatically.*

Exception handling is another area that the exam creation team decided to expand for the SCJP 5 exam. This section discusses the aspects of exceptions that were added for this new version. The intention of Objective 2.6 is to make sure that you are familiar with some of the most common exceptions and errors you'll encounter as a Java programmer.

The questions from this section are likely to be along the lines of, "Here's some code that just did something bad, which exception will be thrown?"

Throughout the exam, questions will present some code and ask you to determine whether the code will run, or whether an exception will be thrown. Since these questions are so common, understanding the causes for these exceptions is critical to your success.

This is another one of those objectives that will turn up all through the real exam (does "An exception is thrown at runtime" ring a bell?), so make sure this section gets a lot of your attention.

Where Exceptions Come From

Jump back a page and take a look at the last sentence of Objective 2.6. It's important to understand what causes exceptions and errors, and where they come from. For the purposes of exam preparation, let's define two broad categories of exceptions and errors:

- **JVM exceptions**   Those exceptions or errors that are either exclusively or most logically thrown by the JVM.
- **Programmatic exceptions**   Those exceptions that are thrown explicitly by application and/or API programmers.

JVM Thrown Exceptions

Let's start with a very common exception, the `NullPointerException`. As we saw in Chapter 3, this exception occurs when you attempt to access an object using a reference variable with a current value of `null`. There's no way that the compiler can hope to find these problems before runtime. Let's look at the following:

```
class NPE {
  static String s;
  public static void main(String [] args) {
    System.out.println(s.length());
  }
}
```

Surely, the compiler can find the problem with that tiny little program! Nope, you're on your own. The code will compile just fine, and the JVM will throw a `NullPointerException` when it tries to invoke the `length()` method.

Earlier in this chapter we discussed the call stack. As you recall, we used the convention that `main()` would be at the bottom of the call stack, and that as `main()` invokes another method, and that method invokes another, and so on, the stack grows upward. Of course the stack resides in memory, and even if your OS gives you a gigabyte of RAM for your program, it's still a finite amount. It's possible to grow the stack so large that the OS runs out of space to store the call stack. When this happens you get (wait for it...), a `StackOverflowError`. The most common way for this to occur is to create a recursive method. A recursive method is one that invokes itself in the method body. While that may sound weird, it's a very common and useful technique for such things as searching and sorting algorithms. Take a look at this code:

```
void go() {    // recursion gone bad
  go();
}
```

As you can see, if you ever make the mistake of invoking the `go()` method, your program will fall into a black hole; `go()` invoking `go()` invoking `go()`, until, no matter how much memory you have, you'll get a `StackOverflowError`. Again, only the JVM knows when this moment occurs, and the JVM will be the source of this error.

Programmatically Thrown Exceptions

Now let's look at programmatically thrown exceptions. Remember we defined "programmatically" as meaning something like this:

Created by an application and/or API developer.

For instance, many classes in the Java API have methods that take `String` arguments, and convert these `Strings` into numeric primitives. A good example of these classes are the so-called "wrapper classes" that we studied in Chapter 3.

At some point long ago, some programmer wrote the `java.lang.Integer` class, and created methods like `parseInt()` and `valueOf()`. That programmer wisely decided that if one of these methods was passed a `String` that could not be converted into a number, the method should throw a `NumberFormatException`. The partially implemented code might look something like this:

```
int parseInt(String s) throws NumberFormatException {
  boolean parseSuccess = false;
  int result = 0;
  // do complicated parsing
  if (!parseSuccess)    // if the parsing failed
    throw new NumberFormatException();
  return result;
}
```

Other examples of programmatic exceptions include an `AssertionError` (okay, it's not an exception, but it IS thrown programmatically), and throwing an `IllegalArgumentException`. In fact, our mythical API developer could have used `IllegalArgumentException` for her `parseInt()` method. But it turns out that `NumberFormatException` extends `IllegalArgumentException`, and is a little more precise, so in this case, using `NumberFormatException` supports the notion we discussed earlier: that when you have an exception hierarchy, you should use the most precise exception that you can.

Of course, as we discussed earlier, you can also make up your very own special, custom exceptions, and throw them whenever you want to. These homemade exceptions also fall into the category of "programmatically thrown exceptions."

A Summary of the Exam's Exceptions and Errors

Objective 2.6 lists ten specific exceptions and errors. In this section we discussed the `StackOverflowError`. The other nine exceptions and errors listed in the objective are covered elsewhere in this book. Table 5-2 summarizes this list and provides chapter references to the exceptions and errors we did not discuss here.

TABLE 5-2   Descriptions and Sources of Common Exceptions.

Exception (Chapter Location)	Description	Typically Thrown
ArrayIndexOutOfBoundsException (Chapter 3, "Assignments")	Thrown when attempting to access an array with an invalid index value (either negative or beyond the length of the array).	By the JVM
ClassCastException (Chapter 2, "Object Orientation")	Thrown when attempting to cast a reference variable to a type that fails the IS-A test.	By the JVM
IllegalArgumentException (This chapter)	Thrown when a method receives an argument formatted differently than the method expects.	Programmatically
IllegalStateException (Chapter 6, "Formatting")	Thrown when the state of the environment doesn't match the operation being attempted, e.g., using a Scanner that's been closed.	Programmatically
NullPointerException (Chapter 3, "Assignments")	Thrown when attempting to access an object with a reference variable whose current value is `null`.	By the JVM
NumberFormatException (Chapter 3, "Assignments")	Thrown when a method that converts a String to a number receives a String that it cannot convert.	Programmatically
AssertionError (This chapter)	Thrown when a statement's boolean test returns `false`.	Programmatically
ExceptionInInitializerError (Chapter 3, "Assignments")	Thrown when attempting to initialize a static variable or an initialization block.	By the JVM
StackOverflowError (This chapter)	Typically thrown when a method recurses too deeply. (Each invocation is added to the stack.)	By the JVM
NoClassDefFoundError (Chapter 10, "Development")	Thrown when the JVM can't find a class it needs, because of a command-line error, a classpath issue, or a missing `.class` file.	By the JVM

Working with the Assertion Mechanism (Exam Objective 2.3)

2.3   Develop code that makes use of assertions, and distinguish appropriate from inappropriate uses of assertions.

You know you're not supposed to make assumptions, but you can't help it when you're writing code. You put them in comments:

```
if (x > 2 && y) {
  // do something
} else if (x < 2 || y) {
  // do something
} else {
  // x must be 2
  // do something else
}
```

You write print statements with them:

```
while (true) {
  if (x > 2) {
    break;
  }
  System.out.print("If we got here " +
                   "something went horribly wrong");
}
```

Added to the Java language beginning with version 1.4, assertions let you test your assumptions during development, without the expense (in both your time and program overhead) of writing exception handlers for exceptions that you assume will never happen once the program is out of development and fully deployed.

Starting with exam 310-035 (version 1.4 of the Sun Certified Java Programmer exam) and continuing through to the current exam 310-065 (SCJP 6), you're expected to know the basics of how assertions work, including how to enable them, how to use them, and how *not* to use them.

Assertions Overview

Suppose you assume that a number passed into a method (say, `methodA()`) will never be negative. While testing and debugging, you want to validate your assumption, but you don't want to have to strip out `print` statements, runtime exception handlers, or `if/else` tests when you're done with development. But leaving any of those in is, at the least, a performance hit. Assertions to the rescue! Check out the following code:

```
private void methodA(int num) {
  if (num >= 0) {
    useNum(num + x);
  } else {  // num must be < 0
            // This code should never be reached!
    System.out.println("Yikes! num is a negative number! "
                       + num);
  }
}
```

Because you're so certain of your assumption, you don't want to take the time (or program performance hit) to write exception-handling code. And at runtime, you don't want the `if/else` either because if you do reach the `else` condition, it means your earlier logic (whatever was running prior to this method being called) is flawed.

Assertions let you test your assumptions during development, but the assertion code basically evaporates when the program is deployed, leaving behind no overhead or debugging code to track down and remove. Let's rewrite `methodA()` to validate that the argument was not negative:

```
private void methodA(int num) {
  assert (num>=0);   // throws an AssertionError
                     // if this test isn't true
  useNum(num + x);
}
```

Not only do assertions let your code stay cleaner and tighter, but because assertions are inactive unless specifically "turned on" (enabled), the code will run as though it were written like this:

```
private void methodA(int num) {
  useNum(num + x); // we've tested this;
                   // we now know we're good here
}
```

Assertions work quite simply. You always assert that something is `true`. If it is, no problem. Code keeps running. But if your assertion turns out to be wrong (`false`), then a stop-the-world `AssertionError` is thrown (that you should never, ever handle!) right then and there, so you can fix whatever logic flaw led to the problem.

Assertions come in two flavors: *really simple* and *simple*, as follows:

Really simple:

```
private void doStuff() {
  assert (y > x);
  // more code assuming y is greater than x
}
```

Simple:

```
private void doStuff() {
  assert (y > x): "y is " + y + " x is " + x;
  // more code assuming y is greater than x
}
```

The difference between the two is that the simple version adds a second expression, separated from the first (boolean expression) by a colon, this expression's string value is added to the stack trace. Both versions throw an immediate `AssertionError`, but the simple version gives you a little more debugging help while the really simple version simply tells you only that your assumption was false.

on the **job**

Assertions are typically enabled when an application is being tested and debugged, but disabled when the application is deployed. The assertions are still in the code, although ignored by the JVM, so if you do have a deployed application that starts misbehaving, you can always choose to enable assertions in the field for additional testing.

Assertion Expression Rules

Assertions can have either one or two expressions, depending on whether you're using the "simple" or the "really simple." The first expression must always result in a `boolean` value! Follow the same rules you use for `if` and `while` tests. The whole point is to assert aTest, which means you're asserting that aTest is `true`. If it is `true`, no problem. If it's not `true`, however, then your assumption was wrong and you get an `AssertionError`.

The second expression, used only with the simple version of an `assert` statement, can be anything that results in a value. Remember, the second expression is used to generate a `String` message that displays in the stack trace to give you a little more debugging information. It works much like `System.out.println()` in that you can pass it a primitive or an object, and it will convert it into a `String` representation. It must resolve to a value!

The following code lists legal and illegal expressions for both parts of an `assert` statement. Remember, expression2 is used only with the simple `assert` statement, where the second expression exists solely to give you a little more debugging detail:

```
void noReturn() { }
int aReturn() { return 1; }
void go() {
  int x = 1;
  boolean b = true;

  // the following six are legal assert statements
  assert(x == 1);
  assert(b);
  assert true;
  assert(x == 1) : x;
  assert(x == 1) : aReturn();
  assert(x == 1) : new ValidAssert();

  // the following six are ILLEGAL assert statements
  assert(x = 1);  // none of these are booleans
  assert(x);
  assert 0;
  assert(x == 1) : ;            // none of these return a value
  assert(x == 1) : noReturn();
  assert(x == 1) : ValidAssert va;
}
```

e x a m
ⓦ a t c h

If you see the word "expression" in a question about assertions, and the question doesn't specify whether it means expression1 (the boolean test) or expression2 (the value to print in the stack trace), then always assume the word "expression" refers to expression1, the boolean test. For example, consider the following question:

An assert expression must result in a boolean *value, true or false?*

Assume that the word 'expression' refers to expression1 of an assert, so the question statement is correct. If the statement were referring to expression2, however, the statement would not be correct, since expression2 can have a result of any value, not just a boolean.

Enabling Assertions

If you want to use assertions, you have to think first about how to compile with assertions in your code, and then about how to run with assertions enabled. Both require version 1.4 or greater, and that brings us to the first issue: how to compile with assertions in your code.

Identifier vs. Keyword

Prior to version 1.4, you might very well have written code like this:

```
int assert = getInitialValue();
if (assert == getActualResult()) {
  // do something
}
```

Notice that in the preceding code, assert is used as an identifier. That's not a problem prior to 1.4. But you cannot use a keyword/reserved word as an identifier, and beginning with version 1.4, assert is a keyword. The bottom line is this:

You can use **assert** as a keyword or as an identifier, but not both.

on the
ⓙob

If for some reason you're using a Java 1.4 compiler, and if you're using assert *as a keyword (in other words, you're actually trying to* assert *something in your code), then you must explicitly enable assertion-awareness at compile time, as follows:*

```
javac -source 1.4 com/geeksanonymous/TestClass.java
```

You can read that as "compile the class TestClass, in the directory com/geeksanonymous*, and do it in the 1.4 way, where* assert *is a keyword."*

Use Version 6 of java and javac

As far as the exam is concerned, you'll ALWAYS be using version 6 of the Java compiler (javac), and version 6 of the Java application launcher (java). You might see questions about older versions of source code, but those questions will always be in the context of compiling and launching old code with the current versions of javac and java.

Compiling Assertion-Aware Code

The Java 6 compiler will use the assert keyword by default. Unless you tell it otherwise, the compiler will generate an error message if it finds the word assert used as an identifier. However, you can tell the compiler that you're giving it an old piece of code to compile, and that it should pretend to be an old compiler! (More about compiler commands in Chapter 10.) Let's say you've got to make a quick fix to an old piece of 1.3 code that uses assert as an identifier. At the command line you can type

```
javac -source 1.3 OldCode.java
```

The compiler will issue warnings when it discovers the word assert used as an identifier, but the code will compile and execute. Suppose you tell the compiler that your code is version 1.4 or later, for instance:

```
javac -source 1.4 NotQuiteSoOldCode.java
```

In this case, the compiler will issue errors when it discovers the word assert used as an identifier.

If you want to tell the compiler to use Java 6 rules you can do one of three things: omit the -source option, which is the default, or add one of two source options:

```
-source 1.6 or -source 6.
```

If you want to use assert as an identifier in your code, you MUST compile using the -source 1.3 option. Table 5-3 summarizes how the Java 6 compiler will react to assert as either an identifier or a keyword.

| TABLE 5-3 | Using Java 6 to Compile Code That Uses assert as an Identifier or a Keyword |

Command Line	If assert Is an Identifier	If assert Is a Keyword
javac -source 1.3 TestAsserts.java	Code compiles with warnings.	Compilation fails.
javac -source 1.4 TestAsserts.java	Compilation fails.	Code compiles.
javac -source 1.5 TestAsserts.java	Compilation fails.	Code compiles.
javac -source 5 TestAsserts.java	Compilation fails.	Code compiles.
javac -source 1.6 TestAsserts.java	Compilation fails.	Code compiles.
javac -source 6 TestAsserts.java	Compilation fails.	Code compiles.
javac TestAsserts.java	Compilation fails.	Code compiles.

Running with Assertions

Here's where it gets cool. Once you've written your assertion-aware code (in other words, code that uses assert as a keyword, to actually perform assertions at runtime), you can choose to enable or disable your assertions at runtime! Remember, assertions are disabled by default.

Enabling Assertions at Runtime

You enable assertions at runtime with

```
java -ea com.geeksanonymous.TestClass
```

or

```
java -enableassertions com.geeksanonymous.TestClass
```

The preceding command-line switches tell the JVM to run with assertions enabled.

Disabling Assertions at Runtime

You must also know the command-line switches for disabling assertions,

```
java -da com.geeksanonymous.TestClass
```

or

```
java -disableassertions com.geeksanonymous.TestClass
```

Because assertions are disabled by default, using the disable switches might seem unnecessary. Indeed, using the switches the way we do in the preceding example just gives you the default behavior (in other words, you get the same result regardless of whether you use the disabling switches). But...you can also selectively enable and disable assertions in such a way that they're enabled for some classes and/or packages, and disabled for others, while a particular program is running.

Selective Enabling and Disabling

The command-line switches for assertions can be used in various ways:

- **With no arguments (as in the preceding examples)**   Enables or disables assertions in all classes, except for the system classes.
- **With a package name**   Enables or disables assertions in the package specified, and any packages below this package in the same directory hierarchy (more on that in a moment).
- **With a class name**   Enables or disables assertions in the class specified.

You can combine switches to, say, disable assertions in a single class, but keep them enabled for all others, as follows:

```
java -ea  -da:com.geeksanonymous.Foo
```

The preceding command line tells the JVM to enable assertions in general, but disable them in the class `com.geeksanonymous.Foo`. You can do the same selectivity for a package as follows:

```
java -ea -da:com.geeksanonymous...
```

The preceding command line tells the JVM to enable assertions in general, but disable them in the package `com.geeksanonymous`, and all of its subpackages! You may not be familiar with the term subpackages, since there wasn't much use of that term prior to assertions. A subpackage is any package in a subdirectory of the named package. For example, look at the following directory tree:

```
com
    |_geeksanonymous
                |_Foo
                |_twelvesteps
                            |_StepOne
                            |_StepTwo
```

This tree lists three directories,

```
com
geeksanonymous
twelvesteps
and three classes:
com.geeksanonymous.Foo
com.geeksanonymous.twelvesteps.StepOne
com.geeksanonymous.twelvesteps.StepTwo
```

The subpackage of `com.geeksanonymous` is the `twelvesteps` package. Remember that in Java, the `com.geeksanonymous.twelvesteps` package is treated as a completely distinct package that has no relationship with the packages above it (in this example, the `com.geeksanonymous` package), except they just happen to share a couple of directories. Table 5-4 lists examples of command-line switches for enabling and disabling assertions.

TABLE 5-4	Assertion Command-Line Switches

Command-Line Example	What It Means
`java -ea` `java -enableassertions`	Enable assertions.
`java -da` `java -disableassertions`	Disable assertions (the default behavior of Java 6).
`java -ea:com.foo.Bar`	Enable assertions in class `com.foo.Bar`.
`java -ea:com.foo...`	Enable assertions in package `com.foo` and any of its subpackages.
`java -ea -dsa`	Enable assertions in general, but disable assertions in system classes.
`java -ea -da:com.foo...`	Enable assertions in general, but disable assertions in package `com.foo` and any of its subpackages.

Using Assertions Appropriately

Not all legal uses of assertions are considered appropriate. As with so much of Java, you can abuse the intended use of assertions, despite the best efforts of Sun's Java engineers to discourage you from doing so. For example, you're never supposed to handle an assertion failure. That means you shouldn't catch it with a `catch` clause and attempt to recover. Legally, however, `AssertionError` is a subclass of `Throwable`, so it can be caught. But just don't do it! If you're going to try to recover from something, it should be an exception. To discourage you from trying to substitute an assertion for an exception, the `AssertionError` doesn't provide access to the object that generated it. All you get is the `String` message.

So who gets to decide what's appropriate? Sun. The exam uses Sun's "official" assertion documentation to define appropriate and inappropriate uses.

Don't Use Assertions to Validate Arguments to a Public Method

The following is an inappropriate use of assertions:

```
public void doStuff(int x) {
  assert (x > 0);                // inappropriate !
  // do things with x
}
```

e x a m

ⓦatch
        If you see the word "appropriate" on the exam, do not mistake that for "legal." "Appropriate" always refers to the way in which something is supposed to be used, according to either the developers of the mechanism or best practices officially embraced by Sun. If you see the word "correct" in the context of assertions, as in, "Line 3 is a correct use of assertions," you should also assume that correct is referring to how assertions SHOULD be used rather than how they legally COULD be used.

A `public` method might be called from code that you don't control (or from code you have never seen). Because `public` methods are part of your interface to the outside world, you're supposed to guarantee that any constraints on the arguments will be enforced by the method itself. But since assertions aren't guaranteed to actually run (they're typically disabled in a deployed application), the enforcement won't happen if assertions aren't enabled. You don't want publicly accessible code that works only conditionally, depending on whether assertions are enabled.

If you need to validate `public` method arguments, you'll probably use exceptions to throw, say, an `IllegalArgumentException` if the values passed to the `public` method are invalid.

Do Use Assertions to Validate Arguments to a Private Method

If you write a `private` method, you almost certainly wrote (or control) any code that calls it. When you assume that the logic in code calling your `private` method is correct, you can test that assumption with an assertion as follows:

```
private void doMore(int x) {
   assert (x > 0);
   // do things with x
}
```

The only difference that matters between the preceding example and the one before it is the access modifier. So, do enforce constraints on `private` methods' arguments, but do not enforce constraints on `public` methods. You're certainly free to compile assertion code with an inappropriate validation of `public` arguments, but for the exam (and real life) you need to know that you shouldn't do it.

Don't Use Assertions to Validate Command-Line Arguments

This is really just a special case of the "Do not use assertions to validate arguments to a public method" rule. If your program requires command-line arguments, you'll probably use the exception mechanism to enforce them.

Do Use Assertions, Even in Public Methods, to Check for Cases that You Know Are Never, Ever Supposed to Happen

This can include code blocks that should never be reached, including the default of a `switch` statement as follows:

```
switch(x) {
   case 1: y = 3; break;
   case 2: y = 9; break;
   case 3: y = 27; break;
   default: assert false; // we're never supposed to get here!
}
```

If you assume that a particular code block won't be reached, as in the preceding example where you assert that x must be either 1, 2, or 3, then you can use `assert false` to cause an `AssertionError` to be thrown immediately if you ever do reach that code. So in the `switch` example, we're not performing a boolean test—we've already asserted that we should never be there, so just getting to that point is an automatic failure of our assertion/assumption.

Don't Use Assert Expressions that Can Cause Side Effects!

The following would be a very bad idea:

```
public void doStuff() {
  assert (modifyThings());
  // continues on
}
public boolean modifyThings() {
  y = x++;
  return true;
}
```

The rule is, an `assert` expression should leave the program in the same state it was in before the expression! Think about it. `assert` expressions aren't guaranteed to always run, so you don't want your code to behave differently depending on whether assertions are enabled. Assertions must not cause any side effects. If assertions are enabled, the only change to the way your program runs is that an `AssertionError` can be thrown if one of your assertions (think: *assumptions*) turns out to be false.

on the **job**

Using assertions that cause side effects can cause some of the most maddening and hard-to-find bugs known to man! When a hot tempered Q.A. analyst is screaming at you that your code doesn't work, trotting out the old "well it works on MY machine" excuse won't get you very far.

CERTIFICATION SUMMARY

This chapter covered a lot of ground, all of which involves ways of controlling your program flow, based on a conditional test. First you learned about `if` and `switch` statements. The `if` statement evaluates one or more expressions to a `boolean` result. If the result is `true`, the program will execute the code in the block that is encompassed by the `if`. If an `else` statement is used and the `if` expression evaluates to `false`, then the code following the `else` will be performed. If no `else` block is defined, then none of the code associated with the `if` statement will execute.

You also learned that the `switch` statement can be used to replace multiple `if-else` statements. The `switch` statement can evaluate integer primitive types that can be implicitly cast to an `int` (those types are `byte`, `short`, `int`, and `char`), or it can evaluate enums.

At runtime, the JVM will try to find a match between the expression in the `switch` statement and a constant in a corresponding `case` statement. If a match is found, execution will begin at the matching case, and continue on from there, executing code in all the remaining `case` statements until a `break` statement is found or the end of the `switch` statement occurs. If there is no match, then the `default` case will execute, if there is one.

You've learned about the three looping constructs available in the Java language. These constructs are the `for` loop (including the basic `for` and the enhanced `for` which is new to Java 6), the `while` loop, and the `do` loop. In general, the `for` loop is used when you know how many times you need to go through the loop. The `while` loop is used when you do not know how many times you want to go through, whereas the `do` loop is used when you need to go through at least once. In the `for` loop and the `while` loop, the expression will have to evaluate to `true` to get inside the block and will check after every iteration of the loop. The `do` loop does not check the condition until after it has gone through the loop once. The major benefit of the `for` loop is the ability to initialize one or more variables and increment or decrement those variables in the `for` loop definition.

The `break` and `continue` statements can be used in either a labeled or unlabeled fashion. When unlabeled, the `break` statement will force the program to stop processing the innermost looping construct and start with the line of code following the loop. Using an unlabeled `continue` command will cause the program to stop execution of the current iteration of the innermost loop and proceed with the next iteration. When a `break` or a `continue` statement is used in a labeled manner, it will perform in the same way, with one exception: the statement will not apply to the innermost loop; instead, it will apply to the loop with the label. The `break` statement is used most often in conjunction with the `switch` statement. When there is a match between the `switch` expression and the case constant, the code following the case constant will be performed. To stop execution, a `break` is needed.

You've seen how Java provides an elegant mechanism in exception handling. Exception handling allows you to isolate your error-correction code into separate blocks so that the main code doesn't become cluttered by error-checking code. Another elegant feature allows you to handle similar errors with a single error-handling block, without code duplication. Also, the error handling can be deferred to methods further back on the call stack.

You learned that Java's `try` keyword is used to specify a guarded region—a block of code in which problems might be detected. An exception handler is the code that is executed when an exception occurs. The handler is defined by using Java's `catch` keyword. All `catch` clauses must immediately follow the related `try` block. Java also provides the `finally` keyword. This is used to define a block of code that is always executed, either immediately after a `catch` clause completes or immediately after the associated `try` block in the case that no exception was thrown (or there was a `try` but no `catch`). Use `finally` blocks to release system resources and to perform any cleanup required by the code in the `try` block. A `finally` block is not required, but if there is one it must immediately follow the last `catch`. (If there is no `catch` block, the `finally` block must immediately follow the `try` block.) It's guaranteed to be called except when the `try` or `catch` issues a `System.exit()`.

An exception object is an instance of class `Exception` or one of its subclasses. The `catch` clause takes, as a parameter, an instance of an object of a type derived from the `Exception` class. Java requires that each method either catches any checked exception it can throw or else declares that it throws the exception. The exception declaration is part of the method's public interface. To declare that an exception may be thrown, the `throws` keyword is used in a method definition, along with a list of all checked exceptions that might be thrown.

Runtime exceptions are of type `RuntimeException` (or one of its subclasses). These exceptions are a special case because they do not need to be handled or declared, and thus are known as "unchecked" exceptions. Errors are of type `java.lang.Error` or its subclasses, and like runtime exceptions, they do not need to be handled or declared. Checked exceptions include any exception types that are not of type `RuntimeException` or Error. If your code fails to either handle a checked exception or declare that it is thrown, your code won't compile. But with unchecked exceptions or objects of type `Error`, it doesn't matter to the compiler whether you declare them or handle them, do nothing about them, or do some combination of declaring and handling. In other words, you're free to declare them and handle them, but the compiler won't care one way or the other. It's not good practice to handle an `Error`, though, because you can rarely recover from one.

Exceptions can be generated by the JVM, or by a programmer.

Assertions, added to the language in version 1.4, are a useful debugging tool. You learned how you can use them for testing, by enabling them, but keep them disabled when the application is deployed. If you have older Java code that uses the word `assert` as an identifier, then you won't be able to use assertions, and you must recompile your older code using the `-source 1.3` flag. Remember that as of Java 6, assertions are compiled as a keyword by default, but must be enabled explicitly at runtime.

You learned how assert statements always include a boolean expression, and if the expression is `true` the code continues on, but if the expression is `false`, an `AssertionError` is thrown. If you use the two-expression `assert` statement, then the second expression is evaluated, converted to a `String` representation and inserted into the stack trace to give you a little more debugging info. Finally, you saw why assertions should not be used to enforce arguments to `public` methods, and why assert expressions must not contain side effects!

TWO-MINUTE DRILL

Here are some of the key points from each certification objective in this chapter. You might want to loop through them several times.

Writing Code Using if and switch Statements (Obj. 2.1)

❑ The only legal expression in an if statement is a boolean expression, in other words an expression that resolves to a boolean or a Boolean variable.

❑ Watch out for boolean assignments (=) that can be mistaken for boolean equality (==) tests:

```
boolean x = false;
if (x = true) { } // an assignment, so x will always be true!
```

❑ Curly braces are optional for if blocks that have only one conditional statement. But watch out for misleading indentations.

❑ switch statements can evaluate only to enums or the byte, short, int, and char data types. You can't say,

```
long s = 30;
switch(s) { }
```

❑ The case constant must be a literal or final variable, or a constant expression, including an enum. You cannot have a case that includes a non-final variable, or a range of values.

❑ If the condition in a switch statement matches a case constant, execution will run through all code in the switch following the matching case statement until a break statement or the end of the switch statement is encountered. In other words, the matching case is just the entry point into the case block, but unless there's a break statement, the matching case is not the only case code that runs.

❑ The default keyword should be used in a switch statement if you want to run some code when none of the case values match the conditional value.

❑ The default block can be located anywhere in the switch block, so if no case matches, the default block will be entered, and if the default does not contain a break, then code will continue to execute (fall-through) to the end of the switch or until the break statement is encountered.

Writing Code Using Loops (Objective 2.2)

❑ A basic `for` statement has three parts: declaration and/or initialization, boolean evaluation, and the iteration expression.

❑ If a variable is incremented or evaluated within a basic `for` loop, it must be declared before the loop, or within the `for` loop declaration.

❑ A variable declared (not just initialized) within the basic `for` loop declaration cannot be accessed outside the `for` loop (in other words, code below the `for` loop won't be able to use the variable).

❑ You can initialize more than one variable of the same type in the first part of the basic `for` loop declaration; each initialization must be separated by a comma.

❑ An enhanced `for` statement (new as of Java 6), has two parts, the *declaration* and the *expression*. It is used only to loop through arrays or collections.

❑ With an enhanced `for`, the *expression* is the array or collection through which you want to loop.

❑ With an enhanced `for`, the *declaration* is the block variable, whose type is compatible with the elements of the array or collection, and that variable contains the value of the element for the given iteration.

❑ You cannot use a number (old C-style language construct) or anything that does not evaluate to a `boolean` value as a condition for an `if` statement or looping construct. You can't, for example, say `if(x)`, unless x is a `boolean` variable.

❑ The `do` loop will enter the body of the loop at least once, even if the test condition is not met.

Using break and continue (Objective 2.2)

❑ An unlabeled `break` statement will cause the current iteration of the innermost looping construct to stop and the line of code following the loop to run.

❑ An unlabeled `continue` statement will cause: the current iteration of the innermost loop to stop, the condition of that loop to be checked, and if the condition is met, the loop to run again.

❑ If the `break` statement or the `continue` statement is labeled, it will cause similar action to occur on the labeled loop, not the innermost loop.

Handling Exceptions (Objectives 2.4, 2.5, and 2.6)

❑ Exceptions come in two flavors: checked and unchecked.

❑ Checked exceptions include all subtypes of Exception, excluding classes that extend RuntimeException.

❑ Checked exceptions are subject to the handle or declare rule; any method that might throw a checked exception (including methods that invoke methods that can throw a checked exception) must either declare the exception using throws, or handle the exception with an appropriate try/catch.

❑ Subtypes of Error or RuntimeException are unchecked, so the compiler doesn't enforce the handle or declare rule. You're free to handle them, or to declare them, but the compiler doesn't care one way or the other.

❑ If you use an optional finally block, it will always be invoked, regardless of whether an exception in the corresponding try is thrown or not, and regardless of whether a thrown exception is caught or not.

❑ The only exception to the finally-will-always-be-called rule is that a finally will not be invoked if the JVM shuts down. That could happen if code from the try or catch blocks calls System.exit().

❑ Just because finally is invoked does not mean it will complete. Code in the finally block could itself raise an exception or issue a System.exit().

❑ Uncaught exceptions propagate back through the call stack, starting from the method where the exception is thrown and ending with either the first method that has a corresponding catch for that exception type or a JVM shutdown (which happens if the exception gets to main(), and main() is "ducking" the exception by declaring it).

❑ You can create your own exceptions, normally by extending Exception or one of its subtypes. Your exception will then be considered a checked exception, and the compiler will enforce the handle or declare rule for that exception.

❑ All catch blocks must be ordered from most specific to most general. If you have a catch clause for both IOException and Exception, you must put the catch for IOException first in your code. Otherwise, the IOException would be caught by catch(Exception e), because a catch argument can catch the specified exception or any of its subtypes! The compiler will stop you from defining catch clauses that can never be reached.

❑ Some exceptions are created by programmers, some by the JVM.

Working with the Assertion Mechanism (Objective 2.3)

❏ Assertions give you a way to test your assumptions during development and debugging.

❏ Assertions are typically enabled during testing but disabled during deployment.

❏ You can use `assert` as a keyword (as of version 1.4) or an identifier, but not both together. To compile older code that uses `assert` as an identifier (for example, a method name), use the `-source 1.3` command-line flag to `javac`.

❏ Assertions are disabled at runtime by default. To enable them, use a command-line flag `-ea` or `-enableassertions`.

❏ Selectively disable assertions by using the `-da` or `-disableassertions` flag.

❏ If you enable or disable assertions using the flag without any arguments, you're enabling or disabling assertions in general. You can combine enabling and disabling switches to have assertions enabled for some classes and/or packages, but not others.

❏ You can enable and disable assertions on a class-by-class basis, using the following syntax:

```
java -ea  -da:MyClass  TestClass
```

❏ You can enable and disable assertions on a package-by-package basis, and any package you specify also includes any subpackages (packages further down the directory hierarchy).

❏ Do not use assertions to validate arguments to `public` methods.

❏ Do not use `assert` expressions that cause side effects. Assertions aren't guaranteed to always run, and you don't want behavior that changes depending on whether assertions are enabled.

❏ Do use assertions—even in `public` methods—to validate that a particular code block will never be reached. You can use `assert false;` for code that should never be reached, so that an assertion error is thrown immediately if the `assert` statement is executed.

SELF TEST

1. Given two files:

```
1. class One {
2.   public static void main(String[] args) {
3.     int assert = 0;
4.   }
5. }
```

```
1. class Two {
2.   public static void main(String[] args) {
3.     assert(false);
4.   }
5. }
```

And the four command-line invocations:

```
javac -source 1.3 One.java
javac -source 1.4 One.java
javac -source 1.3 Two.java
javac -source 1.4 Two.java
```

What is the result? (Choose all that apply.)

A. Only one compilation will succeed

B. Exactly two compilations will succeed

C. Exactly three compilations will succeed

D. All four compilations will succeed

E. No compiler warnings will be produced

F. At least one compiler warning will be produced

2. Given:

```
class Plane {
  static String s = "-";
  public static void main(String[] args) {
    new Plane().s1();
    System.out.println(s);
  }
  void s1() {
    try { s2(); }
    catch (Exception e) { s += "c"; }
  }
  void s2() throws Exception  {
```

```
      s3();  s += "2";
      s3();  s += "2b";
    }
    void s3() throws Exception {
      throw new Exception();
    }
  }
```

What is the result?

A. -

B. -c

C. -c2

D. -2c

E. -c22b

F. -2c2b

G. -2c2bc

H. Compilation fails

3. Given:

```
    try { int x = Integer.parseInt("two"); }
```

Which could be used to create an appropriate catch block? (Choose all that apply.)

A. ClassCastException

B. IllegalStateException

C. NumberFormatException

D. IllegalArgumentException

E. ExceptionInInitializerError

F. ArrayIndexOutOfBoundsException

4. Which are true? (Choose all that apply.)

A. It is appropriate to use assertions to validate arguments to methods marked public

B. It is appropriate to catch and handle assertion errors

C. It is NOT appropriate to use assertions to validate command-line arguments

D. It is appropriate to use assertions to generate alerts when you reach code that should not be reachable

E. It is NOT appropriate for assertions to change a program's state

5. Given:

```
1. class Loopy {
2.    public static void main(String[] args) {
3.       int[] x = {7,6,5,4,3,2,1};
4.       // insert code here
5.          System.out.print(y + " ");
6.       }
7.    }
8. }
```

Which, inserted independently at line 4, compiles? (Choose all that apply.)

A. for(int y : x) {

B. for(x : int y) {

C. int y = 0; for(y : x) {

D. for(int y=0, z=0; z<x.length; z++) { y = x[z];

E. for(int y=0, int z=0; z<x.length; z++) { y = x[z];

F. int y = 0; for(int z=0; z<x.length; z++) { y = x[z];

6. Given:

```
class Emu {
  static String s = "-";
  public static void main(String[] args) {
    try {
      throw new Exception();
    } catch (Exception e) {
        try {
          try { throw new Exception();
          } catch (Exception ex) { s += "ic "; }
          throw new Exception(); }
        catch (Exception x) { s += "mc "; }
        finally { s += "mf "; }
    } finally { s += "of "; }
    System.out.println(s);
} }
```

What is the result?

A. -ic of

B. -mf of

C. -mc mf

D.   `-ic mf of`

E.   `-ic mc mf of`

F.   `-ic mc of mf`

G.   Compilation fails

7. Given:

```
3. class SubException extends Exception { }
4. class SubSubException extends SubException { }
5.
6. public class CC { void doStuff() throws SubException { } }
7.
8. class CC2 extends CC { void doStuff() throws SubSubException { } }
9.
10. class CC3 extends CC { void doStuff() throws Exception { } }
11.
12. class CC4 extends CC { void doStuff(int x) throws Exception { } }
13.
14. class CC5 extends CC {  void doStuff()  { } }
```

What is the result? (Choose all that apply.)

A. Compilation succeeds

B. Compilation fails due to an error on line 8

C. Compilation fails due to an error on line 10

D. Compilation fails due to an error on line 12

E. Compilation fails due to an error on line 14

8. Given:

```
3. public class Ebb {
4.    static int x = 7;
5.    public static void main(String[] args) {
6.       String s = "";
7.       for(int y = 0; y < 3; y++) {
8.          x++;
9.          switch(x) {
10.            case 8: s += "8 ";
11.            case 9: s += "9 ";
12.            case 10: { s+= "10 "; break; }
13.            default: s += "d ";
14.            case 13: s+= "13 ";
```

```
15.          }
16.        }
17.      System.out.println(s);
18.      }
19.    static { x++; }
20. }
```

What is the result?

A. 9 10 d

B. 8 9 10 d

C. 9 10 10 d

D. 9 10 10 d 13

E. 8 9 10 10 d 13

F. 8 9 10 9 10 10 d 13

G. Compilation fails

9. Given:

```
3. class Infinity { }
4. public class Beyond extends Infinity {
5.    static Integer i;
6.    public static void main(String[] args) {
7.      int sw = (int)(Math.random() * 3);
8.      switch(sw) {
9.        case 0: {  for(int x = 10; x > 5; x++)
10.                     it(x > 10000000) x = 10;
11.                   break; }
12.        case 1: {  int y = 7 * i;  break;  }
13.        case 2: {  Infinity inf = new Beyond();
14.                   Beyond b = (Beyond)inf;  }
15.      }
16.    }
17. }
```

And given that line 7 will assign the value 0, 1, or 2 to sw, which are true? (Choose all that apply.)

A. Compilation fails

B. A ClassCastException might be thrown

C. A StackOverflowError might be thrown

D. A NullPointerException might be thrown

E. An IllegalStateException might be thrown

F. The program might hang without ever completing

G. The program will always complete without exception

10. Given:

```
3. public class Circles {
4.    public static void main(String[] args) {
5.       int[] ia = {1,3,5,7,9};
6.       for(int x : ia) {
7.         for(int j = 0; j < 3; j++) {
8.            if(x > 4 && x < 8) continue;
9.            System.out.print(" " + x);
10.           if(j == 1) break;
11.           continue;
12.         }
13.         continue;
14.       }
15.    }
16. }
```

What is the result?

A. 1 3 9

B. 5 5 7 7

C. 1 3 3 9 9

D. 1 1 3 3 9 9

E. 1 1 1 3 3 3 9 9 9

F. Compilation fails

11. Given:

```
3. public class OverAndOver {
4.    static String s = "";
5.    public static void main(String[] args) {
6.       try {
7.          s += "1";
8.          throw new Exception();
9.       } catch (Exception e) { s += "2";
10.      } finally { s += "3"; doStuff(); s += "4";
11.      }
```

```
12.        System.out.println(s);
13.     }
14.    static void doStuff() { int x = 0; int y = 7/x; }
15. }
```

What is the result?

A. 12

B. 13

C. 123

D. 1234

E. Compilation fails

F. 123 followed by an exception

G. 1234 followed by an exception

H. An exception is thrown with no other output

12. Given:

```
3. public class Wind {
4.    public static void main(String[] args) {
5.       foreach:
6.       for(int j=0; j<5; j++) {
7.          for(int k=0; k< 3; k++) {
8.             System.out.print(" " + j);
9.             if(j--3 && k==1) break foreach;
10.            if(j--0 || j==2) break;
11.         }
12.      }
13.   }
14. }
```

What is the result?

A. 0 1 2 3

B. 1 1 1 3 3

C. 0 1 1 1 2 3 3

D. 1 1 1 3 3 4 4 4

E. 0 1 1 1 2 3 3 4 4 4

F. Compilation fails

13. Given:

```
3. public class Gotcha {
4.   public static void main(String[] args) {
5.     // insert code here
6.
7.   }
8.   void go() {
9.     go();
10.  }
11. }
```

And given the following three code fragments:

```
I.    new Gotcha().go();
II.   try { new Gotcha().go(); }
      catch (Error e) { System.out.println("ouch"); }

III.  try { new Gotcha().go(); }
      catch (Exception e) { System.out.println("ouch"); }
```

When fragments I - III are added, independently, at line 5, which are true? (Choose all that apply.)

A. Some will not compile

B. They will all compile

C. All will complete normally

D. None will complete normally

E. Only one will complete normally

F. Two of them will complete normally

14. Given:

```
3. public class Clumsy {
4.   public static void main(String[] args) {
5.     int j = 7;
6.     assert(++j > 7);
7.     assert(++j > 8): "hi";
8.     assert(j > 10): j=12;
9.     assert(j==12): doStuff();
```

```
10.      assert(j==12): new Clumsy();
11.    }
12.    static void doStuff() { }
13. }
```

Which are true? (Choose all that apply.)

A. Compilation succeeds

B. Compilation fails due to an error on line 6

C. Compilation fails due to an error on line 7

D. Compilation fails due to an error on line 8

E. Compilation fails due to an error on line 9

F. Compilation fails due to an error on line 10

15. Given:

```
1. public class Frisbee {
2.    // insert code here
3.       int x = 0;
4.       System.out.println(7/x);
5.    }
6. }
```

And given the following four code fragments:

```
I.   public static void main(String[] args) {
II.  public static void main(String[] args) throws Exception {
III. public static void main(String[] args) throws IOException {
IV.  public static void main(String[] args) throws RuntimeException {
```

If the four fragments are inserted independently at line 4, which are true? (Choose all that apply.)

A. All four will compile and execute without exception

B. All four will compile and execute and throw an exception

C. Some, but not all, will compile and execute without exception

D. Some, but not all, will compile and execute and throw an exception

E. When considering fragments II, III, and IV, of those that will compile, adding a try/catch block around line 6 will cause compilation to fail

16. Given:

```
 2. class MyException extends Exception { }
 3. class Tire {
 4.   void doStuff() {   }
 5. }
 6. public class Retread extends Tire {
 7.   public static void main(String[] args) {
 8.     new Retread().doStuff();
 9.   }
10.   // insert code here
11.     System.out.println(7/0);
12.   }
13. }
```

And given the following four code fragments:

```
I.    void doStuff() {
II.   void doStuff() throws MyException {
III.  void doStuff() throws RuntimeException {
IV.   void doStuff() throws ArithmeticException {
```

When fragments I - IV are added, independently, at line 10, which are true? (Choose all that apply.)

A. None will compile

B. They will all compile

C. Some, but not all, will compile

D. All of those that compile will throw an exception at runtime

E. None of those that compile will throw an exception at runtime

F. Only some of those that compile will throw an exception at runtime

SELF TEST ANSWERS

1. Given two files:

```
1. class One {
2.   public static void main(String[] args) {
3.     int assert = 0;
4.   }
5. }
1. class Two {
2.   public static void main(String[] args) {
3.     assert(false);
4.   }
5. }
```

And the four command-line invocations:

```
javac -source 1.3 One.java
javac -source 1.4 One.java
javac -source 1.3 Two.java
javac -source 1.4 Two.java
```

What is the result? (Choose all that apply.)

A. Only one compilation will succeed

B. Exactly two compilations will succeed

C. Exactly three compilations will succeed

D. All four compilations will succeed

E. No compiler warnings will be produced

F. At least one compiler warning will be produced

Answer:

☑ **B** and **F** are correct. Class One will compile (and issue a warning) using the 1.3 flag, and class Two will compile using the 1.4 flag.

☒ **A, C, D,** and **E** are incorrect based on the above. (Objective 2.3)

2. Given:

```
class Plane {
  static String s = "-";
  public static void main(String[] args) {
    new Plane().s1();
```

```
      System.out.println(s);
    }
    void s1() {
      try { s2(); }
      catch (Exception e) { s += "c"; }
    }
    void s2() throws Exception  {
      s3();   s += "2";
      s3();   s += "2b";
    }
    void s3() throws Exception {
      throw new Exception();
  } }
```

What is the result?

A. -

B. -c

C. -c2

D. -2c

E. -c22b

F. -2c2b

G. -2c2bc

H. Compilation fails

Answer:

☑ **B** is correct. Once s3() throws the exception to s2(), s2() throws it to s1(), and no more of s2()'s code will be executed.

☒ **A, C, D, E, F, G,** and **H** are incorrect based on the above. (Objective 2.5)

3. Given:

```
    try { int x = Integer.parseInt("two"); }
```

Which could be used to create an appropriate catch block? (Choose all that apply.)

A. ClassCastException

B. IllegalStateException

C. NumberFormatException

D. IllegalArgumentException

E. `ExceptionInInitializerError`

F. `ArrayIndexOutOfBoundsException`

Answer:

☑ **C** and **D** are correct. `Integer.parseInt` can throw a `NumberFormatException`, and `IllegalArgumentException` is its superclass (i.e., a broader exception).

☒ **A, B, E,** and **F** are not in `NumberFormatException`'s class hierarchy. (Objective 2.6)

4. Which are true? (Choose all that apply.)

A. It is appropriate to use assertions to validate arguments to methods marked `public`

B. It is appropriate to catch and handle assertion errors

C. It is NOT appropriate to use assertions to validate command-line arguments

D. It is appropriate to use assertions to generate alerts when you reach code that should not be reachable

E. It is NOT appropriate for assertions to change a program's state

Answer:

☑ **C, D,** and **E** are correct statements.

☒ **A** is incorrect. It *is* acceptable to use assertions to test the arguments of `private` methods. **B** is incorrect. While assertion errors can be caught, Sun discourages you from doing so. (Objective 2.3)

5. Given:

```
1. class Loopy {
2.    public static void main(String[] args) {
3.        int[] x = {7,6,5,4,3,2,1};
4.        // insert code here
5.          System.out.print(y + " ");
6.       }
7. } }
```

Which, inserted independently at line 4, compiles? (Choose all that apply.)

A. `for(int y : x) {`

B. `for(x : int y) {`

C. `int y = 0; for(y : x) {`

D. `for(int y=0, z=0; z<x.length; z++) { y = x[z];`

E. `for(int y=0, int z=0; z<x.length; z++) { y = x[z];`

F. `int y = 0; for(int z=0; z<x.length; z++) { y = x[z];`

Answer:

☑ **A, D,** and **F** are correct. **A** is an example of the enhanced `for` loop. **D** and **F** are examples of the basic `for` loop.

☒ **B** is incorrect because its operands are swapped. **C** is incorrect because the enhanced `for` must declare its first operand. **E** is incorrect syntax to declare two variables in a `for` statement. (Objective 2.2)

6. Given:

```
class Emu {
  static String s = "-";
  public static void main(String[] args) {
    try {
      throw new Exception();
    } catch (Exception e) {
        try {
          try { throw new Exception();
          } catch (Exception ex) { s += "ic "; }
          throw new Exception(); }
        catch (Exception x) { s += "mc "; }
        finally { s += "mf "; }
    } finally { s += "of "; }
    System.out.println(s);
  } }
```

What is the result?

A. `-ic of`

B. `-mf of`

C. `-mc mf`

D. `-ic mf of`

E. `-ic mc mf of`

F. `-ic mc of mf`

G. Compilation fails

Answer:

☑ **E** is correct. There is no problem nesting `try` / `catch` blocks. As is normal, when an exception is thrown, the code in the `catch` block runs, then the code in the `finally` block runs.

☒ **A, B, C, D,** and **F** are incorrect based on the above. (Objective 2.5)

7. Given:

```
3. class SubException extends Exception { }
4. class SubSubException extends SubException { }
5.
6. public class CC { void doStuff() throws SubException { } }
7.
8. class CC2 extends CC { void doStuff() throws SubSubException { } }
9.
10. class CC3 extends CC { void doStuff() throws Exception { } }
11.
12. class CC4 extends CC { void doStuff(int x) throws Exception { } }
13.
14. class CC5 extends CC {  void doStuff()  { } }
```

What is the result? (Choose all that apply.)

A. Compilation succeeds

B. Compilation fails due to an error on line 8

C. Compilation fails due to an error on line 10

D. Compilation fails due to an error on line 12

E. Compilation fails due to an error on line 14

Answer:

☑ **C** is correct. An overriding method cannot throw a broader exception than the method it's overriding. Class CC4's method is an overload, not an override.

☒ **A, B, D,** and **E** are incorrect based on the above. (Objectives 1.5, 2.4)

8. Given:

```
3. public class Ebb {
4.   static int x - 7;
5.   public static void main(String[] args) {
6.     String s = "";
```

```
7.      for(int y = 0; y < 3; y++) {
8.        x++;
9.        switch(x) {
10.          case 8: s += "8 ";
11.          case 9: s += "9 ";
12.          case 10: { s+= "10 "; break; }
13.          default: s += "d ";
14.          case 13: s+= "13 ";
15.        }
16.      }
17.      System.out.println(s);
18.    }
19.    static { x++; }
20. }
```

What is the result?

A. 9 10 d

B. 8 9 10 d

C. 9 10 10 d

D. 9 10 10 d 13

E. 8 9 10 10 d 13

F. 8 9 10 9 10 10 d 13

G. Compilation fails

Answer:

☑ **D** is correct. Did you catch the static initializer block? Remember that switches work on "fall-thru" logic, and that fall-thru logic also applies to the default case, which is used when no other case matches.

☒ **A, B, C, E, F,** and **G** are incorrect based on the above. (Objective 2.1)

9. Given:

```
3. class Infinity { }
4. public class Beyond extends Infinity {
5.    static Integer i;
6.    public static void main(String[] args) {
7.      int sw = (int)(Math.random() * 3);
8.      switch(sw) {
9.        case 0: {  for(int x = 10; x > 5; x++)
```

```
10.                        if(x > 10000000) x = 10;
11.                   break; }
12.        case 1: {  int y = 7 * i;  break;  }
13.        case 2: {  Infinity inf = new Beyond();
14.                   Beyond b = (Beyond)inf;  }
15.      }
16.    }
17. }
```

And given that line 7 will assign the value 0, 1, or 2 to sw, which are true? (Choose all that apply.)

A. Compilation fails

B. A ClassCastException might be thrown

C. A StackOverflowError might be thrown

D. A NullPointerException might be thrown

E. An IllegalStateException might be thrown

F. The program might hang without ever completing

G. The program will always complete without exception

Answer:

☑ **D** and **F** are correct. Because i was not initialized, case 1 will throw an NPE. Case 0 will initiate an endless loop, not a stack overflow. Case 2's downcast will *not* cause an exception.

☒ **A, B, C, E,** and **G** are incorrect based on the above. (Objective 2.6)

10. Given:

```
3. public class Circles {
4.   public static void main(String[] args) {
5.     int[] ia = {1,3,5,7,9};
6.     for(int x : ia) {
7.       for(int j = 0; j < 3; j++) {
8.         if(x > 4 && x < 8) continue;
9.         System.out.print(" " + x);
10.        if(j == 1) break;
11.        continue;
12.      }
13.      continue;
14.    }
15.  }
16. }
```

What is the result?

A. 1 3 9

B. 5 5 7 7

C. 1 3 3 9 9

D. 1 1 3 3 9 9

E. 1 1 1 3 3 3 9 9 9

F. Compilation fails

Answer:

☑ **D** is correct. The basic rule for unlabeled continue statements is that the current iteration stops early and execution jumps to the next iteration. The last two continue statements are redundant!

☒ **A, B, C, E,** and **F** are incorrect based on the above. (Objective 2.2)

11. Given:

```
3. public class OverAndOver {
4.    static String s = "";
5.    public static void main(String[] args) {
6.       try {
7.          s += "1";
8.          throw new Exception();
9.       } catch (Exception e) { s += "2";
10.      } finally { s += "3"; doStuff(); s += "4";
11.      }
12.      System.out.println(s);
13.   }
14.   static void doStuff() { int x = 0; int y = 7/x; }
15. }
```

What is the result?

A. 12

B. 13

C. 123

D. 1234

E. Compilation fails

F. 123 followed by an exception

G. 1234 followed by an exception

H. An exception is thrown with no other output

Answer:

☑ **H** is correct. It's true that the value of String s is 123 at the time that the divide-by-zero exception is thrown, but finally() is *not* guaranteed to complete, and in this case finally() never completes, so the System.out.println (S.O.P.) never executes.

☒ **A, B, C, D, E, F,** and **G** are incorrect based on the above. (Objective 2.5)

12. Given:

```
3. public class Wind {
4.   public static void main(String[] args) {
5.     foreach:
6.     for(int j=0; j<5; j++) {
7.       for(int k=0; k< 3; k++) {
8.         System.out.print(" " + j);
9.         if(j==3 && k==1) break foreach;
10.        if(j==0 || j==2) break;
11.       }
12.     }
13.   }
14. }
```

What is the result?

A. 0 1 2 3

B. 1 1 1 3 3

C. 0 1 1 1 2 3 3

D. 1 1 1 3 3 4 4 4

E. 0 1 1 1 2 3 3 4 4 4

F. Compilation fails

Answer:

☑ **C** is correct. A break breaks out of the current innermost loop and continues. A labeled break breaks out of and terminates the current loops.

☒ **A, B, D, E,** and **F** are incorrect based on the above. (Objective 2.2)

13. Given:

```
3. public class Gotcha {
4.   public static void main(String[] args) {
5.     // insert code here
6.
7.   }
8.   void go() {
9.     go();
10.  }
11. }
```

And given the following three code fragments:

```
I.   new Gotcha().go();
II.  try { new Gotcha().go(); }
     catch (Error e) { System.out.println("ouch"); }

III. try { new Gotcha().go(); }
     catch (Exception e) { System.out.println("ouch"); }
```

When fragments I - III are added, independently, at line 5, which are true? (Choose all that apply.)

A. Some will not compile

B. They will all compile

C. All will complete normally

D. None will complete normally

E. Only one will complete normally

F. Two of them will complete normally

Answer:

☑ **B** and **E** are correct. First off, `go()` is a badly designed recursive method, guaranteed to cause a StackOverflowError. Since `Exception` is not a superclass of `Error`, catching an `Exception` will not help handle an `Error`, so fragment III will not complete normally. Only fragment II will catch the `Error`.

☒ **A, C, D,** and **F** are incorrect based on the above. (Objective 2.5)

14. Given:

```
3. public class Clumsy {
4.   public static void main(String[] args) {
5.     int j = 7;
6.     assert(++j > 7);
7.     assert(++j > 8): "hi";
8.     assert(j > 10): j=12;
9.     assert(j==12): doStuff();
10.    assert(j==12): new Clumsy();
11.   }
12.   static void doStuff() { }
13. }
```

Which are true? (Choose all that apply.)

A. Compilation succeeds

B. Compilation fails due to an error on line 6

C. Compilation fails due to an error on line 7

D. Compilation fails due to an error on line 8

E. Compilation fails due to an error on line 9

F. Compilation fails due to an error on line 10

Answer:

☑ **E** is correct. When an `assert` statement has two expressions, the second expression must return a value. The only two-expression `assert` statement that doesn't return a value is on line 9.

☒ **A, B, C, D,** and **F** are incorrect based on the above. (Objective 2.3)

15. Given:

```
1. public class Frisbee {
2.   // insert code here
3.     int x = 0;
4.     System.out.println(7/x);
5.   }
6. }
```

And given the following four code fragments:

```
I.    public static void main(String[] args) {
II.   public static void main(String[] args) throws Exception {
III.  public static void main(String[] args) throws IOException {
IV.   public static void main(String[] args) throws RuntimeException {
```

If the four fragments are inserted independently at line 4, which are true? (Choose all that apply.)

A. All four will compile and execute without exception

B. All four will compile and execute and throw an exception

C. Some, but not all, will compile and execute without exception

D. Some, but not all, will compile and execute and throw an exception

E. When considering fragments II, III, and IV, of those that will compile, adding a try/catch block around line 6 will cause compilation to fail

> **Answer:**
>
> ☑ **D** is correct. This is kind of sneaky, but remember that we're trying to toughen you up for the real exam. If you're going to throw an IOException, you have to import the java.io package or declare the exception with a fully qualified name.
>
> ☒ **E** is incorrect because it's okay to both handle and declare an exception. **A, B,** and **C** are incorrect based on the above. (Objective 2.4)

16. Given:

```
2. class MyException extends Exception { }
3. class Tire {
4.   void doStuff() {  }
5. }
6. public class Retread extends Tire {
7.   public static void main(String[] args) {
8.     new Retread().doStuff();
9.   }
10.  // insert code here
11.    System.out.println(7/0);
12.  }
13. }
```

And given the following four code fragments:

```
I.   void doStuff() {
II.  void doStuff() throws MyException {
III. void doStuff() throws RuntimeException {
IV.  void doStuff() throws ArithmeticException {
```

When fragments I - IV are added, independently, at line 10, which are true? (Choose all that apply.)

A. None will compile

B. They will all compile

C. Some, but not all, will compile

D. All of those that compile will throw an exception at runtime

E. None of those that compile will throw an exception at runtime

F. Only some of those that compile will throw an exception at runtime

Answer:

☑ **C** and **D** are correct. An overriding method cannot throw checked exceptions that are broader than those thrown by the overridden method. However an overriding method *can* throw RuntimeExceptions not thrown by the overridden method.

☒ **A, B, E,** and **F** are incorrect based on the above. (Objective 2.4)

6

Strings, I/O, Formatting, and Parsing

T his chapter focuses on the various API-related topics that were added to the exam for Java 5 and remain in the Java 6 exam. J2SE comes with an enormous API, and a lot of your work as a Java programmer will revolve around using this API. The exam team chose to focus on APIs for I/O, formatting, and parsing. Each of these topics could fill an entire book. Fortunately, you won't have to become a total I/O or regex guru to do well on the exam. The intention of the exam team was to include just the basic aspects of these technologies, and in this chapter we cover *more* than you'll need to get through the String, I/O, formatting, and parsing objectives on the exam.

CERTIFICATION OBJECTIVE

String, StringBuilder, and StringBuffer (Exam Objective 3.1)

3.1 Discuss the differences between the String, StringBuilder, and StringBuffer classes.

Everything you needed to know about Strings in the SCJP 1.4 exam, you'll need to know for the SCJP 5 and SCJP 6 exams. plus, Sun added the *StringBuilder* class to the API, to provide faster, nonsynchronized StringBuffer capability. The StringBuilder class has exactly the same methods as the old StringBuffer class, but StringBuilder is faster because its methods aren't synchronized. Both classes give you String-like objects that handle some of the String class's shortcomings (like immutability).

The String Class

This section covers the String class, and the key concept to understand is that once a String object is created, it can never be changed—so what is happening when a String object seems to be changing? Let's find out.

Strings Are Immutable Objects

We'll start with a little background information about strings. You may not need this for the test, but a little context will help. Handling "strings" of characters is a fundamental aspect of most programming languages. In Java, each character in a string is a 16-bit Unicode character. Because Unicode characters are 16 bits (not the skimpy 7 or 8 bits that ASCII provides), a rich, international set of characters is easily represented in Unicode.

In Java, strings are objects. Just like other objects, you can create an instance of a String with the new keyword, as follows:

```
String s = new String();
```

This line of code creates a new object of class String, and assigns it to the reference variable s. So far, String objects seem just like other objects. Now, let's give the String a value:

```
s = "abcdef";
```

As you might expect, the String class has about a zillion constructors, so you can use a more efficient shortcut:

```
String s = new String("abcdef");
```

And just because you'll use strings all the time, you can even say this:

```
String s = "abcdef";
```

There are some subtle differences between these options that we'll discuss later, but what they have in common is that they all create a new String object, with a value of "abcdef", and assign it to a reference variable s. Now let's say that you want a second reference to the String object referred to by s:

```
String s2 = s;    //  refer s2 to the same String as s
```

So far so good. String objects seem to be behaving just like other objects, so what's all the fuss about?...Immutability! (What the heck is immutability?) Once you have assigned a String a value, that value can never change— it's immutable, frozen solid, won't budge, fini, done. (We'll talk about why later, don't let us forget.) The good news is that while the String object is immutable, its reference variable is not, so to continue with our previous example:

```
s = s.concat(" more stuff");  // the concat() method 'appends'
                              // a literal to the end
```

Now wait just a minute, didn't we just say that Strings were immutable? So what's all this "appending to the end of the string" talk? Excellent question: let's look at what really happened...

The VM took the value of String s (which was "abcdef"), and tacked " more stuff" onto the end, giving us the value "abcdef more stuff". Since Strings are immutable, the VM couldn't stuff this new value into the old String referenced by s, so it created a new String object, gave it the value "abcdef more stuff", and made s refer to it. At this point in our example, we have two String objects: the first one we created, with the value "abcdef", and the second one with the value "abcdef more stuff". Technically there are now three String objects, because the literal argument to concat, " more stuff", is itself a new String object. But we have references only to "abcdef" (referenced by s2) and "abcdef more stuff" (referenced by s).

What if we didn't have the foresight or luck to create a second reference variable for the "abcdef" String before we called s = s.concat(" more stuff");? In that case, the original, unchanged String containing "abcdef" would still exist in memory, but it would be considered "lost." No code in our program has any way to reference it—it is lost to us. Note, however, that the original "abcdef" String didn't change (it can't, remember, it's immutable); only the reference variable s was changed, so that it would refer to a different String. Figure 6-1 shows what happens on the heap when you reassign a reference variable. Note that the dashed line indicates a deleted reference.

To review our first example:

```
String s = "abcdef";    // create a new String object, with
                        // value "abcdef", refer s to it
String s2 = s;          // create a 2nd reference variable
                        // referring to the same String

// create a new String object, with value "abcdef more stuff",
// refer s to it. (Change s's reference from the old String
// to the new String.) ( Remember s2 is still referring to
// the original "abcdef" String.)

s = s.concat(" more stuff");
```

FIGURE 6-1	String objects and their reference variables

Step 1: `String s = "abc";`

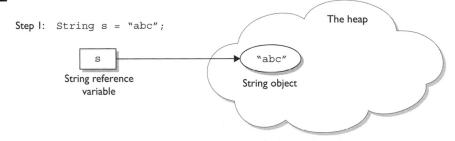

Step 2: `String s2 = s;`

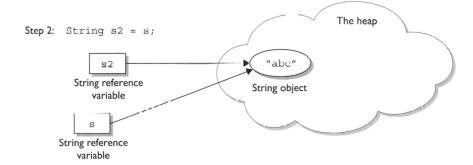

Step 3: `s = s.concat ("def");`

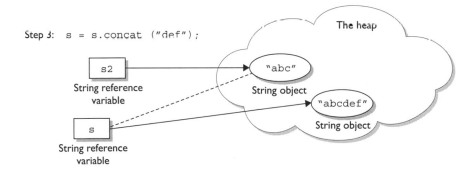

Let's look at another example:

```
String x = "Java";
x.concat(" Rules!");
System.out.println("x = " + x);  // the output is "x = Java"
```

The first line is straightforward: create a new String object, give it the value "Java", and refer x to it. Next the VM creates a second String object with the value "Java Rules!" but nothing refers to it. The second String object is instantly lost; you can't get to it. The reference variable x still refers to the original String with the value "Java". Figure 6-2 shows creating a String without assigning a reference to it.

FIGURE 6-2   A String object is abandoned upon creation

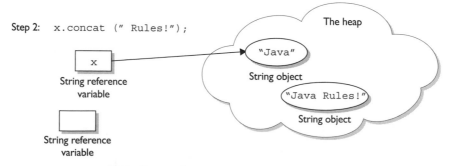

Let's expand this current example. We started with

```
String x = "Java";
x.concat(" Rules!");
System.out.println("x = " + x);    // the output is: x = Java
```

Now let's add

```
x.toUpperCase();
System.out.println("x = " + x);    // the output is still:
                                   // x = Java
```

(We actually did just create a new String object with the value "JAVA", but it was lost, and x still refers to the original, unchanged String "Java".) How about adding

```
x.replace('a', 'X');
System.out.println("x = " + x);    // the output is still:
                                   // x = Java
```

Can you determine what happened? The VM created yet another new String object, with the value "JXvX", (replacing the a's with x's), but once again this new String was lost, leaving x to refer to the original unchanged and unchangeable String object, with the value "Java". In all of these cases we called various String methods to create a new String by altering an existing String, but we never assigned the newly created String to a reference variable.

But we can put a small spin on the previous example:

```
String x = "Java";
x = x.concat(" Rules!");            // Now we're assigning the
                                   // new String to x
System.out.println("x = " + x);    // the output will be:
                                   // x = Java Rules!
```

This time, when the VM runs the second line, a new String object is created with the value of "Java Rules!", and x is set to reference it. But wait, there's more—now the original String object, "Java", has been lost, and no one is referring to it. So in both examples we created two String objects and only one reference variable, so one of the two String objects was left out in the cold. See Figure 6-3 for a graphic depiction of this sad story. The dashed line indicates a deleted reference.

| FIGURE 6-3 | An old String object being abandoned |

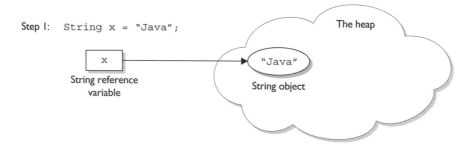

Step I: `String x = "Java";`

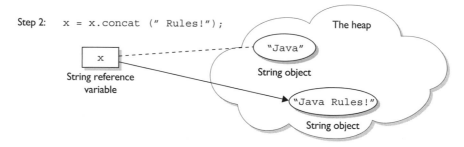

Step 2:   `x = x.concat (" Rules!");`

Notice in step 2 that there is no
valid reference to the "Java" String;
that object has been "abandoned,"
and a new object created.

Let's take this example a little further:

```
String x = "Java";
x = x.concat(" Rules!");
System.out.println("x = " + x);    // the output is:
                                    // x = Java Rules!

x.toLowerCase();                    // no assignment, create a
                                    // new, abandoned String

System.out.println("x = " + x);    // no assignment, the output
                                    // is still: x = Java Rules!
```

```
x = x.toLowerCase();              // create a new String,
                                  // assigned to x
System.out.println("x = " + x);   // the assignment causes the
                                  // output: x = java rules!
```

The preceding discussion contains the keys to understanding Java String immutability. If you really, really get the examples and diagrams, backward and forward, you should get 80 percent of the String questions on the exam correct.

We will cover more details about Strings next, but make no mistake—in terms of bang for your buck, what we've already covered is by far the most important part of understanding how String objects work in Java.

We'll finish this section by presenting an example of the kind of devilish String question you might expect to see on the exam. Take the time to work it out on paper (as a hint, try to keep track of how many objects and reference variables there are, and which ones refer to which).

```
String s1 = "spring ";
String s2 = s1 + "summer ";
s1.concat("fall ");
s2.concat(s1);
s1 += "winter ";
System.out.println(s1 + " " + s2);
```

What is the output? For extra credit, how many String objects and how many reference variables were created prior to the println statement?

Answer: The result of this code fragment is spring winter   spring summer. There are two reference variables, s1 and s2. There were a total of eight String objects created as follows: "spring", "summer " (lost), "spring summer", "fall" (lost), "spring fall" (lost), "spring summer spring" (lost), "winter" (lost), "spring winter" (at this point "spring" is lost). Only two of the eight String objects are not lost in this process.

Important Facts About Strings and Memory

In this section we'll discuss how Java handles String objects in memory, and some of the reasons behind these behaviors.

One of the key goals of any good programming language is to make efficient use of memory. As applications grow, it's very common for String literals to occupy large amounts of a program's memory, and there is often a lot of redundancy within the universe of String literals for a program. To make Java more memory efficient, the JVM sets aside a special area of memory called the "String constant pool." When the compiler encounters a String literal, it checks the pool to see if an identical String already exists. If a match is found, the reference to the new literal is directed to the existing String, and no new String literal object is created. (The existing String simply has an additional reference.) Now we can start to see why making String objects immutable is such a good idea. If several reference variables refer to the same String without even knowing it, it would be very bad if any of them could change the String's value.

You might say, "Well that's all well and good, but what if someone overrides the String class functionality; couldn't that cause problems in the pool?" That's one of the main reasons that the String class is marked `final`. Nobody can override the behaviors of any of the String methods, so you can rest assured that the String objects you are counting on to be immutable will, in fact, be immutable.

Creating New Strings

Earlier we promised to talk more about the subtle differences between the various methods of creating a String. Let's look at a couple of examples of how a String might be created, and let's further assume that no other String objects exist in the pool:

```
String s = "abc";    //  creates one String object and one
                     //  reference variable
```

In this simple case, "abc" will go in the pool and s will refer to it.

```
String s = new String("abc");  // creates two objects,
                               // and one reference variable
```

In this case, because we used the `new` keyword, Java will create a new String object in normal (nonpool) memory, and s will refer to it. In addition, the literal "abc" will be placed in the pool.

Important Methods in the String Class

The following methods are some of the more commonly used methods in the String class, and also the ones that you're most likely to encounter on the exam.

- **charAt()** Returns the character located at the specified index
- **concat()** Appends one String to the end of another ("+" also works)
- **equalsIgnoreCase()** Determines the equality of two Strings, ignoring case
- **length()** Returns the number of characters in a String
- **replace()** Replaces occurrences of a character with a new character
- **substring()** Returns a part of a String
- **toLowerCase()** Returns a String with uppercase characters converted
- **toString()** Returns the value of a String
- **toUpperCase()** Returns a String with lowercase characters converted
- **trim()** Removes whitespace from the ends of a String

Let's look at these methods in more detail.

public char charAt(int index) This method returns the character located at the String's specified index. Remember, String indexes are zero-based—for example,

```
String x = "airplane";
System.out.println( x.charAt(2) );        //  output is 'r'
```

public String concat(String s) This method returns a String with the value of the String passed in to the method appended to the end of the String used to invoke the method—for example,

```
String x = "taxi";
System.out.println( x.concat(" cab") ); // output is "taxi cab"
```

The overloaded + and += operators perform functions similar to the concat() method—for example,

```
String x = "library";
System.out.println( x + " card");      // output is "library card"

String x = "Atlantic";
x+= " ocean";
System.out.println( x );               // output is "Atlantic ocean"
```

In the preceding "Atlantic ocean" example, notice that the value of x really did change! Remember that the += operator is an assignment operator, so line 2 is really creating a new String, "Atlantic ocean", and assigning it to the x variable. After line 2 executes, the original String x was referring to, "Atlantic", is abandoned.

public boolean equalsIgnoreCase(String s) This method returns a boolean value (true or false) depending on whether the value of the String in the argument is the same as the value of the String used to invoke the method. This method will return true even when characters in the String objects being compared have differing cases—for example,

```
String x = "Exit";
System.out.println( x.equalsIgnoreCase("EXIT"));    // is "true"
System.out.println( x.equalsIgnoreCase("tixe"));    // is "false"
```

public int length() This method returns the length of the String used to invoke the method—for example,

```
String x = "01234567";
System.out.println( x.length() );       // returns "8"
```

public String replace(char old, char new) This method returns a String whose value is that of the String used to invoke the method, updated so that any occurrence of the char in the first argument is replaced by the char in the second argument—for example,

```
String x = "oxoxoxox";
System.out.println( x.replace('x', 'X') );    // output is
                                              // "oXoXoXoX"
```

public String substring(int begin)
public String substring(int begin, int end) The substring() method is used to return a part (or substring) of the String used to invoke the method. The first argument represents the starting location (zero-based) of the substring. If the call has only one argument, the substring returned will include the characters to the end of the original String. If the call has two arguments, the substring returned will end with the character located in the nth position of the original String where n is the

second argument. Unfortunately, the ending argument is not zero-based, so if the second argument is 7, the last character in the returned String will be in the original String's 7 position, which is index 6 (ouch). Let's look at some examples:

```
String x = "0123456789";              // as if by magic, the value
                                      // of each char
                                      // is the same as its index!
System.out.println( x.substring(5) );     // output is  "56789"
System.out.println( x.substring(5, 8));   // output is "567"
```

The first example should be easy: start at index 5 and return the rest of the String. The second example should be read as follows: start at index 5 and return the characters up to and including the 8th position (index 7).

public String toLowerCase() This method returns a String whose value is the String used to invoke the method, but with any uppercase characters converted to lowercase—for example,

```
String x = "A New Moon";
System.out.println( x.toLowerCase() );    // output is
                                          // "a new moon"
```

public String toString() This method returns the value of the String used to invoke the method. What? Why would you need such a seemingly "do nothing" method? All objects in Java must have a toString() method, which typically returns a String that in some meaningful way describes the object in question. In the case of a String object, what more meaningful way than the String's value? For the sake of consistency, here's an example:

```
String x = "big surprise";
System.out.println( x.toString() );      // output -
                                          // reader's exercise
```

public String toUpperCase() This method returns a String whose value is the String used to invoke the method, but with any lowercase characters converted to uppercase—for example,

```
String x = "A New Moon";
System.out.println( x.toUpperCase() );    // output is
                                          // "A NEW MOON"
```

public String trim() This method returns a String whose value is the String used to invoke the method, but with any leading or trailing blank spaces removed—for example,

```
String x = "       hi        ";
System.out.println( x + "x" );            // result is
                                          // "     hi     x"
System.out.println( x.trim() + "x");      // result is "hix"
```

The StringBuffer and StringBuilder Classes

The java.lang.StringBuffer and java.lang.StringBuilder classes should be used when you have to make a lot of modifications to strings of characters. As we discussed in the previous section, String objects are immutable, so if you choose to do a lot of manipulations with String objects, you will end up with a lot of abandoned String objects in the String pool. (Even in these days of gigabytes of RAM, it's not a good idea to waste precious memory on discarded String pool objects.) On the other hand, objects of type StringBuffer and StringBuilder can be modified over and over again without leaving behind a great effluence of discarded String objects.

on the Job

A common use for StringBuffers and StringBuilders is file I/O when large, ever-changing streams of input are being handled by the program. In these cases, large blocks of characters are handled as units, and StringBuffer objects are the ideal way to handle a block of data, pass it on, and then reuse the same memory to handle the next block of data.

StringBuffer vs. StringBuilder

The StringBuilder class was added in Java 5. It has exactly the same API as the StringBuffer class, except StringBuilder is not thread safe. In other words, its methods are not synchronized. (More about thread safety in Chapter 9.) Sun recommends that you use StringBuilder instead of StringBuffer whenever possible because StringBuilder will run faster (and perhaps jump higher). So apart from synchronization, anything we say about StringBuilder's methods holds true for StringBuffer's methods, and vice versa. The exam might use these classes in the creation of thread-safe applications, and we'll discuss how *that* works in Chapter 9.

Using StringBuilder and StringBuffer

In the previous section, we saw how the exam might test your understanding of String immutability with code fragments like this:

```
String x = "abc";
x.concat("def");
System.out.println("x = " + x);       // output is "x = abc"
```

Because no new assignment was made, the new String object created with the concat() method was abandoned instantly. We also saw examples like this:

```
String x = "abc";
x = x.concat("def");
System.out.println("x = " + x);       // output is "x = abcdef"
```

We got a nice new String out of the deal, but the downside is that the old String "abc" has been lost in the String pool, thus wasting memory. If we were using a StringBuffer instead of a String, the code would look like this:

```
StringBuffer sb = new StringBuffer("abc");
sb.append("def");
System.out.println("sb = " + sb);       // output is "sb = abcdef"
```

All of the StringBuffer methods we will discuss operate on the value of the StringBuffer object invoking the method. So a call to `sb.append("def");` is actually appending "def" to itself (StringBuffer sb). In fact, these method calls can be chained to each other—for example,

```
StringBuilder sb = new StringBuilder("abc");
sb.append("def").reverse().insert(3, "---");
System.out.println( sb );               // output is  "fed---cba"
```

Notice that in each of the previous two examples, there was a single call to new, concordantly in each example we weren't creating any extra objects. Each example needed only a single StringXxx object to execute.

Important Methods in the StringBuffer and StringBuilder Classes

The following method returns a StringXxx object with the argument's value appended to the value of the object that invoked the method.

public synchronized StringBuffer append(String s)
As we've seen earlier, this method will update the value of the object that invoked the method, whether or not the return is assigned to a variable. This method will take many different arguments, including boolean, char, double, float, int, long, and others, but the most likely use on the exam will be a String argument—for example,

```
StringBuffer sb = new StringBuffer("set ");
sb.append("point");

System.out.println(sb);        // output is "set point"
StringBuffer sb2 = new StringBuffer("pi = ");
sb2.append(3.14159f);
System.out.println(sb2);       // output is  "pi = 3.14159"
```

public StringBuilder delete(int start, int end)
This method returns a StringBuilder object and updates the value of the StringBuilder object that invoked the method call. In both cases, a substring is removed from the original object. The starting index of the substring to be removed is defined by the first argument (which is zero-based), and the ending index of the substring to be removed is defined by the second argument (but it is one-based)! Study the following example carefully:

```
StringBuilder sb = new StringBuilder("0123456789");
System.out.println(sb.delete(4,6));        // output is "01236789"
```

exam
watch

The exam will probably test your knowledge of the difference between String and StringBuffer objects. Because StringBuffer objects are changeable, the following code fragment will behave differently than a similar code fragment that uses String objects:

```
StringBuffer sb = new StringBuffer("abc");
sb.append("def");
System.out.println( sb );
```

In this case, the output will be: "abcdef"

---

public StringBuilder insert(int offset, String s)   This method returns a StringBuilder object and updates the value of the StringBuilder object that invoked the method call. In both cases, the String passed in to the second argument is inserted into the original StringBuilder starting at the offset location represented by the first argument (the offset is zero-based). Again, other types of data can be passed in through the second argument (boolean, char, double, float, int, long, and so on), but the String argument is the one you're most likely to see:

```
StringBuilder sb = new StringBuilder("01234567");
sb.insert(4, "---");
System.out.println( sb );           //   output is  "0123---4567"
```

public synchronized StringBuffer reverse()   This method returns a StringBuffer object and updates the value of the StringBuffer object that invoked the method call. In both cases, the characters in the StringBuffer are reversed, the first character becoming the last, the second becoming the second to the last, and so on:

```
StringBuffer s = new StringBuffer("A man a plan a canal Panama");
sb.reverse();
System.out.println(sb); // output: "amanaP lanac a nalp a nam A"
```

public String toString()   This method returns the value of the StringBuffer object that invoked the method call as a String:

```
StringBuffer sb = new StringBuffer("test string");
System.out.println( sb.toString() );  // output is "test string"
```

That's it for StringBuffers and StringBuilders. If you take only one thing away from this section, it's that unlike Strings, StringBuffer objects and StringBuilder objects can be changed.

Many of the exam questions covering this chapter's topics use a tricky (and not very readable) bit of Java syntax known as "chained methods." A statement with chained methods has this general form:

```
result = method1().method2().method3();
```

In theory, any number of methods can be chained in this fashion, although typically you won't see more than three. Here's how to decipher these "handy Java shortcuts" when you encounter them:

1. Determine what the leftmost method call will return (let's call it x).
2. Use x as the object invoking the second (from the left) method. If there are only two chained methods, the result of the second method call is the expression's result.
3. If there is a third method, the result of the second method call is used to invoke the third method, whose result is the expression's result—for example,

```
String x = "abc";
String y = x.concat("def").toUpperCase().replace('C','x');
//chained methods
System.out.println("y = " + y); // result is "y = ABxDEF"
```

Let's look at what happened. The literal def *was concatenated to* abc, *creating a temporary, intermediate String (soon to be lost), with the value* abcdef. *The* toUpperCase() *method created a new (soon to be lost) temporary String with the value* ABCDEF. *The* replace() *method created a final String with the value* ABxDEF, *and referred* y *to it.*

File Navigation and I/O (Exam Objective 3.2)

3.2   Given a scenario involving navigating file systems, reading from files, or writing to files, develop the correct solution using the following classes (sometimes in combination), from java.io: BufferedReader, BufferedWriter, File, FileReader, FileWriter, PrintWriter, and Console.

I/O has had a strange history with the SCJP certification. It was included in all the versions of the exam up to and including 1.2, then removed from the 1.4 exam, and then re-introduced for Java 5 and extended for Java 6.

I/O is a huge topic in general, and the Java APIs that deal with I/O in one fashion or another are correspondingly huge. A general discussion of I/O could include topics such as file I/O, console I/O, thread I/O, high-performance I/O, byte-oriented I/O, character-oriented I/O, I/O filtering and wrapping, serialization, and more. Luckily for us, the I/O topics included in the Java 5 exam are fairly well restricted to file I/O for characters, and serialization.

Here's a summary of the I/O classes you'll need to understand for the exam:

■ **File**   The API says that the class File is "An abstract representation of file and directory pathnames." The File class isn't used to actually read or write data; it's used to work at a higher level, making new empty files, searching for files, deleting files, making directories, and working with paths.

■ **FileReader**   This class is used to read character files. Its read() methods are fairly low-level, allowing you to read single characters, the whole stream of characters, or a fixed number of characters. FileReaders are usually *wrapped* by higher-level objects such as BufferedReaders, which improve performance and provide more convenient ways to work with the data.

■ **BufferedReader**   This class is used to make lower-level Reader classes like FileReader more efficient and easier to use. Compared to FileReaders, BufferedReaders read relatively large chunks of data from a file at once, and keep this data in a buffer. When you ask for the next character or line of data, it is retrieved from the buffer, which minimizes the number of times that time-intensive, file read operations are performed. In addition,

BufferedReader provides more convenient methods such as `readLine()`, that allow you to get the next line of characters from a file.

■ **FileWriter**   This class is used to write to character files. Its `write()` methods allow you to write character(s) or Strings to a file. FileWriters are usually *wrapped* by higher-level Writer objects such as BufferedWriters or PrintWriters, which provide better performance and higher-level, more flexible methods to write data.

■ **BufferedWriter**   This class is used to make lower-level classes like FileWriters more efficient and easier to use. Compared to FileWriters, BufferedWriters write relatively large chunks of data to a file at once, minimizing the number of times that slow, file writing operations are performed. The BufferedWriter class also provides a `newLine()` method to create platform-specific line separators automatically.

■ **PrintWriter**   This class has been enhanced significantly in Java 5. Because of newly created methods and constructors (like building a PrintWriter with a File or a String), you might find that you can use PrintWriter in places where you previously needed a Writer to be wrapped with a FileWriter and/or a BufferedWriter. New methods like `format()`, `printf()`, and `append()` make PrintWriters very flexible and powerful.

■ **Console**   This new, Java 6 convenience class provides methods to read input from the console and write formatted output to the console.

Stream classes are used to read and write bytes, and Readers and Writers are used to read and write characters. Since all of the file I/O on the exam is related to characters, if you see API class names containing the word "Stream", for instance DataOutputStream, then the question is probably about serialization, or something unrelated to the actual I/O objective.

Creating Files Using Class File

Objects of type File are used to represent the actual files (but not the data in the files) or directories that exist on a computer's physical disk. Just to make sure we're clear, when we talk about an object of type File, we'll say File, with a capital F. When we're talking about what exists on a hard drive, we'll call it a file with a lowercase f (unless it's a variable name in some code). Let's start with a few basic examples of creating files, writing to them, and reading from them. First, let's create a new file and write a few lines of data to it:

```
import java.io.*;            // The Java 6 exam focuses on
                            // classes from java.io
class Writer1 {
  public static void main(String [] args) {
    File file = new File("fileWrite1.txt");    // There's no
                                              // file yet!
  }
}
```

If you compile and run this program, when you look at the contents of your current directory, you'll discover absolutely no indication of a file called `fileWrite1.txt`. When you make a new instance of the class File, *you're not yet making an actual file, you're just creating a filename*. Once you have a File *object*, there are several ways to make an actual file. Let's see what we can do with the File object we just made:

```
import java.io.*;

class Writer1 {
 public static void main(String [] args) {
   try {                         // warning: exceptions possible
     boolean newFile = false;
     File file = new File            // it's only an object
                   ("fileWrite1.txt");
     System.out.println(file.exists());  // look for a real file
     newFile = file.createNewFile();     // maybe create a file!
     System.out.println(newFile);        // already there?
     System.out.println(file.exists());  // look again
   } catch(IOException e) { }
 }
}
```

This produces the output

```
false
true
true
```

And also produces an empty file in your current directory. If you run the code a *second* time you get the output

```
true
false
true
```

Let's examine these sets of output:

■ **First execution**   The first call to `exists()` returned `false`, which we expected...remember `new File()` doesn't create a file on the disk! The `createNewFile()` method created an actual file, and returned `true`, indicating that a new file was created, and that one didn't already exist. Finally, we called `exists()` again, and this time it returned `true`, indicating that the file existed on the disk.

■ **Second execution**   The first call to `exists()` returns `true` because we built the file during the first run. Then the call to `createNewFile()` returns `false` since the method didn't create a file this time through. Of course, the last call to `exists()` returns `true`.

A couple of other new things happened in this code. First, notice that we had to put our file creation code in a try/catch. This is true for almost all of the file I/O code you'll ever write. I/O is one of those inherently risky things. We're keeping it simple for now, and ignoring the exceptions, but we still need to follow the handle-or-declare rule since most I/O methods declare checked exceptions. We'll talk more about I/O exceptions later. We used a couple of File's methods in this code:

■ **boolean exists()**   This method returns `true` if it can find the actual file.
■ **boolean createNewFile()**   This method creates a new file if it doesn't already exist.

Using FileWriter and FileReader

In practice, you probably won't use the FileWriter and FileReader classes without wrapping them (more about "wrapping" very soon). That said, let's go ahead and do a little "naked" file I/O:

```java
import java.io.*;

class Writer2 {
  public static void main(String [] args) {
    char[] in = new char[50];            // to store input
    int size = 0;
    try {
      File file = new File(              // just an object
                "fileWrite2.txt");
      FileWriter fw =
                new FileWriter(file);    // create an actual file
                                         // & a FileWriter obj
      fw.write("howdy\nfolks\n");        // write characters to
                                         // the file
      fw.flush();                        // flush before closing
      fw.close();                        // close file when done
```

```
        FileReader fr =
                new FileReader(file);   // create a FileReader
                                        // object
        size = fr.read(in);            // read the whole file!
        System.out.print(size + " ");  // how many bytes read
        for(char c : in)               // print the array
          System.out.print(c);
        fr.close();                    // again, always close
      } catch(IOException e) { }
    }
  }
}
```

which produces the output:

```
12 howdy
folks
```

Here's what just happened:

1. `FileWriter fw = new FileWriter(file)` did three things:

   a. It created a FileWriter reference variable, `fw`.

   b. It created a FileWriter object, and assigned it to `fw`.

   c. It created an actual empty file out on the disk (and you can prove it).

2. We wrote 12 characters to the file with the `write()` method, and we did a `flush()` and a `close()`.

3. We made a new FileReader object, which also opened the file on disk for reading.

4. The `read()` method read the whole file, a character at a time, and put it into the `char[]` `in`.

5. We printed out the number of characters we read `size`, and we looped through the `in` array printing out each character we read, then we closed the file.

Before we go any further let's talk about `flush()` and `close()`. When you write data out to a stream, some amount of buffering will occur, and you never know for sure exactly when the last of the data will actually be sent. You might perform many write operations on a stream before closing it, and invoking the `flush()` method guarantees that the last of the data you thought you had already written actually gets out to the file. Whenever you're done using a file, either reading it or writing to it, you should invoke the `close()` method. When you are doing file I/O you're using expensive and limited operating system resources, and so when you're done, invoking `close()` will free up those resources.

Now, back to our last example. This program certainly works, but it's painful in a couple of different ways:

1. When we were writing data to the file, we manually inserted line separators (in this case \n), into our data.

2. When we were reading data back in, we put it into a character array. It being an array and all, we had to declare its size beforehand, so we'd have been in trouble if we hadn't made it big enough! We could have read the data in one character at a time, looking for the end of file after each `read()`, but that's pretty painful too.

Because of these limitations, we'll typically want to use higher-level I/O classes like BufferedWriter or BufferedReader in combination with FileWriter or FileReader.

Combining I/O classes

Java's entire I/O system was designed around the idea of using several classes in combination. Combining I/O classes is sometimes called *wrapping* and sometimes called *chaining*. The java.io package contains about 50 classes, 10 interfaces, and 15 exceptions. Each class in the package has a very specific purpose (creating high cohesion), and the classes are designed to be combined with each other in countless ways, to handle a wide variety of situations.

When it's time to do some I/O in real life, you'll undoubtedly find yourself pouring over the java.io API, trying to figure out which classes you'll need, and how to hook them together. For the exam, you'll need to do the same thing, but we've artificially reduced the API. In terms of studying for exam Objective 3.2, we can imagine that the entire java.io package consisted of the classes listed in exam Objective 3.2, and summarized in Table 6-1, our mini I/O API.

TABLE 6-1		java.io Mini API	

java.io Class	Extends From	Key Constructor(s) Arguments	Key Methods
File	Object	File, String String String, String	createNewFile() delete() exists() isDirectory() isFile() list() mkdir() renameTo()
FileWriter	Writer	File String	close() flush() write()
BufferedWriter	Writer	Writer	close() flush() newLine() write()
PrintWriter	Writer	File (as of Java 5) String (as of Java 5) OutputStream Writer	close() flush() format()*, printf()* print(), println() write()
FileReader	Reader	File String	read()
BufferedReader	Reader	Reader	read() readLine()
			*Discussed later

Now let's say that we want to find a less painful way to write data to a file and read the file's contents back into memory. Starting with the task of writing data to a file, here's a process for determining what classes we'll need, and how we'll hook them together:

1. We know that ultimately we want to hook to a File object. So whatever other class or classes we use, one of them must have a constructor that takes an object of type File.

2. Find a method that sounds like the most powerful, easiest way to accomplish the task. When we look at Table 6-1 we can see that BufferedWriter has a `newLine()` method. That sounds a little better than having to manually embed a separator after each line, but if we look further we see that PrintWriter has a method called `println()`. That sounds like the easiest approach of all, so we'll go with it.

3. When we look at PrintWriter's constructors, we see that we can build a PrintWriter object if we have an object of type File, so all we need to do to create a PrintWriter object is the following:

```
File file = new File("fileWrite2.txt");   // create a File
PrintWriter pw = new PrintWriter(file);   // pass file to
                                          // the PrintWriter
                                          // constructor
```

Okay, time for a pop quiz. Prior to Java 5, PrintWriter did not have constructors that took either a String or a File. If you were writing some I/O code in Java 1.4, how would you get a PrintWriter to write data to a file? Hint: You can figure this out by studying the mini I/O API, Table 6-1.

Here's one way to go about solving this puzzle: First, we know that we'll create a File object on one end of the chain, and that we want a PrintWriter object on the other end. We can see in Table 6-1 that a PrintWriter can also be built using a Writer object. Although Writer isn't a *class* we see in the table, we can see that several other classes extend Writer, which for our purposes is just as good; any class that extends Writer is a candidate. Looking further, we can see that FileWriter has the two attributes we're looking for:

1. It can be constructed using a File.
2. It extends Writer.

Given all of this information, we can put together the following code (remember, this is a Java 1.4 example):

```
File file = new File("fileWrite2.txt");   // create a File object
FileWriter fw = new FileWriter(file);     // create a FileWriter
                                          // that will send its
                                          // output to a File
```

```
PrintWriter pw = new PrintWriter(fw);    // create a PrintWriter
                                         // that will send its
                                         // output to a Writer

pw.println("howdy");                     // write the data
pw.println("folks");
```

At this point it should be fairly easy to put together the code to more easily read data from the file back into memory. Again, looking through the table, we see a method called readLine() that sounds like a much better way to read data. Going through a similar process we get the following code:

```
File file =
      new File("fileWrite2.txt");  // create a File object AND
                                   // open "fileWrite2.txt"
FileReader fr =
        new FileReader(file);      // create a FileReader to get
                                   // data from 'file'
BufferedReader br =
        new BufferedReader(fr);    // create a BufferReader to
                                   // get its data from a Reader
String data = br.readLine();       // read some data
```

e x a m

ⓦ a t c h

You're almost certain to encounter exam questions that test your knowledge of how I/O classes can be chained. If you're not totally clear on this last section, we recommend that you use Table 6-1 as a reference, and write code to experiment with which chaining combinations are legal and which are illegal.

Working with Files and Directories

Earlier we touched on the fact that the File class is used to create files and directories. In addition, File's methods can be used to delete files, rename files, determine whether files exist, create temporary files, change a file's attributes, and differentiate between files and directories. A point that is often confusing is that an object of type File is used to represent *either* a *file* or a *directory*. We'll talk about both cases next.

We saw earlier that the statement

```
File file = new File("foo");
```

always creates a File object, and then does one of two things:

1. If "foo" does NOT exist, no actual file is created.

2. If "foo" *does* exist, the new File object refers to the existing file.

Notice that File file = new File("foo"); NEVER creates an actual file. There are two ways to create a file:

1. Invoke the createNewFile() method on a File object. For example:

```
File file = new File("foo");     // no file yet
file.createNewFile();            // make a file, "foo" which
                                 // is assigned to 'file'
```

2. Create a Writer or a Stream. Specifically, create a FileWriter, a PrintWriter, or a FileOutputStream. Whenever you create an instance of one of these classes, you automatically create a file, unless one already exists, for instance

```
File file = new File("foo"); // no file yet
PrintWriter pw =
    new PrintWriter(file);   // make a PrintWriter object AND
                             // make a file, "foo" to which
                             // 'file' is assigned, AND assign
                             // 'pw' to the PrintWriter
```

Creating a directory is similar to creating a file. Again, we'll use the convention of referring to an object of type File that represents an actual directory, as a Directory File object, capital D, (even though it's of type File.) We'll call an actual directory on a computer a directory, small d. Phew! As with creating a file, creating a directory is a two-step process; first we create a Directory (File) object, then we create an actual directory using the following mkdir() method:

```
File myDir = new File("mydir");    // create an object
myDir.mkdir();                      // create an actual directory
```

Once you've got a directory, you put files into it, and work with those files:

```
File myFile = new File(myDir, "myFile.txt");
myFile.createNewFile();
```

This code is making a new file in a subdirectory. Since you provide the subdirectory to the constructor, from then on you just refer to the file by its reference variable. In this case, here's a way that you could write some data to the file myFile:

```
PrintWriter pw = new PrintWriter(myFile);
pw.println("new stuff");
pw.flush();
pw.close();
```

Be careful when you're creating new directories! As we've seen, constructing a Writer or a Stream will often create a file for you automatically if one doesn't exist, but that's not true for a directory:

```
File myDir = new File("mydir");
// myDir.mkdir();                   // call to mkdir() omitted!
File myFile = new File(
            myDir, "myFile.txt");
myFile.createNewFile();            // exception if no mkdir!
```

This will generate an exception something like

```
java.io.IOException: No such file or directory
```

You can refer a File object to an existing file or directory. For example, assume that we already have a subdirectory called existingDir in which resides an existing file existingDirFile.txt, which contains several lines of text. When you run the following code,

```
File existingDir = new File("existingDir");    // assign a dir
System.out.println(existingDir.isDirectory());
```

```
File existingDirFile = new File(
        existingDir, "existingDirFile.txt");  // assign a file
System.out.println (existingDirFile.isFile());

FileReader fr = new FileReader(existingDirFile);
BufferedReader br = new BufferedReader(fr);       // make a Reader

String s;
while( (s = br.readLine()) != null)               // read data
  System.out.println(s);

br.close();
```

the following output will be generated:

```
true
true
existing sub-dir data
line 2 of text
line 3 of text
```

Take special note of what the readLine() method returns. When there is no
more data to read, readLine() returns a null—this is our signal to stop reading the
file. Also, notice that we didn't invoke a flush() method. When reading a file, no
flushing is required, so you won't even find a flush() method in a Reader kind of
class.

In addition to creating files, the File class also lets you do things like renaming
and deleting files. The following code demonstrates a few of the most common ins
and outs of deleting files and directories (via delete()), and renaming files and
directories (via renameTo()):

```
File delDir = new File("deldir");        // make a directory
delDir.mkdir();

File delFile1 = new File(
        delDir, "delFile1.txt");         // add file to directory
delFile1.createNewFile();

File delFile2 = new File(
        delDir, "delFile2.txt");         // add file to directory
delFile2.createNewFile();
```

```
        delFile1.delete();                         // delete a file
        System.out.println("delDir is "
                        + delDir.delete());        // attempt to delete
                                                   // the directory
        File newName = new File(
                delDir, "newName.txt");            // a new object
        delFile2.renameTo(newName);                // rename file

        File newDir = new File("newDir");          // rename directory
        delDir.renameTo(newDir);
```

This outputs

```
delDir is false
```

and leaves us with a directory called `newDir` that contains a file called
`newName.txt`. Here are some rules that we can deduce from this result:

- **delete()** You can't delete a directory if it's not empty, which is why the
  invocation `delDir.delete()` failed.
- **renameTo()** You must give the existing File object a valid new File object
  with the new name that you want. (If `newName` had been `null` we would
  have gotten a NullPointerException.)
- **renameTo()** It's okay to rename a directory, even if it isn't empty.

There's a lot more to learn about using the java.io package, but as far as the
exam goes we only have one more thing to discuss, and that is how to search for a
file. Assuming that we have a directory named `searchThis` that we want to search
through, the following code uses the `File.list()` method to create a String array
of files and directories, which we then use the enhanced `for` loop to iterate through
and print:

```
        String[] files = new String[100];
        File search = new File("searchThis");
        files = search.list();                     // create the list

        for(String fn : files)                     // iterate through it
          System.out.println("found " + fn);
```

On our system, we got the following output:

```
found dir1
found dir2
found dir3
found file1.txt
found file2.txt
```

Your results will almost certainly vary :)

In this section we've scratched the surface of what's available in the java.io package. Entire books have been written about this package, so we're obviously covering only a very small (but frequently used) portion of the API. On the other hand, if you understand everything we've covered in this section, you will be in great shape to handle any java.io questions you encounter on the exam (except for the Console class, which we'll cover next, and serialization, which is covered in the next section).

The java.io.Console Class

New to Java 6 is the `java.io.Console` class. In this context, the *console* is the physical device with a keyboard and a display (like your Mac or PC). If you're running Java SE 6 from the command line, you'll typically have access to a console object, to which you can get a reference by invoking `System.console()`. Keep in mind that it's possible for your Java program to be running in an environment that doesn't have access to a console object, so be sure that your invocation of `System.console()` actually returns a valid console reference and not null.

The `Console` class makes it easy to accept input from the command line, both echoed and nonechoed (such as a password), and makes it easy to write formatted output to the command line. It's a handy way to write test engines for unit testing or if you want to support a simple but secure user interaction and you don't need a GUI.

On the input side, the methods you'll have to understand are `readLine` and `readPassword`. The `readLine` method returns a string containing whatever the user keyed in—that's pretty intuitive. However, the `readPassword` method doesn't return a string: it returns a character array. Here's the reason for this: Once you've got the password, you can verify it and then absolutely remove it from memory. If a string was returned, it could exist in a pool somewhere in memory and perhaps some nefarious hacker could find it.

Let's take a look at a small program that uses a console to support testing another class:

```java
import java.io.Console;

public class NewConsole {
  public static void main(String[] args) {
    Console c = System.console();            // #1: get a Console
    char[] pw;
    pw = c.readPassword("%s", "pw: ");       // #2: return a char[]
    for(char ch: pw)
      c.format("%c ", ch);                   // #3: format output
    c.format("\n");

    MyUtility mu = new MyUtility();
    while(true) {
      name = c.readLine("%s", "input?: ");   // #4: return a String

      c.format("output: %s \n", mu.doStuff(name));
    }
  }
}

class MyUtility {                            // #5: class to test
  String doStuff(String arg1) {
    // stub code
    return "result is " + arg1;
  }
}
```

Let's review this code:

- At line 1, we get a new console object. Remember that we can't say this:

  ```java
  Console c = new Console();
  ```

- At line 2, we invoke readPassword, which returns a char[], not a string. You'll notice when you test this code that the password you enter isn't echoed on the screen.

- At line 3, we're just manually displaying the password you keyed in, separating each character with a space. Later on in this chapter, you'll read about the `format` method, so stay tuned.

- At line 4, we invoke `readLine`, which returns a string.

- At line 5 is the class that we want to test. Later in this chapter, when you're studying regex and formatting, we recommend that you use something like `NewConsole` to test the concepts that you're learning.

The `Console` class has more capabilities than are covered here, but if you understand everything discussed so far, you'll be in good shape for the exam.

CERTIFICATION OBJECTIVE

Serialization (Exam Objective 3.3)

3.3   Develop code that serializes and/or de-serializes objects using the following APIs from java.io: DataInputStream, DataOutputStream, FileInputStream, FileOutputStream, ObjectInputStream, ObjectOutputStream, and Serializable.

Imagine you want to save the state of one or more objects. If Java didn't have serialization (as the earliest version did not), you'd have to use one of the I/O classes to write out the state of the instance variables of all the objects you want to save. The worst part would be trying to reconstruct new objects that were virtually identical to the objects you were trying to save. You'd need your own protocol for the way in which you wrote and restored the state of each object, or you could end up setting variables with the wrong values. For example, imagine you stored an object that has instance variables for height and weight. At the time you save the state of the object, you could write out the height and weight as two `int`s in a file, but the order in which you write them is crucial. It would be all too easy to re-create the object but mix up the height and weight values—using the saved height as the value for the new object's weight and vice versa.

Serialization lets you simply say "save this object and all of its instance variables." Actually it is a little more interesting than that, because you can add, "... unless I've explicitly marked a variable as `transient`, which means, don't include the transient variable's value as part of the object's serialized state."

Working with ObjectOutputStream and ObjectInputStream

The magic of basic serialization happens with just two methods: one to serialize objects and write them to a stream, and a second to read the stream and deserialize objects.

```
ObjectOutputStream.writeObject()    // serialize and write

ObjectInputStream.readObject()      // read and deserialize
```

The java.io.ObjectOutputStream and java.io.ObjectInputStream classes are considered to be *higher*-level classes in the java.io package, and as we learned earlier, that means that you'll wrap them around *lower*-level classes, such as java.io.FileOutputStream and java.io.FileInputStream. Here's a small program that creates a (Cat) object, serializes it, and then deserializes it:

```
import java.io.*;

class Cat implements Serializable { }   // 1

public class SerializeCat {
  public static void main(String[] args) {
    Cat c = new Cat();  // 2
    try {
      FileOutputStream fs = new FileOutputStream("testSer.ser");
      ObjectOutputStream os = new ObjectOutputStream(fs);
      os.writeObject(c);    // 3
      os.close();
    } catch (Exception e) { e.printStackTrace(); }

    try {
      FileInputStream fis = new FileInputStream("testSer.ser");
      ObjectInputStream ois = new ObjectInputStream(fis);
      c = (Cat) ois.readObject();   // 4
      ois.close();
    } catch (Exception e) { e.printStackTrace(); }
  }
}
```

Let's take a look at the key points in this example:

1. We declare that the Cat class implements the Serializable interface. Serializable is a *marker* interface; it has no methods to implement. (In the next several sections, we'll cover various rules about when you need to declare classes Serializable.)

2. We make a new Cat object, which as we know is serializable.

3. We serialize the Cat object c by invoking the `writeObject()` method. It took a fair amount of preparation before we could actually serialize our Cat. First, we had to put all of our I/O-related code in a try/catch block. Next we had to create a FileOutputStream to write the object to. Then we wrapped the FileOutputStream in an ObjectOutputStream, which is the class that has the magic serialization method that we need. Remember that the invocation of `writeObject()` performs two tasks: it serializes the object, and then it writes the serialized object to a file.

4. We de-serialize the Cat object by invoking the `readObject()` method. The `readObject()` method returns an Object, so we have to cast the deserialized object back to a Cat. Again, we had to go through the typical I/O hoops to set this up.

This is a bare-bones example of serialization in action. Over the next set of pages we'll look at some of the more complex issues that are associated with serialization.

Object Graphs

What does it really mean to save an object? If the instance variables are all primitive types, it's pretty straightforward. But what if the instance variables are themselves references to *objects*? What gets saved? Clearly in Java it wouldn't make any sense to save the actual value of a reference variable, because the value of a Java reference has meaning only within the context of a single instance of a JVM. In other words, if you tried to restore the object in another instance of the JVM, even running on the same computer on which the object was originally serialized, the reference would be useless.

But what about the object that the reference refers to? Look at this class:

```
class Dog {
  private Collar theCollar;
  private int dogSize;
  public Dog(Collar collar, int size) {
    theCollar = collar;
    dogSize = size;
```

```
      }
      public Collar getCollar() { return theCollar; }
   }
   class Collar {
      private int collarSize;
      public Collar(int size) { collarSize = size; }
      public int getCollarSize() { return collarSize; }
   }
```

Now make a dog... First, you make a Collar for the Dog:

```
Collar c = new Collar(3);
```

Then make a new Dog, passing it the Collar:

```
Dog d = new Dog(c, 8);
```

Now what happens if you save the Dog? If the goal is to save and then restore a Dog, and the restored Dog is an exact duplicate of the Dog that was saved, then the Dog needs a Collar that is an exact duplicate of the Dog's Collar at the time the Dog was saved. That means both the Dog and the Collar should be saved.

And what if the Collar itself had references to other objects—like perhaps a Color object? This gets quite complicated very quickly. If it were up to the programmer to know the internal structure of each object the Dog referred to, so that the programmer could be sure to save all the state of all those objects...whew. That would be a nightmare with even the simplest of objects.

Fortunately, the Java serialization mechanism takes care of all of this. When you serialize an object, Java serialization takes care of saving that object's entire "object graph." That means a deep copy of everything the saved object needs to be restored. For example, if you serialize a Dog object, the Collar will be serialized automatically. And if the Collar class contained a reference to another object, THAT object would also be serialized, and so on. And the only object you have to worry about saving and restoring is the Dog. The other objects required to fully reconstruct that Dog are saved (and restored) automatically through serialization.

Remember, you do have to make a conscious choice to create objects that are serializable, by implementing the Serializable interface. If we want to save Dog objects, for example, we'll have to modify the Dog class as follows:

```
class Dog implements Serializable {
   // the rest of the code as before
```

```
      // Serializable has no methods to implement
}
```

And now we can save the Dog with the following code:

```
import java.io.*;
public class SerializeDog {
  public static void main(String[] args) {
    Collar c = new Collar(3);
    Dog d = new Dog(c, 8);
    try {
      FileOutputStream fs = new FileOutputStream("testSer.ser");
      ObjectOutputStream os = new ObjectOutputStream(fs);
      os.writeObject(d);
      os.close();
    } catch (Exception e) { e.printStackTrace(); }
  }
}
```

But when we run this code we get a runtime exception something like this

```
java.io.NotSerializableException: Collar
```

What did we forget? The Collar class must ALSO be Serializable. If we modify the Collar class and make it serializable, then there's no problem:

```
class Collar implements Serializable {
    // same
}
```

Here's the complete listing:

```
import java.io.*;
public class SerializeDog {
  public static void main(String[] args) {
    Collar c = new Collar(3);
    Dog d = new Dog(c, 5);
    System.out.println("before: collar size is "
                       + d.getCollar().getCollarSize());
    try {
      FileOutputStream fs = new FileOutputStream("testSer.ser");
```

```
        ObjectOutputStream os = new ObjectOutputStream(fs);
        os.writeObject(d);
        os.close();
    } catch (Exception e) { e.printStackTrace(); }
    try {
        FileInputStream fis = new FileInputStream("testSer.ser");
        ObjectInputStream ois = new ObjectInputStream(fis);
        d = (Dog) ois.readObject();
        ois.close();
    } catch (Exception e) { e.printStackTrace(); }

    System.out.println("after:  collar size is "
                        + d.getCollar().getCollarSize());
  }
}
class Dog implements Serializable {
    private Collar theCollar;
    private int dogSize;
    public Dog(Collar collar, int size) {
        theCollar = collar;
        dogSize = size;
    }
    public Collar getCollar() { return theCollar; }
}
class Collar implements Serializable {
    private int collarSize;
    public Collar(int size) { collarSize = size; }
    public int getCollarSize() { return collarSize; }
}
```

This produces the output:

```
    before: collar size is 3
    after:  collar size is 3
```

But what would happen if we didn't have access to the Collar class source code? In other words, what if making the Collar class serializable was not an option? Are we stuck with a non-serializable Dog?

Obviously we could subclass the Collar class, mark the subclass as Serializable, and then use the Collar subclass instead of the Collar class. But that's not always an option either for several potential reasons:

1. The Collar class might be final, preventing subclassing.
   OR

2. The Collar class might itself refer to other non-serializable objects, and without knowing the internal structure of Collar, you aren't able to make all these fixes (assuming you even wanted to TRY to go down that road).
   OR

3. Subclassing is not an option for other reasons related to your design.

So…THEN what do you do if you want to save a Dog?

That's where the `transient` modifier comes in. If you mark the Dog's Collar instance variable with `transient`, then serialization will simply skip the Collar during serialization:

```
class Dog implements Serializable {
    private transient Collar theCollar;   // add transient
    // the rest of the class as before
}

class Collar {                   // no longer Serializable
    // same code
}
```

Now we have a Serializable Dog, with a non-serializable Collar, but the Dog has marked the Collar `transient`; the output is

```
before. collar size is 3
Exception in thread "main" java.lang.NullPointerException
```

So NOW what can we do?

Using writeObject and readObject

Consider the problem: we have a Dog object we want to save. The Dog has a Collar, and the Collar has state that should also be saved as part of the Dog's state. But…the Collar is not Serializable, so we must mark it `transient`. That means when the Dog is deserialized, it comes back with a null Collar. What can we do to somehow make sure that when the Dog is deserialized, it gets a new Collar that matches the one the Dog had when the Dog was saved?

Java serialization has a special mechanism just for this—a set of private methods you can implement in your class that, if present, will be invoked automatically during serialization and deserialization. It's almost as if the methods were defined in the Serializable interface, except they aren't. They are part of a special callback contract the serialization system offers you that basically says, "If you (the programmer) have a pair of methods matching this exact signature (you'll see them in a moment), these methods will be called during the serialization/deserialization process.

These methods let you step into the middle of serialization and deserialization. So they're perfect for letting you solve the Dog/Collar problem: when a Dog is being saved, you can step into the middle of serialization and say, "By the way, I'd like to add the state of the Collar's variable (an int) to the stream when the Dog is serialized." You've manually added the state of the Collar to the Dog's serialized representation, even though the Collar itself is not saved.

Of course, you'll need to restore the Collar during deserialization by stepping into the middle and saying, "I'll read that extra int I saved to the Dog stream, and use it to create a new Collar, and then assign that new Collar to the Dog that's being deserialized." The two special methods you define must have signatures that look EXACTLY like this:

```
private void writeObject(ObjectOutputStream os) {
  // your code for saving the Collar variables
}

private void readObject(ObjectInputStream is) {
  // your code to read the Collar state, create a new Collar,
  // and assign it to the Dog
}
```

Yes, we're going to write methods that have the same name as the ones we've been calling! Where do these methods go? Let's change the Dog class:

```
class Dog implements Serializable {
  transient private Collar theCollar; // we can't serialize this
  private int dogSize;
  public Dog(Collar collar, int size) {
    theCollar = collar;
    dogSize = size;
  }
  public Collar getCollar() { return theCollar; }
```

```
    private void writeObject(ObjectOutputStream os) {
      //  throws IOException {                          // 1
     try {
      os.defaultWriteObject();                          // 2
      os.writeInt(theCollar.getCollarSize());           // 3
     } catch (Exception e) { e.printStackTrace(); }
    }
    private void readObject(ObjectInputStream is) {
      //   throws IOException, ClassNotFoundException {  // 4
     try {
      is.defaultReadObject();                           // 5
      theCollar = new Collar(is.readInt());             // 6
     } catch (Exception e) { c.printStackTrace(); }
    }
}
```

Let's take a look at the preceding code.

In our scenario we've agreed that, for whatever real-world reason, we can't serialize a Collar object, but we want to serialize a Dog. To do this we're going to implement `writeObject()` and `readObject()`. By implementing these two methods you're saying to the compiler: "If anyone invokes `writeObject()` or `readObject()` concerning a Dog object, use this code as part of the read and write."

1. Like most I/O-related methods `writeObject()` can throw exceptions. You can declare them or handle them but we recommend handling them.

2. When you invoke `defaultWriteObject()` from within `writeObject()` you're telling the JVM to do the normal serialization process for this object. When implementing `writeObject()`, you will typically request the normal serialization process, *and* do some custom writing and reading too.

3. In this case we decided to write an extra int (the collar size) to the stream that's creating the serialized Dog. You can write extra stuff before and/or after you invoke `defaultWriteObject()`. BUT...when you read it back in, you have to read the extra stuff in the same order you wrote it.

4. Again, we chose to handle rather than declare the exceptions.

5. When it's time to deserialize, `defaultReadObject()` handles the normal deserialization you'd get if you didn't implement a `readObject()` method.

6. Finally we build a new Collar object for the Dog using the collar size that we manually serialized. (We had to invoke `readInt()` *after* we invoked `defaultReadObject()` or the streamed data would be out of sync!)

Remember, the most common reason to implement `writeObject()` and `readObject()` is when you have to save some part of an object's state manually. If you choose, you can write and read ALL of the state yourself, but that's very rare. So, when you want to do only a *part* of the serialization/deserialization yourself, you MUST invoke the `defaultReadObject()` and `defaultWriteObject()` methods to do the rest.

Which brings up another question—why wouldn't *all* Java classes be serializable? Why isn't class Object serializable? There are some things in Java that simply cannot be serialized because they are runtime specific. Things like streams, threads, runtime, etc. and even some GUI classes (which are connected to the underlying OS) cannot be serialized. What is and is not serializable in the Java API is NOT part of the exam, but you'll need to keep them in mind if you're serializing complex objects.

How Inheritance Affects Serialization

Serialization is very cool, but in order to apply it effectively you're going to have to understand how your class's superclasses affect serialization.

That brings up another key issue with serialization…what happens if a superclass is not marked Serializable, but the subclass is? Can the subclass still be serialized even if its superclass does not implement Serializable? Imagine this:

```
class Animal { }
class Dog extends Animal implements Serializable {
    // the rest of the Dog code
}
```

Now you have a Serializable Dog class, with a non-Serializable superclass. This works! But there are potentially serious implications. To fully understand those implications, let's step back and look at the difference between an object that comes from deserialization vs. an object created using new. Remember, when an object is constructed using new (as opposed to being deserialized), the following things happen (in this order):

1. All instance variables are assigned default values.
2. The constructor is invoked, which immediately invokes the superclass constructor (or another overloaded constructor, until one of the overloaded constructors invokes the superclass constructor).
3. All superclass constructors complete.
4. Instance variables that are initialized as part of their declaration are assigned their initial value (as opposed to the default values they're given prior to the superclass constructors completing).
5. The constructor completes.

But these things do NOT happen when an object is deserialized. When an instance of a serializable class is deserialized, the constructor does not run, and instance variables are NOT given their initially assigned values! Think about it—if the constructor were invoked, and/or instance variables were assigned the values given in their declarations, the object you're trying to restore would revert back to its original state, rather than coming back reflecting the changes in its state that happened sometime after it was created. For example, imagine you have a class that declares an instance variable and assigns it the int value 3, and includes a method that changes the instance variable value to 10:

```
class Foo implements Serializable {
    int num = 3;
    void changeNum() {  num = 10;   }
}
```

Obviously if you serialize a Foo instance *after* the changeNum() method runs, the value of the num variable should be 10. When the Foo instance is deserialized, you want the num variable to still be 10! You obviously don't want the initialization (in this case, the assignment of the value 3 to the variable num) to happen. Think of constructors and instance variable assignments together as part of one complete object initialization process (and in fact, they DO become one initialization method in the bytecode). The point is, when an object is deserialized we do NOT want any of the normal initialization to happen. We don't want the constructor to run, and we don't want the explicitly declared values to be assigned. We want only the values saved as part of the serialized state of the object to be reassigned.

Of course if you have variables marked transient, they will not be restored to their original state (unless you implement readObject()), but will instead be given the default value for that data type. In other words, even if you say

```
class Bar implements Serializable {
    transient int x = 42;
}
```

when the Bar instance is deserialized, the variable x will be set to a value of 0. Object references marked transient will always be reset to null, regardless of whether they were initialized at the time of declaration in the class.

So, that's what happens when the object is deserialized, and the class of the serialized object directly extends Object, or has ONLY serializable classes in its inheritance tree. It gets a little trickier when the serializable class has one or more non-serializable superclasses. Getting back to our non-serializable Animal class with a serializable Dog subclass example:

```
class Animal {
    public String name;
}
class Dog extends Animal implements Serializable {
    // the rest of the Dog code
}
```

Because Animal is NOT serializable, any state maintained in the Animal class, even though the state variable is inherited by the Dog, isn't going to be restored with the Dog when it's deserialized! The reason is, the (unserialized) Animal part of the Dog is going to be reinitialized just as it would be if you were making a new Dog (as opposed to deserializing one). That means all the things that happen to an object during construction, will happen—but only to the Animal parts of a Dog. In other words, the instance variables from the Dog's class will be serialized and deserialized correctly, but the inherited variables from the non-serializable Animal superclass will come back with their default/initially assigned values rather than the values they had at the time of serialization.

If you are a serializable class, but your superclass is NOT serializable, then any instance variables you INHERIT from that superclass will be reset to the values they were given during the original construction of the object. This is because the non-serializable class constructor WILL run!

In fact, every constructor ABOVE the first non-serializable class constructor will also run, no matter what, because once the first super constructor is invoked, (during deserialization), it of course invokes its super constructor and so on up the inheritance tree.

For the exam, you'll need to be able to recognize which variables will and will not be restored with the appropriate values when an object is deserialized, so be sure to study the following code example and the output:

```
import java.io.*;
class SuperNotSerial {
  public static void main(String [] args) {

    Dog d = new Dog(35, "Fido");
    System.out.println("before: " + d.name + " "
                       + d.weight);
    try {
      FileOutputStream fs = new FileOutputStream("testSer.ser");
      ObjectOutputStream os = new ObjectOutputStream(fs);
      os.writeObject(d);
      os.close();
    } catch (Exception e) { e.printStackTrace(); }
    try {
      FileInputStream fis = new FileInputStream("testSer.ser");
      ObjectInputStream ois = new ObjectInputStream(fis);
      d = (Dog) ois.readObject();
      ois.close();
    } catch (Exception e) { e.printStackTrace(); }

    System.out.println("after:  " + d.name + " "
                       + d.weight);
  }
}
class Dog extends Animal implements Serializable {
  String name;
```

```
Dog(int w, String n) {
  weight = w;              // inherited
  name = n;                // not inherited
}
}
class Animal {             // not serializable !
  int weight = 42;
}
```

which produces the output:

```
before: Fido 35
after:  Fido 42
```

The key here is that because Animal is not serializable, when the Dog was
deserialized, the Animal constructor ran and reset the Dog's inherited weight variable.

---

exam
ⓦatch
*If you serialize a collection or an array, every element must be
serializable! A single non-serializable element will cause serialization to fail. Note also
that while the collection interfaces are not serializable, the concrete collection classes in
the Java API are.*

Serialization Is Not for Statics

Finally, you might notice that we've talked ONLY about instance variables, not
static variables. Should static variables be saved as part of the object's state? Isn't the
state of a static variable at the time an object was serialized important? Yes and no.
It might be important, but it isn't part of the instance's state at all. Remember, you
should think of static variables purely as CLASS variables. They have nothing to
do with individual instances. But serialization applies only to OBJECTS. And what
happens if you deserialize three different Dog instances, all of which were serialized
at different times, and all of which were saved when the value of a static variable
in class Dog was different. Which instance would "win"? Which instance's static
value would be used to replace the one currently in the one and only Dog class that's
currently loaded? See the problem?

Static variables are NEVER saved as part of the object's state…because they do
not belong to the object!

e x a m

ⓦ a t c h

What about DataInputStream and DataOutputStream? They're in the objectives! It turns out that while the exam was being created, it was decided that those two classes wouldn't be on the exam after all, but someone forgot to remove them from the objectives! So you get a break. That's one less thing you'll have to worry about.

on the

Ⓙ o b

As simple as serialization code is to write, versioning problems can occur in the real world. If you save a Dog object using one version of the class, but attempt to deserialize it using a newer, different version of the class, deserialization might fail. See the Java API for details about versioning issues and solutions.

CERTIFICATION OBJECTIVE

Dates, Numbers, and Currency (Exam Objective 3.4)

3.4   Use standard J2SE APIs in the java.text package to correctly format or parse dates, numbers and currency values for a specific locale; and, given a scenario, determine the appropriate methods to use if you want to use the default locale or a specific locale. Describe the purpose and use of the java.util.Locale class.

The Java API provides an extensive (perhaps a little *too* extensive) set of classes to help you work with dates, numbers, and currency. The exam will test your knowledge of the basic classes and methods you'll use to work with dates and such. When you've finished this section you should have a solid foundation in tasks such as creating new Date and DateFormat objects, converting Strings to Dates and back again, performing Calendaring functions, printing properly formatted currency values, and doing all of this for locations around the globe. In fact, a large part of why this section was added to the exam was to test whether you can do some basic internationalization (often shortened to "i18n").

Working with Dates, Numbers, and Currencies

If you want to work with dates from around the world (and who doesn't?), you'll need to be familiar with at least four classes from the java.text and java.util packages. In fact, we'll admit it right up front, you might encounter questions on the exam that use classes that aren't specifically mentioned in the Sun objective. Here are the four date related classes you'll need to understand:

- **java.util.Date** Most of this class's methods have been deprecated, but you can use this class to bridge between the Calendar and DateFormat class. An instance of Date represents a mutable date and time, to a millisecond.

- **java.util.Calendar** This class provides a huge variety of methods that help you convert and manipulate dates and times. For instance, if you want to add a month to a given date, or find out what day of the week January 1, 3000 falls on, the methods in the Calendar class will save your bacon.

- **java.text.DateFormat** This class is used to format dates not only providing various styles such as "01/01/70" or "January 1, 1970," but also to format dates for numerous locales around the world.

- **java.text.NumberFormat** This class is used to format numbers and currencies for locales around the world.

- **java.util.Locale** This class is used in conjunction with DateFormat and NumberFormat to format dates, numbers and currency for specific locales. With the help of the Locale class you'll be able to convert a date like "10/10/2005" to "Segunda-feira, 10 de Outubro de 2005" in no time. If you want to manipulate dates without producing formatted output, you can use the Locale class directly with the Calendar class.

Orchestrating Date- and Number-Related Classes

When you work with dates and numbers, you'll often use several classes together. It's important to understand how the classes we described above relate to each other, and when to use which classes in combination. For instance, you'll need to know that if you want to do date formatting for a specific locale, you need to create your Locale object before your DateFormat object, because you'll need your Locale object as an argument to your DateFormat factory method. Table 6-2 provides a quick overview of common date- and number-related use cases and solutions using these classes. Table 6-2 will undoubtedly bring up specific questions about individual classes, and we will dive into specifics for each class next. Once you've gone through the class level discussions, you should find that Table 6-2 provides a good summary.

TABLE 6-2   Common Use Cases When Working with Dates and Numbers

Use Case	Steps
Get the current date and time.	1. Create a Date: `Date d = new Date();` 2. Get its value: `String s = d.toString();`
Get an object that lets you perform date and time calculations in your locale.	1. Create a Calendar: `Calendar c = Calendar.getInstance();` 2. Use `c.add(...)` and `c.roll(...)` to perform date and time manipulations.

Get an object that lets you perform date and time calculations in a different locale.	1. Create a Locale:
	   `Locale loc = new Locale(language);` or
	   `Locale loc = new Locale(language, country);`
	2. Create a Calendar for that locale:
	   `Calendar c = Calendar.getInstance(loc);`
	3. Use `c.add(...)` and `c.roll(...)` to perform date and time manipulations.

Get an object that lets you perform date and time calculations, and then format it for output in different locales with different date styles.	1. Create a Calendar:
	   `Calendar c = Calendar.getInstance();`
	2. Create a Locale for each location:
	   `Locale loc = new Locale(...);`
	3. Convert your Calendar to a Date:
	   `Date d = c.getTime();`
	4. Create a DateFormat for each Locale:
	   `DateFormat df = DateFormat.getDateInstance(style, loc);`
	5. Use the format() method to create formatted dates:
	   `String s = df.format(d);`

Get an object that lets you format numbers or currencies across many different locales.	1. Create a Locale for each location:
	   `Locale loc = new Locale(...);`
	2. Create a NumberFormat:
	   `NumberFormat nf = NumberFormat.getInstance(loc);`
	   -or- `NumberFormat nf = NumberFormat.getCurrencyInstance(loc);`
	3. Use the format() method to create formatted output:
	   `String s = nf.format(someNumber);`

The Date Class

The Date class has a checkered past. Its API design didn't do a good job of handling internationalization and localization situations. In its current state, most of its methods have been deprecated, and for most purposes you'll want to use the Calendar class instead of the Date class. The Date class is on the exam for several reasons: you might find it used in legacy code, it's really easy if all you want is a quick and dirty way to get the current date and time, it's good when you want a universal time that is not affected by time zones, and finally, you'll use it as a temporary bridge to format a Calendar object using the DateFormat class.

As we mentioned briefly above, an instance of the Date class represents a single date and time. Internally, the date and time is stored as a primitive long. Specifically, the long holds the number of milliseconds (you know, 1000 of these per second), between the date being represented and January 1, 1970.

Have you ever tried to grasp how big really big numbers are? Let's use the Date class to find out how long it took for a trillion milliseconds to pass, starting at January 1, 1970:

```
import java.util.*;
class TestDates {
  public static void main(String[] args) {
    Date d1 = new Date(1000000000000L);  // a trillion!
    System.out.println("1st date " + d1.toString());
  }
}
```

On our JVM, which has a US locale, the output is

```
1st date Sat Sep 08 19:46:40 MDT 2001
```

Okay, for future reference remember that there are a trillion milliseconds for every 31 and 2/3 years.

Although most of Date's methods have been deprecated, it's still acceptable to use the getTime and setTime methods, although as we'll soon see, it's a bit painful. Let's add an hour to our Date instance, d1, from the previous example:

```
import java.util.*;
class TestDates {
  public static void main(String[] args) {
    Date d1 = new Date(1000000000000L);  // a trillion!
```

```
    System.out.println("1st date " + d1.toString());
    d1.setTime(d1.getTime() + 3600000); // 3600000 millis / hour
    System.out.println("new time " + d1.toString());
  }
}
```

which produces (again, on our JVM):

```
1st date Sat Sep 08 19:46:40 MDT 2001
new time Sat Sep 08 20:46:40 MDT 2001
```

Notice that both `setTime()` and `getTime()` used the handy millisecond scale... if you want to manipulate dates using the Date class, that's your only choice. While that wasn't too painful, imagine how much fun it would be to add, say, a year to a given date.

We'll revisit the Date class later on, but for now the only other thing you need to know is that if you want to create an instance of Date to represent "now," you use Date's no-argument constructor:

```
Date now = new Date();
```

(We're guessing that if you call `now.getTime()`, you'll get a number somewhere between one trillion and two trillion.)

The Calendar Class

We've just seen that manipulating dates using the Date class is tricky. The Calendar class is designed to make date manipulation easy! (Well, easier.) While the Calendar class has about a million fields and methods, once you get the hang of a few of them the rest tend to work in a similar fashion.

When you first try to use the `Calendar` class you might notice that it's an abstract class. You can't say

```
Calendar c = new Calendar();   // illegal, Calendar is abstract
```

In order to create a `Calendar` instance, you have to use one of the overloaded `getInstance()` static factory methods:

```
Calendar cal = Calendar.getInstance();
```

When you get a Calendar reference like `cal`, from above, your Calendar reference variable is actually referring to an instance of a concrete subclass of Calendar. You can't know for sure what subclass you'll get (`java.util.GregorianCalendar` is what you'll almost certainly get), but it won't matter to you. You'll be using Calendar's API. (As Java continues to spread around the world, in order to maintain cohesion, you might find additional, locale-specific subclasses of `Calendar`.)

Okay, so now we've got an instance of Calendar, let's go back to our earlier example, and find out what day of the week our trillionth millisecond falls on, and then let's add a month to that date:

```java
import java.util.*;
class Dates2 {
  public static void main(String[] args) {
    Date d1 = new Date(1000000000000L);
    System.out.println("1st date " + d1.toString());

    Calendar c = Calendar.getInstance();
    c.setTime(d1);                                    // #1

    if(Calendar.SUNDAY == c.getFirstDayOfWeek())     // #2
      System.out.println("Sunday is the first day of the week");
    System.out.println("trillionth milli day of week is "
               + c.get(Calendar.DAY_OF_WEEK));       // #3

    c.add(Calendar.MONTH, 1);                         // #4
    Date d2 = c.getTime();                            // #5
    System.out.println("new date " + d2.toString() );
  }
}
```

This produces something like

```
1st date Sat Sep 08 19:46:40 MDT 2001
Sunday is the first day of the week
trillionth milli day of week is 7
new date Mon Oct 08 19:46:40 MDT 2001
```

Let's take a look at this program, focusing on the five highlighted lines:

1. We assign the Date `d1` to the Calendar instance `c`.

2. We use Calendar's SUNDAY field to determine whether, for our JVM, SUNDAY is considered to be the first day of the week. (In some locales, MONDAY is the first day of the week.) The Calendar class provides similar fields for days of the week, months, the day of the month, the day of the year, and so on.

3. We use the DAY_OF_WEEK field to find out the day of the week that the trillionth millisecond falls on.

4. So far we've used setter and getter methods that should be intuitive to figure out. Now we're going to use Calendar's add() method. This very powerful method lets you add or subtract units of time appropriate for whichever Calendar field you specify. For instance:

```
c.add(Calendar.HOUR, -4);       // subtract 4 hours from c's value
c.add(Calendar.YEAR, 2);        // add 2 years to c's value
c.add(Calendar.DAY_OF_WEEK, -2); // subtract two days from
                                // c's  value
```

5. Convert c's value back to an instance of Date.

The other Calendar method you should know for the exam is the roll() method. The roll() method acts like the add() method, except that when a part of a Date gets incremented or decremented, larger parts of the Date will not get incremented or decremented. Hmmm...for instance:

```
// assume c is October 8, 2001
c.roll(Calendar.MONTH, 9);      // notice the year in the output
Date d4 = c.getTime();
System.out.println("new date " + d4.toString() );
```

The output would be something like this

```
new date Fri Jul 08 19:46:40 MDT 2001
```

Notice that the year did not change, even though we added 9 months to an October date. In a similar fashion, invoking roll() with HOUR won't change the date, the month, or the year.

For the exam, you won't have to memorize the Calendar class's fields. If you need them to help answer a question, they will be provided as part of the question.

The DateFormat Class

Having learned how to create dates and manipulate them, let's find out how to format them. So that we're all on the same page, here's an example of how a date can be formatted in different ways:

```
import java.text.*;
import java.util.*;
class Dates3 {
  public static void main(String[] args) {
    Date d1 = new Date(1000000000000L);

    DateFormat[] dfa = new DateFormat[6];
    dfa[0] = DateFormat.getInstance();
    dfa[1] = DateFormat.getDateInstance();
    dfa[2] = DateFormat.getDateInstance(DateFormat.SHORT);
    dfa[3] = DateFormat.getDateInstance(DateFormat.MEDIUM);
    dfa[4] = DateFormat.getDateInstance(DateFormat.LONG);
    dfa[5] = DateFormat.getDateInstance(DateFormat.FULL);

    for(DateFormat df : dfa)
      System.out.println(df.format(d1));
  }
}
```

which on our JVM produces

```
9/8/01 7:46 PM
Sep 8, 2001
9/8/01
Sep 8, 2001
September 8, 2001
Saturday, September 8, 2001
```

Examining this code we see a couple of things right away. First off, it looks like `DateFormat` is another abstract class, so we can't use `new` to create instances of `DateFormat`. In this case we used two factory methods, `getInstance()` and `getDateInstance()`. Notice that `getDateInstance()` is overloaded; when we discuss locales, we'll look at the other version of `getDateInstance()` that you'll need to understand for the exam.

Next, we used static fields from the DateFormat class to customize our various instances of DateFormat. Each of these static fields represents a formatting *style*. In this case it looks like the no-arg version of `getDateInstance()` gives us the same style as the MEDIUM version of the method, but that's not a hard and fast rule. (More on this when we discuss locales.) Finally, we used the `format()` method to create Strings representing the properly formatted versions of the Date we're working with.

The last method you should be familiar with is the `parse()` method. The `parse()` method takes a String formatted in the style of the DateFormat instance being used, and converts the String into a Date object. As you might imagine, this is a risky operation because the `parse()` method could easily receive a badly formatted String. Because of this, `parse()` can throw a `ParseException`. The following code creates a `Date` instance, uses `DateFormat.format()` to convert it into a String, and then uses `DateFormat.parse()` to change it back into a Date:

```
Date d1 = new Date(1000000000000L);
System.out.println("d1 = " + d1.toString());

DateFormat df = DateFormat.getDateInstance(
                              DateFormat.SHORT);
String s = df.format(d1);
System.out.println(s);

try {
  Date d2 = df.parse(s);
  System.out.println("parsed = " + d2.toString());
} catch (ParseException pe) {
  System.out.println("parse exc"); }
```

which on our JVM produces

```
d1 = Sat Sep 08 19:46:40 MDT 2001
9/8/01
parsed = Sat Sep 08 00:00:00 MDT 2001
```

Note: If we'd wanted to retain the time along with the date we could have used the `getDateTimeInstance()` method, but it's not on the exam.

on the
job
The API for DateFormat.parse() explains that by default, the `parse()` *method is lenient when parsing dates. Our experience is that* `parse()` *isn't very lenient about the formatting of Strings it will successfully parse into dates; take care when you use this method!*

The Locale Class

Earlier we said that a big part of why this objective exists is to test your ability to do some basic internationalization tasks. Your wait is over; the Locale class is your ticket to worldwide domination. Both the DateFormat class and the NumberFormat class (which we'll cover next) can use an instance of Locale to customize formatted output to be specific to a locale. You might ask how Java defines a locale? The API says a locale is "a specific geographical, political, or cultural region." The two Locale constructors you'll need to understand for the exam are

```
Locale(String language)
Locale(String language, String country)
```

The language argument represents an ISO 639 Language Code, so for instance if you want to format your dates or numbers in Walloon (the language sometimes used in southern Belgium), you'd use "wa" as your language string. There are over 500 ISO Language codes, including one for Klingon ("tlh"), although unfortunately Java doesn't yet support the Klingon locale. We thought about telling you that you'd have to memorize all these codes for the exam…but we didn't want to cause any heart attacks. So rest assured, you won't have to memorize any ISO Language codes or ISO Country codes (of which there are about 240) for the exam.

Let's get back to how you might use these codes. If you want to represent basic Italian in your application, all you need is the language code. If, on the other hand, you want to represent the Italian used in Switzerland, you'd want to indicate that the country is Switzerland (yes, the country code for Switzerland is "CH"), but that the language is Italian:

```
Locale locPT = new Locale("it");        // Italian
Locale locBR = new Locale("it", "CH");  // Switzerland
```

Using these two locales on a date could give us output like this:

```
sabato 1 ottobre 2005
sabato, 1. ottobre 2005
```

Now let's put this all together in some code that creates a Calendar object, sets its date, then converts it to a Date. After that we'll take that Date object and print it out using locales from around the world:

```
Calendar c = Calendar.getInstance();
c.set(2010, 11, 14);                    // December 14, 2010
                                        // (month is 0-based

Date d2 = c.getTime();

Locale locIT = new Locale("it", "IT");  // Italy
Locale locPT = new Locale("pt");        // Portugal
Locale locBR = new Locale("pt", "BR");  // Brazil
Locale locIN = new Locale("hi", "IN");  // India
Locale locJA = new Locale("ja");        // Japan

DateFormat dfUS = DateFormat.getInstance();
System.out.println("US         " + dfUS.format(d2));

DateFormat dfUSfull = DateFormat.getDateInstance(
                                    DateFormat.FULL);
System.out.println("US full  " + dfUSfull.format(d2));

DateFormat dfIT = DateFormat.getDateInstance(
                                    DateFormat.FULL, locIT);
System.out.println("Italy     " + dfIT.format(d2));

DateFormat dfPT = DateFormat.getDateInstance(
                                    DateFormat.FULL, locPT);
System.out.println("Portugal " + dfPT.format(d2));

DateFormat dfBR = DateFormat.getDateInstance(
                                    DateFormat.FULL, locBR);
System.out.println("Brazil    " + dfBR.format(d2));

DateFormat dfIN = DateFormat.getDateInstance(
                                    DateFormat.FULL, locIN);
System.out.println("India     " + dfIN.format(d2));

DateFormat dfJA = DateFormat.getDateInstance(
                                    DateFormat.FULL, locJA);
System.out.println("Japan     " + dfJA.format(d2));
```

This, on our JVM, produces

```
US       12/14/10 3:32 PM
US full  Sunday, December 14, 2010
Italy    domenica 14 dicembre 2010
```

```
Portugal Domingo, 14 de Dezembro de 2010
Brazil   Domingo, 14 de Dezembro de 2010
India    ??????, ?? ??????, ????
Japan    2010?12?14?
```

Oops! Our machine isn't configured to support locales for India or Japan, but you can see how a single Date object can be formatted to work for many locales.

exam

ⓦatch

Remember that both DateFormat and NumberFormat objects can have their locales set only at the time of instantiation. Watch for code that attempts to change the locale of an existing instance—no such methods exist!

There are a couple more methods in Locale (`getDisplayCountry()` and `getDisplayLanguage()`) that you'll have to know for the exam. These methods let you create Strings that represent a given locale's country and language in terms of both the default locale and any other locale:

```
Calendar c = Calendar.getInstance();
c.set(2010, 11, 14);
Date d2 = c.getTime();

Locale locBR = new Locale("pt", "BR");  // Brazil
Locale locDK = new Locale("da", "DK");  // Denmark
Locale locIT = new Locale("it", "IT");  // Italy

System.out.println("def " + locBR.getDisplayCountry());
System.out.println("loc " + locBR.getDisplayCountry(locBR));

System.out.println("def " + locDK.getDisplayLanguage());
System.out.println("loc " + locDK.getDisplayLanguage(locDK));
System.out.println("D>I " + locDK.getDisplayLanguage(locIT));
```

This, on our JVM, produces

```
def Brazil
loc Brasil
def Danish
loc dansk
D>I danese
```

Given that our JVM's locale (the default for us) is US, the default for the country Brazil is "Brazil", and the default for the Danish language is "Danish". In Brazil, the country is called "Brasil", and in Denmark the language is called "dansk". Finally, just for fun, we discovered that in Italy, the Danish language is called "danese".

The NumberFormat Class

We'll wrap up this objective by discussing the NumberFormat class. Like the DateFormat class, NumberFormat is abstract, so you'll typically use some version of either getInstance() or getCurrencyInstance() to create a NumberFormat object. Not surprisingly, you use this class to format numbers or currency values:

```
float f1 = 123.4567f;
Locale locFR = new Locale("fr");          // France
NumberFormat[] nfa = new NumberFormat[4];

nfa[0] = NumberFormat.getInstance();
nfa[1] = NumberFormat.getInstance(locFR);
nfa[2] = NumberFormat.getCurrencyInstance();
nfa[3] = NumberFormat.getCurrencyInstance(locFR);

for(NumberFormat nf : nfa)
  System.out.println(nf.format(f1));
```

This, on our JVM, produces

```
123.457
123,457
$123.46
123,46 ?
```

Don't be worried if, like us, you're not set up to display the symbols for francs, pounds, rupees, yen, baht, or drachmas. You won't be expected to know the symbols used for currency: if you need one, it will be specified in the question. You might encounter methods other than the format method on the exam. Here's a little code that uses getMaximumFractionDigits(), setMaximumFractionDigits(), parse(), and setParseIntegerOnly():

```
float f1 = 123.45678f;
NumberFormat nf = NumberFormat.getInstance();
System.out.print(nf.getMaximumFractionDigits() + " ");
System.out.print(nf.format(f1) + "   ");

nf.setMaximumFractionDigits(5);
System.out.println(nf.format(f1) + "   ");

try {
  System.out.println(nf.parse("1234.567"));
  nf.setParseIntegerOnly(true);
  System.out.println(nf.parse("1234.567"));
} catch (ParseException pe) {
  System.out.println("parse exc");
}
```

This, on our JVM, produces

```
3   123.457   123.45678
1234.567
1234
```

Notice that in this case, the initial number of fractional digits for the default NumberFormat is three: and that the format() method rounds f1's value, it doesn't truncate it. After changing nf's fractional digits, the entire value of f1 is displayed. Next, notice that the parse() method must run in a try/catch block and that the setParseIntegerOnly() method takes a boolean and in this case, causes subsequent calls to parse() to return only the integer part of Strings formatted as floating-point numbers.

As we've seen, several of the classes covered in this objective are abstract. In addition, for all of these classes, key functionality for every instance is established at the time of creation. Table 6-3 summarizes the constructors or methods used to create instances of all the classes we've discussed in this section.

| TABLE 6-3 | Instance Creation for Key java.text and java.util Classes |

Class	Key Instance Creation Options
util.Date	`new Date();` `new Date(long millisecondsSince010170);`
util.Calendar	`Calendar.getInstance();` `Calendar.getInstance(Locale);`

util.Locale	`Locale.getDefault();`
	`new Locale(String language);`
	`new Locale(String language, String country);`

text.DateFormat	`DateFormat.getInstance();`
	`DateFormat.getDateInstance();`
	`DateFormat.getDateInstance(style);`
	`DateFormat.getDateInstance(style, Locale);`

text.NumberFormat	`NumberFormat.getInstance()`
	`NumberFormat.getInstance(Locale)`
	`NumberFormat.getNumberInstance()`
	`NumberFormat.getNumberInstance(Locale)`
	`NumberFormat.getCurrencyInstance()`
	`NumberFormat.getCurrencyInstance(Locale)`

CERTIFICATION OBJECTIVE

Parsing, Tokenizing, and Formatting (Exam Objective 3.5)

3.5   Write code that uses standard J2SE APIs in the java.util and java.util.regex packages to format or parse strings or streams. For strings, write code that uses the Pattern and Matcher classes and the String.split method. Recognize and use regular expression patterns for matching (limited to: .(dot), *(star), +(plus), ?, \d, \s, \w, [ ], ()). The use of *, + , and ? will be limited to greedy quantifiers, and the parenthesis operator will only be used as a grouping mechanism, not for capturing content during matching. For streams, write code using the Formatter and Scanner classes and the PrintWriter.format/printf methods. Recognize and use formatting parameters (limited to: %b, %c, %d, %f, %s) in format strings.

We're going to start with yet another disclaimer: This small section isn't going to morph you from regex newbie to regex guru. In this section we'll cover three basic ideas:

- **Finding stuff**   You've got big heaps of text to look through. Maybe you're doing some screen scraping, maybe you're reading from a file. In any case, you need easy ways to find textual needles in textual haystacks. We'll use the java.util.regex.Pattern, java.util.regex.Matcher, and java.util.Scanner classes to help us find stuff.

- **Tokenizing stuff**   You've got a delimited file that you want to get useful data out of. You want to transform a piece of a text file that looks like: "1500.00,343.77,123.4" into some individual float variables. We'll show you the basics of using the `String.split()` method and the java.util.Scanner class, to tokenize your data.

- **Formatting stuff**   You've got a report to create and you need to take a float variable with a value of 32500.000f and transform it into a String with a value of "$32,500.00". We'll introduce you to the java.util.Formatter class and to the `printf()` and `format()` methods.

A Search Tutorial

Whether you're looking for stuff or tokenizing stuff, a lot of the concepts are the same, so let's start with some basics. No matter what language you're using, sooner or later you'll probably be faced with the need to search through large amounts of textual data, looking for some specific stuff.

Regular expressions (regex for short) are a kind of language within a language, designed to help programmers with these searching tasks. Every language that provides regex capabilities uses one or more regex *engines*. Regex engines search through textual data using instructions that are coded into *expressions*. A regex expression is like a very short program or script. When you invoke a regex engine, you'll pass it the chunk of textual data you want it to process (in Java this is usually a String or a stream), and you pass it the expression you want it to use to search through the data.

It's fair to think of regex as a language, and we will refer to it that way throughout this section. The regex language is used to create expressions, and as we work through this section, whenever we talk about expressions or expression syntax, we're talking about syntax for the regex "language." Oh, one more disclaimer...we know that you regex mavens out there can come up with better expressions than what we're about to present. Keep in mind that for the most part we're creating these expressions using only a portion of the total regex instruction set, thanks.

Simple Searches

For our first example, we'd like to search through the following *source* String

```
abaaaba
```

for all occurrences (or *matches*) of the *expression*

```
ab
```

In all of these discussions we'll assume that our data sources use zero-based indexes, so if we apply an index to our source string we get

```
source: abaaaba
index:  0123456
```

We can see that we have two occurrences of the expression ab: one starting at position 0 and the second starting at position 4. If we sent the previous source data and expression to a regex engine, it would reply by telling us that it found matches at positions 0 and 4:

```
import java.util.regex.*;
class RegexSmall {
  public static void main(String [] args) {
    Pattern p = Pattern.compile("ab");       // the expression
    Matcher m = p.matcher("abaaaba");        // the source
    while(m.find()) {
      System.out.print(m.start() + " ");
    }
  }
}
```

This produces

```
0 4
```

We're not going to explain this code right now. In a few pages we're going to show you a lot more regex code, but first we want to go over some more regex syntax. Once you understand a little more regex, the code samples will make a lot more sense. Here's a more complicated example of a source and an expression:

```
source: abababa
index:  0123456
expression: aba
```

How many occurrences do we get in this case? Well, there is clearly an occurrence starting at position 0, and another starting at position 4. But how about starting at position 2? In general in the world of regex, the aba string that starts at position 2 will not be considered a valid occurrence. The first general regex search rule is

In general, a regex search runs from left to right, and once a source's character has been used in a match, it cannot be reused.

So in our previous example, the first match used positions 0, 1, and 2 to match the expression. (Another common term for this is that the first three characters of the source were *consumed*.) Because the character in position 2 was consumed in the first match, it couldn't be used again. So the engine moved on, and didn't find another occurrence of aba until it reached position 4. This is the typical way that a regex matching engine works. However, in a few pages, we'll look at an exception to the first rule we stated above.

So we've matched a couple of exact strings, but what would we do if we wanted to find something a little more dynamic? For instance, what if we wanted to find all of the occurrences of hex numbers or phone numbers or ZIP codes?

Searches Using Metacharacters

As luck would have it, regex has a powerful mechanism for dealing with the cases we described above. At the heart of this mechanism is the idea of a *metacharacter*. As an easy example, let's say that we want to search through some source data looking for all occurrences of numeric digits. In regex, the following expression is used to look for numeric digits:

```
\d
```

If we change the previous program to apply the expression \d to the following source string

```
source: a12c3e456f
index:  0123456789
```

regex will tell us that it found digits at positions 1, 2, 4, 6, 7, and 8. (If you want to try this at home, you'll need to "escape" the `compile` method's "\d" argument by making it "\\d", more on this a little later.)

Regex provides a rich set of metacharacters that you can find described in the API documentation for java.util.regex.Pattern. We won't discuss them all here, but we will describe the ones you'll need for the exam:

```
\d   A digit
\s   A whitespace character
\w   A word character (letters, digits, or "_" (underscore))
```

So for example, given

```
source: "a 1 56 _Z"
index:   012345678
pattern: \w
```

regex will return positions 0, 2, 4, 5, 7, and 8. The only characters in this source that don't match the definition of a word character are the whitespaces. (Note: In this example we enclosed the source data in quotes to clearly indicate that there was no whitespace at either end.)

You can also specify sets of characters to search for using square brackets and ranges of characters to search for using square brackets and a dash:

```
[abc]   Searches only for a's, b's or c's
[a-f]   Searches only for a, b, c, d, e, or f characters
```

In addition, you can search across several ranges at once. The following expression is looking for occurrences of the letters a - f or A - F, it's NOT looking for an fA combination:

```
[a-fA-F]   Searches for the first six letters of the alphabet, both cases.
```

So for instance,

```
source:  "cafeBABE"
index:    01234567
pattern:  [a-cA-C]
```

returns positions 0, 1, 4, 5, 6.

In addition to the capabilities described for the exam, you can also apply the following attributes to sets and ranges within square brackets: "^" to negate the characters specified, nested brackets to create a union of sets, and "&&" to specify the intersection of sets. While these constructs are not on the exam, they are quite useful, and good examples can be found in the API for the java.util.regex.Pattern class.

Searches Using Quantifiers

Let's say that we want to create a regex pattern to search for hexadecimal literals. As a first step, let's solve the problem for one-digit hexadecimal numbers:

```
0[xX][0-9a-fA-F]
```

The preceding expression could be stated: "Find a set of characters in which the first character is a "0", the second character is either an "x" or an "X", and the third character is either a digit from "0" to "9", a letter from "a" to "f" or an uppercase letter from "A" to "F" ". Using the preceding expression, and the following data,

```
source:  "12 0x 0x12 0Xf 0xg"
index:    012345678901234567
```

regex would return 6 and 11. (Note: 0x and 0xg are not valid hex numbers.)

As a second step, let's think about an easier problem. What if we just wanted regex to find occurrences of integers? Integers can be one or more digits long, so it would be great if we could say "one or more" in an expression. There is a set of regex constructs called quantifiers that let us specify concepts such as "one or more." In fact, the quantifier that represents "one or more" is the "+" character. We'll see the others shortly.

The other issue this raises is that when we're searching for something whose length is variable, getting only a starting position as a return value has limited value. So, in addition to returning starting positions, another bit of information that a regex engine can return is the entire match or *group* that it finds. We're going to change the way we talk about what regex returns by specifying each return on its own line, remembering that now for each return we're going to get back the starting position AND then the group:

```
source: "1 a12 234b"
pattern: \d+
```

You can read this expression as saying: "Find one or more digits in a row." This expression produces the regex output

```
0 1
3 12
6 234
```

You can read this as "At position 0 there's an integer with a value of 1, then at position 3 there's an integer with a value of 12, then at position 6 there's an integer with a value of 234." Returning now to our hexadecimal problem, the last thing we need to know is how to specify the use of a quantifier for only part of an expression. In this case we must have exactly one occurrence of 0x or 0X but we can have from one to many occurrences of the hex "digits" that follow. The following expression adds parentheses to limit the "+" quantifier to only the hex digits:

```
0[xX]([0-9a-fA-F])+
```

The parentheses and "+" augment the previous find-the-hex expression by saying in effect: "Once we've found our 0x or 0X, you can find from one to many occurrences of hex digits." Notice that we put the "+" quantifier at the end of the expression. It's useful to think of quantifiers as always quantifying the part of the expression that precedes them.

The other two quantifiers we're going to look at are

*   Zero or more occurrences

?   Zero or one occurrence

Let's say you have a text file containing a comma-delimited list of all the file names in a directory that contains several very important projects. (BTW, this isn't how we'd arrange our directories :) You want to create a list of all the files whose names start with `proj1`. You might discover .txt files, .java files, .pdf files, who knows? What kind of regex expression could we create to find these various `proj1` files? First let's take a look at what a part of this text might look like:

```
..."proj3.txt,proj1sched.pdf,proj1,proj2,proj1.java"...
```

To solve this problem we're going to use the regex ^ (carat) operator, which we mentioned earlier. The regex ^ operator isn't on the exam, but it will help us create a fairly clean solution to our problem. The ^ is the negation symbol in regex. For instance, if you want to find anything but a's, b's, or c's in a file you could say

```
[^abc]
```

So, armed with the ^ operator and the * (zero or more) quantifier we can create the following:

```
proj1([^,])*
```

If we apply this expression to just the portion of the text file we listed above, regex returns

```
10 proj1sched.pdf
25 proj1
37 proj1.java
```

The key part of this expression is the "give me zero or more characters that aren't a comma."

The last quantifier example we'll look at is the ? (zero or one) quantifier. Let's say that our job this time is to search a text file and find anything that might be a local, 7-digit phone number. We're going to say, arbitrarily, that if we find either seven digits in a row, or three digits followed by a dash or a space followed by 4 digits, that we have a candidate. Here are examples of "valid" phone numbers:

```
1234567
123 4567
123-4567
```

The key to creating this expression is to see that we need "zero or one instance of either a space or a dash" in the middle of our digits:

```
\d\d\d([-\s])?\d\d\d\d
```

The Predefined Dot

In addition to the \s, \d, and \w metacharacters that we discussed, you also have to understand the "." (dot) metacharacter. When you see this character in a regex expression, it means "any character can serve here." For instance, the following source and pattern

```
source: "ac abc a c"
pattern: a.c
```

will produce the output

```
3 abc
7 a c
```

The "." was able to match both the "b" and the " " in the source data.

Greedy Quantifiers

When you use the *, +, and ? quantifiers, you can fine tune them a bit to produce behavior that's known as "greedy", "reluctant", or "possessive". Although you need to understand only the greedy quantifier for the exam, we're also going to discuss the reluctant quantifier to serve as a basis for comparison. First the syntax:

? is greedy, ?? is reluctant, for zero or once
* is greedy, *? is reluctant, for zero or more
+ is greedy, +? is reluctant, for one or more

What happens when we have the following source and pattern?

```
source:  yyxxxyxx
pattern: .*xx
```

First off, we're doing something a bit different here by looking for characters that prefix the static (xx) portion of the expression. We think we're saying something like: "Find sets of characters that ends with xx". Before we tell what happens, we at least want you to consider that there are two plausible results...can you find them? Remember we said earlier that in general, regex engines worked from left to right, and consumed characters as they went. So, working from left to right, we might predict that the engine would search the first 4 characters (0-3), find xx starting in position 2, and have its first match. Then it would proceed and find the second xx starting in position 6. This would lead us to a result like this:

```
0 yyxx
4 xyxx
```

A plausible second argument is that since we asked for a set of characters that ends with xx we might get a result like this:

```
0 yyxxxyxx
```

The way to think about this is to consider the name *greedy*. In order for the second answer to be correct, the regex engine would have to look (greedily) at the *entire* source data before it could determine that there was an xx at the end. So in fact, the second result is the correct result because in the original example we used the greedy quantifier *. The result that finds two different sets can be generated by using the reluctant quantifier *?. Let's review:

```
source:  yyxxxyxx
pattern:  .*xx
```

is using the greedy quantifier * and produces

```
0 yyxxxyxx
```

If we change the pattern to

```
source:  yyxxxyxx
pattern:  .*?xx
```

we're now using the reluctant qualifier *?, and we get the following:

```
0 yyxx
4 xyxx
```

The greedy quantifier does in fact read the entire source data, and then it works backward (from the right) until it finds the rightmost match. At that point, it includes everything from earlier in the source data up to and including the data that is part of the rightmost match.

on the job

There are a lot more aspects to regex quantifiers than we've discussed here, but we've covered more than enough for the exam. Sun has several tutorials that will help you learn more about quantifiers, and turn you into the go-to person at your job.

When Metacharacters and Strings Collide

So far we've been talking about regex from a theoretical perspective. Before we can put regex to work we have to discuss one more gotcha. When it's time to implement regex in our code, it will be quite common that our source data and/or our expressions will be stored in Strings. The problem is that metacharacters and Strings don't mix too well. For instance. let's say we just want to do a simple regex pattern that looks for digits. We might try something like

```
String pattern = "\d";    // compiler error!
```

This line of code won't compile! The compiler sees the \ and thinks, "Ok, here comes an escape sequence, maybe it'll be a new line!" But no, next comes the d and the compiler says "I've never heard of the \d escape sequence." The way to satisfy the compiler is to add another backslash in front of the \d

```
String pattern = "\\d";    // a compilable metacharacter
```

The first backslash tells the compiler that whatever comes next should be taken literally, not as an escape sequence. How about the dot (.) metacharacter? If we want a dot in our expression to be used as a metacharacter, then no problem, but what if we're reading some source data that happens to use dots as delimiters? Here's another way to look at our options:

```
String p = ".";    // regex sees this as the "." metacharacter
String p = "\.";   // the compiler sees this as an illegal
                   // Java escape sequence
```

```
String p = "\\."; // the compiler is happy, and regex sees a
                  // dot, not a metacharacter
```

A similar problem can occur when you hand metacharacters to a Java program via command-line arguments. If we want to pass the \d metacharacter into our Java program, our JVM does the right thing if we say

```
% java DoRegex "\d"
```

But your JVM might not. If you have problems running the following examples, you might try adding a backslash (i.e., \\d) to your command-line metacharacters. Don't worry, you won't see any command-line metacharacters on the exam!

on the **Job**

The Java language defines several escape sequences, including

> \n *= linefeed (which you might see on the exam)*
> \b *= backspace*
> \t *= tab*

And others, which you can find in the Java Language Specification. Other than perhaps seeing a \n *inside a String, you won't have to worry about Java's escape sequences on the exam.*

At this point we've learned enough of the regex language to start using it in our Java programs. We'll start by looking at using regex expressions to find stuff, and then we'll move to the closely related topic of tokenizing stuff.

Locating Data via Pattern Matching

Once you know a little regex, using the java.util.regex.Pattern (Pattern) and java.util.regex.Matcher (Matcher) classes is pretty straightforward. The Pattern class is used to hold a representation of a regex expression, so that it can be used and reused by instances of the Matcher class. The Matcher class is used to invoke the regex engine with the intention of performing match operations. The following program shows Pattern and Matcher in action, and it's not a bad way for you to do your own regex experiments. Note, you might want to modify the following class by adding some functionality from the Console class. That way you'll get some practice with the Console class, and it'll be easier to run multiple regex experiments.

```
import java.util.regex.*;
class Regex {
  public static void main(String [] args) {
    Pattern p = Pattern.compile(args[0]);
    Matcher m = p.matcher(args[1]);
    System.out.println("Pattern is " + m.pattern());
    while(m.find()) {
      System.out.println(m.start() + " " + m.group());
    }
  }
}
```

This program uses the first command-line argument (args[0]) to represent the regex expression you want to use, and it uses the second argument (args[1]) to represent the source data you want to search. Here's a test run:

```
% java Regex "\d\w" "ab4 56_7ab"
```

Produces the output

```
Pattern is \d\w
4 56
7 7a
```

(Remember, if you want this expression to be represented in a String, you'd use \\d\\w). Because you'll often have special characters or whitespace as part of your arguments, you'll probably want to get in the habit of always enclosing your argument in quotes. Let's take a look at this code in more detail. First off, notice that we aren't using new to create a Pattern; if you check the API, you'll find no constructors are listed. You'll use the overloaded, static compile() method (that takes String expression) to create an instance of Pattern. For the exam, all you'll need to know to create a Matcher, is to use the Pattern.matcher() method (that takes String sourceData).

The important method in this program is the find() method. This is the method that actually cranks up the regex engine and does some searching. The find() method returns true if it gets a match, and remembers the start position of the match. If find() returns true, you can call the start() method to get the starting position of the match, and you can call the group() method to get the string that represents the actual bit of source data that was matched.

exam watch

To provide the most flexibility, `Matcher.find()`, when coupled with the greedy quantifiers ? or *, allow for (somewhat unintuitively) the idea of a zero-length match. As an experiment, modify the previous `Regex.java` class and add an invocation of `m.end()` to the S.O.P. in the while loop. With that modification in place, the invocation

```
java Regex "a?" "aba"
```

should produce something very similar to this:

```
Pattern is a?
0 1 a
1 1
2 3 a
3 3
```

The lines of output `1 1` and `3 3` are examples of zero-length matches. Zero-length matches can occur in several places:

- After the last character of source data (the `3 3` example)
- In between characters after a match has been found (the `1 1` example)
- At the beginning of source data (try `java Regex "a?" "baba"`)
- At the beginning of zero-length source data

on the job

A common reason to use regex is to perform search and replace operations. Although replace operations are not on the exam you should know that the Matcher class provides several methods that perform search and replace operations. See the `appendReplacement()`, `appendTail()`, and `replaceAll()` methods in the Matcher API for more details.

The Matcher class allows you to look at subsets of your source data by using a concept called *regions*. In real life, regions can greatly improve performance, but you won't need to know anything about them for the exam.

Searching Using the Scanner Class   Although the java.util.Scanner class is primarily intended for tokenizing data (which we'll cover next), it can also be used to find stuff, just like the Pattern and Matcher classes. While Scanner doesn't provide location information or search and replace functionality, you can use it to apply regex expressions to source data to tell you how many instances of an expression exist in a given piece of source data. The following program uses the first command-line argument as a regex expression, then asks for input using System.in. It outputs a message every time a match is found:

```
import java.util.*;
class ScanIn {
  public static void main(String[] args) {
    System.out.print("input: ");
    System.out.flush();
    try {
      Scanner s = new Scanner(System.in);
      String token;
      do {
        token = s.findInLine(args[0]);
        System.out.println("found " + token);
      } while (token != null);
    } catch (Exception e) { System.out.println("scan exc"); }
  }
}
```

The invocation and input

```
java ScanIn "\d\d"
input: 1b2c335f456
```

produce the following:

```
found 33
found 45
found null
```

Tokenizing

Tokenizing is the process of taking big pieces of source data, breaking them into little pieces, and storing the little pieces in variables. Probably the most common tokenizing situation is reading a delimited file in order to get the contents of the file moved into useful places like objects, arrays or collections. We'll look at two classes in the API that provide tokenizing capabilities: String (using the `split()` method) and Scanner, which has many methods that are useful for tokenizing.

Tokens and Delimiters

When we talk about tokenizing, we're talking about data that starts out composed of two things: tokens and delimiters. Tokens are the actual pieces of data, and delimiters are the expressions that *separate* the tokens from each other. When most people think of delimiters, they think of single characters, like commas or backslashes or maybe a single whitespace. These are indeed very common delimiters, but strictly speaking, delimiters can be much more dynamic. In fact, as we hinted at a few sentences ago, delimiters can be anything that qualifies as a regex expression. Let's take a single piece of source data and tokenize it using a couple of different delimiters:

```
source: "ab,cd5b,6x,z4"
```

If we say that our delimiter is a comma, then our four tokens would be

```
ab
cd5b
6x
z4
```

If we use the same source, but declare our delimiter to be \d, we get three tokens:

```
ab,cd
b,
x,z
```

In general, when we tokenize source data, the delimiters themselves are discarded, and all that we are left with are the tokens. So in the second example, we defined digits to be delimiters, so the 5, 6, and 4 do not appear in the final tokens.

Tokenizing with String.split()

The String class's `split()` method takes a regex expression as its argument, and returns a String array populated with the tokens produced by the split (or tokenizing) process. This is a handy way to tokenize relatively small pieces of data. The following program uses `args[0]` to hold a source string, and `args[1]` to hold the regex pattern to use as a delimiter:

```
import java.util.*;
class SplitTest {
  public static void main(String[] args) {
    String[] tokens = args[0].split(args[1]);
    System.out.println("count " + tokens.length);
    for(String s : tokens)
      System.out.println(">" + s + "<");
  }
}
```

Everything happens all at once when the `split()` method is invoked. The source string is split into pieces, and the pieces are all loaded into the `tokens` String array. All the code after that is just there to verify what the split operation generated. The following invocation

```
% java SplitTest "ab5 ccc 45 @" "\d"
```

produces

```
count 4
>ab<
> ccc <
><
> @<
```

(Note: Remember that to represent "\" in a string you may need to use the escape sequence "\\". Because of this, and depending on your OS, your second argument might have to be "\\d" or even "\\\\d".)

We put the tokens inside "> <" characters to show whitespace. Notice that every digit was used as a delimiter, and that contiguous digits created an empty token.

One drawback to using the `String.split()` method is that often you'll want to look at tokens as they are produced, and possibly quit a tokenization operation early when you've created the tokens you need. For instance, you might be searching a large file for a phone number. If the phone number occurs early in the file, you'd like to quit the tokenization process as soon as you've got your number. The Scanner class provides a rich API for doing just such on-the-fly tokenization operations.

exam

ⓦatch

Because `System.out.println()` *is so heavily used on the exam, you might see examples of escape sequences tucked in with questions on most any topic, including regex. Remember that if you need to create a String that contains a double quote* " *or a backslash* \ *you need to add an escape character first:*

```
System.out.println("\" \\");
```

This prints

```
" \
```

So, what if you need to search for periods (.) in your source data? If you just put a period in the regex expression, you get the "any character" behavior. So, what if you try \. *? Now the Java compiler thinks you're trying to create an escape sequence that doesn't exist. The correct syntax is*

```
String s = "ab.cde.fg";
String[] tokens = s.split("\\.");
```

Tokenizing with Scanner

The java.util.Scanner class is the Cadillac of tokenizing. When you need to do some serious tokenizing, look no further than Scanner—this beauty has it all. In addition to the basic tokenizing capabilities provided by `String.split()`, the Scanner class offers the following features:

- Scanners can be constructed using files, streams, or Strings as a source.
- Tokenizing is performed within a loop so that you can exit the process at any point.
- Tokens can be converted to their appropriate primitive types automatically.

Let's look at a program that demonstrates several of Scanner's methods and capabilities. Scanner's default delimiter is whitespace, which this program uses.

The program makes two Scanner objects: s1 is iterated over with the more generic next() method, which returns every token as a String, while s2 is analyzed with several of the specialized nextXxx() methods (where Xxx is a primitive type):

```
import java.util.Scanner;
class ScanNext {
  public static void main(String [] args) {
    boolean b2, b;
    int i;
    String s, hits = " ";
    Scanner s1 = new Scanner(args[0]);
    Scanner s2 = new Scanner(args[0]);
    while(b = s1.hasNext()) {
      s = s1.next();   hits += "s";
    }
    while(b = s2.hasNext()) {
      if (s2.hasNextInt()) {
        i = s2.nextInt();   hits += "i";
      } else if (s2.hasNextBoolean()) {
        b2 = s2.nextBoolean();   hits += "b";
      } else {
        s2.next();   hits += "s2";
      }
    }
    System.out.println("hits " + hits);
  }
}
```

If this program is invoked with

```
% java ScanNext "1 true 34 hi"
```

it produces

```
hits  ssssibis2
```

Of course we're not doing anything with the tokens once we've got them, but you can see that s2's tokens are converted to their respective primitives. A key point here is that the methods named hasNextXxx() test the value of the next token but do not actually get the token, nor do they move to the next token in the source data. The `nextXxx()` methods all perform two functions: they get the next token, and then they move to the next token.

The Scanner class has `nextXxx()` (for instance `nextLong()`) and `hasNextXxx()` (for instance `hasNextDouble()`) methods for every primitive type except `char`. In addition, the Scanner class has a `useDelimiter()` method that allows you to set the delimiter to be any valid regex expression.

Formatting with printf() and format()

What fun would accounts receivable reports be if the decimal points didn't line up? Where would you be if you couldn't put negative numbers inside of parentheses? Burning questions like these caused the exam creation team to include formatting as a part of the exam. The `format()` and `printf()` methods were added to java.io.PrintStream in Java 5. These two methods behave exactly the same way, so anything we say about one of these methods applies to both of them. (The rumor is that Sun added `printf()` just to make old C programmers happy.)

Behind the scenes, the `format()` method uses the `java.util.Formatter` class to do the heavy formatting work. You can use the `Formatter` class directly if you choose, but for the exam all you have to know is the basic syntax of the arguments you pass to the `format()` method. The documentation for these formatting arguments can be found in the Formatter API. We're going to take the "nickel tour" of the formatting String syntax, which will be more than enough to allow you to do a lot of basic formatting work, AND ace all the formatting questions on the exam.

Let's start by paraphrasing the API documentation for format strings (for more complete, way-past-what-you-need-for-the-exam coverage, check out the java.util.Formatter API):

```
printf("format string", argument(s));
```

The format string can contain both normal string literal information that isn't associated with any arguments, and argument-specific formatting data. The clue to determining whether you're looking at formatting data, is that formatting data will always start with a percent sign (%). Let's look at an example, and don't panic, we'll cover everything that comes after the % next:

```
System.out.printf("%2$d  +  %1$d", 123, 456);
```

This produces

```
456 + 123
```

Let's look at what just happened. Inside the double quotes there is a format string, then a +, and then a second format string. Notice that we mixed literals in with the format strings. Now let's dive in a little deeper and look at the construction of format strings:

```
%[arg_index$][flags][width][.precision]conversion char
```

The values within [ ] are optional. In other words, the only required elements of a format string are the % and a conversion character. In the example above the only optional values we used were for argument indexing. The 2$ represents the second argument, and the 1$ represents the first argument. (Notice that there's no problem switching the order of arguments.) The d after the arguments is a conversion character (more or less the type of the argument). Here's a rundown of the format string elements you'll need to know for the exam:

arg_index   An integer followed directly by a $, this indicates which argument should be printed in this position.

flags   While many flags are available, for the exam you'll need to know:

- "-"   Left justify this argument
- "+"   Include a sign (ı or -) with this argument
- "0"   Pad this argument with zeroes
- ","   Use locale-specific grouping separators (i.e., the comma in 123,456)
- "("   Enclose negative numbers in parentheses

width   This value indicates the minimum number of characters to print. (If you want nice even columns, you'll use this value extensively.)

precision   For the exam you'll only need this when formatting a floating-point number, and in the case of floating point numbers, precision indicates the number of digits to print after the decimal point.

conversion   The type of argument you'll be formatting. You'll need to know:

- b   boolean
- c   char
- d   integer
- f   floating point
- s   string

Let's see some of these formatting strings in action:

```
int i1 = -123;
int i2 = 12345;
System.out.printf(">%1$(7d< \n", i1);
System.out.printf(">%0,7d< \n", i2);
System.out.format(">%+-7d< \n", i2);
System.out.printf(">%2$b + %1$5d< \n", i1, false);
```

This produces:

```
>  (123)<
>012,345<
>+12345 <
>false +  -123<
```

(We added the > and < literals to help show how minimum widths, and zero padding and alignments work.) Finally, it's important to remember that if you have a mismatch between the type specified in your conversion character and your argument, you'll get a runtime exception:

```
System.out.format("%d", 12.3);
```

This produces something like

```
Exception in thread "main" java.util.IllegalFormatConversionEx-
ception: d != java.lang.Double
```

CERTIFICATION SUMMARY

Strings   The most important thing to remember about Strings is that String objects are immutable, but references to Strings are not! You can make a new String by using an existing String as a starting point, but if you don't assign a reference variable to the new String it will be lost to your program—you will have no way to access your new String. Review the important methods in the String class.

The StringBuilder class was added in Java 5. It has exactly the same methods as the old StringBuffer class, except StringBuilder's methods aren't thread-safe. Because StringBuilder's methods are not thread safe, they tend to run faster than StringBuffer methods, so choose StringBuilder whenever threading is not an issue. Both StringBuffer and StringBuilder objects can have their value changed over and over without having to create new objects. If you're doing a lot of string manipulation, these objects will be more efficient than immutable String objects, which are, more or less, "use once, remain in memory forever." Remember, these methods ALWAYS change the invoking object's value, even with no explicit assignment.

File I/O   Remember that objects of type File can represent either files or directories, but that until you call `createNewFile()` or `mkdir()` you haven't actually created anything on your hard drive. Classes in the java.io package are designed to be chained together. It will be rare that you'll use a FileReader or a FileWriter without "wrapping" them with a BufferedReader or BufferedWriter object, which gives you access to more powerful, higher-level methods. As of Java 5, the PrintWriter class has been enhanced with advanced `append()`, `format()`, and `printf()` methods, and when you couple that with new constructors that allow you to create PrintWriters directly from a String name or a File object, you may use BufferWriters a lot less. The Console class allows you to read non-echoed input (returned in a char[]), and is instantiated using System.console().

Serialization   Serialization lets you save, ship, and restore everything you need to know about a *live* object. And when your object points to other objects, they get saved too. The java.io.ObjectOutputStream and java.io.ObjectInputStream classes are used to serialize and deserialize objects. Typically you wrap them around instances of FileOutputStream and FileInputStream, respectively.

The key method you invoke to serialize an object is `writeObject()`, and to deserialize an object invoke `readObject()`. In order to serialize an object, it must implement the Serializable interface. Mark instance variables `transient` if you don't want their state to be part of the serialization process. You can augment the serialization process for your class by implementing `writeObject()` and `readObject()`. If you do that, an embedded call to `defaultReadObject()` and `defaultWriteObject()` will handle the normal serialization tasks, and you can augment those invocations with manual *reading from* and *writing to* the stream.

If a superclass implements Serializable then all of its subclasses do too. If a superclass doesn't implement Serializable, then when a subclass object is deserialized the unserializable superclass's constructor runs—be careful! Finally, remember that serialization is about instances, so static variables aren't serialized.

Dates, Numbers, and Currency   Remember that the Sun objective is a bit misleading, and that you'll have to understand the basics of five related classes: java.util.Date, java.util.Calendar, java.util.Locale, java.text.DateFormat, and java.text.NumberFormat. A Date is the number of milliseconds since Jan 1, 1970, stored in a `long`. Most of Date's methods have been deprecated, so use the Calendar class for your date-manipulation tasks. Remember that in order to create instances of Calendar, DateFormat, and NumberFormat, you have to use static factory methods like `getInstance()`. The Locale class is used with DateFormat and NumberFormat to generate a variety of output styles that are language and/or country specific.

Parsing, Tokenizing, and Formatting   To find specific pieces of data in large data sources, Java provides several mechanisms that use the concepts of regular expressions (Regex). regex expressions can be used with the java.util.regex package's Pattern and Matcher classes, as well as with java.util.Scanner and with the `String.split()` method. When creating regex patterns, you can use literal characters for matching or you can use metacharacters, that allow you to match on concepts like "find digits" or "find whitespace". Regex provides *quantifiers* that allow you to say things like "find one or more of these things in a row." You won't have to understand the Matcher methods that facilitate replacing strings in data.

Tokenizing is splitting delimited data into pieces. Delimiters are usually as simple as a comma, but they can be as complex as any other regex pattern. The java.util.Scanner class provides full tokenizing capabilities using regex, and allows you to tokenize in a loop so that you can stop the tokenizing process at any point. `String.split()` allows full regex patterns for tokenizing, but tokenizing is done in one step, hence large data sources can take a long time to process.

Formatting data for output can be handled by using the Formatter class, or more commonly by using the new PrintStream methods `format()` and `printf()`. Remember `format()` and `printf()` behave identically. To use these methods, you create a format string that is associated with every piece of data you want to format.

TWO-MINUTE DRILL

Here are some of the key points from the certification objectives in this chapter.

Using String, StringBuffer, and StringBuilder (Objective 3.1)

❏ String objects are immutable, and String reference variables are not.

❏ If you create a new String without assigning it, it will be lost to your program.

❏ If you redirect a String reference to a new String, the old String can be lost.

❏ String methods use zero-based indexes, except for the second argument of `substring()`.

❏ The String class is `final`—its methods can't be overridden.

❏ When the JVM finds a String literal, it is added to the String literal pool.

❏ Strings have a method: `length()`; arrays have an attribute named `length`.

❏ The StringBuffer's API is the same as the new StringBuilder's API, except that StringBuilder's methods are not synchronized for thread safety.

❏ StringBuilder methods should run faster than StringBuffer methods.

❏ All of the following bullets apply to both StringBuffer and StringBuilder:

  ❏ They are mutable—they can change without creating a new object.

  ❏ StringBuffer methods act on the invoking object, and objects can change without an explicit assignment in the statement.

  ❏ StringBuffer `equals()` is not overridden; it doesn't compare values.

❏ Remember that chained methods are evaluated from left to right.

❏ String methods to remember: `charAt()`, `concat()`, `equalsIgnoreCase()`, `length()`, `replace()`, `substring()`, `toLowerCase()`, `toString()`, `toUpperCase()`, and `trim()`.

❏ StringBuffer methods to remember: `append()`, `delete()`, `insert()`, `reverse()`, and `toString()`.

File I/O (Objective 3.2)

❏ The classes you need to understand in java.io are File, FileReader, BufferedReader, FileWriter, BufferedWriter, PrintWriter, and Console.

❏ A new File object doesn't mean there's a new file on your hard drive.

❏ File objects can represent either a file or a directory.

❏ The File class lets you manage (add, rename, and delete) files and directories.

❏ The methods `createNewFile()` and `mkdir()` add entries to your file system.

❏ FileWriter and FileReader are low-level I/O classes. You can use them to write and read files, but they should usually be wrapped.

❏ Classes in java.io are designed to be "chained" or "wrapped." (This is a common use of the decorator design pattern.)

❏ It's very common to "wrap" a BufferedReader around a FileReader or a BufferedWriter around a FileWriter, to get access to higher-level (more convenient) methods.

❏ PrintWriters can be used to wrap other Writers, but as of Java 5 they can be built directly from Files or Strings.

❏ Java 5 PrintWriters have new `append()`, `format()`, and `printf()` methods.

❏ Console objects can read non-echoed input and are instantiated using System.console().

Serialization (Objective 3.3)

❏ The classes you need to understand are all in the java.io package; they include: ObjectOutputStream and ObjectInputStream primarily, and FileOutputStream and FileInputStream because you will use them to create the low-level streams that the ObjectXxxStream classes will use.

❏ A class must implement Serializable before its objects can be serialized.

❏ The `ObjectOutputStream.writeObject()` method serializes objects, and the `ObjectInputStream.readObject()` method deserializes objects.

❏ If you mark an instance variable `transient`, it will not be serialized even thought the rest of the object's state will be.

❏ You can supplement a class's automatic serialization process by implementing the `writeObject()` and `readObject()` methods. If you do this, embedding calls to `defaultWriteObject()` and `defaultReadObject()`, respectively, will handle the part of serialization that happens normally.

❏ If a superclass implements Serializable, then its subclasses do automatically.

❏ If a superclass doesn't implement Serializable, then when a subclass object is deserialized, the superclass constructor will be invoked, along with its superconstructor(s).

❏ DataInputStream and DataOutputStream aren't actually on the exam, in spite of what the Sun objectives say.

Dates, Numbers, and Currency (Objective 3.4)

❑ The classes you need to understand are java.util.Date, java.util.Calendar, java.text.DateFormat, java.text.NumberFormat, and java.util.Locale.

❑ Most of the Date class's methods have been deprecated.

❑ A Date is stored as a `long`, the number of milliseconds since January 1, 1970.

❑ Date objects are go-betweens the Calendar and Locale classes.

❑ The Calendar provides a powerful set of methods to manipulate dates, performing tasks such as getting days of the week, or adding some number of months or years (or other increments) to a date.

❑ Create Calendar instances using static factory methods (`getInstance()`).

❑ The Calendar methods you should understand are `add()`, which allows you to add or subtract various pieces (minutes, days, years, and so on) of dates, and `roll()`, which works like `add()` but doesn't increment a date's bigger pieces. (For example: adding 10 months to an October date changes the month to August, but doesn't increment the Calendar's year value.)

❑ DateFormat instances are created using static factory methods (`getInstance()` and `getDateInstance()`).

❑ There are several format "styles" available in the DateFormat class.

❑ DateFormat styles can be applied against various Locales to create a wide array of outputs for any given date.

❑ The `DateFormat.format()` method is used to create Strings containing properly formatted dates.

❑ The Locale class is used in conjunction with DateFormat and NumberFormat.

❑ Both DateFormat and NumberFormat objects can be constructed with a specific, immutable Locale.

❑ For the exam you should understand creating Locales using language, or a combination of language and country.

Parsing, Tokenizing, and Formatting (Objective 3.5)

❑ regex is short for regular expressions, which are the patterns used to search for data within large data sources.

❑ regex is a sub-language that exists in Java and other languages (such as Perl).

❑ regex lets you to create search patterns using literal characters or metacharacters. Metacharacters allow you to search for slightly more abstract data like "digits" or "whitespace".

❑ Study the \d, \s, \w, and . metacharacters

❑ regex provides for *quantifiers* which allow you to specify concepts like: "look for one or more digits in a row."

❑ Study the ?, *, and + greedy quantifiers.

❑ Remember that metacharacters and Strings don't mix well unless you remember to "escape" them properly. For instance String s = "\\d";

❑ The Pattern and Matcher classes have Java's most powerful regex capabilities.

❑ You should understand the Pattern compile() method and the Matcher matches(), pattern(), find(), start(), and group() methods.

❑ You WON'T need to understand Matcher's replacement-oriented methods.

❑ You can use java.util.Scanner to do simple regex searches, but it is primarily intended for tokenizing.

❑ Tokenizing is the process of splitting delimited data into small pieces.

❑ In tokenizing, the data you want is called tokens, and the strings that separate the tokens are called delimiters.

❑ Tokenizing can be done with the Scanner class, or with String.split().

❑ Delimiters are single characters like commas, or complex regex expressions.

❑ The Scanner class allows you to tokenize data from within a loop, which allows you to stop whenever you want to.

❑ The Scanner class allows you to tokenize Strings or streams or files.

❑ The String.split() method tokenizes the entire source data all at once, so large amounts of data can be quite slow to process.

❑ New to Java 5 are two methods used to format data for output. These methods are format() and printf(). These methods are found in the PrintStream class, an instance of which is the out in System.out.

❑ The format() and printf() methods have identical functionality.

❑ Formatting data with printf() (or format()) is accomplished using *formatting strings* that are associated with primitive or string arguments.

❑ The format() method allows you to mix literals in with your format strings.

❑ The format string values you should know are

  ❑ Flags: -, +, 0, ",", and (

  ❑ Conversions: b, c, d, f, and s

❑ If your conversion character doesn't match your argument type, an exception will be thrown.

SELF TEST

1. Given:

```
import java.util.regex.*;
class Regex2 {
  public static void main(String[] args) {
    Pattern p = Pattern.compile(args[0]);
    Matcher m = p.matcher(args[1]);
    boolean b = false;
    while(b = m.find()) {
      System.out.print(m.start() + m.group());
    }
  }
}
```

And the command line:

```
java Regex2 "\d*" ab34ef
```

What is the result?

A. `234`

B. `334`

C. `2334`

D. `0123456`

E. `01234456`

F. `12334567`

G. Compilation fails

2. Given:

```
import java.io.*;
class Player {
  Player() { System.out.print("p"); }
}
class CardPlayer extends Player implements Serializable {
  CardPlayer() { System.out.print("c"); }
```

```
      public static void main(String[] args) {
        CardPlayer c1 = new CardPlayer();
        try {
          FileOutputStream fos = new FileOutputStream("play.txt");
          ObjectOutputStream os = new ObjectOutputStream(fos);
          os.writeObject(c1);
          os.close();
          FileInputStream fis = new FileInputStream("play.txt");
          ObjectInputStream is = new ObjectInputStream(fis);
          CardPlayer c2 = (CardPlayer) is.readObject();
          is.close();
        } catch (Exception x ) { }
      }
    }
```

What is the result?

A. pc

B. pcc

C. pcp

D. pcpc

E. Compilation fails

F. An exception is thrown at runtime

3. Given:

```
class TKO {
  public static void main(String[] args) {
    String s = "-";
    Integer x = 343;
    long L343 = 343L;
    if(x.equals(L343))  s += ".e1 ";
    if(x.equals(343))  s += ".e2 ";
    Short s1 = (short)((new Short((short)343)) / (new Short((short)49)));
    if(s1 == 7)        s += "=s ";
    if(s1 < new Integer(7+1))  s += "fly ";
    System.out.println(s);
  }
}
```

Which of the following will be included in the output String s? (Choose all that apply.)

A. `.e1`

B. `.e2`

C. `=s`

D. `fly`

E. None of the above

F. Compilation fails

G. An exception is thrown at runtime

4. Given:

```
import java.io.*;

class Keyboard { }
public class Computer implements Serializable {
  private Keyboard k = new Keyboard();
  public static void main(String[] args) {
    Computer c = new Computer();
    c.storeIt(c);
  }
  void storeIt(Computer c) {
    try {
      ObjectOutputStream os = new ObjectOutputStream(
        new FileOutputStream("myFile"));
      os.writeObject(c);
      os.close();
      System.out.println("done");
    } catch (Exception x) {System.out.println("exc"); }
  }
}
```

What is the result? (Choose all that apply.)

A. exc

B. done

C. Compilation fails

D. Exactly one object is serialized

E. Exactly two objects are serialized

5. Using the fewest **fragments** possible (and filling the fewest slots possible), complete the **code** below so that the class builds a directory named "dir3" and creates a file named "file3" inside "dir3". Note you can use each fragment either zero or one times.

Code:

```
import java.io._____

class Maker {
  public static void main(String[] args) {

      _____  _____  _____

      _____  _____  _____

      _____  _____  _____

      _____  _____  _____

      _____  _____  _____

      _____  _____  _____

      _____  _____  _____
  }
}
```

Fragments:

```
File;        FileDescriptor;      FileWriter;      Directory;
try {        .createNewDir();     File dir         File
{ }          (Exception x)        ("dir3");        file
file         .createNewFile();    = new File       = new File
dir          (dir, "file3");      (dir, file);     .createFile();
} catch      ("dir3", "file3");   .mkdir();        File file
```

6. Given that 1119280000000L is roughly the number of milliseconds from Jan 1, 1970, to June 20, 2005, and that you want to print that date in German, using the LONG style such that "June" will be displayed as "Juni", complete the code using the fragments below. Note: you can use each fragment either zero or one times, and you might not need to fill all of the slots.

Code:

```
import java._____

import java._____

class DateTwo {
  public static void main(String[] args) {
    Date d = new Date(1119280000000L);

    DateFormat df = _____

                    _____ , _____ );

    System.out.println(_____
  }
}
```

Fragments:

```
io.*;       new DateFormat(           Locale.LONG
nio.*;      DateFormat.getInstance(   Locale.GERMANY
util.*;     DateFormat.getDateInstance(  DateFormat.LONG
text.*;     util.regex;               DateFormat.GERMANY
date.*;     df.format(d));            d.format(df));
```

7. Given:

```
import java.io.*;
class Directories {
  static String [] dirs = {"dir1", "dir2"};
  public static void main(String [] args) {
    for (String d : dirs) {

      // insert code 1 here

      File file = new File(path, args[0]);

      // insert code 2 here

    }
  }
}
```

and that the invocation

```
java Directories file2.txt
```

is issued from a directory that has two subdirectories, "dir1" and "dir2", and that "dir1" has a file "file1.txt" and "dir2" has a file "file2.txt", and the output is "false true"; which set(s) of code fragments must be inserted? (Choose all that apply.)

A. ```
String path = d;
```

```
System.out.print(file.exists() + " ");
```

B. ```
String path = d;
```

```
System.out.print(file.isFile() + " ");
```

C. ```
String path = File.separator + d;
```

```
System.out.print(file.exists() + " ");
```

D. ```
String path = File.separator + d;
```

```
System.out.print(file.isFile() + " ");
```

8. Given:

```
import java.io.*;

public class TestSer {
  public static void main(String[] args) {
    SpecialSerial s = new SpecialSerial();
    try {
      ObjectOutputStream os = new ObjectOutputStream(
        new FileOutputStream("myFile"));
      os.writeObject(s);  os.close();
      System.out.print(++s.z + " ");

      ObjectInputStream is = new ObjectInputStream(
        new FileInputStream("myFile"));
      SpecialSerial s2 = (SpecialSerial)is.readObject();
      is.close();
```

```
        System.out.println(s2.y + " " + s2.z);
      } catch (Exception x) {System.out.println("exc"); }
    }
  }
  class SpecialSerial implements Serializable {
    transient int y = 7;
    static int z = 9;
  }
```

Which are true? (Choose all that apply.)

A. Compilation fails

B. The output is 10 0 9

C. The output is 10 0 10

D. The output is 10 7 9

E. The output is 10 7 10

F. In order to alter the standard deserialization process you would implement the
   readObject() method in SpecialSerial

G. In order to alter the standard deserialization process you would implement the
   defaultReadObject() method in SpecialSerial

9. Given:

```
3. public class Theory {
4.   public static void main(String[] args) {
5.     String s1 = "abc";
6.     String s2 = s1;
7.     s1 += "d";
8.     System.out.println(s1 + " " + s2 + " " + (s1==s2));
9.
10.    StringBuffer sb1 = new StringBuffer("abc");
11.    StringBuffer sb2 = sb1;
12.    sb1.append("d");
13.    System.out.println(sb1 + " " + sb2 + " " + (sb1==sb2));
14.  }
15. }
```

Which are true? (Choose all that apply.)

A. Compilation fails

B. The first line of output is abc abc true

C. The first line of output is `abc abc false`

D. The first line of output is `abcd abc false`

E. The second line of output is `abcd abc false`

F. The second line of output is `abcd abcd true`

G. The second line of output is `abcd abcd false`

10. Given:

```
3.  import java.io.*;
4.  public class ReadingFor {
5.    public static void main(String[] args) {
6.      String s;
7.      try {
8.        FileReader fr = new FileReader("myfile.txt");
9.        BufferedReader br = new BufferedReader(fr);
10.       while((s = br.readLine()) != null)
11.         System.out.println(s);
12.       br.flush();
13.     } catch (IOException e) { System.out.println("io error"); }
16.   }
17. }
```

And given that myfile.txt contains the following two lines of data:

```
ab
cd
```

What is the result?

A. `ab`

B. `abcd`

C. `ab`
   `cd`

D. `a`
   `b`
   `c`
   `d`

E. Compilation fails

11. Given:

```
3. import java.io.*;
4. public class Talker {
5.    public static void main(String[] args) {
6.       Console c = System.console();
7.       String u = c.readLine("%s", "username: ");
8.       System.out.println("hello " + u);
9.       String pw;
10.      if(c != null && (pw = c.readPassword("%s", "password: ")) != null)
11.         // check for valid password
12.   }
13. }
```

If line 6 creates a valid Console object, and if the user enters *fred* as a username and *1234* as a password, what is the result? (Choose all that apply.)

A. username:
   password:

B. username: fred
   password:

C. username: fred
   password: 1234

D. Compilation fails

E. An exception is thrown at runtime

12. Given:

```
3. import java.io.*;
4. class Vehicle { }
5. class Wheels { }
6. class Car extends Vehicle implements Serializable {  }
7. class Ford extends Car { }
8. class Dodge extends Car {
9.    Wheels w = new Wheels();
10. }
```

Instances of which class(es) can be serialized? (Choose all that apply.)

A. Car

B. Ford

C. Dodge

D. Wheels

E. Vehicle

13. Given:

```
3.  import java.text.*;
4.  public class Slice {
5.    public static void main(String[] args) {
6.      String s = "987.123456";
7.      double d  = 987.123456d;
8.      NumberFormat nf = NumberFormat.getInstance();
9.      nf.setMaximumFractionDigits(5);
10.     System.out.println(nf.format(d) + " ");
11.     try {
12.       System.out.println(nf.parse(s));
13.     } catch (Exception e) { System.out.println("got exc"); }
14.   }
15. }
```

Which are true? (Choose all that apply.)

A. The output is 987.12345 987.12345

B. The output is 987.12346 987.12345

C. The output is 987.12345 987.123456

D. The output is 987.12346 987.123456

E. The try/catch block is unnecessary

F. The code compiles and runs without exception

G. The invocation of parse() must be placed within a try/catch block

14. Given:

```
3.  import java.util.regex.*;
4.  public class Archie {
5.    public static void main(String[] args) {
6.      Pattern p = Pattern.compile(args[0]);
7.      Matcher m = p.matcher(args[1]);
8.      int count = 0;
9.      while(m.find())
10.       count++;
```

```
11.        System.out.print(count);
12.    }
13. }
```

And given the command line invocation:

```
java Archie "\d+" ab2c4d67
```

What is the result?

A. 0

B. 3

C. 4

D. 8

E. 9

F. Compilation fails

15. Given:

```
3. import java.util.*;
4. public class Looking {
5.    public static void main(String[] args) {
6.       String input = "1 2 a 3 45 6";
7.       Scanner sc = new Scanner(input);
8.       int x = 0;
9.       do {
10.         x = sc.nextInt();
11.         System.out.print(x + " ");
12.       } while (x!=0);
13.    }
14. }
```

What is the result?

A. 1 2

B. 1 2 3 45 6

C. 1 2 3 4 5 6

D. 1 2 a 3 45 6

E. Compilation fails

F. 1 2 followed by an exception

SELF TEST ANSWERS

1. Given:

```
import java.util.regex.*;
class Regex2 {
  public static void main(String[] args) {
    Pattern p = Pattern.compile(args[0]);
    Matcher m = p.matcher(args[1]);
    boolean b = false;
    while(b = m.find()) {
      System.out.print(m.start() + m.group());
    }
  }
}
```

And the command line:

```
java Regex2 "\d*" ab34ef
```

What is the result?

A. 234

B. 334

C. 2334

D. 0123456

E. 01234456

F. 12334567

G. Compilation fails

Answer:

☑ **E** is correct. The `\d` is looking for digits. The `*` is a quantifier that looks for 0 to many occurrences of the pattern that precedes it. Because we specified `*`, the `group()` method returns empty Strings until consecutive digits are found, so the only time `group()` returns a value is when it returns 34 when the matcher finds digits starting in position 2. The `start()` method returns the starting position of the previous match because, again, we said find 0 to many occurrences.

☒ **A, B, C, D, F,** and **G** are incorrect based on the above. (Objective 3.5)

2. Given:

```
import java.io.*;
class Player {
  Player() { System.out.print("p"); }
}
class CardPlayer extends Player implements Serializable {
  CardPlayer() { System.out.print("c"); }
  public static void main(String[] args) {
    CardPlayer c1 = new CardPlayer();
    try {
      FileOutputStream fos = new FileOutputStream("play.txt");
      ObjectOutputStream os = new ObjectOutputStream(fos);
      os.writeObject(c1);
      os.close();
      FileInputStream fis = new FileInputStream("play.txt");
      ObjectInputStream is = new ObjectInputStream(fis);
      CardPlayer c2 = (CardPlayer) is.readObject();
      is.close();
    } catch (Exception x ) { }
  }
}
```

What is the result?

A. pc

B. pcc

C. pcp

D. pcpc

E. Compilation fails

F. An exception is thrown at runtime

Answer:

☑ **C** is correct. It's okay for a class to implement Serializable even if its superclass doesn't. However, when you deserialize such an object, the non-serializable superclass must run its constructor. Remember, constructors don't run on deserialized classes that implement Serializable.

☒ **A, B, D, E,** and **F** are incorrect based on the above. (Objective 3.3)

3. Given:

```
class TKO {
  public static void main(String[] args) {
    String s = "-";
    Integer x = 343;
    long L343 = 343L;
    if(x.equals(L343))   s += ".e1 ";
    if(x.equals(343))   s += ".e2 ";
    Short s1 = (short)((new Short((short)343)) / (new Short((short)49)));
    if(s1 == 7)          s += "=s ";
    if(s1 < new Integer(7+1))  s += "fly ";
    System.out.println(s);
  } }
```

Which of the following will be included in the output String s? (Choose all that apply.)

A. `.e1`

B. `.e2`

C. `=s`

D. `fly`

E. None of the above

F. Compilation fails

G. An exception is thrown at runtime

Answer:

☑ **B, C,** and **D** are correct. Remember, that the `equals()` method for the integer wrappers will only return `true` if the two primitive types and the two values are equal. With **C**, it's okay to unbox and use `==`. For **D**, it's okay to create a wrapper object with an expression, and unbox it for comparison with a primitive.

☒ **A, E, F,** and **G** are incorrect based on the above. (Remember that **A** is using the `equals()` method to try to compare two different types.) (Objective 3.1)

4. Given:

```
import java.io.*;

class Keyboard { }
public class Computer implements Serializable {
```

```
      private Keyboard k = new Keyboard();
      public static void main(String[] args) {
        Computer c = new Computer();
        c.storeIt(c);
      }
      void storeIt(Computer c) {
        try {
          ObjectOutputStream os = new ObjectOutputStream(
            new FileOutputStream("myFile"));
          os.writeObject(c);
          os.close();
          System.out.println("done");
        } catch (Exception x) {System.out.println("exc"); }
      }
    }
```

What is the result? (Choose all that apply.)

A. exc

B. done

C. Compilation fails

D. Exactly one object is serialized

E. Exactly two objects are serialized

Answer:

☑ **A** is correct. An instance of type Computer Has-a Keyboard. Because Keyboard doesn't implement Serializable, any attempt to serialize an instance of Computer will cause an exception to be thrown.

☒ **B, C, D,** and **E** are incorrect based on the above. If Keyboard did implement Serializable then two objects would have been serialized. (Objective 3.3)

5. Using the fewest fragments possible (and filling the fewest slots possible), complete the code below so that the class builds a directory named "dir3" and creates a file named "file3" inside "dir3". Note you can use each fragment either zero or one times.

Code:

```
import java.io._____

class Maker {
  public static void main(String[] args) {

    _____   _____   _____

    _____   _____   _____

    _____   _____   _____

    _____   _____   _____

    _____   _____

    _____   _____

    _____   _____   _____

} }
```

Fragments:

```
File;        FileDescriptor;    FileWriter;    Directory;
try {        .createNewDir();   File dir       File
{ }          (Exception x)      ("dir3");      file
file         .createNewFile();  = new File     = new File
dir          (dir, "file3");    (dir, file);   .createFile();
} catch      ("dir3", "file3"); .mkdir();      File file
```

Answer:

```
import java.io.File;
class Maker {
  public static void main(String[] args) {
    try {
      File dir = new File("dir3");
      dir.mkdir();
      File file = new File(dir, "file3");
      file.createNewFile();
    } catch (Exception x) { }
} }
```

Notes: The new File statements don't make actual files or directories, just objects. You need the mkdir() and createNewFile() methods to actually create the directory and the file. (Objective 3.2)

6. Given that 1119280000000L is roughly the number of milliseconds from Jan. 1, 1970, to June 20, 2005, and that you want to print that date in German, using the LONG style such that "June" will be displayed as "Juni", complete the code using the fragments below. Note: you can use each fragment either zero or one times, and you might not need to fill all of the slots.

Code:

```
import java._____
import java._____

class DateTwo {
  public static void main(String[] args) {
    Date d = new Date(1119280000000L);
    DateFormat df = _____

                    _____ , _____ );

    System.out.println(_____
  }
}
```

Fragments:

io.*;	new DateFormat(	Locale.LONG
nio.*;	DateFormat.getInstance(	Locale.GERMANY
util.*;	DateFormat.getDateInstance(	DateFormat.LONG
text.*;	util.regex;	DateFormat.GERMANY
date.*;	df.format(d));	d.format(df));

Answer:

```
import java.util.*;
import java.text.*;
class DateTwo {
  public static void main(String[] args) {
    Date d = new Date(1119280000000L);
  DateFormat df = DateFormat.getDateInstance(
                   DateFormat.LONG, Locale.GERMANY);
    System.out.println(df.format(d));
  }
}
```

Notes: Remember that you must build `DateFormat` objects using static methods. Also remember that you must specify a Locale for a `DateFormat` object at the time of instantiation. The `getInstance()` method does not take a Locale. (Objective 3.4)

7. Given:

```
import java.io.*;

class Directories {
  static String [] dirs = {"dir1", "dir2"};
  public static void main(String [] args) {
    for (String d : dirs) {

      // insert code 1 here

      File file = new File(path, args[0]);

      // insert code 2 here
    }
  }
}
```

and that the invocation

```
java Directories file2.txt
```

is issued from a directory that has two subdirectories, "dir1" and "dir2", and that "dir1" has a file "file1.txt" and "dir2" has a file "file2.txt", and the output is "false true", which set(s) of code fragments must be inserted? (Choose all that apply.)

A. `String path = d;`

   `System.out.print(file.exists() + " ");`

B. `String path = d;`

   `System.out.print(file.isFile() + " ");`

C. `String path = File.separator + d;`

   `System.out.print(file.exists() + " ");`

D. `String path = File.separator + d;`

   `System.out.print(file.isFile() + " ");`

> Answer:
>
> ☑ **A** and **B** are correct. Because you are invoking the program from the directory whose direct subdirectories are to be searched, you don't start your path with a `File.separator` character. The `exists()` method tests for either files or directories; the `isFile()` method tests only for files. Since we're looking for a file, both methods work.
>
> ☒ **C** and **D** are incorrect based on the above. (Objective 3.2)

8. Given:

```
import java.io.*;

public class TestSer {
  public static void main(String[] args) {
    SpecialSerial s = new SpecialSerial();
    try {
      ObjectOutputStream os = new ObjectOutputStream(
        new FileOutputStream("myFile"));
      os.writeObject(s);  os.close();
      System.out.print(++s.z + " ");

      ObjectInputStream is = new ObjectInputStream(
        new FileInputStream("myFile"));
      SpecialSerial s2 = (SpecialSerial)is.readObject();
      is.close();
      System.out.println(s2.y + " " + s2.z);
    } catch (Exception x) {System.out.println("exc"); }
  }
}
class SpecialSerial implements Serializable {
  transient int y = 7;
  static int z = 9;
}
```

Which are true? (Choose all that apply.)

A. Compilation fails

B. The output is `10  0  9`

C. The output is `10  0  10`

D. The output is `10  7  9`

E. The output is `10  7  10`

F. In order to alter the standard deserialization process you would implement the `readObject()` method in `SpecialSerial`

G. In order to alter the standard deserialization process you would implement the `defaultReadObject()` method in `SpecialSerial`

Answer:

☑ **C** and **F** are correct. **C** is correct because `static` and `transient` variables are not serialized when an object is serialized. **F** is a valid statement.

☒ **A, B, D,** and **E** are incorrect based on the above. **G** is incorrect because you don't implement the `defaultReadObject()` method, you call it from within the `readObject()` method, along with any custom read operations your class needs. (Objective 3.3)

9. Given:

```
3. public class Theory {
4.    public static void main(String[] args) {
5.       String s1 = "abc";
6.       String s2 = s1;
7.       s1 += "d";
8.       System.out.println(s1 + " " + s2 + " " + (s1==s2));
9.
10.      StringBuffer sb1 = new StringBuffer("abc");
11.      StringBuffer sb2 = sb1;
12.      sb1.append("d");
13.      System.out.println(sb1 + " " + sb2 + " " + (sb1==sb2));
14.   }
15. }
```

Which are true? (Choose all that apply.)

A. Compilation fails

B. The first line of output is `abc abc true`

C. The first line of output is `abc abc false`

D. The first line of output is `abcd abc false`

E. The second line of output is `abcd abc false`

F. The second line of output is `abcd abcd true`

G. The second line of output is `abcd abcd false`

Answer:

☑ **D** and **F** are correct. While String objects are immutable, references to Strings are mutable. The code `s1 += "d";` creates a new String object. StringBuffer objects are mutable, so the `append()` is changing the single StringBuffer object to which both StringBuffer references refer.

☒ **A, B, C, E,** and **G** are incorrect based on the above. (Objective 3.1)

10. Given:

```
3.  import java.io.*;
4.  public class ReadingFor {
5.    public static void main(String[] args) {
6.      String s;
7.      try {
8.        FileReader fr = new FileReader("myfile.txt");
9.        BufferedReader br = new BufferedReader(fr);
10.       while((s = br.readLine()) != null)
11.         System.out.println(s);
12.       br.flush();
13.     } catch (IOException e) { System.out.println("io error"); }
16.   }
17. }
```

And given that myfile.txt contains the following two lines of data:

```
ab
cd
```

What is the result?

A.   ab

B.   abcd

C.   ab
     cd

D.   a
     b
     c
     d

E.   Compilation fails

Answer:

☑   **E** is correct. You need to call `flush()` only when you're writing data. Readers don't have
    `flush()` methods. If not for the call to `flush()`, answer C would be correct.

☒   **A, B, C,** and **D** are incorrect based on the above. (Objective 3.2)

11.   Given:

```
3. import java.io.*;
4. public class Talker {
5.   public static void main(String[] args) {
6.     Console c = System.console();
7.     String u = c.readLine("%s", "username: ");
8.     System.out.println("hello " + u);
9.     String pw;
10.    if(c != null && (pw = c.readPassword("%s", "password: ")) != null)
11.       // check for valid password
12.  }
13. }
```

If line 6 creates a valid Console object, and if the user enters *fred* as a username and *1234* as a
password, what is the result? (Choose all that apply.)

A.   username:
     password:

B.   username: fred
     password:

C. `username: fred`
    `password: 1234`

D. Compilation fails

E. An exception is thrown at runtime

Answer:

☑ **D** is correct. The `readPassword()` method returns a `char[]`. If a `char[]` were used, answer B would be correct.

☒ **A, B, C,** and **E** are incorrect based on the above. (Objective 3.2)

12. Given:

```
 3. import java.io.*;
 4. class Vehicle { }
 5. class Wheels { }
 6. class Car extends Vehicle implements Serializable {  }
 7. class Ford extends Car { }
 8. class Dodge extends Car {
 9.   Wheels w = new Wheels();
10. }
```

Instances of which class(es) can be serialized? (Choose all that apply.)

A. Car

B. Ford

C. Dodge

D. Wheels

E. Vehicle

Answer:

☑ **A** and **B** are correct. Dodge instances cannot be serialized because they "have" an instance of Wheels, which is not serializable. Vehicle instances cannot be serialized even though the subclass Car can be.

☒ **C, D,** and **E** are incorrect based on the above. (Objective 3.3)

13. Given:

```
 3. import java.text.*;
 4. public class Slice {
 5.   public static void main(String[] args) {
 6.     String s = "987.123456";
 7.     double d  = 987.123456d;
 8.     NumberFormat nf = NumberFormat.getInstance();
 9.     nf.setMaximumFractionDigits(5);
10.     System.out.println(nf.format(d) + " ");
11.     try {
12.       System.out.println(nf.parse(s));
13.     } catch (Exception e) { System.out.println("got exc"); }
14.   }
15. }
```

Which are true? (Choose all that apply.)

A. The output is `987.12345 987.12345`

B. The output is `987.12346 987.12345`

C. The output is `987.12345 987.123456`

D. The output is `987.12346 987.123456`

E. The try/catch block is unnecessary

F. The code compiles and runs without exception

G. The invocation of `parse()` must be placed within a try/catch block

Answer:

☑ **D, F,** and **G** are correct. The `setMaximumFractionDigits()` applies to the formatting but not the parsing. The try/catch block is placed appropriately. This one might scare you into thinking that you'll need to memorize more than you really do. If you can remember that you're formatting the number and parsing the string you should be fine for the exam.

☒ **A, B, C,** and **E** are incorrect based on the above. (Objective 3.4)

14. Given:

```
 3. import java.util.regex.*;
 4. public class Archie {
 5.   public static void main(String[] args) {
 6.     Pattern p = Pattern.compile(args[0]);
```

```
7.       Matcher m = p.matcher(args[1]);
8.       int count = 0;
9.       while(m.find())
10.         count++;
11.      System.out.print(count);
12.    }
13. }
```

And given the command line invocation:

```
java Archie "\d+" ab2c4d67
```

What is the result?

A. 0

B. 3

C. 4

D. 8

E. 9

F. Compilation fails

Answer:

☑ **B** is correct. The "\d" metacharacter looks for digits, and the + quantifier says look for "one or more" occurrences. The `find()` method will find three sets of one or more consecutive digits: 2, 4, and 67.

☒ **A, C, D, E,** and **F** are incorrect based on the above. (Objective 3.5)

15. Given:

```
3.  import java.util.*;
4.  public class Looking {
5.    public static void main(String[] args) {
6.      String input = "1 2 a 3 45 6";
7.      Scanner sc = new Scanner(input);
8.      int x = 0;
9.      do {
10.        x = sc.nextInt();
11.        System.out.print(x + " ");
12.      } while (x!=0);
13.    }
14. }
```

What is the result?

A. `1 2`

B. `1 2 3 45 6`

C. `1 2 3 4 5 6`

D. `1 2 a 3 45 6`

E. Compilation fails

F. `1 2` followed by an exception

Answer:

☑ **F** is correct. The `nextXxx()` methods are typically invoked after a call to a `hasNextXxx()`, which determines whether the next token is of the correct type.

☒ **A, B, C, D,** and **E** are incorrect based on the above. (Objective 3.5)

7

Generics and Collections

G enerics are possibly the most talked about feature of Java 5. Some people love 'em, some people hate 'em, but they're here to stay. At their simplest, they can help make code easier to write, and more robust. At their most complex, they can be very, very hard to create, and maintain. Luckily, the exam creators stuck to the simple end of generics, covering the most common and useful features, and leaving out most of the especially tricky bits. Coverage of collections in this exam has expanded in two ways from the previous exam: the use of generics in collections, and the ability to sort and search through collections.

CERTIFICATION OBJECTIVE

Overriding hashCode() and equals() (Objective 6.2)

6.2   Distinguish between correct and incorrect overrides of corresponding hashCode and equals methods, and explain the difference between == and the equals method.

You're an object. Get used to it. You have state, you have behavior, you have a job. (Or at least your chances of getting one will go up after passing the exam.) If you exclude primitives, everything in Java is an object. Not just an *object*, but an Object with a capital O. Every exception, every event, every array extends from java.lang.Object. For the exam, you don't need to know every method in Object, but you will need to know about the methods listed in Table 7-1.

Chapter 9 covers wait(), notify(), and notifyAll(). The finalize() method was covered in Chapter 3. So in this section we'll look at just the hashCode() and equals() methods. Oh, that leaves out toString(), doesn't it. Okay, we'll cover that right now because it takes two seconds.

The toString() Method   Override toString() when you want a mere mortal to be able to read something meaningful about the objects of your class. Code can call toString() on your object when it wants to read useful details about your object. When you pass an object reference to the System.out.println() method, for example, the object's toString() method is called, and the return of toString() is shown in the following example:

TABLE 7-1	Methods of Class Object Covered on the Exam
Method	**Description**
`boolean equals (Object obj)`	Decides whether two objects are meaningfully equivalent.
`void finalize()`	Called by garbage collector when the garbage collector sees that the object cannot be referenced.
`int hashCode()`	Returns a hashcode int value for an object, so that the object can be used in Collection classes that use hashing, including Hashtable, HashMap, and HashSet.
`final void notify()`	Wakes up a thread that is waiting for this object's lock.
`final void notifyAll()`	Wakes up *all* threads that are waiting for this object's lock.
`final void wait()`	Causes the current thread to wait until another thread calls `notify()` or `notifyAll()` on this object.
`String toString()`	Returns a "text representation" of the object.

```
public class HardToRead {
   public static void main (String [] args) {
     HardToRead h = new HardToRead();
     System.out.println(h);
   }
}
```

Running the HardToRead class gives us the lovely and meaningful,

```
% java HardToRead
HardToRead@a47e0
```

The preceding output is what you get when you don't override the `toString()` method of class Object. It gives you the class name (at least that's meaningful) followed by the @ symbol, followed by the unsigned hexadecimal representation of the object's hashcode.

Trying to read this output might motivate you to override the `toString()` method in your classes, for example,

```
public class BobTest {
   public static void main (String[] args) {
     Bob f = new Bob("GoBobGo", 19);
```

```
        System.out.println(f);
    }
}
class Bob {
    int shoeSize;
    String nickName;
    Bob(String nickName, int shoeSize) {
        this.shoeSize = shoeSize;
        this.nickName = nickName;
    }
    public String toString() {
        return ("I am a Bob, but you can call me " + nickName +
                ". My shoe size is " + shoeSize);
    }
}
```

This ought to be a bit more readable:

```
% java BobTest
I am a Bob, but you can call me GoBobGo. My shoe size is 19
```

Some people affectionately refer to toString() as the "spill-your-guts method,"
because the most common implementations of toString() simply spit out
the object's state (in other words, the current values of the important instance
variables). That's it for toString(). Now we'll tackle equals() and hashCode().

Overriding equals()

You learned about the equals() method in earlier chapters, where we looked at
the wrapper classes. We discussed how comparing two object references using the
== operator evaluates to true only when both references refer to the same object
(because == simply looks at the bits in the variable, and they're either identical or
they're not). You saw that the String class and the wrapper classes have overridden
the equals() method (inherited from class Object), so that you could compare
two different objects (of the same type) to see if their contents are meaningfully
equivalent. If two different Integer instances both hold the int value 5, as far as
you're concerned they are equal. The fact that the value 5 lives in two separate
objects doesn't matter.

When you really need to know if two references are identical, use ==. But when
you need to know if the objects themselves (not the references) are equal, use the
equals() method. For each class you write, you must decide if it makes sense to

consider two different instances equal. For some classes, you might decide that two objects can never be equal. For example, imagine a class Car that has instance variables for things like make, model, year, configuration—you certainly don't want your car suddenly to be treated as the very same car as someone with a car that has identical attributes. Your car is your car and you don't want your neighbor Billy driving off in it just because, "hey, it's really the same car; the `equals()` method said so." So no two cars should ever be considered exactly equal. If two references refer to one car, then you know that both are talking about one car, not two cars that have the same attributes. So in the case of a Car you might not ever need, or want, to override the `equals()` method. Of course, you know that isn't the end of the story.

What It Means If You Don't Override equals()

There's a potential limitation lurking here: if you don't override a class's `equals()` method, you won't be able to use those objects as a key in a hashtable and you probably won't get accurate Sets, such that there are no conceptual duplicates.

The `equals()` method in class Object uses only the `==` operator for comparisons, so unless you override `equals()`, two objects are considered equal only if the two references refer to the same object.

Let's look at what it means to not be able to use an object as a hashtable key. Imagine you have a car, a very specific car (say, John's red Subaru Outback as opposed to Mary's purple Mini) that you want to put in a HashMap (a type of hashtable we'll look at later in this chapter), so that you can search on a particular car and retrieve the corresponding Person object that represents the owner. So you add the car instance as the key to the HashMap (along with a corresponding Person object as the value). But now what happens when you want to do a search? You want to say to the HashMap collection, "Here's the car, now give me the Person object that goes with this car." But now you're in trouble unless you still have a reference to the exact object you used as the key when you added it to the Collection. *In other words, you can't make an identical Car object and use it for the search.*

The bottom line is this: if you want objects of your class to be used as keys for a hashtable (or as elements in any data structure that uses equivalency for searching for—and/or retrieving—an object), then you must override `equals()` so that two different instances can be considered the same. So how would we fix the car? You might override the `equals()` method so that it compares the unique VIN (Vehicle Identification Number) as the basis of comparison. That way, you can use one instance when you add it to a Collection, and essentially re-create an identical instance when you want to do a search based on that object as the key. Of course, overriding the `equals()` method for Car also allows the potential that more than one object representing a single unique car can exist, which might not be safe in your design. Fortunately, the String and wrapper classes work well as keys in hashtables—they override the `equals()` method. So rather than using the actual car instance as the key into the car/owner pair, you could simply use a String that represents the unique identifier for the car. That way, you'll never have more than one instance representing a specific car, but you can still use the car—or rather, one of the car's attributes—as the search key.

Implementing an equals() Method

Let's say you decide to override `equals()` in your class. It might look like this:

```
public class EqualsTest {
  public static void main (String [] args) {
    Moof one = new Moof(8);
    Moof two = new Moof(8);
    if (one.equals(two)) {
       System.out.println("one and two are equal");
    }
  }
}
class Moof {
  private int moofValue;
  Moof(int val) {
     moofValue = val;
  }
  public int getMoofValue() {
     return moofValue;
  }
  public boolean equals(Object o) {
    if ((o instanceof Moof) && (((Moof)o).getMoofValue()
        == this.moofValue)) {
     return true;
    } else {
       return false;
    }
  }
}
```

Let's look at this code in detail. In the `main()` method of EqualsTest, we create two Moof instances, passing the same value 8 to the Moof constructor. Now look at the Moof class and let's see what it does with that constructor argument—it assigns the value to the `moofValue` instance variable. Now imagine that you've decided two Moof objects are the same if their `moofValue` is identical. So you override the `equals()` method and compare the two `moofValues`. It is that simple. But let's break down what's happening in the `equals()` method:

```
1. public boolean equals(Object o) {
2.    if ((o instanceof Moof) && (((Moof)o).getMoofValue()
         == this.moofValue)) {
3.       return true;
4.    } else {
5.       return false;
6.    }
7. }
```

First of all, you must observe all the rules of overriding, and in line 1 we are indeed declaring a valid override of the `equals()` method we inherited from Object.

Line 2 is where all the action is. Logically, we have to do two things in order to make a valid equality comparison.

First, be sure that the object being tested is of the correct type! It comes in polymorphically as type Object, so you need to do an `instanceof` test on it. Having two objects of different class types be considered equal is usually not a good idea, but that's a design issue we won't go into here. Besides, you'd still have to do the `instanceof` test just to be sure that you could cast the object argument to the correct type so that you can access its methods or variables in order to actually do the comparison. Remember, if the object doesn't pass the `instanceof` test, then you'll get a runtime ClassCastException. For example:

```
public boolean equals(Object o) {
    if (((Moof)o).getMoofValue() == this.moofValue){
        // the preceding line compiles, but it's BAD!
        return true;
    } else {
        return false;
    }
}
```

The `(Moof)o` cast will fail if o doesn't refer to something that IS-A Moof.

Second, compare the attributes we care about (in this case, just `moofValue`). Only the developer can decide what makes two instances equal. (For best performance, you're going to want to check the fewest number of attributes.)

In case you were a little surprised by the whole `((Moof)o).getMoofValue()` syntax, we're simply casting the object reference, o, just-in-time as we try to call a method that's in the Moof class but not in Object. Remember, without the cast, you can't compile because the compiler would see the object referenced by o as simply, well, an Object. And since the Object class doesn't have a `getMoofValue()` method, the compiler would squawk (technical term). But then as we said earlier, even with the cast, the code fails at runtime if the object referenced by o isn't something that's castable to a Moof. So don't ever forget to use the `instanceof` test first. Here's another reason to appreciate the short circuit && operator—if the `instanceof` test fails, we'll never get to the code that does the cast, so we're always safe at runtime with the following:

```
if ((o instanceof Moof) && (((Moof)o).getMoofValue()
        == this.moofValue)) {
    return true;
} else {
    return false;
}
```

So that takes care of `equals()`...

Whoa...not so fast. If you look at the Object class in the Java API spec, you'll find what we call a contract specified in the `equals()` method. A Java contract is a set of rules that should be followed, or rather must be followed if you want to provide a "correct" implementation as others will expect it to be. Or to put it another way, if you don't follow the contract, your code may still compile and run, but your code (or someone else's) may break at runtime in some unexpected way.

Be sure you're very comfortable with the rules of overriding so that you can identify whether a method from Object is being overridden, overloaded, or illegally redeclared in a class. The equals() *method in class Boo changes the argument from Object to Boo, so it becomes an overloaded method and won't be called unless it's from your own code that knows about this new, different method that happens to also be named* equals().

The equals() Contract

Pulled straight from the Java docs, the equals() contract says

- It is **reflexive**. For any reference value x, x.equals(x) should return true.
- It is **symmetric**. For any reference values x and y, x.equals(y) should return true if and only if y.equals(x) returns true.
- It is **transitive**. For any reference values x, y, and z, if x.equals(y) returns true and y.equals(z) returns true, then x.equals(z) must return true.
- It is **consistent**. For any reference values x and y, multiple invocations of x.equals(y) consistently return true or consistently return false, provided no information used in equals comparisons on the object is modified.
- For any non-null reference value x, x.equals(null) should return false.

And you're so not off the hook yet. We haven't looked at the hashCode() method, but equals() and hashCode() are bound together by a joint contract that specifies if two objects are considered equal using the equals() method, then they must have identical hashcode values. So to be truly safe, your rule of thumb should be, if you override equals(), override hashCode() as well. So let's switch over to hashCode() and see how that method ties in to equals().

Overriding hashCode()

Hashcodes are typically used to increase the performance of large collections of data. The hashcode value of an object is used by some collection classes (we'll look at the collections later in this chapter). Although you can think of it as kind of an object ID number, it isn't necessarily unique. Collections such as HashMap and HashSet use the hashcode value of an object to determine how the object should be *stored* in the collection, and the hashcode is used again to help *locate* the object in the collection. For the exam you do not need to understand the deep details of how the collection classes that use hashing are implemented, but you do need to know which collections use them (but, um, they all have "hash" in the name so you should be good there). You must also be able to recognize an appropriate or correct implementation of `hashCode()`. This does not mean legal and does not even mean efficient. It's perfectly legal to have a terribly inefficient hashcode method in your class, as long as it doesn't violate the contract specified in the Object class documentation (we'll look at that contract in a moment). So for the exam, if you're asked to pick out an appropriate or correct use of hashcode, don't mistake appropriate for legal or efficient.

Understanding Hashcodes

In order to understand what's appropriate and correct, we have to look at how some of the collections use hashcodes.

Imagine a set of buckets lined up on the floor. Someone hands you a piece of paper with a name on it. You take the name and calculate an integer code from it by using A is 1, B is 2, and so on, and adding the numeric values of all the letters in the name together. A given name will always result in the same code; see Figure 7-1.

FIGURE 7-1	Key	Hashcode Algorithm	Hashcode
	Alex	A(1) + L(12) + E(5) + X(24)	= 42
A simplified	Bob	B(2) + O(15) + B(2)	= 19
hashcode	Dirk	D(4) + I(9) + R(18) + K(11)	= 42
example	Fred	F(6) + R(18) + E(5) + D(4)	= 33

HashMap Collection

Hashcode Buckets [19] [   ] [33] [   ] [42] [   ] [   ]

          "Bob"   "Fred"   "Alex"
                                          "Dirk"

We don't introduce anything random, we simply have an algorithm that will always run the same way given a specific input, so the output will always be identical for any two identical inputs. So far so good? Now the way you use that code (and we'll call it a hashcode now) is to determine which bucket to place the piece of paper into (imagine that each bucket represents a different code number you might get). Now imagine that someone comes up and shows you a name and says, "Please retrieve the piece of paper that matches this name." So you look at the name they show you, and run the same hashcode-generating algorithm. The hashcode tells you in which bucket you should look to find the name.

You might have noticed a little flaw in our system, though. Two different names might result in the same value. For example, the names Amy and May have the same letters, so the hashcode will be identical for both names. That's acceptable, but it does mean that when someone asks you (the bucket-clerk) for the Amy piece of paper, you'll still have to search through the target bucket reading each name until we find Amy rather than May. The hashcode tells you only which bucket to go into, but not how to locate the name once we're in that bucket.

In real-life hashing, it's not uncommon to have more than one entry in a bucket. Hashing retrieval is a two-step process.

1. Find the right bucket (using `hashCode()`***)***

2. Search the bucket for the right element (using `equals()` ***).***

So for efficiency, your goal is to have the papers distributed as evenly as possible across all buckets. Ideally, you might have just one name per bucket so that when someone asked for a paper you could simply calculate the hashcode and just grab the one paper from the correct bucket (without having to go flipping through different papers in that bucket until you locate the exact one you're looking for). The least efficient (but still functional) hashcode generator would return the same hashcode (say, 42) regardless of the name, so that all the papers landed in the same bucket while the others stood empty. The bucket-clerk would have to keep going to that one bucket and flipping painfully through each one of the names in the bucket until the right one was found. And if that's how it works, they might as well not use the hashcodes at all but just go to the one big bucket and start from one end and look through each paper until they find the one they want.

This distributed-across-the-buckets example is similar to the way hashcodes are used in collections. When you put an object in a collection that uses hashcodes, the collection uses the hashcode of the object to decide in which bucket/slot the object should land. Then when you want to fetch that object (or, for a hashtable, retrieve the associated value for that object), you have to give the collection a reference to an object that the collection compares to the objects it holds in the collection. As long as the object (stored in the collection, like a paper in the bucket) you're trying to search for has the same hashcode as the object you're using for the search (the name you show to the person working the buckets), then the object will be found. But...and this is a Big One, imagine what would happen if, going back to our name example, you showed the bucket-worker a name and they calculated the code based on only half the letters in the name instead of all of them. They'd never find the name in the bucket because they wouldn't be looking in the correct bucket!

Now can you see why if two objects are considered equal, their hashcodes must also be equal? Otherwise, you'd never be able to find the object since the default hashcode method in class Object virtually always comes up with a unique number for each object, even if the `equals()` method is overridden in such a way that two or more objects are considered equal. It doesn't matter how equal the objects are if their hashcodes don't reflect that. So one more time: If two objects are equal, their hashcodes must be equal as well.

Implementing hashCode()

What the heck does a real hashcode algorithm look like? People get their PhDs on hashing algorithms, so from a computer science viewpoint, it's beyond the scope of the exam. The part we care about here is the issue of whether you follow the contract. And to follow the contract, think about what you do in the `equals()` method. You compare attributes. Because that comparison almost always involves instance variable values (remember when we looked at two Moof objects and considered them equal if their `int moofValues` were the same?). Your `hashCode()` implementation should use the same instance variables. Here's an example:

```
class HasHash {
  public int x;
  HasHash(int xVal) { x = xVal; }

  public boolean equals(Object o) {
    HasHash h = (HasHash) o; // Don't try at home without
                             // instanceof test
    if (h.x == this.x) {
      return true;
    } else {
      return false;
    }
```

```
    }
    public int hashCode() { return (x * 17); }
}
```

This equals() method says two objects are equal if they have the same x value, so objects with the same x value will have to return identical hashcodes.

e**x**a m
ⓦatch

A hashCode() *that returns the same value for all instances whether they're equal or not is still a legal—even appropriate—*hashCode() *method! For example,*

```
    public int hashCode() { return 1492; }
```

This does not violate the contract. Two objects with an x *value of* 8 *will have the same hashcode. But then again, so will two unequal objects, one with an* x *value of* 12 *and the other a value of* -920. *This* hashCode() *method is horribly inefficient, remember, because it makes all objects land in the same bucket, but even so, the object can still be found as the collection cranks through the one and only bucket—using* equals()*—trying desperately to finally, painstakingly, locate the correct object. In other words, the hashcode was really no help at all in speeding up the search, even though improving search speed is hashcode's intended purpose! Nonetheless, this one-hash-fits-all method would be considered appropriate and even correct because it doesn't violate the contract. Once more, correct does not necessarily mean good.*

Typically, you'll see hashCode() methods that do some combination of ^-ing (XOR-ing) a class's instance variables (in other words, twiddling their bits), along with perhaps multiplying them by a prime number. In any case, while the goal is to get a wide and random distribution of objects across buckets, the contract (and whether or not an object can be found) requires only that two equal objects have equal hashcodes. The exam does not expect you to rate the efficiency of a hashCode() method, but you must be able to recognize which ones will and will not work (work meaning "will cause the object to be found in the collection").

Now that we know that two equal objects must have identical hashcodes, is the reverse true? Do two objects with identical hashcodes have to be considered equal? Think about it—you might have lots of objects land in the same bucket because their hashcodes are identical, but unless they also pass the equals() test, they won't come up as a match in a search through the collection. This is exactly what you'd get with our very inefficient everybody-gets-the-same-hashcode method. It's legal and correct, just slooooow.

So in order for an object to be located, the search object and the object in the collection must have both identical hashcode values and return `true` for the `equals()` method. So there's just no way out of overriding both methods to be absolutely certain that your objects can be used in Collections that use hashing.

The hashCode() Contract

Now coming to you straight from the fabulous Java API documentation for class Object, may we present (drum roll) the `hashCode()` contract:

- Whenever it is invoked on the same object more than once during an execution of a Java application, the `hashCode()` method must consistently return the same integer, provided no information used in `equals()` comparisons on the object is modified. This integer need not remain consistent from one execution of an application to another execution of the same application.

- If two objects are equal according to the `equals(Object)` method, then calling the `hashCode()` method on each of the two objects must produce the same integer result.

- It is NOT required that if two objects are unequal according to the `equals(java.lang.Object)` method, then calling the `hashCode()` method on each of the two objects must produce distinct integer results. However, the programmer should be aware that producing distinct integer results for unequal objects may improve the performance of hashtables.

And what this means to you is...

Condition	Required	Not Required (But Allowed)
`x.equals(y) == true`	`x.hashCode() == y.hashCode()`	
`x.hashCode() == y.hashCode()`		`x.equals(y) == true`
`x.equals(y) == false`		No `hashCode()` requirements
`x.hashCode() != y.hashCode()`	`x.equals(y) == false`	

So let's look at what else might cause a hashCode() method to fail. What happens if you include a transient variable in your hashCode() method? While that's legal (compiler won't complain), under some circumstances an object you put in a collection won't be found. As you know, serialization saves an object so that it can be reanimated later by deserializing it back to full objectness. But danger Will Robinson—remember that transient variables are not saved when an object is serialized. A bad scenario might look like this:

```
class SaveMe implements Serializable{
  transient int x;
  int y;
   SaveMe(int xVal, int yVal) {
      x = xVal;
      y = yVal;
   }
  public int hashCode() {
     return (x ^ y);       // Legal, but not correct to
                           // use a transient variable
   }
  public boolean equals(Object o) {
     SaveMe test = (SaveMe)o;
     if (test.y == y && test.x == x) { // Legal, not correct
        return true;
     } else {
        return false;
     }
   }
}
```

Here's what could happen using code like the preceding example:

1. Give an object some state (assign values to its instance variables).
2. Put the object in a HashMap, using the object as a key.
3. Save the object to a file using serialization without altering any of its state.
4. Retrieve the object from the file through deserialization.
5. Use the deserialized (brought back to life on the heap) object to get the object out of the HashMap.

Oops. The object in the collection and the supposedly same object brought back to life are no longer identical. The object's transient variable will come back with a default value rather than the value the variable had at the time it was saved (or put into the HashMap). So using the preceding SaveMe code, if the value of x is 9 when the instance is put in the HashMap, then since x is used in the calculation of the hashcode, when the value of x changes, the hashcode changes too. And when that same instance of SaveMe is brought back from deserialization, x == 0, regardless of the value of x at the time the object was serialized. So the new hashcode calculation will give a different hashcode, and the equals() method fails as well since x is used to determine object equality.

Bottom line: transient variables can really mess with your equals() and hashCode() implementations. Keep variables non-transient or, if they must be marked transient, don't use them to determine hashcodes or equality.

CERTIFICATION OBJECTIVE

Collections (Exam Objective 6.1)

6.1 Given a design scenario, determine which collection classes and/or interfaces should be used to properly implement that design, including the use of the Comparable interface.

Can you imagine trying to write object-oriented applications without using data structures like hashtables or linked lists? What would you do when you needed to maintain a sorted list of, say, all the members in your Simpsons fan club? Obviously you can do it yourself; Amazon.com must have thousands of algorithm books you can buy. But with the kind of schedules programmers are under today, it's almost too painful to consider.

The Collections Framework in Java, which took shape with the release of JDK 1.2 and was expanded in 1.4 and again in Java 5, and yet again in Java 6, gives you lists, sets, maps, and queues to satisfy most of your coding needs. They've been tried, tested, and tweaked. Pick the best one for your job and you'll get—at the least—reasonable performance. And when you need something a little more custom, the Collections Framework in the java.util package is loaded with interfaces and utilities.

So What Do You Do with a Collection?

There are a few basic operations you'll normally use with collections:

■ Add objects to the collection.

■ Remove objects from the collection.

- Find out if an object (or group of objects) is in the collection.
- Retrieve an object from the collection (without removing it).
- Iterate through the collection, looking at each element (object) one after another.

Key Interfaces and Classes of the Collections Framework

For the exam you'll need to know which collection to choose based on a stated requirement. The collections API begins with a group of interfaces, but also gives you a truckload of concrete classes. The core interfaces you need to know for the exam (and life in general) are the following nine:

Collection	Set	SortedSet
List	Map	SortedMap
Queue	NavigableSet	NavigableMap

The core concrete implementation classes you need to know for the exam are the following 13 (there are others, but the exam doesn't specifically cover them):

Maps	Sets	Lists	Queues	Utilities
HashMap	HashSet	ArrayList	PriorityQueue	Collections
Hashtable	LinkedHashSet	Vector		Arrays
TreeMap	TreeSet	LinkedList		
LinkedHashMap				

Not all collections in the Collections Framework actually implement the Collection interface. In other words, not all collections pass the IS-A test for Collection. Specifically, none of the Map-related classes and interfaces extend from Collection. So while SortedMap, Hashtable, HashMap, TreeMap, and LinkedHashMap are all thought of as collections, none are actually extended from Collection-with-a-capital-C (see Figure 7-2). To make things a little more confusing, there are really three overloaded uses of the word "collection":

- collection (lowercase *c*), which represents any of the data structures in which objects are stored and iterated over.
- Collection (capital C), which is actually the java.util.Collection interface from which Set, List, and Queue extend. (That's right, extend, not implement. There are no direct implementations of Collection.)
- Collections (capital C and ends with *s*) is the java.util.Collections class that holds a pile of `static` utility methods for use with collections.

FIGURE 7-2   The interface and class hierarchy for collections

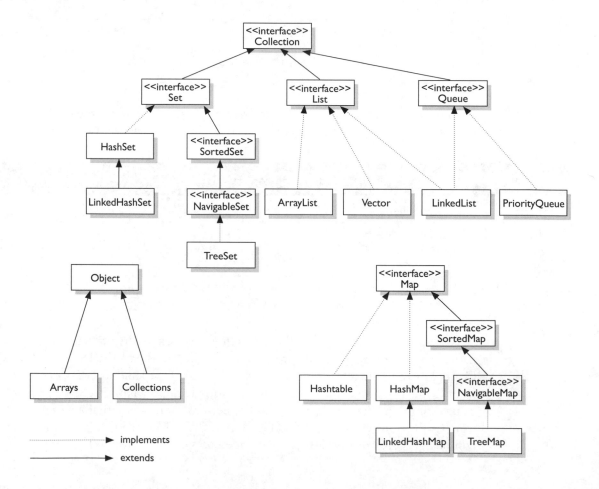

Collections come in four basic flavors:

- **Lists**   *Lists* of things (classes that implement List).
- **Sets**   *Unique* things (classes that implement Set).
- **Maps**   Things with a *unique* ID (classes that implement Map).
- **Queues**   Things arranged by the order in which they are to be processed.

Figure 7-3 illustrates the structure of a List, a Set, and a Map.

FIGURE 7-3

The structure of a List, a Set, and a Map

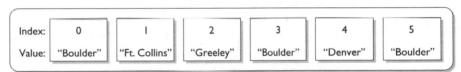

List: The salesman's itinerary (Duplicates allowed)

Set: The salesman's territory (No duplicates allowed)

HashMap: the salesman's products (Keys generated from product IDs)

But there are sub-flavors within those four flavors of collections:

Sorted	Unsorted	Ordered	Unordered

An implementation class can be unsorted and unordered, ordered but unsorted, or both ordered and sorted. But an implementation can never be sorted but unordered, because sorting is a specific type of ordering, as you'll see in a moment. For example, a HashSet is an unordered, unsorted set, while a LinkedHashSet is an ordered (but not sorted) set that maintains the order in which objects were inserted.

Maybe we should be explicit about the difference between sorted and ordered, but first we have to discuss the idea of iteration. When you think of iteration, you may think of iterating over an array using, say, a `for` loop to access each element in the array in order ([0], [1], [2], and so on). Iterating through a collection usually means walking through the elements one after another starting from the first element. Sometimes, though, even the concept of *first* is a little strange—in a Hashtable there really isn't a notion of first, second, third, and so on. In a Hashtable, the elements are placed in a (seemingly) chaotic order based on the hashcode of the key. But something has to go first when you iterate; thus, when you iterate over a Hashtable, there will indeed be an order. But as far as you can tell, it's completely arbitrary and can change in apparently random ways as the collection changes.

Ordered   When a collection is ordered, it means you can iterate through the collection in a specific (not-random) order. A Hashtable collection is not ordered. Although the Hashtable itself has internal logic to determine the order (based on hashcodes and the implementation of the collection itself), you won't find any order when you iterate through the Hashtable. An ArrayList, however, keeps the order established by the elements' index position (just like an array). LinkedHashSet keeps the order established by insertion, so the last element inserted is the last element in the LinkedHashSet (as opposed to an ArrayList, where you can insert an element at a specific index position). Finally, there are some collections that keep an order referred to as the natural order of the elements, and those collections are then not just ordered, but also sorted. Let's look at how natural order works for sorted collections.

Sorted   A *sorted* collection means that the order in the collection is determined according to some rule or rules, known as the sort order. A sort order has nothing to do with when an object was added to the collection, or when was the last time it was accessed, or what "position" it was added at. Sorting is done based on properties of the objects themselves. You put objects into the collection, and the collection will figure out what order to put them in, based on the sort order. A collection that keeps an order (such as any List, which uses insertion order) is not really considered *sorted* unless it sorts using some kind of sort order. Most commonly, the sort order used is something called the *natural* order. What does that mean?

You know how to sort alphabetically—A comes before B, F comes before G, and so on. For a collection of String objects, then, the natural order is alphabetical. For Integer objects, the natural order is by numeric value—1 before 2, and so on. And for Foo objects, the natural order is…um…we don't know. There is no natural order for Foo unless or until the Foo developer provides one, through an interface (*Comparable*)that defines how instances of a class can be compared to one another (does instance a come before b, or does instance b come before a?). If the developer decides that Foo objects should be compared using the value of some instance variable (let's say there's one called `bar`), then a sorted collection will order the Foo objects according to the rules in the Foo class for how to use the bar instance variable to determine the order. Of course, the Foo class might also inherit a natural order from a superclass rather than define its own order, in some cases.

Aside from natural order as specified by the Comparable interface, it's also possible to define other, different sort orders using another interface: *Comparator*. We will discuss how to use both Comparable and Comparator to define sort orders later in this chapter. But for now, just keep in mind that sort order (including natural order) is not the same as ordering by insertion, access, or index.

Now that we know about ordering and sorting, we'll look at each of the four interfaces, and we'll dive into the concrete implementations of those interfaces.

List Interface

A List cares about the index. The one thing that List has that non-lists don't have is a set of methods related to the index. Those key methods include things like `get(int index)`, `indexOf(Object o)`, `add(int index, Object obj)`, and so on. All three List implementations are ordered by index position—a position that you determine either by setting an object at a specific index or by adding it without specifying position, in which case the object is added to the end. The three List implementations are described in the following sections.

ArrayList   Think of this as a growable array. It gives you fast iteration and fast random access. To state the obvious: it is an ordered collection (by index), but not sorted. You might want to know that as of version 1.4, ArrayList now implements the new RandomAccess interface—a marker interface (meaning it has no methods) that says, "this list supports fast (generally constant time) random access." Choose this over a LinkedList when you need fast iteration but aren't as likely to be doing a lot of insertion and deletion.

Vector   Vector is a holdover from the earliest days of Java; Vector and Hashtable were the two original collections, the rest were added with Java 2 versions 1.2 and 1.4. A Vector is basically the same as an ArrayList, but Vector methods are synchronized for thread safety. You'll normally want to use ArrayList instead of Vector because the synchronized methods add a performance hit you might not need. And if you do need thread safety, there are utility methods in class Collections that can help. Vector is the only class other than ArrayList to implement RandomAccess.

LinkedList   A LinkedList is ordered by index position, like ArrayList, except that the elements are doubly-linked to one another. This linkage gives you new methods (beyond what you get from the List interface) for adding and removing from the beginning or end, which makes it an easy choice for implementing a stack or queue. Keep in mind that a LinkedList may iterate more slowly than an ArrayList, but it's a good choice when you need fast insertion and deletion. As of Java 5, the LinkedList class has been enhanced to implement the java.util.Queue interface. As such, it now supports the common queue methods: `peek()`, `poll()`, and `offer()`.

Set Interface

A Set cares about uniqueness—it doesn't allow duplicates. Your good friend the `equals()` method determines whether two objects are identical (in which case only one can be in the set). The three Set implementations are described in the following sections.

HashSet   A HashSet is an unsorted, unordered Set. It uses the hashcode of the object being inserted, so the more efficient your `hashCode()` implementation the better access performance you'll get. Use this class when you want a collection with no duplicates and you don't care about order when you iterate through it.

LinkedHashSet   A LinkedHashSet is an ordered version of HashSet that maintains a doubly-linked List across all elements. Use this class instead of HashSet when you care about the iteration order. When you iterate through a HashSet the order is unpredictable, while a LinkedHashSet lets you iterate through the elements in the order in which they were inserted.

e x a m
ⓦ a t c h
When using HashSet or LinkedHashSet, the objects you add to them must override hashCode()*. If they don't override* hashCode()*, the default* Object. hashCode() *method will allow multiple objects that you might consider "meaningfully equal" to be added to your "no duplicates allowed" set.*

TreeSet   The TreeSet is one of two sorted collections (the other being TreeMap). It uses a Red-Black tree structure (but you knew that), and guarantees that the elements will be in ascending order, according to natural order. Optionally, you can construct a TreeSet with a constructor that lets you give the collection your own rules for what the order should be (rather than relying on the ordering defined by the elements' class) by using a Comparable or Comparator. As of Java 6, TreeSet implements NavigableSet.

Map Interface

A Map cares about unique identifiers. You map a unique key (the ID) to a specific value, where both the key and the value are, of course, objects. You're probably quite familiar with Maps since many languages support data structures that use a key/value or name/value pair. The Map implementations let you do things like search for a value based on the key, ask for a collection of just the values, or ask for a collection of just the keys. Like Sets, Maps rely on the equals() method to determine whether two keys are the same or different.

HashMap   The HashMap gives you an unsorted, unordered Map. When you need a Map and you don't care about the order (when you iterate through it), then HashMap is the way to go; the other maps add a little more overhead. Where the keys land in the Map is based on the key's hashcode, so, like HashSet, the more efficient your hashCode() implementation, the better access performance you'll get. HashMap allows one null key and multiple null values in a collection.

Hashtable   Like Vector, Hashtable has existed from prehistoric Java times. For fun, don't forget to note the naming inconsistency: HashMap vs. Hashtable. Where's the capitalization of *t*? Oh well, you won't be expected to spell it. Anyway, just as Vector is a synchronized counterpart to the sleeker, more modern ArrayList, Hashtable is the synchronized counterpart to HashMap. Remember that you don't synchronize a class, so when we say that Vector and Hashtable are synchronized, we just mean that the key methods of the class are synchronized. Another difference, though, is that while HashMap lets you have `null` values as well as one `null` key, a Hashtable doesn't let you have anything that's `null`.

LinkedHashMap   Like its Set counterpart, LinkedHashSet, the LinkedHash-Map collection maintains insertion order (or, optionally, access order). Although it will be somewhat slower than HashMap for adding and removing elements, you can expect faster iteration with a LinkedHashMap.

TreeMap   You can probably guess by now that a TreeMap is a sorted Map. And you already know that by default, this means "sorted by the natural order of the elements." Like TreeSet, TreeMap lets you define a custom sort order (via a Comparable or Comparator) when you construct a TreeMap, that specifies how the elements should be compared to one another when they're being ordered. As of Java 6, TreeMap implements NavigableMap.

Queue Interface

A Queue is designed to hold a list of "to-dos," or things to be processed in some way. Although other orders are possible, queues are typically thought of as FIFO (first-in, first-out). Queues support all of the standard Collection methods and they also add methods to add and subtract elements and review queue elements.

PriorityQueue   This class is new with Java 5. Since the LinkedList class has been enhanced to implement the Queue interface, basic queues can be handled with a LinkedList. The purpose of a PriorityQueue is to create a "priority-in, priority out" queue as opposed to a typical FIFO queue. A PriorityQueue's elements are ordered either by natural ordering (in which case the elements that are sorted first will be accessed first) or according to a Comparator. In either case, the elements' ordering represents their relative priority.

Table 7-2 summarizes the 11 of the 13 concrete collection-oriented classes you'll need to understand for the exam. (Arrays and Collections are coming right up!)

TABLE 7-2   Collection Interface Concrete Implementation Classes

Class	Map	Set	List	Ordered	Sorted
HashMap	x			No	No
Hashtable	x			No	No
TreeMap	x			Sorted	By *natural order* or custom comparison rules
LinkedHashMap	x			By insertion order or last access order	No
HashSet		x		No	No
TreeSet		x		Sorted	By *natural order* or custom comparison rules
LinkedHashSet		x		By insertion order	No
ArrayList			x	By index	No
Vector			x	By index	No
LinkedList			x	By index	No
PriorityQueue				Sorted	By to-do order

Be sure you know how to interpret Table 7-2 in a practical way. For the exam, you might be expected to choose a collection based on a particular requirement, where that need is expressed as a scenario. For example, which collection would you use if you needed to maintain and search on a list of parts, identified by their unique alphanumeric serial number where the part would be of type Part? Would you change your answer at all if we modified the requirement such that you also need to be able to print out the parts in order, by their serial number? For the first question, you can see that since you have a Part class, but need to search for the objects based on a serial number, you need a Map. The key will be the serial number as a String, and the value will be the Part instance. The default choice should be HashMap, the quickest Map for access. But now when we amend the requirement to include getting the parts in order of their serial number, then we need a TreeMap—which maintains the natural order of the keys. Since the key is a String, the natural order for a String will be a standard alphabetical sort. If the requirement had been to keep track of which part was last accessed, then we'd probably need a LinkedHashMap. But since a LinkedHashMap loses the natural order (replacing it with last-accessed order), if we need to list the parts by serial number, we'll have to explicitly sort the collection, using a utility method.

CERTIFICATION OBJECTIVE

Using the Collections Framework (Objectives 6.3 and 6.5)

6.3   Write code that uses the NavigableSet and NavigableMap interfaces.

6.5   Use capabilities in the java.util package to write code to manipulate a list by sorting, performing a binary search, or converting the list to an array. Use capabilities in the java.util package to write code to manipulate an array by sorting, performing a binary search, or converting the array to a list. Use the java.util.Comparator and java.lang. Comparable interfaces to affect the sorting of lists and arrays. Furthermore, recognize the effect of the "natural ordering" of primitive wrapper classes and java.lang.String on sorting.

We've taken a high-level, theoretical look at the key interfaces and classes in the Collections Framework, now let's see how they work in practice.

ArrayList Basics

The `java.util.ArrayList` class is one of the most commonly used of all the classes in the Collections Framework. It's like an array on vitamins. Some of the advantages `ArrayList` has over arrays are

- It can grow dynamically.
- It provides more powerful insertion and search mechanisms than arrays.

Let's take a look at using an `ArrayList` that contains Strings. A key design goal of the Collections Framework was to provide rich functionality at the level of the main interfaces: List, Set, and Map. In practice, you'll typically want to instantiate an `ArrayList` polymorphically like this:

```
List myList = new ArrayList();
```

As of Java 5 you'll want to say

```
List<String> myList = new ArrayList<String>();
```

This kind of declaration follows the object oriented programming principle of "coding to an interface", and it makes use of generics. We'll say lots more about generics later in this chapter, but for now just know that, as of Java 5, the <String> syntax is the way that you declare a collection's type. (Prior to Java 5 there was no way to specify the type of a collection, and when we cover generics, we'll talk about the implications of mixing Java 5 (typed) and pre-Java 5 (untyped) collections.)

In many ways, `ArrayList<String>` is similar to a `String[]` in that it declares a container that can hold only Strings, but it's more powerful than a `String[]`. Let's look at some of the capabilities that an `ArrayList` has

```
List<String> test = new ArrayList<String>();
String s = "hi";
test.add("string");
test.add(s);
test.add(s+s);
System.out.println(test.size());
System.out.println(test.contains(42));
```

```
System.out.println(test.contains("hihi"));
test.remove("hi");
System.out.println(test.size());
```

which produces

```
3
false
true
2
```

There's lots going on in this small program. Notice that when we declared the
ArrayList we didn't give it a size. Then we were able to ask the ArrayList for
its size, we were able to ask it whether it contained specific objects, we removed an
object right out from the middle of it, and then we rechecked its size.

Autoboxing with Collections

In general, collections can hold Objects but not primitives. Prior to Java 5, a very
common use for the wrapper classes was to provide a way to get a primitive into a
collection. Prior to Java 5, you had to wrap a primitive by hand before you could put
it into a collection. With Java 5, primitives still have to be wrapped, but autoboxing
takes care of it for you.

```
List myInts = new ArrayList();      // pre Java 5 declaration
myInts.add(new Integer(42));        // had to wrap an int
```

As of Java 5 we can say

```
myInts.add(42);                     // autoboxing handles it!
```

In this last example, we are still adding an Integer object to myInts (not an int
primitive); it's just that autoboxing handles the wrapping for us.

Sorting Collections and Arrays

Sorting and searching topics have been added to the exam for Java 5. Both
collections and arrays can be sorted and searched using methods in the API.

Sorting Collections

Let's start with something simple like sorting an ArrayList of Strings alphabetically. What could be easier? Okay, we'll wait while you go find ArrayList's `sort()` method...got it? Of course, ArrayList doesn't give you any way to sort its contents, but the java.util.Collections class does

```
import java.util.*;
class TestSort1 {
  public static void main(String[] args) {
    ArrayList<String> stuff = new ArrayList<String>(); // #1
    stuff.add("Denver");
    stuff.add("Boulder");
    stuff.add("Vail");
    stuff.add("Aspen");
    stuff.add("Telluride");
    System.out.println("unsorted " + stuff);
    Collections.sort(stuff);                           // #2
    System.out.println("sorted   " + stuff);
  }
}
```

This produces something like this:

```
unsorted [Denver, Boulder, Vail, Aspen, Telluride]
sorted   [Aspen, Boulder, Denver, Telluride, Vail]
```

Line 1 is declaring an ArrayList of Strings, and line 2 is sorting the ArrayList alphabetically. We'll talk more about the Collections class, along with the Arrays class in a later section, for now let's keep sorting stuff.

Let's imagine we're building the ultimate home-automation application. Today we're focused on the home entertainment center, and more specifically the DVD control center. We've already got the file I/O software in place to read and write data between the dvdInfo.txt file and instances of class DVDInfo. Here are the key aspects of the class:

```
class DVDInfo {
  String title;
  String genre;
  String leadActor;
  DVDInfo(String t, String g, String a) {
```

```
      title = t;   genre = g;   leadActor = a;
    }
    public String toString() {
      return title + " " + genre + " " + leadActor + "\n";
    }
    // getters and setter go here
  }
```

Here's the DVD data that's in the `dvdinfo.txt` file:

```
Donnie Darko/sci-fi/Gyllenhall, Jake
Raiders of the Lost Ark/action/Ford, Harrison
2001/sci-fi/??
Caddy Shack/comedy/Murray, Bill
Star Wars/sci-fi/Ford, Harrison
Lost in Translation/comedy/Murray, Bill
Patriot Games/action/Ford, Harrison
```

In our home-automation application, we want to create an instance of `DVDInfo` for each line of data we read in from the `dvdInfo.txt` file. For each instance, we will parse the line of data (remember `String.split()`?) and populate `DVDInfo`'s three instance variables. Finally, we want to put all of the `DVDInfo` instances into an ArrayList. Imagine that the `populateList()` method (below) does all of this. Here is a small piece of code from our application:

```
ArrayList<DVDInfo> dvdList = new ArrayList<DVDInfo>();
populateList();    // adds the file data to the ArrayList
System.out.println(dvdList);
```

You might get output like this:

```
[Donnie Darko sci-fi Gyllenhall, Jake
, Raiders of the Lost Ark action Ford, Harrison
, 2001 sci-fi ??
, Caddy Shack comedy Murray, Bill
, Star Wars sci-fi Ford, Harrison
, Lost in Translation comedy Murray, Bill
, Patriot Games action Ford, Harrison
]
```

(Note: We overrode `DVDInfo`'s `toString()` method, so when we invoked `println()` on the ArrayList it invoked `toString()` for each instance.)

Now that we've got a populated ArrayList, let's sort it:

```
Collections.sort(dvdlist);
```

Oops!, you get something like this:

```
TestDVD.java:13: cannot find symbol
symbol  : method sort(java.util.ArrayList<DVDInfo>)
location: class java.util.Collections
    Collections.sort(dvdlist);
```

What's going on here? We know that the Collections class has a sort() method, yet this error implies that Collections does NOT have a sort() method that can take a dvdlist. That means there must be something wrong with the argument we're passing (dvdlist).

If you've already figured out the problem, our guess is that you did it without the help of the obscure error message shown above...How the heck do you sort instances of DVDInfo? Why were we able to sort instances of String? When you look up Collections.sort() in the API your first reaction might be to panic. Hang tight, once again the generics section will help you read that weird looking method signature. If you read the description of the one-arg sort() method, you'll see that the sort() method takes a List argument, and that the objects in the List must implement an interface called Comparable. It turns out that String implements Comparable, and that's why we were able to sort a list of Strings using the Collections.sort() method.

The Comparable Interface

The Comparable interface is used by the Collections.sort() method and the java.util.Arrays.sort() method to sort Lists and arrays of objects, respectively. To implement Comparable, a class must implement a single method, compareTo(). Here's an invocation of compareTo():

```
int x = thisObject.compareTo(anotherObject);
```

The compareTo() method returns an int with the following characteristics:

- negative   If thisObject < anotherObject
- zero   If thisObject == anotherObject
- positive   If thisObject > anotherObject

The sort() method uses compareTo() to determine how the List or object array should be sorted. Since you get to implement compareTo() for your own classes, you can use whatever weird criteria you prefer, to sort instances of your classes. Returning to our earlier example for class DVDInfo, we can take the easy way out and use the String class's implementation of compareTo():

```
class DVDInfo implements Comparable<DVDInfo> {     // #1
  // existing code
  public int compareTo(DVDInfo d) {
    return title.compareTo(d.getTitle());          // #2
} }
```

In line 1 we declare that class DVDInfo implements Comparable in such a way that DVDInfo objects can be compared to other DVDInfo objects. In line 2 we implement compareTo() by comparing the two DVDInfo object's titles. Since we know that the titles are Strings, and that String implements Comparable, this is an easy way to sort our DVDInfo objects, by title. Before generics came along in Java 5, you would have had to implement Comparable something like this:

```
class DVDInfo implements Comparable {
  // existing code
  public int compareTo(Object o) {    // takes an Object rather
                                      // than a specific type
    DVDInfo d = (DVDInfo)o;
    return title.compareTo(d.getTitle());
} }
```

This is still legal, but you can see that it's both painful and risky, because you have to do a cast, and you need to verify that the cast will not fail before you try it.

It's important to remember that when you override equals() **you MUST take an argument of type** Object, **but that when you override** compareTo() **you should take an argument of the type you're sorting.**

Putting it all together, our DVDInfo class should now look like this:

```
class DVDInfo implements Comparable<DVDInfo> {
  String title;
  String genre;
  String leadActor;
  DVDInfo(String t, String g, String a) {
    title = t;  genre = g;  leadActor = a;
  }
  public String toString() {
    return title + " " + genre + " " + leadActor + "\n";
  }
  public int compareTo(DVDInfo d) {
    return title.compareTo(d.getTitle());
  }
  public String getTitle() {
    return title;
  }
  // other getters and setters
}
```

Now, when we invoke Collections.sort(dvdList); we get

```
[2001 sci-fi ??
, Caddy Shack comedy Murray, Bill
, Donnie Darko sci-fi Gyllenhall, Jake
, Lost in Translation comedy Murray, Bill
, Patriot Games action Ford, Harrison
, Raiders of the Lost Ark action Ford, Harrison
, Star Wars sci-fi Ford, Harrison
]
```

Hooray! Our ArrayList has been sorted by title. Of course, if we want our home automation system to really rock, we'll probably want to sort DVD collections in lots of different ways. Since we sorted our ArrayList by implementing the compareTo() method, we seem to be stuck. We can only implement compareTo() once in a class, so how do we go about sorting our classes in an order different than what we specify in our compareTo() method? Good question. As luck would have it, the answer is coming up next.

Sorting with Comparator

While you were looking up the `Collections.sort()` method you might have noticed that there is an overloaded version of `sort()` that takes both a List AND something called a *Comparator*. The Comparator interface gives you the capability to sort a given collection any number of different ways. The other handy thing about the Comparator interface is that you can use it to sort instances of any class—even classes you can't modify—unlike the Comparable interface, which forces you to change the class whose instances you want to sort. The Comparator interface is also very easy to implement, having only one method, `compare()`. Here's a small class that can be used to sort a List of DVDInfo instances, by `genre`.

```
import java.util.*;
class GenreSort implements Comparator<DVDInfo> {
  public int compare(DVDInfo one, DVDInfo two) {
    return one.getGenre().compareTo(two.getGenre());
  }
}
```

The `Comparator.compare()` method returns an `int` whose meaning is the same as the `Comparable.compareTo()` method's return value. In this case we're taking advantage of that by asking `compareTo()` to do the actual comparison work for us. Here's a test program that lets us test both our Comparable code and our new Comparator code:

```
import java.util.*;
import java.io.*;            // populateList() needs this
public class TestDVD {
  ArrayList<DVDInfo> dvdlist = new ArrayList<DVDInfo>();
  public static void main(String[] args) {
    new TestDVD().go();
  }
  public void go() {
    populateList();
    System.out.println(dvdlist);      // output as read from file
    Collections.sort(dvdlist);
    System.out.println(dvdlist);      // output sorted by title

    GenreSort gs = new GenreSort();
    Collections.sort(dvdlist, gs);
    System.out.println(dvdlist);      // output sorted by genre
  }
```

```
public void populateList() {
    // read the file, create DVDInfo instances, and
    // populate the ArrayList dvdlist with these instances
  }
}
```

You've already seen the first two output lists, here's the third:

```
[Patriot Games action Ford, Harrison
, Raiders of the Lost Ark action Ford, Harrison
, Caddy Shack comedy Murray, Bill
, Lost in Translation comedy Murray, Bill
, 2001 sci-fi ??
, Donnie Darko sci-fi Gyllenhall, Jake
, Star Wars sci-fi Ford, Harrison
]
```

Because the Comparable and Comparator interfaces are so similar, expect the exam to try to confuse you. For instance you might be asked to implement the compareTo() method in the Comparator interface. Study Table 7-3 to burn in the differences between these two interfaces.

TABLE 7-3   Comparing Comparable to Comparator

java.lang.Comparable	java.util.Comparator
int objOne.compareTo(objTwo)	int compare(objOne, objTwo)
Returns negative if objOne < objTwo zero if objOne == objTwo positive if objOne > objTwo	Same as Comparable
You must modify the class whose instances you want to sort.	You build a class separate from the class whose instances you want to sort.
Only **one** sort sequence can be created	**Many** sort sequences can be created
Implemented frequently in the API by: String, Wrapper classes, Date, Calendar...	Meant to be implemented to sort instances of third-party classes.

Sorting with the Arrays Class

We've been using the java.util.Collections class to sort collections; now let's look at using the java.util.Arrays class to sort arrays. The good news is that sorting arrays of objects is just like sorting collections of objects. The `Arrays.sort()` method is overridden in the same way the `Collections.sort()` method is.

- `Arrays.sort(arrayToSort)`
- `Arrays.sort(arrayToSort, Comparator)`

In addition, the `Arrays.sort()` method is overloaded about a million times to provide a couple of sort methods for every type of primitive. The `Arrays.sort()` methods that sort primitives always sort based on natural order. Don't be fooled by an exam question that tries to sort a primitive array using a Comparator.

Finally, remember that the `sort()` methods for both the Collections class and the Arrays class are `static` methods, and that they alter the objects they are sorting, instead of returning a different sorted object.

Searching Arrays and Collections

The Collections class and the Arrays class both provide methods that allow you to search for a specific element. When searching through collections or arrays, the following rules apply:

- Searches are performed using the `binarySearch()` method.
- Successful searches return the `int` index of the element being searched.
- Unsuccessful searches return an `int` index that represents the *insertion point*. The insertion point is the place in the collection/array where the element would be inserted to keep the collection/array properly sorted. Because posi-

tive return values and 0 indicate successful searches, the `binarySearch()` method uses negative numbers to indicate insertion points. Since 0 is a valid result for a successful search, the first available insertion point is -1. Therefore, the actual insertion point is represented as (-(insertion point) -1). For instance, if the insertion point of a search is at element 2, the actual insertion point returned will be -3.

■ The collection/array being searched must be sorted before you can search it.

■ If you attempt to search an array or collection that has not already been sorted, the results of the search will not be predictable.

■ If the collection/array you want to search was sorted in natural order, it *must* be searched in natural order. (Usually this is accomplished by NOT sending a Comparator as an argument to the `binarySearch()` method.)

■ If the collection/array you want to search was sorted using a Comparator, it *must* be searched using the same Comparator, which is passed as the second argument to the `binarySearch()` method. Remember that Comparators cannot be used when searching arrays of primitives.

Let's take a look at a code sample that exercises the `binarySearch()` method:

```
import java.util.*;
class SearchObjArray {
  public static void main(String [] args) {
    String [] sa = {"one", "two", "three", "four"};

    Arrays.sort(sa);                                         // #1
    for(String s : sa)
      System.out.print(s + " ");
    System.out.println("\none = "
                       + Arrays.binarySearch(sa,"one"));    // #2

    System.out.println("now reverse sort");
    ReSortComparator rs = new ReSortComparator();            // #3
    Arrays.sort(sa,rs);
    for(String s : sa)
      System.out.print(s + " ");
    System.out.println("\none = "
                       + Arrays.binarySearch(sa,"one"));    // #4
    System.out.println("one = "
                       + Arrays.binarySearch(sa,"one",rs)); // #5
  }
```

```
    static class ReSortComparator
                    implements Comparator<String> {        // #6
      public int compare(String a, String b) {
        return b.compareTo(a);                             // #7
      }
    }
}
```

which produces something like this:

```
four one three two
one = 1
now reverse sort
two three one four
one = -1
one = 2
```

Here's what happened:

Line 1   Sort the sa array, alphabetically (the natural order).

Line 2   Search for the location of element "one", which is 1.

Line 3   Make a Comparator instance. On the next line we re-sort the array using the Comparator.

Line 4   Attempt to search the array. We didn't pass the binarySearch() method the Comparator we used to sort the array, so we got an incorrect (undefined) answer.

Line 5   Search again, passing the Comparator to binarySearch(). This time we get the correct answer, 2

Line 6   We define the Comparator; it's okay for this to be an inner class.

Line 7   By switching the use of the arguments in the invocation of compareTo(), we get an inverted sort.

e x a m
w a t c h

When solving searching and sorting questions, two big gotchas are
* 1. Searching an array or collection that hasn't been sorted.*
* 2. Using a Comparator in either the sort or the search,*
*   but not both.*

Converting Arrays to Lists to Arrays

There are a couple of methods that allow you to convert arrays to Lists, and Lists to arrays. The List and Set classes have toArray() methods, and the Arrays class has a method called asList().

The Arrays.asList() method copies an array into a List. The API says, "Returns a fixed-size list backed by the specified array. (Changes to the returned list 'write through' to the array.)" When you use the asList() method, the array and the List become joined at the hip. When you update one of them, the other gets updated automatically. Let's take a look:

```
String[] sa = {"one", "two", "three", "four"};
List sList = Arrays.asList(sa);                 // make a List
System.out.println("size  " + sList.size());
System.out.println("idx2  " + sList.get(2));

sList.set(3,"six");                             // change List
sa[1] = "five";                                 // change array
for(String s : sa)
  System.out.print(s + " ");
System.out.println("\nsl[1] " + sList.get(1));
```

This produces

```
size 4
idx2 three
one five three six
sl[1] five
```

Notice that when we print the final state of the array and the List, they have both been updated with each other's changes. Wouldn't something like this behavior make a great exam question?

Now let's take a look at the toArray() method. There's nothing too fancy going on with the toArray() method; it comes in two flavors: one that returns a new Object array, and one that uses the array you send it as the destination array:

```
List<Integer> iL = new ArrayList<Integer>();
for(int x=0; x<3; x++)
  iL.add(x);
Object[] oa = iL.toArray();           // create an Object array
Integer[] ia2 = new Integer[3];
ia2 = iL.toArray(ia2);                // create an Integer array
```

Using Lists

Remember that Lists are usually used to keep things in some kind of order. You can use a LinkedList to create a first-in, first-out queue. You can use an ArrayList to keep track of what locations were visited, and in what order. Notice that in both of these examples it's perfectly reasonable to assume that duplicates might occur. In addition, Lists allow you to manually override the ordering of elements by adding or removing elements via the element's index. Before Java 5, and the enhanced for loop, the most common way to examine a List "element by element" was by the use of an Iterator. You'll still find Iterators in use in the Java code you encounter, and you might just find an Iterator or two on the exam. An Iterator is an object that's associated with a specific collection. It lets you loop through the collection step by step. The two Iterator methods you need to understand for the exam are

- **boolean hasNext()**   Returns true if there is at least one more element in the collection being traversed. Invoking hasNext() does NOT move you to the next element of the collection.

- **Object next()**   This method returns the next object in the collection, AND moves you forward to the element after the element just returned.

Let's look at a little code that uses a List and an Iterator:

```
import java.util.*;
class Dog {
  public String name;
  Dog(String n) { name = n; }
}
class ItTest {
  public static void main(String[] args) {
    List<Dog> d = new ArrayList<Dog>();
    Dog dog = new Dog("aiko");
    d.add(dog);
    d.add(new Dog("clover"));
    d.add(new Dog("magnolia"));
    Iterator<Dog> i3 = d.iterator();  // make an iterator
    while (i3.hasNext()) {
      Dog d2 = i3.next();                // cast not required
      System.out.println(d2.name);
    }
    System.out.println("size " + d.size());
    System.out.println("get1 " + d.get(1).name);
    System.out.println("aiko " + d.indexOf(dog));
```

```
        d.remove(2);
        Object[] oa = d.toArray();
        for(Object o : oa) {
          Dog d2 = (Dog)o;
          System.out.println("oa " + d2.name);
        }
    }
}
```

This produces

```
aiko
clover
magnolia
size 3
get1 clover
aiko 0
oa aiko
oa clover
```

First off, we used generics syntax to create the Iterator (an Iterator of type Dog). Because of this, when we used the next() method, we didn't have to cast the Object returned by next() to a Dog. We could have declared the Iterator like this:

```
Iterator i3 = d.iterator();   // make an iterator
```

But then we would have had to cast the returned value:

```
Dog d2 = (Dog)i3.next();
```

The rest of the code demonstrates using the size(), get(), indexOf(), and toArray() methods. There shouldn't be any surprises with these methods. In a few pages Table 7-5 will list all of the List, Set, and Map methods you should be familiar with for the exam. As a last warning, remember that List is an interface!

Using Sets

Remember that Sets are used when you don't want any duplicates in your collection. If you attempt to add an element to a set that already exists in the set, the duplicate element will not be added, and the add() method will return false. Remember, HashSets tend to be very fast because, as we discussed earlier, they use hashcodes.

You can also create a TreeSet, which is a Set whose elements are sorted. You must use caution when using a TreeSet (we're about to explain why):

```
import java.util.*;
class SetTest {
  public static void main(String[] args) {
    boolean[] ba = new boolean[5];
    // insert code here

    ba[0] = s.add("a");
    ba[1] = s.add(new Integer(42));
    ba[2] = s.add("b");
    ba[3] = s.add("a");
    ba[4] = s.add(new Object());
    for(int x=0; x<ba.length; x++)
      System.out.print(ba[x] + " ");
    System.out.println("\n");
    for(Object o : s)
      System.out.print(o + " ");
  }
}
```

If you insert the following line of code you'll get output something like this:

```
Set s = new HashSet();        // insert this code

true true true false true
a java.lang.Object@e09713 42 b
```

It's important to know that the order of objects printed in the second `for` loop is not predictable: HashSets do not guarantee any ordering. Also, notice that the fourth invocation of `add()` failed, because it attempted to insert a duplicate entry (a String with the value `a`) into the Set.

If you insert this line of code you'll get something like this:

```
Set s = new TreeSet();        // insert this code

Exception in thread "main" java.lang.ClassCastException: java.
lang.String
        at java.lang.Integer.compareTo(Integer.java:35)
        at java.util.TreeMap.compare(TreeMap.java:1093)
```

```
          at java.util.TreeMap.put(TreeMap.java:465)
          at java.util.TreeSet.add(TreeSet.java:210)
```

The issue is that whenever you want a collection to be sorted, its elements must
be mutually comparable. Remember that unless otherwise specified, objects of
different types are not mutually comparable.

Using Maps

Remember that when you use a class that implements Map, any classes that you
use as a part of the keys for that map must override the hashCode() and equals()
methods. (Well, you only have to override them if you're interested in retrieving
stuff from your Map. Seriously, it's legal to use a class that doesn't override equals()
and hashCode() as a key in a Map; your code will compile and run, you just won't
find your stuff.) Here's some crude code demonstrating the use of a HashMap:

```java
import java.util.*;
class Dog {
  public Dog(String n) { name = n; }
  public String name;
  public boolean equals(Object o) {
    if((o instanceof Dog) &&
       (((Dog)o).name == name)) {
      return true;
    } else {
      return false;
    }
  }
  public int hashCode() {return name.length(); }
}
class Cat { }

enum Pets {DOG, CAT, HORSE }

class MapTest {
  public static void main(String[] args) {
    Map<Object, Object> m = new HashMap<Object, Object>();

    m.put("k1", new Dog("aiko"));   // add some key/value pairs
    m.put("k2", Pets.DOG);
    m.put(Pets.CAT, "CAT key");
    Dog d1 = new Dog("clover");     // let's keep this reference
```

```
        m.put(d1, "Dog key");
        m.put(new Cat(), "Cat key");

        System.out.println(m.get("k1"));           // #1
        String k2 = "k2";
        System.out.println(m.get(k2));             // #2
        Pets p = Pets.CAT;
        System.out.println(m.get(p));              // #3
        System.out.println(m.get(d1));             // #4
        System.out.println(m.get(new Cat()));      // #5
        System.out.println(m.size());              // #6
    }
}
```

which produces something like this:

```
Dog@1c
DOG
CAT key
Dog key
null
5
```

Let's review the output. The first value retrieved is a Dog object (your value will vary). The second value retrieved is an enum value (DOG). The third value retrieved is a String; note that the key was an enum value. Pop quiz: What's the implication of the fact that we were able to successfully use an enum as a key?

The implication of this is that enums override equals() and hashCode(). And, if you look at the java.lang.Enum class in the API, you will see that, in fact, these methods have been overridden.

The fourth output is a String. The important point about this output is that the key used to retrieve the String was made of a Dog object. The fifth output is null. The important point here is that the get() method failed to find the Cat object that was inserted earlier. (The last line of output confirms that indeed, 5 key/value pairs exist in the Map.) Why didn't we find the Cat key String? Why did it work to use an instance of Dog as a key, when using an instance of Cat as a key failed?

It's easy to see that Dog overrode equals() and hashCode() while Cat didn't.

Let's take a quick look at hashcodes. We used an incredibly simplistic hashcode formula in the Dog class—the hashcode of a Dog object is the length of the instance's name. So in this example the hashcode = 6. Let's compare the following two hashCode() methods:

```
public int hashCode() {return name.length(); }    // #1
public int hashCode() {return 4; }                 // #2
```

Time for another pop quiz: Are the preceding two hashcodes legal? Will they successfully retrieve objects from a Map? Which will be faster?

The answer to the first two questions is Yes and Yes. Neither of these hashcodes will be very efficient (in fact they would both be incredibly inefficient), but they are both legal, and they will both work. The answer to the last question is that the first hashcode will be a little bit faster than the second hashcode. In general, the more *unique* hashcodes a formula creates, the faster the retrieval will be. The first hashcode formula will generate a different code for each name length (for instance the name Robert will generate one hashcode and the name Benchley will generate a different hashcode). The second hashcode formula will always produce the same result, 4, so it will be slower than the first.

Our last Map topic is what happens when an object used as a key has its values changed? If we add two lines of code to the end of the earlier MapTest.main(),

```
d1.name = "magnolia";
System.out.println(m.get(d1));
```

we get something like this:

```
Dog@4
DOG
CAT key
Dog key
null
5
null
```

The Dog that was previously found now cannot be found. Because the Dog.name variable is used to create the hashcode, changing the name changed the value of the hashcode. As a final quiz for hashcodes, determine the output for the following lines of code if they're added to the end of MapTest.main():

```
d1.name = "magnolia";
System.out.println(m.get(d1));                        // #1
d1.name = "clover";
System.out.println(m.get(new Dog("clover")));         // #2
d1.name = "arthur";
System.out.println(m.get(new Dog("clover")));         // #3
```

Remember that the hashcode is equal to the length of the name variable. When you study a problem like this, it can be useful to think of the two stages of retrieval:

1. Use the hashCode() method to find the correct bucket
2. Use the equals() method to find the object in the bucket

In the first call to get(), the hashcode is 8 (magnolia) and it should be 6 (clover), so the retrieval fails at step 1 and we get null. In the second call to get(), the hashcodes are both 6, so step 1 succeeds. Once in the correct bucket (the "length of name = 6" bucket), the equals() method is invoked, and since Dog's equals() method compares names, equals() succeeds, and the output is Dog key. In the third invocation of get(), the hashcode test succeeds, but the equals() test fails because arthur is NOT equal to clover.

Navigating (Searching) TreeSets and TreeMaps

We've talked about searching lists and arrays. Let's turn our attention to searching TreeSets and TreeMaps. Java 6 introduced (among others) two new interfaces: java.util.NavigableSet and java.util.NavigableMap. For the purposes of the exam, you're interested in how TreeSet and TreeMap implement these interfaces.

Imagine that the Santa Cruz–Monterey ferry has an irregular schedule. Let's say that we have the daily Santa Cruz departure times stored, in military time, in a TreeSet. Let's look at some code that determines two things:

1. The last ferry that leaves before 4 PM (1600 hours)
2. The first ferry that leaves after 8 PM (2000 hours)

```
import java.util.*;
public class Ferry {
  public static void main(String[] args) {
    TreeSet<Integer> times = new TreeSet<Integer>();
    times.add(1205);   // add some departure times
    times.add(1505);
    times.add(1545);
    times.add(1830);
    times.add(2010);
    times.add(2100);
```

```
// Java 5 version

TreeSet<Integer> subset = new TreeSet<Integer>();
subset = (TreeSet)times.headSet(1600);
System.out.println("J5 - last before 4pm is: " + subset.last());

TreeSet<Integer> sub2 = new TreeSet<Integer>();
sub2 = (TreeSet)times.tailSet(2000);
System.out.println("J5 - first after 8pm is: " + sub2.first());

// Java 6 version using the new lower() and higher() methods

System.out.println("J6 - last before 4pm is: " + times.lower(1600));
System.out.println("J6 - first after 8pm is: " + times.higher(2000));
    }
}
```

This should produce the following:

```
J5 - last before 4pm is: 1545
J5 - first after 8pm is: 2010
J6 - last before 4pm is: 1545
J6 - first after 8pm is: 2010
```

As you can see in the preceding code, before the addition of the NavigableSet interface, zeroing in on an arbitrary spot in a Set—using the methods available in Java 5—was a compute-expensive and clunky proposition. On the other hand, using the new Java 6 methods `lower()` and `higher()`, the code becomes a lot cleaner.

For the purpose of the exam, the NavigableSet methods related to this type of navigation are `lower()`, `floor()`, `higher()`, `ceiling()`, and the mostly parallel NavigableMap methods are `lowerKey()`, `floorKey()`, `ceilingKey()`, and `higherKey()`. The difference between `lower()` and `floor()` is that `lower()` returns the element less than the given element, and `floor()` returns the element less than *or equal to* the given element. Similarly, `higher()` returns the element greater than the given element, and `ceiling()` returns the element greater than *or equal to* the given element. Table 7-4 summarizes the methods you should know for the exam.

Other Navigation Methods

In addition to the methods we just discussed there are a few more new Java 6 methods that could be considered "navigation" methods. (Okay, it's a little stretch to call these "navigation" methods, but just play along.)

Polling

Although the idea of polling isn't new to Java 6 (as you'll see in a minute, `PriorityQueue` had a `poll()` method before Java 6), it *is* new to TreeSet and TreeMap. The idea of polling is that we want *both* to retrieve *and* remove an element from either the beginning or the end of a collection. In the case of TreeSet, `pollFirst()` returns and removes the first entry in the set, and `pollLast()` returns and removes the last. Similarly, TreeMap now provides `pollFirstEntry()` and `pollLastEntry()` to retrieve and remove key-value pairs.

Descending Order

Also new to Java 6 for TreeSet and TreeMap are methods that return a collection in the reverse order of the collection on which the method was invoked. The important methods for the exam are TreeSet.descendingSet() and TreeMap .descendingMap().

Table 7-4 summarizes the "navigation" methods you'll need to know for the exam.

TABLE 7-4	Important "Navigation" Related Methods

Method	Description
`TreeSet.ceiling(e)`	Returns the lowest element >= e
`TreeMap.ceilingKey(key)`	Returns the lowest key >= key
`TreeSet.higher(e)`	Returns the lowest element > e
`TreeMap.higherKey(key)`	Returns the lowest key > key
`TreeSet.floor(e)`	Returns the highest element <= e
`TreeMap.floorKey(key)`	Returns the highest key <= key
`TreeSet.lower(e)`	Returns the highest element < e
`TreeMap.lowerKey(key)`	Returns the highest key < key
`TreeSet.pollFirst()`	Returns and removes the first entry
`TreeMap.pollFirstEntry()`	Returns and removes the first key-value pair
`TreeSet.pollLast()`	Returns and removes the last entry
`TreeMap.pollLastEntry()`	Returns and removes the last key-value pair
`TreeSet.descendingSet()`	Returns a NavigableSet in reverse order
`TreeMap.descendingMap()`	Returns a NavigableMap in reverse order

Backed Collections

Some of the classes in the java.util package support the concept of "backed collections". We'll use a little code to help explain the idea:

```
TreeMap<String, String> map = new TreeMap<String, String>();
map.put("a", "ant"); map.put("d", "dog"); map.put("h", "horse");

SortedMap<String, String> submap;
submap = map.subMap("b", "g");              // #1 create a backed collection

System.out.println(map + " " + submap);     // #2 show contents

map.put("b", "bat");                         // #3 add to original
submap.put("f", "fish");                     // #4 add to copy

map.put("r", "raccoon");                     // #5 add to original - out of range
// submap.put("p", "pig");                   // #6 add to copy - out of range

System.out.println(map + " " + submap);      // #7 show final contents
```

This should produce something like this:

```
{a=ant, d=dog, h=horse} {d=dog}
{a=ant, b=bat, d=dog, f=fish, h=horse, r=raccoon} {b=bat, d=dog, f=fish}
```

The important method in this code is the `TreeMap.subMap()` method. It's easy to guess (and it's correct), that the `subMap()` method is making a copy of a portion of the TreeMap named `map`. The first line of output verifies the conclusions we've just drawn.

What happens next is powerful and a little bit unexpected (now we're getting to why they're called *backed* collections). When we add key-value pairs to either the original TreeMap or the partial-copy SortedMap, the new entries were automatically added to the other collection—sometimes. When `submap` was created, we provided a value range for the new collection. This range defines not only what should be included when the partial copy is created, but also defines the range of values that can be added to the copy. As we can verify by looking at the second line of output, we can add new entries to either collection within the range of the copy, and the new entries will show up in both collections. In addition, we can add a new entry to the original collection, even if it's outside the range of the copy. In this case, the new entry will show up only in the original—it won't be added to the copy because it's outside the copy's range. Notice that we commented out line #6. If you attempt to add an out-of-range entry to the copied collection an exception will be thrown.

For the exam, you'll need to understand the basics just explained, plus a few more details about three methods from TreeSet—(`headSet()`, `subSet()`, and `tailSet()`), and three methods from TreeMap (`headMap()`, `subMap()`, and `tailMap()`). As with the navigation-oriented methods we just discussed, we can see a lot of parallels between the TreeSet and the TreeMap methods. The `headSet()` / `headMap()` methods create a subset that starts at the beginning of the original collection and ends at the point specified by the method's argument. The `tailSet()` / `tailMap()` methods create a subset that starts at the point specified by the method's argument and goes to the end of the original collection. Finally, the `subSet()` / `subMap()` methods allow you to specify both the start and end points for the subset collection you're creating.

As you might expect, the question of whether the subsetted collection's end points are inclusive or exclusive is a little tricky. The good news is that for the exam you have to remember only that when these methods are invoked with endpoint *and* boolean arguments, the boolean always means "is inclusive?". A little more good news is that all you have to know for the exam is that unless specifically indicated by a boolean argument, a subset's starting point will always be inclusive. Finally, you'll notice when you study the API that all of the methods we've been discussing here have an overloaded version that's new to Java 6. The older methods return either a SortedSet or a SortedMap, the new Java 6 methods return either a NavigableSet or a NavigableMap. Table 7-5 summarizes these methods.

TABLE 7-5	Important "Backed Collection" Methods for TreeSet and TreeMap

Method	Description
`headSet(e, b*)`	Returns a subset ending at element e and *exclusive* of e
`headMap(k, b*)`	Returns a submap ending at key k and *exclusive* of key k
`tailSet(e, b*)`	Returns a subset starting at and *inclusive* of element e
`tailMap(k, b*)`	Returns a submap starting at and *inclusive* of key k
`subSet(s, b*, e, b*)`	Returns a subset starting at element s and ending just before element e
`subMap(s, b*, e, b*)`	Returns a submap starting at key s and ending just before key s

* NOTE: These boolean arguments are optional. If they exist it's a Java 6 method that lets you specify whether the endpoint is exclusive, and these methods return a NavigableXxx. If the boolean argument(s) don't exist, the method returns either a SortedSet or a SortedMap.

Using the PriorityQueue Class

The last collection class you'll need to understand for the exam is the PriorityQueue.
Unlike basic queue structures that are first-in, first-out by default, a PriorityQueue
orders its elements using a user-defined priority. The priority can be as simple as
natural ordering (in which, for instance, an entry of 1 would be a higher priority
than an entry of 2). In addition, a PriorityQueue can be ordered using a Comparator,
which lets you define any ordering you want. Queues have a few methods not found
in other collection interfaces: `peek()`, `poll()`, and `offer()`.

```
import java.util.*;
class PQ {
  static class PQsort
         implements Comparator<Integer> {   // inverse sort
    public int compare(Integer one, Integer two) {
      return two - one;                      // unboxing
    }
  }
  public static void main(String[] args) {
    int[] ia = {1,5,3,7,6,9,8 };             // unordered data
    PriorityQueue<Integer> pq1 =
      new PriorityQueue<Integer>();          // use natural order

    for(int x : ia)                          // load queue
```

```
      pq1.offer(x);
    for(int x : ia)                               // review queue
      System.out.print(pq1.poll() + " ");
    System.out.println("");

    PQsort pqs = new PQsort();                     // get a Comparator
    PriorityQueue<Integer> pq2 =
      new PriorityQueue<Integer>(10,pqs);          // use Comparator

    for(int x : ia)                               // load queue
      pq2.offer(x);
    System.out.println("size " + pq2.size());
    System.out.println("peek " + pq2.peek());
    System.out.println("size " + pq2.size());
    System.out.println("poll " + pq2.poll());
    System.out.println("size " + pq2.size());
    for(int x : ia)                               // review queue
      System.out.print(pq2.poll() + " ");
  }
}
```

This code produces something like this:

```
1 3 5 6 7 8 9
size 7
peek 9
size 7
poll 9
size 6
8 7 6 5 3 1 null
```

Let's look at this in detail. The first `for` loop iterates through the `ia` array, and uses the `offer()` method to add elements to the PriorityQueue named `pq1`. The second `for` loop iterates through `pq1` using the `poll()` method, which returns the highest priority entry in `pq1` AND removes the entry from the queue. Notice that the elements are returned in priority order (in this case, natural order). Next, we create a Comparator—in this case, a Comparator that orders elements in the opposite of natural order. We use this Comparator to build a second PriorityQueue, `pq2`, and we load it with the same array we used earlier. Finally, we check the size of `pq2` before and after calls to `peek()` and `poll()`. This confirms that `peek()` returns the highest priority element in the queue without removing it, and `poll()` returns the highest priority element, AND removes it from the queue. Finally, we review the remaining elements in the queue.

Method Overview for Arrays and Collections

For these two classes, we've already covered the trickier methods you might encounter on the exam. Table 7-6 lists a summary of the methods you should be aware of. (Note: The T[] syntax will be explained later in this chapter; for now, think of it as meaning "any array that's NOT an array of primitives.")

TABLE 7-6	Key Methods in Arrays and Collections

Key Methods in java.util.Arrays	Descriptions
`static List asList(T[])`	Convert an array to a List (and bind them).
`static int binarySearch(Object[], key)` `static int binarySearch(primitive[], key)`	Search a sorted array for a given value, return an index or insertion point.
`static int binarySearch(T[], key, Comparator)`	Search a Comparator-sorted array for a value.
`static boolean equals(Object[], Object[])` `static boolean equals(primitive[], primitive[])`	Compare two arrays to determine if their contents are equal.
`public static void sort(Object[ ] )` `public static void sort(primitive[ ] )`	Sort the elements of an array by natural order.
`public static void sort(T[], Comparator)`	Sort the elements of an array using a Comparator.
`public static String toString(Object[])` `public static String toString(primitive[])`	Create a String containing the contents of an array.

Key Methods in java.util.Collections	Descriptions
`static int binarySearch(List, key)` `static int binarySearch(List, key, Comparator)`	Search a "sorted" List for a given value, return an index or insertion point.
`static void reverse(List)`	Reverse the order of elements in a List.
`static Comparator reverseOrder()` `static Comparator reverseOrder(Comparator)`	Return a Comparator that sorts the reverse of the collection's current sort sequence.
`static void sort(List)` `static void sort(List, Comparator)`	Sort a List either by natural order or by a Comparator.

Method Overview for List, Set, Map, and Queue

For these four interfaces, we've already covered the trickier methods you might encounter on the exam. Table 7-7 lists a summary of the List, Set, and Map methods you should be aware of, **but don't forget the new "Navigable" methods floor, lower, ceiling, and higher that we discussed a few pages back.**

TABLE 7-7   Key Methods in List, Set, and Map

Key Interface Methods	List	Set	Map	Descriptions
boolean **add**(element) boolean **add**(index, element)	X X	X		Add an element. For Lists, optionally add the element at an index point.
boolean **contains**(object) boolean **containsKey**(object key) boolean **containsValue**(object value)	X	X	X X	Search a collection for an object (or, optionally for Maps a key), return the result as a boolean.
object **get**(index) object **get**(key)	X		X	Get an object from a collection, via an index or a key.
int **indexOf**(object)	X			Get the location of an object in a List.
Iterator **iterator**()	X	X		Get an Iterator for a List or a Set.
Set **keySet**()			X	Return a Set containing a Map's keys.
put(key, value)			X	Add a key/value pair to a Map.
remove(index) **remove**(object) **remove**(key)	X X	X	X	Remove an element via an index, or via the element's value, or via a key.
int **size**()	X	X	X	Return the number of elements in a collection.
Object[] **toArray**() T[] **toArray**(T[])	X	X		Return an array containing the elements of the collection.

For the exam, the PriorityQueue methods that are important to understand are offer() (which is similar to add()), peek() (which retrieves the element at the head of the queue, but doesn't delete it), and poll() (which retrieves the head element and removes it from the queue).

exam
watch

It's important to know some of the details of natural ordering. The following code will help you understand the relative positions of uppercase characters, lowercase characters, and spaces in a natural ordering:

```
String[] sa = {">ff<", "> f<", ">f <", ">FF<" }; // ordered?
PriorityQueue<String> pq3 = new PriorityQueue<String>();
for(String s : sa)
  pq3.offer(s);
for(String s : sa)
  System.out.print(pq3.poll() + " ");
```

This produces

```
> f< >FF< >f < >ff<
```

If you remember that spaces sort before characters and that uppercase letters sort before lowercase characters, you should be good to go for the exam.

CERTIFICATION OBJECTIVE

Generic Types (Objectives 6.3 and 6.4)

6.3   Write code that uses the generic versions of the Collections API, in particular the Set, List, and Map interfaces and implementation classes. Recognize the limitations of the non-generic Collections API and how to refactor code to use the generic versions.

6.4   Develop code that makes proper use of type parameters in class/interface declarations, instance variables, method arguments, and return types; and write generic methods or methods that make use of wildcard types and understand the similarities and differences between these two approaches. Write code that uses the NavigableSet and NavigableMap interfaces.

Arrays in Java have always been type safe—an array declared as type String (`String []`) can't accept Integers (or `int`s), Dogs, or anything other than Strings. But remember that before Java 5 there was no syntax for declaring a type safe collection. To make an ArrayList of Strings, you said,

```
ArrayList myList = new ArrayList();
```

or, the polymorphic equivalent

```
List myList = new ArrayList();
```

There was no syntax that let you specify that `myList` will take Strings and only Strings. And with no way to specify a type for the ArrayList, the compiler couldn't enforce that you put only things of the specified type into the list. As of Java 5, we can use generics, and while they aren't only for making type safe collections, that's just about all most developers use generics for. So, while generics aren't just for collections, think of collections as the overwhelming reason and motivation for adding generics to the language.

And it was not an easy decision, nor has it been an entirely welcome addition. Because along with all the nice happy type safety, generics come with a lot of baggage—most of which you'll never see or care about, but there are some gotchas that come up surprisingly quickly. We'll cover the ones most likely to show up in your own code, and those are also the issues that you'll need to know for the exam.

The biggest challenge for Sun in adding generics to the language (and the main reason it took them so long) was how to deal with legacy code built without generics. Sun's Java engineers obviously didn't want to break everyone's existing Java code, so they had to find a way for Java classes with both type safe (generic) and non-type safe (non-generic/pre-Java 5) collections to still work together. Their solution isn't the friendliest, but it does let you use older non-generic code, as well as use generic code that plays with non-generic code. But notice we said "plays," and not "plays WELL."

While you can integrate Java 5 and Java 6 generic code with legacy non-generic code, the consequences can be disastrous, and unfortunately, most of the disasters happen at runtime, not compile time. Fortunately, though, most compilers will generate warnings to tell you when you're using unsafe (meaning non-generic) collections.

The Java 5 exam covers both pre-Java 5 (non-generic) and Java 5 style collections, and you'll see questions that expect you to understand the tricky problems that can come from mixing non-generic and generic code together. And like some of the other topics in this book, you could fill an entire book if you really wanted to cover every detail about generics, but the exam (and this book) covers more than most developers will ever need to use.

The Legacy Way to Do Collections

Here's a review of a pre-Java 5 ArrayList intended to hold Strings. (We say "intended" because that's about all you had—good intentions—to make sure that the ArrayList would hold only Strings).

```
List myList = new ArrayList();   // can't declare a type

myList.add("Fred");              // OK, it will hold Strings

myList.add(new Dog());           // and it will hold Dogs too

myList.add(new Integer(42));     // and Integers...
```

A non-generic collection can hold any kind of object! A non-generic collection is quite happy to hold anything that is NOT a primitive.

This meant it was entirely up to the programmer to be...careful. Having no way to guarantee collection type wasn't very programmer-friendly for such a strongly typed language. We're so used to the compiler stopping us from, say, assigning an int to a boolean reference or a String to a Dog reference, but with collections, it was, "Come on in! The door is always open! All objects are welcome here any time!"

And since a collection could hold anything, the methods that get objects out of the collection could have only one kind of return type—java.lang.Object. That meant that getting a String back out of our only-Strings-intended list required a cast:

```
String s = (String) myList.get(0);
```

And since you couldn't guarantee that what was coming out really was a String (since you were allowed to put anything in the list), the cast could fail at runtime.

So, generics takes care of both ends (the putting in and getting out) by enforcing the type of your collections. Let's update the String list:

```
List<String> myList = new ArrayList<String>();
myList.add("Fred");          // OK, it will hold Strings
myList.add(new Dog());       // compiler error!!
```

Perfect. That's exactly what we want. By using generics syntax—which means putting the type in angle brackets <String>, we're telling the compiler that this collection can hold only String objects. The type in angle brackets is referred to as either the "parameterized type," "type parameter," or of course just old-fashioned "type." In this chapter, we'll refer to it both new ways.

So, now that what you put IN is guaranteed, you can also guarantee what comes OUT, and that means you can get rid of the cast when you get something from the collection. Instead of

```
String s = (String)myList.get(0);   // pre-generics, when a
                                     // String wasn't guaranteed
```

we can now just say

```
String s = myList.get(0);
```

The compiler already knows that `myList` contains only things that can be assigned to a String reference, so now there's no need for a cast. So far, it seems pretty simple. And with the new `for` loop, you can of course iterate over the guaranteed-to-be-String list:

```
for (String s : myList) {
    int x = s.length();
    // no need for a cast before calling a String method! The
    // compiler already knew "s" was a String coming from MyList
}
```

And of course you can declare a type parameter for a method argument, which then makes the argument a type safe reference:

```
void takeListOfStrings(List<String> strings) {
    strings.add("foo");   // no problem adding a String
}
```

The method above would NOT compile if we changed it to

```
void takeListOfStrings(List<String> strings) {
    strings.add(new Integer(42)); // NO!! strings is type safe
}
```

Return types can obviously be declared type safe as well:

```
public List<Dog> getDogList() {
    List<Dog> dogs = new ArrayList<Dog>();
    // more code to insert dogs
    return dogs;
}
```

The compiler will stop you from returning anything not compatible with a List<Dog> (although what is and is not compatible is going to get very interesting in a minute). And since the compiler guarantees that only a type safe Dog List is returned, those calling the method won't need a cast to take Dogs from the List:

```
Dog d = getDogList().get(0);   // we KNOW a Dog is coming out
```

With pre-Java 5, non-generic code, the getDogList() method would be

```
public List getDogList() {
    List dogs = new ArrayList();
     // code to add only Dogs... fingers crossed...
    return dogs; // a List of ANYTHING will work here
}
```

and the caller would need a cast:

```
Dog d = (Dog) getDogList().get(0);
```

(The cast in this example applies to what comes from the List's get() method; we aren't casting what is returned from the getDogList() method, which is a List.)

But what about the benefit of a completely heterogeneous collection? In other words, what if you liked the fact that before generics you could make an ArrayList that could hold any kind of object?

```
List myList = new ArrayList();   // old-style, non-generic
```

is almost identical to

```
List<Object> myList = new
                ArrayList<Object>(); // holds ANY object type
```

Declaring a List with a type parameter of <Object> makes a collection that works in almost the same way as the original pre-Java 5, non-generic collection—you can put ANY Object type into the collection. You'll see a little later that non-generic collections and collections of type <Object> aren't entirely the same, but most of the time the differences do not matter.

Oh, if only this were the end of the story...but there are still a few tricky issues with methods arguments, polymorphism, and integrating generic and non-generic code, so we're just getting warmed up here.

Generics and Legacy Code

The easiest generics thing you'll need to know for the exam is how to update non-generic code to make it generic. You just add a type in angle brackets (<>) immediately following the collection type in BOTH the variable declaration and the constructor call, including any place you declare a variable (so that means arguments and return types too). A pre-Java 5 List meant to hold only Integers:

```
List myList = new ArrayList();
```

becomes

```
List<Integer> myList = new ArrayList<Integer>();
```

and a list meant to hold only Strings goes from

```
public List changeStrings(ArrayList s) { }
```

to this:

```
public List<String> changeStrings(ArrayList<String> s) { }
```

Easy. And if there's code that used the earlier non-generic version and performed a cast to get things out, that won't break anyone's code:

```
Integer i = (Integer) list.get(0); // cast no longer needed,
                                    // but it won't hurt
```

Mixing Generic and Non-generic Collections

Now here's where it starts to get interesting...imagine we have an ArrayList, of type Integer, and we're passing it into a method from a class whose source code we don't have access to. Will this work?

```
// a Java 5 class using a generic collection
import java.util.*;
public class TestLegacy {
    public static void main(String[] args) {
        List<Integer> myList = new ArrayList<Integer>();
                                    // type safe collection
        myList.add(4);
        myList.add(6);
        Adder adder = new Adder();
        int total = adder.addAll(myList);
                            // pass it to an untyped argument
        System.out.println(total);
    }
}
```

The older, non-generics class we want to use:

```
import java.util.*;
class Adder {
    int addAll(List list) {
        // method with a non-generic List argument,
        // but assumes (with no guarantee) that it will be Integers
        Iterator it = list.iterator();
        int total = 0;
        while (it.hasNext()) {
          int i = ((Integer)it.next()).intValue();
          total += i;
        }
        return total;
    }
}
```

Yes, this works just fine. You can mix correct generic code with older non-generic code, and everyone is happy.

In the previous example, the addAll() legacy method assumed (trusted? hoped?) that the list passed in was indeed restricted to Integers, even though when the code was written, there was no guarantee. It was up to the programmers to be careful.

Since the `addAll()` method wasn't doing anything except getting the Integer (using a cast) from the list and accessing its value, there were no problems. In that example, there was no risk to the caller's code, but the legacy method might have blown up if the list passed in contained anything but Integers (which would cause a ClassCastException).

But now imagine that you call a legacy method that doesn't just *read* a value but *adds* something to the ArrayList? Will this work?

```java
import java.util.*;
public class TestBadLegacy {
    public static void main(String[] args) {
        List<Integer> myList = new ArrayList<Integer>();
        myList.add(4);
        myList.add(6);
        Inserter in  = new Inserter();
        in.insert(myList);  // pass List<Integer> to legacy code
      }
}
class Inserter {
    // method with a non-generic List argument
    void insert(List list) {
      list.add(new Integer(42)); // adds to the incoming list
    }
}
```

Sure, this code works. It compiles, and it runs. The `insert()` method puts an Integer into the list that was originally typed as <Integer>, so no problem.

But...what if we modify the `insert()` method like this:

```java
void insert(List list) {
   list.add(new String("42"));  // put a String in the list
                                // passed in
}
```

Will that work? Yes, sadly, it does! It both compiles and runs. No runtime exception. Yet, someone just stuffed a String into a *supposedly* type safe ArrayList of type <Integer>. How can that be?

Remember, the older legacy code was allowed to put anything at all (except primitives) into a collection. And in order to support legacy code, Java 5 and Java 6 allows your newer type safe code to make use of older code (the last thing Sun wanted to do was ask several million Java developers to modify all their existing code).

So, the Java 5 or Java 6 compiler is *forced* into letting you compile your new type safe code even though your code invokes a method of an older class that takes a non-type safe argument and does who knows what with it.

However, just because the Java 5 compiler allows this code to compile doesn't mean it has to be HAPPY about it. In fact the compiler will warn you that you're taking a big, big risk sending your nice protected ArrayList<Integer> into a dangerous method that can have its way with your list and put in Floats, Strings, or even Dogs.

When you called the addAll() method in the earlier example, it didn't insert anything to the list (it simply added up the values within the collection), so there was no risk to the caller that his list would be modified in some horrible way. It compiled and ran just fine. But in the second version, with the legacy insert() method that adds a String, the compiler generated a warning:

```
javac TestBadLegacy.java
Note: TestBadLegacy.java uses unchecked or unsafe operations.
Note: Recompile with -Xlint:unchecked for details.
```

Remember that *compiler warnings are NOT considered a compiler failure*. The compiler generated a perfectly valid class file from the compilation, but it was kind enough to tell you by saying, in so many words, "I seriously hope you know what you are doing because this old code has NO respect (or even knowledge) of your <Integer> typing, and can do whatever the heck it wants to your precious ArrayList<Integer>."

e x a m
w a t c h

Be sure you know the difference between "compilation fails" and "compiles without error" and "compiles without warnings" and "compiles with warnings." In most questions on the exam, you care only about compiles vs. compilation fails—compiler warnings don't matter for most of the exam. But when you are using generics, and mixing both typed and untyped code, warnings matter.

Back to our example with the legacy code that does an insert, keep in mind that for BOTH versions of the insert() method (one that adds an Integer and one that adds a String) the compiler issues warnings. The compiler does NOT know whether the insert() method is adding the right thing (Integer) or wrong thing (String). The reason the compiler produces a warning is because the method is ADDING something to the collection! In other words, the compiler knows there's a chance the method might add the wrong thing to a collection the caller thinks is type safe.

exam

ⓦatch

For the purposes of the exam, unless the question includes an answer that mentions warnings, then even if you know compilation will produce warnings, that is still a successful compile! Compiling with warnings is NEVER considered a compilation failure.
One more time—if you see code that you know will compile with warnings, you must NOT choose "Compilation fails." as an answer. The bottom line is this: code that compiles with warnings is still a successful compile. If the exam question wants to test your knowledge of whether code will produce a warning (or what you can do to the code to ELIMINATE warnings), the question (or answer) will explicitly include the word "warnings."

So far, we've looked at how the compiler will generate warnings if it sees that there's a chance your type safe collection could be harmed by older, non-type-safe code. But one of the questions developers often ask is, "Okay, sure, it compiles, but why does it RUN? Why does the code that inserts the wrong thing into my list work at runtime?" In other words, why does the JVM let old code stuff a String into your ArrayList<Integer>, without any problems at all? No exceptions, nothing. Just a quiet, behind-the-scenes, total violation of your type safety that you might not discover until the worst possible moment.

There's one Big Truth you need to know to understand why it runs without problems—the JVM has no idea that your ArrayList was supposed to hold only Integers. The typing information does not exist at runtime! All your generic code is strictly for the compiler. Through a process called "type erasure," the compiler does all of its verifications on your generic code and then strips the type information out of the class bytecode. At runtime, ALL collection code—both legacy and new Java 5 code you write using generics—looks exactly like the pre-generic version of collections. None of your typing information exists at runtime. In other words, even though you WROTE

```
List<Integer> myList = new ArrayList<Integer>();
```

By the time the compiler is done with it, the JVM sees what it always saw before Java 5 and generics:

```
List myList = new ArrayList();
```

The compiler even inserts the casts for you—the casts you had to do to get things out of a pre-Java 5 collection.

Think of generics as strictly a compile-time protection. The compiler uses generic type information (the <type> in the angle brackets) to make sure that your code doesn't put the wrong things into a collection, and that you do not assign what you get from a collection to the wrong reference type. But NONE of this protection exists at runtime.

This is a little different from arrays, which give you BOTH compile-time protection and runtime protection. Why did they do generics this way? Why is there no type information at runtime? To support legacy code. At runtime, collections are collections just like the old days. What you gain from using generics is compile-time protection that guarantees that you won't put the wrong thing into a typed collection, and it also eliminates the need for a cast when you get something out, since the compiler already knows that only an Integer is coming out of an Integer list.

The fact is, you don't NEED runtime protection...until you start mixing up generic and non-generic code, as we did in the previous example. Then you can have disasters at runtime. The only advice we have is to pay very close attention to those compiler warnings:

```
javac TestBadLegacy.java
Note: TestBadLegacy.java uses unchecked or unsafe operations.
Note: Recompile with -Xlint:unchecked for details.
```

This compiler warning isn't very descriptive, but the second note suggests that you recompile with -Xlint:unchecked. If you do, you'll get something like this:

```
javac -Xlint:unchecked TestBadLegacy.java
TestBadLegacy.java:17: warning: [unchecked] unchecked call to
add(E) as a member of the raw type java.util.List
        list.add(new String("42"));
              ^
1 warning
```

When you compile with the -Xlint:unchecked flag, the compiler shows you exactly which method(s) might be doing something dangerous. In this example, since the list argument was not declared with a type, the compiler treats it as legacy code and assumes no risk for what the method puts into the "raw" list.

On the exam, you must be able to recognize when you are compiling code that will produce warnings but still compile. And any code that compiles (even with warnings) will run! No type violations will be caught at runtime by the JVM, *until* those type violations mess with your code in some other way. In other words, the act of adding a String to an <Integer> list won't fail at runtime *until* you try to treat that String-you-think-is-an-Integer as an Integer.

For example, imagine you want your code to pull something out of your *supposedly* type safe ArrayList<Integer> that older code put a String into. It compiles (with warnings). It runs...or at least the code that actually adds the String to the list runs. But when you take the String-that-wasn't-supposed-to-be-there out of the list, and try to assign it to an Integer reference or invoke an Integer method, you're dead.

Keep in mind, then, that the problem of putting the wrong thing into a typed (generic) collection does not show up at the time you actually do the add() to the collection. It only shows up later, when you try to use something in the list and it doesn't match what you were expecting. In the old (pre-Java 5) days, you always assumed that you might get the wrong thing out of a collection (since they were all non-type safe), so you took appropriate defensive steps in your code. The problem with mixing generic with non-generic code is that you won't be expecting those problems if you have been lulled into a false sense of security by having written type safe code. Just remember that the moment you turn that type safe collection over to older, non-type safe code, your protection vanishes.

Again, pay very close attention to compiler warnings, and be prepared to see issues like this come up on the exam.

e x a m
ⓦatch
When using legacy (non-type safe) collections—watch out for unboxing problems! If you declare a non-generic collection, the `get()` *method ALWAYS returns a reference of type java.lang.Object. Remember that unboxing can't convert a plain old Object to a primitive, even if that Object reference refers to an Integer (or some other wrapped primitive) on the heap. Unboxing converts only from a wrapper class reference (like an Integer or a Long) to a primitive.*

e x a m
w atch

Unboxing gotcha, continued:

```
List test = new ArrayList();
test.add(43);
int x = (Integer)test.get(0);      // you must cast !!

List<Integer> test2 = new ArrayList<Integer>();
test2.add(343);
int x2 = test2.get(0);             // cast not necessary
```

Watch out for missing casts associated with pre-Java 5, non-generic collections.

Polymorphism and Generics

Generic collections give you the same benefits of type safety that you've always had with arrays, but there are some crucial differences that can bite you if you aren't prepared. Most of these have to do with polymorphism.

You've already seen that polymorphism applies to the "base" type of the collection:

```
List<Integer> myList = new ArrayList<Integer>();
```

In other words, we were able to assign an ArrayList to a List reference, because List is a supertype of ArrayList. Nothing special there—this polymorphic assignment works the way it always works in Java, regardless of the generic typing.

But what about this?

```
class Parent { }
class Child extends Parent { }
List<Parent> myList = new ArrayList<Child>();
```

Think about it for a minute.

Keep thinking...

No, it doesn't work. There's a very simple rule here—the type of the variable declaration must match the type you pass to the actual object type. If you declare List<Foo> foo then whatever you assign to the foo reference MUST be of the generic type <Foo>. Not a subtype of <Foo>. Not a supertype of <Foo>. Just <Foo>.

These are wrong:

```
List<Object> myList = new ArrayList<JButton>();  // NO!
List<Number> numbers = new ArrayList<Integer>(); // NO!
// remember that Integer is a subtype of Number
```

But these are fine:

```
List<JButton> myList = new ArrayList<JButton>(); // yes
List<Object> myList = new ArrayList<Object>();   // yes
List<Integer> myList = new ArrayList<Integer>(); // yes
```

So far so good. Just keep the generic type of the reference and the generic type of the object to which it refers identical. In other words, polymorphism applies here to only the "base" type. And by "base," we mean the type of the collection class itself—the class that can be customized with a type. In this code,

```
List<JButton> myList = new ArrayList<JButton>();
```

List and ArrayList are the *base* type and JButton is the *generic* type. So an ArrayList can be assigned to a List, but a collection of <JButton> cannot be assigned to a reference of <Object>, even though JButton is a subtype of Object.

The part that feels wrong for most developers is that this is NOT how it works with arrays, where you *are* allowed to do this,

```
import java.util.*;
class Parent { }
class Child extends Parent { }
public class TestPoly {
    public static void main(String[] args) {
        Parent[] myArray = new Child[3];  // yes
    }
}
```

which means you're also allowed to do this

```
Object[] myArray = new JButton[3];   // yes
```

but not this:

```
List<Object> list = new ArrayList<JButton>();   // NO!
```

Why are the rules for typing of arrays different from the rules for generic typing? We'll get to that in a minute. For now, just burn it into your brain that polymorphism does not work the same way for generics as it does with arrays.

Generic Methods

If you weren't already familiar with generics, you might be feeling very uncomfortable with the implications of the previous no-polymorphic-assignment-for-generic-types thing. And why shouldn't you be uncomfortable? One of the biggest benefits of polymorphism is that you can declare, say, a method argument of a particular type and at runtime be able to have that argument refer to any subtype—including those you'd never known about at the time you wrote the method with the supertype argument.

For example, imagine a classic (simplified) polymorphism example of a veterinarian (AnimalDoctor) class with a method checkup(). And right now, you have three Animal subtypes—Dog, Cat, and Bird—each implementing the abstract checkup() method from Animal:

```
abstract class Animal {
    public abstract void checkup();
}
class Dog extends Animal {
    public void checkup() {   // implement Dog-specific code
      System.out.println("Dog checkup");
    }
}
class Cat extends Animal {
    public void checkup() {   // implement Cat-specific code
      System.out.println("Cat checkup");
    }
}
class Bird extends Animal {
    public void checkup() {   // implement Bird-specific code
      System.out.println("Bird checkup");
    }   }
```

Forgetting collections/arrays for a moment, just imagine what the AnimalDoctor class needs to look like in order to have code that takes any kind of Animal and invokes the Animal checkup() method. Trying to overload the AnimalDoctor class with checkup() methods for every possible kind of animal is ridiculous, and obviously not extensible. You'd have to change the AnimalDoctor class every time someone added a new subtype of Animal.

So in the AnimalDoctor class, you'd probably have a polymorphic method:

```
public void checkAnimal(Animal a) {
    a.checkup(); // does not matter which animal subtype each
                 // Animal's overridden checkup() method runs
}
```

And of course we do want the AnimalDoctor to also have code that can take arrays of Dogs, Cats, or Birds, for when the vet comes to the dog, cat, or bird kennel. Again, we don't want overloaded methods with arrays for each potential Animal subtype, so we use polymorphism in the AnimalDoctor class:

```
public void checkAnimals(Animal[] animals) {
    for(Animal a : animals) {
        a.checkup();
    }
}
```

Here is the entire example, complete with a test of the array polymorphism that takes any type of animal array (Dog[], Cat[], Bird[]).

```
import java.util.*;
abstract class Animal {
    public abstract void checkup();
}
class Dog extends Animal {
    public void checkup() {   // implement Dog-specific code
        System.out.println("Dog checkup");
    }
}
class Cat extends Animal {
    public void checkup() {   // implement Cat-specific code
        System.out.println("Cat checkup");
    }
}
```

```
class Bird extends Animal {
   public void checkup() {      // implement Bird-specific code
      System.out.println("Bird checkup");
   }
}
public class AnimalDoctor  {
    // method takes an array of any animal subtype
    public void checkAnimals(Animal[] animals) {
      for(Animal a : animals) {
        a.checkup();
      }
    }
    public static void main(String[] args) {
       // test it
       Dog[] dogs = {new Dog(), new Dog()};
       Cat[] cats = {new Cat(), new Cat(), new Cat()};
       Bird[] birds = {new Bird()};

       AnimalDoctor doc - new AnimalDoctor();
       doc.checkAnimals(dogs);  // pass the Dog[]
       doc.checkAnimals(cats);  // pass the Cat[]
       doc.checkAnimals(birds); // pass the Bird[]
    }
}
```

This works fine, of course (we know, we know, this is old news). But here's why we brought this up as refresher—this approach does NOT work the same way with type safe collections!

In other words, a method that takes, say, an ArrayList<Animal> will NOT be able to accept a collection of any Animal subtype! That means ArrayList<Dog> cannot be passed into a method with an argument of ArrayList<Animal>, even though we already know that this works just fine with plain old arrays.

Obviously this difference between arrays and ArrayList is consistent with the polymorphism assignment rules we already looked at—the fact that you cannot assign an object of type ArrayList<JButton> to a List<Object>. But this is where you really start to feel the pain of the distinction between typed arrays and typed collections.

We know it won't work correctly, but let's try changing the AnimalDoctor code to use generics instead of arrays:

```
public class AnimalDoctorGeneric  {
```

```
    // change the argument from Animal[] to ArrayList<Animal>
    public void checkAnimals(ArrayList<Animal> animals) {
      for(Animal a : animals) {
        a.checkup();
      }
    }
    public static void main(String[] args) {
        // make ArrayLists instead of arrays for Dog, Cat, Bird
        List<Dog> dogs = new ArrayList<Dog>();
        dogs.add(new Dog());
        dogs.add(new Dog());
        List<Cat> cats = new ArrayList<Cat>();
        cats.add(new Cat());
        cats.add(new Cat());
        List<Bird> birds = new ArrayList<Bird>();
        birds.add(new Bird());
        // this code is the same as the Array version
        AnimalDoctorGeneric doc = new AnimalDoctorGeneric();
        // this worked when we used arrays instead of ArrayLists
        doc.checkAnimals(dogs);  // send a List<Dog>
        doc.checkAnimals(cats);  // send a List<Cat>
        doc.checkAnimals(birds); // send a List<Bird>
    }
}
```

So what does happen?

```
javac AnimalDoctorGeneric.java
AnimalDoctorGeneric.java:51: checkAnimals(java.util.
ArrayList<Animal>) in AnimalDoctorGeneric cannot be applied to
(java.util.List<Dog>)
        doc.checkAnimals(dogs);
            ^

AnimalDoctorGeneric.java:52: checkAnimals(java.util.
ArrayList<Animal>) in AnimalDoctorGeneric cannot be applied to
(java.util.List<Cat>)
        doc.checkAnimals(cats);
            ^

AnimalDoctorGeneric.java:53: checkAnimals(java.util.
ArrayList<Animal>) in AnimalDoctorGeneric cannot be applied to
(java.util.List<Bird>)
        doc.checkAnimals(birds);
            ^

3 errors
```

The compiler stops us with errors, not warnings. You simply CANNOT assign the individual ArrayLists of Animal subtypes (<Dog>, <Cat>, or <Bird>) to an ArrayList of the supertype <Animal>, which is the declared type of the argument.

This is one of the biggest gotchas for Java programmers who are so familiar with using polymorphism with arrays, where the same scenario (`Animal[]` can refer to `Dog[]`, `Cat[]`, or `Bird[]`) works as you would expect. So we have two real issues:

1. Why doesn't this work?
2. How do you get around it?

You'd hate us and all of the Sun engineers if we told you that there wasn't a way around it—that you had to accept it and write horribly inflexible code that tried to anticipate and code overloaded methods for each specific <type>. Fortunately, there is a way around it.

But first, why can't you do it if it works for arrays? Why can't you pass an ArrayList<Dog> into a method with an argument of ArrayList<Animal>?

We'll get there, but first let's step way back for a minute and consider this perfectly legal scenario:

```
Animal[] animals = new Animal[3];
animals[0] = new Cat();
animals[1] = new Dog();
```

Part of the benefit of declaring an array using a more abstract supertype is that the array itself can hold objects of multiple subtypes of the supertype, and then you can manipulate the array assuming everything in it can respond to the Animal interface (in other words, everything in the array can respond to method calls defined in the Animal class). So here, we're using polymorphism not for the object that the array reference points to, but rather what the array can actually HOLD—in this case, any subtype of Animal. You can do the same thing with generics:

```
List<Animal> animals = new ArrayList<Animal>();
animals.add(new Cat());  // OK
animals.add(new Dog());  // OK
```

So this part works with both arrays and generic collections—we can add an instance of a subtype into an array or collection declared with a supertype. You can add Dogs and Cats to an Animal array (`Animal[]`) or an Animal collection (ArrayList<Animal>).

And with arrays, this applies to what happens within a method:

```
public void addAnimal(Animal[] animals) {
    animals[0] = new Dog();  // no problem, any Animal works
                             // in Animal[]
}
```

So if this is true, and if you can put Dogs into an ArrayList<Animal>, then why can't you use that same kind of method scenario? Why can't you do this?

```
public void addAnimal(ArrayList<Animal> animals) {
    animals.add(new Dog()); // sometimes allowed...
}
```

Actually, you CAN do this under certain conditions. The code above WILL compile just fine IF what you pass into the method is also an ArrayList<Animal>. This is the part where it differs from arrays, because in the array version, you COULD pass a Dog[] into the method that takes an Animal[].

The ONLY thing you can pass to a method argument of ArrayList<Animal> is an ArrayList<Animal>! (Assuming you aren't trying to pass a subtype of ArrayList, since remember—the "base" type can be polymorphic.)

The question is still out there—why is this bad? And why is it bad for ArrayList but not arrays? Why can't you pass an ArrayList<Dog> to an argument of ArrayList<Animal>? Actually, the problem IS just as dangerous whether you're using arrays or a generic collection. It's just that the compiler and JVM behave differently for arrays vs. generic collections.

The reason it is dangerous to pass a collection (array or ArrayList) of a subtype into a method that takes a collection of a supertype, is because you might add something. And that means you might add the WRONG thing! This is probably really obvious, but just in case (and to reinforce), let's walk through some scenarios. The first one is simple:

```
public void foo() {
  Dog[] dogs = {new Dog(), new Dog()};
  addAnimal(dogs);  // no problem, send the Dog[] to the method
}
public void addAnimal(Animal[] animals) {
  animals[0] = new Dog();  // ok, any Animal subtype works
}
```

This is no problem. We passed a `Dog[]` into the method, and added a Dog to the array (which was allowed since the method parameter was type `Animal[]`, which can hold any Animal subtype). But what if we changed the calling code to

```
public void foo() {
  Cat[] cats = {new Cat(), new Cat()};
  addAnimal(cats);  // no problem, send the Cat[] to the method
}
```

and the original method stays the same:

```
public void addAnimal(Animal[] animals) {
    animals[0] = new Dog();  // Eeek! We just put a Dog
                             // in a Cat array!
}
```

The compiler thinks it is perfectly fine to add a Dog to an `Animal[]` array, since a Dog can be assigned to an Animal reference. The problem is, if you passed in an array of an Animal subtype (Cat, Dog, or Bird), the compiler does not know. The compiler does not realize that out on the heap somewhere is an array of type `Cat[]`, not `Animal[]`, and you're about to try to add a Dog to it. To the compiler, you have passed in an array of type Animal, so it has no way to recognize the problem.

THIS is the scenario we're trying to prevent, regardless of whether it's an array or an ArrayList. The difference is, the compiler lets you get away with it for arrays, but not for generic collections.

The reason the compiler won't let you pass an ArrayList<Dog> into a method that takes an ArrayList<Animal>, is because within the method, that parameter is of type ArrayList<Animal>, and that means you could put *any* kind of Animal into it. There would be no way for the compiler to stop you from putting a Dog into a List that was originally declared as <Cat>, but is now referenced from the <Animal> parameter.

We still have two questions…how do you get around it and why the heck does the compiler allow you to take that risk for arrays but not for ArrayList (or any other generic collection)?

The reason you can get away with compiling this for arrays is because there is a runtime exception (ArrayStoreException) that will prevent you from putting the wrong type of object into an array. If you send a `Dog` array into the method that takes an `Animal` array, and you add only Dogs (including Dog subtypes, of course) into the array now referenced by `Animal`, no problem. But if you DO try to add a Cat to the object that is actually a `Dog` array, you'll get the exception.

But there IS no equivalent exception for generics, because of type erasure! In other words, at runtime the JVM KNOWS the type of arrays, but does NOT know the type of a collection. All the generic type information is removed during compilation, so by the time it gets to the JVM, there is simply no way to recognize the disaster of putting a Cat into an ArrayList<Dog> and vice versa (and it becomes exactly like the problems you have when you use legacy, non-type safe code).

So this actually IS legal code:

```
public void addAnimal(List<Animal> animals) {
    animals.add(new Dog());   // this is always legal,
                              // since Dog can
                              // be assigned to an Animal
                              // reference
}
 public static void main(String[] args) {
    List<Animal> animals = new ArrayList<Animal>();
    animals.add(new Dog());
    animals.add(new Dog());
    AnimalDoctorGeneric doc = new AnimalDoctorGeneric();
    doc.addAnimal(animals); // OK, since animals matches
                            // the method arg
}
```

As long as the only thing you pass to the addAnimals(List<Animal>) is an ArrayList<Animal>, the compiler is pleased—knowing that any Animal subtype you add will be valid (you can always add a Dog to an Animal collection, yada, yada, yada). But if you try to invoke addAnimal() with an argument of any OTHER ArrayList type, the compiler will stop you, since at runtime the JVM would have no way to stop you from adding a Dog to what was created as a Cat collection.

For example, this code that changes the generic type to <Dog>, but without changing the addAnimal() method, will NOT compile:

```
public void addAnimal(List<Animal> animals) {
  animals.add(new Dog());   // still OK as always
}
public static void main(String[] args) {
  List<Dog> animals = new ArrayList<Dog>();
  animals.add(new Dog());
  animals.add(new Dog());
  AnimalDoctorGeneric doc = new AnimalDoctorGeneric();
  doc.addAnimal(animals); // THIS is where it breaks!
}
```

The compiler says something like:

```
javac AnimalDoctorGeneric.java
AnimalDoctorGeneric.java:49: addAnimal(java.util.List<Animal>)
in AnimalDoctorGeneric cannot be applied to (java.util.
List<Dog>)
        doc.addAnimal(animals);
            ^
1 error
```

Notice that this message is virtually the same one you'd get trying to invoke any method with the wrong argument. It's saying that you simply cannot invoke `addAnimal(List<Animal>)` using something whose reference was declared as List<Dog>. (It's the reference type, not the actual object type that matters—but remember—the generic type of an object is ALWAYS the same as the generic type declared on the reference. List<Dog> can refer ONLY to collections that are subtypes of List, but which were instantiated as generic type <Dog>.)

Once again, remember that once inside the `addAnimals()` method, all that matters is the type of the parameter—in this case, List<Animal>. (We changed it from ArrayList to List to keep our "base" type polymorphism cleaner.)

Back to the key question—how do we get around this? If the problem is related only to the danger of adding the wrong thing to the collection, what about the `checkup()` method that used the collection passed in as read-only? In other words, what about methods that invoke Animal methods on each thing in the collection, which will work regardless of which kind of ArrayList subtype is passed in?

And that's a clue! It's the `add()` method that is the problem, so what we need is a way to tell the compiler, "Hey, I'm using the collection passed in just to invoke methods on the elements—and I promise not to ADD anything into the collection." And there IS a mechanism to tell the compiler that you can take any generic subtype of the declared argument type because you won't be putting anything in the collection. And that mechanism is the wildcard `<?>`.

The method signature would change from

```
public void addAnimal(List<Animal> animals)
```

to

```
public void addAnimal(List<? extends Animal> animals)
```

By saying `<? extends Animal>`, we're saying, "I can be assigned a collection that is a subtype of List and typed for `<Animal>` or anything that *extends* Animal. And oh yes, I SWEAR that I will not ADD anything into the collection." (There's a little more to the story, but we'll get there.)

So of course the `addAnimal()` method above won't actually compile even with the wildcard notation, because that method DOES add something.

```
public void addAnimal(List<? extends Animal> animals) {
      animals.add(new Dog());   // NO! Can't add if we
                                // use <? extends Animal>
}
```

You'll get a very strange error that might look something like this:

```
javac AnimalDoctorGeneric.java
AnimalDoctorGeneric.java:38: cannot find symbol
symbol  : method add(Dog)
location: interface java.util.List<capture of ? extends Animal>
      animals.add(new Dog());
             ^
1 error
```

which basically says, "you can't add a Dog here." If we change the method so that it doesn't add anything, it works.

But wait—there's more. (And by the way, everything we've covered in this generics section is likely to be tested for on the exam, with the exception of "type erasure," for which you aren't required to know any details.)

First, the `<? extends Animal>` means that you can take any subtype of Animal; however, that subtype can be EITHER a subclass of a class (abstract or concrete) OR a type that implements the interface after the word `extends`. In other words, the keyword `extends` in the context of a wildcard represents BOTH subclasses and interface implementations. There is no `<? implements Serializable>` syntax. If you want to declare a method that takes anything that is of a type that implements Serializable, you'd still use `extends` like this:

```
void foo(List<? extends Serializable> list) // odd, but correct
                                            // to use "extends"
```

This looks strange since you would never say this in a class declaration because Serializable is an interface, not a class. But that's the syntax, so burn it in!

One more time—there is only ONE wildcard keyword that represents *both* interface implementations and subclasses. And that keyword is extends. But when you see it, think "Is-a", as in something that passes the instanceof test.

However, there is another scenario where you can use a wildcard AND still add to the collection, but in a safe way—the keyword super.

Imagine, for example, that you declared the method this way:

```
public void addAnimal(List<? super Dog> animals) {
  animals.add(new Dog());  // adding is sometimes OK with super
}
public static void main(String[] args) {
  List<Animal> animals = new ArrayList<Animal>();
  animals.add(new Dog());
  animals.add(new Dog());
  AnimalDoctorGeneric doc = new AnimalDoctorGeneric();
  doc.addAnimal(animals); // passing an Animal List
}
```

Now what you've said in this line

```
public void addAnimal(List<? super Dog> animals)
```

is essentially, "Hey compiler, please accept any List with a generic type that is of type Dog, or a supertype of Dog. Nothing lower in the inheritance tree can come in, but anything higher than Dog is OK."

You probably already recognize why this works. If you pass in a list of type Animal, then it's perfectly fine to add a Dog to it. If you pass in a list of type Dog, it's perfectly fine to add a Dog to it. And if you pass in a list of type Object, it's STILL fine to add a Dog to it. When you use the <? super ...> syntax, you are telling the compiler that you can accept the type on the right-hand side of super or any of its supertypes, since—and this is the key part that makes it work—a collection declared as any supertype of Dog will be able to accept a Dog as an element. List<Object> can take a Dog. List<Animal> can take a Dog. And List<Dog> can take a Dog. So passing any of those in will work. So the super keyword in wildcard notation lets you have a restricted, but still possible way to add to a collection.

So, the wildcard gives you polymorphic assignments, but with certain restrictions that you don't have for arrays. Quick question: are these two identical?

```
public void foo(List<?> list) { }
public void foo(List<Object> list) { }
```

If there IS a difference (and we're not yet saying there is), what is it?

There IS a huge difference. List<?>, which is the wildcard <?> without the keywords extends or super, simply means "any type." So that means any type of List can be assigned to the argument. That could be a List of <Dog>, <Integer>, <JButton>, <Socket>, whatever. And using the wildcard alone, without the keyword super (followed by a type), means that you cannot ADD anything to the list referred to as List<?>.

List<Object> is completely different from List<?>. List<Object> means that the method can take ONLY a List<Object>. Not a List<Dog>, or a List<Cat>. It does, however, mean that you can add to the list, since the compiler has already made certain that you're passing only a valid List<Object> into the method.

Based on the previous explanations, figure out if the following will work:

```
import java.util.*;
public class TestWildcards {
  public static void main(String[] args) {
    List<Integer> myList = new ArrayList<Integer>();
    Bar bar = new Bar();
    bar.doInsert(myList);
  }
}
class Bar {
  void doInsert(List<?> list) {
    list.add(new Dog());
  }
}
```

If not, where is the problem?

The problem is in the list.add() method within doInsert(). The <?> wildcard allows a list of ANY type to be passed to the method, but the add() method is not valid, for the reasons we explored earlier (that you could put the wrong kind of thing into the collection). So this time, the TestWildcards class is fine, but the Bar class won't compile because it does an add() in a method that uses a wildcard (without super). What if we change the doInsert() method to this:

```
public class TestWildcards {
  public static void main(String[] args) {
    List<Integer> myList = new ArrayList<Integer>();
    Bar bar = new Bar();
    bar.doInsert(myList);
  }
}
```

```
class Bar {
   void doInsert(List<Object> list) {
     list.add(new Dog());
   }
}
```

Now will it work? If not, why not?

This time, class Bar, with the doInsert() method, compiles just fine. The problem is that the TestWildcards code is trying to pass a List<Integer> into a method that can take ONLY a List<Object>. And *nothing* else can be substituted for <Object>.

By the way, List<? extends Object> and List<?> are absolutely identical! They both say, "I can refer to any type of object." But as you can see, neither of them are the same as List<Object>. One way to remember this is that if you see the wildcard notation (a question mark ?), this means "many possibilities". If you do NOT see the question mark, then it means the <type> in the brackets, and absolutely NOTHING ELSE. List<Dog> means List<Dog> and not List<Beagle>, List<Poodle>, or any other subtype of Dog. But List<? extends Dog> could mean List<Beagle>, List<Poodle>, and so on. Of course List<?> could be... anything at all.

Keep in mind that the wildcards can be used only for reference declarations (including arguments, variables, return types, and so on). They can't be used as the type parameter when you create a new typed collection. Think about that—while a reference can be abstract and polymorphic, the actual object created must be of a specific type. You have to lock down the type when you make the object using new.

As a little review before we move on with generics, look at the following statements and figure out which will compile:

```
1) List<?> list = new ArrayList<Dog>();
2) List<? extends Animal> aList = new ArrayList<Dog>();
3) List<?> foo = new ArrayList<? extends Animal>();
4) List<? extends Dog> cList = new ArrayList<Integer>();
5) List<? super Dog> bList = new ArrayList<Animal>();
6) List<? super Animal> dList = new ArrayList<Dog>();
```

The correct answers (the statements that compile) are 1, 2, and 5.
The three that won't compile are

■ Statement: List<?> foo = new ArrayList<? extends Animal>();
    Problem: you cannot use wildcard notation in the object creation. So the
    new ArrayList<? extends Animal>() will not compile.

- Statement: `List<? extends Dog> cList =`
  `new ArrayList<Integer>();`

  Problem: You cannot assign an Integer list to a reference that takes only a Dog (including any subtypes of Dog, of course).

- Statement: `List<? super Animal> dList = new ArrayList<Dog>();`

  Problem: You cannot assign a Dog to <? super Animal>. The Dog is too "low" in the class hierarchy. Only <Animal> or <Object> would have been legal.

Generic Declarations

Until now, we've talked about how to create type safe collections, and how to declare reference variables including arguments and return types using generic syntax. But here are a few questions: How do we even know that we're allowed/ supposed to specify a type for these collection classes? And does generic typing work with any other classes in the API? And finally, can we declare our own classes as generic types? In other words, can we make a class that requires that someone pass a type in when they declare it and instantiate it?

First, the one you obviously know the answer to—the API tells you when a parameterized type is expected. For example, this is the API declaration for the java.util.List interface:

```
public interface List<E>
```

The <E> is a placeholder for the type you pass in. The List interface is behaving as a generic "template" (sort of like C++ templates), and when you write your code, you change it from a generic List to a List<Dog> or List<Integer>, and so on.

The E, by the way, is only a convention. Any valid Java identifier would work here, but E stands for "Element," and it's used when the template is a collection. The other main convention is T (stands for "type"), used for, well, things that are NOT collections.

Now that you've seen the interface declaration for List, what do you think the add() method looks like?

```
boolean add(E o)
```

In other words, whatever E is when you declare the List, *that's what you can add to it.* So imagine this code:

```
List<Animal> list = new ArrayList<Animal>();
```

The E in the List API suddenly has its waveform collapsed, and goes from the abstract <your type goes here>, to a List of Animals. And if it's a List of Animals, then the add() method of List must obviously behave like this:

```
boolean add(Animal a)
```

When you look at an API for a generics class or interface, pick a type parameter (Dog, JButton, even Object) and do a mental find and replace on each instance of E (or whatever identifier is used as the placeholder for the type parameter).

Making Your Own Generic Class

Let's try making our own generic class, to get a feel for how it works, and then we'll look at a few remaining generics syntax details. Imagine someone created a class Rental, that manages a pool of rentable items.

```
public class Rental {
    private List rentalPool;
    private int maxNum;
    public Rental(int maxNum, List rentalPool) {
        this.maxNum = maxNum;
        this.rentalPool = rentalPool;
    }
    public Object getRental() {
        // blocks until there's something available
        return rentalPool.get(0);
    }
    public void returnRental(Object o) {
        rentalPool.add(o);
    }
}
```

Now imagine you wanted to make a subclass of Rental that was just for renting cars. You might start with something like this:

```
import java.util.*;
public class CarRental extends Rental {
    public CarRental(int maxNum, List<Car> rentalPool) {
        super(maxNum, rentalPool);
    }
    public Car getRental() {
        return (Car) super.getRental();
    }
```

```
    public void returnRental(Car c) {
      super.returnRental(c);
    }
    public void returnRental(Object o) {
      if (o instanceof Car) {
        super.returnRental(o);
      } else {
        System.out.println("Cannot add a non-Car");
        // probably throw an exception
} } }
```

But then the more you look at it, the more you realize:

1. You are doing your own type checking in the `returnRental()` method.
    You can't change the argument type of `returnRental()` to take a Car,
    since it's an override (not an overload) of the method from class Rental.
    (Overloading would take away your polymorphic flexibility with Rental).

2. You really don't want to make separate subclasses for every possible kind of
    rentable thing (cars, computers, bowling shoes, children, and so on).

But given your natural brilliance (heightened by this contrived scenario), you
quickly realize that you can make the Rental class a generic type—a template for any
kind of Rentable thing—and you're good to go.

(We did say contrived...since in reality, you might very well want to have
different behaviors for different kinds of rentable things, but even that could be
solved cleanly through some kind of behavior composition as opposed to inheritance
(using the Strategy design pattern, for example). And no, design patterns aren't on
the exam, but we still think you should read our design patterns book. Think of the
kittens.) So here's your new and improved generic Rental class:

```
import java.util.*;
public class RentalGeneric<T> {  // "T" is for the type
                                 // parameter
  private List<T> rentalPool;    // Use the class type for the
                                 // List type
  private int maxNum;
  public RentalGeneric(
    int maxNum, List<T> rentalPool) { // constructor takes a
                                      // List of the class type
    this.maxNum = maxNum;
    this.rentalPool = rentalPool;
  }
```

```
    public T getRental() {                          // we rent out a T
      // blocks until there's something available
      return rentalPool.get(0);
    }
    public void returnRental(T returnedThing) { // and the renter
                                                // returns a T
      rentalPool.add(returnedThing);
    }
}
```

Let's put it to the test:

```
class TestRental {
  public static void main (String[] args) {
      //make some Cars for the pool
      Car c1 = new Car();
      Car c2 = new Car();
      List<Car> carList = new ArrayList<Car>();
      carList.add(c1);
      carList.add(c2);
      RentalGeneric<Car> carRental = new
                      RentalGeneric<Car>(2, carList);
      // now get a car out, and it won't need a cast
      Car carToRent = carRental.getRental();
      carRental.returnRental(carToRent);
      // can we stick something else in the original carList?
      carList.add(new Cat("Fluffy"));
  }
}
```

We get one error:

```
kathy% javac1.5 RentalGeneric.java
RentalGeneric.java:38: cannot find symbol
symbol   : method add(Cat)
location: interface java.util.List<Car>
    carList.add(new Cat("Fluffy"));
                ^
1 error
```

Now we have a Rental class that can be *typed* to whatever the programmer chooses, and the compiler will enforce it. In other words, it works just as the

Collections classes do. Let's look at more examples of generic syntax you might find in the API or source code. Here's another simple class that uses the parameterized type of the class in several ways:

```
public class TestGenerics<T> {  // as the class type
   T anInstance;                 // as an instance variable type
   T [] anArrayOfTs;             // as an array type

   TestGenerics(T anInstance) {    // as an argument type
      this.anInstance = anInstance;
   }
   T getT() {                      // as a return type
      return anInstance;
   }
}
```

Obviously this is a ridiculous use of generics, and in fact you'll see generics only rarely outside of collections. But, you do need to understand the different kinds of generic syntax you might encounter, so we'll continue with these examples until we've covered them all.

You can use more than one parameterized type in a single class definition:

```
public class UseTwo<T, X> {
  T one;
  X two;
  UseTwo(T one, X two) {
    this.one = one;
    this.two = two;
  }
  T getT() { return one; }
  X getX() { return two; }

// test it by creating it with <String, Integer>

  public static void main (String[] args) {
    UseTwo<String, Integer> twos =
                    new UseTwo<String, Integer>("foo", 42);

    String theT = twos.getT(); // returns a String
    int theX = twos.getX();   // returns Integer, unboxes to int
  }
}
```

And you can use a form of wildcard notation in a class definition, to specify a range (called "bounds") for the type that can be used for the type parameter:

```
public class AnimalHolder<T extends Animal> { // use "T" instead
                                               // of "?"
  T animal;
  public static void main(String[] args) {
    AnimalHolder<Dog> dogHolder = new AnimalHolder<Dog>(); // OK
    AnimalHolder<Integer> x = new AnimalHolder<Integer>(); // NO!
  }
}
```

Creating Generic Methods

Until now, every example we've seen uses the class parameter type—the type declared with the class name. For example, in the UseTwo<T,X> declaration, we used the T and X placeholders throughout the code. But it's possible to define a parameterized type at a more granular level—a method.

Imagine you want to create a method that takes an instance of any type, instantiates an ArrayList of that type, and adds the instance to the ArrayList. The class itself doesn't need to be generic; basically we just want a utility method that we can pass a type to and that can use that type to construct a type safe collection. Using a generic method, we can declare the method without a specific type and then get the type information based on the type of the object passed to the method. For example:

```
import java.util.*;
public class CreateAnArrayList {
  public <T> void makeArrayList(T t) { // take an object of an
                                       // unknown type and use a
                                       // "T" to represent the type
    List<T> list = new ArrayList<T>(); // now we can create the
                                       // list using "T"
    list.add(t);
  }
}
```

In the preceding code, if you invoke the makeArrayList() method with a Dog instance, the method will behave as though it looked like this all along:

```
public void makeArrayList(Dog t) {
  List<Dog> list = new ArrayList<Dog>();
  list.add(t);
}
```

And of course if you invoke the method with an Integer, then the T is replaced by Integer (not in the bytecode, remember—we're describing how it appears to behave, not how it actually gets it done).

The strangest thing about generic methods is that you must declare the type variable BEFORE the return type of the method:

```
public <T> void makeArrayList(T t)
```

The <T> before void simply defines what T is before you use it as a type in the argument. You MUST declare the type like that unless the type is specified for the class. In CreateAnArrayList, the class is not generic, so there's no type parameter placeholder we can use.

You're also free to put boundaries on the type you declare, for example, if you want to restrict the makeArrayList() method to only Number or its subtypes (Integer, Float, and so on) you would say

```
public <T extends Number> void makeArrayList(T t)
```

e x a m
watch

It's tempting to forget that the method argument is NOT where you declare the type parameter variable T. In order to use a type variable like T, you must have declared it either as the class parameter type or in the method, before the return type. The following might look right,

```
public void makeList(T t) { }
```

But the only way for this to be legal is if there is actually a class named T, in which case the argument is like any other type declaration for a variable. And what about constructor arguments? They, too, can be declared with a generic type, but then it looks even stranger since constructors have no return type at all:

```
public class Radio {
    public <T> Radio(T t) { }  // legal constructor
}
```

e x a m

ⓦatch

If you REALLY want to get ridiculous (or fired), you can declare a class with a name that is the same as the type parameter placeholder:

```
class X { public <X> X(X x) { } }
```

Yes, this works. The X that is the constructor name has no relationship to the <X> type declaration, which has no relationship to the constructor argument identifier, which is also, of course, X. The compiler is able to parse this and treat each of the different uses of X independently. So there is no naming conflict between class names, type parameter placeholders, and variable identifiers.

e x a m

ⓦatch

One of the most common mistakes programmers make when creating generic classes or methods is to use a <?> in the wildcard syntax rather than a type variable <T>, <E>, and so on. This code might look right, but isn't:

```
public class NumberHolder<? extends Number> { }
```

While the question mark works when declaring a reference for a variable, it does NOT work for generic class and method declarations. This code is not legal:

```
public class NumberHolder<?> { ? aNum; }      // NO!
```

But if you replace the <?> with a legal identifier, you're good:

```
public class NumberHolder<T> { T aNum; }      // Yes
```

98% of what you're likely to do with generics is simply declare and use type safe collections, including using (and passing) them as arguments. But now you know much more (but by no means everything) about the way generics works.

If this was clear and easy for you, that's excellent. If it was…painful…just know that adding generics to the Java language very nearly caused a revolt among some of the most experienced Java developers. Most of the outspoken critics are simply unhappy with the complexity, or aren't convinced that gaining type safe collections is worth the ten million little rules you have to learn now. It's true that with Java 5, learning Java just got harder. But trust us…we've never seen it take more than two days to "get" generics. That's 48 consecutive hours.

CERTIFICATION SUMMARY

We began with a quick review of the `toString()` method. The `toString()` method is automatically called when you ask `System.out.println()` to print an object—you override it to return a String of meaningful data about your objects.

Next we reviewed the purpose of `==` (to see if two reference variables refer to the same object) and the `equals()` method (to see if two objects are meaningfully equivalent). You learned the downside of not overriding `equals()`—you may not be able to find the object in a collection. We discussed a little bit about how to write a good `equals()` method—don't forget to use `instanceof` and refer to the object's significant attributes. We reviewed the contracts for overriding `equals()` and `hashCode()`. We learned about the theory behind hashcodes, the difference between legal, appropriate, and efficient hashcoding. We also saw that even though wildly inefficient, it's legal for a `hashCode()` method to always return the same value.

Next we turned to collections, where we learned about Lists, Sets, and Maps, and the difference between ordered and sorted collections. We learned the key attributes of the common collection classes, and when to use which.

We covered the ins and outs of the Collections and Arrays classes: how to sort, and how to search. We learned about converting arrays to Lists and back again.

Finally we tackled generics. Generics let you enforce compile-time type-safety on collections or other classes. Generics help assure you that when you get an item from a collection it will be of the type you expect, with no casting required. You can mix legacy code with generics code, but this can cause exceptions. The rules for polymorphism change when you use generics, although by using wildcards you can still create polymorphic collections. Some generics declarations allow reading of a collection, but allow very limited updating of the collection.

All in all, one fascinating chapter.

TWO-MINUTE DRILL

Here are some of the key points from this chapter.

Overriding hashCode() and equals() (Objective 6.2)

❑ `equals()`, `hashCode()`, and `toString()` are public.

❑ Override `toString()` so that `System.out.println()` or other methods can see something useful, like your object's state.

❑ Use `==` to determine if two reference variables refer to the same object.

❑ Use `equals()` to determine if two objects are meaningfully equivalent.

❑ If you don't override `equals()`, your objects won't be useful hashing keys.

❑ If you don't override `equals()`, different objects can't be considered equal.

❑ Strings and wrappers override `equals()` and make good hashing keys.

❑ When overriding `equals()`, use the `instanceof` operator to be sure you're evaluating an appropriate class.

❑ When overriding `equals()`, compare the objects' significant attributes.

❑ Highlights of the `equals()` contract:

  ❑ Reflexive: `x.equals(x)` is true.

  ❑ Symmetric: If `x.equals(y)` is true, then `y.equals(x)` must be true.

  ❑ Transitive: If `x.equals(y)` is true, and `y.equals(z)` is true, then `z.equals(x)` is true.

  ❑ Consistent: Multiple calls to `x.equals(y)` will return the same result.

  ❑ Null: If `x` is not `null`, then `x.equals(null)` is false.

❑ If `x.equals(y)` is true, then `x.hashCode() == y.hashCode()` is true.

❑ If you override `equals()`, override `hashCode()`.

❑ HashMap, HashSet, Hashtable, LinkedHashMap, & LinkedHashSet use hashing.

❑ An appropriate `hashCode()` override sticks to the `hashCode()` contract.

❑ An efficient `hashCode()` override distributes keys evenly across its buckets.

❑ An overridden `equals()` must be at least as precise as its `hashCode()` mate.

❑ To reiterate: if two objects are equal, their hashcodes must be equal.

❑ It's legal for a `hashCode()` method to return the same value for all instances (although in practice it's very inefficient).

❑ Highlights of the `hashCode()` contract:

   ❑ Consistent: multiple calls to `x.hashCode()` return the same integer.

   ❑ If `x.equals(y)` is `true`, `x.hashCode() == y.hashCode()` is `true`.

   ❑ If `x.equals(y)` is `false`, then `x.hashCode() == y.hashCode()` can be either `true` or `false`, but `false` will tend to create better efficiency.

❑ `transient` variables aren't appropriate for `equals()` and `hashCode()`.

Collections (Objective 6.1)

❑ Common collection activities include adding objects, removing objects, verifying object inclusion, retrieving objects, and iterating.

❑ Three meanings for "collection":

   ❑ **collection**   Represents the data structure in which objects are stored

   ❑ **Collection**   java.util interface from which Set and List extend

   ❑ **Collections**   A class that holds static collection utility methods

❑ Four basic flavors of collections include Lists, Sets, Maps, Queues:

   ❑ **Lists of things**   Ordered, duplicates allowed, with an index.

   ❑ **Sets of things**   May or may not be ordered and/or sorted; duplicates not allowed.

   ❑ **Maps of things with keys**   May or may not be ordered and/or sorted; duplicate keys are not allowed.

   ❑ **Queues of things to process**   Ordered by FIFO or by priority.

❑ Four basic sub-flavors of collections Sorted, Unsorted, Ordered, Unordered.

   ❑ **Ordered**   Iterating through a collection in a specific, non-random order.

   ❑ **Sorted**   Iterating through a collection in a sorted order.

❑ Sorting can be alphabetic, numeric, or programmer-defined.

Key Attributes of Common Collection Classes (Objective 6.1)

❑ ArrayList: Fast iteration and fast random access.

❑ Vector: It's like a slower ArrayList, but it has synchronized methods.

❑ LinkedList: Good for adding elements to the ends, i.e., stacks and queues.

❑ HashSet: Fast access, assures no duplicates, provides no ordering.

❑ LinkedHashSet: No duplicates; iterates by insertion order.

❑ TreeSet: No duplicates; iterates in sorted order.

❑ HashMap: Fastest updates (key/values); allows one `null` key, many `null` values.

❑ Hashtable: Like a slower HashMap (as with Vector, due to its synchronized methods). No `null` values or `null` keys allowed.

❑ LinkedHashMap: Faster iterations; iterates by insertion order or last accessed; allows one `null` key, many `null` values.

❑ TreeMap: A sorted map.

❑ PriorityQueue: A to-do list ordered by the elements' priority.

Using Collection Classes (Objective 6.3)

❑ Collections hold only Objects, but primitives can be autoboxed.

❑ Iterate with the enhanced `for`, or with an Iterator via `hasNext()` & `next()`.

❑ `hasNext()` determines if more elements exist; the Iterator does NOT move.

❑ `next()` returns the next element AND moves the Iterator forward.

❑ To work correctly, a Map's keys must override `equals()` and `hashCode()`.

❑ Queues use `offer()` to add an element, `poll()` to remove the head of the queue, and `peek()` to look at the head of a queue.

❑ As of Java 6 TreeSets and TreeMaps have new navigation methods like floor() and higher().

❑ You can create/extend "backed" sub-copies of TreeSets and TreeMaps.

Sorting and Searching Arrays and Lists (Objective 6.5)

❑ Sorting can be in natural order, or via a Comparable or many Comparators.

❑ Implement Comparable using `compareTo()`; provides only one sort order.

❑ Create many Comparators to sort a class many ways; implement `compare()`.

❑ To be sorted and searched, a List's elements must be *comparable*.

❑ To be searched, an array or List must first be sorted.

Utility Classes: Collections and Arrays (Objective 6.5)

❑ Both of these java.util classes provide

   ❑ A `sort()` method. Sort using a Comparator or sort using natural order.

   ❑ A `binarySearch()` method. Search a pre-sorted array or List.

❏ `Arrays.asList()` creates a List from an array and links them together.

❏ `Collections.reverse()` reverses the order of elements in a List.

❏ `Collections.reverseOrder()` returns a Comparator that sorts in reverse.

❏ Lists and Sets have a `toArray()` method to create arrays.

Generics (Objective 6.4)

❏ Generics let you enforce compile-time type safety on Collections (or other classes and methods declared using generic type parameters).

❏ An ArrayList<Animal> can accept references of type Dog, Cat, or any other subtype of Animal (subclass, or if Animal is an interface, implementation).

❏ When using generic collections, a cast is not needed to get (declared type) elements out of the collection. With non-generic collections, a cast is required:

```
List<String> gList = new ArrayList<String>();
List list = new ArrayList();
// more code
String s = gList.get(0);              // no cast needed
String s = (String)list.get(0);       // cast required
```

❏ You can pass a generic collection into a method that takes a non-generic collection, but the results may be disastrous. The compiler can't stop the method from inserting the wrong type into the previously type safe collection.

❏ If the compiler can recognize that non-type-safe code is potentially endangering something you originally declared as type-safe, you will get a compiler warning. For instance, if you pass a List<String> into a method declared as

```
void foo(List aList) { aList.add(anInteger); }
```

You'll get a warning because add() is potentially "unsafe".

❏ "Compiles without error" is not the same as "compiles without warnings." A compilation *warning* is not considered a compilation *error* or *failure*.

❏ Generic type information does not exist at runtime—it is for compile-time safety only. Mixing generics with legacy code can create compiled code that may throw an exception at runtime.

❏ Polymorphic assignments applies only to the base type, not the generic type parameter. You can say

```
List<Animal> aList = new ArrayList<Animal>();    // yes
```

You can't say

```
List<Animal> aList = new ArrayList<Dog>();        // no
```

❑ The polymorphic assignment rule applies everywhere an assignment can be made. The following are NOT allowed:

```
void foo(List<Animal> aList) { }  // cannot take a List<Dog>
List<Animal> bar() { }            // cannot return a List<Dog>
```

❑ Wildcard syntax allows a generic method, accept subtypes (or supertypes) of the declared type of the method argument:

```
void addD(List<Dog> d) {}  // can take only <Dog>
void addD(List<? extends Dog>) {} // take a <Dog> or <Beagle>
```

❑ The wildcard keyword extends is used to mean either "extends" or "implements." So in <? extends Dog>, Dog can be a class or an interface.

❑ When using a wildcard, List<? extends Dog>, the collection can be accessed but not modified.

❑ When using a wildcard, List<?>, any generic type can be assigned to the reference, but for access only, no modifications.

❑ List<Object> refers only to a List<Object>, while List<?> or List<? extends Object> can hold any type of object, but for access only.

❑ Declaration conventions for generics use T for type and E for element:

```
public interface List<E>  // API declaration for List
boolean add(E o)          // List.add() declaration
```

❑ The generics type identifier can be used in class, method, and variable declarations:

```
class Foo<t> { }       // a class
T anInstance;          // an instance variable
Foo(T aRef) {}         // a constructor argument
void bar(T aRef) {}    // a method argument
T baz() {}             // a return type
```

The compiler will substitute the actual type.

❑ You can use more than one parameterized type in a declaration:

```
public class UseTwo<T, X> { }
```

❑ You can declare a generic method using a type not defined in the class:

```
public <T> void makeList(T t) { }
```

is NOT using T as the return type. This method has a void return type, but to use T within the method's argument you must declare the <T>, which happens before the return type.

SELF TEST

1. Given:

```
public static void main(String[] args) {

    // INSERT DECLARATION HERE
    for (int i = 0; i <= 10; i++) {
      List<Integer> row = new ArrayList<Integer>();
      for (int j = 0; j <= 10; j++)
        row.add(i * j);
      table.add(row);
    }
    for (List<Integer> row : table)
      System.out.println(row);
}
```

Which statements could be inserted at `// INSERT DECLARATION HERE` to allow this code to compile and run? (Choose all that apply.)

A. `List<List<Integer>> table = new List<List<Integer>>();`

B. `List<List<Integer>> table = new ArrayList<List<Integer>>();`

C. `List<List<Integer>> table = new ArrayList<ArrayList<Integer>>();`

D. `List<List, Integer> table = new List<List, Integer>();`

E. `List<List, Integer> table = new ArrayList<List, Integer>();`

F. `List<List, Integer> table = new ArrayList<ArrayList, Integer>();`

G. None of the above

2. Which statements are true about comparing two instances of the same class, given that the `equals()` and `hashCode()` methods have been properly overridden? (Choose all that apply.)

A. If the `equals()` method returns true, the `hashCode()` comparison `==` might return false

B. If the `equals()` method returns false, the `hashCode()` comparison `==` might return true

C. If the `hashCode()` comparison `==` returns true, the `equals()` method must return true

D. If the `hashCode()` comparison `==` returns true, the `equals()` method might return true

E. If the `hashCode()` comparison `!=` returns true, the `equals()` method might return true

3. Given:

```
public static void before() {
  Set set = new TreeSet();
  set.add("2");
  set.add(3);
  set.add("1");
  Iterator it = set.iterator();
    while (it.hasNext())
  System.out.print(it.next() + " ");
}
```

Which statements are true?

A. The `before()` method will print 1 2

B. The `before()` method will print 1 2 3

C. The `before()` method will print three numbers, but the order cannot be determined

D. The `before()` method will not compile

E. The `before()` method will throw an exception at runtime

4. Given:

```
import java.util.*;
class MapEQ {
  public static void main(String[] args) {
    Map<ToDos, String> m = new HashMap<ToDos, String>();
    ToDos t1 = new ToDos("Monday");
    ToDos t2 = new ToDos("Monday");
    ToDos t3 = new ToDos("Tuesday");
    m.put(t1, "doLaundry");
    m.put(t2, "payBills");
    m.put(t3, "cleanAttic");
    System.out.println(m.size());
  }
}
class ToDos{
  String day;
  ToDos(String d) { day = d; }
  public boolean equals(Object o) {
    return ((ToDos)o).day == this.day;
  }
  // public int hashCode() { return 9; }
}
```

Which is correct? (Choose all that apply.)

A. As the code stands it will not compile

B. As the code stands the output will be 2

C. As the code stands the output will be 3

D. If the `hashCode()` method is uncommented the output will be 2

E. If the `hashCode()` method is uncommented the output will be 3

F. If the `hashCode()` method is uncommented the code will not compile

5. Given:

```
12. public class AccountManager {
13.       private Map accountTotals = new HashMap();
14.       private int retirementFund;
15.
16.       public int getBalance(String accountName) {
17.           Integer total = (Integer) accountTotals.get(accountName);
18.           if (total == null)
19.               total = Integer.valueOf(0);
20.           return total.intValue();
21.       }
23.       public void setBalance(String accountName, int amount) {
24.           accountTotals.put(accountName, Integer.valueOf(amount));
25.       }
26. }
```

This class is to be updated to make use of appropriate generic types, with no changes in behavior (for better or worse). Which of these steps could be performed? (Choose three.)

A. Replace line 13 with
```
private Map<String, int> accountTotals = new HashMap<String, int>();
```

B. Replace line 13 with
```
private Map<String, Integer> accountTotals = new HashMap<String, Integer>();
```

C. Replace line 13 with
```
private Map<String<Integer>> accountTotals = new HashMap<String<Integer>>();
```

D. Replace lines 17–20 with
```
int total = accountTotals.get(accountName);
if (total == null)
    total = 0;
return total;
```

E. Replace lines 17–20 with
```
Integer total = accountTotals.get(accountName);
if (total == null)
    total = 0;
return total;
```

F. Replace lines 17–20 with
```
return accountTotals.get(accountName);
```

G. Replace line 24 with
```
accountTotals.put(accountName, amount);
```

H. Replace line 24 with
```
accountTotals.put(accountName, amount.intValue());
```

6. Given:

```
interface Hungry<E> { void munch(E x); }
interface Carnivore<E extends Animal> extends Hungry<E> {}
interface Herbivore<E extends Plant> extends Hungry<E> {}
abstract class Plant {}
class Grass extends Plant {}
abstract class Animal {}
class Sheep extends Animal implements Herbivore<Sheep> {
  public void munch(Sheep x) {}
}
class Wolf extends Animal implements Carnivore<Sheep> {
  public void munch(Sheep x) {}
}
```

Which of the following changes (taken separately) would allow this code to compile? (Choose all that apply.)

A. Change the Carnivore interface to
```
interface Carnivore<E extends Plant> extends Hungry<E> {}
```

B. Change the Herbivore interface to
```
interface Herbivore<E extends Animal> extends Hungry<E> {}
```

C. Change the Sheep class to
```
class Sheep extends Animal implements Herbivore<Plant> {
    public void munch(Grass x) {}
}
```

D. Change the Sheep class to
```
class Sheep extends Plant implements Carnivore<Wolf> {
    public void munch(Wolf x) {}
}
```

E. Change the Wolf class to

```
class Wolf extends Animal implements Herbivore<Grass> {
    public void munch(Grass x) {}
}
```

F. No changes are necessary

7. Which collection class(es) allows you to grow or shrink its size and provides indexed access to its elements, but whose methods are not synchronized? (Choose all that apply.)

A. `java.util.HashSet`

B. `java.util.LinkedHashSet`

C. `java.util.List`

D. `java.util.ArrayList`

E. `java.util.Vector`

F. `java.util.PriorityQueue`

8. Given a method declared as

```
public static <E extends Number> List<E> process(List<E> nums)
```

A programmer wants to use this method like this

```
// INSERT DECLARATIONS HERE

output = process(input);
```

Which pairs of declarations could be placed at `// INSERT DECLARATIONS HERE` to allow the code to compile? (Choose all that apply.)

A. `ArrayList<Integer> input = null;`
   `ArrayList<Integer> output = null;`

B. `ArrayList<Integer> input = null;`
   `List<Integer> output = null;`

C. `ArrayList<Integer> input = null;`
   `List<Number> output = null;`

D.
```
List<Number> input = null;
ArrayList<Integer> output = null;
```

E.
```
List<Number> input = null;
List<Number> output = null;
```

F.
```
List<Integer> input = null;
List<Integer> output = null;
```

G. None of the above

9. Given the proper import statement(s), and

```
13.     PriorityQueue<String> pq = new PriorityQueue<String>();
14.     pq.add("2");
15.     pq.add("4");
16.     System.out.print(pq.peek() + " ");
17.     pq.offer("1");
18.     pq.add("3");
19.     pq.remove("1");
20.     System.out.print(pq.poll() + " ");
21.     if(pq.remove("2")) System.out.print(pq.poll() + " ");
22.     System.out.println(pq.poll() + " " + pq.peek());
```

What is the result?

A. 2 2 3 3

B. 2 2 3 4

C. 1 3 3 4

D. 2 2 3 3 3

E. 4 3 3 3 3

F. 2 2 3 3 4

G. Compilation fails

H. An exception is thrown at runtime

10. Given:

```
3.  import java.util.*;
4.  public class Mixup {
5.    public static void main(String[] args) {
```

```
6.      Object o = new Object();
7.      // insert code here
8.      s.add("o");
9.      s.add(o);
10.   }
11. }
```

And these three fragments:

```
I.   Set s = new HashSet();
II.  TreeSet s = new TreeSet();
III. LinkedHashSet s = new LinkedHashSet();
```

When fragments I, II, or III are inserted, independently, at line 7, which are true? (Choose all that apply.)

A. Fragment I compiles

B. Fragment II compiles

C. Fragment III compiles

D. Fragment I executes without exception

E. Fragment II executes without exception

F. Fragment III executes without exception

11. Given:

```
3. import java.util.*;
4. class Turtle {
5.    int size;
6.    public Turtle(int s) { size = s; }
7.    public boolean equals(Object o) { return (this.size == ((Turtle)o).size); }
8.    // insert code here
9. }
10. public class TurtleTest {
11.    public static void main(String[] args) {
12.       LinkedHashSet<Turtle> t = new LinkedHashSet<Turtle>();
13.       t.add(new Turtle(1));   t.add(new Turtle(2));   t.add(new Turtle(1));
14.       System.out.println(t.size());
15.    }
16. }
```

And these two fragments:

```
I.   public int hashCode() { return size/5; }
II.  // no hashCode method declared
```

If fragment I or II is inserted, independently, at line 8, which are true? (Choose all that apply.)

A. If fragment I is inserted, the output is 2

B. If fragment I is inserted, the output is 3

C. If fragment II is inserted, the output is 2

D. If fragment II is inserted, the output is 3

E. If fragment I is inserted, compilation fails

F. If fragment II is inserted, compilation fails

12. Given the proper import statement(s), and:

```
13.    TreeSet<String> s = new TreeSet<String>();
14.    TreeSet<String> subs = new TreeSet<String>();
15.    s.add("a"); s.add("b"); s.add("c"); s.add("d"); s.add("e");
16.
17.    subs = (TreeSet)s.subSet("b", true, "d", true);
18.    s.add("g");
19.    s.pollFirst();
20.    s.pollFirst();
21.    s.add("c2");
22.    System.out.println(s.size() +" "+ subs.size());
```

Which are true? (Choose all that apply.)

A. The size of s is 4

B. The size of s is 5

C. The size of s is 7

D. The size of subs is 1

E. The size of subs is 2

F. The size of subs is 3

G. The size of subs is 4

H. An exception is thrown at runtime

13. Given:

```
 3. import java.util.*;
 4. public class Magellan {
 5.   public static void main(String[] args) {
 6.     TreeMap<String, String> myMap = new TreeMap<String, String>();
 7.     myMap.put("a", "apple"); myMap.put("d", "date");
 8.     myMap.put("f", "fig"); myMap.put("p", "pear");
 9.     System.out.println("1st after mango: " +   // sop 1
10.       myMap.higherKey("f"));
11.     System.out.println("1st after mango: " +   // sop 2
12.       myMap.ceilingKey("f"));
13.     System.out.println("1st after mango: " +   // sop 3
14.       myMap.floorKey("f"));
15.     SortedMap<String, String> sub = new TreeMap<String, String>();
16.     sub = myMap.tailMap("f");
17.     System.out.println("1st after mango: " +   // sop 4
18.       sub.firstKey());
19.   }
20. }
```

Which of the System.out.println statements will produce the output 1st after mango: p?
(Choose all that apply.)

A. sop 1

B. sop 2

C. sop 3

D. sop 4

E. None; compilation fails

F. None; an exception is thrown at runtime

14. Given:

```
 3. import java.util.*;
 4. class Business { }
 5. class Hotel extends Business { }
 6. class Inn extends Hotel { }
 7. public class Travel {
 8.   ArrayList<Hotel> go() {
 9.     // insert code here
10.   }
11. }
```

Which, inserted independently at line 9, will compile? (Choose all that apply.)

A. `return new ArrayList<Inn>();`

B. `return new ArrayList<Hotel>();`

C. `return new ArrayList<Object>();`

D. `return new ArrayList<Business>();`

15. Given:

```
3.  import java.util.*;
4.  class Dog { int size; Dog(int s) { size = s; } }
5.  public class FirstGrade {
6.    public static void main(String[] args) {
7.      TreeSet<Integer> i = new TreeSet<Integer>();
8.      TreeSet<Dog> d = new TreeSet<Dog>();
9.
10.     d.add(new Dog(1));   d.add(new Dog(2));   d.add(new Dog(1));
11.     i.add(1);            i.add(2);            i.add(1);
12.     System.out.println(d.size() + " " + i.size());
13.   }
14. }
```

What is the result?

A. 1 2

B. 2 2

C. 2 3

D. 3 2

E. 3 3

F. Compilation fails

G. An exception is thrown at runtime

16. Given:

```
3.  import java.util.*;
4.  public class GeoCache {
5.    public static void main(String[] args) {
6.      String[] s = {"map", "pen", "marble", "key"};
7.      Othello o = new Othello();
```

```
8.      Arrays.sort(s,o);
9.      for(String s2: s) System.out.print(s2 + " ");
10.     System.out.println(Arrays.binarySearch(s, "map"));
11.   }
12.   static class Othello implements Comparator<String> {
13.     public int compare(String a, String b) { return b.compareTo(a); }
14.   }
15. }
```

Which are true? (Choose all that apply.)

A. Compilation fails

B. The output will contain a 1

C. The output will contain a 2

D. The output will contain a –1

E. An exception is thrown at runtime

F. The output will contain `"key map marble pen"`

G. The output will contain `"pen marble map key"`

SELF TEST ANSWERS

1. Given:

```
public static void main(String[] args) {
  // INSERT DECLARATION HERE
  for (int i = 0; i <= 10; i++) {
    List<Integer> row = new ArrayList<Integer>();
    for (int j = 0; j <= 10; j++)
      row.add(i * j);
    table.add(row);
  }
  for (List<Integer> row : table)
    System.out.println(row);
}
```

Which statements could be inserted at // INSERT DECLARATION HERE to allow this code to compile and run? (Choose all that apply.)

A. `List<List<Integer>> table = new List<List<Integer>>();`

B. `List<List<Integer>> table = new ArrayList<List<Integer>>();`

C. `List<List<Integer>> table = new ArrayList<ArrayList<Integer>>();`

D. `List<List, Integer> table = new List<List, Integer>();`

E. `List<List, Integer> table = new ArrayList<List, Integer>();`

F. `List<List, Integer> table = new ArrayList<ArrayList, Integer>();`

G. None of the above

Answer:

☑ **B** is correct.

☒ **A** is incorrect because List is an interface, so you can't say new `List()` regardless of any generic types. **D, E,** and **F** are incorrect because List only takes one type parameter (a Map would take two, not a List). **C** is tempting, but incorrect. The type argument `<List<Integer>>` must be the same for both sides of the assignment, even though the constructor new `ArrayList()` on the right side is a subtype of the declared type List on the left. (Objective 6.4)

2. Which statements are true about comparing two instances of the same class, given that the `equals()` and `hashCode()` methods have been properly overridden? (Choose all that apply.)

A. If the `equals()` method returns true, the `hashCode()` comparison `==` might return false

B. If the `equals()` method returns false, the `hashCode()` comparison `==` might return true

C. If the `hashCode()` comparison `==` returns true, the `equals()` method must return true

D. If the `hashCode()` comparison `==` returns true, the `equals()` method might return true

E. If the `hashCode()` comparison `!=` returns true, the `equals()` method might return true

Answer:

☑ **B and D. B** is true because often two dissimilar objects can return the same hashcode value. **D** is true because if the `hashCode()` comparison returns `==`, the two objects might or might not be equal.

☒ **A, C,** and **E** are incorrect. **C** is incorrect because the `hashCode()` method is very flexible in its return values, and often two dissimilar objects can return the same hash code value. **A** and **E** are a negation of the `hashCode()` and `equals()` contract. (Objective 6.2)

3. Given:
```
public static void before() {
   Set set = new TreeSet();
   set.add("2");
   set.add(3);
   set.add("1");
   Iterator it = set.iterator();
     while (it.hasNext())
   System.out.print(it.next() + " ");
}
```

Which statements are true?

A. The `before()` method will print 1 2

B. The `before()` method will print 1 2 3

C. The `before()` method will print three numbers, but the order cannot be determined

D. The `before()` method will not compile

E. The `before()` method will throw an exception at runtime

Answer:

☑ **E** is correct. You can't put both Strings and `ints` into the same TreeSet. Without generics, the compiler has no way of knowing what type is appropriate for this TreeSet, so it allows everything to compile. At runtime, the TreeSet will try to sort the elements as they're added, and when it tries to compare an Integer with a String it will throw a ClassCastException. Note that although the `before()` method does not use generics, it does use autoboxing. Watch out for code that uses some new features and some old features mixed together.

☒ **A, B, C,** and **D** are incorrect based on the above. (Objective 6.5)

4. Given:

```
import java.util.*;
class MapEQ {
  public static void main(String[] args) {
    Map<ToDos, String> m = new HashMap<ToDos, String>();
    ToDos t1 = new ToDos("Monday");
    ToDos t2 = new ToDos("Monday");
    ToDos t3 = new ToDos("Tuesday");
    m.put(t1, "doLaundry");
    m.put(t2, "payBills");
    m.put(t3, "cleanAttic");
    System.out.println(m.size());
} }
class ToDos{
  String day;
  ToDos(String d) { day = d; }
  public boolean equals(Object o) {
    return ((ToDos)o).day == this.day;
  }
  // public int hashCode() { return 9; }
}
```

Which is correct? (Choose all that apply.)

A. As the code stands it will not compile

B. As the code stands the output will be 2

C. As the code stands the output will be 3

D. If the `hashCode()` method is uncommented the output will be 2

E. If the `hashCode()` method is uncommented the output will be 3

F. If the `hashCode()` method is uncommented the code will not compile

> Answer:
>
> ☑ **C** and **D** are correct. If `hashCode()` is not overridden then every entry will go into its own bucket, and the overridden `equals()` method will have no effect on determining equivalency. If `hashCode()` is overridden, then the overridden `equals()` method will view `t1` and `t2` as duplicates.
>
> ☒ **A, B, E,** and **F** are incorrect based on the above. (Objective 6.2)

5. Given:

```
12. public class AccountManager {
13.     private Map accountTotals = new HashMap();
14.     private int retirementFund;
15.
16.     public int getBalance(String accountName) {
17.         Integer total = (Integer) accountTotals.get(accountName);
18.         if (total == null)
19.             total = Integer.valueOf(0);
20.         return total.intValue();
21.     }
23.     public void setBalance(String accountName, int amount) {
24.         accountTotals.put(accountName, Integer.valueOf(amount));
25. } }
```

This class is to be updated to make use of appropriate generic types, with no changes in behavior (for better or worse). Which of these steps could be performed? (Choose three.)

A. Replace line 13 with
```
private Map<String, int> accountTotals = new HashMap<String, int>();
```

B. Replace line 13 with
```
private Map<String, Integer> accountTotals = new HashMap<String, Integer>();
```

C. Replace line 13 with
```
private Map<String<Integer>> accountTotals = new HashMap<String<Integer>>();
```

D. Replace lines 17–20 with
```
int total = accountTotals.get(accountName);
if (total == null)  total = 0;
return total;
```

E. Replace lines 17–20 with
```
Integer total = accountTotals.get(accountName);
if (total == null)  total = 0;
return total;
```

F. Replace lines 17–20 with
```
return accountTotals.get(accountName);
```
G. Replace line 24 with
```
accountTotals.put(accountName, amount);
```
H. Replace line 24 with
```
accountTotals.put(accountName, amount.intValue());
```

Answer:

☑ **B, E,** and **G** are correct.

☒ **A** is wrong because you can't use a primitive type as a type parameter. **C** is wrong because a Map takes two type parameters separated by a comma. **D** is wrong because an int can't autobox to a null, and **F** is wrong because a null can't unbox to 0. **H** is wrong because you can't autobox a primitive just by trying to invoke a method with it. (Objective 6.4)

6. Given:
```
interface Hungry<E> { void munch(E x); }
interface Carnivore<E extends Animal> extends Hungry<E> {}
interface Herbivore<E extends Plant> extends Hungry<E> {}
abstract class Plant {}
class Grass extends Plant {}
abstract class Animal {}
class Sheep extends Animal implements Herbivore<Sheep> {
  public void munch(Sheep x) {}
}
class Wolf extends Animal implements Carnivore<Sheep> {
  public void munch(Sheep x) {}
}
```

Which of the following changes (taken separately) would allow this code to compile? (Choose all that apply.)

A. Change the Carnivore interface to
```
interface Carnivore<E extends Plant> extends Hungry<E> {}
```
B. Change the Herbivore interface to
```
interface Herbivore<E extends Animal> extends Hungry<E> {}
```
C. Change the Sheep class to
```
class Sheep extends Animal implements Herbivore<Plant> {
    public void munch(Grass x) {}
}
```

D. Change the Sheep class to

```
class Sheep extends Plant implements Carnivore<Wolf> {
    public void munch(Wolf x) {}
}
```

E. Change the Wolf class to

```
class Wolf extends Animal implements Herbivore<Grass> {
    public void munch(Grass x) {}
}
```

F. No changes are necessary

Answer:

☑ **B** is correct. The problem with the original code is that Sheep tries to implement `Herbivore<Sheep>` and Herbivore declares that its type parameter E can be any type that extends Plant. Since a Sheep is not a Plant, `Herbivore<Sheep>` makes no sense—the type Sheep is outside the allowed range of Herbivore's parameter E. Only solutions that either alter the definition of a Sheep or alter the definition of Herbivore will be able to fix this. So **A, E,** and **F** are eliminated. **B** works, changing the definition of an Herbivore to allow it to eat Sheep solves the problem. **C** doesn't work because an `Herbivore<Plant>` must have a `munch(Plant)` method, not `munch(Grass)`. And **D** doesn't work, because in **D** we made Sheep extend Plant, now the Wolf class breaks because its `munch(Sheep)` method no longer fulfills the contract of Carnivore. (Objective 6.4)

7. Which collection class(es) allows you to grow or shrink its size and provides indexed access to its elements, but whose methods are not synchronized? (Choose all that apply.)

A. `java.util.HashSet`

B. `java.util.LinkedHashSet`

C. `java.util.List`

D. `java.util.ArrayList`

E. `java.util.Vector`

F. `java.util.PriorityQueue`

Answer:

☑ **D** is correct. All of the collection classes allow you to grow or shrink the size of your collection. `ArrayList` provides an index to its elements. The newer collection classes tend not to have synchronized methods. Vector is an older implementation of `ArrayList` functionality and has synchronized methods; it is slower than `ArrayList`.

☒ **A, B, C, E,** and **F** are incorrect based on the logic described above; Notes: **C**, List is an interface, and **F**, `PriorityQueue` does not offer access by index. (Objective 6.1)

8. Given a method declared as

```
public static <E extends Number> List<E> process(List<E> nums)
```

A programmer wants to use this method like this

```
// INSERT DECLARATIONS HERE
output = process(input);
```

Which pairs of declarations could be placed at `// INSERT DECLARATIONS HERE` to allow the code to compile? (Choose all that apply.)

A. ```
ArrayList<Integer> input = null;
ArrayList<Integer> output = null;
```

**B.** ```
ArrayList<Integer> input = null;
List<Integer> output = null;
```

C. ```
ArrayList<Integer> input = null;
List<Number> output = null;
```

**D.** ```
List<Number> input = null;
ArrayList<Integer> output = null;
```

E. ```
List<Number> input = null;
List<Number> output = null;
```

**F.** ```
List<Integer> input = null;
List<Integer> output = null;
```

G. None of the above

> Answer:
>
> ☑ **B, E,** and **F** are correct.
>
> ☒ The return type of process is definitely declared as a `List`, not an `ArrayList`, so **A** and **D** are wrong. **C** is wrong because the return type evaluates to `List<Integer>`, and that can't be assigned to a variable of type `List<Number>`. Of course all these would probably cause a `NullPointerException` since the variables are still null—but the question only asked us to get the code to compile. (Objective 6.4)

9. Given the proper import statement(s), and

```
13.    PriorityQueue<String> pq = new PriorityQueue<String>();
14.    pq.add("2");
15.    pq.add("4");
```

```
16.     System.out.print(pq.peek() + " ");
17.     pq.offer("1");
18.     pq.add("3");
19.     pq.remove("1");
20.     System.out.print(pq.poll() + " ");
21.     if(pq.remove("2")) System.out.print(pq.poll() + " ");
22.     System.out.println(pq.poll() + " " + pq.peek());
```

What is the result?

A. 2 2 3 3

B. 2 2 3 4

C. 4 3 3 4

D. 2 2 3 3 3

E. 4 3 3 3 3

F. 2 2 3 3 4

G. Compilation fails

H. An exception is thrown at runtime

Answer:

☑ **B** is correct. For the sake of the exam, add() and offer() both add to (in this case), naturally sorted queues. The calls to poll() both return and then remove the first item from the queue, so the if test fails.

☒ **A, C, D, E, F, G,** and **H** are incorrect based on the above. (Objective 6.1)

10. Given:

```
3. import java.util.*;
4. public class Mixup {
5.   public static void main(String[] args) {
6.     Object o = new Object();
7.     // insert code here
8.     s.add("o");
9.     s.add(o);
10.   }
11. }
```

And these three fragments:

```
I.   Set s = new HashSet();
II.  TreeSet s = new TreeSet();
III. LinkedHashSet s = new LinkedHashSet();
```

When fragments I, II, or III are inserted, independently, at line 7, which are true?
(Choose all that apply.)

A. Fragment I compiles

B. Fragment II compiles

C. Fragment III compiles

D. Fragment I executes without exception

E. Fragment II executes without exception

F. Fragment III executes without exception

> **Answer:**
>
> ☑ **A, B, C, D,** and **F** are all correct.
>
> ☒ Only **E** is incorrect. Elements of a TreeSet must in some way implement Comparable.
> (Objective 6.1)

11. Given:

```
3. import java.util.*;
4. class Turtle {
5.    int size;
6.    public Turtle(int s) { size = s; }
7.    public boolean equals(Object o) { return (this.size == ((Turtle)o).size); }
8.    // insert code here
9. }
10. public class TurtleTest {
11.    public static void main(String[] args) {
12.       LinkedHashSet<Turtle> t = new LinkedHashSet<Turtle>();
13.       t.add(new Turtle(1));    t.add(new Turtle(2));    t.add(new Turtle(1));
14.       System.out.println(t.size());
15.    }
16. }
```

And these two fragments:

```
I.   public int hashCode() { return size/5; }
II.  // no hashCode method declared
```

If fragment I or II is inserted, independently, at line 8, which are true? (Choose all that apply.)

A. If fragment I is inserted, the output is 2

B. If fragment I is inserted, the output is 3

C. If fragment II is inserted, the output is 2

D. If fragment II is inserted, the output is 3

E. If fragment I is inserted, compilation fails

F. If fragment II is inserted, compilation fails

> **Answer:**
>
> ☑ **A** and **D** are correct. While fragment II wouldn't fulfill the hashCode() contract (as you can see by the results), it is legal Java. For the purpose of the exam, if you don't override hashCode(), every object will have a unique hashcode.
>
> ☒ **B, C, E,** and **F** are incorrect based on the above. (Objective 6.2)

12. Given the proper import statement(s), and:

```
13.    TreeSet<String> s = new TreeSet<String>();
14.    TreeSet<String> subs = new TreeSet<String>();
15.    s.add("a"); s.add("b"); s.add("c"); s.add("d"); s.add("e");
16.
17.    subs = (TreeSet)s.subSet("b", true, "d", true);
18.    s.add("g");
19.    s.pollFirst();
20.    s.pollFirst();
21.    s.add("c2");
22.    System.out.println(s.size() +" "+ subs.size());
```

Which are true? (Choose all that apply.)

A. The size of s is 4

B. The size of s is 5

C. The size of s is 7

D. The size of subs is 1

E. The size of subs is 2

F. The size of subs is 3

G. The size of subs is 4

H. An exception is thrown at runtime

Answer:

☑ **B** and **F** are correct. After "g" is added, TreeSet s contains six elements and TreeSet subs contains three (b, c, d), because "g" is out of the range of subs. The first pollFirst() finds and removes only the "a". The second pollFirst() finds and removes the "b" from *both* TreeSets (remember they are backed). The final add() is in range of both TreeSets. The final contents are [c,c2,d,e,g] and [c,c2,d].

☒ **A, C, D, E, G,** and **H** are incorrect based on the above. (Objective 6.3)

13. Given:

```
3.  import java.util.*;
4.  public class Magellan {
5.    public static void main(String[] args) {
6.      TreeMap<String, String> myMap = new TreeMap<String, String>();
7.      myMap.put("a", "apple"); myMap.put("d", "date");
8.      myMap.put("f", "fig"); myMap.put("p", "pear");
9.      System.out.println("1st after mango: " +   // sop 1
10.       myMap.higherKey("f"));
11.     System.out.println("1st after mango: " +   // sop 2
12.       myMap.ceilingKey("f"));
13.     System.out.println("1st after mango: " +   // sop 3
14.       myMap.floorKey("f"));
15.     SortedMap<String, String> sub = new TreeMap<String, String>();
16.     sub = myMap.tailMap("f");
17.     System.out.println("1st after mango: " +   // sop 4
18.       sub.firstKey());
19.   }
20. }
```

Which of the System.out.println statements will produce the output 1st after mango: p? (Choose all that apply.)

A. sop 1

B. sop 2

C. sop 3

D. `sop 4`

E. None; compilation fails

F. None; an exception is thrown at runtime

Answer:

☑ **A** is correct. The `ceilingKey()` method's argument is inclusive. The `floorKey()` method would be used to find keys before the specified key. The `firstKey()` method's argument is also inclusive.

☒ **B, C, D, E,** and **F** are incorrect based on the above. (Objective 6.3)

14. Given:

```
3. import java.util.*;
4. class Business { }
5. class Hotel extends Business { }
6. class Inn extends Hotel { }
7. public class Travel {
8.    ArrayList<Hotel> go() {
9.       // insert code here
10.   }
11. }
```

Which, inserted independently at line 9, will compile? (Choose all that apply.)

A. `return new ArrayList<Inn>();`

B. `return new ArrayList<Hotel>();`

C. `return new ArrayList<Object>();`

D. `return new ArrayList<Business>();`

Answer:

☑ **B** is correct.

☒ **A** is incorrect because polymorphic assignments don't apply to generic type parameters. **C** and **D** are incorrect because they don't follow basic polymorphism rules. (Objective 6.4)

15. Given:

```
3. import java.util.*;
4. class Dog { int size; Dog(int s) { size = s; } }
5. public class FirstGrade {
6.   public static void main(String[] args) {
7.     TreeSet<Integer> i = new TreeSet<Integer>();
8.     TreeSet<Dog> d = new TreeSet<Dog>();
9.
10.    d.add(new Dog(1));   d.add(new Dog(2));   d.add(new Dog(1));
11.    i.add(1);            i.add(2);            i.add(1);
12.    System.out.println(d.size() + " " + i.size());
13.  }
14. }
```

What is the result?

A. 1 2

B. 2 2

C. 2 3

D. 3 2

E. 3 3

F. Compilation fails

G. An exception is thrown at runtime

Answer:

☑ **G** is correct. Class Dog needs to implement Comparable in order for a TreeSet (which keeps its elements sorted) to be able to contain Dog objects.

☒ **A, B, C, D, E,** and **F** are incorrect based on the above. (Objective 6.5)

16. Given:

```
3. import java.util.*;
4. public class GeoCache {
5.   public static void main(String[] args) {
6.     String[] s = {"map", "pen", "marble", "key"};
7.     Othello o = new Othello();
8.     Arrays.sort(s,o);
```

```
9.      for(String s2: s) System.out.print(s2 + " ");
10.     System.out.println(Arrays.binarySearch(s, "map"));
11.   }
12.   static class Othello implements Comparator<String> {
13.     public int compare(String a, String b) { return b.compareTo(a); }
14.   }
15. }
```

Which are true? (Choose all that apply.)

A. Compilation fails

B. The output will contain a 1

C. The output will contain a 2

D. The output will contain a –1

E. An exception is thrown at runtime

F. The output will contain `"key map marble pen"`

G. The output will contain `"pen marble map key"`

Answer:

☑ **D** and **G** are correct. First, the `compareTo()` method will reverse the normal sort. Second, the `sort()` is valid. Third, the `binarySearch()` gives –1 because it needs to be invoked using the same `Comparator` (o), as was used to sort the array. Note that when the `binarySearch()` returns an "undefined result" it doesn't officially have to be a -1, but it usually is, so if you selected only G, you get full credit!

☒ **A, B, C, E,** and **F** are incorrect based on the above. (Objective 6.5)

8

Inner Classes

I nner classes (including static nested classes) appear throughout the exam. Although there are no official exam objectives specifically about inner classes, Objective 1.1 includes inner (a.k.a. nested) classes. More important, the code used to represent questions on virtually *any* topic on the exam can involve inner classes. Unless you deeply understand the rules and syntax for inner classes, you're likely to miss questions you'd otherwise be able to answer. *As if the exam weren't already tough enough.*

This chapter looks at the ins and outs (inners and outers?) of inner classes, and exposes you to the kinds of (often strange-looking) syntax examples you'll see scattered throughout the entire exam. So you've really got two goals for this chapter—to learn what you'll need to answer questions testing your inner class knowledge, and to learn how to read and understand inner class code so that you can correctly process questions testing your knowledge of *other* topics.

So what's all the hoopla about inner classes? Before we get into it, we have to warn you (if you don't already know) that inner classes have inspired passionate love 'em or hate 'em debates since first introduced in version 1.1 of the language. For once, we're going to try to keep our opinions to ourselves here and just present the facts as you'll need to know them for the exam. It's up to you to decide how—and to what extent—you should use inner classes in your own development. We mean it. We believe they have some powerful, efficient uses in very specific situations, including code that's easier to read and maintain, but they can also be abused and lead to code that's as clear as a cornfield maze, and to the syndrome known as "reuseless": *code that's useless over and over again*.

Inner classes let you define one class within another. They provide a type of scoping for your classes since you can make one class *a member of another class*. Just as classes have member *variables* and *methods*, a class can also have member *classes*. They come in several flavors, depending on how and where you define the inner class, including a special kind of inner class known as a "top-level nested class" (an inner class marked `static`), which technically isn't really an inner class. Because a static nested class is still a class defined within the scope of another class, we're still going to cover them in this chapter on inner classes.

Unlike the other chapters in this book, the certification objectives for inner classes don't have official exam objective numbers since they're part of other objectives covered elsewhere. So for this chapter, the Certification Objective headings in the following list represent the four inner class *topics* discussed in this chapter, rather than four official exam *objectives*:

■ Inner classes
■ Method-local inner classes
■ Anonymous inner classes
■ Static nested classes

Inner Classes

You're an OO programmer, so you know that for reuse and flexibility/extensibility you need to keep your classes specialized. In other words, a class should have code *only* for the things an object of that particular type needs to do; any *other* behavior should be part of another class better suited for *that* job. Sometimes, though, you find yourself designing a class where you discover you need behavior that belongs in a separate, specialized class, but also needs to be intimately tied to the class you're designing.

Event handlers are perhaps the best example of this (and are, in fact, one of the main reasons inner classes were added to the language in the first place). If you have a GUI class that performs some job like, say, a chat client, you might want the chat-client–specific methods (accept input, read new messages from server, send user input back to server, and so on) to be in the class. But how do those methods get invoked in the first place? A user clicks a button. Or types some text in the input field. Or a separate thread doing the I/O work of getting messages from the server has messages that need to be displayed in the GUI. So you have chat-client–specific methods, but you also need methods for handling the "events" (button presses, keyboard typing, I/O available, and so on) that drive the calls on those chat-client methods. The ideal scenario—from an OO perspective—is to keep the chat-client–specific methods in the ChatClient class, and put the event-handling *code* in a separate event-handling *class*.

Nothing unusual about that so far; after all, that's how you're *supposed* to design OO classes. As *specialists*. But here's the problem with the chat-client scenario: the event-handling code is intimately tied to the chat-client–specific code! Think about it: when the user presses a Send button (indicating that they want their typed-in message to be sent to the chat server), the chat-client code that sends the message needs to read from a *particular* text field. In other words, if the user clicks Button A, the program is supposed to extract the text from the TextField B, *of a particular*

ChatClient instance. Not from some *other* text field from some *other* object, but specifically the text field that a specific instance of the ChatClient class has a reference to. So the event-handling code needs access to the members of the ChatClient object, to be useful as a "helper" to a particular ChatClient instance.

And what if the ChatClient class needs to inherit from one class, but the event handling code is better off inheriting from some *other* class? You can't make a class extend more than one class, so putting all the code (the chat-client– specific code and the event-handling code) in one class won't work in that case. So what you'd really like to have is the benefit of putting your event code in a separate class (better OO, encapsulation, and the ability to extend a class other than the class the ChatClient extends) but still allow the event-handling code to have easy access to the members of the ChatClient (so the event-handling code can, for example, update the ChatClient's private instance variables). You *could* manage it by making the members of the ChatClient accessible to the event-handling class by, for example, marking them `public`. But that's not a good solution either.

You already know where this is going—one of the key benefits of an inner class is the "special relationship" an *inner class instance* shares with *an instance of the outer class*. That "special relationship" gives code in the inner class access to members of the enclosing (outer) class, *as if the inner class were part of the outer class*. In fact, that's exactly what it means: the inner class *is* a part of the outer class. Not just a "part" but a full-fledged, card-carrying *member* of the outer class. Yes, an inner class instance has access to all members of the outer class, *even those marked private*. (Relax, that's the whole point, remember? We want this separate inner class instance to have an intimate relationship with the outer class instance, but we still want to keep everyone *else* out. And besides, if you wrote the outer class, then you also wrote the inner class! So you're not violating encapsulation; you *designed* it this way.)

Coding a "Regular" Inner Class

We use the term *regular* here to represent inner classes that are not

- Static
- Method-local
- Anonymous

For the rest of this section, though, we'll just use the term "inner class" and drop the "regular". (When we switch to one of the other three types in the preceding list, you'll know it.) You define an inner class within the curly braces of the outer class:

```
class MyOuter {
   class MyInner { }
}
```

Piece of cake. And if you compile it,

```
%javac MyOuter.java
```

you'll end up with *two* class files:

MyOuter.class
MyOuter$MyInner.class

The inner class is still, in the end, a separate class, so a separate class file is generated for it. But the inner class file isn't accessible to you in the usual way. You can't say

```
%java MyOuter$MyInner
```

in hopes of running the main () method of the inner class, because a *regular* inner class can't have static declarations of any kind. *The only way you can access the inner class is through a live instance of the outer class!* In other words, only at runtime when there's already an instance of the outer class to tie the inner class instance to. You'll see all this in a moment. First, let's beef up the classes a little:

```
class MyOuter {
   private int x = 7;

   // inner class definition
   class MyInner {
      public void seeOuter() {
         System.out.println("Outer x is " + x);
      }
   } // close inner class definition

} // close outer class
```

The preceding code is perfectly legal. Notice that the inner class is indeed accessing a private member of the outer class. That's fine, because the inner class is also a member of the outer class. So just as any member of the outer class (say, an instance method) can access any other member of the outer class, private or not, the inner class—also a member—can do the same.

OK, so now that we know how to write the code giving an inner class access to members of the outer class, how do you actually use it?

Instantiating an Inner Class

To create an instance of an inner class, *you must have an instance of the outer class* to tie to the inner class. There are no exceptions to this rule: an inner class instance can never stand alone without a direct relationship to an instance of the outer class.

Instantiating an Inner Class from Within the Outer Class Most often, it is the outer class that creates instances of the inner class, since it is usually the outer class wanting to use the inner instance as a helper for its own personal use. We'll modify the MyOuter class to create an instance of MyInner:

```
class MyOuter {
   private int x = 7;
   public void makeInner() {
      MyInner in = new MyInner();  // make an inner instance
      in.seeOuter();
   }

   class MyInner {
      public void seeOuter() {
         System.out.println("Outer x is " + x);
      }
   }
}
```

You can see in the preceding code that the MyOuter code treats MyInner just as though MyInner were any other accessible class—it instantiates it using the class name (new MyInner()), and then invokes a method on the reference variable (in.seeOuter()). But the only reason this syntax works is because the outer class instance method code is doing the instantiating. In other words, *there's already an instance of the outer class—the instance running the* makeInner() *method*. So how do you instantiate a MyInner object from somewhere outside the MyOuter class? Is it even possible? (Well, since we're going to all the trouble of making a whole new subhead for it, as you'll see next, there's no big mystery here.)

Creating an Inner Class Object from Outside the Outer Class

Instance Code Whew. Long subhead there, but it does explain what we're trying to do. If we want to create an instance of the inner class, we must have an instance of the outer class. You already know that, but think about the implications...it means that, without a reference to an instance of the outer class, you can't instantiate the inner class from a static method of the outer class (because, don't forget, in static code *there is no* this *reference*), or from any other code in any other class. Inner class instances are always handed an implicit reference to the outer class. The compiler takes care of it, so you'll never see anything but the end result—the ability of the inner class to access members of the outer class. The code to make an instance from anywhere outside nonstatic code of the outer class is simple, but you must memorize this for the exam!

```
public static void main(String[] args) {
   MyOuter mo = new MyOuter();      // gotta get an instance!
   MyOuter.MyInner inner = mo.new MyInner();
   inner.seeOuter();
}
```

The preceding code is the same regardless of whether the main() method is within the MyOuter class or some *other* class (assuming the other class has access to MyOuter, and since MyOuter has default access, that means the code must be in a class within the same package as MyOuter).

If you're into one-liners, you can do it like this:

```
public static void main(String[] args) {
   MyOuter.MyInner inner = new MyOuter().new MyInner();
   inner.seeOuter();
}
```

You can think of this as though you're invoking a method on the outer instance, but the method happens to be a special inner class instantiation method, and it's invoked using the keyword new. Instantiating an inner class is the *only* scenario in which you'll invoke new *on* an instance as opposed to invoking new to *construct* an instance.

Here's a quick summary of the differences between inner class instantiation code that's *within* the outer class (but not static), and inner class instantiation code that's *outside* the outer class:

■ From *inside* the outer class instance code, use the inner class name in the normal way:

```
MyInner mi = new MyInner();
```

■ From *outside* the outer class instance code (including static method code within the outer class), the inner class name must now include the outer class's name:

```
MyOuter.MyInner
```

To instantiate it, you must use a reference to the outer class:

```
new MyOuter().new MyInner(); or outerObjRef.new MyInner();
```

if you already have an instance of the outer class.

Referencing the Inner or Outer Instance from Within the Inner Class

How does an object refer to itself normally? By using the `this` reference. Here is a quick review of `this`:

■ The keyword `this` can be used only from within instance code. In other words, not within `static` code.

■ The `this` reference is a reference to the currently executing object. In other words, the object whose reference was used to invoke the currently running method.

■ The `this` reference is the way an object can pass a reference to itself to some other code, as a method argument:

```
public void myMethod() {
  MyClass mc = new MyClass();
  mc.doStuff(this);  // pass a ref to object running myMethod
}
```

Within an inner class code, the `this` reference refers to the instance of the inner class, as you'd probably expect, since `this` always refers to the currently executing object. But what if the inner class code wants an explicit reference to the outer class instance that the inner instance is tied to? In other words, *how do you reference the "outer `this`"*? Although normally the inner class code doesn't need a reference to the outer class, since it already has an implicit one it's using to access the members of the outer class, it would need a reference to the outer class if it needed to pass that reference to some other code as follows:

```
class MyInner {
   public void seeOuter() {
      System.out.println("Outer x is " + x);
      System.out.println("Inner class ref is " + this);
      System.out.println("Outer class ref is " + MyOuter.this);
   }
}
```

If we run the complete code as follows:

```
class MyOuter {
   private int x = 7;
   public void makeInner() {
      MyInner in = new MyInner();
      in.seeOuter();
   }
   class MyInner {
      public void seeOuter() {
         System.out.println("Outer x is " + x);
         System.out.println("Inner class ref is " + this);
         System.out.println("Outer class ref is " + MyOuter.this);
      }
   }
   public static void main (String[] args) {
      MyOuter.MyInner inner = new MyOuter().new MyInner();
      inner.seeOuter();
   }
}
```

the output is something like this:

```
Outer x is 7
Inner class ref is MyOuter$MyInner@113708
Outer class ref is MyOuter@33f1d7
```

So the rules for an inner class referencing itself or the outer instance are as follows:

- To reference the inner class instance itself, from *within* the inner class code, use this.
- To reference the "*outer* this" (the outer class instance) from within the inner class code, use NameOfOuterClass.this (example, MyOuter.this).

Member Modifiers Applied to Inner Classes   A regular inner class is a member of the outer class just as instance variables and methods are, so the following modifiers can be applied to an inner class:

- ■ final
- ■ abstract
- ■ public
- ■ private
- ■ protected
- ■ static—*but* static *turns it into a* static *nested class not an inner class*
- ■ strictfp

CERTIFICATION OBJECTIVE

Method-Local Inner Classes

A regular inner class is scoped inside another class's curly braces, but outside any method code (in other words, at the same level that an instance variable is declared). But you can also define an inner class within a method:

```
class MyOuter2 {
    private String x = "Outer2";

    void doStuff() {
        class MyInner {
            public void seeOuter() {
                System.out.println("Outer x is " + x);
            } // close inner class method
        } // close inner class definition
    } // close outer class method doStuff()

} // close outer class
```

The preceding code declares a class, MyOuter2, with one method, doStuff(). But *inside* doStuff(), another class, MyInner, is declared, and it has a method of its own, seeOuter(). The code above is completely useless, however, because *it never instantiates the inner class!* Just because you *declared* the class doesn't mean you created an *instance* of it. So to *use* the inner class you must make an instance of it somewhere *within the method but below the inner class definition* (or the compiler won't be able to find the inner class). The following legal code shows how to instantiate and use a method-local inner class:

```
class MyOuter2 {
    private String x = "Outer2";
    void doStuff() {
        class MyInner {
            public void seeOuter() {
                System.out.println("Outer x is " + x);
            } // close inner class method
        } // close inner class definition

        MyInner mi = new MyInner();  // This line must come
                                     // after the class
        mi.seeOuter();
    } // close outer class method doStuff()
} // close outer class
```

What a Method-Local Inner Object Can and Can't Do

A method-local inner class can be instantiated only within the method where the inner class is defined. In other words, no other code running in any other method—inside or outside the outer class—can ever instantiate the method-local inner class. Like regular inner class objects, the method-local inner class object shares a special relationship with the enclosing (outer) class object, and can access its `private` (or any other) members. However, *the inner class object cannot use the local variables of the method the inner class is in.* Why not?

Think about it. The local variables of the method live on the stack, and exist only for the lifetime of the method. You already know that the scope of a local variable is limited to the method the variable is declared in. When the method ends, the stack frame is blown away and the variable is history. But even after the method completes, the inner class object created within it might still be alive on the heap if, for example, a reference to it was passed into some other code and then stored in an instance variable. Because the local variables aren't guaranteed to be alive as long as the method-local inner class object, the inner class object can't use them. *Unless the local variables are marked* `final`! The following code attempts to access a local variable from within a method-local inner class.

```
class MyOuter2 {
  private String x = "Outer2";
  void doStuff() {
    String z = "local variable";
    class MyInner {
      public void seeOuter() {
        System.out.println("Outer x is " + x);
        System.out.println("Local variable z is " + z); // Won't Compile!
      } // close inner class method
    }   // close inner class definition
  }     // close outer class method doStuff()
}       // close outer class
```

Compiling the preceding code *really* upsets the compiler:

```
MyOuter2.java:8: local variable z is accessed from within inner class;
needs to be declared final
          System.out.println("Local variable z is " + z);
                                                       ^
```

Marking the local variable z as `final` fixes the problem:

```
final String z = "local variable";  // Now inner object can use it
```

And just a reminder about modifiers within a method: the same rules apply to method-local inner classes as to local variable declarations. You can't, for example, mark a method-local inner class `public`, `private`, `protected`, `static`, `transient`, and the like. For the purpose of the exam, the only modifiers you *can* apply to a method-local inner class are `abstract` and `final`, but as always, never both at the same time.

exam ⓦatch

Remember that a local class declared in a `static` *method has access to only* `static` *members of the enclosing class, since there is no associated instance of the enclosing class. If you're in a* `static` *method there is no* `this`, *so an inner class in a* `static` *method is subject to the same restrictions as the* `static` *method. In other words, no access to instance variables.*

CERTIFICATION OBJECTIVE

Anonymous Inner Classes

So far we've looked at defining a class within an enclosing class (a regular inner class) and within a method (a method-local inner class). Finally, we're going to look at the most unusual syntax you might ever see in Java; inner classes declared without any class name at all (hence the word *anonymous*). And if that's not weird enough, you can define these classes not just within a method, but even within an *argument* to a method. We'll look first at the *plain-old* (as if there is such a thing as a plain-old anonymous inner class) version (actually, even the plain-old version comes in two flavors), and then at the argument-declared anonymous inner class.

Perhaps your most important job here is to *learn to not be thrown when you see the syntax*. The exam is littered with anonymous inner class code: you might see it on questions about threads, wrappers, overriding, garbage collection, and... well, you get the idea.

Plain-Old Anonymous Inner Classes, Flavor One

Check out the following legal-but-strange-the-first-time-you-see-it code:

```
class Popcorn {
    public void pop() {
        System.out.println("popcorn");
    }
}
class Food {
    Popcorn p = new Popcorn() {
        public void pop() {
            System.out.println("anonymous popcorn");
        }
    };
}
```

Let's look at what's in the preceding code:

- We define two classes, Popcorn and Food.
- Popcorn has one method, pop().
- Food has one instance variable, declared as type Popcorn. That's it for Food. Food has *no* methods.

And here's the big thing to get

The Popcorn reference variable refers *not* to an instance of Popcorn, but to *an instance of an anonymous (unnamed) subclass of Popcorn.*

Let's look at just the anonymous class code:

```
2. Popcorn p = new Popcorn() {
3.    public void pop() {
4.        System.out.println("anonymous popcorn");
5.    }
6. };
```

Line 2 Line 2 starts out as an instance variable declaration of type `Popcorn`. But instead of looking like this:

```
Popcorn p = new Popcorn(); // notice the semicolon at the end
```

there's a curly brace at the end of line 2, where a semicolon would normally be.

```
Popcorn p = new Popcorn() { // a curly brace, not a semicolon
```

You can read line 2 as saying,

Declare a reference variable, p, of type `Popcorn`. Then declare a new class that has no name, but that is a *subclass* of `Popcorn`. And here's the curly brace that opens the class definition…

Line 3 Line 3, then, is actually the first statement within the new class definition. And what is it doing? Overriding the `pop()` method of the superclass `Popcorn`. This is the whole point of making an anonymous inner class—to *override one or more methods of the superclass!* (Or to implement methods of an interface, but we'll save that for a little later.)

Line 4 Line 4 is the first (and in this case *only*) statement within the overriding `pop()` method. Nothing special there.

Line 5 Line 5 is the closing curly brace of the `pop()` method. Nothing special.

Line 6 Here's where you have to pay attention: line 6 includes a *curly brace closing off the anonymous class definition* (it's the companion brace to the one on line 2), but there's more! Line 6 also has *the semicolon that ends the statement started on line 2*—the statement where it all began—the statement declaring and initializing the `Popcorn` reference variable. And what you're left with is a `Popcorn` reference to a brand-new *instance* of a brand-new, just-in-time, anonymous (no name) *subclass* of Popcorn.

e x a m
watch

The closing semicolon is hard to spot. Watch for code like this:

```
2. Popcorn p = new Popcorn() {
3.   public void pop() {
4.       System.out.println("anonymous popcorn");
5.   }
6. }                     //  Missing the semicolon needed to end
                         //  the statement started on 2!
7. Foo f = new Foo();
```

You'll need to be especially careful about the syntax when inner classes are involved, because the code on line 6 looks perfectly natural. It's rare to see semicolons following curly braces.

Polymorphism is in play when anonymous inner classes are involved. Remember that, as in the preceding Popcorn example, we're using a superclass reference variable type to refer to a subclass object. What are the implications? You can only call methods on an anonymous inner class reference that are defined in the reference variable type! This is no different from any other polymorphic references, for example,

```
class Horse extends Animal{
   void buck() { }
}
class Animal {
   void eat() { }
}
```

```
class Test {
   public static void main (String[] args) {
      Animal h = new Horse();
      h.eat();  // Legal, class Animal has an eat() method
      h.buck();  // Not legal! Class Animal doesn't have buck()
   }
}
```

So on the exam, you must be able to spot an anonymous inner class that—rather than overriding a method of the superclass—defines its own new method. The method definition isn't the problem, though; the real issue is how do you invoke that new method? The reference variable type (the superclass) won't know anything about that new method (defined in the anonymous subclass), so the compiler will complain if you try to invoke any method on an anonymous inner class reference that is not in the superclass class definition.

Check out the following, illegal code:

```
class Popcorn {
   public void pop() {
      System.out.println("popcorn");
   }
}

class Food {
   Popcorn p = new Popcorn() {
      public void sizzle() {
         System.out.println("anonymous sizzling popcorn");
      }
      public void pop() {
         System.out.println("anonymous popcorn");
      }
   };

   public void popIt() {
      p.pop();     // OK, Popcorn has a pop() method
      p.sizzle();  // Not Legal! Popcorn does not have sizzle()
   }
}
```

Compiling the preceding code gives us something like,

```
Anon.java:19: cannot resolve symbol
symbol  : method sizzle  ()
```

```
location: class Popcorn
     p.sizzle();
     ^
```

which is the compiler's way of saying, "I can't find method `sizzle()` in class `Popcorn`," followed by, "Get a clue."

Plain-Old Anonymous Inner Classes, Flavor Two

The only difference between flavor one and flavor two is that flavor one creates an anonymous *subclass* of the specified *class* type, whereas flavor two creates an anonymous *implementer* of the specified *interface* type. In the previous examples, we defined a new anonymous subclass of type `Popcorn` as follows:

```
Popcorn p = new Popcorn() {
```

But if `Popcorn` were an *interface* type instead of a *class* type, then the new anonymous class would be an *implementer* of the *interface* rather than a *subclass* of the *class*. Look at the following example:

```
interface Cookable {
   public void cook();
}
class Food {
   Cookable c = new Cookable() {
     public void cook() {
        System.out.println("anonymous cookable implementer");
     }
   };
}
```

The preceding code, like the Popcorn example, still creates an instance of an anonymous inner class, but this time the new just-in-time class is an implementer of the `Cookable` interface. And note that this is the only time you will ever see the syntax

```
new Cookable()
```

where `Cookable` is an *interface* rather than a `nonabstract` class type. Because think about it, *you can't instantiate an interface*, yet that's what the code *looks* like it's doing. But of course it's not instantiating a Cookable object, it's creating an instance of a new, anonymous, implementer of Cookable. You can read this line:

```
Cookable c = new Cookable() {
```

as, "Declare a reference variable of type `Cookable` that, obviously, will refer to an object from a class that implements the `Cookable` interface. But, oh yes, we don't yet *have* a class that implements `Cookable`, so we're going to make one right here, right now. We don't need a name for the class, but it will be a class that implements `Cookable`, and this curly brace starts the definition of the new implementing class."

One more thing to keep in mind about anonymous interface implementers—*they can implement only one interface*. There simply isn't any mechanism to say that your anonymous inner class is going to implement multiple interfaces. In fact, an anonymous inner class can't even extend a class and implement an interface at the same time. The inner class has to choose either to be a subclass of a named class— and not directly implement any interfaces at all—*or* to implement a single interface. By directly, we mean actually using the keyword `implements` as part of the class declaration. If the anonymous inner class is a subclass of a class type, it automatically becomes an implementer of any interfaces implemented by the superclass.

Argument-Defined Anonymous Inner Classes

If you understood what we've covered so far in this chapter, then this last part will be simple. If you *are* still a little fuzzy on anonymous classes, however, then you should reread the previous sections. If they're not completely clear, we'd like to take full responsibility for the confusion. But we'll be happy to share.

Okay, if you've made it to this sentence, then we're all going to assume you understood the preceding section, and now we're just going to add one new twist. Imagine the following scenario. You're typing along, creating the Perfect Class, when you write code calling a method on a `Bar` object, and that method takes an object of type `Foo` (an interface).

```
class MyWonderfulClass {
   void go() {
      Bar b = new Bar();
      b.doStuff(ackWeDoNotHaveAFoo!); // Don't try to compile this at home
   }
}
interface Foo {
   void foof();
}
class Bar {
   void doStuff(Foo f) { }
}
```

No *problemo*, except that you don't *have* an object from a class that implements Foo, and you can't instantiate one, either, because *you don't even have a class that implements Foo*, let alone an instance of one. So you first need a class that implements Foo, and then you need an instance of that class to pass to the Bar class's doStuff() method. Savvy Java programmer that you are, you simply define an anonymous inner class, *right inside the argument*. That's right, just where you least expect to find a class. And here's what it looks like:

```
1. class MyWonderfulClass {
2.    void go() {
3.       Bar b = new Bar();
4.       b.doStuff(new Foo() {
5.          public void foof() {
6.             System.out.println("foofy");
7.          } // end foof method
8.       }); // end inner class def, arg, and b.doStuff stmt.
9.    } // end go()
10. } // end class
11.
12. interface Foo {
13.    void foof();
14. }
15. class Bar {
16.    void doStuff(Foo f) { }
17. }
```

All the action starts on line 4. We're calling doStuff() on a Bar object, but the method takes an instance that IS-A Foo, where Foo is an interface. So we must make both an *implementation* class and an *instance* of that class, all right here in the argument to doStuff(). So that's what we do. We write

```
new Foo() {
```

to start the new class definition for the anonymous class that implements the Foo interface. Foo has a single method to implement, foof(), so on lines 5, 6, and 7 we implement the foof() method. Then on line 8—whoa!—more strange syntax appears. The first curly brace closes off the new anonymous class definition. But don't forget that this all happened as part of a method argument, so the close parenthesis,), finishes off the method invocation, and then we must still end the statement that began on line 4, so we end with a semicolon. Study this syntax! You will see anonymous inner classes on the exam, and you'll have to be very, very picky about the way they're closed. If they're *argument local*, they end like this:

```
});
```

but if they're just plain-old anonymous classes, then they end like this:

```
};
```

Regardless, the syntax is not what you use in virtually any other part of Java, so be careful. Any question from any part of the exam might involve anonymous inner classes as part of the code.

CERTIFICATION OBJECTIVE

Static Nested Classes

We saved the easiest for last, as a kind of treat :)

You'll sometimes hear static nested classes referred to as *static inner classes*, but they really aren't inner classes at all, by the standard definition of an inner class. While an inner class (regardless of the flavor) enjoys that *special relationship* with the outer class (or rather the *instances* of the two classes share a relationship), a static nested class does not. It is simply a non-inner (also called "top-level") class scoped within another. So with static classes it's really more about name-space resolution than about an implicit relationship between the two classes.

A static nested class is simply *a class that's a static member of the enclosing class*:

```
class BigOuter {
    static class Nested { }
}
```

The class itself isn't really "static"; there's no such thing as a static class. The `static` modifier in this case says that the nested class is *a static member of the outer class*. That means it can be accessed, as with other static members, *without having an instance of the outer class*.

Instantiating and Using Static Nested Classes

You use standard syntax to access a static nested class from its enclosing class. The syntax for instantiating a static nested class from a non-enclosing class is a little different from a normal inner class, and looks like this:

```
class BigOuter {
    static class Nest {void go() { System.out.println("hi"); } }
}
class Broom {
    static class B2 {void goB2() { System.out.println("hi 2"); } }
    public static void main(String[] args) {
        BigOuter.Nest n = new BigOuter.Nest();    // both class names
        n.go();
        B2 b2 = new B2();      // access the enclosed class
        b2.goB2();
    }
}
```

Which produces

```
hi
hi 2
```

---

exam

ⓦatch   *Just as a static method does not have access to the instance variables and nonstatic methods of the class, a static nested class does not have access to the instance variables and nonstatic methods of the outer class. Look for static nested classes with code that behaves like a nonstatic (regular inner) class.*

CERTIFICATION SUMMARY

Inner classes will show up throughout the exam, in any topic, and these are some of the exam's hardest questions. You should be comfortable with the sometimes bizarre syntax, and know how to spot legal and illegal inner class definitions.

We looked first at "regular" inner classes, where one class is a member of another. You learned that coding an inner class means putting the class definition of the inner class inside the curly braces of the enclosing (outer) class, but outside of any method or other code block. You learned that an inner class *instance* shares a special relationship with a specific *instance* of the outer class, and that this special relationship lets the inner class access all members of the outer class, including those marked `private`. You learned that to instantiate an inner class, you *must* have a reference to an instance of the outer class.

Next we looked at method-local inner classes—classes defined *inside* a method. The code for a method-local inner class looks virtually the same as the code for any other class definition, except that you can't apply an access modifier the way you can with a regular inner class. You learned why method-local inner classes cannot use non-`final` local variables declared within the method—the inner class instance may outlive the stack frame, so the local variable might vanish while the inner class object is still alive. You saw that to *use* the inner class you need to instantiate it, and that the instantiation must come *after* the class declaration in the method.

We also explored the strangest inner class type of all—the *anonymous* inner class. You learned that they come in two forms, normal and argument-defined. Normal, ho-hum, anonymous inner classes are created as part of a variable assignment, while argument-defined inner classes are actually declared, defined, and automatically instantiated *all within the argument to a method!* We covered the way anonymous inner classes can be either a subclass of the named class type, or an *implementer* of the named interface. Finally, we looked at how polymorphism applies to anonymous inner classes: you can invoke on the new instance only those methods defined in the named class or interface type. In other words, even if the anonymous inner class defines its own new method, no code from anywhere outside the inner class will be able to invoke that method.

As if we weren't already having enough fun for one day, we pushed on to static nested classes, which really aren't inner classes at all. Known as static nested classes, a nested class marked with the `static` modifier is quite similar to any other non-inner class, except that to access it, code must have access to both the nested and enclosing class. We saw that because the class is `static`, no instance of the enclosing class is needed, and thus the static nested class *does not share a special relationship with any instance of the enclosing class.* Remember, static inner classes can't access instance methods or variables.

✔ TWO-MINUTE DRILL

Here are some of the key points from this chapter.

Inner Classes

❑ A "regular" inner class is declared *inside* the curly braces of another class, but *outside* any method or other code block.

❑ An inner class is a full-fledged member of the enclosing (outer) class, so it can be marked with an access modifier as well as the `abstract` or `final` modifiers. (Never both `abstract` and `final` together— remember that `abstract` *must* be subclassed, whereas `final` *cannot* be subclassed).

❑ An inner class instance shares a special relationship with an instance of the enclosing class. This relationship gives the inner class access to *all* of the outer class's members, including those marked `private`.

❑ To instantiate an inner class, you must have a reference to an instance of the outer class.

❑ From code within the enclosing class, you can instantiate the inner class using only the name of the inner class, as follows:

```
MyInner mi = new MyInner();
```

❑ From code outside the enclosing class's instance methods, you can instantiate the inner class only by using both the inner and outer class names, and a reference to the outer class as follows:

```
MyOuter mo = new MyOuter();
MyOuter.MyInner inner = mo.new MyInner();
```

❑ From code within the inner class, the keyword `this` holds a reference to the inner class instance. To reference the *outer* `this` (in other words, the instance of the outer class that this inner instance is tied to) precede the keyword `this` with the outer class name as follows: `MyOuter.this;`

Method-Local Inner Classes

❑ A method-local inner class is defined within a method of the enclosing class.

❑ For the inner class to be used, you must instantiate it, and that instantiation must happen within the same method, but *after* the class definition code.

❑ A method-local inner class cannot use variables declared within the method (including parameters) unless those variables are marked `final`.

❏ The only modifiers you can apply to a method-local inner class are `abstract` and `final`. (Never both at the same time, though.)

Anonymous Inner Classes

❏ Anonymous inner classes have no name, and their type must be either a subclass of the named type or an implementer of the named interface.

❏ An anonymous inner class is always created as part of a statement; don't forget to close the statement after the class definition with a curly brace. This is a rare case in Java, a curly brace followed by a semicolon.

❏ Because of polymorphism, the only methods you can call on an anonymous inner class reference are those defined in the reference variable class (or interface), even though the anonymous class is really a subclass or implementer of the reference variable type.

❏ An anonymous inner class can extend one subclass *or* implement one interface. Unlike non-anonymous classes (inner or otherwise), an anonymous inner class cannot do both. In other words, it cannot both extend a class *and* implement an interface, nor can it implement more than one interface.

❏ An argument-defined inner class is declared, defined, and automatically instantiated as part of a method invocation. The key to remember is that the class is being defined within a method argument, so the syntax will end the class definition with a curly brace, followed by a closing parenthesis to end the method call, followed by a semicolon to end the statement: `});`

Static Nested Classes

❏ Static nested classes are inner classes marked with the `static` modifier.

❏ A static nested class is *not* an inner class, it's a top-level nested class.

❏ Because the nested class is static, it does not share any special relationship with an instance of the outer class. In fact, you don't need an instance of the outer class to instantiate a static nested class.

❏ Instantiating a static nested class requires using both the outer and nested class names as follows:

```
BigOuter.Nested n = new BigOuter.Nested();
```

❏ A static nested class cannot access non-static members of the outer class, since it does not have an implicit reference to any outer instance (in other words, the nested class instance does not get an *outer* `this` reference).

SELF TEST

The following questions will help you measure your understanding of the dynamic and life-altering material presented in this chapter. Read all of the choices carefully. Take your time. Breathe.

1. Which are true about a static nested class? (Choose all that apply.)
    A. You must have a reference to an instance of the enclosing class in order to instantiate it
    B. It does not have access to non-static members of the enclosing class
    C. Its variables and methods must be static
    D. If the outer class is named MyOuter, and the nested class is named MyInner, it can be instantiated using new MyOuter.MyInner();
    E. It must extend the enclosing class

2. Given:

    ```
    class Boo {
        Boo(String s) { }
        Boo() { }
    }
    class Bar extends Boo {
        Bar() { }
        Bar(String s) {super(s);}
        void zoo() {
        // insert code here
        }
    }
    ```

    Which create an anonymous inner class from within class Bar? (Choose all that apply.)
    A. Boo f = new Boo(24) { };
    B. Boo f = new Bar() { };
    C. Boo f = new Boo() {String s; };
    D. Bar f = new Boo(String s) { };
    E. Boo f = new Boo.Bar(String s) { };

3. Which are true about a method-local inner class? (Choose all that apply.)
    A. It must be marked final
    B. It can be marked abstract

C. It can be marked `public`

D. It can be marked `static`

E. It can access private members of the enclosing class

4. Given:

```
1. public class TestObj {
2.    public static void main(String[] args) {
3.       Object o = new Object() {
4.          public boolean equals(Object obj) {
5.             return true;
6.          }
7.       }
8.       System.out.println(o.equals("Fred"));
9.    }
10. }
```

What is the result?

A. An exception occurs at runtime

B. `true`

C. `Fred`

D. Compilation fails because of an error on line 3

E. Compilation fails because of an error on line 4

F. Compilation fails because of an error on line 8

G. Compilation fails because of an error on a line other than 3, 4, or 8

5. Given:

```
1. public class HorseTest {
2.    public static void main(String[] args) {
3.       class Horse {
4.          public String name;
5.          public Horse(String s) {
6.             name = s;
7.          }
8.       }
9.       Object obj = new Horse("Zippo");
10.      System.out.println(obj.name);
11.   }
12. }
```

What is the result?

A. An exception occurs at runtime at line 10

B. `Zippo`

C. Compilation fails because of an error on line 3

D. Compilation fails because of an error on line 9

E. Compilation fails because of an error on line 10

6. Given:

```
public abstract class AbstractTest {
   public int getNum() {
      return 45;
   }
   public abstract class Bar {
     public int getNum() {
       return 38;
     }
   }
   public static void main(String[] args) {
      AbstractTest t = new AbstractTest() {
         public int getNum() {
            return 22;
         }
      };
      AbstractTest.Bar f = t.new Bar() {
         public int getNum() {
            return 57;
         }
      };
      System.out.println(f.getNum() + " " + t.getNum());
   }
}
```

What is the result?

A. 57 22

B. 45 38

C. 45 57

D. An exception occurs at runtime

E. Compilation fails

7. Given:

```
3. public class Tour {
4.   public static void main(String[] args) {
5.     Cathedral c = new Cathedral();
6.     // insert code here
7.     s.go();
8.   }
9. }
10. class Cathedral {
11.   class Sanctum {
12.     void go() { System.out.println("spooky"); }
13.   }
14. }
```

Which, inserted independently at line 6, compile and produce the output "spooky"? (Choose all that apply.)

A. `Sanctum s = c.new Sanctum();`

B. `c.Sanctum s = c.new Sanctum();`

C. `c.Sanctum s = Cathedral.new Sanctum();`

D. `Cathedral.Sanctum s = c.new Sanctum();`

E. `Cathedral.Sanctum s = Cathedral.new Sanctum();`

8. Given:

```
5. class A { void m() { System.out.println("outer"); } }
6.
7. public class TestInners {
8.   public static void main(String[] args) {
9.     new TestInners().go();
10.   }
11.   void go() {
12.     new A().m();
13.     class A { void m() { System.out.println("inner"); } }
14.   }
15.   class A { void m() { System.out.println("middle"); } }
16. }
```

What is the result?

A. `inner`

B. `outer`

C. `middle`
D. Compilation fails
E. An exception is thrown at runtime

9. Given:

```
3. public class Car {
4.   class Engine {
5.      // insert code here
6.   }
7.   public static void main(String[] args) {
8.     new Car().go();
9.   }
10.  void go() {
11.    new Engine();
12.  }
13.  void drive() { System.out.println("hi"); }
14. }
```

Which, inserted independently at line 5, produce the output "hi"? (Choose all that apply.)

A. `{ Car.drive(); }`
B. `{ this.drive(); }`
C. `{ Car.this.drive(); }`
D. `{ this.Car.this.drive(); }`
E. `Engine() { Car.drive(); }`
F. `Engine() { this.drive(); }`
G. `Engine() { Car.this.drive(); }`

10. Given:

```
3. public class City {
4.   class Manhattan {
5.     void doStuff() throws Exception { System.out.print("x "); }
6.   }
7.   class TimesSquare extends Manhattan {
8.     void doStuff() throws Exception { }
9.   }
10.  public static void main(String[] args) throws Exception {
11.    new City().go();
12.  }
13.  void go() throws Exception { new TimesSquare().doStuff(); }
14. }
```

What is the result?

A. x
B. x x
C. No output is produced
D. Compilation fails due to multiple errors
E. Compilation fails due only to an error on line 4
F. Compilation fails due only to an error on line 7
G. Compilation fails due only to an error on line 10
H. Compilation fails due only to an error on line 13

11. Given:

```
3. public class Navel {
4.    private int size = 7;
5.    private static int length = 3;
6.    public static void main(String[] args) {
7.      new Navel().go();
8.    }
9.    void go() {
10.       int size = 5;
11.       System.out.println(new Gazer().adder());
12.    }
13.    class Gazer {
14.       int adder() { return size * length; }
15.    }
16. }
```

What is the result?

A. 15
B. 21
C. An exception is thrown at runtime
D. Compilation fails due to multiple errors
E. Compilation fails due only to an error on line 4
F. Compilation fails due only to an error on line 5

12. Given:

```
3. import java.util.*;
4. public class Pockets {
5.    public static void main(String[] args) {
6.       String[] sa = {"nickel", "button", "key", "lint"};
7.       Sorter s = new Sorter();
8.       for(String s2: sa) System.out.print(s2 + " ");
9.       Arrays.sort(sa,s);
10.      System.out.println();
11.      for(String s2: sa) System.out.print(s2 + " ");
12.   }
13.   class Sorter implements Comparator<String> {
14.      public int compare(String a, String b) {
15.         return b.compareTo(a);
16.      }
17.   }
18. }
```

What is the result?

A. Compilation fails

B. button key lint nickel
   nickel lint key button

C. nickel button key lint
   button key lint nickel

D. nickel button key lint
   nickel button key lint

E. nickel button key lint
   nickel lint key button

F. An exception is thrown at runtime

SELF TEST ANSWERS

1. Which are true about a static nested class? (Choose all that apply.)
   A. You must have a reference to an instance of the enclosing class in order to instantiate it
   B. It does not have access to non-static members of the enclosing class
   C. Its variables and methods must be static
   D. If the outer class is named MyOuter, and the nested class is named MyInner, it can be instantiated using new MyOuter.MyInner();
   E. It must extend the enclosing class

Answer:

☑ **B and D. B** is correct because a static nested class is not tied to an instance of the enclosing class, and thus can't access the non-static members of the class (just as a static method can't access non-static members of a class). **D** uses the correct syntax for instantiating a static nested class.

☒ **A** is incorrect because static nested classes do not need (and can't use) a reference to an instance of the enclosing class. **C** is incorrect because static nested classes can declare and define non-static members. **E** is wrong because...it just is. There's no rule that says an inner or nested class has to extend anything.

2. Given:

```
class Boo {
    Boo(String s) { }
    Boo() { }
}
class Bar extends Boo {
    Bar() { }
    Bar(String s) {super(s);}
    void zoo() {
    // insert code here
    }
}
```

Which create an anonymous inner class from within class Bar? (Choose all that apply.)
   A. Boo f = new Boo(24) { };
   B. Boo f = new Bar() { };

```
C. Boo f = new Boo() {String s; };
D. Bar f = new Boo(String s) { };
E. Boo f = new Boo.Bar(String s) { };
```

Answer:

☑ **B** and **C**. **B** is correct because anonymous inner classes are no different from any other class when it comes to polymorphism. That means you are always allowed to declare a reference variable of the superclass type and have that reference variable refer to an instance of a subclass type, which in this case is an anonymous subclass of Bar. Since Bar is a subclass of Boo, it all works. **C** uses correct syntax for creating an instance of Boo.

☒ **A** is incorrect because it passes an `int` to the Boo constructor, and there is no matching constructor in the Boo class. **D** is incorrect because it violates the rules of polymorphism; you cannot refer to a superclass type using a reference variable declared as the subclass type. The superclass doesn't have everything the subclass has. **E** uses incorrect syntax.

3. Which are true about a method-local inner class? (Choose all that apply.)
   A. It must be marked `final`
   B. It can be marked `abstract`
   C. It can be marked `public`
   D. It can be marked `static`
   E. It can access private members of the enclosing class

Answer:

☑ **B** and **E**. **B** is correct because a method-local inner class can be `abstract`, although it means a subclass of the inner class must be created if the `abstract` class is to be used (so an `abstract` method-local inner class is probably not useful). **E** is correct because a method-local inner class works like any other inner class—it has a special relationship to an instance of the enclosing class, thus it can access all members of the enclosing class.

☒ **A** is incorrect because a method-local inner class does not have to be declared `final` (although it is legal to do so). **C** and **D** are incorrect because a method-local inner class cannot be made `public` (remember—local variables can't be `public`) or `static`.

4. Given:

```
1. public class TestObj {
2.   public static void main(String[] args) {
3.     Object o = new Object() {
```

```
4.  ·        public boolean equals(Object obj) {
5.               return true;
6.            }
7.         }
8.         System.out.println(o.equals("Fred"));
9.       }
10. }
```

What is the result?

A. An exception occurs at runtime

B. `true`

C. `fred`

D. Compilation fails because of an error on line 3

E. Compilation fails because of an error on line 4

F. Compilation fails because of an error on line 8

G. Compilation fails because of an error on a line other than 3, 4, or 8

Answer:

☑ **G.** This code would be legal if line 7 ended with a semicolon. Remember that line 3 is a statement that doesn't end until line 7, and a statement needs a closing semicolon!

☒ **A, B, C, D, E,** and **F** are incorrect based on the program logic described above. If the semicolon were added at line 7, then answer **B** would be correct—the program would print `true`, the return from the `equals()` method overridden by the anonymous subclass of `Object`.

5. Given:

```
1. public class HorseTest {
2.   public static void main(String[] args) {
3.     class Horse {
4.       public String name;
5.       public Horse(String s) {
6.         name = s;
7.       }
8.     }
9.     Object obj = new Horse("Zippo");
10.    System.out.println(obj.name);
11.   }
12. }
```

What is the result?

A. An exception occurs at runtime at line 10

B. `Zippo`

C. Compilation fails because of an error on line 3

D. Compilation fails because of an error on line 9

E. Compilation fails because of an error on line 10

Answer:

☑ **E.** If you use a reference variable of type `Object`, you can access only those members defined in class `Object`.

☒ **A, B, C,** and **D** are incorrect based on the program logic described above.

6. Given:

```
public abstract class AbstractTest {
    public int getNum() {
        return 45;
    }
    public abstract class Bar {
        public int getNum() {
            return 38;
        }
    }
    public static void main(String[] args) {
        AbstractTest t = new AbstractTest() {
            public int getNum() {
                return 22;
            }
        };
        AbstractTest.Bar f = t.new Bar() {
            public int getNum() {
                return 57;
            }
        };
        System.out.println(f.getNum() + " " + t.getNum());
    }
}
```

What is the result?

A. `57 22`

B. `45 38`

C. `45 57`

D. An exception occurs at runtime

E. Compilation fails

Answer:

☑ **A.** You can define an inner class as abstract, which means you can instantiate only concrete subclasses of the abstract inner class. The object referenced by the variable t is an instance of an anonymous subclass of AbstractTest, and the anonymous class overrides the getNum() method to return 22. The variable referenced by f is an instance of an anonymous subclass of Bar, and the anonymous Bar subclass also overrides the getNum() method (to return 57). Remember that to create a Bar instance, we need an instance of the enclosing AbstractTest class to tie to the new Bar inner class instance. AbstractTest can't be instantiated because it's abstract, so we created an anonymous subclass (non-abstract) and then used the instance of that anonymous subclass to tie to the new Bar subclass instance.

☒ **B, C, D,** and **E** are incorrect based on the program logic described above.

7. Given:

```
3. public class Tour {
4.    public static void main(String[] args) {
5.       Cathedral c = new Cathedral();
6.       // insert code here
7.       s.go();
8.    }
9. }
10. class Cathedral {
11.    class Sanctum {
12.       void go() { System.out.println("spooky"); }
13.    }
14. }
```

Which, inserted independently at line 6, compile and produce the output "spooky"? (Choose all that apply.)

A. Sanctum s = c.new Sanctum();

B. c.Sanctum s = c.new Sanctum();

C. c.Sanctum s = Cathedral.new Sanctum();

D. Cathedral.Sanctum s = c.new Sanctum();

E. Cathedral.Sanctum s = Cathedral.new Sanctum();

Answer:

☑ **D** is correct. It is the only code that uses the correct inner class instantiation syntax.

☒ **A, B, C,** and **E** are incorrect based on the above. (Objective 1.1)

8. Given:

```
 5. class A { void m() { System.out.println("outer"); } }
 6.
 7. public class TestInners {
 8.   public static void main(String[] args) {
 9.     new TestInners().go();
10.   }
11.   void go() {
12.     new A().m();
13.     class A { void m() { System.out.println("inner"); } }
14.   }
15.   class A { void m() { System.out.println("middle"); } }
16. }
```

What is the result?

A. inner

B. outer

C. middle

D. Compilation fails

E. An exception is thrown at runtime

Answer:

☑ **C** is correct. The "inner" version of class A isn't used because its declaration comes after the instance of class A is created in the go() method.

☒ **A, B, D,** and **E** are incorrect based on the above. (Objective 1.1)

9. Given:

```
 3. public class Car {
 4.   class Engine {
 5.     // insert code here
 6.   }
 7.   public static void main(String[] args) {
 8.     new Car().go();
 9.   }
10.   void go() {
11.     new Engine();
12.   }
13.   void drive() { System.out.println("hi"); }
14. }
```

Which, inserted independently at line 5, produce the output "hi"? (Choose all that apply.)

A. `{ Car.drive(); }`

B. `{ this.drive(); }`

C. `{ Car.this.drive(); }`

D. `{ this.Car.this.drive(); }`

E. `Engine() { Car.drive(); }`

F. `Engine() { this.drive(); }`

G. `Engine() { Car.this.drive(); }`

Answer:

☑ **C** and **G** are correct. **C** is the correct syntax to access an inner class's outer instance method from an initialization block, and **G** is the correct syntax to access it from a constructor.

☒ **A, B, D, E,** and **F** are incorrect based on the above. (Objectives 1.1, 1.4)

10. Given:

```
3. public class City {
4.    class Manhattan {
5.      void doStuff() throws Exception { System.out.print("x "); }
6.    }
7.    class TimesSquare extends Manhattan {
8.      void doStuff() throws Exception { }
9.    }
10.   public static void main(String[] args) throws Exception {
11.     new City().go();
12.   }
13.   void go() throws Exception { new TimesSquare().doStuff(); }
14. }
```

What is the result?

A. x

B. x x

C. No output is produced

D. Compilation fails due to multiple errors

E. Compilation fails due only to an error on line 4

F. Compilation fails due only to an error on line 7

G. Compilation fails due only to an error on line 10

H. Compilation fails due only to an error on line 13

Answer:

☑ **C** is correct. The inner classes are valid, and all the methods (including `main()`), correctly throw an Exception, given that `doStuff()` throws an Exception. The `doStuff()` in class `TimesSquare` overrides class `Manhattan`'s `doStuff()` and produces no output.

☒ **A, B, D, E, F, G,** and **H** are incorrect based on the above. (Objectives 1.1, 2.4)

11. Given:

```
3. public class Navel {
4.    private int size = 7;
5.    private static int length = 3;
6.    public static void main(String[] args) {
7.      new Navel().go();
8.    }
9.    void go() {
10.     int size = 5;
11.     System.out.println(new Gazer().adder());
12.   }
13.   class Gazer {
14.     int adder() { return size * length; }
15.   }
16. }
```

What is the result?

A. 15
B. 21
C. An exception is thrown at runtime
D. Compilation fails due to multiple errors
E. Compilation fails due only to an error on line 4
F. Compilation fails due only to an error on line 5

Answer:

☑ **B** is correct. The inner class `Gazer` has access to `Navel`'s `private static` and private instance variables.

☒ **A, C, D, E,** and **F** are incorrect based on the above. (Objectives 1.1, 1.4)

12. Given:

```
3. import java.util.*;
4. public class Pockets {
5.    public static void main(String[] args) {
6.       String[] sa = {"nickel", "button", "key", "lint"};
7.       Sorter s = new Sorter();
8.       for(String s2: sa) System.out.print(s2 + " ");
9.       Arrays.sort(sa,s);
10.      System.out.println();
11.      for(String s2: sa) System.out.print(s2 + " ");
12.   }
13.   class Sorter implements Comparator<String> {
14.      public int compare(String a, String b) {
15.         return b.compareTo(a);
16.      }
17.   }
18. }
```

What is the result?

A. Compilation fails

B. `button key lint nickel`
   `nickel lint key button`

C. `nickel button key lint`
   `button key lint nickel`

D. `nickel button key lint`
   `nickel button key lint`

E. `nickel button key lint`
   `nickel lint key button`

F. An exception is thrown at runtime

Answer:

☑ **A** is correct, the inner class `Sorter` must be declared `static` to be called from the `static` method `main()`. If `Sorter` had been `static`, answer E would be correct.

☒ **B, C, D, E,** and **F** are incorrect based on the above. (Objectives 1.1, 1.4, 6.5)

9
Threads

CERTIFICATION OBJECTIVE

Defining, Instantiating, and Starting Threads (Objective 4.1)

4.1   Write code to define, instantiate, and start new threads using both java.lang.Thread and java.lang.Runnable.

Imagine a stockbroker application with a lot of complex capabilities. One of its functions is "download last stock option prices," another is "check prices for warnings," and a third time-consuming operation is "analyze historical data for company XYZ."

In a single-threaded runtime environment, these actions execute one after another. The next action can happen *only* when the previous one is finished. If a historical analysis takes half an hour, and the user selects to perform a download and check afterward, the warning may come too late to, say, buy or sell stock as a result.

We just imagined the sort of application that cries out for multithreading. Ideally, the download should happen in the background (that is, in another thread). That way, other processes could happen at the same time so that, for example, a warning could be communicated instantly. All the while, the user is interacting with other parts of the application. The analysis, too, could happen in a separate thread, so the user can work in the rest of the application while the results are being calculated.

So what exactly is a thread? In Java, "thread" means two different things:

- An instance of class java.lang.Thread
- A thread of execution

An instance of Thread is just…an object. Like any other object in Java, it has variables and methods, and lives and dies on the heap. But a *thread of execution* is an individual process (a "lightweight" process) that has its own call stack. In Java, there is *one thread per call stack*—or, to think of it in reverse, *one call stack per thread*. Even if you don't create any new threads in your program, threads are back there running.

The main() method, that starts the whole ball rolling, runs in one thread, called (surprisingly) the *main* thread. If you looked at the main call stack (and you can, any time you get a stack trace from something that happens after main begins, but not within another thread), you'd see that main() is the first method on the stack—

the method at the bottom. But as soon as you create a *new* thread, a new stack materializes and methods called from *that* thread run in a call stack that's separate from the `main()` call stack. That second new call stack is said to run concurrently with the main thread, but we'll refine that notion as we go through this chapter.

You might find it confusing that we're talking about code running *concurrently*— as if in *parallel*—given that there's only one CPU on most of the machines running Java. What gives? The JVM, which gets its turn at the CPU by whatever scheduling mechanism the underlying OS uses, operates like a mini-OS and schedules *its* own threads regardless of the underlying operating system. In some JVMs, the Java threads are actually mapped to native OS threads, but we won't discuss that here; native threads are not on the exam. Nor is it required to understand how threads behave in different JVM environments. In fact, the most important concept to understand from this entire chapter is this:

When it comes to threads, very little is guaranteed.

So be very cautious about interpreting the behavior you see on one machine as "the way threads work." The exam expects you to know what is and is not guaranteed behavior, so that you can design your program in such a way that it will work regardless of the underlying JVM. *That's part of the whole point of Java.*

Don't make the mistake of designing your program to be dependent on a particular implementation of the JVM. As you'll learn a little later, different JVMs can run threads in profoundly different ways. For example, one JVM might be sure that all threads get their turn, with a fairly even amount of time allocated for each thread in a nice, happy, round-robin fashion. But in other JVMs, a thread might start running and then just hog the whole show, never stepping out so others can have a turn. If you test your application on the "nice turn-taking" JVM, and you don't know what is and is not guaranteed in Java, then you might be in for a big shock when you run it under a JVM with a different thread scheduling mechanism.

The thread questions are among the most difficult questions on the exam. In fact, for most people they *are* the toughest questions on the exam, and with four objectives for threads you'll be answering a *lot* of thread questions. If you're not already familiar with threads, you'll probably need to spend some time experimenting. Also, one final disclaimer: *This chapter makes almost no attempt to teach you how to design a good, safe, multithreaded application. We only scratch the surface of that huge topic in this chapter!* You're here to learn the basics of threading, and what you need to get through the thread questions on the exam. Before you can write decent multithreaded code, however, you really need to study more on the complexities and subtleties of multithreaded code.

(Note: The topic of daemon threads is NOT on the exam. All of the threads discussed in this chapter are "user" threads. You and the operating system can create a second kind of thread called a daemon thread. The difference between these two types of threads (user and daemon) is that the JVM exits an application only when all user threads are complete—the JVM doesn't care about letting daemon threads complete, so once all user threads are complete, the JVM will shut down, regardless of the state of any daemon threads. Once again, this topic is NOT on the exam.)

Making a Thread

A thread in Java begins as an instance of java.lang.Thread. You'll find methods in the Thread class for managing threads including creating, starting, and pausing them. For the exam, you'll need to know, at a minimum, the following methods:

```
start()
yield()
sleep()
run()
```

The action happens in the run() method. Think of the code you want to execute in a separate thread as *the job to do*. In other words, you have some work that needs to be done, say, downloading stock prices in the background while other things are happening in the program, so what you really want is that *job* to be executed in its own thread. So if the *work* you want done is the *job*, the one *doing* the work (actually executing the job code) is the *thread*. And the *job always starts from a* run() *method* as follows:

```
public void run() {
  // your job code goes here
}
```

You always write the code that needs to be run in a separate thread in a run() method. The run() method will call other methods, of course, but the thread of execution—the new call stack—always begins by invoking run() . So where does the run() method go? In one of the two classes you can use to define your thread job. You can define and instantiate a thread in one of two ways:

- Extend the java.lang.Thread class.
- Implement the Runnable interface.

You need to know about both for the exam, although in the real world you're much more likely to implement Runnable than extend Thread. Extending the Thread class is the easiest, but it's usually not a good OO practice. Why? Because subclassing should be reserved for specialized versions of more general superclasses. So the only time it really makes sense (from an OO perspective) to extend Thread is when you have a more specialized version of a Thread class. In other words, because *you have more specialized thread-specific behavior*. Chances are, though, that the thread work you want is really just a job to be done *by* a thread. In that case, you should design a class that implements the Runnable interface, which also leaves your class free to extend some *other* class.

Defining a Thread

To define a thread, you need a place to put your run() method, and as we just discussed, you can do that by extending the Thread class or by implementing the Runnable interface. We'll look at both in this section.

Extending java.lang.Thread

The simplest way to define code to run in a separate thread is to

- Extend the java.lang.Thread class.
- Override the run() method.

It looks like this:

```
class MyThread extends Thread {
  public void run() {
    System.out.println("Important job running in MyThread");
    }
  }
```

The limitation with this approach (besides being a poor design choice in most cases) is that if you extend Thread, *you can't extend anything else*. And it's not as if you really need that inherited Thread class behavior, because in order to use a thread you'll need to instantiate one anyway.

Keep in mind that you're free to overload the `run()` method in your Thread subclass:

```
class MyThread extends Thread {
  public void run() {
    System.out.println("Important job running in MyThread");
  }
  public void run(String s) {
    System.out.println("String in run is " + s);
  }
}
```

But know this: *The overloaded* `run(String s)` *method will be ignored by the Thread class unless you call it yourself. The Thread class expects a* `run()` *method with no arguments, and it will execute this method for you in a separate call stack after the thread has been started.* With a `run(String s)` method, the Thread class won't call the method for you, and even if you call the method directly yourself, execution won't happen in a new thread of execution with a separate call stack. It will just happen in the same call stack as the code that you made the call from, just like any other normal method call.

Implementing java.lang.Runnable

Implementing the Runnable interface gives you a way to extend any class you like, but still define behavior that will be run by a separate thread. It looks like this:

```
class MyRunnable implements Runnable {
  public void run() {
    System.out.println("Important job running in MyRunnable");
  }
}
```

Regardless of which mechanism you choose, you've now got yourself some code that can be run by a thread of execution. So now let's take a look at *instantiating* your thread-capable class, and then we'll figure out how to actually get the thing *running*.

Instantiating a Thread

Remember, every thread of execution begins as an instance of class Thread. Regardless of whether your `run()` method is in a Thread subclass or a Runnable implementation class, you still need a Thread object to do the work.

If you extended the Thread class, instantiation is dead simple (we'll look at some additional overloaded constructors in a moment):

```
MyThread t = new MyThread()
```

If you implement Runnable, instantiation is only slightly less simple. To have code run by a separate thread, *you still need a Thread instance*. But rather than combining both the *thread* and the *job* (the code in the run() method) into one class, you've split it into two classes—the Thread class for the *thread-specific* code and your Runnable implementation class for your *job-that-should-be-run-by-a-thread* code. (Another common way to think about this is that the Thread is the "worker," and the Runnable is the "job" to be done.)

First, you instantiate your Runnable class:

```
MyRunnable r = new MyRunnable();
```

Next, you get yourself an instance of java.lang.Thread (*somebody* has to run your job...), and you *give it your job!*

```
Thread t = new Thread(r);  // Pass your Runnable to the Thread
```

If you create a thread using the no-arg constructor, the thread will call its own run() method when it's time to start working. That's exactly what you want when you extend Thread, but when you use Runnable, you need to tell the new thread to use *your* run() method rather than its own. The Runnable you pass to the Thread constructor is called the *target* or the *target Runnable*.

You can pass a single Runnable instance to multiple Thread objects, so that the same Runnable becomes the target of multiple threads, as follows:

```
public class TestThreads {
   public static void main (String [] args) {
     MyRunnable r = new MyRunnable();
     Thread foo = new Thread(r);
     Thread bar = new Thread(r);
     Thread bat = new Thread(r);
   }
}
```

Giving the same target to multiple threads means that several threads of execution will be running the very same job (and that the same job will be done multiple times).

The Thread class itself implements Runnable. (After all, it has a `run()` *method that we were overriding.) This means that you could pass a Thread to another Thread's constructor:*

```
Thread t = new Thread(new MyThread());
```

This is a bit silly, but it's legal. In this case, you really just need a Runnnable, and creating a whole other Thread is overkill.

Besides the no-arg constructor and the constructor that takes a Runnable (the target, i.e., the instance with the job to do), there are other overloaded constructors in class Thread. The constructors we care about are

- `Thread()`
- `Thread(Runnable target)`
- `Thread(Runnable target, String name)`
- `Thread(String name)`

You need to recognize all of them for the exam! A little later, we'll discuss some of the other constructors in the preceding list.

So now you've made yourself a Thread instance, and it knows which `run()` method to call. *But nothing is happening yet.* At this point, all we've got is a plain old Java object of type Thread. *It is not yet a thread of execution.* To get an actual thread—a new call stack—we still have to *start* the thread.

When a thread has been instantiated but not started (in other words, the `start()` method has not been invoked on the Thread instance), the thread is said to be in the *new* state. At this stage, the thread is not yet considered to be *alive*. Once the `start()` method is called, the thread is considered to be *alive* (even though the `run()` method may not have actually started executing yet). A thread is considered *dead* (no longer *alive*) after the `run()` method completes. The `isAlive()` method is the best way to determine if a thread has been started but has not yet completed its `run()` method. (Note: The `getState()` method is very useful for debugging, but you won't have to know it for the exam.)

Starting a Thread

You've created a Thread object and it knows its target (either the passed-in Runnable or itself if you extended class Thread). Now it's time to get the whole thread thing happening—to launch a new call stack. It's so simple it hardly deserves its own subheading:

```
t.start();
```

Prior to calling `start()` on a Thread instance, the thread (when we use lowercase `t`, we're referring to the *thread of execution* rather than the Thread class) is said to be in the *new* state as we said. The new state means you have a Thread *object* but you don't yet have a *true thread*. So what happens after you call `start()`? The good stuff:

■ A new thread of execution starts (with a new call stack).

■ The thread moves from the *new* state to the *runnable* state.

■ When the thread gets a chance to execute, its target `run()` method will run.

Be *sure* you remember the following: You start a *Thread*, not a *Runnable*. You call `start()` on a Thread instance, not on a Runnable instance. The following example demonstrates what we've covered so far—defining, instantiating, and starting a thread:

```
class FooRunnable implements Runnable {
   public void run() {
      for(int x - 1; x < 6; x++) {
         System.out.println("Runnable running");
      }
   }
}

public class TestThreads {
   public static void main (String [] args) {
      FooRunnable r = new FooRunnable();
      Thread t = new Thread(r);
      t.start();
   }
}
```

Running the preceding code prints out exactly what you'd expect:

```
% java TestThreads
Runnable running
Runnable running
Runnable running
Runnable running
Runnable running
```

(If this isn't what you expected, go back and re-read everything in this objective.)

---

exam
Watch

There's nothing special about the `run()` *method as far as Java is concerned. Like* `main()`, *it just happens to be the name (and signature) of the method that the new thread knows to invoke. So if you see code that calls the* `run()` *method on a Runnable (or even on a Thread instance), that's perfectly legal. But it doesn't mean the* `run()` *method will run in a separate thread! Calling a* `run()` *method directly just means you're invoking a method from whatever thread is currently executing, and the* `run()` *method goes onto the current call stack rather than at the beginning of a new call stack. The following code does not start a new thread of execution:*

```
Thread t = new Thread();
t.run();  // Legal, but does not start a new thread
```

So what happens if we start multiple threads? We'll run a simple example in a moment, but first we need to know how to print out which thread is executing. We can use the `getName()` method of class Thread, and have each Runnable print out the name of the thread executing that Runnable object's `run()` method. The following example instantiates a thread and gives it a name, and then the name is printed out from the `run()` method:

```
class NameRunnable implements Runnable {
    public void run() {
        System.out.println("NameRunnable running");
        System.out.println("Run by "
          + Thread.currentThread().getName());
```

```
       }
    }
}
public class NameThread {
    public static void main (String [] args) {
      NameRunnable nr = new NameRunnable();
      Thread t = new Thread(nr);
      t.setName("Fred");
      t.start();
    }
}
```

Running this code produces the following, extra special, output:

```
% java NameThread
NameRunnable running
Run by Fred
```

To get the name of a thread you call—who would have guessed—getName() on the Thread instance. But the target Runnable instance doesn't even *have* a reference to the Thread instance, so we first invoked the static Thread.currentThread() method, which returns a reference to the currently executing thread, and then we invoked getName() on that returned reference.

Even if you don't explicitly name a thread, it still has a name. Let's look at the previous code, commenting out the statement that sets the thread's name:

```
public class NameThread {
    public static void main (String [] args) {
      NameRunnable nr = new NameRunnable();
      Thread t = new Thread(nr);
      // t.setName("Fred");
      t.start();
    }
}
```

Running the preceding code now gives us

```
% java NameThread
NameRunnable running
Run by Thread-0
```

And since we're getting the name of the current thread by using the static Thread.currentThread() method, we can even get the name of the thread running our main code,

```
public class NameThreadTwo {
  public static void main (String [] args) {
    System.out.println("thread is "
      + Thread.currentThread().getName());
  }
}
```

which prints out

```
% java NameThreadTwo
thread is main
```

That's right, the main thread already has a name—*main*. (Once again, what are the odds?) Figure 9-1 shows the process of starting a thread.

FIGURE 9-I

Starting a thread

```
public static void main(String [] args) {
    //  running

    //  some code

    //  in main()

    method2();

    //  running

    //  more code
}
static void method2() {
  Runnable r = new MyRunnable();

  Thread t = new Thread(r);

  t.start();

  //  do more stuff

}
```

main

stack A

method2
main

stack A

run

stack B
(thread t)

method2
main

stack A
(main thread)

1) main() begins

2) main() invokes method2()

3) method2() starts a new thread

Starting and Running Multiple Threads

Enough playing around here; let's actually get multiple threads going (more than two, that is). We already had two threads, because the main() method starts in a thread of its own, and then t.start() started a *second* thread. Now we'll do more. The following code creates a single Runnable instance and three Thread instances. All three Thread instances get the same Runnable instance, and each thread is given a unique name. Finally, all three threads are started by invoking start() on the Thread instances.

```
class NameRunnable implements Runnable {
    public void run() {
        for (int x = 1; x <= 3; x++) {
            System.out.println("Run by "
                    + Thread.currentThread().getName()
                    + ", x is " + x);
        }
    }
}
public class ManyNames {
    public static void main(String [] args) {
        // Make one Runnable
        NameRunnable nr = new NameRunnable();
        Thread one = new Thread(nr);
        Thread two = new Thread(nr);
        Thread three = new Thread(nr);

        one.setName("Fred");
        two.setName("Lucy");
        three.setName("Ricky");
        one.start();
        two.start();
        three.start();
    }
}
```

Running this code might produce the following:

```
% java ManyNames
Run by Fred, x is 1
Run by Fred, x is 2
Run by Fred, x is 3
```

```
Run by Lucy, x is 1
Run by Lucy, x is 2
Run by Lucy, x is 3
Run by Ricky, x is 1
Run by Ricky, x is 2
Run by Ricky, x is 3
```

Well, at least that's what it printed when we ran it—this time, on our machine. But the behavior you see above is not guaranteed. This is so crucial that you need to stop right now, take a deep breath, and repeat after me, "The behavior is not guaranteed." You need to know, for your future as a Java programmer as well as for the exam, that there is nothing in the Java specification that says threads will start running in the order in which they were started (in other words, the order in which start() was invoked on each thread). And there is no guarantee that once a thread starts executing, it will keep executing until it's done. Or that a loop will complete before another thread begins. No siree Bob. Nothing is guaranteed in the preceding code except this:

Each thread will start, and each thread will run to completion.

Within each thread, things will happen in a predictable order. But the actions of different threads can mix together in unpredictable ways. If you run the program multiple times, or on multiple machines, you may see different output. Even if you don't see different output, you need to realize that the behavior you see is not guaranteed. Sometimes a little change in the way the program is run will cause a difference to emerge. Just for fun we bumped up the loop code so that each run() method ran the for loop 400 times rather than 3, and eventually we did start to see some wobbling:

```
public void run() {
    for (int x = 1; x <= 400; x++) {
        System.out.println("Run by "
                + Thread.currentThread().getName()
                + ", x is " + x);
    }
}
```

Running the preceding code, with each thread executing its run loop 400 times, started out fine but then became nonlinear. Here's just a snip from the command-line output of running that code. To make it easier to distinguish each thread, we put Fred's output in italics and Lucy's in bold, and left Ricky's alone:

Run by Fred, x is 345
Run by Ricky, x is 313
Run by Lucy, x is 341
Run by Ricky, x is 314
Run by Lucy, x is 342
Run by Ricky, x is 315
Run by Fred, x is 346
Run by Lucy, x is 343
Run by Fred, x is 347
Run by Lucy, x is 344
... it continues on ...

Notice that there's not really any clear pattern here. If we look at only the output from Fred, we see the numbers increasing one at a time, as expected:

Run by Fred, x is 345
Run by Fred, x is 346
Run by Fred, x is 347

And similarly if we look only at the output from Lucy, or Ricky. Each one individually is behaving in a nice orderly manner. But together—chaos! In the fragment above we see Fred, then Lucy, then Ricky (in the same order we originally started the threads), but then Lucy butts in when it was Fred's turn. What nerve! And then Ricky and Lucy trade back and forth for a while until finally Fred gets another chance. They jump around like this for a while after this. Eventually (after the part shown above) Fred finishes, then Ricky, and finally Lucy finishes with a long sequence of output. So even though Ricky was started third, he actually completed second. And if we run it again, we'll get a different result. Why? Because it's up to the scheduler, and we don't control the scheduler! Which brings up another key point to remember: Just because a series of threads are started in a particular order doesn't mean they'll run in that order. For any group of started threads, order is not guaranteed by the scheduler. And duration is not guaranteed. You don't know, for example, if one thread will run to completion before the others have a chance to get in or whether they'll all take turns nicely, or whether they'll do a combination of both. There is a way, however, to start a thread but tell it not to run until some other thread has finished. You can do this with the `join()` method, which we'll look at a little later.

A thread is done being a thread when its target `run()` *method completes.*

When a thread completes its `run()` method, the thread ceases to be a thread of execution. The stack for that thread dissolves, and the thread is considered dead. (Technically the API calls a dead thread "terminated", but we'll use "dead" in this chapter.) Not dead and gone, however, just dead. It's still a Thread *object*, just not a *thread of execution*. So if you've got a reference to a Thread instance, then even when that Thread instance is no longer a thread of execution, you can still call methods on the Thread instance, just like any other Java object. What you can't do, though, is call `start()` again.

Once a thread has been started, it can never be started again.

If you have a reference to a Thread, and you call `start()`, it's started. If you call `start()` a second time, it will cause an exception (an IllegalThreadStateException, which is a kind of RuntimeException, but you don't need to worry about the exact type). This happens whether or not the `run()` method has completed from the first `start()` call. Only a new thread can be started, and then only once. A runnable thread or a dead thread cannot be restarted.

So far, we've seen three thread states: *new*, *runnable*, and *dead*. We'll look at more thread states before we're done with this chapter.

The Thread Scheduler

The thread scheduler is the part of the JVM (although most JVMs map Java threads directly to native threads on the underlying OS) that decides which thread should run at any given moment, and also takes threads *out* of the run state. Assuming a single processor machine, only one thread can actually *run* at a time. Only one stack can ever be executing at one time. And it's the thread scheduler that decides *which* thread—of all that are eligible—will actually *run*. When we say *eligible*, we really mean *in the runnable state*.

Any thread in the *runnable* state can be chosen by the scheduler to be the one and only running thread. If a thread is not in a runnable state, then it cannot be chosen to be the *currently running* thread. And just so we're clear about how little is guaranteed here:

The order in which runnable threads are chosen to run is not guaranteed.

Although *queue* behavior is typical, it isn't guaranteed. Queue behavior means that when a thread has finished with its "turn," it moves to the end of the line of the runnable pool and waits until it eventually gets to the front of the line, where it can be chosen again. In fact, we call it a runnable *pool*, rather than a runnable *queue*, to help reinforce the fact that threads aren't all lined up in some guaranteed order.

Although we don't *control* the thread scheduler (we can't, for example, tell a specific thread to run), we can sometimes influence it. The following methods give us some tools for *influencing* the scheduler. Just don't ever mistake influence for control.

Methods from the java.lang. Thread Class Some of the methods that can help us influence thread scheduling are as follows:

```
public static void sleep(long millis) throws InterruptedException
public static void yield()
public final void join() throws InterruptedException
public final void setPriority(int newPriority)
```

Note that both sleep() and join() have overloaded versions not shown here.

Methods from the java.lang.Object Class   Every class in Java inherits the following three thread-related methods:

```
public final void wait() throws InterruptedException
public final void notify()
public final void notifyAll()
```

The `wait()` method has three overloaded versions (including the one listed here).

We'll look at the behavior of each of these methods in this chapter. First, though, we're going to look at the different states a thread can be in.

CERTIFICATION OBJECTIVE

Thread States and Transitions (Objective 4.2)

4.2   *Recognize the states in which a thread can exist, and identify ways in which a thread can transition from one state to another.*

We've already seen three thread states— *new, runnable,* and *dead*—but wait! There's more! The thread scheduler's job is to move threads in and out of the *running* state. While the thread scheduler can move a thread from the running state back to runnable, other factors can cause a thread to move out of running, but *not* back to runnable. One of these is when the thread's `run()` method completes, in which case the thread moves from the running state directly to the dead state. Next we'll look at some of the other ways in which a thread can leave the running state, and where the thread goes.

Thread States

A thread can be only in one of five states (see Figure 9-2):

  ■ **New**   This is the state the thread is in after the Thread instance has been created, but the `start()` method has not been invoked on the thread. It is a live Thread object, but not yet a thread of execution. At this point, the thread is considered *not alive*.

- **Runnable**   This is the state a thread is in when it's eligible to run, but the scheduler has not selected it to be the running thread. A thread first enters the runnable state when the start() method is invoked, but a thread can also return to the runnable state after either running or coming back from a blocked, waiting, or sleeping state. When the thread is in the runnable state, it is considered *alive*.

- **Running**   This is it. The "big time." Where the action is. This is the state a thread is in when the thread scheduler selects it (from the runnable pool) to be the currently executing process. A thread can transition out of a running state for several reasons, including because "the thread scheduler felt like it." We'll look at those other reasons shortly. Note that in Figure 9-2, there are several ways to get to the runnable state, but only *one* way to get to the running state: the scheduler chooses a thread from the runnable pool.

FIGURE 9-2

Transitioning between thread states

- **Waiting/blocked/sleeping**   This is the state a thread is in when it's not eligible to run. Okay, so this is really three states combined into one, but they all have one thing in common: the thread is still alive, but is currently not eligible to run. In other words, it is not *runnable*, but it might *return* to a runnable state later if a particular event occurs. A thread may be *blocked* waiting for a resource (like I/O or an object's lock), in which case the event that sends it back to runnable is the availability of the resource—for example, if data comes in through the input stream the thread code is reading from, or if the object's lock suddenly becomes available. A thread may be *sleeping* because the thread's run code *tells* it to sleep for some period of time, in which case the event that sends it back to runnable is that it wakes up because its sleep time has expired. Or the thread may be *waiting*, because the thread's run code *causes* it to wait, in which case the event that sends it back to runnable is that another thread sends a notification that it may no longer be necessary for the thread to wait. The important point is that one thread does not *tell* another thread to block. Some methods may *look* like they tell another thread to block, but they don't. If you have a reference t to another thread, you can write something like this:

```
t.sleep();   or      t.yield()
```

But those are actually static methods of the Thread class—*they don't affect the instance* t; instead they are defined to always affect the thread that's currently executing. (This is a good example of why it's a bad idea to use an instance variable to access a static method—it's misleading. There *is* a method, suspend(), in the Thread class, that lets one thread tell another to suspend, but the suspend() method has been deprecated and won't be on the exam (nor will its counterpart resume()). There is also a stop() method, but it too has been deprecated and we won't even go there. Both suspend() and stop() turned out to be very dangerous, so you shouldn't use them and again, because they're deprecated, they won't appear on the exam. Don't study 'em, don't use 'em. Note also that a thread in a blocked state is still considered to be *alive*.

■ **Dead**   A thread is considered dead when its run() method completes. It may still be a viable Thread object, but it is no longer a separate thread of execution. Once a thread is dead, it can never be brought back to life! (The whole "I see dead threads" thing.) If you invoke start() on a dead Thread instance, you'll get a runtime (not compiler) exception. And it probably doesn't take a rocket scientist to tell you that if a thread is dead, it is no longer considered to be *alive*.

Preventing Thread Execution

A thread that's been stopped usually means a thread that's moved to the dead state. But Objective 4.2 is also looking for your ability to recognize when a thread will get kicked out of running but *not* be sent back to either runnable or dead.

For the purpose of the exam, we aren't concerned with a thread blocking on I/O (say, waiting for something to arrive from an input stream from the server). We *are* concerned with the following:

- Sleeping
- Waiting
- Blocked because it needs an object's lock

Sleeping

The `sleep()` method is a `static` method of class Thread. You use it in your code to "slow a thread down" by forcing it to go into a sleep mode before coming back to runnable (where it still has to beg to be the currently running thread). When a thread sleeps, it drifts off somewhere and doesn't return to runnable until it wakes up.

So why would you want a thread to sleep? Well, you might think the thread is moving too quickly through its code. Or you might need to force your threads to take turns, since reasonable turn-taking isn't guaranteed in the Java specification. Or imagine a thread that runs in a loop, downloading the latest stock prices and analyzing them. Downloading prices one after another would be a waste of time, as most would be quite similar—and even more important, it would be an incredible waste of precious bandwidth. The simplest way to solve this is to cause a thread to pause (sleep) for five minutes after each download.

You do this by invoking the static `Thread.sleep()` method, giving it a time in milliseconds as follows:

```
try {
  Thread.sleep(5*60*1000);  // Sleep for 5 minutes
} catch (InterruptedException ex) { }
```

Notice that the `sleep()` method can throw a checked InterruptedException (you'll usually know if that is a possibility, since another thread has to explicitly do the interrupting), so you must acknowledge the exception with a handle or declare. Typically, you wrap calls to `sleep()` in a `try/catch`, as in the preceding code.

Let's modify our Fred, Lucy, Ricky code by using `sleep()` to *try* to force the threads to alternate rather than letting one thread dominate for any period of time. Where do you think the `sleep()` method should go?

```
class NameRunnable implements Runnable {
  public void run() {
    for (int x = 1; x < 4; x++) {
      System.out.println("Run by "
        + Thread.currentThread().getName());
```

```
            try {
              Thread.sleep(1000);
            } catch (InterruptedException ex) { }
        }
    }
}

public class ManyNames {
    public static void main (String [] args) {

        // Make one Runnable
        NameRunnable nr = new NameRunnable();

        Thread one = new Thread(nr);
        one.setName("Fred");
        Thread two = new Thread(nr);
        two.setName("Lucy");
        Thread three = new Thread(nr);
        three.setName("Ricky");

        one.start();
        two.start();
        three.start();
    }
}
```

Running this code shows Fred, Lucy, and Ricky alternating nicely:

```
% java ManyNames
Run by Fred
Run by Lucy
Run by Ricky
Run by Fred
Run by Lucy
Run by Ricky
Run by Fred
Run by Lucy
Run by Ricky
```

Just keep in mind that the behavior in the preceding output is still not guaranteed. You can't be certain how long a thread will actually run *before* it gets put to sleep, so you can't know with certainty that only one of the three threads will be in the runnable state when the running thread goes to sleep. In other words, if there are two threads awake and in the runnable pool, you can't know with certainty that the least recently used thread will be the one selected to run. *Still, using* `sleep()` *is the best way to help all threads get a chance to run!* Or at least to guarantee that one thread doesn't get in and stay until it's done. When a thread encounters a sleep call, it *must* go to sleep for *at least* the specified number of milliseconds (unless it is interrupted before its wake-up time, in which case it immediately throws the InterruptedException).

---

e x a m

ⓦ a t c h

Just because a thread's `sleep()` *expires, and it wakes up, does not mean it will return to running! Remember, when a thread wakes up, it simply goes back to the runnable state. So the time specified in* `sleep()` *is the minimum duration in which the thread won't run, but it is not the exact duration in which the thread won't run. So you can't, for example, rely on the* `sleep()` *method to give you a perfectly accurate timer. Although in many applications using* `sleep()` *as a timer is certainly good enough, you must know that a* `sleep()` *time is not a guarantee that the thread will start running again as soon as the time expires and the thread wakes.*

Remember that `sleep()` is a static method, so don't be fooled into thinking that one thread can put another thread to sleep. You can put `sleep()` code anywhere, since *all code is being run by *some* thread. When the executing code (meaning the currently running thread's code) hits a `sleep()` call, it puts the currently running thread to sleep.

EXERCISE 9-1

Creating a Thread and Putting It to Sleep

In this exercise we will create a simple counting thread. It will count to 100, pausing one second between each number. Also, in keeping with the counting theme, it will output a string every ten numbers.

1. Create a class and extend the Thread class. As an option, you can implement the Runnable interface.

2. Override the `run()` method of Thread. This is where the code will go that will output the numbers.

3. Create a `for` loop that will loop 100 times. Use the modulo operation to check whether there are any remainder numbers when divided by 10.

4. Use the `static` method `Thread.sleep()` to pause. (Remember, the one-arg version of `sleep()` specifies the amount of time of sleep in milliseconds.)

Thread Priorities and yield( )

To understand `yield()`, you must understand the concept of thread *priorities*. Threads always run with some priority, usually represented as a number between 1 and 10 (although in some cases the range is less than 10). The scheduler in most JVMs uses preemptive, priority-based scheduling (which implies some sort of time slicing). *This does not mean that all JVMs use time slicing.* The JVM specification does not require a VM to implement a time-slicing scheduler, where each thread is allocated a fair amount of time and then sent back to runnable to give another thread a chance. Although many JVMs do use time slicing, some may use a scheduler that lets one thread stay running until the thread completes its `run()` method.

In most JVMs, however, the scheduler does use thread priorities in one important way: If a thread enters the runnable state, and it has a higher priority than any of the threads in the pool and a higher priority than the currently running thread, *the lower-priority running thread usually will be bumped back to runnable and the highest-priority thread will be chosen to run.* In other words, at any given time the currently running thread usually will not have a priority that is lower than any of the threads in the pool. *In most cases, the running thread will be of equal or greater priority than the highest priority threads in the pool.* This is as close to a guarantee about scheduling as you'll get from the JVM specification, so you must never rely on thread priorities to guarantee the correct behavior of your program.

on the job

Don't rely on thread priorities when designing your multithreaded application. Because thread-scheduling priority behavior is not guaranteed, use thread priorities as a way to improve the efficiency of your program, but just be sure your program doesn't depend on that behavior for correctness.

What is also *not* guaranteed is the behavior when threads in the pool are of equal priority, or when the currently running thread has the same priority as threads in the pool. All priorities being equal, a JVM implementation of the scheduler is free to do just about anything it likes. That means a scheduler might do one of the following (among other things):

- Pick a thread to run, and run it there until it blocks or completes.

- Time slice the threads in the pool to give everyone an equal opportunity to run.

Setting a Thread's Priority A thread gets a default priority that is *the priority of the thread of execution that creates it*. For example, in the code

```
public class TestThreads {
  public static void main (String [] args) {
    MyThread t = new MyThread();
  }
}
```

the thread referenced by t will have the same priority as the *main* thread, since the main thread is executing the code that creates the MyThread instance.

You can also set a thread's priority directly by calling the setPriority() method on a Thread instance as follows:

```
FooRunnable r = new FooRunnable();
Thread t = new Thread(r);
t.setPriority(8);
t.start();
```

Priorities are set using a positive integer, usually between 1 and 10, and the JVM will never change a thread's priority. However, the values 1 through 10 are not guaranteed. Some JVM's might not recognize ten distinct values. Such a JVM might merge values from 1 to 10 down to maybe values from 1 to 5, so if you have, say, ten threads each with a different priority, and the current application is running in a JVM that allocates a range of only five priorities, then two or more threads might be mapped to one priority.

Although *the default priority is 5*, the Thread class has the three following constants (static final variables) that define the range of thread priorities:

```
Thread.MIN_PRIORITY   (1)
Thread.NORM_PRIORITY  (5)
Thread.MAX_PRIORITY   (10)
```

The yield( ) Method   So what does the static Thread.yield() have to do with all this? Not that much, in practice. What yield() is *supposed* to do is make the currently running thread head back to runnable to allow other threads of the same priority to get their turn. So the intention is to use yield() to promote graceful turn-taking among equal-priority threads. In reality, though, the yield() method isn't guaranteed to do what it claims, and even if yield() does cause a thread to step out of running and back to runnable, *there's no guarantee the yielding thread won't just be chosen again over all the others!* So while yield() might—and often does—make a running thread give up its slot to another runnable thread of the same priority, there's no guarantee.

A yield() won't ever cause a thread to go to the waiting/sleeping/ blocking state. At most, a yield() will cause a thread to go from running to runnable, but again, it might have no effect at all.

The join( ) Method

The non-static join() method of class Thread lets one thread "join onto the end" of another thread. If you have a thread B that can't do its work until another thread A has completed *its* work, then you want thread B to "join" thread A. This means that thread B will not become runnable until A has finished (and entered the dead state).

```
Thread t = new Thread();
t.start();
t.join();
```

The preceding code takes the currently running thread (if this were in the main() method, then that would be the main thread) and *joins* it to the end of the thread referenced by t. This blocks the current thread from becoming runnable until after the thread referenced by t is no longer alive. In other words, the code t.join() means "Join me (the current thread) to the end of t, so that t must finish before I (the current thread) can run again." You can also call one of the overloaded versions of join() that takes a timeout duration, so that you're saying, "wait until thread t is done, but if it takes longer than 5,000 milliseconds, then stop waiting and become runnable anyway." Figure 9-3 shows the effect of the join() method.

FIGURE 9-3   The `join()` method

Output	Key Events in the Threads' Code

```
A is running
A is running
A is running
A is running
A is running         Thread b = new Thread(aRunnable);
A is running ─────── b.start();
A is running
B is running         // Threads bounce back and forth
B is running
A is running
B is running
A is running
A is running
B is running
B is running
A is running
B is running
A is running ─────── b.join();  // A joins to the end
B is running                    // of B
B is running
B is running
B is running
B is running
B is running
B is running
B is running ─────── // Thread B completes !!
A is running ─────── // Thread A starts again !
A is running
A is running
A is running
A is running
A is running
```

doStuff()

Stack A is running

doStuff()   doOther()

Stack A is running   Stack B is running

doOther()

Stack B

doStuff()

Stack A

Stack A joined to Stack B

So far we've looked at three ways a running thread could leave the running state:

- **A call to `sleep()`**   Guaranteed to cause the current thread to stop executing for at least the specified sleep duration (although it might be *interrupted* before its specified time).

- **A call to `yield()`**   Not guaranteed to do much of anything, although typically it will cause the currently running thread to move back to runnable so that a thread of the same priority can have a chance.

- **A call to `join()`**   Guaranteed to cause the current thread to stop executing until the thread it joins with (in other words, the thread it calls `join()`

on) completes, or if the thread it's trying to join with is not alive, however, the current thread won't need to back out.

Besides those three, we also have the following scenarios in which a thread might leave the running state:

- The thread's `run()` method completes. Duh.

- A call to `wait()` on an object (we don't call `wait()` on a *thread*, as we'll see in a moment).

- A thread can't acquire the *lock* on the object whose method code it's attempting to run.

- The thread scheduler can decide to move the current thread from running to runnable in order to give another thread a chance to run. No reason is needed—the thread scheduler can trade threads in and out whenever it likes.

CERTIFICATION OBJECTIVE

Synchronizing Code (Objective 4.3)

4.3   Given a scenario, write code that makes appropriate use of object locking to protect static or instance variables from concurrent access problems.

Can you imagine the havoc that can occur when two different threads have access to a single instance of a class, and both threads invoke methods on that object…and those methods modify the state of the object? In other words, what might happen if *two* different threads call, say, a setter method on a *single* object? A scenario like that might corrupt an object's state (by changing its instance variable values in an inconsistent way), and if that object's state is data shared by other parts of the program, well, it's too scary to even visualize.

But just because we enjoy horror, let's look at an example of what might happen. The following code demonstrates what happens when two different threads are accessing the same account data. Imagine that two people each have a checkbook for a single checking account (or two people each have ATM cards, but both cards are linked to only one account).

In this example, we have a class called Account that represents a bank account. To keep the code short, this account starts with a balance of 50, and can be used only for withdrawals. The withdrawal will be accepted even if there isn't enough money in the account to cover it. The account simply reduces the balance by the amount you want to withdraw:

```
class Account {
   private int balance = 50;
   public int getBalance() {
      return balance;
   }
   public void withdraw(int amount) {
      balance = balance - amount;
   }
}
```

Now here's where it starts to get fun. Imagine a couple, Fred and Lucy, who both have access to the account and want to make withdrawals. But they don't want the account to ever be overdrawn, so just before one of them makes a withdrawal, he or she will first check the balance to be certain there's enough to cover the withdrawal. Also, withdrawals are always limited to an amount of 10, so there must be at least 10 in the account balance in order to make a withdrawal. Sounds reasonable. But that's a two-step process:

1. Check the balance.

2. If there's enough in the account (in this example, at least 10), make the withdrawal.

What happens if something separates step 1 from step 2? For example, imagine what would happen if Lucy checks the balance and sees that there's just exactly enough in the account, 10. *But before she makes the withdrawal, Fred checks the balance and also sees that there's enough for his withdrawal.* Since Lucy has verified the balance, but not yet made her withdrawal, Fred is seeing "bad data." He is seeing the account balance *before* Lucy actually debits the account, but at this point that debit is certain to occur. Now both Lucy and Fred believe there's enough to make their withdrawals. So now imagine that Lucy makes *her* withdrawal, and now there isn't enough in the account for Fred's withdrawal, but he thinks there is since when he checked, there was enough! Yikes. In a minute we'll see the actual banking code, with Fred and Lucy, represented by two threads, each acting on the same Runnable, and that Runnable holds a reference to the one and only account instance—so, two threads, one account.

The logic in our code example is as follows:

1. The Runnable object holds a reference to a single account.

2. Two threads are started, representing Lucy and Fred, and each thread is given a reference to the same Runnable (which holds a reference to the actual account)

3. The initial balance on the account is 50, and each withdrawal is exactly 10.

4. In the run() method, we loop 5 times, and in each loop we

   ■ Make a withdrawal (if there's enough in the account).

   ■ Print a statement *if the account is overdrawn* (which it should never be, since we check the balance *before* making a withdrawal).

5. The makeWithdrawal() method in the test class (representing the behavior of Fred or Lucy) will do the following:

   ■ Check the balance to see if there's enough for the withdrawal.

   ■ If there is enough, print out the name of the one making the withdrawal.

   ■ Go to sleep for 500 milliseconds—just long enough to give the other partner a chance to get in before you actually *make* the withdrawal.

   ■ Upon waking up, complete the withdrawal and print that fact.

   ■ If there wasn't enough in the first place, print a statement showing who you are and the fact that there wasn't enough.

So what we're really trying to discover is if the following is possible: for one partner to check the account and see that there's enough, but before making the actual withdrawal, the other partner checks the account and *also* sees that there's enough. When the account balance gets to 10, if both partners check it before making the withdrawal, both will think it's OK to withdraw, and the account will overdraw by 10! Here's the code:

```
public class AccountDanger implements Runnable {
    private Account acct = new Account();
    public static void main (String [] args) {
        AccountDanger r = new AccountDanger();
        Thread one = new Thread(r);
        Thread two = new Thread(r);
        one.setName("Fred");
        two.setName("Lucy");
```

```
        one.start();
        two.start();
      }
    public void run() {
      for (int x = 0; x < 5; x++) {
        makeWithdrawal(10);
        if (acct.getBalance() < 0) {
          System.out.println("account is overdrawn!");
        }
      }
    }
  }
    private void makeWithdrawal(int amt) {
      if (acct.getBalance() >= amt) {
          System.out.println(Thread.currentThread().getName()
                    + " is going to withdraw");
          try {
            Thread.sleep(500);
          } catch(InterruptedException ex) { }
          acct.withdraw(amt);
          System.out.println(Thread.currentThread().getName()
                    + " completes the withdrawal");
      } else {
          System.out.println("Not enough in account for "
                    + Thread.currentThread().getName()
                    + " to withdraw " + acct.getBalance());
      }
    }
  }
}
```

So what happened? Is it possible that, say, Lucy checked the balance, fell asleep,
Fred checked the balance, Lucy woke up and completed *her* withdrawal, then Fred
completes *his* withdrawal, and in the end they overdraw the account? Look at the
(numbered) output:

```
% java AccountDanger
 1. Fred is going to withdraw
 2. Lucy is going to withdraw
 3. Fred completes the withdrawal
 4. Fred is going to withdraw
 5. Lucy completes the withdrawal
 6. Lucy is going to withdraw
 7. Fred completes the withdrawal
 8. Fred is going to withdraw
 9. Lucy completes the withdrawal
```

```
10. Lucy is going to withdraw
11. Fred completes the withdrawal
12. Not enough in account for Fred to withdraw 0
13. Not enough in account for Fred to withdraw 0
14. Lucy completes the withdrawal
15. account is overdrawn!
16. Not enough in account for Lucy to withdraw -10
17. account is overdrawn!
18. Not enough in account for Lucy to withdraw -10
19. account is overdrawn!
```

Although each time you run this code the output might be a little different, let's walk through this particular example using the numbered lines of output. For the first four attempts, everything is fine. Fred checks the balance on line 1, and finds it's OK. At line 2, Lucy checks the balance and finds it OK. At line 3, Fred makes his withdrawal. At this point, the balance Lucy checked for (and believes is still accurate) has actually changed since she last checked. And now Fred checks the balance *again*, before Lucy even completes her first withdrawal. By this point, even Fred is seeing a potentially inaccurate balance, because we know Lucy is going to complete her withdrawal. It is possible, of course, that Fred will complete his before Lucy does, but that's not what happens here.

On line 5, Lucy completes her withdrawal and then before Fred completes his, Lucy does another check on the account on line 6. And so it continues until we get to line 8, where Fred checks the balance and sees that it's 20. On line 9, Lucy completes a withdrawal (that she had checked for earlier), and this takes the balance to 10. On line 10, Lucy checks again, sees that the balance is 10, so she knows she can do a withdrawal. *But she didn't know that Fred, too, has already checked the balance on line 8 so he thinks it's safe to do the withdrawal!* On line 11, Fred completes the withdrawal he approved on line 8. This takes the balance to zero. But Lucy still has a pending withdrawal that she got approval for on line 10! You know what's coming.

On lines 12 and 13, Fred checks the balance and finds that there's not enough in the account. But on line 14, Lucy completes her withdrawal and BOOM! The account is now overdrawn by 10—*something we thought we were preventing by doing a balance check prior to a withdrawal.*

Figure 9-4 shows the timeline of what can happen when two threads concurrently access the same object.

FIGURE 9-4

Problems with
concurrent access

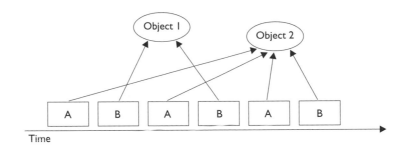

Thread A will access Object 2 only

Thread B will access Object 1, and then Object 2

This problem is known as a "race condition," where multiple threads can access the same resource (typically an object's instance variables), and can produce corrupted data if one thread "races in" too quickly before an operation that should be "atomic" has completed.

Preventing the Account Overdraw   So what can be done? The solution is actually quite simple. We must guarantee that the two steps of the withdrawal—checking the balance and *making* the withdrawal —are never split apart. We need them to always be performed as one operation, even when the thread falls asleep in between step 1 and step 2! We call this an "atomic operation" (although the physics is a little outdated, in this case "atomic" means "indivisible") because the operation, regardless of the number of actual statements (or underlying byte code instructions), is completed *before* any other thread code that acts on the same data.

You can't guarantee that a single thread will stay running throughout the entire atomic operation. But you *can* guarantee that even if the thread running the atomic operation moves in and out of the running state, *no other running thread will be able to act on the same data.* In other words, If Lucy falls asleep after checking the balance, we can stop Fred from checking the balance until *after* Lucy wakes up and completes her withdrawal.

So how do you protect the data? You must do two things:

- Mark the variables `private`.
- Synchronize the code that modifies the variables.

Remember, you protect the variables in the normal way—using an access control modifier. It's the method code that you must protect, so that only one thread at a time can be executing that code. You do this with the `synchronized` keyword.

We can solve all of Fred and Lucy's problems by adding one word to the code. We mark the `makeWithdrawal()` method `synchronized` as follows:

```
private synchronized void makeWithdrawal(int amt) {
  if (acct.getBalance() >= amt) {
    System.out.println(Thread.currentThread().getName() +
                        " is going to withdraw");
    try {
      Thread.sleep(500);
    } catch(InterruptedException ex) { }
    acct.withdraw(amt);
    System.out.println(Thread.currentThread().getName() +
                        " completes the withdrawal");
  } else {
    System.out.println("Not enough in account for "
                        + Thread.currentThread().getName()
                        + " to withdraw " + acct.getBalance());
  }
}
```

Now we've guaranteed that once a thread (Lucy or Fred) starts the withdrawal process (by invoking `makeWithdrawal()`), the other thread cannot enter that method until the first one completes the process by exiting the method. The new output shows the benefit of synchronizing the `makeWithdrawal()` method:

```
% java AccountDanger
Fred is going to withdraw
Fred completes the withdrawal
Lucy is going to withdraw
Lucy completes the withdrawal
Fred is going to withdraw
Fred completes the withdrawal
Lucy is going to withdraw
Lucy completes the withdrawal
Fred is going to withdraw
Fred completes the withdrawal
Not enough in account for Lucy to withdraw 0
Not enough in account for Fred to withdraw 0
Not enough in account for Lucy to withdraw 0
Not enough in account for Fred to withdraw 0
Not enough in account for Lucy to withdraw 0
```

Notice that now both threads, Lucy and Fred, always check the account balance *and* complete the withdrawal before the other thread can check the balance.

Synchronization and Locks

How does synchronization work? With locks. Every object in Java has a built-in lock that only comes into play when the object has synchronized method code. When we enter a synchronized non-static method, we automatically acquire the lock associated with the current instance of the class whose code we're executing (the this instance). Acquiring a lock for an object is also known as getting the lock, or locking the object, locking *on* the object, or synchronizing on the object. We may also use the term *monitor* to refer to the object whose lock we're acquiring. Technically the lock and the monitor are two different things, but most people talk about the two interchangeably, and we will too.

Since there is only one lock per object, if one thread has picked up the lock, no other thread can pick up the lock until the first thread releases (or returns) the lock. This means no other thread can enter the synchronized code (which means it can't enter any synchronized method of that object) until the lock has been released. Typically, releasing a lock means the thread holding the lock (in other words, the thread currently in the synchronized method) exits the synchronized method. At that point, the lock is free until some other thread enters a synchronized method on that object. Remember the following key points about locking and synchronization:

- Only methods (or blocks) can be synchronized, not variables or classes
- Each object has just one lock.
- Not all methods in a class need to be synchronized. A class can have both synchronized and non-synchronized methods.
- If two threads are about to execute a synchronized method in a class, and both threads are using the same instance of the class to invoke the method, only one thread at a time will be able to execute the method. The other thread will need to wait until the first one finishes its method call. In other words, once a thread acquires the lock on an object, no other thread can enter any of the synchronized methods in that class (for that object).

- If a class has both `synchronized` and non-`synchronized` methods, multiple threads can still access the class's non-`synchronized` methods! If you have methods that don't access the data you're trying to protect, then you don't need to synchronize them. Synchronization can cause a hit in some cases (or even deadlock if used incorrectly), so you should be careful not to overuse it.

- If a thread goes to sleep, it holds any locks it has—it doesn't release them.

- A thread can acquire more than one lock. For example, a thread can enter a `synchronized` method, thus acquiring a lock, and then immediately invoke a `synchronized` method on a different object, thus acquiring that lock as well. As the stack unwinds, locks are released again. Also, if a thread acquires a lock and then attempts to call a `synchronized` method on that same object, no problem. The JVM knows that this thread already has the lock for this object, so the thread is free to call other `synchronized` methods on the same object, using the lock the thread already has.

- You can synchronize a block of code rather than a method.

Because synchronization does hurt concurrency, you don't want to synchronize any more code than is necessary to protect your data. So if the scope of a method is more than needed, you can reduce the scope of the synchronized part to something less than a full method—to just a block. We call this, strangely, a *synchronized block*, and it looks like this:

```
class SyncTest {
  public void doStuff() {
    System.out.println("not synchronized");
    synchronized(this) {
      System.out.println("synchronized");
    }
  }
}
```

When a thread is executing code from within a `synchronized` block, including any method code invoked from that `synchronized` block, the code is said to be executing in a synchronized context. The real question is, synchronized on what? Or, synchronized on which object's lock?

When you synchronize a method, the object used to invoke the method is the object whose lock must be acquired. But when you synchronize a block of code, you specify which object's lock you want to use as the lock, so you could, for example, use some third-party object as the lock for this piece of code. That gives you the ability to have more than one lock for code synchronization within a single object.

Or you can synchronize on the current instance (`this`) as in the code above. Since that's the same instance that `synchronized` methods lock on, it means that you could always replace a `synchronized` method with a non-synchronized method containing a `synchronized` block. In other words, this:

```
public synchronized void doStuff() {
    System.out.println("synchronized");
}
```

is equivalent to this:

```
public void doStuff() {
    synchronized(this) {
        System.out.println("synchronized");
    }
}
```

These methods both have the exact same effect, in practical terms. The compiled bytecodes may not be exactly the same for the two methods, but they *could* be—and any differences are not really important. The first form is shorter and more familiar to most people, but the second can be more flexible.

So What About Static Methods? Can They Be Synchronized?

`static` methods can be synchronized. There is only one copy of the static data you're trying to protect, so you only need one lock per class to synchronize static methods—a lock for the whole class. There is such a lock; every class loaded in Java has a corresponding instance of java.lang.Class representing that class. It's that java.lang.Class instance whose lock is used to protect the `static` methods of the class (if they're `synchronized`). There's nothing special you have to do to synchronize a `static` method:

```
public static synchronized int getCount() {
    return count;
}
```

Again, this could be replaced with code that uses a `synchronized` block. If the method is defined in a class called MyClass, the equivalent code is as follows:

```
public static int getCount() {
    synchronized(MyClass.class) {
        return count;
    }
}
```

Wait—what's that `MyClass.class` thing? That's called a *class literal*. It's a special feature in the Java language that tells the compiler (who tells the JVM): go and find me the instance of Class that represents the class called MyClass. You can also do this with the following code:

```
public static void classMethod() {
    Class cl = Class.forName("MyClass");
    synchronized (cl) {
        // do stuff
    }
}
```

However that's longer, ickier, and most important, *not on the SCJP exam*. But it's quick and easy to use a class literal—just write the name of the class, and add `.class` at the end. No quotation marks needed. Now you've got an expression for the Class object you need to synchronize on.

EXERCISE 9-2

Synchronizing a Block of Code

In this exercise we will attempt to synchronize a block of code. Within that block of code we will get the lock on an object, so that other threads cannot modify it while the block of code is executing. We will be creating three threads that will all attempt to manipulate the same object. Each thread will output a single letter 100 times, and then increment that letter by one. The object we will be using is StringBuffer.

We could synchronize on a String object, but strings cannot be modified once they are created, so we would not be able to increment the letter without generating a new String object. The final output should have 100 As, 100 Bs, and 100 Cs all in unbroken lines.

1. Create a class and extend the Thread class.

2. Override the `run()` method of Thread. This is where the `synchronized` block of code will go.

3. For our three thread objects to share the same object, we will need to create a constructor that accepts a StringBuffer object in the argument.

4. The `synchronized` block of code will obtain a lock on the StringBuffer object from step 3.

5. Within the block, output the StringBuffer 100 times and then increment the letter in the StringBuffer. You can check Chapter 6 for StringBuffer methods that will help with this.

6. Finally, in the `main()` method, create a single StringBuffer object using the letter A, then create three instances of our class and start all three of them.

What Happens If a Thread Can't Get the Lock?

If a thread tries to enter a `synchronized` method and the lock is already taken, the thread is said to be blocked on the object's lock. Essentially, the thread goes into a kind of pool for that particular object and has to sit there until the lock is released and the thread can again become runnable/running. Just because a lock is released doesn't mean any particular thread will get it. There might be three threads waiting for a single lock, for example, and there's no guarantee that the thread that has waited the longest will get the lock first.

When thinking about blocking, it's important to pay attention to which objects are being used for locking.

- Threads calling non-`static` `synchronized` methods in the same class will only block each other if they're invoked using the same instance. That's because they each lock on `this` instance, and if they're called using two different instances, they get two locks, which do not interfere with each other.

- Threads calling `static` `synchronized` methods in the same class will always block each other—they all lock on the same Class instance.

- A `static` `synchronized` method and a non-`static` `synchronized` method will not block each other, ever. The `static` method locks on a Class instance while the non-`static` method locks on the `this` instance—these actions do not interfere with each other at all.

■ For synchronized blocks, you have to look at exactly what object has been used for locking. (What's inside the parentheses after the word synchronized?) Threads that synchronize on the same object will block each other. Threads that synchronize on different objects will not.

Table 9-1 lists the thread-related methods and whether the thread gives up its lock as a result of the call.

TABLE 9-1   Methods and Lock Status

Give Up Locks	Keep Locks	Class Defining the Method
wait ()	notify() (Although the thread will probably exit the synchronized code shortly after this call, and thus give up its locks.)	java.lang.Object
	join()	java.lang.Thread
	sleep()	java.lang.Thread
	yield()	java.lang.Thread

So When Do I Need to Synchronize?

Synchronization can get pretty complicated, and you may be wondering why you would want to do this at all if you can help it. But remember the earlier "race conditions" example with Lucy and Fred making withdrawals from their account. When we use threads, we usually need to use some synchronization somewhere to make sure our methods don't interrupt each other at the wrong time and mess up our data. Generally, any time more than one thread is accessing mutable (changeable) data, you synchronize to protect that data, to make sure two threads aren't changing it at the same time (or that one isn't changing it at the same time the other is reading it, which is also confusing). You don't need to worry about local variables—each thread gets its own copy of a local variable. Two threads executing the same method at the same time will use different copies of the local variables, and they won't bother each other. However, you do need to worry about static and non-static fields, if they contain data that can be changed.

For changeable data in a non-static field, you usually use a non-static method to access it. By synchronizing that method, you will ensure that any threads trying to run that method *using the same instance* will be prevented from simultaneous access. But a thread working with a *different* instance will not be affected, because it's acquiring a lock on the other instance. That's what we want—threads working with the same data need to go one at a time, but threads working with different data can just ignore each other and run whenever they want to; it doesn't matter.

For changeable data in a `static` field, you usually use a static method to access it. And again, by synchronizing the method you ensure that any two threads trying to access the data will be prevented from simultaneous access, because both threads will have to acquire locks on the Class object for the class the `static` method's defined in. Again, that's what we want.

However—what if you have a non-`static` method that accesses a `static` field? Or a `static` method that accesses a non-`static` field (using an instance)? In these cases things start to get messy quickly, and there's a very good chance that things will not work the way you want. If you've got a `static` method accessing a non-`static` field, and you synchronize the method, you acquire a lock on the Class object. But what if there's another method that also accesses the non-`static` field, this time using a non-`static` method? It probably synchronizes on the current instance (`this`) instead. Remember that a `static` synchronized method and a non-`static` synchronized method will not block each other—they can run at the same time. Similarly, if you access a static field using a non-`static` method, two threads might invoke that method using two different `this` instances. Which means they won't block each other, because they use different locks. Which means two threads are simultaneously accessing the same `static` field—exactly the sort of thing we're trying to prevent.

It gets very confusing trying to imagine all the weird things that can happen here. To keep things simple: in order to make a class thread-safe, methods that access changeable fields need to be synchronized.

Access to static fields should be done from `static` synchronized *methods. Access to non-*`static` *fields should be done from non-*`static` synchronized *methods.* For example:

```
public class Thing {
    private static int staticField;
    private int nonstaticField;
    public static synchronized int getStaticField() {
        return staticField;
    }
    public static synchronized void setStaticField(
                                    int staticField) {
```

```
            Thing.staticField = staticField;
        }
        public synchronized int getNonstaticField() {
            return nonstaticField;
        }
        public synchronized void setNonstaticField(
                                         int nonstaticField) {
            this.nonstaticField = nonstaticField;
        }
    }
```

What if you need to access both static and non-static fields in a method? Well, there are ways to do that, but it's beyond what you need for the exam. You will live a longer, happier life if you JUST DON'T DO IT. Really. Would we lie?

Thread-Safe Classes

When a class has been carefully synchronized to protect its data (using the rules just given, or using more complicated alternatives), we say the class is "thread-safe." Many classes in the Java APIs already use synchronization internally in order to make the class "thread-safe." For example, StringBuffer and StringBuilder are nearly identical classes, except that all the methods in StringBuffer are synchronized when necessary, while those in StringBuilder are not. Generally, this makes StringBuffer safe to use in a multithreaded environment, while StringBuilder is not. (In return, StringBuilder is a little bit faster because it doesn't bother synchronizing.) However, even when a class is "thread-safe," it is often dangerous to rely on these classes to provide the thread protection you need. (C'mon, the repeated quotes used around "thread-safe" had to be a clue, right?) You still need to think carefully about how you use these classes, As an example, consider the following class.

```
import java.util.*;
public class NameList {
    private List names = Collections.synchronizedList(
                                       new LinkedList());
    public void add(String name) {
        names.add(name);
    }
    public String removeFirst() {
        if (names.size() > 0)
            return (String) names.remove(0);
        else
            return null;
```

```
        }
    }
```

The method `Collections.synchronizedList()` returns a List whose methods are all `synchronized` and "thread-safe" according to the documentation (like a Vector—but since this is the 21st century, we're not going to use a Vector here). The question is, can the NameList class be used safely from multiple threads? It's tempting to think that yes, since the data in names is in a synchronized collection, the NameList class is "safe" too. However that's not the case—the `removeFirst()` may sometimes throw a NoSuchElementException. What's the problem? Doesn't it correctly check the `size()` of names before removing anything, to make sure there's something there? How could this code fail? Let's try to use NameList like this:

```
public static void main(String[] args) {
    final NameList nl = new NameList();
    nl.add("Ozymandias");
    class NameDropper extends Thread {
        public void run() {
            String name = nl.removeFirst();
            System.out.println(name);
        }
    }
    Thread t1 = new NameDropper();
    Thread t2 = new NameDropper();
    t1.start();
    t2.start();
}
```

What might happen here is that one of the threads will remove the one name and print it, then the other will try to remove a name and get `null`. If we think just about the calls to `names.size()` and `names.get(0)`, they occur in this order:

Thread `t1` executes `names.size()`, which returns 1.
Thread `t1` executes `names.remove(0)`, which returns `Ozymandias`.
Thread `t2` executes `names.size()`, which returns 0.
Thread `t2` does not call `remove(0)`.

The output here is

```
Ozymandias
null
```

However, if we run the program again something different might happen:

Thread t1 executes names.size(), which returns 1.
Thread t2 executes names.size(), which returns 1.
Thread t1 executes names.remove(0), which returns Ozymandias.
Thread t2 executes names.remove(0), which throws an exception because the list is now empty.

The thing to realize here is that in a "thread-safe" class like the one returned by synchronizedList(), each *individual* method is synchronized. So names.size() is synchronized, and names.remove(0) is synchronized. But nothing prevents another thread from doing something else to the list *in between* those two calls. And that's where problems can happen.

There's a solution here: don't rely on Collections.synchronizedList(). Instead, synchronize the code yourself:

```
import java.util.*;
public class NameList {
    private List names = new LinkedList();
    public synchronized void add(String name) {
        names.add(name);
    }
    public synchronized String removeFirst() {
        if (names.size() > 0)
            return (String) names.remove(0);
        else
            return null;
    }
}
```

Now the entire removeFirst() method is synchronized, and once one thread starts it and calls names.size(), there's no way the other thread can cut in and steal the last name. The other thread will just have to wait until the first thread completes the removeFirst() method.

The moral here is that just because a class is described as "thread-safe" doesn't mean it is *always* thread-safe. If individual methods are synchronized, that may not be enough—you may be better off putting in synchronization at a higher level (i.e., put it in the block or method that *calls* the other methods). Once you do that, the original synchronization (in this case, the synchronization inside the object returned by Collections.synchronizedList()) may well become redundant.

Thread Deadlock

Perhaps the scariest thing that can happen to a Java program is deadlock. Deadlock occurs when two threads are blocked, with each waiting for the other's lock. Neither can run until the other gives up its lock, so they'll sit there forever.

This can happen, for example, when thread A hits synchronized code, acquires a lock B, and then enters another method (still within the synchronized code it has the lock on) that's also synchronized. But thread A can't get the lock to enter this synchronized code—block C—because another thread D has the lock already. So thread A goes off to the waiting-for-the-C-lock pool, hoping that thread D will hurry up and release the lock (by completing the synchronized method). But thread A will wait a very long time indeed, because while thread D picked up lock C, it then entered a method synchronized on lock B. Obviously, thread D can't get the lock B because thread A has it. And thread A won't release it until thread D releases lock C. But thread D won't release lock C until after it can get lock B and continue. And there they sit. The following example demonstrates deadlock:

```
1. public class DeadlockRisk {
2.    private static class Resource {
3.       public int value;
4.    }
5.    private Resource resourceA = new Resource();
6.    private Resource resourceB = new Resource();
7.    public int read() {
8.       synchronized(resourceA) { // May deadlock here
9.          synchronized(resourceB) {
10.            return resourceB.value + resourceA.value;
11.         }
12.      }
13.   }
14.
15.   public void write(int a, int b) {
16.      synchronized(resourceB) { // May deadlock here
17.         synchronized(resourceA) {
18.            resourceA.value = a;
19.            resourceB.value = b;
20.         }
21.      }
22.   }
23. }
```

Assume that read() is started by one thread and write() is started by another. If there are two different threads that may read and write independently, there is a risk of deadlock at line 8 or 16. The reader thread will have resourceA, the writer thread will have resourceB, and both will get stuck waiting for the other.

Code like this almost never results in deadlock because the CPU has to switch from the reader thread to the writer thread at a particular point in the code, and the chances of deadlock occurring are very small. The application may work fine 99.9 percent of the time.

The preceding simple example is easy to fix; just swap the order of locking for either the reader or the writer at lines 16 and 17 (or lines 8 and 9). More complex deadlock situations can take a long time to figure out.

Regardless of how little chance there is for your code to deadlock, the bottom line is, if you deadlock, you're dead. There are design approaches that can help avoid deadlock, including strategies for always acquiring locks in a predetermined order.

But that's for you to study and is beyond the scope of this book. We're just trying to get you through the exam. If you learn everything in this chapter, though, you'll still know more about threads than most experienced Java programmers.

CERTIFICATION OBJECTIVE

Thread Interaction (Objective 4.4)

4.4   Given a scenario, write code that makes appropriate use of wait, notify. or notifyAll.

The last thing we need to look at is how threads can interact with one another to communicate about—among other things—their locking status. The Object class has three methods, wait(), notify(), and notifyAll() that help threads communicate about the status of an event that the threads care about. For example, if one thread is a mail-delivery thread and one thread is a mail-processor thread, the mail-processor thread has to keep checking to see if there's any mail to process. Using the wait and notify mechanism, the mail-processor thread could check for mail, and if it doesn't find any it can say, "Hey, I'm not going to waste my time checking for mail every two seconds. I'm going to go hang out, and when the mail deliverer puts something in the mailbox, have him notify me so I can go back to runnable and do some work." In other words, using wait() and notify() lets one thread put itself into a "waiting room" until some *other* thread notifies it that there's a reason to come back out.

One key point to remember (and keep in mind for the exam) about wait/notify is this:

wait (), notify (), and notifyAll () *must be called from within a synchronized context! A thread can't invoke a wait or notify method on an object unless it owns that object's lock.*

Here we'll present an example of two threads that depend on each other to proceed with their execution, and we'll show how to use wait () and notify () to make them interact safely and at the proper moment.

Think of a computer-controlled machine that cuts pieces of fabric into different shapes and an application that allows users to specify the shape to cut. The current version of the application has one thread, which loops, first asking the user for instructions, and then directs the hardware to cut the requested shape:

```
public void run(){
    while(true){
        // Get shape from user
        // Calculate machine steps from shape
        // Send steps to hardware
    }
}
```

This design is not optimal because the user can't do anything while the machine is busy and while there are other shapes to define. We need to improve the situation.

A simple solution is to separate the processes into two different threads, one of them interacting with the user and another managing the hardware. The user thread sends the instructions to the hardware thread and then goes back to interacting with the user immediately. The hardware thread receives the instructions from the user thread and starts directing the machine immediately. Both threads use a common object to communicate, which holds the current design being processed.

The following pseudocode shows this design:

```
public void userLoop(){
    while(true){
        // Get shape from user
        // Calculate machine steps from shape
        // Modify common object with new machine steps
```

```
            }
        }

        public void hardwareLoop(){
            while(true){
                // Get steps from common object
                // Send steps to hardware
            }
        }
```

The problem now is to get the hardware thread to process the machine steps as soon as they are available. Also, the user thread should not modify them until they have all been sent to the hardware. The solution is to use wait() and notify(), and also to synchronize some of the code.

The methods wait() and notify(), remember, are instance methods of Object. In the same way that every object has a lock, every object can have a list of threads that are waiting for a signal (a notification) from the object. A thread gets on this waiting list by executing the wait() method of the target object. From that moment, it doesn't execute any further instructions until the notify() method of the target object is called. If many threads are waiting on the same object, only one will be chosen (in no guaranteed order) to proceed with its execution. If there are no threads waiting, then no particular action is taken. Let's take a look at some real code that shows one object waiting for another object to notify it (take note, it is somewhat complex):

```
1.   class ThreadA {
2.       public static void main(String [] args) {
3.           ThreadB b = new ThreadB();
4.           b.start();
5.
6.           synchronized(b) {
7.               try {
8.                   System.out.println("Waiting for b to complete...");
9.                   b.wait();
10.              } catch (InterruptedException e) {}
11.              System.out.println("Total is: " + b.total);
12.          }
13.      }
14.  }
15.
16.  class ThreadB extends Thread {
17.      int total;
```

```
18.
19.      public void run() {
20.          synchronized(this) {
21.              for(int i=0;i<100;i++) {
22.                  total += i;
23.              }
24.              notify();
25.          }
26.      }
27.  }
```

This program contains two objects with threads: ThreadA contains the main thread and ThreadB has a thread that calculates the sum of all numbers from 0 through 99. As soon as line 4 calls the `start()` method, ThreadA will continue with the next line of code in its own class, which means it could get to line 11 before ThreadB has finished the calculation. To prevent this, we use the `wait()` method in line 9.

Notice in line 6 the code synchronizes itself with the object b—this is because in order to call `wait()` on the object, ThreadA must own a lock on b. For a thread to call `wait()` or `notify()`, the thread has to be the owner of the lock for that object. When the thread waits, it temporarily releases the lock for other threads to use, but it will need it again to continue execution. It's common to find code like this:

```
synchronized(anotherObject) { // this has the lock on anotherObject
    try {
        anotherObject.wait();
        // the thread releases the lock and waits
        // To continue, the thread needs the lock,
        // so it may be blocked until it gets it.
    } catch(InterruptedException e){}
}
```

The preceding code waits until `notify()` is called on `anotherObject`.

```
synchronized(this) { notify(); }
```

This code notifies a single thread currently waiting on the `this` object. The lock can be acquired much earlier in the code, such as in the calling method. Note that if the thread calling `wait()` does not own the lock, it will throw an `IllegalMonitorStateException`. This exception is not a checked exception, so you don't have to *catch* it explicitly. You should always be clear whether a thread has the lock of an object in any given block of code.

Notice in lines 7–10 there is a try/catch block around the wait() method. A waiting thread can be interrupted in the same way as a sleeping thread, so you have to take care of the exception:

```
try {
   wait();
} catch(InterruptedException e) {
   // Do something about it
}
```

In the fabric example, the way to use these methods is to have the hardware thread wait on the shape to be available and the user thread to notify after it has written the steps. The machine steps may comprise global steps, such as moving the required fabric to the cutting area, and a number of substeps, such as the direction and length of a cut. As an example they could be

```
int fabricRoll;
int cuttingSpeed;
Point startingPoint;
float[] directions;
float[] lengths;
etc..
```

It is important that the user thread does not modify the machine steps while the hardware thread is using them, so this reading and writing should be synchronized. The resulting code would look like this:

```
class Operator extends Thread {
   public void run(){
      while(true){
         // Get shape from user
         synchronized(this){
            // Calculate new machine steps from shape
            notify();
         }
      }
   }
}
class Machine extends Thread {
   Operator operator; // assume this gets initialized
```

```
public void run(){
    while(true){
        synchronized(operator){
            try {
                operator.wait();
            } catch(InterruptedException ie) {}
            // Send machine steps to hardware
        }
    }
}
```

The machine thread, once started, will immediately go into the waiting state and will wait patiently until the operator sends the first notification. At that point it is the operator thread that owns the lock for the object, so the hardware thread gets stuck for a while. It's only after the operator thread abandons the synchronized block that the hardware thread can really start processing the machine steps.

While one shape is being processed by the hardware, the user may interact with the system and specify another shape to be cut. When the user is finished with the shape and it is time to cut it, the operator thread attempts to enter the synchronized block, maybe blocking until the machine thread has finished with the previous machine steps. When the machine thread has finished, it repeats the loop, going again to the waiting state (and therefore releasing the lock). Only then can the operator thread enter the synchronized block and overwrite the machine steps with the new ones.

Having two threads is definitely an improvement over having one, although in this implementation there is still a possibility of making the user wait. A further improvement would be to have many shapes in a queue, thereby reducing the possibility of requiring the user to wait for the hardware.

There is also a second form of wait() that accepts a number of milliseconds as a maximum time to wait. If the thread is not interrupted, it will continue normally whenever it is notified or the specified timeout has elapsed. This normal continuation consists of getting out of the waiting state, but to continue execution it will have to get the lock for the object:

```
synchronized(a){ // The thread gets the lock on 'a'
    a.wait(2000); // Thread releases the lock and waits for notify
    // only for a maximum of two seconds, then goes back to Runnable
    // The thread reacquires the lock
    // More instructions here
}
```

When the `wait()` *method is invoked on an object, the thread executing that code gives up its lock on the object immediately. However, when* `notify()` *is called, that doesn't mean the thread gives up its lock at that moment. If the thread is still completing synchronized code, the lock is not released until the thread moves out of synchronized code. So just because* `notify()` *is called doesn't mean the lock becomes available at that moment.*

Using notifyAll( ) When Many Threads May Be Waiting

In most scenarios, it's preferable to notify *all* of the threads that are waiting on a particular object. If so, you can use `notifyAll()` on the object to let all the threads rush out of the waiting area and back to runnable. This is especially important if you have several threads waiting on one object, but for different reasons, and you want to be sure that the *right* thread (along with all of the others) gets notified.

```
notifyAll(); // Will notify all waiting threads
```

All of the threads will be notified and start competing to get the lock. As the lock is used and released by each thread, all of them will get into action without a need for further notification.

As we said earlier, an object can have many threads waiting on it, and using `notify()` will affect only one of them. Which one, exactly, is not specified and depends on the JVM implementation, so you should never rely on a particular thread being notified in preference to another.

In cases in which there might be a lot more waiting, the best way to do this is by using `notifyAll()`. Let's take a look at this in some code. In this example, there is one class that performs a calculation and many readers that are waiting to receive the completed calculation. At any given moment many readers may be waiting.

```
1.    class Reader extends Thread {
2.        Calculator c;
3.
4.        public Reader(Calculator calc) {
5.            c = calc;
```

```
 6.      }
 7.
 8.      public void run() {
 9.          synchronized(c) {
10.              try {
11.                  System.out.println("Waiting for calculation...");
12.                  c.wait();
13.              } catch (InterruptedException e) {}
14.              System.out.println("Total is: " + c.total);
15.          }
16.      }
17.
18.      public static void main(String [] args) {
19.          Calculator calculator = new Calculator();
20.          new Reader(calculator).start();
21.          new Reader(calculator).start();
22.          new Reader(calculator).start();
23.          calculator.start();
24.      }
25.  }
26.
27.  class Calculator extends Thread {
28.      int total;
29.
30.      public void run() {
31.          synchronized(this) {
32.              for(int i=0;i<100;i++) {
33.                  total += i;
34.              }
35.              notifyAll();
36.          }
37.      }
38.  }
```

The program starts three threads that are all waiting to receive the finished calculation (lines 18–24), and then starts the calculator with its calculation. Note that if the run() method at line 30 used notify() instead of notifyAll(), only one reader would be notified instead of all the readers.

Using wait( ) in a Loop

Actually both of the previous examples (Machine/Operator and Reader/Calculator) had a common problem. In each one, there was at least one thread calling wait(), and another thread calling notify() or notifyAll(). This works well enough as long as the waiting threads have actually started waiting before the other thread executes the `notify()` or `notifyAll()`. But what happens if, for example, the Calculator runs first and calls `notify()` before the Readers have started waiting? This could happen, since we can't guarantee what order the different parts of the thread will execute in. Unfortunately, when the Readers run, they just start waiting right away. They don't do anything to see if the event they're waiting for has already happened. So if the Calculator has already called `notifyAll()`, it's not going to call `notifyAll()` again—and the waiting Readers will keep waiting forever. This is probably *not* what the programmer wanted to happen. Almost always, when you want to wait for something, you also need to be able to check if it has already happened. Generally the best way to solve this is to put in some sort of loop that checks on some sort of conditional expressions, and only waits if the thing you're waiting for has not yet happened. Here's a modified, safer version of the earlier fabric-cutting machine example:

```
class Operator extends Thread {
  Machine machine; // assume this gets initialized
  public void run() {
    while (true) {
      Shape shape = getShapeFromUser();
      MachineInstructions job =
                       calculateNewInstructionsFor(shape);
      machine.addJob(job);
    }
  }
}
```

The operator will still keep on looping forever, getting more shapes from users, calculating new instructions for those shapes, and sending them to the machine. But now the logic for `notify()` has been moved into the `addJob()` method in the Machine class:

```
class Machine extends Thread {
  List<MachineInstructions> jobs =
                       new ArrayList<MachineInstructions>();

  public void addJob(MachineInstructions job) {
    synchronized (jobs) {
      jobs.add(job);
      jobs.notify();
```

```
      }
    }
  public void run() {
    while (true) {
      synchronized (jobs) {
        // wait until at least one job is available
        while (jobs.isEmpty()) {
          try {
            jobs.wait();
          } catch (InterruptedException ie) { }
        }
        // If we get here, we know that jobs is not empty
        MachineInstructions instructions = jobs.remove(0);
        // Send machine steps to hardware
      }
    }
  }
}
```

A machine keeps a list of the jobs it's scheduled to do. Whenever an operator adds a new job to the list, it calls the addJob() method and adds the new job to the list. Meanwhile the run() method just keeps looping, looking for any jobs on the list. If there are no jobs, it will start waiting. If it's notified, it will stop waiting and then recheck the loop condition: is the list still empty? In practice this double-check is probably not necessary, as the only time a notify() is ever sent is when a new job has been added to the list. However, it's a good idea to require the thread to recheck the isEmpty() condition whenever it's been woken up, because it's possible that a thread has accidentally sent an extra notify() that was not intended. There's also a possible situation called *spontaneous wakeup* that may exist in some situations—a thread may wake up even though no code has called notify() or notifyAll(). (At least, no code you know about has called these methods. Sometimes the JVM may call notify() for reasons of its own, or code in some other class calls it for reasons you just don't know.) What this means is, when your thread wakes up from a wait(), you don't know for sure why it was awakened. By putting the wait() method in a while loop and re-checking the condition that represents what we were waiting for, we ensure that *whatever* the reason we woke up, we will re-enter the wait() if (and only if) the thing we were waiting for has not happened yet. In the Machine class, the thing we were waiting for is for the jobs list to not be empty. If it's empty, we wait, and if it's not, we don't.

Note also that both the `run()` method and the `addJob()` method synchronize on the same object—the jobs list. This is for two reasons. One is because we're calling `wait()` and `notify()` on this instance, so we need to synchronize in order to avoid an IllegalThreadState exception. The other reason is, the data in the jobs list is changeable data stored in a field that is accessed by two different threads. We need to synchronize in order to access that changeable data safely. Fortunately, the same `synchronized` blocks that allow us to `wait()` and `notify()` also provide the required thread safety for our other access to changeable data. In fact this is a main reason why synchronization is required to use `wait()` and `notify()` in the first place—you almost always need to share some mutable data between threads at the same time, and that means you need synchronization. Notice that the `synchronized` block in `addJob()` is big enough to also include the call to `jobs.add(job)`—which modifies shared data. And the `synchronized` block in `run()` is large enough to include the whole `while` loop—which includes the call to `jobs.isEmpty()`, which accesses shared data.

The moral here is that when you use `wait()` and `notify()` or `notifyAll()`, you should almost always also have a `while` loop around the `wait()` that checks a condition and forces continued waiting until the condition is met. And you should also make use of the required synchronization for the `wait()` and `notify()` calls, to also protect whatever other data you're sharing between threads. If you see code which fails to do this, there's usually something wrong with the code—even if you have a hard time seeing what exactly the problem is.

TABLE 9-2	Key Thread Methods		
Class Object	**Class Thread**		**Interface Runnable**
wait ()	start()		run()
notify()	*yield()*		
notifyAll()	*sleep()*		
	join()		

CERTIFICATION SUMMARY

This chapter covered the required thread knowledge you'll need to apply on the certification exam. Threads can be created by either extending the Thread class or implementing the Runnable interface. The only method that must be overridden in the Runnable interface is the run() method, but the thread doesn't become a *thread of execution* until somebody calls the Thread object's start() method. We also looked at how the sleep() method can be used to pause a thread, and we saw that when an object goes to sleep, it holds onto any locks it acquired prior to sleeping.

We looked at five thread states: new, runnable, running, blocked/waiting/sleeping, and dead. You learned that when a thread is dead, it can never be restarted even if it's still a valid object on the heap. We saw that there is only one way a thread can transition to running, and that's from runnable. However, once running, a thread can become dead, go to sleep, wait for another thread to finish, block on an object's lock, wait for a notification, or return to runnable.

You saw how two threads acting on the same data can cause serious problems (remember Lucy and Fred's bank account?). We saw that, to let one thread execute a method, but prevent other threads from running the same object's method, we use the synchronized keyword. To coordinate activity between different threads, use the wait(), notify(), and notifyAll() methods.

✓ # TWO-MINUTE DRILL

Here are some of the key points from each certification objective in this chapter. Photocopy it and sleep with it under your pillow for complete absorption.

Defining, Instantiating, and Starting Threads (Objective 4.1)

- ❑ Threads can be created by extending Thread and overriding the `public void run()` method.
- ❑ Thread objects can also be created by calling the Thread constructor that takes a Runnable argument. The Runnable object is said to be the *target* of the thread.
- ❑ You can call `start()` on a Thread object only once. If `start()` is called more than once on a Thread object, it will throw a RuntimeException.
- ❑ It is legal to create many Thread objects using the same Runnable object as the target.
- ❑ When a Thread object is created, it does not become a *thread of execution* until its `start()` method is invoked. When a Thread object exists but hasn't been started, it is in the *new* state and is not considered *alive*.

Transitioning Between Thread States (Objective 4.2)

- ❑ Once a new thread is started, it will always enter the runnable state.
- ❑ The thread scheduler can move a thread back and forth between the runnable state and the running state.
- ❑ For a typical single-processor machine, only one thread can be running at a time, although many threads may be in the runnable state.
- ❑ There is no guarantee that the order in which threads were started determines the order in which they'll run.
- ❑ There's no guarantee that threads will take turns in any fair way. It's up to the thread scheduler, as determined by the particular virtual machine implementation. If you want a guarantee that your threads will take turns regardless of the underlying JVM, you can use the `sleep()` method. This prevents one thread from hogging the running process while another thread starves. (In most cases, though, `yield()` works well enough to encourage your threads to play together nicely.)
- ❑ A running thread may enter a blocked/waiting state by a `wait()`, `sleep()`, or `join()` call.

❑ A running thread may enter a blocked/waiting state because it can't acquire the lock for a synchronized block of code.

❑ When the sleep or wait is over, or an object's lock becomes available, the thread can only reenter the runnable state. It will *go* directly from waiting to running (well, for all practical purposes anyway).

❑ A dead thread cannot be started again.

Sleep, Yield, and Join (Objective 4.2)

❑ Sleeping is used to delay execution for a period of time, and no locks are released when a thread goes to sleep.

❑ A sleeping thread is guaranteed to sleep for at least the time specified in the argument to the `sleep()` method (unless it's interrupted), but there is no guarantee as to when the newly awakened thread will actually return to running.

❑ The `sleep()` method is a `static` method that sleeps the currently executing thread's state. One thread *cannot* tell another thread to sleep.

❑ The `setPriority()` method is used on Thread objects to give threads a priority of between 1 (low) and 10 (high), although priorities are not guaranteed, and not all JVMs recognize 10 distinct priority levels—some levels may be treated as effectively equal.

❑ If not explicitly set, a thread's priority will have the same priority as the priority of the thread that created it.

❑ The `yield()` method *may* cause a running thread to back out if there are runnable threads of the same priority. There is no guarantee that this will happen, and there is no guarantee that when the thread backs out there will be a *different* thread selected to run. A thread might yield and then immediately reenter the running state.

❑ The closest thing to a guarantee is that at any given time, when a thread is running it will usually not have a lower priority than any thread in the runnable state. If a low-priority thread is running when a high-priority thread enters runnable, the JVM will usually preempt the running low-priority thread and put the high-priority thread in.

❑ When one thread calls the `join()` method of another thread, the currently running thread will wait until the thread it joins with has completed. Think of the `join()` method as saying, "Hey thread, I want to join on to the end of you. Let me know when you're done, so I can enter the runnable state."

Concurrent Access Problems and Synchronized Threads (Objective 4.3)

❑ `synchronized` methods prevent more than one thread from accessing an object's critical method code simultaneously.

❑ You can use the `synchronized` keyword as a method modifier, or to start a synchronized block of code.

❑ To synchronize a block of code (in other words, a scope smaller than the whole method), you must specify an argument that is the object whose lock you want to synchronize on.

❑ While only one thread can be accessing synchronized code of a particular instance, multiple threads can still access the same object's *unsynchronized* code.

❑ When a thread goes to sleep, its locks will be unavailable to other threads.

❑ `static` methods can be `synchronized`, using the lock from the java.lang.Class instance representing that class.

Communicating with Objects by Waiting and Notifying (Objective 4.4)

❑ The `wait()` method lets a thread say, "there's nothing for me to do now, so put me in your waiting pool and notify me when something happens that I care about." Basically, a `wait()` call means "wait me in your pool," or "add me to your waiting list."

❑ The `notify()` method is used to send a signal to one and only one of the threads that are waiting in that same object's waiting pool.

❑ The `notify()` method can NOT specify which waiting thread to notify.

❑ The method `notifyAll()` works in the same way as `notify()`, only it sends the signal to *all* of the threads waiting on the object.

❑ All three methods—`wait()`, `notify()`, and `notifyAll()`—must be called from within a `synchronized` context! A thread invokes `wait()` or `notify()` on a particular object, and the thread must currently hold the lock on that object.

Deadlocked Threads (Objective 4.3)

❑ Deadlocking is when thread execution grinds to a halt because the code is waiting for locks to be removed from objects.

❑ Deadlocking can occur when a locked object attempts to access another locked object that is trying to access the first locked object. In other words, both threads are waiting for each other's locks to be released; therefore, the locks will *never* be released!

❑ Deadlocking is bad. Don't do it.

SELF TEST

The following questions will help you measure your understanding of the material presented in this chapter. If you have a rough time with some of these at first, don't beat yourself up. Some of these questions are long and intricate, expect long and intricate questions on the real exam too!

I. The following block of code creates a Thread using a Runnable target:

```
Runnable target = new MyRunnable();
Thread myThread = new Thread(target);
```

Which of the following classes can be used to create the target, so that the preceding code compiles correctly?

A. `public class MyRunnable extends Runnable{public void run(){}}`

B. `public class MyRunnable extends Object{public void run(){}}`

C. `public class MyRunnable implements Runnable{public void run(){}}`

D. `public class MyRunnable implements Runnable{void run(){}}`

E. `public class MyRunnable implements Runnable{public void start(){}}`

2. Given:

```
3.  class MyThread extends Thread {
4.      public static void main(String [] args) {
5.          MyThread t = new MyThread();
6.          Thread x = new Thread(t);
7.          x.start();
8.      }
9.      public void run() {
10.         for(int i=0;i<3;++i) {
11.             System.out.print(i + "..");
12.         }
13.     }
14. }
```

What is the result of this code?

A. Compilation fails

B. 1..2..3..

C. 0..1..2..3..

D. 0..1..2..

E. An exception occurs at runtime

3. Given:

```
3.   class Test {
4.      public static void main(String [] args) {
5.         printAll(args);
6.      }
7.      public static void printAll(String[] lines) {
8.         for(int i=0;i<lines.length;i++) {
9.            System.out.println(lines[i]);
10.           Thread.currentThread().sleep(1000);
11.        }
12.     }
13.  }
```

The `static` method `Thread.currentThread()` returns a reference to the currently executing Thread object. What is the result of this code?

A. Each String in the array `lines` will output, with a 1-second pause between lines

B. Each String in the array `lines` will output, with no pause in between because this method is not executed in a Thread

C. Each String in the array `lines` will output, and there is no guarantee there will be a pause because `currentThread()` may not retrieve this thread

D. This code will not compile

E. Each String in the `lines` array will print, with at least a one-second pause between lines

4. Assume you have a class that holds two `private` variables: a and b. Which of the following pairs can prevent concurrent access problems in that class? (Choose all that apply.)

A. ```
public int read(){return a+b;}
public void set(int a, int b){this.a=a;this.b=b;}
```

B. ```
public synchronized int read(){return a+b;}
public synchronized void set(int a, int b){this.a=a;this.b=b;}
```

C. ```
public int read(){synchronized(a){return a+b;}}
public void set(int a, int b){synchronized(a){this.a=a;this.b=b;}}
```

D. ```
public int read(){synchronized(a){return a+b;}}
public void set(int a, int b){synchronized(b){this.a=a;this.b=b;}}
```

E. ```
public synchronized(this) int read(){return a+b;}
public synchronized(this) void set(int a, int b){this.a=a;this.b=b;}
```

F. ```
public int read(){synchronized(this){return a+b;}}
public void set(int a, int b){synchronized(this){this.a=a;this.b=b;}}
```

5. Given:

```
1.  public class WaitTest {
2.     public static void main(String [] args) {
3.        System.out.print("1 ");
4.        synchronized(args){
5.           System.out.print("2 ");
6.           try {
7.              args.wait();
8.           }
9.           catch(InterruptedException e){}
10.       }
11.       System.out.print("3 ");
12.    }
13. }
```

What is the result of trying to compile and run this program?

A. It fails to compile because the `IllegalMonitorStateException` of `wait()` is not dealt with in line 7

B. `1 2 3`

C. `1 3`

D. `1 2`

E. At runtime, it throws an `IllegalMonitorStateException` when trying to wait

F. It will fail to compile because it has to be synchronized on the `this` object

6. Assume the following method is properly synchronized and called from a thread A on an object B:

```
wait(2000);
```

After calling this method, when will the thread A become a candidate to get another turn at the CPU?

A. After object B is notified, or after two seconds

B. After the lock on B is released, or after two seconds

C. Two seconds after object B is notified

D. Two seconds after lock B is released

7. Which are true? (Choose all that apply.)

   A. The `notifyAll()` method must be called from a synchronized context

   B. To call `wait()`, an object must own the lock on the thread

   C. The `notify()` method is defined in class `java.lang.Thread`

   D. When a thread is waiting as a result of `wait()`, it releases its lock

   E. The `notify()` method causes a thread to immediately release its lock

   F. The difference between `notify()` and `notifyAll()` is that `notifyAll()` notifies all waiting threads, regardless of the object they're waiting on

8. Given the scenario: This class is intended to allow users to write a series of messages, so that each message is identified with a timestamp and the name of the thread that wrote the message:

```
public class Logger {
    private StringBuilder contents = new StringBuilder();
    public void log(String message) {
        contents.append(System.currentTimeMillis());
        contents.append(": ");
        contents.append(Thread.currentThread().getName());
        contents.append(message);
        contents.append("\n");
    }
    public String getContents() { return contents.toString(); }
}
```

How can we ensure that instances of this class can be safely used by multiple threads?

   A. This class is already thread-safe

   B. Replacing `StringBuilder` with `StringBuffer` will make this class thread-safe

   C. Synchronize the `log()` method only

   D. Synchronize the `getContents()` method only

   E. Synchronize both `log()` and `getContents()`

   F. This class cannot be made thread-safe

9. Given:

```
public static synchronized void main(String[] args) throws
  InterruptedException {
    Thread t = new Thread();
    t.start();
    System.out.print("X");
    t.wait(10000);
    System.out.print("Y");
}
```

What is the result of this code?

A. It prints X and exits

B. It prints X and never exits

C. It prints XY and exits almost immeditately

D. It prints XY with a 10-second delay between X and Y

E. It prints XY with a 10000-second delay between X and Y

F. The code does not compile

G. An exception is thrown at runtime

10. Given:

```
class MyThread extends Thread {
   MyThread() {
     System.out.print(" MyThread");
   }
   public void run() {
     System.out.print(" bar");
   }
   public void run(String s) {
      System.out.print(" baz");
   }
 }
 public class TestThreads {
   public static void main (String [] args) {
     Thread t = new MyThread() {
       public void run() {
         System.out.print(" foo");
       }
     };
     t.start();
 } }
```

What is the result?

A. foo

B. MyThread foo

C. MyThread bar

D. foo bar

E. foo bar baz

F. bar foo

G. Compilation fails

H. An exception is thrown at runtime

11. Given:

```
public class ThreadDemo {
    synchronized void a() { actBusy(); }
    static synchronized void b() { actBusy(); }
    static void actBusy() {
        try {
            Thread.sleep(1000);
        } catch (InterruptedException e) {}
    }
    public static void main(String[] args) {
        final ThreadDemo x = new ThreadDemo();
        final ThreadDemo y = new ThreadDemo();
        Runnable runnable = new Runnable() {
            public void run() {
                int option = (int) (Math.random() * 4);
                switch (option) {
                    case 0: x.a(); break;
                    case 1: x.b(); break;
                    case 2: y.a(); break;
                    case 3: y.b(); break;
                }
            }
        };
        Thread thread1 = new Thread(runnable);
        Thread thread2 = new Thread(runnable);
        thread1.start();
        thread2.start();
    }
}
```

Which of the following pairs of method invocations could NEVER be executing at the same time? (Choose all that apply.)

A. `x.a()` in thread1, and `x.a()` in thread2

B. `x.a()` in thread1, and `x.b()` in thread2

C. `x.a()` in thread1, and `y.a()` in thread2

D. `x.a()` in thread1, and `y.b()` in thread2

E. `x.b()` in thread1, and `x.a()` in thread2

F. `x.b()` in thread1, and `x.b()` in thread2

G. `x.b()` in thread1, and `y.a()` in thread2

H. `x.b()` in thread1, and `y.b()` in thread2

12. Given:

```
public class TwoThreads {
    static Thread laurel, hardy;
    public static void main(String[] args) {
        laurel = new Thread() {
            public void run() {
                System.out.println("A");
                try {
                    hardy.sleep(1000);
                } catch (Exception e) {
                    System.out.println("B");
                }
                System.out.println("C");
            }
        };
        hardy = new Thread() {
            public void run() {
                System.out.println("D");
                try {
                    laurel.wait();
                } catch (Exception e) {
                    System.out.println("E");
                }
                System.out.println("F");
            }
        };
        laurel.start();
        hardy.start();
    }
}
```

Which letters will eventually appear somewhere in the output? (Choose all that apply.)

A. A

B. B

C. C

D. D

E. E

F. F

G. The answer cannot be reliably determined

H. The code does not compile

13. Given:

```
 3. public class Starter implements Runnable {
 4.    void go(long id) {
 5.       System.out.println(id);
 6.    }
 7.    public static void main(String[] args) {
 8.       System.out.print(Thread.currentThread().getId() + " ");
 9.       // insert code here
10.    }
11.    public void run() { go(Thread.currentThread().getId()); }
12. }
```

And given the following five fragments:

```
I.   new Starter().run();
II.  new Starter().start();
III. new Thread(new Starter());
IV.  new Thread(new Starter()).run();
V.   new Thread(new Starter()).start();
```

When the five fragments are inserted, one at a time at line 9, which are true? (Choose all that apply.)

A. All five will compile

B. Only one might produce the output 4 4

C. Only one might produce the output 4 2

D. Exactly two might produce the output 4 4

E. Exactly two might produce the output 4 2

F. Exactly three might produce the output 4 4

G. Exactly three might produce the output 4 2

14. Given:

```
3. public class Leader implements Runnable {
4.    public static void main(String[] args) {
5.       Thread t = new Thread(new Leader());
6.       t.start();
7.       System.out.print("m1 ");
8.       t.join();
9.       System.out.print("m2 ");
10.   }
11.   public void run() {
12.       System.out.print("r1 ");
13.       System.out.print("r2 ");
14.   }
15. }
```

Which are true? (Choose all that apply.)

A. Compilation fails

B. The output could be r1 r2 m1 m2

C. The output could be m1 m2 r1 r2

D. The output could be m1 r1 r2 m2

E. The output could be m1 r1 m2 r2

F. An exception is thrown at runtime

15. Given:

```
3. class Dudes {
4.    static long flag = 0;
5.    // insert code here
6.       if(flag == 0) flag = id;
7.       for(int x = 1; x < 3; x++) {
8.          if(flag == id) System.out.print("yo ");
9.          else System.out.print("dude ");
10.      }
11.   }
12. }
13. public class DudesChat implements Runnable {
14.    static Dudes d;
15.    public static void main(String[] args) {
16.       new DudesChat().go();
17.    }
18.    void go() {
19.       d = new Dudes();
```

```
20.        new Thread(new DudesChat()).start();
21.        new Thread(new DudesChat()).start();
22.    }
23.    public void run() {
24.       d.chat(Thread.currentThread().getId());
25.    }
26. }
```

And given these two fragments:

```
I.  synchronized void chat(long id) {
II. void chat(long id) {
```

When fragment I or fragment II is inserted at line 5, which are true? (Choose all that apply.)

A. An exception is thrown at runtime

B. With fragment I, compilation fails

C. With fragment II, compilation fails

D. With fragment I, the output could be yo dude dude yo

E. With fragment I, the output could be dude dude yo yo

F. With fragment II, the output could be yo dude dude yo

16. Given:

```
3. class Chicks {
4.    synchronized void yack(long id) {
5.       for(int x = 1; x < 3; x++) {
6.          System.out.print(id + " ");
7.          Thread.yield();
8.       }
9.    }
10. }
11. public class ChicksYack implements Runnable {
12.    Chicks c;
13.    public static void main(String[] args) {
14.       new ChicksYack().go();
15.    }
16.    void go() {
17.       c = new Chicks();
18.       new Thread(new ChicksYack()).start();
19.       new Thread(new ChicksYack()).start();
20.    }
21.    public void run() {
```

```
22.        c.yack(Thread.currentThread().getId());
23.    }
24. }
```

Which are true? (Choose all that apply.)

A. Compilation fails

B. The output could be 4 4 2 3

C. The output could be 4 4 2 2

D. The output could be 4 4 4 2

E. The output could be 2 2 4 4

F. An exception is thrown at runtime

17. Given:

```
 3. public class Chess implements Runnable {
 4.    public void run() {
 5.       move(Thread.currentThread().getId());
 6.    }
 7.    // insert code here
 8.       System.out.print(id + " ");
 9.       System.out.print(id + " ");
10.    }
11.    public static void main(String[] args) {
12.       Chess ch = new Chess();
13.       new Thread(ch).start();
14.       new Thread(new Chess()).start(),
15.    }
16. }
```

And given these two fragments:

```
I.   synchronized void move(long id) {
II.  void move(long id) {
```

When either fragment I or fragment II is inserted at line 7, which are true? (Choose all that apply.)

A. Compilation fails

B. With fragment I, an exception is thrown

C. With fragment I, the output could be 4 2 4 2

D. With fragment I, the output could be 4 4 2 3

E. With fragment II, the output could be 2 4 2 4

SELF TEST ANSWERS

1. The following block of code creates a Thread using a Runnable target:

```
Runnable target = new MyRunnable();
Thread myThread = new Thread(target);
```

Which of the following classes can be used to create the target, so that the preceding code compiles correctly?

A. `public class MyRunnable extends Runnable{public void run(){}}`
B. `public class MyRunnable extends Object{public void run(){}}`
C. `public class MyRunnable implements Runnable{public void run(){}}`
D. `public class MyRunnable implements Runnable{void run(){}}`
E. `public class MyRunnable implements Runnable{public void start(){}}`

Answer:

☑ **C** is correct. The class implements the Runnable interface with a legal `run()` method.

☒ **A** is incorrect because interfaces are implemented, not extended. **B** is incorrect because even though the class has a valid `public void run()` method, it does not implement the Runnable interface. **D** is incorrect because the `run()` method must be `public`. **E** is incorrect because the method to implement is `run()`, not `start()`. (Objective 4.1)

2. Given:

```
3.   class MyThread extends Thread {
4.      public static void main(String [] args) {
5.         MyThread t = new MyThread();
6.         Thread x = new Thread(t);
7.         x.start();
8.      }
9.      public void run() {
10.        for(int i=0;i<3;++i) {
11.           System.out.print(i + "..");
12.   } } }
```

What is the result of this code?

A. Compilation fails

B. 1..2..3..

C. 0..1..2..3..

D. 0..1..2..

E. An exception occurs at runtime

Answer:

☑ **D** is correct. The thread `MyThread` will start and loop three times (from 0 to 2).

☒ **A** is incorrect because the Thread class implements the Runnable interface; therefore, in line 5, Thread can take an object of type Thread as an argument in the constructor (this is NOT recommended). **B** and **C** are incorrect because the variable `i` in the `for` loop starts with a value of 0 and ends with a value of 2. **E** is incorrect based on the above. (Objective 4.1)

3. Given:

```
3.    class Test {
4.        public static void main(String [] args) {
5.            printAll(args);
6.        }
7.        public static void printAll(String[] lines) {
8.            for(int i=0;i<lines.length;i++){
9.                System.out.println(lines[i]);
10.               Thread.currentThread().sleep(1000);
11.    } } }
```

The `static` method `Thread.currentThread()` returns a reference to the currently executing Thread object. What is the result of this code?

A. Each String in the array `lines` will print, with exactly a 1-second pause between lines

B. Each String in the array `lines` will print, with no pause in between because this method is not executed in a Thread

C. Each String in the array `lines` will print, and there is no guarantee there will be a pause because `currentThread()` may not retrieve this thread

D. This code will not compile

E. Each String in the `lines` array will print, with at least a one-second pause between lines

Answer:

☑ **D** is correct. The `sleep()` method must be enclosed in a `try/catch` block, or the method `printAll()` must declare it throws the `InterruptedException`.

☒ **E** is incorrect, but it would be correct if the `InterruptedException` was dealt with (**A** is too precise). **B** is incorrect (even if the `InterruptedException` was dealt with) because all Java code, including the `main()` method, runs in threads. **C** is incorrect. The `sleep()` method is `static`, it always affects the currently executing thread. (Objective 4.2)

4. Assume you have a class that holds two `private` variables: a and b. Which of the following pairs can prevent concurrent access problems in that class? (Choose all that apply.)

```
A.  public int read(){return a+b;}
    public void set(int a, int b){this.a=a;this.b=b;}
B.  public synchronized int read(){return a+b;}
    public synchronized void set(int a, int b){this.a=a;this.b=b;}
C.  public int read(){synchronized(a){return a+b;}}
    public void set(int a, int b){synchronized(a){this.a=a;this.b=b;}}
D.  public int read(){synchronized(a){return a+b;}}
    public void set(int a, int b){synchronized(b){this.a=a;this.b=b;}}
E.  public synchronized(this) int read(){return a+b;}
    public synchronized(this) void set(int a, int b){this.a=a;this.b=b;}
F.  public int read(){synchronized(this){return a+b;}}
    public void set(int a, int b){synchronized(this){this.a=a;this.b=b;}}
```

Answer:

☑ **B** and **F** are correct. By marking the methods as `synchronized`, the threads will get the lock of the `this` object before proceeding. Only one thread will be setting or reading at any given moment, thereby assuring that `read()` always returns the addition of a valid pair.

☒ **A** is incorrect because it is not synchronized; therefore, there is no guarantee that the values added by the `read()` method belong to the same pair. **C** and **D** are incorrect; only objects can be used to synchronize on. **E** fails—it is not possible to select other objects (even `this`) to synchronize on when declaring a method as `synchronized`. (Objective 4.3)

5. Given:

```
1.  public class WaitTest {
2.      public static void main(String [] args) {
3.          System.out.print("1 ");
4.          synchronized(args){
```

```
5.              System.out.print("2 ");
6.              try {
7.                  args.wait();
8.              }
9.              catch(InterruptedException e){}
10.         }
11.         System.out.print("3 ");
12.  }  }
```

What is the result of trying to compile and run this program?

A. It fails to compile because the `IllegalMonitorStateException` of `wait()` is not dealt with in line 7

B. `1 2 3`

C. `1 3`

D. `1 2`

E. At runtime, it throws an `IllegalMonitorStateException` when trying to wait

F. It will fail to compile because it has to be synchronized on the `this` object

Answer:

☑ **D** is correct. 1 and 2 will be printed, but there will be no return from the `wait` call because no other thread will notify the main thread, so 3 will never be printed. It's frozen at line 7.

☒ **A** is incorrect; `IllegalMonitorStateException` is an unchecked exception. **B** and **C** are incorrect; 3 will never be printed, since this program will wait forever. **E** is incorrect because `IllegalMonitorStateException` will never be thrown because the `wait()` is done on `args` within a block of code synchronized on `args`. **F** is incorrect because any object can be used to synchronize on and `this` and `static` don't mix. (Objective 4.4)

6. Assume the following method is properly synchronized and called from a thread A on an object B:

```
wait(2000);
```

After calling this method, when will the thread A become a candidate to get another turn at the CPU?

A. After object B is notified, or after two seconds

B. After the lock on B is released, or after two seconds

C. Two seconds after object B is notified

D. Two seconds after lock B is released

Answer:

☑ **A** is correct. Either of the two events will make the thread a candidate for running again.

☒ **B** is incorrect because a waiting thread will not return to runnable when the lock is released, unless a notification occurs. **C** is incorrect because the thread will become a candidate immediately after notification. **D** is also incorrect because a thread will not come out of a waiting pool just because a lock has been released. (Objective 4.4)

7. Which are true? (Choose all that apply.)

    A. The `notifyAll()` method must be called from a synchronized context

    B. To call `wait()`, an object must own the lock on the thread

    C. The `notify()` method is defined in class `java.lang.Thread`

    D. When a thread is waiting as a result of `wait()`, it releases its lock

    E. The `notify()` method causes a thread to immediately release its lock

    F. The difference between `notify()` and `notifyAll()` is that `notifyAll()` notifies all waiting threads, regardless of the object they're waiting on

Answer:

☑ **A** is correct because `notifyAll()` (and `wait()` and `notify()`) must be called from within a synchronized context. **D** is a correct statement.

☒ **B** is incorrect because to call `wait()`, the thread must own the lock on the object that `wait()` is being invoked on, not the other way around. **C** is wrong because `notify()` is defined in `java.lang.Object`. **E** is wrong because `notify()` will not cause a thread to release its locks. The thread can only release its locks by exiting the synchronized code. **F** is wrong because `notifyAll()` notifies all the threads waiting on a particular locked object, not all threads waiting on *any* object. (Objective 4.4)

8. Given the scenario: This class is intended to allow users to write a series of messages, so that each message is identified with a timestamp and the name of the thread that wrote the message:

```
public class Logger {
    private StringBuilder contents = new StringBuilder();
    public void log(String message) {
        contents.append(System.currentTimeMillis());
        contents.append(": ");
        contents.append(Thread.currentThread().getName());
```

```
            contents.append(message);
            contents.append("\n");
        }
        public String getContents() { return contents.toString(); }
    }
```

How can we ensure that instances of this class can be safely used by multiple threads?

A. This class is already thread-safe

B. Replacing `StringBuilder` with `StringBuffer` will make this class thread-safe

C. Synchronize the `log()` method only

D. Synchronize the `getContents()` method only

E. Synchronize both `log()` and `getContents()`

F. This class cannot be made thread-safe

Answer:

☑ **E** is correct. Synchronizing the `public` methods is sufficient to make this safe, so **F** is false. This class is not thread-safe unless some sort of synchronization protects the changing data.

☒ **B** is not correct because although a `StringBuffer` is synchonized internally, we call `append()` multiple times, and nothing would prevent two simultaneous `log()` calls from mixing up their messages. **C** and **D** are not correct because if one method remains unsynchronized, it can run while the other is executing, which could result in reading the contents while one of the messages is incomplete, or worse. (You don't want to call `getString()` on the `StringBuffer` as it's resizing its internal character array.) (Objective 4.3)

9. Given:

```
public static synchronized void main(String[] args) throws
  InterruptedException {
    Thread t = new Thread();
    t.start();
    System.out.print("X");
    t.wait(10000);
    System.out.print("Y");
}
```

What is the result of this code?

A. It prints X and exits

B. It prints X and never exits

C. It prints XY and exits almost immediately

D. It prints XY with a 10-second delay between X and Y

E. It prints XY with a 10000-second delay between X and Y

F. The code does not compile

G. An exception is thrown at runtime

Answer:

☑ **G** is correct. The code does not acquire a lock on t before calling t.wait(), so it throws an IllegalMonitorStateException. The method is synchronized, but it's not synchronized on t so the exception will be thrown. If the wait were placed inside a synchronized(t) block, then the answer would have been **D**.

☒ **A, B, C, D, E,** and **F** are incorrect based the logic described above. (Objective 4.2)

10. Given:

```
class MyThread extends Thread {
    MyThread() {
        System.out.print(" MyThread");
    }
    public void run() { System.out.print(" bar"); }
    public void run(String s) { System.out.print(" baz"); }
}
public class TestThreads {
    public static void main (String [] args) {
        Thread t = new MyThread() {
            public void run() { System.out.print(" foo"); }
        };
        t.start();
} }
```

What is the result?

A. foo

B. MyThread foo

C. MyThread bar

D. foo bar

E. foo bar baz

F. bar foo

G. Compilation fails

H. An exception is thrown at runtime

Answer:

☑ **B** is correct. The first line of main we're constructing an instance of an anonymous inner class extending from `MyThread`. So the `MyThread` constructor runs and prints `MyThread`. Next, `main()` invokes `start()` on the new thread instance, which causes the overridden `run()` method (the `run()` method in the anonymous inner class) to be invoked.

☒ **A, C, D, E, F, G,** and **H** are incorrect based on the logic described above. (Objective 4.1)

11. Given:

```
public class ThreadDemo {
    synchronized void a() { actBusy(); }
    static synchronized void b() { actBusy(); }
    static void actBusy() {
        try { Thread.sleep(1000); }
        catch (InterruptedException e) {}
    }
    public static void main(String[] args) {
        final ThreadDemo x = new ThreadDemo();
        final ThreadDemo y = new ThreadDemo();
        Runnable runnable = new Runnable() {
            public void run() {
                int option = (int) (Math.random() * 4);
                switch (option) {
                    case 0: x.a(); break;
                    case 1: x.b(); break;
                    case 2: y.a(); break;
                    case 3: y.b(); break;
                }
            }
        };
        Thread thread1 = new Thread(runnable);
        Thread thread2 = new Thread(runnable);
        thread1.start();
        thread2.start();
    }
}
```

Which of the following pairs of method invocations could NEVER be executing at the same time? (Choose all that apply.)

A. `x.a()` in thread1, and `x.a()` in thread2

B. `x.a()` in thread1, and `x.b()` in thread2

C. `x.a()` in thread1, and `y.a()` in thread2

D. `x.a()` in thread1, and `y.b()` in thread2

E. `x.b()` in thread1, and `x.a()` in thread2

F. `x.b()` in thread1, and `x.b()` in thread2

G. `x.b()` in thread1, and `y.a()` in thread2

H. `x.b()` in thread1, and `y.b()` in thread2

Answer:

☑ **A, F,** and **H. A** is a right answer because when `synchronized` instance methods are called on the same *instance*, they block each other. **F** and **H** can't happen because `synchronized` `static` methods in the same class block each other, regardless of which instance was used to call the methods. (An instance is not required to call `static` methods; only the class.)

☒ **C** could happen because `synchronized` instance methods called on different instances do not block each other. **B, D, E,** and **G** could all happen because instance methods and `static` methods lock on different objects, and do not block each other. (Objective 4.3)

12. Given:

```
public class TwoThreads {
    static Thread laurel, hardy;
    public static void main(String[] args) {
        laurel = new Thread() {
            public void run() {
                System.out.println("A");
                try {
                    hardy.sleep(1000);
                } catch (Exception e) {
                    System.out.println("B");
                }
                System.out.println("C");
            }
        };
        hardy = new Thread() {
            public void run() {
                System.out.println("D");
                try {
                    laurel.wait();
                } catch (Exception e) {
                    System.out.println("E");
                }
                System.out.println("F");
```

```
                    }
                };
                laurel.start();
                hardy.start();
            }
    }
```

Which letters will eventually appear somewhere in the output? (Choose all that apply.)

A. A

B. B

C. C

D. D

E. E

F. F

G. The answer cannot be reliably determined

H. The code does not compile

Answer:

☑ **A, C, D, E,** and **F** are correct. This may look like `laurel` and `hardy` are battling to cause the other to `sleep()` or `wait()`—but that's not the case. Since `sleep()` is a static method, it affects the current thread, which is `laurel` (even though the method is invoked using a reference to `hardy`). That's misleading but perfectly legal, and the Thread `laurel` is able to sleep with no exception, printing A and C (after at least a 1-second delay). Meanwhile `hardy` tries to call `laurel.wait()`—but `hardy` has not synchronized on `laurel`, so calling `laurel.wait()` immediately causes an `IllegalMonitorStateException`, and so `hardy` prints D, E, and F. Although the *order* of the output is somewhat indeterminate (we have no way of knowing whether A is printed before D, for example) it is guaranteed that A, C, D, E, and F will all be printed in some order, eventually—so **G** is incorrect.

☒ **B, G,** and **H** are incorrect based on the above. (Objective 4.4)

13. Given:

```
3. public class Starter implements Runnable {
4.    void go(long id) {
5.        System.out.println(id);
6.    }
7.    public static void main(String[] args) {
8.        System.out.print(Thread.currentThread().getId() + " ");
9.        // insert code here
```

```
10.   }
11.   public void run() { go(Thread.currentThread().getId()); }
12. }
```

And given the following five fragments:

```
I.    new Starter().run();
II.   new Starter().start();
III.  new Thread(new Starter());
IV.   new Thread(new Starter()).run();
V.    new Thread(new Starter()).start();
```

When the five fragments are inserted, one at a time at line 9, which are true? (Choose all that apply.)

A. All five will compile

B. Only one might produce the output 4 4

C. Only one might produce the output 4 2

D. Exactly two might produce the output 4 4

E. Exactly two might produce the output 4 2

F. Exactly three might produce the output 4 4

G. Exactly three might produce the output 4 2

Answer:

☑ **C and D are correct.** Fragment I doesn't start a new thread. Fragment II doesn't compile. Fragment III creates a new thread but doesn't start it. Fragment IV creates a new thread and invokes `run()` directly, but it doesn't start the new thread. Fragment V creates *and* starts a new thread.

☒ **A, B, E, F,** and **G** are incorrect based on the above. (Objective 4.1)

14. Given:

```
3. public class Leader implements Runnable {
4.    public static void main(String[] args) {
5.      Thread t = new Thread(new Leader());
6.      t.start();
7.      System.out.print("m1 ");
8.      t.join();
9.      System.out.print("m2 ");
10.   }
```

```
11.    public void run() {
12.       System.out.print("r1 ");
13.       System.out.print("r2 ");
14.    }
15. }
```

Which are true? (Choose all that apply.)

A. Compilation fails

B. The output could be `r1 r2 m1 m2`

C. The output could be `m1 m2 r1 r2`

D. The output could be `m1 r1 r2 m2`

E. The output could be `m1 r1 m2 r2`

F. An exception is thrown at runtime

> **Answer:**
>
> ☑ **A** is correct. The `join()` must be placed in a try/catch block. If it were, answers B and D would be correct. The `join()` causes the main thread to pause and join the end of the other thread, meaning `"m2"` must come last.
>
> ☒ **B, C, D, E,** and **F** are incorrect based on the above. (Objective 4.2)

15. Given:

```
3. class Dudes {
4.    static long flag = 0;
5.    // insert code here
6.      if(flag == 0) flag = id;
7.      for(int x - 1; x < 3; x++) {
8.         if(flag == id) System.out.print("yo ");
9.         else System.out.print("dude ");
10.      }
11.    }
12. }
13. public class DudesChat implements Runnable {
14.    static Dudes d;
15.    public static void main(String[] args) {
16.       new DudesChat().go();
17.    }
18.    void go() {
19.       d = new Dudes();
```

```
20.        new Thread(new DudesChat()).start();
21.        new Thread(new DudesChat()).start();
22.    }
23.    public void run() {
24.        d.chat(Thread.currentThread().getId());
25.    }
26. }
```

And given these two fragments:

```
I.  synchronized void chat(long id) {
II. void chat(long id) {
```

When fragment I or fragment II is inserted at line 5, which are true? (Choose all that apply.)

A. An exception is thrown at runtime

B. With fragment I, compilation fails

C. With fragment II, compilation fails

D. With fragment I, the output could be yo dude dude yo

E. With fragment I, the output could be dude dude yo yo

F. With fragment II, the output could be yo dude dude yo

Answer:

☑ **F** is correct. With fragment I, the chat method is synchronized, so the two threads can't swap back and forth. With either fragment, the first output must be yo.

☒ **A, B, C, D,** and **E** are incorrect based on the above. (Objective 4.3)

16. Given:

```
3. class Chicks {
4.    synchronized void yack(long id) {
5.      for(int x = 1; x < 3; x++) {
6.        System.out.print(id + " ");
7.        Thread.yield();
8.      }
9.    }
10. }
11. public class ChicksYack implements Runnable {
12.    Chicks c;
13.    public static void main(String[] args) {
14.      new ChicksYack().go();
15.    }
```

```
16.    void go() {
17.      c = new Chicks();
18.      new Thread(new ChicksYack()).start();
19.      new Thread(new ChicksYack()).start();
20.    }
21.    public void run() {
22.      c.yack(Thread.currentThread().getId());
23.    }
24. }
```

Which are true? (Choose all that apply.)

A. Compilation fails

B. The output could be 4 4 2 3

C. The output could be 4 4 2 2

D. The output could be 4 4 4 2

E. The output could be 2 2 4 4

F. An exception is thrown at runtime

Answer:

☑ **F** is correct. When run() is invoked, it is with a new instance of ChicksYack and c has not been assigned to an object. If c were static, then because yack is synchronized, answers C and E would have been correct.

☒ **A, B, C, D,** and **E** are incorrect based on the above. (Objective 4.3)

17. Given:

```
3. public class Chess implements Runnable {
4.    public void run() {
5.      move(Thread.currentThread().getId());
6.    }
7.    // insert code here
8.      System.out.print(id + " ");
9.      System.out.print(id + " ");
10.   }
11.   public static void main(String[] args) {
12.     Chess ch = new Chess();
13.     new Thread(ch).start();
14.     new Thread(new Chess()).start();
15.   }
16. }
```

And given these two fragments:

```
I.   synchronized void move(long id) {
II.  void move(long id) {
```

When either fragment I or fragment II is inserted at line 7, which are true? (Choose all that apply.)

A. Compilation fails

B. With fragment I, an exception is thrown

C. With fragment I, the output could be 4 2 4 2

D. With fragment I, the output could be 4 4 2 3

E. With fragment II, the output could be 2 4 2 4

Answer:

☑ C and E are correct. E should be obvious. C is correct because even though move() is synchronized, it's being invoked on two different objects.

☒ A, B, and D are incorrect based on the above. (Objective 4.3)

EXERCISE ANSWERS

Exercise 9-1: Creating a Thread and Putting It to Sleep

The final code should look something like this:

```
class TheCount extends Thread {
    public void run() {
        for(int i = 1;i<=100;++i) {
            System.out.print(i + "  ");
            if(i % 10 == 0)  System.out.println("Hahaha");
            try { Thread.sleep(1000); }
            catch(InterruptedException e) {}
        }
    }
    public static void main(String [] args) {
        new TheCount().start();
    }
}
```

Exercise 9-2: Synchronizing a Block of Code

Your code might look something like this when completed:

```
class InSync extends Thread {
  StringBuffer letter;
  public InSync(StringBuffer letter) { this.letter = letter; }
  public void run() {
    synchronized(letter) {        // #1
      for(int i = 1;i<=100;++i) System.out.print(letter);
      System.out.println();
      char temp = letter.charAt(0);
      ++temp;             // Increment the letter in StringBuffer:
      letter.setCharAt(0, temp);
    }        // #2
  }
  public static void main(String [] args) {
    StringBuffer sb = new StringBuffer("A");
    new InSync(sb).start();  new InSync(sb).start();
    new InSync(sb).start();
  }
}
```

Just for fun, try removing lines 1 and 2 then run the program again. It will be unsynchronized—watch what happens.

10

Development

- Use Packages and Imports

- Determine Runtime Behavior
  for Classes and Command-Lines

- Use Classes in JAR Files

- Use Classpaths to
  Compile Code

✓ Two-Minute Drill

Q&A Self Test

Y ou want to keep your classes organized. You need to have powerful ways for your classes to find each other. You want to make sure that when you're looking for a particular class you get the one you want, and not another class that happens to have the same name. In this chapter we'll explore some of the advanced capabilities of the java and javac commands. We'll revisit the use of packages in Java, and how to search for classes that live in packages.

CERTIFICATION OBJECTIVES

Using the javac and java Commands
(Exam Objectives 7.1, 7.2, and 7.5)

7.1   *Given a code example and a scenario, write code that uses the appropriate access modifiers, package declarations, and import statements to interact with (through access or inheritance) the code in the example.*

7.2   *Given an example of a class and a command-line, determine the expected runtime behavior.*

7.5   *Given the fully-qualified name of a class that is deployed inside and/or outside a JAR file, construct the appropriate directory structure for that class. Given a code example and a classpath, determine whether the classpath will allow the code to compile successfully.*

So far in this book, we've probably talked about invoking the java and javac commands about 1000 times; now we're going to take a closer look.

Compiling with javac

The javac command is used to invoke Java's compiler. In Chapter 5 we talked about the assertion mechanism and when you might use the -source option when compiling a file. There are many other options you can specify when running javac, options to generate debugging information or compiler warnings for example. For the exam, you'll need to understand the -classpath and -d options, which we'll cover in the next few pages. Here's the structural overview for javac:

```
javac [options] [source files]
```

There are additional command-line options called `@argfiles`, but you won't need to study them for the exam. Both the `[options]` and the `[source files]` are optional parts of the command, and both allow multiple entries. The following are both legal `javac` commands:

```
javac -help
javac -classpath com:. -g Foo.java Bar.java
```

The first invocation doesn't compile any files, but prints a summary of valid options. The second invocation passes the compiler two options (`-classpath`, which itself has an argument of `com:.` and `-g`), and passes the compiler two `.java` files to compile (`Foo.java` and `Bar.java`). Whenever you specify multiple options and/or files they should be separated by spaces.

Compiling with -d

By default, the compiler puts a `.class` file in the same directory as the `.java` source file. This is fine for very small projects, but once you're working on a project of any size at all, you'll want to keep your `.java` files separated from your `.class` files. (This helps with version control, testing, deployment...) The `-d` option lets you tell the compiler in which directory to put the `.class` file(s) it generates (d is for destination). Let's say you have the following directory structure:

```
myProject
      |
      |--source
      |        |
      |        |-- MyClass.java
      |
      |-- classes
               |
               |--
```

The following command, issued from the `myProject` directory, will compile `MyClass.java` and put the resulting `MyClass.class` file into the `classes` directory. (Note: This assumes that MyClass does not have a package statement; we'll talk about packages in a minute.)

```
cd myProject
javac -d classes source/MyClass.java
```

This command also demonstrates selecting a .java file from a subdirectory of the directory from which the command was invoked. Now let's take a quick look at how packages work in relationship to the -d option.

Suppose we have the following .java file in the following directory structure:

```
package com.wickedlysmart;
public class MyClass { }

myProject
    |
    |--source
    |     |
    |     |--com
    |          |
    |          |--wickedlysmart
    |                    |
    |                    |--MyClass.java
    |
    |--classes
    |     |
    |     |--com
    |          |
    |          |--wickedlysmart
    |                    |
    |                    |-- (MyClass.class goes here)
```

If you were in the source directory, you would compile MyClass.java and put the resulting MyClass.class file into the classes/com/wickedlysmart directory by invoking the following command:

```
javac -d ../classes com/wickedlysmart/MyClass.java
```

This command could be read: "To set the destination directory, cd back to the myProject directory then cd into the classes directory, which will be your destination. Then compile the file named MyClass.java. Finally, put the resulting MyClass.class file into the directory structure that matches its package, in this case, classes/com/wickedlysmart." Because MyClass.java is in a package, the compiler knew to put the resulting .class file into the classes/com/wickedlysmart directory.

Somewhat amazingly, the `javac` command can sometimes help you out by building directories it needs! Suppose we have the following:

```
package com.wickedlysmart;
public class MyClass { }

myProject
      |
      |--source
      |      |
      |      |--com
      |             |
      |             |--wickedlysmart
      |                        |
      |                        |--MyClass.java
      |
      |--classes
      |      |
```

And the following command (the same as last time):

```
javac -d ../classes com/wickedlysmart/MyClass.java
```

In this case, the compiler will build two directories called `com` and `com/wickedlysmart` in order to put the resulting `MyClass.class` file into the correct package directory (`com/wickedlysmart/`) which it builds within the existing `.../classes` directory.

The last thing about `-d` that you'll need to know for the exam is that if the destination directory you specify doesn't exist, you'll get a compiler error. If, in the previous example, the `classes` directory did NOT exist, the compiler would say something like:

```
java:5: error while writing MyClass: classes/MyClass.class (No
such file or directory)
```

Launching Applications with java

The `java` command is used to invoke the Java virtual machine. In Chapter 5 we talked about the assertion mechanism and when you might use flags such as `-ea` or `-da` when launching an application. There are many other options you can specify when running the `java` command, but for the exam, you'll need to understand the `-classpath` (and its twin `-cp`) and `-D` options, which we'll cover in the next few pages. In addition, it's important to understand the structure of this command. Here's the overview:

```
java [options] class [args]
```

The `[options]` and `[args]` parts of the `java` command are optional, and they can both have multiple values. You must specify exactly one class file to execute, and the `java` command assumes you're talking about a `.class` file, so you don't specify the `.class` extension on the command line. Here's an example:

```
java -DmyProp=myValue MyClass x 1
```

Sparing the details for later, this command can be read as "Create a *system property* called `myProp` and set its value to `myValue`. Then launch the file named `MyClass.class` and send it two String *arguments* whose values are x and 1."

Let's look at system properties and command-line arguments more closely.

Using System Properties

Java has a class called `java.util.Properties` that can be used to access a system's persistent information such as the current versions of the operating system, the Java compiler, and the Java virtual machine. In addition to providing such default information, you can also add and retrieve your own properties. Take a look at the following:

```
import java.util.*;
public class TestProps {
  public static void main(String[] args) {
    Properties p = System.getProperties();
    p.setProperty("myProp", "myValue");
    p.list(System.out);
  }
}
```

If this file is compiled and invoked as follows:

```
java -DcmdProp=cmdVal TestProps
```

You'll get something like this:

```
. . .
os.name=Mac OS X
myProp=myValue
. . .
java.specification.vendor=Sun Microsystems Inc.
user.language=en
java.version=1.6.0_05
. . .
cmdProp=cmdVal
. . .
```

where the . . . represent lots of other name=value pairs. (The *name* and *value* are sometimes called the *key* and the *property*.) Two name=value properties were added to the system's properties: myProp=myValue was added via the setProperty method, and cmdProp=cmdVal was added via the -D option at the command line. When using the -D option, if your value contains white space the entire value should be placed in quotes like this:

```
java -DcmdProp="cmdVal take 2" TestProps
```

Just in case you missed it, when you use -D, the name=value pair must follow *immediately*, no spaces allowed.

The getProperty() method is used to retrieve a single property. It can be invoked with a single argument (a String that represents the name (or key)), or it can be invoked with two arguments, (a String that represents the name (or key), and a default String value to be used as the property if the property does not already exist). In both cases, getProperty() returns the property as a String.

Handling Command-Line Arguments

Let's return to an example of launching an application and passing in arguments from the command line. If we have the following code:

```java
public class CmdArgs {
  public static void main(String[] args) {
    int x = 0;
    for(String s : args)
      System.out.println(x++ + " element = " + s);
  }
}
```

compiled and then invoked as follows

```
java CmdArgs x 1
```

the output will be

```
0 element = x
1 element = 1
```

Like all arrays, `args` index is zero based. Arguments on the command line directly follow the class name. The first argument is assigned to `args[0]`, the second argument is assigned to `args[1]`, and so on.

Finally, there is some flexibility in the declaration of the `main()` method that is used to start a Java application. The order of `main()`'s modifiers can be altered a little, the String array doesn't have to be named `args`, and as of Java 5 it can be declared using var-args syntax. The following are all legal declarations for `main()`:

```
static public void main(String[] args)
public static void main(String... x)
static public void main(String bang_a_gong[])
```

Searching for Other Classes

In most cases, when we use the `java` and `javac` commands, we want these commands to search for other classes that will be necessary to complete the operation. The most obvious case is when classes we create use classes that Sun provides with J2SE (now sometimes called Java SE), for instance when we use classes in `java.lang` or `java.util`. The next common case is when we want to compile a file or run a class that uses other classes that have been created outside of what Sun provides, for instance our own previously created classes. Remember that for any given class, the `java` virtual machine will need to find exactly the same supporting classes that the `javac` compiler needed to find at compilation time. In other words, if `javac` needed access to `java.util.HashMap` then the `java` command will need to find `java.util.HashMap` as well.

Both `java` and `javac` use the same basic search algorithm:

1. They both have the same list of places (directories) they search, to look for classes.

2. They both search through this list of directories in the same order.

3. As soon as they find the class they're looking for, they stop searching for that class. In the case that their search lists contain two or more files with the same name, the first file found will be the file that is used.

4. The first place they look is in the directories that contain the classes that come standard with J2SE.

5. The second place they look is in the directories defined by classpaths.

6. Classpaths should be thought of as "class search paths." They are lists of directories in which classes might be found.

7. There are two places where classpaths can be declared:

   A classpath can be declared as an operating system environment variable. The classpath declared here is used by default, whenever `java` or `javac` are invoked.

   A classpath can be declared as a command-line option for either `java` or `javac`. *Classpaths declared as command-line options override the classpath declared as an environment variable, but they persist only for the length of the invocation.*

Declaring and Using Classpaths

Classpaths consist of a variable number of directory locations, separated by delimiters. For Unix-based operating systems, forward slashes are used to construct directory locations, and the separator is the colon (:). For example:

```
-classpath /com/foo/acct:/com/foo
```

specifies two directories in which classes can be found: `/com/foo/acct` and `/com/foo`. In both cases, these directories are absolutely tied to the root of the file system, which is specified by the leading forward slash. It's important to remember that when you specify a subdirectory, you're NOT specifying the directories above it. For instance, in the preceding example the directory `/com` will NOT be searched.

A very common situation occurs in which `java` or `javac` complains that it can't find a class file, and yet you can see that the file is IN the current directory! When searching for class files, the `java` and `javac` commands don't search the current directory by default. You must *tell* them to search there. The way to tell `java` or `javac` to search in the current directory is to add a dot (.) to the classpath:

```
-classpath /com/foo/acct:/com/foo:.
```

This classpath is identical to the previous one EXCEPT that the dot (.) at the end of the declaration instructs `java` or `javac` to *also* search for class files in the current directory. (Remember, we're talking about class files—when you're telling `javac` which `.java` file to compile, `javac` looks in the current directory by default.)

It's also important to remember that classpaths are searched from left to right. Therefore in a situation where classes with duplicate names are located in several different directories in the following classpaths, different results will occur:

```
-classpath /com:/foo:.
```

is not the same as

```
-classpath .:/foo:/com
```

Finally, the `java` command allows you to abbreviate `-classpath` with `-cp`. The Java documentation is inconsistent about whether the `javac` command allows the `-cp` abbreviation. On most machines it does, but there are no guarantees.

Packages and Searching

When you start to put classes into packages, and then start to use classpaths to find these classes, things can get tricky. The exam creators knew this, and they tried to create an especially devilish set of package/classpath questions with which to confound you. Let's start off by reviewing packages. In the following code:

```
package com.foo;
public class MyClass { public void hi() { } }
```

We're saying that MyClass is a member of the com.foo package. This means that the fully qualified name of the class is now com.foo.MyClass. Once a class is in a package, the package part of its fully qualified name is *atomic*—it can never be divided. You can't split it up on the command line, and you can't split it up in an import statement.

Now let's see how we can use com.foo.MyClass in another class:

```
package com.foo;
public class MyClass { public void hi() { } }
```

And in another file:

```
import com.foo.MyClass;    // either import will work
import com.foo.*;

public class Another {
  void go() {
    MyClass m1 = new MyClass();                        // alias name
    com.foo.MyClass m2 = new com.foo.MyClass();  // full name
    m1.hi();
    m2.hi();
  }
}
```

It's easy to get confused when you use import statements. The preceding code is perfectly legal. The import statement is like an alias for the class's fully qualified name. You define the fully qualified name for the class with an import statement (or with a wildcard in an import statement of the package). Once you've defined the fully qualified name, you can use the "alias" in your code—but the alias is referring back to the fully qualified name.

Now that we've reviewed packages, let's take a look at how they work in conjunction with classpaths and command lines. First we'll start off with the idea that when you're searching for a class using its fully qualified name, that fully qualified name relates closely to a specific directory structure. For instance, relative to your current directory, the class whose source code is

```
package com.foo;
public class MyClass { public void hi() { } }
```

would *have* to be located here:

```
com/foo/MyClass.class
```

In order to find a class in a package, you have to have a directory in your classpath that has the package's leftmost entry (the package's "root") as a subdirectory.

This is an important concept, so let's look at another example:

```
import com.wickedlysmart.Utils;
class TestClass {
  void doStuff() {
    Utils u = new Utils();                       // simple name
    u.doX("arg1", "arg2");
    com.wickedlysmart.Date d =
               new com.wickedlysmart.Date();   // full name
    d.getMonth("Oct");
  }
}
```

In this case we're using two classes from the package `com.wickedlysmart`. For the sake of discussion we imported the fully qualified name for the `Utils` class, and we didn't for the `Date` class. The *only* difference is that because we listed `Utils` in an `import` statement, we didn't have to type its fully qualified name inside the class. In both cases the package is `com.wickedlysmart`. When it's time to compile or run `TestClass`, the classpath will have to include a directory with the following attributes:

- A subdirectory named `com` (we'll call this the "package root" directory)
- A subdirectory in `com` named `wickedlysmart`
- Two files in `wickedlysmart` named `Utils.class` and `Date.class`

Finally, the directory that has all of these attributes has to be accessible (via a classpath) in one of two ways:

1. The path to the directory must be absolute, in other words, from the root (the file system root, not the package root).

   or

2. The path to the directory has to be correct relative to the current directory.

Relative and Absolute Paths

A classpath is a collection of one or more paths. Each path in a classpath is either an absolute path or a relative path. An absolute path in Unix begins with a forward slash (/) (on Windows it would be something like c:\). The leading slash indicates that this path is starting from the root directory of the system. Because it's starting from the root, it doesn't *matter* what the current directory is—*a directory's absolute path is always the same*. A *relative* path is one that does NOT start with a slash. Here's an example of a full directory structure, and a classpath:

```
/ (root)
    |
    |--dirA
        |
        |-- dirB
             |
             |--dirC


-cp dirB:dirB/dirC
```

In this example, `dirB` and `dirB/dirC` are relative paths (they don't start with a slash /). Both of these relative paths are meaningful *only* when the current directory is `dirA`. Pop Quiz! If the current directory is `dirA`, and you're searching for class files, and you use the classpath described above, which directories will be searched?

`dirA? dirB? dirC?`

Too easy? How about the same question if the current directory is the root (/)? When the current directory is `dirA`, then `dirB` and `dirC` will be searched, but not dirA (remember, we didn't specify the current directory by adding a dot (.) to the classpath). When the current directory is root, since dirB is not a direct subdirectory of root, no directories will be searched. Okay, how about if the current directory is dirB? Again, no directories will be searched! This is because dirB doesn't have a subdirectory named dirB. In other words, Java will look in dirB for a directory named dirB (which it won't find), without realizing that it's already in dirB.

Let's use the same directory structure and a different classpath:

```
/ (root)
     |
     |--dirA
          |
          |-- dirB
               |
               |--dirC


-cp /dirB:/dirA/dirB/dirC
```

In this case, what directories will be searched if the current directory is dirA? How about if the current directory is root? How about if the current directory is dirB? In this case, both paths in the classpath are absolute. It doesn't matter what the current directory is; since absolute paths are specified the search results will always be the same. Specifically, only dirC will be searched, regardless of the current directory. The first path (/dirB) is invalid since dirB is not a direct subdirectory of root, so dirB will never be searched. And, one more time, for emphasis, since dot (.) is not in the classpath, the current directory will only be searched if it happens to be described elsewhere in the classpath (in this case, dirC).

CERTIFICATION OBJECTIVE

JAR Files (Objective 7.5)

7.5 *Given the fully-qualified name of a class that is deployed inside and/or outside a JAR file, construct the appropriate directory structure for that class. Given a code example and a classpath, determine whether the classpath will allow the code to compile successfully.*

JAR Files and Searching

Once you've built and tested your application, you might want to bundle it up so that it's easy to distribute and easy for other people to install. One mechanism that Java provides for these purposes is a JAR file. JAR stands for Java Archive. JAR files are used to compress data (similar to ZIP files) and to archive data.

Here's an application with classes in different packages:

```
test
   |--UseStuff.java
   |--ws
       |--(create MyJar.jar here)
       |--myApp
           |--utils
           |      |--Dates.class        (package myApp.utils;)
           |--engine
                  |--rete.class          (package myApp.engine;)
                  |--minmax.class          "           "
```

You can create a single JAR file that contains all of the files in myApp, and also maintains myApp's directory structure. Once this JAR file is created, it can be moved from place to place, and from machine to machine, and all of the classes in the JAR file can be accessed, via classpaths, by java and javac, without ever unJARing the JAR file. Although you won't need to know how to make JAR files for the exam, let's make the current directory ws, and then make a JAR file called MyJar.jar:

```
cd ws
jar -cf MyJar.jar myApp
```

The jar command will create a JAR file called MyJar.jar and it will contain the myApp directory and myApp's entire subdirectory tree and files. You can look at the contents of the JAR file with the next command (this isn't on the exam either):

```
jar -tf MyJar.jar
```

(which produces something like)

```
META-INF/
META-INF/MANIFEST.MF
myApp/
myApp/.DS_Store
myApp/utils/
```

```
myApp/utils/Dates.class
myApp/engine/
myApp/engine/rete.class
myApp/engine/minmax.class
```

Here are some rules concerning the structure of JAR files:

■ **The jar command creates the** META-INF **directory automatically.**
■ **The jar command creates the** MANIFEST.MF **file automatically.**
■ **The jar command won't place any of your files in** META-INF/.
■ **As you can see above, the exact tree structure is represented.**
■ java **and** javac **will use the JAR like a normal directory tree.**

Back to exam stuff. Finding a JAR file using a classpath is similar to finding a package file in a classpath. The difference is that when you specify a path for a JAR file, *you must include the name of the JAR file at the end of the path*. Let's say you want to compile UseStuff.java in the test directory, and UseStuff.java needs access to a class contained in myApp.jar. To compile UseStuff.java say

```
cd test
javac -classpath ws/myApp.jar UseStuff.java
```

Compare the use of the JAR file to using a class in a package. If UseStuff.java needed to use classes in the myApp.utils package, and the class was not in a JAR, you would say

```
cd test
javac -classpath ws UseStuff.java
```

Remember when using a classpath, the last directory in the path must be the super-directory of the *root* directory for the package. (In the preceding example, myApp is the root directory of the package myApp.utils.) Notice that myApp can be the root directory for more than one package (myApp.utils and myApp.engine), and the java and javac commands can find what they need across multiple *peer* packages like this. So, if ws is on the classpath and ws is the super-directory of myApp, then classes in both the myApp.utils and myApp.engine packages will be found.

exam
ⓦatch

When you use an import statement you are declaring only one package. When you say `import java.util.*;` *you are saying "Use the short name for all of the classes in the* `java.util` *package." You're NOT getting the* `java.util.jar` *classes or* `java.util.regex` *packages! Those packages are totally independent of each other; the only thing they share is the same "root" directory, but they are not the same packages. As a corollary, you can't say* `import java.*;` *in the hopes of importing multiple packages—just remember, an* `import` *statement can import only a single package.*

Using .../jre/lib/ext with JAR files

When you install Java, you end up with a huge directory tree of Java-related stuff, including the JAR files that contain the classes that come standard with J2SE. As we discussed earlier, java and javac have a list of places that they access when searching for class files. Buried deep inside of your Java directory tree is a subdirectory tree named `jre/lib/ext`. If you put JAR files into the ext subdirectory, java and javac can find them, and use the class files they contain. You don't have to mention these subdirectories in a classpath statement—searching this directory is a function that's built right into Java. Sun recommends, however, that you use this feature only for your own internal testing and development, and not for software that you intend to distribute.

exam
ⓦatch

It's possible to create environment variables that provide an alias for long classpaths. The classpath for some of the JAR files in J2SE can be quite long, and so it's common for such an alias to be used when defining a classpath. If you see something like `JAVA_HOME` *or* `$JAVA_HOME` *in an exam question it just means "That part of the absolute classpath up to the directories we're specifying explicitly." You can assume that the* `JAVA_HOME` *literal means this, and is pre-pended to the partial classpath you see.*

Using Static Imports (Exam Objective 7.1)

7.1 Given a code example and a scenario, write code that uses the appropriate access modifiers, package declarations, and import statements to interact with (through access or inheritance) the code in the example.

Note: In Chapter 1 we covered most of what's defined in this objective, but we saved static imports for this chapter.

Static Imports

We've been using `import` statements throughout the book. Ultimately, the only value `import` statements have is that they save typing and they can make your code easier to read. In Java 5, the `import` statement was enhanced to provide even greater keystroke-reduction capabilities...although some would argue that this comes at the expense of readability. This new feature is known as *static imports*. Static imports can be used when you want to use a class's `static` members. (You can use this feature on classes in the API and on your own classes.) Here's a "before and after" example:

Before static imports:

```
public class TestStatic {
  public static void main(String[] args) {
    System.out.println(Integer.MAX_VALUE);
    System.out.println(Integer.toHexString(42));
  }
}
```

After static imports:

```
import static java.lang.System.out;            // 1
import static java.lang.Integer.*;             // 2
public class TestStaticImport {
  public static void main(String[] args)  {
    out.println(MAX_VALUE);                     // 3
    out.println(toHexString(42));               // 4
  }
}
```

Both classes produce the same output:

```
2147483647
2a
```

Let's look at what's happening in the code that's using the static import feature:

1. Even though the feature is commonly called "static import" the syntax MUST be import static followed by the fully qualified name of the static member you want to import, or a wildcard. In this case we're doing a static import on the System class out object.

2. In this case we might want to use several of the static members of the java.lang.Integer class. This static import statement uses the wildcard to say, "I want to do static imports of ALL the static members in this class."

3. Now we're finally seeing the *benefit* of the static import feature! We didn't have to type the System in System.out.println! Wow! Second, we didn't have to type the Integer in Integer.MAX_VALUE. So in this line of code we were able to use a shortcut for a static method AND a constant.

4. Finally, we do one more shortcut, this time for a method in the Integer class.

We've been a little sarcastic about this feature, but we're not the only ones. We're not convinced that saving a few keystrokes is worth possibly making the code a little harder to read, but enough developers requested it that it was added to the language.

Here are a couple of rules for using static imports:

■ You must say import static; you can't say static import.

■ Watch out for ambiguously named static members. For instance, if you do a static import for both the Integer class and the Long class, referring to MAX_VALUE will cause a compiler error, since both Integer and Long have a MAX_VALUE constant, and Java won't know which MAX_VALUE you're referring to.

■ You can do a static import on static object references, constants (remember they're static and final), and static methods.

CERTIFICATION SUMMARY

We started by exploring the `javac` command more deeply. The `-d` option allows you to put class files generated by compilation into whatever directory you want to. The `-d` option lets you specify the destination of newly created class files.

Next we talked about some of the options available through the `java` application launcher. We discussed the ordering of the arguments `java` can take, including `[options] class [args]`. We learned how to query and update system properties in code and at the command line using the `-D` option.

The next topic was handling command-line arguments. The key concepts are that these arguments are put into a String array, and that the first argument goes into array element 0, the second argument into array element 1, and so on.

We turned to the important topic of how `java` and `javac` search for other class files when they need them, and how they use the same algorithm to find these classes. There are search locations predefined by Sun, and additional search locations, called *classpaths* that are user defined. The syntax for Unix classpaths is different than the syntax for Windows classpaths, and the exam will tend to use Unix syntax.

The topic of packages came next. Remember that once you put a class into a package, its name is atomic—in other words, it can't be split up. There is a tight relationship between a class's fully qualified package name and the directory structure in which the class resides.

JAR files were discussed next. JAR files are used to compress and archive data. They can be used to archive entire directory tree structures into a single JAR file. JAR files can be searched by `java` and `javac`.

We finished the chapter by discussing a new Java 5 feature, static imports. This is a convenience-only feature that reduces keying long names for `static` members in the classes you use in your programs.

...

 # TWO-MINUTE DRILL

Here are the key points from this chapter.

Using javac and java (Objective 7.2)

❑ Use -d to change the destination of a class file when it's first generated by the javac command.

❑ The -d option can build package-dependent destination classes on-the-fly if the *root* package directory already exists.

❑ Use the -D option in conjunction with the java command when you want to set a system property.

❑ System properties consist of name=value pairs that must be appended directly behind the -D, for example, java -Dmyproperty=myvalue.

❑ Command-line arguments are always treated as Strings.

❑ The java command-line argument 1 is put into array element 0, argument 2 is put into element 1, and so on.

Searching with java and javac (Objective 7.5)

❑ Both java and javac use the same algorithms to search for classes.

❑ Searching begins in the locations that contain the classes that come standard with J2SE.

❑ Users can define secondary search locations using classpaths.

❑ Default classpaths can be defined by using OS environment variables.

❑ A classpath can be declared at the command line, and it overrides the default classpath.

❑ A single classpath can define many different search locations.

❑ In Unix classpaths, forward slashes (/) are used to separate the directories that make up a path. In Windows, backslashes (\) are used.

❑ In Unix, colons (:) are used to separate the paths within a classpath. In Windows, semicolons (;) are used.

❑ In a classpath, to specify the current directory as a search location, use a dot (.)

❑ In a classpath, once a class is found, searching stops, so the order of locations to search is important.

Packages and Searching (Objective 7.5)

❑ When a class is put into a package, its fully qualified name must be used.

❑ An import statement provides an alias to a class's fully qualified name.

❑ In order for a class to be located, its fully qualified name must have a tight relationship with the directory structure in which it resides.

❑ A classpath can contain both relative and absolute paths.

❑ An absolute path starts with a / or a \.

❑ Only the final directory in a given path will be searched.

JAR Files (Objective 7.5)

❑ An entire directory tree structure can be archived in a single JAR file.

❑ JAR files can be searched by `java` and `javac`.

❑ When you include a JAR file in a classpath, you must include not only the directory in which the JAR file is located, but the name of the JAR file too.

❑ For testing purposes, you can put JAR files into `.../jre/lib/ext`, which is somewhere inside the Java directory tree on your machine.

Static Imports (Objective 7.1)

❑ You must start a static import statement like this: `import static`

❑ You can use static imports to create shortcuts for `static` members (static variables, constants, and methods) of any class.

SELF TEST

1. Given:

```
1. // insert code here
2. class StatTest {
3.   public static void main(String[] args) {
4.     System.out.println(Integer.MAX_VALUE);
5.   }
6. }
```

Which, inserted independently at line 1, compiles? (Choose all that apply.)

A. `import static java.lang;`

B. `import static java.lang.Integer;`

C. `import static java.lang.Integer.*;`

D. `import static java.lang.Integer.*_VALUE;`

E. `import static java.lang.Integer.MAX_VALUE;`

F. None of the above statements are valid import syntax

2. Given:

```
import static java.lang.System.*;
class _ {
  static public void main(String... __A_V_) {
    String $ = "";
    for(int x=0; ++x < __A_V_.length; )
      $ += __A_V_[x];
    out.println($);
  }
}
```

And the command line:

```
java _ - A .
```

What is the result?

A. `-A`

B. `A.`

C. `-A.`

D. _A.

E. _-A.

F. Compilation fails

G. An exception is thrown at runtime

3. Given the default classpath:

```
/foo
```

And this directory structure:

```
foo
  |
  test
    |
    xcom
        |--A.class
        |--B.java
```

And these two files:

```
package xcom;
public class A { }

package xcom;
public class B extends A { }
```

Which allows B.java to compile? (Choose all that apply.)

A. Set the current directory to xcom then invoke
    `javac B.java`

B. Set the current directory to xcom then invoke
    `javac -classpath . B.java`

C. Set the current directory to test then invoke
    `javac -classpath . xcom/B.java`

D. Set the current directory to test then invoke
    `javac -classpath xcom B.java`

E. Set the current directory to test then invoke
    `javac -classpath xcom:. B.java`

4. Given two files:

```
a=b.java
c_d.class
```

Are in the current directory, which command-line invocation(s) could complete without error? (Choose all that apply.)

A. `java -Da=b c_d`

B. `java -D a=b c_d`

C. `javac -Da=b c_d`

D. `javac -D a=b c_d`

5. If three versions of `MyClass.class` exist on a file system:

Version 1 is in `/foo/bar`
Version 2 is in `/foo/bar/baz`
Version 3 is in `/foo/bar/baz/bing`

And the system's classpath includes

```
/foo/bar/baz
```

And this command line is invoked from `/foo`

```
java -classpath /foo/bar/baz/bing:/foo/bar MyClass
```

Which version will be used by `java`?

A. `/foo/MyClass.class`

B. `/foo/bar/MyClass.class`

C. `/foo/bar/baz/MyClass.class`

D. `/foo/bar/baz/bing/MyClass.class`

E. The result is not predictable

6. Given two files:

```
1. package pkgA;
2. public class Foo {
3.    int a = 5;
4.    protected int b = 6;
5. }
```

```
1.  package pkgB;
2.  import pkgA.*;
3.  public class Fiz extends Foo {
4.    public static void main(String[] args) {
5.       Foo f = new Foo();
6.       System.out.print("  " + f.a);
7.       System.out.print(" " + f.b);
8.       System.out.print(" " + new Fiz().a);
9.       System.out.println(" " + new Fiz().b);
10.   }
11. }
```

What is the result? (Choose all that apply.)

A. 5 6 5 6

B. 5 6 followed by an exception

C. Compilation fails with an error on line 6

D. Compilation fails with an error on line 7

E. Compilation fails with an error on line 8

F. Compilation fails with an error on line 9

7. Given:

```
3.  import java.util.*;
4.  public class Antique {
5.    public static void main(String[] args) {
6.       List<String> myList = new ArrayList<String>();
7.       assert (args.length > 0);
8.       System.out.println("still static");
9.    }
10. }
```

Which sets of commands (javac followed by java) will compile and run without exception or error? (Choose all that apply.)

A. javac Antique.java
   java Antique

B. javac Antique.java
   java -ea Antique

C. javac -source 6 Antique.java
   java Antique

D. javac -source 1.4 Antique.java
   java Antique

E. javac -source 1.6 Antique.java
   java -ea Antique

8. Given:

```
3.  import java.util.*;
4.  public class Values {
5.     public static void main(String[] args) {
6.        Properties p = System.getProperties();
7.        p.setProperty("myProp", "myValue");
8.        System.out.print(p.getProperty("cmdProp") + " ");
9.        System.out.print(p.getProperty("myProp") + " ");
10.       System.out.print(p.getProperty("noProp") + " ");
11.       p.setProperty("cmdProp", "newValue");
12.       System.out.println(p.getProperty("cmdProp"));
13.    }
14. }
```

And given the command line invocation:

```
java -DcmdProp=cmdValue Values
```

What is the result?

A. null myValue null null

B. cmdValue null null cmdValue

C. cmdValue null null newValue

D. cmdValue myValue null cmdValue

E. cmdValue myValue null newValue

F. An exception is thrown at runtime

9. Given the following directory structure:

```
x-|
  |- FindBaz.class
  |
  |- test-|
          |- Baz.class
          |
          |- myApp-|
                   |- Baz.class
```

And given the contents of the related .java files:

```
1. public class FindBaz {
2.   public static void main(String[] args) { new Baz(); }
3. }
```

In the test directory:

```
1. public class Baz {
2.   static { System.out.println("test/Baz"); }
3. }
```

In the myApp directory:

```
1. public class Baz {
2.   static { System.out.println("myApp/Baz"); }
3. }
```

If the current directory is x, which invocations will produce the output `"test/Baz"`? (Choose all that apply.)

A. `java FindBaz`

B. `java -classpath test FindBaz`

C. `java -classpath .:test FindBaz`

D. `java -classpath .:test/myApp FindBaz`

E. `java -classpath test:test/myApp FindBaz`

F. `java -classpath test:test/myApp:. FindBaz`

G. `java -classpath test/myApp:test:. FindBaz`

10. Given the following directory structure:

```
test-|
     |- Test.java
     |
     |- myApp-|
              |- Foo.java
              |
              |- myAppSub-|
                          |- Bar.java
```

If the current directory is test, and you create a .jar file by invoking this,

```
jar -cf MyJar.jar myApp
```

then which path names will find a file in the .jar file? (Choose all that apply.)

A. Foo.java

B. Test.java

C. myApp/Foo.java

D. myApp/Bar.java

E. META-INF/Foo.java

F. META-INF/myApp/Foo.java

G. myApp/myAppSub/Bar.java

11. Given the following directory structure:

```
test-|
     |- GetJar.java
     |
     |- myApp-|
              |-Foo.java
```

And given the contents of GetJar.java and Foo.java:

```
3. public class GetJar {
4.    public static void main(String[] args) {
5.       System.out.println(myApp.Foo.d);
6.    }
7. }
```

```
3. package myApp;
4. public class Foo { public static int d = 8; }
```

If the current directory is "test", and myApp/Foo.class is placed in a JAR file called MyJar.jar located in test, which set(s) of commands will compile GetJar.java and produce the output 8? (Choose all that apply.)

A. ```
   javac -classpath MyJar.jar GetJar.java
   java GetJar
   ```

B. ```
   javac MyJar.jar GetJar.java
   java GetJar
   ```

C. ```
   javac -classpath MyJar.jar GetJar.java
   java -classpath MyJar.jar GetJar
   ```

D. ```
   javac MyJar.jar GetJar.java
   java -classpath MyJar.jar GetJar
   ```

12. Given the following directory structure:

```
x-|
  |- GoDeep.class
  |
  |- test-|
          |- MyJar.jar
          |
          |- myApp-|
                   |-Foo.java
                   |-Foo.class
```

And given the contents of GoDeep.java and Foo.java:

```
3. public class GoDeep {
4.   public static void main(String[] args) {
5.     System.out.println(myApp.Foo.d);
6.   }
7. }
```

```
3. package myApp;
4. public class Foo { public static int d = 8; }
```

And MyJar.jar contains the following entry:

```
myApp/Foo.class
```

If the current directory is x, which commands will successfully execute GoDeep.class and produce the output 8? (Choose all that apply.)

A. `java GoDeep`

B. `java -classpath . GoDeep`

C. `java -classpath test/MyJar.jar GoDeep`

D. `java GoDeep -classpath test/MyJar.jar`

E. `java GoDeep -classpath test/MyJar.jar:.`

F. `java -classpath .:test/MyJar.jar GoDeep`

G. `java -classpath test/MyJar.jar:. GoDeep`

SELF TEST ANSWERS

1. Given:

```
1. // insert code here
2. class StatTest {
3.   public static void main(String[] args) {
4.     System.out.println(Integer.MAX_VALUE);
5.   }
6. }
```

Which, inserted independently at line 1, compiles? (Choose all that apply.)

A. `import static java.lang;`

B. `import static java.lang.Integer;`

C. `import static java.lang.Integer.*;`

D. `import static java.lang.Integer.*_VALUE;`

E. `import static java.lang.Integer.MAX_VALUE;`

F. None of the above statements are valid import syntax

Answer:

☑ **C** and **E** are correct syntax for static imports. Line 4 isn't making use of `static imports`, so the code will also compile with none of the imports.

☒ **A, B, D,** and **F** are incorrect based on the above. (Objective 7.1)

2. Given:

```
import static java.lang.System.*;
class _ {
  static public void main(String... __A_V_) {
    String $ = "";
    for(int x=0; ++x < __A_V_.length; )
      $ += __A_V_[x];
    out.println($);
  }
}
```

And the command line:

```
java _ - A .
```

What is the result?

A. `-A`

B. `A.`

C. `-A.`

D. `_A.`

E. `_-A.`

F. Compilation fails

G. An exception is thrown at runtime

> Answer:
>
> ☑ **B** is correct. This question is using valid (but inappropriate and weird) identifiers, static imports, var-args in main(), and pre-incrementing logic.
>
> ☒ **A, C, D, E, F,** and **G** are incorrect based on the above. (Objective 7.2)

3. Given the default classpath:

```
/foo
```

And this directory structure:

```
foo
  |
  test
     |
     xcom
        |--A.class
        |--B.java
```

And these two files:

```
package xcom;
public class A { }

package xcom;
public class B extends A { }
```

Which allows `B.java` to compile? (Choose all that apply.)

A. Set the current directory to `xcom` then invoke
   ```
   javac B.java
   ```

B. Set the current directory to `xcom` then invoke
   ```
   javac -classpath . B.java
   ```

C. Set the current directory to `test` then invoke
   ```
   javac -classpath . xcom/B.java
   ```

D. Set the current directory to `test` then invoke
   ```
   javac -classpath xcom B.java
   ```

E. Set the current directory to `test` then invoke
   ```
   javac -classpath xcom:. B.java
   ```

Answer:

☑ **C** is correct. In order for `B.java` to compile, the compiler first needs to be able to find `B.java`. Once it's found `B.java` it needs to find `A.class`. Because `A.class` is in the `xcom` package the compiler won't find `A.class` if it's invoked from the `xcom` directory. Remember that the `-classpath` isn't looking for `B.java`, it's looking for whatever classes `B.java` needs (in this case `A.class`).

☒ **A, B,** and **D** are incorrect based on the above. **E** is incorrect because the compiler can't find `B.java`. (Objective 7.2)

4. Given two files:

   ```
   a=b.java
   c_d.class
   ```

   Are in the current directory, which command-line invocation(s) could complete without error? (Choose all that apply.)

   A. `java -Da=b c_d`

   B. `java -D a=b c_d`

   C. `javac -Da=b c_d`

   D. `javac -D a=b c_d`

Answer:

☑ **A** is correct. The -D flag is NOT a compiler flag, and the name=value pair that is associated with the -D must follow the -D with no spaces.

☒ **B, C,** and **D** are incorrect based on the above. (Objective 7.2)

---

5. If three versions of `MyClass.class` exist on a file system:

> Version 1 is in `/foo/bar`
> Version 2 is in `/foo/bar/baz`
> Version 3 is in `/foo/bar/baz/bing`

And the system's classpath includes

> `/foo/bar/baz`

And this command line is invoked from `/foo`

> `java -classpath /foo/bar/baz/bing:/foo/bar MyClass`

Which version will be used by `java`?

A. `/foo/MyClass.class`

B. `/foo/bar/MyClass.class`

C. `/foo/bar/baz/MyClass.class`

D. `/foo/bar/baz/bing/MyClass.class`

E. The result is not predictable.

Answer:

☒ **D** is correct. A -classpath included with a `java` invocation overrides a system classpath. When `java` is using any classpath, it reads the classpath from left to right, and uses the first match it finds.

☒ **A, B, C,** and **E** are incorrect based on the above. (Objective 7.5)

6. Given two files:

```
1. package pkgA;
2. public class Foo {
3.   int a = 5;
4.   protected int b = 6;
5. }
```

```
1. package pkgB;
2. import pkgA.*;
3. public class Fiz extends Foo {
4.    public static void main(String[] args) {
5.       Foo f = new Foo();
6.       System.out.print("  " + f.a);
7.       System.out.print(" " + f.b);
8.       System.out.print(" " + new Fiz().a);
9.       System.out.println(" " + new Fiz().b);
10.   }
11. }
```

What is the result? (Choose all that apply.)

A. `5 6 5 6`

B. `5 6` followed by an exception

C. Compilation fails with an error on line 6

D. Compilation fails with an error on line 7

E. Compilation fails with an error on line 8

F. Compilation fails with an error on line 9

Answer:

☑ **C, D,** and **E** are correct. Variable `a` (default access) cannot be accessed from outside the package. Since variable `b` is protected, it can be accessed only through inheritance.

☒ **A, B,** and **F** are incorrect based on the above. (Objectives 1.1, 7.1)

7. Given:

```
3. import java.util.*;
4. public class Antique {
5.    public static void main(String[] args) {
6.       List<String> myList = new ArrayList<String>();
```

```
 7.        assert (args.length > 0);
 8.        System.out.println("still static");
 9.     }
10. }
```

Which sets of commands (javac followed by java) will compile and run without exception or error? (Choose all that apply.)

A. `javac Antique.java`
   `java Antique`

B. `javac Antique.java`
   `java -ea Antique`

C. `javac -source 6 Antique.java`
   `java Antique`

D. `javac -source 1.4 Antique.java`
   `java Antique`

E. `javac -source 1.6 Antique.java`
   `java -ea Antique`

Answer:

☑ **A** and **C** are correct. If assertions (which were first available in Java 1.4) are enabled, an AssertionError will be thrown at line 7.

☒ **D** is incorrect because the code uses generics, and generics weren't introduced until Java 5. **B** and **E** are incorrect based on the above. (Objective 7.2)

8. Given:

```
 3. import java.util.*;
 4. public class Values {
 5.    public static void main(String[] args) {
 6.       Properties p = System.getProperties();
 7.       p.setProperty("myProp", "myValue");
 8.       System.out.print(p.getProperty("cmdProp") + " ");
 9.       System.out.print(p.getProperty("myProp") + " ");
10.       System.out.print(p.getProperty("noProp") + " ");
11.       p.setProperty("cmdProp", "newValue");
12.       System.out.println(p.getProperty("cmdProp"));
13.    }
14. }
```

And given the command line invocation:

```
java -DcmdProp=cmdValue Values
```

What is the result?

A. `null myValue null null`

B. `cmdValue null null cmdValue`

C. `cmdValue null null newValue`

D. `cmdValue myValue null cmdValue`

E. `cmdValue myValue null newValue`

F. An exception is thrown at runtime

Answer:

☑ **E** is correct. System properties can be set at the command line, as indicated correctly in the example. System properties can also be set and overridden programmatically.

☒ **A, B, C, D,** and **F** are incorrect based on the above. (Objective 7.2)

9. Given the following directory structure:

```
x-|
  |- FindBaz.class
  |
  |- test-|
          |- Baz.class
          |
          |- myApp-|
                   |- Baz.class
```

And given the contents of the related .java files:

```
1. public class FindBaz {
2.   public static void main(String[] args) { new Baz(); }
3. }
```

In the test directory:

```
1. public class Baz {
2.   static { System.out.println("test/Baz"); }
3. }
```

In the myApp directory:

```
1. public class Baz {
2.   static { System.out.println("myApp/Baz"); }
3. }
```

If the current directory is x, which invocations will produce the output `"test/Baz"`? (Choose all that apply.)

A. `java FindBaz`

B. `java -classpath test FindBaz`

C. `java -classpath .:test FindBaz`

D. `java -classpath .:test/myApp FindBaz`

E. `java -classpath test:test/myApp FindBaz`

F. `java -classpath test:test/myApp:. FindBaz`

G. `java -classpath test/myApp:test:. FindBaz`

Answer:

☑ **C** and **F** are correct. The `java` command must find both `FindBaz` and the version of `Baz` located in the test directory. The `"."` finds `FindBaz`, and `"test"` must come before `"test/myApp"` or `java` will find the other version of `Baz`. Remember the real exam will default to using the Unix path separator.

☒ **A, B, D, E,** and **G** are incorrect based on the above. (Objective 7.2)

10. Given the following directory structure:

```
test-|
     |- Test.java
     |
     |- myApp-|
             |- Foo.java
             |
             |- myAppSub-|
                         |- Bar.java
```

If the current directory is test, and you create a .jar file by invoking this,

```
jar -cf MyJar.jar myApp
```

then which path names will find a file in the .jar file? (Choose all that apply.)

A. `Foo.java`

B. `Test.java`

C. `myApp/Foo.java`

D. `myApp/Bar.java`

E. `META-INF/Foo.java`

F. `META-INF/myApp/Foo.java`

G. `myApp/myAppSub/Bar.java`

Answer:

☑ **C** and **G** are correct. The files in a .jar file will exist within the same exact directory tree structure in which they existed when the .jar was created. Although a .jar file will contain a META-INF directory, none of your files will be in it. Finally, if any files exist in the directory from which the `jar` command was invoked, they won't be included in the .jar file by default.

☒ **A, B, D, E,** and **F** are incorrect based on the above. (Objective 7.5)

11. Given the following directory structure:

```
test-|
     |- GetJar.java
     |
     |- myApp-|
             |-Foo.java
```

And given the contents of GetJar.java and Foo.java:

```
3. public class GetJar {
4.    public static void main(String[] args) {
5.       System.out.println(myApp.Foo.d);
6.    }
7. }

3. package myApp;
4. public class Foo { public static int d = 8; }
```

If the current directory is "test", and myApp/Foo.class is placed in a JAR file called MyJar.jar located in test, which set(s) of commands will compile GetJar.java and produce the output 8? (Choose all that apply.)

A. ```
javac -classpath MyJar.jar GetJar.java
java GetJar
```

B. ```
javac MyJar.jar GetJar.java
java GetJar
```

C. ```
javac -classpath MyJar.jar GetJar.java
java -classpath MyJar.jar GetJar
```

D. ```
javac MyJar.jar GetJar.java
java -classpath MyJar.jar GetJar
```

> **Answer:**
>
> ☑ **A** is correct. Given the current directory and where the necessary files are located, these are the correct command line statements.
>
> ☒ **B** and **D** are wrong because javac MyJar.jar GetJar.java is incorrect syntax. **C** is wrong because the -classpath MyJar.java in the java invocation does not include the test directory. (Objective 7.5)

12. Given the following directory structure:

```
x-|
  |- GoDeep.class
  |
  |- test-|
          |- MyJar.jar
          |
          |- myApp-|
                   |-Foo.java
                   |-Foo.class
```

And given the contents of GoDeep.java and Foo.java:

```
3. public class GoDeep {
4.    public static void main(String[] args) {
5.       System.out.println(myApp.Foo.d);
6.    }
7. }

3. package myApp;
4. public class Foo { public static int d = 8; }
```

And MyJar.jar contains the following entry:

```
myApp/Foo.class
```

If the current directory is x, which commands will successfully execute GoDeep.class and produce the output 8? (Choose all that apply.)

A. `java GoDeep`

B. `java -classpath . GoDeep`

C. `java -classpath test/MyJar.jar GoDeep`

D. `java GoDeep -classpath test/MyJar.jar`

E. `java GoDeep -classpath test/MyJar.jar:.`

F. `java -classpath .:test/MyJar.jar GoDeep`

G. `java -classpath test/MyJar.jar:. GoDeep`

Answer:

☑ **F** and **G** are correct. The `java` command must find both `GoDeep` and `Foo`, and the `-classpath` option must come before the class name. Note, the current directory (.), in the `classpath` can be searched first or last.

☒ **A, B, C, D,** and **E** are incorrect based on the above. (Objective 7.5)

A

About the CD

Threaded: Whe CD-ROM included with this book comes complete with MasterExam and the electronic version of the book. The software is easy to install on any Windows 98/ NT/2000/XP/Vista computer and must be installed to access the MasterExam feature. You may, however, browse the electronic book directly from the CD without installation. To register for a second bonus MasterExam, simply click the Bonus Material link on the Main Page and follow the directions to the free online registration.

System Requirements

Software requires Windows 98 or higher and Internet Explorer 5.0 or above and 20 MB of hard disk space for full installation. The Electronic book requires Adobe Acrobat Reader.

Installing and Running MasterExam

If your computer CD-ROM drive is configured to auto run, the CD will automatically start up upon inserting the disk. From the opening screen you may install MasterExam by pressing the MasterExam buttons. This will begin the installation process and create a program group named "LearnKey." To run MasterExam, choose Start | Programs | LearnKey. If the auto run feature did not launch your CD, browse to the CD and click RunInstall.

MasterExam

MasterExam provides you with a simulation of the actual exam. The number of questions, types of questions, and the time allowed are intended to be an accurate representation of the exam environment. You have the option to take an open-book exam, including hints, references, and answers; a closed-book exam; or the timed MasterExam simulation.

When you launch MasterExam, a digital clock display will appear in the upper-left corner of your screen. The clock will continue to count down to zero unless you choose to end the exam before the time expires. To register for a second bonus MasterExam, simply click the Bonus Material link on the Main Page and follow the directions to the free online registration.

Electronic Book

The entire contents of the Study Guide are provided in PDF format. Adobe's Acrobat Reader has been included on the CD.

Help

A help file is provided through the Help button on the main page in the lower-left corner. Individual help features are also available through MasterExam and LearnKey's Online Training.

Removing Installation(s)

MasterExam is installed on your hard drive. For best results for removal of programs use the Start | Programs | LearnKey | Uninstall options to remove MasterExam.

If you want to remove the Real Player, use the Add/Remove Programs icon from your Control Panel. You may also remove the LearnKey training program from this location.

Technical Support

For questions regarding the technical content of the electronic book, or MasterExam, please visit www.osborne.com or e-mail customer.service@mcgraw-hill.com. For customers outside the 50 United States, e-mail international_cs@mcgraw-hill.com.

LearnKey Technical Support

For technical problems with the software (installation, operation, removing installations), and for questions regarding any LearnKey Online Training content, please visit www.learnkey.com or e-mail techsupport@learnkey.com.

INDEX

J

Just As I Am

Just As I Am

THE AUTOBIOGRAPHY OF BILLY GRAHAM

Billy Graham

HarperCollins*Publishers*Ltd

FIRST EDITION

Canadian Cataloguing in Publication Data
Graham, Billy
Just as I am: the autobiography of Billy Graham
ISBN 0–00–255412–7
1. Graham, Billy
2. Evangelists - United States - Biography.
I. Title
BV3785.G69A3 1997   269'.2'092   C95–932436–4

97 98 99 00 01 ❖ RRDH 10 9 8 7 6 5 4 3 2 1

This book is gratefully dedicated to every person
who has faithfully supported our ministry
over the years.

Contents

Preface

To be honest, I never thought I would write this book.

For one thing, I felt I was simply too busy for such an extended project. Not only my preaching but my responsibilities as chief executive officer of the Billy Graham Evangelistic Association have always demanded a tremendous amount of time and decision making. I have always been focused on the future, rather than trying to remember what happened half a lifetime ago. How could I justify canceling a busy schedule to write about the past?

For another thing, I knew it would be beyond my ability to write such a work alone. I would need the help of others, but where would I ever find them? And how could we ever encompass a lifetime of ministry in only one volume?

Most of all, if anything has been accomplished through my life, it has been solely God's doing, not mine, and He—not I—must get the credit.

But a number of friends still urged me to undertake this task. Not only was it important for the historical record, they contended, but they felt there were lessons to be learned from the ministry God had entrusted to us. I recalled how much I had learned from reading the writings and studying the lives of the great men and women of the past. At my age, I thought of the next generation, who might be encouraged by such a book to believe that God can do in their generation what He did in ours. I came to see that in its own way this book could be a ministry also.

As I say in more detail at the end of the book, I also found the right people to assist me—although the shortcomings are solely my responsibility, not theirs.

This book has taken ten years to write. My biggest problem was always carving out the time to work on it. During those years, not only have I continued to preach the Gospel on every continent, both in person and on television, but I have had to deal with numerous problems, including several illnesses and accidents.

I soon realized it was impossible to include in this book everything we have been involved in during more than half a century of ministry, and one of the hardest parts has been deciding what to leave out. As I look back over the hundreds of Crusades we have been privileged to hold, they tend to come together in my memory as one. Every one had its unique character, of course; but time and space don't allow me to cover more than a few Crusades and a few other events that were especially memorable.

Even as I write these words, I think of the many individuals to whom I owe an enormous debt because of their help or their friendship, and yet whose names are not mentioned in these pages. I want them to know of my genuine gratitude to them in any case.

I have tried to be as accurate as possible in summarizing events and conversations, researching them thoroughly and recounting them carefully. However, I have come to realize how memories fade over the years. We have all heard the illustration of the blind men who were asked to describe an elephant, each coming up with a wildly different description because they were all touching a different part of the animal. I realize that my memory may differ occasionally from that of others; the best I can do is record events as I recall them.

Finally, I want to add a few words about my calling as an evangelist. The word *evangelist* comes from a Greek word meaning "one who announces Good News." Its verb form occurs over fifty times in the Greek New Testament. An evangelist, then, is like a newscaster on television or a journalist writing for a newspaper or magazine—except that the evangelist's mission is to tell the good news of the Gospel. (The word *Gospel* actually means "Good News.")

In the Bible, an evangelist is a person sent by God to announce the Gospel, the Good News; he or she has a spiritual gift that has never been withdrawn from the Church. Methods differ, but the central truth remains: an evangelist is a person who has been called and especially equipped by God to declare the Good News to those who have not yet accepted it, with the goal of challenging them to turn to Christ in repentance and faith and to follow Him in obedience to His will. The evangelist is not called to do *everything* in the church or in the world that God wants done. On the contrary, the calling of the evangelist is very specific.

Nor is the evangelist free to change the message, any more than a newscaster is free to change the news. The main thrust of our message is centered in Christ and what He has done for us by His death and resurrection, and the need for us to respond by committing our lives to Him. It is the message that Christ came to forgive us and give us new life and hope as we turn to Him.

Through these pages, the reader will discover how I have sought (however imperfectly) to follow Christ. But if through these pages someone learns what it means to follow Christ, or gains a new vision of God's plan for this world, then the effort has been worth it.

BILLY GRAHAM
JANUARY 1997

Introduction:
Between Two Presidents

HARRY S. TRUMAN 1950, KIM IL SUNG 1992

It was July 14, 1950, and I was about to make a fool of myself.

At the urging of my friends Congressman Joe Bryson of South Carolina and Congressman Herbert C. Bonner of North Carolina, John McCormack, who was the influential representative from Massachusetts, had arranged an appointment for me with President Truman. It had not been easy for them, however.

In May 1950, Congressman Bryson had written Congressman McCormack that I would be in Washington on June 2, 3, and 6. He asked whether an appointment could be made for me with the President on any of those days. The President's secretary wrote back to McCormack promptly, saying that the schedule was full. "It will be quite some time before we will be able to make any additions to the President's calendar," the secretary added.

My friends persevered, however. I will never know exactly what happened behind the scenes; perhaps Mr. McCormack called the President's attention to the Crusade we had held in his hometown of Boston several months before.

Whatever the reason, less than three weeks later Congressman McCormack received another letter from the President's secretary, suggesting "that you ask Dr. Graham if it would be convenient for him to call here at the Executive Office at 12:00 Noon on Friday, July 14th."

And then, five days later, war broke out in Korea.

On June 25, 1950, troops from North Korea invaded South Korea. Kim Il Sung, North Korea's Communist president, was determined to reunite the Korean Peninsula, which had been divided (with U.S. approval) at the thirty-eighth parallel after World War II.

When I heard the news, I sent President Truman a telegram urging him to stand firm against President Kim Il Sung's military and ideological threat.

"MILLIONS OF CHRISTIANS PRAYING GOD GIVE YOU WISDOM IN THIS CRISIS. STRONGLY URGE SHOWDOWN WITH COMMUNISM NOW. MORE CHRISTIANS IN SOUTHERN KOREA PER CAPITA THAN ANY PART OF WORLD. WE CANNOT LET THEM DOWN."

Three weeks later, I was on my way to meet the President.

Apart from the fact that Truman was a fellow Baptist and a fellow Democrat—which meant practically the same thing in the South, where I grew up—I did not know much about him.

Did he know much about us? It was doubtful, although I had written him a couple of times since he came to office.

Several years earlier, I wrote to tell him about Youth for Christ, the organization that had employed me as an evangelist since 1945. I wanted him to help us start a ministry in the American-occupied zone in Germany; his approval would be necessary, or so some friends in Congress had told me. In my mind's eye I pictured the President giving careful and prolonged personal attention to my request. But that, of course, was not the case; he probably never saw my letter.

In February 1949, shortly after his inauguration, I wrote to the White House asking the President's secretary to assure President Truman "that over 1,100 students here at these Northwestern Schools are praying daily that God will give him wisdom and guidance in the strenuous days lying ahead."

The invitation to the White House was for me alone, but I corralled my colleagues Grady Wilson, Cliff Barrows, and Jerry Beavan into flying with me to Washington from the Winona Lake, Indiana, Bible conference at which I had been preaching. When we arrived at the capital, we checked in at the Mayflower Hotel. We slept fitfully.

First thing the following morning, I telephoned our contact to ask if I might bring along my three companions. After a noticeable pause, which I thought was a prelude to the answer no, the voice on the telephone agreed.

What should we wear? We had been praying about that issue since receiving Congressman McCormack's telegram of July 11, but we did not have a great deal to choose from. In the end, we went with what we had been wearing at the Bible conference.

I was just a tanned, lanky thirty-one-year-old, crowned by a heavy thatch of wavy blond hair, wearing what *Time* magazine would later describe as a "pistachio-green" suit (I remember it as cream-colored) with rust-colored socks and a hand-painted tie. My three colleagues were similarly attired. But was there something missing, we asked ourselves.

We had seen a picture of the President on vacation in Florida, wearing white buck shoes. That was it! Grady already had a pair. I sent him to the nearest Florsheim store to buy white bucks for Cliff and me. So how could we go wrong? After all, the President was a haberdasher himself.

"What time is it?" I kept asking. "We don't want to be late."

My watch was broken; fortunately, Cliff's watch was working.

Better early than late, we left the hotel. The White House was too close to take a cab so we walked down Connecticut Avenue and across Lafayette Square, turning a few heads, I guess. People probably thought we were a barbershop quartet out for a stroll.

When we arrived at the side gate of the White House, we passed through the security guards and checkpoints easily enough. The President's secretary then took us in hand, informing us that our visit would last exactly twenty minutes.

Promptly at noon, we were ushered into the Oval Office. From the look on President Truman's face, the chief executive of our nation must have thought he was receiving a traveling vaudeville team. He welcomed us cordially enough, though, with handshakes all around. Then he said he had heard some good things about our meetings.

I told him about Los Angeles the previous fall, where we preached in a huge tent but, initially, attracted virtually no mention in the press. Then newspaper tycoon William Randolph Hearst, for no apparent reason, had directed his editors to focus on what was going on inside the tent. Almost overnight we became nationally known. During the fifty days of meetings there, attendance snowballed to a total of 350,000, an unheard-of crowd for an evangelistic gathering in those days.

Then I told him about Boston, where we had meetings at the end of 1949, followed by an extensive New England tour in the early months of 1950. By this time, the newspapers were spotlighting us everywhere we went. After our rally on Boston Common on Sunday, April 23, officials had estimated the crowd at 50,000. On that day, against the backdrop of the revelation that the Soviet Union was building a nuclear arsenal, I had publicly called on the President of the United States to proclaim a day of national repentance and prayer for peace.

Mr. Truman nodded as though he remembered the incident.

Then I reaffirmed my support for his swift reaction to Kim Il Sung's invasion of South Korea, even though the recent news from the battlefields had not been all that encouraging.

Our allotted time was quickly running out, and what I really wanted to talk to him about was faith. I did not know how to begin.

"Mr. President," I blurted out, "tell me about your religious background and leanings."

"Well," he replied in his Missouri accent, "I try to live by the Sermon on the Mount and the Golden Rule."

"It takes more than that, Mr. President. It's faith in Christ and His death on the Cross that you need."

The President stood up. Apparently, our twenty minutes were up. We stood up too.

"Mr. President, could we have prayer?"

"It can't do any harm," he said—or something similar.

I put my arm around the shoulders of the President of the United States of America and prayed.

"Amen," Cliff exclaimed during the prayer. "Do it, Lord!"

When we left the Oval Office, I looked at the clock; my prayer had taken another five minutes.

When we stepped outside the White House, reporters and photographers from the press corps pounced on us.

"What did the President say?"

I told them everything I could remember.

"What did you say?"

Again I told them everything I could remember.

"Did you pray with the President?"

"Yes, we prayed with the President."

"What did he think about that?" someone called out.

Before I could respond, an enterprising photographer asked us to kneel on the lawn and reenact the prayer. The press corps roared its approval.

I declined to repeat the words we had prayed in the Oval Office, but I said that we had been planning to thank God for our visit anyway, and now was as good a time as any. The four of us bent one knee of our pastel summer suits, and I led the prayer of thanksgiving as sincerely as I could, impervious to the popping flashbulbs and scribbling pencils.

It began to dawn on me a few days later how we had abused the privilege of seeing the President. National coverage of our visit was definitely not to our advantage. The President was offended that I had quoted him without authorization, Drew Pearson observed in his syndicated column, and now I was persona non grata at the White House. And Pearson was right. Mr. Truman never asked me to come back.

A White House staff memorandum in late 1951 stated it bluntly: "At Key West the President said very decisively that he did not wish to endorse Billy Graham's Washington revival meeting and particularly he said he did not want to receive him at the White House. You remember what a show of himself Billy Graham made the last time he was here. The President does not want it repeated."

I did visit Mr. Truman many years later at his home in Independence, Missouri. I recalled the incident and apologized profusely for our ignorance and naiveté.

"Don't worry about it," he replied graciously. "I realized you hadn't been properly briefed."

After our gaffe, I vowed to myself it would never happen again if I ever was given access to a person of rank or influence.

Forty-two years later—April 2, 1992—I was, in the minds of some, about to make a fool of myself again, this time in another capital, Pyongyang.

North Korea was a place few people from the West had ever visited. Politically and diplomatically, it was considered one of the most isolated nations on earth. Technically, the United States and North Korea were still at war, and there was almost no contact between them. The Korean War had ended some four decades before, but only with an armistice, not a peace treaty. Now it was rumored that North Korea was developing its own nuclear arms program.

Before leaving the United States, I had asked President Bush if he thought it was wise for me to go. He and others cautioned me about the risks we might be taking, including the danger of being used for propaganda purposes. Yet he encouraged me to go anyway. He even asked me to deliver a brief message of greeting if I was received by President Kim.

On the other hand, some felt it was foolish for me to journey to a country so openly hostile to my own. And it would be especially foolish to meet with President Kim, others contended, given that millions of people—especially in South Korea, where we had many friends—would draw the conclusion that just by meeting with him, I would be giving support to his political and social policies.

Furthermore, under President Kim—the same Communist leader who had been President Truman's adversary during the Korean War (and whom I had urged President Truman to resist with all his power)—North Korea had become the most nonreligious nation on earth. President Kim had even proclaimed North Korea the first completely atheistic state in the world, although recently two churches—where I would preach—had been opened in Pyongyang.

As I recount in more detail later in these pages, we were driven through the countryside to the President's residence about twenty miles outside the city. In the reception room, President Kim greeted me with a warm embrace as cameras clicked. Though just turning eighty, he had only a few streaks of gray in his black hair. He wore spectacles, but his intelligent eyes flashed behind them. In a dark business suit, white shirt, and deep maroon tie, he looked like an international business executive. He could not have been more cordial.

Among my token gifts to him were a copy of my first book, *Peace with God,* and a copy of the Bible, both of which I had inscribed to him personally.

In return, President Kim gave me the first volumes of his autobiography, the conclusion of which he was still working on. In those volumes, I later learned about his boyhood, including the fact that his mother was a Christian.

Before our private meeting began, President Kim commented to the media that the warmth of early spring stirred his hope that a new spring was coming in relations between our two countries. Subsequent developments would cast a temporary chill over our hopes for that, but I am sure his kind reception of our little group was meant as a friendly gesture politically as well as personally.

In our private meeting, I conveyed President Bush's greeting to him, and he in turn gave me a message to convey back to the President. Subsequent events indicated that our visit might have been a first step toward better relations. When we went to Hong Kong, en route back to America, reporters and cameramen—including a large number from South Korea—jammed the press conference. They clamored repeatedly for details about our private conversation, demanding to know the message President Kim had asked me to deliver to President Bush. I could not help but recall the fiasco on the White House lawn four decades before. I politely but firmly refused.

No two heads of state—President Harry Truman and President Kim Il Sung—could have been further apart ideologically and politically. Yet those two Presidents are like bookends on my shelf of memories. Between them stand volumes of varied contacts and conversations with my fellow human beings—a few leaders like them, but mostly very ordinary people like myself.

1918–1943

Foundations

1

Down on the Farm

Day after day, the tall, spare farmer leaned on the board fence and searched the sky for clouds. In front of him, rows of corn were stunted, brown for lack of rain. He shoved his hat back on his head, exposing a strip of white forehead above a sun-browned face. No rain meant no crops. His shoulders slumped. His feet shuffled up the hot, dusty path back to the farmhouse, where I watched from the open door. My heart sank as I read the concern in his weary face. That man was my dad. . . .

When I was a boy growing up, Park Road outside Charlotte, North Carolina, was little more than a rutted dirt lane cutting across acres of farmland. Our white frame house with green trim sat back from the road and overlooked sprawling pastures dotted with our family's dairy herd, set against the tranquil backdrop of trees and low hills. There I was born on November 7, 1918, four days before the armistice that ended World War I and one year to the day after the Bolshevik Revolution in Russia.

This was not the first house built on the site. A log cabin on acreage bought after the Civil War in Sharon Township, between the villages of Pineville and Matthews, was built by my grandfather William Crook Graham, a hard-drinking, hard-cursing veteran

3

whose service with the Sixth South Carolina Volunteers left him with a Yankee bullet in his leg for the rest of his life.

My Aunt Eunice said the extent of her father's religion was to be an honest man. Fortunately, his wife, a God-fearing Scotswoman named Maggie McCall, influenced the character formation of their eight daughters and three sons by teaching them precepts and principles from the Scriptures. They all grew up to be deeply religious, and a number of their grandchildren became preachers—I being the first.

The first death in our immediate family was that of my maternal grandmother, Lucinda Coffey. Grandmother talked often about her husband, Ben Coffey, who had been badly wounded while serving with the Eleventh North Carolina Regiment, Pettigrew's Brigade, which led the advance on Gettysburg from the west on July 1, 1863. Shrapnel almost severed his left leg. While he was lying on the battlefield, a bullet grazed his right eye, blinding it forever. Doctors were forced to amputate his wounded leg some time later. On August 1, the company commander wrote a letter of commendation: "Benny was such a good boy; . . . a better soldier never lived." His comrades testified to his concern for spiritual values. I never knew him; he died in 1916 at the ripe old age of seventy-four.

When Grandmother Coffey died, I was in elementary school, and my sister Catherine and I were called out of school. The manner of her dying became a legacy of faith for our family. She sat up in bed and almost laughingly said, "I see Jesus. He has His arms outstretched toward me. And there's Ben! He has both of his eyes and both of his legs." She was buried among many other members of our family in the large Steele Creek Presbyterian churchyard.

For a child of the Roaring Twenties who reached adolescence in the Depression of the early thirties, rural life probably offered the best of all worlds. As Scottish Presbyterians believing in strict observance of moral values, we stayed relatively uncontaminated by the Great Gatsby lifestyle of the flapper era, with its fast dancing and illegal drinking. And being farmers, we could manage to live off the land when the economy nose-dived in the 1929 stock market crash, even though my father lost his savings—$4,000—in the failed Farmers' and Merchants' Bank in Charlotte.

Not that those were not anxious times. Yet it never occurred to me or my parents to think of the rigors of dairy farming as hardships. We all simply believed in hard work. The fact was that the South had never fully recovered economically from the Civil War and Reconstruction. It is strange to realize now, in light of Charlotte's present prosperity, that the region of my boyhood only sixty years ago was unbelievably poor.

In the Depression, our dairy farm barely survived when milk got down to 5¢ a quart. After the stock market crash of 1929, and the bank holiday that President Franklin D. Roosevelt ordered in 1933 under his National Industrial Recovery Act, my father nearly went broke. At first he was confident that his bank in Charlotte would reopen, but it did not. He couldn't even write a check to pay his bills. He had to start over from scratch. It took him months to recover from the blow.

Yet business reverses never stifled my father's sense of humor. While he had cause to be melancholy or depressed, he was anything but that. There were down moments, of course, when the rains did not come and the crops did not grow, or when a prize cow died. But in spite of the hardships, he found much to laugh about. People loved to come to our place from all around the neighborhood just to hear him tell his jokes. His dry sense of humor kept us laughing by the hour.

Growing up in those years taught us the value of nickels and dimes. My father early on illustrated for me the merits of free enterprise. Once in a while when a calf was born on the farm, he turned it over to my friend Albert McMakin and me to raise. When it got to the veal stage, we marketed it ourselves and split the proceeds.

We were not out of touch with what was going on elsewhere, but our newspaper carried mostly local stories. Radio was still in its infancy. Once my father made his first crystal set, he tuned in pioneer station KDKA from Pittsburgh. We gathered around the squawking receiver, holding our breath. When, after Daddy had done a lot of fiddling with the three tuning dials, something intelligible broke through the static, we all shouted, "That's it! We have it!"

Later we were among the first in our neighborhood to have a radio in our car. When my folks went into a store to shop, I stretched out on the back seat and listened to those mysterious sounds—distorted broadcasts marvelously relayed by wireless from Europe. They had a hollow echo as if coming to us through a magic seashell. I was particularly fascinated by the oratorical style of speeches shouted in an almost hypnotic voice by a man in Germany named Adolf Hitler. He frightened me in some way, even though I did not understand his language.

However, there were more important things to think about in my boyhood North Carolina universe. It centered on the three hundred acres inherited from my grandfather by my father and his brother Clyde, where they ran Graham Brothers Dairy. Father handled the business affairs and the farm itself, with Mother doing the bookkeeping at our kitchen table. Uncle Clyde looked after the milk-processing house.

My father's younger brother and dedicated business partner, Uncle Clyde seemed to depend on Daddy for nearly all the decisions having to do with the farm. The first few years of my life, he lived with us. He always liked a good laugh. He once placed an order with a traveling salesman for a whole case of wonder tonic that was supposed to restore his lost hair. He was only moderately disappointed when it failed to live up to its promise.

Even though a bachelor, he never had any women friends that we knew about. Yet when he decided to build a house across the road from us, my mother jokingly said, "Maybe he's planning to get married!"

Little did we know! I'd had a teacher in the second grade by the name of Jennie Patrick. She came from a prominent family in South Carolina. I would never have dreamed that Uncle Clyde was secretly courting her! One day when he was pulling out of the driveway, all dressed up for a change, my father stopped him.

"Where are you going, Clyde?" Daddy asked in astonishment.

"I'm going to get married," he stammered with a blush and a smile.

That was the only announcement we had—and the only preparation my mother had—that Uncle Clyde's bride would be arriving soon.

6

Aunt Jennie proved to be a marvelous cook, and of course she had a special affection for me because I had been one of her pupils. She and Uncle Clyde eventually had two sons who grew up sharing the devout convictions of their parents. One of them, Ed, became one of the finest pastors I have ever known, with the largest Presbyterian congregation in the western part of North Carolina. His older brother, Clyde, worked at Ivey's department store in Charlotte, where he was promoted a number of times through the years.

In the "Wild West" years, the eldest Graham brother, my Uncle Tom, went off to Oklahoma, where he married a full-blooded Cherokee woman. He did well for himself in cotton gins. Each summer when they came back to North Carolina for a two-week visit, driving the biggest car I had ever seen (with every kind of gadget on it), they stayed at our house. He was tall and heavyset, and how he and the equally ample Aunt Belle could sleep in that three-quarter-size bed in our guest room remained one of the unsolved mysteries of my childhood.

Our barns had tin roofs. On rainy days, I liked to sneak away into the hay barn and lie on a sweet-smelling and slippery pile of straw, listening to the raindrops hit that tin roof and dreaming. It was a sanctuary that helped shape my character. Whenever I visit a bustling city anywhere in the world now, I like to retreat from noisy boulevards into an open church building and just meditate in the cool, dim quietness. At our home in the Blue Ridge Mountains, my favorite spot is a little path above the house where I walk alone and talk with God.

We always had a collie—at least one—and what would any farm be without plenty of cats? Not knowing any better, I once took a cat and shut it in the doghouse with the dog. They hated each other with some ancient instinct when they went in, but after spending the night inside they came out as friends forever. Maybe that is where the seeds of some of my ecumenical convictions got planted, wanting to help people at odds with each other find ways to get along together.

When I was quite little, I kept pet goats. I had them pull me and my sister Catherine (who was a couple of years younger than I) around in my cart while we played dairy farm and pretended to be helping Daddy haul hay. One long-horned, red-haired goat named Billy Junior was a favorite of mine, but he attacked Catherine several times. She was quieter than the rest of us; maybe she seemed more vulnerable to the goat.

We were fortunate to have Catherine with us. As an infant, she swallowed an open safety pin. The unusual and complicated surgical procedure that had to be performed to close the pin inside her and remove it made medical news in our part of the country. Since my parents were at the hospital a lot of the time, I had to stay at my Aunt Lill's house in town. We just had to wait to see whether Catherine would survive.

I had one narrow brush with death myself as a child. Once when I was sick, Mother thought she was giving me cough medicine, but she gave me iodine instead. If it had not been for a quick phone call to Aunt Jennie, who suggested some thick cream from the dairy to counteract the iodine, I might have died.

When I got too big for the goat cart, I rode my bike down the road, followed by a procession of goats and dogs (but never the proud cats), to the amusement of our few neighbors and the people who passed by in buggies and cars. My father kept a riding horse, Mamie, for us children. And as we got older, we rode the mules—Mag, Emma, and Bessie—bareback, sometimes standing up on the backs of the gentler mules.

It was a happy moment for me when, at almost six, I discovered that my folks had gotten me a baby brother. When Melvin got big enough to play with me, we bonded for a lifetime. We moved from the clapboard house with outside plumbing to a compact, two-story brick house with indoor plumbing that my father built for $9,000 when I was about nine. Melvin and I shared a room without much in it besides our twin beds and a white dresser.

Every day Daddy and Uncle Clyde worked hard from before dawn until after dark, with the help of several hired hands. I, and later Melvin too, joined them as we each got strong enough to be more of a help than a hindrance. Being older, I got initiated into the barn and dairy routines before Melvin did. My six-year seniority helped me stay in charge of things at first, but then my reedy growth and his developing bulk evened the score.

When I left home to attend college, Melvin inherited my room for himself. At one stage, he got into weight-lifting, and when he dropped those weights, the whole house shook. My parents thought his exercise program was tremendous, because he was getting so muscular. That made him a strong candidate for world-class plowing and other heavy farm duties. When I pumped my arms and invited Catherine to feel my muscles, she could find only little bumps. She giggled, but I already knew I was no Atlas.

Whether it was cows or horses or land, Daddy was a good horse trader, as the expression went, even when he was trading cows. He often took me along on his short trips away from home for the regular ritual of trading with people who wanted to buy one of our cows. On one such venture to a farm perhaps five miles from our own, I broke in as my father was telling the man all the good qualities of the animal under discussion.

"Daddy, that cow really kicks when you're milking her," I reminded him. "She's very temperamental."

He had some unforgettable instructions for me on the way home about my not interrupting his future business negotiations!

Family outings were few and far between, due to the lack of both money and leisure time. The only luxuries my parents allowed were indulged in on an occasional Saturday night. We all piled into the car and drove to the nearby country grocery store, or maybe even into Charlotte to Niven's Drugstore. On those glorious occasions, Daddy bought us ice-cream cones or soft drinks—never both. We sat in the car with Mother, enjoying our treat while he went into the barbershop for his shave.

Mother and Daddy seldom went to "entertainments." About once a year, they attended a neighborly social at a community hall a mile away, where there would be a potluck picnic and plenty of music. My father's favorite song was "My Blue Heaven." As for the movies, they went to see Will Rogers, Marie Dressler, and Wallace Beery. For that matter, so did we kids: we went as a whole family. This was in the days before censorship restrictions, and there was a surprising amount of nudity on the screen. Once the preview of a coming attraction suddenly flashed a breathtaking shot of a woman swimming nude. My mother reached over and grabbed my hand, commanding, "Close your eyes!" I wasn't old enough to be shocked, but I was admittedly curious.

We always looked forward to spending two or three days each year on what was called a vacation. Usually we went to the beach. It took us from about four in the morning to two in the afternoon to drive either to Wilmington or to Myrtle Beach. After we got there, my father would inquire at various boardinghouses to see which was the cheapest. He usually was able to get board and room for about $1 a night per person.

My mother also liked to go to the Magnolia Gardens near Charleston, South Carolina. We saw the flowers, spent the night, and headed home. For me the best part was that we usually went along with Aunt Ida and her husband, Tom Black, and their several kids, including cousin Laura, who was more like a sister to us. They lived about four miles down the road from us and ran a dairy of their own.

The first long trip I can remember taking was to Washington, D.C., four hundred miles away. Cousin Frank Black drove the car, but he did not want to spend much time sight-seeing because he had to get back to his girlfriend. I think we went through the entire Smithsonian Institution—not the extensive complex it is today—in forty minutes. We did take the time, though, to climb every one of those steps up the Washington Monument.

One summer my father and Uncle Tom Black decided to take us all—two carloads—to Oklahoma to visit Uncle Tom Graham and Aunt Belle and the cousins out West in Tahlequah, Oklahoma. It was a hair-raising trip. Most of the roads we traveled weren't paved; they were simply topped with gravel. It took us two or three days to drive to Oklahoma, and we had several tire blowouts on the way. One night in Arkansas, we had to stop along a desolate stretch of clay road to repair a tire. We had gotten separated from the other car, which was being driven by cousin Ervin Stafford; he had gone to school in Tahlequah and knew the country.

While my father fixed the tire, we kids waited in the quiet darkness, more than a little frightened. We thought we saw strange creatures peering out at us from behind the trees. A car came by and stopped.

"Where y'all from?" the driver asked.

"North Carolina," Daddy answered.

"Y'all better be careful," the stranger said. "This road attracts robbers and cutthroats. You could get robbed or even killed here."

My father got that flat tire fixed in record time! But it was still a hard trip for a twelve-year-old. Daddy insisted on not paying more than $1 for a place to stay. Even in those days that was cheap.

Finally we arrived in Oklahoma, headquarters of the Cherokee Nation, home for those Cherokee who had survived the terrible march of the "Trail of Tears." We had a wonderful two or three days with my uncle and his family in Tahlequah.

The variety of adventures made those some of my happiest years, even though when I grew big enough to help with chores, the work was truly hard. To this day, I can clearly remember the hours working in Mother's garden, guiding the plow, and following the hind end of a mule to put the fertilizer on after the seeds had been sown. In the spring, summer, and fall, we had many acres of corn, wheat, rye, and barley, as well as the vegetable acreage, and Melvin, the McMakins, and I all worked in those fields. When that Big Ben alarm clock went off at two-thirty in the morning, I wanted to slam it to the floor and burrow back under the covers. But heavy footsteps thudded in the quiet hallway outside my upstairs bedroom, where I had taken my apple and the white tomcat to bed with me seemingly only minutes before. That sound told me that my father was on the move and expected me to hustle down the hill to rouse Pedro, one of the hired hands. Besides that, I knew there would be no breakfast until after we had finished the milking. I rolled out in a hurry.

Joe McCall, another of our workers, would usually call the cows in with his "Whooee, whooee, whooee!" Each one headed instinctively for her own stall, where we would fasten the stanchions around her neck and, if she was one of the rambunctious ones, put kickers—restraining chains—on her hind legs. I would then set my three-legged stool and tin milk pail on the floor under her working end, press my head against her warm belly, and get to work on the udder "faucets," trying not to get hit in the eyes with her switching tail while I milked.

I repeated the process in twenty stalls each morning; and each afternoon, as soon as I got home from school, I milked the same twenty of our cows again. The job took my flexible fingers about two hours—a very commendable rate of around five minutes per cow.

That was followed by wielding a shovel to clean out the fresh, warm manure, and by generally straightening things up inside the cow barn. The other hands and I brought in fresh hay from the hay barn next door, or silage from one of our two silos, and refilled the feed troughs.

Carrying the five-gallon milk cans over to the milk-processing house where my Uncle Clyde worked was a favorite ritual for me. In the earliest years, before I was old enough to help with the milking, I watched the muscular men settle those huge, silvery cans down into the clear water of the spring to get them cool before bottling the milk for delivery to the homes in town.

I especially loved to watch Reese Brown work. He was the foreman on our place for fifteen years, perhaps the highest-paid farmhand in Mecklenburg County (at $3 to $4 a day), which made a few other farmers critical of my father. Reese was one of Daddy's best personal friends. A black man who had served with distinction as an Army sergeant during World War I, he had great intelligence. Physically, he was one of the strongest men I ever knew, with a tremendous capacity for working hard. Everyone respected him, and I thought there was nothing Reese did not know or could not do. If I did something he thought was wrong, he did not mind correcting me. He also taught me to respect my father and was almost like another uncle to me. I used to play with his children and eat his wife's fabulous buttermilk biscuits in the tenant house that was their home.

With the whole milking process finished about five-thirty, it was time to eat in the warm and appetizing breakfast room. While we worked in the barns, Mother chopped wood for the stove, did household tasks, and cooked for the hungry men. Now, with my sister Catherine and the maid helping her, she ladled out grits and gravy, fresh eggs, ham or bacon, and hot homemade rolls—a traditional farm breakfast—with all the milk we non-coffee drinkers wanted. Susie Nickolson, the black woman who worked for Mother for twenty years, was like a second mother to us children. It was a busy but easygoing time.

After all my heavy labor in the fresh air at daybreak, followed by Mother's good food, I was ready for almost anything—except school. With only three or four hours of sleep some nights, I often felt tired in my classes. I think fatigue contributed to my course grades being as poor as they were. I had made mostly A's when I was in elementary school, but in high school I was at the C level.

Maybe that was why I failed French in the tenth grade. Every day the following summer, classmate Winston Covington, whom I called Wint, and I had to drive over in his car to spend two hours with a teacher who sat us down and tutored us in French.

For that matter, the classroom was traumatic on my very first day in elementary school. Mother had packed my lunch and told me I was to eat it at recess. She did not say there would be *two* recesses! The first came at ten in the morning and lasted only ten minutes; by the time the bell rang for us to return to class, I had finished my lunch. The second, longer recess was the official lunchtime, and I had nothing to eat. I was mighty hungry by dismissal time at three o'clock and must have rushed out of the building. The principal did not like my haste and yanked my car in reprimand.

At home, from my earliest years, Mother encouraged me in the habit of reading. The exploits of Robin Hood in Sherwood Forest entranced me. I read the whole Tom Swift series, and the Rover Boys. Among my favorite adventure reading were the Tarzan books; they came out every few months. I could hardly wait for the next one to be issued, and my mother would always buy it for me. In the woods in back of our house, I tried to imitate Tarzan's vine-swinging antics and distinctive yell, much to the amusement of Catherine.

Mother saw to it that there was more serious reading too. Before I was ten, she had made me memorize the Westminster (Presbyterian) Shorter Catechism. Once I was visiting an aunt who ordered us to spend some time reading the Bible. In about ten minutes, I went back to her and boasted, "I just read a whole book in the Bible." She thought I was a remarkable boy. (I had discovered the Epistle of Jude, the shortest book in the New Testament. One page!) Mother also prodded me to read *The Book of Knowledge,* an encyclopedia.

Dr. W. B. Lindsay, the minister in our church, was a sweet and godly man. He reminded me of a mortician, though, because as far as I knew, he never told a humorous story. I found his sermons biblical but boring. Still, I shared our family's respect for him. He was what I supposed a saint should be. Discouraging thought, since I felt so far from sainthood! Dr. Lindsay's wife . . . well, I could have given *her* a cheer! She sat in the front pew and shook her watch at her husband when it was time for him to quit preaching.

One day, though, in vacation Bible school, I threw a Bible across the room to someone who wanted one. Mrs. Lindsay, looming like a locomotive, steamed over to me and boomed, "Don't you *ever* do that again! That book is God's Word."

There was not much about Dr. Lindsay's church to make it lively for me, not even in the youth group. We sang only metrical psalms—that is to say, only hymns taken from the Book of Psalms—in the services on the Sabbath (we were too strict to say "Sunday"). We did not always get back to church for the evening meeting; it was about a ten-mile trip in the Model A Ford over two parallel mud ruts. To make up for that, Mother liked to gather us around her to listen to a Bible story on Sunday afternoons before the milking.

One unpleasant complication about high school was a change in the school system that required us country kids to transfer from the Woodlawn School to the Sharon School at the edge of town. We newcomers glared at the students who were already there, and they glared back. It took at least six months for us to get adjusted to each other. That first year at Sharon, I got into more fistfights and wrestling matches than in all the rest of my schooldays put together. And a couple of times I got beaten.

Immediately after school each day, I returned home for the afternoon milking, putting on my old clothes and heading right out to the barn. My father usually had at least two or three men helping us, and I would get to talk to them and hear all the events of the day and swap stories with them. Then, after chores, there was baseball practice, and homework, and church activities, and get-togethers with my friends.

During summer vacations, there was no more leisure. In addition to the regular milking and other chores on the farm, I had to help our deliveryman Tom Griffin on our dairy route in Charlotte, which was then a city of more than 50,000. He was always a lot of fun, entertaining me with tales of incredible encounters with some of his customers; some of those stories would be rated R or X today. I remember delivering four quarts of milk every day to the home of Randolph Scott. He would later become a famous film actor; as adults, he and I occasionally played golf together, and I preached at his funeral.

Life on our small dairy farm was far from a sheltered existence. The natural cycles of birth and death were commonplace and un-avoidable. Dogs, cats, cows. One morning we found a holstein lying dead and swollen on the bank of Sugar Creek, which ran through the middle of our place. A textile mill somewhere upstream was dis-charging poisonous waste into the creek, making it useless for swim-ming and deadly for drinking. We had to build a fence to keep the cattle away from it.

Whenever a cow died, we hitched up the mules and dragged the carcass to a far corner of the pasture, where we buried it. The rest of the herd followed along with us, mooing mournfully as if they could feel bereavement. At least our cow burials lacked the flowery fuss I had observed at the few human funerals I had already attended.

There was a graveyard not too far from where we lived. One day—this was when I was a little boy—my father and I walked by it when we were hunting. It was almost dark. I had to reach up and hold tight to his hand. Even when I grew older, I used to lie awake at night and wonder what would happen to me if I died. It upset me to pray, "If I should die before I wake, I pray the Lord my soul to take." It only strengthened my distaste for the possibility of ever be-coming an undertaker.

Driving cars was every boy's obsession. I started as early as eight, when Reese Brown coached me in driving our GMC truck.

By ten or twelve, I had graduated to our little Model T Ford. We did not bother with a learner's permit (or even a driver's license) back then in our part of the world.

When I was in the ninth grade, I started asking my father for the car to go to a basketball game, or maybe out on an evening date, thus launching a driving career that nearly came to an abrupt end. One night out on Park Road, I was showing off with some of my buddies. My closest schoolfriends were Sam Paxton, Wint Covington, and Julian Miller. Somehow I steered the car into heavy mud. In minutes that goo came up over the fenders. I had gone into a sinkhole. With considerable embarrassment, I went to a nearby house to phone my father and ask him to bring a team of mules to pull the car out. He made it perfectly clear to me that he was upset.

I might have had some tendencies toward crowd-pleasing wildness when I got behind a steering wheel. I sure tried to make that car go as fast as possible, especially when I had a girlfriend along with me. Certainly, that was the case more than once with a particular girl—one who liked to stand up in the bright yellow convertible, which I sometimes borrowed from one of our relatives, and vigorously clang a cowbell as I chugged merrily down some country lane.

What about girls? I especially liked Jeanne Elliott, whose mother prepared lunches in the school cafeteria for the few kids who could afford to eat there. She made a fruit punch that was delicious! I went with Jeanne off and on through my high school days, but we were only buddies and did not have dates together in a formal sense.

I dated several girls and enjoyed holding hands and kissing like the rest of the kids, but I never went further. At times I entertained the same thoughts and desires as other adolescents my age, but the Lord used my parents' strong love, faith, and discipline—as well as their teaching and example—to keep me on the straight and narrow path. It never really seemed right to me to have sex with anybody but the woman I would marry.

Once in my senior year, when we were in a night rehearsal of a school play at Sharon High, one of the girls in the cast coaxed me aside into a dark classroom. She had a reputation for "making out" with the boys. Before I realized what was happening, she was begging me to make love to her.

My hormones were as active as any other healthy young male's, and I had fantasized often enough about such a moment. But when it came, I silently cried to God for strength and darted from that classroom the way Joseph fled the bedroom of Potiphar's philandering wife in ancient Egypt.

My sexual restraint could not be attributed to ignorance of the facts of life. Naturally, all of us boys discussed those appealing topics that our parents did not. I had an added tutor in Pedro; he was a pretty rough character, though really good-natured. He confided in me all his erotic experiences with women, probably embellished for my wide-eyed benefit.

It was Pedro who tried to teach me to chew tobacco. The day my father caught me with a chaw in my cheek became Pedro's last day to work for us! And me—I got a thrashing to remember. My experience with cigarettes was similarly aborted by Daddy. He smoked only the proverbial "good 5¢ cigar."

When it came to alcohol, though, he was an absolute teetotaler. He came up with an unusual way to give Catherine and me the cure before we even had a chance to get the habit. At repeal of the Prohibition Amendment, Daddy brought home some beer and took the two of us children into the kitchen. He gave us each a bottle and ordered us to drink it. *All* of it. I was around fifteen, I guess, and assumed that there had to be a method to his madness. Both of us instantly hated the taste of the brew and registered our disgust in no uncertain terms.

"From now on," Daddy said, "whenever any of your friends try to get you to drink alcohol, just tell them you've already tasted it and you don't like it. That's all the reason you need to give."

His approach was more pragmatic than pious, but it worked. And it helped keep me fit for my favorite pastime, baseball. I made the team only as a substitute, playing sometimes when someone was sick. It turned out that I was a fairly good fielder because of my long reach. I was not a good hitter, though; I batted from the left side of the plate, cross-handed somehow, the same way I later played golf.

I did not know if my father's being chairman of the local school board (though he never had but a third-grade education himself) had anything to do with Coach Eudy's choice to put me at first base.

I preferred to imagine that it was determined only by my athletic merits. Maybe at some point I even dreamed about a sports career, but the talent for baseball obviously was not there. I did make it into the *Charlotte Observer* once, though; playing basketball for Sharon High School, I got into a game as a sub, and somehow my name made it into a sports column.

The main game I played at home (along with occasionally tossing horseshoes with my father in the shade of a big oak tree) was pitching ball at lunchtime and in the evenings after chores with the husky McMakin boys—Albert, Wilson, and especially Bill. Although Bill was a couple of years older than I, he became my closest friend on the farm. The two of us did a lot of fishing and hunting together.

The McMakin family had a remarkable influence on my life as far as morality and hard work were concerned. Redheaded, fast-talking Mr. McMakin raised the most beautiful tomatoes in the county, as well as other kinds of vegetables, for sale in the markets in Charlotte. I worked for him as much as for my father, and I enjoyed doing it. One summer Albert helped me raise thirteen of those prize tomato plants myself, in anticipation of earning the proceeds.

Ironically, I was not much aware of a professional baseball-player-turned-preacher who was then in the heyday of his evangelistic ministry. His name was Billy Sunday. Daddy took me to hear him in Charlotte when I was five years old. I was overwhelmed by the huge crowd and properly subdued by my father's warning to keep quiet during the service lest the preacher call out my name and have me arrested by a policeman!

In about 1930, I gave my first speech. I portrayed Uncle Sam in a pageant at Woodlawn School, with a long beard and a tailcoat. My mother was a nervous wreck after teaching me the speech and listening to me practice it until I knew it word perfect. My knees shook, my hands perspired, and I vowed to myself that I would never be a public speaker! But Mrs. Boylston, the principal of Woodlawn, told Mother I had a gift for it.

My sister Jean, the last of my siblings, was born in 1932. She was still a child when I left for college, but I remember she was a beautiful little girl. I vividly remember the alarm that gripped our hearts when she contracted polio about the time Ruth and I got married—and our gratitude to God when she recovered.

My father and mother were strong-willed people. They *had* to be, or they could not have endured the hardships and setbacks of farming in the twenties and thirties. They accepted hardship and discipline in their own lives, and they never hesitated when necessary to administer physical discipline to us. Sometimes I got it for teasing Catherine or tricking Melvin into trouble, but usually it was for misdemeanors of my own.

In all the strictness of my upbringing, there was no hint of child abuse. While my parents were swift to punish when punishment was deserved, they did not overload me with arbitrary regulations that were impossible to respect. In fact, they were very open. My parents never once told me to be in at a certain time when I went out on a Friday or Saturday night date. I knew that I had to be up by three in the morning and that if I stayed out past midnight I would get only a couple of hours of sleep.

I learned to obey without questioning. Lying, cheating, stealing, and property destruction were foreign to me. I was taught that laziness was one of the worst evils, and that there was dignity and honor in labor. I could abandon myself enthusiastically to milking the cows, cleaning out the latrines, and shoveling manure, not because they were pleasant jobs, certainly, but because sweaty labor held its own satisfaction.

There had to have been tensions between Daddy and Mother, from time to time, that we children were not supposed to see. I suppose my parents occasionally disappointed each other, and certainly they sometimes disagreed about serious as well as trivial things. But in any quarrels between them that I witnessed, I never heard either of them use a word of profanity. My mother and father (mostly my mother) could storm at each other once in a while when provoked, but they weathered every tempest and sailed on, together.

When they read the family Bible in our home, they were not simply going through a pious ritual. Mother told us that they had established a family altar with daily Bible reading the very first day they were married. They accepted that book as the very Word of God, seeking and getting heavenly help to keep the family together.

19

Every time my mother prayed with one of us, and every time my parents prayed for their sons and daughters, they were declaring their dependence on God for the wisdom and strength and courage to stay in control of life, no matter what circumstances might bring. Beyond that, they prayed for their children, that they might come into the kingdom of God.

2

The 180-Degree Turn

In 1934, Charlotte, North Carolina, had the reputation of being one of the leading churchgoing cities in the United States, but at the approach of Dr. Mordecai Fowler Ham, it began to tremble.

A stately, balding man with a neatly trimmed white mustache, wearing eyeglasses that made him look like a dignified schoolteacher and sporting impeccable clothes, Ham was in fact a strong, rugged evangelist. He had a great knowledge of the Bible and had educated himself in a number of other areas as well. He remained in the city for eleven weeks, preaching every night and every morning, except Mondays.

A few Charlotte ministers and several members of a group called the Christian Men's Club (which had been organized by Billy Sunday at the close of his meetings in 1924) had invited Dr. Ham to preach in a 5,000-seat tabernacle. Actually, the tabernacle was a sprawling, ramshackle building constructed of wood over a steel frame with a sawdust groundcover, especially built for the occasion on property at the edge of town, on Pecan Avenue, adjoining the Cole Manufacturing Company.

Mordecai Ham had been pastor of the First Baptist Church in Oklahoma City, a leading congregation in the Southern Baptist Convention. He had once studied law and had been a traveling salesman before his ordination to the ministry. He arrived in Charlotte under a considerable cloud of controversy. One charge leveled against him was that he was anti-Semitic, but I had no way of knowing if that was true; I did not even know what that term meant then. Part of the controversy was along denominational lines. The Baptists in the South generally supported him, but denominations like Methodists and Presbyterians did not care much for either his message or his style.

He did not mince words about sin, either in the abstract or in its specific expressions in the local community. His candid denunciations of various evils got reported widely in the newspapers. People were drawn to the meetings, maybe out of curiosity to begin with. I did not attend, however, and everything I heard or read about him made me feel antagonistic toward the whole affair. It sounded like a religious circus to me.

There were two newspapers in Charlotte at that time. My best friend was Julian Miller, and his father, a churchgoing man, was editor of the morning paper, the *Charlotte Observer.* Julian's dad generally treated Dr. Ham with more respect, while the editor of the afternoon paper, the *Charlotte News,* frequently had a negative article about him.

At first my mother and father did not take a position one way or the other about Dr. Ham.

My father had been reared as a Methodist, in the best old mourner's-bench revivalist tradition. One of my earliest recollections is Daddy's attending the Dilworth Methodist Church. As an eighteen-year-old in 1908, he had driven his horse and buggy three miles one Sunday night to attend an evangelistic meeting in the one-room Butt's Chapel (where the Dilworth Methodist Church met then) at the edge of Charlotte. This was in spite of a friend's warning him, "If you don't want to get religion, don't go in there."

The way my father told it, he had been out late to a dance the night before and did not feel up to churchgoing on Sunday morning. "I was under conviction from the time I hit the door," he remembered. "Well, when the preacher dismissed the congregation, I sat on. A couple of members came back to me and wanted to know if they could help me. I said, 'I don't know what's wrong with me. I'm in bad shape.' They said, 'Come up and let us pray with you.' They did, but I went on for about ten days and nights, unable to eat or sleep. I cared nothing for this world nor anything the world had to offer. I wanted something that the world couldn't give, and I believed that I would know it when I got it. That was what I was looking for."

The spiritual struggle went on for days but finally came to an end. As my father told it: "One night, just as I turned off Park Road—the road I lived on—onto Worthington Avenue, God saved me, and my eyes were opened and old things passed away, and all things became new. I will never forget that moonlit night."

When he walked into the meeting house, the preacher saw the change on his face, called him up front, put his arm around my father's shoulders, and announced, "Here is a young man whom God has called to preach, I'm sure."

Despite his strict moral code and rigidly ethical behavior, churchgoing seemed to be more a part of my father's self-discipline than a joyful commitment. His Christian faith became nominal, which I supposed was about the same as minimal. My Uncle Simon Barker, Aunt Lill's husband, who had been soundly converted, used to spend hours talking to him about religion. He listened patiently enough to Uncle Simon's exposition of various Scriptures while smoking his big cigar. There were times when he seemed to be bored; there were times when he seemed to be interested. I did not understand everything they said, but it made a strong impression on me.

About that time, just a few weeks after my sister Jean was born in 1932, my father suffered a near-fatal accident. Reese Brown was using a mechanical saw to cut wood for the boiler down behind the milk-processing house when my father came up to ask him a question. The racket from the saw made it hard for Reese to hear, so he turned a little to listen. In a split second, the saw caught a piece of wood and flung it with terrific force right into my father's mouth, smashing his jaw and cutting his head almost back to his brain. They rushed him, bleeding nearly to death, to the hospital.

For days the outcome was uncertain. Mother summoned her friends to intensive prayer. After he was stabilized, surgeons rebuilt my father's face, which left him looking a bit different; but eventually his recovery was complete. Both my parents ascribed the full recovery to God's special intervention in answer to prayer. After that episode, what Uncle Simon said seemed to make more sense to my father. He got much more serious about his spiritual life.

I have no doubt it was partly that experience that prompted Father to support the Christian businessmen in Charlotte who wanted to hold one of their all-day prayer meetings in our pasture in May 1934. The group had held three similar meetings since they started praying together eighteen months earlier. My mother invited the ladies to the farmhouse for their own prayer meeting.

That afternoon, when I came back from school and went to pitch hay in the barn across the road with one of our hired hands, we heard singing.

"Who are those men over there in the woods making all that noise?" he asked me.

"I guess they're some fanatics that have talked Daddy into using the place," I replied.

Years later my father recalled a prayer that Vernon Patterson had prayed that day: that out of Charlotte the Lord would raise up someone to preach the Gospel to the ends of the earth.

At that time, in 1934, it certainly wasn't obvious that that someone might be me. My father knew that I went along with the family to church every week only "grudgingly, or of necessity," to use a biblical phrase. I believe he sincerely wanted me to experience what he had felt a quarter-century earlier. In fact, he privately hoped and prayed that his firstborn son might someday fulfill the old Methodist evangelist's prophecy by becoming a preacher in his stead.

The church outside Charlotte in which my mother had been reared (and in which my grandfather had been an elder) was Steele Creek Presbyterian, called the largest country church in America at that time. My parents' later membership in the Associate Reformed Presbyterian Church in Charlotte was a compromise between them, encouraged by her sisters, who attended there. (The ARP, as it was called, traced its roots back to a very strict group that had seceded from the Church of Scotland in the eighteenth century.) Later Mother also came into fellowship with some Plymouth Brethren neighbors, and under their influence she studied the Scriptures more deeply than before.

In addition, she read the writings of noted Bible teachers Arno C. Gaebelein, Harry A. Ironside of the Moody Memorial Church in Chicago, and Donald Grey Barnhouse, a renowned preacher who pastored Tenth Presbyterian Church in Philadelphia. I could see that she took their writings seriously, but whenever she talked to me about the things they said in their magazines, I thought it was nonsense.

A local minister told Mother she would go crazy reading the Book of Revelation, the last book in the New Testament, but it was while reading about the Second Coming of Christ that a sense of her own religious conversion became meaningful to her. All of this spiritual development was going on quietly in her life for about two years before the Ham meetings in Charlotte.

At the beginning of the Ham-Ramsay meetings, even my mother was somewhat skeptical. Yet she sincerely desired to hear the visiting evangelist for her own spiritual nurture, and she wanted to encourage my father in his search for certainty of salvation. They went, and both found what they were seeking. "My experience," Daddy said, "is that Dr. Ham's meetings opened my eyes to the truth."

He commented on the dissatisfaction he had felt previously in simply moving his membership from one church to another. The Gospel had a new reality for him that made a marked difference in his life from then on.

Mother, in her quietly pointed fashion, got to the nub of the issue: "I feel that Dr. Ham's meetings did more, especially for the Christians, than any other meetings we've had here."

Despite my parents' enthusiasm, I did not want anything to do with anyone called an evangelist—and particularly with such a colorful character as Dr. Ham. Just turning sixteen, I told my parents that I would not go to hear him.

One day a few weeks into his campaign, I read in the *Charlotte News* about his charge regarding immoral conditions at Central

High School in Charlotte. Apparently, the evangelist knew what he was talking about. He claimed to have affidavits from certain students that a house across the street from the school, supposedly offering the boys and girls lunch during noon recess, actually gave them some additional pleasures.

When the scandalous story broke, rumors flew that a number of angry students, on a night yet to be determined, were going to march on the tabernacle and demonstrate right in front of the platform. Maybe they would even do some bodily harm to the preacher. That stirred up my curiosity, and I wanted to go just to see what would happen. But how could I save face after holding out for nearly a month? That was when Albert McMakin stepped in.

"Why don't you come out and hear our fighting preacher?" he suggested.

"Is he a *fighter?*" I asked. That put a little different slant on things. "I *like* a fighter."

Albert added the incentive of letting me drive his old vegetable truck into town for the meeting, loaded with as many folks, white and black, as he could get to go along. We all sat in the rear of the auditorium to see the show, with a few thousand other people—one of the largest crowds I had ever been in.

As soon as the evangelist started his sermon, he opened his Bible and talked straight from his text. He talked loudly, even though there was an amplifying system. I have no recollection of what he preached about, but I was spellbound. In some indefinable way, he was getting through to me. I was hearing another voice, as was often said of Dwight L. Moody when he preached: the voice of the Holy Spirit.

Bumping along in the truck on the way home, I was deep in thought. Later, after I stretched out on my back in bed, I stared out the window at a Carolina moon for a long time.

The next night, all my father's mules and horses could not have kept me from getting to that meeting. From then on, I was a faithful attendant, night after night, week after week.

The tabernacle was well filled all the time. One reason for the good attendance was Dr. Ham's choice of lively topics, like the Second Coming of Christ. Mother had read about the Second

Coming in the Book of Revelation, of course, but I did not recall having heard of it. He also preached on subjects such as money, infidelity, the Sabbath, and drinking.

I had never heard a sermon on Hell, either, though I was familiar with some people's use of that term as a swear word. Certainly our clergyman, Dr. Lindsay, never mentioned that it was a real place, even though I know he believed there was a Hell. But Dr. Ham left no doubt about it in anybody's mind!

That was not to say Dr. Ham neglected or minimized the great love of God. He just put it against a background of sin and judgment and Hell in a novel way that fascinated me. His words, and his way with words, grabbed my mind, gripped my heart. What startled me was that the same preacher who warned us so dramatically about the horrible fate of the lost in the everlasting lake of fire and brimstone also had a tremendous sense of humor and could tell stories almost as good as my father's.

I became deeply convicted about my sinfulness and rebellion. And confused. How could this evangelist be talking to me, of all people? I had been baptized as a baby, had learned the Shorter Catechism word perfect, and had been confirmed in the Associate Reformed Presbyterian Church with the full approval of the pastor and elders. I had gotten into mischief once in a while, but I could hardly be called wicked. I resisted temptations to break the moral code my parents had so strictly instilled in me. I was a good milker in the dairy barn and never complained about any of the nasty work, such as shoveling manure. I was even the vice president of my youth group in our church (although, granted, it wasn't a particularly vital organization).

So why would the evangelist always be pointing his bony finger at *me?*

One thing that echoed in my mind was Dr. Ham's singing, right in the middle of his sermon, "The toils of the road will seem nothing, when I get to the end of the way."

He had an almost embarrassing way of describing sins and shortcomings, and of demanding, on pain of divine judgment, that we mend our ways. I was so sure he had singled me out one night that I actually ducked behind the wide-brimmed hat of the lady sitting in front of me. Yet, as uncomfortable as I was getting to be, I simply could not stay away.

At the meetings, I struck up an acquaintance with a likable student from the notorious Central High School, Grady Wilson. He was already a Christian, but he was having some problems of his own under Dr. Ham's preaching. He had an older, unconverted brother, Thomas Walter, called T.W. by everybody, a big fellow who could be pretty rough. I would not call him a bully, at least not to his face, but I could safely describe him as burly. T.W. could certainly have had a job as a bouncer!

Grady and I had both decided on a strategy to avoid the frontal attack by Dr. Ham. We had signed up for the choir, which sat on the platform behind the preacher. Neither of us could sing, but we could move our mouths or hold a hymnbook in front of our faces for camouflage. As choir members, we were safe from Dr. Ham's accusatory stare.

Another person who was very important to me at the time of the Ham meetings was my first cousin Crook Stafford. He lived in town and had a job as an accountant. Some years my senior, he always went out of his way to be kind and thoughtful to me as we were growing up. He not only encouraged me to go to the tabernacle in the evenings, but he would drive out and get me if I had no one to take me. He also was in the choir.

What was slowly dawning on me during those weeks was the miserable realization that I did not know Jesus Christ for myself. I could not depend on my parents' faith. Christian influence in the home could have a lasting impact on a child's life, but faith could not be passed on as an inheritance, like the family silver. It had to be exercised by each individual.

I could not depend on my church membership either. Saying "I believe" in the Apostles' Creed every Sunday, or taking the bread and wine of Communion, could so easily become nothing but rote and ritual, without power in themselves to make me any different.

Nor could I depend on my own resolution to do better. I constantly failed in my efforts at self-improvement. Nobody needed to tell me *that*.

As a teenager, what I needed to know for certain was that I was right with God. I could not help but admit to myself that I was purposeless and empty-hearted. Our family Bible reading, praying, psalm-singing, and churchgoing—all these had left me restless and resentful. I had even tried, guiltily, to think up ways of getting out of all those activities as much as I could. In a word, I was spiritually dead.

And then it happened, sometime around my sixteenth birthday. On that night, Dr. Ham finished preaching and gave the Invitation to accept Christ. After all his tirades against sin, he gave us a gentle reminder: "But God commendeth his love toward us, in that, while we were yet sinners, Christ died for us" (Romans 5:8, KJV). His song leader, Mr. Ramsay, led us all in "Just As I Am"—four verses. Then we started another song: "Almost Persuaded, Now to Believe."

On the last verse of that second song, I responded. I walked down to the front, feeling as if I had lead weights attached to my feet, and stood in the space before the platform. That same night, perhaps three or four hundred other people were there at the front making spiritual commitments. The next night, my cousin Crook Stafford made his decision for Christ.

My heart sank when I looked over at the lady standing next to me with tears running down her cheeks. I was not crying. I did not feel any special emotion of any kind just then. Maybe, I thought, I was not supposed to be there. Maybe my good intentions to be a real Christian wouldn't last. Wondering if I was just making a fool of myself, I almost turned around and went back to my seat.

As I stood in front of the platform, a tailor named J. D. Prevatt, who was a friend of our family with a deep love for souls, stepped up beside me, weeping. Putting his arms around me, he urged me to make my decision. At the same time, in his heavy European accent, he explained God's plan for my salvation in a simple way. That explanation was addressed to my own mental understanding. It did not necessarily answer every question I had at the moment—and it certainly did not anticipate every question that would come to me in the months and years ahead—but it set forth simply the facts I needed to know in order to become God's child.

My tailor friend helped me to understand what I had to do to become a genuine Christian. The key word was *do*. Those of us standing up front had to decide to *do* something about what we knew before it could take effect.

He prayed for me and guided *me* to pray. I had heard the message, and I had felt the inner compulsion to go forward. Now came the moment to commit myself to Christ. Intellectually, I accepted Christ to the extent that I acknowledged what I knew about Him to be true. That was mental assent. Emotionally, I felt that I wanted to love Him in return for His loving me. But the final issue was whether I would turn myself over to His rule in my life.

I checked "Recommitment" on the card I filled out. After all, I had been brought up to regard my baptism and confirmation as professions of faith too. The difference was that this time I was doing it on *purpose,* doing it with *intention*. For all my previous religious upbringing and church activity, I believe that that was the moment I made my real commitment to Jesus Christ.

No bells went off inside me. No signs flashed across the tabernacle ceiling. No physical palpitations made me tremble. I wondered again if I was a hypocrite, not to be weeping or something. I simply felt at peace. Quiet, not delirious. Happy and peaceful.

My father came to the front and put his arm around my shoulders, telling me how thankful he was. Later, back home, when we went to the kitchen, my mother put her arm around me and said, "Billy Frank, I'm so glad you took the stand you did tonight."

That was all.

I went upstairs to my room. Standing at the window, I looked out across one of the fields that was glowing in the moonlight.

Then I went over to my bed and for the first time in my life got down on my knees without being told to do so. I really wanted to talk to God. "Lord, I don't know what happened to me tonight," I prayed. "*You* know. And I thank You for the privilege I've had tonight."

It took a while to fall asleep. How could I face school tomorrow? Would this action spoil my relationships with friends who were not interested in spiritual matters? Might Coach Eudy, who had publicly expressed his dislike of Dr. Ham, make fun of me? Perhaps. I felt pretty sure, though, that the school principal, Connor Hutchinson, whose history lessons I enjoyed, would be sympathetic.

But the hardest question of all remained to be answered: What, exactly, had happened to me?

All I knew was that the world looked different the next morning when I got up to do the milking, eat breakfast, and catch the schoolbus. There seemed to be a song in my heart, but it was mixed with a kind of pounding fear as to what might happen when I got to class.

The showdown at school was not too bad. For one thing, most of the students had not heard about what I had done at the Ham meeting the night before. Besides that, the change I felt so strongly inside me did not make me look or sound any different. I was still Billy Frank to them, and their attitude did not change. Studies and ball games and dates and chores on the farm—all these stayed pretty much the same. I was still just a high-spirited schoolboy.

I invited Sam Paxton, Wint Covington, and some of my other friends from high school to go with me to the Ham meetings. They did go once or twice, but somehow they did not respond as I had.

"I understand we have Preacher Graham with us today," one of my teachers said to the class some days later. Everybody laughed. She was making fun of me, and I felt some resentment. Then I remembered what Dr. Ham had said: when we come to Christ, we're going to suffer persecution.

It would take some time before I understood what had happened to me well enough to explain it to anybody else. There were signs, though, that my thinking and direction had changed, that I had truly been converted. To my own surprise, church activities that had bored me before seemed interesting all of a sudden—even Dr. Lindsay's sermons (which I took notes on!). The choir sounded better to me. I actually wanted to go to church as often as possible.

The Bible, which had been familiar to me almost since infancy, drew me now to find out what it said besides the verses I had memorized through the years. I enjoyed the few minutes I could take when I was by myself each morning and evening for quiet talking to God in prayer. As one of Mr. Ramsay's former choir members, I was even singing hymns while I milked the cows!

31

Before my conversion, I tended to be touchy, oversensitive, envious of others, and irritable. Now I deliberately tried to be courteous and kind to everybody around me. I was experiencing what the Apostle Paul had described: "The old has gone, the new has come!" (2 Corinthians 5:17). Mother especially, but other family members too, thought there was a difference. Most remarkable of all—to me at least—was an uncharacteristic enthusiasm for my studies! (It was about this time that I read Gibbon's *Decline and Fall of the Roman Empire*.)

Looking back now, I'm sure I spent entirely too much time working on the farm and playing baseball during my boyhood, and not enough time with the books. But what good would school do for me if I was going to be a farmer?

Purpose was still missing from my outlook on life in general. Although I had been converted, I did not have much of a concept of my life coming under some kind of divine plan. In the remaining year and a half of high school, I had no inkling of what my life work was to be. The future was foggy at best. But I could tell from my changed interests and new satisfactions that spiritual growth was going on.

In the following year, other revivalists and evangelists came through Charlotte. I went to hear most of them. Two or three were invited to stay in our home. Jimmie Johnson was one. Just out of college, he was young and handsome, and his devotion to Christ flashed in his dark eyes as he preached the Gospel in all of its power to the crowds that came to hear him.

One weekend we drove Jimmie out to Monroe, North Carolina, where he was to speak in a little jail. When preaching to prisoners, he always liked to give young Christians a chance to help out. This time, without warning, he picked on me. "Here's a fellow who'll tell you what it's like to be converted," he said, nodding at me with a smile of encouragement.

I tried, with my knees knocking. The ten or so prisoners looked off into the distance or picked their teeth for the two or three minutes I spoke. Jimmie claimed that I did quite well, once I got going. It was the first public utterance I had given of my faith, but it reinforced my conviction that I would never become a preacher.

Another time we went with a group to a home for wayward girls, where I gave a brief testimony. After the service, several of the girls made a profession of faith. I was surprised to recognize one of them; she had lived for some time with a tenant family on our farm. She promised to live a Christian life. I had only $5 in my pocket, and I thought it only right to give it to her.

Out of Jimmie Johnson's youth revival in the Methodist church in Charlotte there developed a Tuesday night Bible-study group of young people, the Fellowship Club. Some 20 to 30 boys and girls from different Charlotte churches were invited to the large home of "Mommy" Jones, wife of a telephone company executive, who taught the Bible in her own lovable and dynamic way. We studied outside on her screened porch in the summer and in the living room in the winter. Afterward we crowded into her old-fashioned kitchen to eat wheat biscuits and jam and drink milk or coffee, chattering about what we had learned and generally having a good time. Grady, T.W., and I were nearly always there.

In my changing outlook, I did not feel entirely at home with some of my friends, though I still liked them all. I'd had several girl-friends over the years, sometimes two at once, but I decided I had to quit going with my current one. She had not accepted Christ and wasn't in sympathy with me.

When Grady announced one day that he felt the Lord was calling him to be a preacher, we all were as proud as could be. He had gotten two or three sermons from Jimmie and had practiced them. When he got a chance to speak at a small mission church across the tracks in Charlotte, I took a friend along to hear him. There were about 20 people in the audience.

Grady did not have a watch, so he borrowed mine. He announced his text and said that he was going to preach on "Four Great Things God Wants You to Do."

After nearly a half-hour of speaking, he said, "We now come to the second thing."

I sat there very proud that Grady knew so much of the Bible. He never once looked at my watch—he talked for an hour and a half—but all the while he was preaching, he kept winding it until he had wound the stem right off. He claimed it was because I had been holding hands with his girlfriend.

Jimmie and Fred Brown, another evangelist who stayed in our home, were graduates of Bob Jones College in Cleveland, Tennessee. They did a good job of convincing me I should go on to college somewhere.

I vaguely supposed I would try to get into the University of North Carolina, though I wondered whether that institution would accept me in view of my mediocre high school grades. But when the founder and president of Jimmie and Fred's college, Dr. Bob Jones himself, spoke at our high school in my senior year, my folks decided it would be best for me to go there. We did not know at the time that it was not accredited. T.W. had already started there, and Grady also decided to enroll.

Dr. Bob was an old-fashioned Methodist who had not only been offered the appointment to become a bishop but also often told us he could have been governor of Alabama if he had wanted to. He was a very dramatic orator. Fiftyish and over six feet tall, he charmed us students with his witty stories and quick answers to our questions. It was obvious that he loved young people. Earlier, as an evangelist drawing large crowds, he had determined to found a college where students could get a higher education in a vigorously Christian setting. He received large love offerings from his audiences, which was the way traveling evangelists were supported in those days, and had saved them up until at last he was able to found his college.

Influence from a totally different direction came through Albert McMakin, who had first taken me to hear Mordecai Ham. After years of working with his father and brothers on our farm, he got himself a job with the Fuller Brush Company. By our standards, he was making fairly good money as a field manager in his South Carolina territory. Just before I graduated from high school in 1936, he asked, in his slow southern drawl, if I would be willing to join him in selling brushes through the summer.

It seemed like a perfect way to make some money for college. My father was in a financial position to help me some, but I knew I would also have to work part-time. Daddy didn't think much of the plan, maybe because he pictured losing a fast milker. Finally, though, he said, "If you want to go, go." He and Mother had a great deal of confidence in Albert, both as a worker and as a strong Christian. (Maybe more confidence in him than in me!)

As soon as I graduated with my twenty-five Sharon High School classmates in May, Albert and I set out together. But after my first week or two, I told him I was getting lonesome way down there in South Carolina, so far from home. "How about if we ask a couple of my friends to come with us?" I suggested. He readily agreed.

With enthusiasm I spelled out my plan to my high school buddies Wint Covington and Sam Paxton. They turned the opportunity down because they had already made other plans for the summer. Then I talked to my new friends Grady and T.W. They both accepted, so the three of us joined Albert on the road to sell brushes.

South Carolina had one of the lowest per-capita incomes of any state back then. Staying in boardinghouses, where a room and meals cost $1 a day, we ate at the same table with a lot of coarse-talking, rough-living traveling salesmen. I'm afraid some of their uncouth attitudes rubbed off on me. One day in Lancaster, the boardinghouse biscuits were so hard we could barely bite into them. I got upset and fast-pitched a biscuit right back through the kitchen door at the cook.

Justice had its day, though. At one house where I stopped to sell, I rang and rang the bell. The lady did not come to the door, but she did go to the upstairs window. She saw me down there on the step, and next thing I knew, she had dumped a whole pail of water right on top of me!

In Monroe, North Carolina, one night, T.W. and I were sharing a room in a cheap little hotel; Grady and Albert were in another room. I woke up with the sensation of something crawling on me. "Turn on the light," I called to T.W. "I got him!"

We thought at first it was a big mosquito, but it was a bedbug. Neither he nor I had ever seen one before. We went downstairs and reported it to the desk clerk before checking out with all our stuff, not caring to stay and get bedbug-eaten all night.

It happened that our friend Jimmie Johnson was holding a revival meeting in that same town in a specially built wooden tabernacle, sawdust shavings and all. Newly roomless, we headed for the revival. After the crowd left, T.W. and I lay down, piling some shavings under our soiled shirts to make a pillow. We did not sleep much, though—and not at all after the flies started buzzing around us about five in the morning.

The Fuller Brush Company's sales strategy was sound, but sometimes it backfired. The trainers told us always to try to get our foot in the door and hold it there so that the customer couldn't close it. It was a good theory, maybe, but I came the hard way to learn the meaning of "footsore."

And then there was the matter of the giveaway item, usually a bottle brush or a utility brush. We salesmen had to pay 10¢ apiece for them, which was a lot of money in those Depression days. We would give the lady a choice. She could have whichever one she wanted, and it was absolutely free. What the trainers did not tell us, and what infuriated Grady especially, was that some women who answered the door grabbed the free brush and *then* slammed the door shut, foot or no foot!

T.W. gives me credit for being the best salesman of the four of us. Perhaps it was that he and Grady liked to play a lot on the side. They would make house calls for a while and then take off to fish or swim for the rest of the day. Still, we would get back to the boardinghouse about the same time in the afternoon and compare notes on what local girls we would try to get dates with that night. Albert did not date, however; he was a married man going on twenty-five.

While the Wilson boys indulged in their recreation, I kept plugging along with my sample case of Fuller brushes, knocking on doors from sunrise to sunset in the little towns and villages of eastern South Carolina. We would stay three or four days in each town if necessary, covering all the white homes and then all the black homes.

My approach was to say to the housewife, "Well, I haven't come here to sell you anything. I've come to give you a brush." She always wanted to see that. So I emptied my case and laid out all of the brushes—I always kept the free samples on the bottom. She saw that array, and maybe pointed to one or another and said, "You know, I've never seen a brush like that before. What *is* that one?" And a sale was in the making.

One day, though, T.W. overdid it. He had studied the sales manual backward and forward, and the idea got into his mind that a certain bristle comb was made of bear hair that had been bleached. At one house he launched into his usual talk: "Now if you'll just look at *this*. No wonder so many movie stars use this particular bristle comb. Notice the alternate rows of bristles. This brush is made out of the best boar-bear bristles that money can buy."

"Excuse me," she interrupted. "Did you say 'boar-bear'? I thought a boar was a hog."

"Oh, yes, there's a boar-hog, but these bristles are boar-bear, from Russia."

To T.W.'s credit, he went to the local library later that afternoon to look up *boar-bear*. Of course, he couldn't find it. When he went back to deliver the brush, he confessed to the woman. "I was wrong. You don't even have to buy that brush you ordered. I don't know what made me say what I did, but you're right: a boar *is* a hog. It must have been the bleaching process that threw me off."

Her reply taught him something that all of us tried to remember after that. "Young man," she said, "because you're honest, I want to buy a couple more of your bristle combs."

Every day we had to send our orders in to the company. Then the brushes would come by mail, and we had to revisit each town to make deliveries—and collect the money. That was the catch! Some women ordered quite a lot of brushes and then forgot that they had done so (or failed to tell their husbands). I learned that the best time to make deliveries was at suppertime or a little after. The people were generally at home then, and the husband and wife could work it out together.

Boar or bear or whatever, I was convinced that Fuller brushes were the best product money could buy, and I was dedicated to the proposition that every family ought to have Fuller brushes as a matter of principle. But I was almost eighteen, and the question was, Should I plan to be doing this kind of thing for the rest of my life? I had gotten off the farm and was headed for college. But why? What lay down the road?

That summer's experience selling Fuller brushes taught me a lot about myself, about human nature, and about communicating a message to people even if I had to talk my way in and out of all kinds of situations. I did not win any awards or honors from the company, but in the poorer areas that I was assigned to (the company seemed to reserve the best sections for their top people), I had done well enough to earn sometimes as much as $50 or $75 in a week, almost a fortune then for a teenager. And being away from my parents, learning to make my own way, gave me self-confidence.

I learned a lot about prayer too. I developed a practice of praying about every call as I walked up to the door, asking God to give me an opportunity to witness for Christ. At times I was somewhat headstrong about this, and not really sensitive to the leading of the Holy Spirit. Albert got complaints from some of our customers that I was trying to give them a hard sell about Christ as much as about Fuller brushes. He rightly cautioned me to be more discerning.

Under Albert's mature spiritual influence, we four used to have prayer meetings in our shabby lodgings, reading the Bible together as well. I'm sure that fellowship built into us a kind of accountability to each other that helped us resist a lot of the temptations that traveling salesmen regularly face.

As summer faded into fall, I kept asking myself, What are you going to be when you grow up?

I was looking forward to registration day at Bob Jones College, but I still liked squatting on a milking stool in the cow barn.

The first evangelist I had ever heard, Billy Sunday, had been a ball player before he became a preacher. The second one, Mordecai Ham, had been a traveling salesman before he became a preacher. I had done both: played ball and sold stuff on the road.

I had been converted for two years now, but surely the Lord wouldn't require me to follow in their steps and become a preacher too! Hadn't I ruled out that profession, along with undertaker, a long time ago?

3

Called to Preach

BOB JONES COLLEGE 1936, FLORIDA BIBLE INSTITUTE 1937–1940

GRIPING NOT TOLERATED!

That was the sign on the wall of the dormitory room welcoming me to Bob Jones College. My father had driven the Wilson boys and me across the Appalachians to Cleveland in east Tennessee in September 1936. Every one of the three hundred students there faced the same stark warning on the wall of his or her room. Grady and I did not know whether to believe it or not.

Dr. Bob Jones, Sr., the school's founder, who had won our hearts when he spoke at Sharon High School back home, believed in Authority (his) and Discipline (ours), with capital letters. A military academy could not have been more strict.

My father and mother had never been exactly lax in enforcing their rules on us children, as I could vouch for personally. But now I found myself in an environment so rigidly regimented that it shocked me. Our social life was restricted. Dating had to be scheduled and was governed by the dean's code book. When you did date, you could not sit on the same sofa or chair as the girl. You were chaperoned and watched like a hawk. Outside of approved dating times, you could not stop to talk to your girlfriend. On certain evenings, though, you were allowed to sit in the lobby and talk (but only for fifteen minutes), and you could always write notes.

Even our intellectual life was subject to regulation. Teaching in every subject was dogmatic, and there was little chance to raise questions. Dr. Bob's interpretation of doctrine, ethics, and academics was the only one allowed. Very few students ever questioned his authority to his face. But sometimes, stretched out on the double-decker bunks in our tiny four-bedded rooms with the grim motto confronting us, we did discuss it—though always with fear in our voices.

To make matters worse, we also loved Dr. Bob (as we often called him). Sometimes as intimidating as a bull, he could also be as tender as a child. We could not help but sense that he had our best interests at heart in all the policies he imposed. His religious convictions and genuine devotion to the Lord kindled a deep respect in my heart.

"I've made all the mistakes in evangelism," he often said. "There are no more to be made." That was memorable, but he never elaborated on what they were. Almost every day he spoke to us in the compulsory chapel service, and we enjoyed his homespun philosophy tartly expressed.

"If the Devil is going your way, ride the Devil," he would say.

"If a hound dog is barking for Jesus Christ, I'm for the hound dog."

As I looked forward to a few days of Christmas vacation, I tried to sort things out in my mind. I am not sure I could have defined in detail just what was bothering me about Bob Jones College. After all, I had nothing to compare it with. But I disliked the overwhelming discipline, which often seemed to have little rationale behind it. And I disliked being told what to think without being given the opportunity to reason issues through on my own or to look at other viewpoints. Coming down with the flu did not help.

One of my roommates, Wendell Phillips, had become a good friend in those early months. Frustrated with the rules and faced with the possibility of being "shipped" (expelled) by the college, Wendell quit and drove to Florida where he had been reading about a school that was reported to have excellent Bible teachers—although he had also considered Moody Bible Institute in Chicago, where he had gone to school the previous year. Knowing how unhappy I was at Bob Jones, he now urged me, by letters and at least one phone call, to join him.

I surely knew I was not fitting in where I was. I asked for an interview with Dr. Bob in his office and told him about my discontent and my thoughts of leaving. His voice booming, he pronounced me a failure and predicted only more failure ahead. I left his office disillusioned and dejected.

Naturally, I assumed the problem was more with me than with the college. "I know I've been converted," I wrote to Mother. "I know that I know Jesus Christ, but I've lost my feeling. I can't seem to get anywhere in prayer. I don't feel anything."

"Son, God is testing you," she wrote back. "He tells us to walk not by feeling but by faith, and when you don't feel anything, God may be closer to you than ever before. Through the darkness and through the fog, put your hand up by faith. You'll sense the touch of God."

And I did. But the deep struggle was to continue for weeks.

The family's Christmas plans all along had been to take Catherine, Melvin, little Jean, and me on a trip to Florida, where Mother's older sister Sissy, along with Uncle Bo and my cousin Mildred, had bought a large rooming house in the heart of Orlando. They hoped I would get enough time off from school to make the trip.

Still sick from the flu and confused in my thinking, I headed south with them. By then my parents had heard about Florida Bible Institute from a small ad in *Moody Monthly*. I also talked with a Plymouth Brethren Bible teacher named Chambers who was staying at our house just then, and he counseled me to consider transferring there.

Once in Florida, I immediately acquired a taste for the warmer climate and the palm trees. Raising oranges and cattle appealed to a lifelong farmboy like myself. And Orlando's many lakes attracted me too. I made up my mind to leave Bob Jones College when I returned there in January.

While we were in Orlando, Daddy did something unusual: he encouraged little Jean (who was four) to get up on the table in front of the guests and "preach" to them. She was so cute, with her beautiful blond hair, that they stopped to pay attention. I don't know why Daddy put her up to it, but Jean was serious about her message and told the guests that they needed to come to Jesus. I guess you could say she was the first preacher in our family.

Back in Charlotte, Mother wrote to the president of Florida Bible Institute, asking him for information about the start of the second semester, courses offered, costs, and so on. She added a postscript asking him to send a copy to me at Bob Jones College. Dr. Watson, the president, replied by return mail: "In view of the fact that he is already in school at the Bob Jones College, we do not feel like writing him to explain our school to him as we do not wish to be misunderstood and have it appear in any way whatsoever that we are even suggesting that he make another change from another school to ours."

Mother wrote back to him that our interest in the Florida school was prompted by friends of ours in Charlotte and by its advertisement in *Moody Monthly* magazine, along with the favorable impression Florida made on the family when we visited at Christmas.

She also sent a letter from our family physician, which had been copied to Dr. Jones, explaining my need for a less strenuous environment. In a veiled allusion to Wendell Phillips and myself, she told Dr. Watson that she would "leave it entirely with you as well as other faculty members, sincerely believing they will not be permitted to 'run around' except in the Lord's work."

Every day after lunch, I found out later, both Mother and Daddy went upstairs to their bedroom, got down on their knees, and prayed for me in line with Paul's concern for his young associate Timothy, using the beloved cadences of the King James Version of the Bible: "Study to shew thyself approved unto God, a workman that needeth not to be ashamed, rightly dividing the word of truth" (2 Timothy 2:15). When I received the news from Florida that I had been admitted, I was overjoyed.

Riding in my father's 1937 green Plymouth, we arrived at the campus of Florida Bible Institute one morning late in January. It was located in Temple Terrace, fifteen miles east of Tampa. After the damp and dismal autumn in the mountains of east Tennessee, western Florida seemed like Paradise to me. The Institute itself was housed in a Spanish-style country-club hotel with several outbuildings. All had creamy pink stucco and tiled roofs, with wrought-iron railings along red-brick steps. Surrounded by a horseshoe-shaped eighteen-hole golf course on the banks of the Hillsborough River, the buildings were part of an exclusive residential subdivision that went broke in 1929. The family stayed for lunch before driving back to Charlotte.

The next day the lady who supervised the dining room ("Gibby," the students called her) hailed me from across the room.

"Say, can you drive a car?" she asked hopefully.

"Yes, ma'am."

"Well, I have a station wagon full of tourists who are supposed to be taken on a tour of Tampa, and I've nobody to drive them. Will you do it?"

"But I've never been to Tampa," I protested. "How can I take them on a tour of the city?"

It was the height of the annual Gasparilla celebration—Gaspar was a pirate who had once captured Tampa—and there would be extra traffic and lots of crowds.

"Well, tell them something," she said in desperation.

When I brought them back to the campus late in the afternoon, they all seemed happy. I did not know whether they had seen the main attractions, but I had done my best to explain the virtues of Tampa (as I was seeing them myself for the first time). After all, anybody could point out a post office when there was a big sign on the building. And I did remember a few things from a Chamber of Commerce brochure I had read before arriving in Tampa.

Only a few houses had been built in Temple Terrace by the time of the stock market crash, and some of them had been left deserted ever since. One of the men who lived there was J. W. Van DeVenter, who wrote "I Surrender All" and a number of other familiar Gospel songs. In another house lived a doctor who came to see the students when they were sick. Mainly, though, the broad, paved streets ran mile after mile through barren blocks.

A former Christian and Missionary Alliance (CMA) minister from North Carolina, Dr. W. T. Watson, had taken over the bankrupt property and started Florida Bible Institute as a nondenominational institution. It had forty women and thirty men students when

I arrived. We all lived and ate and had our classes in the hotel complex. There was still plenty of room left over for "paying customers"—ministers and Christian laypeople (well-to-do Yankees, as I saw them) who took advantage of the Institute's comfortable quarters and reasonable rates in winter months. It cost a lot less than hotels and was far superior to tourist camps and trailer parks. Perhaps as many as fifty people from the North would spend the entire winter there; others came and went. Every room had twin beds and a private bath, and some included sitting areas—suites, really.

We students were the workforce that ran the place, waiting on tables, cooking, washing dishes in the kitchen, doing the housekeeping, and handling grounds maintenance—all for 20¢ an hour. But those were good wages, because Dr. Watson, who had come from a poor home, managed to keep school fees down to $1 a day, all-inclusive. My father was paying my expenses and providing my pocket money, so I was affluent compared to some of the other students. I worked like everybody else, though, mainly to be part of the action and to expend some of my surplus nervous energy. I became the school's first "automatic dishwasher," or so they told me. My pace in the soapsuds races kept four girls busy with their dish towels.

My achievements were not all glorious, however. One day I was serving the head table. The Christian Church denomination, having rented all the facilities at the Institute for a time, was in the process of holding its summer conference. As I was about to pour steaming hot coffee into a cup, a man in a white suit raised his arm to make a point. When that arm hit the coffee pot, he screamed! He knocked it right out of my hand and into the lap of the lady in a white dress sitting next to him—and *she* screamed! I snatched a napkin and desperately tried to dry both people off.

"Get away!" he yelled. "Get away!"

I preferred the outdoor chores anyway—tasks like hedge-trimming and lawn maintenance. A real bonus job for many of us fellows was caddying on the golf course. Legendary preachers whom I had only heard about materialized right on the fairways and greens of our campus, and I could walk beside them as they made their rounds on the course, carrying their golf bags and spotting where their balls landed.

44

Preachers got reduced rates in exchange for speaking in our chapel and classes or at Dr. Watson's independent church in St. Petersburg, the Gospel Tabernacle. That church had started in a ragged tent in the early twenties, but it now occupied a building seating 4,000 people. Many of those visiting preachers made a lasting impression on me in their own individual ways.

World-renowned evangelist Gipsy Smith, probably in his seventies by then, came and stayed for weeks at a time. I asked him for his autograph, but he turned me down. I felt hurt by the rebuff. Later, when we became good friends, I did get his autograph, and I promised myself that if anyone was ever kind enough to ask me for my autograph, I would gladly give it if I possibly could.

William Evans, former director of the Bible department at Moody Bible Institute, particularly impressed my schoolmate Roy Gustafson, who would years later become a member of our evangelistic Team. Roy copied many things Evans said and did—his hand movements, his tone of voice. One day in class, or so the story goes, Roy's roommate, Charles Massey, fell asleep beside Roy while Evans was lecturing.

"Wake that boy up there!" shouted Evans.

"Dr. Evans," responded Roy, "you put him to sleep; *you* wake him up."

For carrying his golf clubs around the course, Dr. Evans tipped me $1 and told me to apply myself to my studies so that someday I would be in a position to give a tip too.

E. A. Marshall spent every winter there, fascinating all of us with his maps and flannelgraphs of the Holy Land that explained where everything in the Bible had happened.

W. B. Riley and his wife from First Baptist Church in Minneapolis came down every year too; he was also founder and president of Northwestern Schools. His wife took time to help us students put together our yearbook, since she supervised the excellent one put out at Northwestern Schools. My previous Fuller Brush salesmanship won me a place on the yearbook staff, drumming up advertising from local businesses.

Another speaker was the highly intellectual A. B. Winchester from Canada. He had a memorable phrase he repeated frequently throughout his lectures and sermons: "My Bible says. . . ."

This visiting faculty also included such men as W. R. Newell, E. R. Neighbor, Theodore Elsner, A. C. Gaebelein, Donald G. Barnhouse, Oswald J. Smith, E. J. Pace, Homer Rodeheaver, and Harry Rimmer. They were not names in the headlines, but in conservative Christian circles they were the Who's Who of evangelicals; they exerted a lot of good influence. And they were colorful personalities with a highly individual flair in their public speaking.

It was wonderful to be in the company of these men and women, and with such others as the general superintendents of the Christian and Missionary Alliance, Methodist preachers, and a whole host of people from other denominations. That exposure broadened my view of the Church.

Wendell, my former roommate, and Woodrow Flynn, my present roommate (who had also attended Bob Jones College for a time), quickly introduced me all around to my new classmates, and I soon had a sense of belonging to a wonderful new family. I knew I was where I ought to be. This was confirmed in an early letter home: "Mother, words can't express Florida Bible Institute. . . . I love it here. I'm working a little every day so as to help a little on my way. I'm stronger and feel so much better."

The curriculum was largely Bible courses, or subjects related to the Bible (for example, church history). It also offered me the saturation I wanted in the study of God's Word. I came to believe with all my heart in the full inspiration of the Bible.

One thing that thrilled me was the diversity of viewpoints we were exposed to in the classroom, a wondrous blend of ecumenical and evangelical thought that was really ahead of its time. Our teachers came from different backgrounds and denominations, exhibiting to us what harmony could be present where Christ and His Word were loved and served. In their teaching, they were not afraid to let us know about other philosophies and even about views critical of Christianity. Dr. Watson had actually dropped the word *Fundamentalist* from the name of the school after its first two years because it had come to connote such a negative image in the public mind.

We were encouraged to think things through for ourselves, but always with the unique authority of Scripture as our guide. So many of the questions that I had to keep bottled up previously could now be freely aired and wisely answered. I could stretch my mind without feeling that I was doing violence to my soul.

The faculty's openness, and the diversity of visiting lecturers, instilled in me a fresh enthusiasm for the Lord and a burst of energy to get involved in His work. I still had no clear plan of action for my life, however. I was as carefree and happy-go-lucky as ever—maybe more so—in this subtropical playground of the Lord's.

The Institute was committed to equipping all of us for Christian witness in the world, even if not as preachers. So students were sent out regularly, both as individuals and in teams, to churches, missions, trailer parks, jails, street corners, and just about any other place that would have them. What we lacked in finesse we made up in youthful exuberance. In the course of student assignments that came my way, I spoke almost regularly at the well-populated trailer parks in the winter months and at The Stockade, Tampa's jail.

The dean of men was the Reverend John Minder, a red-haired giant. His mother, who was from Switzerland, lived with him and inspired me a great deal. The fact that Minder was a bachelor freed him to give a lot of time to each student, as well as to his pastoral duties at the Tampa Gospel Tabernacle (CMA), which he had founded—as Dr. Watson had his St. Petersburg church—while in his early twenties. He saw me for what I was—a spindly farmboy with lots of nail-biting energy, a mediocre academic record, and a zeal to serve the Lord that exceeded my knowledge and skills.

I enthusiastically took his courses in pastoral theology and hermeneutics (or Bible interpretation), and I responded instinctively and positively to his gentle counseling approach, so different from the authoritarian ways I had just experienced in Tennessee. Instead of resenting his advice, I wanted to hear everything he could tell me about life and service. He did not dictate how to think and what to do; rather, he opened my thinking to consider the perfect trustworthiness of God, and to rest in that.

One day not long after I arrived, Dr. Watson called a meeting of the whole school to tell us there was a financial crisis and that he had nowhere to turn for funds. Under his leadership, we spent almost the entire day in prayer. At the end of the day, Dr. Watson stepped back into the prayer meeting to make a special announcement. He had just received a telegram from a man in the North named Kellogg, who said he had been strangely burdened that day to send a check to the school. That check was for $10,000! We were convinced our prayers had been answered, as the Scriptures promised, even above what we had dared to expect.

In early spring of 1937, at Easter, Dr. Minder invited me to accompany him on the 150-mile ride to his summer conference grounds at Lake Swan in northern Florida, a 150-acre property owned by his family. While there on a cold, blustery Saturday, we got together in nearby Palatka with his friend Cecil Underwood, a lay preacher who was pastoring Peniel Baptist Church five miles to the west.

Out of the blue, Mr. Underwood asked Dean Minder if he would mind preaching for him the following evening at a small Baptist church in Bostwick, for which Mr. Underwood had taken responsibility.

"No," he answered, "Billy is going to preach."

I was stunned. My repertoire at the time consisted of about four borrowed sermons, which I had adapted and practiced but never preached. This would be different from the old Fellowship Club meetings in Charlotte. There I just got up and "let them have it." But in a strange church—a Baptist one at that—what would I do?

When I told Mr. Underwood that I had never preached a formal sermon in front of a church audience, he and Dean Minder both laughed.

"We'll pray for you," said Mr. Underwood, "and God will help you."

"All right," I agreed rather hesitantly.

What else could I say to the dean of my school? But I was so frightened that I spent the night studying and praying instead of sleeping. I did the same most of the next day, practicing aloud. By evening I felt confident that any one of my sermons should be good for at least twenty or thirty minutes.

The meeting room was small, with a potbellied iron stove near the front to take the chill off that cold, windy night. The song leader, who chewed tobacco, had to go to the door every so often to spit outside; he could have used the stove just as conveniently. The congregation of about 40 included ranchers and cowboys in overalls and their women in cotton wash dresses.

When the moment came to walk to the pulpit in the tiny Bostwick Baptist Church, my knees shook and perspiration glistened on my hands. I launched into sermon number one. It seemed to be over almost as soon as I got started, so I added number two. And number three. And eventually number four. Then I sat down.

Eight minutes—that was all it took to preach all four of my sermons! Was this the stuff of which those marvelous preachers at Florida Bible Institute were made?

Believe it or not, though, when I got back to campus I felt that I had grown spiritually through the experience. But at the same time I was concerned: I could not get away from a nagging feeling in my heart that I was being called by God to preach the Gospel. I did not welcome that call. Whatever glimmer of talent Dr. Minder might have thought he saw in me was certainly Raw, with a capital R.

I practiced for when the time would again come to preach in public. My roommate, Woodrow Flynn, was a great sermonizer and would preach his outlines to me in our cold room in front of the little stove. I used outlines of sermons borrowed from great published preachers like Dr. Lee Scarborough of Texas. I would paddle a canoe across the Hillsborough to a little island where I could address all creatures great and small, from alligators to birds. If they would not stop to listen, there was always a congregation of cypress stumps that could neither slither nor fly away. The loudness of my preaching was in direct proportion to their unresponsiveness, so the trees got my voice at full blast.

Once some fishermen, wandering within earshot, paused in amazement at this bellowing beanpole of a boy who seemed to rise from the river. Too often a few of my fellow students would line the opposite bank at my return to cheer me on with comments like, "How many converts did you get today, Billy?"

One day Dr. Watson was walking down a corridor of the men's residence building when he overheard a similar practice session. Drawn toward the open door of my room, he looked in to see me shouting a sermon at his four-year-old son, Bobby, whom I had perched on top of the high antique dresser, perhaps to prevent his escape.

Things were bound to get better, though. Woodrow recalled one of my earliest speaking experiences in a rural Methodist church where I was teamed with him as organist and Wendell as song leader.

In full swing, physically and vocally, I was telling my audience about the ancient world's wait for Christ, as the great Dwight L. Moody had presented it in a sermon.

"A thousand years went by, and no Christ!"

Dramatic pause.

"Two thousand years rolled by, and no Christ!"

Dramatic pause.

It was during just such a dramatic pause, after I had gotten to "seven thousand years," that Wendell, from his seat on the platform behind me, hissed, "Shut up!"

Indignant, I asked him on the way home, "What did you mean saying, 'Shut up,' when I was preaching?"

"Well," he said, "according to Archbishop Ussher's chronology of Genesis, there have been but six thousand years since Adam was created."

"I was going to at least ten thousand years," I replied, "because that was good preaching!"

Despite my awkward debut in Bostwick at Easter, Dr. Minder invited me to speak to his Sunday night youth group at the Tampa Gospel Tabernacle. Then came the moment when he asked me to preach at a regular service. I was downright frightened. Woodrow was lying on his bunk in our room when I told him about it. "And I haven't even got a sermon!" I concluded in despair.

He sat up and, then and there, commenced to preach me one of his own on Belshazzar, the ancient pagan monarch in Daniel 5. I liked it and told him I would use it. But I was not counting on having to repeat to the congregation the handwriting on the wall that made the king turn pale in verse 25: *"Mene, Mene, tekel, upharsin"* was not the kind of phraseology that came easily to a Carolina farmboy. *"Meany, meany, tickle, upjohn"* was the way it came out of my mouth. It sure tickled my buddies, but I didn't think it was all that funny.

When I returned to the Institute after summer vacation that first year, I little guessed that I would face my severest test before the schoolyear was over, when a beautiful girl complicated my life. Emily Cavanaugh—I had been smitten with love at the first sight of her soon after arriving at Florida Bible Institute, spending as much time with her as I could that first year. And I was not the only fellow on campus so afflicted. Wendell had been the first to alert me to the jewel that was Emily. It was something about her dark hair and sparkling eyes.

A chance to be near Emily happened every Sunday night. The several of us who went to Dr. Minder's youth group at the Tampa Gospel Tabernacle converged on the Cavanaughs' nearby house for supper before the meeting. I got in the habit of suggesting that we go back there afterward for our dessert, my favorite being Jell-O with fruit in it.

Sometimes Emily and others would go along on my preaching assignments or to young people's events, riding in the used 1929 Chevrolet coupe I had picked up for $75 (or later in the 1931 Oldsmobile for which I went into debt for $225, payable at $10 a month). But there was so much to do on campus—canoeing, volleyball, Ping-Pong, tennis—that we really never had to leave it for our social contacts. Emily and I used to double on the tennis court with my good friend Charles Massey and a girl from Michigan he went with occasionally.

What I did not notice was the growing friendship between Emily and Charles, who was a sophisticated senior with plans to go on to Harvard. In my own infatuation, I was sure she was the woman God meant for me to marry. So I proposed to her . . . in writing . . . during the first summer vacation! She told me she would have to think about it. I could not imagine why.

During the fall semester of that second year, it seemed she was growing more favorable to the idea, and my hopes soared along with my assumptions. One night after we attended a service together at a black church, she indicated that she would say yes to my letter. From then on, I guess I considered us engaged, even though I had not given her a ring. After the turn of the year, though, she seemed to be having second thoughts, and they apparently lingered through the spring.

At the close of school each spring, we celebrated Class Night, *the* social event of the year. On that May day in 1938, Dr. Minder took several of us fellows to Larson's Florist in Tampa to get flowers for our dates. This was a real splurge for most of us, with our limited finances. The going rate was 25¢ for a corsage, but I insisted on a 50¢ corsage for Emily!

When she did not wear my flowers to the party, I was perplexed. During a break in the festivities, we walked down to the river and sat in a swing hanging from a tree branch. I asked her to explain. She did not hesitate to tell me, quite gently but firmly, that she was in love with Charlie and would not marry me.

Charles Massey was one of the best preachers I ever heard as a student. In fact, on my very first weekend in Florida, I listened to his superb preaching at a student street meeting in Sulphur Springs—a meeting at which Roy Gustafson played his trumpet. I used to look forward to any chance of hearing Charles when I was not on an assignment myself.

But *Emily* and Charles? Incredible!

That woeful night in the spring of 1938 when she called it quits between us was Paradise Lost for me. In my despondency, I looked up Dr. Minder after my fellow students had gone back to their dorm rooms. I wept out my misery to his understanding ears.

But my problem was deeper than losing a girlfriend, and in my heart I admitted it. The issue was not trying to do something to please her and win her back. Her new boyfriend had wooed and won her fair and square. The issue was doing what pleased the Lord. If I refused that, could I expect the future to hold any happiness?

For some weeks, triggered by a profoundly searching sermon in chapel, I paced those deserted, echoing streets of Temple Terrace. In the moonlight, a soft southern breeze stirred the wispy Spanish moss that draped the trees on the golf course. I never felt so alone in my life—or so close to God. I walked through the late-night hours, struggling with the Holy Spirit over the call of God to be a minister. That was the last thing I wanted to be, and I had used all kinds of rationalizations to convince God to let me do something else.

I had the same sense of uncertainty in Charlotte nearly four years before, standing in the sawdust shavings of Mordecai Ham's tabernacle. There I did what I felt I should do: commit my eternal destiny to the saving grace of God in Jesus Christ. But was I now being asked to commit the rest of my life on earth to serving Him in a way that I did not particularly relish?

In the eighteen months since arriving at Florida Bible Institute, I exercised some gifts and began to develop some skills that I did not know I had. I knew that I loved to tell people the good news of God's salvation in Jesus Christ. On Sundays I often preached on the streets of Tampa, sometimes as many as five or six times a day.

But in those days, the greatest ministry that God opened up to me was the trailer parks. One of them, the largest (or close to it) in the country, was known as Tin Can Trailer Park. Two ladies there had gotten the concession to hold religious services on Sunday nights, but they had no preacher; they asked me if I would come. The crowds ran anywhere from 200 to 1,000. They would take up a collection, which I think the ladies kept and used for some worthy project, and they would give me $5—a tremendous help to my meager budget.

Many people responded to my preaching by confessing faith in Christ and being converted. My teachers and classmates seemed to affirm that this ministry was good and right for me. But did I want to preach for a lifetime? I asked myself that question for the umpteenth time on one of my nighttime walks around the golf course. The inner, irresistible urge would not subside. Finally, one night, I got down on my knees at the edge of one of the greens. Then I prostrated myself on the dewy turf. "O God," I sobbed, "if you want me to serve you, I will."

The moonlight, the moss, the breeze, the green, the golf course—all the surroundings stayed the same. No sign in the heavens. No voice from above. But in my spirit I knew I had been called to the ministry. And I knew my answer was yes.

From that night in 1938 on, my purpose and objectives in life were set. I knew that I would be a preacher of the Gospel. I did not yet know how or when, however.

My next preaching assignment seemed a long time in coming. I so badly wanted to preach, but nobody asked me to. The schoolyear was over. Students had left for the summer. I decided to stay on in Tampa, hoping to help Dr. Minder with the conferences at Lake Swan or to be kept busy with pulpit engagements while I worked at odd jobs on the campus. I applied to one church after another, but they either did not have openings or did not want an inexperienced student. A week went by, and I began to wonder nervously whether I had been truly called to preach or not.

Then, on one Saturday afternoon when I was down by the river cutting grass, I saw Mr. Corwin wandering about the campus. He operated the West Tampa Gospel Mission in the Hispanic section and always used Institute people to assist him. I had begun to think he would never ask me.

I dropped to my knees behind a bush and prayed, "Dear Lord, please let me preach at his mission tomorrow."

When I looked up, the kindly old man was coming right toward me. "Mr. Graham, a student had to cancel his appointment at the last minute," he said. "Would you mind coming to my mission to preach for me tomorrow?"

Having accepted Mr. Corwin's invitation gladly, the next day I spoke to a couple dozen Hispanic teenagers in Tampa, talking as loudly as I could for them. Whether it was my volume or my message I wasn't sure, but Mr. Corwin was impressed enough to ask me back the next Saturday, and many times after that.

Talking to those young men had given me a full head of steam. I asked Mr. Corwin after the mission service if I could go out and preach on the street. That day I preached seven sermons outdoors, and I continued to do that every weekend for the next two schoolyears, usually in front of saloons.

On Saturday nights, I would speak in the Tampa Gospel Mission off Franklin Street to whoever wandered in; Brunette Brock, Dr. Watson's secretary, and some other musicians from school helped me out from time to time.

I was also invited to preach on a Sunday morning at a small Methodist church some forty miles from Tampa, where Roy Gustafson and a musical trio from school were conducting a week of meetings. Then came the big break I had been longing for.

Dr. Minder's old friend Cecil Underwood arranged for me to preach for a week of evenings at East Palatka Baptist Church. And not only in the church but also over radio station WFOY in nearby

St. Augustine, live every morning. By now I had prepared and practiced about fifteen sermons—full-length ones—and I was ready to go!

During my stay in Palatka I lived in his home. I walked the streets practicing my sermons. I found a nearby church that was empty during the day and fine-tuned my sermons in there. By the time evenings came around, I was worn out from preaching to those empty pews.

Every night a congregation of 150 filled the church building. I became irritated at some of the young people who always sat in the back pews and cut up during the services. I scolded them from the pulpit and even threatened to go back there and throw them out bodily.

At that, the son of a leading member of the church jumped up, shook his fist at me, and stalked out, slamming the screen door behind him. I let the people know I could do other things besides preach, threatening that if there was a repeat performance of that behavior, I would give the boy a whipping. I think he came back two nights later. Fortunately, I wasn't challenged to make good on my threat.

Despite my immaturity, the Lord graciously moved 80 people to profess conversion that week, and many of them joined the church. I could not doubt that His hand was on me, which made me practice my sermons all the harder every day. I was so keyed up that I could hardly sleep at night, and yet I had to drive on a rural road the twenty-eight miles from Palatka to St. Augustine and back in the morning in order to preach on the radio.

A by-product of my Palatka experience was my third baptism! In accordance with their Presbyterian covenant theology, my parents had presented their infant son for baptism by sprinkling in 1919 at Chalmers Memorial Church back home. I had never questioned the validity of that solemn act of commitment on their part, born of a heart desire to have their child identified with the household of faith. Years later as a youngster, after studying the catechism, I was "confirmed" in the faith by declaring my personal allegiance to the Lord. That background contributed to my checking

"Recommitment" when I went forward in the Mordecai Ham meetings; that, I feel, was the moment when I truly put my trust in Christ as my Savior and was born again.

In Florida I had become convinced that I should be baptized by immersion and had arranged quietly for Dr. Minder to do that. It was an adult act, following my conscious conversion, and signified my dying to sin and rising again to a new life in Christ, as Paul described it in Romans 6.

But preaching in Southern Baptist churches raised a problem for me. Cecil Underwood pointed out that for Southern Baptists to invite preachers from other denominations—especially Presbyterians—into their pulpits was like defying a sacred tradition. Although he did not care one way or the other, not being a strict denominationalist himself, he thought that if I did not want to have a row with the deacons, I would be wise to be immersed under Southern Baptist auspices.

I pondered the question and prayed. It certainly seemed redundant, if not superfluous, to be baptized a third time. I did not believe there was anything magical or automatic about another baptism, as far as changing my heart. Baptism was only, to use the standard terminology, an outward sign of an inward grace. I knew that God had already made me a member of the Body of Christ, visibly expressed on earth in the Church, and that human labels could not affect my standing with Him one way or the other. On the other hand, I did not want anything to be a stumbling block or barrier in the minds of those I was seeking to reach.

In late 1938, therefore, Cecil Underwood immersed me in Silver Lake, with people from the church on the shore to witness the ordinance. I waded down into the water, where he lowered me under and lifted me out in less than three seconds. I waded ashore again and went into a little shanty bathhouse to change into dry clothes.

Early in 1939, Woodrow came to me and said, "I think you ought to be ordained. That would give you a standing in the Baptist Association and be of great benefit to you in many ways."

Woodrow and I talked it over and prayed about it. We agreed to get in touch with Cecil Underwood, who was still pastor at Peniel

Baptist Church near Palatka. Cecil was glad to call together four or five neighboring pastors to form an ordination council. On a Sunday in February after I preached at one of the churches, we went to Peniel for the two o'clock session.

The little white frame church, about four windows long, was hot, and I was nervous. The handful of rural Southern Baptist pastors took their responsibility seriously, and under Cecil's considerate direction commenced to question me in a kindly way about my background and beliefs.

One brother took it on himself to probe a bit into my theological views. After all, he must have reasoned, they were dealing here with a youngster who only recently had seen the light and converted from Presbyterian to Baptist. I am afraid my patience ran short. "Brother," I said, "you've heard me preach around these parts, and you've seen how the Lord has seen fit to bless. I'm not an expert on theology, but you know what I believe and how I preach, and that should be enough to satisfy you."

He chuckled, along with the others, and reckoned it was so. They approved me for ordination, and the service was held that night in the Peniel church. Cecil presided, and Woodrow preached the ordination sermon on the text, "Thou therefore endure hardness, as a good soldier of Jesus Christ" (2 Timothy 2:3, KJV).

I knelt on the little platform in front of a small congregation and was encircled by a half-dozen country preachers. I felt the light touch of their outstretched fingers and calloused hands on my blond head and bony shoulders as they prayed me into their distinguished fellowship. When I stood up again, I was an ordained Southern Baptist minister in the St. John's River Association.

Being ordained meant lots of things. Now I had sanction to perform weddings, conduct funerals, and officiate in church activities not open to me before. Far more important, though, by that simple act of ordination I was henceforth "set apart" for the preaching of the Gospel. Ordination did not elevate me to superiority over my fellow Christians who sat in the pews and listened, even if I stood in a high pulpit. On the contrary, it specially designated me to be their servant, their shepherd, for Christ's sake. It was meant to nurture in me humility, not pride.

After another profitable schoolyear, the summer of 1939 brought me new and larger opportunities. I was promoted to a two-week evangelistic series in Welaka Baptist Church, surely the longest I would ever have been at one place. Welaka was a fishing village on the St. John's River, with a reputation as a rough and tough place. Again the Lord was generous in drawing nightly crowds, and several people responded to the appeal to receive Christ. In the process, I was developing the basics of my own preaching style and my approach to giving the Invitation to come to Christ. For all of these meetings in north Florida, I stayed in the home of Cecil Underwood. While he was out working, painting houses, I would walk the streets around his house practicing my sermons and praying.

Then John Minder gave me an incredible opportunity. He needed to spend some time away that summer and asked me to be his summer replacement at the large Tampa Gospel Tabernacle. For six weeks, I would have my own church, preaching at all the regular services and carrying out pastoral responsibilities.

The embarrassments of Bostwick and Belshazzar faded into memory as I moved into the Tampa parsonage next door to the church. The neighbors were largely Cuban immigrants, most of them Roman Catholics in name if not in practice. I visited faithfully in home after home, inviting people to church. Surprisingly, many came, and listened, and responded.

I went to the Tampa hospitals and prayed for the sick. I held the hands of the dying and learned how much love and compassion a pastor must have toward his people.

And I preached. And practiced. Every Saturday I went into the empty sanctuary and rehearsed aloud the sermon I would preach the next day. Sometimes I had an audience of one, the janitor, who seemed to feel quite free to make suggestions.

One night in the parsonage, I woke up suddenly. Someone was breaking into the house. I was all alone, of course, and tensely aware that someone was in the next room. In the closet, I kept my old .22 rifle, left over from my hunting days on the farm. I eased out of bed, got the gun, put a cartridge in it, and shot it through the door into the ceiling of the next room. That loud bang was followed almost instantly by the bang of the back door as the intruder fled.

Apart from that, Dr. Minder found things pretty much in one piece when he got back. To my amazement, he appointed me to become his assistant pastor for the next year, while I was completing my education.

I was vice president of the young people's ministry for the Christian and Missionary Alliance churches in the state of Florida, and all the CMA churches had invited me, in that role, to visit and speak to their young people. This had given me many contacts all over Florida and southern Georgia. For the balance of the summer, I did more preaching through these contacts, including Dr. Watson's huge church in St. Petersburg. I went back to school for my final year, rejoicing in the evidence that God's call was valid.

Then came a blow, the kind that was most damaging to the spirit of a young Christian. Dr. Watson was accused of moral indiscretions—*falsely* accused, I was certain. He was a man of God and one of my spiritual fathers. I did not believe for one minute that the evidence supported the charges against him. It was all circumstantial. Even the testimony of the accusers was not unanimous. The chief accuser was an employee of the school who himself had come under suspicion on a separate matter and might have been motivated by revenge. Dr. Minder and I were among the majority who stood by Dr. Watson.

The whole affair seared my soul with sorrow, both for his own pain and for the damage to the school. A few faculty and maybe a fourth of the students left. The campus was under a pall. As president of the senior class, I did what I could—which was negligible—to improve morale. Dreadful as the experience was, I was grateful that the dark cloud passed over Florida Bible Institute while I was there. It was a big learning experience for me in many ways, and it taught me to be very careful myself.

In May 1940, I graduated from Florida Bible Institute. At Class Night just before commencement that spring, one of the girls, Vera Resue, read the traditional "prophecy"—a passage that she had composed for the occasion: "Each time God had a chosen human instrument to shine forth His light in the darkness. Men like Luther, John and Charles Wesley, Moody, and others were ordinary men, but men who heard the voice of God. Their surrounding conditions were as black as night, but they had God. 'If God is for us, who can be against us?' (Romans 8:31). It has been said that Luther revolutionized the world. It was not he, but Christ working through him. The time is ripe for another Luther, Wesley, Moody, _____. There is room for another name in this list. There is a challenge facing us."

I did not think my name was the one to be added to that list, but I did know that I was a human instrument and that God had chosen me to preach.

During that summer after graduation, classmate Ponzi Pennington and I went north to York, Pennsylvania, where pastor Ralph Boyer had invited me to preach in his church for a week in July.

We did not dare drive that far in my decrepit 1931 Oldsmobile, whose tire blowouts, broken piston rods, and exhausted spark plugs were enough to try the patience of Job. So we left it in Charlotte and borrowed my father's 1937 Plymouth.

The meetings in York went well. We were invited for one week, and the series was extended for a second week. In our room at the YMCA, I had to think up and pray through more messages, since I had already preached all my evangelistic sermons. There was a good response to the Gospel, even though my heavy accent made it difficult for some people to understand me. I tried speaking louder than usual, but a few still did not get what I was saying. I wanted to blame the poor communication on their spiritual deafness, but it had to have been my dialect.

While in York, we drove up to New York and spent a day at the World's Fair. It was the first time I ever saw television. They had a camera there, and as you walked by, you could see yourself on a screen. We never thought it would amount to anything, though. It seemed too incredible!

On our way back from York, on the Skyline Drive in Virginia, a farmer in a pickup truck pulled out in front of us without warning, forcing me off the road and into a ditch. He towed us into Galax, where we waited six hours for the car to be repaired. It took all my money, and as I was fishing the bills out of my wallet, I heard faint echoes of my father talking, telling me how many automobile mishaps I'd had and how he'd had to come rescue me with the mules. When I told him in person, however, he understood and mercifully traded my old blue Oldsmobile in for a new car for himself; the green Plymouth he gave to me.

As for me, the certainty about a call to preach motivated me to desire further education. An accredited college of liberal arts seemed to be the next step. I had a particular one in mind because of two visitors to Temple Terrace in the winter of my senior year.

4

Northern Exposure

While I was a student at Florida Bible Institute, a Chicago attorney, Paul Fischer, stayed in the Institute's hotel section with a business friend, Elner Edman, and Mr. Edman's mother. Fischer's brother Herman was chairman of the board at Wheaton College, just west of Chicago, and Edman's brother Ray was a history professor and interim president at the school. After hearing me preach, they talked to me about getting further training at Wheaton College.

I had heard of the school, of course, but Chicago and its suburbs were in another world from the South. Would the college even admit me from a Bible institute, and with the kind of grades my high school transcript would show? Would I ever survive in frigid Illinois?

Paul Fischer astonished me when he offered to pay my tuition at Wheaton for the first year, and Elner Edman volunteered to help with other expenses. As to being admitted, I could hardly have had more influential references. Things began to look hopeful.

Another force in my favor, which I really did not know about at the time, was Mother's prayers. Four years before, she had heard Wheaton's former president, Dr. James Oliver Buswell, preach at a church in Charlotte. She was so impressed that she prayed from then on that someday I would go to Wheaton College. My parents also became acquainted with Dr. Jim Graham, a former missionary to China; he was then a professor of Bible at Wheaton.

With some misgivings and anxiety, I applied for admission and was accepted. Thus it was that I drove to Wheaton in September 1940 and began college. Many of my Florida Bible Institute credits were not accepted; the few credits that were accepted gave me second-semester freshman rank.

Wheaton College had been founded in 1860 by a staunch anti-slavery Congregationalist minister from New England, Jonathan Blanchard. It was a fully accredited college of liberal arts and sciences, with several substantial buildings and a highly qualified faculty. Students, including the first blacks I had ever gone to school with, came from Christian homes in most of the forty-eight states and from many foreign countries as well. The college had a strong four-year Bible requirement, regardless of a student's major, and that was appealing to me.

Though it did not call itself *fundamentalist*, this venerable institution at the time demanded rigid adherence to a code of conduct that prohibited staff as well as students from using tobacco or alcohol in any form, dancing, card playing, or joining secret societies. The college also had scriptural convictions, with a conservative theological statement of faith that had been drafted in the mid-twenties. Trustees and faculty had to sign it every year as a condition of employment. All these requirements gave Wheaton a reputation in the collegiate world of being rather narrow and bluenose, but the integrity of instruction in all disciplines was widely respected.

In the eighty years of its existence, only three men had preceded V. Raymond Edman as president: the founder; his son Charles Albert Blanchard; and a controversial Presbyterian clergyman, James Oliver Buswell, who had really put Wheaton on the academic map.

"Prexy" Edman won my heart at once. Crossing campus one of my first days there, I was greeted by a person I did not recognize. "Hi, Bill!" he said. "How's everything in North Carolina?"

I found out the next day he was the president of the college. Perhaps his brother had told him about me after his visit to Temple Terrace, but I was still amazed that he knew my first name and what I looked like.

On Wheaton's elm-shaded suburban campus twenty-five miles due west of Chicago's downtown Loop, I felt like a hick. Born and bred on a farm in the South, I doubted there was anybody in the entering class as green as I was. In the first six weeks, missing the old friends in sunny Florida and the recent exhilaration of preaching, I was so miserable that I began to wonder if I had made a mistake.

The only student I knew when I first arrived at Wheaton was Howard Van Buren, who had been a neighbor of ours in Charlotte. He was a year or two ahead of me, a brilliant student who later became a noted heart surgeon.

At twenty-one years of age, I was older than most of my classmates, which did not help my self-image. I was sure they were staring at my Li'l Abner appearance, what with out-of-style clothes and brogan shoes. I decided to do something about it. One day, tagging along with some other students, I went to Chicago's Maxwell Street, a kind of open-air flea market. On Monday mornings, if you were the first there and a sharp bargainer, you could talk the merchants down to about a third of the asking price. For $4.95 I bought a beautiful turquoise tweed suit and wore it proudly to a football game in October. Then it started to rain. The pants legs shrank up my ankles, and the seat of the pants became so tight that I burst the seam. I couldn't get home fast enough!

When I talked at my customary rapid clip, people looked at me curiously, as if my heavily accented drawl were a foreign language. At six-foot-two, I was too tall to fade into the background. When I went out for the wrestling team, probably at about the 160-pound class, I looked like a python on the mat. Two defeats in intercollegiate matches ended that career. As colder weather came, I went along with my new friends and tried to learn to ice-skate on the frozen lagoon in North Side Park. Unable to keep my ankles straight, I gave up after a number of falls.

I declared a major in anthropology, a subject I had barely heard of before. Why did I not major in Bible or public speaking, since I was committed to being a preacher? There were three good reasons.

First, with such a full Bible background at Florida Bible Institute, I was able to take a validation exam and transfer several hours of Bible credits. With that background, I now wanted to get as broad a liberal arts education as I could before going on to seminary for a professional degree. My choice of courses at Wheaton reflected this, ranging from classical Greek to economics to geology.

Second, I considered the remote possibility that I might end up on the mission field. Anthropology would give me empathy for people in social settings different from my own and an understanding of social customs and primitive religions. A focus on anthropology would give me a liberal arts education in the best sense, obliterating any condescending notions I might have toward people from backgrounds other than my own. (There was one more reason I took anthropology. I was told it was an easy course and that the professor could not always read the students' writing on the tests!)

Third, Alexander Grigolia. The head of the college's new anthropology department was popular among the students. "Don't leave Wheaton without a course in Grigolia" became a favorite saying. Short and rotund, with flashing dark eyes and an accent that hinted at his Russian birth, he had received one Ph.D. in Germany and another at the University of Pennsylvania; he had a medical degree tucked in there somewhere too. In a corner of his crowded little office, ever watchful, stood his faithful colleague Josephine, with whom I was quick to make acquaintance; she was a full-sized human skeleton.

Dr. Grigolia ardently convinced us that the origins of the human race were not up from the ape but down from the hand of God, as Genesis recorded. His humorous mistakes in the King's English were a continuous source of merriment. Once when he was at the blackboard and a couple of students were whispering to each other, he said, without turning around, "Would someone please pipe down him?"

As for my initial homesickness, the Lane family soon came to my rescue. Dr. Mortimer B. Lane taught courses in government and economics at the college. Before that, when he was in government service, he and his wife and their seven children lived in Switzerland. Quite well-off, they entertained students in their large, comfortable Victorian home near the campus. They welcomed me as one of their own. Early on Sunday mornings, as Plymouth

Brethren, they hosted a small local assembly in their house. I began to attend that quiet communion service with students from other churches.

One of the few students on campus to have a car of his own, I was soon drafted by the Student Christian Council, which sent student Gospel teams out to churches and missions on weekends. They assigned me to go with a singing quartet and preach at a church at Terre Haute in southern Indiana. I leaped at the chance to give my first sermon since arriving at Wheaton.

The quartet must have liked what they heard. Their report back to the council director opened a flood of requests for me to speak here and there. Lest my dismal academic history repeat itself, I turned down most of the invitations, at least at first. I had pledged myself to give priority to studies, and my 87 percent average at the end of the first semester proved that it had paid off.

Downtown, about a mile from the school, a church met on Sundays in the Masonic Lodge hall on Wesley Street. Dr. Edman had preached there when he was teaching history at the college; but when he was named president in 1940, he discontinued his ministry with the United Gospel Tabernacle, known locally as "The Tab" or "The Tabernacle." The congregation was filling in with student-supply preachers, and I was invited to speak one Sunday. The $15 honorarium they gave me was generous and much appreciated.

Repeat invitations to the Tab followed. In their Sunday crowd of 300, packing that hall to capacity, were business and professional people, college students, and (most intimidating of all) professors—men such as philosopher Gordon Clark, biologist Russell Mixter, and scientist Roger Voskuyl, who would work on the Manhattan Project.

In the summer of 1941, the Tab called me to be their regular pastor when I returned to college in the fall. Dr. Edman, who by then had become my friend and counselor, advised me to think it through carefully. After much prayer, I decided to accept the position.

After my first year at Wheaton, I returned to Charlotte, where I was honored by the home folks with an invitation to preach for a week of meetings at the Sharon Presbyterian Church. I was nervous at first. It surely was another case where dependence on the Lord was my only hope. And it was another case where He proved

Himself faithful beyond imagination. Good crowds turned out for the services, they listened respectfully, and a number of people made commitments to Christ that week.

When I returned to Wheaton for the fall semester, I tackled my pastorate at the Tab with enthusiasm. I had to prepare and preach two sermons every week and lead a prayer meeting on Wednesday nights. What I lacked in content I made up in volume.

My responsibilities at the Tab did, however, turn out to be detrimental to my studies. To do more preaching, I had to do less studying, and the dilemma really developed there. I missed a great deal in the classroom.

On Sunday evening, December 7, 1941, someone told me that Pearl Harbor had been attacked. I had no idea where Pearl Harbor was—I had never heard of it. Then, on my way from the Tab back to my room, I heard from a newsboy hawking a special edition of the *Chicago Tribune* that the United States was at war with Japan.

I got into my car and drove over to the Lane house. Students and friends who gathered there on Sundays were usually up on all the latest happenings in the world. As I entered the front door, Howard Van Buren met me and told me the grim story of Japan's surprise attack on our naval base.

The next morning, Dr. Edman called the whole student body together for a special chapel service. Prexy had been a soldier in the trenches in World War I. He knew, as General Sherman had said, that war was hell; he also knew that some of his students would die before it was over.

My first thought was to volunteer. Not that I felt I would make a good fighting man. Indeed, as a cadet in the Army training program on campus, I had nearly cut one fellow's head off with my bayonet when I made a sudden wrong turn during a drill. But, as an ordained Baptist minister, I knew there had to be a place in the Chaplains' Corps for a person like me.

I wrote immediately to the War Department to ask about the possibility of becoming a chaplain. They said I would have to finish college and then take a seminary course.

In the next three semesters, schoolwork took on a new seriousness, and the pastoral ministry to members of the Tab's congregation deepened along with the preaching. Life and death were not abstractions to us anymore, and the Wheaton township of seven thousand shared with the rest of the nation the anxiety and pain and grief of war.

Yes, Wheaton was both a spiritual and an intellectual turning point in my life. It also became a turning point in another significant way.

1943–1949

A Ministry Begins

5

Ruth

"Saturday nights I dedicate to prayer and study, in preparation for the Lord's day."

What kind of a romance could a college man have with a woman who said a thing like that? Dating Ruth Bell had to be creative. And I did my best. For example, on one occasion we took a long walk in the countryside surrounding Wheaton to a graveyard, where we read tombstone epitaphs! It was a far cry from careening through Charlotte in a jalopy.

Ruth, born in China, had spent her first seventeen years in Asia. Her father, Dr. L. Nelson Bell, was a medical missionary in the eastern Chinese province of Northern Kiangsu, and her family lived in the hospital compound. Theirs was a hard existence, and certainly not a sheltered one. She remembers it as a happy, interesting childhood with strict but loving parents, among happy Christians, both fellow missionaries and Christian Chinese friends and helpers. But they were all exposed to everything from monsoons, sandstorms, and epidemics to bandit attacks and civil war. For high school, Ruth went to the Foreign School in Pyongyang, Korea (now North Korea).

In more ways than one, she was one of the belles of Wheaton campus. This I learned during my first term from a fellow I met at the Lane home, Johnny Streater. To pay his way through college, Johnny ran his own trucking service. For a price, he would haul anything in his little yellow pickup. I gladly accepted his offer of work at 50¢ an hour and spent many afternoons at hard labor, moving furniture and other items around the western Chicago suburbs.

Johnny was a little older than I and had been in the Navy before coming to Wheaton. He had a vision for the mission field and felt that God had called him to serve in China, where he intended to go as soon as he graduated. He told me about a girl in the junior class—one of the most beautiful and dedicated Christian girls he had ever met. Sounded like my type. I paid attention.

One day we were hanging around in our sweaty work clothes in front of Williston Hall, the girls' dorm, getting ready to haul some furniture for a lady in Glen Ellyn, the next town over, when Johnny let out a whoop. "Billy, here's the girl I was telling you about," he said. "It's Ruth Bell."

I straightened up, and there she was. Standing there, looking right at me, was a slender, hazel-eyed movie starlet! I said something polite, but I was flustered and embarrassed. It took me a month to muster the courage to ask her out for a date.

The Christmas holidays were fast approaching, and the combined glee clubs were presenting Handel's *Messiah*. One day in the library in Blanchard Hall, I saw Ruth studying at one of the long tables. Johnny Streater and Howard Van Buren urged me to make my pitch to her right there. The expression of the librarian at the desk turned to a frown as we whispered among ourselves. Undaunted, I sauntered nonchalantly across to Ruth and scribbled my proposal for a date to the concert. To my surprise and delight, she agreed to go.

That Sunday afternoon was cold and snowy. With Ruth Bell sitting beside me in Pierce Chapel, I did not pay much attention to the music. Afterward we walked over to the Lane house for a cup of tea, and we had a chance to talk. I just could not believe that anyone could be so spiritual and so beautiful at one and the same time.

Ruth went back to her room (she told me later), got on her knees, and told the Lord that if she could spend the rest of her life serving Him with me, she would consider it the greatest privilege imaginable. So why did she make it so hard for me to get her to say yes out loud?

If I had not been smitten with love at the first sight of Ruth Bell, I would certainly have been the exception. Many of the men at Wheaton thought she was stunning. Petite, vivacious, smart, talented, witty, stylish, amiable, and unattached. What more could a fellow ask for?

Add to that the fact that her Virginia-based parents and their missionary companions were all in China under the auspices of the Southern Presbyterian denomination. Not the Associated Reformed Presbyterian Church I had grown up in, but close enough.

"Billy, hold your horses!" I fell so head-over-heels in love with her that Johnny had to caution me. "You're going too fast."

And there was one minor problem that kept coming up. She wanted me to go with her as a missionary to Tibet! My mind was not closed to such a possibility. Not completely. After all, I had chosen to major in anthropology with just such a contingency in mind. But missionary work was a lot more comfortable to consider in the global abstract than in the Tibetan concrete.

In that list of good adjectives I just assigned to Ruth, I omitted one: *determined.*

She felt that God had called her to be a missionary to the remote borders of Tibet just as strongly as I felt that He had called me to preach the Gospel. In my case, though, there was not a geographical stipulation.

Ruth was deeply impressed by the life of Amy Carmichael, that single—and indeed singular—woman whom God had called to devote herself utterly to the children of Dohnavur, in southern India.

She reinforced her case by telling me about Mildred Cable, who had rejected the young man she loved because marriage to him would have cut across her call from God to do pioneer work in China.

Two things I felt sure of: first, that Ruth was bound to get married someday; and second, that I was the man she would marry. Beyond that, I did not try to pressure her or persuade her—that is to say, not *overly* much. I let God do my courting for me.

But as the months went by, I asked her to at least consider me. It would not have been right to let her assume that what seemed to be my heroic understanding of her concerns was a lack of interest or expectation on my part. We had lots of discussions about our relationship. I wouldn't call them arguments exactly, but we certainly did not see eye to eye.

In the meantime, Ruth enjoyed the social life at Wheaton, as I did, with many friends. One day she went canoeing on the Fox River in St. Charles, about ten miles west of Wheaton, with classmates Harold Lindsell, Carl Henry, and Carl's fiancée, Helga. Somehow the canoe capsized, and Ruth went under. Since both men were staunch Baptists, I suspected them of wanting to immerse the pretty Presbyterian missionary kid from China!

Because I was already an ordained Baptist minister, our divided denominational allegiance was another topic of conversation between us. Ruth stuck to her convictions.

"We've both got such strong wills or minds or something, I almost despaired of ever having things go peacefully between us," she wrote to her parents, "but I wouldn't want him any other way, and I *can't* be any other way. But you know, it's remarkable how two strong minds (or wills) like that can gradually begin to sort of fuse together. Or maybe we're learning to give in and don't realize it."

I was making some adjustments, certainly. At the Lane house one evening, I was so busy talking at the supper table that I ate three helpings of macaroni and cheese before I woke up to the fact that I had told Ruth I hated macaroni and cheese. That incident encouraged her to hope she could feed me anything and get away with it!

One Sunday evening after church, I walked into the parlor of the Gerstung home, where I was rooming, and collapsed into a chair. That dear professor of German and his wife, with three young boys of their own, were getting accustomed to my moods and always listened patiently. This time I bemoaned the fact that I did not stand a chance with Ruth. She was so superior to me in culture and poise. She did not talk as much as I did, so she seemed superior in her intelligence too. "The reason I like Ruth so much," I wrote home to Mother, "is that she looks and reminds me of you."

By now I had directly proposed marriage to Ruth, and she was struggling with her decision. At the same time, she encouraged me to keep an open mind about the alternative of my going to the mission field. She was coming to realize, though, that the Lord was not calling me in that direction.

One day I posed a question to Ruth point-blank: "Do you believe that God brought us together?"

She thought so, without question.

"In that case," I said, "God will lead me, and you'll do the following."

She did not say yes to my proposal right then and there, but I knew she was thinking it over.

A test of our bond came when her sister Rosa was diagnosed as having tuberculosis. Ruth dropped out of school in the middle of my second semester to care for her. Rosa was placed in a hospital in New Mexico, and Ruth stayed with her the next fall too.

That summer I returned home and preached in several churches in the South. Ruth's parents had returned from China on a furlough—actually, the Japanese had invaded the mainland, so the Bells were not sure if they could ever return—and had settled temporarily in Virginia, their home state.

While I was in Florida, preaching in Dr. Minder's church, I got a thick letter from Ruth postmarked July 6, 1941. One of the first sentences made me ecstatic, and I took off running. "I'll marry you," she wrote.

When I went back to my room, I read that letter over and over until church time. On page after page, Ruth explained how the Lord had worked in her heart and said she felt He wanted her to marry me. That night I got up to the pulpit and preached. When I finished and sat down, the pastor turned to me.

"Do you know what you just said?" he asked.

"No," I confessed.

"I'm not sure the people did either!"

After I went to bed, I switched my little lamp on and off all night, rereading that letter probably another dozen times.

At the close of a preaching series just after that at Sharon Presbyterian Church in Charlotte, those dear people gave me, as I recall, an offering of $165. I raced right out and spent almost all of it on an engagement ring with a diamond so big you could almost see it with a magnifying glass! I showed it off at home, announcing that I planned to present it to Ruth over in Montreat in the middle of the day. But daytime was not romantic enough, I was told.

Ruth was staying part of that summer at the cottage of Buck Currie and his wife, whom she called uncle and aunt, and their niece Gay. Buck was the brother of Ed Currie, one of Ruth's father's fellow missionaries in China. Their house on Craigmont Road in Black Mountain was built near a stream and had swings that went out over the water.

As I turned off the main road and drove toward the house, which was some distance off, I saw a strange creature walking down the road. She had long, straight hair sticking out all over, an awful-looking faded dress, bare feet, and what looked to be very few teeth. I passed her by, but when I suddenly realized it was Ruth playing a trick on me—her teeth blacked out so that she looked toothless—I slammed on the brakes. She got in and we went on to the Currie house deep in the woods.

I had the ring with me.

We went up to what is now the Blue Ridge Parkway. The sun was sinking on one side of us and the moon rising on the other. I kissed Ruth on the lips for the first time. I thought it was romantic, but she thought, or so she told me later, that I was going to swallow her.

"I can't wear the ring until I get permission from my parents," she said apologetically.

They were away, so she sent them a telegram: "Bill has offered me a ring. May I wear it?"

"Yes," they wired back, "if it fits."

Later in that summer of 1941, Ruth decided to visit her parents. She took a train to Waynesboro, Virginia, where I was to join her. I had to go, of course, to meet them. No, to do more than that—to pass inspection. I drove my Plymouth from Charlotte through North Carolina, stopping on the way to give a brief message on a Christian radio station. About five miles out of Waynesboro, I stopped and changed into a suit and tie. I finally found the small brick house; and when I pulled up, Ruth rushed out to greet me. She had expected me to hug and kiss her, but I was so nervous about meeting her parents that I froze.

Dr. and Mrs. Bell came out right behind her. That night we all had dinner together with Dr. Bell's mother. I enjoyed it, though I was still tense. Dr. Bell had booked a room for me at the General Wayne Hotel, and I was surprised (and relieved) in the morning to find that the $3 room charge had been paid.

When I went to visit Ruth later in the morning, Dr. Bell asked if we would like to follow him and Mrs. Bell to Washington, D.C., where he had several appointments. We did, and we enjoyed a memorable walk down by the Potomac River. Only later did I learn that he had gone to warn the State Department about the danger of the Japanese and their increasing military power. Dr. Bell said he could not get anyone in Washington to take him seriously, though—except Congressman Walter Judd, who himself had been a missionary to China.

Ruth was the woman of my dreams, but the delightful in-laws I would gain in the process would make our eventual marriage all the better.

Our relationship deepened in the next year. I was studying, working on the truck with Johnny Streater, and preaching regularly at the Tab. I began to listen to Torrey Johnson's *Midwest Bible Hour* on Sunday afternoons at five o'clock, and to *Songs in the Night,* a forty-five-minute program on WCFL, Chicago's most powerful radio station, on Sunday nights.

During this time, after Rosa got better and Ruth returned to Wheaton, there came into Ruth's mind a serious doubt about me, centered on my uncertainty about my calling (if any) to the mission field. She even reached the point of feeling that we ought to quit dating and not see each other for a while. I said I would appreciate having the ring back, in that case. She could not accept that, though. She was emotional about the ring and would not give it back to me. And that was the end of her doubt.

But we did not move ahead with any haste. Although we were engaged, we felt that it was right for us not to get married until after our graduation.

During the next academic year, 1941–42, I changed where I lived, now rooming with Ken Hansen and Lloyd Fesmire. Ruth roomed with Helen Stam. Lloyd and I both admired the other's girl greatly, and Helen would later become Lloyd's wife.

The early months of 1943 found Ruth making trips to Oak Park or to the downtown Chicago Loop to shop for her trousseau. I could not get all that excited about the shopping, but when her folks offered to give us silver tableware as a wedding gift, I decided to go along with her to Peacock's Jewelry. And it was a good thing too. The pattern she chose had knives and forks in two sizes, and I talked her into getting one of each in the super size for me to use; they cost 20¢ extra.

In addition to Ruth's shopping and finishing up her senior year at college (with an earnest plea to her parents to pray that she would pass the comprehensive exams in the spring), she joined me on Sunday mornings, first at the Lane home for a Plymouth Brethren meeting, then later at the Tab, where I preached.

But I too had schoolwork to finish, and I think she was exasperated by the fact that I was on the road so often. After telling her folks about my coming itinerary in Flint, Michigan; Rockford, Illinois; and then "Wisconsin or Pennsylvania or somewhere," she wrote, "I can't keep control of him much less keep track of him."

Already she sensed what kind of future we faced together. "I'm a rotten sport when it comes to his leaving. It's no fun. I never thought about this side of it. What is it going to be like after we're married? I probably won't see as much of him then, as I do *now*."

Something loomed immediately ahead, though, that made Ruth and me both expect me to stay put a little more.

One day a big Lincoln Continental pulled up in front of the house where I was rooming. Out of it popped a young man who bounded up the steps and asked to see me. He turned out to be president of Hitchcock Publishing Company in Chicago and treasurer of the National Gideon Association, the group that distributed Bibles to hotels.

His name was Bob Van Kampen, and he wanted to sound me out about becoming pastor of the church where he was a deacon, Western Springs Baptist Church, about twenty miles southeast of

Wheaton. Since my work at the Tab had been an extracurricular, part-time thing, I felt ready to consider a change.

In January 1943, midway through my senior year, I began to feel the responsibility of supporting a wife. I was also attracted by the proximity of the University of Chicago, with its strong anthropology department offering advanced-study opportunities. Hence, I accepted the call to Western Springs; I had already preached there as a student, and I could begin work there after college commencement. In my enthusiasm, however, I forgot to consult my bride-to-be! She let me know in no uncertain terms that she did not appreciate such insensitivity. And I could not blame her.

Both Ruth and I felt sure the pastorate would be a temporary thing. For me, it was a possible stepping-stone to qualifying for the Army chaplaincy. I made this priority clear to the church in Western Springs, and they accepted the condition. They even gave me the freedom to travel occasionally to evangelistic meetings. In the next months, I preached there several times, and Ruth was introduced to people as "our pastor's future wife." She had her own reasons for viewing the placement as temporary—"since we're planning on going to the mission field as soon as we can," she wrote home. For that reason, we asked the church to find us a furnished apartment so that we would not get encumbered with a lot of possessions.

In June 1943, Ruth and I graduated from Wheaton College in the same class. (Although she was a junior when I entered as a second-semester freshman, we ended up graduating in the same class. She fell behind because of the time she took out for Rosa's illness, while I advanced because the school later transferred some additional credits from Florida Bible Institute.) During the ceremony, she sat in front of me. When she received her diploma, I laughingly whispered, "At long last!" She turned around, and I could see that she was not amused. Even so, she made a cute little face at me.

Ruth's parents had moved from Virginia to a house on the Presbyterian conference grounds at Montreat, North Carolina, just east of Asheville. We were married there in August, on the night of Friday the thirteenth, with a full moon in the sky. In Gaither Chapel at eight-thirty in the evening, amid candles and clematis, my beloved Florida mentor, Dr. John Minder, pronounced us husband and wife. Dr. Kerr Taylor, close friend of the Bells and former missionary to China, assisted him in the ceremony. Sophie Graham (no relation), a missionary from Haichow, China, played the piano and accompanied Roy Gustafson in two solos before the ceremony. Andrew Yang from Chinkiang, China, sang two solos during the service. All the details took up two columns on the social-news page of the Asheville paper; that was because Dr. Bell was well known in the area. It was the most memorable day of my life.

For a wedding present, my father had already given me $50. I had $25 of my own saved up. That meant I had $75 to pay for a honeymoon and get us back to Chicago.

The first night we went to the Battery Park Hotel in Asheville; that cost us $5 for the night. I had wanted Ruth to have the best, but the Grove Park Inn would have cost $20. I couldn't sleep in the bed, so after Ruth fell asleep, I got up quietly, lay down on the floor, and dropped right off. (I had suffered from insomnia all through school, and Chief Whitefeather, who had come through town once and given his Christian testimony, had suggested that I sleep on the floor. He promised that though it would take a couple of weeks to get used to, it would help my problem, and he was right.) The next morning, when Ruth woke up, I was gone . . . or at least appeared to be gone. It took a few minutes for her to find me on the floor, sleeping like a baby.

We then drove to Boone, where we went to a private home that let out rooms; ours cost $1. To get to the bathroom at night, we had to go through two other rooms where people were sleeping. At the end of our stay, Ruth confided in the lady of the house that we were on our honeymoon.

"Yes, I know," she said. "I've been sweeping up the rice every day."

We ate out at little sandwich places and played golf. Ruth knew nothing about the game, and I knew little more, in spite of the caddying I had done in Florida. There were many people behind us on the course each time, and we did not know we were supposed to let them play through.

One time we decided to splurge. We ate a meal at Mayview Manor, *the* place to eat in town. Lunch was $3. My money was going fast. But we decided, just for one night, to spend $2 at the Boone Hotel.

Then we went back to my family's home in Charlotte, but there was no room for us. My sister Catherine was getting married; Jean had a room, and so did Melvin. So we slept on the floor in what my mother called her sunroom.

Our trip back to Chicago, after our brief honeymoon in the Blue Ridge Mountains near home, was uneventful. "Hit two starlings, that was all," Ruth recorded. "Everything else we ran over had already been run over before." Like most travelers in those days, we had along a trusty thermos bottle filled with Dr. Pepper and crushed ice, plus a supply of cheese and crackers and raisin wafers.

We stopped at a hotel in Indianapolis and got a small, dirty room. After the maid changed the soiled bed linens, we still had to scrub the ring out of the tub ourselves. Then, in the dimly lighted and thickly carpeted restaurant downstairs, the host would not admit me without my jacket (packed in the car) or Ruth with her pigtails. We were as disgusted as could be at the management, and as happy as could be with each other!

When we arrived at 214 South Clay Street, Hinsdale, Illinois—the furnished apartment found for us by someone at Western Springs—our landlady, Mrs. Pantke, had our four upstairs rooms tidy, with a welcoming bouquet of flowers from her own garden. We unloaded the car and stowed everything away in less than an hour, including more than two bushels of canned goods that the church people had brought in. Ruth served us supper using all her lace, china, crystal, and silver. Then I did dishes while she rushed through a bath and pressed her travel suit so that we could get to the church in time for our reception.

The small group in the Western Springs church—fewer than a hundred members—had been able to construct only the basement of what they hoped someday would become a church building. It was not a very impressive place to meet. Ruth thought of it, in those war days, as an air-raid shelter. But the congregation really put themselves out to make us feel welcome. After hearing various speeches, we were handed an envelope with a gift of $48 in it. In addition, Ruth received two dozen red roses and I was presented with a huge bouquet made out of fresh vegetables. They even had a wedding cake for us to cut.

The aftermath was anything but romantic. Soon Ruth came down with a sore throat and a 101-degree fever. I nursed her as well as I could, cooking my own meals and eating them on the floor in the bedroom so I could be near her. Her temperature was higher the next day. I put her in the Seventh Day Adventist hospital because I had to go out of town for the week; it was for a speaking engagement in Ohio substituting for Dr. Edman that I felt I had to take. She recovered quickly and was discharged. By the time I got home at seven on Friday morning, she had the apartment straightened up from my mess.

As newlyweds in a first pastorate, Ruth and I were pretty typical lovebirds, I guess. We took hikes in the sunshine and in the rain, especially enjoying the arboretum nearby. On rare occasions, I went golfing and Ruth caddied for me. It was a major excursion to go into Chicago to see movies at Telenews, an all-newsreel theater on North State Street.

On the spur of the moment late one Monday, which was my day off, I took Ruth out for supper at a restaurant in La Grange. I was wearing my battered Li'l Abner brogans, and Ruth was in her loafers and sport coat. While we waited for an empty table, a lot of the people pouring in—and quite a crowd it was—stopped and shook hands with us, saying how glad they were to see us there. Then it dawned on me that there was a youth banquet upstairs at which I had been invited to speak—an invitation that I had declined. We ducked out in a hurry.

Our old car was in bad shape and needed about $100 worth of repairs. But I got a good trade-in allowance from a local dealer on a 1942 maroon Pontiac. Our budget was given a big break by the fact that the church paid the $55 in monthly rent directly to the Pantkes. That meant that by law our dwelling was considered a church parsonage; therefore, the money paid toward rent wasn't chargeable to us for income tax purposes. That kept our total income so low that we did not even have to file a return. Ruth thought that put us in a class with tramps, but we were the happier for it.

We lived in downtown Hinsdale, a block or two from the Burlington railroad tracks. We enjoyed hamburgers and Cokes when we stepped out for a newspaper, and hot gingerbread and Postum when we stayed in. Sometimes we listened to a murder mystery or *Henry Aldrich* or *Truth or Consequences* on the radio while we ate supper by candlelight. While I studied, Ruth looked up sermon illustrations for me in old *Reader's Digest* magazines.

I needed to do a lot of studying, as well as work on my sermons. I was still blithely mixing my metaphors, as in this letter I once wrote to Ruth's parents after we returned from vacationing down South: "Things were so piled up here in my absence that I have had quite a time catching up, but at last I can see daylight. It was hard to come back from a month of do-nothing and get down to brass tacks, but I am again in the rut."

I had addressed them fondly for the first time as Mother and Dad in that letter; for the rest of his life, though, I generally referred to my father-in-law as Dr. Bell.

Occasionally Ruth's sense of humor landed us in hot water, even with her parents. One day she sent one of her regular postcards home to her folks in North Carolina, keeping them informed on developments with the newlyweds. It was postmarked October 26, 1943, about ten weeks into our marriage. At the very bottom and squeezed up along the left side, she penned an apparent afterthought: "Guess what? Bill and I are going to have an addition to our family. He's not so enthusiastic. Says it will be too much trouble, but I think it will be fun. More later. Adoringly, Ruth."

The rejoicing in the Bell household down South immediately prompted her doctor father to send us by return mail a glowing letter of congratulations—a classic of paternal pride, love, and fatherly advice. What second thoughts they might have had about their son-in-law, I could not imagine, but Dr. Bell assured us of their prayers.

For the *three* of us. For Ruth. For me. And for "Junior," the name Ruth gave the alley cat we had just adopted!

Instantly remorseful over her little joke, Ruth followed up the postcard the next day with a letter of explanation. It crossed her father's in the mail. The damage was done.

I did not let her off easily. "Now they will never believe you," I scolded her. "You've forfeited the privilege of ever getting another letter like that from your father when the real thing comes!"

She promised her folks that the next time she announced an addition to the family, it would not have whiskers and a long tail.

I rubbed it in. "Just think of your mother and daddy praying for a cat!"

Things could only get better after that.

In spite of my rough edges, the church people could not have been nicer to us. Attendance began to grow steadily, getting into the 90s by October and passing 100 two months later—about double the previous average.

It was still a basement church with high windows that we could not see out of. In the winter, visibility was obscured because of snow; in the summer, the weeds interfered. The "sort of junky" building, as Ruth described it, was redecorated free of charge by a member who was in the business, and the building committee met constantly to discuss completion plans. I preached twice on Sundays and attended youth meetings in members' homes after the evening service. In addition to a midweek prayer meeting, Ruth and I both taught Child Evangelism classes on Wednesday afternoons. She went with me on many pastoral calls.

One day, as I was driving down the street, a man driving in the opposite direction pulled up next to me.

"You're Billy Graham?" he asked.

"Yes, sir."

"I'm Torrey Johnson," he said by way of introduction.

"Oh, yes," I responded enthusiastically. "I've heard you lots of times on the radio."

"I'd like to talk with you," he said.

"Certainly, any time," I agreed.

He called on the phone a little later. "I've got too many things on my plate, with a large, growing church and my main radio program on Sunday afternoon," he said. "I have another radio program called *Songs in the Night*, and I'd like to give that to you. I've prayed about it and thought about it, and I think you're the one who should have it."

I said I would think and pray about it too, and I would have a talk with the deacons at my church.

"Okay," he said, "call me when you've made a decision."

So I took it to the deacons at the church. It would cost $150 a week for the radio time on WCFL in Chicago, a station heard in the Midwest and into the South and East. A big decision! Little did I realize that it was one of the turning points of my life.

Ruth did not like the idea at first. Ministry at the Village Church—I had suggested the change of name from Western Springs Baptist Church because there were mainly Lutherans and Congregationalists (but very few Baptists) in the surrounding area—already was demanding more than enough of my time and strength. She figured I would be in the Army chaplaincy before long, and right after the war we would be on the mission field.

Initially, the church board rejected the idea due to lack of money. But when the needs for financing and staffing were provided, God's answer seemed clear to go ahead. Bob Van Kampen agreed to provide the start-up funding. The quartet from the Wheaton College women's glee club who had sung with me from time to time agreed to come on Sunday nights and sing for the live forty-five-minute program.

The first thing I wanted to do was to get a marquee name on the program. It was unlikely that listeners would have heard of our church, or of me. But what about George Beverly Shea, the handsome bass baritone who at that time was a staff announcer at the Moody Bible Institute's station, WMBI?

In my bold fashion, I headed to Moody and went to the radio station office located on the top floor of the main building. There I asked for Mr. Shea. I could see him through the glass door of his office, but a secretary said he was busy in a meeting. Well, I did not want to waste a trip to Chicago, and I believed as much in the importance of his being on our program as I did in the Fuller brushes I had sold not so many years before. So I waited until I saw his door open for a moment, and then I brushed past his secretary.

"Mr. Shea," I said, "I'm sorry to intrude, but I just have a quick proposal for you."

"Yes?"

"My name is Billy Graham, and I'm pastor of the Village Church in Western Springs."

"I've heard of you," he offered.

"Torrey Johnson has asked us to take over his Sunday night radio show," I said, too frightened to be flattered by Shea's recognition of my name, "and I'm convinced that the program would be most successful if you'd agree to appear on it."

"Well, I don't know . . ."

I plunged on, outlining how I saw his singing fitting into the forty-five-minute program. I think he agreed to give it a try only because he could see that that was the only way he was going to get rid of me.

We did not have a typewriter, let alone a secretary, so Ruth helped me write the scripts. The program consisted of vignettes about three minutes long, in which the preacher would say a few things, and then there was a song. I preached for the radio program for the first time in early December, and several weeks later, following our Sunday evening service, we started broadcasting live from our basement church in Western Springs. We signed on with the program's same theme song, "Songs in the Night," inspired by Job 35:10, with lyrics by George Graves and music by Wendell P. Loveless.

Our church, which sat only 125 at the most, was filled for the first broadcast. Very few people except our own congregation knew that Bev Shea would be there. But one visitor was an emotionally troubled woman who had been following him around obsessively for some months. He was embarrassed by all her attention. At the end of the program, Bev whispered to me and asked if I could sneak him out.

I knew of an exit through the furnace room in back. We had to balance our way across a single plank in the dark to make our way through. Bev fell off, but he made his escape.

I built my radio talks around the events of the day. Keeping up with current events through newspapers and radio news programs, I began each message with a reference to something people would have been hearing and talking about that very day. Then I moved into a biblical message, showing that God and the Scriptures are relevant to every problem.

That first broadcast really put our church on the map. People started piling into our little building on Sunday nights to watch the show, and we got letters from listeners all over the Midwest. The

Chicago Tribune sent a reporter out to write a story about our radio ministry. My filling station attendant in Hinsdale gave me $1 to support the program. A poor woman sent us 10¢. A carload of people listening as they rode took up a collection for us on the spot. When I went over the books with the chairman of the radio committee at the end of the first two months, our average income from listeners had been $105.07 per week. The Lord kept the budget in the black with other contributions.

To add to the excitement, station WMBI signed us up to broadcast our regular Sunday morning service from the church during March and April of 1944. One of our listeners wrote in to request fifty copies of my latest sermon—mixed metaphors and all. I was swamped by all the incoming mail, which I had to handle personally. We asked for volunteers. Only one showed up, a young woman from Knoxville, Tennessee, whose husband had a defense job nearby.

The year-end flurry of activity kept us from going south at Christmas, our first time away from our families at the holiday season. It made us terribly homesick to hear our landlords downstairs playing Christmas carols on their old Victrola while they bustled around trimming the house and wrapping packages. My cousin Steve Hunter, who was stationed at nearby Great Lakes Naval Training Station, came on Christmas Eve to spend the weekend with us; Ruth made us both hang up our stockings. And the Lanes invited us to Wheaton for Christmas dinner at their house.

By the middle of April, with an increasing number of people not only attending the church but coming to faith in Christ, Ruth and I began to feel that we might be there for several years. But two factors were working to redirect our lives.

First, there was discontent among a few of the deacons about my going away for evangelistic meetings so frequently. Of course, they had agreed to those meetings when I accepted their call, and the church letterhead listed me as "pastor/evangelist." At the same time, they probably were justified, because I was accepting a number of invitations to speak in several surrounding states.

Second, from my standpoint, preaching throughout the Midwest made me restless with the pastorate. It seemed to me, perhaps because of the war, that the whole world was ripe for the Gospel. I wanted to be moving, traveling, preaching, anywhere and everywhere. Ruth soon began to realize, as she later told me, that her life was going to be one of good-byes. Already it seemed I was gone as much as I was home.

That pattern was made even worse when I got another call from Torrey Johnson. He was heading a committee to start what was to be called Chicagoland Youth for Christ. The plan was to reach the flood of servicemen and young people who hit Michigan Avenue in Chicago on Saturday nights. The first meeting was to be held in Orchestra Hall, which sat about 3,000 and was internationally noted for its concerts. He asked me to preach an evangelistic message that first night.

Many of Torrey's friends and advisers were against my participation because I was so little known. There were many famous preachers from all over the country who might have been more likely choices, but Torrey was interested in only one thing—someone to preach the Gospel and invite young people to receive Christ. He believed I was the one for the task. I was honored and overwhelmed.

That first Saturday night—May 27, 1944—proclaiming the Gospel live before a large crowd (the auditorium was nearly full), I was tense, *very* tense, but I found I had great liberty in speaking. When 40 came forward to receive Christ, it was one of the most humbling and spiritually encouraging moments of my life up to that time.

Other Saturday night Youth for Christ (YFC) rallies were springing up in Indianapolis, Philadelphia, and Detroit, and I was asked to go to each. When I filled in for Torrey Johnson on short notice in Detroit, I took my first plane ride.

Nevertheless, my constant absences understandably caused some concern in my Western Springs congregation. Things came to a head when I got back from a week of preaching services in Columbus, Ohio, in March 1944.

Good Presbyterian that she was, Ruth could not tolerate those Baptists "running their preacher," she wrote home. "You can't have a lot of respect for a pastor who is just a button for everyone to push."

Still, I was probably out of line. I got upset when someone remarked that the church would have to cut my pay if I went off much more. *What* pay? Thinking of my very modest salary of $40 a week, I told them that I was their pastor, not their employee, and that if they deducted 1¢, they could start looking for another man. They were not used to that kind of straight talk, and maybe it was good for them. But to this day I am not sure it was right for me to say it.

Harder to take than that, though, was the superior attitude some of them had toward the new believers and people from other denominations who were coming our way. It was a judgmental attitude based on different lifestyles and associations. Take, for example, the concert pianist and orchestra conductor who was married to a former chorus girl—not the right type for our congregation, some thought. By contrast, Ruth and I found such people refreshing; we enjoyed their enthusiasm and earnestness in their newfound Christian life. They helped us to believe more than ever in the power of the Gospel to produce the more abundant life the Bible described.

One Sunday night, I bluntly (and perhaps brashly) told the people from the pulpit that some of them needed to confess the sin of troublemaking. I told them I would get the job done in Western Springs that God had brought me there for, regardless of their attitudes and opposition. Nobody talked back. But there remained an underlying tension that contributed to my restlessness about staying.

There were plenty of opportunities to leave for greener pastures. There was a big church in Fort Wayne, Indiana, that wanted me to come as pastor. And one in Chicago with an office staff, great music, a large salary, and a home for the pastor. As I recall, even Wheaton College got into the act, with a request for me to become one of their field representatives. None of the opportunities, however, seemed compelling enough for me to forsake our suburban basement flock, nor did I sense that God was calling me to do so.

But a couple of things happened to shorten the pastorate.

I was accepted into the Army's chaplaincy program. I would have passed my previous physical in Chicago and joined up earlier but for the humiliating fact that I was three pounds underweight. I had requested a couple more months to fatten up. The Army granted the extension.

The second thing was completely beyond my control. Ruth had just gotten home from a visit to Montreat in September 1944, and I had worked hard to get the apartment in order, adding gladiolus in the dining room, carnations in the living room, and rosebuds in the bedroom. That was enough domestic activity to make any man sick! And I was. In bed. It seemed like a toothache, but one worse than I had ever experienced. Dr. Richard Matthies made a tentative diagnosis that sounded ridiculous to a twenty-six-year-old man and his wife.

Mumps?

Mumps it was. Ruth applied hot packs, but they did nothing to alleviate the pain. She thought I looked funny, but I felt frantic. That very night, attorney James Bennett was to speak in our church. A funeral was scheduled for Wednesday afternoon. The night of the funeral, I was to begin two weeks of meetings at a church in Roseland, on Chicago's South Side. But mumps would keep me in bed for at least two weeks, it was estimated.

That did it! I had put on the three pounds the Army wanted, but now, because of the mumps, I could not go to Harvard, where the chaplaincy school was located.

Ruth, daughter of a doctor, thought it was hilarious. "I spent all morning telephoning, and others called, such as Mrs. Armour," she wrote to her folks. "She just howled when I said Bill had the mumps. So did I. Everybody does when you say *mumps*." Since I was bedridden, Ruth went on to say, "I guess to be impressive I should say, 'Graham's maid speaking.'"

She talked about our plans to be in Montreat for Christmas: "The specialist said Bill's throat has a form of nervous paralysis," she wrote to her parents. "It's improving. The mumps will help him forget it." She updated them a few days later, reporting that it was definitely mumps, on both sides, and said "Ha, ha" when she told of feeding me mainly liquids and strained baby foods, and giving me a bath in bed.

Before long, however, no one was laughing. The fever raged, and the two weeks stretched into two months as mumps turned into orchitis. People prayed on my behalf, and Dr. Matthies exerted his skills to keep me alive.

A radio listener who had heard of my plight sent Ruth and me a check for $100 to finance a recovery vacation in Florida. We gratefully accepted and left as soon as I was able, which was in December. I had lost a lot more than the three pounds I had gained for the Army (indeed, a lot more than was healthy for my already slight frame), and my eyes were dark and hollow. The doctors warned us that because of the orchitis, we probably would not be able to have children. I needed desperately to regain my strength, and Florida seemed like Heaven to me.

We rented rooms in a small, inexpensive hotel on Seventy-ninth Street in Miami, about a mile from the beach. Soon we discovered that Torrey Johnson and his family were renting on the same street, but closer to the beach. I looked him up and thanked him for his confidence in me and for all the opportunities he had sent my way. He invited me fishing. . . .

6

Youth for Christ

At the end of 1944, when I was still recovering from the aftereffects
of mumps, Torrey Johnson took me fishing off the Florida coast. I
was looking forward to a relaxing day in the sun, but once we were
on the ocean, he launched into an idea that had been boiling inside
him for weeks. The early success of Chicagoland Youth for Christ
had awakened in him a dream he could hardly contain.

During the war, he argued, servicemen and -women on weekend leave from their bases often went for a fling in nearby cities.
Many Christians wanted to give them an alternative to the taverns
and honky-tonks. They organized Saturday night youth rallies in
several cities, quite independent of each other, that drew large
crowds. Snappy Gospel music, interesting testimonies, and (most of
all) short, youth-oriented sermons combined to attract thousands of
lonely, insecure, and frightened teenagers and young adults. While
still at Western Springs, I had spoken at several such youth rallies.
From Torrey's point of view, the big one had been in Chicago, where
I was the first speaker in Orchestra Hall.

As we sat bobbing in the boat, Torrey began selling me on his
blueprint for evangelism—and my part in it. He wanted to help

organize youth rallies throughout the United States, Canada, and eventually the world. He planned to call the movement Youth for Christ International. He would get his Midwest Bible Church in Chicago to let him work half-time; the other half he would spend raising money to open a YFC office downtown. I almost immediately agreed with him that this plan was of God.

"But you'll need more money than that," I said.

"I'll leave that to Bill Erny," he replied confidently. "He'll get it done."

Bill Erny was a businessman who knew about money. He was also the only one who could talk straight to Torrey, giving him advice and counsel and saying no to him when necessary.

But how could I say yes to Torrey? In an informal way, independent YFC groups were already flourishing. Roger Malsbary had charge of the group in Indianapolis; Walter Smyth was coordinating in Philadelphia; George Wilson was responsible in Minneapolis; and Jack Wyrtzen handled New York—you could hear him on the radio, opening with the words, "From Times Square . . ."

But there was no real coordination among these groups, said Torrey. They had sprung up independent of each other and were only loosely connected. What he wanted to do was bring them all together to form a national organization, with perhaps twenty-five to fifty organizational components. "I think you're the man to be our first full-time employee," he said. "Would you pray about becoming our national—and international—organizer?"

I was learning to trust God for every step of my life. I generally prayed about everything, but it seemed unnecessary to pray about *this* opportunity! My strength was returning, and I was ready to travel, ready to preach, ready to evangelize. I wouldn't be much of an organizer or paperwork man, I told Torrey, but I could not hide my enthusiasm. It was all I talked about with Ruth for the next several weeks. Finally, we decided that I should take the job.

But what would I do about my year-old pastorate? And what about my pending chaplaincy? Having seen my ministry expanding, the board of deacons at Western Springs graciously (and a few of them joyfully) accepted my resignation. The Army's chief of chaplains granted me a discharge, since the end of the war seemed in sight, agreeing with my logic that I could make a far greater contribution to the spiritual well-being of servicepeople by organizing and preaching at youth rallies than I could serving as a chaplain.

And so it was, in January of 1945, that I walked into the first-ever office of YFC in Chicago, on Wells Street in the Loop. I felt excited and exhilarated: this was where I belonged, and I could not wait to get started. But the office was a sorry excuse for corporate headquarters—a couple of bare rooms alongside the elevated train tracks, furnished with boxes. Maybe there was even a chair.

With me was Amy Anderson, Torrey's longtime secretary. One day early on she came to the door of my office. "There are two people here from Jackson, Mississippi: Dr. and Mrs. Overton," she told me. In they came.

"We want to start a youth meeting in our town. Would you come help us?" they asked.

I didn't have to think twice, because it was the only invitation I'd had. I said yes.

Of course, I felt no temptation to bask among those comforts of the Wells Street office. When more invitations came, as they soon did, I was glad to be out of town most of the time. Torrey worked from his office at the church. I was a traveling salesman again—not displaying a case of brushes this time, just brandishing my Bible.

At the beginning of 1945, in addition to Atlanta and Norfolk, I was preaching all over the Midwest. One day, as I was boarding a train with Al Smith, who was leading my singing, someone handed me a telegram from Chicago. I put it in my pocket, got onto the train, and was well on my way to Indianapolis before pulling it out. The doctor's dire warnings about my possible inability to become a father were proved false: Ruth was expecting! I was elated at the news! I could hardly wait to get there so that I could send her a telegram and wire her some flowers.

Good as the news was, it meant we had to make some major changes. We were more in love with each other than ever, and the idea of living apart, even temporarily, caused me a lot of heartache. But working full-time with Youth for Christ would keep me on the road for more than half the time. Ruth did not want to stay alone in

Chicago while I was away, especially now that she was pregnant, we agreed that she would be much better off among friends and family in familiar surroundings. We went back to North Carolina and moved in with her parents in the little, close-knit mountain community of Montreat. Her father was practicing medicine in nearby Asheville, and we were grateful she could be with them while I was on the road. Although we felt sure it was what the Lord was prompting us to do, we knew it was only a temporary, though happy, arrangement.

At that time, the military had priority on everything. To civilians like us, planes were available only on a standby basis. A very generous businessman, Mr. Walter Block of Kenosha, Wisconsin, gave an Air Travel Card to Torrey and one to me. As long as I was with YFC, I had that card and could charge a ticket to his account.

Sometimes I traveled by air, but mostly I went by Greyhound bus or by train. Because the railroads gave clergy of all denominations half-price tickets, I could take the Northwestern Railroad anywhere, have a bunk, and get some sleep for half of what the others were paying. I traveled across the country in those days, stopping in cities of all sizes.

Typical of the earliest YFC meetings was one in Atlanta's City Auditorium on February 24, 1945, where I was introduced to the crowd of 5,000 as "the director of the *Songs in the Night* broadcast in Chicago." I doubt if anyone in Atlanta had ever heard of the program. But with me on this night were a chalk artist, an Army major general, several servicemen who gave their Christian testimonies, and musicians galore—guitarist, pianist, soloist, sextet, trio, and the Salvation Army band! The press reported that this new movement, only a year old, was active in three hundred American cities.

For several months, Ruth was able to join me in various places. That made the traveling life more bearable. While we were in Atlanta, Ruth noticed a change in me.

"Every time we pass a 'kiddie shop,'" she wrote to her parents, "Bill wants to stop and window-shop. He notices every little baby in sight now, and he used to ignore them completely. Guess I ought to write a book on *Preacher Will Be a Papa*." (She had recently read the book entitled *Papa Was a Preacher*.)

As the months went by, Ruth grew bigger and bigger. She enjoyed shopping for maternity clothes. By June she could just squeeze into a size fourteen. From Pittsburgh, where I was preaching, she wrote home. She called my being with her "the nicest honeymoon we've had yet."

"Bill has to speak only once a day, which makes it nice." I hoped she meant nice for us to have time together, not nice that she had to listen to only one sermon a day!

In early July we were together in Ocean City, New Jersey, where I was preaching. We enjoyed some time sunning ourselves at the beach, but Ruth described her particular problem in a letter to her sister Rosa in Montreat: "Have the front of me toasted fairly nicely. But getting the other side is something else. A hard flat beach and I don't fit face to face. Bill suggested I scoop out a hole for my tummy."

That trip to Ocean City produced another amusing incident, as Ruth described in a hastily written letter to her parents: "When we first got there, we put some clothes in the cleaners with the promise we could get them in three days. The third day we were busy so we called for them the fourth. Found the place locked up and the man off on a two weeks' vacation. So Monday morning before we left we called on the police and after half an hour of pleading, got them to go down and break in for us. There was much ringing of burglar alarms and looks of amazement from the shoppers (it being on the main street) and loss of dignity on the part of the cops who had to climb ladders, open transoms, shut off the alarm and glare at wisecrackers who'd stick their necks in at the door and warn the cops if they didn't get out they'd have to call the police. But they were good sports and seemed to enjoy it. Found Bill's jacket and my green mesh dress but no yellow coat anywhere. Left money with the assistant pastor to have it mailed when the wretched proprietor returns."

On that same trip, we included a side excursion to New York City over the Fourth of July. Ruth noted that the Statue of Liberty looked as she expected, "only she was facing the wrong direction." Harry Emerson Fosdick's Riverside Church, a bastion of theological liberalism, was "impressive in a pagan sort of way"; it was devoid of any Christian symbol, even a cross.

Everywhere, through contact persons in various cities, I met with local pastors and lay leaders to form committees and plan rallies. In the first year, this took me from coast to coast (with plenty of places in between) and to most of the provinces of Canada, mostly by train. Additional preaching opportunities ranged from Moody Church in Chicago to Princeton Seminary in New Jersey.

Unfamiliar as I was with pregnancy timetables, I did not take Ruth all that seriously as she walked with me to the car on September 21, 1945. She did not want me to make this trip. She wanted desperately for me to be with her when the baby came.

"Bill, the pains have already begun."

"No, I don't think so," I replied confidently, as if I knew anything about labor.

"Yes, they have. The baby will be here soon!"

But I predicted it might take another two or three weeks. I kissed her good-bye and headed for a speaking engagement in Mobile, Alabama.

That evening, Virginia Leftwich Graham was born into the world, the daughter we would forever call Gigi and who enriched our lives immeasurably.

When I arrived home from Alabama and looked down at the baby in the bassinet that Ruth had trimmed with her wedding veil, I could only repeat over and over, "Hello, darling! Hello, precious!"

Proud parents that we were, we thought our daughter was perfect, from her shapely head to her pudgy toes. Her eyes were the largest Ruth had ever seen in a baby, and the way Gigi stared wide-eyed at her mother made Ruth think, This child has seen more, knows more, than I. If the poet Wordsworth was right about our arriving in this world with "intimations of immortality," that was true in Gigi's case.

When Gigi was a few months old, Ruth left her in the Bells' care from time to time and came along with me to places from Minnesota to Massachusetts. It was nice for both of us, but it emotionally pulled Ruth in two directions at once.

EUROPE 1946–1947

In March and April of 1946, Torrey led a group of six men—me among them—to Great Britain and the Continent to launch YFC there. For most of us, it was our first trip abroad.

The trip over was something of a fiasco. The military-type DC–4 plane with bucket seats left out of Chicago in the morning. Hearst newspaperman Wesley Hartzell was with us, as was Stratton Shufelt, music director of Moody Church in Chicago. Charles Templeton—a Toronto YFC organizer and pastor of Toronto's Avenue Road Church, one of the largest congregations in the city— was with us, and I remember how sick he got on the trip.

We stopped in Toronto and Montreal, and we were supposed to stop in Gander, Newfoundland. But as we neared Gander, the pilot announced over the loudspeaker system that because of a heavy snowstorm, we were going instead to a small U.S. airfield nearby.

Apparently thinking that the plane's passengers were a vaude-ville troupe, the social director at the military base hastily scheduled a late-night performance. Torrey didn't tell him we were a Youth for Christ team! The audience in the packed theater whistled and cheered during the first part of the meeting as Chuck told stories. They roared at Strat Shufelt's rendition of "Shortnin' Bread." But when Torrey appeared on the stage, they started to yell.

"Where are the girls?" I heard. "Show us the legs!"

When Strat sang again, they booed.

Backstage we had prayer, and then I had to go out and face them. I apologized for not being the entertainment they had ex-pected and gave my testimony.

The base commander was furious and wanted to throw us in jail, but eventually we were able to resume our trip.

Meantime, in London, Gavin Hamilton had organized a group of evangelical pastors to greet us and listen to our talk on Youth for Christ work in America. But our plane, after being refueled at Shannon, Ireland, was diverted to Scotland because of bad weather over London. As a result, we had to travel down to London by train and arrived late for the meeting.

The pastors seemed patient, though, and they asked each one of us to give a talk. None of us had spoken to a British audience before. I had some advantage because the majority of them had some connection with the Plymouth Brethren; I had met with Brethren in Wheaton and knew their methods and terminology. So when I got up, I told them that Dr. H. A. Ironside, pastor of Moody Church in Chicago, had a saying: any real evangelical theologian always milked the Plymouth Brethren cow!

Among evangelicals in England, Dr. Ironside was well known as one of the great preachers in the world, though I don't think he was ever ordained. He had been a Brethren and had been a missionary to the Native Americans in Arizona and New Mexico, and he knew the Bible better than anybody I think I ever met. I remember sitting beside him once at the Moody Church, where he was to speak at a Youth for Christ meeting. He went sound asleep and began to snore, and when it was his time to speak, I just nudged him with my elbow. He got up, opened the Bible, and spoke from the passage he had opened to at random. It was tremendous!

Alan Redpath, pastor of Duke Street Church in Richmond, a suburb of London, was impressed with my words and came up afterward to ask if I would preach for him on Sunday. I said I was happy to do it.

To rest after the long plane ride, we spent several nights at Hildenborough Hall, run by Tom Rees, Britain's leading evangelist. He and his wife, Jean, had developed the Hall as a large conference building for young people. The speaker that particular evening was Stephen Olford, and we were invited to attend the meetings and to each give a word.

Chuck Templeton and I went around together all the time on that trip; we roomed together and had a lot of fun, becoming real pals. A Canadian, he impressed us all with his knowledge of the history and culture of places like Ireland.

The travels of Odysseus held no more wonders than ours for us, as we visited England, Scotland, Ireland, Sweden, and Norway. Everywhere we traveled, we were joined by local church leaders who contributed mightily not only to our success but also to our survival.

The whole city of London looked to us as if it had been destroyed. St. Paul's Cathedral was still standing; so were the Houses of Parliament, although they had been bombed. The people were in a happy mood. The war was finished; no longer did the sirens wail, sending people hustling into the Underground. The British still ruled one-fifth of the world: India, Canada, and Australia were still being run by the Colonial Office.

We stayed mostly in homes and run-down hotels wherever we went.

To cover all the territory, we split up into teams, and this led to diverse adventures. We were there less than a year after the end of World War II, and we encountered shortages, hardships, and rationing everywhere. Food especially preoccupied us, as it did most people there. There was envy for the Dublin team, who enjoyed fruit juice and real coffee for breakfast, along with ham and eggs. Wes observed that the only eggs in London were in museums; in Britain, he added, "everything edible has become extinct, and cold plaster of paris has become an acceptable substitute for ice cream." He and Torrey reveled in the huge smorgasbord featured on a Danish steamer.

The team visiting Stockholm and Oslo held sixteen meetings in four days, with crowds of up to 4,500 and a couple of thousand turned away. In Norway especially, where people were still recovering from the oppressive Nazi occupation, enthusiasm for YFC ran high.

During the first three weeks, I was in the group that toured Great Britain from one end to the other, holding three and four meetings a day, almost every one packed to capacity. We might be in a public hall on a Saturday night, in a fashionable church on a Sunday night, and in a moviehouse on a weekday night after the film. The people, still reeling from the war, were starved for hope and hungry for God.

After a whirlwind tour of Holland, Denmark, Belgium, and France with Chuck Templeton during the next three weeks, we finally headed home.

Right after we got back to the United States, we had a board meeting of Youth for Christ at a hotel in Swampscott, Massachusetts. A scant two weeks after that, I preached at the first of a half-dozen rallies spread over the summer from Toronto to San Antonio, and from New Jersey to Oregon, as well as at a couple of youth conferences.

Gavin Hamilton urged me to come and hold campaigns in Great Britain. He would be glad to stay over there, he said, and set up the meetings. I felt in my heart that my future was in this type of evangelism. Torrey pointed out that it would cost a lot of money, however, and said I would have to raise it all myself.

I asked Ruth to leave our year-old daughter, Gigi, with the extended family of grandparents, aunts, and uncles in Montreat and join me as soon as she could. I asked Strat Shufelt if he would come with me as song leader, since he was well known in Britain. He was a handsome man with a lot of charisma, and he loved the Lord with all his heart. He and his wife, Marge, agreed to go with me; but two or three weeks before we were to leave, he called to say they just couldn't leave their two little girls.

So I turned to Jack Shuler's song leader, Cliff Barrows. He and his wife, Billie, said they would be thrilled to go. From time to time, Cliff and I had crossed paths; I had seen him lead the singing at Winona Lake, for example, and thought he had done a fine job. So Cliff and Billie Barrows came to my rescue. During this summer of 1946, I recruited them to form a team, with Cliff to lead the singing, Billie to play the piano, me to do the preaching. Ruth would do the praying while I preached. (Right from the start, Cliff, in order to distinguish between me and his wife, called me Bill.)

We had no idea how long we would be gone.

We got on a ship in New York and sailed to Southampton, where Gavin met us, along with a young Methodist preacher, Joe Blinco, and a leading evangelical layman in that part of England, Oliver Stott. They had already set up meetings in Southampton's Methodist Central Hall.

After arriving in England early in October, we conducted rallies throughout England and Wales. In the early part of the tour, we spent a weekend in Wales in the home of a non-Christian couple who gave us the best they had, which wasn't much on the husband's meager income of £3 or £4 per week. That visit gave us a real appreciation for the hardships they endured. For breakfast we had a heated tomato, along with a hot drink that was more chicory than coffee. Later in the day, we had some chicken soup (though I'm not sure a chicken had ever passed through it), along with some bread. George Wilson was with us to handle the arrangements and finances for YFC, and he and I had a single bed to sleep in. So we took turns: halfway through the night, we exchanged places, the one who had been sleeping on the floor moving up to the bed. It was very cold, especially for the one on the floor, because there was no heat whatsoever.

Ruth did not feel free to join me until December 9. From behind a fence at the London airport, as I waited for the passengers to get through customs, I jokingly shouted to Ruth that the customs inspector was going to put her in jail. It did not seem funny to her at the time!

Although she got a warm, husbandly reception from me, she got a damp, chilly one from England. At one of the first meetings she attended, the fog inside the church was so thick that it looked as if everyone were smoking. From the platform, I could not even see the back of the church. Despite the presence of a potbellied barrel with some hot coals in it where the transept and main aisle crossed, it was as bitter cold inside the church as outside.

And Ruth had difficulty adjusting to the food rationing most British had to endure. When she first tasted the powdered scrambled eggs, she thought she would choke; these eggs had never seen a chicken, she managed to say. And the sausages were made out of bread. But outside of London, the people gave us eggs and bacon, probably their whole week's ration. And everybody still seemed to have plenty of tea.

In Reading one evening, the building was packed with people. Halfway through my sermon, I heard a voice of protest coming from someone in the middle of the church. The speaker was a minister wearing an ecclesiastical collar; I could not tell his denomination, for all British ministers wore such collars. "I don't believe a word of it," he shouted, claiming that I was teaching heresy.

When a woman in the balcony stood up and got into a public argument with the minister, his wife got hold of his coat and tried to pull him down. He kept on shouting, though, trying all the while to free himself from his wife's grasp. The ushers got hold of him finally and led him from the church.

I knew that the Anglican Church was the state church, and the most important church in Britain, but I had very little knowledge of its history. What I did know I had learned in a church history course taught by Dr. Minder at Florida Bible Institute. This was one of my first times to preach in an Anglican church.

It was at that church that I met John Cordle, who had driven down from London in a car whose windows had been broken in. When I rode back with him, the car's interior was ice cold. We had to hold pieces of cardboard in the window spaces to keep from freezing to death.

At Bradford one evening, we held a meeting in the local theater after the movie. The chairman of the meeting happened to be a certain Mr. Bradford. When Ruth entered the unlighted doorway, she itched to turn on bright spotlights and to pass out handbills to the people passing by; unfortunately, neither option was available to her. Taking a seat as Billie began the piano prelude, Ruth counted an audience of 6 grown people (including herself), 4 youngsters, and a big black cat snoozing on the back of a seat.

The stage curtain was not rolled up far enough to conceal the advertisements painted on it:

LEG TROUBLES

VARICOSE VEINS

RHEUMATISM

SAY IT WITH FLOWERS

SNACK BAR

On the stage backdrop, in gaudy greens, yellows, and reds, was painted a garden scene that looked to Ruth like rows of green mausoleums leading to a central fountain.

But people steadily dribbled in until there was a respectable attendance by the time Billie Barrows had finished her prelude. Under Cliff's direction, they sang the lively old Charles Wesley hymn "And Can It Be?" When I invited them to receive Christ after my sermon on the rich young ruler, 23 came forward for counseling and prayer with the 4 of us.

Ruth was somewhat more impressed at the local Baptist church, which seated 1,000. Before the recently hired minister had arrived, Sunday attendance had averaged 9 in the morning and 20 at night. Yet 100 showed up for our morning service. Ruth's enthusiasm for the whole enterprise grew as we saw people respond to the Word of God.

With forty, perhaps fifty rallies behind us by mid-December, we were very tired and ready for a break. Somewhere Ruth saw an ad featuring a palm tree waving in southern France. Since we were chilled to the bone, we immediately made reservations. We took off from London for the hour-and-a-half flight to Paris on December 16, landing on an airstrip that was covered, where there had been bomb craters, with heavy net wire over the soft brown earth.

We were fortunate to get a taxi driver for our sight-seeing; he was a Russian expatriate and could speak GI American. He said, "Hokay, Jackson," to everything, so we called him Jackson. (His real name was something like Leon Poustilnik.) He took us out to Versailles Palace, where Ruth thought the guide looked as if he had been there since the days of Louis XIV. At the old Roman amphitheater in Nîmes, south of Paris, she wondered whether the structure might ever be used again as a place for throwing Christians to the lions. In that historic area where so many Huguenots had been slain, we met with fellow believers and enjoyed eating with them and smiling at them, but very little conversation; we did not really know each other's language. But we had a refreshing time; we prayed together, they in French and we in English.

With tremendous anticipation, we headed for Nice to spend Christmas. Our first glimpse of the beautiful Mediterranean was through the train windows en route from Marseilles. On the other side of the tracks, though, along the coast, ruins of houses flattened by the war alternated with pillboxes.

Our spirits really took a dive when we learned that the hotel we had planned to stay in could not (or would not) honor our reservations. Without a word of warning from our travel agent, we had been bumped to the Balmoral Hotel in Monte Carlo. We knew very little about the tiny principality tucked along the shore between

My embarrassing experience on the White House lawn after meeting with President Truman, July 14, 1950. *From left:* Jerry Beavan, Cliff Barrows, Billy Graham, Grady Wilson.

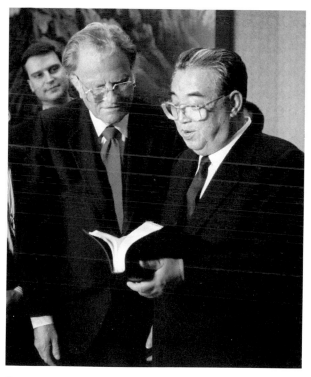

Pyongyang, North Korea, April 2, 1992: presenting a Bible to President Kim Il Sung. *Left:* my son Ned.

My first known photograph at six months, with my mother, Morrow Graham.

With my father, Frank Graham, and my sister Catherine in Blowing Rock, North Carolina, August 20, 1925.

I was born on November 7, 1918, in the downstairs bedroom of this frame farmhouse outside Charlotte, North Carolina.

With my sister
Catherine in our
goat cart.

*On extreme
left, in black
robe:* At age
six, graduating
from Sunday
school primary
department.

The main milking barn on the Graham farm, where I milked cows twice a day.

Morrow and Frank Graham in later years.

The W. F. Graham family in 1962, shortly before my father's death. With mother and father are *(from left)* Catherine, Billy, Melvin, and Jean.

The Graham family in Florida during Christmas, 1936, shortly before I enrolled in Florida Bible Institute.

Perhaps the earliest photograph of me preaching, about 1939, at Swan Lake Bible Conference, Melrose (near Palatka), Florida.

At Florida Bible Institute, with Dean John Minder and visiting friend Jimmie Johnson.

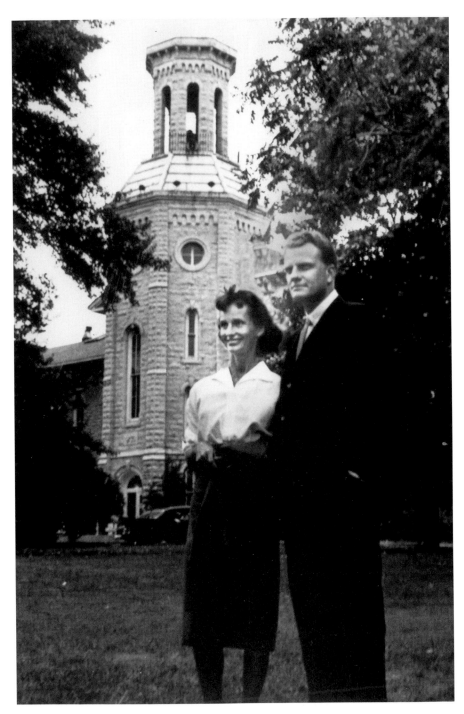

With Ruth Bell at Wheaton College, Illinois, shortly after our engagement, 1941.

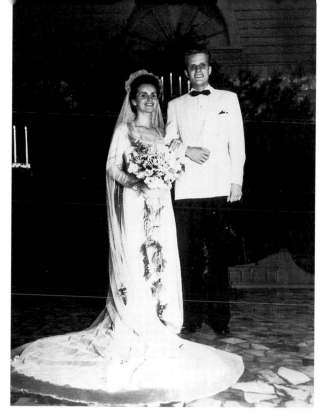

With Ruth on our
wedding day, August 13,
1943, Montreat
Presbyterian Church,
Montreat, North
Carolina.

The young pastor and his
wife, Western Springs,
Illinois, about 1944.

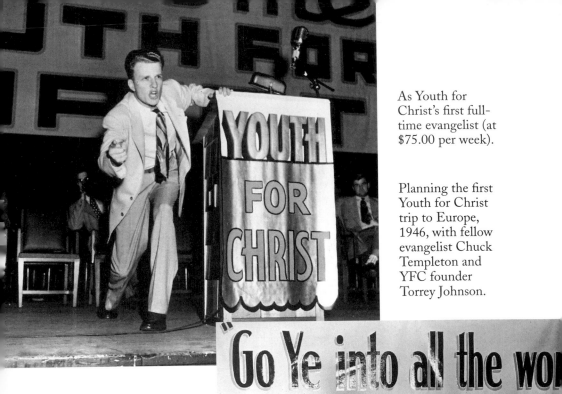

As Youth for Christ's first full-time evangelist (at $75.00 per week).

Planning the first Youth for Christ trip to Europe, 1946, with fellow evangelist Chuck Templeton and YFC founder Torrey Johnson.

America's youngest college president with vice president T. W. Wilson, Northwestern Schools, Minneapolis, Minnesota, about 1949.

France and Italy, but we knew enough to ask ourselves how an evangelistic team could find rest in a gambling resort. Ruth and Billie were especially appalled.

At the Balmoral's front desk, I flinched when I found out that the bill would run $5 per day for two persons, including meals. We just could not afford that. But then I had an inspiration. We were carrying with us a large quantity of women's nylon stockings. Why, I did not know, but Mr. Cole, a hosiery manufacturer in North Carolina, knowing of the shortages in Europe, had given them to me for whatever eventuality. I gingerly inquired of the hotel manager if he might just consider a payment under the barter system—my contribution being something that not only would be of interest to his wife but also was impossible to obtain anywhere else in Europe.

His eyes were overjoyed when he heard my proposition, but his voice was subdued. He just might consider it, he said, if word did not get around to the other guests. As a pastor, I told him, I knew the meaning of confidentiality. Each morning, then, in the privacy of his office, I presented him with a pair of nylons, and each morning he marked our bill, which included not only our room but also three meals, paid. Ten pairs for ten days. And ten more pairs for Cliff and Billie's room.

So began our life of "luxury" in Monte Carlo, overlooking the Mediterranean, where rarities like fruit, butter, and eggs were available. And there was wine in abundance, which Ruth thought was the nastiest stuff she had ever tasted. She was astonished to see children drinking it instead of milk. For five or six days I walked past pineapples for sale, wishing I could have one to eat. Billie, Cliff, Ruth, and I joined in praying for that fruit, which was selling at the time for the equivalent of $5 a pineapple. (We never did try one.) That's not the only flavor we craved: for a chocolate soda—if we could have found such a treat along the Riviera—we would gladly have traded two pairs of nylons. Then poor Billie Barrows came down with the flu and couldn't enjoy food of any kind for a time.

The blissful quiet of Christmas Eve was shattered five minutes before midnight with a cannon blast that nearly blew us out of bed. Was it war all over again? No, it was just some friendly fire—blast after blast every minute until midnight, when the explosions were replaced by the ringing of all the church bells, summoning the Monegasques to Mass. After services, the people drank and danced in the streets until dawn, but we slept through most of their celebration.

On Christmas afternoon, Ruth and I took a horse and buggy ride toward the Italian border. Everywhere along the way we saw evidence of the war; building after building was pockmarked with shell holes. It was a sobering reminder of the suffering so many had experienced so recently. And everywhere, because they had no money, girls were trying to sell themselves, which grieved us both greatly. We were deeply burdened and prayed daily for the people of Europe who had suffered so much and now had so little.

Further meetings had been scheduled in Great Britain early in the new year. A couple of days after Christmas, we headed north, with stopovers in Geneva and elsewhere in Switzerland. Coffee on the Swedish airliner was the genuine article, and we were happy with a hotel room that overlooked the Rhône River. It was nice to see Kleenex again, and chewing gum. Ruth exclaimed with delight when we were served bottled Cokes at lunch!

On January 3, 1947, we took the train to Paris for a day's sightseeing before an evening flight to London. At the station, the redcap responded rudely to Ruth. We four Americans, and an Indian army major who had shared our compartment, traded heated comments with the Frenchman through two Dutch travelers who came to our rescue as interpreters. Ruth thought it might be a good thing to meet more such obnoxious people; it would be a way of getting our blood pressure pumped up and thus getting warm enough to fight off the damp and the cold in England!

Where was Jackson, our Russian taxi driver, when we needed him? He finally appeared and showed us some more sights. We were disappointed at not being able to see the Bastille. It had been torn down 150 years earlier, he informed us—but that was news to us. At Napoleon's Tomb, the guide told us men to take off our hats in respect to the emperor's memory. And we managed to stop in a shop where Cliff and I bought inexpensive rabbit-fur coats for our wives.

Due to fog in London, our plane flight was canceled. We had to make reservations for the train to Calais the next morning, where we would get the ferry to England. After Jackson drove us to the station, he gave me some francs for our breakfast on the train. I gave him a Gospel of John, praying that he would read it (or at least use it to practice his English).

Riding through northern France, we again saw more war damage—buildings and bridges in ruins, and fields pitted with shell holes, craters, foxholes, and machine-gun nests. Crossing the English Channel, we saw the white cliffs of Dover, made so famous in the popular wartime song.

The creature comforts we had been reintroduced to on the Continent were still pretty much lacking in the English Midlands that winter. There was no central heat in the Westleigh Hotel, where we stayed. The common bath at the end of the drafty hall was also unheated. The small gas heater in our room ran only on the endless insertion of penny coins. Ruth huddled beside it in her robe, getting scorched on one side and frostbitten on the other. She moved away a little when Billie Barrows came in to say that Cliff had stuck his fountain pen too near their heater; it had caught fire and burned up before he could put the flame out.

Overcrowding in the hotel forced some rearrangements. The manager shifted Ruth and me to his private sitting room, which had a daybed with four thin blankets. Ruth had to put on a sweater and two pairs of pants under her pajamas, and she slept with her slippers on. She was still cold, so she got up and added her wool robe and her rabbit-fur coat. I had on long wool underwear, flannel pajamas, wool socks, a heavy wool sweater, and a big overcoat. No wonder so many Britons had such ruddy cheeks in those days!

Gigi was just a year old and staying with the Bells in Montreat. We never tired of getting reports about her, but poor Ruth reached a point where she wrote in desperation to her folks from Paris. "I closed my eyes yesterday just to picture her, and you know, it was hard for me to remember just how she looks even. In a way it does not seem like I have a little girl at all."

After two months, Ruth felt she had to return home to our little daughter, Gigi, for whom she had longed every day. I still had two more months of meetings scheduled in Great Britain, so she would fly home alone on February 4. Our meetings had already started in

Ireland by the day of her departure—we were staying in a tiny rooming house on the coast about fifteen miles out of Dublin, and the icy wind blew from morning to night. I had the flu and I had to kiss her good-bye without being able to take her to the airport. I was very lonely when she left and got a little homesick. But Ruth's letters cheered me up.

When she arrived back in Montreat, she was overjoyed when Gigi greeted her with "Mama! Mama!" But Ruth quickly found out that Gigi was calling any young woman "Mama" and any young man "Daddy."

I was very worried at that time about our finances: we were down almost to our last dollar. I wrote a letter to industrialist R. G. LeTourneau. He was the only wealthy man I knew in America who might give us consideration. I told him our predicament, adding that it would take $7,000 to finish the job. Two weeks later, a letter came from him with a cashier's check for exactly that amount.

In Birmingham for a series of meetings, some of us stayed at the home of the Eric Hutchings family. Cliff and Billie Barrows were guests of Mr. and Mrs. A.G.B. Owen, wonderful Christians. Mr. Owen was wealthy, best known for the fast automobiles he built; the two couples became close friends.

R. G. LeTourneau himself came to one of our meetings. He had built a factory near Newcastle to produce earth-moving equipment for Britain's postwar rebuilding process. He had sent his brother-in-law, a preacher, to scout the initial prospects. On that brother's advice, the plant was built, and apparently it wasn't a success. LeTourneau had come to see for himself.

By airmail Ruth sent some vitamin and mineral pills her father had had specially prepared for me. "Now, darling," she admonished me, "please—for a change—do what the doctor says."

Ruth was bothered also by something not completely unrelated to the illness I was battling when she left. She thought I was unwise to push myself so hard in the Lord's service. "I think sometimes it is easier to drive ourselves to actual death than it is to take ourselves firmly in hand and make ourselves do the wise thing," she wrote from home. "Without sounding funny, it is better to rest awhile above the earth than to rest forever beneath it." Then her theology came to her rescue. "While we do not expect to rest forever beneath it, so far as your present usefulness would be concerned, you may as well be."

I wrote to her, of course, but before she received my answering letter, she wrote me another. That one really caught me off-guard. It was about our marriage. Her intuition told her that I was feeling guilty and that I was worried there might be an estrangement between us, caused by my obsession with the ministry and my repeated absences.

"In your thinking we have grown apart due to the wide separation of our ways and interests," she wrote. "But I feel closer to you than ever before. . . . Wherever you are, I go with you in mind and heart—praying for you continually. You, with your broader sphere of service, your worldwide circle of friends, your unlimited interests and responsibilities, would find it more difficult to be with me in mind and heart and prayers. . . . Don't judge my heart-following of all your goings and comings by your interest in and understanding of my two-by-four world. And since my body was able to follow my heart for two months, the world you travel will seem much more personal and real to me. Your problems, thrills, heartaches, and glorious victories—much more my very own. . . . Take good care of your precious self. There is so much yet to be done for God, and so much love yet unexplored and unexperienced for us." She was right—and more than that, I marveled at her sensitivity and insight.

Ruth had been writing poetry since her girlhood in China. I am not sure when she wrote this poem, but people can read between the lines to understand how heartfelt were those convictions she expressed to me in her letter.

Love
without clinging;
cry—
if you must—
but privately cry;
the heart will adjust
to the newness of loving
in practical ways:
cleaning
and cooking
and sorting out clothes,
all say, "I love you,"
when lovingly done.

So—
love
without clinging;
cry—
if you must—
but privately cry;
the heart will adjust
to the length of his stride,
the song he is singing,
the trail he must ride,
the tensions that make him
the man that he is,
the world he must face,
the life that is his.

So—
love
without clinging;
cry—
if you must—
but privately cry;
the heart will adjust
to being the heart,
not the forefront of life;
a part of himself,
not the object—
his wife.

So—
love!

I returned home from our European tour at the beginning of April 1947, having been gone for six months, knowing that Ruth and I had weathered the slight tension in our relationship. Those months had also been a time of spiritual challenge and growth. My contact with British evangelical leaders during this and subsequent trips, especially with Stephen Olford, deepened my personal spiritual life. I was beginning to understand that Jesus Himself was our victory, through the Holy Spirit's power. I developed an even deeper hunger for Bible study and new biblical insights for my messages. I quoted the Bible more frequently than ever before.

At a YFC rally in Minneapolis, Minnesota, back in February 1945—only a month after I had joined Torrey Johnson's new venture—a man heard me preach who was now about to change my life radically. And that, incidentally, would lead me into great confusion about a great many things.

111

7

College President

NORTHWESTERN SCHOOLS 1948–1952

I had been with Youth for Christ for only a year or so when the venerable evangelical leader and educator Dr. W. B. Riley invited me to speak at a fundamentalist conference sponsored by his Northwestern Schools in Minneapolis.

I enplaned in Seattle. In Vancouver I had to switch planes, this time to a Lockheed Lodestar, in the pouring rain. Above the clouds in the moonlight, we could see the beautiful Canadian Rockies. After a few hours in the air, however, somewhere over Alberta, the stewardess came back and saw that I was the only one of the fourteen passengers who was still awake.

"We're having some difficulty," she whispered.

"What is it?"

"All the airports within the range of our fuel are closed because of snow," she explained.

"So we're going back to Vancouver?"

"We don't have enough fuel."

"What are we going to do?" I asked.

"That's what the pilot is trying to figure out right now."

I was, to say the least, nervous. Then the intercom crackled loudly enough to wake everyone up. The pilot announced that he had located a radio tower and was in communication with the ground. He was being told to set the plane down as soon as possible. The storm was worsening. There was an open field somewhere below, he understood. He found a hole in the clouds and dived through it.

"It's going to be bumpy," he said. "We're going to have to use our own lights to see what we're doing. It's a plowed field, but with the snow cover I won't know which way the furrows are running. I'll leave the wheels up, and we'll slide in the snow."

The stewardess told us to lean forward and bury our head between our knees.

The pilot reassured us that we were so low on fuel that there should be no fire.

When we landed, we bumped hard. People screamed and hollered as we came to an abrupt stop. Several of the passengers suffered severe bruises from the seatbelts, but no one was killed or seriously injured. I too had some bruises but was otherwise all right.

We spent what was left of the night in the plane. The pilot's radio must have been working; he was in touch with a small town nearby. People there promised to send out a wagon with a team of horses at first light. The wagon took us to a waiting bus, and the bus took us the rest of the way to town. There the airline put us up in a boardinghouse. I was so shaken from the ordeal that I collapsed into bed and went right to sleep, although it was late morning. About an hour later, I was awakened by loud knocking. At the door was a Canadian Mountie.

"I need you to come with me," he said.

"Why?" I asked.

"A bank robber was registered in this room last night. Until we can be sure who you are, you'll have to remain at the station with me."

Fortunately, the pilot and the stewardess were able to identify me as a fellow passenger.

I eventually made it to Minnesota and spoke as scheduled. Dr. Riley startled me by saying privately that he believed I was God's man to replace him as president of Northwestern Schools.

Dr. Riley had established Northwestern in 1902 as a response to requests from young people in his congregation to give them systematic, intensive Bible study. Later he incorporated into his Bible school a liberal arts college and a theological seminary.

He was now in his middle eighties, and I was in my late twenties. I didn't take his offer seriously.

This was not my first contact with Dr. Riley. Back in February 1945, the venerable clergyman and educator had sat on the platform in the old Minneapolis Auditorium as I preached at a Youth for Christ rally. Some 44 people responded to the Invitation that night, and he shared our joy. Next morning, he phoned one of his personal assistants at the school to ask who I was. Later he remembered that he had met me at Florida Bible Institute in the late thirties; he used to come south in the winter with Mrs. Riley and stay on the campus both as tourist and guest lecturer.

For more than forty years, he had pastored First Baptist Church, a large church in downtown Minneapolis, making it one of the great preaching stations of the Midwest. He was an intellectual, a deep student of the Bible, and a man who spoke with authority and had the respect of liberals and fundamentalists alike. In vigorous contention with his denomination, then called the Northern Baptist Convention, he battled theological liberalism on many fronts, including the educational. William Jennings Bryan was reported to have called him "the greatest Christian statesman in the American pulpit."

Dr. Riley had the persuasive charisma of an Old Testament prophet: his figure was stately, his snow-white hair wavy, his nose hawkish, his eyes burning. To that charisma was added the formidable combination of his being both a scholar and a renowned preacher. He was a graduate of Southern Baptist Seminary and was looked upon as a national leader, especially among theological conservatives.

In my more thoughtful and prayerful moments, I thought it might be just possible to become president of Northwestern. The lure was to lead an educational institution in a different direction from most of the other Bible schools and Christian colleges in the United States. The sort of school I envisioned was one from which we might send young people on fire with Jesus Christ and evangelism to the ends of the world.

What Dr. Riley wanted was a young man like he himself had been sixty years before—someone who could instill Northwestern students with a passion to win people to Christ. He also wanted someone who had the potential for nurturing student recruitment, prayer support, and fund-raising among a broad constituency. With my nationwide Youth for Christ contacts and my growing visibility as an evangelist, it must have seemed to him that I met all his qualifications. That there might be educational and administrative deficiencies in me apparently did not bother him; he felt that a properly equipped staff and faculty could make up for those to a large extent. He also had a strong board, with fifty directors.

The matter came to a head late in the summer of 1947. I was speaking at the annual Northwestern Bible conference at Medicine Lake, not far from Minneapolis. It was a rainy afternoon when I got word that Dr. Riley wanted to see me. I made the trip as quickly as I could to his suburban home in Golden Valley. His wife, Marie, led me over to where he was lying on a couch. Raising his head from the pillow, the eighty-six-year-old man fixed his clear eyes on me and lifted a frail hand in my direction. With great certainty in his voice, he announced that I would wear his mantle as Elisha had worn the Old Testament prophet Elijah's.

His words seemed like a patriarchal blessing. When he died, he seemed to be saying, I must succeed him as president of the college he had founded four decades before. He insisted on at least designating me as the school's vice president at large, whatever that meant.

"But Dr. Riley, I can't accept this responsibility. God hasn't shown it to me. But if it'll ease you, I'll take it on an interim basis until the board can find a permanent president."

That seemed to satisfy him, and he relaxed. But I left his side with a troubled heart and walked out into the rain to think.

Stalin had already broken the agreements made at Yalta and Potsdam; the Communists were attempting to take over China; and we were well into the Atomic Age. Surely, I felt, the Gospel of Christ was the answer to the predicament of humanity, because it was authentic, adequate, and available. It alone pointed the way to individual peace, social harmony, life adjustment, and spiritual satisfaction.

I believed I was called to spread the Gospel. I also thought that through Christian education we could train men and women with a passion to present that Gospel. Did that mean that through education I could multiply my ministry? I felt so. My dilemma was deep and produced a feeling of uncertainty.

Despite his declining health, Dr. Riley presided at a Northwestern Schools board meeting on October 1, 1947. I was present at his request, and he called on me to make a statement.

"I have no clear indication from the Lord that I am to succeed Dr. Riley," I said in part. "God called me into evangelism. I have a definite responsibility and commitment to Youth for Christ for the present. However, if it would . . . be . . . any help, I would be glad to become *interim* president in case of an emergency until the board could make some disposition of the office. . . . My position at the moment is that I am only Vice President at large."

I didn't know how I could have made my position any clearer.

At midnight on December 5, 1947, George Wilson called me at a Youth for Christ meeting in Hattiesburg, Mississippi. "Dr. Riley has died," he informed me.

I was asked to preach at his funeral. Fortunately, my British friend Stephen Olford was visiting with me. I asked him to take over my speaking schedule. I traveled at once to Minnesota, preparing the funeral sermon on the plane. I decided to preach on the first eighty-six words of the first Psalm; Dr. Riley had died at age eighty-six, and Psalm 1, on the importance of God's Word, so aptly described him.

A prominent local pastor who led a prayer at the service later announced that *he* should have preached at the funeral and that he was the obvious successor to the presidency. Dr. Riley had had other ideas, he added disdainfully, and had recruited this young man.

That pastor was probably right. My bachelor's degree in anthropology from Wheaton College hardly qualified me to become a college president—the youngest one in the nation, I later learned—only four years after graduating myself. That was probably what a lot of the other board members and faculty thought too. At the next board meeting, however, the directors dutifully followed the founder's mandate and named me interim president. (The board had fifty members, which I found too large for efficiency, but it included a number of leading businessmen, doctors, and other professionals.)

I walked into the middle of existing emergencies on campus and created a few of my own. My second day on the job, the librarian came into my office and said that she couldn't possibly make ends meet any longer on her small monthly salary. I agreed wholeheartedly and wrote out a slip for the treasurer, authorizing an immediate increase. Word of my generosity spread like wildfire through faculty ranks! Those underpaid folks had to do so much moonlighting through speaking engagements and other work that they were away from campus almost as much as I intended to be. A pay raise was merited for everyone.

My enlightened generosity would have been a bold stroke, winning me instant acceptance by the faculty, if the school had had the money. But it didn't. In fact, it needed a major infusion of cash. After decades of operating in Jackson Hall, the educational building belonging to First Baptist Church, Dr. Riley had decided to build an administrative and academic headquarters three blocks away, overlooking a little lake in Loring Park. Most of the money he raised was sunk into the excavation and the foundation pilings. At the time of his death, the project lacked funds for completion. The most urgent item on my presidential agenda was to raise money to finish the building.

Settling into an executive office and running a school's daily routines neither appealed to me nor suited my temperament. I was twenty-nine years old. My wife and two young daughters—Anne Morrow Graham was born in May 1948, a few months after I joined Northwestern—were at home in North Carolina. I myself was on the road at least one-fourth of the time from coast to coast as an itinerant evangelist holding youth rallies and organizing local Youth for Christ groups. Ruth had no desire to move to Minneapolis. I had the *vision* for Northwestern, but not the stomach. It did not help any that Ruth kept reminding me that I was called by God to be an evangelist, not an educator.

To keep an eye on things while I was at the school, Marie Riley, officially as the dean of women and unofficially as the founder's widow, understandably took a rather proprietary stance; wonderfully qualified, she kept her managerial hand on every aspect of the institution. She symbolized the authority that in her late husband had been almost absolute. If it had not been for her deep commitment to the Lord, her great talent and ability, and the warmth with which she always greeted me, I could not have handled the job.

One of the great encouragements I had during this time was inheriting Dr. Riley's longtime secretary, Luverne Gustavson. Because she knew everything about the school, had known Dr. Riley, and could find filed letters in which he had outlined his thinking on policies and people, she was a great help to me.

To keep an eye on things while I was away, I thought of my old friend T.W. Wilson. I began pressuring him to leave his own effective ministry with Youth for Christ to come help me as vice president. His educational credentials were no more impressive than mine. Physically, though, he was a big man who was not afraid to speak up for his convictions. He had been trained under Bob Jones and had been on his board and in YFC. That, along with his spiritual warmth and congenial sense of humor, rounded out the qualifications I thought were necessary for an assistant. I had many friends at the school and in Minnesota. But I had years of well-founded confidence in T.W., not only as a friend but as a watchdog when I was away.

So he and his wife, Mary Helen, moved from their comfortable home in the South to the stern climate of Minnesota. That was more than I was willing to do; I stayed at an old hotel whenever I was in the city. But I was traveling constantly. Mainly for our children's sake, Ruth wanted to stay near her parents in Montreat; I went there as often as I could.

One night, as I was lying awake in North Carolina, I realized that we needed a catchy slogan that would illustrate what we wanted Northwestern to be. The Lord gave me the words "Knowledge on fire." I took them back with me, and everybody seemed to feel they were exactly the slogan we needed.

Absentee president though I was for much of the time during the next few years, I was aware that good progress in enrollment and finances at Northwestern camouflaged lingering campus unrest. The board did not know what to make of me. I had ideas, lots of them, and a few of them might even have been good for the school. But I wanted them to be put into practice immediately.

"I am finding that schools are not made overnight," I wrote to a minister friend in Michigan. "It takes much blood, sweat, tears, and prayer to make an institution. The school has been going through a great transitory period; it has growing pains. New ideas, new horizons, new attitudes, and new objectives are not always easy." I went on to make reference to "jealous hearts . . . hurling criticisms at Northwestern that are totally unjustified." I asked him for ideas on how I could get out of this responsibility.

Another sore spot with some of the ultrafundamentalist board members was the Council of Churches' sponsorship of my fall 1948 Crusade in Augusta, Georgia. It was the first time an interdenominational ministerial organization had given us all-out support. While some of the men on the board did not like it, I saw great new possibilities for evangelism in this development.

A crisis in the school's building fund made me forever skittish about wearing the two hats of evangelist and fund-raiser. For the first six months of my tenure as president, those two roles posed no conflict of interest for me. I felt that I could raise money for the school's programs and departments while conducting youth rallies around the country. During that time, I accepted no salary from Northwestern; Youth for Christ was still paying my regular salary. Nevertheless, public perception was just the opposite, and that became a troublesome factor in ministry financing.

I soon had to cut down my traveling schedule with Youth for Christ. Board, faculty, and students became increasingly close to my heart—especially the young people, as I listened to their exuberant singing in chapel services, or heard testimonies of the Lord's blessing in their Christian outreach assignments, or had a chance for spirited conversation with individuals and small groups. I was a scant ten years older than many of them, and I felt more like their brother than their elder.

I already had two Wilsons in my life, the brothers T.W. and Grady. At Northwestern I added a third, George—no relation to the first two. He was a layman, the business manager at Northwestern as well as the owner of a Christian bookstore downtown. He also had

119

been director of the Youth for Christ rallies in Minneapolis, the largest YFC in America, averaging perhaps 10,000 at each rally. He had a remarkable youth ministry of his own, and his enthusiasm for Northwestern was a gift of God to my work there. In addition, he had a terrific personality and a lot of humor, as I had learned during our travels together in England.

To those virtues was added a tremendous loyalty. "George Wilson will devote himself completely to just one person," Dr. Riley had warned. "He's been loyal that way to me. When I'm gone, he'll transfer that loyalty to you." He never spoke a truer word.

George always exercised a sharp sense of stewardship over the funds God entrusted to us, meager as they might be. That made him a terrific bargain-hunter on the school's behalf. He got twenty-three old pianos from historic Fort Snelling, outside Minneapolis, for a few dollars each. The majority weren't worth fixing up as musical instruments; he had them made into podiums for classrooms.

When I assumed the interim presidency, George Wilson and his friend Loren Bridges, who was a sergeant in the Marine Corps and a radio expert, had already looked into the possibility of establishing a radio station at the school. The Christian Businessmen's Committee in Minneapolis was in the process of establishing one of its own. Every time George and Loren had approached Dr. Riley, however, he had turned them down. I, on the other hand, was enthusiastic and gave them permission to proceed as quickly as possible.

Under the leadership of the dean of the school and T.W., the students were asked to give as much money as they could toward the radio station. I went out to call on some friends of the school to help raise the rest. George stayed right in the middle of the project with his tremendous enthusiasm. Not too long thereafter, radio station KTIS was established, and I had the privilege of being the first voice on the air; I spoke for fifteen minutes each day.

Funds for completing Memorial Hall were also successfully raised. On moving day, a truly memorable day, students, faculty, and staff carried all the books—each volume numbered in sequence for its respective place on the shelves—in a procession down Harmon Place to the library in the new building. The new campus was in full operation.

Faculty salaries had been raised, and finances in general were on a sound basis. To help meet expenses, we nearly doubled the tuition charge, and still enrollment expanded. But when I tried to cut expenses to stay within the budget, I almost had a faculty rebellion on my hands. How we wrestled in prayer over all our problems! We had prayer meetings at every turn—something I had learned at Florida Bible Institute. What we needed, God provided because of His grace, not because we deserved it.

As you will see later, within the next few years much happened to expand my evangelistic ministry, and I became more convinced than ever that full-time evangelism was God's plan for me. Because of that conviction, in June 1950 I resigned from the Northwestern presidency, but the board of directors would not accept my resignation.

At Christmastime in 1951, I did an awful lot of soul-searching back home in the solitude of the North Carolina mountains. The board, faculty, and students at Northwestern were as cooperative as anyone could ask, but the school was suffering in several areas without a full-time president on duty to make executive decisions. Back home with Ruth and our three girls—Ruth Bell Graham, who was nicknamed Bunny, had been born in December 1950—I went off by myself almost every day for prayer and study. I reread and pondered the great Bible passages that had motivated me for years, in the Book of Acts and in prophets like Daniel and Ezekiel. My decision was unavoidable.

In February 1952, I tried again. This time the board accepted the resignation.

I sincerely felt that I was leaving the institution in much better condition than I found it. Our difficult progress toward accreditation was well under way. Enrollment had climbed from 700 to 1,200—the highest level in its half-century of existence; that total included several foreign students we had invited to come tuition-free as we met them in our overseas rallies. Most of them were students aflame for a world on fire, just as our school's slogan advocated.

Admittedly, I was never completely happy at Northwestern or totally convinced that I was in the will of God. As I look back, however, I can see that many good things came of my time there, especially in the experience I gained in management and finances and in working with a board. The years there also gave me a greater under-standing of young people. All of this would be valuable to me in fu-ture years.

There was some understandable unhappiness with me when I left the school. I took with me some of my friends and staff into our new organization, the Billy Graham Evangelistic Association. For example, I took George Wilson, who had been Northwestern's busi-ness manager; Luverne Gustavson, who had been Dr. Riley's and then my own private secretary; Betty Lowry, an administrative whiz; and Jerry Beavan, who had been registrar at the school.

During those years as president of Northwestern, was I, as some critics were quick to report, thoughtless and insensitive? Some of both, I had to admit. But the historic Los Angeles and New England Crusades took place during my tenure, and the world seemed to be opening up to evangelism in an unprecedented way. Maybe some of my decisions and actions would have been different if I had reflected longer. But things were happening so fast that there was hardly time to think. Three months after I resigned, I wrote to a Baptist editor friend. "There is no doubt that I made mis-takes and I believe the Lord has forgiven. However, there were many other elements that entered in that the public probably will never know."

The college's new president told me that those of the old fac-ulty he had met did not agree with all of my self-assessment. All I could say to him was, "Well, there are a lot of things that I remem-ber that they don't remember!"

"I am feeling the best I've ever felt in my life," I wrote to my parents on June 23, 1952, in the middle of a memorable Crusade in Jackson, Mississippi. "Getting the School off my mind has been a tremendous relief."

8

A Growing Outreach

Following our first citywide Campaign in September 1947, in
Grand Rapids, Michigan—back then we used the label *Campaign*
rather than *Crusade*—we held a number of others; but Augusta,
Modesto, and Altoona now stand out in my mind for various reasons, and I recall Forest Home for the most important reason of all.

AUGUSTA

It was October 1948, and we were in Augusta, Georgia, about to
conclude a fairly successful two-and-a-half-week citywide Campaign. Though I had recently taken on the presidency of Northwestern Schools, I was still on the road a great deal, speaking at
YFC rallies, conferences, and evangelistic campaigns.

Our Augusta Campaign clearly was not having any impact on
the people in the hotel. An automobile dealers' convention was in
town that Saturday night, and around one in the morning a wild
party erupted in the next room, awakening me from a deep sleep.
Grady came to my room to complain.

"I can't sleep."

"I can't either, and tomorrow's a big day," I said to him. "I'm going over there to put a stop to this."

I wrapped my bathrobe around me and went out and pounded on their door.

"Whad'ya want?" asked the drunken man who responded to my knock.

"I want to speak to this crowd!"

I had intended just to tell my neighbors to stifle the noise, but I guess the preacher in me took over. I yelled for silence into the crowd of thirty or forty carousing men and women behind him. Startled, they quieted down.

"I'm a minister of the Gospel," I began.

Pin-drop silence. This was a bunch of South Carolina auto dealers who knew a Bible Belt evangelist when they saw one, even in his bathrobe.

"I'm holding a revival Campaign in this town. Some of you may have read about it in the paper."

Not a reasonable assumption.

"I daresay most of this crowd are church members. Some of you are deacons and elders. Maybe even Sunday school teachers. I know your pastors would be ashamed of you, because you're certainly not *acting* like Christians."

I got bolder: "I know God is ashamed of you."

"That's right, preacher," one of them piped up. "I'm a deacon."

"And I'm a Sunday school teacher," a woman confessed.

Well, I stood there and preached an evangelist's sermon to that crowd. I don't know what happened to the party after I left, but there was no more noise for the rest of the night.

That was not my usual pattern, of course, although I have endured more noisy hotel rooms than I care to remember. But sometimes an evangelist has to be bold, and sometimes he comes across as brash!

Those meetings in Augusta were part of a series of Campaigns that marked a new departure for us. My first years with Youth for Christ had been a whirlwind of activity: I spoke at YFC rallies and churches all across North America and Europe. In February of that year, for example, I spoke forty-four times for YFC in several midwestern states, not including various church services and other related events.

However, I was beginning to think and pray about new opportunities for full-scale citywide Campaigns. Some of these were youth-oriented and closely tied to YFC. Others were invitations to hold citywide Campaigns separate from YFC, targeting the whole community. The first of these not related to YFC had been in late 1947 in my hometown of Charlotte; Augusta was our second.

As it turned out, we followed several principles in Augusta that would become the established pattern for our work in later years.

The first was to work for as broad church involvement as possible. Our citywide Campaign in Augusta was officially sponsored by the city's ministerial association—a sort of council of churches. Such extensive sponsorship never happened before; in all previous cities, a few churches, or in some cases only one church invited us to hold meetings. In Augusta we had all-out support from virtually the entire Christian community, under the chairmanship of the pastor of First Presbyterian Church, Dr. Cary Weisiger.

Perhaps an event that occurred a few months before that Campaign, in late summer, had given me a greater desire to work with as many churches as possible. I had attended the founding session of the World Council of Churches in Amsterdam. Christianity was taking on a new worldwide dimension for me. Dr. Willem Visser 't Hooft, who was the secretary of the newly formed council, had invited me as an observer from Youth for Christ and had treated me very warmly.

Like many, I was concerned that some extreme theological liberals—persons who would not hold all the tenets of the Apostles' Creed, which was my own basic creed—had been given prominence. Nevertheless, I was impressed by the spiritual depth and commitment of many of the participants. Furthermore, at the local level in a city such as Augusta, I could see a great advantage in a united effort that brought all the churches together around the preaching of the Gospel.

Second, we stressed that prayer was an indispensable element in preparation for a Campaign, and we sought to organize in advance as much prayer as possible. In the months before we arrived, I was told, several hundred prayer meetings brought people together in churches and neighborhoods to ask God's blessing.

Third, special care was taken to avoid problems with finances. Money had to be raised to take care of Campaign expenses, but it needed to be done in a way that did not bring suspicion or hostility to the effort. Long before the Campaign in Augusta ended, audiences contributed enough to pay all the budgeted expenses. At that point, the sponsors stopped taking an offering at the meetings. At the last meeting, as was customary in those days, a love offering was gathered for Cliff Barrows and me. (Bev Shea we paid a weekly fee, and Grady Wilson did not come to every Campaign, but he received a stipend when he was able to come.)

Fourth, we learned the value of publicity and the importance of being honest and careful in talking about our efforts. The local committee had run ads in the newspaper, letting the public know the facts of time and place. (Such ads were essential, since our early Campaigns seldom rated any coverage in the news section.) However, some of the ad copy concerned me, because it placed emphasis on individuals rather than on the Gospel message. "Hear These Famous Religious Workers," one ad exhorted, greatly exaggerating our importance. Bev Shea was the only one who was famous; he had hordes of radio fans—in Des Moines!

On the other hand, we saw that systematic advertising clearly could increase interest in a Campaign. Ads announcing our theme as "Christ for This Crisis" seemed to stimulate media interest in the meetings. I wanted to let people know that the Gospel had a uniquely dynamic relevance to life as they experienced it here and now. Newspapers began to report on the meetings daily, with good summaries of the high points in my sermons. All of us had opportunities to speak on local radio programs too.

One newspaper article said that in my next sermon I would hold the Bible in one hand and a newspaper in the other. I don't know whether that was literally true, but it did symbolize my constant effort to show the timeliness of God's eternal truths. In preaching the Gospel, I could also comment on everything current—the Communist threat, moral and social issues in the newspapers, Judgment Day.

MODESTO

Immediately after the Augusta Campaign, Cliff Barrows, Grady Wilson, and I drove across the country toward Modesto, California, which was near Cliff's boyhood home, for another citywide Campaign scheduled to begin in late October . . . and therein lay a tale.

Cliff and I had bought same-model Buicks. Cliff's was pulling a trailer called the "Bonnie B. Special," named for his baby daughter. Because I had a commitment in Augusta just after the Campaign, I could not leave right away. Grady decided to travel with me. We agreed to let Cliff go first, promising to meet him at a prearranged spot in Texas, where Grady would swap cars and share the rest of the drive with Cliff.

But we never saw Cliff! After waiting for a time at our scheduled meeting place, we gave up and went on without him, stopping (it seemed) at every Buick place on the road to inquire about a fellow driving a Buick pulling a trailer. At some point, we learned that he was only about six hours ahead of us, but we needed to stop for three or four hours' sleep. Besides, the oil light on the dash told me that something was wrong; I had to get the oil pump fixed. By the time we stopped at the Buick place in Albuquerque, we knew that Cliff had to be way ahead of us. When we finally got to Cliff's father's home in Ceres, just outside of Modesto, we found a smiling Cliff waiting for us; he had arrived an hour before.

A large tent had been erected for the event. Right from the first, we were encouraged by the response. Some nights we had to turn hundreds of people away because of lack of space. Some of the Modesto leaders even urged us to stretch the original two weeks into three. I had to decide against it, however, due to pressing responsibilities at Northwestern.

But Modesto not only encouraged us to continue citywide Campaigns, it also provided the foundation for much of our future work in another way. From time to time Cliff, Bev, Grady, and I talked among ourselves about the recurring problems many evangelists seemed to have, and about the poor image so-called mass evangelism had in the eyes of many people. Sinclair Lewis's fictional character Elmer Gantry unquestionably had given traveling evangelists a bad name. To our sorrow, we knew that some evangelists were not much better than Lewis's scornful caricature.

One afternoon during the Modesto meetings, I called the Team together to discuss the problem. Then I asked them to go to their rooms for an hour and list all the problems they could think of that evangelists and evangelism encountered.

When they returned, the lists were remarkably similar, and in a short amount of time, we made a series of resolutions or commitments among ourselves that would guide us in our future evangelistic work. In reality, it was more of an informal understanding among ourselves—a shared commitment to do all we could to uphold the Bible's standard of absolute integrity and purity for evangelists.

The first point on our combined list was money. Nearly all evangelists at that time—including us—were supported by love offerings taken at the meetings. The temptation to wring as much money as possible out of an audience, often with strong emotional appeals, was too great for some evangelists. In addition, there was little or no accountability for finances. It was a system that was easy to abuse—and led to the charge that evangelists were in it only for the money.

I had been drawing a salary from YFC and turning all offerings from YFC meetings over to YFC committees, but my new independent efforts in citywide Campaigns required separate finances. In Modesto we determined to do all we could to avoid financial abuses and to downplay the offering and depend as much as possible on money raised by the local committees in advance.

The second item on the list was the danger of sexual immorality. We all knew of evangelists who had fallen into immorality while separated from their families by travel. We pledged among ourselves to avoid any situation that would have even the appearance of compromise or suspicion. From that day on, I did not travel, meet, or eat alone with a woman other than my wife. We determined that the Apostle Paul's mandate to the young pastor Timothy would be ours as well: "Flee . . . youthful lusts" (2 Timothy 2:22, KJV).

Our third concern was the tendency of many evangelists to carry on their work apart from the local church, even to criticize local pastors and churches openly and scathingly. We were convinced, however, that this was not only counterproductive but also wrong from the Bible's standpoint. We were determined to cooperate with all who would cooperate with us in the public proclamation of the Gospel, and to avoid an antichurch or anticlergy attitude.

The fourth and final issue was publicity. The tendency among some evangelists was to exaggerate their successes or to claim higher attendance numbers than they really had. This likewise discredited evangelism and brought the whole enterprise under suspicion. It often made the press so suspicious of evangelists that they refused to take notice of their work. In Modesto we committed ourselves to integrity in our publicity and our reporting.

So much for the Modesto Manifesto, as Cliff called it in later years. In reality, it did not mark a radical departure for us; we had always held these principles. It did, however, settle in our hearts and minds, once and for all, the determination that integrity would be the hallmark of both our lives and our ministry.

After the Campaign, Cliff, Grady, and I drove back east. One night we stopped somewhere out in the desert for a break. The stars seemed so close, it felt like we could reach out and touch them. They were so beautiful that we lay on our backs a long time, just talking and praying.

The next day, one of us said, "Let's race to the top of this mountain and back to see who can win." That was our last race; it frightened us too much when Grady collapsed and began to spit up blood. Cliff was the strongest of the three of us and would always win at any sport—except golf!

At the time, the transition to full-scale citywide Campaigns didn't seem to us to be a major break. It was instead a natural development of our YFC work; in reality, most of our YFC rallies were citywide and involved local committees. The primary differences were that the YFC rallies were limited mainly to youth, and they did not directly involve the churches the way our regular evangelistic Campaigns would.

MIAMI AND BALTIMORE

A series of meetings chaired by Ira Eshleman in Miami in early 1949 gave us even greater encouragement to develop more citywide

129

Campaigns. Those meetings were a struggle financially, but we were able to meet in the Municipal Auditorium.

In this and every other citywide Campaign for some years after that, we devoted one night to missions. My message that night would be on missions and the need for missionaries, and I would encourage the young people to consider dedicating their lives to missionary service. To support that message, we would give the entire offering from that service to missions.

On mission night in Miami, Ira stepped into the elevator at the Everglades Hotel and asked Grady and me a question: "Can you explain why we're giving an offering to missions?" he asked with a smile. "I haven't been paid a thing!"

"Well," said Grady mockingly, "what about *my* salary?"

And the two teased each other for the rest of the night.

One day Ira took me to Fort Lauderdale, which was then just a small village outside of Miami. "If I were you and could get any money," he said, "I would invest it in land all through here. It's going to become a great city one day."

"Ira," I said, "I don't want to get into any business. I'll just rely on the Lord to pay my way."

At the urging of the local leadership, we extended the Campaign from two weeks to three. A thirteen-day series in May in Baltimore's old Lyric Theatre, which seated 3,000 people, gave us similar encouragement.

DEATH OF AN UNCLE

Uncle Tom Graham died in June 1949. I was in Kansas City with Bev Shea and Al Metzker preparing for a Youth for Christ rally to be held on June 11, which was a Saturday night. Our Crusade in Altoona was scheduled to begin the next day. When I learned that Uncle Tom had died, I asked Grady to begin the Altoona meetings for me. The funeral was to be the day after the rally, on Sunday, so we would have to fly out in order to make it on time. Tahlequah, Oklahoma, was well off the beaten path. I asked Al to see if he could get us a private plane. The best he could do was a single-engine Stinson Reliant. Early Sunday morning, Bev and I set out.

When we arrived at the airport, we had a plane, but no one to fly it. The best we could do was a student pilot.

After we took off, I asked the young man how long the trip would take.

"Maybe an hour," he answered. "Maybe an hour and a half."

We hadn't been airborne all that long when the young pilot made a casual observation. "I don't know if we have any fuel. The gauge isn't working."

He, Bev, and I began to look for a place to land. Fortunately, we spotted a small runway in the middle of nowhere. The young man brought the plane down ably enough, but when we got out, there was nobody around.

"It's Sunday," said Bev. "Everybody must be in church."

The young man went over to a parked car, siphoned the gas right out of its tank, and transferred the fuel to our airplane in one smooth sweep. I just stood there watching—apparently, he had done this sort of thing before. Bev and the pilot were clamoring for me to get on board and get out of there. I reached into my pocket, pulled out some bills, and ran to stick them under the car's windshield wiper. Then, without looking back, I ran for the plane, hoping that what I had left would be enough to cover the gas and the inconvenience.

Airborne again, I noticed that the engine seemed to be asthmatic, wheezing when it should be whirring. I leaned forward and asked the pilot a simple question. "Is car gasoline good for a plane engine?"

"It can't hurt," came the reply.

"It can't hurt," repeated Bev with a nod.

We soon flew into a rainstorm. To cover my anxiety, I talked to the pilot again.

"What do you do for a living?" I asked him.

"I lay carpet."

"He lays carpet," repeated Bev with another doubtful nod.

The worse the storm became, the more I talked.

"By the way, how long have you been flying?"

"Well, I've been working at it, off and on, for six months," he said proudly.

"I suppose you have your pilot's license?"

"Oh, yes, sir, I have my pilot's license," he assured me.

"And you have your license to carry passengers?"

"Well, no, sir, I don't have that yet," he admitted.

"Don't have that yet," repeated Bev, nodding in my direction.

"Have you ever flown this plane before?" I asked, suspecting the answer.

"Not *this* plane," he said.

"Not *this* plane," repeated Bev, this time shaking his head.

Bev and I would have jumped if only we could have found the chutes.

We landed two more times, each time to pick up more fuel—real plane fuel, not gasoline—but we seemed to be getting no nearer to Tahlequah. Bev and I resigned ourselves to the inevitable; we were never going to get to the funeral. At the same time, we decided that we were not going to board that plane again. We walked down the road toward what we hoped was a village or a town.

Our prayers were quickly answered. A man drove up in an ancient Chevy. "I run this little airport," he said. "When I heard the plane, I decided to come back here to find out what was wrong." He drove us back to the airport, filled the plane's tank, and gave the pilot directions. Bev and I decided to try again after all.

Our hopes rose when we spotted a runway that seemed to match the description given by our airport rescuer. The pilot buzzed the cattle off the strip and then made his descent onto the grass—which was apparently higher than the pilot had figured. We jolted down and then rolled to a quick stop. I got out and walked around the plane. The propeller and both the wheels were choked with thick clumps of green strands.

As I looked at this problem, a word of warning was shouted from the plane. I turned around and saw a heifer with horns charging right at me. I made it over the barbed wire fence just in time, but not without a couple of scratches. When I turned around again, I noticed some farm folks who had been watching our antics in the field. I knew the answer was no, but I had to ask the question anyway.

"Is this the airport for Tahlequah?"

"No, sir, it's over on the other side of town," the man said.

It seemed that there were two airports in Tahlequah. Since we were expected at the real airport and the bystanders could offer us no ground transportation, we decided to fly across town.

I went back over the fence to the field and explained the situation. After we had cut away as much of the grass as we could from the wheels and propeller, the pilot was able to turn the plane around and take off.

Not many minutes later we saw the paved runway of the other airport and noticed some cars screeching to a stop. They had heard our plane and came to pick us up. As they drove us to the church, they told us that the funeral service had already started. The minister received us with great excitement. And there was my uncle, lying in front, with the casket open. Bev went to the piano, where he sat down and readied himself to play. I sat down where the minister indicated I should, opened my Bible, and got ready to speak.

"Do you know, ladies and gentlemen," said the kindly old preacher, "what a privilege it is to have George Beverly Shea here with us today?!"

As I said, Bev was the celebrity!

"Instead of Mr. Shea's singing just one song," asked the preacher, "why don't we prevail upon him to sing two or three?"

Bev sang three songs, I finally said a few words, and we buried my uncle with dignity and love.

Back at the airport, Bev and I made a deal. If the prop did not start at the first catch, we were going back on the train. It caught, though, and we flew back, with barely a wheeze, to Kansas City. We even had a beautiful sunset. It certainly felt good to get on a full-size airliner—a DC–4, as I recall—to fly to Altoona.

ALTOONA

There was more, much more, to learn about how to run a successful Campaign, as we soon discovered. Some of it we learned in Altoona, Pennsylvania.

We did not keep statistics systematically in those days. Besides, numbers by themselves are never a true indication of what God

133

accomplishes. But if ever I felt I conducted a Campaign that was a flop, *humanly* speaking, Altoona was it!

The community itself seemed apathetic, competing ministerial associations squabbled over trivia, and organization for the Campaign was poor. There were other problems that we had not encountered before to any extent. Altoona was a center of extreme fundamentalism (and also strong liberalism), and some people yelled out in the meetings, not out of enthusiasm but to condemn me for fellowshipping with Christians they considered too liberal (and for other perceived faults). One unfortunate woman in the choir had mental problems and shouted out repeatedly in the middle of one sermon, disrupting the service. When she refused to quiet down, Cliff and Grady finally had to eject her, but she kept coming back. We could not help but sense that Satan was on the attack.

Not surprisingly, the attendance was small when compared to the turnout we had just had in Baltimore, and the results were insignificant by my own measurement.

Altoona was an industrial town built on coal, and I left it discouraged and with painful cinders in my eyes. In fact, I pondered whether God had really called me to evangelism after all. Maybe Altoona was sending me a signal that I had better give full time to my job as president of Northwestern Schools. At a minimum, it called into question our desire to expand from youth-oriented rallies into citywide Campaigns.

It was not the first time I had considered leaving evangelism for education. At the same time, I still was not sure I was cut out to be a college president. I will never forget one good-looking student who decided that he wanted to go to Northwestern. Not long thereafter, I saw him on the campus and greeted him. He put his arm around me—I guess he felt he knew me because we had talked at the meetings—and welcomed me home. "Billy, you old bag of bones," he said to me, "we're so glad to have you back!" That was the sort of respect I generated in some of the students.

The Augusta experience at the outset of the 1948–49 academic year left no doubt in my heart that God was blessing our work in evangelism. But back in Minneapolis, when Northwestern Schools opened for the fall 1948 term, we had the largest enrollment in the institution's history. It thrilled me to have a part in equipping so many promising young people for ministry in church and society. Their combined outreach with the Gospel in years to come would far exceed anything I could ever envision for myself.

By the spring of 1949, I gave serious consideration to taking a two-year leave of absence from Northwestern to work toward a Ph.D. A bachelor of arts degree hardly seemed adequate for a college president, and it did not help Northwestern in its pursuit of accreditation. I wrote to several universities to find out what would be involved in graduate study in religion, anthropology, history, or philosophy. Their answers were not encouraging. What with residence requirements and all the study I would have to do in foreign languages, it would take forever. Still, the prospect attracted me. An advanced degree, I felt, would not hurt wherever life took me, either as a college president or as an itinerant evangelist.

To have or not to have an advanced degree was not my only dilemma. My very faith was under siege. For one thing, my friend and partner in preaching on that memorable trip to the British Isles and Europe in 1946, Chuck Templeton, had resigned from his church in Toronto to enroll at Princeton Theological Seminary. I talked with him two or three times that winter of 1948–49—his first year as a graduate student—and discovered that he was undergoing serious theological difficulties, particularly concerning the authority of the Scriptures. My respect and affection for Chuck were so great that whatever troubled him troubled me also.

I had similar questions arising from my own broadened reading habits. I wanted to keep abreast of theological thinking at mid-century, but brilliant writers such as Karl Barth and Reinhold Niebuhr really made me struggle with concepts that had been ingrained in me since childhood. They were the pioneers in what came to be called neo-orthodoxy. While they rejected old liberalism, the new meanings they put into some of the old theological terms confused me terribly. I never doubted the Gospel itself, or the deity of Christ on which it depended, but other major issues were called into question.

The particular intellectual problem I was wrestling with, for the first time since my conversion as a teenager, was the inspiration and authority of the Scriptures. Seeming contradictions and problems with interpretation defied intellectual solutions, or so I thought. Could the Bible be trusted completely?

If this doubt had sprung up in my student days, as it did for so many, it might have been taken as a normal development. But neo-orthodoxy's redefinition of inspiration to allow for a Bible prone to mistakes and to subjective interpretations certainly should not have been an option for someone in my position. I was not a searching sophomore, subject to characteristic skepticism. I was the president of a liberal arts college, Bible school, and seminary—an institution whose doctrinal statement was extremely strong and clear on this point. I professed to believe in the full inspiration of the Scriptures. But did I believe in the same sense that my predecessor, Dr. Riley, had believed?

Feeling a little hypocritical, I began an intensive study of this question. I read theologians and scholars on all sides of the issue. I also turned to the Bible itself. Paul had written to Timothy, "All scripture is given by inspiration of God" (2 Timothy 3:16, KJV). (I knew that the New Testament Greek term that translates as "inspiration" literally meant "God-breathed writings.") There was an impenetrable mystery to that concept, as with all things pertaining to God. Yet the basic meaning was clear: the Bible was more than just another human book.

The Apostle Peter said, "For the prophecy came not in old time by the will of man: but holy men of God spake as they were moved by the Holy Ghost" (2 Peter 1:21, KJV). Jesus Himself said, "Heaven and earth shall pass away, but my words shall not pass away" (Matthew 24:35, KJV). The internal testimony of the Scriptures to their own inspiration and authority was unequivocal. So was Jesus' own view of the Scriptures.

The disturbing conversations with Chuck Templeton, my confused reaction to studying influential and sometimes contradictory theologians, the quandary over a career in education versus a ministry in evangelism, and most recently the fiasco in Altoona—all these were the intellectual, spiritual, and emotional baggage I was carrying in the summer of 1949 as we began to prepare for Los Angeles, the largest citywide Campaign to date.

FOREST HOME

One of God's hidden stratagems to prepare me for Los Angeles was an engagement I had made for late summer that I was not enthusiastic about keeping. At the end of August, the annual College Briefing Conference met at Forest Home, a retreat center east of Los Angeles. In my role as the then-youngest college president in America, I had agreed to speak, but after Altoona I did not feel I had much to say.

Head of the conference was Miss Henrietta Mears, director of religious education at First Presbyterian Church of Hollywood. From a wealthy background, she was always dressed in the latest fashion, and she wore tasteful makeup and fine jewelry. Always positive, she had a great love for down-and-outs. She was a former high school chemistry teacher in Minneapolis and had been a key worker in the Sunday school at Dr. Riley's First Baptist Church. Some twenty years before, she accepted an invitation to serve at the Hollywood church. Within three years of her arrival, she had built a dynamic Christian education program, with the Sunday school enrollment rising from a fairly respectable Presbyterian 450 to an absolutely awesome 4,500; it was the talk of the West Coast. In the class she herself taught for college students, weekly attendance ran to 500 men and women who were devoted to "Teacher," as she was called. Her enthusiasm for the Lord Jesus Christ was contagious.

Other speakers included her own pastor at Hollywood Presbyterian, Dr. Louis Evans; my good friend and fellow seeker Chuck Templeton, who had just finished his first year at Princeton seminary; and evangelist-scholar J. Edwin Orr, who had received his Ph.D. from Oxford University and was an authority on religious revivals. As always, I felt intimidated by so many bright and gifted leaders, which just added to my generally low spirits at the time. I would just as soon have been at Forest Lawn, the famous Los Angeles cemetery, as at Forest Home.

During the week, I had times of prayer and private discussion with Miss Mears at her cottage. Rarely had I witnessed such Christian love and compassion as she had for those students. She had faith in the integrity of the Scriptures, and an understanding of Bible truth as well as modern scholarship. I was desperate for every insight she could give me.

By contrast, Chuck Templeton had a passion for intellectualism that had been stimulated by his studies. He made no attempt to hide his feelings about me. "Billy, you're fifty years out of date. People no longer accept the Bible as being inspired the way you do. Your faith is too simple. Your language is out of date. You're going to have to learn the new jargon if you're going to be successful in your ministry."

My friend Bob Evans, who had been at Wheaton with me, was also at Forest Home. He overheard Chuck say, "Poor Billy, I feel sorry for him. He and I are taking two different roads."

This cut me to the quick; the friendship and fellowship we had enjoyed meant a great deal to me. Ironically, the Christian Business Men's Committee of Greater Los Angeles (which was taking a great step of faith in having an unknown evangelist like me) had invited Chuck to speak in July at a "booster dinner" for the Campaign.

I ached as if I were on the rack, with Miss Mears stretching me one way and Chuck Templeton stretching me the other. Alone in my room one evening, I read every verse of Scripture I could think of that had to do with "thus saith the Lord." I recalled hearing someone say that the prophets had used the phrase "the Word of the Lord said" (or similar wording) more than two thousand times. I had no doubts concerning the deity of Jesus Christ or the validity of the Gospel, but was the Bible completely true? If I was not exactly doubtful, I was certainly disturbed.

I pondered the attitude of Christ toward the Scriptures. He loved those sacred writings and quoted from them constantly. Never once did He intimate that they could be wrong. In fact, He verified some of the stories in the Old Testament that were the hardest to believe, such as those concerning Noah and Jonah. With the Psalmist, He delighted in the law of the Lord, the Scriptures.

As that night wore on, my heart became heavily burdened. Could I trust the Bible? With the Los Angeles Campaign galloping

138

toward me, I had to have an answer. If I *could not* trust the Bible, I could not go on. I would have to quit the school presidency. I would have to leave pulpit evangelism. I was only thirty years of age. It was not too late to become a dairy farmer. But that night I believed with all my heart that the God who had saved my soul would never let go of me.

I got up and took a walk. The moon was out. The shadows were long in the San Bernardino Mountains surrounding the retreat center. Dropping to my knees there in the woods, I opened the Bible at random on a tree stump in front of me. I could not read it in the shadowy moonlight, so I had no idea what text lay before me. Back at Florida Bible Institute, that kind of woodsy setting had given me a natural pulpit for proclamation. Now it was an altar where I could only stutter into prayer.

The exact wording of my prayer is beyond recall, but it must have echoed my thoughts: "O God! There are many things in this book I do not understand. There are many problems with it for which I have no solution. There are many seeming contradictions. There are some areas in it that do not seem to correlate with modern science. I can't answer some of the philosophical and psychological questions Chuck and others are raising."

I was trying to be on the level with God, but something remained unspoken. At last the Holy Spirit freed me to say it. "Father, I am going to accept this as Thy Word—by *faith!* I'm going to allow faith to go beyond my intellectual questions and doubts, and I will believe this to be Your inspired Word."

When I got up from my knees at Forest Home that August night, my eyes stung with tears. I sensed the presence and power of God as I had not sensed it in months. Not all my questions were answered, but a major bridge had been crossed. In my heart and mind, I knew a spiritual battle in my soul had been fought and won.

Despite all the negotiations and arrangements we had already entered into with the Christian Business Men's Committee of Greater Los Angeles, I still had a frightening lack of assurance that the Lord really was leading us to Los Angeles.

I had been away from home so much that year that I hated to be leaving again, even though Ruth was going to attempt to join me later. The first week in September, she and I took a short vacation drive up in the northwoods of Minnesota.

We returned to Minneapolis in time for a weekend faculty retreat at Northwestern Schools, where the fall semester was about to begin. I knew that the faculty and students had a right to expect me on campus. I also knew, though, that T.W., Dean Ed Hartill, and Mrs. Riley could capably handle everything for at least a while.

Some of my negative praying would have made even God gloomy, I guessed, if He had not known ahead what He was going to do for the glory of His name.

1949–1955

Turning Points

9

Watershed

If the amount of advance press coverage was any indication, the Los Angeles Campaign was going to be a failure. Not that the local organizing committee hadn't tried. They had employed Lloyd Doctor, public relations director for the local Salvation Army, to drum up interest. One day shortly before the meetings opened, he persuaded a handful of reporters to attend the first press conference I had ever conducted. Next day we eagerly scanned the newspapers to see the stories those reporters had written.

Nothing.

As far as the media were concerned, the Los Angeles Campaign—by far our most ambitious evangelistic effort to date—was going to be a nonevent.

Later Lloyd got me a brief appointment with the mayor of Los Angeles, and the *Los Angeles Times* carried a small back-page picture and story of that meeting. Except for the ads that the committee ran in the church section, that was virtually the only press exposure we got for the first couple of weeks.

The invitation to hold meetings in Los Angeles originally came from a group of businessmen who called themselves "Christ for

143

Greater Los Angeles," representing about two hundred churches. They had already sponsored several such Campaigns with other evangelists, all of which were reasonably successful. Now they wanted me to preach and to bring Cliff Barrows and George Beverly Shea. I agreed but insisted on several stringent conditions.

First, they were to try to broaden church support to include as many churches and denominations as possible. Second, they were to raise their budget from $7,000 to $25,000, in order to invest more in advertising and promotion. Third, they were to erect a much larger tent than they had planned; our limited experience in citywide Campaigns had already taught us that the crowds seemed to grow as the days went on.

The men from Los Angeles initially agreed to every point except raising the budget. They were convinced it would be impossible to come up with such a large amount.

They had a point. In those days, Campaigns were modest efforts. Even at the biggest meetings, it was unusual to hear of more than 50 people responding to the Invitation to receive Christ. Any evangelist preaching before more than 2,000 people was considered highly successful. The Christ for Greater Los Angeles committee undoubtedly felt that their commitment to raise $7,000 was an ambitious step in the right direction.

To many of those seasoned, older Christians, I came across as brash. But I found myself drafting a Los Angeles scenario bigger and bolder than anything I had imagined before. Besides insisting on the budget increase, I set yet another seemingly impossible condition: the committee had to put the public leadership and the platform duties of the Campaign entirely in the hands of local clergy. The committee, I felt, represented too limited an evangelical constituency to make an impact.

I consulted with Cliff, and he agreed. I wrote back to our hosts and told them we would be forced to cancel if they could not see their way clear to step out in faith and take that financial risk.

"I stand upon the brink of absolute fear and trembling when I think we might come to Los Angeles with only a small handful of churches," I wrote in February 1949. "The city of Los Angeles will not be touched unless the majority of the churches are actively back of this campaign."

My limited experience had already shown me that without the cooperation of the local churches and their pastors, not only would attendance suffer but so would the follow-up of new Christians.

One of my objectives was to build the church in the community. I did not simply want the audience to come from the churches. I wanted to leave something behind in the very churches themselves.

Even as I imposed these conditions on the long-suffering committee, I doubted that they could comply. Yet I burned with a sense of urgency to move forward: "I'm convinced . . . that if a revival could break out in the city of Los Angeles," I wrote to Mr. Claude Jenkins, secretary of the committee, "it would have repercussions around the world. Let's not stop at anything to make this the meeting that God could use as a spark to send a flame of revival through the nation. Your responsibilities are tremendous. Let's go forward by prayer."

Initial reports from Los Angeles indicated that I was stirring up a hornet's nest. Some opponents circulated distorted and false stories about my being a self-promoting money-grabber. The kind of conditions I was insisting on certainly might have fueled that fire. And getting the committee's agreement would take a miracle. I was soon humbled when I found out what truly big men they were in the depth of their devotion to evangelism: they agreed to do what we had asked. The Campaign was set to begin in the last week of September and run for three weeks.

Just before the Campaign began, Henrietta Mears invited me to her home in Beverly Hills to speak to the Hollywood Christian Group. That occasion gave me an opportunity for lengthy discussions with well-known actors and actresses.

One man at the meeting, Stuart Hamblen, impressed me tremendously. He was rough, strong, loud, and earthy. Every inch of his six-foot-two frame was genuine cowboy, and his 220 pounds seemed all bone and muscle. His name was legendary up and down the West Coast for his popular radio show, heard every afternoon for two hours. He said he would invite me on as a guest. I took an instant liking to him and coveted him for Christ. Only half-jokingly, he said he could fill the tent if he gave his endorsement.

In the months ahead, I would meet other Hollywood celebrities of the time, especially in visits to Miss Mears's "out of this world" home, as Ruth described it—people such as Tim Spencer (who wrote a number-one song on the hit parade, "Room Full of Roses"), Mickey Finn, Jon Hall, Connie Haines, and Jane Russell. Edwin Orr led these meetings, so they were both intellectually stimulating and spiritually stirring. Many of these stars were so earnest about learning the Word of God and translating it into daily living that Ruth felt they put to shame our Thursday afternoon prayer meetings back home in the Bible Belt.

I was inspired especially by the testimony of actress Colleen Townsend, who had a contract with Twentieth Century–Fox and whose picture had just been on the cover of *Life* magazine. She was one of the most dedicated Christians I had met, and yet she was working in the film industry—an industry that was anathema to many of the supporters of the Crusade. She became engaged to Louis Evans, Jr., whose father was pastor of Hollywood's First Presbyterian Church. They would actively participate in the tent meetings. It was she who thoughtfully wrote a note to Ruth after meeting me at Forest Home. "Billy mentioned how much he'd like to have you here," she said, "so I thought I'd just drop you a note of added encouragement."

Ruth did come, a month earlier than she intended. She wanted to be with me for my birthday on November 7 but got mixed up on the date and arrived on October 7 instead! "I tell you, I have a brain tumor," she wrote back to North Carolina. "I've never felt so foolish in my life, and got ribbed good and properly." Gigi had been left in the care of Grandmother Bell in Montreat, and Anne was staying with her Aunt Rosa and Uncle Don Montgomery in Los Alamos, New Mexico. (Bunny hadn't yet been born, of course.)

I was overjoyed to have Ruth with me so soon. Having gotten to California well ahead of the September 25 starting date to allow time for getting acquainted with the leaders and the special challenges of the area, I had been missing her terribly.

The attendance at our early Los Angeles meetings averaged about 3,000 each night and 4,000 on Sunday afternoons, so the tent was never filled to capacity.

I sensed that interest was building, though, and the crowds were getting larger. However, I found that I was preaching mainly to Christians. As Ruth observed in a letter home to her folks in October, "It isn't easy to get unconverted to a tent."

Nevertheless, I was preaching with a new confidence and fervor. I had always been loud and enthusiastic (and some said authoritative). But since my pivotal experience in the mountain woods at Forest Home, I was no longer struggling internally. There was no gap between what I said and what I knew I believed deep in my soul. It was no coincidence that the centerpiece of the 150-foot platform in the tent, right in front of the pulpit, was a replica of an open Bible—twenty feet high and twenty feet wide.

Stuart Hamblen did indeed invite me to be a guest on his radio show. I hesitated at first. Would the Campaign committee want me on that kind of program, sponsored by a tobacco company, even if Hamblen was the number-one radio personality on the West Coast?

The more I thought about it, the more intriguing the idea seemed. Hadn't Christ Himself spent time with sinners? Hadn't He been criticized by the religious leaders of His day for that very thing? Why should I not take the risk? I said yes.

On his show, he surprised me by telling all his listeners, in his own rough-and-ready manner, to "go on down to Billy Graham's tent and hear the preaching." Even more surprising, to his listeners as well as to me, was his next remark: "I'll be there too!"

The first night Stuart attended, we would find out later, he became deeply convicted of his own sins and the need for Christ to save him. Not understanding what was going on in his soul, he became angry and stalked out. For two or three nights he stayed away. Then he came back. Each time he showed up, he had the same reaction, getting so mad once that he actually shook his fist at me as he walked out of the tent.

We were approaching the scheduled closing-night meeting— Sunday, October 16—of our three-week Campaign. During the week before that final meeting, since there was evident blessing, some committee members advocated extending the Campaign a short time. Others thought it should stop as planned; the choir, the counselors, and other workers were tired, and we might risk an anticlimax. The budget had been met, and now the organizers just took love offerings for Cliff and me. Everybody was confident the tent would be filled on the closing Sunday to give us a truly grand finale to an excellent series of meetings.

Should the Campaign be extended? It was not simply for the committee to decide. We needed a clear sense of direction from the Lord. Grady, Cliff, Bev, and I prayed together over and over again as the last week wore on. At last we decided to follow the example of Gideon in the Old Testament and put out a fleece, asking God to give us a decisive sign of His purpose.

It came at four-thirty the next morning.

I was awakened in my room at the Langham Hotel by the jangling of the telephone. In a voice broken by tears, a man begged to see me right away. It was Stuart Hamblen. I woke up Grady and Wilma Wilson, and they went with Ruth into another room to pray.

By the time I was up and dressed, Stuart and his praying, godly wife, Suzy, were at my door. We talked together and prayed, and the rugged cowboy gave his life to Christ in a childlike act of faith. He came forward in the next service. The first thing he did after he received Christ was to call his father, who was an old-fashioned Methodist preacher in west Texas. I could hear his father shout with joy over the phone!

It would not be long before Stuart put his vibrant experience into a song that was inspired by a conversation he'd had with John Wayne: "It Is No Secret [What God Can Do]." That still remains one of the favorites people like to hear Bev Shea sing. Shortly after, he wrote another testimony song, "This Ole House," which I think was number one for several weeks on the national radio show *Your Hit Parade*.

Years later, when we were back in Los Angeles for a Crusade at the Coliseum, Cliff, Grady, Bev, and I went to Stuart's home for breakfast. "Billy," Stuart said at one point, "it's terrible that these planes come over the stadium while you're trying to preach. I'm a member of the President's Club of Western Airlines, and I think I'll call the president. If he won't do anything about it, I think I'll get my old longhorn rifle out and see if I can't stop those planes from here!"

That very night I was telling the crowd how Stuart was willing to get his longhorn rifle out to bag a few of the low-flying airplanes . . . when there was a terribly loud bang at the other end of the stadium.

148

"Stuart, is that you?" I called out.

The crowd roared.

That night back in 1949, Cliff and I knew that we had our answer about continuing the Campaign. Clearly, the Lord had unfinished business to do in the lives of people who were just beginning to hear about the meetings and think about the Gospel. We told the committee that the Campaign had to go on, and they agreed.

But for how long? During the next week—the first week of our extension—we were thrilled to hear Stuart Hamblen give his testimony over his radio program, telling listeners how Christ had changed his life. People were talking about it all along the West Coast. Did this justify *another* extension of the Campaign?

Cliff and I had not experienced such mounting interest and enthusiasm during our previous Campaigns. In our uncertainty about what to do, we agreed that the best thing was to put out the fleece again, as Gideon had done, and ask the Lord for another sign. We were relatively inexperienced young men with a lot to learn. (Cliff was four and a half years younger than I.) Our wives were coping with our unpredictable lifestyles, but we wanted to be considerate of their feelings too. Would God give us another clear indication what to do?

When I arrived at the tent for the next meeting, the scene startled me. For the first time, the place was crawling with reporters and photographers. They had taken almost no notice of the meetings up until now, and very little had appeared in the papers. I asked one of the journalists what was happening.

"You've just been kissed by William Randolph Hearst," he responded.

I had no idea what the reporter was talking about, although I knew the name. Hearst, of course, was the great newspaper owner. I had never met the man, but like most Americans I had read his papers. The next morning's headline story about the Campaign in the *Los Angeles Examiner,* followed by an evening story in the *Los Angeles Herald Express*—both owned by Hearst—stunned me. The story was picked up by the Hearst papers in New York, Chicago, Detroit, and San Francisco, and then by all their competitors. Until then, I doubt if any newspaper editor outside the area had heard of our Los Angeles Campaign.

Puzzled as I was, my curiosity was never satisfied. Hearst and I did not meet, talk by phone, or correspond as long as he lived. Supposedly, he had sent a message to his editors, "Puff Graham," but there were so many stories about how we might have come to his notice and about why he might have been interested in promoting us that I did not know which, if any, was true. One of the more intriguing ones was that Hearst and his controversial partner, Marion Davies, disguised themselves and attended a tent meeting in person. I doubted it.

Time magazine pulled out all the rhetorical stops in its November 14, 1949, issue: "Blond, trumpet-lunged North Carolinian William Franklin Graham Jr., a Southern Baptist minister who is also president of the Northwestern Schools in Minneapolis, dominates his huge audience from the moment he strides onstage to the strains of *Send the Great Revival in My Soul.* His lapel microphone, which gives added volume to his deep, cavernous voice, allows him to pace the platform as he talks, rising to his toes to drive home a point, clenching his fists, stabbing his finger at the sky and straining to get his words to the furthermost corners of the tent."

The newspaper coverage was just the beginning of a phenomenon. As more and more extraordinary conversion stories caught the public's attention, the meetings continued night after night, drawing overflow crowds. Something was happening that all the media coverage in the world could not explain. And neither could I. God may have used Mr. Hearst to promote the meetings, as Ruth said, but the credit belonged solely to God. All I knew was that before it was over, we were on a journey from which there would be no looking back.

A veteran police officer in Medford, Oregon, who had attended a Los Angeles meeting at the start of the third week, wrote to me shortly after he got home: "I am glad you have continued on. . . . and I pray God will continue to bless you and your good work there." He added a postscript explaining the gift he had enclosed: "A small token to help you—and keep spreading that tent out."

That was exactly what we had to do. As November began with a further extension of the Campaign, headlines as far away as Indiana screamed, "OLD-TIME RELIGION SWEEPS LOS ANGELES." Reporters were comparing me with Billy Sunday; church leaders were quoted as saying that the Campaign was "the greatest religious revival in the history of Southern California."

One evening when the Invitation was given, I noticed a giant of a man, tears rolling down his cheeks, coming up with his wife to receive Christ. I did not know who he was, but I asked Cliff to have the audience sing one more verse of the final song to give them time to reach the front. Reporters recognized him, and the next day's newspaper made a big thing of it: "EVANGELIST CONVERTS VAUS, SOUND ENGINEER IN VICE PROBE." Jim Vaus was the electronics wizard who had allegedly served as reputed mobster Mickey Cohen's personal wiretapper.

A few days after his conversion, Jim came to visit me.

"Billy, I told Mickey Cohen what happened to me. Instead of his getting angry, he said, 'Jim, I'm glad you did it. I hope you stick to it.'"

There was a contract out on Jim's life, but apparently it was not from Cohen.

"Billy, would you be willing to talk to Mickey if I could arrange it?" he asked.

"I'll go anywhere to talk to anybody about Christ," I shot back without thinking.

By arrangement, then, we slipped out of the tent by a back exit after the meeting one night, in order to avoid the press, and got away undetected in Jim's car. As he drove toward Mickey Cohen's home, I had mixed feelings—a little uncertainty and hesitation, to be sure, yet a deep-down boldness as well, because I knew I was going to witness to a well-known mobster in the name of Jesus Christ.

As we drove up to an unimpressive house in the exclusive Brentwood section of Los Angeles, I noticed a car parked across the street with a man sitting in it.

When we got out of our car in the driveway, Cohen opened the front door to greet us. I was surprised to see how short he was. He reminded me of Zacchaeus in the New Testament, the undersized tax collector who shinnied up a tree in order to see Jesus over the heads of the crowd (*see* Luke 19:1–10). Looking straight at me with curiosity in his big brown eyes, he invited us in.

151

"What'll you have to drink?" Cohen asked.

"I'll have a Coca-Cola," I replied.

"That's fine," he said. "I think I'll have one too."

He went to get the drinks himself. Apparently, there was no one else in the house.

Jim told Mickey again how he had accepted Christ and planned to change his entire life; he described the peace and joy he now had.

Then I explained to Mickey, as simply and forthrightly as I could, the Gospel from A to Z. As we talked, I prayed inwardly (as I did when preaching to thousands in the tent) that God would help me to find the right words.

Mickey responded with some items about his own life, especially mentioning the charitable organizations he had supported and the good works he had done. Although he was of a different religious belief than I, he told me he respected me and certainly respected what Jim Vaus had done. Before we left, we had a prayer.

"WIRETAPPER IN CONFESSION AS EVANGELIST TRIES TO SAVE COHEN."

That was one paper's headline the next day. Without my knowledge or approval, the story of that visit had been leaked to the press—perhaps by the man I had seen in the car parked across the street, perhaps by a reporter who had been tipped off by someone in the Campaign organization, perhaps even by Cohen himself (who had a reputation for promoting his own notoriety).

Cohen denied the story. "I think the whole thing is a publicity stunt," one newspaper reported him as saying, "and that's what I'm tryin' to avoid—publicity. . . . I don't want to meet the guy. I haven't got time."

Lies of that magnitude were startlingly new to me, but I could not be discouraged about them. Ruth's mother wrote to us about a prayer Gigi had offered on Cohen's behalf: "Dear Jesus, thank You for the meetings, and dear Jesus, thank You for Mickey Cohen. Make him good and make him let Jesus put His blood in his heart."

As the Campaign went into its fifth week, we rearranged the seating to accommodate 3,000 more chairs. When that wasn't enough, crowds overflowed into the street. We added an extension, doubling the size of the 480-foot-long tent. Reporters were on hand to cover every meeting, and press accounts were positive.

The Associated Press put it on their priority "A" wire that went throughout the world. Both *Life* and *Time* magazines carried major stories. And the *Los Angeles Times* (the main competitor to the Hearst-owned papers) picked up the Campaign in a big way, of course.

People came to the meetings for all sorts of reasons, not just religious ones. No doubt some were simply curious to see what was going on. Others were skeptical and dropped by just to confirm their prejudices. Many were desperate over some crisis in their lives and hoped they might get a last chance to set things right. A few, we learned, were even sentenced to attend by a Los Angeles County judge, a woman who strongly supported the ministry and thought a night in the tent might do convicted offenders more good than a night in jail.

A minister from Yucca Valley took a leave of absence from his church so that he could be night watchman at the tent after each meeting ended. "Johnny" was the name he wanted us to call him by. He slept under the platform to keep an eye on the place. One night he heard something rattling the chain at the entrance.

"Who goes there?" he called out.

"Just me," came the reply.

"What do you want?"

"I just want to find Jesus."

Johnny led him to Christ right then and there.

As for Northwestern, I sent reports regularly to my secretary, Luverne Gustavson, in Minneapolis. Sometimes, forgetful of the two-hour time difference between California and Minnesota, I phoned George Wilson at his home at two in the morning, his time, to tell him what had happened at that night's meeting.

Back in Los Angeles, we asked the Lord for yet another signal. Should we extend the meetings to a sixth week? Attendance was still growing, but I did not want numerical success to become our standard for discerning the will of God. We did not dare go forward without His direction.

A fierce storm was heading toward Los Angeles from the Pacific. If it hit the coast, it would wreak havoc on our huge tent and the thousands of folding chairs. We prayed that if God wanted us to continue, the storm would not reach Los Angeles. The next morning the newspapers reported that the storm had dissipated at sea, much to the surprise of the meteorologists. We entered the sixth week with high hopes and grateful hearts but with sagging shoulders. I had never preached so much or so hard in all my life. I had run out of sermons in my stockpile and was having to prepare a new one every day. That took up to six or eight hours. Increasingly, I forgot about illustrations and applications, though I knew they were supposed to be necessary to good sermon construction. In some of these later messages, I used mostly Scripture references. I had two or three old Bibles from which I clipped out passages to paste onto my outline. Then, from the platform, I read these as part of my sermon without having had to write them out longhand.

A movie star who was not a Christian offered me this word of spiritual wisdom: "Billy, you can't compete with us in entertainment. We know all the ropes. If you get up there and preach what's in the Bible, I'll be on hand every night." I tried to follow that advice.

On one or two nights at the height of the Campaign, we had new believers give their testimonies of what Christ had done for them. Their words made such an impression that afterward I sensed the Holy Spirit was already speaking to many, so I simply gave a brief explanation of the Gospel and an Invitation to receive Christ, and people came forward.

One night a man took a taxi from a tavern to the tent and ran down the aisle while I was preaching. I asked Grady to take him into the auxiliary prayer tent and then invited anyone who wanted to join them to come forward. Scores did, even though the sermon wasn't finished. The man put his faith in Christ and began a new life by the grace of God.

Long after the crowds left, people drifted in singly or in pairs. Some were simply wanderers in the night; others, too troubled to sleep, were seeking something in that odd sanctuary. Johnny, the pastor-watchman, seated them in a row at the front and read Scripture to them, gave them the Gospel, and prayed for them.

154

Occasionally, I invited others to preach for me. T.W. came two or three times from Minneapolis. One night Bob Pierce, founder of World Vision and Samaritan's Purse, spoke for me. I introduced them, and then I would come back to the pulpit and give the Invitation.

Besides the sermon preparation, I desperately needed time for prayer to unload my burdens to the Lord and to seek His direction for the preaching and for other ministry opportunities. Some mornings as early as five o'clock, I would go to Grady's room to ask him to pray with me. Some time after the third week, he had to leave for a previous Campaign commitment back in the Midwest, but Cliff and Bev stayed with me to encourage me and do all they could to ease the load.

Under the leadership of a Lutheran spiritual leader, Armin Gesswein, organized prayer meetings were going on all over Southern California as well as in other parts of the country. Students were praying in Christian colleges, businesspeople were praying in offices, families were praying in their homes, and congregations were gathering for special prayer meetings. "The mightiest force in the world," as Frank Laubach called prayer, undergirded me and brought the blessing of God from Heaven to Los Angeles. (Laubach was a great advocate of teaching people how to read and write in areas of the world where education could not be taken for granted.)

Faithfully, day after day, 40 to 50 women prayed together on our behalf and then attended the meetings, sitting just in front of the platform each night with their faces full of expectant faith that God was about to work again.

The increasing media exposure brought a never-ending stream of requests for special appearances that often had me speaking three or four additional times each day: civic gatherings, churches, evangelism parties in the mansions of the rich and famous, school assemblies, and one-on-one interviews by the score.

When newsreels of the Campaign started appearing in theaters, people began to recognize us on the street. Of course, we had no staff to handle all the calls, letters, and telegrams that overwhelmed us in a daily avalanche. The word *burnout* was not in the popular vocabulary yet, but I was getting perilously close to that condition.

Before the end of that sixth week, I did not need to put out another fleece to find out whether I could continue the pace. That colorful writer for *Time* magazine had described me earlier as "trumpet-lunged" and having a "cavernous voice." In the final weeks, though, I often felt too weak to stand at the pulpit, and some of my platform-pacing was necessary to keep myself from toppling over when I stood still. I had lost a lot of weight thus far in the Campaign; dark rings circled my eyes. Cliff and Bev (who had to commute back to Chicago one day each week for his radio broadcast) felt the strain too, as did our long-suffering wives. Billie Barrows at the piano worked as hard as any of us, and Lorin Whitney tirelessly played the organ. Ruth herself stayed up long hours each night counseling people. None of us would leave the little counseling tent until every person had been personally talked to.

Drained as I was, physically, mentally, and emotionally, I experienced God's unfailing grace in perpetual spiritual renewal. I wanted the Campaign to close, but I was convinced that God wanted it to continue. All my personal reserves were used up; I had to put my entire dependence on the Lord for the messages to preach and the strength to preach them. "[God's] strength is made perfect in weakness," Paul wrote, "for when I am weak, then am I strong" (2 Corinthians 12:9, 10, KJV). It seemed that the weaker my body became, the more powerfully God used my simple words.

There was another concern. My job was to be president of Northwestern Schools, and all of this Los Angeles ministry coincided with the first term of the academic year. Back in Minneapolis, students were wondering if their president was ever going to come home. Newspaper clippings were pasted up on a board to keep them informed, and they were praying for the Campaign, of course, thrilled at each report of what the Lord was accomplishing. Nevertheless, a few board members were murmuring about the school's absentee president. Dr. Riley's widow, Marie, had reason to question her late husband's wisdom in appointing me his successor as president.

And there was still another concern: my family and the personal price they were paying while I was in Los Angeles. Ruth's sister and brother-in-law, Rosa and Don Montgomery, came from

New Mexico to join us for the closing week, bringing Anne, who had been staying with them. "Whose baby is this?" I asked when I saw the child in Rosa's arms, not recognizing my own daughter. And the baby went to sleep crying for her aunt, not her mother.

But as the eighth week approached in Los Angeles, we all knew that the end had to come. Not that the blessings were diminishing. It was then that Louis Zamperini was converted. He was the U.S. track star who had pulled a flag bearing the Nazi swastika down from the Reichstag during the 1936 Berlin Olympic Games. Later, in the Second World War, he was shot down in the Pacific and drifted on a liferaft for forty-seven days. He survived attacks by Japanese pilots who swooped down on him for target practice. Finally, the Japanese captured him and put him in prison for two years. Although he was a famous athlete and war hero, he came home feeling unhappy, disillusioned, and broken in spirit. One night he wandered into our tent in Los Angeles with his wife and accepted Christ, and his life was transformed.

Finally, a closing day came for the 1949 Los Angeles Campaign, a month late. In anticipation, a pastors' breakfast on Wednesday of the final week at the Alexandria Hotel drew 500 ministers and other Christian workers. They planned to spend one hour together but stayed for four, listening to testimonies by Hamblen, Vaus, Zamperini, and Harvey Fritts, who starred in a popular television show as "Colonel Zack." In his report on the event, Claude Jenkins indicated that some people thought the breakfast was the spiritual highlight of the Campaign.

On Sunday afternoon, November 20, two hours before the start of the final meeting, 11,000 people packed the tent to standing room only. Thousands milled about in the streets, unable to get in. Hundreds left because they couldn't hear. On the platform with me were 450 fellow ministers, to whom now fell the awesome challenge of shepherding those who had come forward through the weeks.

For that time, the statistics were overwhelming. In eight weeks, hundreds of thousands had heard, and thousands had responded to accept Christ as Savior; 82 percent of them had never been church members. Thousands more, already Christians, had come forward to register various fresh commitments to the Lord. Someone calculated that we had held seventy-two meetings. I had preached sixty-five full sermons and given hundreds of evangelistic talks to small groups, in addition to talks on the radio.

That evening, exhausted after the final meeting, T.W., Ruth, and I got on the Santa Fe *Super Chief* train, hoping to get a couple of days of rest traveling back to Minneapolis. We were greeted by the conductor and the porter as though we were some kind of celebrities. A strange experience, believe me.

As we knelt together to pray before climbing into our berths, we were both grateful and afraid. We could hardly find words to express to the Lord our thanks for His many mercies to us personally, and for His blessing on the Los Angeles Campaign. But we feared that we did not have the capacity to live up to our responsibilities. People were expecting so much from us now.

When the train stopped briefly in Kansas City, we were met by a couple of reporters. When we got to Minneapolis, the press was again there to interview us, along with some Twin Cities pastors and faculty and students from Northwestern Schools. Until then it had not fully registered with me how far-reaching the impact of the Los Angeles Campaign had been. I would learn over the next few weeks that the phenomenon of that Los Angeles tent Campaign at Washington and Hill Streets would forever change the face of my ministry and my life. Overnight we had gone from being a little evangelistic team, whose speaker also served with Youth for Christ and Northwestern Schools, to what appeared to many to be the hope for national and international revival. Everywhere we turned, someone wanted us to come and do for them what had been done in Los Angeles. What they didn't know, however, was that *we* had not done it. I was still a country preacher with too much on my plate. Whatever this could be called and whatever it would become, it was *God's* doing.

In the middle of all the press hoopla in Minneapolis, one of George Wilson's little girls ran up and handed me a rose.

"Uncle Billy," she said, "we prayed for you."

And of course I had my own two little daughters praying for me every night. That put it all in perspective. That was the whole secret of everything that had happened: God had answered prayer.

10

Whirlwind

BOSTON, COLUMBIA, NEW ENGLAND, THE TEAM 1950

Was Los Angeles a flash in the pan, a quirk, a unique event caused by better organization or greater advertising? Or was it the symptom of something deeper, a new hunger for spiritual reality? Boston, the next Campaign—scheduled to begin less than six weeks after the close of the Los Angeles meetings—would provide the answer.

Discussions about going to Boston had taken place long before the Los Angeles meetings. The Evangelistic Association of New England (a fellowship of evangelical pastors) had asked me to hold a New Year's Eve service in Mechanics Hall, and Dr. Harold John Ockenga had invited me to preach for a week afterward in the historic Park Street Church in downtown Boston.

Though I was intimidated by Boston's reputation as the educational and cultural capital of the United States, I took the opportunity to conduct a Campaign there as a gift from God.

BOSTON

"EVANGELIST HERE TO VIE WITH NEW YEAR'S FUN," read the headline in the *Boston Herald* on December 30, 1949. The accompanying story went on to say, somewhat skeptically, that I

159

was "a youthful evangelist who thinks he can outrival the convivial lures of New Year's Eve with a Mechanic's Building religious rally tomorrow night."

Not everyone in Boston renounced traditional New Year's Eve observances, of course, but that first meeting of the Campaign unexpectedly drew a capacity crowd.

"Although hotels, night clubs and bars in the city were crowded last night," reported the *Boston Sunday Globe,* "the largest gathering in all of Greater Boston packed Mechanics Building to hear Rev. Billy Graham, crusader for Christ. . . ."

The announced sermon topics for the opening weekend were phrased to catch interest: "Will God Spare America?" "Must We Fight?" "The New Social Order." But people soon found out that my theme was always the same: God's redemptive love for sinners, and the need for personal repentance and conversion. The topics were timely, but the basic message was eternal. "I doubt that mankind will ever see the year 2000," the *Boston Globe* quoted me as saying. "Our wild, sinful way of living in this country must be a stench in the holy nostrils of God."

I hadn't expected our arrival to cause much controversy, but it did. Many in Boston considered me a throwback to Puritan times, hopelessly out of date. Some extreme liberal and Unitarian clergy said I was setting back the cause of religion a hundred years. I replied that I did indeed *want* to set religion back—not just a hundred years but nineteen hundred years, to the Book of Acts, where first-century followers of Christ were accused of turning the Roman Empire upside down.

Quite a lot of publicity was given to my taking issue publicly with Harvard's distinguished professor of anthropology Dr. Earnest A. Hooton, for his defense of a "mercy killing" and his attack on a God who would call such an act murder. As a college major in his field, I had read his famous book, *Up from the Ape,* and I respected his scholarship. But his attitude toward religion and the Ten Commandments struck me as intellectually arrogant.

As our support swelled, the meetings were extended. After two nights with Dr. Ockenga, we left Park Street Church and went back to Mechanics Hall for as long as it was available. We then moved

160

briefly to the Opera House and concluded at the 13,000-seat Boston Garden on Monday, January 16. Crowds were unprecedented; thousands had to be turned away on some occasions. After more than doubling the original schedule to seventeen days, we at last ran out of available meeting spaces.

Response to the Invitation at each service overwhelmed us physically. There had been no significant training of counselors in advance of the meetings. Hence, all of us on the Team—including Grady, Cliff, Bev, and myself—met with individual inquirers, helped by volunteers who stepped forward on the spur of the moment.

Heartening to us also was the response of the Roman Catholic Church, remarkable especially in light of the fact that the landmark decisions on ecumenism of the Second Vatican Council were still years away. "BRAVO BILLY!" read the editorial headline in the *Pilot*, the official newspaper of the Boston Archdiocese. "We are 'not amused' by his critics, some unfortunately among the Protestant cloth. . . . If, as some people seem to think, the non-Catholic Christian congregations of New England are disintegrating, we are not such bigots as to rejoice therein."

Should we leave Boston, or should we stay? That was the question. After much thought and prayer, we decided to leave. If we had stayed for six weeks or six months more, might God have sent a sweeping revival to New England like the Great Awakening in an earlier century? On the train leaving the city of the baked bean and the cod, my misgivings almost made me get off at the next stop. So many doors of opportunity stood ajar all over the region, even at the renowned New England universities, beckoning us to walk in.

In the end, I continued on to Toronto to fulfill a scheduled engagement. One thing was clear to me, though. We should follow up as soon as possible with a Campaign that would go beyond Boston into the rest of New England.

In my closing sermon of the Boston Campaign, I mentioned having talked to an unnamed underworld figure. When we arrived in Niagara Falls on our way to Toronto, the police were waiting and the Boston newspapers were calling. It seemed that the multimillion-dollar robbery of the Brink's Boston express office had occurred on January 17, the day after the Campaign closed. The law officers thought I knew something about it. But the underworld figure I had in mind was Jim Vaus on the West Coast. Their interrogation gave Grady and me some much-needed comic relief.

COLUMBIA, SOUTH CAROLINA

In late winter of 1950, we held our first major southern Crusade in Columbia, South Carolina. Governor Strom Thurmond invited Ruth and me to come and stay in the governor's mansion as his guests.

One day while there, we received a call from a Mr. Howland, the head of the Atlanta office of *Time* and *Life*, saying that the founding editor and publisher, Henry Luce, wanted to come down and spend two or three days with us. Mr. Luce, it seemed, had received a letter from his friend, senior statesman and financier Bernard Baruch, who was vacationing at Hobcaw Barony, his plantation near Charleston. The morning newspaper in Columbia, the *State*, was carrying my sermons each day, and Mr. Baruch had been reading them. He had told Mr. Luce that this was something he thought America needed and that he should send some of his people to get acquainted with me. Henry Luce decided to come himself.

We were meeting in the Township Auditorium, seating about 3,800. Most of the ministers in the city were supporting the Campaign. Helping us tremendously was fellow Wheatonite Don Hoke, by then a professor at Columbia Bible College.

The night Mr. Luce came, I was very tense because I had announced I was going to preach on divine judgment. I thought to myself, "Henry Luce will be turned off by my sermon on judgment." But the more I thought about it, the more I felt certain that the Holy Spirit had led me to speak on that subject, regardless of who would be in attendance. As I preached it, I felt a tremendous sense of God's power, and a number of people responded to the Invitation. Mr. Luce himself responded in a way. He decided that his magazines would not only carry newsworthy articles about our work but also support us editorially. It seemed his parents had been missionaries in China, as Ruth's had been, and their spiritual legacy to him was evident in some of his attitudes.

One of the most important developments from our South Carolina meetings was the growth of our Team, a group of dedicated people who would strengthen our work for years to come.

Willis Haymaker first joined our Team in Columbia to help us with organization. His credentials were impressive; a former banker, he had worked for Billy Sunday, Gipsy Smith, and Bob Jones (father and son). He arranged a variety of small gatherings for us and re-served and dispensed blocks of tickets for cooperating churches during the Campaign. It was Willis, in his preliminary work in Columbia, who urged us to drop the word *Campaign* in favor of *Crusade*. The word *Campaign*, Willis pointed out, had been used for many years by evangelists, and was associated in the public mind with outmoded (or even sensationalist) ways of doing things. A new word was needed, he felt, and we agreed on *Crusade*.

Willis's wisdom and experience soon became indispensable. Not only did he know how to organize a Crusade, but he was also upbeat and enthusiastic. He would go before us into a city to analyze the situation and see if we should hold a Crusade there. Then, once we decided to go, he would set up the office and enlist key people to organize every detail. He would also call on the local Catholic bishop or other clerics to acquaint them with Crusade plans and invite them to the meetings; they would usually appoint a priest to attend and report back. This was years before Vatican II's openness to Protestants, but we were concerned to let the Catholic bishops see that my goal was not to get people to leave their church; rather, I wanted them to commit their lives to Christ.

At Columbia we were also joined for the first time by Tedd Smith, a Canadian recently graduated from the Royal Conservatory of Music in Toronto. He had been secretary and pianist for Chuck Templeton both in his church and with Youth for Christ. In the early days, when we traveled, he would often act as my secretary as well as my pianist, and he was a great typist. One of his vital but unrecognized tasks was to make sure there was always a glass of warm water for me at the pulpit when I got up to speak; ice water only tightens the throat muscles.

For our closing meeting in Columbia, we booked the University of South Carolina stadium for a big open-air meeting. With

40,000 in attendance, the meeting made national news, and both *Life* and *Time* carried stories on it. What had begun in Los Angeles and continued in Boston now took the South by storm.

After the Crusade, Governor Strom Thurmond provided us with a state police escort for a hastily prepared two-week preaching tour of the state. That itinerary included a return to Bob Jones University (relocated by then in Greenville, South Carolina), where I was introduced to a crowded auditorium by Bob Jones, Jr. My sermon, which was on Belshazzar that day, was also carried live on the campus radio station, WMUU (acronym of World's Most Unusual University).

The day after the end of our whirlwind tour, I flew back to Boston, determined to pick up where we had left off a couple of months before.

NEW ENGLAND

At the end of March 1950, a circulation war was raging among Boston's five daily newspapers. They chose to make us a focal point of their competition, sending fifteen or twenty reporters with us everywhere. In addition, *Look* magazine sent senior reporter Lewis Gillenson to cover us, and both the United Press International and the Associated Press sent correspondents. It had been a long time since religion had gotten such press attention in Boston, if it ever had (although the city editor of the *Boston Post* wrote to wool merchant Allan Emery, Jr., that the paper had covered earlier evangelistic meetings by Billy Sunday, Gipsy Smith, and J. Wilbur Chapman).

I did not know how to conduct myself in front of the reporters. Sometimes in my innocence I made statements on politics and foreign affairs that were outside my jurisdiction as a preacher. But experience was gradually teaching all of us to be more careful.

Once I sent Grady to preach for me in Fall River, Massachusetts, because I had a touch of the flu. That afternoon one of the Boston newspapers carried a headline based on Grady's effort to impress them that I really was sick. "GRAHAM CARRIES GOSPEL DESPITE DEATH PERIL." Even though we got a good laugh out of it, we took the lesson seriously. It was not necessary for us to exaggerate anything.

An intensive twenty-day itinerary beginning on March 27 took us to about fifteen cities, with many one-night rallies. In addition, Grady preached in a dozen places, and Cliff led at least one Saturday afternoon children's service. Grady and Jack Wyrtzen substituted for me on two occasions when I was sick, and I myself preached at least twenty times. In addition, there were the constant automobile trips to new destinations, and new committees to meet once we got there. But what a work God did during this tour of New England! Of the many thousands of people who attended the meetings in churches, school and municipal auditoriums, sports stadiums, and theaters (and even an airplane hangar in Houlton, Maine), hundreds of them made commitments to Jesus Christ. Everywhere, despite often bitterly cold or rainy weather, overflow crowds packed surrounding streets and waited until I came out and gave a short sermon for them. Police escorts did a great job of getting us through.

Although we held meetings during 1950 in a wide range of settings in the Northeast, it was the opportunities at New England universities—among them, MIT, Brown, Harvard, Yale, Amherst, Vassar, Wellesley, and the University of Massachusetts—that touched me most deeply. They had an impact on me in at least two ways.

First, they demonstrated beyond doubt that in spite of what often appeared to be a lack of seriousness, many students were open to the Gospel and would give it a respectful hearing. We were such celebrities all over this area that the students were fascinated by and curious about who we were and what we had to say. It was more than that, however. I detected, in fact, a deep-seated spiritual hunger on the part of many. The anxieties of the Atomic Age and the moral decline and confusion evidenced by the recently released first Kinsey report were causing many thoughtful students to reevaluate their lives and give more thought to their need for a spiritual foundation.

Second, my appetite for more opportunities to speak in university settings had been sharpened. I always felt the power of the Holy Spirit in these student meetings. I didn't claim to be an intellectual, nor did I have the academic training to answer every philosophical question that might be raised. But I had come to realize that there was absolutely no need to apologize for the Gospel of Jesus Christ in academic settings. The Gospel could more than hold its own. It alone dealt with the deepest questions of the human mind. It alone met the deepest yearnings of the human heart. As someone once commented to me, the Gospel wasn't so much examined and rejected on most university campuses as it was ignored.

In spite of my deep desire to give more time to universities, however, I had relatively little opportunity to do so during the next couple of years. Following our 1949 and 1950 meetings, there was an explosion in invitations to hold citywide Crusades. In responding to those invitations, I was kept in constant motion.

What could we do for the closing meeting in Boston in order to accommodate those reportedly wanting to attend from all over New England? The decision was made to use the Boston Common. (We called it a Peace Rally because war clouds were gathering in the Far East, and we felt the word *peace* was something everyone could rally around.)

The prospect of preaching on the historic Boston Common was numbing to me for a number of reasons.

A big open space in the heart of a city was a far cry from, say, a junior high school auditorium in Portsmouth, New Hampshire. Would enough people show up to make a respectable crowd?

Staging the meeting outside posed a weather problem too. I have never been quite sure who controls the weather. Although we always prayed for clear skies, I had had to preach in all kinds of storms.

Then there was the question of my own stamina. The Lord tells us to be anxious for nothing (*see* Philippians 4:6), but that's always been a hard lesson for me to learn.

It was raining when I got up that Sunday morning. Pouring! I gathered the Team in my hotel room. "Let's pray and ask God to clear the sky, if it's His will," I urged.

When we were finished, my anxiety lifted. I had complete peace of heart, even when the newspapers phoned about noon to ask if we were going to cancel the meeting because of the bad weather.

"No," I said. "The sun will be shining by the time the meeting begins at three o'clock." They laughed. So did my friends.

At two o'clock, as the first hymn was being sung, the rain stopped. One hour later, when I stepped to the pulpit to preach, a sun-drenched crowd—reported by the *Boston Post* to be 50,000 strong—smiled up at me.

I remembered reading that George Whitefield had preached there in 1740 to many thousands of people without benefit of an amplification system. What a voice he must have had! Incidentally, I borrowed Whitefield's topic for my sermon that day: "Shall God Reign in New England?"

At that time, Protestantism in New England was weak, due in part to theological differences within some denominations, the influence of Unitarian ideas in other denominations, and the strength of the Roman Catholic Church. In spite of all that, a number of Roman Catholic priests and Unitarian clergy, together with some of their parishioners, came to the meetings along with those from evangelical churches. With my limited evangelical background, this was a further expansion of my own ecumenical outlook. I now began to make friends among people from many different backgrounds and to develop a spiritual love for their clergy.

Three people from Boston brought a surge of gratitude to my heart during those days.

The first was Harold Ockenga, who was, as I have said, the distinguished minister of Park Street Church in Boston. He intimidated me because of his intellectual caliber, with his Ph.D. from the University of Pittsburgh; but his intellectualism made him a perfect fit for ministry in that academic citadel. I felt that I was no match for him in any way; indeed, I worried that with my simple preaching I might be an embarrassment to his sophistication and scholarship. As we got to know each other, I came to realize that Harold was a rare blend of intellectual ability and deep personal piety.

Harold was looked on as *the* evangelical intellectual leader, not only in New England but also in the United States. He had just been elected the first president of the new National Association of Evangelicals. One of his close friends and colleagues at Park Street Church was Allan Emery, Jr. (the wool merchant mentioned earlier); a generation earlier, Allan's father had been chairman of the Billy Sunday meetings.

Stopping by Park Street Church one day during our April meetings in 1950, I knocked on the door of Harold's office. There was no response, although I thought I heard a faint sound inside. I opened the door and walked in. The sound I had heard came again; it was someone sobbing. At first I could not see anyone. Then, behind the desk, I found Harold prostrate on the floor, praying brokenly with tears. Though he was not an emotional type, the burden he had carried so long for the spiritual and moral needs of New England had wrung the weeping from him.

I vividly remember another incident with Harold during those days. Rockwell Cage Gymnasium at the Massachusetts Institute of Technology was filled with students for our meeting. As the service began, some waved beer and whiskey bottles in the air and generally let it be known that they did not take kindly to an evangelist on the campus. A few, we even heard, were planning a prank. During the service, someone was going to hobble in on crutches, shouting, "I'm healed! I'm healed!" and then throw his crutches in the air.

Harold was scheduled to introduce me.

"Harold," I hastily whispered to him, "give me the most intellectual introduction you've ever given anybody. Maybe that will calm them down."

He responded to my plea with an extended introduction that was nothing less than a masterpiece, not only drawing on his awesome command of the English language but touching on some of the major philosophical and intellectual trends of the day, and then setting my address within the context of MIT's recent centennial and the school's tradition of objective scientific inquiry.

When I spoke, there were no disruptions, and I have seldom had a more attentive audience.

"This has been an age in which we have humanized God and deified man, and we have worshiped at the throne of science. We thought that science could bring about Utopia," I declared. "We must have a spiritual awakening similar to that which we had under Wesley and Whitefield," I added, as I urged them to commit their lives to Christ.

The second person God placed in my life in Boston was John Bolten. He was a German industrialist who had amassed his wealth after World War I. A cultured man and a fine musician, John would sit at the piano with tears flowing down his cheeks as he played Bach, Beethoven, and other German composers, some of whom his family had been personal friends with.

Along with many other industrialists and businessmen in Germany during that period, John was acquainted with Adolf Hitler. When Hitler's anti-Jewish policies became open and violent, however, a group of leading businessmen decided to withdraw their support. John felt forced to leave Germany in 1928, leaving behind his industrial empire.

In 1929 John emigrated to Boston, where he slowly but steadily rebuilt his fortune. Harold Ockenga had a great influence on John during those years. At one of our 1950 meetings, John recommitted his life to Christ, and in the following years he became a firm friend and golfing partner to me, as well as a supporter who paid a lot of our bills. His knowledge of the Bible was encyclopedic, and we often spent hours praying or talking about the meaning of certain biblical passages. At my suggestion, he later became a member of the board of *Christianity Today* magazine in its early years, and I always valued his wise and thoughtful counsel.

One day John said something that touched me where I was most vulnerable. Despite the Los Angeles boost and the current vigorous response to the Gospel in New England, I still thought the recent nationwide interest in our ministry was a meteoric flash across the religious sky that would fizzle as fast as it had flared.

Indeed, secretly one side of me rather hoped it would. I loved evangelism, and I felt at home in the pulpit ministry. But the nationwide publicity was unnerving. I did not feel equal to the responsibilities it demanded. I almost wanted to escape to academe.

"Billy," John said to me one day as we walked across the Boston Common, "I can envision you preaching in the great stadiums of the capital cities of the world. I believe the world is ripe and ready to listen to a voice of authority like yours. They are in need of the Gospel. You are the man to give it to them."

Incredible! This intellectual and business tycoon was surely out of his element. But whether he was right about me or not, he opened a new dimension for me to think and pray about. And from that moment on, whenever John spoke, I listened.

The third Bostonian who influenced me was Allan Emery, Jr. I had met him in our student days at Wheaton, and during the New England meetings I was able to pick up the friendship again. He was the son of one of the world's largest wool merchants; his home in the heart of Boston was a replica of Mount Vernon. The thing that made Allan special to me was his deep love for Christ, his humility and sense of humor, his business ability, and his experience as a ship commander during World War II. Some years later, Allan became chairman of the executive committee of the Billy Graham Evangelistic Association. For many years now, he has given of himself unstintingly for this ministry.

For many good reasons—some having to do with people such as these; others dealing more directly with issues—it was hard to leave New England the second time.

The California and New England experiences had shocked us with undeniable proof that thousands of people in this country were spiritual seekers, ready to listen to the Gospel and willing to respond.

But what were people looking for that they didn't already have?

The euphoria of military victories in Europe and the Far East should have left most of us feeling self-sufficient and optimistic—hardly the ideal climate for a religious revival. But instead, we were headed for anxiety and apathy. For one thing, we worried about a mushroom cloud drifting on the horizon of history over the ghost cities of Japan, and about a red star rising in eastern Europe. Under this double threat to our security and happiness, what purpose was left in life? We didn't seem to have either an exhilarating sense of national destiny or a satisfying sense of personal identity. Even the Korean War, with the kind of negative invigoration of the spirit most international conflicts bring, let people down on that point. Our American men and women in the armed forces were losing their lives overseas again, and few seemed to know why.

What we saw in 1950 were the early stirrings of a wide-reaching spiritual search—stirrings that helped to create an unaccustomed audience for the Gospel. Disillusioned and disconnected people seemed willing to try anything. It was a morally promising but exceedingly perilous time.

It was a trying time for me personally because I was not a profound analyst by nature, nor could I claim a gift of prophecy. All I knew how to do was to preach the essential Gospel as revealed in the New Testament and experienced by millions across the centuries. It was the "old, old story of Jesus and His love," as a hymn writer put it, but maybe it caught fresh attention because it was such an unfamiliar story to so many.

All of these social and religious currents swirled around us as we headed from New England to Portland, Oregon.

11

Building for the Future

PORTLAND, FILMS, RADIO (*The Hour of Decision*),
THE BILLY GRAHAM EVANGELISTIC ASSOCIATION,
ATLANTA 1950

Almost half a century later it is impossible to re-create the nonstop activity and excitement that engulfed us during those months following our meetings in Los Angeles and Boston. At times I felt almost as if we were standing in the path of a roaring avalanche or a strong riptide, and all we could do was hold on and trust God to help us. Not only were we unaccustomed to the crowds and the publicity, but unexpectedly we found ourselves facing a new (and happy) problem: a flood of invitations urging us to hold Crusades in many of the larger cities of the United States.

In response to these pleas, we committed ourselves to extended Crusades in two cities during the second half of 1950: Portland, Oregon, and Atlanta, Georgia. Little did we imagine the impact they would have on our future ministry.

PORTLAND

Three hundred churches and a number of Christian laypeople had invited us to the Northwest's beautiful City of Roses, beginning in July 1950. Although the local council of churches stayed aloof toward this

172

largely unknown evangelist from the South, the Lord greatly used Dr. Frank Phillips to prepare the way for us. A veterinarian whom I had spent a week with in 1948 and had talked into starting a Youth for Christ rally in Portland, Frank proved to be so effective for YFC that he was appointed executive vice president of YFC International at its Chicago headquarters. Health reasons sent him back to Portland to direct YFC there, and to put together our Crusade.

A temporary wooden tabernacle seating 12,000 people, constructed for $40,000 with lots of volunteer labor from men, women, and children, turned out to be too small on several occasions: a total of more than 500,000 people attended the six-week Crusade. Some 9,000 inquirers signed decision cards when they talked with counselors.

Frank saw to it that people with special needs were thoughtfully considered. He made arrangements for a local pastor, Willis Ethridge, to sign for the deaf; this was a first for us. And Crusade participants added their own contribution: newspaper reports said that three deaf and mute participants used their fingertips to pass the songs and sermon along to some blind folks by spelling out words on their palms and cheeks, much as Anne Sullivan had done for Helen Keller as a child.

Another first in Portland: we tried separate meetings for men and women on the subject of problems in the American home. Some 11,000 showed up for the first one, which was for men; I told the audience not to tell the women what I had told them. Out of curiosity, I think, 30,000 packed the tabernacle and the surrounding circus lot for the women's session, listening via an outdoor public address system. Such a massive turnout had some of the women sitting in trees and even on the tabernacle roof. Police had to detour traffic around the jammed streets.

So many parents were attending the Crusade meetings that five satellite tents had to be set up. In those, volunteers could care for up to 300 crib babies and young children. Other volunteers helped 3,000 drivers find parking spaces for their cars each night.

At noontime we held meetings in a small downtown park, where hundreds of people gathered, huddling under their umbrellas to listen when it poured rain.

Once, on a Saturday afternoon, Cliff filled the tabernacle with 8,000 children, vividly dramatizing for them stories from the Old Testament—Naaman the leper among them.

At the closing "Crusade for Freedom" rally in Multnomah Stadium on Labor Day, September 4, the governors of Washington and Oregon were present to bring greetings to a crowd estimated at 22,000. (Governor Arthur Langlie of Washington became one of my best political friends and one of the links between me and Eisenhower in the years to come.) At the Invitation, 1,200 came forward.

Statistics are never the full story of any Crusade. I have mentioned these only because at that early stage in our ministry, they verified for me a groundswell of public responsiveness to the Gospel. With each new Crusade experience, I was increasingly driven to the conclusion that it was not a fluke. Instead, it was the Lord letting us in on a special moving of the Holy Spirit in America. With that conviction, I was open to three unforeseen developments.

MAKING FILMS

The first such development had to do with films in evangelism.

While still a student at Wheaton College, I thought that someone ought to make evangelistic motion pictures. The one and only religious film I had seen was amateurish and unlikely to appeal to unchurched people.

Our first effort in that direction came in connection with the Portland Crusade in 1950. Bob Pierce had told me about a filmmaker named Dick Ross, who had accompanied him on a trip to China and prepared a documentary that was well received in churches.

"You ought to have one of your Crusades filmed," Bob urged me.

After some discussion, the local committee in Portland invited Dick to send a small crew to make a sixteen-millimeter color film about the Crusade, which could be shown in churches in the Northwest. Dick had a small production company called Great Commission Films.

Eventually, his company merged with the company we ourselves had already set up, Billy Graham Films. (We later changed the name to World Wide Pictures. I felt that my name might discourage some people from attending.) We constructed a building in Burbank, just across from the Walt Disney Studios. *The Portland Story* was the first of about two hundred films we have done.

Soon after the Portland Crusade, Dick and I got to talking about the use of films in evangelism. "Why," I asked, "don't we do a fictional story that would be a dramatic picture, totally Christian and evangelical and evangelistic, appealing to young people?"

Our next Crusade was scheduled to be in Fort Worth in early 1951, and we decided to make the film there. We centered the film's story around the conversion of a rodeo rider in that Crusade. Redd Harper and Cindy Walker agreed to star in *Mr. Texas,* which we made on a low budget. In a fit of brashness, we rented the Hollywood Bowl for the world premiere. The outdoor arena seated 25,000 people; 5,000 more sat on the hillside. The audience included some of Hollywood's best-known film executives, among them Cecil B. DeMille, Frank Freeman, and Walter Wanger.

A few months earlier, I had been invited to Paramount Studios to have lunch with that company's president, Frank Freeman, whose wife was a deeply spiritual person. There I met DeMille; he was in preproduction for the remake of his 1923 classic, *The Ten Commandments.* Also at the lunch were Anthony Quinn, Barbara Stanwyck, Betty Hutton, and Bob Hunter, a Paramount executive who was a committed Christian and treasurer of Hollywood's First Presbyterian Church.

During the lunch, Frank made me a proposition: "Billy, MGM has employed an evangelist by the name of Clifford to act in one of their films. But we at Paramount think that your name and ability would be far superior, and I'd like to ask you to consider doing a film with us."

I looked him straight in the eye, with the others listening, and told him that God had called me to preach the Gospel and that I would never do anything else as long as I lived. And then I related my own experience with Christ for the benefit of all those at the table.

At Jerry Beavan's suggestion, we hired twenty-five searchlights to crisscross the sky for the *Mr. Texas* premiere, outdoing anything the film capital had seen before. As I look back, I blush at our brazenness—not just in that lighting effort but in the whole

175

project—and at the extent to which our youthful zeal sometimes outraced our knowledge. As soon as the showing started, we realized that the loudspeakers were too far away from some of the audience; and the sound was not synchronized exactly between the forty-foot screen and the top tier of seats a thousand feet away. Then the projector broke down.

I wanted the earth to open up and swallow me, I was so embarrassed! I hastily called some of our Team to one side. We fervently prayed that God would help the technicians get the projector started. After five minutes, the movie came on again, and we were able to watch the remainder without incident. To my utter amazement, when I gave the Invitation at the end of the film, 500 people responded. The whole incident impressed on us the risks of taking things for granted, particularly when dealing with something as complex as film.

Nevertheless, I was so excited about this new step in our ministry that I took a copy of the film with me to London to show to the great British filmmaker J. Arthur Rank, whom I had met on a previous visit. He watched the screening patiently and then spoke diplomatically. "Well, you know, the thing you're trying to get over comes across. It's not technically a good film, but the message comes across."

He was right, of course—the movie left much to be desired—and it irked me that we had not done a professionally acceptable job. Arthur Rank's comments made me determined to do our future films to the highest standard possible. And yet *Mr. Texas* is being shown in many parts of the world still, and I continually come across people who came to Christ as a result of seeing it.

RADIO—*The Hour of Decision*

The second development had much more immediate consequences for us.

Some months before, in Boston, I heard over the radio that Dr. Walter A. Maier, the great Lutheran theologian and radio preacher from St. Louis, had died of a heart attack. I was so jolted that I knelt in my hotel room and prayed that God might raise up someone to take his place on the radio. In those days, radio was still king; television's impact was just beginning to be felt. There were only a few evangelical programs on national radio, and none seemed to have a wide audience among nonbelievers. Dr. Maier and Charles Fuller were virtually the only preachers on national radio at the time.

Early that summer, while I was preaching at a conference led by Walter Smyth in New Jersey, Cliff and I stopped for lunch one day at a roadside diner and were greeted by a big, smiling man whose eyes grew large as he studied me.

"Hallelujah!" he shouted, grabbing and pumping my hand. "What an answer to prayer! I was just sitting here praying that I might meet Billy Graham, and in you walk! I didn't even know you were on the East Coast."

He introduced himself as Dr. Theodore Elsner, a preacher from Philadelphia.

"I have a great burden on my heart," he said. "It's a message that I believe is from the Lord. Billy, you must go on national radio. You know Dr. Maier is dead, and you're the man God could use to touch America through radio."

I did not know what to think.

Dr. Elsner urged me to contact Fred Dienert, his son-in-law, and Walter Bennett, a Christian who was also a radio agent. Impressed though I was by this abrupt meeting, I did not look up either Mr. Dienert or Mr. Bennett; indeed, I pretty much forgot the whole idea. I was so busy that I could not imagine adding anything else to my plate.

A few weeks later I was speaking at a conference in Michigan. Two well-dressed strangers approached and introduced themselves as Fred Dienert and Walter Bennett. I did not know whether Dr. Elsner had spoken with them since he had met me, but their mission was to interest me in a national radio program.

I was still president of Northwestern Schools, still active with YFC, and spinning in a whirlwind of national interest in our evangelistic Crusades. I told Fred and Walter that I appreciated their interest but simply could not do a radio program at the time. My closest advisers—Cliff, Bev, and Grady—concurred: it was out of the question.

Now, in Portland, these two extremely persistent men repeatedly lay in ambush to catch me. All they wanted, they claimed, was five minutes of my time. I got so irritated with their pestering that sometimes I took a back elevator to avoid them. I finally told Grady to let them know I was not interested in their scheme to get me into broadcasting. *Leave me alone* was my message.

But as I came out of the hotel one night, there they were.

"We want to say good-bye," one of them said. "We're leaving tonight for Chicago."

"All right, fellows," I said laughingly, "if before midnight tonight I should get $25,000 for the purpose of a radio broadcast, I'll take that as an answer to prayer and be willing to do a national broadcast."

The thought was so incredible to them that they laughed along with me before heading for the airport.

More than 17,000 people were at the meeting that night. Just before introducing my friend Bob Pierce for a brief report on his travels in the Far East, I told them about the burden Walter and Fred had for broadcasting the Gospel, and the $25,000 condition I had laid down. The audience joined in my laugh. After Bob spoke, I preached and then extended the Invitation to receive Christ. Afterward, in the little room set aside for me in the tabernacle, a number of people dropped by to greet me. Several of them said they believed God had spoken to them during the service about helping us go on national radio. They began to leave cash, checks, and pledges. I couldn't believe it!

"Billy," said Frank Phillips when everybody had left, "people have given us $24,000 tonight for radio!"

Their confidence and generosity were enough to make me weep. But how could this be God's answer? It was $1,000 short. I told Grady, Cliff, Ruth, and Frank that maybe the Devil could give us that much to mislead us. We agreed to say nothing to anyone else about the funds and went out to eat.

It was our custom to have supper after the service. That night we went to a little Japanese sukiyaki place across the street. (Ruth continued to cultivate my taste for Oriental food.) We got back to the hotel about eleven-thirty.

"There are two letters here for you, Mr. Graham," said the desk clerk.

Postmarked two days earlier, they were from people I hardly knew—businessmen Howard Butt and Bill Mead. Both said they believed we should go on the radio and that they wanted to be the first to contribute. And each enclosed a $500 check!

Stunned, I bowed my head and said a silent prayer. Emotion so overcame me that I could not think straight. Clearly, the funds had come from God. Then, when I turned to go to the elevator, who should be standing in the lobby but Walter and Fred! They had been at the airport, they said, but something had told them not to get on the plane.

I put my hands on a shoulder of each man. "Sign us up for radio for at least thirteen weeks," I told them. "God has answered prayer. We have the $25,000. We'll take this as a step of faith."

I was not kidding about that, since the total estimated cost, at $7,000 per week, would be $91,000—an astronomical amount that was nowhere in sight. Not in *my* sight, anyway.

Walter and Fred arrived in New York on a Saturday to conclude the contract, and they found only one person in the ABC offices, a junior executive. He informed them that the ABC board had just made a decision not to allow any more religious programming on the network.

Walter and Fred protested strenuously: "You *promised* it. We've guaranteed this young man, Billy Graham, that he has a network. To change your minds now is very unfair to us. Get hold of the board."

"That's impossible," he said. "They're all playing golf."

"Well, get them on the golf course."

"I can't do that," he said, digging in his heels. "You'll have to wait till Monday."

"We are *not* coming back on Monday," they said firmly. "We'll sit here until this thing is resolved."

Seeing their determination, the man finally reached one of the board members on the eighteenth hole and explained the situation. The board's decision was reversed on the spot, and *The Hour of Decision* was saved.

In mid-August we signed a contract for thirteen weeks with the American Broadcasting Company to go on their coast-to-coast network, with a target starting date during our upcoming Atlanta Crusade.

That was the beginning of my lifelong friendship with Walter and Fred. The Walter Bennett Agency handled everything for us, both initially and through the years. Walter had great business ability and was very skilled in negotiating contracts for us. Fred was Walter's partner, and over the years he not only personally handled all of our advertising and other related matters in radio and television, but also became a liaison with my publishers. On an even deeper and more personal level, he and his wife, Millie, went on vacation with Ruth and me for many years. He is in Heaven now, and I continue to miss him.

When we were considering going on radio, some people suggested that we adopt a folksy or informal format. But I analyzed the styles of those who had the highest ratings at the time—newsmen such as Walter Winchell, Drew Pearson, and Gabriel Heater, as well as the late Dr. Maier, whom I admired greatly. All four were fast and intense speakers. That fitted my own natural style.

From the first, I decided to use a lot of current illustrations from national and international affairs as well as from social issues. I wanted to bring the Bible to bear on those matters, concentrating on a direct presentation of the Gospel with a clear call to decision. For a while, I even had a news Teletype machine in our house so I could keep abreast of the latest events for these messages.

Listener response immediately confirmed that we were meeting a need in people's lives. Within two years, we were receiving three to four thousand letters a week. This correspondence was the beginning of our mailing list. The programs quickly became self-sustaining with a minimum of comment about finances. In 1954 we extended *The Hour of Decision* to the NBC network as well, bringing the total to eight hundred stations; that did not include foreign and shortwave.

NBC had a policy against selling time for religious broadcasting, but the network made an exception through the personal interest of NBC's founder and president, General David Sarnoff. I met him, seemingly by accident, in Hawaii.

When we were on the ship returning us from Japan and Korea in early 1953, we met a Jewish businessman named Jack Lewis. He invited us to a party he was giving, during which a woman performed a hula dance. When she found out who I was, she apologized, fearing that she had offended me. I told her I had been to Hawaii before and knew that the hula was part of their ancient culture. It turned out that she was the wife of the owner of Honolulu's morning newspaper. After our arrival in the islands, she invited me to a dinner party at their home. General Sarnoff and his wife were there, and afterward they offered to take me back to the hotel. On the way, the general asked, "Is there anything I can do for you?"

"Yes, sir." I could tell he was surprised at my quick answer. "I'd like to go on NBC with my radio program."

"I'll see what I can do," he said.

Apparently true to his word, we soon were on NBC every Sunday evening.

Often we broadcast live from various places where we were holding Crusades, from the front lines during the Korean War to the Hollywood Bowl.

THE BILLY GRAHAM EVANGELISTIC ASSOCIATION

One final development during the Portland Crusade came about as a direct result of the money we collected to start our radio evangelism.

Grady Wilson and I had a problem.

Underneath his bed in the hotel in Portland, Oregon, was a shoebox filled with $25,000 in cash, checks, and pledges.

But what could we do with the money?

Offerings for all of our Campaigns and Crusades had always been collected by the local sponsoring committee and placed in a bank account set up by that group. But the money in the shoebox had been collected for a purpose that had nothing to do with the 1950 Portland Crusade and therefore could not be deposited in the local Crusade account. As I told the crowd that evening, the collection would go toward radio.

Needless to say, the money needed to be deposited in a bank right away. Either one of us could open a local account under his own name and deposit the money in it, of course, but he would be subject to income tax on the full amount.

The larger problem, we had begun to realize, was that we had no formal organization. We had simply been known as the Graham-Barrows Campaigns, but we had never formed a separate corporation or opened a bank account in that name. For that matter, we did not even have a board of directors. To make things worse, if we did go on the air nationwide, people would probably send us contributions to purchase more radio time. But then we would be dealing with a larger number of donors and larger amounts of money.

From time to time, we talked about establishing a separate nonprofit organization for our work. George Wilson, our business manager at Northwestern Schools, had even made some preliminary inquiries with an attorney. I called George from Portland and told him our desperate, if happy, problem. He suggested that we go ahead with formal incorporation, and almost immediately he filed documents in St. Paul, the capital of Minnesota, establishing the Billy Graham Evangelistic Association (often abbreviated BGEA).

George was the one who chose the name, although I protested strongly. George protested just as strongly that the new organization needed to be identified with my name, since I was the major evangelist. Forty-seven years later, I still wish my name were not so visible. It is God's organization, not mine, and if we ever lose sight of that fact, God will withdraw His blessing from our work.

The incorporation papers required a statement of purpose. George put it in simple and direct language: "To spread and propagate the Gospel of the Lord Jesus Christ by any and all . . . means." That was our purpose up to that time, and since that time it has continued to be our purpose.

The first directors were Cliff Barrows, Grady Wilson, George Wilson, and myself; a few years later, Bev Shea was also added. Across the street from Northwestern Schools, George rented 620 square feet of office space, more than enough for any imaginable needs the new corporation might have. He hired accountant Mary

Cook as our first employee; she and her husband had come from Portland to work at Northwestern.

I called Walter Bennett in Chicago and asked him to become our agent to buy radio time. Then I asked if he and Fred Dienert would go to Minneapolis to sit down with George and help get us organized.

Almost immediately after the first broadcast from the Atlanta Crusade on November 5, 1950, mail and donations began to pour into the Minneapolis office—although in that first program we did not even ask for donations. Within weeks we were processing hundreds of letters every day, each needing a thank-you letter and, if a gift was enclosed, a receipt.

For our broadcast time, we chose Sunday afternoons at three. In some towns, traffic at that hour was so light, we were told, that police assumed everybody was inside listening to Billy Graham.

Soon George resigned from Northwestern to become BGEA's full-time business manager. We also added our first secretary, Lorrayne Edberg. Later, a former student at Northwestern, Esther Hawley LaDow, began working for us and served faithfully in the BGEA office as George's executive assistant and in other capacities until her retirement four decades later. My own personal secretary at Northwestern, Luverne Gustavson, had not only a good business head but also a strong feel for Christian ethics; she too would soon join BGEA.

As far as numbers went, Portland was a successful Crusade. As the Lord said to ancient Israel, "I know the plans I have for you" (Jeremiah 29:11), and "As the heavens are higher than the earth, so are my ways higher than your ways and my thoughts than your thoughts" (Isaiah 55:9). That prophetic message related very specifically to Portland in a special way. I spoke to the press club there at the close of the Crusade.

"This may be God's last revival in Portland," I said to them. "I'm going on the basis of the fact that very few great citywide revivals ever come to a city over once a generation. I seriously doubt if the old America is going to exist another generation unless we have a turning to Christ. If we don't have a turning to religion in this country, I do not believe that we can stand. And I would include, of course, Portland in that."

ATLANTA

From the cool climate of the great Northwest in the summer of 1950, we headed to Minneapolis for some large rallies. Then, in the late autumn, we headed for Atlanta, a city that evangelist Dwight L. Moody had described as "harder to break for God than hard-rock gravel."

The first thing to go wrong took place on October 26. A gunman fatally shot the general secretary of the central YMCA on Luckie Street and then took refuge in our Crusade office in that same building. He ordered our two young secretaries to call the police and to keep everyone else away from him or he would use his gun again. We were all thankful that the incident ended without them being hurt. "GUNMAN MENACES NEWSMAN AT GRAHAM CRUSADE OFFICE" ran the next headline of the *Atlanta Journal.*

A misunderstanding spawned another problem. It was our custom to hold a weekly private, closed meeting with the clergy during our Crusades, during which I brought a brief message to encourage them, reported on Crusade progress, and made some off-the-record remarks about the local religious scene as I observed it.

In November, as we approached the climax of the six-week Crusade, at one of those meetings in St. Mark's Methodist Church I told 80 fellow preachers that worldliness in the churches indicated a need for rededication on the part of ministers. A retired minister present, who wrote religious reports for the *Atlanta Constitution,* wrote up his personal version of the meeting for the paper. One of that paper's columnists picked the topic up and created a mild furor with the headline "BILLY GRAHAM'S 'STINGING SLAP' AT AT-LANTA MINISTERS IS VIEWED AS REGRETTABLE."

Although I was determined not to reply to criticisms, this was something I had to address. After all, we had been invited to Atlanta by 135 churches from many denominations, both white and black— a group headed by Dr. Paul James of the Baptist Tabernacle—and by numerous Christian laypeople headed by Charles Outlaw. Furthermore, Methodist Bishop Arthur Moore was a staunch supporter of the Crusade. In a letter to the editor of the *Constitution* I reaffirmed my pledge never again to "preach" at preachers in this way.

The day after the closing meeting on December 10, the *Atlanta Constitution*, accompanying its wrap-up story of the Crusade, printed two pictures side by side. In the first, I was grinning broadly and waving good-bye as I stepped into a car for my departure to South Carolina. In the next, two Crusade ushers, with a uniformed police sergeant between them, could barely wrap their arms around four bulging money sacks. "GRAHAM 'LOVE OFFERING' COLLECTED AT FINAL SERVICE," read the caption.

I was horrified by the implication. Was I an Elmer Gantry who had successfully fleeced another flock? Many might just decide that I was.

We had already publicized one fiscal-policy safeguard. Newspaperman Morgan Blake, an active Crusade worker, had published a detailed story on our audit procedures, debunking the rumor that I had demanded a guarantee of $100,000 as a condition of my coming to Atlanta. He pointed out that all collections were transported immediately to the Fulton National Bank, which counted the money the next morning for deposit in the local Crusade committee's account.

Other Team members received an honorarium for their work out of that, but Cliff and I received nothing personally except for our living expenses while in Atlanta. Instead, as was traditional in evangelistic work, love offerings were designated for the two of us at the close of the Crusade. I received 60 percent and Cliff 40 percent.

I was embarrassed to discover that this offering in Atlanta was larger than the sum most clergy made in an entire year. Ruth and I gave away about a third of our portion. With the rest, we finished remodeling our mountain home and bought a wooded tract of land up on the mountain, where we now live.

Riding back to Montreat in the car, I promised myself that such a misunderstanding would never happen again. We had to find some other way to support ourselves than through love offerings. Cliff agreed with me.

I got in touch with a wise older friend, Dr. Jesse M. Bader, evangelism secretary for the former Federal Council of Churches. "You've incorporated your ministry," he said, "so let the board put you on the payroll as a salaried employee." The salary, he urged, should compare favorably with that of a typical minister in any average large-city church. We put his recommendation into action, and that has been our guideline ever since.

If one day of the Atlanta Crusade can be singled out as a red-letter day, it would have to be November 5, 1950. That Sunday afternoon, live from Ponce de Leon Park, we went on the ABC radio network with our first nationwide broadcast of *The Hour of Decision*. Cliff led a thousand-voice choir, Bev sang, Grady read Scripture, and I preached. Tedd Smith was at the piano, and Paul Mickelson from California took over at the organ for Bill Berntsen, who'd been with us in Portland but had had to return to his teaching duties at Northwestern Schools, where he was head of the music department. Our potential audience was 9 million listeners. For that first *Hour of Decision* broadcast from Atlanta, a scheduling problem at the station in Minneapolis, of all places, pitted our lineup against truly awesome competition from a new NBC radio program called *The Big Show*. Its initial broadcast was also on November 5, originating at Radio City in New York and featuring Tallulah Bankhead, Fred Allen and Portland Hoffa, Jimmy Durante, José Ferrer, Frankie Laine, Ethel Merman, Danny Thomas, Mindy Carson, and Meredith Willson's orchestra. Talk about a David and Goliath confrontation! Yet our ratings turned out to be surprisingly strong.

The year 1950 ended as it had started, with a New Year's Eve rally at Mechanics Hall in Boston. On the whole, the press was friendlier than they had been during our first visit a year before. The *Boston Post* heralded our arrival on December 29 with this headline on the first page: "BILLY GRAHAM IS IN HOPEFUL MOOD." The subhead read, "Fiery Preacher Here for Weekend Revival Encouraged by Trend of Leaders to Prayer."

The accompanying picture showed me standing with my arm around Mother at the Bellevue Hotel; it was the first time she had been with me at a citywide Crusade outside of North Carolina. My father had refused to make the trip, saying that Boston was too cold for his southern blood.

It was now a year since we had completed the Los Angeles Crusade, which had thrust us into the national media spotlight. So much had happened so fast. Clearly, it had been the year of the whirlwind. Cumulative attendance at the meetings had passed the 1.5 million mark, with nearly 50,000 recorded inquirers. It was the Lord's doing, and it was marvelous in our eyes. But if things went on at this rate, where might they lead? I needed time to catch my breath and my balance, both. Invitations flooded in, and with eight Crusades scheduled, ranging from three days to six weeks, we were booked every month in 1951. As our calendar began to fill up even further ahead, 1952 was starting to shape up much the same. Our main concern, of course—whether at a Crusade or on the radio or at some other speaking engagement—continued to be the souls of people.

Clearly, the Lord was setting our course for the immediate future. In the one year between Los Angeles and Atlanta, we had developed an organization, a radio broadcast, a film ministry, a financial policy, and a compatible Team. Now we needed to find out if all these things would work.

12

The General Who
Became President

PRESIDENT DWIGHT D. EISENHOWER

It was 1952, and I was on the most farfetched mission I could imagine.

Some time before, I'd had dinner with a friend from Fort Worth, Texas—oil baron Sid Richardson, whom I affectionately called Mr. Sid—and we had discussed General Dwight D. Eisenhower as a possible candidate in the 1952 election. Mr. Sid had urged me to contact Eisenhower and encourage him to run. During Eisenhower's short tenure as president of Columbia University, his speeches had marked him as a conservative, but nobody knew his party affiliation. Rumors said Harry Truman hoped he would run as a Democrat.

In spite of Mr. Sid's confidence in me, I had no illusions about being able to persuade Eisenhower to run. After all, he had been telling both parties for years that he was not interested. And I was not interested in being sidetracked by politics! Though a registered Democrat (a sort of birthright in the part of the South where I came from), I always voted for the man and not the party.

I wrote the same thing in a letter to Mr. Sid, which he forwarded to Eisenhower in France, where he was serving as Commander at the Supreme Headquarters of the Allied Powers in

Europe (SHAPE). In it I stressed the need for a man like the general to become president. "The American people have come to the point where they want a man with honesty, integrity, and spiritual power," I wrote to Mr. Sid. "I believe the General has it. I hope you can persuade him to put his hat in the ring."

On November 8, 1951, Eisenhower wrote to me, cordially reacting to the case I had presented in my letter to Mr. Sid, and reaffirming his refusal to make a partisan declaration. A month later, I wrote directly to him for the first time. A district judge, I told him, had "confided in me that if Washington were not cleaned out in the next two or three years, we were going to enter a period of chaos that could bring about our downfall. Sometimes I wonder who is going to win the battle first—the barbarians beating at our gates from without, or the termites of immorality from within." I assured him of my prayers for God to "guide you in the greatest decision of your life. Upon this decision could well rest the destiny of the Western World."

Nobody could accuse me of understatement. I even brashly told him that I had "been in Europe six times since the end of World War II, and I know something of your dilemma." Back then I was not averse to publicly criticizing the U.S. State Department for its many blunders, but how foolish and presumptuous that appears now!

I was told that Eisenhower said to Mr. Sid, "That was the damnedest letter I ever got. Who is this young fellow?"

"I'll send him over so you can meet him," Mr. Sid replied.

Meanwhile, Eisenhower's letter to me sharpened my desire to see him become president under whatever label he chose. I was heartened that he told me to "continue to press and fight for the old-fashioned virtues of integrity, decency, and straightforwardness in public life." He continued, "I applaud your efforts to support high moral standards and to remind us of the priceless privileges of freedom in our political, economic, and religious life."

I felt that the country would be fortunate to have a national leader who espoused such principles. I was pleased, therefore, when Mr. Sid arranged for me to meet General Eisenhower in Europe.

Shortly after the Washington Crusade in early 1952, I traveled by ship to Europe, going by way of England—where Ruth and I, Cliff and Billie, and T.W. stopped at the invitation of the British

Evangelical Alliance to hold discussions with British clergy about a possible Crusade—and Germany, for other Crusade explorations. Then on to Paris. By this time it was March.

As our taxi pulled up in front of SHAPE, I was tense. Leaving Cliff and our close friend Bob Evans to wait for me, I was escorted by a military aide past various guardposts to the office of the commander of the Allied forces.

General Eisenhower welcomed me warmly, with an outstretched hand and a wide smile. He was younger looking than I had expected, and more down-to-earth. Although he was in uniform, his office looked like that of a corporate executive, with walnut-paneled walls, a walnut desk, and green carpeting to match his chair. (Columbia University had sent both desk and chair from his office on the New York City campus.)

We talked about our mutual friend, Sid Richardson. I explained that Mr. Sid often introduced me to people he thought I should know.

The General shared some of his religious experiences as a boy. His parents had been River Brethren, a small but devoutly pious group in the Mennonite tradition. They had read the New Testament in the original Greek and had taught their sons to memorize Scripture, just as my parents had taught me.

He asked me about the Washington Crusade in the National Guard Armory and the message I was preaching. I considered that an especially perceptive question. Most people assumed they knew what preachers were all about, but the General was interested enough to probe my basic message. He listened intently and confessed that he and his wife, Mamie, rarely attended military chapel services, even during wartime.

We talked about the Korean War and about the gains Communists were making around the world. And of course we talked about the following November's election.

"General Eisenhower," I said, "I must tell you that no matter how much I might be for you privately, I couldn't issue a public political statement."

"I'm glad to hear you say that," he said. "I wouldn't expect you to."

In more than two hours together, at no time did he hint that he would run. Still, I left feeling that I had met the next president of the United States.

Four months later, in Chicago, the Republican Convention nominated General Eisenhower, with Senator Richard Nixon as his running mate. To my surprise, a call came from Frank Carlson, a senator from Kansas whom I had gotten to know during our Washington Crusade; he told me that General Eisenhower wanted to see me. Mystified, I traveled immediately to Chicago to meet with him at the Blackstone Hotel. Apparently, Carlson had sold Eisenhower on the idea that I could contribute a religious note to some of his campaign speeches.

"Would you be willing?" Eisenhower asked.

"Of course I want to do anything I can for you," I said, "but as I told you last spring, I have to be careful not to publicly disclose my preferences or become embroiled in partisan politics."

"I understand," he said. "But would you be able to come and see me in Denver next month? Plan on spending a few days."

In August we were together at the Brown Palace Hotel in Denver for several sessions. During these, I gave him some Scripture verses I thought he might find helpful. Once I absentmindedly addressed him as "Congressman." I quickly recovered but said "Senator." By the time I got around to "General," he was laughing and I was red-faced.

"Why don't you just call me Ike," he said, but I never could. It was "Mr. President" when he was in office, and "General" when he was not.

I respected his desire to inject a spiritual tone into his campaign, and the moment came when I felt free to talk to him about his own faith.

"General, do you still respect the religious teaching of your father and mother?" I asked.

"Yes," he said, adding softly, "but I've gotten a long way from it."

I also felt free to present the Gospel to him and to clarify again the message that I preached. He told me that he had become disillusioned with the church early on when some preachers seemed to detour from spiritual essentials to merely social or even secular matters.

"Frankly," I said, "I don't think the American people would be happy with a president who didn't belong to any church or even attend one."

"As soon as the election is over, I'll join a church," he said. "But I'm not going to do it in order to get elected. I don't want to use the church politically."

"What denomination do you have in mind?" I asked.

"I've thought about that," he said. "I suppose Presbyterian, because Mamie is Presbyterian. Do you know any good Presbyterian churches in Washington?"

I recommended a couple, including National Presbyterian, where the pastor had been a wartime chaplain on the European front. He made a note of the name. In the course of our meetings in Denver, I gave him a red-leather Bible, which I inscribed to him on the flyleaf. In later years, some articles mentioned that he kept a red Bible by his bedside during his presidency.

When Eisenhower won the election in November, I was asked by the press to pray for the President-elect in front of newsreel cameras. It had been only two years since the Truman fiasco, when photographers had asked me to pray on the White House lawn. I agreed, but I took care not to repeat what had taken place privately between Eisenhower and me, but I gladly prayed that the new President be given wisdom, confidence, strength, humility, and a deep dependence on God. I urged Americans to close ranks behind him and to pray for him.

Shortly after the election, an opportunity for ministry arose that effectively removed me from any further direct involvement with General Eisenhower before his inauguration.

For months I had been receiving letters from missionaries, chaplains, GIs, and Korean religious leaders asking if I could come to Korea. Bob Pierce, the founder of World Vision, also urged me to go. The war was in full swing, but as much as I wanted to comply, going seemed impossible. Back then our schedule was made up almost two years in advance, and I hesitated to cancel anything already established.

The year 1952 had already proved the most strenuous in my ministry. We had held more Crusades and scheduled more meetings, and I had preached more sermons than ever. We were involved in radio, television, and film, and I was even writing a book.

My schedule for the months of November and December included a Crusade in Albuquerque and a series of TV programs in Hollywood. I hoped to take the last two weeks of December off to relax with my family in the mountains of North Carolina. How could I possibly squeeze in a Korean tour?

Before the Albuquerque meetings, Ruth was able to join me in Florida, and we had a couple of days to ourselves. As she and I settled into a little hotel room for a couple of days, I suddenly turned to her. "Darling, what would you think about my going to Korea to spend Christmas with our troops?" I asked.

Since Ruth had been born in China and had attended high school in Korea, she knew and loved the land and its people. "I think it would be wonderful," she said without hesitation.

"It's hard to think about a Christmas away from home," I said.

"We'll manage," she assured me.

Knowing that she was behind me, I asked Bob Pierce and Grady Wilson to see how quickly they could make the arrangements. We three would be the only ones going. We would fly out of Albuquerque after the Crusade and rest a few days in Honolulu before the long, grueling flight to the Far East. Grady had told us that a doctor had prescribed sleeping pills for him, to allow him to sleep on the plane.

Somehow Ruth—never one to turn down an opportunity for a practical joke—got hold of those sleeping pills and replaced them with empty capsules she had gotten at a pharmacy and filled with hot mustard powder, sharing her plan with Bob and me. Grady did not pull them out until he, Bob, and I finally left Honolulu to head for our next stop, Tokyo. We settled into the special beds on the Boeing Stratocruiser. Grady asked Bob and me if we wanted one of his sleeping pills. We both said yes and pretended to take them.

About halfway through the night, I noticed that Grady was still awake.

"Can't you sleep?" I whispered.

"I've got terrible heartburn," he said. "I just took another sleeping pill. The first one didn't work!"

Our first stop was Japan, and I will never forget seeing that beautiful coastline from the air. This was part of the area my wife knew so well and about which she had told me so much. We were several hours late, but as we got off the plane, we were greeted by well-wishers singing Christian songs in English and carrying a sign that read, "WELCOME BILLY GRAHAM TO JAPAN."

The red tape of getting us into a war zone was monumental. But once we got over there, we were delighted to find that we had the support of the U.S. military. I hadn't been in Tokyo but two or three days when I got an invitation to see General Mark Clark, commander of U.N. and U.S. Army forces in the Far East. He was so warm and gracious that I immediately felt at home. He said he had read about our work and knew us by reputation.

"I want to give you the field rank of major general. When you go to Korea, I want you to go to all the military sites you have time for, and I'll see to it that you have everything you need."

He rolled out the red carpet for us, providing transportation, lodging, and entrée to every spot we wanted to visit. That proved to be of great benefit, allowing us to get around in a difficult area. While the missionaries set up meetings for us, often it was the military who provided sound systems or lighting or carpentry or transportation.

While in Japan, I heard a rumor that years earlier the emperor had made an astounding statement to General Douglas MacArthur. "I'll make Japan a Christian nation," he said.

MacArthur thought about it for a day or two before he responded. "No, then Japan wouldn't be truly Christian. The people must come to Christ voluntarily."

So then, instead of the emperor proclaiming Christianity as the official state religion, General MacArthur sent out an appeal to the United States for ten thousand missionaries and ten million Bibles. American churches responded with perhaps a thousand missionaries and two or three million Bibles.

Years later, when I was visiting General MacArthur in his suite in New York's Waldorf-Astoria Hotel, he confirmed the story. Many people have wondered what would have happened had MacArthur accepted the emperor's offer.

At a banquet in Tokyo, Japan, I addressed 750 missionaries in what some said was the largest meeting ever of missionaries in the field. Never had I felt less worthy to stand before an audience. These were the true warriors of the Cross. They had left their homes and loved ones to battle on the front lines for the Gospel. God spoke to me through their example, and I would never be the same.

The missionaries were tired, discouraged, and in need of a laugh. That night I shared with them the practical joke Ruth had pulled on Grady with the sleeping pills. They loved it, nearly falling off their chairs laughing. Grady, sitting at the head table, was hearing this for the first time. He turned several shades of red; for once his sense of humor abandoned him. But when he saw Ruth again back in the States, he had to laugh; it was the first time, he said, that he had taken a mustard plaster internally.

My first opportunity to meet American GIs was in Tokyo General Hospital. I was moved as I saw the wounded. We talked to men whose spines had been crushed and who were paralyzed for life. We talked to others who had had their skulls split open. One boy had lost both eyes, an arm, and a leg, yet he greeted me with a smile. I would never forget those valiant men.

I preached in several meetings before leaving Japan. I felt great liberty in speaking, and this confirmed in my heart that God had indeed sent us. Then we left for Korea. It was sunset as we approached the coastline. I could see why Korea was called the Switzerland of the Far East; the mountains were blanketed with snow. Little villages with their thatched-roof houses reflected the rosy tint of the setting sun. It was a picture of tranquillity. Only when we were on the ground and could see all the armaments, the devastation, and the poverty did we realize the enormity of the war.

My first contact with the Korean people made me realize why my wife loved them so. They smiled when there was little to smile about, and they were deeply grateful for even the smallest gift.

Over the next two weeks, I would travel under military supervision and in military transportation, preaching all over Korea, seeing how the Korean people existed in the towns and villages, and meeting the American GIs who represented us in the conflict. It seemed that everywhere we went there was despair and fear and danger. And yet every meeting, from gatherings at makeshift platforms near the fighting areas to more formal meetings in various cities, was packed with eager, enthusiastic audiences. Many hundreds responded to the Invitation to receive Christ and be converted.

We had not been in Korea long before we developed a real affection for the children. Each night in our street meetings in the city of Pusan, the southernmost city in Korea, three or four hundred children sat right in front. From my seat on the platform, I would wink and smile at them during the preliminaries, causing them to cover their giggles with their hands. In the children's hospitals and foundling homes, we saw babies sleeping on the floor.

One night we had to walk what seemed like several miles in sticky, ankle-deep mud to reach "the Lighthouse," a home for blind children. I had the unforgettable experience of hearing a little blind fellow stand and sing in English "The Love of God":

> The love of God is greater far
> Than tongue or pen can ever tell;
> It goes beyond the highest star,
> And reaches to the lowest hell;
> The guilty pair, bowed down with care,
> God gave His Son to win;
> His erring child He reconciled,
> And pardoned from his sin.
>
> Oh love of God, how rich and pure!
> How measureless and strong!
> It shall forevermore endure
> The saints' and angels' song. . . .

At the Oriental Missionary Society on the outskirts of Pusan, seminary students huddled in frigid, unheated classrooms, studying ten to twelve hours a day, eating and sleeping in the same room they studied in. Prayer was a hallmark of these believers.

Young and new to the international scene, I wrote more than one unflattering entry in my diary: "I am certain that some of our leaders are going to have to answer to Almighty God for the terrible suffering and death of this land. Every soldier we have lost, every civilian who has died or been murdered is the result of the scandalous decision by the men who sold us down the river in the secret agreements at the peace tables."

I had never been so weary. I slept through heavy gunfire nearby, slept on a bumpy, noisy nighttime train passing through ambush territory, and still felt as if I were living on adrenaline all the time. On our way from Pusan to Seoul, we were inside a train car that had an open flatcar ahead and behind it, filled with soldiers. We were told to pile our luggage around us because guerrillas would shoot at anything that moved. Just a few days before, a newspaperman traveling through that area had his fingers shot off as he slept!

One highlight was preaching to 2,500 a night in the unheated but huge and beautiful Young Nak Presbyterian Church in Seoul, pastored by Han Kyung Chik. Many GIs got special leave to come from the front lines. I can never forget the sight of American soldiers alongside Koreans at the front of the church, responding to the Invitation. Korean pastors would grip my hand in their humble, gracious way and in tears thank us for coming to encourage them.

My first sermon on the front lines saw me on a newly built platform graced by a painting done by a soldier forty miles away. Troops had carried the painting (which depicted Christ watching over an exhausted soldier) to us overnight, and it stood next to me as I preached. I did not use humor or stories to break the ice that night. I dove right into the Gospel, and hundreds responded. I felt the Spirit of God in that meeting. Men of every rank came forward, many in tears—and they were tough, rugged men!—to receive Christ.

In the evacuation hospitals, we saw more of the horrible effects of war. On the way to one hospital, Grady was in one helicopter and I was in another. General Jenkins, who was escorting us, shot a wild boar from the airship and radioed down to his mess sergeant where to find it so that we could have it for dinner. Before we landed, however, we were assailed by flak from the ground. The copter pilots had to fly low and hide us behind trees and ridges. For some reason, I was not scared and didn't assume it was the end for me. The more dangerous it was, the more I sometimes felt I was really doing something for the Lord.

At a base camp, I spoke to the officers. Then, in the moonlight, we rode by jeep two or three miles to another camp. The password that day was "Christmas card," I later learned. If a guard said "Christmas" to you, you had to respond "card." These passwords changed every day. When we were stopped by guards on the way, the general with us found that he had forgotten the password! The guards pointed their rifles at him and shone a flashlight in his face, demanding identification. He had to work hard to convince them that he was who he said he was.

It was thirty degrees below zero, and we were grateful for the clothing that the military had supplied: big gloves, thick boots, military hats with the chaplain's cross, and even heavy underwear.

In a field hospital about a mile behind the front lines on Christmas Eve, we went from bed to bed, bringing greetings and trying to encourage the wounded. One young man was so mangled that he lay face down on a canvas-and-steel contraption. A doctor whispered to me, "I doubt he'll ever walk again."

"Mr. Graham, could I see your face?" asked the young man. "We've all been praying for you and looking forward to your coming. I won't be able to be at the service." So I lay on the floor beneath him and looked up into his hollow eyes, still stunned with his fate. I prayed with him.

"Sir," said the young man to General Jenkins, who was escorting me, "I fought for you, but I've never seen you. Could I see *your* face?"

The general got down on all fours, slid under that bed as best he could, and talked with the young man. I saw a tear fall from the soldier onto the general's cheek.

When we walked from the bleeding, broken, dying men of that hospital into the crisp, clean, thirty-below-zero air of Christmas Eve, I felt sadder, older, and more aware of the needs and suffering not only in Asia but also in the entire world.

At one of our Christmas Day services, I got to meet and have pictures taken with Major John Eisenhower, son of the President-elect. I found him both delightful and appreciative of our visit. His father had just recently been there.

I wired his father from Korea that I would like to see him on my return. Eisenhower invited me to visit him at the Commodore Hotel in New York City five days before the inauguration. He asked me to bring the pictures of his son to show him.

We wrapped up our Korean trip on December 25. Soon after our return, I headed for New York for my scheduled meeting with Eisenhower. After I briefed him on the trip, he got to the real reason for our meeting. "I'd like to quote one or two passages from the Bible in my inaugural speech," he said.

I suggested several references, among which was the one he chose, 2 Chronicles 7:14 (KJV): "If my people, which are called by my name, shall humble themselves, and pray, and seek my face, and turn from their wicked ways; then will I hear from heaven, and will forgive their sin, and will heal their land." He would rest his hand on that passage when he took the oath of office.

The General stepped to a window in the Commodore Hotel and looked out across the city as we talked. "I think one of the reasons I was elected was to help lead this country spiritually," he said. "We *need* a spiritual renewal."

I told him I could not agree more and suggested that he make one of his first official acts the proclamation of a national day of prayer. He said he would. Eisenhower's own spiritual pilgrimage had moved rapidly. Prior to the inaugural ceremony at the Capitol, he arranged a worship service for his incoming administration.

I was as astounded as anyone else, though, when at the conclusion of the inaugural address he read a prayer he had written himself for the occasion. It was traditional, of course, to have various clergy give official prayers. But here was the President himself, praying his own prayer.

Rumor had it that I wrote the prayer for him, or had at least helped. But I did not even know he was considering a prayer, and it bothered me that such reports persisted. Years later I wrote Mamie Eisenhower to recount how I had suggested only some Scripture verses as her husband had requested. In her typically gracious way, she sent me a handwritten note: "Please do not give . . . that newspaper account another thought. Of course I personally saw Ike write his own little prayer, so why worry about what other folks say."

As soon as Eisenhower assumed office, he proved that he was as good as his word. He proclaimed a national day of prayer, as promised, and joined the National Presbyterian Church. That church affiliation was no perfunctory ritual. When the President made his intentions known, Pastor Ed Elson told him they must first spend an hour a day together for five days for religious instruction. Eisenhower complied humbly and became grounded in what it means to be a Christian and a Presbyterian before he was baptized into church membership. On the day of his baptism, the congregation sang "What a Friend We Have in Jesus"; Eisenhower later told Bev Shea that it was his favorite hymn.

My official interactions with President Eisenhower were always warm and friendly, but they were also mostly formal. I was never invited to the private quarters of the White House, for instance. (Nor, for that matter, was Vice President Nixon.) Our meetings were always in the Oval Office. We did, however, enjoy some golf together.

One day Grady Wilson and I were playing golf with Richard Nixon at the Burning Tree Country Club near Washington. We were told that the President and his partners were playing ahead of us. When I was in the clubhouse shower afterward, Grady dashed in. "The President wants to see you," he said.

I stepped out of the shower and grabbed a towel. For the next several minutes, I stood there, dripping, chatting with the President of the United States, who was wearing white tie and tails on his way to a state dinner.

"You're probably the only preacher in history who's talked to the President and the Vice President of the United States so informally," chuckled Nixon as we rode back to the city later.

Subsequent golf games with Eisenhower himself are happy memories. I can still see the President jumping in glee one day when his partner, who happened to be Grady, sank a fifty-foot putt on the eighteenth hole at Palm Springs, clinching their victory over my partner and me. Golf gave me not only a way to relax but also, when played with well-known people, a chance to exercise my ministry in a relaxed, informal way. Golf games (and other informal encounters) with the President bonded us more closely at the spiritual level. I became more and more impressed with his character and the intensity of his growing faith, which he not only formally confessed but also applied to policies and programs.

Civil rights, for example. He saw the need for decisive action to end racial discrimination. A crisis flared in Little Rock in September 1957 when Arkansas Governor Orval Faubus called in National Guard troops to bar black children from the public schools. By that time, Eisenhower already had strong convictions based in part on his study of the 1955 bus boycott in Montgomery, Alabama.

He and I talked and corresponded about the issue. His executive order to eliminate racial segregation in the armed forces left no doubt what side he was on. The whole nation needed healing.

I expected the clergy to take the lead. Because of stands I had taken against segregated seating in our Crusades from the early days, Eisenhower knew I was active within my own sphere. Before he sent federal troops into Little Rock to enforce the law, he phoned me in New York—where we had been holding the Madison Square Garden Crusade—to ask what I thought.

"I think you've got no alternative," I said. "The discrimination must be stopped."

An hour later, Richard Nixon phoned and asked the same thing. Some might say I was advising the President on a political issue. I did not see it that way, though. He saw fit to ask my opinion, as I was sure he did of many other counselors. I also believed there were important moral and spiritual issues at stake. I hope he was at least encouraged to know that he was in my prayers concerning this fateful decision.

My deep convictions on racial integration got a direct challenge when I was asked shortly afterward by the Little Rock Ministerial Association to come to help unite the city by preaching in Little Rock's large War Memorial Stadium. I called my old Christian friend Congressman Brooks Hays from Arkansas and asked his advice.

"You don't want to call for the chaplain too early in these things," he said. "Do it, but wait a year."

I took his advice. In September 1959, I went to Little Rock to preach. The previous year, I had preached to an integrated audience in Clinton, Tennessee. Senator Estes Kefauver and columnist Drew Pearson had challenged me to come. I said I would if they would come with me and sit on the platform. The White Citizens' Council there made some very strong statements against me and the event. It was reported they said that I would never get out of town alive. That convinced me of the rightness of my going.

In Little Rock, I again insisted on fully integrated seating. It could have been lighting the fuse to a powder keg, but nothing blew up that night. We held the meeting with a capacity crowd of blacks and whites intermingled throughout the stadium. Governor Orval Faubus came and could not find a seat; finally, he sat on the steps leading down into the stadium, way in the back.

PRESIDENTIAL PRAYER BREAKFASTS

During Eisenhower's administration, several of us helped start what was then called the Presidential Prayer Breakfast (now the National Prayer Breakfast). This is how it began.

In the early 1950s, while we were in Portland, Oregon, I met a remarkable man by the name of Abraham Vereide. He talked to me about having regular prayer groups of businessmen, something he had already started in Seattle. When we arrived in Seattle for our Crusade a year later, Vereide came nightly to the meetings. Before or after each meeting, he would come around to see me, talking about the burden that he had to reach political leaders with the Gospel. He also came to my hotel room several times, talking about starting an annual Presidential Prayer Breakfast.

My part was to encourage him and also, as his plans became firm, to help him get President Eisenhower to the first prayer breakfast. The President was extremely reluctant. In fact, he turned down a request conveyed by Senator Frank Carlson. When I went to see him, he turned me down also, though he promised to think more about it. He eventually called or wrote to Senator Carlson to say he would come to the first one but would not promise to come to another one; he did not want to set a precedent.

At my Denver meeting with Eisenhower, he had introduced me to hotel magnate Conrad Hilton. That introduction was providential; Hilton was to become a financial sponsor of the annual Presidential Prayer Breakfasts in Washington for several years; after that, Bill Jones paid for the breakfasts. But the driving force was always Abraham Vereide, with (later) Dr. Richard Halverson, the distinguished chaplain to the Senate, and Doug Coe. Out of the first fifteen Prayer Breakfasts, I brought the main address in almost all of them, always using them as an opportunity to preach the Gospel and even giving a clear Invitation to follow Christ.

Eisenhower's faith did not go untested. Physical ailments included heart and stroke problems, among other maladies. God saw fit to preserve him, however, and I believe Eisenhower's faith was deepened through these experiences. Well into his term there were also moments when he pondered his spiritual state. In August 1955, I was awakened in a Washington hotel room late one Sunday night by a call from Sid Richardson in Fort Worth.

"Billy, I've had a terrible time tracking you down," he said. "The President wants to see you, and the White House couldn't locate you. I'll let them know where you are."

The next morning I was informed that a car would come by to take me to the President's farm in Gettysburg. I had hoped to fly to Charlotte later in the day to spend some time with my parents prior to a speaking engagement there that evening. I called them to say my plans had changed, but that I still hoped to keep the speaking commitment. I had no idea what President Eisenhower wanted, but all the way there I prayed that God would help me say the right thing.

When I arrived, the President opened the car door for me himself. At first it seemed that this would be just a social visit. We had a quiet lunch together and then went upstairs to pray with Mamie, who was sick in bed. Then he asked if I would like to tour the famous Gettysburg battlefield.

I told him both of my grandfathers had fought there.

"Do you know which group they were with—North or South Carolina?"

I called my mother from his home, and she told me the company that her father, Ben Coffey, had been in. So Eisenhower took me to the place he thought that company might have served while part of Pickett's Charge.

When we arrived at the battlefield, we switched from the car to a golf cart, with the Secret Service in another cart behind. President

Eisenhower narrated as he drove. As a student of the Civil War, and especially of the Battle of Gettysburg, he pointed out things I never knew before.

Back at the house, in his little den, he paced in front of the fireplace. I sensed that the real reason for my visit would soon be made clear.

"Billy, do you believe in Heaven?" he asked.

"Yes, sir, I do."

"Give me your reasons."

With my New Testament open, I gave the President a guided tour through the Scriptures that spoke of the future life.

"How can a person know he's going to Heaven?" he asked.

I explained the Gospel to him all over again, as I had on previous occasions. I sensed he was reassured by that most misunderstood message: salvation is by grace through faith in Christ alone, and not by anything we can do for ourselves.

As our day wound to a close, I told President Eisenhower that I had to speak in Charlotte that night. If I was not going to make the plane in Washington, I should call and postpone.

"You can fly straight to Charlotte in my Aero Commander," he offered.

I accepted gratefully, but after a full day and with the rush to get going, I failed to make a visit to the restroom. I didn't realize until in flight that I needed to use the facilities very badly, and there were none on the small plane. In desperation, I asked the pilot to land for a few minutes in Greensboro, a hundred miles north of Charlotte. He did—and it seemed that every person in that little airport recognized me as I hurried through! When I came out, I had to shake hands with many of them before I could get back on the plane. That necessary detour had properly humbled me for the evening's talk!

Shortly afterward, President Eisenhower suffered a heart attack, from which he slowly recovered. Given his earlier questions about Heaven, perhaps he had anticipated his illness.

He knew another truth that too few people understand. Peace between nations depends on goodwill between individuals. He personalized that sentiment at the end of one of my visits to him at the Walter Reed Army Hospital years later in 1968.

"Billy, I want you to do me a favor," he said. "Nixon and I have had our differences. There have been misunderstandings, at least on my part. Now he's going to be President, and my grandson is going to marry his daughter. I want to straighten things out. I think you're the one to help."

"I'll do my best, sir," I promised.

Eisenhower did not tell me the particulars of their differences, although I thought I knew. One sore spot had been Eisenhower's tardiness in endorsing Nixon in the 1960 campaign against Kennedy.

"I'd like to see Nixon, if he'd be willing to come and see me. Would you ask him?"

I was invited to Mr. Nixon's apartment in New York for dinner that very evening. Over steaks in front of the fireplace, I passed along Eisenhower's request.

"I'll call him in the morning and see him tomorrow," Nixon said.

I never learned the details of their reconciliation, but I have no doubt that it took place. Both men were eager to put their differences behind them.

Not long afterward, in December of 1968, I had a private meeting at Walter Reed with Eisenhower. The details of our conversation were so intimate and sacred that I never hinted of them until after his death; then I asked Mamie's permission to reveal them, which she gave willingly.

As my scheduled twenty minutes with him extended to thirty, he asked the doctor and nurses to leave us. Propped up on pillows amidst intravenous tubes, he took my hand and looked into my eyes. "Billy, you've told me how to be sure my sins are forgiven and that I'm going to Heaven. Would you tell me again?"

I took out my New Testament and read to him again the familiar Gospel verses, the precious promises of God about eternal life. Then, my hand still in his, I prayed briefly.

"Thank you," he said. "I'm ready."

I knew he was. As I stood to leave, he grinned and waved.

"Billy, are you going to visit our boys in Vietnam again?" he asked.

"Yes, sir," I replied.

"Do me a favor and tell 'em there's an old doughboy back here praying for them."

"I will, General."

A few months later, when I was in the office of Foreign Secretary Abba Eban in Israel, I was handed a note saying that Eisenhower had died in Washington. I took the next available flight to New York and called President Nixon in Washington. He told me Mamie Eisenhower wanted to see me.

At a hotel in Washington, where she was receiving foreign guests, Mamie welcomed me warmly and asked me to sit beside her. I never understood why she wanted me there just then, instead of a government dignitary or one of her family, but it was an honor to comfort her.

Dwight Eisenhower was one of the great men in our history, and it was a privilege to know him.

13

Breakthrough in Britain

LONDON 1954

"A Labour member of Parliament announced today that he would challenge in Commons the admission of Billy Graham to England on the grounds the American evangelist was interfering in British politics under the guise of religion."

The captain of the SS *United States* received this news report by radio just a couple of days before we were due to dock at Southampton, England. The first steward brought me a copy. I was thankful that the captain hadn't included it in the daily news sheet that was distributed to all the passengers.

The message seemed simple enough on the surface, but at the same time it was mystifying and sent us to our knees. Was one of the most important Crusades we had ever undertaken up to this time about to collapse because we would not even be permitted to get off the ship?

We were confident we had done as much as we could, humanly speaking, to prepare for the Crusade, but we also knew that Satan would not allow a mission like this to go forth unopposed. Was the door now closing in our faces just as we were on the threshold?

Perhaps no decision in our ministry up to this time had been as difficult as this one: the decision to hold a Crusade in London, which at the time was billed as the world's largest city.

Since our first visit with Youth for Christ back in 1946 and 1947, Great Britain had had a special place in my thinking. For one thing, some of the great revivals in history, under the preaching of men like Whitefield and Wesley, had taken place in Britain. And Dwight L. Moody had had a remarkable ministry there in the latter part of the nineteenth century.

In addition, God had opened doors for us during our previous visits. During that extended tour in 1946 and 1947, we had called together in Birmingham 100 leaders from different churches; out of that four-day conference had come the British Youth for Christ movement. Tom Livermore, an Anglican clergyman, had been elected president, and many others had become involved, such as A. W. Goodwin-Hudson, who was later co–adjutor bishop of Sydney, Australia, and Birmingham industrialist Alfred Owen.

The publicity generated by our 1949 meetings in Los Angeles—as well as the documentary film about us, which was widely circulated in Britain—had further aroused the curiosity of many British evangelicals.

During the Washington, D.C., Crusade in January and February of 1952, two prominent British Christian leaders—one a clergyman, one a future member of Parliament—visited the meetings and talked with me about the possibility of a Crusade in London. A few weeks later, in March, I addressed a meeting of more than 750 British clergymen in the Assembly Hall of Church House, Westminster, the administrative headquarters of the Church of England; that gathering was held under the auspices of the British Evangelical Alliance. I had been asked to speak that day on our Crusade ministry in the United States.

In the reception line before the buffet luncheon at that March gathering, I met such national Christian leaders as the bishop of Barking, Hugh R. Gough (who later became the Archbishop of Sydney, Australia); Dr. D. Martyn Lloyd-Jones, one of Britain's outstanding preachers; General Sir Arthur Smith (who presided at the meeting), commander of forces protecting London during the blitz and later chairman of the Evangelical Alliance; and the Reverend Colin Kerr, whom I had gotten to know in 1946, vicar of St. Paul's Church, Portman Square, and prebendary of St. Paul's Cathedral.

I spoke for about ninety minutes, describing the new interest in evangelism and the Gospel that we had detected in America. In addition, I set forth some of the principles that guided us, including our commitment to work *with* the churches and not apart from them. The part of the speech that apparently made the deepest impression on my audience was my honest discussion of the major criticisms of mass evangelism, including the danger of false emotion, the potential overemphasis on finances, and the problem of converts who did not last. I addressed each of these as openly as possible and then outlined the specific ways we had worked to overcome them.

The substance of my message was later reprinted by the Evangelical Alliance and widely distributed across Britain. Following the address, I answered questions for about an hour. The next day, I met with a group of leaders who wanted to discuss the possibility of a Crusade in more detail. The upshot was a tentative invitation to hold meetings in London sometime during 1954.

A highlight of that 1952 trip was my being guest speaker at the Royal Albert Hall with the great British evangelist Tom Rees. Because the meeting was recorded for broadcast overseas by the British Broadcasting Corporation (BBC) and on the British Forces Network in Germany, the printed program carried some detailed instructions for the audience in the hall: "It is of the utmost importance that the hymns do not drag. The congregation, especially those in the balcony, are earnestly requested not to take their time from the organ or the choir, but to watch the conductor."

The choir of 1,200 had thrilled Cliff particularly, and he was glad they taped the service; we could replay parts of it later on *The Hour of Decision*.

Ruth went along with me to England for those meetings, which was a special encouragement to me.

Later in 1952, John Cordle and Mr. F. Roy Cattell, the secretary of the Evangelical Alliance of Britain, came to the United States to try to talk me into accepting their invitation to hold a

Crusade. They impressed me with their burden for England; they expressed themselves eloquently about the social and spiritual problems there since the war.

Part of our meeting was held in Ruth's hospital room in Asheville as we awaited the arrival of our fourth child. I loved my three daughters—Anne, Gigi, and Bunny—with all my heart, but we were hoping and praying for a boy this time. When Ruth's labor pains began in earnest, the nurse took her out. A couple of hours later another nurse came to tell me that we had a son. I was thrilled and emotional, but I also felt terribly guilty that I had not been with her, but with those two men. We named our son William Franklin Graham III, but we would call him Franklin. I went out into the hall and was so excited that I soon forgot about London and our British visitors! Eventually, in a lengthy letter, I accepted the invitation for a London Crusade to begin on March 1, 1954.

Our plans for widely publicizing the Crusade staggered our London committee. I was convinced that in a huge city like London, only a massive publicity effort would bring the event to the public's attention; anything less would be lost in the constant barrage of commercial advertising. We budgeted $50,000 for publicity, an unheard-of amount.

In the months before the Crusade began, striving for simplicity and clarity (and using only my photograph and the slogan HEAR BILLY GRAHAM), thousands of posters and hundreds of thousands of handbills were distributed in the greater London area. In addition, groups all over England and around the world were praying for the success of these meetings.

We had been encouraged by being able to secure Harringay Arena, a 12,000-seat indoor stadium in the north of London; it was customarily the site of greyhound races, hockey games, boxing matches, and circuses. Though barnlike and without glamour, it seemed the only suitable building. When the arena management optioned it to the committee for a maximum of three months, even our most ardent supporters gasped. Most believed that three or four weeks was the maximum length of time we should plan for.

Having committed themselves with the three-month option, the London organizing committee still wasn't used to the idea of arranging and publicizing a massive religious effort or with investing thousands of pounds in an outreach led by an untested American evangelist. I could not blame them. Around that time, a noted British evangelical leader, returning from Africa, was killed in the crash of a British Comet, the first all-jet commercial airplane. Planning a welcome-home reception for him, a group of evangelicals in London had spent hundreds of pounds. Alas for them, the sum was not refundable. What would happen, the London committee asked Jerry Beavan (who was serving as the Crusade's associate director under Roy Cattell), if something similar happened to Billy Graham? Would the tens of thousands of pounds already spent for publicity, reserving the arena, and so forth be lost?

Jerry told them we never worried about such problems. He encouraged them to believe that "God would see us through." His encouragement wasn't enough, though. The committee continued to worry. Something of an impasse developed.

Then Arthur Goodwin-Hudson, who was vicar of St. Mary Magdalene, London, thought to recommend to Jerry a young insurance man connected with Lloyd's of London, John Mercer. Using his contacts and his persuasive skills, Mercer managed to put together something that had never been written before, at least to our knowledge: an insurance policy to guarantee the timely arrival of a person for a specific public event. The premium was large, but the organizing committee took great comfort in knowing that they were protected financially. Their enthusiasm restored, they renewed their support of the Crusade.

The London meetings were being set up by Roy Cattell. I asked Jerry to go over several months earlier to assist Mr. Cattell with the preparations. Willis Haymaker went over with him, to help organize worldwide prayer support; Dawson Trotman and Lorne Sanny went over to conduct counseling classes. Letters were exchanged weekly between those advance men and the Team at home, and almost every week I was on the phone with Jerry in London getting the latest news, making decisions, and giving suggestions and ideas.

As for the economics of the Crusade, we knew, weeks before we left for England, that we did not have adequate reserves or adequate pledges. I asked the entire Team going to London—including myself—to work for just their expenses and a $50 weekly honorarium for the next few weeks. Without exception, they all agreed. Early in 1954, before embarking for London, we took a tour of West Coast cities (including Seattle, Portland, and Hollywood), partly to raise money for the forthcoming British meetings and to encourage prayer in support of that project.

In early February, when I was in Washington, D.C., Senator Alton Lennon of North Carolina gave a luncheon for me in the Vandenburg Room of the United States Senate. I outlined the possibilities and responsibilities of our forthcoming London Crusade to the senators and congressmen who were present. Then I asked if they would consider sending over a Republican senator and a Democratic senator to bring greetings from the United States Senate on the Crusade's opening night. They were a little surprised at my request. However, it was finally decided that Democratic Senator Stuart Symington of Missouri and Republican Senator Styles Bridges of New Hampshire would go. Both of them said that they and any other representatives that would make the trip would be doing official work in London as well.

Early 1954 gave me very little time at home in Montreat. Ruth maintained in her counsel and advice to me that my studies should consist primarily of filling up spiritually; she believed, as I did, that God would give me the message and bring to remembrance in my preaching the things I had studied. This was always the most effective preaching, we had discovered: preaching that came from the overflow of a heart and mind filled not only with the Spirit but with much reading. Hence, I picked each sermon topic carefully, read myself full, wrote myself empty, and read myself full again on the subject.

When I wasn't studying or spending time with the family, I spent hours walking the mountain trails near my home, getting into shape. Travel had always been grueling for me—the farther the trip, the worse the fatigue. And so I walked, praying the whole way that God's will would be done in London.

There was a cottage near us in Montreat called Chapman Home, the residence of the late J. Wilbur Chapman, one of America's great evangelists in the early part of the century. I often sat on the front porch there for hours. In the solitude and beauty of the mountains, I meditated and prayed. Sometimes Ruth joined me, and we watched the scenery change colors in the sweep of the sun or the flash of a rainstorm moving up that valley into the high mountains. I would pray and pray and pray, believing deep in my soul that God would bless and honor His Word if I preached it faithfully.

And yet I was also filled with fear. In my entire life, I had never approached anything with such a feeling of inadequacy as I did London. If God did not do it, it could not be done. But was I, as some critics suggested, too young at age thirty-five for such an awesome responsibility? I felt I was, but I also knew that I was doing what God had called me to do. In my flesh, I too often dwelled on the question, Who do you think you are? Yet all the while, God kept reminding me to dwell on Whom I knew Him to be: the Almighty God.

As Ruth and I traveled to New York to board the SS *United States*, I put on a brave smile for the media, but I had to quietly remind myself of the spiritual truth I had learned so long ago: in my weakness, I was made strong by God's grace.

Before boarding, I called on my friend Henry Luce at *Time* and *Life* magazines to ask for advice. He had one suggestion: "If you can get even an inch of coverage in the *Daily Mirror* or one of the other big London dailies, that will help."

Already in England there were dire predictions that the Crusade would be a failure. The British were suspicious of Americans coming over to save them. They had not been impressed by flashy American preachers before. "Billy Graham will fall . . . on his face in London," one editor wrote. "Billy Graham will return to the United States with his tail between his legs," a bishop promised.

In February the *Daily Worker*, which represented the British Communist Party, ran the headline ATOM BOMB GOSPELLER. "We should be able to get some quiet fun out of Mr. Billy Graham when he gets here," the article said. "His mission is to cause a religious revival on the strength of scores of thousands of pounds provided by wealthy backers. . . . He will try to persuade us that the more atom bombs America piles up, the more certain is the victory of the Prince of Peace."

The Crusade was supported by a thousand churches in greater London, two-thirds of them Anglican. Many pastors probably went along reluctantly, expecting no great good and praying that no significant harm would result. British church attendance was at a hundred-year low, and there were few signs of the religious upsurge that was already appearing in the United States.

Back on board the SS *United States* . . .

Each morning our little party—Grady Wilson, Dawson Trotman (who had been over earlier to set up counseling for the Crusade), Dr. Paul Rees (pastor of First Covenant Church in Minneapolis), Paul Maddox, Dr. and Mrs. Wade Freeman, Ruth, and I—met for prayers and Bible study. I enjoyed spending the rest of the day with Ruth or studying. Every afternoon, Ruth and I took a vigorous walk around the deck, and I was feeling better physically than at any other time in my ministry.

On Sunday morning, at the invitation of the captain, I preached at a service for the passengers, holding tight to the little pulpit and microphone as the ship rocked and rolled. Most of the ship's passengers and many of the crew came, overtaxing the ball-room. It was the next morning when the captain relayed to us the message that a member of Parliament was planning to challenge in the House of Commons my admission into England.

In hours I had a fuller picture—and it was not encouraging. Under a banner headline two days before in the *London Daily Herald*, reading "APOLOGISE, BILLY—OR STAY AWAY," journalist Hannen Swaffer had written that a calendar, supposedly distributed all over the United States by the Billy Graham Evangelistic Association, included the following statement urging people to pray for the forthcoming London Crusade: "What Hitler's bombs could not do, Socialism, with its accompanying evils, shortly accomplished."

It was, he said, a direct, highly political insult to the Labour Party, with its fourteen million supporters, for in Britain the term *Socialist* was almost synonymous with the term *Labour Party*. "Billy Graham has more gravely libelled us than anyone has dared to do since the war," he wrote. "It is a foul lie . . . [and] I urge the Bishop of

Barking [the Crusade's most visible church supporter] to disown all this ignorant nonsense before the Big Business evangelist whom he sponsors opens his Crusade. . . . And I urge him to call Billy Graham to repentance before he has the effrontery to start converting us!"

At once the uproar splashed across the front pages of London's other newspapers. The coverage was ironic. Up to this point, hardly a line had been written in a single British newspaper about the upcoming meetings, even though Christians throughout the Commonwealth and the United States had been praying for the Crusade's success for some time.

Frantically, I checked by radio telephone with Jerry in London and also contacted our Minneapolis office to discover the underlying facts. Slowly, the picture emerged. It seemed that the draft text for a brochure urging prayer and financial support of the London Crusade had been written in the United States by someone unfamiliar with Britain. The printer's proof had indeed used the world *socialism* (although with a small *s;* the newspaper had changed it to a capital *S*, giving it a more political connotation). But as soon as a copy was shown to one of our British supporters, he immediately spotted the possible misunderstanding and changed the word to *secularism*. Unfortunately, however—through one of those mix-ups that occasionally happen in any organization—the printer in Minneapolis had apparently used an uncorrected version to prepare our annual calendar. Although only two hundred copies were printed before the mistake was caught and corrected, somehow—I never discovered how—one of those copies had landed in the hands of Mr. Swaffer.

As soon as we knew the facts, Jerry issued an explanation to the press. Both George Wilson and I accepted full responsibility and wired apologies to members of Parliament, attempting to explain the error and expressing regret for any misunderstanding we had caused.

When the *United States* docked briefly the next day in Le Havre, France, a hoard of reporters and photographers came on board, swarming all around us. I tried to be as careful and as pleasant as possible, telling them I would try to straighten out the entire problem when I arrived in England.

One member of that press corps was a reporter from the *London Daily Herald,* whom I asked to send my warmest greetings to his colleague Hannen Swaffer. Swaffer, who was a Spiritualist (and apparently opposed to Christianity) was unmollified, but the offended Labour member of Parliament, Mr. Geoffrey de Freitas, accepted our apologies; several days later, I met with him and some of his colleagues to apologize in person.

Upon our arrival at Southampton, a tug full of press representatives—twenty-five reporters and a dozen photographers—pulled alongside the liner. There was no doubt they were after my scalp. One well-known movie star was on board with us, but I think only one reporter interviewed her. There was nothing to do but pray for wisdom and be as courteous and gracious as we could.

The reporters raised questions about the calendar furor, of course, but their curiosity went far beyond that issue. They wanted to know, for example, if I carried around a special jug of water for baptism! And they made great sport of the fact that I wore no clerical collar but instead had on a tie with some red in it.

Many of the reporters crowded around my wife as well, some wanting to know if she wore makeup. One of them confided to Ruth that he was disappointed in me. "We had expected bright hand-painted ties, flashy socks, and a sort of mass hysteria, but your husband is quite an ordinary chap," he complained.

As we stepped on shore, we were immediately on television.

"Who invited you over here, anyway?"

"Don't you think you're more needed in your own country?"

"What do you plan to do about Russia?"

The ordinary people of Great Britain, though, were warm and welcoming. As we went through customs, an official greeted us. "Welcome to England, and good luck, sir," he said. "We need you." I'll never forget his warm handshake.

Outside the customs hall a great crowd of people from all over southern England was waiting.

"I'm praying for you, sir," a dockworker said to me.

"God bless you, sir," said a soldier.

It was great to see Cliff Barrows, Luverne Gustavson, and other Team members who had driven down from London to welcome us. They returned directly to London; and by the time they got back, about seven-thirty, the evening papers already had our pictures on the front page. Whatever awaited us in the days to come, we at least knew the British press was no longer ignoring us!

That night Ruth and I, along with Grady Wilson and Paul Rees (who were going to be preaching throughout the London area during the Crusade), spent the night not far from Southampton at the home of an old friend, Oliver Stott. As we boarded our third-class train compartment for London the next day, the conductor had a good word for me. "I'm not much on religion," he said, "but I could do with some."

Our Team met for Bible reading and prayer. Clearly, we were in a serious situation, with news coming in that many supporters had already deserted us because of the bad press. Those who still stood by us were being abused by both the press and their fellow clergy. I had no idea what to expect.

When we arrived at Waterloo Station that Wednesday, we were overwhelmed by the number of people. The newspaper coverage the next day said that the group that had gathered to welcome us was the biggest crowd since the arrival in 1924 of Mary Pickford and Douglas Fairbanks. One newspaper headline said, "FILM STARS— SO WHY NOT BILLY?" When we stepped into the tightly packed throng, cheers rose, but the pressure of the crowd was fearsome. We thought we might be crushed or that somebody might be hurt, but the mood was reassuring: everyone had a wonderful smile, and the air was filled with shouts of "God bless you; welcome to England." Suddenly, the crowd began singing a hymn.

The press descended on us again just outside the station. One of the reporters wanted to know if I didn't think that this tremendous crowd at Waterloo was made up of religious fanatics.

"Not unless you consider some of your leading clergymen, leading generals, members of Parliament, and the good Christian people who have been praying for these meetings," I managed to say in the crush, "not unless you consider *them* fanatics."

I had gotten separated from Ruth by the crowd. She too was surrounded by reporters asking questions.

"Is your husband difficult to live with?"

"Do you have to handle him with kid gloves?"

"Do you ever feel a twinge of jealousy over the attention your husband receives?"

Jerry had tried in advance of our arrival to get the police to assign more officers to the station, but they had declined, saying that they expected only a small crowd to greet us. They had to call in more officers eventually, though—I could hear the sirens wailing just after we got there. But it took us twenty minutes to navigate the hundred yards between the station and the waiting cars. If Donn Moomaw, a former all-American football player for the University of Southern California whom we brought in to help with the Crusade, had not led the way, I doubt that we would have made it! Luverne, who had also come to the station to meet us, was pressed against a fence that soon began to sway alarmingly, but she finally found Ruth and got a taxi with her.

We stayed at the Stratford Court hotel just off Oxford Street. It had one distinction: it was probably the smallest and cheapest hotel in London. We had chosen it deliberately, knowing that criticisms would result if we appeared extravagant.

The only luxury we enjoyed while in London was given us courtesy of the Ford Motor Company. They furnished us with two small automobiles with chauffeurs for our use the entire time we were in Britain. This came about largely because of the help of two people: our friend Horace Hull, an automobile dealer in Memphis, Tennessee, and Ernie Breech, the executive vice president of the Ford Motor Company. We had met Mr. Breech during our recent five-week crusade in Detroit. A number of top people from the car companies had come to that Crusade, and Mr. Breech had entertained us in his home.

After the crowds at the Stratford Court dispersed and the reporters left, we had a closed meeting of the Team at six o'clock in the lounge. I talked to them on how they should act as Americans in Britain. General Wilson-Haffenden, chairman of the Crusade committee, said some words as well. Then we discussed a newspaper article, published just that day, that had been extremely unkind to the bishop of Barking. In the *London Daily Herald*, Hannen Swaffer had asked how any bishop of the Church of England could possibly support such an evangelist as Billy Graham. We had just requested prayer for the bishop when in he walked.

"Don't bother to pray for the bishop," said General Wilson-Haffenden. "He's where Christ put him. You get busy and pray for Hannen Swaffer."

"Don't worry about me, Billy," agreed the bishop. "If for a few days the newspapers have made you appear a fool for Christ's sake, I shall be only too happy to appear a fool with you."

In spite of my anxiety, I enjoyed a deep sense of God's presence. We were told that 800 of the faithful had spent the previous night in an unheated building, praying on their knees for the Crusade.

A press conference had been arranged for the next morning at Central Hall, Westminster. About 150 journalists and photographers jostled for position—one of the biggest press conferences for any person in years, one of the committee members told me. I began with a prepared statement on why we were coming to Britain.

"I have come to preach Christ," I stated. "You may ask me, 'Do you feel this is a message we need in Britain?' I should answer that it is the message the whole world needs. . . . I am calling for a revival that will cause men and women to return to their offices and shops to live out the teaching of Christ in their daily relationships. I am going to preach a gospel not of despair but of hope—hope for the individual, for society, and for the world."

Afterward they asked me a whole range of questions, from my personal opinion of Senator Joseph McCarthy to whether or not I believed in Hell. With every question, I prayed that God would give me the right answer.

That evening saw Ruth and me in formal dress for the first time in our lives. The Lord and Lady Luke of Pavenham gave a dinner in our honor at Claridge's hotel. Some of the guests arrived in Rolls-Royces; we were pleased to drive up in our small Ford. The engraved invitations read, "Full dress and decorations."

Before we knew it, we were shaking hands and introducing ourselves.

I had not met our hosts before that evening. When I was introduced to Lord Luke, I was surprised to find him young, jovial, and handsome. I told him that I had expected an English lord to be old and have a long beard, and he laughed with great delight. He put me immediately at ease in what could have been an awkward or intimidating situation.

The next day I addressed 1,000 ministers at a luncheon. Who paid for it? Sid Richardson—who had never given us money before. He had sent me a check along with this note: "I'm glad you're going to England. Those people over there like to drink—here's some entertaining money." The check was for $25,000! We used Mr. Sid's gift to subsidize this and similar gatherings.

That evening I was guest of honor in the House of Commons. The press coverage about the calendar had aroused much interest, and everyone wanted to get a look at this foreign intruder. Henry Luce had encouraged me to try to get a brief story in one of the papers, but I knew the coverage to date was not the kind he'd had in mind. I could not wait until Monday when the long-awaited Crusade would get under way. In the end, in God's providence, the entire flap over the misprinted calendar got us publicity far beyond anything we could have imagined.

During those days, I was slowed down much of the time with a sore throat, resting as much as I could between appearances and engagements in an effort to regain my voice in time for the Crusade itself. The Hungarian valet at our hotel gave me a bit of advice in his broken English. "Dr. Graham, leave windows open night and day, even if cold." There was little heat in the hotel, but I was desperate. I left the windows open, as he suggested, and soon I was feeling better.

On Sunday we decided to go to church as a Team. We chose to attend All Souls, Langham Place. We had never heard of it before, nor had we ever met the rector, John Stott, though later he became one of my best friends.

Even now, more than forty years later, Monday, March 1, 1954, remains one of the most memorable days of my ministry. I kept my schedule clear and spent the entire day praying and studying in my room. There seemed to be a lot of interest and support for our Crusade, but the press coverage and the controversy had given me deep doubts about whether people would come. And if they *did* come, would they respond to my style of preaching? By the afternoon, I had developed a headache. Then came a phone call I did not want.

Senator Symington informed me that he and Senator Bridges were in London as planned but had decided against appearing on the Crusade platform with me. "It might be misunderstood," he said, "if we endorsed your meetings from the platform. I don't think we had better come. We've accepted a dinner invitation this evening with Foreign Secretary Anthony Eden, and we may see you later on in your schedule."

I was disappointed, but I understood his position and told him so. Later I learned that American Ambassador Aldrich had said that it might not look right if they attended. Given the ruckus that had resulted from our calendar miscue, I could see why the U.S. Senate—and the American Ambassador to Great Britain—might want to distance themselves from us, at least for the present.

One newspaper account that day—the day of the first meeting—referred to me as having "all the tricks of the modern demagogue."

"Only the people seem to be for Billy," another wrote, making it appear that we had been abandoned by the government, the leaders, and the clergy.

When I hung up from my call with Senator Symington, I fell to my knees with a sinking feeling. "Lord," I prayed, "I can only commit the entire matter to You. I know that what You want to happen will happen. It's out of my hands."

A few hours of turmoil later, I took a call from Jerry at Harringay Arena. He sounded down, and by now I myself was nearly despairing. I saw sleet outside and asked if the weather was the same where he was.

"I'm afraid so," he said. "Only a few people have trickled in so far. By now we should be half-filled."

I sighed. "How about the press?"

"Oh, they're here," he said. "Right now it seems there's more of them than us. They're taking pictures of the empty seats."

In my soul, I was willing to become a laughingstock if that was what was supposed to happen, but the prospect was terrifying.

Half an hour later, Jerry called back with the news that there were now about 2,000 people in the massive arena. That meant that 10,000 seats were still empty.

"What do you think?" I asked.

"It looks like we've had it," he replied.

When it was time for us to leave the hotel, Ruth and I got on our knees and had a last prayer. I could envision people all over the world praying for us. For the first time, my gloom lifted and I had confidence that whatever happened that night, God would be glorified.

During the half-hour ride to the arena, Ruth and I sat holding hands. I had often been caught in traffic heading to our meetings, but that night we arrived in good time and saw no lines of cars or people.

"Honey," I said to her, "let's just go and face it and believe God had a purpose in it."

As we reached the door, Willis Haymaker rushed out to meet us.

"The arena is jammed!" he said.

"What do you mean, jammed? We didn't see anybody as we approached."

"The main entrance is on the other side. Most of the traffic and people came from that direction. The place is full and running over, and hundreds are outside."

As we walked in, people were already singing. I stepped into a small office for my last-minute preparations, and there stood Senators Symington and Bridges! "Billy, we couldn't let you down," Senator Symington said, shaking my hand. "The foreign secretary understood and excused us."

There was still the problem of the reporters and photographers, though. As we stood on the platform, I noticed that the first two or three rows were filled with press representatives, and many of them had yet to sit down. I thought of the New Testament story of Zacchaeus, the tax-gatherer mentioned in Luke 19, who couldn't see Jesus "for the press" of the crowd. Would the press be in the way here as well? But I decided that there was nothing worse than apathy and indifference, and since the press had already generated much of the interest, they could be forgiven for their high profile.

I reported to the audience that prayer groups all over the world were focusing their attention on London for these meetings—

including, we heard, 35,000 groups in India. Now *that* was newsworthy! All of our preparation, promotion, and programming, and even my preaching itself—necessary as those things were—were nothing compared with the prayer power around the world. We were engaged in a spiritual battle for Britain, and we needed intercession for divine intervention. Periodically during our Crusade, we scheduled all-night prayer meetings that lasted from 10:30 P.M. to 6:00 A.M. in venues all over the city.

Our two senators brought greetings, and we listened to several wonderful musical offerings.

"Do you think I ought to give an Invitation to receive Christ the first night?" I asked the bishop of Barking between songs.

"Of course," he said, gripping my hand.

I preached on the topic "Does God Matter?" Nearly 200 came forward at the Invitation, and they seemed to represent every stratum of society. The unemotional British, as the newspapers had called them, had tears streaming down their cheeks as they came to Christ. One onlooker later commented on how struck he was by the sound of shoes creaking on the wood floor.

Photographer Carl Mydens of *Time* magazine went with his camera into the room where scores of counselors were leading converts as they prayed to receive Christ. When he realized what was going on, he backed out. "This isn't the place for a photographer; this is too intimate and too holy," he said.

As sleet turned to snow, snarling public transportation, we wondered what the second night would bring. To our great relief, more than 10,000 showed up. That included 1,000 in the choir Cliff led in singing stately old hymns and the favorite Gospel songs of the British.

In the United States, there had just been a shooting in the House of Representatives, and two congressmen had been injured. I requested special prayer for them. That incident gave a backdrop for my message on the universality of human sin, and the need we all have for God's forgiveness.

Even my clergy critics found it hard to argue with that theme and the response it was producing. In the following days, support came from unexpected quarters. The world-famous Methodist minister Dr. Leslie Dixon Weatherhead wrote a generous newspaper article giving his impressions after attending the first week of the Crusade. In that article, he pledged his own prayers for us and urged critics to go to the services and "listen without prejudice."

By Saturday night that first week, the arena was jammed to capacity an hour before the service was to begin. I went out and spoke to the crowd outside. The police said that between 30,000 and 35,000 people were outside. There were 1,000 from Wales alone, we were told. From then on, we had two services on weekends to take care of the crowd.

By the end of the first month, the Crusade had gathered such momentum that the building was jammed anywhere from a half-hour to two hours in advance of the service. People were clamoring for the free tickets, which were distributed in a variety of ways before each of the meetings. The socialites of the city were coming; bishops were beginning to sit on the platform; and the newspapers had become friendly and were giving the Crusade all-out support, with William Hickey of the *London Daily Express* writing one of the first sympathetic columns. This was the Lord's doing, and it was marvelous in our eyes.

I was also getting opportunities to speak on the BBC. By this time, French, Italian, and other European newspapers, television stations, and radio programs were interested, and the story of the Crusade was being carried around the world. The Associated Press was sending two stories daily back to the United States, and Eugene Patterson of the United Press was assigned full-time to cover the story. Invitations were pouring in to our London office from all over England. I was invited to address the directors of Lloyd's of London; Mr. Astor, the chairman of the board of the *Times* (London), invited me to lunch with his editors; and Hugh Cuttlepp, the editor of the *Daily Mirror* (London), invited me to lunch at Brown's Hotel. Now it seemed that all of London was listening to the Gospel. Before the Crusade was over, we would speak to 2 million people.

One night Charlie Riggs and the London committee had a meeting at which they prayed that God would give them the opportunity to reach beyond London to more of the nation of England. (Although I'd had speaking opportunities on the BBC, my Crusade meetings themselves were not carried on British radio or television.) Bob Benninghoff, an ABC network engineer, happened to overhear them and began thinking about how that might be accomplished. He found that during World War II, the General Post Office had constructed telephone-type message lines throughout the country—lines that they called landline relays. Over these, they broadcast messages about the war to people everywhere.

Somehow the committee negotiated to get hold of those lines and encouraged local churches and groups to broadcast the services in their own villages and towns, often in public halls or theaters. As the idea caught on, four hundred lines went out from Harringay, and 400,000 listeners received the audio signal from the Crusade.

I was also invited to address the various schools and colleges of the University of London, including the London School of Economics.

"This is the first time a minister has been on this platform," said the professor who introduced me to the crowd. "This school was founded on secularism," he added pointedly. That resulted in strong applause.

I tried to break the ice with a little humor, but with little success, I felt. Then when it was time for me to turn serious, a student crashed through an upstairs window and stood scratching himself like an ape. I joined in the laughter.

"He reminds me of my ancestors," I said. Everybody roared. "Of course, my ancestors came from Britain," I added.

That brought down the house. Now on the same wavelength as my audience, I felt free to preach the Gospel.

As the Crusade gained momentum, I found myself becoming more and more dependent on God. I knew that all we had seen happening in Britain was the work of God. If we got in the way or began to take credit for what was happening, God's blessing would be withdrawn. I knew it was also due to the work of the many dedicated people on our Team. I was merely the preacher, the messenger. None of what was happening could have happened apart from God and all the help we had.

The wear and tear were beginning to show on me, however. By the six-week mark, I had lost fifteen pounds. Sleep was elusive, as always, and my eyes looked dark and hollow. It was great to have Ruth with me, though. She had more stamina than I. Many evenings I would rush back from Harringay and collapse into bed, only to have her arrive hours later, having stayed to counsel and pray with people until the arena was empty. One of the greatest joys for me was that she could stay in England the entire time. Her encouragement, her counsel, and her prayer supported me more than anything else.

One night she told me about an overly friendly man who had approached her in Hyde Park.

"I'm busy tonight," she told him.

He asked her out for the next night.

"I'm busy then too."

And the next?

"Yes, I'm busy then too."

"Just what is it that keeps you busy every night?" he asked in exasperation.

"I go to hear Billy Graham speak at Harringay Arena."

"You wouldn't be *related* to Billy Graham, would you?"

"Yes, I'm his wife."

"Oh, my . . ."

A columnist for the *Daily Mirror* (London), Bill Connor, under the name Cassandra, wrote a devastatingly clever article against me; it appeared the day we arrived in Britain. I wrote him a note telling him that while I didn't agree with him, his column had been very well done. He wrote back that he would like to meet me. His conditions were that we come together on neutral ground; he suggested a pub called the Baptist's Head. A pub sounded less than neutral to me, but he insisted that I could have a soft drink while he had his beer. I accepted. We met for lunch there, and I believe Mr. Connor got a different view of me than he had expected. I got a different view of him as well, when he picked me up in a Rolls-Royce.

"I thought you and your paper represented the working class," I said.

"Shhhh! Don't say anything," he replied. "This is the boss's car."

That afternoon he put me into his next column: "When [Billy Graham] came into *The Baptist's Head* . . . he was absolutely at home—a teetotaler and an abstainer able to make himself completely at his ease in the spit and sawdust department, . . . a very difficult thing to do. Billy Graham looks ill. He has lost [fifteen pounds] in this nonstop merciless Crusade. . . . But this fact he can carry back to North Carolina with him. . . . It is that in this country, battered and squeezed as no victorious nation has ever been before and disillusioned almost beyond endurance, he has been welcomed with an exuberance that almost makes us blush behind our precious Anglo-Saxon reserve. . . . I never thought that simplicity could cudgel us sinners so damned hard. We live and we learn."

The Archbishop of Canterbury invited us to tea at Lambeth Palace. I accepted, of course, but was very nervous about it. "Honey," Ruth reassured me, "any man who has six sons must be quite ordinary."

How right she was. Dr. Geoffrey Fisher was a charming and delightful man, wholly without pretense. He became a great friend, although not all of the Anglican clergy approved of our method of evangelism. By meeting with us he was giving tacit approval to our work.

In his book documenting the Harringay meetings, Frank Colquhoun gave an example of one clergyman's reluctance to accept me: "A rector in central London found fault with Graham's belief in 'sudden conversions.' He said in a Sunday evening sermon: 'I do not know of a single case in the whole Bible of a sudden, complete conversion.' Oddly enough he was preaching in a church dedicated to St. Paul (whose conversion in all conscience was sudden enough)— and to a congregation of thirteen."

A whole book could have been written on the stories we heard of people whose lives were changed by Christ. Repeatedly, in various parts of the world, I have met people who came to Christ during those days, and who are continuing to serve Christ, often as dedicated laypeople. When we returned to London for a Crusade at Earls Court in 1966, we had 52 Anglican clergymen sitting on the platform one night, all of whom had been converted in the Harringay meetings twelve years before. While working on this chapter, I was in California for our 1995 Sacramento Crusade. During our time there, I met two pastors now serving in that state who had come to Christ during Harringay.

California is also home to one of our long-time Team members, Bill Brown; he headed our World Wide Pictures unit for many years. In 1954 the name of Joan Winmill was well known on the London stage, and she had a brilliant future ahead of her. But down inside, she was miserable and on the brink of suicide. One night at Harringay she gave her life to Christ, and she was transformed. A year later she married Bill Brown, whom she had met through the Crusade; since then she has been a steadfast witness to Christ's power to change lives. Her autobiographical story, *No Longer Alone,* was made into a feature-length film that God has used to bring many to a commitment to Christ.

Richard Carr-Gomm was already a believer, but during the London meetings he realized that he needed to rededicate his life to Christ in a deeper way. He never could have anticipated how God would lead him, however. At the time he was captain of the Queen's Guard at Buckingham Palace; in time he sensed that God was calling him to leave that prestigious position and devote his life instead to the poor. Noticing the loneliness of many older people, he began to scrub floors to help them, then bought a home and invited four of them to live with him. In time he established the Abbeyfield Society, which owns one thousand homes for the elderly, and later founded the Carr-Gomm Society, which uses many volunteers to help the staff of the two hundred homes it oversees.

Most people who came forward did not have the public visibility of Joan Winmill or Richard Carr-Gomm, of course. They were simply ordinary people moved by the extraordinary love of Christ.

One night Ruth was asked to help a woman who was standing in the hallway outside the counseling room. At first the woman showed no response when Ruth asked if she could help her. Gradually, however, her story came out. For many weeks she and her husband had planned to come to London for a vacation and to attend the Harringay meetings. Just the week before, however, he had died suddenly. In bitterness, she had come to London anyway, but life seemed utterly empty without her husband, who had been a strong Christian. Ruth tried to assure her of God's love and presence, even in times of great heartache, but she felt totally inadequate to say anything that would take away the widow's pain. Twelve years later,

Ruth received a letter from that woman. "You won't remember me," it read. "My husband had died suddenly the week before, and I came to London to end everything. But in the meeting, as I listened to the message, God spoke to me. . . . My life is busy—am still singing in the Salvation Army Songsters, and trying to love and serve my Lord!"

Many other stories told of lives that had been changed through the power of Christ. A doctor confessed that he had been ruled by his passions, even to the point of filling his waiting room with pornographic literature. After giving his life to Christ, he immediately gathered the pornography up and threw it into the Thames. He became an active layman in London.

A committed Communist came to Christ one night, and in the six months after his conversion read the Gospel of John a hundred times.

The assistant manager of our hotel cynically watched the lives of our Team during our first days in London, assuming that it was all a show. But he began to realize not only that we were genuinely happy but that we had something he did not have, and that he longed for. One night, after one of the meetings, Dawson Trotman led him to Christ in his hotel room. Later the assistant manager said, "My doubts and fears and the sense of futility have all gone."

Another night a man came very reluctantly to the meeting and was very vocal in his scorn of all that was taking place. When Bev Shea got up to sing, he made yet another wisecrack. But halfway through Bev's song, "He's Got the Whole World in His Hands," the man became serious. As Bev quietly sang the words, "He's got the tiny little baby in His hands," the man bowed his head. At the Invitation, he came forward to open his heart to Christ, later telling his counselor that his child was at home seriously ill and that it was Bev's song that had touched his heart.

One night Charlie Riggs was supervising the landline relay meetings at the Trocadero Cinema, located in a crime-ridden area of South London. A gang of tough youths arrived outside determined to break up the meeting. They were stopped at the door by a broad-shouldered Christian police officer named Tony.

"You fellows are a bunch of cowards," he told them boldly. "If not, you would all accept Christ as your Savior."

"*You're* not a Christian, are you?" one of them asked in disbelief. "I've never heard of a Christian copper. How'd you get to be that way?"

So with his back against the wall, Tony shared with them how Christ had saved him and changed his life.

With that, one youth stepped forward. "What do you have to do to become a Christian?" he asked.

Tony told him how he could accept Christ, warning him that it would take courage.

"I've got the courage, and I'd like to become a Christian," he replied while his fellow gang members watched.

Tony led the young man into the theater just as the Invitation was being given.

Some incidents had their humorous side. One evening I preached from John 11 on the miracle of the raising of Lazarus from the dead—and an undertaker was converted!

Richard Bewes, later the rector of All Souls, Langham Place, told me some years afterward of a man who arrived late; the doors of the arena had been locked because of the crowd. Loitering nearby was a "teddy boy," one of London's rebellious youth, who asked if he needed help. The man said he wanted to get in, but the door was locked. After the teddy boy calmly picked the lock, the man went in and was converted.

One night a friend of ours noted two men who came in and sat near the back. They apparently did not know each other but within minutes had loudly agreed on two things: they did not like Americans, and they especially did not like American evangelists. They had come to see the show, they agreed, just so they could make fun of it. But the Holy Spirit spoke to them both. When the Invitation was given, one of them turned to the other and said, "I'm going forward." The other one said, "I am too. And here's your wallet back—I'm a pickpocket."

We had hundreds of other meetings in all kinds of interesting places throughout the greater London area and in the rest of England. For example, more than 12,000 people gathered at the foot of Nelson's Column in Trafalgar Square on April 3 to hear me preach. Even larger was the crowd at our Good Friday afternoon service at Hyde Park. Across the street from the park was the Odeon, one of the leading cinemas in London; during the morning, after each movie showing, I spoke to the audience for five minutes. Traffic came to a standstill in London because Hyde Park was surrounded by what the newspapers said was the largest religious crowd since the end of the war.

We had optioned Harringay Arena for three months, expecting the Crusade to last perhaps six weeks, but we could not bring ourselves to shut the meetings down with more and more people thronging to hear the simple Gospel message.

Many of our friends and supporters in the United States traveled to England to be a part of the Crusade. Among them were Roy Rogers and his wife, Dale Evans. They spoke at a children's meeting at the dog track next door to Harringay; an estimated 10,000 adults showed up with 40,000 boys and girls. Roy Rogers rode his cowboy horse, Trigger, around the track, showing off his tricks. But when he and Dale spoke, it was a simple and straightforward witness to their faith in Christ.

Henrietta Mears, the great Christian educator and Bible teacher who had been so instrumental in my spiritual growth in Los Angeles, also came to see what God was doing in London. During her visit, we made sure she was invited to one of the formal functions held in our honor at the Dorchester Hotel, then considered the most prestigious hotel in London. Once again the invitation read, "Full dress and decorations."

Miss Mears, a warm, fashionable woman who was welcomed in the highest society of the United States, regaled those at her table with interesting stories. I was proud that she was such a hit. At one point in the evening, Ruth and I went over to chat with her.

"You look very lovely tonight," I said.

She smiled and pulled us closer. "I didn't have a formal thing in my suitcase and had no time to shop," she whispered. "I'm wearing my nightgown!"

Invaluable to me during that trip (and throughout the early years of the BGEA) was Paul Maddox. Paul had been U.S. chief of chaplains in the European theater during World War II. He acted as my personal assistant, helping to coordinate my schedule and making sure I was always where I was supposed to be. Paul also acted as a gatekeeper (as it were), buffering me from problems that could better be handled by someone else, while being sure I saw the people I really needed to see and made the decisions only I could make. He was a man with a great love for people and was in turn greatly loved by the Team. Paul also had a dry sense of humor that defused more than one awkward situation. In the military he had learned to wait on generals, and he had a true servant's heart—willing to do anything to take some of the load off of me, even shining my shoes or taking my suits out to be pressed.

In London I had to prepare new messages constantly, and that was where my secretary, Luverne, was so helpful. Of the seventy-two major addresses I preached in the evenings, at least fifty of them were prepared the day they were delivered. Early in the morning and late at night, I studied and wrote my outline; then I dictated the message and asked Luverne to type up the notes. Often I would receive the final draft of the outline just before I stepped up to the pulpit. I felt the presence and power of the Holy Spirit in preparing those talks, and when I got up, I felt increasingly a greater power that refreshed me.

Several weeks into the Crusade, I was approached by a friend I had met during my Youth for Christ tour a few years before, the Reverend Canon Tom Livermore, by this time director of YFC in England. He gave me a book by an old Puritan preacher, Dr. Watson; it contained a series of sermons on the Ten Commandments. I adapted them into messages that I preached each night for ten successive nights, adding my own illustrations and evangelistic focus.

When we no longer had access to Harringay Arena—the twelve weeks were up—we were forced to end the London Crusade. I was exhausted; in three months I had lost thirty pounds. And the rest of the Team was also exhausted. Bev had been singing every night; Cliff had been leading the musicians and directing the choir every night. The pace we endured was grueling, and yet with that pace came the joy of being exactly where we were supposed to be, doing what we were supposed to be doing, and seeing God bless our endeavor all the way.

We planned to have the last meeting on Saturday, May 22, at Wembley Stadium, which seated 100,000. So many had been turned away from Harringay that we began taking reservations from groups who wanted to be sure to join us for that last meeting. But would we really see 100,000 people at one meeting?

Soon enough we knew the truth: Wembley would not hold the masses asking to come. So we also secured the second-largest facility, White City Stadium. We would hold a two-hour meeting there and then bus our Team to Wembley for the grand finale.

At White City Stadium alone, we had one of our largest crowds ever: 65,000. As we prepared to depart, we were told that traffic was already so jammed around Wembley that we should look into going there by helicopter. But there was no time to make new arrangements. We piled our Team onto a bus, and with the help of the police made our way through the traffic. Half an hour before the meeting, Wembley's gates were closed; all 100,000 seats were filled. Someone escorted me to a high perch from which I could see the entire place through a window. It was amazing!

I was tempted for a brief moment to depart from my chosen sermon topic, "Choose This Day Whom You Will Serve." With so many dignitaries and intellectuals in the audience—including Princess Marina, mother of the present Duke of Kent (who was at that time the Duchess of Kent), and her guests in the Royal Box—I wondered whether I should try to be erudite and academic. But then I reminded myself that I must not try to be impressive.

As I looked down on that great crowd, I noticed activity on the soccer field. The gates had been reopened, and another 22,000 were allowed to rush in and sit on the hallowed playing field, shoulder to shoulder in the frigid temperature under a black sky.

Cliff led the great choir as sleet stung the faces of singers and audience alike. Tens of thousands of umbrellas came to life all over the stadium. I half-expected the crowd to begin a mass exodus, but no one moved. Something bonded us in that weather—all of us together, shoulders hunched against the elements, squinting through the torrents, listening to the music. Bev sang, and then I preached in utter simplicity. Once I began, I was grateful that I had not succumbed to the temptation to try to be something I was not.

233

Some 2,000 people waded through the mud to respond to the Invitation. The Archbishop of Canterbury pronounced the benediction, and the people sang "To God Be the Glory."

As we exited the platform, the Archbishop told Grady, "We may never again see a sight like that this side of Heaven."

Grady, so moved that he forgot protocol, threw his arm around Dr. Fisher. "That's right, Brother Archbishop!" he agreed enthusiastically.

As soon as the meeting was over, we went to a holding area where we greeted many of the local committee members and special guests and said good-bye to them all. Then police escorted us through the crowds to the bus, which was now surrounded by thousands of people. They were shouting their thanks and singing hymns. For a moment, I feared that the pressure of the crowd might overturn us. Ruth was beaming and said later that her sadness at the end of the great Crusade was balanced by gratitude and joy over all that had taken place.

As the bus slowly wended through the crowd, I stood up and asked the Team to join me in thanking God for what He had done. Bev sang softly the doxology: "Praise God from Whom All Blessings Flow." The Team picked up the words, and we all sang as the bus passed through the shouting, waving people. I have never forgotten that moment.

Toward the end of the Crusade, a minister who wrote a regular column in the *Sunday Graphic,* the Reverend Frank Martin, commented that he had attended three of the meetings and drawn a couple of fascinating conclusions: first, "that religion is alive and a powerful issue," and second, "that religion can be warm, personal, invigorating." He found my evangelistic approach to be unsophisticated but not boring. Obviously, he was not one of our most enthusiastic supporters, but I was deeply touched by his final statement: "Thank you, Billy. You've done us a power of good. Come again soon."

In writing a report of the Crusade for a magazine in the United States, Paul Rees, who had helped us enormously in London, listed six factors that he believed contributed to the historic impact of the

London Crusade: the power of prayer, the authority of the Word of God, the effectiveness of organization and promotion, the beneficial effect of teamwork, the link with local churches, and the spiritual vacuum waiting to be filled.

We were scheduled to leave for Scotland for a brief holiday the evening of Tuesday, May 25. That morning I received an unexpected call from Jock Colville, secretary to Prime Minister Winston Churchill.

"Would you be available," he asked, "to join Mr. Churchill for lunch here tomorrow noon?"

"I'm honored," I said, "but it would be impossible. We are leaving this evening for Scotland." Turning down an invitation from Winston Churchill—that showed how exhausted I was!

Half an hour later the phone rang again. "Would you be able to meet with Mr. Churchill at noon today?" asked Mr. Colville. "He has a lunch scheduled at twelve-thirty with the Duke of Windsor, who is flying over from Paris, but he can see you before that."

I hardly had time to get nervous! Much later I learned from Mr. Colville's own writings that Mr. Churchill had himself been nervous about the meeting. Apparently, the prime minister had paced the room, asking, "What do you talk about to an evangelist?"

When I arrived at Number 10 Downing Street, I was reminded discreetly by Mr. Colville that the prime minister had precisely twenty minutes. After I was announced, I was shown into a large, dimly lit cabinet room. Mr. Churchill rose from his chair and shook my hand. I had not realized what a short man he was; I towered over him. He motioned with an unlit cigar for me to sit next to him. It would be just the two of us, apparently. I noticed that three London afternoon dailies were spread out on a table next to him.

"Well, first," he said, in the marvelous voice I had heard so many times on the radio and in the newsreels, "I want to congratulate you for these huge crowds you've been drawing."

"Oh, well, it's God's doing, believe me," I said.

"That may be," he replied, squinting at me, "but I daresay that if I brought Marilyn Monroe over here, and she and I together went to Wembley, we couldn't fill it."

I laughed, trying to imagine the spectacle.

"Tell me, Reverend Graham, what is it that filled Harringay night after night?"

"I think it's the Gospel of Christ," I told him without hesitation. "People are hungry to hear a word straight from the Bible. Almost all the clergy of this country used to preach it faithfully, but I believe they have gotten away from it." (I had heard that Mr. Churchill had written a book while he was a reporter in South Africa, in which he stated that he believed the Bible was inspired of God.)

"Yes," he said, sighing. "Things have changed tremendously. Look at these newspapers—filled with nothing but murder and war and what the Communists are up to. You know, the world may one day be taken over by the Communists."

I agreed with him, but I did not feel free to comment on world politics. I merely nodded, and he continued: "I'll tell you, I have no hope. I see no hope for the world."

"Things do look dark," I agreed. I hesitated, not wanting to repeat the gaffe I had committed with President Truman just a few years before by being too direct about religion in our conversation. We talked at length about the world situation, and then, as if on cue, the prime minister looked me in the eye. "I am a man without hope," he said somberly. "Do you have any real hope?"

He might have been talking geopolitically, but to me this sounded like a personal plea. In the notes I jotted after the meeting, I recalled he referred to hopelessness no fewer than nine times. His bouts with depression are now well documented, although I was not aware of them at the time.

"Are you without hope for your own soul's salvation?"

"Frankly, I think about that a great deal," he replied.

I had my New Testament with me. Knowing that we had but a few minutes left, I immediately explained the way of salvation. I watched carefully for signs of irritation or offense, but he seemed receptive, if not enthusiastic. I also talked about God's plan for the future, including the return of Christ. His eyes seemed to light up at the prospect.

At precisely twelve-thirty, Mr. Colville knocked. "Sir Winston, the Duke of Windsor is here for your luncheon," he said.

"Let him wait!" Mr. Churchill growled, waving Mr. Colville off and turning back to me. "Go ahead."

I went on for about another fifteen minutes, then asked if I could pray.

"Most certainly," he said, standing up. "I'd appreciate it."

I prayed for the difficult situations the prime minister faced every day and acknowledged that God was the only hope for the world and for us individually.

Mr. Churchill thanked me and walked me out. As we shook hands he leaned toward me. "Our conversations are private, aren't they?"

"Yes, sir," I said, having decided after the Truman fiasco that I would never again quote a leader during his or her lifetime.

What was the impact of Harringay?

First and foremost, we left London confident that thousands of lives had been touched with the transforming message of Jesus Christ. We knew that even among those who made no decision during the meetings, seeds had been planted that would bear fruit in God's timing.

Second, we left London confident that the churches had been strengthened, not only by the influx of new converts but also by the opportunity to participate in what God was doing in their city and catch a new vision of His will. A few years later, Maurice A. P. Wood, principal of Oak Hill Theological College (Anglican) in the London area, stated that the majority of his students were either Billy Graham counselors or convert-inquirers from the Crusade.

I was humbled at what the Archbishop of Canterbury wrote after our departure in a letter printed in the *Canterbury Diocesan Notes:* "That the blessing of the Holy Spirit has been upon this campaign cannot be doubted.... The mission has beyond doubt brought new strength and hope in Christ to multitudes, and won many to him; and for this God is to be praised. It has given an impetus to evangelism for which all Churches may be thankful to God."

Then he added a challenge: "As we thank God for what this had meant to so many, the Churches must take a lesson out of it for themselves. So often they do not begin far enough back. They expect people to understand whole sentences of church life and doctrine before they have been taught the letters of the Christian alphabet and the words of one syllable. It is the natural mistake of the keen teacher. Dr. Graham has taught us all to begin again at the beginning in our Evangelism and speak by the power of the Holy Spirit of sin and of righteousness and of judgment."

Third, the London meetings gave us a greater vision of what God could do in a major city. I knew that God was not limited, but at the same time I had sometimes wondered if the challenges and problems of the great cities of the world were simply too overwhelming, and the task too massive for the message of the Gospel through mass evangelism to make any impact.

There was a fourth effect from Harringay, although we did not fully realize it at the time. If our 1949 meetings in Los Angeles marked a decisive watershed for our ministry in the United States, the London Crusade in 1954 did the same for us internationally. News of what had happened at Harringay traveled like lightning around the world, challenging Christians to believe that the particular place where God had put them was not beyond hope, but that He was still at work. As invitations poured in to hold Crusades on every continent, we knew that our ministry could no longer be limited mainly to the English-speaking world.

14

Impact in Europe

Immediately after the final London meeting on May 22, 1954, we took a quick trip to Glasgow to rest and to meet with ministers about a possible Crusade there the following year. Then Cliff, Grady, Jerry, and I left by ship from Tilbury, England, for Sweden, where we had a brief but refreshing rest before embarking on an intensive series of meetings on the Continent. I had seldom felt so relieved and relaxed as I did on that ship. There was an orchestra of Swedish students on board; they played and sang Scandinavian songs. It was a marvelous few days.

BARNSTORMING THROUGH EUROPE

Jerry Beavan and Bob Evans, a friend from Wheaton College days who had founded the Greater Europe Mission a few years before and knew Europe intimately, had laid out a plan to hold a series of fairly modest meetings—many one-day rallies—in several of the major continental cities, often under the sponsorship of a new group, the European Evangelical Alliance. But the torrent of publicity coming out of London changed all that. The chosen venues could not handle the crowds that were now expected. With virtually no notice, they had to switch to the largest locations they could find.

Helsinki

Our whirlwind tour across Europe began with our arrival at Helsinki's harbor on June 16. There we were astounded to find several thousand people packing the dock area and waving handkerchiefs. The national radio network carried my greetings live across the country. We had the strong support of the Lutheran bishop of Helsinki, E. G. Gulin, even though the state-supported Lutheran Church was not officially involved.

That evening an overflow crowd jammed the Helsinki Exhibition Hall. The next evening—with the summer sun shining almost as brightly as at noon—30,000, said to be the largest crowd ever gathered in Finland for a religious event, attended our meeting at the city's Olympic Stadium. Rather nervously, George Beverly Shea sang his "I'd Rather Have Jesus" in Finnish; he'd had the tongue-twisting words written out phonetically for him by a local pastor. So successful was he that he adopted that practice of singing in the native tongue in many of our international Crusades.

Stockholm

On to Stockholm, Sweden.

During a stopover in Gothenburg en route to Finland, a reporter had given me something of a warning: "So many of you Americans think we Swedes are Christians because almost all of us are baptized. . . . The truth is we are deeply pagan underneath. You will get little response from us."

A few days later, after our Helsinki meetings, a large crowd, estimated variously by the press as anywhere from 45,000 to 100,000, filled Skansen Park, an open-air area in Stockholm; the meeting was carried live by the national radio network. A second rally took place the next evening in the city's main stadium, with many turned away for lack of space. We were heartened by the response, although we did sense that secularism had become firmly entrenched in the hearts and minds of many Swedes.

Copenhagen

On June 21 we flew from Stockholm into Copenhagen.

An afternoon meeting for clergy in the cathedral drew 2,000 people. With only a small percentage of the Danish population actively involved with any church, I knew that many of the clergy were discouraged. I sought to point them to the biblical mandate for evangelism and to the reality of the spiritual hunger we were seeing everywhere we went. I myself was frustrated by the passive attitude I had detected among some of the clergy in Europe. I challenged the audience to be more aggressive in proclaiming the Gospel: "It's up to you to carry the Gospel out to the masses, not to wait with empty seats in your churches for the people to come to *you!*"

That evening 5,000 people filled the city's largest auditorium; several thousand others were connected to the meeting by an audio link to several churches and a nearby tennis arena. After that meeting was over, the local committee took me to another meeting they had scheduled at midnight, this one in an open square sometimes used as a vegetable market. In spite of the lateness of the hour and the rain, 15,000 more people came to stand and hear the Word of God. At the end of the message, I asked those who wanted to commit their lives to Christ to wave their handkerchiefs. Their response looked like a sea of white. We then directed those people to a church at one corner of the square, where counselors spoke and prayed with 1,000 of them.

During the time we were in Scandinavia, we saw 200,000 attend the meetings in Helsinki, Stockholm, and Copenhagen, with thousands professing a commitment to follow Christ.

Amsterdam

The next day, June 22, we flew into Amsterdam, where Jerry and Bob had laid out for us a packed schedule that lasted for only eight hours. In that time we had a large meeting with clergy, a press conference, and a public rally in the city's Olympic Stadium. Unlike other secularized areas of Europe, Holland still retained a measure of active church life, particularly among the various Reformed churches.

241

During the weeks before the meeting in Amsterdam, we had been alternately attacked and defended in the Dutch press, the lively comments often reflecting the theological divisions within the churches. One liberal pastor wrote disdainfully of our planned meeting as a "dismal religious circus" and attacked me as "primitive" for quoting the Bible as the Word of God. He was answered by others, including the distinguished theologian G. C. Berkouwer, professor of systematic theology at the Free University of Amsterdam. While there, I also saw Willem Visser 't Hooft, who had gone out of his way to befriend and support me a few years before when the World Council of Churches was formed. All of this focused public attention on our brief visit and probably brought many more people to the public meeting—and to Christ.

The Amsterdam meeting filled all 40,000 seats in the stadium, with Cliff Barrows leading a choir of 2,400. Dan Piatt, European director of The Navigators, had trained 1,000 counselors. (The Navigators is an American organization started by Dawson Trotman during World War II to work with American service personnel in both evangelism and discipleship training. The methods they developed in training people to do evangelism and in helping new Christians to grow spiritually greatly influenced our own counselor-training and follow-up programs in the years to come.) But even after the training, the counselors were still unprepared for the overwhelming response. Nevertheless, they pressed on, doing what they could, encouraging those who made commitments to grow in their faith through prayer and Bible study, as well as involvement in a Christian church.

Each of these meetings during that whirlwind week in Scandinavia and Holland convinced us that something extraordinary was happening—something that could not be explained only by publicity or curiosity over what had happened in London. Millions in Europe could be called confirmed secularists, although wherever there was a state church, there was some understanding of God and some knowledge of stories from the Bible in their background. Countless people, however, obviously had a spiritual hunger and an openness to the Gospel that was almost overwhelming.

Berlin

On June 23, we moved on to Germany. Accompanying us was German-born industrialist John Bolten, who had recommitted his life to Christ during our 1950 meetings in Boston. Exactly a year before our German meetings, something had happened to focus the message I was preaching; and John was part of that change.

In 1953 he had been with us during a series of Crusade meetings in Dallas's Cotton Bowl. One night my preaching did not seem to have spiritual depth or power, although a number of people did come forward at the Invitation. After the meeting, John and I took a walk together, and he confronted me.

"Billy," he said, "you didn't speak about the Cross. How can anyone be converted without having at least one single view of the Cross where the Lord died for us? You must preach about the Cross, Billy. You must preach about the blood that was shed for us there. There is no other place in the Bible where there is greater power than when we talk or preach about the Cross."

At first I resisted his rebuke. The Cross and its meaning were, more often than not, a part of my sermons. But that night I could not sleep, and before morning came I knew he was right. I made a commitment never to preach again without being sure that the Gospel was as complete and clear as possible, centering on Christ's sacrificial death for our sins on the Cross and His resurrection from the dead for our salvation.

Back to Germany . . .

Our 1954 visit unleashed a torrent of publicity in the national press—some favorable, but much of it highly critical. One paper labeled me "God's machine gun"; another, "God's flame-thrower." The Communist press in East Germany outdid itself in attacking me as a lackey of American capitalism, a tool of greedy Texas oilmen, a spymaster for the Office of Strategic Services.

The meetings began with a service for U.S. Army personnel in Frankfurt on our first day. A reporter from Germany's largest mass-circulation magazine, *Der Spiegel*, cornered John and me. She was a beautiful woman of about thirty-five, and she had only one question.

"Mr. Graham, what do you think about sex?" she asked.

"Sex is the most wonderful thing on this earth," I replied, "as long as God is in it. When the Devil gets in it, it's the most terrible thing on this earth."

She wrote my response down, but she looked disconcerted at what I was saying and quickly turned away without so much as a thank-you. To my knowledge, the brief interview never appeared in print.

The following evening, we had a public service, our first to an all-German audience. Some 34,000 people filled Düsseldorf's Rhine Stadium. The local sponsors, skeptical that anyone would respond, had resisted the attempts of The Navigators' representative, Bob Hopkins, to train counselors and ushers; they said they would not be needed. After the Invitation, Bob hurriedly recruited some Christian airmen from a nearby U.S. base to help direct people to the tent set aside for inquirers. Twice as many people came for counseling as could be accommodated in the tent.

It was midnight when we finally got back to our hotel. About two in the morning, I had to call Jerry Beavan and Bob Evans to ask them for help. They came immediately and found me writhing in agony on my bathroom floor. I wondered if I had been poisoned, or was dying, or both. John, who had been born ten miles from Düsseldorf, woke up a local doctor (who, it turned out, was a Christian and had been at the meeting that evening). He gave me a painkilling shot, then got me to a local specialist the next morning.

The X rays showed a kidney stone. The agony lingered, and the doctors insisted I enter the hospital for a complete physical examination. However, our next scheduled meeting was going to be our largest, in Berlin's Olympic Stadium, where Hitler's rhetoric had inflamed the hearts and minds of his followers slightly over a decade before. I told the doctors I was determined to preach in Berlin even if they had to carry me in on a stretcher. From that moment on, I refused the painkillers the doctors offered me. I did not want to be groggy when I preached in Berlin.

"Why is God doing this to me? Or is it Satan?" I asked John that night as he sat by my bedside. "I can't understand it!"

Then, as we talked, it occurred to me that God was humbling me, making me depend on Him and not on myself, so that He alone would get the glory. The dangers of depending on my own strength and abilities were very real, I knew. I recalled again God's word to Isaiah: "For mine own sake, even for mine own sake, will I do it: . . . and I will not give my glory unto another" (Isaiah 48:11, KJV).

Berlin's local committee, unlike the organizers at some of the other stops on this tour, had prepared for six months to make sure every detail was covered in the arrangements. The Lutheran bishop of East and West Berlin, Otto Dibelius, had given strong support to the event. Thousands of posters blanketed the city.

In spite of a steady rain, 80,000 poured into the stadium—a record for any postwar event, or so we were told at the time. According-ing to the *Manchester Dispatch*, "There has been no such crowd since the days of Hitler." From the offering, which contained a large amount of East German currency, we could tell that perhaps as many as 20,000 people had come from the Eastern Zone.

I began my message with an allusion to Hitler's use of that same stadium: "Others have stood here and spoken to you," I said. Then I raised my Bible. "Now God speaks to you." I then spoke on Jesus' story of the rich young ruler found in Mark 10.

Because of stadium regulations, we could not have people come forward to the platform. Five days later, on a ship in the Atlantic heading for home, came a radio phone message from Berlin: 16,000 Germans had filled out decision cards. This swamped the follow-up program headed by Peter Schneider of the Berlin YMCA. He orga-nized a series of meetings in churches scattered around Berlin to help those who had made a commitment to Christ to become grounded in the Bible. Many of them, he later discovered, were un-clear about the meaning of the Invitation. The idea of making a personal decision or commitment to Christ was foreign to their background in the Lutheran state church, but large numbers were brought to a full commitment during the follow-up process. One of those was Peter Schneider's future wife, Margot.

Paris

After Berlin came Paris a few days later. We were already planning a full Crusade there for the next year, so we held no public meetings, though we did meet with clergy to help prepare for the upcoming event.

As we looked back over this whirlwind tour of the Continent—lasting almost exactly two weeks—we could not help but be overwhelmed by the response we had seen almost everywhere—a response we could attribute only to God. For millions in Europe, the crushing devastation of war and the failure of secularism and rationalism to prevent the greatest slaughter in history were creating a new openness to Christ. We left determined to make Great Britain and the Continent a major part of our ministry in the future.

HARVESTING IN SCOTLAND, AND BEYOND

We did not wait long to return.

Less than a year later—an interval marked mainly by extended Crusades and other opportunities in the United States—we went back, this time to Scotland. The invitation came from a broad-based committee for an effort known as "Tell Scotland," sponsored by the Church of Scotland. There was a huge debate about the invitation in both the press and the Church of Scotland General Assembly; the latter voted that Tell Scotland would be the instrument, and that Tom Allan, who was highly respected in the Church of Scotland, would be the chairman. Most meetings would be held in Glasgow, with single rallies in other major cities.

On March 12, 1955, we sailed from New York on the French liner *Liberté*. I told reporters at our departure that in my view our forthcoming meetings were more important than any diplomatic or political mission. Given the intensity of the work to come, I was grateful for the blessed leisure of the ocean voyage. I usually had breakfast in bed, met with Team members at eleven for a prayer meeting, took lunch, studied until four, and then got some exercise on deck.

On Sunday I was invited by the captain to preach in the ship's theater. Such had been the international coverage of our meetings that I was already pretty well known to everyone on board the ship; they filled the theater that morning. Our colleague Howard Butt, who was introduced as a Texas millionaire, led the temporary congregation in the Lord's Prayer. He forgot part of it, confusing everybody. He explained to me afterward, with a smile, that he knew I was pressed for time and he thought an abbreviated version of the prayer would help!

We arrived in Plymouth, England, at six in the morning. As the tender bearing us to shore pulled away from the ship, we could hear the strains of "This Is My Story, This Is My Song" floating toward us. A large group of people had gotten up early and waited in the cold morning to greet us. Before we could get off the tender, the press tumbled on board and asked me all kinds of questions, from my reaction to the hydrogen bomb to what I thought of Princess Margaret. The Lord helped me through it. Their coverage turned out to be pretty favorable—much more so than the year before.

On the two-hundred-mile trip by car to London, somewhere between Plymouth and Bournemouth we had a coffee break at an inn on the coast; the town parson greeted us warmly there. We spent a lot of our driving time in prayer, with a renewed burden for Great Britain to come to Christ. Lunch was at Bournemouth, which I remembered from eight years before. When I went to the restroom in the hotel, a man followed me in, saying that he needed God. I gave him the Gospel in essence, and he promised to attend our Wembley meeting in London after the Glasgow Crusade.

Jerry was not very reassuring about the prospects in Scotland. There was a feeling among some people there that the Crusade had been so overorganized and overpromoted that the meetings themselves might be an anticlimax. A local debate over our coming had at least shaken a lot of people out of indifference. It didn't help, though, that Lorne Sanny had the flu, Bev Shea couldn't speak above a whisper, and Willis Haymaker had laryngitis.

We had dinner that night in London at the home of Mr. Joynson-Hicks, a member of Parliament who served as the British attorney for several Hollywood film companies. He and his wife were perfect hosts, even letting our shivering Texan, Howard Butt, have that English rarity, a hot bath; just taking off his shoes and putting his feet up by the fireplace hadn't done it for Howard.

In London many old friends came down to the station to see us off on the train for Glasgow. When a little girl about seven—our Anne's age—waved to me, a lump came into my throat as I thought of my children back home. A picture that had been taken of Gigi kissing me good-bye in Montreat was in all the British papers and stirred a lot of warmhearted comment.

The photographers and reporters were becoming a nuisance. On the train to Glasgow, when reporters tried to interview me in the corridor, I said goodnight and shut the door to my compartment.

Before I went to bed, I felt a great burden of prayer. In my pajamas, I got on my knees and prayed for the meetings in Glasgow, particularly for the press conference the next day; I asked that the Lord would give me wisdom. A verse kept coming to mind: "So he fed them according to the integrity of his heart; and guided them by the skilfulness of his hands" (Psalm 78:72, KJV). I also prayed that the Lord would give me a good rest; I had been having difficulty sleeping the last few nights and was tired. No sooner had I prayed and crawled into bed than I went sound asleep.

At six-thirty the next morning, I was awakened by the porter with a cup of tea. As our train stopped in the first Scottish village, scores of people at the station greeted us with hymns. I got out of bed, put on my overcoat, and looked out the window. The well-wishers all laughed when I told them I was not dressed to come outside. During the next two hours to Glasgow, I saw more people standing along the way, waving to us and singing. Apparently, the newspapers had revealed the precise train we would be on. They were "angels unaware," I thought, whom the Lord had sent to cheer my tense spirit.

A fresh concern to communicate the Gospel message had been stirring for two years among many Scottish Christians. Our All-Scotland Crusade, beginning on March 21, 1955, was to be just a part of the harvesting from the faithful sowing and nurturing of the spiritual seed done by those Christians, as I told the 1,000 clergymen who gathered at Glasgow's St. Andrew's Hall to welcome us.

Before the meetings began, I was to address a gathering of clergy, theological professors, and theological students. That was a bit intimidating. I asked Dr. John Sutherland Bonnell, the distinguished Scottish-born pastor of Fifth Avenue Presbyterian Church in New York, to accompany me. As he looked over the crowd, he leaned over and whispered, "This is probably the greatest gathering of theological minds in modern Scottish history." That didn't help me to relax!

The main meetings were held in Glasgow's Kelvin Hall. I took encouragement from the city's ancient motto, inscribed over the entrance: *Let Glasgow Flourish by the Preaching of the Word and the Praising of His Name.* Some Scottish church leaders had advised against giving an Invitation at the meetings, saying that the Scots had no tradition of coming forward in an evangelistic meeting; besides, they were far too reserved to do so.

The first night, Kelvin Hall was filled to capacity; normally, it held 8,000 or 9,000 people, but it had been renovated to hold several thousand more. I felt a strong closeness with the audience that I could explain only as the power of the Holy Spirit. But when I gave the Invitation at the end of the sermon, not a soul moved. My advisers, I admitted, had been right. I bowed my head in prayer, and moments later, when I looked up, people were streaming down the aisles, some with tears in their eyes.

The meetings in Glasgow lasted for six weeks. We took every opportunity we could to extend the mission to people who might not ordinarily come to the main meetings. For example, we preached to thousands of steelworkers and dockers at the John Brown Shipyard. Other meetings ran the gamut from mills and factories to the homes of the wealthy. The Scots were particularly fascinated by Howard Butt, attracted both by his image as a wealthy Texas businessman and by his clear-cut testimony to Christ.

In Scotland we had the support of several prominent people, which helped gain entrée into social and business circles. John Henderson, member of Parliament, went with us everywhere and became a good friend; Hugh Fraser, founder of the House of Fraser department store chain in Great Britain, likewise was very supportive and had us to his home for gatherings with other leading businesspeople.

Our time in Scotland included a number of other unique events. I was invited to many of the colleges and universities, and following the Glasgow Crusade I was asked to address the Church of Scotland General Assembly, which meets annually. The latter was a very formal occasion, and I had forgotten to bring the proper clothing from London. The day in question was a holiday, and Paul Maddox could not find a store open that carried formal wear; eventually, I had to call Hugh Fraser, who let us into one of his stores.

Ruth and I also attended an elaborate dinner as guests of the Duke of Hamilton, held in the banquet hall of Mary, Queen of Scots, at the Palace of Holyroodhouse in Edinburgh. Almost everyone I met at that dinner seemed to be a lord or lady.

"Your Grace," I said to one of the handsome young men dressed in black tie and tux, "I don't believe I've met you."

"No, sir, you haven't," he said, somewhat amused. "I'm your waiter this evening."

I assured him that I was still happy to meet him.

"And you might like to know, sir," he added, "that *Your Grace* is reserved for dukes and archbishops."

Overwhelmingly, however, we were mostly with ordinary people like ourselves, not with the wealthy or influential. We took advantage of every opportunity to speak before all kinds of groups, whatever their social position. I was especially concerned to reach out to working people, who I felt had often been alienated from the churches.

One of my British-born associates, Joe Blinco, was a workingman himself and therefore knew the workingman's language inside out. He went to all kinds of meetings. He had a volatile spirit, though, and on one occasion, at a tumultuous gathering of jeering, working-class people like himself, he got so mad that he told them, "Okay, so *go* to Hell!"

More than any previous Crusade, the Glasgow meetings attracted large numbers of nonchurched people, in part through the implementation of a program we called "Operation Andrew." Although the basic concept had been in place in other Crusades, Lorne Sanny and Charlie Riggs refined its operation in Glasgow. It took its name from the disciple Andrew in the New Testament, who brought his brother Simon Peter to Christ (*see* John 1:40–42). Through this program, individuals were encouraged to make a deliberate effort to pray for those they knew who were unchurched or uncommitted and to bring them personally to the meetings. Lorne and Charlie also refined the process for recruiting and training our counselors more effectively.

The response was far beyond anything we could ever have anticipated. Using telephone lines during Easter week from Kelvin Hall, Church of Scotland evangelist D. P. Thomson helped us to organize rallies in thirty-seven locations; over 1,000 people later attended follow-up classes from these meetings. Nor was the Crusade's impact limited to Scotland. On Good Friday, the BBC beamed on radio and television a special sermon I had prepared on the meaning of the Cross. It had what was said to be the largest audience for a single program since the coronation of the Queen.

We later discovered that the Queen herself had watched the program. Two or three days later, one of her equerries came to see me, conveying an invitation to preach at Windsor Castle the week after the London Crusade. He stressed that the engagement must be kept confidential, however, or it would have to be canceled. I told only Ruth.

During this holy but hard time, letters to Ruth were my safety valve. In the intimacy of our partnership in the ministry, as well as our mutual love and respect, I could express myself to her as to few others. I smarted under grievous criticisms from fundamentalists, and I minced no words in telling her how I felt: "Some of the things they say are pure fabrications. . . . I do not intend to get down to their mud-slinging and get into endless arguments and discussions with them. . . . We are too busy winning souls to Christ and helping build the church to go down and argue with these . . . publicity-seekers."

I continued in the same vein: "If a man accepts the deity of Christ and is living for Christ to the best of his knowledge, I intend to have fellowship with him in Christ. If this extreme type of fundamentalism was of God, it would have brought revival long ago. Instead, it has brought dissension, division, strife, and has produced dead and lifeless churches."

The fact that I was in Christian work didn't make it any easier, humanly speaking, to be away from Ruth and the children. Right after I got to Scotland, I expressed my yearning for her company in a letter that might have pressured her as much as I hope it pleased her: "You have no idea how lonesome it is without you! In thinking about my message tonight, I'd give anything if you were here to talk it over with. You are the only one that ever really understands my dilemma in the choice of messages. Your advice is the only one that I really trust. You have no idea how often I have listened to your advice and it has been as if it were spoken from the Lord. During the past year, I have learned to lean on you a great deal more than you realize. I'll be counting the days till you arrive."

I guess I must have let my feelings for Ruth show in public. The Scottish reporters asked me how many letters I had received from her, and how many times I had written to her. They even wanted to know how much perfume she put on her letters for me to smell!

"Hurry on over," my associate Lee Fisher wrote to Ruth. "Bill's about to languish away. He tries to act like he's self-sufficient, but he's a perfect fool about your coming."

In Glasgow, though, criticism took a back seat to rejoicing in Crusade blessings. My personal joy reached new heights when Ruth came over to join me for the last two weeks of the Crusade; it had been only a month since I had left home, but it seemed like a year. She brought with her nine-year-old Gigi, who was old enough to appreciate a visit to another country. Gigi immediately got a crush on our Scottish chauffeur. It was my first experience of functioning as evangelist and daddy at the same time.

The meetings in those last weeks were carried by telephone lines to locations all over the British Isles. The final meeting in Kelvin Hall drew a capacity crowd on Thursday night, with another 6,000 listening outside in the streets over loudspeakers. Then, on Saturday, 100,000 people jammed every available space—sitting and standing—at Hampden Park, Glasgow's main soccer stadium.

Dr. Tom Rees put it well: "London broke the ice; Glasgow swam in a warmer current."

At Hampden Park and elsewhere, the St. John Ambulance Brigade was on duty for first aid. When they received a call for help while I was preaching, they ran to whomever was in distress and brought him or her back to their station, which was under the platform. One night especially it seemed to us that a lot of people were in distress. Grady went down to find out what was going on and discovered that the primary restorative used by the first aid workers was a shot of brandy. While down there, Grady claimed he saw one woman come back three times!

We reached a half-million more people in our six weeks in Glasgow and at single rallies in Aberdeen and Inverness than the 2 million we had touched in twelve weeks in London. And the response to the Gospel by recorded inquirers, which numbered some 38,000 in London, went beyond 52,000 in Scotland. As mass figures, these were somewhat numbing, but they were indeed "vital statistics" when you heard the individual stories.

Like the woman who told her hairdresser that she owed her new permanent to Billy Graham. Her husband, after being converted at the Crusade, brought home all of his paycheck instead of holding out much of it for drinking and gambling.

Or like the cabby who was led to Christ by my old friend Dr. John R. Rice, editor of *The Sword of the Lord* newspaper. Rice had enthusiastically participated in the Crusade for a week after an American businessman gave him an airplane ticket to fly over. When he got back, he described his Scotland visit in *The Sword* as "seven miracle days."

Or like the devout, churchgoing husband and wife in a small Irish town, listening over the radio to the Crusade broadcast from Kelvin Hall; they decided on the spot to trust "the Man on the Cross" for their salvation and held to their decision in the face of strong local criticism and family opposition.

Sometimes we hear about the impact of a Crusade only much later. Almost forty years after this particular Crusade, in 1991, I returned to Scotland for a Crusade in several cities. Two years later, in 1993, I addressed a Scottish School of Evangelism on television via satellite from the United States. At the school, the Moderator of the Church of Scotland, the Right Reverend Hugh Wiley, introduced me. In his remarks, he noted that in 1955 he had hoped to hear me in person in Kelvin Hall but was able only to listen on landline at Elgin. But my words had crystallized the commitment of his parents to Christ and hastened his own response to the claims of Jesus Christ, resulting in his call to full-time service in the church.

Almost immediately after Glasgow, we had another Crusade in London, at Wembley Stadium. It rained every single night except the last, which was the coldest night of the year!

In the months following Glasgow and Wembley, we held rallies throughout West Germany, at the largest stadiums and arenas available in the cities of Frankfurt, Wiesbaden, Kaiserslautern, Mannheim, Stuttgart, Nürnberg, Darmstadt (where I had the privilege of meeting with the great hero of resistance to the Nazis, Lutheran pastor Martin Niemöller), and Dortmund.

Other meetings were scheduled in Oslo, Norway; Gothenburg, Sweden; Århus, Denmark; and Rotterdam, the Netherlands. I also made visits to Zürich, Stockholm, and Copenhagen. Before returning to the United States, I preached at a worship service at the U.S. military installation at Verdun in France and addressed for the first time the Baptist World Alliance meeting in England.

COLLEGES AND UNIVERSITIES

Ever since my days at Northwestern Schools, youth in general and college students in particular have been a special concern for Ruth and me. In fact, this concern went back to our days with Youth for Christ. As we evaluated and prayed over invitations to speak and preach, colleges and universities often took priority.

I have often felt inadequate in such settings. At the same time, I have discovered that in the midst of the contradictory philosophies and ideologies competing for attention on the average university campus, there is something compelling (and even life-changing) for many students about the person of Jesus Christ. Many of them have developed a vaunted intellectual approach to life. But of these, few have ever seriously examined the record of Jesus' life or considered the evidence for His claim to be the One who alone can give ultimate meaning to life and death.

I have already described our spring 1950 tour of New England, which included speaking engagements at a number of colleges and universities. Our experiences there convinced us that we needed to devote more time to campuses in the future, but during the next few years our Crusade schedule was so intense that we had little time, except for schools in the Crusade cities.

Princeton Seminary 1953

One exception was an invitation to speak at Princeton Theological Seminary in February 1953. I almost did not accept it. How could I address ministerial students at one of the most respected seminaries in the United States when I had not been to seminary myself?

As houseguests of President and Mrs. John Mackay, Ruth and I were treated with unrestrained warmth. And even though the students were not predisposed toward our ministry, I couldn't have asked for more respectful treatment. That did not mean they were not candid or direct during the question periods following my talks; they certainly were! These were dedicated and intelligent students, not about to be taken in by the cult of personality that they perceived the media had developed around me. (Perhaps they were disarmed by finding out that the so-called cultism concerned me more than it did them.)

At that time, the Scottish-born Dr. Mackay was a giant in American church circles. The unhurried private talks we had together revealed to me that he was a man who had a deep heart for God. He also seemed to appreciate the opportunity to talk about his deepest concerns with someone outside his immediate context.

His comments in a letter written after our visit were encouraging: "Your presence on this campus has meant more for the spiritual life of Princeton Seminary and for the creation of a spirit of unity in the student body than anything that has taken place during the nearly seventeen years that I have been President."

Cambridge University 1955

Of a much different nature was our experience the first time we held an extended series of meetings focused on one specific university. Those meetings took us back once again to Great Britain.

Following our meetings in London in 1954, we received an invitation to hold an eight-day mission at Cambridge University under the auspices of the student-led Cambridge Inter-Collegiate

Christian Union (CICCU); it had 800 members out of the university's student body of 8,000. After much prayer, we accepted the invitation for November 1955.

Unexpectedly, the invitation unleashed a storm of controversy in nothing less than the editorial pages of the *Times*. Between August 15 and August 27, the newspaper printed twenty-eight letters to the editor about the proposed mission. So intense was the interest in the topic of our visit that the paper later reprinted those letters in a separate booklet. The series of letters began with one from a liberal Anglican clergyman from Durham, Canon H. K. Luce.

"The recent increase of fundamentalism among university students cannot but cause concern to those whose work lies in religious education," he wrote. "Is it not time that our religious leaders made it plain that while they respect, or even admire, Dr. Graham's sincerity and personal power, they cannot regard fundamentalism as likely to issue in anything but disillusionment and disaster for educated men and women in this twentieth-century world?"

The issue was complicated by the fact that the CICCU's student leaders had obtained permission to use the official university church, Great St. Mary's, for the meetings. "This does not mean that the University Church endorses fundamentalist views," the church's vicar, Mervyn Stockwood, wrote to the *Times*.

We later became good friends, Mervyn and I, in spite of our theological disagreements. But during the next ten days, a flurry of letters went back and forth in the pages of the newspaper. Some ranking clergymen and scholars, including some affiliated with Cambridge, strongly defended the mission; others just as strongly decried it. Still others attempted to define the exact theological meaning of the term *fundamentalist;* it didn't have quite as negative a connotation in Great Britain as it had in America, referring in England mainly to someone who held to the essential tenets of the historic Christian faith as found in Scripture.

"Does not Canon Luce," one writer chided, "underestimate the intelligence of undergraduates who, one may suppose, have reached an age when they begin to sift knowledge gained and to form their own opinions?"

In late August, I expressed my doubts in a letter to my trusted friend John Stott, vicar of All Souls, Langham Place, in London; as an undergraduate at Cambridge, he had won a double first (modern languages and theology). "I have been deeply concerned and in much thought about our Cambridge mission this autumn," I wrote John candidly. "I do not know that I have ever felt more inadequate and totally unprepared for a mission. As I think over the possibility for messages, I realize how shallow and weak my presentations are. In fact, I was so overwhelmed with my unpreparedness that I almost decided to cancel my appearance, but because plans have gone so far perhaps it is best to go through with it. . . . However, it is my prayer that I shall come in the demonstration and power of the Holy Spirit, though I am going to lean heavily on you, Maurice, and the others."

A copy of my letter to John Stott went to another close friend and supporter, the bishop of Barking, Hugh Gough, himself a Cambridge man. Hastily, he wrote me a letter of encouragement from on board ship as he was about to depart from Canada: "I can well understand your feelings of apprehension about Cambridge, but Billy do not worry. God has opened up the way so wonderfully & has called you to it & so all will be well. . . . Do not regard these men as 'intellectuals.' Appeal to their conscience. They are sinners, needing a Savior. Conviction of sin, not intellectual persuasion, is the need. So many preachers fail at this point when they speak to university men. So, Billy, keep to the wonderful clear simple message God has qualified you to preach."

In spite of his admonition, I worked as diligently as I knew how to put the Gospel into an intellectual framework in eight messages.

Rumor had it that traditional interschool rivalry with Oxford University would lead some Oxford "blues" to kidnap me. The day I was to arrive at Cambridge—Saturday, November 5, 1955—was Guy Fawkes Day; the holiday commemorated the foiling of the Gunpowder Plot in 1605, a plan by Catholics to blow up Parliament and kill the king. As celebrated in England in general, and no doubt at Cambridge as well, Guy Fawkes was burned in effigy, "pennies for the Guy" were collected by children, and fireworks were set off. Kidnapping me might just top off the festivities.

So a plan was hatched with the help of some members of the CICCU to make sure no kidnapping took place. They had formed, it appeared, a miniature Scotland Yard in order to safeguard my movements. And they were having fun with it: one of them was dressed as Sherlock Holmes; another, as Dr. Watson.

On the appointed day, Lord Luke, whom I had first met during the 1954 London Crusade, picked me up and drove me to a village near Cambridge. I quickly changed to the unmarked CICCU car and was driven via back roads to town. At a certain street, we were to look for a proctor (a university employee dressed in black and wearing a bowler hat whose job was to enforce discipline, sometimes even to act as a bouncer). If he waved to the right, there was trouble and we were to keep going straight. If he waved to the left, we were to proceed directly to the hall, where I was to meet the masters of the colleges. When we found him, he waved left, and I arrived without incident at the university's gorgeous setting—a winding river (the Cam), spreading lawns, and ancient buildings.

On Saturday I spoke to the senior members of the university in the afternoon and to the CICCU in the evening. Among the professors I met privately with that day was C. S. Lewis. A decade before, he had captured the imagination of many in England and the United States with his remarkable little book *The Screwtape Letters;* in 1947 he had been on the cover of *Time* magazine.

John Stott was very anxious for me to meet Professor Lewis and went with me. Lewis was not as well known in the United States as he would become in later years, particularly after his death in 1963. But I had read *Screwtape,* and Ruth would later read the *Chronicles of Narnia* series.

We met in the dining room of his college, St. Mary Magdalene's, and we talked for an hour or more. I was afraid I would be intimidated by him because of his brilliance, but he immediately put me at my ease. I found him to be not only intelligent and witty but also gentle and gracious; he seemed genuinely interested in our meetings. "You know," he said as we parted, "you have many critics, but I have never met one of your critics who knows you personally."

For the first three nights of the public meetings, beginning on Sunday, November 6, I felt as if I were in a straitjacket on the platform, and very little happened. Great St. Mary's was packed beyond capacity with students in academic gowns; students also filled two other churches, which were equipped to carry the meetings by public address system. One-fourth of the student body attended each evening, listening intently, but there seemed to be little spiritual impact.

Then, on my knees with a deep sense of failure, inadequacy, and helplessness, I turned to God. My gift, such as it was, was not to present the intellectual side of the Gospel. I knew that. What those students needed was a clear understanding of the simple but profound truths of the Gospel: our separation from God because of sin; Christ's provision of forgiveness and new life; and our hope because of Him.

Finally, on Wednesday night, I threw away my prepared address and preached a simple Gospel message on the meaning of the Cross of Christ. That night more than 400 Cambridge students stayed behind to make their commitment to Christ. (On the advice of the CICCU students, I used a different approach at Cambridge from that used in most of our Crusades; I asked those who wanted to receive Christ to stay behind after the end of the meeting.) For the rest of the week, I strove to be as simple and yet as direct as possible, and the response continued to surprise us all. I also enjoyed the informal discussions we held in many of the residence halls, where students felt free to ask all kinds of questions.

John Stott was one of 30 missioners who joined us during the week, speaking in the various Cambridge colleges; others included Dr. Paul Rees and Dr. David Cowie from the United States, the Reverend Tom Allan from Scotland, and the Reverend Maurice Wood from England itself.

The Cambridge mission of 1955 opened my eyes as well as my heart to the opportunities for campus evangelism. Immediately afterward we went to Oxford, where the visit originally scheduled to last a few days was extended to a week.

Those months overseas in 1955 convinced me that our ministry henceforth had to be worldwide. But could Crusade evangelism be effective in non-Western countries, which were the home of the world's great non-Christian religions? We would never know the answer to the question without trying.

On January 15, 1956, we headed for India and other Asian destinations.

1956–1967

To the Ends of the Earth

15

Into Asia

When we toured Japan and Korea during the Korean War, most of our meetings were held for the United Nations forces stationed there, especially the American troops. I was fascinated by what I saw of Asia's culture, and Korea's wartime devastation and poverty had moved me greatly, but I knew that we had only begun to glimpse Asia's rich diversity and complexity. Now, as 1955 drew to a close, we found ourselves preparing for a much more extended journey among the teeming populations and cultures of that vast region.

INDIA

"Billy Graham was cutting through India like Gabriel in a gabardine suit." That was the way *Time* described me in the February 13, 1956, issue. It was nice to get some coverage in the Luce magazine, but I preferred the Associated Press wirephoto of me astride an elephant in Kottayam, looking far from angelic as I held on for dear life to the tough hide behind those huge floppy ears.

For years now, even as far back as my anthropology studies at Wheaton, I had been fascinated by India, with its vast multireligious and multicultural population of (at that time) over 400 million people, and I had prayed that someday God might open the door for us to go there.

Plans for an extended series of meetings in India actually crystallized in my thinking during the week-long May 1955 Crusade in London's Wembley Stadium, which was a follow-up to the Harringay meetings of the previous year. Between 50,000 and 60,000 Londoners trekked to the chilly stadium in Wembley each evening, in spite of the fact that it poured rain five of the seven nights—weatherwise, one of our bleakest Crusades ever.

One morning during those Wembley meetings, I asked Jack Dain to join me at the Kensington Palace Hotel for breakfast. A former lay missionary in northern India and an officer in an Indian Gurkha regiment during the war, Jack was now serving as Overseas Secretary for the Evangelical Alliance in London. (He later was ordained and became an Anglican bishop in Australia, where he assisted us greatly in some of our visits there.) I told him that I had recently received an invitation from all the major Protestant denominations in India to hold a series of meetings.

Grabbing his napkin—neither of us had a blank piece of paper—Jack quickly sketched a map of India and marked six cities scattered around the country that he felt would be the most strategic for us to visit: Bombay, Madras, Kottayam, Palamcottah, New Delhi, and Calcutta. Each one of the six cities, he pointed out, had a small established Christian population that would provide a foundation for preparations and follow-up.

Shortly before leaving the United States for India—and just a half-year after that meeting with Jack—I was able to meet with Secretary of State John Foster Dulles for a briefing on relations between the United States and India. He felt that it was especially important for me to know that the visit to India of Soviet leaders Khrushchev and Bulganin two months earlier had had as its sole purpose drawing India into closer ties with the Communist bloc.

On January 15, 1956, we left for India from New York. The Team for this trip was a small one, but it did include a Christian newspaper reporter from Chattanooga, George Burnham, self-described as "an ex-alcoholic." Six hundred newspapers had signed up to carry George's stories, and later he wrote a book about the trip.

It took us a couple of days by plane to cover the eight thousand miles to India. Grady Wilson, Jerry Beavan, and John Bolten were accompanying me. John was upset by the length of the flight, but he had no recourse but to settle down. During a stopover in Athens (at three in the morning, local time), we began talking about the Apostle Paul's visit to that ancient center of culture and philosophy, remembering how the apostle had adopted a special approach in his sermon on Mars Hill (*see* Acts 17) in order to build a bridge to his pagan audience and win a hearing for the Gospel.

"Billy," John said, "you are on your way to India, a country that has no conception of God. You will need a special approach to break into people's thinking, because they know nothing of the Bible or of God. Do you have such an approach in mind?"

Admitting that I didn't, I suggested that we make that issue a matter of concentrated prayer.

Shortly after taking off from our next stopover, which was Cairo—we had already been traveling about thirty hours—we flew near Mt. Sinai, where God had entrusted the Ten Commandments to Moses. Off in the distance we could see Israel, where Jesus had been born and lived. Suddenly it came to me: Jesus had been born in the one part of the world where the three great continents of Asia, Africa, and Europe intersect.

That was the answer to our prayer for an approach to the people of India.

"I am not here to tell you about an American or a Britisher or a European," I said everywhere we went. "I am here to tell you about a Man who was born right here in your part of the world, in Asia. He was born at the place where Asia and Africa and Europe meet. He had skin that was darker than mine, and He came to show us that God loves all people. He loves the people of India, and He loves you."

We could see people's eyes light up as they realized that Christianity was not exclusively for Europeans or the white race but that Christ came for all.

Bombay

When we arrived in Bombay on January 17, 1956, the situation was not promising. In violent political riots unrelated to our visit, just

265

before our arrival, two people were killed outside the stadium where we were scheduled to hold a meeting. The riots got worldwide headlines, but it was not the kind of publicity we needed! When, as part of those same ongoing riots, a rock-throwing mob attacked the police station after several Christian leaders had conferred there with government officials, it was clear that our own event had to be canceled, although I met privately with ministers and other Christian workers. Alone in my hotel room afterward, all I could do was cry out to God to help me love those people as Christ did.

Out on the street, as one mob swirled by, I asked a young man with a rock in his hand why he was rioting.

"I don't know," he replied. "Someone told me to."

Later I saw some young men beating an old shopkeeper who had refused to close his stall. Altogether, we later learned, fifty people were killed during the riots, and hundreds were injured in violent clashes between the rioters and the police.

Although I had read about the destitution of India frequently enough, nothing could have prepared me for the overwhelming poverty we saw on every hand.

Later, in my diary, I recorded my reaction: "It was one of the most heartbreaking scenes that I had seen since I left Korea [during the Korean War]. . . . The missionaries and others, and even the Indian leaders, had warned us already not to give money. . . . It's a most difficult thing, however, to turn your back on such poverty as this. Some of them may be able to do it, but I can't. I gave as many rupees as I possibly could to as many people as I saw in need. However, the missionaries and Indian leaders were right—we soon collected a great crowd who were begging and screaming and fighting for money. Only with considerable effort were we able to break away from the dangerous near-riot I had caused."

But there was at least one light moment in Bombay. Outside my hotel one day, I saw a man with two bags go out into the middle of the street. From one bag he let out a cobra, which immediately wrapped itself into a coil and struck out at everyone who approached. He let out a mongoose from another bag, which went right after the cobra. During the tussle that followed, the man took up a collection from the crowd.

I went outside to take in the scene more closely. Standing next to me was a congenial American. He invited me back into the hotel for a cup of tea. He was Reuben Youngdahl, pastor of the largest Lutheran church in Minnesota, and we became good friends.

Madras

At our next stop, Madras, the city was jammed with people who had traveled long distances to participate in our meetings. I read, for instance, that 100 people from Hyderabad had ridden the train for days to get there. With the translators standing beside me—Mr. Titus for the Telugu and Mr. J. Victor Manogarom for the Tamil—I preached to integrated crowds of 40,000 in which all the rigid lines of caste and gender were temporarily ignored. We also had two choirs—one for each language—which repeated each number (including the "Hallelujah Chorus"), adding to the length of the service.

At one point in my address, I knew that I had said something awry. Talking about Jesus, I had said, "He's alive!" Mr. Titus promptly rendered that in Telugu, but Mr. Manogarom faltered. I repeated the expression several times. Finally, he uttered, *"Avan poikaran."* The Tamils gasped. As I learned afterward, the best Mr. Manogarom could make of my North Carolina accent was, "He was a liar!" No great harm was done, for the mistake evened itself out in the next few sentences.

As I continued, I tried to assure my listeners that it was wrong to think of Christianity as a *Western* religion. It had been in India long before America was discovered, going back as far as a visit by the Apostle Thomas in A.D. 52, according to tradition. Out of 100,000 who heard me speak in three days, 4,000 recorded their decisions for Christ. We could have used more counselors, but we made up for that shortcoming by distributing twelve thousand copies of the Gospel of John. Such a result witnessed to the spiritual power generated by the twenty-four-hour prayer chains that had preceded our visit.

Rooms in the city were at a premium during our Crusade meetings. Hundreds slept in the streets at night and camped at the meeting site all day. Our morning services were at seven; the evening ones, at six. In addition to those services, we also met with a variety of different groups at other locations. One day, for example, I spoke to a student gathering of 7,500 out of which 250 responded to the Invitation to commit their lives to Christ. Many were from non-Christian backgrounds.

In both Bombay and Madras, I had some opportunity to observe the practices of Hinduism, one of the dominant religions in India. In Bombay we watched the funeral of an old man whose body was placed on a pile of wood and burned. As the flames died down, the son took a stick and punched a hole in the skull, hoping to release the man's spirit. In Madras we visited a Hindu temple dedicated to the worship of Siva—a form of worship that was (I discovered as soon as I entered the temple) phallic. We also watched people offer their sacrifices to the priests. I recorded my reaction in my diary: "We stood and watched it and almost wept, longing that these people might know the forgiveness that is in Christ."

In my messages, I did not directly attack the views of those who adhered to other religions; I was not in India to stir up controversy. Instead, I concentrated on presenting in a positive way the message of Christ as simply and forcefully as possible. Throughout my ministry to date, I had seen that the message of Christ, if accepted, had the power to replace false ideas and beliefs. However, it was necessary at times in India to explain that Christ wasn't just another deity who could be added to the list of thirty thousand gods and goddesses already worshiped by Hindus in general. He was uniquely God in human flesh, and He alone was worthy of our worship and commitment.

Our visit to Madras gave me a glimpse into something else that I found upsetting: the Ugly American. One day in our hotel, Jerry saw three half-drunk Americans loudly berating and abusing the mail clerk, a kindly little man who had been very helpful to us. In my diary, I recorded my heated reaction: "These are the types of American tourists that are giving us a bad name and making people hate us all over the world. . . ."

Kottayam

In Kottayam, at the southern tip of India, the support for our presence was almost unbelievable. Any doubts I might have had about the relevancy of the Cross in a cultural setting so different from everything I had known were instantly dispelled.

Girls with baskets, working as a labor of love, had carved out the entire side of a hill into a giant amphitheater with three levels so that the people could sit comfortably on the ground; in accordance with Indian custom, which we were not in a position to change, women had to sit on a different level from the men. From where we were staying we could see the greenest rice paddies I have ever seen, and beyond *that*—after a dotting of little green houses—was the jungle, with all of its palms. I can imagine few places in the world more beautiful.

Kottayam itself had a population of only 50,000, yet a preliminary service that had gotten almost no publicity drew 25,000 people. The next night, at the first scheduled meeting, 75,000 people came. Three days later—the crowds having continued to grow with each passing day—the final crowd was 100,000. In our few days there, a third of a million people heard the Gospel.

They were all dressed in white, and tens of thousands of them brought along large palm leaves to sit on. Those traveling from a distance, in order not to rely on the local stores, brought their own food. As for the Team, we were fearful after hearing stories about foreigners who had gotten sick because they were not acclimated to India's food and hygiene. Most of us, therefore, ate enormous quantities of bananas every day of the trip, and we peeled them ourselves. I myself had few problems, but I wrote in my diary that "I've eaten so many bananas until I feel like I'm going to turn into a banana."

Jerry, Paul Maddox, and I were staying in the nearby house of Bishop Jacob, a tall, gray haired, commanding figure who was clearly loved and respected as the leader of the Church of South India. At first I liked the idea of staying in a private residence. Then the bishop casually let it drop that some snake charmers had captured twenty-six cobras in his yard the week before! He tried to quiet our fears by assuring us that cobras seldom came into the house.

Our first night with Bishop Jacob, I was awakened about four in the morning by amplified music blaring outside. I had been dreaming I was on an airplane, and when this booming started, I thought the plane had crashed. When I looked out of my window,

I realized that the music was coming from the roughly 5,000 people who had already gathered for a prayer service.

Palamcottah

Attendance figures were comparable in the other cities we visited. In Palamcottah crowds were waiting to cheer us, but they almost turned over our car as we tried to make our way to the cathedral for a meeting of women. At a later meeting for ministers in the same cathedral, I had to crawl out a window after speaking because the crowd was so great, both inside and outside.

I also became aware there of another problem that concerned me very deeply. "Jack Dain," I wrote in my diary, "is fearful that many of the Hindus are beginning to accept me as a god. Many of them fall down and practically worship me as I come by. Many of them try to get in my shadow. I told them time after time, very much as Peter, that I am not a god but a man."

One of the most moving experiences for me personally during our stay in Palamcottah was a side trip we took to a place called Dohnavur, made famous by the work of one of the century's great Christians, Amy Carmichael. Ruth and I had treasured Miss Carmichael's devotional writings for years and prayed for her work among youth who had been abandoned by their parents and dedicated to a life of sacred prostitution in a Hindu temple. Although Miss Carmichael had died a few years before, the loving family spirit among those who lived and worked in Dohnavur moved me to tears. In the room where she had breathed her last, I was asked to pray. I started but could not continue. I had to ask John Bolten to finish for me.

New Delhi

In New Delhi, 15,000 people gathered on the grounds of the YMCA. We were honored by the presiding of a Christian government leader, Minister of Health (Princess) Rajkumari Amrit Kaur, daughter of a prince. She had been in British prison with Jawaharlal Nehru, where they became friends; he later made her a cabinet officer in his government. Rajkumari was the person who had the most influence in our coming to New Delhi, and she opened many doors for us. She also entertained us at a dinner with a number of influential people.

Through her influence I also had the privilege of meeting Prime Minister Nehru. This assisted us in other ways, because once you have been received by the head of state in a country like India, mayors and governors are more likely to welcome you to their area.

Bald except for a fringe of white hair, Nehru wore that famous jacket to which his name was given, with a high open collar and buttons all down the front.

It was a very awkward interview initially. When we first sat down, he did not say anything. He simply waited for me to speak.

I thanked him for seeing me and said that I knew many Americans respected him, although they did not fully realize the great problems he faced. He made no response; he just sat there twiddling a letter opener in his hands. Not quite knowing what to do next, I embarked on a summary of our Indian trip. Once again he made no response.

After a few moments of silence, I decided to tell him what Christ had meant to me and how He had changed my life. Immediately, Mr. Nehru's attitude changed, and he began asking questions and making well-informed comments about Christianity in India. He added that he was not opposed to the work of missionaries, although those who became involved in political matters (as some apparently had done in northern India) would not be welcome. He even commended us on our trip, saying in sincerity that he thought we had done good work. I appreciated the comment.

After thirty-five minutes, we ended on a very cordial note.

One day in New Delhi I was in a taxi that turned a corner rapidly and accidentally hit a baboon, which screamed and then lay still. A crowd gathered immediately and began to throw stones at the car, and the driver said we must get out of there at once or we could be killed. Animals are sacred in the Hindu religion, and I was very concerned that if the Indian people thought I had killed an animal it might close the door to any future ministry there. Nevertheless, I was impressed by how friendly and loving the Indian people can be, and whenever I am asked what country I would like to go back to, I reply "India."

In New Delhi, my interpreter into Hindustani was a scholar by the name of Dr. Akbar Abdul-Haqq. His father had walked all over that part of India, staff in hand, proclaiming Islam; but while in a mission hospital for medical treatment, he had forsaken his Islamic priesthood and been converted to Christ. Dr. Abdul-Haqq himself was a Methodist who had received his doctorate from Northwestern University in Chicago; he was head of the Henry Martyn School of Islamic Studies in Aligarh, India. He admitted that he was not particularly supportive of my visit at first, and for two or three weeks turned down the strong request that he be my interpreter. But after the first night, seeing the responsiveness of the Indian people to the biblical Gospel, he made a confession: "I believe God has called me tonight to be an evangelist."

Several months later, he joined our Team as an associate evangelist and has had a great impact on many lives, not only in his native India but throughout the world, especially in universities.

By now I had developed a certain amount of skill in preaching through interpreters. That was due in part to Dr. Oswald J. Smith, the noted preacher from Peoples Church in Toronto. In the late 1940s, when he and I were in Europe, he showed me the value of short sentences and a fairly rapid delivery when preaching through an interpreter. I also learned the importance of having an interpreter who was a Christian and knew Scripture thoroughly, since I often spontaneously interpolated Scripture passages and thoughts in my sermons that were not included in my prepared text.

Christians made up a large part of those Indian audiences, I was sure, but there were many Hindus too, who simply recognized Christ as a great religious figure alongside Buddha. That did not make them Christians, though.

I knew I was not qualified to pass judgment on some of the things I heard and saw, so I tried to be complimentary as much as possible. I thought the sari worn by Indian women was a beautiful garment, for example, and told them I was taking one home to Ruth.

THE PHILIPPINES

In mid-February we left India and met with missionaries in Bangkok, Thailand; in the whole of that country at that time, there were not more than a few hundred Christians and just a handful of missionaries. When I returned there years later, I was grateful to see that the churches were growing.

After Bangkok we went to Manila for a couple of days. That required another cultural adjustment as we coped with a different variety of circumstances. I was grateful to be invited by President Magsaysay for a pleasant conversation together at the palace.

It was not Communists who opposed our visit to the Philippines; it was the Catholic Archbishop of Manila, who told his people to stay away from the meeting. As is often the case, the climate of controversy got people's attention. I think the Archbishop's opposition contributed more to the Manila experience than all the careful planning, which one paper thought rivaled that for a bullfight.

In this land that had only 700,000 Protestants, the 25,000-seat Rizal Stadium was absolutely jammed, both in the stands and on the grounds. Ours was the largest Protestant-sponsored meeting in the history of the Philippines; several government leaders attended. Cliff directed 1,000 people in the choir, and somewhere in the neighborhood of 5,000 responded to the Invitation. We later learned that 30 percent of those who had committed themselves to Christ that day were Catholics. In that era, we—Protestants and Catholics—were slowly growing in our understanding of each other and of our mutual commitment to those teachings we hold in common.

My experience in the Philippines, and in other countries where the Roman Catholic Church had significant influence, taught me that most people were not going to take us seriously if we spent all our time debating our differences instead of uniting at the Cross.

HONG KONG, FORMOSA (TAIWAN), JAPAN, AND KOREA

The last two weeks in February were a whirlwind as we held meetings in Hong Kong, in Formosa (now Taiwan), in three Japanese cities—Tokyo, Yokohama, and Osaka—and in Seoul, Korea. I enjoyed meeting Generalissimo and Madame Chiang Kai-shek in Taipei, Formosa, and Prime Minister Hatoyama in Tokyo, where he postponed his appearance at a session of Parliament for a half-hour in order to accommodate me.

In Japan we also had the opportunity to hold meetings for American armed services personnel, with senior officers in attendance from the Army, the Navy, and the Air Force. The Army even hosted a luncheon for us. We held pastors' conferences as well and met at one point with 1,200 missionaries.

We could hardly get inside the 15,000-seat Kokusai Stadium in Tokyo for one of our meetings because of an overflow crowd of several thousand waiting outside in the bitterly cold weather. At that meeting, there were a thousand decisions for Christ.

When we returned home, after a stopover rally in Honolulu on March 11, I knew beyond a doubt that the Far East would feature in our future plans somehow.

On my return to the United States, I went through Washington and brought President Eisenhower and Vice President Nixon up to date on the details of my visit to India. I mentioned that when Soviet leader Khrushchev had given Nehru a magnificent white horse, that fact was reported on the front page of all the Indian newspapers. But when Secretary of State John Foster Dulles offered India $50 million, that offer appeared only as a small item at the back of Indian newspapers. I felt the average person in India had no concept of $50 million but could readily understand and appreciate a white horse. Hence, I suggested to the president that we give not only wheat, but also a distinctive white train to deliver it from one end of India to another, so the people would know the gift came from the United States.

"I want you to talk to Dulles about it," said the President. I did so, but nothing came of the suggestion.

However, Dulles kept me a long time because he wanted to hear every detail of our visit to Asia as well as my impressions of India and Nehru. He also wanted to talk with me on a personal matter. Before becoming secretary of state, he was active in the Federal Council of Churches, an antecedent to the National Council of Churches. He told me that his son Avery had just decided to become a Jesuit priest.

My conviction about the place of Asia in our ministry turned out to be true. Since that first tour, we have returned to India and other parts of Asia repeatedly. Many of those trips are still fresh in my memory, as if they happened only yesterday, although the details of all but a few are too copious to include in these pages.

I recall, for example, the closing service of our Crusade in Seoul, Korea, in 1973. Well over 1 million people crowded Yoido Plaza on an island in the Han River; that was the largest live audience we ever addressed at one time. (The number was not an estimate; the people were grouped in squares, and hence easily countable; and there was electronic tabulation too.) My interpreter, Billy Kim, had just graduated from Bob Jones and had received a letter from Dr. Bob warning that if he interpreted for me, his support from America would be cut off. However, Billy Kim did interpret for me and said that he had never seen a Korean audience so still and so attentive. There were no toilet facilities on the vast grounds. After the meeting, when the people left, there were little spots all over the landscape. What sacrifices they had made to come!

And I recall our visits to Taiwan and Hong Kong, which fell within a few weeks of each other in late 1975. Our Crusade director for Asia, Henry Holley, masterfully managed to organize preparations for both Crusades in spite of the enormous logistical problems. Our return visit to Hong Kong in 1990 was carried by satellite and video to more than thirty countries throughout Asia, with interpretation into forty-eight languages. Further Crusades in Manila (1977), Singapore (1978), and Japan (1980, 1994) also stand out in my memory.

INDIA REVISITED

One trip to India, in 1972, deserves more than passing mention for several reasons.

President Nixon, at the request of the American consul in New Delhi, had personally asked me to seek an interview with Prime Minister Indira Gandhi, in part to find out from her what kind of ambassador she wanted from America. He asked me to notice every single thing about her—the movement of her hands, the expression on her face, how her eyes looked. "When you've finished the interview," he said to me, "go to the American embassy and dictate your report to me."

And so, when I visited with Mrs. Gandhi in the Indian capital, I put the question to her. She told me she wanted someone who understood economics, who had the ear of the President, and who had influence in Congress. This I reported to the President. He later appointed Daniel Patrick Moynihan. Whether my report influenced the President's decision, I never learned.

Our purpose in going to India was to preach in Nagaland, an isolated area tucked in the mountainous, jungle-covered northeast corner of India near the Burmese border. The area was home to a dozen separate tribes, each with its own dialect and often with a history of headhunting. Tensions among Nagaland's tribes, and an armed guerrilla movement bent on independence from India, made it a highly unstable area. During Akbar Abdul-Haqq's crusade five years before in Nagaland's largest town (and capital), Kohima, three people had been killed during an assassination attempt against the Indian government's chief representative.

On one hand, because of Nagaland's instability, very few foreigners were granted government permission to visit the area. On the other hand, Nagaland was home to one of the largest concentrations of Christians in India; at the time of our visit, more than half the population of 500,000 were Christians, almost all living in villages. November 1972 marked the hundredth anniversary of the coming of Baptist missionaries to Nagaland, and we were invited to Kohima as part of that celebration.

Almost miraculously, the Indian government in New Delhi granted a permit for us to enter Nagaland in late November. This permission was in response to an appeal from a delegation headed by the Reverend Longri Ao and other church leaders from Nagaland. (Assisting them was a gifted young Indian clergyman named Robert Cunville, who was head of the North East India Christian Council and had been invited to be director of youth evangelism for the World Council of Churches; he later joined our Team as an evangelist and has had a wide ministry not only in India but in many other parts of the world as well.) Nevertheless, by the time we got to Bangkok on our way to India, news came of renewed guerrilla activity in the area, with several soldiers killed in an ambush.

Reluctantly, I decided to cancel the trip; I feared that the tens of thousands of people expected to travel to Kohima would be too tempting a target for the guerrillas to resist. Others also urged me to cancel because they were afraid I would be an easy target for assassination, something I had never paid much attention to in the past. Finally—just a few days before our scheduled arrival in Kohima—I asked Walter Smyth to release a press statement in New Delhi announcing the cancellation.

When word reached our hosts, they were deeply concerned and immediately called to prayer the thousands already gathering in Kohima. Most had come several days' journey on foot, bringing their own food and bedding.

Early the next morning, I answered an insistent knock from two men at my Bangkok hotel door. One was a Nagaland layman, Lhulie Bizo, who happened to be traveling through Bangkok when he heard of our decision; the other was a former American missionary to Nagaland, Neal Jones. They strongly urged me to reverse the decision, pointing out the great harm that would be done to the churches if the meetings were canceled. They challenged me to trust God for the safety of the meetings. Believing that God had sent them, we agreed to continue with the original plans and went on to Calcutta that afternoon to arrange the final details.

I was met at the airport by the American consul. He was a friend of Mother Teresa's, and he took me to visit her in the home where she and her co-workers ministered to Calcutta's dying. I was deeply touched not only by her work but also by her humility and Christian love. She mentioned that she had held five dying people in her arms the night before and talked with them about God and His love as they were dying. When I asked her why she did what she did, she quietly pointed to the figure of Christ on the Cross hanging on her wall.

From Calcutta, Cliff, Tedd Smith, singer Archie Dennis, Charlie Riggs, T.W. Wilson, and I flew to Dimapur. Then we were driven the last three hours up a rough, twisting, dusty mountain road to Kohima. We were in convoy, with well-armed troops ahead and behind us. Brush along the roadside, favorite cover for armed guerrillas, had been cleared away by the Christians. A week or two before, on this very road, a fatal ambush had taken place.

Kohima, at 7,000 feet above sea level, had a population of about 30,000. There was no access to the capital except by car and helicopter. The countryside was lush with greenery, where I was told I could find banana trees, snakes, and Bengal tigers—everything a good dense jungle should have.

As we rounded a curve about three or four miles from Kohima, we came upon crowds of people—tens of thousands of them lining the road to welcome us. They waved and hit the sides of the vehicles with their hands. I got out and started shaking hands with the people, but other hands, the hands of police, grabbed me and pulled me back into the car; the officers felt I was in great danger.

A few hours later, when we arrived at the soccer field at which we were scheduled to hold our meetings, there were 90,000 people already inside, with thousands more outside. They were arranged by tribe, and each tribe had its own interpreter with a public address system pointed to their area. As I spoke, I paused after each sentence. There followed a cacophony of sound as all seventeen bullhorns blared at once, each in a different dialect.

After that, we were taken to a government house to spend the night. The chief minister of the cabinet of Nagaland had arranged a dinner for us. At that dinner, the schedule for the next day was discussed.

"We have early-morning Bible studies," he said. "Of course, we would like you to preside, but because you have several other things during the day, if you want to send one of your associates, we'll accept that."

"Maybe Charlie or Cliff could take that meeting," I replied. "By the way, how many people do you expect?"

"About 100,000," he said without hesitation.

"Well, I believe I'll take that meeting after all," I managed to say.

When Charlie, Cliff, and I were shown to our quarters in the government house, we were introduced to Nihuli; he was the person who would handle our baggage, make us tea, and do whatever else needed doing. He took our shoes to wipe the mud off them.

"We can do that," I told him.

"No, please let me," he said.

As he was brushing the shoes, I asked him about the early-morning service. I especially wanted to know, I said, who would be teaching the Bible before I arrived.

He didn't reply. When I pressed him further, he admitted that it was he who would be teaching the Bible to that huge crowd. The man cleaning my shoes had just taught me a lesson on the servant attitude and spirit of ministering so often adopted by Christ Himself. I have never forgotten it.

When I went to bed that evening, I could already hear the crowd assembling and praying in the darkness.

Next morning, as I looked down from the platform, I saw that many of the people were attired in tribal dress. On their faces they wore different colors, and in their hands they carried spears and guns. Some of them, from as far away as Nepal and China, had walked for two weeks to hear me interpreted in perhaps fourteen, perhaps as many as seventeen, languages.

Charlie, T. W., and Cliff also assisted in teaching the classes. During the Wednesday morning service, gunfire broke out nearby. The crowd stayed calm, but one man had been killed a short distance away. We knew permission to stay longer might not be granted.

At the final service that afternoon, more than 100,000 people jammed into the stadium in the hot sun, with many thousands more outside. At a closing reception that evening in the chief government minister's home, we sampled some local delicacies. Cliff asked for a second helping of the hors d'oeuvres.

"What kind of meat is this?" he inquired.

"Dog meat."

"And what are these?" he asked, pointing.

"Fried hornets."

"Oh," he said, looking a bit queasy. After that, Cliff only pushed the food around on his plate.

Mrs. Gandhi had told me that she would be following the trip with great personal interest and warned me of some particular dangers. She ordered two helicopters to pick us up at the conclusion of our meetings. It was Thanksgiving Day back in the United States, so they had put some cold chicken on board for us. The helicopters were Russian-built and had a huge fuel tank sitting in the middle of the cabin like an old country stove. When we took off, the machine vibrated terribly; the blades didn't seem to synchronize. The pilot, who sported a handlebar mustache, noticed that I was somewhat tense.

"We'll be flying over one of the most dense jungles in India, and there are lots of tigers down there, Dr. Graham," he said. "You may even get to see one of them. But don't worry. We'll get you through."

As we bumped along above some of the most rugged jungle in the world, I could not help but praise God for the privilege of allowing us to share in the lives of those remarkable people. We were grateful that several years later a treaty brought a measure of peace to the region.

At Dimapur we boarded a plane for the flight to New Delhi. When we got up to cruising altitude, the pilot asked me to come up front and see him. As I entered the cockpit, he turned around and kissed my hand. As a Hindu, he apparently saw me as a holy man and wanted to show respect. He pointed out that it was a beautiful evening and we would be able to see Mt. Everest. "It will be out of our way," he said, "but if you would like to see it, we will go that way."

I said I would very much like to.

He turned the plane and went two hundred miles out of the way to show me the absolutely magnificent sight just at sunset (although I have to admit I was never quite sure which of the many peaks was Everest!). Then he banked sharply and resumed his course for New Delhi.

IRAN

On our return to the United States, we had a stopover in Tehran, the capital of Iran, where I visited with the shah. As I stepped out of the car at the hotel afterward, I was surrounded by an angry group of students. Why, they wondered, had I, a well-known Christian, gone to see the shah? I did not know much about religion in Iran; I did know, though, that in addition to Islam there were still some Nestorians in the country, survivors of an ancient form of Christianity dating back many centuries.

"This is an Islamic country, and we are going to make this an Islamic state," they shouted. "The shah is standing in our way, and America is behind the shah."

I told them that the shah had been kind enough to invite me to visit him if ever I was in Iran. I did not get into an argument with them. I really didn't know enough of their political situation to get into even a *discussion*. I did manage to tell them of Persia in biblical times, especially of Queen Esther. They quieted down eventually and finally left the hotel. But they made me aware for the first time of dissent in that country. And I was reminded once again of how difficult it was for a visitor to grasp the politics of a country other than his own.

Later, during a visit to Washington, I heard a late-night knock on my hotel-room door. It was Daniel Patrick Moynihan.

"I want to thank you for appointing me ambassador to India," he said.

"I didn't have you appointed," I protested. "I just passed on to Mr. Nixon a message from Mrs. Gandhi."

"I'm sure you had me appointed," Moynihan insisted. "I'm a Catholic," he went on, "but would you have a prayer with me?"

I was in my pajamas; but he got down on his knees and I got down on mine, and I prayed with him that God would lead and direct and help him in his new responsibilities.

16

The Power of the Printed Page

"My Answer," Books, *Christianity Today, Decision*

The exposure the media gave us during the first few years of the 1950s was unquestionably decisive in bringing our work before the public. And yet all along, another question kept surfacing in my mind: If the media could be used to promote our ministry of evangelism, could it not also be used directly for evangelism?

As I have already noted, this led us first into radio and films. Before long, however, we turned our attention to the printed page. Once a radio program or a film is over, its impact is largely finished. Books and magazines, however, go places a spoken sermon will never reach, and they can continue to have an impact long after their author is gone.

WRITING A NEWSPAPER COLUMN

Only a few months after *The Hour of Decision* radio program started in 1950, the *Chicago Tribune–New York News* syndicate approached Walter Bennett about the possibility of my writing a daily syndicated column dealing with practical problems from the standpoint of the Bible. The interested parties then came to see me in

Montreat. After some discussion, I said I was willing if they would allow others to assist me in writing the column, under my supervision, whenever I could not do it personally. They replied that most columnists faced the same problem and agreed that I or my wife (or someone else I trusted) would approve each one and that each one would represent my own answer to the question of the day. Thus the "My Answer" column was born, with a daily circulation soon exceeding 20 million readers.

Homer Rodeheaver, who had been Billy Sunday's song leader, told me about a gifted man named Lee Fisher who was directing his youth ranch. We approached Lee, and soon he and his wife, Betty, moved to Montreat. For many years, Lee helped me with suggested scripts for the column; he also did background research for sermons and other messages. My father-in-law, Dr. L. Nelson Bell, also helped me greatly in this area. Other staff people, including Dr. Robert Ferm (the former dean of Houghton College) and his wife, Dr. Lois Ferm, the Reverend Bob Featherstone, Dr. John Akers, and our associate evangelist Dr. John Wesley White, have also put their gifts of scholarship and editing at my disposal over the years.

It has always been helpful to talk over with others an article or special speech while I was drafting it. At the same time, I have always adapted and digested material until it was part of me. And I have never been able to have others help me do my evangelistic sermons, nor have I had others ghostwrite the books I have written. Sometimes, though, I have used others to provide research and help organize my thoughts, provide a rough draft, and edit the final manuscript. I have always acknowledged these talented people in my books.

VENTURING INTO BOOKS

During a Crusade in Dallas in 1952, an editor with Doubleday, Clement Alexander, heard me and felt that my messages might be turned into a book. When I told him I did not think of myself as a writer, he said they could assign someone in their organization to assist me. We reached an agreement, but unfortunately, that person turned out to be in spiritual and intellectual turmoil personally and did not understand my perspective. After a short time, I took the project in hand myself.

I worked on that first book, on and off, for the better part of a year. I dictated the first draft in about ten days on an Ediphone, a machine using bulky wax cylinders. It was one of those times in my life when I sensed the direction of God in an extraordinary way. I wrote it out of a burning conviction that a book presenting the Gospel in a simple but comprehensive way was what people who had little or no religious background needed. Ruth was my greatest helper in giving me ideas; she has always been a storehouse of illustrations and stories. I sent that first draft to a few people, including my friend Dr. Donald Grey Barnhouse, for suggestions. The final draft I got into the publisher's hands by August 1953. *Peace with God*, as it was titled, was published in late October and became an immediate bestseller. Millions of copies have been distributed in the intervening years, and it has now been translated into fifty languages.

The royalties from almost every book I have written—about a dozen and a half to date—have been given to various Christian organizations and ministries. Occasionally, a small portion has been set aside for our children's, and now our grandchildren's, education.

ENVISIONING *Christianity Today*

In mainline denominations where a significant number of leaders had liberal leanings, many rank-and-file clergy and lay leaders held more orthodox views and felt discontentment with the status quo. But they had no flag to follow. They had no counterbalance to the views presented in publications such as *The Christian Century*.

Joe Blinco, Cliff, and I often met these concerned Christians when we visited homes during Crusades; we spent hours talking with them, sometimes sitting on the floor for our "bull sessions." Back then I had the strength and stamina to stay up to all hours in lively discussions with pastors and theologians. I wanted to call these servants back to the Bible, back to the priority of evangelism and missions, back to a freshened ethical understanding of the ways to relate our Christian faith to the issues of the day.

For seventy years, Protestant liberalism had enjoyed a platform through *The Christian Century* magazine. Founded in 1884 by the Disciples of Christ denomination, it became a force in religious journalism in 1908 when Chicago clergyman Charles Clayton Morrison took it over. For the next four decades, it was a flagship of Protestant liberal theology, social action, and even politics. With equal vigor, it judged as outdated, even obnoxious, the views of conservative Christianity—or *fundamentalism,* as they labeled it. As Dr. Martin Marty, a distinguished church historian at the University of Chicago who has been long associated with *The Christian Century,* wrote at its centennial, "The editors saw fundamentalism as a backwoods, over the hill, jerkwater phenomenon that had already outlived its time."

Partly because of the efforts of *The Christian Century,* conservative Christianity had fallen into disrepute. The nineteenth-century evolutionary theories of Charles Darwin had spilled over into other fields of learning, including theology, where it threatened the traditional views of the integrity and authority of the Bible. Conservatives (who were more often called *evangelicals*) of that era fought to define and defend the "fundamentals" of the faith; hence, the term *fundamentalist.*

The Christian Century waged war on the liberal side, contending that Scripture was open to what it called "higher" criticism. In this view, the Bible, although it had religious value, was not the inspired Word of God or the objective standard of truth for our faith and practice. Instead, it was a book of human origin, to be approached the same way any other human book was approached—which is to say, critically and even skeptically.

The periodical's philosophy was progressive, inclusive, optimistic, and relatively humanistic, within a loose framework of Christian concepts. "Modernism" was the vaunted label it wore. It counted on human effort to bring in the kingdom of God on earth. Even the magazine's title expressed its founders' optimism that human nature was basically good and that the twentieth century would be a time of unparalleled progress and peace. The primary mission of the church was to help shape this "Christian century" through direct and indirect social action. At the same time, theological distinctives were down-played and evangelism was redefined—or dismissed as unimportant or irrelevant to the work of the church.

The Christian Century guided the thinking of a large number of American clergy and, in turn, their church members. But the Depression and war were hard for liberals to coordinate with their optimistic philosophy. Even Morrison himself began rethinking his position. On November 8, 1939, he wrote the following in the magazine: "I had baptized the whole Christian tradition in the waters of psychological empiricism and was vaguely awaking to the fact that, after this procedure, what I had left was hardly more than a moralistic ghost of the distinctive Christian reality."

With World War II followed so closely by the Korean War, general disillusionment became epidemic. Many clergy were desperate for tenable alternatives. However, "fightin' fundamentalism" was not what they were looking for.

About two o'clock one night in 1953, an idea raced through my mind, freshly connecting all the things I had seen and pondered about reaching a broader audience. Trying not to disturb Ruth, I slipped out of bed and into my study upstairs to write. A couple of hours later, the concept of a new magazine was complete. I thought its name should be *Christianity Today*. I worked out descriptions of the various departments, editorial policies, even an estimated budget. I wrote everything I could think of, both about the magazine's organization and about its purpose. I stated that it should have the best news coverage of any religious magazine and even specified that it should be located in Washington, D.C., which might give it a measure of authority in the minds of some; that crucial location would also keep its editors and staff in contact with the latest news. I wanted it also to be a focal point for the best in evangelical scholarship, for I knew that God was already beginning to raise up a new generation of highly trained scholars who were deeply committed to Christ and His Word.

My idea that night was for a magazine, aimed primarily at ministers, that would restore intellectual respectability and spiritual impact to evangelical Christianity; it would reaffirm the power of the Word of God to redeem and transform men and women. As I had witnessed, the Gospel of Jesus Christ had that effect everywhere around the world.

A relatively short time passed before the magazine became a reality. When it did, in 1956, I believe a force was released that has helped change the profile of the American church. It was to become another example of the power of the press.

The idea also came to me that night that we should raise enough money in the beginning to send a free subscription to every pastor and every seminary student and professor in the United States, and a stack of them to every seminary, Bible school, and Christian college in the country. I was convinced that most clergy didn't care where their reading material came from if it was *good* material; many of them were already used to receiving gift subscriptions.

I was not the man to be the editor, though. Such a magazine would require spiritual and intellectual leadership and professional skills I didn't have. We needed someone who could win the respect and support of weary and wandering preachers and seminary professors, the kind Martin Marty called "chastened liberals."

The first man I shared my vision with was my father-in-law, Dr. Bell. His wisdom served as a compass. It amazed me to learn that a similar idea for a magazine had often occurred to him. He became a key person in developing *Christianity Today*. One of the first things he did was to take soundings about the magazine idea among ministers and professors; he found the reaction overwhelmingly positive.

Next I turned to Dr. Wilbur Smith, a well-known evangelical leader and professor at the recently established Fuller Theological Seminary in Pasadena. I flew to California and outlined my plan to him. To my surprise, he began to weep. "You know," he said, "I've been dreaming and praying about something like this for years." Although he eventually declined my invitation to serve as editor, he gave invaluable counsel.

Dr. Bell already had extensive experience in writing and editing, having been instrumental in starting a magazine called *The Presbyterian Journal,* which had been organized to uphold biblical theology and practice within the Presbyterian Church in the United

States. Later he gave up his successful surgical practice in Asheville, North Carolina, to work full-time at the task of launching *Christianity Today*. He also became its executive editor, commuting regularly to Washington from his home in Montreat and writing "A Layman and His Faith," a regular (and very popular) column in the magazine.

Eventually, Dr. Bell and I shared my vision with J. Howard Pew, chairman of the board of directors of the Sun Oil Company. I met him for the first time not long before conceiving the idea for *Christianity Today*. He had been asking me to come to Philadelphia to meet with him and spend the night. I had never heard of him, and I declined. Then he sent me a check for our work in the amount of $25,000, along with a message: "When you come and spend the night with me, I'll have another check for $25,000 for you." Needless to say, *that* got my attention! After that (and my visit to Philadelphia; yes, I flew up there!), we got to know each other very well. I came to have great affection and admiration for him, not because he had a great deal of money but because he was a man of God and a man of wisdom who wanted to see his wealth used wisely for the cause of Christ.

Early on in our relationship, I mentioned that we were thinking of starting a magazine, and I made bold to ask him a direct question: "Would you contribute heavily to that?"

He smoked his cigar and looked out the window. "Well, I'll talk to my sisters [Mabel and Ethel] about it. I think we can do it."

In the magazine's early years, he supported *Christianity Today* generously; in fact, without his support I have no doubt the project would have failed. He was very conservative politically and didn't always agree with some of the editorials in the magazine, but never once did he threaten to withdraw his support or attempt to control its editorial policy.

Another strong supporter was Maxey Jarman, a Southern Baptist layman from Nashville, Tennessee, with business interests in New York and elsewhere. He not only helped financially but also offered sound advice.

Another early consultant was Dr. Harold Ockenga, minister of the historic Park Street Church in Boston, whose friendship I talk of in an earlier chapter. "I wish we could organize an editorial board," I wrote him, "and start a magazine that would be precisely like *The Christian Century*, except from an evangelical viewpoint. . . . We should avoid extremes, both to the right and left. We should discuss all issues objectively and not from a biased viewpoint."

The choice of an editor became one of the thorniest problems.

A college acquaintance, Harold Lindsell, wrote to me from Fuller Seminary to recommend one of his teaching colleagues and our mutual friend from Wheaton days, Dr. Carl F. H. Henry. Carl had been in the Wheaton College graduate school when I was at Wheaton. "He has tremendous insight into the application of the Gospel to the social problems of the day," wrote Dr. Lindsell, "and he also has an awareness of the weaknesses of fundamentalism along with a keen insight into the problems of neoorthodoxy, liberalism, and conservative Christianity."

I had some questions about Carl, though. He had professional journalism experience, but I had read some of his recent work and told Harold that it "has a tendency to be rather heavy. . . . and though I am a minister of average intelligence, it has been very difficult for me to follow." That was an understatement! I thought *The Christian Century* did a good job of representing the liberal cause in popular language, and I coveted the same effectiveness in our journal.

My frequent references here to *The Christian Century* underscore how much we respected that magazine as a promoter of its viewpoint. While I felt it represented a dying cause, not for a moment did I underestimate its influence. Nor did I take lightly its journalistic standards, and I desperately hoped we would be able to do as good a job for evangelicals as it had done for liberals.

I did not want our magazine to be divisive. Harold strengthened my determination on that count: "One cannot be a member of the body of Christ in a vertical relationship without also having a horizontal relationship with his fellow believers who are members of the same body," he wrote. "Division is sin and nothing will obscure that fact, even though it may presently be stressed more by the ecumenical movement than it is being stressed by our conservative brethren. The divisive approach is death and it cannot hope to succeed. . . ."

While I was in the United Kingdom for several months in 1955, Dr. Bell kept me informed of the project's progress by phone and mail. I read between the lines. I had some anxiety about disagreements between him and some of the other principals, especially those I had in mind to be members of the board of directors. I prayed every day about the project. The men who would make up the board were friends of mine, but many of them didn't know each other. I felt that they would unite behind the project, and I knew that I would have their confidence in the beginning in a way others would not. I was anxious that we not get conflicting opinions and break into small segments of thought.

I wrote to Mr. Pew (with a copy to Dr. Bell) on April 13, 1955: "These campaigns that thrill and excite the clergy for a short period and show them what God can do with old-fashioned theology must be followed through with a periodical that will give them a reason for the hope that is in them. . . . The Lord seemingly has given me the vision for this paper and I am desperately afraid of its getting out of hand."

I went on to name ten men to a board of directors, with myself as chairman. This had been furthest from my intention at the start. In fact, I had not even wanted my name associated with the enterprise in a prominent way; the connotations some people had of Crusade evangelism might prejudice them before they gave the magazine a fair reading. We wanted to appeal to all kinds of people. In addition, the magazine I had envisioned might have to take strong positions with which I would not want to be totally identified.

Dr. Bell allayed any misgivings in his reply to me in Glasgow. He wrote that my letter was "like a breath of fresh, cool air. I do not believe anyone but yourself can bring these very strong-minded people into the homogeneous group that we must have."

The top spot on the first *Christianity Today* masthead—editor—carried the name Carl F. H. Henry. It had taken some doing to get it there! Ever since Harold had first mentioned his name, Carl had emphasized that he was not seeking the job. He even wrote to Dr. Bell listing several reasons why he should not be considered. Nevertheless, he was the right man for the position.

As for the contributing editors, I suggested to Carl a lot of people I had met in my travels throughout the world—people he wouldn't necessarily have known. Among these were English and Australian leaders and World Council of Churches people whom I knew to be evangelical. And of course Carl included some whom he knew were real theologians.

The hallmark distinguishing *Christianity Today* was a commitment to the trustworthiness of Scripture as the Word of God, with all of the ramifications of that commitment. Of supreme importance to me also was our editorial strategy. Instead of using the stick of denunciation and criticism, we would present a positive and constructive program. We would attempt to lead and love rather than vilify, criticize, and beat. Conservative Christians had failed with the big-stick approach; now it was time to take a more gentle and loving direction. Thousands of young ministers and theological students in churches and seminaries were ready to be led, but at any pushing, probing, and fighting they would rebel. We would not compromise the essentials of our faith, but we would use a positive approach to gain the same objectives that conservative Christians had failed to win using other means for twenty years. We knew that not everyone, especially extreme fundamentalists, would follow the magazine. However, it was my vision that the magazine be pro-church and pro-denomination and that it become the rallying point of evangelicals within and without the large denominations.

On October 10, 1956, I was in Louisville, Kentucky, staying at the Brown Hotel during our Crusade there, when an airmail letter from Dr. Bell arrived: "My dear Bill. 285,000 copies of the first issue of *Christianity Today* finished rolling off the presses in Dayton at 2 A.M. today."

That first issue, dated October 15, carried three articles dealing with critical theological issues, in addition to several editorials and book reviews. The distinguished Dutch theologian G. C. Berkouwer contributed an article on "The Changing Climate in European Theology"; Presbyterian theologian Addison Leitch wrote on "The Primary Task of the Church"; my contribution was more modest, a heartfelt essay on "Biblical Authority in Evangelism."

The lead editorial on "Why *Christianity Today?*" set the tone for everything we were attempting to do: "*Christianity Today* has its origin in a deepfelt desire to express historical Christianity to the present generation. Neglected, slighted, misrepresented—evangelical

291

Christianity needs a clear voice, to speak with conviction and love, and to state its true position and its relevance to the world crisis. A generation has grown up unaware of the basic truths of the Christian faith taught in the Scriptures and expressed in the creeds of the historic evangelical churches. . . . *Christianity Today* is confident that the answer to the theological confusion existing in the world [today] is found in Christ and the Scriptures."

I was thrilled at the initial reactions. A Lutheran minister in New York City told a conference that as a result of reading the magazine, he had gotten on his knees and rededicated his life to God. A young Baptist minister told a denominational gathering that the article on the authority of the Bible in evangelism had caused him to have the same experience I had in 1949, accepting the Bible as the Word of God. Professors at both the Presbyterian and Southern Baptist seminaries in Louisville gave excellent reactions too.

Not long afterward, I visited a Catholic theological school. There I noticed a stack of copies of *Christianity Today*, which had been sent to the school free of charge.

"Is that magazine read and studied by the students much?" I asked the man showing me around.

"More than any other," he replied.

The BGEA contributed heavily to the initial cost and for many years continued to put several thousand dollars per month into the magazine. But early on, *Christianity Today* came to a point where it faced bills amounting to $90,000 but had only $15,000 in the bank. Although the BGEA wanted to help more, we were already beginning to incur heavy expenses connected with the Crusade we planned for Madison Square Garden in 1957.

Carl Henry was troubled that the board would face what he called a "rescue operation" at its January 1957 meeting. We needed about $200,000 more than we anticipated. If there were to be serious cutbacks, Carl said, he couldn't consider a second year with the magazine.

Dr. Bell wrote to him at once: "You have the qualities none of the rest of us have and we would be completely lost without your guiding hand."

That Carl stuck with it relieved and delighted all of us. By the end of our first year of publication, we had claimed our niche in religious journalism. I sent a note to Carl: "I thank God every day that you have seen fit to take this as your responsibility. I believe you are making the greatest possible contribution to the entire church at this critical hour."

A few years after we began publication of *Christianity Today*, we became involved in two magazines in Britain.

I had heard that the *Church of England Newspaper*, which leaned toward the evangelical point of view, was going to close because of a lack of finances. It was a stock company, and I asked Jerry Beavan to see if he, acting on my behalf, could purchase the majority stock; he did so. My plan was to sell it to a group of evangelicals or to a wealthy evangelical businessman. We didn't publicize our involvement, and later Sir Alfred Owen took over our interest.

We then purchased a struggling magazine in Great Britain called *The Christian*. Our goal was to make it similar to *Christianity Today*. It had been started in the previous century and covered extensively Dwight L. Moody's ministry in Britain; by 1962 it was on the point of being closed by its owners, the publishers Marshall, Morgan, and Scott. Tom Allan, our friend from Glasgow, briefly came on as editor and also manager of our London office, but soon he suffered a heart attack from which he never recovered.

Dr. James D. Douglas of Scotland, a well-known editor and theologian, then took the helm. Jim turned *The Christian* into a relevant and respected evangelical periodical that made a significant impact during the seven years it was published. In spite of concerted efforts, however, its paid circulation seldom went above 15,000; the BGEA was forced to subsidize it heavily. We closed it rather abruptly in 1969. Admittedly, we caused some hurt feelings, and in retrospect I wish we had dealt with the closing in a more sensitive way. However, I am grateful that in time other British publications rose up to fill the gap.

In the subsequent decades, we have had many personnel changes at *Christianity Today*, and worldwide Christianity has seen much movement. Carl served as editor until 1968; he was followed by a succession of distinguished editors, including Harold Lindsell, Kenneth Kantzer, and Gilbert Beers, before the magazine moved to the editorial-team approach that it presently uses. In addition, regular contributors from all over the world give input and alert the editorial staff to new trends and events. Today the organization incorporates a number of other publications directed at specific groups, including pastors, youth, and families.

The road, however, has not been consistently easy. Some years ago, the board discovered that because of unwise business decisions (including an attempt to start a book club without thoroughly researching the matter), *Christianity Today* was facing a very large deficit of $900,000. A young publishing executive who was with Youth for Christ, Harold Myra, was brought in with the mandate to place the magazine on a businesslike basis with a break-even budget. He oversaw the magazine's move from Washington to Carol Stream, Illinois; that relocation saved a significant amount of money. Under his leadership, *Christianity Today* and its companion publications are among the best managed in the publishing industry, secular or religious.

Dr. Clayton Bell, senior pastor of Highland Park Presbyterian Church in Dallas, has continued his father's commitment to the magazine by serving as executive chair of the board of directors.

The magazine has changed through the years. Evangelicals are no longer an ignored minority. In fact, our greatest danger may come from our public visibility and influence. *Christianity Today* seeks to speak to these and other contemporary issues. I have always urged the editorial staff to deal with them in an openly biblical and theological way. I pray that the magazine will never depart from its founding commitment to high biblical and theological scholarship. All over the globe, people are desperate to hear a voice of biblical authority and to find a stable spiritual standard.

FOUNDING *Decision* MAGAZINE

Before *Christianity Today* came to be, Bob Pierce mentioned to me that his organization, World Vision, had started a magazine to tell supporters about his work and to encourage them to pray. "It's almost doubled our income," he told me, adding that when people were informed regularly about an organization's work, they were more likely to support it with their gifts and prayers. "Billy, something like this would help your work tremendously," he assured me.

My thought was that any magazine we did should be a vehicle primarily for evangelistic and devotional articles, not a "house organ" to raise financial support. Yet we were doing so many other things that a magazine just seemed beyond us. Furthermore, there were already a few good magazines being printed from an evangelical perspective, such as Donald Grey Barnhouse's *Revelation* (later *Eternity*) and Moody Bible Institute's *Moody Monthly*. And George Wilson opposed the idea; a periodical would require a new staff with skills in journalism, as well as a strong financial commitment.

However, as plans began developing for *Christianity Today* in the mid-1950s, my thoughts turned more and more to the possibility of another magazine. I felt that we needed two publications: one on an intellectual and theological level for clergy and lay leaders, and another, more popular magazine to help ordinary Christians in their witness and daily walk. I wanted the latter to include articles with an evangelistic emphasis, as well as devotional messages, simple Bible studies, stories of conversions and changed lives, and news of our Crusades.

In April 1958, we were in San Francisco for a seven-week Crusade at the Cow Palace. *Christianity Today* had assigned Sherwood Wirt, a local Presbyterian pastor who had been a professional journalist, to cover the meetings for them; he later wrote a book on that Crusade. Woody, as he came to be known to us all, was once a theological liberal but had become a thorough-going evangelical several years before. He held a Ph.D. from the University of Edinburgh and had experience as a military chaplain and minister to university students. I was impressed by both his writing skills and his quiet spirit. He accepted our offer to become the first editor of our new magazine. We debated various titles, including *World Evangelism*, but George Wilson came up with the name *Decision*, which we adopted.

Decision magazine began publication with the November 1960 issue; it had a print run of 299,000 copies at its inception.

"The basic purpose of this magazine," I wrote in the first issue, "will be twofold: to provide spiritual food for Christians, and to publish evangelistic messages and articles aimed at reaching the secular mind and winning the nonbeliever to Christ."

We have adhered to those goals ever since.

Within a year, we added separate editions for Australia and England. By 1962 circulation had passed the 1 million mark. George reported that at one time requests for the magazine subscriptions were coming in at the rate of 10,000 a day. Within the next few years, several foreign-language editions were added, as well as an edition in Braille. By the time *Decision* celebrated its tenth anniversary, circulation had passed 4 million. One spin-off was the School of Christian Writing, which Woody established in 1963 to train budding Christian writers through intensive workshops.

Woody was editor until his retirement sixteen years later. His successor, Roger Palms, has continued Woody's tradition of journalistic excellence and spiritual relevance.

The response to *Decision* more than convinced us that it was meeting a need in many people's lives. Not only does it go to individuals, but through the years bulk copies have gone to prisons, hospitals, and overseas mission groups.

We have often heard stories of unexpected or unusual ways God has used *Decision*. Some people, for example, used their copies as wrapping paper for small gifts they mailed into a country that was one of the most closed and restrictive in the world. Unsuspecting customs officials apparently never caught on to the real reason for the wrapping.

Speaking of crumpled paper, I must tell also of the well-dressed man who one day entered BGEA's London office. He told Maurice Rowlandson, the manager, that he had been manager of a bank until his life was ruined by alcohol. He lost his family and job, eventually ending up as a vagrant on the streets of London. One day he was rummaging through a trash barrel looking for something to eat when he came across a discarded copy of *Decision*. Intrigued by the cover story, he read the magazine straight through, and as a result turned his life over to Christ. Now, a year later, he had been reconciled to his family and was once again working in a bank.

When George Wilson heard that story, he wryly suggested to Maurice that he stuff a copy of *Decision* into every London trash bin!

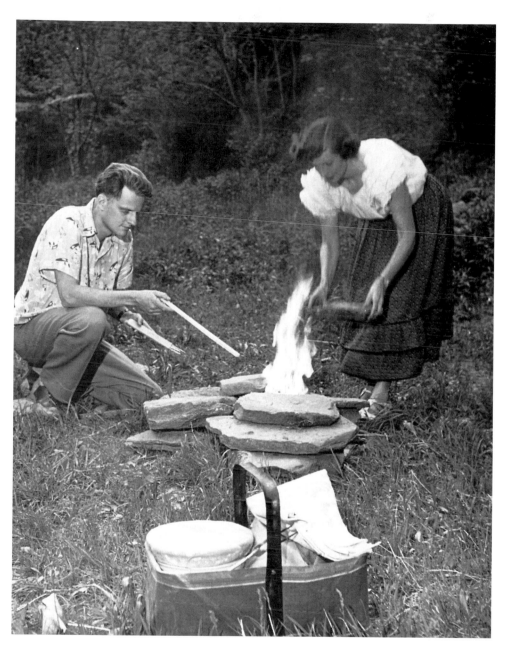

The young couple on a picnic near Montreat.

Ruth and the newborn Nelson Edman Graham (Ned), with *(from left)* Franklin, Bunny, Gigi, Anne, and Billy, 1958.

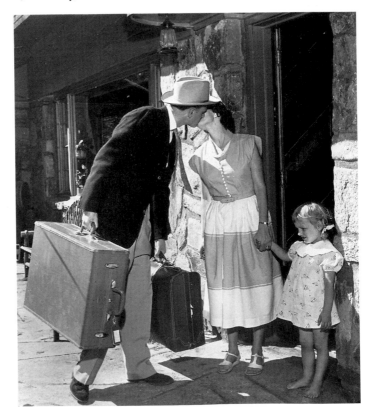

Leaving on another trip and saying good-bye to Ruth as Bunny looks on, mid-1950s. Back then, my trips often lasted several months.

With my sons, Ned *(left)* and Franklin, in the yard of our home, 1965.

Relaxing with a game of baseball. I always batted left-handed but played golf right-handed.

From left: Gigi, Anne, Bunny, Ruth, and me at home with Belshazzar, our Great Pyrenees dog.

The Los Angeles evangelistic campaign, corner of Washington and Hill Streets, fall 1949, was the beginning of our national press coverage and recognition.

The closing meeting of the sixteen-week New York Crusade, Times Square, September 1, 1957.

Preaching to 40,000 people at the Canadian National Exhibition in Toronto, Ontario, Canada, September 1967.

Preaching in Harlem,
New York, August 1, 1957.

Enjoying lemonade and a lively discussion in
an English pub with newspaper columnist
"Cassandra," during the 1954 London Crusade.

Leaving Number 10 Downing Street after meeting
with Prime Minister Winston Churchill, following
the 1954 London Crusade.

Putting on a flak jacket before preaching to American troops in Korea, Christmas day, 1952.

With President and Mrs. Eisenhower at National Presbyterian Church, Washington, D.C. At right is the Reverend E.L.R. Elson, the church's pastor.

The Team, 1953. *Front, from left:* George Beverly Shea, Billy Graham, Cliff Barrows; *rear:* Grady Wilson, Paul Mickelson, Tedd Smith, Lorne Sanny.

Live from the Atlanta, Georgia, Crusade, the first radio broadcast of *The Hour of Decision*, November 5, 1950.

Monitoring the first broadcast of *The Hour of Decision*, 1950. *From left:* George Wilson, Walter Bennett, Fred Dienert.

With the associate evangelists, 1964. *Front, from left:* Grady Wilson, Joe Blinco, Howard Jones, John Wesley White, Akbar Abdul-Haqq. *Rear:* Roy Gustafson, Billy Graham, T. W. Wilson, Leighton Ford, Ralph Bell.

With my father-in-law and mentor, Dr. L. Nelson Bell, 1972.

17

Marathon in Manhattan

NEW YORK 1957

Taking a brief break from the June 1955 Paris Crusade, Grady and I were playing a few holes of golf on a course near Versailles. He looked at his watch. We were running late for a meeting back in Paris, so we cut our game short, hurried back to the locker room, and changed our clothes. As we were running out to the car, I heard someone calling my name.

"Dr. Graham, I heard you on television last night," he said, "and my wife and I were very interested. I'm playing golf, and we have only two in our party. Would you and your friend like to join us?"

"Sir, I would like to very much," I replied.

It was the Duke of Windsor. Few faces were as familiar to the public at that time as his, due to his abdication of the British throne to marry an American, Mrs. Simpson. He also had the reputation of living a rather meaningless life, and I could not help but wonder if that was true.

"But unfortunately I have a commitment in town," I added. "Let me call to see if I can get it postponed."

When I called Bob Evans, I discovered that my commitment *could not* be changed. As I went back to apologize to the duke, someone handed me a cable that apparently had been forwarded to the golf club. It was from George Champion, vice president of the Chase Manhattan Bank, who headed the evangelism department of the Protestant Council of New York. The council had voted to extend an invitation to us to hold a Crusade in New York during the summer of 1957.

No other city in America—perhaps in the world—presented as great a challenge to evangelism. My old friend Jesse Bader of the Department of Evangelism of the National Council of Churches had said once that "evangelistic work in New York is like digging in flint." In a message to our supporters, I acknowledged that "humanly speaking, New York is the most unlikely city in the western hemisphere for successful evangelism."

One reason New York would be so challenging was its incredible diversity, with some sixty major ethnic groups in its population—more Italians than Rome, more Irish than Dublin, more Germans than Berlin, more Puerto Ricans than San Juan. At least one out of every ten Jews in the world lived there as well. Protestants were a distinct minority, making up only 7.5 percent of the population; many of them were only nominally committed to the Christian faith. According to our findings before the Crusade, 58 percent of New Yorkers claimed no religious identity at all.

New York was the business, financial, communication, and entertainment hub of the nation. It was also the headquarters of the United Nations, founded only a decade before. Everything that happened in New York literally touched the whole world. If New York could be reached with the Gospel of Christ, the effects would be felt in many other cities as well.

As I said in one sermon during that Crusade, New York is "the most strategic center in the world. We could have this many people [for a meeting] in Louisville, Kentucky; we could have this many people in Oklahoma City; we could have this many people even in Chicago; and it wouldn't mean as much as New York City. . . . It becomes a stage on which we can do evangelism to the whole nation, to the whole world."

This, I had come to believe, was also a biblical pattern for evangelistic strategy. The Apostle Paul preached in all kinds of places, including some that were insignificant, humanly speaking. But under the guidance of the Holy Spirit, he had concentrated on the great cities of the Roman Empire, sensing the enormous impact that they had beyond their own areas. To the Christians in Rome he said, "Your faith is being reported all over the world" (Romans 1:8).

"No one can read the Bible even casually without sensing that God has a special interest in cities," I wrote in *This Week* magazine shortly before the New York Crusade opened. "His love for Nineveh caused Him to send the prophet Jonah to warn the city of its coming destruction. Christ wept over Jerusalem."

Jack Wyrtzen, who had an extensive evangelistic outreach to youth in New York City, had been urging me for years to come to New York. In fact, I had already turned down two previous invitations, in 1951 and 1954. This invitation, however, was different, since it represented a much broader base of church support than the previous ones had.

The official sponsor was an independent executive committee of both clergy and laity; it had been appointed by the Protestant Council of New York and represented a cross section of the city's churches and institutions. The chairman of the committee was Roger Hull, executive vice president of the Mutual Life Insurance Company of New York. Included on the executive committee were such people as banker George Champion, industrialist and philanthropist Cleveland Dodge, business executive Edwin Chinlund (who was treasurer of the Macy's department stores and served as the Crusade treasurer), Dr. Gardner Taylor of Concord Baptist Church, Dr. John Sutherland Bonnell of Fifth Avenue Presbyterian Church, Dr. Richard Hildebrand of the African Methodist Episcopal Church, and the Reverend Dan Potter, executive director of the Protestant Council. The council represented some seventeen hundred churches in the New York area; many churches that weren't part of the council also cooperated.

Quite unexpectedly, we were able to get an option on Madison Square Garden for the summer months of 1957. The Crusade itself was scheduled to begin on May 15. Our initial plan was to conclude the Crusade six weeks later, on June 30.

I was not sure we had the organizational depth for such an effort. One possibility as director of the Crusade was Betty Lowry of Minneapolis, a highly dedicated and competent person who had directed almost single-handedly our Oklahoma City Crusade in

June 1956; but Betty felt she could not take the project on for health reasons. Instead, Jerry Beavan took the position; I felt his experience with us in London and elsewhere would be invaluable. In early 1957, however—less than four months before the Crusade was to begin—Jerry resigned from the BGEA for personal reasons.

Suddenly, I found myself virtually directing the Crusade over the telephone; instead of talking two or three times a week with the local staff about preparations, as I normally did in other Crusades, I found myself on the phone every day.

My first thought after Jerry left was to prevail again on Betty Lowry to assume the position, but Roger Hull urged me instead to appoint Charlie Riggs. A tough roustabout in the Pennsylvania oil-fields before coming to Christ, Charlie had been active in The Navigators and was deeply involved in our own counselor-training classes.

Dawson Trotman, the head of The Navigators (who had spent nine months in developing our counseling and follow-up program), had drowned the previous summer in a tragic boating accident at Schroon Lake, New York. His loss just as we were preparing for New York was immense, and Charlie had been filling the gap in his place, assisting Lorne Sanny, who had already taken over The Navigators.

Roger had gotten to know Charlie fairly well and respected not only his organizational ability and practical good sense but also his spiritual character. "He knows the Scripture, and he knows the Lord. Charlie Riggs is the man," Roger stated with finality. "If anything happens in New York for God, it's got to be by prayer. And Charlie Riggs is a man of prayer."

Charlie later said that it "wasn't my particular cup of tea," but he graciously took on the responsibility and did a magnificent job. In later years, Charlie—returning to his primary interest—directed our counseling and follow-up department, teaching tens of thousands of people across the world the basic principles of the Christian life and practical ways to share Christ with others.

Problems of a different sort came from the opposition that arose over our plans for New York City. One source was the liberal wing of Christianity. The magazine *The Christian Century* grumbled

that "the Billy Graham campaign will spin along. . . . and an audience gladly captive to its own sensations is straining for the grand
entrance . . . whether or not the Holy Spirit is in attendance."

More thoughtful was the objection raised by one of the nation's
leading liberal theologians, Dr. Reinhold Niebuhr of New York's
Union Theological Seminary. I appreciated his commitment to social concern but could not agree with his scorn of evangelism. In an
article in *Life* magazine, he termed me "obviously sincere" but added
that the message we preached was "too simple in any age, but particularly so in a nuclear one with its great moral perplexities. . . .
Graham offers Christian evangelism even less complicated answers
than it has ever before provided."

I let it be known that I wanted to meet Dr. Niebuhr. George
Champion called him to see if he would see me, but he declined.
Not used to giving up easily, George then called the chairman of the
Union Theological Seminary board, who was also a leading banker.
The chairman promised that there would be no difficulty in arrang-
ing such a meeting, but he came back (as George later said,) "with
his tail between his legs"; Niebuhr simply refused to see me.

Opposition also came from a few in the Roman Catholic and
Jewish communities, although I had made it clear I was not going to
New York to speak against other traditions or to proselytize people
away from them. My goal instead was to preach the Gospel of Jesus
Christ as it was presented in the Bible and to call men and women
to commit their lives to Him.

During the Crusade, I met with various Jewish groups and individuals. One of these was Rabbi Marc Tanenbaum, with whom I
began a lifelong friendship. His advice through the years as an official with the American Jewish Committee and his personal warmth
meant much to me. Many of Jewish background did come to the
meetings at Madison Square Garden, and some openly declared
their commitment to Jesus as their Messiah.

To my knowledge, the only vocal opposition from the Roman Catholic community came from a single article in a limited-
circulation Catholic magazine. The author, an official with the
National Catholic Welfare Conference (NCWC) in Washington, D.C., wrote, "Catholics are not permitted to participate in

Protestant religious services." He went on to state that for faithful Catholics, "Billy is a danger to the faith."

Such a statement seems harsh in light of present-day Protestant-Catholic relations, but four decades ago the situation was much different. The breakthroughs in ecumenical relations heralded by the Second Vatican Council were still several years away, and in all fairness, many Protestants likewise had strong anti-Catholic views. For me the central issue has always been Christ and our commitment to Him, not our loyalty to an ecclesiastical system, important as the church is to our spiritual growth and service.

The NCWC statement attracted attention, however, precisely because it was almost the only comment on the Crusade from a Roman Catholic source. No ranking member of the Catholic hierarchy spoke out against the Crusade, and I suspect many Catholics knew of my friendship with various Catholic leaders. Cardinal Cushing of Boston had been particularly friendly to me. He wryly told the press after our meeting several years before that if he had half a dozen Billy Grahams, he would not worry about the future of his church! Many Catholics did come to the meetings, a good number stepping forward to personally commit their lives to Christ.

Much more painful to me, however, was the opposition from some of the leading fundamentalists. Most of them I knew personally, and even if I did not agree with them on every detail, I greatly admired them and respected their commitment to Christ. Many also had been among our strongest supporters in the early years of our public ministry. Their criticisms hurt immensely, nor could I shrug them off as the objections of people who rejected the basic tenets of the Christian faith or who opposed evangelism of any type. Their harshness and their lack of love saddened me and struck me as being far from the spirit of Christ.

The heart of the problem for men like Bob Jones, Carl McIntire, and John R. Rice was the sponsorship of the Crusade by the Protestant Council of New York. The council, they contended, included many churches and clergy who were theologically liberal and who denied some of the most important elements of the biblical message. It was not the first time some of them had raised their objections to my growing ecumenism, of course, but the New York

Crusade marked their final break with our work. I studied and prayed over their criticisms, wanting to accept their indictments if they were right. But I came to the firm conclusion that they were not, and that God was leading us in a different direction. Ruth like-wise studied the whole matter; we discussed the issue and prayed over it frequently. Her conclusion was the same as mine.

In addition, my study of the major evangelists in history also showed me that the issue was not new; every one of them—from Whitefield and Wesley to Moody and Sunday—had to contend with similar criticisms, both from the right and from the left.

Early in our work, I had tried to answer any such attacks, but I eventually decided the only course was to ignore them. The critics showed no inclination to change, and at any rate I did not have time to devote to such arguments. In a 1955 letter to Carl McIntire about an article he had written opposing our work, I admitted that "I felt a little resentment and I got on my knees and asked God to give me love in my heart. . . . Beloved friend, if you feel led of the Spirit of God to continue your attacks upon me, rest assured I shall not an-swer you back nor shall I attempt to harm one hair of your head. . . . My objective is to glorify our Lord Jesus Christ by the preaching of His Word to sinners."

A year before the New York meetings, one of our Team mem-bers, Dr. Ralph Mitchell, had an extended discussion with Bob Jones. He came away convinced that Bob Jones would never change his position, which was that our work was not of God. Ralph con-cluded by writing me, "You must not concern yourself unduly about such critics. . . . Nevertheless, it is a fresh challenge to all of us in the whole Association to be much more in prayer." I agreed wholeheart-edly and asked God to keep us from being diverted from His work by such critics. Occasionally, my father-in-law, Dr. Bell, attempted to answer such attacks, but with little success. I often felt like Nehemiah when his enemies tried to get him to stop rebuilding the walls of Jerusalem and come down to discuss the project; he replied that he was too busy building the wall (see Nehemiah 6:1–4).

My own position was that we should be willing to work with all who were willing to work with us. Our message was clear, and if someone with a radically different theological view somehow decided to join with us in a Crusade that proclaimed Christ as the way of salvation, he or she was the one who was compromising personal convictions, not we.

The more vocal the opposition, however, the more the supporting churches in the New York area rallied to our side. God had a way of taking our problems and turning them to His own advantage.

Following a month-long Crusade in Louisville, Kentucky, in October 1956, I accepted only occasional speaking engagements and no further extended Crusades until the New York meetings the following May. The main exception was a series of meetings at Yale University, where the longtime chaplain, Sidney Lovett, had invited me to speak for four evenings in February.

Like many of America's older colleges and universities, Yale was founded as a Christian institution. One of its early presidents, Timothy Dwight, was a distinguished Christian leader; and during its first century, I heard, Yale sent 40 percent of its graduates into the ministry. Now that strong spiritual heritage has been largely forgotten.

Following the pattern set at Cambridge University, our Yale meetings included a number of assistant missioners, including Dr. Samuel Shoemaker, rector of Calvary Episcopal Church in Pittsburgh, and the Reverend Robert Raines, son of a Methodist bishop in Indiana. Each evening after the main meeting, I went to various campus fraternities for question-and-answer sessions that sometimes lasted past midnight.

One day the head of the psychology department invited me to have lunch with about twenty members of his department. They all sat with their box lunches on one side of the room, while I sat on the other; I felt at first as if I were a mental patient undergoing examination! They were especially interested in what I meant by *conversion;* and to our mutual surprise, there was much agreement between us, at least as far as the psychological benefits of authentic conversion were concerned.

Thomas Ruhm, a writer for a student publication called *Ivy Magazine,* commented that he doubted if my experiences at Cambridge and Oxford had prepared me "for Yale's cultivated general indifference toward religion." Chaplain Lovett, however, reported later that his office had follow-up contact with three hundred students who stayed for the after-meetings.

In ways I couldn't have foreseen, the Yale meetings helped prepare me for the New York Crusade. One way was through people I met in New Haven who worked in New York or had influential contacts there—people who threw their support behind the Crusade. Another was through the comment of a student, who brought home to me in a fresh way the need for absolute clarity in presenting the Gospel message: "Mr. Graham, we hear a lot about what Christ has done for us, the value of religion, and what personal salvation is. But nobody tells us how to find Christ." As the New York Crusade approached, I was more determined than ever to make that clear.

My time during the months leading up to the Crusade was spent in study, of course, but I also knew I needed rest and exercise to be prepared physically for the demanding road ahead of us. Those were days of peace, relaxing in the spring sun and spending time with Ruth and the children.

"I shall miss the children during the next few weeks," I wrote in the diary I was keeping at the time. "I have come to love this mountain top and would like nothing better than for the Lord to say that I should stay here the rest of my life. I do not naturally like to go out to the wars. It is so peaceful and restful here. But duty calls. I must put on the whole armor of God and go forth to meet the foe."

Much of my time was spent in spiritual preparation—praying, reading the Scriptures, and talking with Ruth and members of our Team and board (as well as with some others) about the task before us. We knew that millions of Christians around the world were already praying for the meetings in New York, and this gave me a deep sense of peace in spite of the uncertainties we faced.

"There are many of my friends who have predicted that the New York Crusade could end in failure," I wrote in my diary. "From the human viewpoint and by human evaluation it may be a flop. However, I am convinced in answer to the prayers of millions that in the sight of God and by Heaven's evaluation it will be no failure. God will have His way." Then I added, "I have prayed more over this assignment and wept more over the city of New York than any other city we have ever been to. Now it is in God's hands."

The time to leave for New York was rapidly approaching. Dorothy Kilgallen, a nationally syndicated gossip columnist and television personality, had been asking for some time to interview Ruth and me. Some thought she would be nice to us in person and then do a hatchet job on us on paper, but we invited her to Montreat anyway. She spent several days in our home, interviewing us. Her series of articles surprised everyone. They were some of the kindest and most supportive we had ever received. The Hearst papers carried her columns on us for five days in a row. "To Billy Graham," she wrote in the second one, "Heaven is a definite place, like Chicago. He can't point it out on the map, but he knows it has pearly gates and streets of gold, and he is headed there as surely as if the one-way ticket were crackling in his pocket."

The result of these and other articles was that our press buildup in New York was growing even before we left home.

Before leaving—we would both be going to New York, though leaving separately—Ruth and I took our last stroll to see our four sheep and to lie on the grass, talking, quoting Scripture, and praying together. What a wonderful companion she has always been, so full of Scripture for every occasion and event!

By the time I left on the train for New York on May 9, I felt in the best physical and spiritual shape I had been in for a long time.

On the way to New York, we stopped in Washington for a meeting with President Eisenhower. As Grady and I sat waiting in a reception room, a reporter from *Newsweek* came over to tell us the magazine had originally planned to have a cover story he had written that week on presidential aide Sherman Adams, but—he noted with a wry smile—the editors were setting it aside for a cover story on us and the New York Crusade.

President Eisenhower greeted me with, "Hello there, my friend," and listened intently for half an hour to my summary of the plans for the meetings in Madison Square Garden. He said it would be a wonderful thing if people all over the world could learn to love each other. I agreed, stating my conviction that people had a capacity to love in the fullest sense only when they opened their lives to Christ's love and transforming power. He heartily agreed. As I was leaving, he called me back to have our photograph taken together; that was, I think, one way he felt he could indirectly endorse what we were doing. I also chatted briefly with Vice President Nixon, who also indicated his support for the meetings.

At four-thirty the next morning, Paul Maddox, Grady, and I got up. Ruth was scheduled to be on the early train from Asheville, and we were going to join her at Union Station. Her train was delayed, however. By the time it arrived, Ruth had been awake since two, reading her Bible and praying. We both fell sound asleep until Paul Maddox brought some toast and coffee to our compartment on the train. It tasted wonderful—a bit of calm before the storm.

We arrived at New York's Pennsylvania Station forty minutes late. Roger Hull and other members of our committee and staff, as well as about twenty-five photographers, spotted us. I recalled President Truman's remark that photographers were the only people in the world who could order him around.

As we made our way through the station, many people waved. One man shouted, "God bless you, Billy!" Another man grabbed me and whispered in my ear, "We sure need you!" Still another said, "I'm a Catholic, but we're backing you." These greetings all encouraged me, especially in light of New York's reputation (undeserved, we decided by Crusade's end) as a cold, unfriendly city.

When we finally arrived at the New Yorker hotel, where I would stay for the whole Crusade, we found a score of reporters patiently waiting for us. "There is a notable difference in the press from what it used to be," Ruth wrote in her diary. "They are more respectful, friendlier. It may not last or it may—but thank God for it, while it does."

That evening I went to be interviewed by Walter Cronkite for his CBS television news show, recorded for broadcast the following night. He was an amiable host, and we had a great time, sitting together in a room overlooking Times Square. He asked the kind of leading questions I love to answer, about our work, our objectives, the message we preached, and what we had to offer New York.

The news staff then screened some film clips that they had taken around Times Square and Broadway, and Walter asked me to comment on them. I observed that thousands of frustrated and bewildered people there who were searching for reality, could find it if they would give their lives to Christ.

On the way back to the hotel afterward, we were joined by David Zing, a writer for *Look* magazine, and his photographer. We had a hot dog together in a little place along Times Square.

I saw every media setup as a welcome chance to get out the Gospel, but we certainly could not engineer those opportunities ourselves. We had no advance agents or press corps in our organization. Betty Lowry single-handedly ran the Crusade "press room," if it could be called that, and provided coffee for all visitors. In New York, I stayed on my knees about the media more than about any other single thing, including my sermons. Far more people would read the newspaper and magazine stories than would hear me preach in person. My prayer was that the Holy Spirit would guard our statements to the press and use the coverage to glorify Christ.

First thing I did the next morning, Sunday, after Ruth and I had breakfast, was to make two radio broadcasts: one was a tape to be flown out to a group of ministers in Los Angeles for their Tuesday meeting, describing to them the New York Crusade prospects; the other, an interview for a network of about 250 stations in the Midwest. After the taping, Lorne Sanny, Mel Dibble, Ruth, and I went to church at Calvary Baptist on West Fifty-seventh Street, across from Carnegie Hall, to hear John Wimbish preach.

That night, with some hesitancy, I went to appear on *The Steve Allen Show*. Did I have any business appearing on an entertainment variety program? Well, 40 million people might be watching on NBC-TV. I went on with the other guests: singer Pearl Bailey, actor Dean Jones, and actress Tallulah Bankhead.

Miss Bankhead startled me when she grabbed my hand. "I've been looking forward to meeting you for a long time," she said. She was extremely warm and cordial, urging Ruth and me to come over to her apartment for tea. She planned to attend as many of the meetings as possible, she said—and definitely on "opening night." That term made it sound as if we were one of the theatrical attractions in town.

Pearl Bailey said the same thing when she shook hands, mentioning that her father was a minister, that God was her agent, and that she believed in prayer and the Bible. As I talked, I sensed that many of these people were looking for some deeper meaning in life.

Then, amid all the celebrities, someone squeezed my arm. "God bless you," said an anonymous floor director. "I'm a Christian too. See you Wednesday night."

As on the previous night, we were joined after the show by a couple of men from *Life* magazine—writer Dick Billings and photographer Cornell Capa, who talked about taking his now-famous photographs a year earlier in Ecuador following the martyrdom of five American missionaries by Stone Age tribesmen. They took me for a walk, this time along Times Square, and we enjoyed some more hot dogs.

The next two days were almost nonstop media appearances. First was the Bill Leonard show, *Eye on New York,* for which we made five programs in succession to use each day that week. At eleven that morning, I was on ABC-TV with John Cameron Swayze. At two that afternoon, it was interview time with *New York Mirror* columnist Sidney Fields. Even when the Crusade executive committee met at four-thirty in the afternoon, photographers from *Look, Life,* and *Ebony* magazines were snapping pictures.

Tuesday matched Monday, starting with a forty-five-minute radio show with Martha Deane, sponsored by the *New York Times* on station WOR. At noon Ruth and I arrived at the Waldorf-Astoria Hotel to be interviewed by Tex and Jinx McCrary on their coast-to-coast NBC television show; they actually allowed me to preach a short message at the end.

One of the people we faced in our first days in the city was a beautiful Indian woman journalist who asked Ruth why I didn't stay in the South and straighten out the race problem. Assuring her the problem was universal, Ruth had to bite her tongue to keep from asking what the journalist was doing about the caste system in her homeland.

The media attention was hard for Ruth, since she is such a private person. All the focus in New York, she said, made her feel like a beetle under a stone as the stone was removed. "And behind it all," she wrote, "lurking in the background, is that fear that somewhere in this avalanche of publicity we will stumble and disgrace Him." Even five months before the Crusade, she wrote of the stress: "It's silly to bewail this publicity. It may be a cross. It may be an opportunity. It may be both. Our hearts' deepest desire is that in it all, *He* may be glorified and accomplish His purpose."

Nevertheless, we both realized the importance of the media and had learned to live with it. In my diary I wrote, "It is strange how one has gotten used to publicity. I used to so terribly resent the invasion of our privacy; now we have learned to live with it and have dedicated it many times to the Lord. I realize that the same press that has made us known could ruin us overnight."

On Tuesday night, after a dedication service for the Team and Crusade workers at the Garden, I intended to visit as many of the all-night prayer meetings as possible, but because I was so fatigued, I decided to go back to the hotel. In came Billings and Capa again, wanting more pictures for the next week's *Life* magazine story. So out we went, and they snapped pictures while I walked up Broadway in the rain. Twenty-four blocks later, we were at Calvary Baptist Church again. There, among other journalists, was a photographer from *Match* magazine who had flown over from Paris to cover the Crusade. There were also reporters from Sweden, Holland, and Australia. I described the walk in my diary that night: "I never dreamed that the day would come when a preacher could walk, in non-clerical clothes, down any street in New York and be recognized. This can only be of God. The responsibility is so overwhelming that I can hardly relax. My heart is in agony continually lest I make one false step that would bring any disrepute to Christ."

Wednesday, with our scheduled opening of the Crusade that evening, offered no letup. After Ruth and I had breakfast and devotions together in our room, George Wilson came by to get me to NBC-TV for an appearance with Dave Garroway. When I walked into the studio, another guest met me—actress Gloria Swanson. We had about a half-hour of intense discussion, and she promised to come to the meetings. When it was time for the taping, my old friend

Dave Garroway asked clear questions that led to the Gospel. Outside the studios, I made another television program for NBC.

When we went down the steps into the old Madison Square Garden arena, news photographers' flashbulbs were popping all around us. My heart kept saying, over and over, "O God, let it be to Thy glory. Let there be no self."

That first meeting will always remain in my memory as one of the highlights of our ministry. As nearly as I could see against the spotlights, the 19,500-seat arena was filled. Cliff had done a splendid job of training the 1,500-voice choir, and Bev was in top form, singing one of our favorite hymns, "How Great Thou Art"; he later calculated that he sang it ninety-nine times during the Crusade. Bev was halfway through another song to the crowd jammed into Madison Square Garden when he suddenly realized it was perhaps a bit inappropriate for the setting; he was singing, "I Come to the Garden Alone."

"We have not come to put on a show or an entertainment," I said as I greeted the audience. "We believe that there are many people here tonight who have hungry hearts. All your life you've been searching for peace and joy, happiness, forgiveness. I want to tell you, before you leave Madison Square Garden this night of May 15, you can find everything that you have been searching for, in Christ. He can bring that inward, deepest peace to your soul. He can forgive every sin you've ever committed. . . . Forget me as the speaker. Listen only to the message that God would have you to retain from what is to be said tonight."

I then spoke on God's call to repentance and faith as recorded in the first chapter of Isaiah. At the Invitation, 704 people came forward.

The first man was Jack Lewis, whom Jerry and I had met on board a ship returning from the Orient to Honolulu a year before. Jack was a prominent businessman from a Jewish background whose exuberance over his newfound faith delighted the whole Team in the following weeks. With him that night was a young German-born scholar named Henry Kissinger, who returned several times to the meetings over the course of the summer.

As I sat in our room late that night, after a glorious first meeting at the Garden, I barely had the energy to write in my diary. I penned just a brief entry: "When have we seen such opportunities in our generation? It should cause all Christians to rejoice. It has greatly humbled me. The press today has been remarkable. Almost every paper with front-page stories of the plans and programs for tonight."

My adrenaline was flowing overtime, but I was fatigued. Ruth could see that. "I don't know when I've seen him so tired," she wrote in her diary after the first meeting. "He has had too tight a schedule."

When I entered the Garden that first night, almost the first thing I saw was 300 members of the press and several newsreel cameras in operation. I knew that the message I was about to give would be carried to the world.

The next morning, the *New York Times* devoted three pages to the opening service, reprinting my sermon word for word. Most of the other five daily papers gave extensive coverage as well, and most of their columnists wrote about the meeting. Dr. Bonnell said he had never seen anything like it during his twenty-three years in New York City.

The *Journal-American* ran a cartoon on its editorial page depicting a boxing ring at the Garden (which was indeed a perennial venue for world-championship bouts). The cartoon had the Devil seated in one corner—beaten, disheveled, and discouraged. To rouse him, his handlers were giving him a bottle of whiskey labeled "Old Nick." Me they represented as a big, strong, muscular prizefighter— what a stretch of the imagination *that* was!—having won the first round. The accompanying column on the front page said, "And tonight he waits for Satan's backlash."

Momentum continued to build during the next few days. Attendance dipped the second night to around 14,000; it almost invariably did in any Crusade, but this was higher by several thousand than the second night in London. We were encouraged by this. By the end of the week, however, the arena was jammed nightly, and hundreds were being turned away. As crowds grew, in addition to the main service inside I began to preach to the crowds that waited patiently outside on Forty-ninth Street and Eighth Avenue, which became a common occurrence during the course of the Crusade. Some nights as many as 8,000 gathered outside, so we had a small platform built from which Bev could sing and I could preach.

Newspaper coverage likewise continued to be favorable; extended news reports and excerpts from the sermons were carried by most papers and wire services throughout the city and abroad. The *New York Herald Tribune* allowed me space on the front page every day to write anything I wanted.

The Associated Press had planned to send out two stories a day during the entire Crusade. George Cornell, along with an assistant, had been assigned to cover it. One night he put his pen down and came forward himself. His executive editor then told him he was making a change in Cornell's assignment. "You've become too close to it and can't write objectively," the editor claimed.

I wrote to some editor friends of mine, saying I was sure that if they got people to request coverage, the Associated Press would provide it. And that's exactly what happened.

Normally, we did not hold Crusade meetings on Sundays, but in New York we made an exception; one reason was that very few churches had Sunday evening services. After some weeks with a Crusade meeting each night, we had to give our Team members some rest. We decided not to have services on Mondays from then on.

The first Sunday evening—the fifth day of the Crusade—an estimated 21,000 people jammed the huge arena (1,500 more than the stated capacity); that encouraged us greatly. That afternoon Mayor Robert Wagner had put Erling Olsen (of the Crusade committee) and me into a convertible and driven us to Brooklyn for the annual Norwegian Independence Day festival, where we found people of Norwegian descent wearing their colorful national costumes. Some 40,000 filled Leif Eriksson Square as I spoke to them, with hundreds raising their hands to indicate their desire to commit their lives to Jesus Christ. This was the first of several mass rallies we held around the city; that included one noontime meeting with an estimated 30,000 on Wall Street (a meeting that completely blocked traffic) and several open-air services in Harlem that attracted many thousands.

Our goal was to reach out to as many people as possible in all kinds of situations—many of whom would never come to one of our Crusade meetings.

Howard Jones, a gifted black pastor from Cleveland who joined our Team about that time, also held dozens of meetings throughout the metropolitan area. When one detractor claimed that very few blacks were attending the Crusade services, Dan Potter had a very careful survey made; he discovered that the proportion was almost identical to the city's demographics. At the same time, we wanted to do more to encourage black participation.

One night civil rights leader Dr. Martin Luther King, Jr., whom I was pleased to count a friend, gave an eloquent opening prayer at the service; he also came at my invitation to one of our Team retreats during the Crusade to help us understand the racial situation in America more fully.

We also held a special service in Madison Square Garden one Saturday afternoon for Spanish-speaking people, the first time I had spoken through an interpreter in the United States. At each service, Willis Haymaker arranged special sections for the handicapped— the blind, the deaf, and those in wheelchairs. Willis's warmth, prayers, and depth of spirituality contributed as much as anything else to our effectiveness in New York.

Most days began to follow a routine pattern. Charlie or Cliff usually appeared at my hotel room or talked on the telephone with me early to go over the day's schedule. I often spoke three or four times a day in addition to the Crusade service in the evening—perhaps a luncheon with business leaders, a visit to a university, a meeting at the United Nations, a gathering in someone's home designed to reach out to neighbors or friends with the Gospel, a tour of the Bowery, with its tragic clusters of men whose lives had been wrecked by alcohol. Since New York also hosted scores of conventions, I often was invited to speak to them. Opportunities seemed limitless, and our Team—augmented by a number of well-known ministers, including Paul Rees, Tom Allan, and Samuel Shoemaker—spoke in almost every kind of situation. Some of our Team, Grady especially, seemed to be going all the time.

One day Ruth and I attended a Father's Day luncheon at the Waldorf-Astoria Hotel, where I was honored as Father of the Year in the field of religion. I had the opportunity to meet Mickey Mantle, the great baseball player. I sat down beside him, and we got to know each other for the first time.

Another day we had lunch with Dr. Norman Vincent Peale and his wife, Ruth; his preaching on "the power of positive thinking" had made him familiar to millions. Mrs. Peale did a magnificent job heading up the women's prayer groups for the Crusade, and Dr. Peale was warmly supportive of the meetings. Although our emphasis in preaching differed, I found him a deeply committed believer with a genuine concern that men and women give their lives to Christ.

Another memorable luncheon took place about ten days into the Crusade, at the Long Island estate of Jane Pickens Langley, a leading socialite whose husband had been president of the New York Stock Exchange. Investment banker E. F. Hutton sent his chauffeured limousine to get Ruth and me, along with my sister Jean and her husband, Leighton Ford, whom she married in 1953. Mrs. Langley had about 50 guests for lunch; an additional 150 joined us afterward for a meeting on the spacious lawn. The house itself was a well-maintained early-American structure. Ruth, who loves antiques and old architecture, wrote in her diary, "A place like that makes me right weak in the knees." The gathering was a veritable Who's Who of New York society, with familiar names such as Vanderbilt, Whitney, Paley, and Cushing sprinkled among the guests. We ate outside, then adjourned to the area on the lawn where chairs had been set up for the guests.

I had not realized until we arrived that I was expected to speak, but at the appropriate moment I took about twenty-five minutes to explain what an evangelist was and why we had accepted the invitation to come to New York. I then spoke on the meaning of the Gospel and answered questions for over half an hour on everything from the Crusade's finances to the meaning of Christ as the way of salvation. Two people came up afterward to say they had already gone forward at the Madison Square Garden meetings. One of those was Eleanor Searle Whitney, whose exuberant personality, vibrant testimony to faith in Christ, and unforgettable hats made her a favorite of our Team.

That same night, a Saturday, we broke our usual pattern; the meeting was scheduled for Forest Hills Tennis Stadium, in the borough of Queens. I went over there straight from the Langleys, but as the meeting began, we realized that the stadium was directly under the flight path for planes landing at LaGuardia Airport.

Erling Olsen immediately called the control tower, and by the time I got up to preach, the flight path had been shifted enough to enable us to be heard.

Almost without exception, however, I refused to take engagements in the afternoon, often lying propped up in bed, concentrating on the evening sermon and preparing myself spiritually for the challenge of preaching. In fact, it has almost always been my custom during Crusades to lie down for a couple of hours before each meeting to rest, think, and pray. About an hour before I am to leave I have a sandwich and usually a cup of tea. Those who have not spoken or preached to any great extent may not realize how demanding and exhausting speaking can be, physically, emotionally, and spiritually. Many nights in New York I would leave the podium drenched in perspiration and be barely able to undress when I got back to my hotel room. My resolve to keep a daily diary flagged; the last two entries were two weeks apart; and then I finally gave up.

Shortly after the Crusade started, our Methodist associate evangelist from England, Joe Blinco, and other Team members took responsibility for speaking to the people in the counseling room, where inquirers were directed after the Invitation. Normally, I liked to meet with the inquirers, but I already could sense that I was going to have to guard my physical strength.

In some ways, the most important outcome of those first weeks in Madison Square Garden was our decision to broadcast the Saturday night service live across the nation over the ABC television network. My old friend Charles Crutchfield from Charlotte, who managed a television station there, urged us to consider the idea. Leonard Goldenson of ABC, who had helped us several years before with *The Hour of Decision,* agreed to carry the program for four weeks in June, until the scheduled end of the Crusade on June 30.

The cost seemed astronomical—$50,000 per week—but we sensed that God was leading us to step out in faith, trusting Him for contributions to cover the expense. The New York committee was doubtful about the experiment; but I called my friend J. Howard Pew, and he agreed (albeit reluctantly) to underwrite up to half the amount if it became necessary; and we signed the contract.

This wasn't our first experiment with television in connection with the New York Crusade; and in that connection, the name Mel

Dibble comes up. He had a national variety program emanating every Saturday night from Cincinnati. His mother had been a wonderful Bible teacher.

Once when I spoke in Cincinnati, Mel and his wife, Ruth, were brought by a friend to the meeting, which was already full. As they turned to leave, a stage door opened and someone recognized Mel, calling him by his stage name, Mel Martin. He invited the group in and seated Mel on the platform behind Dr. Donald Grey Barnhouse, much to Mel's embarrassment. At the conclusion of the meeting, Dr. Barnhouse challenged Mel on his commitment, but Mel said he needed to leave immediately.

Dr. Barnhouse persisted, convincing Mel and his wife to stop by our hotel. By the time the three of them got there, Grady and I were already dressed for bed. We talked, though, and Mel came under conviction—but then said he needed to leave. I challenged him further: "God loves you and has a purpose and plan for your life, but you must surrender your life to Him."

In response Mel did surrender his life to Christ. Dr. Barnhouse, an extremely conservative man, became so emotional that he grabbed Mel and hugged him. Mel ended up in excruciating pain. The fountain pen in his pocket was being crushed into his ribs!

During the New York Crusade, Mel hosted a daily fifteen-minute, late-night television program with other Team members in the New York area, and listeners were invited to call in at the close of each telecast. We had thirteen or fourteen telephone lines set aside for counseling, and calls routinely came in until two or three o'clock in the morning; indeed, Team members often stayed up all night taking calls following those telecasts. In the first two weeks of the Crusade, Cliff Barrows announced on *The Hour of Decision* that one hundred and fifty people had indicated they were committing their lives to Christ through the telephone counseling.

"We know we cannot solve all of life's problems in one phone call," Betty Lowry told the *Journal-American* a week into the Crusade, "but we do know of cases where we've been able to help."

Cliff was a whirlwind of activity, not only leading the choir every night and acting as the Crusade's genial and enthusiastic master of ceremonies, but also overseeing many of the special projects and programs we were doing, including *The Hour of Decision*.

On Saturday, June 1, we aired our first ABC telecast. We were up against two of the most popular programs on television, *The Perry Como Show* and *The Jackie Gleason Show*. Network officials were surprised when the Trendex ratings came in a few days later; the *Herald Tribune* said the program "provided the ABC network with its highest rating to date for the time period opposing the Como and Gleason shows." It then quoted an ABC executive as saying that "the rating means that approximately 6.5 million viewers watched Dr. Graham, enough to fill Madison Square Garden to capacity every day for a whole year."

Response from viewers was quick in coming. "We're still averaging over 10,000 letters a day," I wrote to Dr. Bonnell in July, after the telecasts had been going for several weeks. "Many of them are from ministers testifying that new people are turning up at their churches and that attendance for July is higher than at any [previous] time."

Furthermore, although we spoke only briefly on the air about our need for money to continue the broadcasts, contributions from the very first more than covered the costs.

Altogether we had fourteen live telecasts during the summer as the Crusade was extended, with some 35,000 favorable letters the first week alone, many of them from people who had made a decision for Christ right in their own homes.

"I have begun to feel that perhaps we are holding the Madison Square Garden meetings almost entirely so we could have this telecast," I wrote in my diary a few days after the first one. "Madison Square Garden is a world-renowned stage from which to speak to America."

The Crusade initially had been scheduled to end on June 30, but with the meetings running at capacity (or beyond) almost every night, the Crusade committee quickly decided to extend it by three weeks, with a closing rally planned for Yankee Stadium on July 20. From my standpoint, the decision to extend wasn't so easy; by the end of those first six weeks, I was already physically depleted.

I also had run out of sermons and was having to prepare a new one every day. Some nights during those later weeks, I sat on the platform and prayed silently, "O God, *You* have to do it. I can't do it.

I just *can't* do it." And yet when I stood up, all of a sudden the words would begin to come—God giving strength and spiritual power in a way that could not be explained in human terms.

The final service in Yankee Stadium on July 20 was truly unforgettable. The stadium was jammed with a record crowd of 100,000 people, with another 20,000 outside who could not get in. The heat was fierce—93 degrees outside and 105 degrees on the platform—and how anyone (including me) managed to concentrate is still beyond my imagination. Vice President Nixon came and sat on the platform with us, extending greetings to the audience from President Eisenhower. That was the first time a national political leader of his prominence had attended one of our Crusades.

At that point we faced the decision whether or not to extend the services yet again. A few committee members thought we should not continue. Yankee Stadium was a fitting end, they felt, and anything else would seem like an anticlimax. Noting that hundreds were still coming forward, Dan Potter said to Charlie Riggs, "How can we stop when a new church is being born into the kingdom of God every night?"

"The main points against continuing concern the climax and dangers to our reputations," I told the committee. "Pentecost was a great climactic experience, but the followers of Jesus didn't stop until they were thrown out of the city. Calvary was the greatest climax in our history, but the Lord didn't stop there. As far as our reputations are concerned, that should not be a vital point. Christ made Himself of no reputation." After much prayer, the committee voted to continue.

"I, too, had certain doubts about continuing . . . but in my period of prayer I could not get any peace about closing even though I am sure the crowds are going to drop off . . . dramatically," I wrote to George Champion a few days later. "Yet for some unknown and mysterious reason I believe the Lord would have us carry on."

I was not an accurate prophet, as it turned out; crowds in the Garden continued almost without interruption. When the next deadline approached, the committee had little trouble in deciding to extend the Crusade for as long as Madison Square Garden was available; that was until the Labor Day weekend.

So many people were coming forward that we found we were not equipped to process the number of decision cards we were getting. A former Air Force colonel, Bob Root, was called in to reorganize the effort, using mainly volunteers after every service. His efficiency set the pattern for all our Crusades in the future.

An event this size had its own share of problems—some sad, some humorous.

Once during the early weeks, we had to warn in the press against phony "Crusade workers" who were going door to door in a couple of areas of the city to solicit funds for the Crusade. (We have never raised money in any Crusade by that method, relying instead on the local finance committee to raise the necessary funds.)

Several hours before the service was to begin on another night, a janitor found a note claiming that a bomb had been planted inside the Garden. The police were called immediately, but they found no bomb.

One night burglars broke into the Crusade office and stole about $2,000—a first in our Crusade experience, and one that we would rather have bypassed.

On another evening, a drunk began ranting during the service. Grady and Leighton Ford were dispatched to ease him out, but in order to reach him, they had to go out onto a fire escape high above the streets; once they did, they found themselves locked out. An usher finally responded to their banging and let them back in. Now within reach of the poor inebriate, they convinced him to leave. But when Grady and Leighton came back inside, another man with a rather wild-eyed look was standing in the aisle with a dozen Bibles in his hands, telling them that God had told him to preach that night instead of Billy Graham. Eventually, they persuaded him that he had it wrong; perhaps, they suggested, he was supposed to preach the next night. He left satisfied and apparently never returned.

The closing event for the New York Crusade was a massive rally in Times Square on Sunday evening, September 1. Police blocked off all the surrounding streets, increasing the space available to listeners. I had not prepared a sermon, so I took what I saw on the Broadway theater marquees and applied the words to the Gospel.

The crowd was tremendous. The first estimate sent out over the wire was 200,000 people. Radio commentator Paul Harvey put that same figure out over the air. When I got back to my hotel, I called a good friend of mine at one of the newspapers to ask what he thought the figure was. More like 75,000, he said, and I responded that that seemed about right. *Life* magazine, whose photographers took pictures of the crowd from a number of vantage points, counted the people in their photographs and came up with 60,000; but they admitted later that they had missed one crowded street entirely.

Whatever the exact figure, it was a fitting end to the longest Crusade we would ever hold. Altogether, more than 2 million people attended the Crusade meetings and other events during the sixteen weeks we were in New York, with more than 61,000 inquirers (in addition to the 35,000 who wrote to us indicating a decision as a result of the telecasts). A million and a half letters flooded our Minneapolis office in response to the television broadcasts alone— an influx so great that George Wilson had to expand our staff and equipment rapidly.

What was accomplished?

On the surface, of course, the mammoth city of New York seemed unchanged, as I was the first to admit to the press. But beneath that surface, many people had been touched by the message of the Cross, and any evaluation had to begin with the countless lives that were changed by an encounter with the living Christ. The stories of dramatic conversions were virtually endless.

One night a plainly dressed woman stood in the inquiry room with tears running down her cheeks as she asked Christ to come into her life. When her counselor asked if there was anything else she wanted to share, she replied that she was very afraid of her son. "He drinks a lot," she said, "and I'm afraid he may beat me when he finds out I've become a Christian." Before the counselor could speak, a voice nearby called out, "It's okay, Mom. I'm here too."

One evening, among the hundreds coming forward were a priest and a prostitute.

Another night a man from Little Rock, Arkansas, named Jimmy Karam came to Christ. His picture had been in *Life* magazine because of his active opposition to the civil rights movement, but his life was changed as Christ's love replaced the anger in his heart.

The wife of a French diplomat wrote us after coming forward: "The joy, the thrill of Christ. I just didn't know you could be so happy."

A wealthy man accepted Christ and began bringing anywhere from 20 to 40 guests a night to the meetings, even buying them dinner at a restaurant beforehand.

The *Wall Street Journal* reported that Bible sales were up dramatically in New York City during the Crusade. It also noted that the owner of a bar near Madison Square Garden had sent four of his bartenders on their vacations early because his business had declined so much.

Presbyterian seminary student Lane Adams had been a professional night-club entertainer before his conversion; we recruited him to work specifically with those in the performing arts in New York. Many came to Christ as a result, and a group calling themselves the New York Christian Arts Fellowship was formed, with famed opera singer Jerome Hines as president. One actor who came forward turned down a Hollywood movie contract so he could stay in New York and take his friends to the meetings.

Black actress and singer Ethel Waters slipped into the meeting and rededicated herself to Christ one night. When Cliff learned she was in the audience, he asked her if she would be willing to do a solo, which she did. She then joined the choir. As Ethel often related afterward, because of her generous size, they had to remove the armrest between two seats to accommodate her. She sat anonymously in their midst night after night for the rest of the Crusade. She later became a fixture in many of our Crusades, singing a song that touched the hearts of millions: "His Eye Is on the Sparrow."

Even after the Crusade ended, we heard reports of people who continued to come to Christ. Sometimes seed that is sown takes a long time to grow.

One man we heard about attended a Madison Square Garden meeting but left unmoved. Some weeks later, he attended a rodeo in the same arena. As he was sitting there, the Holy Spirit brought to his mind the Crusade service, and in the middle of the rodeo he silently bowed his head and gave his life to Christ.

God worked in other ways also. Seminary student Michael Cassidy from South Africa stood in the inquiry room in the Garden almost overwhelmed by what he was witnessing. Could this happen elsewhere? he asked himself, and sensed God answering yes. A few years later, after graduating from Fuller Theological Seminary, Michael founded an organization called African Enterprise to reach Africa for Christ, and he has been greatly used as an evangelist himself.

At the same time, the New York Crusade pointed up a bottle-neck in our work. Sadly, many of the churches failed to reach out to new converts and help them in their newfound faith. Some months later, Robert Ferm—who with his wife, Lois, ably assisted me for many years in research and contacts with pastors—spent a month in New York interviewing pastors and inquirers. He found that at least 75 percent of the converts had received no personal contact from a church—nothing more than a letter or phone call, if that. And yet remarkably, the majority of them were still continuing in their faith.

Dan Potter remarked that he almost never visited a New York church during the next five years without having people come up and tell him of their conversion during the Crusade. In our future Crusades, we continued to work diligently on follow-up, especially seeking ways to encourage and train churches to seize the opportunities and challenges of new converts.

New York also had an unforeseen impact on our own ministry. Through the medium of television, an estimated 96 million people had seen at least one of the meetings from Madison Square Garden. That experience showed us that God was opening the door to a new medium for the furtherance of the Gospel. The televised meetings also resulted in a flood of invitations to other major cities under broad sponsorship, including Chicago.

The meetings had an impact on me personally as well. I now knew that no city and no area—no matter how difficult on the surface—was entirely closed to the Gospel message through so-called mass evangelism. But New York also took a toll on me physically. I left drained; I had lost twenty or more pounds. I have said in later years that something went out of me physically in the New York Crusade that I never fully recovered. Never again would we attempt anything as extensive in length.

My exhaustion was caused not just by the intensive schedule. A doctor who was also an evangelist once told me that the hardest work a person can do is preach an evangelistic sermon. Whether that is true or not, I don't know. What I *do* know is that evangelistic preaching is physically and emotionally draining. One reason it is draining for me is that I am constantly driving for commitment. Another reason is that speaking of matters with eternal consequences is a great responsibility, and I am always afraid I won't make the message clear or will say something that is misleading.

From the moment I stand up to speak to a crowd, I am thinking about that person whose life is being crushed by heartache or alcohol or family problems, and I want to make the hope of the Gospel as clear as possible to him or her. Sometimes I pick out someone in the audience who seems to be especially burdened and preach directly to that person. Preaching also involves us in a spiritual battle with the forces of evil. I am always deeply conscious that I am absolutely helpless and that only the Holy Spirit can penetrate the minds and hearts of those who are without Christ. When I am speaking from the Bible, I know there is also another voice speaking to the people, and that is the voice of the Holy Spirit. I am reminded often of Jesus' parable of the seed and the sower (*see* Mark 4:1–20), knowing that all I am doing is sowing seed. It is God—and only God—who can make that seed bear fruit.

We returned to New York several times after that 1957 Crusade. Our 1970 Crusade in Shea Stadium particularly reached areas outside Manhattan. A series of meetings on Long Island and at the Meadowlands (across the river in New Jersey) in 1990 and 1991 brought large numbers of people from the city itself, as well as from surrounding metropolitan areas. In 1991 a one-day rally in Central Park drew a quarter of a million people together to hear the Gospel—the largest audience we ever addressed in North America. On the bus going back to the hotel after Central Park, one of my grandchildren noticed vendors on the sidewalk selling T-shirts saying, "Billy Blessed Us." I trust this was true; but if so, it was solely because of God's grace.

18

To Earth's Ends

As the people at the 1957 Crusade in New York poured down toward the front to make commitments, I prayed two things over and over.

First, "Lord, help these people to receive You in answer to the prayers of the people—and do not let me get any credit."

Second, "I am willing to take any kind of tiredness, disease, or whatever it is, for this one night, for you to win these people."

As the end of the Crusade came, I wondered if I would ever be up to holding another full-scale Crusade.

But news of the Crusade's impact spurred the prayers and sharpened the hopes of Christians elsewhere. Even before the New York Crusade ended, invitations from cities in this country and abroad passed the one hundred mark. All we could do was pray that God would give us the strength and the wisdom to discern His will.

AUSTRALIA

One invitation in particular captured my interest. For some reason I could not fully understand, although I believed it was the leading of the Holy Spirit, I had developed an overwhelming burden to visit the distant continent of Australia.

During our London Crusade in 1954, I had become particularly aware of Australia's spiritual needs, in part through the contact we had there with some church leaders from Australia. Then, in late 1955, an Australian Presbyterian evangelist, Harold Whitney, met with us during our meetings in Ocean Grove, New Jersey; afterward he traveled to England and Scotland to evaluate the impact of our Crusades there. On his return, he wrote a book urging his fellow Australian churchmen to invite us as part of a Tell Australia movement, to be patterned after the Tell Scotland Campaign.

Most influential in my thinking, however, was the strong support of the Anglican Archbishop of Sydney, Howard Mowll, whom I first met during the meetings of the World Council of Churches in Evanston, Illinois, in 1954, where I was an observer. He was unquestionably one of the finest Christian leaders I have ever known, enormously respected in Australia by all denominations; regrettably, he passed away shortly before our 1959 meetings began. Archbishop Mowll spearheaded the preliminary invitation from a broad cross section of clergy in 1955, then followed it up with a strong personal letter in July 1957, during our New York meetings. In response, I asked Jerry Beavan, although he had left our full-time Team, to travel to Australia and New Zealand to assess the situation.

Jerry brought back a number of formal invitations, from Melbourne, Sydney, Adelaide, Canberra, Perth, and Brisbane—cities containing at least half of Australia's population; there were invitations from New Zealand as well. His report spoke realistically of the possible barriers to evangelism in that part of the world, but as we prayed and studied the situation, we sensed God was leading us to accept.

Accordingly, in May 1958, Jerry and Crusade associate Bill Brown moved to Sydney to direct the Crusade preparations there. Walter Smyth, a former Youth for Christ director in Philadelphia who now headed our film distribution work, moved to Melbourne after directing our San Francisco Crusade in the early summer of 1958. Dates were set for meetings in Australia and New Zealand from February through June 1959. It would be the longest series of meetings we had ever held outside the United States.

I knew it was going to be very difficult for me personally. Ruth could not be with us for even part of the time, due to the distances and our growing young family. Our fifth child, Ned, had been born early in the previous year. His birth was the only one I witnessed. The doctor allowed me into the delivery room to hold Ruth's hand and pray with her during the birth. Of course, I had seen the birth of animals before, but the birth of a child was a unique and moving experience for me. When the doctor told me it was a boy, I prayed that he would grow up to be a man of God. The thought of leaving Ned and the other children for five or six months was almost more than I could bear.

Cliff faced exactly the same situation. Because he and Billie had committed themselves to this ministry, he was willing to leave his family to go with me on that long trip; but the separation was still wrenching.

The Australian preparations were unquestionably the most thorough we had undertaken to date. We drew not only on our experiences during the last decade but also on the insights of the Australian committees and leaders. Never before, for example, had we organized such a comprehensive series of neighborhood prayer meetings—5,000 in Sydney alone.

Committees were developed to deal with outreach to all kinds of specialized groups, from doctors, trade unionists, and university students to Australia's Aborigine and New Zealand's Maori populations. Christians who were professional social workers formed special counseling teams to help those with difficult social or emotional problems.

Australia was just beginning to draw large numbers of immigrants from non-English-speaking backgrounds. To serve that new population, in each city we provided translation via headphones for those who did not understand English. Some services were also translated into pidgin English and put on tapes that were carried into the jungles of New Guinea.

The Australian clergy insisted on having special counselors and counseling materials for children as well. Our counseling directors, Charlie Riggs and Dan Piatt, were at first slow to agree, what with all the other pressures on them; but like most everything else we tried in Australia, these materials became standard practice in our later Crusades.

Of special significance was the system of telephone landlines we developed to reach hundreds of far-flung towns and outback settlements. About 650,000 people attended the audio meetings served by those landlines, in everything from churches and theaters to bunkhouses on vast cattle ranches (or *stations,* as they are called in Australia); these additional meetings resulted in 15,000 registered commitments. The use of Operation Andrew and extensive chartered bus reservations for groups also exceeded anything we had ever done.

The major obstacle we faced in this Crusade was that to the average Australian, I was little more than a vague name; most knew nothing of our message or methods. To overcome this in advance of the meetings, the local committees asked us to blanket the nation with broadcasts of *The Hour of Decision.* In addition, copies of our films—especially the documentaries we had done in London and New York—were shown all over the country.

One day shortly before leaving for Australia, Grady and I were playing golf. He noticed that I kept missing the ball—even more than usual, that is! I soon noticed something distorted in my vision: when I looked at the ground, it seemed to be wavy or ridged. Suddenly, I had a sharp pain in my left eye and lost its peripheral vision. Doctors diagnosed a rare but serious problem called angiospastic edema of the macula, which they traced directly to strain and overwork. Failure to rest until it healed, they warned, could lead to permanent blindness.

As a result, we were forced to postpone the beginning of the Australia visit by two weeks and to reschedule all the dates as best we could. Through the generosity of a friend, Grady and I went to a quiet spot in Hawaii, Hana on the island of Maui, which was near the home of Charles Lindbergh. Also staying there were Charles Laughton and his actress wife, Elsa Lanchester, with whom we got acquainted. We ate in the little dining room and enjoyed sitting by ourselves on the black-sand beach. I was grateful that Ruth was able to join me; and through the generosity of another friend, Wilma Wilson was able to join Grady. It would be four months before we would see our wives again.

Another bonus was that Dr. V. Raymond Edman—the president of Wheaton College who had been such a continuing encouragement to me—came over to Maui to lead us in a series of Bible studies. I have never forgotten the spiritual as well as physical refreshment of those days. In spite of the change in plans, we sensed that God's hand was in the whole situation. Gradually, my vision improved, although I still had only 30 percent vision in that left eye when we landed in Australia. On the orders of my doctors, I tried to restrict my schedule to the main meeting and only one or two additional events a day.

Melbourne

Our first city was Melbourne. In spite of the enthusiasm of the local committee, which was led by the dean of the Anglican cathedral, Dr. Stuart Barton Babbage, Walter and others on our staff were cautious. Because Melbourne was known as a conservative, wealthy city with a tradition of education and culture, Walter was afraid we would meet with indifference or even opposition. A few years before, another American evangelist had been forced to cut his campaign short and leave the country because of active opposition there.

After our first meeting on February 15, however, it was obvious that the Melbourne committee had been correct. That first night, both the indoor stadium we had rented and an adjoining temporary annex were jammed to capacity. Additional thousands were standing outside in the rain; after the main service, I went out and spoke to them. As in New York, preaching twice—once to the crowd inside, once to those outside—became standard practice while we were in that stadium.

I appreciated the blunt but cordial honesty of one well-known Melbourne columnist, Eric Baume: "What is the difference between Dr. Billy Graham and some of our local hot-gospellers? He insults no one; he exhorts all; his heart of wondrous sympathy beats in his face. And I, as an infidel, but a convinced Theist, will not hear a word against him. . . . I, personally, cannot accept all he preaches. But that does not debar me from thanking him for coming to Australia."

It was increasingly apparent that the indoor stadium, even with the help of the annex, was inadequate. After five days, we moved to the Sidney Myer Music Bowl, a beautiful outdoor amphitheater set in a large park with a dramatic, aluminum bandshell shaped something like a giant parasail or kite. Tens of thousands of people could sit in the open air on the sloping ground—and did, with attendance reaching as high as 70,000.

During this time, we also went on television with a special program Cliff directed, offering a phone-in number at the end of the show for people desiring spiritual counseling. The second night our meeting was telecast, 10,000 callers overwhelmed the Melbourne exchange's automated system, with hundreds of those callers professing faith in Jesus Christ. Offering phone counseling in conjunction with television broadcasts later became a regular part of our televised Crusades in the United States.

After some days, however, we were forced to move from the Myer Music Bowl; it had already been committed to the city's annual Moomba Festival. The only facility available was a rough open-air structure at the Agricultural Showgrounds, located on the fringe of the city. Dr. Babbage later picturesquely described it as "probably the least suitable surroundings for the preaching of the Gospel that could have been devised. . . . Amplified sound reverberated like an echo machine around the straggling stands. Some nights sulfurous smoke belching from the funnels of shunting trains in the nearby saleyards blended with the stench of adjoining abattoirs to form a misty pall that drifted clingingly over the whole arena." To add to the bleak picture, Melbourne's weather turned unseasonably cold, with drenching rains flooding the area and turning the ground into a quagmire.

And yet people continued to come—up to 25,000 a night. When the four-week Crusade drew to a close, over half a million had come to the Melbourne meetings, with 22,000 inquirers coming forward at the Invitation.

The final service was held in the Melbourne Cricket Ground, a huge facility that had been expanded to a capacity of 105,000 for the 1956 Olympic Games. Two hours before we were scheduled to begin, I went up to the plush area where the directors of the Cricket Ground had gathered. When I asked for their projection, they predicted a crowd of perhaps 50,000. Not long after that, the manager of the grounds sent word that the place would be filled to capacity. When every seat was filled, he had the gates locked and sent word to the directors that thousands more were clamoring to get in. The directors decided on the spot to do something unprecedented; they opened the gates and allowed the crowd to invade the sacred precincts of the cricket pitch, on which only players were supposed to tread. The final crowd estimate—143,750—not only broke the record for the stadium but was also the largest audience I had addressed up to that time.

Tasmania and New Zealand

Following the Melbourne meetings, we embarked on a series of brief stops in Tasmania and New Zealand. In Hobart, the capital of Tasmania, an electrical failure cut off the floodlights and plunged the platform and much of the arena into a faint dimness. The crowd could barely see the platform, and I could sense them growing restless. When I got up to preach, I tried talking to them about the delicious Tasmanian apples that I had been enjoying. Still the restlessness continued. At that point, a small boy walked up the steps of the platform, paused to ask Bev a question, then stepped forward and presented me with a fine, big apple. His openness delighted the crowd, and from that moment on I had their undivided attention.

In Wellington, on New Zealand's North Island, I spoke at the university. Among many other things, I touched on the reality of Hell. After that meeting—in fact, it was shortly before midnight, and Cliff and I, who were sharing adjoining rooms, were almost ready for bed—we heard a loud knock on our door. There stood one of the students, and he was angry—*very* angry.

"What do you mean coming over here from America and talking about Hell? I don't believe in Hell, and you have no right to come over here and talk about it!"

"Let me ask you a question," I responded. "Suppose you went to Auckland to catch a plane for Sydney. And suppose they told you there was a 10 percent chance the plane would not make it but was going to crash. Would you get on?"

"No," he replied, "I wouldn't."

"Well, what if there were only a 5 percent chance the plane wasn't going to make it? Would you get on then?"

"No, of course not."

331

"Now suppose there's only a 10 percent chance—or even just a 5 percent chance—that Jesus was right and there *is* a Hell. Do you think there's at least a 5 percent chance that He might have been right?"

"Well, yes, I suppose there is."

"Then is it worth taking the risk and ignoring those odds?"

"No. No, it isn't," he admitted reluctantly.

"Then will you receive Christ and begin to follow Him?"

He paused for a moment. "No, I can't, because I find that's not my problem. My real problem is that I don't want to live up to the standard that Jesus demands." He thought his problem was an intellectual one, but in reality, as with so many other people, his problem was one of the will. Before he left, Cliff and I prayed with him, but we never knew if he ever came to Christ.

In Australia and New Zealand, we made use of our associate evangelists more than ever before. In New Zealand, for example, Grady preached in Auckland, the country's largest city, and found a very warm reception. Leighton Ford, a highly effective evangelist as well as my brother-in-law, spoke in Wellington to large crowds, in spite of blustery weather. Christchurch, founded by the English on South Island, responded equally well to Joe Blinco, who had grown up in a non-Christian home in northern England and had a real gift for communicating with people of all backgrounds. These associates would preach for a week, perhaps for two; then I would close the series with a final meeting. They also spoke in schools, prisons, factories, and dockyards—anyplace I was unable to include in my schedule. Altogether, one-fifth of the nation's population attended a Crusade meeting.

Sydney

At Sydney University, I had a direct confrontation with the Devil. As I talked to 4,000 students about the necessity of faith, we all heard a sudden, loud bang and saw a puff of white smoke. A figure appeared dressed in a flaming-red costume, complete with horns and a tail. When he walked up to me, I laughed and shook his hand. I took a small Bible out of my pocket, and with one hand on the zealous impersonator's shoulder, I outlined the Gospel to him. After

I left the meeting, he told his fellow students that he still didn't believe in Jesus. The next day, the *Sydney Daily Mirror* put a picture of us on the front page.

At the final meeting in Sydney, on May 10, the crowd of 150,000 broke attendance records for the Sydney Showground and the adjoining Sydney Cricket Ground. In addition, an estimated 1 million-plus people listened to that service over radio and via land-line broadcasts in homes, churches, and halls all over Australia—in places with such intriguing names as Bunbury, Manjimup, Pingelly, and Wubin. But rather than confirming the popularity of the visiting Team, interest indicated to me, as I told the people, "absolute proof of Australia's great spiritual hunger."

That final meeting in Sydney was really two simultaneous meetings. The setup at the Showground was duplicated at the adjoining Cricket Ground—speakers' dais, choir risers, and so on—and both sites had a thousand-voice choir. Both sessions began at three in the afternoon. Bev and other program participants shuttled between the two places by car; to preach to both audiences, I did the same. I was expected to shorten my sermons under those circumstances, but I'm not sure that I did. The results were very encouraging. St. Stephen's Presbyterian Church, for example, received six hundred people to follow up.

Perth, Adelaide, and Brisbane

Perth was a continent away, in Western Australia. To accommodate the swelling crowds in that city, seating at the Claremont Showgrounds had to be supplemented by more than a mile of planks laid across a thousand kerosene cans, almost a thousand ammunition cases, and a thousand gasoline drums. Grady had begun the Crusade, and I came at the end. One night, at the Invitation, an archbishop wanted to come forward. Grady suggested that such an action might be confusing to his flock and counseled the man personally.

At Adelaide, attendance held well above average throughout the Crusade; Joe was particularly effective with students at a meeting in the university's Union Hall. At Brisbane, Leighton addressed large audiences at the Milton Tennis Courts on weeknights; I preached at the Exhibition Ground for the closing weekend meetings, which were carried by landline relays to seventy towns and cities in Queensland.

It was in Adelaide that I met Rupert Murdoch for the first time. He was virtually unknown outside Australia and was just starting his career in publishing, but his quiet intensity impressed me. We later became friends, and he has been very supportive of our work through his publications in many parts of the world.

By the end of our final Australian meeting, which was in Brisbane in May, three and one-third million people had attended the meetings in person (including the meetings led by associates), and there had been 150,000 inquirers.

During our long time away, Cliff and I both missed our families intensely. Billie sent Cliff a photograph of one of his young daughters, but it didn't help much since it showed her sitting in the picture window of her home, crying for her daddy.

Billie herself had her spirits buoyed when a friend sent her a television set on which she could see a newscast of her husband and me trekking about Australia. But before she could turn it on, she had to climb up on the roof of their home to erect the antenna!

We did have a bit of leisure time in the midst of our heavy schedule. Lee Fisher and I played golf together frequently. He was a jack of all trades, able to do many things well, including play a number of musical instruments. He had been an evangelist; but after the death of his wife, he took a tour of the world, during which he did not live for the Lord. When he got back, he developed a stutter, which he thought was God's judgment on him for his disobedience. He married again and returned to the Lord. He had a great sense of humor and even managed to improve my golf game.

Once, between meetings, we decided to take advantage of a day off. Cliff, Paul Maddox, Walter Smyth, and I drove to a resort development called Surfers' Paradise. Somewhere along the road, we pulled up at a beautiful stretch of sandy ocean beach. We were all alone, as far as the eye could see—or so we thought. We had a time of prayer and Bible reading. Then Cliff and I went swimming. We were enjoying being pounded by the waves when all of a sudden we heard Walter and Paul yelling, "Sharks! Get out—sharks!" We looked out and saw fins coming toward us. Apparently, we had not quite reached Surfers' Paradise.

Religion became front-page news across Australia. However, the real story of the Australian Crusade was written in the lives of Australians who would never be the same because of their encounter with Christ.

I heard about one man who was a safecracker, actively involved with a gang planning a theft. He decided to come to a meeting, and there he gave his life to Christ. Later he and his counselor met with the gang to tell them what had happened to him and explain why he would no longer be part of their plans.

Another night I was preaching on the home. A divorced man was there with the girlfriend who had been the cause of the breakup of his marriage. The message penetrated his heart, and as he looked up during the Invitation, he saw his former wife going forward to give her life to Christ. With tears of remorse, he went and stood beside her, becoming reconciled not only to God but to the wife he had rejected.

One man who came forward in Sydney had embezzled a large sum from the bank where he worked. Though it hadn't been detected, he confessed the next morning to the bank manager, offering to make restitution even though he knew he faced almost certain dismissal and prosecution. The manager was so impressed with the man's change of heart that he not only kept him on staff but went to the Crusade that night and gave his own life to Christ.

And then there was Ron Baker. He had almost everything going against him, including functional illiteracy and a speech impediment brought on by a violently abusive childhood. An alcoholic and a confirmed gambler, Ron was also deeply involved in witchcraft. He stopped by his local bar every night, arriving home some hours later drunk and in a foul mood. He abused his poor wife; she threatened divorce.

By profession Ron was a bus driver, and on several nights during the Crusade, he was assigned by his employer to drive delegations to the meetings. Disgusted, he traded routes with another driver. One night, working late, he missed his nightly visit to the bar altogether and arrived home cold sober. A friend to whom he was indebted was there to invite him to the meetings. His wife urged him to go, saying that she had attended the Crusade four days before and made her own commitment to Christ. Although that news sent Ron into a towering rage, his friend was able to quiet him down again and eventually convinced him to attend—but only on the condition that they sit as far away from the platform as possible.

"I thought that the message was the greatest load of garbage I had ever heard," Ron wrote later. But God was at work. God spoke to him that night, and he made his own commitment to Christ. He struggled with his alcoholism for two years, but gradually Christ changed him from within. He began to study, and with the help of a Christian speech therapist, he overcame his impediment. Sensing his call to Christian service, Ron went to Bible college and then seminary. A few years later, as an ordained pastor, he formed his own evangelistic team; since then he has had a powerful ministry as an evangelist throughout Australia and in other parts of the world.

In New Zealand, a man with deep family and financial problems got into his car, determined to commit suicide by running it into a bridge abutment outside town. As he drove, he turned on the radio and found it was tuned to the Crusade broadcast. The message on the Twenty-third Psalm arrested his attention, and he drove instead to the local Crusade office, where someone led him to Christ.

Stories like this could be repeated from any other Crusade, but I never tire of hearing them. I have never ceased to be thrilled at the transformation that comes when a person opens his or her life to Jesus Christ.

However, God alone must get the glory, for only He can penetrate the hardness of our hearts and bring us to faith and commitment and new life. As I said on our last day in Brisbane, "For what has happened in Australia, I want to give the glory and praise to God. . . . I hope you will soon forget about us except to pray for us. When you take pictures and applaud, I know it is from your heart, but you're applauding the wrong person, you're taking pictures of the wrong person; I'm here to represent Jesus Christ, the King of kings and the Lord of lords: to Him be the glory and the praise and the honor."

Heading Home

From Australia we went to Europe, where Ruth and I were reunited in Paris. Before leaving for home, we crossed the English Channel to London; I wanted to hold a press conference there to let the English know about our meetings in Australia. However, the press seemed lethargic, uninterested in anything we had done Down Under. But when I told them that Ruth and I had walked across Hyde Park and that with all the couples locked in intimate embrace, it looked like a bedroom, the press perked up. Almost before we got outside, or so it seemed, the newspapers were already on the street, with my Hyde Park remark as the headline! That headline even sparked a hot debate in Parliament.

A few days later, somewhat embarrassed, Ruth and I met with Queen Elizabeth in Buckingham Palace for tea. As always, she was very interested in our work, expressing special pleasure as we recounted what God had done in Australia, over which she was the earthly sovereign. She did not mention the headline, nor did I.

Since 1959 we have returned to Australia three times—in 1968, 1969, and 1979. In addition, several of our associate evangelists have had frequent ministry there. In 1996 my son Franklin held Crusades in several Australian cities, including Sydney and Brisbane, and he has received a number of invitations to return.

AFRICA

At the beginning of 1960, most of the countries on the vast continent of Africa were still under foreign colonial domination; some, like Nigeria, were due to receive independence later in the year. The cry of freedom was on the lips of people everywhere. And yet we also detected a great deal of nervousness: with the colonial structures collapsing and the old ways of life disappearing, no one knew exactly what the future would hold.

Africa in those days was undergoing great economic and social change. Old ways of life were disappearing forever as millions moved from small villages and tribal areas to the continent's few mushrooming cities. Relative prosperity in some regions was creating new classes and new expectations. The old social structures were being challenged by a new generation of leadership. Many knowledgeable people with whom I talked said that a philosophical and political vacuum was developing across the continent.

337

By 1958 we had accepted invitations for a trip to that great continent beginning in January 1960. After much prayer, we decided on eleven countries: Liberia, Ghana, Nigeria, and the Congo in western Africa; Northern and Southern Rhodesia (now Zambia and Zimbabwe); Kenya, Tanganyika (now part of Tanzania), Ruanda-Urundi (now Rwanda and Burundi), and Ethiopia in eastern Africa; and Egypt in northern Africa. We also scheduled brief stopover meetings in several other countries—informal gatherings at airports, for example, where we would preach.

Jerry Beavan, Howard Jones, and Charlie Riggs crisscrossed the continent arranging the meetings and training counselors. Paul Maddox helped take care of the myriad details that were involved in our complex travel arrangements. Grady Wilson, Cliff Barrows, and Joe Blinco accompanied us to preach in places that I could not visit.

Some countries, such as Sudan, remained closed to us for political or religious reasons. Churches in another nation, South Africa, strongly urged us to come, but I refused; the meetings could not be integrated, and I felt that a basic moral principle was at stake.

Liberia

Liberia, a democracy founded by freed American slaves in the early nineteenth century, was our first stop in Africa on January 19. As we landed, I wondered if it might be the last stop I would ever make. One of the plane's four motors was spurting dark smoke. With sirens wailing, airport fire engines raced toward us. The combustion, I was happy to see, subsided before we reached the terminal.

Vice President William R. Tolbert met us. A noted Baptist leader, he stopped at a small church on the fifty-mile drive into Monrovia. We had a brief prayer session there, sang a hymn, and recited the Twenty-third Psalm.

Liberia's president, William V. S. Tubman, was also a professing Christian, a Methodist; so it was not too surprising that our Liberian visit was the first ever that was government-sponsored rather than church-sponsored. We were housed in the government's official guest house, and we were received by the president in the gleaming-white executive mansion. He expressed his hope that his people's souls would be refreshed through the ministry of our meetings.

Dr. Tolbert accompanied me everywhere, even presiding at our meetings in Monrovia's Antoinette Tubman Stadium.

My associate Howard Jones had already started the Crusade when we arrived. He and his wife, Wanda, were establishing a home in Monrovia. That would enable him to preach regularly on the powerful new Sudan Interior Mission radio station ELWA in Monrovia and to conduct evangelistic crusades all over Africa. The radio station was located on a beautiful beach; fronting it were some lovely missionary homes and a school for children.

In the week preceding our arrival, Howard preached to large audiences. I preached the final two nights of the Crusade, with many thousands in attendance, resulting in 1,000 inquirers. It was an encouraging start to our African journey.

President Tubman invested me, while in the country, as a Grand Commander of the Humane Order of African Redemption, the nation's second-highest honor. The title *commander* was misapplied, I was sure, but the words *humane* and *redemption* meant a great deal to me, in view of my pursuit of God's calling for my life. I knew that Africa could move in any of several directions—Communist, Islamic, animistic, or Christian—and I was there to promote the last.

Ghana

Only three years earlier, Ghana had become the first African nation to get free of European colonialism. It was a small country, but it had many tribes and languages. One Ghanaian I met stood in the middle of the road and said, "I can't understand the people across that hill, and they can't understand us (or the people across the next hill to them)."

The reception I got in Ghana was quite different from my reception in Liberia. An editorial writer in Prime Minister Kwame Nkrumah's party newspaper said I should address my messages only to the European Christians living in that country; they were, in his words, "the worst form of oppressors and hypocrites history has ever recorded."

The Crusade had already been opened in the capital of Accra before my arrival by Leighton Ford. Among the 14,000 people who came to hear me preach in Accra Stadium, many understood

English, but I had two interpreters anyway. I explained that I was not a politician; I was an ambassador of Jesus Christ. And I tried to be diplomatic: I expressed admiration for the leadership (but deliberately kept silent about the policies) of Ghana's prime minister—the nation's founding father, whom I looked forward to meeting in a day or so.

I repeated what I had said in India: that Christ was not a white man; he was a Middle Easterner, darker than I and lighter than they. I pointed out to them that when Jesus fell while carrying His cross, it was an African, Simon of Cyrene, who was pressed into service to carry it for Him. Jesus' parents, I noted, had fled to Africa after He was born.

Many people in other parts of Africa and elsewhere had grave concerns about Mr. Nkrumah, fearing he was turning Ghana into a dictatorship. The prime minister's strong language against the European colonial powers and his strong nationalism were undergirded by an aggressive personality cult that in some eyes bordered on the idolatrous. Carved on his statue in the center of Accra was a blatant parody of Jesus' words in the Sermon on the Mount: "Seek ye first the political kingdom, and all other things shall be added unto it."

The time might soon come, one Ghanaian pastor told us, when "Ghana's Christians may have to choose between Christ and the nation."

Mr. Nkrumah received me cordially when I visited him in his official residence. It was, I believe, my first experience with a political leader who held such a tight rein on the hearts and minds of his people. I knew I could not hope to sort out all the political crosscurrents involved with his philosophy, nor was that my calling. I was, however, deeply concerned about the future of the Christian church under his rule.

After the preliminary courtesies were over, I told Mr. Nkrumah I knew he was concerned for the future of his people and that every truly great nation cherished religious freedom. I expressed the hope that this would be the case with his nation as well. He assured me it would be, as long as churches refrained from interference in political affairs. I knew that Christian believers would need great wisdom to avoid difficulties in the future.

Worried as I was about this matter, I was blindsided by an altogether different issue in Ghana. At that time, many Africans were in a rage about an atomic test blast planned by the French in the Sahara Desert. Ghanaians feared that the harmattan wind from the north would waft radioactive dust over their land. Local reporters did everything they could to squeeze a comment out of me.

My silence—partly a result of an effort to abide by Mr. Nkrumah's injunction against meddling in politics—made them jump on me all the more. Ghanaian reporters, in saying that I was a good actor and a good psychologist, implied that I was little more; the Associated Press quoted one of them as saying, "Nkrumahism is the highest form of Christianity." The reporters even turned my own words against me. As journalist Tom McMahan, who accompanied us, wrote in his account of our trip, *Safari for Souls,* they declared that "Christian civilization is today busily dragging Christ to Golgotha, and an African . . . is bearing the cross for the son of man. This African is Kwame Nkrumah."

The whole issue was, I knew, a complex one, and I doubted that I could avoid offending people on one side or the other no matter what I said. The controversy did not follow us elsewhere, fortunately.

Our audience my second (and final) night in Accra was only a third of what it had been for my first meeting; the response to the Invitation, though, was nearly the same on both nights.

The drive to our next stop, Kumasi, a city northwest of Accra, was spectacular; the road was flanked by giant mahogany trees. We were warmly received in Kumasi by citizens wearing colorful tribal clothing. Some 8,000 had gathered, but a torrential tropical downpour shorted out the public address system, and the crowd had no alternative but to disperse. Afterward we were invited to a buffet dinner given in our honor. Most of our Team members were completely soaked and had no change of clothing or shoes. Five of them—all over six feet tall—were forced to borrow trousers from a much shorter missionary and had to appear at the buffet barefoot.

We were thankful, though, that this was the only meeting in our entire trip that we had to cancel.

Nigeria and the Congo

The flight from Ghana to Lagos, Nigeria, in the middle of the night was one of the most harrowing I've ever taken. The Ghana Airlines DC–3, an old Dakota plane, had previously been owned by several other airlines, their names still visible under successive coats of paint.

An English lord in Bermuda shorts was sitting beside me on the plane; I tried to witness to him, but he was not interested in the slightest.

In mid-flight the pilot, who was European, came back to talk to the non-Africans on the plane. While he was chatting, the aircraft entered a violent thunderstorm. As he returned to the cockpit, the lightning flashed razor-bright. The plane shook, rattled, and rolled; in fact, it did everything but turn over. I didn't think the wings could possibly remain attached to the fuselage.

The Englishman grew as nervous as I, and he asked me to repeat what I had said about salvation earlier. I asked him if he would receive Christ. He said he would give it a thought.

Charlie Riggs was sitting across the aisle from me, trying to talk above the storm to a well-dressed African. But the African was yelling back; certain that we would crash in the storm, he was praying that we would not crash over water; if his body could not be found, his heirs would not inherit.

When we arrived in Lagos on January 27, Grady was already in Nigeria, holding preliminary meetings. At one place, he was told that some Europeans had been killed the night before. His Nigerian hosts had the questionable taste to put him up in the very tent one of those Europeans had died in. Grady got a big knife for himself and kept it by his side during the night. Fortunately, he spent a peaceful night (aside from his own anxiety) and did not have to face the ethics of whether he should actually use it.

We faced hostility, however, from another source. At our first Crusade meeting in Lagos, with 25,000 people present, pamphlets written in the Yoruba language were distributed without our consent to the crowd. Originating from the office of the chief Muslim missionary in West Africa, they essentially denied all biblical teachings about Jesus. We objected, and the hostile literature did not show up again. The Muslim leader attended our services, but we did not accept his challenge to a public debate. I was not there to argue; I just wanted to preach the Gospel.

With independence forthcoming in the fall of 1960, Nigeria was nervously looking forward to an uncertain future. While talking drums reverberated between the villages, television antennas were rising in the cities of Nigeria. So, as I spoke to 40,000 at the second service, I urged the need for building spiritual and moral strength in the nation.

I felt the excitement of the transition in all six Nigerian cities we visited—Lagos, Ibadan, Kontagora, Kaduna, Enugu, and Jos— especially in the 5,000 inquirers who came forward to make commitments at our meetings.

From Lagos, we traveled to Ibadan, the largest city in Nigeria, and the Nigerian headquarters for several mission agencies, including the Sudan Interior Mission. There we met the local king, an old man on a big throne surrounded by his court. He entertained us royally. While there I spoke at University College, which was built along the British design. The architect was English, and hence the buildings were designed to withstand cold weather. But we were close to the equator, the temperature nearing one hundred degrees. The auditorium was beautiful, and it easily held a thousand students, but I nearly burned to a crisp.

I gave the college audience the Gospel. Some of my listeners were disgusted with what I was saying, but others were receptive. When I asked for hands to be lifted up at the Invitation, several hundred people responded.

The day following our meetings in Ibadan, we traveled to the town of Kontagora, situated in the Muslim-dominated area of northern Nigeria. There I was privileged to say a few words and help dedicate a new hospital given by the Southern Baptist Foreign Mission Board, on which I was serving at the time; we were told there was only one fully trained doctor for every 200,000 people in that part of the country.

Our next stop was the city of Kaduna, a district capital. While there we visited a nearby village of conical mud huts whose residents were Christians. As we drove there, a missionary told us that the villagers had been threatened a few years earlier after they had constructed a tiny church. One day a gang of toughs invaded with machetes. The village leader, a Christian for only four years, boldly stopped them: "Young men, over there are our crops. You may burn them if you wish. Yonder are our homes. You may tear them down if you must." Then he opened his robe and bared his neck. "Here are our lives," he said. "You can kill us, but you cannot take our Christ from us." And the invaders fled.

When we arrived, I discovered that the villagers had constructed a "brush arbor"—a shelter made of poles and brush that would accommodate about 100 people—for our meeting. It was full, some of them having walked fifteen miles to participate. As I spoke, I knew I had gained far more from them and their dedication to Christ than I could ever give them.

Kaduna was the Muslim headquarters for Nigeria. Because it also had the major airport in that area, it was where all the planes came to refuel. The noise from the sky was continuous and often deafening during our stay there.

The sultan was considered the king of Kaduna. He was a big man in flowing white robes before whom his people knelt to conduct their business. I had a ninety-minute interview with him. He already knew all about me and what I was doing. I told him about my faith and what Christ meant to me.

"Within ten years," he said to me, "you Christians will be pushed into the sea. We are going to take over all of Africa."

"That's in God's hands," I replied.

He agreed with that.

About six months later I read in a newspaper that he was dead; an assassin had slit his throat from ear to ear.

After meetings in Kaduna and Enugu, we went to Jos. I was able to speak at a public meeting. At a large mission rest station there, we met with missionaries and others who had been in Africa for a number of years. Our hosts told us about their mission work, and I felt very humbled by their dedication.

After preaching one day in Brazzaville, Republic of Congo, we flew almost across the continent to Salisbury, Southern Rhodesia, where we changed to an old leased plane to go to Livingstone, near Victoria Falls, for a few days of rest.

"We can fly high and have a smooth flight," said the pilot, trying to be helpful, "or we can fly low and take a chance on seeing some animals."

"Fly low," said Cliff and I at the same time.

"But you probably won't see any," warned the pilot with the voice of experience.

Low it was, and extremely bumpy. Howard Jones tried to sink into the baggage, he was so nervous. But we did see several herds of water buffaloes, zebras, giraffes, and elephants, including one giant herd of two hundred. We couldn't hear them, but we could see that they were roaring and trumpeting at us.

"That was the most game I've ever seen in one day in all my years of flying this country," the pilot said when we finally landed.

Rhodesia

When we got to Livingstone, at the southern border of Northern Rhodesia, we registered at a small hotel. The next morning, I opened the window, and there on a tree sat a dozen baboons; they were so close, I could reach out and touch them. What friendly creatures, I thought, but I was admonished by our host that one should never open a window like that. The baboons could come right in, make themselves at home, and tear the room asunder.

Cliff and I wanted to see nearby Victoria Falls—on the Zambezi River at the border between Northern and Southern Rhodesia—close up. We were persuaded that the best way to do that was to take a $5 ride in a small, French, pre–World War II trimotor. The pilot took us up the Zambezi through the mist rising up from the falls, allowing us to look down through rainbows at one of the great natural wonders of the world. Then he took us down the Zambezi, flying so low that he ruffled the water. Every time he came to a hippo—both Cliff and I swore to this afterward—the pilot had to pull back a little on the stick to avoid hitting the animal. It wasn't a relaxing flight for a couple of itinerant evangelists, but in retrospect it was exciting and indeed exhilarating.

Although I was supposed to be resting during our few days there, I couldn't help but accept the local pastor's invitation in Livingstone—named after the pioneer missionary and explorer David Livingstone, who had discovered Victoria Falls—to preach one evening. And I was glad I did; the people were warm and receptive.

From Victoria Falls, we flew—in a 1931-vintage biplane—to Bulawayo, one of Southern Rhodesia's largest cities, for a multiracial meeting, said to be the largest one held in that country to date.

We held similar meetings in Salisbury (now Harare, Zimbabwe), where some of the Europeans urged us not to provide any translation into the African languages. We refused, knowing that a lack of translation would discourage black attendance, as it was intended to do. It was deeply moving to watch hundreds of blacks and whites come forward together at the Invitation. The discourtesy, disdain, and paternalistic attitudes toward the Africans by some of the white population in Rhodesia was very disturbing to me. We bent over backward to stress that God's love extended equally to all, regardless of race or background.

In Salisbury we were the houseguests of the British governor-general. Also staying with him was Commonwealth Secretary Sir Alec Douglas-Home, who later became the prime minister of Great Britain. We immediately became good friends and crossed paths a number of times in later years.

One night, listening to the BBC World Service on my portable shortwave radio, I heard the announcer say that a demonstration had broken out against Grady Wilson, who had been speaking in Kitwe, Northern Rhodesia. I was relieved to hear that Grady was fine but was concerned for the next meeting; I was due to speak there the following night.

The meetings in Kitwe were being held in a crude facility with tin sides and a tin roof. Grady showed me around and tried to prepare me for the mood I would encounter. "You'll hear the demonstrators when they're about a mile away," Grady said. "They'll start marching here just about the time you're ready to give the Invitation. When rocks start hitting the tin roof and walls, be ready to leave. We'll have a way out all organized for you."

Sure enough, that was exactly what happened. As soon as I gave the Invitation, the tin roof began to resound. We slipped out and got back to the hotel safely. But the irony was that the demonstrators had no idea who we really were. They thought we were part of a United Nations delegation there to discuss the political future of the country!

Tanganyika, Kenya

One of our briefest visits in Africa was also one of the most spectacular in terms of the setting: the town of Moshi on the slopes of Africa's tallest mountain, Mt. Kilimanjaro. As I looked over the audience of 35,000, which filled the grass field and even climbed nearby trees, I could see the majestic white-capped peak, 19,340 feet high, on one side in the distance. On the other side, only several hundred yards away, were the white spires of the local mosque, by far the most splendid building in town. My interpreter was a schoolteacher named Festo Kivengere, a personal friend who later became an outstanding Anglican bishop and one of the finest speakers and preachers in Africa.

Later, in a couple of Land Rovers and with a guide, we went through one of the game preserves. At one point, we came upon a pride of lions just finishing off a zebra carcass in the middle of the road. Our African driver said it was wiser to wait until they were finished than risk antagonizing them by interrupting their meal. We readily agreed.

We went back from Moshi to Nairobi, which was a convenient center from which we traveled to other places for meetings. We also held public meetings in Nairobi at the agricultural fairgrounds and had a ministers' meeting there arranged by the Anglican bishop of Mombasa.

Ruanda-Urundi

A harrowing experience occurred later on a flight from Kenya to Usumbura, the capital of Ruanda-Urundi. Because no scheduled air service was available for the last lap of that journey, Jerry Beavan was forced to charter an aged DC–3. It wasn't supposed to go over 12,000 feet because the cabin was unpressurized. The mountains, though, went up to 14,000 feet; as a result, we found ourselves gasping for breath. Then we ran into clouds so dense that we could barely see the wingtips. Shortly afterward, the pilot came back to tell us that both radios had gone out. He couldn't tell where we were, he said, and we didn't have enough fuel to turn back. I asked everyone to gather round for a time of prayer. We had several reporters along, from *Time,* the Associated Press, and *Life;* they gave the loudest amens as I prayed. Finally, a hole in the clouds appeared, revealing Lake Victoria below. The pilot dove through the clouds and finally got his bearings; he was then able to land without further incident.

When we taxied up to the terminal, several thousand people made a rush for the plane to welcome us, many of them wearing Watusi native dress and carrying spears. But we noticed that some of them were also waving banners and signs; once again we had been confused with another group, this time a visiting United Nations delegation led by Dag Hammarskjöld, who later became a friend of mine. I met some of the city's leadership but almost didn't get to speak at our own meeting; the local governor took almost half an hour to introduce me!

Ethiopia

Ethiopia's 20 million people were ruled by Emperor Haile Selassie, whose ancient dynasty claimed to be descended from a union between King Solomon and the Queen of Sheba. Ethiopia's Orthodox Church, which was formerly the Coptic Church, traditionally traced its lineage back to the Ethiopian eunuch who was converted to Christ during an encounter with Philip the evangelist, recorded in Acts 8.

Because the emperor was involved in every detail of Ethiopian life, it was necessary for our Team to gain his permission before any meetings could be held. We knew, though, that Protestant churches and missionaries were restricted almost exclusively to the remote rural areas. Our contacts in Addis Ababa had no access to the royal family or the higher levels of government. The year before this trip, 1959, I had sent a cable to the emperor during our Crusade in Indianapolis, but we had no way of knowing if it ever arrived or was seen by him.

Some months later, when Charlie and Jerry visited Addis Ababa on their advance-planning trip, the missionaries dispiritedly told them that the way was closed, short of a miracle. But as they prayed just before leaving, one Ethiopian pastor raised his voice and quoted from the Old Testament Book of Esther. He recalled the occasion when God had awakened the king of Persia in the middle of the night, setting in motion a series of events that ultimately saved the Jewish nation from extinction. "O God," he then prayed, "if you can awaken a king in the middle of the night, then you can get the message about this invitation to His Majesty."

Charlie and Jerry had already packed their bags. As they left to check out of the hotel, in walked a man from Scandinavia who immediately recognized Jerry and greeted him with a big hug. Torrey Mosvold had been on our Crusade committee in Oslo a few years before. After they told him their problem, he said, "Well, maybe I have come to the kingdom for such a time as this—" another quotation from the Book of Esther!

He then explained that he had business interests in Ethiopia and would that very day be having lunch with Emperor Haile Selassie's son, the crown prince. Three days later, Jerry and Charlie received a cable in Cairo, stating that not only had His Majesty granted permission for the meetings, but he was also giving our Team the use of the royal stadium. Furthermore, he planned to order all schools to be closed and all young people, including his grandchildren, to go to our meetings.

When we finally arrived in Addis Ababa, I had a high fever and a sore throat and had to be taken to the only hospital in the city— one run by the Seventh Day Adventists. My temperature soon returned to normal, and I was able to preach again.

An estimated 10,000 came to the first meeting, with almost half staying for counseling afterward. It was the greatest response of our African trip.

His Majesty also received me at his palace, which was not, I discovered, a place for the fainthearted. Scattered around the palace grounds—and greeting me as I walked in—were a number of domesticated lions. They were not on leashes, but at least they were well enough fed not to want to nibble on a visiting American evangelist.

Egypt

Our final major stop in Africa was Cairo—but first we had to get there. Our flight began innocently enough, but somewhere over the desert we encountered a terrible dust storm, with pebbles hitting the side of the plane like machine-gun bullets. It lasted only thirty-five or forty minutes; while we were in it, though, it seemed like an eternity.

In spite of the strong Islamic influence in Cairo, the government gave permission for our meeting. To meet the letter of the law, it was held on mission property owned by the United Presbyterian Church. The local organizers had constructed a fantastic tent for the meeting; measuring 150 by 175 feet, it was made of some type of crimson quilted material that looked like animal skins.

Some 10,000 people jammed the tent. People were literally sitting on top of each other, and many were standing; in fact, two ambassadors, I was told, had to stand. Many in the audience came from a Muslim background, but when the Invitation was given, about 2,000 stayed behind for half an hour's instruction in what it meant to be a Christian. Seldom have I sensed the presence of God so deeply in a meeting.

I had the opportunity of meeting a variety of dignitaries and church leaders while in Cairo. Among them was the Wahby family; they had come up from Alexandria to attend the meeting. Dr. Wahby was moderator of the Presbyterian Church in Egypt at the time. In future years, I would cross paths with him and his family again. I also will never forget standing with Cliff in the shadow of the pyramids, making our weekly *Hour of Decision* radio program.

What did we learn from our first visit to the African continent?

For one thing, I came away with an overwhelming impression that God was at work in Africa and that, with the movement for independence sweeping across the continent, conditions were ripe for an unparalleled spiritual awakening.

At the same time, I also learned firsthand that the struggle for Africa's soul was not over. I knew that Africa could be plunged into spiritual warfare as well as social chaos, with animistic and tribal ways clashing with everything from Islam to Western consumerism.

I was fascinated also by the amazing diversity and pride among the people I met, whether in urban boardrooms or jungle clearings or village bazaars. At the same time, I was deeply concerned about some of the attitudes I had seen among both whites and blacks. In addition, I was troubled by the failure of many of the colonial powers to train the African people in skills of leadership and practical business.

A further result of the trip was a deeper awareness of the hurt and pain that America's racial problems were causing all across Africa. Many African Christians, on learning about racial segregation in American churches, were confused. They could not see American Christianity as the model for the oneness of the Body of Christ. How could they think otherwise when they heard that a person of color was barred from entering certain churches in the United States?

I came away more determined than ever to do what I could as an evangelist to combat the grim legacy of racism in my own country. Almost the first thing I did upon returning home was to endorse the formation of a new biracial committee of one hundred citizens in my native Charlotte to grapple with racial reconciliation; that city was in the midst of a series of demonstrations and lunch-counter sit-ins.

I was also struck by the fact that all the missionaries I encountered were white. I greatly admired them, but I kept asking myself, Where are the missionaries from our great black denominations in the United States?

At the same time, I left Africa with a prayer of deep gratitude for the faith and sacrifice of those who had gone before us, bringing the light of the Gospel to the world's largest continent. We were only following a trail others had blazed.

Thinking about those trailblazers reminded me again of the prophetic words of David Livingstone, the Scottish missionary to the heart of Africa, which I had read to our Team just before leaving New York: "Future missionaries will see conversions following every sermon. We prepare the way for them. May they not forget the pioneers who worked in the thick gloom with few rays to cheer except such as flow from faith in God's promise. We work for a glorious future which we are not destined to see."

I will never forget meeting with 25 missionaries crowded into a small room during a brief refueling stop in Asmara, Eritrea, near the close of our trip in Africa. They listened eagerly as Joe Blinco and I told of what we had seen God do during the last few weeks. Then I asked each of them to tell us about their work. I sensed that most of them were somewhat embarrassed, for we had just been talking about the large crowds and the unexpected response we had seen almost everywhere. But one by one they quietly told of their work. Some of them had been laboring for years, with almost nothing in the way of tangible results. And yet they each had a deep sense that this was where God had called them; and that was all they needed to know. Tears welled up in our eyes as we prayed with them in the attitude of 1 Corinthians 3: "Neither he who plants nor he who waters is anything, but only God, who makes things grow. . . . We are God's fellow workers. . . ."

Africa has changed greatly since our 1960 visit, and parts of it are hardly recognizable from those days. Since then our Team has returned on several occasions. Ruth and I are thrilled that our older son, Franklin, has also become deeply involved in Africa, largely through the organization he heads, Samaritan's Purse. As I note elsewhere in these pages, Samaritan's Purse is committed to giving emergency aid in the name of Christ to those who face some kind of disaster, usually working alongside local churches or mission organizations. From famine relief in Ethiopia and Mozambique to medical care in war-torn Rwanda, Franklin has carried on much of my own vision for Africa and its people.

JORDAN AND ISRAEL

From Egypt we flew to Jordan for an eight-day trip to that Middle Eastern kingdom and Israel. A false rumor the year before—an allegation that I had raised funds in America for the support of Israel—seemingly had barred the door to Jordan. By the time we got there, however, Roy Gustafson, something of a Middle East expert whom I had sent on ahead several weeks before, had arranged everything.

In Amman I was received by King Hussein, who was quite young. The next day, the main Jordanian newspaper carried a picture of the two of us on the front page, which erased any lingering suspicions about the rumor. The king invited me to stay in his palace, but because of our schedule I could not.

I was surprised to be told that 15 percent of the population of Jordan was non-Arab. I also visited historic cities.

When we crossed over the Allenby Bridge separating Jordan and Israel, there were two hundred reporters and photographers awaiting me. A deputy official from the Israeli foreign office intercepted me, welcoming me nervously. He said that the foreign minister, Mrs. Golda Meir, wanted to see me immediately—before I talked to the press. I agreed, but I hated to leave the reporters more or less standing outside wondering what was happening as I was whisked away to her home.

I found Mrs. Meir to be one of the most knowledgeable and delightful people I have ever met. Hopeful (I suspect) that I would have a fuller understanding of their views before meeting with the press, she and her associates briefed me on the situation in Israel.

For all the goodwill, though, a great controversy arose over our planned use of an auditorium in Tel Aviv. The *Jerusalem Post* had asked, before our arrival, "Why is Billy Graham coming here to proselytize?" Concerned about it in the middle of the night at the King David Hotel in Jerusalem, I asked Grady to wake Roy up and bring him to my room. I was very worried about the press conference scheduled for the next day, and I wanted to get my ducks in a row. We discussed the auditorium controversy and prayed about it.

Just prior to our visit, cables addressing the auditorium issue had been exchanged between Prime Minister David Ben-Gurion (who was in America to receive an honorary doctorate from Brandeis University and to hold crucial conversations with the U.S. State Department) and the local officials who were dealing with our Team. I was not aware until later of all the stipulations that were being imposed by Israeli authorities on my planned preaching in Tel Aviv—for example, that Christian meetings must be held on property owned by a Christian group. Cliff and the sponsoring committee declined these stipulations but were able to arrange for the meeting to be held in an Arab Christian church in nearby Haifa, much to everyone's relief. The church normally seated about 600, but 1,200 crowded in and others listened over a loudspeaker in the garden. We also held a meeting in the YMCA auditorium in Jerusalem, and I had a cordial discussion with the chief rabbi of Jerusalem as well.

The next morning—still in Jerusalem—thirty minutes before the press conference, Cliff, Jerry, and I met with a representative of Israel's State Department. We sat around a table, drinking tea. He was nervous about the possible embarrassment his country would suffer if I were to say, in answer to a question, that I had been denied the use of the Tel Aviv stadium. I assured him I did not take their refusal as a personal insult.

That press conference, which was held in the King David Hotel, was by far the largest of our entire trip. I told the reporters in attendance that I had an opening statement. In it, I gave four reasons why I had come to Israel:

- First, to see, as every tourist did, the places that were sacred to Christians, Muslims, and Jews.

- Second, to report to the 50,000 Christians in Israel what was happening in the church in other parts of the world, since they had been praying for our meetings in Africa and elsewhere.

- Third, to preach God's Word to the whole world. This was just one more historic and strategic region I had wanted to visit in fulfillment of that commission.

- Fourth, to say thank you to the people of Israel. I told the gathered press, "I want to thank you for proselytizing me, a Gentile, who has committed his life to a Jew who was born in this country and reared up here in Nazareth. I want to thank you for being the nation through whom Jesus was brought to this earth in the divine plan of God. And I want to thank you as one who has given my life to a Jew who, as a man living upon this earth, claimed to be God." That, I said, was the message of hope we had been sharing around the world.

There was a fifth reason too, though I don't think I shared it at the press conference. I have always believed that the Jews were God's special people, chosen to preserve the Hebrew Scriptures through the centuries and to prepare the way for the coming of Jesus.

When I finished my statement, there was a long silence among the reporters.

The headline in the next edition of the *Jerusalem Post* was something like "BILLY GRAHAM THANKS ISRAEL FOR PROSELYTIZING HIM."

As for the meeting itself, I preached Christ as Savior and Lord, but I also honored the official request not to give a public Invitation for the Gospel. Instead, I concluded the sermons this way: "We're going to dismiss the meeting now. For those of you who want to talk privately about what it means to be a Christian, we'll be back in ten minutes; and we'd be happy to talk with you."

When the meetings turned from public to private in this way, the protocol was preserved. Several hundred were present at each after-meeting. Many of these took their stand for Christ then, in spite of what it might cost them personally, socially, and even economically.

Jesus and Paul were also respectful of civil authority. Neither of them forced a confrontation with the Roman government on religious grounds, godless and decadent as it was, nor is that my calling as an evangelist.

Behind us when we left for home at the end of March, the scheduled "safari for souls" in Africa and our visit in the Middle East had stretched to include meetings in twenty-five cities and seventy-five villages in over a dozen countries. We had averaged a plane flight every two and a half days for ten weeks. Thankfully, we had few problems with sickness. In many places during that Crusade, we stayed in missionary homes, which were better than hotels. Our hosts gave us their best, which we were grateful for although it was often very modest. Local leaders came to dinner with us, bringing their food with them; we were often not quite sure what we were eating, but we ate it with thanksgiving nonetheless.

Less than three months after returning home, we opened our National Capital Crusade in Washington, D.C. Against the backdrop of the recent African and Middle Eastern experience, I preached in the inner courtyard of the Pentagon to 7,000 civilian workers and military personnel. My message? It was the same I had preached all across Africa and in the Middle East: following Christ was the only way to lasting peace.

19

Into All the World

A couple of years before our African trip, following the 1957 New York meetings, we held major Crusades—often lasting two to four weeks apiece—in a number of U.S. cities: San Francisco, Sacramento, Charlotte, Indianapolis, Washington, Minneapolis, Philadelphia, and all across the state of Florida. We also returned to Europe for meetings and rallies in Switzerland, Germany, England, and Northern Ireland. The schedule included dozens of other engagements as well—everything from speaking at a high school in a small town near our home in North Carolina to the annual Christmas services at West Point and Annapolis.

Now it was time for us to turn our full attention southward, but we had to move with great caution. Why?

First, in almost every country of Latin America, Protestants were a tiny minority. For example, when we preached in Quito, Ecuador, Protestants numbered less than 2,000 out of a population of 280,000.

Second, relations between Roman Catholics and Protestants had seldom been cordial in that part of the world; in some places, particularly in rural areas, there had been occasional discrimination, even violence.

Today it may be hard to recall the sharp divisions and contro-versies that sometimes marked Protestant-Catholic relations back then—even during John F. Kennedy's presidential campaign in 1960—but they were real; and in no place were they stronger than in Latin America. The Second Vatican Council, with its acceptance of Christians from other traditions as "separated brethren," had not yet been held. (Its first session opened in October 1962, just as we were concluding our final Latin American meetings.)

Nor was the fault always on the Catholic side, I knew. Often Latin American Protestants were guilty of intolerance, negative preaching, and inflammatory language. I had no intention of adding fuel to the fire. In fact, whenever possible during our trip south (as well as on other tours), I tried to meet with local Catholic leaders, to the occasional consternation of some of our hosts.

My goal, I always made clear, was not to preach against Catholic beliefs or to proselytize people who were already commit-ted to Christ within the Catholic Church. Rather, it was to proclaim the Gospel to all those who had never truly committed their lives to Christ. Large numbers of people in Latin America, I knew, were only nominal believers.

A third reason we needed to proceed with caution had to do with the political instability in many countries. Because most of the governments were not democratic, we knew it would be difficult to gain permission for large public gatherings.

But Ken Strachan, who lived in Costa Rica (and whose wife, Elizabeth, was one of Ruth's closest friends), was constantly urging me to go. He was the most respected Protestant leader in Latin Amer-ica, as was his father before him, who had founded the Latin America Mission. Ken held the same view I did: that there needed to be a coming together in some way and some form between Catholics and Protestants. He worked toward that end, much to the displeasure of some of his colleagues in the Latin America Mission.

Ken was a thoroughgoing evangelical and had a terrific net-work. He worked through all the Protestant organizations (and as many Catholic organizations as he could) throughout Latin Amer-ica. He was so highly respected that when people got a letter from him about our coming, they paid attention.

THE CARIBBEAN

Partly in response to all those invitations, we toured a number of the Caribbean countries in 1958. The crowds everywhere, I was pleased to discover, were overwhelming. And there was a good reason for that: many people on the islands had been listening to me for years over the radio. Our program came on at six in the morning (before they went to work) and at six in the evening (after they had returned home). They might not have recognized my face, but they knew my voice.

Our largest audience was in Barbados. Grady had started the Crusade there, along with singer Ethel Waters. Ethel was making a deep impression on the local population with her call for love and harmony between the white and black races.

Someone had arranged for me to stay without charge at a posh club, the St. James; but when I realized that the local population was not too kindly disposed toward the tourist hotels and resented the displays of wealth and moral laxness among the tourists, I decided to stay instead in a small, unpretentious hotel.

Before I could sign in, however, the British governor-general invited me to be his guest at the official residence. Although I accepted with genuine gratitude, it was an old place, and not very comfortable. As we drove past the Hilton Hotel on our way to the meetings, I admit I looked at it with longing eyes.

The governor-general, Sir Robert Arundell, we were given to understand, was not too enthusiastic about our visit to Barbados, but he went to each meeting. Apparently, from his friends and contacts in London, he had heard a few good words about us.

I was scheduled to preach at the closing service. That evening he drove me to the meeting place in his Rolls-Royce, one of five cars in our party. The crowd was dense, and the streets were narrow. If it hadn't been for the police escort—a little truck that boasted a bell instead of a siren—we would never have gotten there.

The crowd pressed upon us, clapping and shouting. As we arrived at the back of the platform the pianos began to play "God Save the Queen." We stood at attention through the last note and then were escorted by the chief of police to our seats.

The crowd stretched as far as the eye could see. Jerry Beavan put attendance at 60,000; the police estimated 75,000. Lady Arundell felt that half the island—or 100,000 people—had come. It was one of our largest crowds to date. Two thousand cars were parked at the edges of the crowd, and their passengers remained inside; but the amplification system was one of the best we had ever used, and they could hear every word through their open car windows. In that huge crowd, we could sense the presence and power of the Holy Spirit.

As we left the meeting, the governor-general got a rude shock. Surrounded by people, our car was rocked back and forth. He called for the police, who finally got the crowd away from the car and gave us an escort back to the official residence. I tried to reassure him, explaining that the people were just happy—they were waving and shouting, "God bless you!"—but he thought they were drunk.

We visited most of the Caribbean islands during that trip. In addition, we held rallies of a day or two's length in cities in Venezuela, Panama, Costa Rica, Guatemala, and Mexico. It was an exhausting time, so when Jerry—at a brief break in the schedule—told us he had made reservations for us to relax at a nice, quiet hotel on one of the islands, we were delighted. But instead of a pleasant time of relaxation, we had exactly the reverse. The spartan hotel had no beach. The food was bad. We had to boil our drinking water. From that moment on, with tongue in cheek, we thanked Jerry at every opportunity for his thoughtfulness and hospitality!

Shortly after taking off from the island's grass runway for the brief trip to Trinidad, one of our little plane's two engines began to sputter, but we made it safely to our destination. On landing, we went directly to the Pan American Airlines guest house for a night's rest before leaving early the next morning for Panama.

Oddly enough, a year and a half later, in mid-1960, a similar thing happened on our flight to Rio de Janeiro to attend the Baptist World Alliance. We were flying from Puerto Rico with a stop scheduled in Belém, Brazil, where the plane would refuel. The trouble began late at night. We had sleepers, and I was up in my bunk resting. Stephen Olford and Grady were also in theirs; Martin Luther King, Jr., was with us and was sitting up reading. One of the

DC–7's motors caught fire, and the captain announced that we would be making an emergency landing in Trinidad. While the other passengers milled about waiting for instructions, I knew exactly what to do: "Let's get a taxi and go straight to the Pan American guest house we stayed in before," I suggested. It was good to have a familiar haven at one or two in the morning.

We had boarded that plane for Rio de Janeiro, as I said, in Puerto Rico, where we all had stopped for a couple of days' rest before the conference. We had stayed at the Hilton Hotel there and done a lot of swimming and praying together. I had known Martin Luther King, Jr., for several years. His father, who was called Big Mike, called him Little Mike. He asked me to call him just plain Mike.

When we got to Rio, I gave the closing address for the Baptist World Alliance in the Maracanã Stadium; it is one of the largest in the world, with a capacity of 200,000 people, including standees. While in Rio, I gave a dinner at the Copacabana Hotel, which—though I didn't realize it then—was owned by my father-in-law's brother, who had built a business empire down there. The dinner was in honor of Mike, and I invited Southern Baptist leaders from the United States to come. I wanted to build a bridge between blacks and whites in our own South, and this seemed like a good opportunity to move toward that goal. Our Texas businessman friend Howard Butt joined us for dinner. When the meal was over and we had made all our speeches, I said a final word: "I'd like to thank our host, Howard Butt, for this marvelous—and expensive—dinner." That was the first time Howard had heard he was the host!

During our brief stay in Rio, some Mississippi Baptists came up to Grady to welcome him. As they were talking, Mike came by and slapped Grady on the shoulder and greeted him warmly. Our friendly relationship with Mike made the point with my Baptist friends.

SOUTH AMERICA

In 1959, the year before we accepted the invitation to go to South America for meetings in 1962, a band of Communist revolutionaries under Fidel Castro and Che Guevara came to power in Cuba. Two years later, the United States severed diplomatic relations with

360

Castro, setting the stage for his close economic and military alliance with the Soviet Union. Cuba soon embarked on an aggressive program to export Castro's revolutionary (and antichurch) ideas to other Latin American countries. The abortive Bay of Pigs invasion (1961) and the Cuban missile crisis (1962) not only focused the United States' attention on its neighbors to the south but also sent shock waves through almost every Latin American government.

Back to 1960. In that year, we received a formal appeal urging us to come to South America as soon as possible: "The rapid social and political changes which [South America] is undergoing," a group of leading pastors from several countries wrote to me, "demonstrate convincingly that we ought to take advantage of the present hour. We cannot overlook the devastating inroads which foreign political ideologies are making."

Shortly afterward, we accepted invitations to make two extended trips to South America during 1962—the first in January and February, the second in September and October. Although my goals were not political, I could not ignore the possibility that the changing political situation might soon end any opportunities for open evangelism in these countries.

The first tour lasted slightly over a month. Bill Brown and Charlie Riggs went before us to make arrangements and to teach counselor-training classes. Working with them was Charles Ward, a very knowledgeable and seasoned missionary living in Quito, Ecuador. Chuck worked in evangelism with The Evangelical Alliance Mission (TEAM) and later joined our staff and represented us for many years throughout the Spanish-speaking world (along with Norm Mydske, an energetic and able man who also worked with TEAM for many years and later became our director of Latin American ministries).

As we had done in Africa, we utilized several of our associate evangelists—including Grady, Joe Blinco, Leighton Ford, and Roy Gustafson—to begin the Crusades in the main cities. We had a full musical team with us, including Cliff Barrows, Tedd Smith, and Ray Robles, a baritone soloist who was known in much of Latin America.

Russ Busby also came along to document the trip photographically. This was his first international trip since joining our Team. Formerly a portrait photographer by trade, he had also done some

361

work with The Navigators. At one stage in his long career with us, President Johnson tried to lure him away to become the official White House photographer. Russ declined, saying he felt God had called him to our ministry.

Venezuela

We began the South American tour on January 20 and 21 in Caracas, a modern and beautiful city that reminded me in some ways of San Francisco; it was pleasantly cool at an altitude of three thousand feet. Two meetings were held in the large Nuevo Circo Bull Ring. The first night, I came through the entrance that the matador traditionally used; the next night, I came out where the bull always entered the ring. The crowd applauded both times.

Like most Latin Americans, the Venezuelans were spontaneous and effervescent. Those first nights, though, during the preliminaries, it distracted me to see them talking and moving around. But when I stood up to preach from the Bible, they became quiet and attentive, something I could explain only as the work of the Holy Spirit in answer to prayer. Veteran missionaries expressed gratitude for the 18,000 people who came those two nights; hundreds of inquirers went forward, exceeding our expectations for the Crusade. We found the political situation very tense, however: there were riots in several areas of the country during our stay. The day we left Caracas, sixteen people were killed by gunfire in broad daylight, and the U.S. Embassy was bombed. An hour after our car left the city for the airport, the police banned all automobile traffic.

We flew from Caracas to Maracaibo for two nights of meetings. The Maracaibo Basin, we were told, was the third-largest oil-producing area in the world, and the source of much of Venezuela's wealth. Our friend J. Howard Pew, president of Sun Oil in Philadelphia, arranged for one of his company's boats to take us on a tour of Lake Maracaibo, where thousands of wells were located—a forest of oil derricks rising out of the water. I had never seen anything like it before. In Maracaibo proper, we found the political situation very volatile, although the tension did not seem to affect attendance at the public meetings. Eleven radio stations carried the message to the whole country.

My first day in Maracaibo, I was invited to address the state legislature. When we drove up to the legislative building, we could see that a crowd had gathered for some kind of demonstration, apparently against the government. Half of the legislators did not show up; they were too afraid to come, I was told. The only ones who did come were the left-wingers and the Communists.

I was also invited to a smaller midday meeting, as I recall, in another building nearby. The man who invited me seemed to be a Christian leader, so I agreed to go on condition I could preach the Gospel. When we arrived at the meeting, we could see that everything was very secretive, although—since none of us knew Spanish—we couldn't tell what the people were talking about.

I was introduced to the perhaps 50 people in attendance by a man who had two pearl-handled pistols tucked into his belt. He reminded me of characters in the old cowboy movies Ruth and I enjoyed watching occasionally on television.

When I got up to speak, I could see soldiers out front unloading guns from trucks. Not long into my remarks, a rock smashed through a window, followed by a bullet or two. We ducked under the table. *Newsweek* said I was praying the Lord's Prayer; I don't remember what I was praying, but the man who introduced me said we had better get out. Our escort told us we would have to stay in a back room for a time, however; he needed to size things up for himself. On our way down the narrow hall, three young girls ran toward us. "*Yanqui no! Castro si!*" they yelled as we passed each other.

While waiting in the back room with the lights out, I made a suggestion to Russ: "Why don't you go out and get some pictures of what's happening? They might be some of the best pictures of your life."

"No, thank you," he said firmly. "They might be the *last* pictures of my life!"

At last our escort reappeared and told us we would have to sneak out through a side door into an alley. Although we had no way of knowing if it was a trap, we followed him anyway. He had one last thing to say: "If anyone starts shooting at you, just stop. Don't move: they're very poor shots, and if you start moving, they might hit you!"

No one was in the alley when we emerged, and moments later our car came around the corner to get us. Five minutes after we left, we heard later, the demonstration outside turned more violent; windows were broken in, doors were knocked down, the place was peppered with bullets, and at least one man was wounded. We never were sure exactly what the demonstration was all about. That evening we drove back over there to see what it looked like after the shooting. It was as quiet as it could be.

Colombia

Our next stop took us to Barranquilla, Colombia. We heard, shortly before our arrival, that the mayor had canceled our permission to use the municipal baseball stadium; but the local committee hurriedly obtained the grounds of a local Presbyterian school. The mayor's ruling caused such an uproar in the community over the issue of religious freedom that many people who might not otherwise have heard of the event came out of curiosity, and it turned out to be among our largest meetings in the northern part of South America.

When we arrived in Bogotá, we were greeted by a police escort and a limousine that saw us safely to the hotel.

While I was in Bogotá, a former president of Colombia told me that although most Colombians identified themselves with the Catholic Church, only a small percentage actually practiced their faith. Some years later, during a visit we made to the Vatican, a number of church officials expressed the same concern to me about Catholics whose commitment to Christ was only nominal; one of them told me it was the greatest challenge facing the Roman Catholic Church today.

From Bogotá we flew to Cali. Lee Fisher, Cliff Barrows, and I were together on the plane. Among our fellow passengers were two Colombian students from Yale who were going home for the holidays—one behind us, the other in the front. They began to throw things at each other. At first I didn't mind—though I was getting hit on the side of the head with magazines, the exchange seemed fairly friendly—but things got out of hand when they began to yell and get unruly.

The co-pilot came back and talked to them, but rather than toning things down, they talked back to him. A very strong man, the co-pilot hauled them up front and handcuffed them to a seat. He and the pilot then turned the plane around and headed back to Bogotá, where the police took the troublemakers off the plane.

One of the most important people on the South American trip was my interpreter, Dr. José Fajardo. A member of the Cumberland Presbyterian denomination, he was brought by the BGEA to the United States to study; he was an excellent interpreter and a real man of God. I did not know the importance of Cali in José's mind at that time, but it was his hometown, and he was anxious that the meetings be successful.

And they were: we spoke in the soccer stadium to crowds that seemed eager to hear the Gospel. On closing night, after the meeting was concluded, guerrillas came down from the mountains and killed fourteen people not far from where we were staying. We had been warned that we were in a dangerous situation; now it was clear that we were.

A girl I had dated at Wheaton came to see us in Cali. For decades she and her husband had been doing pioneer missionary work at a spot some hundred miles from Cali. She was crippled now and in a wheelchair.

I encountered many other acquaintances on that trip. Wherever I went, throughout Latin America, I met missionaries I had known in other times and places—Youth for Christ, Wheaton, Northwestern Schools, my days on the Southern Baptist Foreign Mission Board—and those encounters gave me a whole new appreciation of what the missionaries were doing (and what they were up against).

Ecuador

In Quito, Chuck Ward and his wife, Margaret, had us over to their house for a memorable evening of fellowship. Among their guests were three of the widows of the missionaries who had been killed five years before by the Auca Indians in the Ecuadorian jungle; several of those missionaries were graduates of Wheaton College. Few events in recent years had attracted so much coverage in both the secular and religious press. The story of their martyrdom for Christ had challenged hundreds of young men and women to give their lives to missionary service.

In Quito, which was ten thousand feet above sea level, I had trouble preaching; because there was less oxygen in the air, I felt a bit breathless even when talking in normal conversation. For our next meeting, we descended to sea level in Guayaquil. That meeting was larger than our first assembly in Ecuador—and a great relief to my lungs.

Peru and Chile

Further meetings in Lima, Peru, and Santiago, Chile, brought us down the western side of South America. Elections in Peru were only a few months away at the time of our visit. Already we could sense tension in the air as conflicting parties demonstrated.

In Lima we were once again in a large bull ring. It turned out to be a good venue, accommodating the large crowds who attended. Seldom had I seen a greater contrast among people in one meeting: wealthy businesspeople sat side by side with impoverished Indian peasants as they all listened to the Gospel of Christ.

Dan Piatt was with us in Peru, and he and I had a chance to play golf one afternoon. It was a very cloudy day, so we both took off our shirts. I was already suntanned from the rest of the trip, but Dan was white as snow. He got so sunburned that he became sick and could not come to the meeting that night.

Between Lima and Santiago, there was only one jet flight a week, a Boeing jet, offered by Air France. As we took off, I was a little nervous about all the surrounding mountains.

The pilot broke in soon after takeoff to say, "They want us to fly over the city of Antofagasta as a salute." He explained that Antofagasta was celebrating some kind of anniversary. With that bit of warning he made a steep dive over the city, flying very low. I did not think he could pull up without tearing the wings off, but he did, just trimming the treetops—or so it seemed. And then he did it two more times!

When we arrived in Santiago for the final meetings of our trip, scheduled for February 16 and 17, I was struck by how similar the city seemed to European cities; it reminded me a great deal of Geneva, in particular. Our activities in Santiago included a colorful, mile-long parade of some 8,000 evangelical Christians. The procession wound enthusiastically through the streets to the grounds of Parque Cousino, where the meetings were held.

John Bolten was there with us; he owned a lot of property in Chile. He took us out to a magnificent golf course, where we enjoyed a bit of relaxation.

From Santiago we flew across the Andes to Buenos Aires, in order to make our airline connection for the long flight home. We found ourselves on an Argentine airliner; it was a Comet, the last of a fleet of five, I was told.

"What happened to the other four?" I asked an airline employee.

"They crashed in service," he answered.

Because the Argentine pilots seemed to be having some difficulty with this type of aircraft, the French manufacturer had sent an experienced pilot to sit in the cockpit during flights. This seemed only moderately reassuring, given the fate of the other planes in the original fleet.

I was sitting in the aisle seat of the front passenger row, which had three seats on each side of the aisle. To my immediate left, in the middle seat on my side of the aisle, was a heavyset woman; we were jammed against each other.

The door between the passenger section and the cockpit was open, and I could see what was going on up front. As we went down the runway, the Argentine crew was apparently a little slow reacting. Just before it was too late, the French pilot hurriedly leaned over and pulled back on the stick, sending us into the sky. I will always remember the Andes as the most beautiful mountains in the world.

Cumulative attendance during this Latin American trip totaled quarter of a million people, with 9,000 inquirers. Measured against the standards set by Crusades in certain other parts of the world, that outcome was not large. However, as I noted at that time on *The Hour of Decision,* "I have never seen such spiritual hunger in all of our travels around the world. . . . We learned once again that spiritual hunger is no respecter of persons. It exists among the rich as well as the poor, and the truth of the Gospel appeals to men universally."

I was grateful for the statement one U.S. Catholic newspaper made as it reviewed our first South American trip: "Never once, at least in our memory, has [Billy Graham] attacked the Catholic Church. . . . In view of past history [in South America], where violence has so often prevailed, it is well to remember that the slightest disturbance could easily make tempers flare again. Billy Graham seems to sense this."

Beyond doubt, God was at work in South America, and we now looked forward eagerly to the second South American trip, scheduled for later in the year, following Crusades in Chicago and Fresno.

CHICAGO

Sandwiched between our two trips to South America in 1962 was the significant Crusade in Chicago, held in the new McCormick Place arena. In some ways, the Chicago Crusade was just as pivotal for our ministry as the New York Crusade of 1957 had been.

On the one hand, Chicago was seen as the center of evangelical strength in America, what with the presence of Moody Bible Institute, Wheaton College (where just a few years earlier we held a memorable areawide Crusade at Centennial Field), and many other evangelical institutions. Of course, I myself had strong ties in the Chicago area, dating back to my days at Wheaton as a student, in Western Springs as a pastor, and all over the whole area as a representative of Youth for Christ. On the other hand, Chicago was also a center of social and theological liberalism, represented by the University of Chicago, Northwestern University, *The Christian Century*, and several major liberal seminaries.

Under these conditions, a broad-based invitation from the Windy City for a Crusade was difficult to secure, and for a number of good reasons.

First, most of the mainline churches in Chicago were liberal (and therefore refused to support us); one of the few exceptions was Fourth Presbyterian Church, one of the largest in Chicago.

Second, the city was a major Roman Catholic center; in those pre-Vatican II days, we had little open support from the Roman Catholic community, although a number of Catholics (including some priests) attended the meetings.

Third, the media were not particularly open to us; the religion editor at the main newspaper, the *Chicago Tribune*, was a graduate of a major liberal seminary, and he ignored us for the most part.

Fourth, we were unable to buy television time in the Chicago area in spite of the fact that Walter Bennett, the advertising executive who arranged all of our television schedules, had his offices there.

Our chairman of the 1962 Crusade was Herbert J. Taylor, chairman of Club Aluminum and one of the godliest gentlemen I have ever known. Every morning before he went to his office, he recited the Sermon on the Mount. An active Rotarian (and the international president of Rotary Clubs in 1954–55), it was he who devised the Rotarian four-way test [of things we think, say, or do]—a formulation that has since become famous. Unfortunately for us, Taylor was not able to bring a wide spectrum of support from the business community to the Crusade; while business support in New York had been massive, support in Chicago was weak.

All the evangelical churches and organizations in Chicago, however, came to our support. Night after night McCormick Place was filled to capacity. Three-quarters of a million people attended over a three-week period, with some 16,500 decisions for Christ. In addition, I squeezed in a visit to the recruits at the Great Lakes Naval Training Station.

The final rally, jammed with more than 100,000 people, was held in Soldier Field on one of the hottest days I have ever experienced. The temperature was well over one hundred degrees. Though I did preach, I had to cut my sermon short because of the heat. That decision had a consequence I had not foreseen. We were recording the meeting for later release on national television, but by shortening my message, I left a hole in the hour-long program. As a result, I had to return that night to the stadium, now empty and dark (and not that much cooler!) to speak off the cuff for seven minutes. What appeared to be a technological disaster, though, actually turned out to be a dramatic close to the program; the response was one of the highest we have ever received from a television broadcast.

We would return to Chicago for other Crusades and events in future years. One night in 1971, for example, inside the mammoth McCormick Place, Mayor Richard J. Daley welcomed us to the city and then remained with us on the platform for the service. In the audience were some 30,000 young people.

After Bev had sung the second hymn of the evening, while Cliff was leading the massed choir in a great anthem of praise, a police officer rushed on stage and whispered in the mayor's ear, "They're coming!"

Earlier in the day, some Satan worshipers had let it be known that they were coming to the meeting with the intention of storming the platform and stopping the proceedings. Sure enough, here they were. They burst past the ushers and hurried down the aisles, all the while chanting something of their own.

"Don't worry about a thing, Dr. Graham," the mayor said. "My police will handle it."

We had never called the police before to handle a meeting disturbance, and I didn't want this to be the first time. "Mr. Mayor, let me try it another way," I urged.

I went to the microphone and interrupted the choir's song. "There are three hundred, or four hundred, Satan worshipers here tonight," I announced. "They've said that they're going to take over the platform. Now I'm going to ask you Christian young people to do something. Don't hurt them. Just surround them and love them and sing to them and, if you can, just gradually move them toward the doors."

Thankfully, to our great relief, that's just what happened. Hundreds of the Christian young people, pointing their fingers up, which is the Christian One Way sign, began to surround them, singing and shouting, "Jesus loves you!" and "God is love!"

"My," said the mayor, "I ought to have you in all these riots we're having around here!"

As one newspaper the following morning put it, "The hell raisers were routed by Jesus' power."

The success of that Crusade resulted in a renewed flood of invitations to Los Angeles in 1963, San Diego in 1964, and Seattle in 1965. It also encouraged committees in other midwestern cities to extend invitations to us; Columbus and Omaha in 1964 and Kansas

City in 1967. Chicago also convinced us that the meetings in New York in 1957 were not a fluke and that America's largest cities were open to evangelism in an unprecedented way. Invitations came to us all the time, and one of the biggest loads I had to carry during that period was where to go next.

SOUTH AMERICA

The second Latin American tour took place in the fall of 1962. Once again our associate evangelists began Crusades in most cities before we arrived for the closing sessions.

Brazil

We opened on September 25 with a six-day Crusade in São Paulo, Brazil. The city—named, I could not help but recall, after Christianity's greatest evangelist, the Apostle Paul—had some 350 Protestant churches giving support to the Crusade. The closing meeting, with a 200-piece orchestra accompanied by a 1,000-voice choir, drew 65,000 to the city's main stadium.

I have always remembered the São Paulo meetings for another, more personal reason. Less than a month before, on August 28, my father had passed away, and this was my first public ministry since his death. He had suffered declining health for several years due to a series of strokes. His death was not unexpected, and yet I felt his absence very keenly even a hemisphere away from home.

My father was always so proud of me. In his last days, he sat in the S&W Cafeteria near their home in Charlotte and greeted people. The owner, Mr. Sherrill, considered my father something of an attraction. He was glad for him to sit there for a couple of hours; people knew him and would come in to say hello. There was something about this picture that appealed to me, probably because I felt that my father was a man of love.

My mother cared for him during his declining years, but Melvin, Catherine, and Jean, all of whom lived in Charlotte, also took major responsibility for his care.

When he died, the *New York Times* printed an obituary with a photograph of that humble and loving man, and to this day I thank God for all he meant to me.

371

Paraguay and Argentina

The São Paulo meetings were followed by a series of one- or two-day meetings in Asunción, Paraguay; Córdoba and Rosario, Argentina; and Montevideo, Uruguay. In each city, Chuck Ward arranged for a welcoming rally at the airport; this was meant to create public interest in the meetings and to unite the local believers who were supporting the effort.

At one place, I recall, our plane was three and a half hours late taking off. I was certain that everyone at the other end would give up and leave before we arrived. Instead, an enthusiastic crowd of 2,000 people greeted us. I expressed surprise to one leader, but he just shrugged. "Oh, you know how relaxed we Latins are about time," he said. "If you'd shown up when you were scheduled to arrive, hardly anyone would have been here!"

The flight had been a rough one, stormy all the way over jungles, mountains, and wild country. The aircraft we were in—it was an old British Viscount turboprop, as I recall—was not all that sturdy. Again, to be honest, I was nervous! It didn't help that the pilot announced, as we were circling for a final approach to the runway, "If you look to your left, you'll see the British Comet plane that crashed last week."

Paraguay's longtime president, General Alfredo Stroessner, received me. I was criticized later by some back in the United States for trying to be diplomatic in my comments about him instead of condemning him outright for his alleged human rights abuses; however, I knew that those matters were already being raised by our ambassador, William P. Snow, with whom I also met. I took the opportunity to share my faith in Christ with Stroessner. He assured us of his support for the meetings. He had, we understood, a German Lutheran background, although I had no reason to believe he was a practicing Christian.

Unfortunately, however, there was strong opposition from other sources in Paraguay. These opponents clearly had considerable influence, even trying to force the local press to boycott us. In fact, the only person who showed up for our scheduled press conference was a radio technician who came to run a tape recorder; not a single reporter was there. The technician turned his tape recorder on, however, and I answered questions about the Crusade posed by members of the local committee. Two radio stations carried the interview later, we heard.

Furthermore, we learned that those opposing the Crusade were organizing a massive counterdemonstration just a few blocks from the outdoor soccer stadium where our meetings were being held. That demonstration, designed for popular appeal—with everything from a parade of 15,000 students in the afternoon to a gigantic free music and folk-dancing festival—was scheduled to start at 7:00 P.M., half an hour before our closing rally was due to begin. Needless to say, this caused a great deal of consternation among the supporters of the Crusade. They redoubled their prayers.

Lee, Grady, and I, who were rooming together in a hotel, had a lot of prayer about the meeting that night. Suddenly, without warning, a storm came up just out of nowhere. It was so fierce that it broke the glass doors in our hotel room, sending shattered pieces all over our room and forcing the three of us into the farthest corner to ride out the vicious winds.

That morning Russ Busby and Dick Lederhaus of World Wide Pictures had flown two hundred miles east to photograph Iguaçú Falls, one of South America's great natural wonders. With the storm approaching, their pilot refused to take off for the return flight.

The local Crusade committee had already blanketed the city with leaflets and posters advertising both the Crusade with Joe Blinco and the closing meeting, at which I was to speak. In response, the counterdemonstration printed several hundred thousand leaflets advertising their evening festival, to be dropped over the city from airplanes that afternoon. But just as the planes were being loaded, the storm, with hail and winds clocked at ninety miles an hour, perhaps including a tornado, unexpectedly hit the city of 300,000, uprooting trees and knocking out electrical power. It also scattered the paraders who were beginning to assemble and destroyed preparations at the festival site, damaging even the statue of the Virgin Mary that had been brought out of the cathedral for the parade. The planes themselves were damaged and would have been unable to take off even had the storm let up in time, and the leaflets were drenched beyond reclamation.

But by five o'clock the sun was out again, and as the time approached for our meeting, electrical power was restored to the arena. In spite of the fact that some roads were blocked by fallen trees, several thousand people came. The local committee felt that God had answered their prayers in a decisive and unmistakable way. It was the first time, we later learned, that an evangelical Protestant meeting had been held on public property in Paraguay's five hundred years of history. One small Mennonite church with only 40 members received 70 referrals of people who had made commitments to Christ during the Crusade.

The next day, when Russ and Dick returned to Asunción, they said the airport looked like a war zone. The government imposed a curfew on the city to prevent looting.

From Asunción we continued across the border to Córdoba and Rosario, Argentina's second-largest city, with cold winds coming off the arid Patagonia that forced me to preach in a heavy coat and muffler. In Rosario I spoke to students at the Catholic university, the area's largest, and received a very warm welcome from them. The Catholics had a reverence for the Bible; we did not have to convince them Who created the world and Who Christ was.

Uruguay

On to Montevideo. Joe Blinco held a separate Crusade in Uruguay among people who were descended from the Waldensians; this particular group were nineteenth-century refugees from religious persecution in Italy.

The vice chairman of the Crusade in Montevideo was the pastor of the city's largest Methodist church, the Reverend Emilio Castro (not a relation of the Cuban dictator). He stayed by my side throughout our visit, taking me everywhere in his little car. He had a social burden, not so much for Uruguay (since at one time it had been among the most prosperous nations in the hemisphere) but for the rest of Latin America. The sharp disparity between the rich and the poor, and the overwhelming poverty in both the cities and the countryside, deeply troubled me as well. In later years, after Emilio

Castro became prominent in the World Council of Churches, we did not always agree on all theological points. On social affairs and social conscience, though, he did sharpen my thinking.

Our Team appreciated Montevideo, but perhaps for a less-than-spiritual reason. Long-distance telephone rates were lower in Uruguay than elsewhere in Latin America (although still very expensive), so we finally got to call our families back in the States. The system in those days was actually a radio telephone; one person would speak, concluding with the word *over*, and then let the other person speak. It was awkward and didn't make for the most spontaneous conversation, but I was delighted to hear Ruth's voice anyway.

Back to Argentina

The trip concluded with an eight-day Crusade in Buenos Aires, one of the most beautiful cities in Latin America (and the largest in Argentina). Two thousand people had been trained as counselors— Charlie Riggs had taught them standing in a boxing ring, the best facility available—and in spite of a severe economic crisis in Argentina (some government workers hadn't been paid in months), the Crusade's full budget was raised in advance; no offerings needed to be taken. (In fact, we took no offerings anywhere in South America, to avoid any hint of financial motivation.)

I was invited to meet with members of the Argentine cabinet, because the relationship between the United States and Cuba was reaching boiling point. Argentina's defense minister asked me if I would come into his office. "I want you to convey to the President of the United States that we have two aircraft carriers," he told me, "and we will put them both at the disposal of the United States if it comes to war. It would be a tragedy if Castro should move any further than he has. His popularity is such that it affects us here."

Shortly after my return to the United States, I was invited to the White House to see President Kennedy. Secretary of State Dean Rusk was there as well. They wanted me to brief them about my tour of the Latin American countries. Needless to say, I relayed the offer made by Argentina's defense minister, but I never learned what use, if any, was made of the information.

What did I learn from the South American tours?

First, everywhere we went, we sensed a deep spiritual hunger and a yearning for a personal relationship with Christ. We came away committed to further ministry there.

Second, we came away with a new sense of the importance of Latin America and of its potential for the future. At the same time, I was struck by the widespread poverty we saw almost everywhere, and by the sharp division between the wealthy and the poor. I could see the potential for explosive social change and even chaos.

Since that trip, we've returned a number of times to various areas, eventually visiting almost every country in South America. (My doctors advised me against attempting to preach in La Paz, Bolivia; its altitude of twelve thousand feet was too high for my voice.)

In 1974 we returned to Brazil for a five-day Crusade in Rio de Janeiro. A quarter-million people gathered for the concluding meeting in Maracanã Stadium, a record for that facility. During the service, I could hear people beating on the locked doors as tens of thousands more tried to get in. The closing meeting was televised on all the networks across the country on the orders of the president; Crusade director Henry Holley was told that up to 50 million people saw the program. When we were ready to leave the stadium, the police escort was reluctant to open the gates for fear the crowd, in their enthusiasm, might riot.

MEXICO

Also memorable was our Crusade in Mexico in 1981. The organizers in Mexico City, our first stop, had been given permission to use the Olympic Stadium for the meetings; it seated 80,000. At the last minute, however, permission was withdrawn by the authorities. We were forced instead to use a much smaller basketball arena in the center of the city, which had no parking facilities. It was damaged in the earthquake a few years before and had not been used since, but the authorities assured us it was safe.

To make matters worse, publicity had already gone out directing people to the other stadium. But somehow word of the change got out, and even on the first night there was an overflow crowd of thousands. We then scheduled two services each day; people exited out one side of the arena as the second crowd entered from the opposite side.

We then went to the city of Villahermosa, a booming oil town near the Guatemalan border. It had an old western frontier feel about it; the people still carried guns in their belts. The church leaders there were some of the kindest people we have ever worked with. The meetings were held in a baseball stadium. Every night on our way there, we passed scores and scores of farm trucks on their way to the Crusade, jammed with people standing tightly packed in the truckbeds. When we gave the Invitation each night, so many people came forward that we couldn't get off the platform until the counseling was completed.

Our 1991 Crusade in Buenos Aires—a decade after the Mexico visit just described—marked a milestone of a different sort, with an extensive outreach to millions, via satellite and video, in twenty Spanish-speaking countries in Central and South America as well as Mexico and the Caribbean.

Since then, I have rejoiced in the many signs that God is still at work in that part of the world.

20

First Steps Behind the Iron Curtain

MOSCOW 1959, POLAND 1966, YUGOSLAVIA 1967

And again we need to go back in time, this time to trace our initial foray behind the Iron Curtain.

MOSCOW

In 1959 a close friend of mine on the West Coast, a Los Angeles businessman by the name of Bill Jones, invited Grady and me to go to the Soviet Union as tourists. He had been there a number of times and came back with remarkable stories of quietly taking Bibles into Russia and discreetly meeting with Christians.

I had been in Australia for several months. Ruth and Grady's wife, Wilma, joined us in Paris, and we flew to London. After a few days of relaxation, Bill, Grady, and I flew to Brussels, where we were to catch an Aeroflot plane to Moscow. I was a little hesitant to go on their airline, but Bill thought it would be wise to do so. We filled out our forms and got on the plane.

The stewardess was a pleasant, sturdily built Russian woman. "Please fasten your seatbelts," she announced in heavily accented English, "and if we get airborne, you can unfasten them!"

We arrived safely at the airport in Moscow. While we were going through immigration, a young woman with a bright smile inspected my passport. Then, looking around to make sure no one was watching, she silently pointed upward, giving the Christian One Way sign.

This was my first encounter with one of the countless silent believers in the Soviet Union. One time I stood with a crowd on Victory Day watching the people lay a wreath at their Tomb of the Unknown Soldier. A stranger wearing a whole string of medals on his chest came close to me. Without speaking a word, he used the tip of his cane to scratch a cross in the dirt at our feet.

Another time I was standing in front of our hotel in a cold drizzle when a bus pulled up. A woman looked out the bus window right at me. Then, on a foggy patch on the window, she rubbed a cross with her finger.

Many things impressed me on our taxi rides and walks in Moscow: the general cleanliness of the city, the lack of outdoor advertising signs (although propaganda posters were common), the intellectual reading matter at the newsstands. Looking at the symbolic red star rising high above the Kremlin, I was startled to see also the Cross of Christ topping the spires of former churches—buildings that in 1959 were serving largely as museums. Visiting Lenin's Tomb, I pondered how his embalmed body could inspire endless lines of viewers. The inspiration for *my* faith was the empty tomb of the risen Christ.

In the popular playground and propaganda platform of Gorky Park, I saw one poster in which the hammer and sickle had crushed Uncle Sam, depicted with his ever-present dollar sign.

One of the people I got to know on that trip was American reporter and writer Harrison Salisbury, Moscow correspondent for the *New York Times*. He was kind enough to accompany us a great deal of the time; he explained the things we were seeing and commented on the things we were doing. The Soviets frowned on public displays of sex, he said. I thought of Harvard professor Pitirim Sorokin's warning that an obsession with sex could destroy the United States faster than Communism.

I had tea with some students at Moscow University. Work meant more to them than play, I learned; 10 million Russian youth were studying English. At the crowded Baptist church—the only Protestant church for Moscow's 7 or 8 million people—my companions and I attended three two-hour services and heard six strong biblical sermons through interpreters! The authorities would not let me preach, the pastor explained apologetically. (Baptists and other Protestant denominations had been forced by Stalin to unite, and they were all called Baptists, although there were still theological tensions within the Baptist Union.)

This was not my first contact with Baptist leaders from the Soviet Union. In late July 1955, I met a Soviet Baptist leader who was representing his church at a meeting of the Baptist World Alliance in London. In October 1955, I responded to his invitation to preach in his church in Moscow, suggesting December of that year—or, if that date was not suitable, sometime in 1956.

"Naturally, I shall not mention political matters while visiting your great country," I wrote to him. "I shall come to preach the Gospel and to promote better relations between the American and Russian people. It is my prayer that such a trip would contribute to the prospects and possibilities of world peace."

No invitation arrived in response.

My intentions were good, but I naively thought going to the Soviet Union from the United States was as simple as going from the United States to the United Kingdom. Nor did I fully realize then the extent to which churches in such societies were forced to cooperate with government authorities; no church could issue such an invitation without their approval.

Lenin Stadium, named after V. I. Lenin, the founder of the Communist Soviet state, was empty the day Grady and I wandered in as tourists. A scratchy recording of Rosemary Clooney was being played over the loudspeaker system. The sight of the empty arena— the location of so many showcase events for the Soviet system— moved me deeply. As we sat gazing out over its vast expanse, I bowed my head and prayed that someday God would open the door for us to preach the Gospel in Moscow and elsewhere in eastern Europe.

And yet for decades, it seemed as if that was one prayer God would never answer, an unrealistic pipedream that could never come true. The barriers were too great, the wall erected by Communism against religion too impregnable. Not that Communist officials would have welcomed me anyway, for I was an avowed and vocal anti-Communist, blasting Communism in one 1953 sermon as "the greatest enemy we have ever known." I did not preach many sermons specifically on the subject, but when I did refer to Communists or Communism from the pulpit, I branded them as enemies of the Gospel.

About that time in Washington, D.C., Senator Joseph McCarthy was holding sensational hearings about alleged anti-American subversion. *McCarthyism* entered the American vocabulary as a word describing the making of unsubstantiated charges against alleged Communists and Communist sympathizers. I think McCarthy tried to contact me once, but I never had any correspondence with him, I never exchanged telegrams with him, and I never talked to him on the phone. Nor did I want to. I was shocked at some of his tactics, even though at the time I agreed that bona fide Communists needed to be exposed. But McCarthy went too far: in many quarters, the paranoia and panic engendered by the rigor of his investigation spread unfounded suspicion and slander.

In those tense times, I frequently mentioned and preached on the various social and political problems plaguing our country, and I probably spoke about Communism more than most others. I believed that the leaders of Communism, especially in the Soviet Union, had vowed world conquest; many of their published statements said as much.

Like millions of others, I honestly feared the spread of Communism to the United States and elsewhere, whether by a fifth column inside society or by armed aggression. After all, the West was still reeling under the knowledge that the Soviet Union had duplicated the atomic and hydrogen bombs.

For all of my early anti-Communist diatribes, however, I certainly did not see myself as a crusader against Communism like Senator McCarthy or Father Charles Coughlin, the vocal Catholic priest who had a national radio program during the 1930s and was often criticized for his extreme right-wing political views. But I couldn't preach the Gospel of Jesus Christ without clashing head-on with the various philosophies and ideologies that were vehemently opposed to Christianity—especially Communism. I quoted Lenin: "There will come times when we talk peace, there will come times when we talk war, but always toward world revolution."

My own comment was this: "We are dealing with a treacherous and vicious enemy who has the supernatural forces of evil behind him."

The scant reliable information that got out to the world through what Sir Winston Churchill first called the Iron Curtain was enough to terrify all of us. Often Jews and Christians were special objects of oppression and persecution in the Soviet bloc. Most abhorrent to me was its current militant atheism and its antireligious policies and persecutions.

Atheism as official policy was openly organized to stamp out religion. As one Soviet commissar of education put it, "We hate Christians; even the best of them must be regarded as our enemies." I knew that my fellow Christians in the Soviet Union and elsewhere were forbidden to declare their faith publicly or to give religious instruction to their children privately. When they defied Communist policies about religion, they often were exiled to Siberia, interned in the Gulag, or killed for their faith.

On the other hand, I have always admired the Soviet people. Nothing I said, even in my most intemperate denunciations of Communism, was intended to be a wholesale condemnation of the Russian people who bravely endured so much. As I was careful to point out, "Pure Communists were only a minority wherever they operated; most of the people under Communist rule were victims rather than disciples."

While in Moscow on that first visit as a tourist, I noted the haunted, tired look on people's faces, along with fear, insecurity, and what I interpreted in some settings as spiritual hunger and emptiness. Those in the churches, though, showed devotion and determination. They *had* to; it was not easy to join an evangelical congregation. Anyone eighteen and over seeking membership was put on probation for eighteen months to three years and could not be a smoker or drinker. Although I had little direct contact with the

Russian Orthodox Church during the 1959 trip, I knew that many Orthodox believers also paid a price for their commitment.

I left Moscow in 1959 with a dream, a hope, and a prayer that someday I, along with many others, might proclaim the Gospel throughout that vast country. At the same time, I had to admit that, humanly speaking, it seemed impossible. As it turned out, a visit to the Soviet Union would have to wait until after a series of visits many years later to other central and eastern European Communist countries, including Yugoslavia, Hungary, Poland, East Germany, and Czechoslovakia.

POLAND

Poland in the mid-sixties seemed to us to be wide open to a visit. Its religious life had remained comparatively strong under Communism, due to the determination and courage of Poland's Roman Catholic majority. The year 1966 marked the millennium of Poland's nationhood and of its Christianity, rooted in the conversion of Mieszko I in A.D. 966.

In the August issue of *Decision* magazine, an optimistic preview of our trip specified the dates (September 28 to October 5), gave the names of sponsors and committees, and listed the locations where we would appear. It mentioned publication of five thousand copies of a special edition of my book *Peace with God* for Polish distribution. It said we would pay a visit to the infamous concentration camp at Auschwitz, as a mark of respect for the millions who were put to death there and in similar camps in World War II.

Only twenty-four hours before our scheduled departure, we learned that we could not go after all. Internal political tangles among the Polish government, the Roman Catholic Church in Poland, and Polish evangelical leaders had resulted in the denial of our visas from the Polish Embassy in Washington. The advance publicity we had released had undoubtedly worked against us as well.

Two lessons emerged from that disappointment.

First, we realized that the emissaries of Christ's kingdom needed to be as careful and thorough in their research as any earthly government when approaching a foreign power. By acting on inadequate information, we put ourselves in a humiliating position and worked a real hardship on the evangelical Christian community in Poland.

Second, we were confirmed in our belief that God had not given up on Communist Europe. There was still a core of vital believers there. Although this visit collapsed, many people were fervently praying that someday the door would open for us.

YUGOSLAVIA

Less than a year later, in July 1967, I preached for the first time inside a Communist country, although technically it was not behind the Iron Curtain. Marshal Tito's Yugoslavia, which had maintained a feisty independence from Moscow's domination of eastern Europe, presented an image of relatively enlightened socialism. Although restrictions and repression prevailed for the twenty years following World War II, things began to loosen up in that country.

After a week-long Crusade at Earls Court in London, which ended on July 1, 1967, we stopped for a one-day rally in Turin, Italy, then crossed over by car to Zagreb, the capital of Croatia, where we had been invited by a committee of Yugoslavian Protestant churches. The contrast-rich landscape—from the long Adriatic coastline, across the rugged mountains, to the rich interior farmlands and forests of the Danube plain—symbolized the diverse groups who would attend the meetings.

The Catholic Church in Zagreb generously allowed us to use a field they owned; it overlooked an army hospital they operated. This outdoor location, while open to the elements, was large enough to handle the crowds we were expecting. Remarkable too was the shared presence on the platform of both Orthodox and Catholic leaders.

The sponsoring group's chairman, Dr. Josip Horak, who was also president of the Yugoslavian Baptist Convention, was exuberant: "Never before have gathered so many Protestants, and it is the first open-air meeting since the war," he said as he welcomed us. "We couldn't dream that something like this can happen in our country."

More than 7,000 stood in a steady, drenching rain for the two meetings. Many had traveled all night by train; others had taken a three-day bus ride from Macedonia; some had come from as far away as Hungary, Czechoslovakia, and Romania.

"I don't believe I've seen people anywhere in the world stay in pouring rain like this to hear the Gospel," I said to them. "I'll never forget this." Walter Smyth and T.W., who were with me, agreed it was a thrilling sight. Response to the Gospel Invitation also encouraged us. It stirred me to see strong men and women embrace each other with tears of joy at what God had wrought in those few hours.

Equally inspiring was the Friday night prayer meeting I attended at a little Baptist church upon our arrival in Zagreb. People so packed the small, hot room that I wondered if there would be enough oxygen! After responding to their request for a brief message, I concluded this way: "We are gathered to pray for the Crusade that begins tomorrow. . . . Nothing . . . will unite us . . . like praying together. I want to join you in prayer. I cannot understand your language, but we both know the language of Heaven. It is the language that God the Holy Spirit speaks to our hearts. . . . And so I can join you at the throne of grace."

The people at that meeting smiled when I told them, through the interpreter, that our prayers would be joined by those of thousands of fellow believers all over the world, who were likewise praying for the Zagreb meetings.

At a press conference in Chicago shortly after we returned from Yugoslavia, reporters seemed to be more curious than usual.

Had Yugoslavian officials opposed the meetings? they wondered.

No, I replied, because Yugoslavia's constitution allowed a certain degree of religious freedom, provided religion was exercised only in private ways and on church premises.

Would I like to do the same thing in the Soviet Union?

Yes, if allowed to, I said, and I added that we might eventually see one of the greatest religious awakenings of all time in that country.

In typical American fashion, reporters questioned the meetings' success in terms of attendance and response statistics.

"If I can talk with one person about Christ," I replied, "and get him to say yes to Jesus Christ, I consider that to be a very successful meeting."

The blessing God gave us in Yugoslavia increased my longing to penetrate with the Gospel deeper into the strongholds of atheistic Communism. Even though our schedule was filled years in advance, I kept my heart open to any firm possibility to preach in eastern Europe. At the same time, the political climate in those nations gave little hope for change, and all we could do was pray.

1960–1976

World in Upheaval

21

The Thousand Days

PRESIDENT JOHN F. KENNEDY

As Grady Wilson and I got on the train in Cincinnati bound for Chicago in late April 1960, we were approached by a young man who introduced himself as Pierre Salinger. Senator Jack Kennedy, he said, wanted a statement from me on the Roman Catholic issue and tolerance in the election for their use in the West Virginia Democratic primary, which would take place two weeks later. Hubert Humphrey, they felt, was giving him a tight race there.

Later during the trip he came back to me and argued his case earnestly and charmingly, but I said no. I was afraid some might interpret anything I said on the subject as an implied political endorsement. Nevertheless, he was courteous when he said good-bye to me in Chicago.

A few days later, in Minneapolis, I received a phone call from someone who identified himself as John Kennedy. In spite of the man's New England accent, I seriously doubted that it was he. He wanted me to say that the religious issue should play no part in the campaign and that I would not hesitate to vote for a Catholic if he was qualified. I gave the voice on the phone the same answer I had given to Salinger.

389

I did not think I saw any serious problem with a Catholic in the White House. Many Protestants, however, did have concerns, including some in my own Southern Baptist denomination. Baptists had a long tradition of stressing the separation of church and state. The idea of having a president who might owe a degree of allegiance to a religious leader who was also head of a foreign political state—Vatican City—concerned some of them greatly.

In my boyhood, Democrats in our part of North Carolina had voted against Catholic Al Smith of New York and for the victorious Republican candidate, Herbert Hoover, partly because of that same religious issue. We schoolchildren celebrated the 1928 election outcome without knowing why.

While I turned down Mr. Salinger's request, I also refused the insistent demands of some Protestants to come out against a Catholic candidate. As it turned out, Kennedy did not need my help; he swept the West Virginia primary on May 10.

I was still in something of a bind, though. While I did not want to appear to endorse Kennedy, neither did I want to seem prejudiced against him on religious grounds. In Kennedy's hometown of Boston, I had enjoyed good rapport with Cardinal Richard J. Cushing for ten years, and I felt sincerely that it was important in our Crusades to foster good church relationships.

I did not agree with some Catholic teachings and church practices, but warm acquaintance and fellowship with many in that church had long since laid to rest whatever prejudices I might have had. In addition, Hubert Humphrey, whom I had met first in Minneapolis, had introduced me to Senator Jack Kennedy some time before. One couldn't help but like Kennedy personally. As far as his own spiritual commitment was concerned, I really had no idea. There were rumors in Washington about his personal life, but I didn't pay too much attention to them, since gossip of all sorts was rampant there.

In the Kennedy-Nixon contest, my position was further complicated by my known friendship with Vice President Nixon. Frankly, I thought Nixon's eight years in the Eisenhower administration qualified him better than Kennedy's terms in the House and

Senate. A lot of people cross-examined me for a clue to my preference (which, apart from the sectarian factor, should have been fairly obvious), but I didn't want to say much, lest a seeming denominational bias should skew perceptions.

Once Kennedy and Nixon officially became their parties' candidates that summer, I felt constant pressure to make an endorsement. Had I been foolish enough to declare myself, it would have been for Mr. Nixon. In May I spoke at the Southern Baptist Convention and made thinly veiled allusions to my preference, without giving Nixon my outright endorsement. I might have fueled some partisan flames, though, with those allusions. In retrospect, only divine intervention kept me from answering the press on that issue, especially during an eight-day Washington, D.C., Crusade in June of 1960.

From then until early October, as the presidential campaign roared into high gear, attendance at the Baptist World Alliance in Rio de Janeiro and a series of Crusades in Europe kept me outside of the United States. It was a great relief to have the Atlantic Ocean between me and American politics.

While overseas, I received a letter from Dr. Norman Vincent Peale, pastor of New York's Marble Collegiate Church and probably America's best-known clergyman at the time. He had already strongly endorsed Nixon, who occasionally attended his church. Peale wanted me to go public on our mutual friend's behalf and asked if he could talk with me about it personally while he was vacationing in Europe. I invited him to Montreux, Switzerland, where I was conducting an evangelism strategy conference with about thirty evangelical leaders. He came and addressed the group briefly, and he and I chatted privately about the U.S. presidential race. I told him that I would think and pray about his request but that I still preferred to stay out of the fray.

One of the conferees, Clyde Taylor, then secretary of the World Evangelical Fellowship, invited Dr. Peale to attend a Washington conference of religious leaders who would be discussing the campaign. I encouraged Peale to go, privately glad that I would still be in Europe and therefore unable to attend. From

Europe I wrote privately to both Kennedy and his running mate, Lyndon Baines Johnson, explaining why I was not going to vote for them. It seemed only fair in view of my friendship with the competing candidates.

The press was not admitted to the Washington conference, but when Dr. Peale came out of the meeting room, reporters asked him for his comments. He read the statement the group had formulated, which contained no explicit statement about either candidate but did express serious reservations about electing a Catholic president in light of the Constitution's separation of church and state. While the group's intention was to deal with the issue on a philosophical (instead of a political) level, their effort backfired and they were branded by some as anti-Catholic. Unfortunately, Dr. Peale was unfairly blamed for the whole situation, and he was hurt both personally and professionally. Later I apologized to him for whatever I might have inadvertently contributed to his problem by urging him to attend the Washington meeting.

When I got back to the States in early October, I went to see Henry Luce at the Time & Life Building in New York City. "I want to help Nixon without blatantly endorsing him," I said. "Any ideas?"

Luce rested his hands behind his head. "Why don't you write an article about Nixon the man, as you know him? If it works, we'll use it in *Life* magazine."

"I don't know."

"Don't write whom you're going to vote for. Just what you think of Nixon as a man."

I wasn't comfortable with the idea, but I went back to our home in the mountains and started writing; the article came easily in one afternoon.

As soon as he got it, Luce called. "Billy, this is just what we want," he said. "I'm running it this coming week—going to feature it."

Pleased as I was that Luce liked the article, I was soon miserable. It was two weeks before the election, and Ruth was upset, totally opposed to my going public on a political subject. What was I getting myself and my friends into? Others who had learned about the piece called me to protest, including Governor Luther Hodges of North Carolina and Governor Frank Clement of Tennessee.

Everybody seemed to agree that it was a serious mistake, but it seemed too late to do anything about it.

On Thursday—the night the magazine went to press—Ruth and I got on our knees and asked the Lord to stop publication if it was not His will. Neither of us felt comfortable with it.

The next day Henry Luce phoned. "Billy, last night I couldn't sleep," he said. "At midnight I pulled your article."

God had intervened!

"Mr. Luce, I'm so relieved, I just can't tell you."

"Well, it was a good piece, but I suppose this is the better part of wisdom."

"Listen," I said impulsively, "what if I wrote you an article on why every Christian ought to vote? I could get it to you right away."

There was silence on the other end for a moment.

"Billy, I don't think so. I appreciate it, but no. That's a nice thought, but it wouldn't have the same punch. Thank you anyway."

For some reason I wrote the article anyway and sent it to him the next day. He called.

"I like the new piece, more than I thought I would. But I need to tell you what I've decided. I'm going to run the first one after all, next issue, a week before the election."

"No, sir, I believe God stopped that," I told him, explaining about our prayers.

"I can't argue with that," he said. "All right, I'll run the second one."

He did, and it received a gratifying response from readers.

Right after the election, I received a phone call from my friend Senator George Smathers of Florida, who told me that the President-elect wanted to talk with me. "I've suggested that we have a game of golf together," he said.

I was delighted. The catch was what my friend Nixon would think, depressed as he was over losing the election. I called him.

"He's the President-elect," Nixon said. "Every time he asks you, you have to go. *I* would go, so don't think anything of it."

On the evening I arrived in Florida, Mrs. Jacqueline Kennedy had just given birth to their son, John; so my meeting with her husband had to be postponed.

Ten days before the inauguration, in January of 1961, Smathers phoned again. "Could you come to Palm Beach to Jack Kennedy's father's house next Monday to have lunch and play golf?"

When I arrived at the Kennedy family estate, the charismatic young President-elect called to me from the window of the bedroom where he was changing clothes. "My father's out by the pool. He wants to talk to you."

After we shook hands and sat down, Joseph Kennedy came straight to the point: "Do you know why you're here?"

"Not exactly, sir," I admitted.

"When I was in Stuttgart, Germany, with the president of Notre Dame University, we saw signs all around that you were preaching there, so we decided to go and see what was happening. What we saw astonished us. You were preaching through an interpreter to 60,000 people. Many responded to your call at the end. When we visited the pope three days later, we told him about it. He said he wished he had a dozen such evangelists in our church. When Jack was elected, I told him that one of the first things he should do was to get acquainted with you. I told him you could be a great asset to the country, helping heal the division over the religious problem in the campaign."

I felt he had greatly overestimated my influence with the public (and had perhaps overlooked God's place in our ministry). However, I assured him that I wanted to do what I could.

Golf was the next order of the day. After a light lunch, at which Jack asked me to pray, he introduced me to his wife, Jackie. I thought her more beautiful in person than in newspaper and magazine pictures.

Jack himself drove us to the Seminole Golf Club at the wheel of a Lincoln convertible, with me in the front seat and George Smathers in the back. He waved at people as they recognized him, and we chatted all the way.

At the club, Kennedy and I rode in one golf cart, Smathers and Billy Reynolds (the aluminum company president, who joined us at the club) in another. When I stood at the first tee, I was nervous as a cat. I did not hit the ball far and wound up with a double bogey.

"I thought you played better than that," Kennedy joked.

"Well, sir, when I'm not playing with the President-elect, I usually do."

He laughed, and I felt more relaxed.

We played only fourteen holes. On the last hole I sank a long putt.

"I made $40 on that putt," shouted Reynolds.

I had a hunch there was something going in the way of a bet on the side, but they had concealed it from me.

In the clubhouse afterward, we got into a lively discussion. Kennedy aired his view that the sixties would be filled with challenges, promises, and problems. As we sat relaxing with soft drinks, he began to talk about Vietnam. Kennedy agreed with Eisenhower's domino theory. "If Laos goes," he said, "all of Southeast Asia will go. Then India. We're going to have to do something about it. Eisenhower's got a number of people over there. We can't allow Vietnam to fall to the Communists."

That was the first time I heard that Vietnam—that far-off country in the Orient—was such a problem. It all sounded so remote to me.

On the way back to the Kennedy house, the President-elect stopped the car and turned to me. "Do you believe in the Second Coming of Jesus Christ?" he asked unexpectedly.

"I most certainly do."

"Well, does *my* church believe it?"

"They have it in their creeds."

"They don't preach it," he said. "They don't tell us much about it. I'd like to know what you think."

I explained what the Bible said about Christ coming the first time, dying on the Cross, rising from the dead, and then promising that He would come back again. "Only then," I said, "are we going to have permanent world peace."

"Very interesting," he said, looking away. "We'll have to talk more about that someday." And he drove on.

Kennedy then asked me to go with him to a party he had been invited to at a private home. I accepted but felt self-conscious in my golfing clothes in front of about 100 people, including many well-known socialites who wintered in Palm Beach.

Then the President-elect popped another surprise on me. "Billy, there are about 300 media people at the Washington Hotel I haven't seen since I've been down here. I've got to say a word to them. Would you mind going with me?" I felt honored.

At the hotel I sat among the press, prepared to listen to the President-elect's comments. He started by saying that he had been playing golf with me and joked about our scores. Then the surprise: "I want to present to you Dr. Billy Graham, who's going to answer some questions."

That was the first I'd heard about *that!* I went up to the podium, and the press dived into the religious controversy that had been so prominent during the campaign—and about which I had kept quiet. Though Mr. Kennedy was using me for his own purposes, I did not mind finally speaking out.

"I don't think that Mr. Kennedy's being a Catholic should be held against him by any Protestant," I said. "They should judge him on his ability and his character. We should trust and support our new President."

If I had said that before the election, I am convinced I would have been in trouble. But the statement seemed justified now. I was interviewed for a half-hour or more, Kennedy sitting off to one side.

As we left the hotel, he asked me where I wanted to go. I told him that my wife and I were staying at the Holiday Inn at Vero Beach some distance up the coast.

"We'll send you back in our plane," he offered.

At the airport, then, I boarded the Kennedy plane, the *Caroline.* As we were landing after the brief flight, I noticed that the place did not look like Vero Beach. I told the pilot so. A man came running out and told us that we had landed at the Ft. Pierce airport, some fifteen miles short of our destination. We took off again and landed a few minutes later in Vero Beach.

One of Kennedy's accomplishments was the Peace Corps, whose humanitarian services overseas paralleled a part of what Christian missionaries had been doing for generations, minus the spiritual emphasis and the lifetime commitment.

"I think the Peace Corps is important," he once told me, "not so much to help other countries, though that is important, but to give American young people something to do."

He was right. Within a few weeks of its launching, hundreds had volunteered for the Peace Corps, indicating that the young and the restless were looking for something meaningful to which to commit: within five years of its founding more than 15,000 were serving in fifty-two countries.

I became good friends with R. Sargent Shriver, head of the Peace Corps, and later we made a documentary film together on the problem of poverty in the Appalachian Mountains. One day he offered to pick me up in Montreat. He showed up with a helicopter and landed in our front yard, which is little more than a shelf on the side of the mountain. The landing was a success, but the rotors blew our lawn furniture down the mountainside.

In one remote area, we landed to get some footage. We went up to a shack where we met a mountain woman. Sarge asked her if she had a $20 bill in her possession. She shook her head. If she *did* have a $20 bill, he asked, what would she do with it?

She thought for a moment and then said, "I'd look around and find somebody who needed it worse than me, and I'd give it to him."

I think Sarge got a new appreciation of the character and pride of the people who live in Appalachia. The documentary, by the way, was something of a success; it was shown all over the United States by various agencies, including the National Council of Churches.

The dawn of the 1960s was a terribly difficult time for any world leader. I was encouraged that President Kennedy took the trouble to attend the annual Presidential Prayer Breakfast each of his three years in Washington. I was the speaker each of those years. I learned later that Mr. Kennedy had reportedly said I was the only Protestant clergyman with whom he felt comfortable.

At one of those breakfasts, sitting beside me, he asked me what religious group was predominant in settling North Carolina and the South. I told him the Scotch-Irish Presbyterians, Lutherans, Moravians, Baptists, and Methodists.

"When did the Catholics come?" he wondered.

"Later" was all I could tell him, adding that there were a lot of Catholics in the South now.

When he stood to make his remarks, to my surprise he used that snippet of information as an illustration.

Several times during the Kennedy years I was invited to the White House, though never to a state dinner or to his personal quarters. I remember several occasions in the Oval Office—one visit especially, when he asked me to tell how I talked through an interpreter. Apparently, he had seen me on a TV program talking through an interpreter in Latin America and had liked the style and method, which was sentence by sentence. The only other alternative was to give the speech in its entirety in English and then have an interpreter repeat it in the foreign language.

During the height of the Cuban missile crisis, Secretary of State Dean Rusk accepted a speaking engagement from a Presbyterian group in Montreat. I went to hear him. One of his aides called and said he would like to visit our home, so we invited him up. During the hour or so we enjoyed coffee together, he had to excuse himself to call Washington two or three times. At one point, he filled me in briefly on the tense standoff with Cuba and the Soviet Union.

"Billy, what do you think we ought to do?" he asked.

"I think we'd better stand firm."

"So do I," he agreed.

During his shockingly short term, President Kennedy endeared himself to me in several ways. One day in Washington in late 1961 the President invited Grady Wilson and me into his office. We informed him of our upcoming five-week Crusade in Latin America beginning in January.

"I'm going down there before that," Kennedy said. "I'll be your John the Baptist."

"Don't forget," Grady said, "that he lost his head!"

That didn't dissuade the President, who laughed and repeated his offer: "What can I do for you?"

We told him we were having problems getting into Colombia, where some leaders warned of riots if we held large meetings. Our missionary friends there were praying that God would reopen the door. The President turned to an adviser and told him simply, "Take care of that." What happened behind the scenes I will never know, but we got into Colombia without further problems, and attendance at our meetings (which proceeded without incident) was as high as 20,000. The Catholic President of the United States had indeed made a good John the Baptist.

The last time I was with Kennedy was at the 1963 National Prayer Breakfast. I had the flu.

"Mr. President, I don't want to give you this bug that I've got, so I'm not going to talk right at your face."

"Oh, I don't mind," he said. "I talk to a lot of people all day long who have got all kinds of bugs."

After I gave my short talk, and he gave his, we walked out of the hotel to his car together, as was always our custom. At the curb, he turned to me.

"Billy, could you ride back to the White House with me? I'd like to see you for a minute."

"Mr. President, I've got a fever," I protested. "Not only am I weak, but I don't want to give you this thing. Couldn't we wait and talk some other time?"

It was a cold, snowy day, and I was freezing as I stood there without my overcoat.

"Of course," he said graciously.

His hesitation at the car door, and his request, haunt me still. What was on his mind? Should I have gone with him? It was an irrecoverable moment.

John Connally (a Democrat at the time) invited me to Texas to participate in his inauguration as governor on January 15, 1963. In late fall of that year, when I was back preaching in Houston, the governor came to my hotel room. He confided that he was concerned about President Kennedy's forthcoming trip to Texas in November. He said that there was much hostility against the President in Texas and he feared a lukewarm, or even a negative, response.

Arizona Senator Barry Goldwater was the front-runner for the Republican nomination for president in the 1964 election, and his conservative cause appeared to be developing a large groundswell in

Texas. Kennedy planned his visit to build Democratic unity and help shore up the Democratic resistance.

Sometime toward the end of the second week in November, I unaccountably felt such a burden about the presidential visit to Dallas that I decided to phone our mutual friend, Senator Smathers, to tell him I really wanted to talk to the President. His secretary told me Senator Smathers was on the Senate floor and would call me back. Instead, he sent me a telegram that the President would get in touch with me directly. He thought I wanted to talk about the President's invitation to another golf game in Florida that weekend; the game was off, he said, and would have to be rescheduled.

But all I wanted to tell him and the President was one thing: "Don't go to Texas!"

I had an inner foreboding that something terrible was going to happen. I told this to T.W. and Calvin Thielman, pastor of the Montreat Presbyterian Church, while we were on the golf course one day (and before I put through the call to Smathers). But was such a strange feeling enough to justify the President's attention?

In the early afternoon of November 22, I was playing golf with T.W., Lee Fisher, and Cliff Barrows at the local course in Black Mountain, North Carolina. We had just teed off for the fifth hole right next to the road when Loren Bridges, manager of WFGW, the Christian radio station we owned there, drove up and shouted that the President had been shot. Just then, the Black Mountain golf pro, Ross Taylor, came running out, shouting the same news.

We rushed to the WFGW studio, where dispatches were clacking over the wires. Loren handed me the latest Associated Press Teletype copy. The report was sketchy; hard information about the President's condition was not available yet.

I asked Calvin Thielman to go on the air with me to pray for Kennedy and his family and to read Scripture. I also asked T.W. to call a friend of ours who was a doctor at Parkland Memorial Hospital in Dallas to get the latest word.

As Calvin and I went on the air, T.W. came to the control room window and held a scrap of paper up against the glass. "He's dead," it said.

I dared not break such news to western North Carolina until a public announcement was made, which Walter Cronkite did over CBS three or four minutes later. Then, Calvin and I spoke of the President and prayed for his family and for the new President, Lyndon Baines Johnson.

At President Kennedy's funeral the following Monday in St. Matthew's Cathedral in Washington, I was invited to sit among friends of the Kennedy family. The question on everybody's mind was, Why did it happen? Like everyone else, I was touched by the sight of the Kennedy children, Caroline and John, Jr. When John and I got acquainted decades later, I was struck by his resemblance to his father, in both personality and ability.

A different thought had haunted me the day before, when I stood in the Capitol Rotunda about thirty feet from Jackie and the family and watched the tearful faces of national and world leaders filing by. My friend Jim Bishop had just written a newspaper column about his last interview with Kennedy. It was hard not to think about his poignant quote from the late President: "There's so little time and so much to do."

Harking back to our Palm Beach conversation only three years before, I became very thoughtful as I listened to Cardinal Cushing read the powerful New Testament statement on Christ's Second Coming from 1 Thessalonians 4:16: "For the Lord himself shall descend from heaven with a shout, with the voice of the archangel, and with the trump of God: and the dead in Christ shall rise first" (KJV). Leaving the cathedral with Paul Miller—a friend and supporter of our work from Rochester, New York, who was head of the Gannett newspaper chain—I prayed that this would be true for John F. Kennedy.

Some months later, as part of a fund-raising event for the Kennedy Library at Harvard, the University of North Carolina invited me to speak at their stadium. Senator Ted Kennedy came to that event, along with his mother, Rose Kennedy. The clan matriarch was exceptionally gracious. "You know, I often listen to you," she said. "Even though we are Catholic, I have never heard you say anything we don't agree with in the Bible."

I was grateful for her kind words, but they also underlined a truth I had come to realize during the debates a few years before over having a Catholic in the presidency. The only hope for finding common ground among Christians of diverse backgrounds and viewpoints was to focus on the Word of God, the ultimate authority for our faith.

22

Tall Timber from Texas

PRESIDENT LYNDON B. JOHNSON

"You and Ruth must be here for our library dedication May 22." That was retired President Lyndon Johnson's handwritten post-script at the bottom of a typewritten note to me dated February 23, 1971—slightly more than two years after leaving office.

For that occasion in Austin, we were invited by President Nixon to accompany him on Air Force One. I gave the invocation. After the ceremony, LBJ took Ruth and me out to his ranch in the hill country. Over the years, we had enjoyed many good visits with him and Lady Bird on that sprawling land under the vast Texas sky, and we were glad to be back.

He and I walked down to the oak trees edging the Pedernales River, which flanked the family cemetery. Usually effervescent, he struck me as subdued that day. We stood in the shade and watched the water flow by.

"Billy," he said at last, "one day you're going to preach at my funeral. You'll stand right here under this tree. I'll be buried right there." He pointed to the spot in the family cemetery. "You'll read the Bible, of course, and preach the Gospel. I want you to." He paused for a moment. "But I hope you'll also tell folks some of the things I tried to do."

When the time came, I did not find it a hard assignment. Ours was that kind of friendship. At the graveside service on January 25, 1973—less than two years after that conversation—I described him as "history in motion" and "a mountain of a man with a whirlwind for a heart . . . [whose] thirty-eight years of public service kept him at the center of the events that have shaped our destiny." If anything, those words, as I look at them now, were an understatement.

LBJ was a powerful, gigantic personality whose charisma dominated a room the minute he entered it. The focus of attention and even the balance of power automatically shifted to him. He could be coarse and charming at the same time, and even profanely poignant. Almost every time he swore in my presence, he would quickly turn and say, "Excuse me, Preacher."

Although many have commented on his complex character, perhaps I saw a side of that complexity that others did not see, for LBJ had a sincere and deeply felt, if simple, spiritual dimension. But while he was serious about it, I could hardly call him pious.

Yet I was beside him many times as he knelt by his bedside, in his pajamas, praying to One mightier than he. I saw strength in that, not weakness. Great men know when to bow.

On Sunday, December 15, less than three weeks after President Kennedy's funeral, the telephone rang just as I was preparing to leave for Annapolis, where I was to speak in the chapel of the United States Naval Academy. "This is Lyndon," the President's familiar voice boomed, adding that he wanted me to come by the White House. The next day, we spent several hours together, talking and swimming in the White House pool. The earthshaking events of the last few weeks had clearly sobered him. We prayed together, and I asked God to give him special grace and wisdom in the difficult days ahead. Afterward he invited me to offer a prayer of thanks at a small dinner honoring the executive staff of the *New York Herald Tribune*.

As the new President in February 1964, he spoke at the National Prayer Breakfast: "No man can live where I live, nor work at the desk where I work now, without needing and seeking the strength and support of earnest and frequent prayer." Those were not the words of a desperate man on a sinking ship. They revealed faith in a Friend who could help.

The spiritual side to his character wasn't surprising in light of his family heritage. One of his cherished family mementos was a faded, yellowed letter that he displayed on the wall of his White House office. It was from the legendary Texas hero of San Jacinto, General Sam Houston, to Johnson's great-grandfather, a frontier evangelist who had led the general to personal faith in Jesus Christ. It was after his conversion that Houston assumed political leadership. The President was proud to point it out to visitors and tell them the story behind it.

At his inauguration in 1965, he invited me to preach at an early-morning service in the National City Christian Church. The crowd included the Supreme Court justices, senators, congressional representatives, governors, and mayors of every city with a population over 100,000. I closed my sermon with the Houston letter, and the President gave me the thumbs-up sign.

LBJ's grandfather had been a professor of Bible at Baylor University. His mother, Rebekah Baines Johnson, often read the Bible to her young son, and her letters were a stirring testament of faith. Inscriptions on many of the tombstones in the little family graveyard beside the Pedernales confirmed that witness. His forebears were Southern Baptists, but he joined the Christian Church at some point because it was nearest to his home. Lady Bird was Episcopalian. He frequently attended her church or other denominational churches, including Catholic. Being a Texan, he respected the considerable influence of the state Baptist paper, *The Baptist Standard,* on the thinking of its more than 200,000 subscribers.

LBJ's practice of churchgoing during his presidency, rain or shine, was an example to many. Though probably the busiest man in America, he sometimes went to services two or three times a week. His faith fortified him when he was facing surgery. I watched him on TV; he was laughing with the nurses and the intern as they wheeled him down the hospital corridor. And the first thing he did when he recovered from the operation was to go back to church. He might have been motivated partly by sentiment for his family legacy of preachers, Bible teachers, and evangelists; but I had every reason to think it was much more than that.

In November 1965, President and Mrs. Johnson attended the closing service of our Houston Crusade, the first chief executive to attend a Crusade while in office. He was not embarrassed to be counted among believers. Six years later, in 1971, when the Texas legislature passed a resolution inviting us to hold a Crusade in Austin in 1973 while they were in session, he wrote to tell me that he and Lady Bird were planning to be with us, not at the Austin Crusade (which never did take place) but at the Dallas Crusade later that year.

"I want to endorse that Resolution," he added, "and if you are able to accept you will hear me saying 'Amen' from the front row at Memorial Stadium."

I knew he was not a saint. When I spoke warmly about his spiritual convictions, I was not forgetting his inconsistencies and transgressions. Did he intimidate me? Maybe just the opposite: I think I intimidated him a little. He liked having an old-fashioned Baptist preacher around for personal as well as political reasons, but I did not avoid taking issue with him or probing his soul whenever I thought it necessary.

At a gathering of police chiefs in Kansas City in September 1967, for example, I was present to hear his address. That evening when I spoke at our Crusade meeting in the Municipal Stadium, I said I disagreed with some of the things he had said that morning. I went on to say, "I'm going to tell you what I believe the Bible teaches." The media picked that up in a hurry. A preacher setting the President straight, and in public at that!

LBJ phoned me the next day.

"What's the matter with you?" he grumbled. "I thought you were my friend."

"I am," I replied, "but I can't always agree with everything you say."

He changed the subject and didn't bring it up again.

I remember one particular weekend that I spent with him. LBJ had given me his assurance that my visit would not get publicity, because he knew I did not want to appear to be involved in the upcoming presidential campaign. That short visit was an eye-opener to me about modern political campaigning. One morning, as we were having a short discussion in his bedroom after having had prayer together, someone came in and handed him a note.

"Read that," he said, passing it on to me.

406

I glanced at it briefly. It was an intelligence report for the day before on his opponent, Senator Barry Goldwater. It contained almost every move Goldwater had made, from breakfast to bedtime. His blood pressure. Whom he had talked to, and what about. It was unbelievable—and unsettling—to realize what goes on behind the scenes in politics.

The Sunday afternoon before election Tuesday, I flew from Washington to Charlotte and then started the drive home. I turned the car radio on. When I heard our daughter Anne quoted as having endorsed Goldwater, I was so shocked that I stopped in Shelby and called Ruth from a pay phone.

"Ruth, what's this about Anne? We're for Johnson."

"Well, Anne's not," she replied.

Oh, no, I thought, with a sinking feeling. We were deep in politics, whether we liked it or not!

When I arrived home, Ruth told me that Anne, our sixteen-year-old high school student, had gone the night before with friends to a Republican rally in Greenville, South Carolina. Someone must have identified her there, and CBS shoved a microphone in front of her.

"Here's Billy Graham's daughter. What do you say?"

"Yeah, Goldwater! All the way with Barry!"

Monday afternoon our phone rang. It was President Johnson, wanting to speak to Anne Graham. She was not home.

"I'll speak to Billy then," he said.

What now? I wondered.

"Billy, you congratulate Anne," he said. "I'm glad to see young people getting involved in politics. I'm glad she's independent, got a mind of her own. I've got an independent daughter too. She's getting ready to join the Catholic Church."

Father to father, we clicked. Later Luci talked with me about the reasons for her decision, which were largely, it seemed to me, related to her plans to marry a Catholic.

LBJ was impulsive and unpredictable. His speech could be as overbearing as his behavior. From my reading about past presidents, I would say he was in the same mold as Andrew Jackson—rough and brilliant, with plenty of natural ability. In an earlier generation, he would have qualified as one of Theodore Roosevelt's Rough Riders.

As with the other presidents, I tried to stop calling him by his first name when he took office. When I occasionally slipped up, he gave me a funny look, which prompted me instantly to correct myself. I wanted to be careful because of what had allegedly happened when he was pulled over for speeding in Texas. The instant the officer recognized Johnson, or so the story goes, he exclaimed, "My God!"

"And don't you forget it!" the President reportedly barked back.

Once T.W. and I flew with him on the presidential plane from Washington to Atlantic City, where he was to speak to a national gathering of 30,000 schoolteachers and administrators.

"Now, the reason I brought Billy Graham with me," the President explained to the assembly, "is because the ceiling was so low at the airport. When I heard it was almost zero-zero, I thought I'd better have Billy with me."

We had landed safely with a 100-foot ceiling, and 150-foot visibility. It was not to *my* credit, though. We all prayed—and prayed hard.

I used to do that also when LBJ took the steering wheel of his car to drive me around his ranch. He seemed to think his vehicle had only one speed: high. It seemed as if all four wheels were never on the road at the same time. Hills, canyons, rocks, scrub brush, riverbeds—it was all like interstate to him. Rough terrain never slowed him down.

On the many occasions when I saw him fill a station wagon with the children of ranch hands or neighbors, hand out jelly beans, and drive out to track the deer running across his property, laughing and joking with the kids all the time, perhaps he was a little more restrained.

Once he lost his temper with Grady Wilson when we were out riding in his Lincoln convertible on just such a deer hunt. Grady was yelling—whether with the exhilaration of the chase or with panic at the President's driving, I don't know—when suddenly LBJ slammed on the brakes. "Grady, just shut up!" he said. "You make me sick! If you make one more sound, you can go back and ride with Jack Valenti or the Secret Service in the other car!"

In reality, LBJ liked Grady and much appreciated his gift for telling funny stories nonstop. Once when we were swimming with the President in the White House pool, Grady spun a yarn that made LBJ laugh out loud. "Write that down," he said to special assistant Bill Moyers, who was standing nearby. "I want to remember that one."

One night Grady and I were sleeping in the same room on the Johnson ranch. In the middle of the night, I heard snoring so loud it shook the frame building. I threw a pillow at Grady and whispered as loud as I could, "Shut up and turn over!" But Grady was already awake. It was not he who was snoring; it was the President in the bedroom under us.

One time when Ruth and I were visiting the ranch, LBJ took Lady Bird and us for a boat ride. It seemed he went the same speed on the water as in a car. As he careened around water-skiers—his wife shouting, "Lyndon, slow down!"—I thought he was going to capsize and kill us all.

By the time we got back it was dark, but he had another suggestion: "While they're getting dinner ready, let me take you for a ride in a car I've got out here." I was still a little shaky from the boat ride, but Ruth and I climbed into the vehicle, and he took off at full throttle. We sped along the riverbank. Without warning, he swerved right into the Pedernales. For a second, I believed he was suicidal. But the engine kept going, and so did we. The car turned out to be an amphibious vehicle that carried us along on the current like a boat.

"Most people jump out when we hit the water," Johnson complained, as Ruth remembered it.

"You're the President," she said to him. "I figured you knew what you were doing!"

Johnson loved to catch people off-guard or throw them off-balance, and not only while driving on the ranch. He pointed to a mutual friend of ours one day and said, in mock horror, "I went to a party for White House staff at this churchgoing Baptist's home the other day, and he never served one drop of alcohol. Can you imagine bringing the cabinet and the staff all the way out to his house and giving them nothing to drink?"

That friend was Marvin Watson, a Texas business executive who served as special assistant to President Johnson before being appointed postmaster general. He would eventually serve on the board of BGEA while president of Dallas Baptist University.

I was the President's guest at the White House around federal budget time one year. As he excused himself to attend an evening cabinet meeting, he said, "Billy, I don't know how long I'll be in there. You take these pencils and see if you can trim a few billion off this budget while I'm gone."

I opened the thick notebook and reviewed the American government budget. By the time he returned, I had actually inflated it a little, thinking he needed to spend a little more here and a little more there. He roared. "You'd have made a good congressman!" he said.

He could also be kind and generous, very solicitous when it came to our comfort and well-being. If he found out I was staying at a hotel in Washington, he would call to say, "There'll be a car there in fifteen minutes. Your hotel is over here."

One Saturday evening when we were visiting, the Johnsons had to go out. That left Ruth and me alone at the White House. Nobody else was there (it seemed), and most of the lights were out. Ruth and I walked all over the place, turning lights on wherever we could find a switch. That was as much power as I ever exercised in the White House.

In 1964 the Scripps Howard newspapers came out with a front-page story announcing that I was giving serious consideration to running for president. Some Republicans phoned me to say they had enough support to nominate me. I did not think they knew what a good friend of Lyndon Johnson's I was, or they would have thought twice before talking to me.

My father-in-law, Dr. Bell, got in touch with me in a hurry. "It's on all the newscasts," he said. "You've got to call a press conference and stop it. It must be T.W.'s fault. He talked you into considering this."

So much for family support. When Ruth called me later, she echoed her father's message.

T.W. had nothing to do with it, of course. I had been urged by a few friends to think about it, but how it leaked out, I would never know. First thing the next morning, I convened a press conference.

"Under no circumstances am I going to run for president," I said. "A number of groups have promised support if I would run, but no amount of pressure can make me yield at any point. I've never hinted to anybody that I would run for president. Like General Sherman, if nominated I will not run; if elected I will not serve. God called me to preach."

Ruth and I were having lunch with the President and Lady Bird at the White House when the 1964 Democratic convention was starting in Atlantic City. He handed me a list of fourteen names. "Now who would you choose as a running mate?" he asked.

I started to answer, but then winced in pain. Instead of taking the hint, I asked Ruth why she had kicked me.

"Yes, Ruth, why?" asked the President.

She turned to me. "You should limit yourself to moral and spiritual advice, not political advice."

"Ruth," said the President, "that's exactly right."

When Ruth and Lady Bird left the room after lunch, Johnson closed the door behind them. "All right," he said, "now what do you *really* think?"

I smiled and pointed to one name on his list, more guessing than advising. He nodded. The Hubert Humphrey decision had already been made.

At the first Presidential Prayer Breakfast during the Johnson presidency, I told LBJ that Calvin Thielman, pastor of the Montreat Presbyterian Church, was in the audience. "He worked for you as a seventeen-year-old student in Texas as your campaign manager in Lamar County when you were first elected to the Senate," I explained. (Johnson had won by a scant eighty-seven votes, earning him the nickname "Landslide Johnson.")

"Really? I'd like to meet him," said the President.

I made the introductions. Before they parted, LBJ said to him, "I remember hearing there was a young fellow who worked hard for me in Lamar County. Come by the White House while you're here."

That was the beginning of a good, strange, and at times humorous relationship between Johnson and Thielman. At Johnson's request, Calvin even made three trips to Vietnam as an observer; while there, he preached and also visited missionaries and volunteer agencies.

411

As for my preacher relationship to Johnson, it became very direct at times. At his ranch one evening, he and I sat in his convertible, watching a glorious sunset.

"Mr. President, have you ever personally, definitely received Jesus Christ as your Savior?"

He gazed out across the landscape. "Well, Billy, I think I have."

I waited quietly for more.

"I did as a boy at a revival meeting." He paused. "I did reading one of the sermons in my great-grandfather's book of evangelistic sermons." Another pause. "I guess I've done it *several* times."

"When someone says that, Mr. President," I said carefully, "I don't feel too sure of it."

He looked at me with a puzzled expression.

"It's a once-for-all transaction," I said. "You receive Christ and He saves you. His Spirit bears witness with your spirit that you're a child of God."

He nodded. I did not feel that this was the time to say more, but I knew he would be thinking about what I had said.

Hardly ever did I leave him without his saying, "Preacher, pray for me." Then he would get down on his knees, whether we were in the ranch house or the White House.

Johnson's dream was the Great Society, of course, much of it made up of the programs Kennedy had not been able to get through Congress. I am convinced that LBJ genuinely loved the minorities and the poor. He wanted to correct injustice, to see everybody in America housed and fed. "That's what I think Jesus would do," was an expression I heard from him more than once. He thought the best expression of his faith was to help humankind.

I was heartsick to read in later biographies of his apparent moral failures. Whatever he might have been guilty of, I was sure he loved Lady Bird and his daughters, Lynda and Luci. His wife in turn was loving and loyal to a larger-than-life husband. He knew he could depend on her because she had tremendous strength of her own. Lady Bird was one of the most remarkable First Ladies ever.

Some years later, when I was in Austin, I phoned her to say hello. She and Luci then drove to the airport in person to pick me up and take me to their home. Lady Bird had a strength and dignity that were never adequately portrayed to the American people. And she could be direct with her husband too. Once when we happened to be with them for dinner, he informed her of a staff appointment he had made, and I saw her drop her fork. "Lyndon, no! You're asking for trouble." It's been my experience that all the First Ladies have had more influence on their husbands than most people have realized.

Powerful and savvy as LBJ was, no doubt he sometimes sacrificed principle for expediency, cutting corners on ethics. After thirty-eight years in public service, he was worn down, despite his gusto and bravado. Stacks of briefs piled high around him every day, demanding to be read before the next morning's endless conferences and calls. I watched Johnson struggle with all that.

And the daily speeches. I observed him one day walking down the little colonnade alongside the White House Rose Garden, where so many ceremonies take place. Someone handed him a fistful of cards containing the remarks he was to make in five minutes. He reviewed and edited them while he walked.

Working with speechwriters consumed a lot of his time. I was in his bedroom one morning when there were several writers clustered around him. He was really letting them have it: "You guys are trying to get me to say things I don't believe. This is *my* speech, not yours! You're trying to make a liberal of me! I don't believe all that junk! Now go back and rewrite the thing!" Every word could have been heard down to the end of the corridor.

And then there were the omnipresent media representatives. I read somewhere that when McKinley was President, there were only two White House reporters. Franklin Roosevelt could fit the White House press corps into the Oval Office. At a presidential press conference today, the man at the podium is the target of scores of reporters.

Across the years, some people have urged me to run for the Senate or for governor of North Carolina. President Johnson asked me if I would like to be appointed ambassador somewhere or take a job in his administration. One day, when I was swimming with

President Johnson and columnist Marianne Means at Camp David (John Chancellor and Ruth had gone bowling), LBJ spoke pointedly about the forthcoming presidential elections. "Billy, I want you to run for president," he said. "I'll put my whole organization behind you."

I am sure he was joking, but there was a certain seriousness in his expression and tone, and he pressed me on the issue.

"I appreciate it," I replied, "but God has called me to preach, and I'll never do anything else as long as I live."

I admit I was flattered by such suggestions. I confess I even entertained a split-second *What if?* But God kept me convinced that His calling was superior to any earthly appointment. For some Christians I admired and respected, His call unquestionably was to public service through elective office. More power to them. The ultimate issue is obedience to God's plan for each of us.

I tried to be a spiritual counselor to Lyndon Johnson, but I was not his confessor. He said to me that he had done a lot of things of which he was ashamed, although he refused to go into detail. He was, however, able to express his belief: "I believe I am saved and that I will spend eternity in Heaven." Nothing I knew personally about him contradicted that. Christ came to save sinners, not the righteous, as He Himself said (*see* Luke 5:32).

One thing the President did confide in me, though, a full year before his term ended, was his decision not to run again. Protests against the Vietnam War—a war he had inherited—had taken their toll on his morale. But that was not the chief factor. Nor was the candidacy of Robert Kennedy. LBJ was not afraid of any competitor except one: death.

Like Winston Churchill, LBJ often received visitors while in bed. He would read, keep his eyes on three TVs, and have a private conversation, all at the same time.

"Billy," he said one morning in his bedroom, "most all my relatives and ancestors died in their sixties of heart trouble. I've already had one heart attack, and I have chest pains now that I don't tell my doctor about." I listened with growing anxiety. "I'm not going to run next time because it wouldn't be fair to the American people. It wouldn't be fair to my family. It wouldn't be fair to me."

Needless to say, I kept that confidential.

President Johnson and I often talked about the Vietnam War, but never about the military strategy involved. He felt we had to get out of it, and he asked me, along with everyone else he knew, just how such a thing could be accomplished.

"Every time I see a casualty list," he once said to me about the servicemen, "I feel for their fathers and mothers, and sometimes I call them on the phone just to talk to them personally."

I made two trips to Vietnam to preach to the troops with a few members of my Team during LBJ's presidency, in 1966 and again in 1968, both during the Christmas season. When I arrived in Vietnam during one of our trips, reporters climbed all over me, trying to learn whether or not I supported the President's policy. My answer was always the same: "My only desire is to minister to our troops by my prayers and spiritual help wherever I can."

Once we paid a visit to Admiral Richardson's aircraft carrier, *Kitty Hawk*. The weather was bad throughout our stay, but a couple of pilots were willing to take us up. The takeoff provided an incredible feeling—what our singer Jimmie McDonald later described as "the world's largest slingshot."

Bob Hope asked us to join up with him and his company who were in Vietnam with their Christmas program. When we reached the spot where we were supposed to land, the pilots told us they had no idea where the airstrip was. The cloud cover was hanging so low that the mountain peaks stuck up all around us. I heard the crew debating what to do over my headset.

"Captain, I don't know whether we ought to try to land here," I said as calmly as I could. "If I was going to preach the Gospel, I'd say let's go in no matter what the weather. But it's just the Bob Hope show. I'm just going to tell a joke or something, and I'm not all that eager to smash into a mountain just for that."

"Mr. Graham," said one of the pilots, "I come from a long list of living cowards. I'm not going to go down there if I don't think I can make it." He did make it, through a hole in the clouds, and I did appear in a skit.

After each show, Bob and his troupe went back to the safety of Bangkok. I and my group, which included Cliff and Bev, stayed in

Vietnam. Some wit was quick to quip that the difference between Bob and me was that he had the hope but I had the faith.

Another flight, this one skittering over the treetops, was just as hair-raising. The weather was worse that time, and only one volunteer—a colonel—came forward to fly the Team to some spots near the front. The plane was a two-motor job with a big hole in the back. At one point, the colonel and I both let out a roar when a mountain appeared right in front of the windscreen. He pulled back on the stick as hard as he could, and I heard the back of the plane scrape the treetops. We finally made an impossible landing at a remote site, and not a moment too soon for my taste. I led a short service with the troops, and Bev sang a hymn. Then the colonel made an impossible takeoff for another spot fifteen minutes away. And so it went throughout the day. I was in a state of perpetual fright, but Bev? He just sat back, singing songs.

The last weekend the Johnsons were in the White House, before Nixon's first inauguration in 1969, Ruth and I were their only guests. Our daughter Anne and her husband, Danny Lotz, joined us as we walked together through quiet rooms emptied of personal possessions. After the Johnsons came back from a good-bye function, we watched a movie together, *The Shoes of the Fisherman;* it was about a fictitious pope, played by Anthony Quinn, who tried to bring peace to the world. In the previous four years, I had watched a lot of movies with President Johnson, but he almost always slept through them. After this particular one, I went to the back of the little White House theater and asked the projectionist to save the film. I wanted Mr. Nixon to see it too.

We attended church together, and on Monday I gave an inaugural prayer at the Capitol. As the distinguished guests on the platform followed President Nixon out after the swearing in, the two Johnson girls, Lynda and Luci, broke protocol when they stopped in the line and kissed me.

Some said I was instrumental in the transfer of authority from Johnson to Nixon. As a friend to both, I might have said or done some things that helped in the transition, but I served in no official or even implied capacity.

I will always treasure a letter Johnson wrote to me when he got back to Texas: "No one will ever fully know how you helped to lighten my load or how much warmth you brought into our house. . . . My mind went back to those lonely occasions at the White House when your prayers and your friendship helped to sustain a President in an hour of trial." If that was so, it was a great privilege for me.

Once out of office, Johnson was much more relaxed. On one occasion in 1970, we were driving all over his ranch, as usual, raising dust because of a long dry spell. "Billy," he said, "how about offering a little prayer for rain?" I took him seriously and prayed briefly. No sooner had I finished than a couple drops hit the windshield. In minutes it was raining so hard that the former President stopped the car and turned to me again. "Billy, we're gonna have a flood! I've got two pumps down in the river that are gonna wash away! See if you can't stop it!" I laughed and assured him it was out of my hands.

In the 1972 election, Johnson, in my opinion, was secretly in favor of Nixon. He called me one day just after the Democratic running mates—George McGovern and Sargent Shriver—had visited him at the ranch. "Billy, they're just now leaving," he said. "I want to tell you some things to pass on to our mutual friend."

He meant Nixon, of course, and his major piece of advice was that Richard Nixon should aggressively ignore McGovern during the campaign. "Tell him to respond to nothing McGovern says. Act as if he's not even a factor."

Some would say LBJ was being a disloyal Democrat, but I suspect he considered his party's 1972 ticket too liberal to fully support.

LBJ's premonition of his own death was right on the mark. He died of heart disease early in 1973. Lady Bird called and asked which service I would like to speak at, the funeral in Washington or the burial in Austin. I told her of his request, and we settled on the burial.

After the state funeral in Washington, which President Nixon attended, Johnson's body was flown to Texas. I met Lady Bird in Austin. At her request, I rode with her and the Johnson daughters to the ranch two hours away. It was bitterly cold, and I put on long underwear under my suit and wore a heavy topcoat. I rode in the back seat between Lady Bird and Lynda and nearly burned up!

On our way out of the city, hundreds of people lined the roads, many of them holding signs. One banner brought tears to our eyes.

417

Two white students held one side of the banner, and two black students the other. "FORGIVE US, MR. PRESIDENT," it read. Student protests over the Vietnam War had grieved Johnson's heart and had helped end his administration four years before under a cloud of unfinished business in Southeast Asia.

At the grave site, John Connally delivered the eulogy. I gave a short sermon, in which I spoke of President Johnson's accomplishments and pointed to the hope we have in Christ because of His resurrection from the dead. As I spoke my tribute and shared God's words of comfort, I looked at the flag-draped casket under the oaks by the Pedernales and thought, Here, indeed, was a Texan who was tall timber.

Like every other administration, his will get mixed reviews from historians. But historians will never be able to ignore LBJ. His Great Society did not accomplish all that he had hoped, but for him personally it was more than a dream. He wanted to harness the wealth and knowledge and greatness of this nation to help the poor and the oppressed here and around the world. That hope must be revived by every President and kept alive in the hearts of all citizens.

23

Reaching Out to a Broken World

MIAMI ROCK FESTIVAL, UNIVERSITIES, IRELAND AND SOUTH
AFRICA, TELEVISION AND FILMS, DISASTERS 1960S–1970S

MIAMI ROCK FESTIVAL

It was eleven o'clock on a Sunday morning, but I was most definitely
not in church. Instead, to the horror of some, I was attending the
1969 Miami Rock Music Festival.

America in 1969 was in the midst of cataclysmic social upheaval. Stories of violent student protests against the Vietnam War
filled the media. Images from the huge Woodstock music festival
that took place just six months before the Miami event near Bethel,
New York—for many a striking symbol of the anti-establishment
feelings of a whole generation of rebellious youth—were still firmly
etched in the public's memory.

Concert promoter Norman Johnson perhaps hoped my presence would neutralize at least some of the fierce opposition he had
encountered from Miami officials. Whatever his reasons, I was delighted for the opportunity to speak from the concert stage to young
people who probably would have felt uncomfortable in the average
church, and yet whose searching questions about life and sharp
protests against society's values echoed from almost every song.

"I gladly accept your kind invitation to speak to those attending the Miami Rock Festival on Sunday morning, December 28," I wired him the day before Christmas. "They are the most exciting and challenging generation in American history."

As I stepped onto the platform that Sunday morning, several thousand young people were lolling on the straw-covered ground or wandering around the concert site in the warm December sun, waiting for such groups as the Grateful Dead and Santana to make their appearance. A few were sleeping; the nonstop music had quit around four that morning.

In order to get a feel for the event, for a few hours the night before I put on a simple disguise and slipped into the crowd. My heart went out to them. Though I was thankful for their youthful exuberance, I was burdened by their spiritual searching and emptiness.

A bearded youth who had come all the way from California for the event recognized me. "Do me a favor," he said to me with a smile, "and say a prayer to thank God for good friends and good weed." Every evening at sunset, he confided to me, he got high on marijuana and other drugs.

"You can also get high on Jesus," I replied.

That Sunday morning, I came prepared to be shouted down, but instead I was greeted with scattered applause. Most listened politely as I spoke. I told the young people that I had been listening carefully to the message of their music. *We reject your materialism,* it seemed to proclaim, *and we want something of the soul.* Jesus was a nonconformist, I reminded them, and He could fill their souls and give them meaning and purpose in life. "Tune in to God today, and let Him give you faith. Turn on to His power."

Afterward two dozen responded by visiting a tent on the grounds set up by a local church as a means of outreach. During the whole weekend, the pastor wrote me later, 350 young people made commitments to Christ, and two thousand New Testaments were distributed.

As I have reflected on my own calling as an evangelist, I frequently recall the words of Christianity's greatest evangelist, the Apostle Paul: "It has always been my ambition to preach the gospel where Christ was not known . . ." (Romans 15:20). Paul not only

420

spoke in houses of worship, but also felt equally at home preaching to crowds in the central marketplace in Athens, small groups on a riverbank or in a jail cell in Philippi, curiosity-seekers in a rented public hall in Ephesus, and fellow passengers on the deck of a sinking ship off the Italian coast. I once told an interviewer that I would be glad to preach in Hell itself—if the Devil would let me out again!

My visit to the Miami Rock Festival was not an attempt to add variety to my schedule. True, it was not a typical setting for our ministry, but neither was it an *unexpected* setting, especially in light of the times. In some ways, in fact, it was symbolic of much of our ministry during the 1960s and early 1970s.

No doubt future historians will debate endlessly about the causes of the social upheaval that shook America during that tumultuous period, particularly among the youth. The word *counterculture* entered our national vocabulary during that time, as a whole generation questioned the values and ideals of their parents, often searching for meaning in bizarre ways—or giving up the search altogether. The tragic assassinations of President Kennedy in 1963 and five years later of his brother Robert and Dr. Martin Luther King, Jr., led to widespread disillusionment and cynicism. The growing civil rights movement made us aware of America's moral failure in the area of racial equality and enlisted many in the fight to end segregation, often through demonstrations and protests. The sexual revolution and the rise of the drug culture likewise influenced an entire generation.

On the international front, events like the Cuban missile crisis and the seemingly endless war in Vietnam contributed to an atmosphere of fear, uncertainty, confusion, and even mindless escapism. The political upheaval surrounding Watergate likewise undermined the confidence of many youth in traditional institutions and values.

As I look back, our schedule during those years was as packed as at any other time in our ministry, with large-scale Crusades in dozens of cities across the world, from Los Angeles and Seoul to Rio de Janeiro and Hong Kong. Much of my time, in fact, was spent overseas, often visiting, in depth, areas that we had only touched earlier. Nevertheless, the rootlessness of the sixties generation burdened me greatly, and I was determined to do whatever I could to point young people to the One who alone gives lasting meaning and purpose to life.

Whether it was at a rock festival in Miami, a spring break on the Ft. Lauderdale beaches, or a university mission, almost everywhere we went we sensed a deep hunger for spiritual reality on the part of many young people. Not all were open to the Gospel, of course, but we still saw God redirect the path of many who found in Christ the answer to their search.

UNIVERSITY CAMPUSES

When I announced plans to spend a part of the winter of 1963–64 holding missions on university campuses, I received one hundred invitations in the next ten days, two hundred more in the next few weeks. Invitations also came from half the theological seminaries in America. I wished I could have been ten men; even then I could never have covered them all. In the end, I accepted only Harvard, Princeton, Wellesley, the University of Michigan, and a few smaller colleges near my home that year, with others the next year.

As the sixties wore on and student unrest accelerated on many campuses, I determined once again to spend as much time as possible at universities, in spite of our commitment to a full schedule of Crusades. On some campuses, we joined with Campus Crusade for Christ, which Bill and Vonette Bright founded (partly at my urging) years before.

"Billy," he told me one night in Hollywood, where he lived, "I don't know what to do with my life."

"What's your interest?" I asked him.

"Well, I'm really interested in students, and Vonette is as well."

"Well, I'd give my life to the students," I suggested.

Bill has often said that I wrote him a check for $1,000 to help him and his wife get their program started. I don't remember ever having $1,000 during those early years, but I will take his word for it.

In 1967 he and I spoke at the University of California at Los Angeles and at the Berkeley campus of the University of California. With InterVarsity and Campus Crusade staff and students saturating the campuses, interest was high. When I spoke at UCLA, 6,000 students came to one meeting, the largest gathering to hear a speaker in the school's history up to that point. Some 8,000 showed up for one outdoor meeting at the Greek Theater at Berkeley. Although Berkeley was a hotbed of student unrest, there were only a few demonstrators; most students listened with rapt attention.

A year later, in 1968, I found myself speaking to another group of students in a much different setting. The American Ambassador to France, Sargent Shriver, asked me if I would come to his official residence in Paris and meet with some of the student leaders from the University of the Sorbonne and elsewhere.

"I think it will be an interesting evening," he said cautiously.

I flew over and stayed up talking with the students until the early hours of the morning. Some had been leaders in the student riots. Cynical about the answers society had given them, they were searching elsewhere for answers and adopting new and seemingly attractive philosophies like existentialism. Some of them, at least, were beginning to be disillusioned about everything. The ambassador's wife, Eunice, sat fascinated through the early part of the discussions and went upstairs to bring her young children down to eavesdrop. After Ambassador Shriver and I went outside to say a final good-bye to the students, he turned to me and summed the evening up: "You know, Billy, the basic problem these young people are facing is religious."

I agreed, adding that the same could be said about students almost anywhere. The basic questions of life are ultimately religious in nature.

Who am I?
Where did I come from?
Where am I going?
Is there any meaning to my life?

Only the God who created us can give us an ultimate answer to those questions.

Since those student missions in the 1960s, I have spoken at dozens and dozens of colleges, seminaries, and universities—

423

everywhere from the military academies at West Point, Annapolis, and Colorado Springs, to the John F. Kennedy School of Government at Harvard, to Kim Il Sung University in Communist-dominated North Korea.

Perhaps nowhere has the potential embodied in the youth of our world been demonstrated more forcefully than at some of the special events at which I spoke during the 1970s. I recall, for example, the following: Explo '72, with 80,000 students in Dallas's Cotton Bowl, sponsored by Campus Crusade for Christ; Spree-e '73 in London and Eurofest '75 in Brussels, both of which we helped sponsor and which drew tens of thousands of youth from all over Europe for challenge, inspiration, and intensive training in evangelism; and the Brazilian youth congress Generation '79, with 5,000 gathering in São Paulo.

Of a slightly different nature is the Urbana Missions Conference, held every three years over Christmas break on the campus of the University of Illinois by InterVarsity Christian Fellowship. Still ongoing, this event now brings as many as 18,000 university students together from across the world—with many more having to be turned away for lack of space—to focus on the challenge of world missions.

One personal incident at an Urbana conference is worth recounting. I was one of several speakers at a plenary session that year. My left leg began to hurt during the session, and I kept lifting it and twisting it in an attempt to relieve the pressure.

Sitting down front was a medical student who sent a note to the platform asking to see me. I turned the note over to David Howard, director of the convention. The pain got worse, and after I finished talking, I left the platform.

"I think you may have something wrong with your leg," said the young doctor. "Let me examine it."

He sat me down on a chair and gave my leg a thorough exam.

"Who's your doctor?" he asked.

"Dr. Rollie Dickson of the Mayo Clinic."

"Call him right away."

T.W. was with me and made the call. My doctor talked first with the medical student, asking him to lift my leg in all directions.

Final 1962 Chicago Crusade meeting at Soldier Field,
where 116,000 people gathered in over 100-degree heat.

With President John F. Kennedy in West Palm Beach,
Florida, for a game of golf, January 1961. In the backseat
is Florida Senator George Smathers.

Discussing my impressions
of her country with the
Prime Minister of India,
Mrs. Indira Gandhi, 1973.

In Israel,
1969, with
Prime Minister
Golda Meir.

Being welcomed in 1964 by Cardinal Richard J. Cushing of Boston, the first ranking Roman Catholic cleric to extend recognition to our ministry.

Arriving in Chicago with Dr. Martin Luther King, Jr., 1962, after a plane trip together from Florida.

At the Kremlin with Politburo member Boris Ponomarev, 1984.

Meeting with Prime Minister Margaret Thatcher of Great Britain, 1989.

Preaching in the pouring rain to troops
in Vietnam, December 1966.

Speaking at the infamous Wall of Death at
the former Nazi concentration camp of
Auschwitz, Poland, 1978.

Answering questions at the John F.
Kennedy School of Government,
Harvard University, 1982.

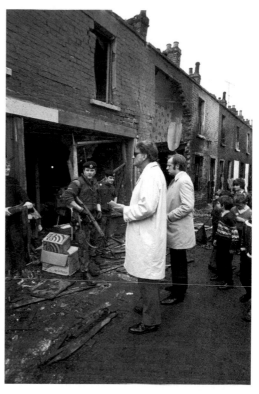

Visiting the Indian state of
Andhra Pradesh, December
1977, where 100,000 lost
their lives in a devastating
cyclone and tidal wave.

On the streets of Belfast, Northern Ireland,
minutes after a bomb blast killed several
people, 1972.

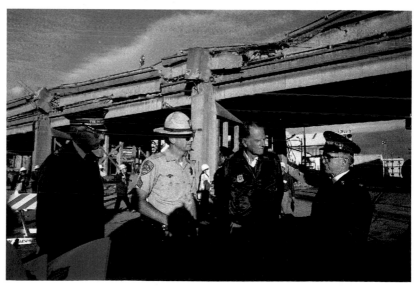

Touring earthquake-damaged areas of Northern California,
October 1989. Behind is a collapsed section of Interstate
Highway 880 in Oakland.

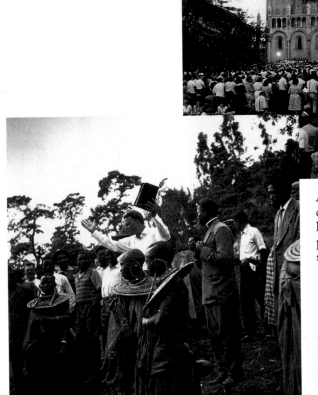

A first in Communist-dominated Europe: crowds legally gathering on public property for an evangelistic service, Pécs, Hungary, 1985.

Preaching to an impromptu gathering of people from the Masai tribe during the 1960 African tour.

Closing meeting of the 1973 Seoul, Korea, Crusade in Yoido Plaza with more than 1 million people, the largest audience in our ministry.

Some 250,000 people gather to hear the gospel in Central Park, New York, 1991.

Metropolitan (later Patriarch) Alexei listens as I preach in the Orthodox Cathedral in Tallinn, Estonia, 1984.

A crowd estimated at 150,000 welcomes us to the Orthodox Cathedral in Timisoara, Romania, 1985.

Following our discussions, Chinese Premier Li Peng escorts Ruth and me to our car, 1988.

Japanese Christians welcome us to their country for a series of Crusades, 1980. *Left:* Team members Walter Smyth and Henry Holley.

Singing with school children at the Great Wall of China, 1988.

Franklin, Ruth, and I visit Ruth's childhood home in Huaiyin, China, during our 1988 trip.

Then my doctor asked to speak with me. "I don't want you to leave that chair," he said. "I want you to be taken back by stretcher to your quarters, and we'll send a hospital plane for you. We think you have thrombophlebitis."

My son Ned was with me also, and when the plane from Minnesota arrived, he and T.W. and the medical student, Victor Wahby, boarded with me. As it turned out, I had met his family during our meetings in Egypt, where his father was a leader in the Presbyterian Church. When we arrived in Rochester, it was so cold—twenty degrees below zero—that the pilot took the plane inside the hangar before letting us out.

We were met by Dr. Dickson and cardiologist Dr. Schirger, who rushed me to the hospital and determined that I did indeed have thrombophlebitis, a blood clot in the deepest vein, close to the bone. If it had broken free, it could have gone immediately to the brain.

With his successful diagnosis, the student doctor from Egypt so impressed the staff at the Mayo Clinic that they later accepted his application for advanced study.

AREAS OF CONFLICT

"A great social revolution is going on in the United States today," I said, introducing Dr. Martin Luther King, Jr., to the audience in Madison Square Garden one night during the 1957 New York Crusade.

With the benefit of four decades of hindsight, we know how far-reaching that revolution would prove to be, but at the time we could not see the future and few realized just how radically the civil rights movement would eventually change the face of America. Nor is it easy for later generations to realize what the racial situation was in much of the United States before the precedent-setting 1954 Supreme Court decision outlawing segregated schools.

I cannot point to any single event or intellectual crisis that changed my mind on racial equality. Growing up in the rural South, I had adopted the attitudes of that region without much reflection, though as I have said, aside from my father, I admired no one as much as Reese Brown, the black foreman on our dairy farm. As a boy, I also loved reading the Tarzan adventure books by Edgar Rice Burroughs, although even at the time it bothered me that white people were consistently portrayed in them as superior to blacks. At Wheaton College, I made friends with black students, and I recall vividly one of them coming to my room one day and talking with deep conviction about America's need for racial justice. Most influential, however, was my study of the Bible, leading me eventually to the conclusion that not only was racial inequality wrong but Christians especially should demonstrate love toward all peoples.

In 1953, during our Crusade in Chattanooga, Tennessee, I went into the building as the people were beginning to gather one night and personally tore down the ropes separating the white from the black sections—ropes that had been mandated according to the custom in those days by the local committee. My action caused the head usher to resign in anger right on the spot (and raised some other hackles), but I did not back down.

Civil rights were very much in the forefront in America during the 1960s and early 1970s. As the issue unfolded, I sometimes found myself under fire from both sides, extreme conservatives castigating me for doing too much and extreme liberals blaming me for not doing enough. In reality, both groups tended to stand aloof from our evangelistic Crusades, but those people who actively supported us understood very well our commitment to doing what we could through our evangelism to end the blight of racism.

Early on, Dr. King and I spoke about his method of using non-violent demonstrations to bring an end to racial segregation. He urged me to keep on doing what I was doing—preaching the Gospel to integrated audiences and supporting his goals by example—and not to join him in the streets. "You stay in the stadiums, Billy," he said, "because you will have far more impact on the white establishment there than you would if you marched in the streets. Besides that, you have a constituency that will listen to you, especially among white people, who may not listen so much to me. But if a leader gets too far out in front of his people, they will lose sight of him and not follow him any longer." I followed his advice.

Few events galvanized the whole issue of civil rights or caused such strong feelings on both sides as did the 1965 Selma March and the violence that followed in its wake. Shortly afterward, in April, President Johnson suggested that I go to Alabama as a gesture of peace and goodwill, and in April we held several rallies around the state, including one at Tuskegee Institute.

During the long summer of 1965, America seemed on the brink of chaos. Immediately after the riots in the Watts neighborhood of Los Angeles, I toured the area with Dr. E. V. Hill, a respected black pastor in Watts (who later became a member of the BGEA board) and other community leaders. No doubt extremists on both sides exploited the situation for their own goals, but I was sickened by the violence and the widespread destruction we saw on every hand. There were no easy answers, I knew, but Dr. Hill and I both agreed that any solution that omitted the need for spiritual renewal could bring only temporary relief. Hatred and racism are fundamentally moral and spiritual problems.

Ireland

Much of my time during the 1960s and early 1970s was spent overseas. Two trips in particular brought us to nations torn by chronic strife and division.

The first was our visit to Ireland in 1972. Long a hotbed of religious and political conflict between Protestants and Catholics, Northern Ireland was a virtual war zone as a result of bombings and armed attacks by the Provisional Wing of the Irish Republican Army (IRA).

After careful investigation by Walter Smyth (who had spent some of his boyhood years in Belfast) and others, we responded to an invitation from a broad-based group of Protestant pastors to make a private visit to Northern Ireland. No Crusade meetings would be possible, for security reasons (although I did preach in one church), but we felt that an expression of goodwill toward both sides might do something to defuse the dangerous situation.

We went to Northern Ireland only days after finishing a Crusade in Birmingham, Alabama. The progress in racial harmony we saw there between our 1965 rallies and this Crusade seven years later encouraged us to believe that even in difficult places with long histories of conflict, love and goodwill have the power to overcome the barriers of the past.

We arrived in Belfast on a Saturday night, and the next morning I joined our friend, Graham Lacey, a British businessman, and Arthur Blessitt, an American evangelist who was carrying a large cross through the streets of Great Britain and Ireland as a demonstration of Christ's love and concern. We went for a walk along Falls Road and Shankill Road, often seen as dividing lines between the warring factions. We had no security guards or police with us. The newspapers had displayed my picture prominently, so people knew who I was.

"How will I know if they're going to accept us?" I asked Arthur.

"Well, if they don't, you'll get a bullet in the back!"

His answer was hardly reassuring, but we prayed and committed the time to the Lord. Along the way, we stopped to talk with individuals about Christ and His love, and to pray. In the Catholic Falls Road area, we came upon a public house with an open door. When we looked in, the Sunday morning drinkers recognized me from the newspapers and television and invited us in.

I told them who we were and why we had come into the Catholic district, to tell them how much God loved them. Some of them laughed at me; others whispered noisily to their neighbors at the tables; but still others, who probably should have been in church at that very moment instead of in the pub, seemed to take the words of Jesus Christ to heart. When I finished, they sent us on our way with applause and a good wish for our safety.

Not too much further down the road, we encountered a roadblock manned by the British. We did not see the soldiers, but we saw their steely rifles poking through the sandbags.

Shortly afterward, we heard a mighty explosion. We could not see its flash, but we certainly felt its impact. People poured out into the streets and ran in the direction of the noise. We joined the crowd and soon came upon the dreadful sight: bodies and pieces of bodies blown apart by a bomb. Three of the dead were apparently known terrorists handling the bomb, but certainly others were innocent bystanders.

We tried to bring some measure of comfort to the chaotic scene. Several of the people recognized me. I was not wearing clerical garb, of course, but they insisted on calling me "Father," begging me to give the last rites to the dead and the dying. It was not a time for theological distinctions: I knelt by each one and prayed for them. One woman said I was the first Protestant clergyman she had met. Many thanked us for coming.

At that moment the soldiers arrived, and one of them advised us to leave the scene as quickly as possible. More trouble was sure to develop. So we turned around and retraced our steps without further incident—without a bullet in the back—but with a profound sense of sadness at what had occurred.

During the next few days, we met with a wide variety of people, including the governor, the Lord Grey of Naunton. In a meeting sponsored by both the Catholic and Protestant chaplains, students at Queen's University listened attentively as I spoke about the power of Christ to change lives and fill hearts with love. Jim Douglas, our journalist friend from Scotland, said later that from his experience of British student behavior, he fully expected the crowd to break into catcalls and jeers at any moment; but the students could not have been more attentive.

Especially memorable was a private meeting with Cardinal Conway, the Roman Catholic primate, at the Archbishop's palace in Armagh. Protestant leaders had also been invited, and they confirmed what I had heard from others: that in spite of the division between Protestants and Catholics, the complex troubles in Ireland were not basically religious but rather were historical and political in nature.

Afterward we went by train to Dublin, in the Republic of Ireland. We were overwhelmed by the warmth of our reception: 2,000 invited guests came to an evening meeting at the Royal Dublin Concert Hall, and Chief Justice O'Dalaigh presided at a breakfast for 450 the next morning. At one meeting, the emcee—a Catholic priest—told how he had come to Christ through reading my book *Peace with God.* Another meeting—this one at Milltown Park, the headquarters of the Jesuit order in Ireland, brought together clergy from all denominations.

429

Of special interest was a secret meeting I had with the leader of the Official Wing of the IRA. The police advised against it, but I decided to go through with it anyway. Walter Smyth and I were taken out the back door of our hotel and bundled into a car driven by two men with beards. Shortly afterward, we switched cars and were driven to a house in a working-class section of the city. Although not evident from the outside, the building had originally consisted of four or five adjacent row houses in which the interior had been gutted and rebuilt to form a large and comfortable home. The IRA leader we met there talked for almost an hour about the history of the conflict in Ireland. Then we had tea, and I spoke about what Christ had done for me and how I believed He could bring healing to the people of Northern Ireland if they would turn humbly to Him.

South Africa

The next year, 1973, we went to South Africa. I had been invited there several times before—the first time being in my Youth for Christ days—but I had always refused to go; that country's strict apartheid policy meant that our audiences would have to be segregated.

In the early 1970s, our friend Michael Cassidy, the founder of African Enterprise, detected some slight changes in his nation's policy and began to pursue the possibility of a congress on evangelism patterned after the 1966 Berlin Congress. He eventually was able to gain permission for a fully integrated conference embracing all races and virtually all Protestant denominations in South Africa, and I was invited by the organizing committee to speak twice at the event.

On March 13, the South African Congress on Mission and Evangelism convened in the coastal resort city of Durban for ten days. All 700 of us, regardless of race, stayed in the same hotel; some said it was the largest interracial meeting held to that date in South Africa.

At first I planned to speak only at the congress, but to almost everyone's surprise, Cassidy was able to secure permission for a fully integrated evangelistic rally. I will never forget Saturday afternoon,

March 17, when 45,000 people of all races—half the people non-white—jammed King's Park Rugby Stadium and spilled over most of the playing field. Some of the committee members were almost overcome with joy by the sight of white ushers escorting nonwhites to their seats.

"Christianity is not a white man's religion," I stated, "and don't let anybody ever tell you that it's white or black. Christ belongs to *all* people!" I went on to proclaim Christ as the only answer to the deepest needs of the human heart. At the Invitation, 3,300 people completely filled the only open space in front of the platform; additional hundreds could not be reached by counselors. Local papers said it was the largest multiracial crowd of any type in South Africa's history. The main Durban newspaper the next day carried the headline "APARTHEID DOOMED," summarizing my statement at the press conference.

Durban's record was broken slightly over a week later in Johannesburg, on Sunday, March 25. Some 60,000 filled Wanderers Stadium—the previous stadium record was less than 40,000—and again blanketed much of the playing field. Many came from dozens of the segregated townships around Johannesburg, including Sharpeville and Soweto. The music, including a Zulu quartet, reflected the diversity of the crowd. The entire service was carried live throughout the nation over government radio, in English and Afrikaans. (Television did not exist then in that country.) At the end of the service, more than 4,000 came forward to indicate their commitment to Christ. While we were in Johannesburg, professional golfer Gary Player went out of his way to welcome us to a multiracial reception at his home.

I left South Africa convinced that apartheid was un-Christian and unworkable. At the same time, I knew that South Africa's problems would not be solved instantly, any more than those in Northern Ireland or the United States. People sometimes assume that an evangelistic Crusade is somehow a failure if the problems in a city or nation are not suddenly solved, but complex and long-standing problems are seldom solved overnight. Nevertheless, a start had been made, and for that we thanked God.

TELEVISION

If the 1960s and early 1970s were years of upheaval in society, they also brought changes and expansion in the outreach of the Billy Graham Evangelistic Association. Chief among these changes was the growth in our use of the media.

Radio, books, and films have all had an important part in extending our ministry, but by far the most significant in the long term has been television. More than one critic has pointed out the limitations and pitfalls of television. No doubt television also has been used to promote lifestyles and points of view that are opposed to what the Bible teaches. At times, in fact, I have wondered if we have not reached the state described by the prophet Jeremiah: "Are they ashamed of their loathsome conduct? No, they have no shame at all; they do not even know how to blush" (Jeremiah 6:15).

All of that, however, does not rule out television as an incredibly powerful vehicle for shaping character and influencing people, for good or for evil. Like most technologies, television in itself is morally neutral; it is what we do with it, or fail to do with it, that makes the difference.

Our first systematic efforts in television were initiated in 1951. Cliff, Bev, and I used the studios of KTTV in Los Angeles to produce a half-hour program in a format called Kinescope, which we then placed on as many stations as we could. Television was still in its infancy, however, and after a few years we discontinued the broadcasts, mainly because of the time involved in making a weekly program—particularly with our London meetings approaching.

Our first telecast to a whole nation took place in 1955 in Great Britain, when the BBC carried our Good Friday message from Glasgow's Kelvin Hall throughout Britain. As I noted in an earlier chapter, we first telecast live in the United States from New York, during the Madison Square Garden Crusade in 1957.

Following the New York meetings, we continued to obtain television time wherever possible for live broadcasts from Crusades in the United States. Color television was in its infancy, but we were not far behind; we began to cover the televised Crusades in color.

Two years later, in 1959, we telecast the Crusade from Melbourne, Australia, back to the United States. Because Australia did not yet have color television, we had to import a huge amount of equipment from a Toronto company in order to handle the color. Our telecasts were the first TV programs ever produced in color in Australia.

Because a Crusade meeting usually runs for two hours and a telecast for one, by 1964 we realized that it was better to tape and edit programs for later release rather than to continue broadcasting live. Cliff became adept at building in musical and other features that would appeal to viewers. Soon we expanded our television outreach to as many stations as possible, not restricting ourselves to one network but purchasing prime time whenever it was available. Our recent pattern has been to go on television four times a year for two or three nights during prime time. We still purchase time in each market on whatever channels are available to us.

In light of television's high cost, I have been grateful we have not attempted a weekly program. Because we generate programs only intermittently, we do not require our own TV production facilities or staff. Instead, we contract with other people to oversee production and editing, using the finest technology to achieve the highest quality possible. It has been a pleasure to work with some of these people for many years. Among them is Danny Franks—internationally respected for his work with numerous major television productions—who oversees the lighting for our Crusades and television. Since 1985 we have also included closed-captioned capabilities for our hearing-impaired viewers.

FILMS

Almost all of our early films were intended to be shown in churches. But we could not sit back and wait for the unchurched to come to church, so in time we began to do films that could be shown in theaters—full-length features with a spiritual message. These included *Two-a-Penny*, starring British pop star Cliff Richard; *Joni*, starring Joni Eareckson Tada as herself; and *The Hiding Place*, with Julie Harris and Jeannette Clift George. They were dramatic films—

433

stories of youth and sex, pop culture and rebellion, physical handicaps, and wartime civilian heroism and tragedy—dealing with moral and spiritual problems from the Bible's standpoint.

Most successful was *The Hiding Place*, the true story of Corrie ten Boom and her family during the Second World War. Committed to hiding Jews who were fleeing from Hitler's terror in Holland, the ten Boom family underwent terrible suffering. When they were discovered, Corrie and her sister, Betsie, were imprisoned in the Nazi death camp of Ravensbrück; Betsie died there. Corrie is one of the great Christian heroines of the century. We met her in Switzerland, and her story made such an impression on Ruth that she recommended it to writers John and Elizabeth Sherrill. They jumped at it; and the book and film that followed brought home the horror of those days and the triumph of Christ's love in the midst of virulent hatred.

All that came home to us during the film's 1975 world premiere at the Beverly Theater, at the corner of Beverly Drive and Wilshire Boulevard. Shortly before the film was to start, someone threw a tear-gas canister into the theater, forcing the crowd to evacuate. The showing had to be postponed. We held an impromptu street meeting out in front while the police and fire departments attempted to find out what had happened. I spoke to the crowd and prayed.

At a reception later that evening, Corrie ten Boom spoke in her distinctive Dutch accent: "People asked me tonight, 'What did you feel about this [tear-gas] bomb that was falling?' I was touched. I was sad. Do you know why? Not only because there was in some way disappointment for people who had hoped to see the film but because on that bomb was the *Hakenkreuz,* the [Nazi] swastika. . . . What we have to do is love these people who hate us—love them, pray for them. These people are wounded people who have hate in their hearts. They need forgiveness. They need the Lord. . . . That is the answer we must give."

In God's providence, the furor over the tear-gas canister created enormous interest in the film. It premiered the following night without incident and has become the most widely seen motion picture we've ever produced.

Another of our films from this period deserves special mention. As plans began to take shape for the 1964–65 New York World's Fair, we were approached by the fair's chief planner, Robert Moses, about the possibility of having some type of exhibit. It sounded like an unusual opportunity; at least 50 million people were expected to attend the fair's two-year run.

We determined to go ahead. As our plans developed, however, I began to have second thoughts. For one thing, the whole fair seemed overwhelming. Someone calculated that if people spent only twelve minutes at every exhibit, it would take them two weeks to see the whole fair. In addition, I doubted if we could raise the funds to build a separate pavilion, staff it for two years, and develop a film that would be adequate for an event this massive. I wrestled with the decision for months. In a moment of discouragement—I was ill at the time—I wrote the BGEA board telling them I thought we should cancel. Dr. Edman, the president of Wheaton College whose wisdom I respected so much, immediately wrote back that he thought I was wrong. He saw this opportunity as "a great challenge put before us by our Lord." He also told me that Dwight L. Moody's greatest impact may have been through the extensive campaign he ran in connection with the 1893 Chicago World's Fair.

So we went ahead, developing a seventy-millimeter widescreen Todd-AO film entitled *Man in the Fifth Dimension*. (The name came from the film's theme: life has a fifth dimension to it, the dimension of the spiritual.) Using spectacular photography to tell the story of God's creation and His love in Christ, scriptwriter Jim Collier and director Dick Ross put together a presentation of the Gospel that touched thousands of lives.

Our pavilion included an exhibit area, which 5 million people visited in the course of the fair, and a 400-seat auditorium where the film was shown hourly, complete with translations into six major languages. Pavilion director Dan Piatt reported that the film was seen by 1 million people.

World Wide Pictures became the largest producer of religious films in the world, with translations into dozens of languages. Someone once calculated that at any hour of the day or night, a

WWP film is being shown somewhere in the world. In the last few years, the head of our international film ministry, Paul Kurtz, has been able to get some of our films on television and in theaters in the former Soviet Union and in countries in eastern Europe. For all of this, we give thanks to God.

At the same time, the film work admittedly has been one of the most difficult parts of my ministry. For one thing, motion pictures by their nature are enormously expensive to make, especially if they are done well. Almost all of our pictures (with the exception of *The Hiding Place* and perhaps a few others) have had to be heavily subsidized by the BGEA. The task of constantly raising money for these was never easy. And occasionally, we faced organizational snafus and difficulties.

In the early years, Ruth reviewed every script; often we held up production until we were convinced that the Gospel message came through with clarity. In recent years, Cliff Barrows has taken fuller responsibility for World Wide Pictures, working first with Dick Ross's successor, Bill Brown, and then overseeing WWP's move from Burbank to Minneapolis.

One film we were involved with—we did not produce it but obtained it after completion—starred Johnny Cash and his wife, June Carter Cash . . . and therein lies a tale.

In 1971 June dreamed she saw her husband on a mountain with a Bible in his hand, talking about Jesus. The next year, they made a movie about the life of Jesus called *The Gospel Road.* Holiday Inns expressed interest in sponsoring it as a TV special, but the corporation wanted artistic as well as financial control. The Cashes said no; they wanted to tell the story their way. That meant they had to finance it themselves.

Johnny got his friends together—Kris Kristofferson and the Statler Brothers, among others—to write songs that would tell the story of Jesus. June played Mary Magdalene; Johnny himself narrated. Robert Elfstrom, who had directed the television special "Johnny Cash: The Man and His Music," was the cinematographer; he also took the role of Jesus.

A few months and a million dollars later, the Cashes sold the work to Twentieth Century–Fox. I had seen a rough cut of it, and from time to time I asked Johnny how the movie was coming. He finally told me it had been sold.

But the news wasn't good: the Hollywood studio was having trouble marketing the movie.

"Well, Johnny," I said to him, "we'll just buy it from them."

The studio wanted to get its money back, of course, but eventually they came down on their price. As I recall, they sold it to us for about $250,000. Since then, it has been one of the best evangelistic film tools that the BGEA has had, with hundreds of prints in circulation. Missionaries are using it in video vans in Africa, India, and elsewhere.

WORLD EMERGENCY FUND

One footnote to our work during the 1960s and early 1970s was the formation in 1973 of a special fund within the BGEA to bring humanitarian aid to places facing natural disasters or other emergencies. For many years we made it a practice to give away a large part of our undesignated income for the support of other evangelistic enterprises and organizations in various parts of the world, including those trying to meet emergency needs. In 1973 we named our effort the World Emergency Fund.

Over the years, I became more and more convinced of the importance of demonstrating our love through acts of compassion. I knew Jesus' parable of the Good Samaritan, of course, and had always believed in our responsibility to do whatever we can as individuals to help those in need.

As I studied and traveled, however, I came to realize that we had a larger responsibility. My travels brought me face to face with the stark reality of human suffering and with the fact that many millions of people live on the knife-edge of starvation or chronic illness or disaster. We also realized that compassionate help often opened the door to opportunities in evangelism, as people saw Christ's love in action.

I recall, for example, the earthquake in Guatemala in 1976. At the time, Ruth and I were in Mexico, where she was recovering from an illness. As soon as I heard of the disaster, I contacted our board to see what we could do through the World Emergency Fund. Then we arranged to travel to the devastated areas. The president of Guatemala put two helicopters at our disposal. His son traveled with us, along with Cliff and a friend of ours, the Argentine-born evangelist Luis Palau.

When we touched down in San Martín Jilotepeque, we saw at once that virtually every building had been destroyed. Of the town's 18,000 residents, 3,800 were dead in the ruins. Another 4,000 were badly wounded, but there was almost no medical help. Ruth and I felt utterly helpless as we watched thousands wandering about in a daze looking for food or lost relatives.

Back in Guatemala City, I spoke to 500 Christian leaders and missionaries to assure them of our prayers and support. We were meeting in the partially destroyed Central Presbyterian Church. Even as I was talking, a sharp aftershock hit and pieces of the ceiling began to fall on us. The clergy got up and ran out, thinking it might be another earthquake. Later that day, I was invited to speak on the national television network. The BGEA, through the World Emergency Fund, flew in a dozen planeloads of food and medicine to help with the relief effort. As in almost every other emergency situation where we have tried to help, we worked with established organizations and local Christian agencies to ensure that the supplies went where they were most needed.

Just as heartbreaking in its effects, but far more extensive, were the cyclone and tidal wave in India in late 1977. A wall of water eighteen feet high and fifty miles wide had swept inland for upward of thirty miles, completely destroying almost everything in its path. Hundreds of coastal villages in the state of Andhra Pradesh were wiped out, and 100,000 people lost their lives. In one village, only six dogs survived.

In God's providence, we were in the country for a series of Crusades when news came of the disaster. No outsiders—not even journalists—were being allowed in. President Reddy, whom I had met on another occasion (and who was from Andhra Pradesh himself), graciously granted us permission to see the site and supplied a helicopter to take us there. Most villages in that part of India were surrounded by thick, tall thorn bushes to keep out wild animals. As we looked down, we could see bright bits of color snagged by the thorns surrounding dozens of villages. These were fully clothed bodies—thousands of them—already beginning to decompose in the humid tropical heat. When we landed, a man ran up to me and grabbed me by the legs, shouting and refusing to let go. "Kill us or help us rebuild," he kept saying.

We took his cry literally. Through the World Emergency Fund, we provided for the rebuilding of one village—285 cement-block homes and a 500-seat church; this became a model for the rebuilding of other villages. The Andhra Pradesh Christian Relief and Rehabilitation Committee oversaw the project. In 1980 Walter Smyth and my son Franklin went to India for the formal dedication of the new town. Against my wishes, the inhabitants insisted on calling it "Billy Graham Nagar [Village]."

The BGEA's World Emergency Fund continues to minister in places of need: famine-ravaged Ethiopia, war-torn Rwanda, the 1989 earthquake in San Francisco, and the areas of South Carolina and Florida decimated by Hurricane Hugo and Hurricane Andrew. In such instances, we often give the money through organizations like the Salvation Army, the Red Cross, and Samaritan's Purse. We have visited many of these disaster areas personally to try to bring hope and encouragement in the name of Christ. We know we cannot do everything that needs to be done, but in a world that is never free of turmoil, Christ calls us to do what we can.

24

My Quaker Friend

PRESIDENT RICHARD M. NIXON

Richard Nixon had tears streaming down his face. It was October 3, 1967, and we were standing in the simple Friends meeting house in East Whittier, California. The Quaker minister and I had just conducted a funeral service for his mother, Hannah. I had already delivered a eulogy for the crowd who attended. The people had filed by the closed casket for the last time and left. The casket was then reopened, and his wife, Pat, and daughters, Julie and Tricia, gathered around. I stretched my arms around their shoulders while the son tearfully expressed his tribute to his mother and the loss he felt at her death. Then I offered a prayer for their comfort.

Almost twenty years before, after our 1949 Los Angeles Crusade, I met Hannah Nixon when I preached in Whittier. She was a godly woman who reared her family to fear the Lord and honor His Word. She told me that her late husband once took his three young sons to Los Angeles to hear evangelist Paul Rader from Chicago. That evening, at the Invitation to commit their lives to Christ, Richard and his brothers walked forward.

In his youth, Richard taught a Bible class in the Whittier Friends meeting and sung in the choir. He played the piano for

Sunday school each Sunday morning and went to Christian Endeavor youth meetings each Sunday night. His spiritual legacy from that quiet Quaker tradition of "friendly persuasion" helped shape the way he looked at the world. These experiences made him a very private person, one who was not prone to exhibit his deep feelings. Tears in public were rare for him. Who knows how many more he shed in private.

From the start of our acquaintance, when he was the freshman senator from California, this godly heritage probably did as much as anything to make us compatible.

Our friendship began one day in 1950 or 1951, when I was in Washington, D.C. North Carolina Senator Clyde Hoey had invited me to join him for lunch. A patrician southern gentleman with a mane of white hair almost to his shoulders, he was born and reared about sixty miles from my home. As we ate together in the Senate dining room, he pointed out to me several legislators in the room whose names I was familiar with from the headlines.

"There's young Richard Nixon from California."

"I've met his mother," I replied.

"Would you like to meet him?"

At my assent, Senator Hoey sent a waiter to ask Nixon to come over to our table at his convenience.

He soon joined us. His warm smile and firm handshake impressed me.

"You've held some wonderful meetings in our state and are well known there," he said, looking me right in the eye. "As a matter of fact, my mother has written me about you."

We had chatted only a few minutes before he asked me an unexpected question: "Do you play golf?"

"Yes, sir, I try."

"We're going to play a round at Burning Tree this afternoon, and we need another partner. Would you join us?"

I was delighted with that outing. Because he knew the course so well, he gave me suggestions on almost every shot. Maybe because of that, our score was fairly even. When we finished the game, he drove me to his home and introduced me to Pat and to his little daughters.

It was not just friendship that put me in Nixon's camp mentally as he rose to national prominence, although we were good friends. I sincerely thought his two terms of administrative experience and privileged access to information as Vice President in the White House environment made him well qualified to succeed Eisenhower. I knew he had a tremendous grasp of world affairs and from our many conversations together I knew he had formulated a well-studied philosophy of American government. He exhibited both courage and patience, which gave him a long-range view of domestic and international problems. However, I kept my thoughts concerning his suitability for the presidency to myself, except in a few private conversations. I also saw him as a modest and moral man with spiritual sensitivity. I had heard of the controversies in California politics, but I formed my own opinions of him based on first-hand observation of the man.

Looking back these forty-five years later, considering all that has intervened, I wonder whether I might have exaggerated his spirituality in my own mind. But then, in my presence, he always made ready references to his mother's faith and the Bible that she loved so much. Where religion was concerned with him, it was not always easy to tell the difference between the spiritual and the sentimental. In retrospect, whenever he spoke about the Lord, it was in pretty general terms.

At the time Nixon was defeated by Kennedy in 1960, many commentators felt he had been hurt by those celebrated television debates. Others questioned the accuracy of the election results, believing that Nixon might actually have won. As a matter of fact, I was told Eisenhower offered to impound all the ballot boxes in several states for a recount. Nixon refused.

I did not publicly endorse Nixon in the 1960 election, but I reluctantly gave in to a plea from James Byrnes, former secretary of state (and then governor of South Carolina), to pray at a Nixon rally in Columbia, South Carolina. Many people took it as an implied endorsement.

Two years later, he lost his bid to become governor of California. There too, although I still wanted to maintain political neutrality, I inadvertently lined up on his side before the election. Nixon seemed lackluster about campaigning. His publicist, Paul Keyes, was discouraged. They were not getting much photographic coverage, and he thought the news photographers might be interested in a shot of the candidate and me together. I consented. A picture was taken of the two of us playing golf at the Riviera Country Club in Bel Air, near Los Angeles—a game that had been scheduled before the photo request came through. The next morning the picture appeared on the front page of the *Los Angeles Times*. Neither of us ever wondered out loud if my public identification with him was more of a jinx than a boost to his cause, but it certainly crossed my mind.

He was so devastated after those defeats that some who knew him best questioned whether he would ever pull out of it. One day he and I were walking together on the Riviera course where we were playing golf with Grady and actor Randolph Scott. On that occasion, Nixon was one of the most disconsolate people I had ever seen. His shoulders were stooped as if the world had caved in on him.

Impulsively, I flung my arm around him. "Dick, I believe you'll have another chance at the presidency," I said. "The world situation is getting worse. There'll come a time when the American people will call on you. You have the ability and the training to be president of the United States. Don't give up."

"No," he said in a low voice, "it's finished. After two straight defeats, it's not likely I'll ever be nominated for anything again, or be given another chance. I'm just going back into law practice."

In the next election year, 1964, when the Republicans nominated Barry Goldwater to run against President Lyndon Johnson, Nixon brought a magnificent speech to the Republican convention, pleading for party unity. He toured the country making speeches for Goldwater. At a whistle-stop in Bangor, Maine, where I was preaching at the time, I went out to the little airport to hear him speak. When he learned that I was there, he sent for me. I met him in a private area, and he spent an hour with me, much to the bewilderment and displeasure of the local Republican hierarchy.

"I doubt if Goldwater can win," he confided in me, "but I'm going to do everything I can to help him."

As the 1968 election loomed on the horizon, Nixon's name surfaced among the prospective Republican candidates. I had no leanings toward any of the announced Democratic hopefuls. If Lyndon Johnson had not told me a year earlier that he would not seek reelection, it would have put me in a quandary as to which friend to vote for.

En route home from a trip in December 1967, I received a message in Atlanta that Nixon wanted to see me in Key Biscayne, Florida. I had the flu and was running a high temperature, but I phoned home and told Ruth of the change in our plans. She had gotten used to such changes; at least she tolerated them.

Dick was staying in a cottage at the Key Biscayne Hotel as guest of the owner. He vacated his front bedroom for me when we arrived, taking the back one for himself. His friend Bebe Rebozo was staying at the hotel too. As was often the case during our conversations, I read Scripture to him and had prayer.

We attended the Key Biscayne Presbyterian Church together on Sunday morning and watched a muddy Green Bay Packers football game on television in the afternoon. Then he asked me to walk with him on the beach. I was feeling weak from the fever (which, as I was soon to learn, was developing into pneumonia), but I dragged myself along anyway.

He was musing about a bid for the presidency and wanted to know what I thought he should do. It was only two months since we had been together at his mother's funeral. Maybe he was remembering how she had said to him on her deathbed, "Dick, don't quit."

We walked as far as the lighthouse, a couple of miles round-trip, and got back none too soon for me. I was about ready to collapse.

I had no intention of advising him what decision to make. The assassination of Jack Kennedy a few years earlier, the seemingly endless and morale-draining war in Vietnam, the campus demonstrations against that war, the takeovers of buildings by radical students, the draft-card burnings that fall—all these combined to throw us into a national crisis. It was daunting in the extreme for anyone who considered seeking the leadership of the country.

"You still haven't told me what to do," he said to me two days later as I was leaving.

"If you don't run, you will always wonder if you should have," I said to him. "I will pray for you, that the Lord will give you the wisdom to make the right choice."

Nixon remembered that day (although somewhat differently) in his memoirs and also in a personal letter to John Pollock, one of my biographers, to whom he wrote, "He [Nixon meant me] was ill at the time, but when we took our long two-mile walk to the lighthouse at Key Biscayne, he was insistent that, because of the problems the country faced abroad and my experience in international affairs, I had an obligation to run.

"He made it clear that he was not against Lyndon Johnson; they were good friends. But he felt that the country was in crisis in 1968 and that Johnson because of the division among his own advisers would be unable to provide the leadership that was needed. . . . Whether the issue was foreign or domestic, he always had a point of view and expressed it articulately and effectively. I think one of the reasons he felt free to do so was that he knew I would not disclose his personal views to others unless he had publicly expressed them."

That might have been how Nixon remembered the walk and the talk, but that was not the way I remembered the incident.

Nixon's candidacy materialized seven months later. Frankly, it muffled those inner monitors that had warned me for years to stay out of partisan politics. Even though our Crusade ministry demanded my time and energy all across this country as well as overseas, I could not completely distance myself from the electoral process that was involving such a close friend. As far as his attitude was concerned, he was more cautious than I: he strongly admonished me not to make any public endorsement of him or to associate with the campaign in any way. He thought that any politicking on my part would have negative repercussions for our ministry.

In 1960 Nixon sought recommendations for a running mate from many friends and advisers. In response to his question, I urged him to consider Congressman Walter Judd from Minnesota. A former missionary to China, he was an expert in foreign policy and a strong intellectual foe of Communism. But one day, when Nixon and I were riding in the back seat of his car, he gave me his reasons for not taking my suggestion. I did not think they were valid. If he had followed my advice, maybe he could have beaten Kennedy. There were some who thought his choice of Henry Cabot Lodge was detrimental.

I struck out the next time around too. Before the 1968 Republican convention, Nixon invited me to come to New York and have dinner with him in his apartment. As we sat in front of the fireplace, he floated a few names of vice-presidential prospects for my reaction—Nelson Rockefeller, John Lindsay, and others, maybe twenty in all. The cons outweighed the pros for most of them, in my opinion. Then I set forth my favored choice, Senator Mark Hatfield of Oregon, a devout evangelical whose liberal Republicanism would give a good ideological balance to the ticket. "I believe he would be a devoted and loyal vice president," I said. "He certainly would appeal to the strong Christian vote, Catholic as well as Protestant."

Nixon didn't say much in response. Although I brought the issue up again in subsequent conversations before the convention, he dodged making a commitment.

In Miami on the night he was nominated, he invited me to meet him at the hotel. He took me by the arm and led me to the room where the choice of a vice president would be discussed and decided.

"You'll enjoy this," he said. "This will be a little bit of history."

I was surprised that he had waited this long before making his decision. I had heard of smoke-filled rooms where political deals were made, but this surely didn't fit the stereotype in my mind. Maybe it was a Republican version: a huge oval room with elegant carpeting, draperies, furniture, and crystal chandelier. The five senators, five representatives, three governors, and various party leaders all matched the surroundings. One writer listing all the dignitaries present put me in a category by myself: "sidekick."

Nixon went around the room and asked everyone their opinion. Many names for vice president were bandied about. Nixon then turned to me and looked me squarely in the eye. "Billy, what do you think?" he asked.

There was a sudden quiet in the room. No doubt people were wondering why I had been invited. Well, that made it unanimous! Nevertheless, I spoke my piece. "Dick, you know that I've always been for Senator Hatfield," I reminded him, listing my reasons again. That was that. I went back to my hotel.

What followed a few hours later was like a verbal Ping-Pong game.

About six-thirty the next morning, Nixon phoned me.

"I haven't made up my mind, but I've got to make the announcement this morning. How about offering a prayer for me?"

I readily promised him I would. It was more to my liking to talk to the Lord about all of this than to dialogue with a group of political professionals. It wasn't the first such prayer I had made. I called Hatfield, who was staying with Bob Green and his wife, Anita Bryant, in Miami, and told him what I had just heard.

"I don't think it's going to be me," he said, although I sensed that he would have been glad to accept.

About an hour later, the phone rang again. It was Nixon, saying that Spiro Agnew had been chosen and asking if I would call Hatfield to tell him the decision.

Like every other American outside the state of Maryland, I asked the question of questions: "Spiro who?"

Nixon then told me his reasons for that choice, none of which was persuasive to me. I was puzzled that so brilliant a tactician as Nixon would wait till the last minute and then choose somebody completely unknown to the electorate.

The phone rang yet again. This time it was my longtime acquaintance Herbert Klein, who was also a Nixon adviser (and who later became Nixon's communications director at the White House). "Dick wanted me to call you," he said, "and say that he hasn't decided after all. It's still between Hatfield and Agnew. You're to call Hatfield and tell him that he's still in the running."

When Mark got my call, he was as surprised as I was.

The eventual final announcement that Agnew was the choice came much later than the press had expected. I felt a real letdown in my heart; indeed, I even felt a little sick. I had nothing personal against Governor Agnew; I had never met him. All I knew about him—admittedly some negative things—I had heard a few days earlier from David Brinkley on the television news. Nevertheless, I could not help but feel disappointed, for I knew that Hatfield would have brought a positive moral and spiritual influence to the office.

That night at the convention, Nixon made his acceptance speech. Then I was brought out to the podium to render the service for which I had been invited: I gave the closing prayer. Then I slipped away from the platform as quickly as possible and hurried back to the Key Biscayne Hotel. (The owner, Bob Mackle, was gracious enough to let me stay there for free whenever I was in south Florida; he often moved out of his personal home on the beach to let me or Mr. Nixon stay there.)

The next night Nixon decided to move to that hotel. "I don't know whom I should eat with tonight," he said to some of his staff. "But if I eat with Billy Graham, everyone will understand, and there'll be no criticism."

So he, Bebe Rebozo, T.W., and I ate together in the hotel restaurant. A lot of people came by to congratulate the new candidate.

A few weeks later, I attended the Democratic convention in Chicago, at their invitation. I did not want people to think I was favoring one party over the other; everyone knew of my friendship with both Nixon and Johnson, and many wondered whom I actually favored. I gave one of the prayers on the night when President Johnson was scheduled to address the assembly.

From my room in the old Stevens Hotel on Michigan Avenue, I watched antiwar demonstrators and assorted radical protesters creating all kinds of mayhem. Mayor Richard Daley's riot police met them right in front of the television cameras. "The whole world is watching!" they screamed in unison.

Sitting backstage with leaders of the Democratic party—I had more friends in the Democratic party than I did in the Republican party; being a southerner, I knew most of them—I shared their apprehension of worse things happening. The mood was so ominous that Lyndon Johnson's staff had kept in constant phone contact from the White House, waiting to learn whether it was safe for him to come to Chicago and give his scheduled speech. Since it was his birthday, as well as his swan song as President, everyone was looking forward to honoring him. I was especially pleased at the prospect of sharing my friend's special night. But in the end, it seemed the only prudent thing for him to do was to stay in Washington.

On that memorable and historic evening, when it was apparent that President Johnson could not come to his own convention, I was scheduled to lead a prayer and then Anita Bryant was to sing. During my prayer, the noise barely died down in the convention. As in most political conventions, up until that point most speakers were ignored by the majority of the people; they were busy debating, visiting, arguing, making deals. Delegates were even having caucuses on the floor. After my prayer, when Anita Bryant got up to sing, it grew quiet; people gave her more attention than they did me, and a good round of applause. But a pall still hung over the convention—something that was darker than mere political pessimism.

The Democrats wound up nominating as their presidential candidate another longtime friend of mine, Hubert Humphrey of Minnesota (then serving as Vice President under Lyndon Johnson). The coming election would pose a personal conflict of loyalties for me after all.

As the postconvention campaigns got under way, I thought I was pretty clever at concealing my presidential choice. After our final Crusade of 1968 ended in Pittsburgh around Labor Day, I tried to follow events at a discreet distance.

On the day of the election, I called Nixon and wished him well.

"Please come to New York," he said, "and watch the election returns with me tonight."

"I'm not sure I ought to do that," I replied. "There will be so much press there. But I'll come and stay in a nearby hotel. If you lose, I'll come over to your hotel and pray with you and your family."

"Okay," he agreed.

T.W. and I left for New York immediately and checked in at the Hilton. Nixon was at the Waldorf Towers.

Final election results were delayed in coming because the voting was so close. I went to bed before the verdict was in. Next morning, after the results became apparent, Bebe Rebozo called. "Nixon wants you to come before he talks to the press," he said. "He wants to talk to you."

T.W. and I immediately got a cab to the hotel. Rebozo met us and led us into Nixon's suite. Only he, Pat, Tricia, and Julie were in the room. The first thing I did was to congratulate them for the victory.

Nixon suggested that we all stand in a circle and hold hands. He asked me to pray. I thanked the Lord for what I believed was God's plan for the country: that Nixon should lead us in the next four years. I prayed also for each member of the family and gave thanks for the spiritual heritage of his mother, Hannah.

He had something to ask before letting me go. He took me over to the window and spoke in a low voice. "Billy, you know we're in a terrible mess in Vietnam. President Johnson has ordered a stop in the bombing, and I think it's a great mistake. We are on the verge of victory in Vietnam. If we stop the bombing now, we are going to be in big trouble. We've got to find a way out of that war. While we have plans, we need prayer that God will help us to find a way."

In early December, I left to spend the Christmas holidays visiting our troops in Vietnam. I got back just in time for the inauguration. Nixon wanted me to do all the prayers at the swearing-in ceremony, but I objected.

"Dick, you've got to have all faiths represented, or you're going to have trouble."

"No, I just want you," he insisted.

Eventually, Nixon gave in to the ecumenical idea, and I suggested other clergy, including my friend and supporter Rabbi Edgar Fogel Magnin, of the large Jewish synagogue on Wilshire Boulevard in Los Angeles.

Nixon had asked me for a five- or ten-minute prayer. I did not pray that long—I think my words ran to four minutes—although *Time* magazine described the prayer as a mini–inaugural speech!

My ecumenical strategy was undercut again when Nixon insisted that I preach a week later, on January 26, at the first White House worship service of his administration. That would be followed days later by the National Prayer Breakfast, which he planned to attend. I was scheduled to speak again on that occasion, which would have meant a number of times in a row, and I protested. (Some of the press were already calling me chaplain to the White House, a title I neither sought nor wanted.) Bill Jones, my business friend from Los Angeles, had other thoughts: "As long as I pay the bills for the breakfast," he said, "Billy Graham will be the speaker." I did speak, but because the program was running late, I cut my talk down to just one of my four points. Everyone had come to hear President Nixon.

Nixon was nervous about the first White House church service. Cliff was with me, and Bev was to sing. That morning the President ran downstairs and looked into the East Room every few minutes to see how many people were coming and who they were. Then he rushed back upstairs to us, sitting down at the piano and playing hymns while Bev sang.

Nevertheless, this church service, destined to become a White House tradition during Nixon's administration, was criticized by some as an infraction of church-state separation.

"It's the most popular thing we have," White House staffer Lucy Winchester was quoted in the *New York Times Magazine* as saying. She felt that mainstream Americans could relate to a president at prayer. I spoke at four of those services, as did Norman Vincent Peale. (Nixon had attended Peale's Marble Collegiate Church when he was in New York City, and Julie and David had been married there by Dr. Peale in December 1968. Although Julie had invited me to participate in that wedding, I couldn't since I was in Vietnam.) Other speakers included leading Protestant, Roman Catholic, and Jewish clergy.

Shortly after that first White House worship service, Ruth and I were on Fiji, a layover on our flight to New Zealand. "It was Sunday," she remembered, "so we decided to walk to the nearest church service. They were repairing the big church, so we met on the verandah of a little house. The week before, we had been at the White House for the worship service. The contrast was so startling, and yet it made the little service out there all the sweeter. Just a hundred years ago, they were headhunters."

I could see value in a president's having some trusted friends without a personal agenda who could function unofficially and informally as a sounding board for his ideas. This seemed to be his plan for me. In one of his first weeks in the White House, I told him that if he ever wanted to talk to someone who would never quote him without authorization, I would be glad to be such a person. The presidency was a lonely spot.

As he settled into his new role, Nixon—whom I no longer addressed as Dick but as Mr. President—took me up on my offer. In the interest of confidentiality, I stopped keeping written notes of our conversations. But, unknown to me, he did keep a record, not only of our conversations but also of staffers' suggestions that might involve me. He might have taped some of our conversations as well, again without my knowledge or consent. I could wish it otherwise. Some of these exchanges—whether including me directly or involving me peripherally—are on public record in the media or open for inspection in libraries. Some of them appear in Nixon's own books.

For example, several of Nixon's memos to H. R. Haldeman alluding to my activities have been published: encouraging him to invite my friend Johnny Cash to perform country music at the White House, commenting on media coverage of demonstrations, and so on. Nixon also made it clear to Haldeman that he wanted to nurture whatever influence I might have with certain religious leaders. Needless to say, this was not discussed with me at the time.

It was naive of me, I suppose, to think that such a close relationship with a president would never be used to serve his political ends. But searching my soul now, I honestly believe my intentions were uncomplicated by personal aims or ambitions.

But occasionally I felt concern about some of Nixon's staff. Haldeman knew that I was somewhat concerned about the fact that he and John Ehrlichman were Christian Scientists; as such, they did not believe in the reality of sin or human depravity. Perhaps that caused Haldeman, later in his published diary, to give a negative slant to some of the comments he claimed I made, many of which I never did.

Elsewhere Nixon recounted our being together at his mother's funeral, our walking on the beach at Key Biscayne, my saying I thought it was his destiny to be President, his receiving a mild rebuke from me about his overblown words when he welcomed back our first moon-walkers, my making a videotape at his request in support of voluntary integration at public schools in the South, even my suggesting casually—and in vain—that he use a TelePrompTer for his speeches.

Advice-giving, however, was a two-way street between us. He told me in all three of his bids for the presidency not to endorse him or any other candidate. "Don't let politics divert you from what you're doing," he said to me in 1960 as we waited at the tee at the Riviera Country Club. "Your ministry is more important than my election."

Once he warned me not to identify myself with the Moral Majority because of the political baggage accompanying that movement. He felt very strongly, as he wrote later, that needed changes in government could come about only through changing people—and that was religion's bailiwick. Nevertheless, he seemed to have concern about the mixing of religion and politics in movements like the Moral Majority, and I understood his concern.

One day, while visiting the President, I told him that I was going back to the Far East for some meetings.

"I've got an idea," he said. "While you're there, maybe you could meet with all those missionaries that live and work there, and get their ideas as to how we could end this war." He was almost obsessed with the idea of ending it as quickly as possible. I thought he was right in that goal and agreed to listen for ideas while overseas.

When I arrived in the Far East in March 1969, I asked some of the missionaries to meet me in Bangkok, which was neutral territory. We convened there for three days, during which they expressed their viewpoints. We prayed a good deal too, of course.

They were old Vietnamese hands, many of them, having been in the country for decades. Some seemed to feel that the only way to end the war was to "Vietnamize" it—that is, to let the south invade the north from the sea, with American air-power coverage, and to take Haiphong and then Hanoi. Others—those of a more pacifist frame of mind—thought the United States should just pull out.

One thing was certain: businesses were making millions on the war, and the South Vietnamese, receiving many millions of American dollars in aid, were becoming afflicted with such American moral evils as fraud, materialism, and graft.

"We don't know how to fight this kind of war," said a military man to me as we flew in a helicopter over the edge of Cambodia, where I could see smoke rising all around.

When I returned home, I composed a thirteen-page confidential report to the President. I noted that most of the missionaries were a hawkish bunch, pro-American and pro-Nixon. They feared the outcome of the Paris peace talks. They lamented that American troops, many of them, were hooked on some form of narcotics. They loathed the American businesses that generated corruption among the Vietnamese. And they saw the importation of American consumer goods as destroying Vietnamese culture. What use—if any—he made of the report I never learned.

I was a kind of listening post for Nixon on many occasions, but one time at least I turned the tables on him. I initiated a discussion with the President and Henry Kissinger with a group of distinguished black clergymen, conservative and liberal. Other than that, I never made it a practice to attend Washington briefings myself, although I was often invited.

Some nights Nixon would call at our house in Montreat just to talk. Once, about one o'clock in the morning, he asked me to put Ruth on the extension phone. He was depressed about the Cambodian crisis, and he told us things about his personal faith that moved us deeply.

The essential bond between us was not political or intellectual; rather, it was personal and spiritual. Less than two weeks before the election in 1968, I was in New York when he came off the campaign trail to spend a day of rest in his Fifth Avenue apartment. I called and invited him to go with me to Calvary Baptist Church on West Fifty-seventh Street. There we heard Pastor Stephen Olford, whose spiritual insights often blessed me, preach a powerful evangelistic sermon on "The Gospel in a Revolutionary Age." It was a plea for national as well as personal repentance and conversion. Nixon said afterward, "The press go with me everywhere, and that was a great message for them to hear!"

Nixon showed his friendliness to me in many personal ways. He came to our home on the mountain. He often referred to the pineapple tea my mother served him when he visited her at home in Charlotte; and he couldn't forget the fried chicken and apple pie served at our home by our longtime resident housekeeper and friend, Beatrice Long.

In our games of golf together, he was always willing to coach me. "Now, Billy, your first shot ought to be here," he might advise, "so that you'll have a clear shot into the green for your second shot." When he gave up the game in order to have more time to read and study, my interest in golf tapered off also, and for much the same reason.

One last golf story. One day I was playing with him while he was Vice President. "Dick," I remarked casually, "I used a certain set of golf clubs in France when we were there last year, and I hit the ball better than I ever have in my life. I tried to buy them, since they were used clubs, but the pro wouldn't sell them to me." At Christmas that year, those very clubs were Dick's gift to me. He had sent to southern France for them.

And he remembered birthdays. Often, when there was something about me or the family in the papers, he would thoughtfully call on the phone. After he saw our picture in the paper with newborn Ned, he wrote to Ruth that our baby was "a very captivating young man." When something big was at stake, like my trip to China in 1988 (years after he had left the White House), he helped set it up through the crucial contacts he had there in government circles.

Nixon's manner in conversation was very instructive to me. For one thing, he had a quality of attentiveness I have noticed also in royalty. When he talked with someone, he often looked them right in the eye, listened intently to what they said, and made them feel they were the only person in the world. He was very good at drawing people out with questions. "What do you think?" he asked me times without number. "Do you agree with that?" "Let's sit and talk a bit." "I want to throw a few ideas at you and see what you think." Rarely did he reveal his own convictions.

One time, before Nixon became President, Ruth and I were invited to Jack Paar's home in New York with the Nixons. At the end of a rather long evening we returned to the Nixons' apartment on Fifth Avenue. We spent a few minutes together, but it was getting late and we had to leave. Dick saw us to the elevator—why the freight elevator, I can't remember, but it was hung with quilted padding—and we pressed the button. As I recall, on its way down the elevator stalled between floors and refused to budge, so I rang and rang the emergency bell. Dick finally heard it and immediately summoned the doorman, who came and helped Ruth and me climb out. There is no dignified way to crawl out of a stalled elevator, but Dick by that time was in his pajamas and a bathrobe, so I suppose we were all glad no one was there with a camera!

And there was Watergate, which some people thought rubbed off on my reputation. When my name did come up slightly in the proceedings, I called my North Carolina neighbor, Senator Sam Ervin.

"Senator Sam," I said, "why did you allow my name to come up in the Watergate hearings? You know what they said about me wasn't true."

"I'll correct it," he responded.

And he did that, in no uncertain terms.

The Watergate break-in, an undeniable personal and national tragedy, should never have happened in the first place. And it should have been laid to rest long before now. If the Lord were as unforgiving to us sinful and disobedient humans as we are to each other, even the best among us wouldn't stand a chance at the Great Judgment. It may not be in the Bible, but there is God's own truth in Alexander Pope's proverb, "To err is human, to forgive divine."

The whole library of literature that has been written detailing the Watergate break-in and the subsequent cover-up has not explained for me what came over President Richard Nixon at that time. I deliberately chose the words *came over* because I cannot accept in my heart that his conduct and conversation during that crisis sprang from the deep wells of his character. The evidence on the tapes and the testimony of many associates leave no doubt that he was culpable. I did not absolve him—but neither did I judge him.

To me, the Watergate affair seemed to be a brief parenthesis in a good man's lengthy political career—a parenthesis that I couldn't understand. Nixon held such noble standards of ethics and morality for the nation. "The hope of America," he once said to me, "is the working people." Furthermore, he held a high view of the presidency as a public trust. The tarnishing of that office by Watergate probably caused him more pain than what happened to his own reputation.

At Nixon's second inauguration in 1973, Bill Marriott, founder and head of the Marriott hotel and restaurant chain, was chair of the gala affair, as he had been in 1969. He had become one of my closest friends and had appointed me honorary chair of the inauguration symphony concert at the Kennedy Center. For that event, Ruth and I dressed up in our best. We arrived early, for a small preconcert reception, and sat with the Agnews and the Charlton Hestons for a while.

Mr. and Mrs. Nelson Rockefeller were at the small reception too. I had known Nelson since my early days with Youth for Christ; Bob Van Kampen was a good friend of his and had introduced us over lunch. Nelson's second wife, "Happy," motioned for me to come to her table. As I stood there, all of a sudden she thrust a glass of champagne in my hand. Seeing the photographers moving into position, I immediately passed the glass to Ruth, thanked Mrs. Rockefeller, and said I did not take champagne on such occasions.

"You're as clever as I've heard," she said with a laugh.

When President and Mrs. Nixon arrived, Ruth and I went to greet them officially. Later I told Ruth that I did not think Nixon looked at all well; he did not look himself. His eyes betrayed that something was wrong. I had no clue at that time, however, that Watergate was beginning to burden him.

He and Pat sat directly in front of Ruth and me at the concert. When I reached over his shoulder and handed him a program, he shoved it aside, letting it fall to the floor. Pat leaned over and whispered something in his ear. He turned around and profusely apologized to me.

In His Sermon on the Mount, Jesus said, "Do not judge, or you too will be judged" (Matthew 7:1). Most of us fail to read what He said next: "For in the same way you judge others, you will be judged, and with the measure you use, it will be measured to you" (verse 2).

On the day the contents of the White House tapes were made public and I heard the President's words, I was deeply distressed. The thing that surprised and shook me most was the vulgar language he used. Never, in all the times I was with him, did he use language even close to that. I felt physically sick and went into the seclusion of my study at the back of the house. Inwardly, I felt torn apart.

I did not shrink from commenting publicly on Watergate. I wrote two op-ed pieces on it at the request of the *New York Times,* gave a long interview to *Christianity Today,* and spoke about it freely on *The Hour of Decision* radio broadcasts and appearances on such television programs as the *Today* show. I called the whole affair sordid, describing it as a symptom of a deeper moral crisis that affected other nations besides our own.

Lots of people did not like what I said. One minister in Arizona wrote to me in December 1973 to tell me that my remarks—I had said that cheating, lying, and betrayal of trust were "mistakes"—were "insipid." I thought they were sins in God's sight, of course, not just mistakes, but at that date a lot of people were being damned by rumors, judged before all the evidence was in.

I did not have to distance myself from Watergate; I wasn't close to it in the first place. The President had not confided in me about his mounting troubles, and after the full story eventually broke, he all but blocked my access to him during the rest of his presidency. As I have said, I wanted to believe the best about him for as long as I could. When the worst came out, it was nearly unbearable for me.

He and I discussed Watergate only once, at his home in San Clemente about two or three months after his resignation. He told me nothing, however, that had not already been said publicly.

The problem with Watergate was not so much the break-in as the cover-up. Nixon was trying to protect the men who had worked with him faithfully and for a long time. He tried to use his office, prestige, and power to save them; but in so doing, a cancer began to develop in the President and on the presidency itself.

During most of the hearings and other Watergate matters in 1973, we were in Korea, South Africa, England, and Switzerland. One journalist suggested that I had fled America because of Watergate and gone into hiding in Europe! That was not true at all; those events had been planned years in advance.

While in Lausanne, I received a letter from Pat Nixon asking if I would bring the 1973 Christmas message at the White House service in December. I accepted. Most of the President's inner circle were present at that service. I preached on repentance and made my message as strong as I possibly could, although I mentioned no names.

In a *Christianity Today* interview published on January 4, 1974, I answered a number of questions on the subject of Watergate. At that point, I did not know all the allegations against the White House. Nor, indeed, did the public. I could not pass judgment on any of the alleged culprits without knowing more facts, but I readily admitted that a misguided obsession to change the world might have driven Nixon partisans to wrong actions. Younger men heady with power and privilege would be especially vulnerable to such action.

One thing I did keep urging upon Nixon privately was to be more forthright in his expression of spiritual conviction. That came through in a reproving letter I wrote to him after he spoke at the National Prayer Breakfast in February 1974; Nixon later reprinted that letter in his book *From: The President*. "While I know you have a personal and private commitment, yet at some point many are hoping and praying that you will state it publicly. . . . In taking such a stand you would find the deepest personal satisfaction in your own life."

I had some misgivings about Nixon's religious understanding, based on what glimpses I got, but then he was a layman in such matters, not a biblical scholar. I've never doubted the reality of his spiritual concern, though, or the sincerity of his identification with the evangelical position toward the authority of the Bible and the person of Christ. He told me, "I believe the Bible from cover to cover."

Shortly before the 1968 election, I welcomed the Nixons and Mark Hatfield's wife, Antoinette, to the Crusade in Pittsburgh. Then, on May 28, 1970, he came as President to give a word of greeting at our Crusade in Neyland Stadium at the University of Tennessee in Knoxville. His remarks were not as forthright a witness for Christ as I had wished for, but I rationalized that he was extremely tired from carrying many burdens. In our pluralistic society, he also probably felt he had to be very careful not to alienate people of other faiths at that delicate point in history.

In the crowd of 75,000 that night were 300 antiwar protesters sitting together. When Nixon began speaking, they stood up as a group and chanted, "Peace now! Peace now!" When he paused, they quieted down, only to start up again the instant he did. He outlasted them after a few minutes of this and finished his remarks.

Then our beloved Ethel Waters got up to sing. She wagged her finger at that group and spoke to them with a humility and authority uniquely her own. "You chillun there, you hush now!" she shouted. "If I was sittin' by you," she said, bringing her hands together with a loud slap, "I'd give you a smack!" The audience was stunned. "Then I would hug you and tell you that I loved you," she added.

Her sweet spirit won out. Several of that group came forward, Charlie Riggs noticed, when I gave a Gospel Invitation at the close of the meeting. One of the leaders of that protesting group was converted to Christ and later worked in several Christian organizations.

When the offering plate was passed that night, President Nixon found himself with an empty wallet. With some sleight of hand, I managed to slip him all the bills in my pocket. It was quite a feat—no one in the vast stadium seemed to notice it. I myself forgot about it until, months later, I received a "Dear Billy" letter from the White House, dated October 2.

"A number of presidents have looked to you for spiritual sustenance over the years," he wrote, "but I suspect I was the first to hit you for a loan. . . . I deeply appreciated the emergency financing which you quickly arranged for me that evening in Knoxville. I only wish that all the money problems that confront me could be handled that efficiently.

"While deficit financing can be useful in a pinch, the time always comes when the deficit must be funded. In keeping with my concern for fiscal responsibility, I am hereby repaying your loan of May 28."

Another disruptive episode occurred when Nixon came to Charlotte on October 15, 1971, honoring me by attending "Billy Graham Day" there—an event sponsored by the city. He and I stood in an open convertible that moved slowly through town. The streets were jammed on both sides. I reached out to take people's hands.

"You'll break your hand that way," said Nixon. "Hold your hand out sideways so that you will just barely touch people in the direction you're going."

We completed the drive without incident but encountered hecklers—antiwar demonstrators, for the most part—outside the coliseum, where I was scheduled to speak. Although we felt some tension, the protest didn't escalate into violence.

In my comments that day, I referred to his impending trip to China, which proved to be so history-making. I said of the Great Wall, built mainly in the third century B.C., that "for defensive purposes the wall proved to be a gigantic failure. When China's enemies wanted to breach it, they didn't have to knock it down. All they did was to bribe the gatekeeper."

460

Then I spoke of our nation's need for inner spiritual and moral commitment and strength. Senator Sam Ervin was there on the platform, as was John Connally, who was then secretary of the treasury. I deeply appreciated that day, more than I can ever tell. Many of my high school classmates were there, and most of my friends from the Charlotte area. It was a great and wonderful moment for my family.

I appreciated Nixon's coming to events such as these—the Knoxville Crusade as well as the more personal celebration—as my friend. He certainly knew and appreciated what our Crusades were about. Before his mother's funeral service, he talked with me for a few minutes about her faith.

"Dick, do you have that same kind of faith?" I asked.

"I believe I do," he said quietly.

"That's the only way you can be guided in life, and it's the only way you can get to Heaven," I said, and then I prayed for him. He later told me that was one of the great moments of his life, and I believe he meant it.

Although I often prayed in his presence, I never heard him pray himself, except for grace at mealtimes. That was his Quaker way, to keep piety private. "We sit in silence," he explained to me. His daughter Julie described him to John Pollock as "a very reserved person anyway." He was private about many things he believed—almost the exact opposite of Lyndon Johnson in temperament.

When the Nixon Presidential Library was dedicated at Yorba Linda, California, in 1990, the organizers offered to fly me from Los Angeles in a helicopter to lead a prayer. That night, at the banquet for 1,000 guests at the Century Plaza Hotel to honor the Nixons' fiftieth wedding anniversary, I gave another prayer at his request. Three years later, fulfilling a promise I had made to him several months earlier, I flew back from working on a book in Europe to conduct the memorial service for his loyal and lovely wife at the library in Yorba Linda.

The service for Pat was primarily for the family and some of their closest friends. As I walked into the little garden in front of the house where Nixon was born, he broke down and cried. I put my arm around him, and we walked to where he was to be seated. He and Pat had loved each other very much. I remembered going

461

on a plane with her to participate in the inauguration of the new president of Liberia; on that flight, she told one or two of us of her great and deep love for him. "He's my man," she said proudly.

Like all human relationships, mine with Richard Nixon was bittersweet. Our laughter was interspersed with tears. We shared both delights and doubts. I prayed for him in agony and in ecstasy. Our disagreements were honest, yet our friendship was close.

On April 19, 1994, I was in New York to attend a small dinner hosted by the North Korean ambassador to the U.N., Kim Jong Su; he had assisted us in arranging our visit to his country earlier in the year. T.W. was staying with me at the Marriott Hotel. My son Ned, who was living in Seattle, called to tell me that he had just heard on the news that Nixon had had a stroke at his home in New Jersey. I immediately tried to find out where he was. I tried to reach Tricia and Julie. Unable to reach them, I then called the White House, but neither the operator nor the secretary to the President knew anything more about it. I asked to speak to President Clinton, who had only just heard the news and did not yet know which hospital in the New York area Nixon had been taken to. I told him I would go over and see Dick as soon as we learned where he was. He promised to call me as soon as he knew, and in a few minutes he was back on the phone to give me the details.

When I arrived at the hospital, television cameras were already being set up. I went in the emergency entrance and was met by a hospital official who took me straight to Tricia. In a room next to the alcove where the doctors were at work on her father, I talked with her, quoting some Scripture and praying with her. Then we talked about the family, especially about her father and all that he meant to those who knew him.

When Julie arrived from Philadelphia about an hour later, we had another time of prayer. Then I told them that I was going back home to North Carolina, where I would wait for further news. I asked them to please keep in touch with me.

The next evening, Tricia called to tell me that her father would not last long. She and her sister both wanted me to officiate at the service in California; Dick himself had expressed the same wish to me some twenty years before. Tricia suggested that if I had the time,

I should go to Yorba Linda to help in the arrangements and to get adjusted to the three-hour time difference from the East Coast. I immediately left for California.

When the time of the funeral was announced, President Clinton called me and asked how I thought the family would feel if he and Hillary were to come. I said I was sure they would be honored but I would have to check. Tricia and Julie agreed that they would be more than welcome. I called the President back, and he said they would be there.

This changed the situation. I was officiating on behalf of the family, of course, but now it was becoming more of a state funeral. Immediately, I was in touch with the military personnel who were handling the complex details of the service. By now hundreds of dignitaries and heads of state were expected to attend.

T.W. and I checked into the Fullerton Marriott Hotel, not far from the Nixon Library in Yorba Linda, where the service was to be held. Since there were to be so many speakers, someone suggested I cut my remarks to six minutes. Military chaplain Bill Perry, however, who was in charge of the program, came to my hotel room and graciously insisted—in point of fact, he ordered—that I stick to my original planned time of fourteen minutes.

I remembered one of my last conversations with Nixon. It was in New York some months earlier. When I called, he suggested lunch. We ate at a table outside the restaurant, watching all the cars go by and talking philosophy and theology.

"Dick," I said at one point, "we don't have many years left, you and I, and I pray that we're both ready to meet the Lord. The Scripture says, 'Prepare to meet God'; if either of us is not prepared, we had better get ready."

Then once again I outlined the Gospel for him—though of course he already knew it well.

Before his funeral in California, 40,000 people filed by his casket in the rain. The following morning, it fell to my lot to do something quite out of character for me: I was to be the official greeter of the family members, the American presidents, and the many other distinguished guests. As they arrived, I escorted them into the library, where they were served coffee.

The service itself was personally difficult for me, not just because of the media attention but because I, like so many others that day, was saying good-bye to a man whose friendship I had valued across the years.

Several of the speakers alluded to his complex personality and the difficulties that had led to his resignation from the presidency.

"Today is a day for his family, his friends, and his nation to remember President Nixon's life in totality," President Clinton said in his remarks. "To them let us say, 'May the day of judging President Nixon on anything less than his entire life and career come to a close.'"

The overwhelming emphasis was on the former President's positive contributions, including his dramatic breakthroughs in foreign policy.

As for my own remarks, I was determined not only to express my own personal reflections on Mr. Nixon himself but also to speak directly to the family and to the others gathered there about the Christian hope of life beyond the grave. "The world has lost a great citizen, America has lost a great statesman, and those of us who knew him have lost a personal friend," I said. "His public service kept him at the center of the events that have shaped our destiny."

Then, as the service reached its conclusion, I strayed somewhat from my prepared text. I looked out at the five living presidents and their wives who were sitting there and all the other dignitaries who were present, and speaking to them (as well as to the Nixon family and to myself) I reminded them that someday every one of us will be lying in a casket.

"John Donne said that there is a democracy about death. 'It comes equally to us all, and makes us all equal when it comes.' I think today every one of us ought to be thinking about our own time to die, because we too are going to die and we are going to have to face Almighty God with the life that we lived here.

"There comes a time when we have to realize that life is short, and in the end the only thing that really counts is not how others see us here, but how God sees us, and what the record books of Heaven have to say. . . ."

"For the believer who has been to the Cross, death is no frightful leap into the dark, but is an entrance into a glorious new life. . . .

"For the believer, the brutal fact of death has been conquered by the resurrection of Jesus Christ.

"For the person who has turned from sin and has received Christ as Lord and Savior, death is not the end.

"For the believer there is *hope* beyond the grave. . . .

"Richard Nixon had that hope, and today that can be our hope as well."

25

The Healer from Michigan

President Gerald Ford

History has not given him a lot of credit yet, but in my view President Gerald Ford helped save the integrity of this country's democratic institutions after Watergate. In spite of the bitter campaign he and Jimmy Carter had fought, President Carter was able to say in his 1977 inaugural address that he wanted to thank his predecessor "for all he's done to heal our land." I agree completely with that assessment.

I cannot remember when I first met him. I knew him for years while he was in Congress. Certainly, most times I went to Capitol Hill, I saw him. I knew him to be a professing Christian, and we had several times of prayer together. He was always warm, friendly, and outgoing to me.

A lot of us Christians saw him as a spiritual leader as well as a political one. He came from Grand Rapids, Michigan, where I had held one of my first citywide Campaigns and where many people had strong ties with the Reformed churches that originally came from Holland. His roots were in that soil, and he brought its values with him. As a representative, he lived in a modest house in Alexandria, picking up the morning paper from his doorstep just like millions of other men and women. Even in the White House, he kept in touch with those spiritual roots: a mutual friend back in Grand Rapids, Billy Zeoli, a Christian filmmaker, served as a kind of counselor to him, stopping by the White House periodically to give him a verse of Scripture and pray.

Gerald Ford inherited one of the worst situations any man ever faced going into the presidency: because of their disappointment and dismay over Watergate and its cover-up, a high percentage of the American people had lost faith in the Oval Office. I wanted Ford to initiate the healing by pardoning Richard Nixon. Although I had personal reasons as well, I believed that a pardon would be good for the office of the presidency.

When the former President went back to his home in San Clemente, California, he developed thrombophlebitis, a dangerous disease of the leg veins. I myself had had it and knew how life-threatening it could be. The blood clot in his leg eventually traveled to other parts of his body, and for a time he hung between life and death.

When he lay in the hospital so ill, Ruth got a friend to charter a small plane and fly it back and forth past the hospital at Long Beach. Behind it trailed a banner that said "NIXON—GOD LOVES YOU AND SO DO WE." He saw it from his hospital window, we learned, but he did not know its source until later. We would like to think it was an encouragement to him.

Ruth and I were staying in Pauma Valley, California, in a little cottage we had been given just over the mountains from Palm Springs. Situated on the Pauma Valley golf course (which itself lay at the edge of an orange grove), it was only three and a half rooms—but we loved it. (After the children were grown, we decided to give it away so that it could be sold and the money used for the Lord's work.)

From Pauma Valley, I phoned Bob Finch, one of Ford's close political advisers, to talk to him about my friend's situation: "Bob, if Nixon has to go through a Watergate trial, perhaps even a prison sentence, just the thought of it might kill him."

Bob suggested that I call Herb Klein; at the time editor of the *San Diego Union*, he had been communications director in the

Nixon White House. I explained the reasons I favored a pardon, including the possibility that it would save Nixon's life. I also expressed my conviction that drawn-out trial proceedings—which is the way Washington usually does things—could keep President Ford from effectively governing the country. Herb agreed with my assessment.

"Billy," he added, "you're the only one that I think Ford would listen to at this time. Why don't you call him directly and see what he says?"

This surprised me. Reluctantly, I decided to follow through on his suggestion, although I knew that others also were surely urging the President to take action, one way or the other.

In none of this did I confer with Nixon. In fact, during the last days he was in office, I could not get near him or even talk to his secretary or his children. He had given an order, one of his friends told me later, to keep Billy Graham away from him. I never asked him about that in our many subsequent conversations, but I am convinced he was trying to spare me from being tarred with Watergate.

Acting on Herb Klein's suggestion, I called Anne Armstrong at the White House and told her my concerns. She agreed to pass them on to Ford's chief of staff, General Alexander Haig. That afternoon, General Haig phoned me and we talked for about ten minutes. He too seemed to agree with me and said President Ford would call on Sunday morning.

I stuck by the phone in Pauma Valley on Sunday morning and did receive a call from the President. "Well, it's a tough call, a tough decision," said President Ford after listening to me. "There are many angles to it. I'm certainly giving it a lot of thought and prayer."

"Mr. President, I'm praying for you constantly," I replied.

He said he would get back to me. Later someone from the White House—Anne Armstrong, as I recall—phoned. "You'll be interested to know," she said, "that the President is going to have a statement about the Nixon pardon in a day or two."

When the pardon came, the expected furor broke loose. Millions of people were gratified; in spite of everything, Nixon still stood rather high in public opinion. On the other hand, his enemies—and he had made plenty of them through the years—were extremely unhappy. Many bitter editorials were written, and Ford's public approval rating fell by twenty or twenty-five percentage points. Some people later claimed that the pardon contributed to his loss in the presidential race that followed, though in my judgment it didn't. I believe he lost mainly because people wanted a new administration without all the lingering weight of Watergate.

Years earlier I became acquainted with Leon Jaworski of Houston, Texas, the special prosecutor in the Watergate trials. I believed him to be a fair man and a committed Christian. He told me some of the things that had gone on behind the scenes, some of the agonizing decisions he'd had to make. That information strengthened my assurance that Ford had done the right thing, and the pardon did succeed to some extent in helping us put Watergate behind us.

As if all that were not enough, President Ford faced international tensions in the Far East and the Middle East, as well as inflation at home. I watched on television the rescue helicopters landing on top of the American Embassy in Saigon, sensing the desperation of the people who were scrambling to get on board. Having worked for the departing Americans, those who were left behind probably faced trial and imprisonment (or execution) at the hands of the North Vietnamese. Scenes like that must have affected our commander in chief far more deeply than they did a civilian like me. But I *was* affected. I had been in that embassy several times and could visualize it. I knew of the devotion of so many thousands of South Vietnamese to the United States. I too felt strongly the tragedy of Vietnam.

During those days, some missionary friends called to say they were sending a DC–6 to Saigon to pick up any Protestant pastors who might want to be evacuated to the United States. I gave them my support. Meanwhile in Saigon, knowing that safe passage out of the country was imminent, the pastors prayed all that night for guidance. Before the plane landed, they had decided it was their duty to stay and minister to the people as best they could, facing whatever persecution might come their way.

One day in 1977, President Ford came to Charlotte to play golf in the Kemper Open. Jim Kemper and I had been acquaintances for a long time, and he had invited me to play with the President in the

Pro-Am part of the tournament. We had played together before and had a great time. He was a pretty fair golfer, but people never knew where his tee shot would go. On this occasion, his ball hit one or two people in the crowd. But he was always able to laugh good-naturedly at the cartoons and jokes about his golf game.

I was distracted by the group of reporters who followed us around. That was to be expected, I thought, with the President of the United States as my partner. But when we got back to the club-house, the journalists seemed to turn their attention to me and my relationship with Ford and Nixon.

On another occasion, President Ford went to Charlotte to give a speech, and the sponsors asked me to lead a prayer before he spoke. They took me to the platform and Ruth to seats reserved for special guests. A young protester stood in front of Ruth in the packed audience and held up a sign that blocked her view of the President. She reached up quick as lightning, jerked the sign down, and put it under her feet. When he asked her to give it back, she refused. He was escorted away by the police.

Little did she dream that the man would get a lawyer and sue her. It made the newspapers everywhere.

A day or two later, President Ford called her up. "Ruth, you should leave things like that to the Secret Service and to the police!"

Some weeks later, the trial was held and the judge dismissed the charges.

The President called her back. "Ruth, I think what you did was a very courageous thing. Thank you."

Years later, Gerald Ford admitted to me that he had initially questioned the wisdom of some of my ventures, particularly some of my trips into eastern Europe. He specifically criticized me for going to Romania, which had a poor record in human rights. But when he watched one of our televised reports from there and saw the crowds that had assembled to hear the preaching of the Gospel, he changed his mind.

"When I first read that Billy Graham was going to a Communist-dominated country, I had reservations," he told one interviewer a few years later. And yet I think Ford came to see the value of that trip: "There is no doubt . . . [Graham] reignited the flame of religious belief and conviction. And that in turn has unquestionably had a political impact on what is taking place."

The personal rapport Ford and I enjoyed extended to family concerns too. Jerry's greatest asset was his wife, Betty. Together they reared a fine family. Several times we wrote back and forth about his son Michael, who attended Gordon-Conwell Theological Seminary (of which I was a board member) and Wake Forest University in North Carolina. Ruth and I tried to work out a visit with Michael while he was living so close, but it never did work out. The President asked me to do something of great personal importance to him, and I let him down: I allowed my busyness to interfere.

When my own security became a problem in some of our Crusades—I had received some death threats—we contacted Chuck Vance; he was at that time the President's son-in-law and had his own security firm. Chuck and his wife, Susan, had me to their home two or three times for coffee or tea.

Following his presidency, the Fords moved to the Palm Springs area of California. We have not seen them very often, because my schedule rarely takes me to the West Coast anymore.

However, during his presidency, we were invited to several social events in Washington. On one occasion, at one of the dinners during Ford's presidency, I sat beside Grace Kelly, Princess Grace of Monaco. We were chatting, but at the same time I was stalling. I was looking in despair at the elaborate place setting of knives, forks, and spoons. She would surely know the correct one with which to start.

"Dr. Graham, are you watching me?" she asked.

"Yes," I said, caught in the act.

"But I'm watching you," she said back. "I'm waiting for *you* to start!"

Another memorable White House visit during the Ford administration was a state dinner in honor of Queen Elizabeth and Prince Philip. Big round tables had been set under a huge tent on the lawn. I sat beside violinist Yehudi Menuhin. I asked him how he practiced when he traveled and mentioned in passing that the father of one of my sons-in-law had once rented Menuhin's house in Switzerland.

He asked me about my work, and I told him what I believed and talked about the Gospel.

The Queen made an excellent speech, after which we all filed into the East Room of the White House for the evening's entertainment, comedian Bob Hope. This old friend and sometime golf partner approached me on the way in.

"Billy, I don't have anything to say tonight. My mind has gone blank, and I don't have any prepared monologue as I normally do. Would you mind if I just tell about you and me playing golf? The Queen knows you, so maybe I could get a few laughs from her."

Knowing Bob, I was never surprised by anything he came up with. That evening he recounted how I would kneel in the sand traps (he claimed), presumably to pray my way out. He described how I would walk on water at those hazards! Yet, he said, *he* always won. "Would you like to know the secret of my winning?" he asked, glancing at the Queen.

"I cheat!"

He got the roar of laughter he always did.

Before that dinner, I made my way through a reception line in front of the West Wing by the Rose Garden. As I was talking with television commentator Barbara Walters and Elton Rule, then president of the American Broadcasting Company, I was approached by insurance tycoon John MacArthur; he was escorting his sister-in-law, actress Helen Hayes.

"Billy," John asked, "do you remember that university I wanted to build for you years ago? If we'd gone ahead with it, we would've had a great institution by this time. You made a mistake in not accepting it."

He was referring to an offer he had made some years before to donate a large tract of land in Florida to us and completely build and endow a university—but only if I would be its president.

"John, I don't think so," I said. "I was going by what I believe the Lord wanted me to do."

In the serious decisions of his presidency, I can't help but feel that that is what a decent and caring Jerry Ford also was trying to do.

1977–1997

New Frontiers

26

Openings in the Curtain

At the start of the 1970s there seemed to be little hope that the Cold War would ever thaw. A host of discouraging factors—from the development of frightening new weapons of mass destruction to repeated failures at the negotiating table—only made the gulf between East and West seem wider.

And the door also seemed closed to any further ministry by us in Communist countries. Our visit to Yugoslavia in 1967 had been encouraging, but Yugoslavia was not part of the Soviet bloc, and before long we could not help but wonder if that first visit to a Communist country would also prove to be our last.

HUNGARY

During the July 1972 Crusade in Cleveland, Ohio, I met Dr. Alexander S. Haraszti, a Hungarian-born surgeon who practiced in Atlanta, Georgia; in addition to his medical degree, he had a doctorate in linguistics and a degree in theology. He had a brilliant mind and a Slavic cultural background. He once told me that he memorized the New Testament by the time he was twenty-one. He had a

475

photographic memory, it seemed, and yet he was the most voluminous note-taker I have ever met.

In 1956, long before I met Dr. Haraszti, he translated my book *Peace with God* into Hungarian. Shortly thereafter, he immigrated to the United States. Then, in 1972, he brought a delegation from Hungary to see me during the Cleveland Crusade. He had an obsession, which he considered to be a burden from the Lord, for me to preach in eastern Europe, starting in Hungary and culminating in Moscow.

Alex knew eastern Europe intimately, not only its history but also the unwritten and sometimes very subtle dynamics of how people in that part of the world thought and acted. In addition—unlike most expatriates from Communist countries—he had maintained good relations with church leaders there and also understood Communist policies and protocol. As we developed our strategies for that part of the world, he soon became indispensable.

We also sought advice, of course, from others who were familiar with the church situation in Hungary and eastern Europe. One was our daughter Anne's brother-in-law, Dr. Denton Lotz, who traveled extensively all over eastern Europe on behalf of the American Baptist Convention (and later became head of the Baptist World Alliance). Another was Joseph Steiner, whom Ruth and I had met while vacationing in the south of France. A native of Hungary, Joe was a missionary with Trans World Radio, beaming Gospel programs into eastern Europe from Monte Carlo, Monaco. As a youth Joe's goal was to become a member of Hungary's diplomatic corps, but during the 1956 uprising, he fled to the United States. One night in 1957 he came to the Crusade in Madison Square Garden and gave his life to Christ. He soon realized that God had indeed called him to be a diplomat—as an ambassador of Christ.

A Russian-born couple at Trans World Radio, Rose and Nick Leonovich, also helped us understand the situation in eastern Europe and the Soviet Union. Our friend Dave Foster, who lived in Switzerland and traveled extensively in Europe, was especially knowledgeable about the churches and parachurch organizations working in the Communist countries, and he passed along their insights.

In April 1977, Alex arranged for Walter Smyth to preach in Hungary. While there they also conferred with officials about a possible visit by me to that country. Alex continued the negotiations, and on August 13, my thirty-fourth wedding anniversary, he hand-delivered to me in Montreat an official invitation signed by the Right Reverend Sandor Palotay, president of the Council of Free Churches of Hungary. We were on our way in two weeks. Remembering the aborted Poland trip, we spent many hours in study and briefings on Hungary before we left. We also did not announce the visit until we had full approval to do so from Hungarian authorities.

Just a few weeks before the invitation arrived, Dr. John Akers had come to assist me on special projects, and immediately I asked him to help on the Hungarian trip. A Presbyterian minister and theologian with a doctorate from the University of Edinburgh, John had been a Bible professor and academic dean at Montreat-Anderson College near where we lived.

I felt that there were a number of things about us and our ministry of which Dr. Haraszti might not be aware, such as the possibly negative reactions in America to our eastern European visits. And I knew I was unaware of some of his methods and strategies. Dr. Akers made an effective bridge between us, and I felt that if anyone in our organization could negotiate with diplomatic officials, he was the one.

The common perception in the West was that religious life was virtually nonexistent in eastern Europe and that what little remained had to be carried out secretly and under constant threat of persecution. In reality, though, that period had passed in Hungary. A limited number of churches were permitted, both Protestant and Catholic, although their activities were closely regulated by a government agency called the State Office for Church Affairs.

Despite this slight openness to religious matters, last-minute negotiations for the 1977 visit proved very difficult. Walter and Alex spent the days just before our visit in Budapest hammering out final arrangements, while our small Team gathered in Vienna for final preparations before flying to Hungary—although at this stage we still were not certain the visit would take place. Hungarian authorities were extremely nervous about permitting a foreign evangelist to preach, and local church officials had little (if any) latitude in making decisions without prior government approval.

At no stage, however, did the authorities place any restrictions on what I could preach. We made it clear that I would be preaching the same Gospel message I had preached all over the world and that I would not be commenting on strictly political issues.

At the airport in Budapest, Mr. Palotay's formal greeting to me included references to peace and trust between our nations. I responded with a reference to Isaiah's amazement over the "new thing" the Lord was doing (Isaiah 43:19). It also was my privilege to convey personal greetings to the people of Hungary, especially its believers, from President Jimmy Carter, with whom I had talked just before I left the United States.

We had been warned that we could not assume our conversations were secure and that our hotel rooms would probably be bugged, so we were prepared to be circumspect in what we said. When we arrived in Budapest, Mr. Palotay informed us that our entire Team would be housed in a large, old, government-run hotel located on beautiful Margit Island in the Danube River. It was isolated from the rest of the city. Furthermore, he said, Team members would be required to share rooms, "because hotel space in Budapest is at a premium." Some suspected that the real reason for putting two in a room was to overhear Team members talking among themselves.

The head of the independent television crew accompanying our Team balked at the cramped arrangements and promptly called the modern Hilton Hotel in Budapest, where he had no trouble securing single rooms for his whole crew. When he announced that they would be moving to another hotel, Mr. Palotay informed him in no uncertain terms that if they did, they would be on the next plane out of the country. They stayed.

Our first meeting was in a crowded Baptist church in Budapest. At the end of my sermon, I was puzzled by the unfamiliar sound of numerous clicks; for a minute I thought people were gnashing their teeth at me! Instead the sound was, I discovered, from people cutting off their personal tape recorders. This was the case in all the meetings in Hungary: services were being recorded so that the Gospel could be passed all around the country.

The most memorable Hungarian meeting took place outside of Budapest, at the Baptist-run Tahi Youth Camp on Sunday morning, September 4. Although the authorities had permitted no public announcement of the meeting, even from church pulpits, news spread by word of mouth. Officials had predicted a maximum turnout of 2,000 people. To their surprise—and ours—attendance was at least 15,000 (police reports said 30,000), with people massed on the hillside under the trees. In that exhilarating setting, with Alex beside me as interpreter, I reinforced a double emphasis in my preaching.

First and foremost, as always, was the simple declaration of humanity's desperate need for a Savior from sin and judgment and of God's loving provision for that salvation through His Son Jesus Christ. My text was the ever-powerful words of John 3:16. When I gave the customary Invitation to come to Christ, many hundreds responded by lifting their hands.

The other emphasis was my expressed desire to build bridges of understanding between nations. I did not mean simple détente or an uneasy peaceful coexistence. It was not enough, I felt, only to keep our distance from each other, to glare and gesture across political fences that were fragile barricades at best. We needed to get to know each other person to person, as President Eisenhower had advocated, so that we could accept each other in spite of our differences. And religion needed to be part of any cultural exchange program working toward that goal—right along with the arts and education. In my view, the greatest unifying force in the world was the fellowship of Christians, people whose faith in Christ brought them together in the family of God.

By God's grace, I was able to say things like that privately to certain government leaders in Hungary too. Some of their comments in response took me by surprise. The deputy prime minister told me frankly that he recognized the church could be useful in helping to build a unified and moral society. The head of the Central Committee of the Hungarian Workers Party, I was told, had even quoted the words of Jesus—"He who is not against us is with us"—when referring to the Christian believers. "I prefer a believer who is a good worker to an atheist who is a bad worker," the Hungarian government's secretary of state for church affairs, Imre Miklos, told me.

The Roman Catholic bishop of Pecs, Dr. Jozsef Cserhati, explained to me that the church had accepted the fact that it would not destroy the government, and the government had accepted the fact that it would not destroy the church. (Incidentally, throughout my week in Hungary, I had opportunities for cordial private visits with him and other Catholic, Protestant, and Jewish leaders.)

In addition to the preaching occasions, Ruth and I especially enjoyed getting out among the people. A cruise on the beautiful Danube—it was not blue, as I had always imagined, but the muddy brown of a working river—as guests of American ambassador Philip Kaiser and his wife; a visit to a cooperative farm at Hortobagy, where I felt right at home feeding sugar lumps to the horses and eating goulash (delicious!); a tour of the magnificent Parliament building and a huge electronics factory—these helped give us a feeling for the vitality and warmth of the Hungarians.

We found out to our surprise that there was quite a bit of traffic in Budapest, sometimes leading to jams. We did not expect to see so many trucks and cars, although Hungary had the highest standard of living in eastern Europe.

I was almost speechless when Mr. Palotay, on behalf of the Council of Free Churches, presented me with a magnificent gift at the farewell reception. It was a five-by-eight-foot painting, done by ninety-four-year-old Hungarian artist John Remsey, of the disciples' miraculous catch of fish as recorded in Luke. The artist had given human eyes to each fish, and to me it immediately symbolized our ministry of "fishing for men."

In ways more significant than we could fully comprehend at the time, the visit to Hungary was not simply an introduction to the Soviet bloc countries. It was also an initiation into the culture and ways of working with authoritarian Communist governments.

At the end of the trip, however, we were not at all certain we would be able to visit any other Communist-dominated countries in the future. Hungary was generally held to be the most liberal country in eastern Europe and in many ways was unique because of its relative openness. As I had done after the Yugoslavia visit, I could not help but wonder if we would ever be able to preach again in this part of the world.

POLAND

As Poland's featureless landscape unfolded beneath our Russian-built Polish LOT Airlines plane, I could not help but recall how often that country had borne the brunt of foreign invasion. I could see why. The land appeared completely flat, devoid of natural barriers to stop an invading force. No wonder Hitler's tanks had been able to storm across the entire country in a few days' time.

In 1978 the country was still a battleground, although of a different sort—not of competing armies but of competing ideologies. More than any other place in Communist central or eastern Europe, the institutional church in Poland had remained strong. And yet I also knew that Christians in Poland were besieged on every hand, their faith sorely tested on a daily basis.

Our invitation—one year after our visit to Hungary—came from the Polish Ecumenical Council, representing the Protestants in the population. Although Protestants were only a tiny minority by comparison, they attempted to maintain good relations with the Roman Catholic majority and also sought to take advantage of their own limited freedom. Again Dr. Alexander Haraszti was our point man. "Come and preach the same Gospel here that you have preached all over the world," the Polish representatives said.

The invitation materialized only after several visits by Dr. Haraszti to Poland, as well as repeated contacts with the Polish Embassy in Washington by Drs. Haraszti, Akers, and Smyth. The Polish ambassador at the time, Romuald Spasowski, gave us a magnificent dinner at the embassy after the visit; he later caused a stir by defecting to the United States after the imposition of military rule during the rise of the Solidarity movement.

Much of Alex's time was spent educating church and state officials about our ministry and our goals. He pointed to the Hungarian visit to illustrate what might be accomplished. He promised that I was not going to use the visit as a platform for anti-Communist or antigovernment statements; my goals would be strictly religious.

He also had to allay the fears of some Roman Catholic officials that I was anti-Catholic and would tell the people to leave the Catholic Church. Unknown to us at the time—at least until we arrived at the Warsaw airport—was an action taken by Poland's Catholic episcopate in May or June, supporting my visit and inviting me to preach in four of Poland's major cathedrals. This turnabout seemed little short of miraculous.

But why was the Communist government really permitting a church group to invite us? That was the question we asked ourselves about every invitation to eastern Europe—and a question we often could not answer in any conclusive way. We could only speculate on the possible reasons—and we always did, hoping to avoid being wrongfully used for political purposes.

In Poland's case, its government probably hoped to enhance its public image in the United States by appearing to grant religious freedom to their citizens while at the same time maintaining a degree of independence from the Soviet Union.

We also suspected, with some justification, that some of the hard-line Communist officials hoped to use an American Protestant evangelist to weaken the strong authority of the Roman Catholic Church. If so, it was a naive hope; I would not have done or said anything that might be taken as anti-Catholic.

During the month of October, we went to six major cities, proclaiming the Gospel from a variety of pulpits and platforms (including Roman Catholic, Baptist, Reformed, and Lutheran) to many thousands of attentive listeners. As in Hungary, state regulations prohibited any religious activity on nonchurch property, so all meetings had to be confined to churches. That was not a serious problem, however, since some of the largest cathedrals in Europe were located in Poland. Unlike our experience in Hungary, some limited advance announcement within churches was permitted, and in at least one Polish city we saw printed posters on church doors.

Cliff Barrows, who was traveling with us, helped with the arrangement of the program and led some of the music. Several of our Team preached in other cities also. Ruth, along with Walter Smyth's wife, Ethel, shared the joy of ministering to groups of women in various cities and towns.

People who kept statistics told me that I myself preached or spoke forty-seven times during that month, not only sermons preached in lengthy services in church buildings but also messages and greetings to groups of Protestant, Catholic, Orthodox, and Jewish leaders. Even civic, government, business, and educational leaders gathered to hear what an American clergyman had to say. Both the secretary of the Polish United Workers Party and the deputy prime minister received me most cordially for private visits.

My interpreter was the Reverend Zdzislaw Pawlik, a Polish Baptist Church leader; he spoke excellent English and had a delightful sense of humor. Most of our Team found his first name unpronounceable, so he told us to call him Fred.

Our first stop was Warsaw. After visiting various cultural and historic sites and preaching in the Warsaw Baptist Church, we went to the eastern city of Białystok, close to the Soviet border. On the way, the driver of our hired bus was caught in a radar speed trap on the edge of a small town; it made us feel right at home! We preached in the modern Baptist church, situated on a large piece of property on the outskirts of the city. In the late October cold, thousands gathered both inside and outside to hear us.

Returning to Warsaw that night, our bus stopped briefly at the infamous Nazi concentration camp of Treblinka, some fifty miles from the capital city; by the end of World War II, 800,000 Jewish men, women, and children had been put to death there. It was eight or nine at night, too late for guides. The place was pitch-black and seemed totally isolated from civilization, adding to the sense of horror at what had taken place there. We read by flashlight the inscription on the monument at the entrance and paused to pray that such a horrible thing would never happen again.

In the western city of Poznan, I spoke in the large Catholic cathedral. Although I had occasionally spoken in Catholic churches (at funerals, for example) and had even received an honorary degree from Belmont Abbey College in North Carolina in 1967, this was the first time I had ever been invited to preach a full evangelistic sermon in a Roman Catholic church.

A few days later, I spoke again in a Catholic church, this time in the huge Cathedral of Christ the King in the coal-mining city of

Katowice in southern Poland. The massive building was jammed with about 10,000 people standing shoulder to shoulder. Bishop Bednorz introduced me to the gathering, and then I preached. Pointing to the modern sculpture of a cross hanging over the altar, I spoke from the Bible on the meaning of the Cross and explained why the death of Christ on the Cross and the resurrection were central for Christians of all backgrounds. After the conclusion of the service, "A Mighty Fortress Is Our God," Martin Luther's Reformation hymn, sounded forth from the magnificent organ in the loft at the rear of the cathedral.

In Cracow, permission to preach in the baroque splendor of St. Ann's Church had been given to me earlier by Cardinal Karol Wojtyla, with whom I was scheduled to have tea. But when I arrived in the city, the cardinal was not there. Pope John Paul I had died quite unexpectedly, and Cardinal Wojtyla had rushed to Rome for a meeting of the College of Cardinals, the body that would elect the new pope. When our plane had landed in Warsaw, I later learned, the plane carrying Cardinal Wojtyla was at the end of the runway, ready to take off for Rome. St. Ann's Church was overflowing for our service; some had traveled from East Germany to urge us to visit their country.

As in Hungary, I observed the constructive witness of devout Christians in their neighborhoods and workplaces. Yes, they suffered from discrimination and restriction in some ways because of their faith, but they were indomitable. Their dependability on the job and their demonstration of brotherly love in daily life had an impact that honored the name of Christ. With their fellow Poles, they shared a tenacious survival spirit that had preserved a national identity throughout a difficult history.

The religious devotion in that largely Catholic country impressed me. We visited various shrines and churches, including in Czestochowa the shrine of the Black Madonna, Poland's most famous icon, dating back to 1382, which was housed in a basilica that was the most renowned Catholic shrine in central Europe. We were guests of the gracious abbot there. He invited me to come some year to preach at the annual pilgrimage, where upward of 1 million people would be present.

By stark contrast, human depravity and suffering never hit me harder than when Ruth and I viewed the grim sites of Auschwitz and Birkenau, the twin concentration camps where approximately 4 million perished in the gas chambers during World War II. The incredible horror that took place there will always be burned into my heart and mind.

Without question, the Jews suffered the most in those camps, being shipped not only from Poland itself but from throughout the Nazi empire. Many died before they even got there, unable to survive the brutal journey in boxcars and cattle cars. Other persecuted groups lost their lives there as well, including Polish patriots and political and religious leaders from various countries. Later, back in Cracow, I met with leaders from the small remaining Jewish community, a practice I have followed in many other countries.

As we toured the appalling death camp of Auschwitz, Ruth and I laid a wreath of red and white carnations at the Wall of Death, where firing squads had executed some 20,000, and we knelt in prayer. At this very spot, just before the Allies captured the prison camp toward the end of World War II, Nazi authorities had carefully removed the blood-soaked sand at the base of the shooting wall, hoping to conceal their crime. I shivered with more than cold as I stood at that wall, and it was one of the few times in my life that I was so choked with emotion I could hardly speak.

"Auschwitz . . . stands as a warning for all humanity . . . that man is still capable of repeating and even multiplying the barbarism of Auschwitz," I said. "I . . . call upon Christians everywhere to work and pray for peace. . . . The issues we face are not only political; they are also moral."

We were followed around the camp by a large group of press people with cameras and microphones. The click of the cameras, Ruth told me later, gave her the eerie feeling that guns were being cocked behind us; for one brief moment, she felt that we were the condemned.

For several years, I had been making statements on peace, although the press had seldom picked them up. Visits to places like Auschwitz, though, made me reflect long and hard on the hawkish sentiments of my youthful years. I felt that I needed to speak out even more concerning the need for efforts toward international peace in the nuclear age.

On the one hand, I believed in the inevitability of war throughout human history. My reason was simple: human rebellion against God alienated us from each other—and still does. But on the other hand, I was becoming more and more appalled at the frightening capacity of nuclear and biochemical weapons to produce global genocide. On one occasion, military experts from the Pentagon had briefed me at my home on the unimaginable dangers we faced from nuclear war. For another thing, I was becoming more sensitive to the numerous biblical injunctions for us to work for peace and to live at peace with each other as far as possible (*see* Romans 12:18). Peace was a moral issue and not just a political issue, and we were to be instruments of His peace whenever possible.

On our last day back in Warsaw, before departing from Poland, I made a few remarks about my impressions of eastern European Christianity at a press conference: "I have come to see that the church can and does exist in every kind of society, including those with Communist governments. I also have discovered that many Christians in these countries have a depth of commitment that puts me to shame. I also am convinced that there are changes taking place within the countries of eastern Europe as they discover that those who are true followers of Jesus Christ are seeking to be loyal and constructive citizens and workers. I believe, as time passes, Christians in these countries will be seen more and more as an asset to their societies, and as a consequence the governments will give more and more recognition to churches and to individual Christians.

"That is not to say," I added, "that there will not be problems in the future, but I am optimistic about the trends I see from personal observation."

In what I suppose was yet another tactical afterthought, I closed my formal statement to the press with these words: "If I receive official invitations from recognized church bodies in other countries in this part of the world, I certainly would give them very careful and prayerful consideration."

By the way, Cardinal Wojtyla never did return to his post in Cracow; it was he whom the other cardinals elected to be the successor pope. He took the name John Paul II. His election was announced shortly after our final press conference in Warsaw. When I got off the plane in Paris, I was besieged by reporters wondering if we had met in Cracow; they even wanted me to tell them how to pronounce his name!

BACK TO POLAND AND HUNGARY

Both Poland and Hungary welcomed us back in January 1981 to confer on me undeserved academic honors.

In Warsaw, on January 6, the Christian Theological Academy gave me an honorary Doctor of Theology degree in recognition of the 1978 preaching mission. That evening we were the guests of honor at a dinner hosted by the churches of Poland. Many changes had resulted from the 1978 mission, notably the formation of vital follow-up discipleship groups involving hundreds of Catholics and Protestants. Not surprisingly, then, they described stronger cooperation among diverse Polish Christian communions.

I sat beside a monsignor who told me about his own spiritual background. Some years before, he had been in Chicago, riding a bus, when a black lady sitting in the seat behind him tapped him on the shoulder.

"Excuse me, sir, but have you ever been born again?"

He was somewhat taken aback, but he did manage a reply: "I'm a priest."

"That isn't the question I asked. I asked if you have ever been born again."

The priest thought about her question all the way back to his residence. He got out his Bible and turned to the passage in John 3 where Jesus told Nicodemus he must be born again. Having read and reread that passage, the priest knelt beside his bed and prayed. He told me he didn't know what to call that incident—recommitment, rededication, or new birth—but for him it was the beginning of a new relationship with God.

A few days later, on January 9, an honorary doctorate was given me by the Reformed Theological Academy of Debrecen, Hungary. Founded in 1538, it is the oldest Protestant seminary in the world. My co-hosts were Bishop Tibor Bartha of the Hungarian Reformed Church and Imre Miklos, secretary of state for church affairs of the Hungarian government (who had been extremely helpful to us during our 1977 visit). On a special train to Debrecen, provided for us by the government, I had an unparalleled opportunity to explain evangelical beliefs to a number of government officials and church leaders who were accompanying us to the ceremony.

I noted to myself that the rails on that journey must have been almost perfect; there was hardly a bump or a shake of the train. The special train itself was extremely comfortable. We were in the private car often used by Prime Minister Janos Kadar. It was one of the coldest evenings I could remember, and when we got to Debrecen, we found that we were lodged in unheated quarters. The Hungarians were used to the cold, but we weren't. I went to bed with my clothes on, under all the blankets and quilts they gave me, and still I was cold! Journalist Ed Plowman had to decide whether to put the short bedclothes over his feet or over his bald head; he ended up sleeping in his hat. In the dark I turned on my flashlight, trying to read and to pronounce the many names of the people I would be meeting the next day.

At a formal academic ceremony steeped in centuries-old tradition, Bishop Bartha conferred the degree on me. The event was in the academy's main auditorium, with the faculty in full academic regalia (as was I). The audience included not only students and pastors but also a number of Communist officials. The American ambassador had driven from Budapest for the ceremony. In accepting the degree, I had to give a brief statement in Latin, which I read from a note held unobtrusively in my hand. I wasn't sure exactly what I said—and I doubt that Bishop Bartha understood my fractured Latin pronunciation either!

When we left Hungary, we set off on a brief trip to the Vatican. Years before, I had visited the city-state as a tourist, but on this trip I was to be received by Pope John Paul II, my first visit with a pope. We were met by a contingent of Swiss Guards, in their colorful medieval uniforms, and escorted into a private elevator leading to the papal apartments. Our first reaction was that the magnificence of the public areas of the Vatican was surpassed, if anything, by that of the private areas.

The person meeting with the pope ahead of us was Archbishop Pio Laghi, who had just been named papal nuncio to Washington, D.C. As he left the papal chamber, he paused to chat with us for a few minutes, warmly expressing the hope that we could meet in Washington when he took up his duties there.

As I was ushered into his quarters, Pope John Paul II greeted me, and we shook hands warmly. I found him extremely cordial and very interested in our ministry, especially in his homeland. After only a few minutes, I felt as if we had known each other for many years. He was very interested in an album of pictures taken during our Japan Crusade a few months before; he was scheduled to make his first trip there shortly.

He also expressed great delight at the small gift I had brought him, a woodcarving of a shepherd with his sheep, done by a North Carolina craftsman. We recalled together Jesus' words in John 10:14, 16. "I am the good shepherd; I know my sheep, and my sheep know me. . . . I have other sheep that are not of this sheep pen. I must bring them also." In turn the pope gave me a medallion commemorating his papacy and several magnificently bound volumes.

About a year later, an invitation to preach in Moscow arrived. Before accepting it, however, I had to settle in my own heart and mind a very serious question: Was it really from God?

27

The Sunday School
Teacher from Georgia

PRESIDENT JIMMY CARTER

It was May 1975. I was in Jackson, Mississippi, for a Crusade, and Governor Bill Waller had invited me for lunch.

"Jimmy Carter is over at the statehouse shaking hands with everybody and telling them he's running for president," he said to me. "Of course, he doesn't stand a chance of getting elected. But would you like to go over there? We'll take him to his next appointment at a TV station."

I readily agreed, but not just out of curiosity. I had had some contact with Jimmy Carter over the years and looked forward to renewing our acquaintance.

Governor Waller put the candidate in the front seat of his official limousine with his driver. We sat in back. As we started out, Carter turned around and flashed us the smile that would become his national trademark.

"I know you fellows think I'm crazy," he said, "but I'm going to be the next president of the United States."

I did not think he was crazy, of course. But to be honest, I was inclined to agree with the governor. A rural Georgia peanut farmer,

490

governor of a southern state with almost no national or international exposure and relatively little experience in national affairs ... it seemed impossible.

On that day in Jackson, my mind went back to the first time I had ever heard of Jimmy Carter. It was in 1966, as we were planning for an evangelistic outreach in Americus, Georgia. This would not be a preaching mission but a mission using an evangelistic film we had produced; that film would be shown for several days in a local theater.

As always, we insisted that the meetings be completely integrated. While this was no longer a new thing in much of the South, in that part of rural Georgia it was by no means the customary practice. Some even urged us to cancel our plans or face a potentially explosive situation. The issue was so critical, in fact, that we could not get a Christian leader in Americus to be chairman of the outreach. We were stymied but determined to hold our position.

At the last minute, a successful farmer and state senator from a nearby community stepped in and courageously volunteered to be chairman of the effort. His name was Jimmy Carter.

"When I went to the major churches," Carter recalled, "none of them would let us in. So because of that, we went to the basement of an abandoned school building, and that's where we had our planning meetings."

Once the outreach began, he stood night after night before the audiences at the end of each showing, inviting those who were searching for spiritual answers to life's problems to come forward for counseling.

Although he and I hadn't yet met, I wrote a note after the film mission to thank him, both for caring and for daring to help.

Later, in 1972, he recalled this experience while addressing the United Methodist General Conference. He admitted that he had not been especially keen on taking the chairmanship, adding that our film, *The Restless Ones*, hadn't particularly impressed him. He also reported, however, that "the first interracial religious effort in the history of our county" resulted in 565 people coming forward at the Invitation, with 137 of those indicating that they were accepting Christ as Savior. Carter gave credit for this response not to the film or his own efforts but to the Holy Spirit.

A few years after the Americus meetings, in January 1971, Jimmy Carter became the governor of Georgia, and we met personally for the first time. In spite of his heavy responsibilities, he willingly accepted the invitation to serve as honorary chair of our Atlanta Crusade. We had an interesting series of meetings in the Atlanta Stadium. Almost every night, he sat on the platform with us to indicate his support for the event. The next year, on March 1, 1972, I spoke at the annual Governor's Prayer Breakfast in Atlanta and spent the night as his guest in the executive mansion. It was then that I got to know him and his wife, Rosalynn, better. Through these contacts, I grew to like him as a person and to respect both his intelligence and his genuine and unashamed Christian commitment.

Carter's unexpected rise to national prominence and his successful pursuit of the Democratic nomination focused media attention on his personality and his political views. It also spotlighted his Southern Baptist roots and religious commitment. His quiet work across the years as a deacon and Sunday school teacher in his home church in Plains, and his self-identification as a "born-again" Christian, became part of his public identity.

Suddenly the phrase *born again* appeared everywhere. The media demonstrated everything from curiosity and respect to misunderstanding, quiet mockery, and even derision. Because I knew from my own experience that reporters often felt uncomfortable dealing with religious issues and unfamiliar terminology, I sympathized with Carter's attempts to explain his religious commitment without sounding "holier-than-thou."

At first the attention on born-again faith seemed to open the door to a number of opportunities for me to explain the Gospel. I found myself answering questions about the expression *born again* in media interviews, for example. It was a term I frequently used in preaching. I had even written a book entitled *How to Be Born Again,* which had been well received by the public. The term was taken from one of the most familiar passages in the New Testament, the third chapter of the Gospel of John. In it Jesus told a noted religious teacher of his day named Nicodemus about the necessity and promise of spiritual renewal—a renewal (or spiritual rebirth) that comes as we turn in faith to Christ.

As time went on, however, the term *born again* was trivialized and came to mean almost anything. Advertisers used it to tout their products; politicians and pundits used it to speak of anyone who had changed his or her mind about something; pop psychologists and trendy cultists used it to identify any kind of "religious" experience, no matter how mysterious or strange. Soon I began to avoid the term almost completely, emphasizing instead the literal meaning of the original Greek term, which translates "born from above" or "born into God's family."

The injection of the religious issue into the 1976 campaign concerned me. On the one hand, I was delighted to hear a presidential candidate speak so openly with the press and the public about his personal faith. On the other hand, I knew Gerald Ford to be a man of deep conviction also, even if his own religious background was much different and less public. Religious conviction alone was not the most reliable guide as to who would be the best or most effective leader.

Jimmy Carter did not present himself as perfect or pious; in fact, the media were quick to pick up his own references to sinfulness in his heart. Neither did he compromise his understanding of the Gospel by verbal dodging or double-talk. He took a political risk by being so forthright about his faith; in the end, though, I believe his candor worked in his favor. After the disillusionment of Watergate, the American people were attracted by Carter's summons to a moral revival.

With his election, some people speculated that I would become a regular fixture around the White House. Although we never talked directly about it, I sensed that President Carter agreed with my feeling that such visibility on my part could easily have been misunderstood by the public, leading to the suspicion that I was somehow taking advantage of our shared faith to influence political decisions or secure favors or influence for the evangelical movement.

I recalled the caution that John Kennedy had exercised during his presidency in this regard. Somewhat like the Carter election, Kennedy's campaign had been marred by religious charges. Some had even contended that Roman Catholic clerics would have ready access to the White House and would use their favored position for political influence. Such was not the case, however; indeed, Kennedy went out of his way to avoid any overt signs of closeness to the Roman Catholic hierarchy. As an example, when Cardinal Cushing—an old family friend—made his occasional visits to the White House, he slipped in without publicity or even press knowledge.

But President Carter and I did have some personal contacts, cordial though infrequent, during the four years he was in office (1977–1981). He was a faithful supporter of the National Prayer Breakfast. During his tenure, I attended the one in 1977 and spoke at the one in 1979.

Ruth and I were privileged to be overnight guests of the Carters at the White House. For several hours, we reminisced about our southern backgrounds and talked about national affairs. Little Amy Carter sat quietly watching the television set. Much of the time that evening, however, we shared our mutual faith in Jesus Christ and discussed some of the issues that sometimes divide sincere Christians. When the four of us prayed together at the close of the evening, we sensed a spirit of oneness and Christian love among us. Rosalynn Carter was frequently pictured in the press with a serious face, but we found her to be a woman with a warm and caring heart.

Two incidents stick out in my memory from the years of the Carter administration.

The first was a personal matter having to do with the sister of one of our sons-in-law. Although born in America, she had been raised in Europe. For some reason, however, she had no passport of any nationality. When she turned eighteen, she applied for an American passport but was turned down, apparently for bureaucratic reasons or legal technicalities. We tried every avenue we knew to help her, but to no avail. One of our North Carolina senators finally told me that only an act of Congress, or an act of the president of the United States, could change the situation.

One day, as I was talking with President Carter on the telephone, I mentioned our dilemma. He listened intently and then said, "Send the details to my secretary." I promptly did as he asked.

About a week later, the President himself called the girl involved. "You are a citizen of the United States, and your passport is being sent to you," he said. "You will never have to worry about this again."

We were very grateful for his help and his personal concern, touched that he had handled such a matter himself. His personal interest in people was unquestionably one of his strongest traits. When I was at the Mayo Clinic one time, he called simply to inquire about my health and to cheer me up.

The second matter involved our 1977 visit to Hungary. It was unprecedented for a Communist government to allow an evangelist from the West to preach, and I sensed that our visit might create a slight opening for better relations between Hungary and the United States. As the time for the trip approached, I contacted President Carter to inform him of the trip. He assured me not only of his interest but also of his prayers. He asked that I deliver his greetings to the people I would meet, especially his fellow Christian believers, which I did.

In preparing for that trip, we learned that Hungary's greatest national symbol—the ancient crown of St. Stephen, first king of Hungary, enthroned in the year 1000—had been stored in the United States at Fort Knox since World War II. America's possession of this emblem of patriotic pride was a real sore spot in Hungarian-American relations. The return of the crown was a major condition for improvement in relations between the two countries, according to the American ambassador to Hungary, Philip Kaiser. I asked his advice about the request for the return to Hungary of the crown of St. Stephen; he was very much in favor of whatever we could do.

The Carter administration, I knew, was already giving thought to the crown case. Many Hungarian-Americans, deeply suspicious of Hungary's Communist government, understandably opposed its return. It was admittedly a complex question: by returning the crown, the United States would be granting undeserved legitimacy to a government it did not support. It was a dilemma for the President in both political and diplomatic terms.

When I arrived back in Washington after the Hungarian trip, I made an appointment with President Carter. At the last minute, a priority engagement surfaced for him. In his absence, I talked with Vice President Walter Mondale, who was courteous and sympathetic to my suggestion that the crown be returned, since that gesture might move Hungary toward closer contact with the West. I also raised with him the question of changing the trade status of Hungary. When I was interviewed after my return on *Good Morning America*, I said frankly that I thought our trade restrictions against Hungary should be lifted. This could, I felt, encourage greater liberalization there. However, I stressed to Mr. Mondale that I did not want the White House to think I was being political or trying to tell the administration what to do; they understood the issues far better than I.

The matter of St. Stephen's crown had been brought to the attention of the U.S. government by several prominent Americans before I spoke up. Whether my support of its return was a significant thing with Mr. Carter or Mr. Mondale, I do not know. I do know that later I was given credit for it by the authorities in Hungary.

The crown soon found its way back to Budapest, where it was put on public display in the national museum, and shortly thereafter our government did negotiate Most Favored Nation trade status for Hungary. Perhaps these steps opened the door for better relations between our two countries and eventual change in Hungary.

My last contact with President Carter during his time in office came on Sunday, December 7, 1980, when Senator Mark Hatfield asked me to preach at the small Baptist church across from his home in Georgetown. "I thought I'd invite the President and Mrs. Carter to come," he told me on the phone. (A month earlier, Carter had lost the presidential election to Ronald Reagan.)

Hatfield called the White House, and the Carters did come. Vice President-elect George Bush and his wife, Barbara, also came to the service. Afterward we all walked across the street to the Hatfields' apartment where Mark and his wife, Antoinette, presided at a lunch for us all. We swapped stories, but mainly we discussed the Bible. In spite of his recent election defeat, President Carter could not have been warmer or more friendly to the Bushes or the rest of us.

Many leaders, I am afraid, place their religious and moral convictions in a separate compartment and do not think of the implications of their faith on their responsibilities. Jimmy Carter, however, was not like that. His deep-seated commitment to human rights around the world was an example of this. His determination to do something about the complex problems in the Middle East also came in part from his Christian convictions concerning peace. And that determination bore fruit: few diplomatic events in recent decades have been as dramatic as his breakthrough agreement with Prime Minister Begin and President Sadat in the Camp David Accords.

Since leaving office, Mr. Carter has continued to carry out his responsibilities as a Christian as he understands them, whether in his efforts on behalf of international understanding and peace or his work with Habitat for Humanity. Other political leaders would do well to learn from his moral and spiritual ideals.

Since his presidency, he and I have maintained occasional contact, and I value his continued friendship. Just before his trip to North Korea in June 1994, he called me and we had an extended conversation about his plans. Relations between the United States and North Korea had reached a stalemate over fears about that country's nuclear program. Tensions were rising to a dangerous level. He was not sure if he could have any impact and had not completely decided about accepting the invitation to go.

I had just been to Pyongyang for the second time and had spent several hours with President Kim Il Sung. President Kim had been very warm to me personally, in spite of our differences in background, and I felt that he sincerely wanted to move forward in establishing better relations. I told Mr. Carter this and urged him to go. I felt that his warm personality would meet with a positive response from President Kim, and it did.

When my plans for another Crusade in Atlanta in 1994 first began to take shape, Jimmy Carter gladly agreed to serve as the honorary chairman. He was on the platform the opening night in October, in the new Georgia Dome, and spoke for several minutes to the audience. It was a remarkable Crusade, drawing strong support from both the African-American and white communities.

Historians will, I suspect, be kinder to President Carter than some of his contemporaries were. A man of faith and sterling integrity, he was undoubtedly one of our most diligent Presidents, persistent and painstaking in his attention to his responsibilities.

28

Moscow and Beyond

We were grateful for the doors God had opened for us in Hungary
and Poland. Even if we never made any further visits to eastern
Europe, those trips would have been worth the effort, both in evangelism and in encouraging the churches. But all along our prayer was
that another door would open—the door to the hardest and most
strategic place of all: the Soviet Union. Preaching there, we were
convinced, would have reverberations all over that part of the world.

MOSCOW

In 1982 the Russian Orthodox Church planned what it called the
"World Conference of Religious Workers for Saving the Sacred Gift
of Life from Nuclear Catastrophe." In spite of its cumbersome
name, the May event was to be a church-sponsored international
peace conference. It would draw to Moscow several hundred representatives from all the major world religions, not just Christianity.

After numerous contacts in Moscow and Washington (with
Alexander Haraszti, Walter Smyth, and John Akers), the head of the

Russian Orthodox Church, Patriarch Pimen of Moscow and All Russia, extended an invitation for me to address the gathering.

The invitation presented serious problems. It was no secret that peace conferences in eastern Europe were ill-disguised showcases for Soviet propaganda. In fact, they were generally assumed to be controlled behind the scenes by Soviet authorities. In addition, they almost inevitably took on a decidedly political and anti-American tone, supporting Soviet policies uniformly and uncritically. There was no guarantee this one would be any different, in spite of its religious sponsorship. If I accepted, would I be an unwitting tool of Communist propaganda?

Alex was able to negotiate three major points in advance.

First, if I went, I would be only an observer, not a full delegate. That way, if any pro-Soviet final statement was adopted by the assembly, I would not be part of it.

Second, he insisted that if I spoke at the conference, I would have complete freedom to speak from the Bible on an appropriate topic of my choice. ("The Christian Faith and Peace in a Nuclear Age" was the title I chose.)

Third, after some discussion, in addition to speaking at the conference, I would be allowed to preach in two Moscow churches, one Orthodox and one Baptist.

These three concessions gave me some comfort. Nevertheless, I have seldom been so unsettled about accepting an invitation. Perhaps it was not from God but was Satan's way of diverting me or bringing disrepute to the Gospel. For some weeks, Ruth and I debated and prayed—even as I spent time preparing a tentative draft of my conference message.

I contacted former President Richard Nixon for advice about the invitation. He repeated what others had already said: that the Communists would certainly attempt to use my presence for propaganda purposes. Unhesitatingly, though, he urged me to go, and he helped us in many ways.

Publisher Rupert Murdoch agreed, as did some other knowledgeable leaders I consulted. The head of PepsiCo, Don Kendall, who had extensive experience in the Soviet Union, likewise urged me to go. Henry Kissinger was recuperating from a heart operation, but he invited me to come to Boston to discuss the issue with him. He read the draft of my message and urged me to make a more forceful statement on human rights. I gratefully accepted his suggestion.

Some people I spoke with were concerned because it was not a distinctively *Christian* conference. Others viewed my acceptance of the invitation—coming as it did from a Communist nation—as a serious compromise with the forces of atheism.

Even some on the executive committee of the BGEA board informally suggested that I not make the trip. I always took seriously their combined wisdom, and very rarely had I ever overridden their advice. This was one time I did, however, feeling strongly that if the Lord was directing me, He would look out for His own interests, no matter what happened.

There was a further consideration, however. Alex was convinced that if I turned down the invitation, I would never receive another invitation of any kind to the Soviet Union or anywhere else in eastern Europe. They would be offended by my refusal, and the Soviet government—which had to approve any invitation—would never give its approval again.

The American ambassador to Moscow, Arthur Hartman, strongly opposed my participation. Convinced that the Soviets would use me for propaganda purposes, he registered his objections both with Alex and with his superiors in Washington. But I was confident that my propaganda for Christ would prove stronger than their propaganda. As the Bible says, "Greater is he that is in you, than he that is in the world" (1 John 4:4, KJV).

"Perhaps the Communists in the Soviet Union will try to use me," I told one friend, "but I'm also going to use them, to preach the Gospel."

A few weeks before I left for Moscow, Vice President George Bush called me in New York, where some of us were meeting at the Essex Hotel to discuss the whole situation. He expressed his concerns and read me the statement from Ambassador Hartman, but he did not tell me to cancel.

Later, on a Sunday shortly before I was due to depart, I was a luncheon guest of the Bushes, along with Arthur Ochs Sulzberger, publisher of the *New York Times*. We had been invited to the official vice-presidential residence on the Naval Observatory grounds. "I don't think the Reagans are busy at lunchtime today," the Vice President told us. "I'll call them and invite them over." They arrived in about half an hour, and we had a good discussion about my proposed Russian trip as well as other subjects. I will never forget President Reagan's enjoyment and patience as he played with the Sulzberger children.

At one point, President Reagan took me aside. "You know what's been in the press," he said. "I believe that God works in mysterious ways. I'll be praying for you every mile of the way."

By the beginning of May, after the trip had been announced, the BGEA office in Minneapolis was receiving anywhere from 10,000 to 15,000 letters a day; criticism of the forthcoming trip to Moscow was amounting to less than one-half of 1 percent.

On Friday, May 7, 1982, we arrived in Moscow to a crowded press conference, where we were welcomed by government officials as well as leaders from the Russian Orthodox and Protestant churches. Afterward, as I was going down the stairs to the waiting cars, an American reporter who had come especially for the event thrust into my hands a piece of paper. It was a list of "Soviet prisoners of conscience," and he demanded that I speak out publicly concerning their plight. I had seen similar lists before; indeed, I already had one with me.

I certainly hoped to be able to share my concerns about alleged abuses of religious freedom privately with high-level Soviet officials. They alone could change the situation. On the other hand, I knew that if I publicly castigated the Soviet government for its policies, I would never have another chance to meet privately with the only people—the leaders—who could bring about change.

Later I presented my list to a ranking official and expressed my concern for those who were being treated unfairly because of their faith. My Russian church hosts strongly applauded my quiet, behind-the-scenes approach. Unfortunately, many in the West never did understand our strategy.

The next evening, our hosts took me to visit (but not to preach in) three Russian Orthodox churches that held Saturday evening services. Each was packed with people standing shoulder to shoulder. (Russian Orthodox churches have no pews or chairs.) One reason Moscow churches were so packed was that the authorities sharply restricted the number that were permitted to be open. The splendid liturgical music and the obvious devotion of the worshipers moved me greatly.

Offhandedly, I commented to a television reporter from North Carolina that he had certainly never seen churches in Charlotte jammed on a Saturday evening. (Of course, most American churches don't hold services on Saturday evening.) My point was that Soviet believers had a depth of devotion not found among many American Christians; they were willing to sacrifice their Saturday evening to prepare their hearts for worship on Sunday. That offhand comment was picked up by the reporter but unfortunately was taken out of context: somehow the phrase "on a Saturday evening" got dropped from stories that were printed in the United States, making it sound as if I had claimed that more people went to church in Moscow than in Charlotte or any other American city!

The next day, Sunday, I was up early to preach in the Moscow Baptist Church, the same church I had attended as a tourist in 1959. The service was originally scheduled for late in the day, but word had leaked out, and the authorities, fearing a huge crowd, forced the church at the last minute to reschedule the service for early morning. Nevertheless, the building was still jammed, its aisles and doorways absolutely crammed with people standing shoulder to shoulder. Constantly throughout the service, small groups would leave to permit others to take their place.

One of the pastors of the church, the Reverend Mikhail Zhidkov, interpreted for me. He and the general secretary of the Baptists in the Soviet Union, the Reverend Alexei Bichkov, had met with me in Hungary in 1977 and since then had worked diligently with the Russian Orthodox Church and the government to gain an invitation for us.

During my sermon, I was told later, a woman from a dissident group unfurled from the balcony a banner protesting the Soviet government's treatment of believers. Within seconds other church members quietly expelled her, because her behavior could have caused them difficulty in their relations with the government. Later

503

some of the international press demanded to know why I had not stopped preaching and made some sympathetic comment. I told them I hadn't noticed the banner and was unaware of the incident at the time. I suspect some of them did not believe me.

At the close of my sermon, I was whisked out the door to be driven immediately to preach at the Cathedral of the Epiphany, the church of the Russian Orthodox patriarch. As we rushed away to the next service—we were running late and the Orthodox service was already in progress—I did not notice the several hundred people I was later told were standing behind a barricade about a block away from the Baptist church, people who had apparently not been permitted to come near the building. No one called my attention to them at the time; I only wish I had been able at least to greet them.

Patriarch Pimen introduced me about halfway through the Divine Liturgy. Surrounded by bearded Orthodox clergy wearing black robes, I rose and looked out at the sea of faces in front of me. Standing in front of an elaborate golden icon screen, I began to preach. I was a bit uneasy at first because there was no podium available; I didn't have a place to rest my sermon notes or lay my Bible down. Then, only a minute or two into my sermon, people began to shout. For a moment, I feared that some kind of demonstration was breaking out. However, the worshipers were only calling for my interpreter to speak louder; there was no effective sound system in the huge cathedral. It was my first experience preaching in an Orthodox service, and I was honored to be there. The steadfastness of Russia's Orthodox believers even in the worst of times remains one of the great examples of courage in the history of the church.

The other formal speaking opportunity came at the peace conference itself. I attended only one morning and one afternoon session of the five-day conference; the rest of my time was filled with private meetings with officials and other events.

The speaker before me, who I think was a Syrian delegate, was supposed to take ten minutes; he took forty. As his speech grew longer and longer, I hastily began to make cuts on the manuscript of my talk. Metropolitan Filaret of Minsk and Byelorussia (*metropolitan* is the title given to the leader of an ecclesiastical province within the Orthodox Church) saw me scribbling and whispered, "Give your full speech."

When I finally rose, I spoke from the Bible on peace. I stated frankly that although I was aware that many of them came from non-Christian backgrounds, I was speaking to them as a Christian, noting that "everything I have ever been, or am, or ever hope to be in this life or the future life, I owe to Jesus Christ."

I made it clear that I was not a pacifist, nor did I support unilateral disarmament; nations and peoples had a right to defend themselves against an aggressor. I then pointed out that the Bible dealt with peace in three dimensions: peace with God through Christ, peace within ourselves, and peace with each other. God was concerned about all three aspects, I said, and none was to be ignored if we were to have true peace.

In addition, I noted that the arms race was not just a political issue, but a moral and spiritual issue as well. For that reason, Christians had a responsibility to be peacemakers in whatever ways God opened for them, although we knew our ultimate hope for lasting peace was only in the kingdom of God. Then I suggested a series of steps toward peace that religious leaders could take, beginning with a call for repentance: "Let us call the nations and the leaders of our world to repentance. . . . No nation, large or small, is exempt from blame for the present state of international affairs."

I also declared that "we should urge all governments to respect the rights of religious believers as outlined in the United Nations Universal Declaration of Human Rights. We must hope that someday all nations (as all those who signed the Final Act of Helsinki declared) 'will recognize and respect the freedom of the individual to profess and practice, alone or in community with others, religion or belief acting in accordance with the dictates of his own conscience.'"

I deliberately included the exact wording of the Helsinki Accord (as the Final Act of Helsinki is usually called), hoping it might stir the conscience of the Soviet government, which had signed the agreement but was widely judged to be ignoring some of its provisions. The speech seemed to be well received; the audience responded with applause that grew into a standing ovation.

Unfortunately, some of the speakers, as we had feared, did take a highly political and pro-Soviet stance, even speaking openly against policies of the American government. I was seated on the rostrum in full view of the audience. In the midst of one particularly abusive statement, I protested by deliberately taking off my translation headset.

Later I met with Boris Ponomarev, chairman of the Foreign Affairs Committee of the Supreme Soviet of the USSR and a member of the Politburo. I told him that if the conference continued to be blatantly anti-American, it would lose all credibility and become a negative influence in Soviet-American relations. The next day, I was told, the tone changed.

That visit with Mr. Ponomarev was one of the most unexpected events of my life. Before going to the Soviet Union I had prayed that I might have an opportunity to meet with someone on that level, although—humanly speaking—I knew it was almost impossible. As I was driven through the Kremlin gate reserved for officials, I knew that we were entering the very center of Soviet power, but the thought did not alarm me or make me nervous. I had the feeling that God was with me, and I knew the Lord was going to give me the words to say and the boldness to speak about Christ. Throughout our meeting I was praying for my host, and I felt (as I have on similar occasions) a surge of inner strength and confidence, similar to that which often comes to me when I am preaching, and which I can only attribute to the Holy Spirit.

We sat at a round table in his high-ceilinged office, which had gray damask-covered walls with matching drapes and upholstery and a glittering crystal chandelier. Some Soviet church leaders told me later that I was probably the first foreign clergyman he, or any other member of the Politburo, had ever met, and certainly one of the few Americans. I found him to be quite different from the Western stereotype of a Soviet official. He was gentle, courteous, thoughtful, and well-informed on America and its views.

I was not there representing my country, I told him, although I did have a concern for better relations. We discussed in some detail the problems and barriers between our two nations. We discussed also the plight of two Siberian Pentecostal families who were living as refugees in the basement of the American Embassy in Moscow, having taken refuge there when they were denied permission to emigrate from the Soviet Union. I urged him and his colleagues to find a solution to their problem. As I have always tried to do in meetings with political leaders, I also sought to share my own convictions as a Christian.

Afterward he personally escorted me on a tour of the Kremlin. He showed me around President Leonid Brezhnev's office, just down the hall from his; Brezhnev himself lay dying in a clinic elsewhere. As we continued the tour, doors seemed to open automatically and people bowed dutifully. He introduced me to staff in several offices, all of whom greeted me with great courtesy—not surprising, considering who my guide was.

I found the Kremlin offices to be sumptuously appointed and elegant in an old-fashioned way. As for the people working there, I sensed a certain pride; they knew they were working in one of the great power centers of the world. After leaving the Kremlin, I told one of my associates that I seriously doubted that those Soviet leaders would ever start a nuclear war; they would not want to lose their perks and comforts.

Although my hosts were very reluctant, I was determined to visit the Siberian Pentecostals at the American Embassy. Their situation had become a major and highly visible irritant in relations between the United States and the USSR, although I wanted to visit them not for political reasons but as a pastor.

"Why does he insist on visiting those people?" the man assigned to accompany us during our stay in Moscow asked Alex and John in exasperation. "Why does he want to do something that will probably close the door on his ever coming here again?" Their answer—that I wanted to pay a pastoral visit on my fellow believers—probably was incomprehensible to him. Nevertheless, we persevered, and plans were finally made for a visit to the embassy one evening.

That man was a most unlikely helper. I knew that the KGB kept a close watch on foreign guests and could, if they chose to, make great difficulty. In our pre-trip negotiations, therefore, I requested that a man "who knew how to get things done" be assigned to accompany us. The gentleman who showed up spoke excellent English and had full power to act, though he never acknowledged any ties to the KGB (nor did we ask). We never had any problems with arrangements as a result. He was with us throughout our 1982 trip and joined us once again in 1984.

The press got wind of the embassy visit and was waiting for us there, perhaps hoping I would do something to embarrass myself or my hosts. As our car approached, several dozen journalists were clustered around the embassy's archway. One of their own, a seasoned correspondent for one of the major American networks, had quietly tipped me off in advance. "You're doing this in exactly the right way, unofficial and low-key, not saying a word about it," he told me. "When we reporters start clamoring for a statement from you, I will be yelling louder than all the rest. Don't answer me, or any of us. Just keep quiet or say, 'No comment.'"

For almost an hour, I waited in an embassy office upstairs while John and Alex tried to work out some ground rules with the Pentecostals for the visit. For a while, it looked as if the meeting was off; one woman in the group was demanding full press coverage of my visit inside their living quarters. When I put my foot down firmly against making the visit into a media event, she wanted to let photographers at least shoot pictures through the basement windows. I could sympathize with her, but I did not want a pastoral visit to be turned into a media circus. Finally, they reluctantly agreed to a private visit.

Actually, my conversations concerning their case with government officials had not been altogether hopeless. I had based my plea for the Siberian Seven, as they were being called by the media, on the urgent need for improving relations between our two countries. One of the Soviet officials I spoke with did indicate that he thought the problem would be resolved in due time. But they viewed the Pentecostals as lawbreakers, not as refugees, he said. He pointed out that we handled religious leaders in America the same way when they disobeyed our laws; he cited the example of Martin Luther King's being jailed for alleged civil disobedience. I did not report this to the Siberians in the American Embassy basement, of course, but I thought there might be a pinpoint of light at the end of their tunnel.

The Seven (now down to six—one had already returned to Siberia) spent much of the hour and a half I was with them plying me with questions about the Bible. A few of their questions were highly political, trying to get me to identify the Antichrist of

Scripture with the Communism of the Soviet government—a position they seemed to take.

As the moment approached for my departure, we all got on our knees and prayed together. Then I went to each one and embraced them, which I could not have done in front of the cameras without it appearing to be a show.

The Siberian Seven were like the tip of an iceberg compared to the Jews in the Soviet Union who were being denied emigration. One of the conditions I set for going to the conference was to be able to meet with Soviet Jewish leaders. Before leaving home, I discussed the situation of Russian Jews with my friend Rabbi Marc Tanenbaum of the American Jewish Committee, who had urged me to take the trip. In Moscow I met in private with the chief rabbi and other Jewish leaders in Moscow's lone synagogue. When we arrived at the synagogue, the building was surrounded by dozens of muscular men in ill-fitting suits; I assumed they were police, unsuccessfully trying to look unobtrusive.

A few of the Western press persisted in trying to get me to criticize the Soviet government in public. When I refused, they attempted to portray me as naive, or even as a Communist sympathizer. During a trip we took outside Moscow to the ancient and historic Orthodox monastery of Zagorsk, it was raining, and we were running late. A police escort had cleared the way for us very efficiently, helping us to meet our schedule. Afterward I thanked them for their assistance. The next day an Amsterdam newspaper carried a photo of me with them, saying I was shaking the hands of the police who were persecuting Christians and thanking them for what they did!

More serious were some misquotes, or partial quotes taken out of context, of statements I had made concerning religious freedom in the Soviet Union. On one occasion, for example, I said that there was "a measure of religious freedom" in the Soviet Union, which was true. Some Western papers, however, reported that I had claimed there was complete religious freedom.

Later, as we were about to depart from the airport at the end of the trip, one reporter asked me again about my impressions of church life in the Soviet Union. Casually I mentioned that unlike Great Britain and other European countries that had a "state church," the Soviet Union had a "free church." Then we were interrupted, and I did not have a chance to see if he understood the distinction I was drawing.

Unfortunately, he was not familiar with the technical meaning of these terms. In Europe the term *state church* or *established church* refers to a denomination that is officially sanctioned and supported by the government; the Anglican Church in England and the Lutheran Church in Germany are good examples. The term *free church* indicates denominations that generally operate without government support. Some reporters assumed incorrectly that I was saying that the church in the Soviet Union was free of any state control and had full freedom.

We left Moscow for London, where I was to receive the Templeton Prize for Progress in Religion, a recognition that I was honored and humbled to receive. The presentation ceremony by Prince Philip was to take place at Buckingham Palace. It immediately became clear, however, that some of my alleged remarks while in Moscow had stirred up a firestorm in the Western press.

A hastily called news conference in London did little to quiet the storm, nor did a brief television interview by satellite to America on a program that included an unannounced participant who was militant about human rights to the point of vocal confrontation. In some ways, of course, I was handicapped by not being able to reveal the confidential discussions about human rights I'd had with officials in Moscow.

When Ruth and I arrived at Buckingham Palace, we were escorted up a wide, grand staircase and down a long hall to the room where the presentation was to take place. Ruth—who has the poet's eye for detail—recalls the sumptuous draperies and appointments, as well as a huge Aubusson carpet, which seemed to stretch forever. At the moment of presentation, Prince Philip picked up the check for $200,000—the largest monetary prize of any type at that time—and handed it not to me but to Ruth, saying with a hearty laugh that he assumed that she handled the family purse strings. Later I had to ask her for the check back to endorse it. (We had already decided to donate it to the cause of world evangelization; much of it was used for scholarships and travel grants for Third World evangelists who would attend the International Conference for Itinerant Evangelists the following year in Amsterdam.)

Immediately after the presentation ceremony, which was followed by a dinner hosted by Sir John Templeton and a speech by me in connection with the Templeton Prize, I left for New York. On arrival, there was another crowded press conference and a barrage of sharp questions. Knowing something of what I had tried to do behind the scenes, Rabbi Marc Tanenbaum spoke in my defense, not only supporting our Soviet trip but commending me for my relationship with the Jewish people. Nevertheless, many people saw only the initial reports and missed the clarifications. The controversy smoldered for a long time afterward.

It distressed me particularly to learn that Aleksandr Solzhenitsyn was offended by comments I allegedly made. He and I had met in 1974, when he received the Nobel Prize for Literature. He had sent a messenger to me in Europe inviting me to join him in Stockholm. I stayed in his hotel, and we had good conversation together. I felt confident that both he and his wife were sincere believers in Christ.

In 1983, however, when he received the Templeton Award for Progress in Religion (the year after I was the recipient, and the year after the Moscow peace conference), his acceptance speech included a somewhat derogatory allusion to "last year's winner." I was saddened over this misunderstanding with someone for whom I had the greatest respect.

By the grace of God, we weathered all the criticism and controversy. In retrospect, I was still convinced it had been God's will for me to go, and I took comfort in the promise of Proverbs 16:7: "When a man's ways are pleasing to the Lord, he makes even his enemies live at peace with him." It saddened me, though, that some of the critics never relented. And the question came back to haunt me: Would this be the end of our ministry in this part of the world?

As it turned out, the May 1982 trip to Moscow was a signal to other Communist-dominated countries that they could now invite us without risking a frown from the Kremlin. During the summer, invitations arrived from East Germany and Czechoslovakia, among the most restrictive governments in that part of the world.

EAST GERMANY

In October 1982, we arrived in the German Democratic Republic, as East Germany was officially known, for a preaching mission.

A lot had changed since I was in Berlin years before, when one East German newspaper cartoon had pictured me with a Bible in one hand and an atomic bomb in the other. One byline-hungry reporter had written that I'd been seen in an East Berlin nightclub—or so he claimed—with a blonde by the name of Beverly Shea. (The only Beverly Shea I ever traveled with was our Crusade soloist, George Beverly Shea!)

Now, however, the authorities were apparently welcoming us, although the East German government had a reputation for taking a hard line in its treatment of the church. During my first meetings in West Berlin almost three decades before, large numbers from the East had traveled to the West to attend the meetings. But since August 1961, that mobility was no longer possible; the construction of the Berlin Wall had effectively cut Germany into two parts.

Furthermore, although the eastern part of Germany was the land of Luther, the course of its churches had been very difficult under Communism. Some churches were still permitted to exist, but only under strict government supervision, including restrictions on open evangelism.

And I felt uncertain about the Lutheran Church itself. These East German Lutherans were the people of Luther and Bonhoeffer, great heroes of reform and resistance in church history. Now they had to walk a tightrope in relations with a hostile, atheistic government. I wondered if they would feel resentful toward, or at least nervous about, a Baptist from the West.

My fears proved groundless. The media were respectful, if not enthusiastic, and our meetings got good coverage, at least for a Communist-dominated land. Church and state officials likewise welcomed me, and the president of the East German Parliament received me. For the most part, the Lutherans themselves could not have been more hospitable.

I preached my first sermon from Martin Luther's pulpit in the City Church of Wittenberg on Sunday morning. I used the text made famous by Luther himself: "The just shall live by faith" (Romans 1:17, KJV). Afterward we toured the historic town with the mayor.

Then we visited Wittenberg's Castle Church, where Luther had nailed his Ninety-five Theses to the door in 1517, thus beginning the Protestant Reformation. We also saw the little room where he gave his table talks—I have read and laughed at and pondered them for years—and visited his grave.

In the evening, we drove to Dresden's Lutheran Church of the Cross, largest in Saxony, where 7,000 people, mostly under the age of twenty-five, jammed every space.

During one of the fiercest and most deadly Allied bombing campaigns of World War II, most of Dresden, including that Lutheran church, had been almost destroyed. But it need not have been so, the Germans told me with some bitterness; Dresden had little strategic value. Since then the church had been meticulously restored. That evening every available space was taken, with hundreds crowded around the pulpit. As the meeting progressed, a thick haze fogged the air from lack of ventilation; and a fine rain of plaster or paint chips descended from the ceiling, apparently loosened by the heat or humidity.

When I saw the high number of young people in the audience, attentive to the message and singing Christian hymns, I could not help but think that the Communists in East Germany had already lost the ideological battle for their minds and souls. Nearly a third of them responded when I gave the Invitation after my sermon.

The next day, in Dresden, I addressed the Synod of Saxony, reputed to be the most sophisticated and intellectual Lutheran body in the world. When I walked in, I shook hands with those charged with greeting me. They were cold and unfriendly, which I thought was strange, especially coming from clergy. Perhaps their reaction had something to do with the government officials accompanying me; after all, the clergy had to wrestle with those officials regularly over the laws pertaining to religious matters. Nevertheless, I felt my irritation rising.

"When I came in here," I said to the group bluntly, "those who greeted me were as unfriendly as any group of clergy I've addressed

513

anywhere else in the world. When I shook hands with you, your eyes were cold. I don't think this is the way Christians should be, even though we may disagree theologically and in other matters." I added that the first thing we should learn as ministers was to love each other (no matter what our differing emphases). I said that I hoped they sensed a spirit of Christian love from me, and thanked them for inviting me to speak.

Out of a full heart, I told them about my visit to the Luther sites in Wittenberg and how much his life and thought had influenced me. The next year they would be celebrating the five hundredth anniversary of his birth, and I confessed how that knowledge had affected me as I stood at his grave: "I am now ten months older than he was when he died, and look at all he accomplished. It made me feel very small."

After I finished my remarks, I invited their questions. By the time I left the meeting, with their standing ovation ringing in my ears, I felt there truly was nothing but love in their hearts.

I preached in four other East German cities: Görlitz, Stendal, Stralsund, and Berlin. I also paid a memorable visit to the Sachsenhausen concentration camp, where many Christians, along with tens of thousands of Jews, had been killed for their faith. As part of that visit, there was to be a wreath-laying ceremony. At first some of the local Christian leaders were reluctant to participate, since the ceremony had been organized by the local Communist officials rather than by our hosts. Dr. Haraszti, however, quickly pointed out that if they did not participate, the Communists would take their place. They joined me in laying the wreath.

Compared with West Germany, East Germany appeared drab and colorless, although there was a surprising amount of automobile traffic and an apparently higher standard of living than in most other eastern European countries. Some of our Team toured a church-run home for the mentally retarded and were impressed by the love and patience of the staff. Their guide said the churches were glad to demonstrate the love of Christ in this way, and that the government allowed the churches to do this work because it had no interest in caring for those who would never become productive workers.

Several times we drove along the Berlin Wall. Our government hosts pointedly avoided mentioning it, although they were quite ready to point out the other local attractions. Once or twice, however, the pastor sitting next to me discreetly nudged me and nodded toward the ugly barrier.

Another pastor told us how he had been only a few days away from leaving East Germany when the wall went up, making it impossible for him and his family to depart. He said God had given him peace about it; he believed that God had called him to minister in East Berlin and that it would have been disobedient of him to leave.

Still another pastor pointed to the giant modern television tower the government had erected in East Berlin several years before. Near its top was a huge globe-shaped structure housing a restaurant and other facilities. The remarkable thing was that once it was finished, the people discovered that sunlight always reflected off the globe in the shape of a cross! The authorities had tried everything they could think of to prevent this optical phenomenon (known as *asterism*), even covering the dome with paint. But nothing worked. "No matter how hard they try, they can't get rid of the cross," the pastor who had pointed out the tower commented wryly.

While in East Berlin, we met a number of people who had come over from West Berlin to attend the meetings. (Although travel out of East Berlin was tightly restricted, people from West Berlin could visit in East Berlin with comparative ease.) Among them was my longtime friend and interpreter in West Germany, Peter Schneider, and his wife, Margot. Dr. Irmhild Barend, editor of the German edition of *Decision* magazine, also joined us. They, like countless other Christians in West Germany, had prayed for years that God would open the door for us in East Germany.

CZECHOSLOVAKIA

Czechoslovakia had a history of being much more restrictive on the churches than Hungary, Poland, or East Germany. In spite of repeated efforts, our trip there did not materialize until almost the last minute. When I heard that the trip was on, Walter Smyth and I decided to fly from Berlin to Vienna for a few days' rest and preparation before going on to Prague.

As we drove to East Berlin's Schönefeld Airport, we could see fog rolling in. We were able to take off as scheduled, however. The pilot pointed out Prague as we flew over, but we couldn't see the ground for the fog. Why hadn't we taken the train? I wondered.

As we began to circle Vienna, the fog over the Danube was impenetrable. The plane descended toward what I hoped was a runway. I kept looking out the window, but I couldn't see or feel anything until we actually touched down.

The next day was Walter's seventieth birthday. His wife, Ethel, had given us a birthday card for him, and we took him to dinner in one of Vienna's old picturesque restaurants. It was one of the few moments of relaxation during that whirlwind schedule.

While I was resting in Vienna, most of our Team went by air from East Berlin to Prague and flew right into trouble. Customs officials appeared to have no knowledge of our trip and refused to allow our television or sound equipment into the country. In fact, they impounded it until officials from the government office overseeing church affairs secured its release.

A few days later, we too found ourselves in Czechoslovakia, for meetings in Prague, Brno, and Bratislava. The churches lived under heavy restrictions, yet God providentially arranged for me to be interviewed on Prague television for a nationwide prime-time program; the interview was also carried over the radio and reported in newspapers. Local church leaders told me the Gospel cause had never received such high visibility in their country.

Our hosts were the Baptist Union of Czechoslovakia, whose churches were mostly small. Some of their leaders still carried emotional scars from their oppression by the government and were intimidated by their contacts with officials.

One of the most delightful Christians I met there was a pastor who had been an international tennis champion. He had been imprisoned some years before, he told us, but a week later they threw him out of jail. He asked his captors why.

"Because a prison is supposed to be a jail," they said, "and you're making it a happy place!"

"I was only teaching the Bible and praying," he explained to us with a wry smile.

In most Czechoslovakian churches, the crowds were so large and the buildings so small that we could not give an Invitation for people to come forward for counseling, nor were we permitted to print special literature to help new believers. In one church, however, the pastor was determined to extend an Invitation anyway and have counselors meet with people at the close of the meeting. I will never forget one young man—probably still in his teens, and wearing a Czech military uniform—who came forward.

"That took real courage," one of the pastors traveling with us commented with tears in his eyes. "He will pay a price for making a public commitment to Christ. Yes, it will be hard for him, and he will need our prayers."

The trip, although brief, was memorable; and it was an encouragement to the churches, which felt it might help them in their relations with the government.

THE SOVIET UNION

In 1984 the substantial invitation I had been waiting for arrived, to conduct a twelve-day preaching mission in September in four Soviet cities, endorsed by both the Russian Orthodox Church and the All-Union Council of Evangelical Christians-Baptists. In Washington the Soviet Union's veteran ambassador, Anatoly Dobrynin, supported the invitation; he even invited me to lunch at the Soviet Embassy.

However, when the invitation came, I was not at all certain I should accept it. Would attempts again be made, as in 1982, to manipulate the visit for propaganda purposes? I found myself in almost as much turmoil and indecision as I had faced then.

I weighed my response as Ruth and I sought a short rest in the south of France in June 1984, after the close of a Crusade in Norwich during the multicity outreach known as Mission England. On the cliffs above the Mediterranean shore, I took long walks alone after lunch each day, praying out loud and meditating. Then I sat on a rock or a bench and pondered some more. I talked with friends of mine at Trans World Radio in Monte Carlo (which beamed religious programs into the Soviet Union) and with a few other Christians I had come to know along the Mediterranean. Almost unanimously, they thought it was a trip I should take. From his extended discussions in Moscow, Dr. Haraszti was convinced that the 1984 trip would not be a repeat of the 1982 visit; he felt, on the contrary, that we would be given unprecedented opportunities to preach. Still, I was not certain.

One afternoon, staring out at the sea, I thought of the Apostle Paul, who had traveled those same waters centuries before to bring the Gospel to the very seat of world power—Rome, where the infamous Nero held sway as emperor. With all his heart, Paul longed to preach the Gospel in the very shadow of the imperial eagle.

That night before I went to bed, I read a familiar Scripture, 1 Corinthians 9:20, 21, in *The Living Bible:* "When I am with the Jews I seem as one of them so that they will listen to the Gospel and I can win them to Christ. When I am with Gentiles who follow Jewish customs and ceremonies I don't argue, even though I don't agree, because I want to help them. When with the heathen I agree with them as much as I can, except of course that I must always do what is right as a Christian. And so, by agreeing, I can win their confidence and help them too."

Those words kept spinning over and over in my mind before I fell asleep. During the night, I woke up with those words clearly in my mind. They seemed to be God's direct answer to my quandary. When morning came, I told Ruth that I had a settled peace about going.

Symbolic of the ecumenical spirit I found on this trip was the warm welcome I received on September 9 at Moscow's Sheremet-yevo Airport from Baptist and Orthodox leaders. An international contingent of journalists also met us. Some of them asked sharply worded questions about our previous trip, but on the whole I sensed a friendlier spirit.

During the next twelve days, I spoke fifty times (only twenty-three engagements were on the original schedule!) at churches and in other settings in all four cities on the itinerary: Leningrad (now St. Petersburg), Tallinn (in Estonia), Moscow, and Novosibirsk (in Siberia). Accompanying me was my son Franklin, who had recently been ordained to the Gospel ministry. I wished that Grady Wilson could have been with us—we had been tourists together when we visited Moscow twenty-five years before—but this time his health did not permit him to travel.

In the following days, both domestic and foreign media coverage was unparalleled for a religious spokesman visiting the Soviet Union. Ed Plowman from Washington, our press coordinator, noted, however, that none of the Western journalists reported my call for opening more churches and distributing more Bibles. TASS, the official Soviet news agency, as well as other Soviet media, covered the visit, omitting my religious comments but selectively including statements about peace.

In private talks with authorities, I urged a more enlightened attitude toward the religious community and specifically a greater tolerance for dissidents, such as the Sakharovs, whose case was world-renowned. In some of these behind-the-scenes conversations, discussion tended to be quite frank and thorough. In addition, what no one outside of my staff knew was that I had conceived on my own initiative a letter that I hoped and prayed I would get a chance to present to Boris Ponomarev, my acquaintance at the Politburo from our previous trip.

As for the preaching, the audiences that overflowed the churches and cathedrals I preached in welcomed the Gospel with great joy. Their smiles and tears were mixed as they waved to me or stretched their arms through the crowds to shake my hand or give me a flower.

The grandmothers, with their babushka-covered heads, seemed to predominate. But the congregations were not made up solely of old women, as a casual observer might have supposed. Photographer Carl Mydens, who was covering our trip for *Time* magazine, let me in on a secret. Under many a matronly kerchief were young women and girls—he was right, I saw when I looked closely—with their ruddy cheeks and radiant smiles and sparkling eyes. We also saw many men and even a number of children in the services.

Within the Soviet Union, I had the invaluable assistance of Father Vladimir Sorokin, rector of the Orthodox Theological Academy and dean of the Orthodox cathedral in Leningrad. He had been with me on the 1982 visit, and our initial rapport had blossomed into real friendship. At the end of our extensive mission in the Soviet Union, Father Sorokin gave me a lesson in evangelistic preaching.

"You've listened to me preach a lot of sermons now," I said to him. "Please give me any critique you might have."

"This is what we need in the Soviet Union," he replied. "We need your emphasis in our churches." His response was gracious, but he added one thing: "Put more emphasis on the resurrection. The Roman Catholic Church puts its emphasis on the Cross, and that's fine. So do we. But we put the main emphasis on the resurrection because without that event the Cross has no meaning."

Leningrad

Although we landed in Moscow, our first preaching stop was Leningrad, second-largest city in the USSR. Its long waterways reminded me of Venice.

Around 600 students and faculty members at the Russian Orthodox Theological Academy filled all the seats and lined the walls of the auditorium. I shared with them the conditions I found common to people's hearts everywhere: emptiness, loneliness, guilt, and fear of death. Then I reminded them of the Gospel answer to all those, and our responsibility to make the Gospel clear in our preaching. I was humbled when Father Sorokin told me that the message had been taped and would be used for classes in homiletics (preaching).

Ten times as many people heard the first evangelistic message of the trip in Holy Trinity Orthodox Cathedral, where I preached a sermon titled "The Glory of the Cross." About half that many poured into the much smaller Baptist church to hear my sermon on Psalm 23.

The Lord gave us opportunities to meet with civic leaders in the Leningrad Peace Committee as well as with Jewish leaders at the synagogue. I was deeply stirred when I visited the Leningrad War Memorial; and when I laid a wreath at Piskaryovskoye Cemetery, where the 400,000 who had died during the nine-hundred-day Nazi siege of the city had been buried in common graves, I was almost overcome.

Tallinn

Our next stop, picturesquely situated on the Baltic Sea and the Gulf of Finland, was Tallinn, the capital of Estonia—a city with a population of half a million.

Shortly before our arrival, we were informed that an additional stop would be added to the schedule: a wreath-laying at a war memorial. Upon investigation, Alex discovered that it was a monument commemorating the Soviet "liberators" who occupied Estonia. A visit there would have made it look as if I—unlike the American government—supported the Soviet occupation of the Baltic states. We refused to add the stop, and the matter was dropped.

The vice president of Estonia's Supreme Soviet, Madame Meta Vannas, invited me to meet with her and other members of the Presidium, along with officials of the Council for Religious Affairs and certain church leaders, including Metropolitan Alexei, who later succeeded Patriarch Pimen as head of the Russian Orthodox Church. "There's nothing more important," Madame Vannas said, "than to know each other and understand each other." At the same time, she was sharply critical of President Reagan's recent comment that the Soviet Union was an "evil empire."

I gave them my own Christian testimony; and when I spoke of God's love, one of them asked me a question: "Do you love Communists?"

"Yes," I answered, "every one of them. And Jesus Christ also loves them."

That was the message I preached later that day in the historic Oleviste Baptist Church, the largest of its denomination in the Soviet Union. The meeting was personally moving for me because my son Franklin read the Scripture and gave the opening prayer, marking the first time we had participated together in a service. The sermon was interpreted into Estonian in the main sanctuary, and translation into Russian was provided for an overflow crowd in an adjoining chapel.

When I preached on Moses at the Orthodox Cathedral of Alexandr Nevsky, with Metropolitan Alexei standing by in his gold crown and gold robe, I pointed to Jesus Christ as our leader and the only door to true peace.

Moscow Again

In Moscow's Resurrection Cathedral, the Orthodox faithful overflowed the building to stand through the three-hour Divine Liturgy and then listen to me preach. Metropolitan Filaret even added the ordination of a deacon to the lengthy proceedings! In the 5,200-member Moscow Baptist Church, we had another lengthy service—two hours, at least. I tried to shorten my sermons in the Soviet Union, especially since translation doubled the time of delivery.

Parenthetically, the selection of an interpreter is always critical on a foreign trip. This was especially true in the Soviet Union since we did not want to risk any misunderstandings. Across the years, we had developed a set of criteria for interpreters, including not only a thorough understanding of both English and the local language but also a comprehensive knowledge of the Bible.

Occasionally, however, we were unable to find someone who met all the criteria. On one occasion in the Soviet Union, a person traveling with us who understood both English and Russian wryly told one of our staff afterward that he had been doubly blessed by the service because he had heard two different sermons—the one I preached and the one the interpreter preached! To my knowledge, however, this was the only time it happened there.

Novosibirsk, Siberia

After the Moscow weekend, we took off for Siberia, a name often synonymous with exile and suffering. What joys awaited us!

We flew across four time zones from Moscow to Novosibirsk, the largest city in Siberia. The warm reception given by the Orthodox archbishop and Baptist regional superintendent did not fit any stereotype we might have had of frigid Siberia. I preached to 2,000 in the very plain Baptist church on the wooded outskirts of the city (with many standing on benches and crates and peering in through the windows) and in the iconic splendor of the Orthodox cathedral, whose wooden herringbone exterior resembled the stave churches of Norway.

Novosibirsk still had something of a frontier feel about it. Already the cold September nights and the golden leaves falling from the trees gave hints of the hard winters Siberians endure. We also got the impression that Novosibirsk was a long way from Moscow—not just in distance, but in the independent spirit of its people. Regulations coming down from Moscow clearly were subject to local interpretation. Having Christians representing an unregistered church (that is, one not officially approved by the government) at an official luncheon that included government leaders would have been unheard of in Moscow.

Several miles to the south, at the famed Academic City—one of the Soviet Union's premier research institutes—I enjoyed a vigorous dialogue with Dr. Anatoly P. Derevyanko, head of the anthropology department. We discussed the probability that the first human to set foot in America came from Siberia. He acknowledged that he was an atheist.

"Have you ever found a tribe or a group of people anywhere in the world who doesn't believe in God, or some type of higher being?" I asked.

He thought for a moment. "No, I don't believe we have."

"Then if man is a worshiping creature," I asked him, "why is it you believe in atheism? Doesn't this universal belief in a higher being suggest that there must be a God?"

He smiled. "Well, I think I'll have to get some of my colleagues to help me out on that!"

After several days in Siberia, we flew into the four-hour sunset back to Moscow. By the generosity of the archbishop, I carried with me two symbols—a traditional fur hat and a beautiful gilded Orthodox icon—to remind me of our shared humanity and faith.

Moscow Yet Again

In 1884, the year after Karl Marx died, a movement was born in Russia that would outlast Soviet Communism. Now, a century later, the Baptists were celebrating the centennial jubilee of their denomination, and they invited me to speak to their gathering.

I tried to encourage them by pointing out spiritual truths that never changed, regardless of the conditions under which we ministered: God and His Word, the moral law, human nature, social responsibilities, God's promise to be with us in all circumstances, and God's way of salvation.

In Moscow, as in Leningrad at the start of the trip, I met with Jewish leaders, including Adolph Shayevich, chief rabbi of Moscow. Our meeting in the synagogue was scheduled early in the morning. Several American reporters and photographers went with us.

"Do you want to use my cap?" asked one of the photographers diplomatically, reminding me of the Jewish custom to cover one's head in a place of worship. I accepted his offer.

Then came an invitation to the Kremlin.

On the next to the last day of our trip, I was once again whisked through one of the Kremlin gates and welcomed by Boris Ponomarev. He still held the important position of chairman of the Foreign Affairs Committee of the Supreme Soviet of the USSR and was still a member of the Politburo. Although Ponomarev was not as well known in the West as Andrey Gromyko or other foreign ministry officials, his position meant that he oversaw all foreign policy matters.

We met in the same office where we had met in 1982. A cut-glass bowl filled with a variety of fresh fruit remained undisturbed at the center of the round table throughout the meeting, even though a knife and linen napkin were laid on a saucer beside each of us.

We sat across from each other, both of us wearing dark blue suits and dark ties. In his mid-seventies, he was small in stature, with thinning hair that grayed at the temples. But his eyes were like little cobalt jets that fixed on me with a penetration that might have made me squirm if he had not been so congenial.

After a few minutes of picture-taking, the media people were dismissed, leaving us to begin our serious conversation. Mr. Ponomarev spoke to me through his interpreter for about forty minutes, cordially but uncompromisingly expounding the Soviet position on foreign policy. His mind seemed rapier sharp, and he exuded a quiet self-confidence, as would be expected of a Politburo member with life tenure.

When he finished, I requested permission to speak from my prepared letter, not reading it word for word, since it was so long, but citing the high spots. I expressed appreciation for the opportunity I had been given to come to the Soviet Union, stating that my primary purpose was to have fellowship with my fellow Christians and to proclaim the Gospel of Jesus Christ. I then took note of the strained relationship between our two countries and the danger it presented to the whole world. My desire, I said, was to build bridges between our nations, and I expressed the hope that our peoples could get to know each other through cultural, educational, commercial, and religious exchanges; this could, I stated, defuse much of the tension between us.

Then I tackled a series of issues that had direct bearing on human rights and religious freedom. I noted that America had many millions of religious believers and that as long as they felt their fellow believers were being oppressed by the Soviet government, the chance of better relations between our countries was very slim.

Furthermore, I pointed out that religious believers were some of the USSR's best citizens—honest, hard-working, not prone to the common Soviet problems of absenteeism, alcohol, and theft. Americans, therefore, found it hard to understand why Christians in the USSR could not practice and propagate their beliefs as freely as nonbelievers. I urged that the process of opening new churches and the printing of Bibles be speeded up, and that Jewish emigration from the Soviet Union, the training of rabbis, and the teaching of Hebrew to Jews who desired it be permitted.

In closing, I underscored something I had said repeatedly in other conversations: "We must not only talk about how much we need peace; we must also establish suitable conditions for peace. Improving the situation of believers in the Soviet Union would be one of the most important steps you could take in that direction."

There was one more thing that I wanted to tell him before I was through. I sketched briefly my boyhood and youth on the farm in North Carolina, where I had been bored by the religion of my parents. "However," I said, "through a series of circumstances, I came to know Jesus Christ as my personal Lord and Savior."

The call to be an evangelist motivated me to plunge ahead.

"I have peace with God in my heart. If I die, I know I'm going to Heaven. God has given me the ability to love, to be more tolerant, to be more understanding, and to work toward peace in our world—within families, between races, and between nations."

He listened courteously (and I believed attentively).

"I only say this to show you that it is because of my relationship with Christ that I stand before you today and offer you my hand of friendship and a renewed dedication to work for better understanding and peace in our world."

How long had I been talking? With everything having to be relayed through an interpreter, I was not sure. He did not show any restlessness or impatience, however.

I then handed him the letter I had stayed up a whole night to draft. John Akers and Alex Haraszti had gone over it repeatedly, and then I stayed up most of another night redoing it.

With the letter in his hand, Ponomarev looked at me and said soberly and sincerely, "We will discuss this with our colleagues." He then thanked me for coming.

During a subsequent visit to the Kremlin a few years later, I ran into Mr. Ponomarev outside one of the buildings. Retired by then, he greeted me very cordially as an old friend.

Did that letter or our various contacts with ranking officials have any impact? Shortly after my 1984 visit, God gave me some encouragement in a letter from Georgi Arbatov—the first correspondence I ever received from a ranking Communist official. He was head of the Institute of United States and Canada Studies, a research and policy think tank. His English was excellent, and he came to our country often. Some thought his affability made him dangerously persuasive. I couldn't help but like him, however.

His letter was dated October 10, about three weeks after I had seen Ponomarev. Arbatov was quite upbeat about the effect of our visit and sent along a copy of a favorable article in the newspaper *Izvestia*. He expressed regret that we hadn't had more time to talk about issues of mutual interest. "For the time being, as a substitute," he wrote, "I am reading some of your books." He added that his wife had read one of them "with great interest."

Maybe he was just being flattering. But if he was sincere, I found encouragement in this statement: "I couldn't agree with you more when you say that life is a glorious opportunity if it is used to condition us for eternity."

What the trip was all about came during the farewell dinner given for us by the All-Union Council when Dr. Alexei Bichkov handed over to me a letter written by a woman who had made her commitment to Christ during our 1982 visit.

My final appearance in Moscow during that 1984 visit was in Patriarch Pimen's Cathedral of the Epiphany—with its beautiful blue walls, white columns, and gold-topped domes—on the morning of our last day. As many as 5,000 people jammed the cathedral, and this time, unlike in my 1982 visit, everyone could hear the message; a special sound system had been installed for the service. I preached on the topic "You Must Be Born Again."

"The greatest need in the world," I said, "is the transformation of human nature. We need a new heart that will not have lust and greed and hate in it. We need a heart filled with love and peace and joy, and that is why Jesus came into the world."

In his response, the patriarch said that it was the kind of preaching they needed in their churches. He invited me publicly to come back to preach in other cities of the Soviet Union.

As we drove from the cathedral, I asked Metropolitan Filaret, "Do you think His Holiness meant that invitation?"

Impulsively, he put his hand on my knee. "Oh, of course he meant it. We all mean it. We want you to come. You have a wide-open door in our country. You have been a tremendous inspiration to us all."

At the airport, Vice Minister Fitsev from the Council for Religious Affairs was there to see me off, representing the government.

"You're welcome at any time," he said in his gruff but cordial way. "We want you to come."

When he learned that I was flying out on Aeroflot, the Soviet airline, he laughed, adding, "Oh, then you'll be in our hands until you get to Paris!"

In an earlier era, I might have thought that sounded ominous.

527

29

Leading with Wit and Conviction

President Ronald Reagan

Ronald Reagan is one of the most winsome men I have ever known. Our long friendship really started one day in 1953, when I was playing golf in Phoenix. Mrs. Loyal Davis, wife of a prominent Chicago surgeon, came up to me on the course.

"I want you to get to know my new son-in-law," she said.

I asked who he was.

"Ronald Reagan."

"You mean the film star?"

She confirmed that he had married her daughter, Nancy, some months before.

Ron (as most of his friends called him) and I actually met later that year in Dallas. Both of us spoke at a benefit to raise money for retired film stars. Ron had been president of the Screen Actors Guild and was at that time a very strong Democrat.

But that day it was an older preacher who really got his attention. Dr. W. A. Criswell, pastor of First Baptist Church in Dallas, the largest congregation of its denomination, was sitting on one side of Ron, just opposite me. Dr. Criswell bluntly told him he had never seen a movie in his life and never intended to, adding that he thought the whole industry was of the Devil.

Reagan rose to the challenge. He explained to the distinguished Baptist leader just how movies were made and pointed out that many of them had a wholesome message. When he finished, Dr. Criswell thought for a moment and then spoke. "I'm going to start going to some movies, and I'll tell my congregation that it's not a sin to see certain types of movies."

Ron had not only changed a man's mind, but he had done it with charm, conviction, and humor—traits I would see repeatedly as I got to know him.

In the next two decades, my travels took me to California with some frequency, and often our paths crossed. As our friendship grew, I not only admired his quick wit and warm personality, but I also came to respect his keen insight and tough-minded approach to broad political issues. I also found him very interested in our work, even giving me friendly advice from time to time.

Once, when we were both going on a television talk show—a "roast" with singer-actor Dean Martin—he asked me, "Do you know what kind of program this is?"

"Yes, I think so," I replied.

"Well, they may try to embarrass you," he warned. "Be careful."

I appreciated his counsel. I'd had enough experience to know that some people take delight in trying to embarrass a clergyman. They seated me beside Zsa Zsa Gabor, the glamorous actress, but no one made any attempt to embarrass me. I suspect Ron may have dropped a hint to them beforehand.

In 1971 I was invited by the Democratic leadership of the California legislature to address a joint session when Ron was the Republican governor. After that session, I had lunch with him and his cabinet. Our discussion on that occasion was almost entirely on the Bible and its teachings.

In May 1980, while campaigning for the presidency, Ron was traveling through Indiana. I was holding a Crusade in Indianapolis at the time, and he asked me to come out to his hotel to have breakfast. I went and was met by Ed Meese. During the course of our conversation, Ron did something that he had never done before: he asked me if, when he went to North Carolina, I would say a positive word about him. The polls did not look too good for him there; at that moment he was at the 50 percent level.

"Ron, I can't do that," I had to reply. "You and I have been friends for a long time, and I have great confidence in you. I believe you're going to win the nomination and be elected President. But I think it would hurt us both, and certainly hurt my ministry, if I publicly endorsed any candidate."

He understood and readily agreed.

I went outside and found T.W. chatting with several of Reagan's aides.

"I hope you'll come on to church with us," Ed Meese said.

"Ed, I can't do that," I said apologetically. "I've got to preach this afternoon. If I were to go with you now, it would be perceived as an endorsement. I just can't do it."

He looked peeved, but I nonetheless thought that he understood my concern to be strictly neutral in the political race, in spite of my friendship with the Reagans.

After his election to the presidency, Reagan asked me to join him in the inauguration ceremonies on January 20, 1981, which I was honored to do. He invited me to speak at the first official event of the day, which was a prayer service at St. John's Episcopal Church across from the White House—for the President-elect and the Vice President-elect and their families.

I walked into St. John's about half an hour early. The only two people there were Frank Sinatra and his wife, Barbara.

"Frank, I'll bet this is the first time you've ever been the first one in church!" I said.

He laughed. "I try to go as often as I can."

Later I joined President Reagan on the platform during the administering of the oath of office; his pastor, the Reverend Donn Moomaw—who back in 1954 had worked with us in the London Crusade and now pastored the Bel Air Presbyterian Church in California—offered the prayers.

On being reelected four years later, he once again asked me to participate in the inaugural ceremonies, beginning with a prayer service at which I spoke in Washington's National Cathedral. As it turned out, terrible weather with bitter cold forced the cancellation of the public ceremonies at the Capitol and the inaugural parade. The oath of office had to be administered indoors in the Capitol Rotunda.

During the eight years of Reagan's administration, we saw each other a number of times. I especially appreciated his kindness in inviting Ruth and me to several state dinners for visiting foreign leaders.

On March 3, 1983, we were privileged to accept an invitation to such a dinner in San Francisco. The guests of honor were Britain's Queen Elizabeth and Prince Philip. In spite of the miserable weather, we had a wonderful time. During the evening, someone was sent to invite us on behalf of the Queen to a reception the next night on board the royal yacht *Britannia*. We accepted, and as Ruth and I boarded, a man with several stripes on his uniform sleeve saluted and whispered, "Wembley '55." During the course of that evening alone, Ruth and I heard of several others who had made commitments to Christ during our various Crusades in England.

Knowing of Ruth's deep interest in China, President Reagan invited us in July of 1985 to a state dinner honoring the Chinese president, Li Xiannian. Due to a Crusade I was holding in Anaheim, California, I was unable to attend, but the President thoughtfully seated Ruth on his left at the dinner, with President Li on his right. I have no doubt this helped us when we began negotiations for our trip to China three years later.

In November of 1985 he invited us again to a state dinner, this one in honor of Prince Charles and Princess Diana. We were greatly disappointed (and somewhat embarrassed, since we considered such an invitation a "command performance") that we were unable to accept the invitation. Again it was due to a long-standing speaking engagement to proclaim the Gospel. I wrote the Queen's secretary explaining why we had had to decline.

In December 1987, the Soviet Union's General Secretary Mikhail Gorbachev and his wife, Raisa, visited Washington for a summit conference. We were invited to some of the festivities. During the welcoming ceremony on the White House lawn, Ruth and I, standing next to Henry Kissinger, were close enough to see the expressions on the faces of the Reagans and the Gorbachevs. Several thousand people had gathered, including hundreds of photographers and reporters. I could not help but wonder how the President, at age seventy-six, could stand up to such physical pressure.

He had gone to the Kennedy Center the night before and now faced a grueling and important summit conference.

That was a busy day for Ruth and me too, with lunch at the Bushes (right before the Vice President went to the treaty-signing ceremony) and a reception at the Soviet Embassy.

Arriving at the White House later for the state dinner, we saw many old friends and made some new ones, including Meadowlark Lemon, the former Harlem Globetrotter, who impressed me as a warm and distinguished person. Many people came up to us and said they had seen our Denver Crusade telecast the night before.

In the receiving line, the President seemed delighted when he greeted us and told General Secretary Gorbachev a little bit about us. (He did not know that we had just come from the Soviet Embassy.) Mr. Gorbachev greeted me very warmly again. Nancy kissed us both, and then we met Mrs. Gorbachev.

In November 1988, President Reagan's last official guest for a state dinner was Prime Minister Margaret Thatcher of England; in 1981 she had been his first such guest. He had invited us then, and he invited us again. It was a hectic day. Ruth had forgotten her evening bag and had to go buy another for the dinner that evening. Then we bought some flowers and stopped in to see our friend Mrs. J. Willard Marriott, who insisted we stay for lunch; we talked about her children, including her son, Bill, Jr., with whom I had developed a genuine friendship, and her grandchildren. We also spoke about our memories of her husband, who had been such a warm friend to us (and whose funeral I had spoken at three years before).

We arrived for the state dinner that night at the same time as football legend Rosey Grier and businessman Malcolm Forbes. Mr. Forbes could not have been friendlier as we talked about his boat trip to China, which had taken place about the same time as our visit the previous spring. The boat, which he had docked up the Huangpu River, was named *The Capitalist Tool.* The name was a cause of much amusement.

"You totally overshadowed my trip," he said laughingly. "You were on television, in the newspapers, and so on. We barely made it on the news at all, except in Hong Kong!"

In the reception line, the President turned to tell Mrs. Thatcher who we were. She told him I had already visited her at Number 10 and she knew we were going back to England to preach the following summer.

To my surprise, I found I had been placed at the table on Mrs. Reagan's left, with Mr. Thatcher on her right.

"I've listened to you all my life, it seems," said actress Loretta Young, who was also sitting at our table. "If you appear on television, my children come and tell me you're on."

At this dinner, Ambassador Charles Price's wife, Carol, gave me a bit of good advice. She was seated to my left, which was toward my bad ear. At one point, she turned to me and asked, "Are you having a hard time hearing me?"

I admitted that I was, explaining that the hearing problem was new to me and that I didn't know how to handle it.

"You should have told me so that I could have raised my voice," she chided. "Don't be bashful about a problem like that."

This last state dinner for the Reagans was nostalgic, with tears in many eyes. When Mrs. Thatcher paid a tribute to Nancy, Nancy reached over and squeezed my hand.

I talked to a number of British people that evening. One lady from Scotland said she had gone to Kelvin Hall to hear us in Glasgow when she was a little girl.

Then we went upstairs, where Michael Feinstein sang and played George Gershwin and Irving Berlin songs. Mrs. Thatcher had said that Mr. Reagan brought a new spiritual atmosphere to America. Ruth later wished that there had been some music played or some other remarks made about spiritual things.

One night in Washington, after Ruth and I had already gone to bed in our room at the Madison Hotel, the phone rang. It was the First Lady.

"Are you all asleep?" she asked.

"Just about."

"We're in bed too," she said, "but we want to see you both and talk to you. Can you come over here?"

I said we would.

"We'll have a car in front of the hotel in fifteen minutes."

We scrambled back into our clothes and rode over to 1600 Pennsylvania Avenue, whose two chief occupants were in their pajamas and in bed themselves. We had a great time talking with them for at least a couple of hours. As usual, it was mostly reminiscing about our families or personal concerns.

During the years before Ron was elected to public office, I had often detected a spiritual side to him. For example, I remember once when I gave a small dinner party at the Beverly Hilton Hotel and invited him. He brought up the subject of the Second Coming of Christ. The same subject came up with him on other occasions as well.

I have been told that where he grew up, in Dixon, Illinois, he did some preaching himself in his late teens. At the time, he was a member of the Christian Church, which was somewhat like the Baptist Church. I kept forgetting to ask him about it, however, something that I now regret.

One night when I was staying at the White House, Nancy and the President got into a discussion about the question of salvation—who was going to be saved and who was going to be lost. He gave her his views on conversion and the new birth right out of the Bible. She turned to me.

"Billy, is that right?"

I said it was and expanded a little further.

They were both interested in understanding more about the Scriptures, especially Ron. He often asked me questions about the biblical view on important topics. Abortion was one such issue he wrestled with. I always stressed the Bible's teaching on the sacredness of human life, both of the unborn and of the born. We talked about other current issues, but always in terms of principles, not what specific policies or programs should be adopted or scrapped.

A lot of Christians were confused and upset that President Reagan did not go to church regularly in Washington during his two terms. Strange as it might seem, I was one of the people who suggested to him that he might stay away. We discussed it together shortly after he was shot in 1981.

"You know," he said to me, "when we go anywhere now, we have to have tremendous security, and it breaks up a church service. When the President comes in, the attention is on him rather than on the sermon or the service. I'm not sure I feel comfortable with that."

"Ron," I said, forgetful for once of the proper way to address the President, "I think that maybe you ought not to try to go to church for a while. I think almost everybody will understand. Not only are you in danger, but you're endangering other people. Wait until this thing [his being shot] has quieted down, and until the Secret Service has gotten a little better organized."

"You know," I added, "you can have a service here just for the few of you and some of the staff in the theater downstairs, or you can revert back to what Nixon did, having a service in the East Room of the White House. I think most people would understand."

Eventually, the Reagans did resume going to National Presbyterian Church in Washington. Dr. Louis Evans, who (before Donn Moomaw) had been their pastor at Bel Air in California, made some structural alterations to accommodate the President's needs. As a result, the Reagans could come in at the rear without disrupting the service and sit in the balcony, unnoticed by the congregation.

Ron did ask my advice on two other matters that I felt had moral or spiritual dimensions, although they also dealt with policy.

First, the Vatican. Reagan was the first American President to appoint a full ambassador to the Vatican. Before he made that appointment, he asked my view. I told him I thought it would probably be a good thing—in spite of a number of potential problems concerning the separation of church and state—and wrote an extended confidential letter outlining my reasons. Among other things, I told him I did not think it necessarily violated the separation of church and state. For whatever reasons, Mr. Reagan went ahead with the plan. Later my letter was leaked to the press. It caused some consternation among my Baptist friends.

Second, in April 1985, both Nancy and Ron were deeply concerned over the furor created when Chancellor Helmut Kohl scheduled them to visit a German cemetery. After accepting the engagement, they discovered that a number of S.S. troops had been buried there, along with thousands of other Germans. Nancy asked if I had any suggestions on how they should handle it.

"Yes, I have one," I said. "I'd get some top Jewish rabbis and ask them to help your husband prepare his speech."

I personally called my friend Rabbi Marc Tanenbaum of the American Jewish Committee. I understood later that he went to Washington and helped the Reagans. That German visit, instead of being a negative experience, turned out to be a positive one, in my opinion.

Etched indelibly in my memory—and that of every American—will always be the March day in 1981 that President Reagan was shot outside the Washington Hilton Hotel. I was at home when I learned of it. The first person to call me was Jesse Helms, our senior senator from North Carolina.

"Billy, I think you ought to go up there and be available for spiritual encouragement and prayer."

About half an hour later I got a call from one of the President's aides saying that they were unable to locate Donn Moomaw, who was thought to be at a conference in Bermuda. They asked me how soon I could come to Washington. I told them I could be ready almost immediately. I got a private plane to National Airport, where I was met by a White House car.

When I saw Nancy the next day, she was calm, but I could sense the anxiety and concern she felt by the tears in her eyes and the extra hug she gave me. I was reminded again of the great love they had for each other; frequently, I had seen them holding hands or just touching each other, and I knew he depended on her greatly, not only for emotional support and encouragement but also for advice. A few minutes later, Frank and Barbara Sinatra came in. Nancy rehearsed all the events for us from her point of view. Then the pastor of National Presbyterian Church, Louis Evans, and his wife, Colleen, came in. Within an hour, Donn Moomaw and his wife arrived.

We sat and talked together about Ron and got the latest information on him. For the first time, I realized how near death he had come the day before. Before we left, Lou Evans turned to me.

"Billy, I think you should lead us in prayer."

We all held hands. I prayed as fervently as I knew how, asking the Lord to raise up our friend. During the prayer, Frank Sinatra said amen twice.

I had read that the Hinckleys, whose son shot the President, were Christians; I called them in Colorado and assured them of my prayers too, because I knew their hearts must have been breaking.

When stories later came out about Nancy's having consulted an astrologer on family and national issues after the assassination attempt, I was amazed. I had never seen her as a gullible or experimental person in her spiritual understanding and could not help but feel it was a momentary lapse caused by anxiety and stress. I called her on the phone at the time and talked frankly to her about it.

"Nancy, surely you didn't really look into astrology, especially for something as important as the dates when the cabinet should meet."

"Billy," she responded, "what you've read is only part of the story. It's 90 percent untrue, but there is possibly 10 percent truth in it," she admitted. I urged her to seek her guidance from the Lord instead.

A few years later, in 1988 or 1989, we were having lunch at the White House with a group of people. Robert Strauss sat on one side of Nancy, and I on the other. (Bob Strauss was one of the closest friends that I had in the Democratic Party in Washington, and over the years he often gave me very helpful advice.) She confided in both of us that she was going to write a book in response to Donald Regan's recently published book, which was sharply critical of her.

"Nancy, don't do it," I said. "It will turn on you. You don't need to get back at Regan and these other people who have hurt you. If you do it at all, wait five or ten years when people aren't so close to it and so tender about it."

Strauss supported me.

When she insisted that she would do it immediately, I cautioned that she was going to regret it. Both my hunches came true. The book project backfired, to her regret.

Many times when I was with the Reagans, they brought up their daughter Patti Davis. I could see that they were both burdened and sometimes discouraged about their rocky relationship with her. We had prayer for her often. After it was announced that Ron had Alzheimer's disease, Patti published her book *Angels Don't Die*. In it she complimented both her parents, but especially her father, for what he had taught her about spiritual and moral values.

In the forty years since first meeting Ronald Reagan, he has taught me a lot, not so much through words as by example. His optimistic spirit was contagious. I have often been a worrier (if biting my fingernails was any sign), even though I know underneath it all that God is in charge.

But I have always found Reagan's attitude to be upbeat. I thought that attitude affected the country psychologically and won him much admiration even among his critics. It wasn't just a stiff-upper-lip attitude; rather, it was genuine cheeriness and good humor—part of his charisma. As a good example, when he was shot he quipped, "I forgot to duck." That spirit was infectious, and the nation was the better for it.

On June 14, 1989, after his presidential term was over, the Queen of England honored Reagan. I was in England at the time; he called me about thirty minutes after the ceremony.

"Guess what?" he said. "I've just been knighted!"

"Well, congratulations, Sir Ronald!" I said.

He laughed. His reaction was a blend of seriousness and humor—grateful for what the honor represented, and yet refusing to take himself too seriously.

After he left office, we stayed close to Ron and Nancy. His life in retirement was packed with travel and engagements and a multitude of responsibilities. Still, loyal friend that he was, he found time to talk to me on the telephone or send me an occasional handwritten letter inquiring about my health and assuring Ruth and me of his and Nancy's prayers. I have seen them in California from time to time and several times have attended Bel Air Presbyterian Church with them.

I also saw him at the funeral for Richard Nixon on April 27, 1994, where he joined the other former presidents and President Clinton in paying tribute. I could tell, however, that some of the old sparkle was gone, and I was very saddened when they announced some months later that he had been diagnosed with Alzheimer's disease. At the same time, their openness and courage in the face of this debilitating illness have been an inspiration to us all.

While he was President, Ronald Reagan bestowed on me one of the highest honors I could ever imagine. On February 23, 1983, he presented me with the Presidential Medal of Freedom, the highest civilian honor our government gives to an American, for service to the nation. I felt unworthy of the honor, and still do. But whatever else it means, it will always remind me of the generosity and friendship of a remarkable man and a warm and enduring personal friend, Ronald Wilson Reagan.

30

A New Day Dawning

ROMANIA, HUNGARY, RUSSIA 1985–1992

Very few people—including me—ever imagined that Communism in eastern Europe and the Soviet Union would collapse almost overnight. For years I had been saying privately that Soviet-style Communism was both unworkable and unnatural and couldn't last indefinitely. But as we approached the mid-1980s, no one could have predicted that in half a dozen years the Berlin Wall would be torn down and the Soviet Union disbanded.

And yet as we traveled to that part of the world, we were already seeing definite signs by 1985 that change was taking place. I was convinced it was only a matter of time before those first trickles became a torrent.

ROMANIA

On the surface, nothing seemed further from that conviction when we took our trip in 1985 to Romania, a year after touring the Soviet Union.

In 1977 I asked Walter Smyth to go to Bucharest with a humanitarian gift from the BGEA World Emergency Fund to help Romania recover from a disastrous earthquake. While there, he opened the discussion with church and government leaders about the prospect of a visit. Four years later, Alex Haraszti followed up with a series of trips, sometimes traveling in unheated trains during fierce winter blizzards. Conversations also were held with the Romanian Embassy in Washington.

One complication was Romania's human rights situation. In 1975, in an effort to nudge Romania toward a more open policy, the United States had granted the Most Favored Nation (MFN) trading status, guaranteeing favorable tariff treatment on goods imported into the United States. (The term was something of a misnomer, since *most* nations trading with the United States had that same status.) Each year Romania's MFN status came up before Congress for renewal, and each year some groups contended it should be withdrawn because of human rights violations. The desire to keep that crucial status was almost certainly a major reason why Romania opened the door for us: it was trying to impress its American critics with the freedom it gave (or seemed to give) to religious believers.

Our visit was also complicated by the situation in Transylvania, an area of Romania that had been part of Hungary. The government's strenuous attempts to integrate the Hungarian ethnic minority into Romanian culture—a process that included suppressing the Hungarian language and Hungarian cultural customs—continued to meet with much opposition, both in Transylvania and from the Hungarian government. Because several cities on our tour were in Transylvania, we found both the Romanian government and the local ethnic Hungarian leaders attempted to pull us into the controversy—something I was determined to resist.

The Baptists had a strong and growing ministry in Romania; they were joined in the invitation to us by the dominant Romanian Orthodox Church, in addition to the Roman Catholic Church, the Reformed Church, and various smaller denominations—fourteen different groups in all. Even the Jewish synagogue in Bucharest welcomed me; on the eve of Rosh Hashanah, I was introduced by Rabbi Rosen and spoke to the congregation from Psalm 23.

The entire visit, however, took place in an atmosphere of tense political pressures, protracted negotiations, and even broken promises. Almost every evening, Alex and John were up past midnight attempting to hammer out details of the following day's schedule with our government contact. One night, after a particularly difficult session, John said he was afraid I was going to be declared persona non grata and expelled from the country.

The seven-city tour was marked by massive crowds, in excess of 100,000 at some stops—by far the largest we saw anywhere in eastern Europe. Everywhere we went, we found ample evidence of spiritual hunger and openness.

Our first evangelistic meeting was near the northwestern city of Suceava, in the beautiful mountainous region of Moldavia, not far from the Soviet border. Here Metropolitan Teoctist of the Romanian Orthodox Church took me on a tour of several ancient Orthodox monasteries. They were unlike the cathedrals I was familiar with in western Europe, where elaborate stained-glass windows depicted biblical passages and figures. In Romania the monasteries did not have stained glass but instead had equally elaborate paintings or frescoes, also based on biblical themes, on the outside walls. The paint had lasted for hundreds of years, just as brilliant now as when it had first been brushed on.

One in particular I remember. (I even used it later as a sermon illustration.) Called "The Ladder of Heaven," it portrayed the final judgment. Angels were assisting pilgrims on their way up an inclined ladder leading to Heaven, while demons clung to their heels and tried to pull them off the ladder into the lake of fire. We also visited the monastery at Putna, where Stephen the Great (1457–1504), Moldavia's heroic king, was entombed.

On a beautiful day—Sunday, September 8—some miles outside Suceava, I preached at the Verona monastery. It was one of the annual festivals of the Romanian Orthodox Church. As we traveled there, we passed thousands of people streaming to the event, many of them walking or in carts or wagons drawn by animals. The large walled courtyard of the old monastery was filled, with people even climbing trees to listen; and thousands more outside the walls were able to hear via the special sound system installed within the courtyard.

Next we traveled to the Transylvanian city of Cluj-Napoca. On the way to the service in a Reformed church that evening, we were greeted by 15,000 people lining the streets many blocks from the church, with thousands more crowded into the square in front. Walter and John got separated from us and were almost trampled by people rushing toward the church; the police had to rescue them. Some 8,000 people jammed the church, but no loudspeakers were permitted outside. Immediately afterward, we went to St. Michael's Roman Catholic Church for another service, with 3,500 packed inside and an estimated 5,000 outside; again speakers were not permitted outside the church, in spite of our vigorous protests.

Romanian authorities had promised that we would be permitted to place loudspeakers outside all the host churches, and also that we could run television relays to large screens in other churches. Our friend David Rennie from London, a businessman in the field of electronics, had come with a team of experts especially to supervise these installations. In each city, however, permission was withdrawn by the authorities. Alex theorized later that the Romanian authorities had simply not believed that people would come to hear the Gospel and had therefore felt free to make promises they wouldn't have to keep. But when the crowds did come, the authorities became thoroughly alarmed. Perhaps they feared that if they permitted loudspeakers at one location, even larger crowds would gather at the next.

Church officials in Oradea and Arad managed to put loudspeakers in place anyway. At one place, I heard, a police officer told a man who was stringing wire to some loudspeakers to take them down.

"*You* take them down," said the man with a shrug. "They'll kill me if I do it."

The crowd of thousands, already assembled hours in advance, clearly was not going to allow the speakers to be removed without a struggle. They stayed in place.

In spite of this official attitude, the assistance provided to us was little short of astonishing. The government gave us the use of two airplanes from the state-run airline—one to carry our equipment and television crew, the other to carry our Team. We had

543

police escorts everywhere to get us through the crowds. Even so, because of the crush of the crowd, we feared for our lives in Timisoara. There were an estimated 150,000 people that night in front of the cathedral.

Coming out of the packed Orthodox cathedral that evening, we were absolutely mobbed. Many in the crowd were upset because the loudspeakers that they could see outside were dead; apparently, the authorities had cut the wires. The people, forced to stand outside for the entire service, unable to hear anything, wanted me to preach from the cathedral steps. But without amplification, I could not do so; nor would the police have allowed it.

As we came down the steps, the crush of the crowd was so great that I didn't know if we could make it. The people were very warm and friendly, though; even if I couldn't preach to them, they wanted to see or to touch us. Most of our Team made it down the long steps to the waiting cars. I couldn't help but think of my secretary, Stephanie Wills, who—along with the Romanian woman accompanying her and a woman from the American Embassy—was caught in that mass behind me. Finally, quite shaken up, they made it back to the hotel.

When we returned to Bucharest at the end of our trip, President Ceauşescu, alarmed and surprised by the favorable public reaction, abruptly canceled my visit with him; I was received instead by a lesser official. Ceauşescu apparently was afraid that if he received me, some people might think he approved of what had happened. He may also have interpreted the huge crowds as a cloaked demonstration against his regime. In some ways I was sorry; I had been looking forward to sharing my faith in Christ with him.

HUNGARY

A few days later, we returned once again to Hungary. The contrast with Romania was startling, for almost immediately, Hungarian officials went out of their way to give us two unprecedented opportunities.

First, however, they expressed great concern over some of my alleged statements, which had appeared in the Romanian government's news service; those statements made it sound as though I supported Romania's policies toward the ethnic Hungarian minority in Transylvania. We hurriedly produced the full text of my remarks, however, and the officials realized that the Romanian news reports had misquoted me.

On September 21, in the southern city of Pecs, I participated in a first for us in eastern Europe: an unrestricted outdoor Gospel meeting. To meet the legal technicality of holding the event on church grounds, I preached over a powerful public address system from the steps of the Roman Catholic cathedral. Bishop Cserhati introduced me. The crowd stretched farther than I could see, well beyond the limits of church property. Halfway down the street loomed a gigantic Diamond Vision TV screen. The sponsors had been permitted to import it from England for this occasion, enabling people several blocks away from the church to see close up in broad daylight.

An even more astounding breakthrough occurred the next day back in Budapest; we were given use of a 12,500-seat public sports arena in the center of the city. It was the first time in many decades, to our knowledge, that a public venue had been used for an evangelistic meeting in eastern Europe. I couldn't explain that in any other way than God's doing. Perhaps his unwitting agent might have been Janos Berecz, the third-ranking official in Hungary's government. I had developed a pleasant acquaintance with him on a previous visit. Although a Communist, he collected miniature Bibles and other books as a hobby. I gave him several old miniature Bibles, including a few Russ Busby had found in London.

Four hours before the start of the September 22 meeting, every seat in the indoor arena was taken; many had to stay outside to listen over loudspeakers. The Hungarians' love of music is legendary, and a large choir, accompanied by a volunteer symphony orchestra, had been recruited for the event from virtually every Christian denomination. Even without special political insight, I felt that eastern Europe was on the brink of massive change.

THE SOVIET UNION

Four years after our 1984 tour, we returned to the Soviet Union, this time to join with others in the celebration of the thousandth anniversary of the Russian Orthodox Church in June 1988. Although the schedule was crammed with services and other meetings, the heady climate of *glasnost* and *perestroika* under General Secretary Mikhail Gorbachev added new dimensions to everything.

In some ways, I wasn't surprised at the changes Mr. Gorbachev was making. Some months before, while he was in Washington for a state visit, I met him and was impressed by his charm and his new perspectives. As soon as I entered the Russian Embassy for a small reception in December 1987, former Soviet Ambassador Dobrynin made a beeline for me, wanting to make sure that I met Gorbachev.

"Oh, yes, I have heard about you," he said as he greeted me warmly. "You've been in our country, and when you come back, we will welcome you again."

Gorbachev spoke to all of us at that 1987 reception for over an hour. I was seated only a few feet in front of him at a small round table, with former Secretary of State Cyrus Vance on one side of me and Soviet Foreign Minister Eduard Shevardnadze on the other.

A reporter asked me afterward if I had noticed anything special about Gorbachev's eyes at that close range. They were not cold eyes, I replied, but warm and dancing. Gorbachev spoke with animation and laughed, I added, and he impressed me as being sincere.

What also caught my attention was that three times, when speaking to us about the need for a sense of values or a moral base for his proposed reforms, he used the word *spiritual*. "You know," one U.S. senator said to me later, "he was talking about religion." And when Gorbachev stepped off the plane in Washington at the beginning of that visit, he said, "May God help us."

Not by any stretch of the imagination did this imply that he was a Christian. But in his secularist or Marxist way, it seemed to me he reflected a hazy yearning for the kingdom of God. So many of his phrases, as he described what the Soviet Union could become through *glasnost* and *perestroika*, sounded almost biblical.

As Gorbachev was concluding, I became a little uneasy; we were due at the White House for the state dinner soon, and I still had to go dress in my tuxedo. As it turned out, Ruth and I were among the last to arrive for the dinner.

The 1988 celebration in Russia commemorated the time a thousand years ago when Prince Vladimir of Rus, founder of modern Russia, embraced Christianity and promptly ordered all his subjects to be baptized in the Dnieper River near Kiev.

From then until the Bolshevik Revolution, Orthodox Christianity was the official Russian state religion. Now the Russian Orthodox Church was celebrating its millennium. I gladly accepted the Orthodox invitation to participate in their celebration; all who professed to believe and follow Christ deserved whatever encouragement in the faith we could give.

I did not accept without a few misgivings, though. For one thing, some Ukrainians in America were sensitive about developments in their homeland and did not look too favorably on my projected visit to Kiev, Orthodoxy's birthplace. Furthermore, my more conservative American colleagues were still troubled by what struck them as compromises I was making with a nondemocratic government and a nonevangelical religious body.

That a religious anniversary could be celebrated at all in the Soviet Union was certainly a sign of the changing times. In fact, during his visits to Moscow to prepare for our trip, Alex Haraszti had perceived a sharp split within the Soviet government over whether the thousandth anniversary should be acknowledged or totally ignored. At the very most, it was argued by some, it should be downplayed. I am convinced that the final decision to give public prominence to the occasion did much to foster later changes in that society.

At the churches where I spoke, old restrictions were overthrown. Loudspeakers were set up outside to carry the message to people who could not get in, reaching even the people a block or more away.

Far from restricting religious observances to church facilities, the government gave permission to hold two main events of the millennial commemoration at the Bolshoi Theater in Moscow and the Shevchenko Theater in Kiev. At the Bolshoi, Mrs. Raisa Gorbachev sat in the first row, just four seats away from the pulpit, while I gave my address. And for the first time, a religious event—the millennial celebration—was featured extensively in the Soviet media.

In recognition of our presence, the Kremlin arranged for us to be received by the longtime foreign minister, Andrey Gromyko. He spoke to us in the Presidium council chamber about the impact of new policies on church life. At an appropriate moment afterward, we were able to distribute the Russian Bibles we had brought along for high-level officials, each handsomely bound in leather and personalized with the name of a Politburo member embossed on the cover. Both Mr. Gromyko and Mr. Gorbachev were among those who were given personal copies.

The next day our caravan of cars traveled the forty or fifty miles to Zagorsk to visit a special council meeting of the Holy Synod of the Orthodox Church. The ancient monastery in Zagorsk has been cherished for centuries as the center of Russia's spiritual life. There Patriarch Pimen, host of the millennial celebration, greeted us warmly, although he was ill and clearly in failing health. Mr. Konstantin Kharchev, the new head of the government's Council for Religious Affairs, was present too and to my surprise thanked me for urging liberalization of government policy toward churches. I had done little, but it was encouraging to hear him say that a common desire for higher moral principles was leading to a new era of church and state cooperation.

"We have never found ultimate truth," he said wistfully. "I would like to believe it exists somewhere."

"Ultimate truth," I responded, "*does* exist in the Person who said, 'I am the way, the truth, and the life'" (John 14:6, KJV).

I gave him a Bible and told him I would pray for him.

From Moscow we flew to Kiev in a Russian-built plane (similar to a 727) that looked as if it were falling apart. A number of church leaders attending the millennial celebration were on board. I remember sitting on the floor talking with Cardinal John O'Connor of New York about the way Protestant–Roman Catholic relations had changed.

The largest audience I spoke to in the Soviet Union was at the Cathedral of St. Vladimir in Kiev, where 15,000 people not only packed the huge building but also spilled out into the surrounding courtyard. That service received coverage on national radio and television and in the two official newspapers, *Pravda* and *Izvestia*. The metropolitan there extended me every courtesy.

A fascinating sidelight did not make the newspapers. In the course of preparing for the service, church officials realized that the electrical system in the cathedral wouldn't be up to the demands of the television lights and the special sound system that were to be installed both inside and outside the building. At the request of those church officials, therefore, and almost certainly with the permission of political and military authorities in Moscow, the Red Army trucked in one of its large portable generators and parked it outside the church.

As the congregation approached the cathedral that evening, their eyes must have popped at the sight of military vehicles around the cathedral—and at the friendliness of the military personnel. If the Christians were amazed, so were the Red Army technicians, I suspect! This sort of church-state cooperation surely was a first in the Soviet Union.

In Kiev I spoke also at the little Baptist church that normally held several hundred. A few thousand were packed inside and around the whole neighborhood outside the church. We could hardly get our car through the crowd to the building.

Later about fifteen of us met with members of the Politburo of the Ukraine. The prime minister, a woman, sat with us and answered our questions. She said immediately—for the benefit of her colleagues and the tape recorders, I suspect—that she was a Communist and an atheist. Afterward, though, she took me aside and conversed in excellent English.

"You know, Dr. Graham, I always go on a certain day to see my mother, who lives beyond the Baptist church where you preached. I'm always amazed as I pass that church that it's so filled with young people."

She paused.

"I have my driver stop the car sometimes just so I can watch them."

She paused again.

"There's something about the Baptists that attracts young people."

A RETURN TO HUNGARY

One year after the millennial celebration in Russia, we returned once again to Hungary, in July 1989. In what can only be described as a miracle, we went to hold a huge evangelistic rally in Hungary's largest outdoor stadium. Months in advance, we were permitted to send one of our Crusade preparation teams there to help organize the details of the meeting. We also were permitted to translate and publish our counseling materials and to advertise the meeting—the sort of preparations we always made for Crusade meetings back in the States.

All attendance records were broken at that rally; every seat was taken, and people also packed the grassy perimeter of the playing field. Statistics never tell the whole story, of course, but everyone was astonished that an estimated 110,000 people attended.

When the Invitation was given, 35,000 people jammed the playing field and overflowed onto the running track. Never in our ministry had such a high percentage responded. The sponsors had been optimistic; 25,000 counseling packets had been prepared in advance. The supply ran out, of course, and in the crush of the crowd no one could get through to pass them out. Instead, people just tossed them over their heads to those behind. Despite that seeming chaos, about 20,000 inquirers managed to turn in, or mail in, cards with their names and addresses for follow-up by the Hungarian churches.

My four visits to Hungary in twelve years absolutely fixed my conviction that the Holy Spirit was releasing a spiritual force in that part of the world that was bound to challenge the atheistic philosophy that had dominated nations in that region for decades.

MOSCOW

In July 1991, I was in Moscow again. In the intervening three years since the 1988 millennial celebration, a virtual revolution had taken

550

place in the Soviet Union. Old ideas and old restrictions were swept aside in every area of life, including religion. Things that would have been impossible—even inconceivable—a few years before were now a reality.

This time I presided at an evangelism training conference that the BGEA sponsored. The Orthodox Church did not participate officially, although it was Patriarch Pimen (recently deceased) who, in a way, had invited me to conduct evangelism training in the Soviet Union. When he was lying ill at the Zagorsk monastery in 1988, he asked me to pray with him. I sat by his side for a long time and held his hand. He told me again, as he had on an earlier visit, that he wanted his priests to learn how to preach evangelistic sermons. I prayed for him as my brother in Christ.

Pimen's successor, Patriarch Alexei II, the Estonian who had welcomed us when he was metropolitan in Tallinn, was cautious about giving his official endorsement to our training conference. He was new in office and facing an evangelical Protestant resurgence that worried some of his own bishops and priests. But he was as cordial as ever toward me, sending a messenger to ask if I could meet with him that Saturday. Regrettably, it was my departure day, and my schedule simply couldn't be stretched any further.

If ever there was a miracle, the Moscow School of Evangelism was it. More than 4,900 Soviet Protestant pastors, lay preachers, and teachers gathered to hear a number of speakers from various countries on evangelism. Among them were my son Franklin and my daughter Anne Graham Lotz. We convened in an atmosphere of optimism that was almost intoxicating. Delegates went into the streets and onto buses, boldly witnessing for Christ, open Bibles in their hands—an amazing sign of the changes taking place.

And there were other signs of growing religious freedom throughout the country: the importation of Bibles and other Christian literature was rising almost to flood level, and Soviet children were again allowed to attend churches and to receive religious instruction.

The Moscow School of Evangelism wasn't without its difficulties, however. In fact, we were not certain it would even be held until almost the last minute. We had arranged for the use of an indoor sports arena next to Lenin Stadium, as well as for housing and food for our delegates at the nearby Moscow State University, but negotiations over the details continued up to our arrival. Some officials, having cast off the old ways of doing things, were now much more concerned about money (especially hard currency). As a result, disagreements arose over financial arrangements that we considered morally and legally questionable.

From Europe en route to Moscow, we had many telephone conversations with members of our executive committee and staff, and with John Corts, our chief operating officer, with whom the primary responsibility rested. Some of our staff and legal counsel joined us in Europe, where we spent two days in prayer and discussion. We affirmed that if the contract could not be negotiated in a totally legal and ethical way, we would cancel even at this late date. I realized that scores of delegates were already on their way from outside Moscow, and there would be great disappointment. It was one of the low spiritual and emotional moments in my ministry. However, at the last minute the arrangements worked out—honorably and ethically.

The conference itself was almost beyond belief. Seldom have I seen such eagerness to learn the Bible and to develop practical skills for evangelism. A surprising number of the participants were highly educated people—schoolteachers, engineers, artists, and other professionals—who grew up under atheism but became Christians within the last year or so. Previously, most Christians in the Soviet Union had been barred from higher education and from positions of influence.

Although I was busy with the conference, I also had several unprecedented opportunities with the media. The top interviewer over the main channel, Channel One, gave me a good going-over, asking penetrating questions about God and the nature of faith. I sensed that he was inquiring from a personal as well as a professional standpoint. Curiosity about religion seemed widespread: for the first time, people in the street felt free to talk about religion, and many openly expressed their longing for some type of spiritual reality.

The last day of the conference General Secretary Gorbachev received me in his office for about forty minutes, the first time I had been with him in that setting. Our two-minute appearance together before the television cameras was shown throughout the USSR in all eleven time zones on a top-rated news show. The subject of spiritual values in society was uppermost in our conversation. A friend of mine who headed the All-Union Council of Evangelical Christians-Baptists, the Reverend Grigori Komendant, was at my side. Serving as chairman of the Moscow School of Evangelism, he could hardly believe that, for the first time in his remembrance, a Soviet evangelical leader was inside the Kremlin freely talking with the head of state.

On July 13, the day before I left for America, I was unexpectedly invited to meet with Boris Yeltsin at his office in the Kremlin. We talked together for an hour. I got the impression that he was even more interested in the religious side of things than Mr. Gorbachev. He did not hesitate to tell me that he no longer was a Communist. I thought he sounded pleased when he volunteered that his three granddaughters all wore crosses now.

Only a few weeks after we left the Soviet Union, old-line Communist leaders attempted a coup. For several days, the fate of democratic reform in the USSR hung in the balance. I could not help but thank God for the opening He had given us for training so many during the School of Evangelism. What might they be facing in the future?

As an anxious world watched, the coup collapsed on August 21, with a minimum of bloodshed. Three days later, General Secretary Gorbachev, at Yeltsin's insistence, disbanded the Central Committee of the Communist Party of the Soviet Union, effectively ending not only Gorbachev's own leadership but also seven decades of Marxist rule.

A new day had truly dawned, not only politically but also religiously, in what had once been the world's strongest bastion of atheism. And with those changes, new opportunities for the proclamation of the Gospel opened up.

Almost immediately after the failed coup, we were approached by Russian church leaders about the possibility of holding a full-scale evangelistic Crusade in Moscow and perhaps several other cities. Sensing that God had opened the door, we accepted the invitation for October 1992.

For logistical reasons, we felt it best to concentrate on Moscow. Difficulties in transportation and communication, we realized, would make it almost impossible to undertake the massive organization required for such an extensive effort in more than one city.

The preparations had their own set of difficulties. For one thing, most Russian church leaders had very little experience in organizing any sort of outreach to the larger public. In addition, many things—such as the rapid printing of materials and the availability of office supplies—were enormously difficult, if not impossible. (We ended up having most of the printing done in Finland.) Renting office space and obtaining housing for our Crusade staff was a complex process as well, since most buildings were still under government ownership.

Even communication between our office in Moscow and our home base in Minneapolis was uncertain. One or two enterprising firms from the West had managed to leapfrog the notoriously unreliable Russian telephone system by setting up satellite connections and running fiber-optic cables to offices through the Moscow sewer system. Nevertheless, Blair Carlson, who headed our pre-Crusade preparation staff, found that his satellite telephone kept breaking down at the wrong time.

There likewise were problems securing an adequate facility. The 38,000-seat Olympic Stadium, a massive covered arena constructed especially for the 1980 Olympics, finally turned out to be the ideal venue.

Although advertising in post-Communist Russia was still in its infancy, we managed to obtain a number of prominent billboards; ours was the largest nongovernment advertising campaign to date. Leaflets describing the meetings and giving a brief Gospel message, 3.2 million of them, were delivered to every Moscow mailbox. Thirty training centers were organized for weekly Bible studies following the Crusade, supplementing the work of the small number of churches in Moscow.

Every night the covered Olympic Stadium was packed beyond capacity. Overflow crowds in the thousands stood outside in the chilly, late-October air to watch over a large-screen television. At the final meeting, on a Sunday afternoon, an estimated 50,000 people jammed the stadium; an additional 20,000 watched outside.

I worked diligently in my sermons to make the Gospel as clear and as simple as possible. Most of those listening, I knew, had virtually no knowledge of the Bible or of Christ. And yet I also tried to set forth as forcefully as possible Christ's call to leave the past behind and to become His followers.

As many as 7,000 people signed up for the choir, and at every service we also had special music by various Russian Christian musical groups. On Saturday night, the soaring voices of a magnificent men's chorus resounded throughout the huge, overflowing stadium, triumphantly echoing the familiar strains of one of America's best-loved hymns of faith, the "Battle Hymn of the Republic."

> In the beauty of the lillies,
> Christ was born across the sea,
> With a glory in His bosom
> that transfigures you and me;
> As He died to make men holy,
> let us live to make men free,
> While God is marching on.
>
> Glory! Glory, hallelujah!
> Glory! Glory, hallelujah!
> Glory! Glory, hallelujah!
> Our God is marching on.

In spite of the familiar English words and the familiar stirring melody, this was not America. Nor were these American singers. They were the Russian Army Chorus, known for many decades as the Red Army Chorus—a group recognized all over the world not only for their musical talent but also for their role as one of the Soviet Union's chief propaganda tools!

Later in the service, I watched in awe as over half the audience—one of the highest percentages in my entire ministry—surged forward at the Invitation (even before Viktor Hamm could finish his translation into Russian!) to commit their lives to Jesus Christ.

After the final service, I stood in my hotel room overlooking the Kremlin and watched the snow falling and the lights illuminating the beautiful towers and churches of the Kremlin and Red Square. I couldn't help but think back to the prayer I had uttered in Lenin Stadium when Grady and I first visited Moscow as tourists in 1959, asking God for an opportunity to preach the Gospel in that nation. Over thirty years had passed, and Grady was now in Heaven, but now, beyond doubt, God had answered our prayer.

31

Broadening the Vision

CONFERENCES AND CONGRESSES
(MONTREUX, BERLIN, LAUSANNE, AMSTERDAM)
1960–1986

I will never forget him. . . .

Several thousand of us had crowded into the huge hall, part of Amsterdam's RAI Center complex. It had been converted into a massive dining room, with long tables on which were served pre-packaged meals in aluminum containers. The event was the 1986 International Conference for Itinerant Evangelists, the second such conference we had held. It marked the culmination of a dream I'd had for many years: to bring together evangelists from all over the world for training and inspiration.

Ruth and I sat down and shook his hand. From his clothes, we suspected that he came from a poor country and had very little. But his face had a gentleness and joy about it that were immediately apparent; it also revealed the sense of purpose and commitment I had seen often during the opening days of the conference.

This evangelist and the others in the hall were on the cutting edge—men and women from some of the hardest places on earth, many bearing the physical and psychological scars of persecution. Many of them, I knew, had spent time in prison for their faith.

"Where are you from?" I inquired.

"I am from Botswana."

In response to my gentle prodding, he told us something about his ministry. He said he traveled, often on foot, from village to village, preaching the Gospel of Christ to anyone who would listen. It was, he admitted, discouraging at times, with frequent opposition and very little response.

"Are there many Christians in Botswana?" I asked.

"A few," he replied. "Only a very few."

"What is your background? Did you go to a Bible school or get any education to help you?"

"Well, actually," he said, "I got my master's degree from Cambridge University."

I was immediately ashamed that I had stereotyped him as an uneducated man. I was also humbled, not only because he was far better educated than I was but because of something else: any man returning to his underdeveloped homeland of Botswana with a coveted Cambridge degree would have virtually unlimited opportunities for political power, social position, and economic advancement. And yet this man was completely content to follow Christ's calling for him as an evangelist. He could truly say, in the Apostle Paul's words, that "whatever was to my profit I now consider loss for the sake of Christ" (Philippians 3:7).

Who could say what impact for Christ a man like this would have in the Africa of the future? I said a silent prayer of gratitude for his dedication, and for the opportunity God had given us to bring together such a unique group from across the world, about 8,000 itinerant evangelists from one hundred and seventy-four countries, for training and encouragement.

This 1986 Amsterdam conference, and its predecessor in 1983, were the culmination of a series of international conferences with which we had been involved for more than two decades; all had as their central theme the evangelistic task of the Church.

As our ministry expanded in the 1950s, my travels brought me into contact with a wide variety of Christian leaders and organizations. Some of them were strongly committed to evangelism and were reaching their cultures with the message of Christ. Many, however, lacked training and had little contact with those who were doing evangelism in effective and creative ways. Furthermore, I came to realize, many churches and leaders had lost sight of the priority of evangelism; some were even ignoring evangelism altogether.

This had not always been the case. In the nineteenth century, evangelism was a central concern of the Church, with thousands of missionaries going to the ends of the earth and making Christianity a truly worldwide movement. This explosion in evangelism—the greatest in the history of the Church—was accompanied by the establishment of schools, hospitals, literacy programs, and indigenous churches and denominations. For the first time in history, the goal of world evangelization seemed to be in reach.

In 1910 church leaders came together—under the slogan "the evangelization of the world in this generation"—in Edinburgh, Scotland, for a historic conference on missions and evangelism. One of the conference conveners was John R. Mott, who had come to Christ as a student under Dwight L. Moody. Their emphasis was on uniting together to evangelize the world, and Edinburgh 1910 influenced a whole generation of youth who committed themselves to world missions. The modern ecumenical movement, which traces its roots back to this time, was born out of the vision for worldwide evangelism conceived by John Mott, Robert Speer, and their colleagues. The founding of the International Missionary Council in 1921—a direct result of Edinburgh 1910—seemed to offer even greater hope of reaching the goal. Other winds were blowing, however, and in time the vision of worldwide evangelism faded.

I respected the attempts of the original architects of the World Council of Churches (founded in 1948) to bring many segments of the Church into a harmonious relationship. A cornerstone of the ecumenical movement's concern was expressed in Jesus' prayer for his disciples in John 17:21—"that all of them may be one, Father." But that prayer was directly related to the evangelistic imperative for the Church, for Jesus continued in the same verse, "May they also be in us *so that the world may believe*" (italics mine). I feared that in some circles, however, the preoccupation with unity was overshadowing a commitment to evangelism and biblical theology.

Perhaps God wanted to use our ministry to reaffirm the priority of biblical evangelism for the Church and to call Christians of different backgrounds to commit themselves to the cause of evangelism. In fact, we had discovered that the only word that would bring some of them together was *evangelism*.

This concern grew, and in time we called together a select group of evangelical leaders from various parts of the world to discuss the issue. I set forth several goals for such a gathering in a letter to a friend in Scotland, the Reverend Tom Allan, in December 1958. (In addition to being pastor of one of Glasgow's most prestigious churches, Tom was also a member of the Department of Evangelism of the World Council of Churches.) These goals would guide us throughout the conferences we would call in the next two and a half decades.

I added: "I believe there is a desperate need for such a conference at this time of confusion and the necessary readjustment of evangelism and missions in the face of changing conditions. Perhaps out of this conference could come . . . a new unity among the Lord's people to get the job of world evangelization done in our generation."

MONTREUX

Our first efforts were modest. In 1960, 33 Christian leaders from twelve countries gathered at my invitation in Montreux, Switzerland, from August 16 to 18. (Following that small conference, we held Crusades in Bern, Zurich, Basel, and Lausanne before going on to Germany for three Crusades.) We invited, among others, John Stott from Great Britain and Clyde Taylor from the United States. All of the participants were people who had been supportive of our Crusades in various places and had become personal friends and advisers.

The theme of the informal gathering was "God's Strategy in Missions and Evangelism." I was the chairman, and as our time together went along, I would ask different people to bring devotions or to speak the next day. We discussed the problems and opportunities for evangelism in a world that seemed to be moving rapidly toward secularization.

560

At the peaceful lakeside setting, we all sensed a deepening spirit of unity among us, and a fresh commitment to do what we could to promote the cause of evangelism. At the same time, no formal document came forth from that gathering, nor were there firm plans for any further meetings.

About four years later, Dr. Victor Nelson came by my hotel room one day when I was speaking in Nova Scotia, Canada. Victor was a wise and valued colleague who had retired from a fruitful ministry as a Presbyterian pastor to join our organization in Minneapolis; at the time of our conversation, he was coordinating Crusades in Canada for some of our associate evangelists. I respected his counsel greatly.

"Billy, if you just puddle-jump from Crusade to Crusade all over the world," he said bluntly, "you'll never accomplish what you could and should accomplish. You not only need to do this work yourself, but you need to multiply your efforts. You need to train others to do effective evangelistic work also."

I knew he was right. In spite of an almost nonstop Crusade schedule, I sensed that we needed to work toward an international conference on evangelism.

BERLIN

Part of the problem was that there was no real worldwide network—formal or informal—of evangelicals or evangelists. A beginning had been made in 1951 with the founding of the World Evangelical Fellowship. Its membership was limited, however; and many evangelicals, particularly in the traditional mainline churches, were not associated with it.

Some of us thought it would be strategic to convene a conference in Rome. I asked George Wilson and Stan Mooneyham of my staff to investigate. They reported that Rome had excellent meeting facilities, with simultaneous translation capabilities available at a reasonable cost. Tom Allan, however, wisely counseled us against Rome. He pointed out that the conference might be perceived as anti-Catholic; at the very least, it would run the risk of being overshadowed by the deliberations of Vatican II, currently in session. In the end we chose Berlin, which by this time was tragically divided by the concrete wall. There we would be meeting at a symbolic crossroads of clashing ideologies, expounding Christ as the only answer to the universal desire for hope and peace.

One concern I had was sponsorship. The Billy Graham Evangelistic Association would have to finance and organize the event, I realized, but the conference would have more impact (and might possibly draw a larger cross section of Christian leaders), if someone else officially sponsored it.

Then the thought occurred to me, Why not ask *Christianity Today* to sponsor it? The magazine had already gained worldwide prestige among both Protestants and Catholics. I met with its editor, Dr. Carl Henry, and laid before him my burden and vision. After we prayed, Carl seized the opportunity.

Now a whole new set of organizational problems had to be worked through in a very short time. Those who sat with Carl to put the program together included Bob Evans, founder of the Greater Europe Mission, and Clyde Taylor (who was a strategic thinker), secretary of the World Evangelical Fellowship. In the end, BGEA organized it and raised the money. We formally titled the event the World Congress on Evangelism, but we generally referred to it simply as the Berlin Congress or Berlin '66.

As word spread of the planned Congress, a few people began what I thought was a studied, perhaps even demonic, campaign to discredit it. One American in Berlin who represented the United Church of Christ as a "fraternal worker"—a man later withdrawn by his denomination—aggressively lobbied against us.

Dr. Kurt Scharf, a newly consecrated bishop of the German Lutheran Church, somehow got the impression that the projected Congress was going to be vigorously "anti-Communist and anti-ecumenical." One of our representatives cleared up this erroneous view with the bishop, who then agreed to bring greetings at the opening of the Congress. His one proviso was that I not make any political statements at the Crusade that was scheduled beforehand.

It certainly was not my intention to be political. But the concern was shared elsewhere, even among our supporters. For example, the Reverend E. L. Golonka, who as a native of Poland understood eastern Europe very well, strongly warned me about the dangers of giving the impression that any evangelistic and missionary activities were "connected with the official policies of the United States and West German governments."

Whom should we invite as participants to the Congress? We carefully formulated general guidelines, but they did not automatically resolve every issue.

For example, the growing charismatic movement, much of it associated with Pentecostal denominations, was somewhat outside mainstream evangelicalism. We did not bar these denominations from our Crusades, but we did not particularly encourage their participation either; some of their ecstatic manifestations were controversial and disruptive within the broader Christian community. I felt that my longtime friend Oral Roberts, world renowned for his preaching and healing ministry as well as for the development of the university bearing his name in Tulsa, Oklahoma, should be included among the delegates. I was not ready to assign him a place on the program, but I was convinced that his presence would mark the beginning of a new era in evangelical cooperation.

Although we tried to have participants from numerous denominations, we made it clear that they were being invited as *individuals*, on the basis of their own unique ministry, not as official representatives of their denominations. This gave them the liberty to be themselves without having to worry about reporting back to any constituency or hierarchy.

We decided to include observers as well—people who were not avowed evangelicals (or even, in some cases, avowed Christians). One of these was Rabbi Arthur Gilbert from the Anti-Defamation League of B'nai B'rith. Following the Congress, just before Christmas that year, he wrote to me and said, "I want to tell you . . . particularly during this Blessed Season, how meaningful an experience it was for me to attend the World Evangelical Congress. I was moved by the depth of spirit demonstrated by the participants, and I was particularly delighted to see that a sensitivity for man's social needs accompanied a commitment to the proclamation of the Gospel."

Holding the Congress in Berlin could not help but remind us that only twenty years or so had passed since the horrors of the Holocaust. Around the time of the Congress I wrote to the chairman of the board of trustees of the Jewish Information Society of America: "I cannot possibly believe that a true Christian would ever be involved in anything anti-Semitic."

The theme of Berlin '66 was "One Race, One Gospel, One Task." Stan Mooneyham, Dr. Victor Nelson, and others from our staff, as well as several on loan from other organizations, moved to Berlin to organize details of the event, which was to be held in the city's recently completed Kongresshalle. Carl Henry was the official chairman; I was designated honorary chairman.

Altogether about 1,200 delegates from one hundred countries came together for the opening ceremonies on October 26, 1966. Some of them were well known in evangelical circles, such as Corrie ten Boom, the valiant Dutch woman whose thrilling story of survival and forgiveness during the Nazi Holocaust was later put on film by our own World Wide Pictures. Others were virtually unknown, never having traveled outside their own countries.

Two attendees drew special attention. They were members of the primitive Auca Indian tribe from the jungles of Ecuador. In 1956 they and their fellow tribesmen speared to death five young American missionaries who had ventured into their forest to bring them the Gospel. Because of the subsequent witness of Rachel Saint, sister of one of the martyrs, and of Elisabeth Elliot, widow of another, they and several other members of their tribe came to faith in Christ. Now, only ten years after the slayings, they were in Berlin—barefoot still, but adding their voices to the praise of God and urging us to greater zeal for winning a lost world to the Savior.

What had happened to our Auca brothers, all of us in Berlin knew, was what God wanted to happen to every tribe and tongue and people and nation in the world. These men were vivid reminders of God's transforming power.

We decided that we should include a well-known world leader as a speaker to call attention to the world scope of the Congress. However, we couldn't think of anybody in that category who was an evangelical Christian, in the usual meaning of that term. Finally, we invited His Imperial Majesty Haile Selassie I, Emperor of Ethiopia and Protector of the ancient Ethiopian Orthodox Church. His eloquent greeting set the tone for the Congress: "However wise or however mighty a person may be, he is like a ship without a rudder if he is without God. . . . Therefore, O Christians, let us arise and, with the spiritual zeal and earnestness which characterized the Apostles and the early Christians, let us labor to lead our brothers and sisters to our Savior Jesus Christ who only can give life in its fullest sense."

In my opening address, I reminded the delegates of the 1910 Edinburgh conference. "One of the purposes of this World Congress on Evangelism is to make an urgent appeal to the world church to return to the dynamic zeal for world evangelization that characterized Edinburgh fifty-six years ago," I stated. "The evangelistic harvest is always urgent. The destiny of men and of nations is always being decided. Every generation is crucial; every generation is strategic. But we are not responsible for the past generation, and we cannot bear full responsibility for the next one. However, we do have *our* generation! God will hold us responsible at the Judgment Seat of Christ for how well we fulfilled our responsibilities and took advantage of our opportunities."

One compelling illustration of the challenge facing the Church was a thirty-foot-high clock in the Kongresshalle's foyer; second by second it recorded the net gain in the world's population. It indicated to us that during the Berlin Congress, the population of the world increased by 1,764,216 people for whom Christ died and who needed to hear the message of Christ before they themselves died.

On Sunday, October 30—the day before the 449th anniversary of the start of the Protestant Reformation under Martin Luther—the delegates joined 10,000 others from Berlin in marching from Wittenberg Square to the Kaiser Wilhelm Memorial Church. Coordinated by staff member Gil Stricklin, press coverage of that event and the whole Congress was extensive.

The Berlin Congress issued a final statement underlining its theme of "One Race, One Gospel, One Task." That statement said, in part, "Our goal is nothing short of the evangelization of the human race in this generation."

It went on to condemn as sin the divisions caused by racism: "In the name of Scripture and of Jesus Christ we condemn racialism wherever it appears. We ask forgiveness for our past sins in refusing to recognize the clear command of God to love our fellowmen with a love that transcends every human barrier and prejudice."

It concluded with an appeal for a renewed commitment to evangelism: "Recognizing that the ministry of reconciliation is given to us all, we seek to enlist every believer and to close the ranks of all Christians for an effective witness to our world. . . . Our responsibility is to see that every one is given the opportunity to decide for Christ in our time."

What was accomplished at the Berlin Congress? Beyond forging a new unity among evangelicals, the Congress served as a catalyst for a number of new efforts in evangelism. Bill Bright once told me that the Berlin Congress had given him the vision for Campus Crusade for Christ, which he had founded some years before, to become worldwide in its outreach.

Father John Sheerin, an observer at the Congress and editor of *The Catholic World* in New York, wrote, "I have been impressed by the broadening and widening perspectives, the obedience to the Great Commission, and the concentration on and reverence for the Bible."

One reporter who had come to the Congress with a very negative view said later, "In spite of myself I am deeply impressed and deeply moved."

Especially gratifying was the response from some German Lutheran leaders. In November, after the Congress, I received a letter from the bishop of Berlin, the venerable Otto Dibelius, who was a past president of the World Council of Churches. "Both the Congress and the preceding Crusade [were] challenging in the best sense of the word," he wrote, "and most meaningful to the thousands who attended."

Certainly a major contribution of the Berlin Congress lay in its emphasis on the theology of evangelism. The Congress papers were later collected in two volumes and widely distributed, thus extending the impact of the event beyond its original participants.

In his book *The Battle for World Evangelism,* Dr. Arthur Johnston summarized another result of the 1966 Congress: "Evangelicalism could now be seen as a significant international body, capable of even greater evangelistic exploits, in an age of technology and population explosion."

The Berlin Congress resulted in several regional conferences, including gatherings in Singapore (1968), Minneapolis (1969), Bogotá (1969), and Amsterdam (1971). Local leaders provided the organization and program for each of these.

The Minneapolis event—the U.S. Congress on Evangelism—grew out of a group of delegates from the Twin Cities area, particularly several Lutheran pastors, who had begun meeting regularly for prayer after the 1966 Congress. Some 5,000 delegates from across the country attended the U.S. Congress on Evangelism.

Black evangelicals in the United States organized a Congress on Evangelism in Kansas City in 1970. This was the first such conference to focus specifically on African-American evangelism. The host pastor was Dr. John W. Williams, a prominent black churchman who for many years until his death was a valued member of the BGEA board of directors and a distinguished leader in the NAACP.

The European Congress on Evangelism in 1971 drew 1,000 carefully selected delegates from thirty-six countries to Amsterdam's RAI Center for a thorough examination of the theology and practice of evangelism and the challenges facing the churches of Europe.

LAUSANNE

The impact made by the Berlin Congress caused some people to urge us to consider a second international conference. They felt that we must not lose the momentum built up by Berlin. I was reluctant to consider such an event. The Berlin Congress had involved a great deal of work, drawing staff time and effort from our Crusade ministry; furthermore, I knew that the difficult task of raising finances over and above our regular budget would fall mainly on the BGEA. And yet there were compelling reasons to convene another conference.

One reason lay in the debates raging in some religious circles, particularly within the World Council of Churches (WCC), over the precise meaning of *evangelism*. Many prominent leaders in the WCC sought to uphold a biblical understanding of evangelism, but the ecumenical movement by and large was moving in another direction. For example, in contrast to Berlin, the 1968 Fourth Assembly of the World Council of Churches, held in the Swedish university city of Uppsala—an assembly that I attended as an observer—tended to redefine the good news of the Gospel in terms of restructuring society instead of calling individuals to repentance and faith in Christ.

A 1973 Bangkok conference sponsored by the WCC's Commission of World Mission and Evangelism carried the process further, focusing even more strongly on social and political justice to the exclusion of the redemptive heart of the Gospel to a lost world. Implicit in much of the discussion at that conference was the assumption that Christ had already given salvation to every human being (a belief known as *universalism*), so that there was no need for humans to repent or believe in Christ in order to be saved. Such a view not only cut the nerve of evangelism, it also rejected the clear teaching of Scripture. This trend alarmed evangelicals, who found themselves grasping for a more thorough understanding of a biblical theology of evangelism.

In January 1970, I called together a group of 15 Christian leaders from various parts of the world to meet in Washington, D.C., to consider the advisability of another world Congress. Our feeling then was that the time was not right.

In December 1971, I called together a slightly larger group in White Sulphur Springs, West Virginia, to consider the question once again. I also sent a letter to 150 influential evangelicals throughout the world, asking for their advice. This time the consensus was different: we felt that the Holy Spirit was now directing us to sponsor another conference.

In subsequent meetings, various committees were set up, and the decision was made by the BGEA to hold a world Congress in the summer of 1974. Particularly important was the appointment of a committee to plan the conference. Care was taken to make it as representative as possible; the days of white, Western paternalism had to end. A committee of 28 people from sixteen nations was finally appointed; about half were from the Third World.

I asked Bishop Jack Dain of Australia to act as executive chairman and Dr. Donald Hoke, veteran missionary to Japan and president of Tokyo Christian College, to be coordinating director of the conference. Paul Little of InterVarsity Christian Fellowship took the assignment of program director, working closely under the program committee, which consisted of Leighton Ford as chairman, Victor Nelson, Harold Lindsell, Samuel Escobar, and Don Hoke. Warwick Olson from Australia was named director of communications. I was designated honorary chairman, with the understanding that no statement would be issued from the conference without my approval.

Our preference was to hold the conference somewhere in the Third World. Unfortunately, our staff discovered that there simply was no facility in the Third World that could host such a large and complicated gathering. At the suggestion of Dr. Robert Denny, general secretary of the Baptist World Alliance (which held its worldwide assemblies every five years), we then focused on Europe.

After careful study, we selected the Palais de Beaulieu conference center in Lausanne, Switzerland. The conference center had auditorium space for 4,000 people as well as facilities for simultaneous translation, and there were ample rooms for the dozens of small groups and workshops we were planning.

Advisory committees were set up in each country to nominate delegates, following guidelines set forth by the executive committee. Among those guidelines was an emphasis on younger leaders, who would have a lifetime of ministry ahead of them.

The planning was not without its problems. Well-known businessman and Christian lay leader Maxey Jarman from Nashville undertook the task of raising special funding for the event. In spite of his energetic efforts, however, many people could not grasp the strategic significance of the conference. In the end, the BGEA had to fund three-fourths of the budget.

As the conference date approached, costs began to soar, in large part because of the Arab oil embargo and skyrocketing plane fares.

At one stage, I was on the verge of canceling the Congress. Ruth, however, persuaded me otherwise. "Don't cancel it," she urged. "You may never be able to have a conference like this again. Go forward, even if you have to borrow the money."

Don Hoke and Jack Dain were both very able men, but both were strong-willed and with different cultural backgrounds. Occasionally, when things got too strained between them, I had to ask Victor Nelson to intervene. From time to time, I had to fly over myself to work on numerous policy decisions that had to be made! I was concerned to involve the executive committee as much as possible.

Inevitably, other problems arose that we couldn't possibly have envisioned. A few are worth mentioning here.

One speaker threatened to pull out when we placed the British intellectual and writer Malcolm Muggeridge on the program. Muggeridge, a fairly recent convert to the Christian faith, was not as versed on theological distinctions as this speaker felt he should be. And yet Muggeridge gave a brilliant analysis of the intellectual climate of the world in which we lived and received the only standing ovation of the Congress.

There also was the delegation who, when they arrived at the Palais de Beaulieu, refused at first to enter because the flag of a country hostile to them was flying on one of the many flagpoles outside.

One day during the conference, the food was so indigestible that Jack Dain took a plate to the caterer, who was not part of the Palais de Beaulieu staff, thrust it under his nose, and bluntly said he wouldn't feed that stuff to his dog. The food improved immediately.

And then there was the personal problem I faced when I arrived in Lausanne. Ruth and I were taken to a spacious suite in the most palatial hotel in the city, overlooking the lakefront. I knew it was being provided without cost to the conference. (I assumed that the hotel was offering it as a courtesy for the business the conference was generating; later I discovered that an American businessman was actually paying for it.) But I felt very uncomfortable there, since most of the delegates lived extremely modest lives and would be staying in far simpler hotels. A day or so later Ruth and I moved to a much smaller hostelry.

Nevertheless, given the scope of the conference, we were very thankful that the problems were not greater. One reason, I was convinced, was that the prayer committee, working under Millie Dienert, had organized strong prayer support in virtually every country.

The conference—officially designated the International Congress on World Evangelization (or ICWE), but commonly called Lausanne '74—was held July 16 through 25. The theme was "Let the Earth Hear His Voice." There were 2,473 official delegates from 150 countries, with another 1,300 people participating as observers, guests, or consultants; in addition, several hundred journalists attended. With only two days to prepare, Maurice Rowlandson, director of our London office, managed to organize the entire registration process and train the several hundred young people who had volunteered as stewards or ushers.

In my opening address, I noted the uniqueness of the Congress: "Never before have so many representatives of so many evangelical Christian churches in so many nations and from so many tribal and language groups gathered to worship, pray, and plan together for world evangelization. Assembled here tonight are more responsible leaders, from more growing national churches of Asia, Africa, and Latin America, than have ever met before."

In that keynote address, I also tried to set forth the reasons for the Congress. I traced its lineage back to other historic conclaves dealing with missions and evangelism, and I noted the pressing need to develop evangelistic strategies for our generation. I outlined also why some evangelistic movements of the past had lost their cutting edge. "If there's one thing that the history of the Church should teach us," I said, "it is the importance of a theology of evangelism derived from the Scriptures."

In addition, I reviewed the challenges that evangelism was facing in a world often gripped by crisis. I likewise underlined the single focus of the Congress: "Here at Lausanne, let's make sure that Evangelization is the one task which we are unitedly determined to do."

Because of our conviction that our lives and our thinking must be shaped by God's Word, every morning session began with a devotional Bible study led by various Bible teachers.

Many of the plenary addresses explored the Bible's teaching on evangelism, including such topics as the nature of God, the work of Christ, conversion, the uniqueness of Christ, the lostness of humanity, the mission of the Church, and the authority of the Bible.

Workshops dealt with everything from evangelizing people living in high-rise apartment buildings to evangelizing in the midst of government hostility. Delegates from each country hammered out strategies for evangelism within their own society. All addresses and reports were edited by Dr. J. D. Douglas of Scotland and printed in a volume that ran fifteen hundred pages.

What was the impact of those ten days in Lausanne?

As had happened after the Berlin Congress, reports began pouring in of new movements and new strategies that were helping Christians reach out to others with the Gospel. Two years after Lausanne, Don Hoke reported that at least twenty-five new evangelistic organizations or missions were formed in Europe alone as a direct result of that conference. I heard of one tribe in Bolivia that had twenty churches in 1974. Those evangelists involved in reaching the area put into practice some of the things they learned in Lausanne, and by 1980 the number of churches grew to one thousand.

As a follow-up to Lausanne '74, Congresses on evangelism, often with little or no involvement by us, were held in such places as India, Hong Kong, Singapore, and even Cuba. One of them, the 1976 Pan-African Christian Leadership Assembly in Nairobi, Kenya, brought together Christian leaders from all across the continent, in spite of the racial and political differences that often divided their countries and even their churches.

I was the only American speaker at that conference. It was held in Nairobi's new Kenyatta indoor arena. President Kenyatta's daughter, the mayor of Nairobi, gave a luncheon in my honor one day. I sat beside her on that occasion, and I remember asking her what kind of meat was being served. "It's our best monkey meat," she replied proudly. Admittedly it was delicious.

In some ways, the most far-reaching impact of Lausanne '74 came from its final document, known as the Lausanne Covenant. Each evening of the conference, a group of about 40 people met to go over the proposed document line by line. John Stott was deeply involved in it (though he did not write it, as some later assumed), as were Leighton Ford and others. I then reviewed the group's progress after each session. The final result, translated into many languages, has since come to be looked upon as a classic statement on evangelism.

Particularly important was the paragraph on the nature of evangelism. "To evangelize," it stated in part, "is to spread the good news that Jesus Christ died for our sins and was raised from the dead according to the Scriptures, and that as the reigning Lord he now offers the forgiveness of sins and the liberating gift of the Spirit to all who repent and believe. . . . The results of evangelism include obedience to Christ, incorporation into his church and responsible service in the world."

Throughout my ministry, I have resisted, as a matter of principle, signing manifestos or documents or petitions of any sort; they can be the cause of unforeseen problems and misunderstandings. My only exception, as I recall, was the Lausanne Covenant. It remains one of the major contributions of Lausanne '74.

One outgrowth of the Lausanne conference was the formation of a permanent committee to carry on the vision and work of Lausanne. That group, known as the Lausanne Committee for World Evangelization (LCWE), was formed to act as a catalyst for evangelistic strategies and programs on a continuing basis.

To be honest, when the question of forming an ongoing organization came up in the executive committee, I did not vote for the proposal, although the majority did. I had made it clear from the beginning that it was not our purpose to set up an organization. Nevertheless, I didn't oppose it openly. They asked me if I would chair the committee, but I declined. They then invited Jack Dain to be chairman, and I agreed to be honorary chairman.

In the following years—under first Jack's and then Leighton Ford's direction—the Lausanne Committee for World Evangelization did much good in training leaders and refining strategies for evangelism. For several years the BGEA joined in supporting it until it could gain financial help from other sources. My own ministry has kept me from being involved to any significant degree in recent years.

AMSTERDAM

Berlin and Lausanne were unquestionably highlights of our work; and yet, in the back of my mind, those two Congresses were actually something of a diversion from what I really yearned to do: call together men and women from across the world who were involved, as I was, in itinerant or traveling evangelism.

My Crusades overseas had left me humbled by the quality of Christian leadership in other cultures. What struck me most was that countless anonymous evangelists were rendering heroic service to the Gospel, often under the most difficult and dangerous circumstances. I yearned to do something to encourage them, and perhaps to give them some tools they could adapt to their own situations.

After much research and prayer, a plan to sponsor what we called the International Conference for Itinerant Evangelists (ICIE) began to form. The gathering would be different from Berlin and Lausanne, where the delegates were primarily leaders in evangelism. This next conference would be for the foot soldiers, not the generals.

Our goal was to find at least 3,000 men and women who were involved in itinerant evangelism. Although we did not know where we would find them—no one had ever attempted to draw up a list of those involved in itinerant evangelism—we knew that most would be coming from the developing world. That meant their participation would have to be heavily subsidized. Some of them would be able to pay almost nothing because of their own personal poverty or the currency restrictions in their home countries.

The budget would have to be raised over and above our normal ministry expenses. Although we had a large gift of $1 million from one individual to be used toward this conference, most of the budget (which totaled about $9 million, as I recall) came from small donations. (We later calculated that the average gift was around $15.)

As we had done before, we surveyed a number of possible locations. In the end, we chose Amsterdam's RAI Center, one of the few places that could accommodate such a large number of people. The fact that Holland had few visa restrictions contributed to our decision. If we had chosen a country requiring visas of most participants, we would have added enormously to the cost and complexity of the effort.

The logistics of such a conference, we knew, would be staggering. Even getting word to some of the evangelists would be difficult. Many would never have traveled outside their country, and the vast cultural differences between those from so many different countries would challenge even the most thorough organizational efforts.

The BGEA's experienced international director, Dr. Walter Smyth, was chairman, with Werner Burklin as executive director and Bob Williams as associate director. Paul Eshleman came on loan to us from Campus Crusade for Christ as program director, with Leighton Ford as chairman of the program committee. Millie Dienert was asked to enlist prayer support, a critical part of the effort. John Corts had charge of follow-up, planning ways to maximize the impact of the conference after the participants returned to their countries. Departments were set up to deal with everything from transportation and accounting to translation and printing; dozens of staff from many countries moved to Amsterdam to plan every detail as thoroughly as possible.

In some ways, the biggest challenge was selecting those who would come. Victor Nelson and his staff started out with about 1,000 names of men and women who we knew were involved in some type of itinerant evangelism. As time went on, we uncovered more than 10,000. We had never dreamed there were that many evangelists in the world. We developed a process to review all applications to be sure that those who were invited were actively involved in itinerant evangelism and would profit from attending such a conference.

Before the conference opened, I went to The Hague, where I was welcomed by Queen Beatrix. I also spoke to the church leaders of Amsterdam, many of whom understandably had no idea what would happen at the conference because they had never experienced anything like it.

I've seldom felt smaller or less important in my life than when I stood on the platform of the RAI Center's Zuidhal on July 12, 1983, for our opening convocation. I saw the flags of 133 nations flying, representing the registered audience of 4,000 evangelists and 1,200 guests and observers. Most were listening on earphones to simultaneous translation of the proceedings into one of ten languages.

Spread out before me was a rainbow of men and women with far greater dedication and gifts than I would ever have. They were black and yellow and brown and red and white; from rural villages and towns and sophisticated cities on every continent and from the islands of the sea; speaking a multitude of tongues and little-known dialects as their first language. It was a microcosm of the human race. The largest number came from India; the second-largest, from Nigeria; the third-largest, from Brazil.

Cliff did a masterful job as master of ceremonies and choral director. Ruth was confined to a wheelchair at the time, waiting for a hip operation, but she did not miss a single session. The prayer times moved us especially. Some delegates just bowed their heads, or leaned forward, or stood with arms outstretched; others knelt by their seats or bent low on the floor. Given all the languages being spoken in the prayers, it was thrilling to realize that God could understand them all.

Various men and women spoke or led workshops. I felt that our daughter Anne Graham Lotz was speaking directly to me when she told the huge assembly, "It is not only your words, it is your life which is an evangelistic message to the world." That thought haunts me even as I write these memoirs, because here in these pages my life is exposed. Where it has been inconsistent with the message I have been preaching, I must repent and ask God's forgiveness.

Even those who didn't speak publicly had stories to tell. One African youth preached all along the first leg of his journey—a sixteen-hundred-mile walk from Zambia to Malawi. He joined fellow Africans from thirty-three countries who made up a quarter of the total attendance at Amsterdam 1983. An itinerant evangelist to Stone Age animists in Irian Jaya (northern West Irian) sold all the pigs that were his means of livelihood in order to raise money to attend the conference. That income got him only as far as Jakarta, however; a special offering from ICIE staff in Amsterdam helped make up the balance he needed.

Delegates, some of them arriving barefoot and without a change of clothes, were overwhelmed with gratitude when they visited the conference clothing center. There they found shirts, pants, dresses, and children's togs—five hundred tons in all—distributed free of charge under the auspices of our son Franklin's organization, Samaritan's Purse.

Twenty-five trained counselors were available to help participants deal with personal and family problems (as well as spiritual concerns) in confidential, private sessions.

Books and study aids were given to delegates who could not afford to purchase them; each one went away with a canvas bag filled with a small library of books to help them study the Bible, prepare evangelistic messages, and do their work more effectively. Some received, without cost, equipment that they needed—such things as overhead projectors, film projectors, tape recorders, sound systems or megaphones, and bicycles. Recognizing that many isolated areas had neither electricity nor a ready and cheap supply of batteries, some received a cassette recorder that generated its own electricity by turning a handle. It was not unusual to see participants making their way back to their hotels and dormitories in sophisticated Amsterdam with their gifts stacked high on top of their heads.

From the kitchens of KLM Royal Dutch Airlines at Amsterdam's Schiphol Airport, prepackaged individual meals, including fifty diverse dietetic trays, were loaded onto ten trucks for transport twice each day to the sprawling conference center miles away. The caterers thought that one evangelist from a Third World country had strange dietary needs when he asked for a supply of *large vultures;* it was some time before they realized he was saying *lunch vouchers!* Another evangelist salvaged all the cast-off trays he could for use back home as roof tiles for huts.

But clothing, supplies, and food weren't what the International Conference for Itinerant Evangelists was all about.

Two hundred workshops dealt with everything from reaching business and political leaders to studying the Bible and organizing a Crusade. In a special program for wives, Ruth and others gave talks stressing the indispensable role of supportive spouses and praying mothers.

Among the countless memorable statements made by speakers was one from BGEA associate evangelist Dr. Akbar Abdul-Haqq of

India. "If the Bible had been available in an Arabic translation at the time of the prophet Muhammad," he said, "the history of the world would have been greatly different."

As at Lausanne '74, we decided in advance to issue a final document from the 1983 conference. I asked Dr. Kenneth Kantzer of Trinity Evangelical Divinity School to chair a small committee of scholars and theologians during the conference (including Dr. Arthur Johnston, Dr. Robert Evans, Dr. James Douglas, and Dr. John Akers) to draft a brief but comprehensive statement directed specifically to the needs of evangelists.

The result, known as the Amsterdam Affirmations, consisted of fifteen concise but clear statements affirming our commitment to Christ and to the Great Commission, and to purity and integrity in our lives and ministries. The final affirmation was a plea to all Christians: "We beseech the body of Christ to join with us in prayer and work for peace in our world, for revival and a renewed dedication to the biblical priority of evangelism in the church, and for the oneness of believers in Christ for the fulfillment of the Great Commission, until Christ returns."

At the conclusion of the conference, the participants stood in a solemn moment of rededication. As each affirmation was read, they responded in their own language with the words, "This I affirm."

A year later, I wrote an interpretative commentary on the Amsterdam Affirmations. This book, entitled *A Biblical Standard for Evangelists*, has been distributed across the world.

"These itinerant evangelists are the most important ambassadors and messengers on earth," I said at the close of the conference. "They are a mighty army of proclaimers, energized by the power of the Holy Spirit, spreading out across the world with a renewed vision to reach their own people for Christ."

I never imagined the full implication of my own words until the second International Conference for Itinerant Evangelists (Amsterdam '86) convened in July three years later in the same RAI Center outside the city. From the opening ceremony—with its torchbearers, parade of flags, and lighting of an Olympics-style "flame of salvation"—the multinational, multiracial, multilingual, multidenominational throng sang, prayed, studied, and witnessed as one in Christ.

The delegates represented almost every conceivable kind of evangelism. Two Dutch women were evangelists to prostitutes. An Indian Airlines flight operations officer was an evangelist to lepers in Madras. Another from Singapore was an evangelist to primitive peoples in the islands off Indonesia. Still others proclaimed the Gospel amid the civil war in Sri Lanka, or under severe restrictions in eastern Europe, or against life-threatening opposition in places like Lebanon. The majority were in their thirties and forties. None had been at the first conference three years earlier; 80 percent had never attended an international conference.

In some ways, the decision to hold a second conference for itinerant evangelists was not difficult. For one thing, of those who had applied to the first conference, 8,000 had been turned away for lack of space or financing. In addition, as word of our first conference spread, more and more evangelists were discovered. To our amazement, 50,000 names of men and women involved in itinerant evangelism were finally collected.

Many of them, we realized, held secular jobs—they had no other way to support themselves—and yet they often gave more time to evangelism than some of their counterparts in the West. Others were pastors because in their cultures they would not otherwise be recognized as legitimate evangelists. Two hundred and twenty-five selection committees were set up in various countries to make preliminary nominations, and then our staff followed a careful process in making the final selections. Some decisions were heartbreaking: there were 3,500 applications from India alone, yet we were able to take only 500. In the end, about 8,000 delegates came to the 1986 conference.

It was an enormous challenge. Werner Burklin, director of the 1986 conference, commented that doubling the number of delegates had probably quadrupled the work; and he was undoubtedly right. For the previous conference, we had dealt primarily with one airline; in 1986 we dealt with twenty-five. In 1983 thirty-five hotels had been used; in 1986 the number rose to eighty-five. In addition, we turned a huge exhibition hall at Jaarbeurs, about twenty-five miles away in Utrecht, into a massive dormitory for 4,000 participants. Dan Southern, one of our longtime Crusade directors, oversaw arrangements for the conference, including the facility at Jaarbeurs; his assistant, Mark Jarvis, calculated that the money saved by using that facility instead of hotels allowed another 3,000 participants to come to the conference. I visited it twice, and the sense of fellowship among those who were housed there was absolutely contagious.

Our budget for the 1986 conference ran close to $21 million; that was over and above our annual BGEA ministry budget. About 80 percent of the participants came from underdeveloped countries and required very substantial support. One evangelist wrote that although his monthly income (which was all he had to support his family) was the equivalent of $10, he promised to raise $100 toward the cost of bringing himself to Amsterdam.

We heard of many examples of sacrificial giving. One woman in America who was very poor walked the highways to collect aluminum cans so that she could give toward the project. Our own employees in Minneapolis held bake sales, garage sales, and other fund-raising events in their spare time to support the conference. Many of the staff in Amsterdam walked to work instead of riding the bus, donating the savings to scholarships for evangelists. Miraculously, the money all came in before the conference opened.

Again Samaritan's Purse set up a center to give clothing and other items to those with special needs. Up to ten garments for each person were available from a total of one hundred thousand items collected by Dutch Christians. Ruth and dozens of other volunteers helped Franklin's staff. One day Ruth found a wedding dress piled on top of a rack of men's clothing and took it over to Gwen Gustafson, who was supervising the women's section.

"Just a minute," Gwen said, hurrying from the room. In a few minutes she returned with a man from Africa who had been praying for a wedding dress for his daughter.

Ruth's heart was touched by a black woman evangelist who walked in barefoot, her feet swollen. Unable to find shoes in her own country, this woman had been traveling and preaching barefoot. The volunteers found two pairs of shoes that fit her.

Ruth also saw a small man whose left leg was painfully crippled. Traveling around to preach must have been extremely difficult for him, she knew. Franklin got him some crutches and arranged for him to see a doctor who could help him.

A very large evangelist found a suit to go with his new shirt and tie, but no shoes were big enough. The next day he was seen on the street all dressed up in his new wardrobe—and walking barefoot.

The gift of a white shirt to every participant especially pleased many. One participant said it would have taken him years to earn enough to buy such a garment.

Inevitably, with such a cross section of cultures, there were occasional conflicts that showed our human frailties. One group from a country torn by ethnic conflict objected strenuously because a representative of another ethnic group was chosen to carry their nation's flag in the opening ceremonies. A delegation from one of the Communist countries refused at first to carry their flag, fearful because they had not explicitly received their government's permission to do so. Alex Haraszti, who was working with the delegations from the Soviet bloc countries, eventually persuaded them to do so, pointing out that if they failed to join in the ceremonies, they would surely bring embarrassment to their country.

Some cultural differences had their humorous side. One group from a very poor country had never seen an elevator before. At first they refused to enter, calling it "the disappearing room." When the doors closed, the elevator was full of people; when the doors opened again, the elevator was empty!

One hundred interpreters were kept busy day and night translating plenary addresses, workshops, seminars, even individual counseling sessions into sixteen languages. A Chinese interpreter from Canada put it this way: "When the speaker gets excited, I get excited. It's almost like preaching myself."

Twenty-two international musical groups and soloists, coordinated by Tom Bledsoe, carried out the multicultural emphasis in wide-ranging indigenous styles.

As at the first conference, busloads of delegates spent a Sunday afternoon witnessing for Christ in parks, on beaches, and at other public places.

Frank Thielman, son of Dr. Calvin Thielman, the Presbyterian pastor in Montreat, went to the park with a group of others who sang together and then began to share their faith.

"Why are you so stupid?" an irate woman demanded of Frank in English.

"Ma'am?" asked Frank.

"Why are you all being so dumb—so stupid?"

"What do you mean?"

"Following this Billy Graham."

"I'm not following Billy Graham."

"Who do you follow then?"

"I follow Jesus Christ."

"Ridiculous!" she exclaimed. "Haven't you read any books? Haven't you been to school?"

"Yes, ma'am."

"Where did you study?" she asked scornfully.

"Well, I'm a graduate student at Cambridge University."

She shook her head in amazement and walked away, her stereotype of Christians at least shaken, if not shattered.

Our film crew was working on a new dramatic film entitled *Caught*. Set in Amsterdam, it told the story of a young American caught in a web of rebellion, confusion, and drugs. The crew was in the city's notorious red-light district shooting some background scenes when a man came up begging for money to buy an obscene object. Instead of rebuking him, one man said they could not do that but they would like to share Jesus with him. The man wound up kneeling right on the street, tearfully asking God for forgiveness.

One day I put on my favorite disguise—baseball cap, dark glasses, and casual clothes—and walked from my hotel to nearby Vondel Park. There I sat on the grass with a group of Indonesians who were witnessing to a group of Dutch young people. Some of the young folks were laughing, but others were listening seriously.

The closing communion service of Amsterdam '86 was led by Anglican Bishop Maurice Wood, assisted by my Presbyterian friend Don Hoke. At its conclusion, the six torchbearers rekindled their torches from the central flame they had ignited on opening night. Lifting the torches high, they carried them from the meeting to symbolize carrying the light of Christ to all the continents of the world.

As convener and honorary chairman of the conference, I hoped the participants would return home with my words ringing in their ears. "Our primary motive," I told them, "is the command of our Commander in Chief, the Lord Jesus Christ. . . . We are under orders. Our Lord has commanded us to go, to preach, to make disciples—and that should be enough for us."

32

A Leader with
Experience and Energy

PRESIDENT GEORGE BUSH

It was January 16, 1991. I had just showered and changed clothes when Barbara Bush tapped on my door with her cane.

"Welcome!" she said. "How about pushing me down to the Blue Room, and we'll watch television together?"

I came out of the Lincoln Bedroom, where I was staying, and pushed her wheelchair down the hall. She was still recovering from a fall off a sled while romping with her grandchildren; her injured leg was stretched out stiffly in front of her.

I had arrived at the White House only a short time earlier. That morning I had received an urgent phone call asking if I could come to Washington immediately and have lunch with the President.

Was it a private lunch? I asked.

I was told yes. It would be at the White House; just the Bushes would be there, but Secretary of State James Baker might drop in.

It was impossible on such short notice to get from North Carolina to Washington, I replied. An hour or two later, another call arrived asking if I could come instead for dinner. No reason was given for the urgency, and I was somewhat perplexed. Rumors of an impending war in the Persian Gulf in response to Iraq's invasion of Kuwait had been flying about for days, but I had no way of knowing if there was any connection.

In the Blue Room, which was made cozy with family pictures and personal mementos, we watched CNN. One or two of the family were there with us, and a bit later Susan Baker, the secretary of state's wife, came in and sat down. All of a sudden, the commentators in Baghdad, Peter Arnett and Bernard Shaw, exclaimed that anti-aircraft fire was going up; that meant, they said, that there must be a raid on.

I turned to Barbara. "Is this the beginning of the war?" I asked.

She did not say anything, but from the way she looked, I was certain that it was.

About fifteen minutes later, the President came into the room and sat down with us to watch television. He confirmed that the war had started.

"I think we should pray for those men and women and for this situation," I said.

We prayed about what was happening in Kuwait and Iraq, asking that it would be a short war, that few casualties would be suffered, and that the Lord would have His way.

Dinner was announced, and the three of us went in to eat. I was asked to say grace.

The President told us he had to make a speech to the American people in a few minutes. During dinner he received a copy of the speech he had hastily prepared. He read through it again and noted a few more things he wanted to include. "I want it to be exactly right," he said.

He left to appear on television, and we returned to the TV set to watch him. Then, some minutes after the telecast, he rejoined Barbara and me and several others in the Blue Room and sat down on the couch.

I told him he had delivered an excellent speech, adding, "I think you clarified the situation."

"I know in my heart I've done right," he replied.

He then asked me if I would be willing to conduct a prayer service the next morning for the cabinet, some of the congressional leaders, and several hundred Marines at Fort Myer.

Of course, I said yes.

When the chief of chaplains called later in the evening, he wanted my ideas about the program and what we should call it. I suggested "A Program for Peace."

The next morning, after his sternly uncompromising television announcement the night before, the president of the United States knelt before the Lord in a chapel at Fort Myer, a military compound across the Potomac River in Virginia, about a fifteen-minute ride from the White House.

Not knowing exactly what was ahead for me or for the nation, I talked on the three kinds of peace outlined in the Bible, as I had in Moscow during our 1982 visit there. I talked about the peace we find *with* God (outlining what a Christian is and how we can find peace with God through the Prince of Peace as we receive Christ into our hearts); the peace *of* God we can experience within us (as He brings peace in the turmoil, stress, and strain of life); and the peace God brings *between individuals and nations* (a peace that we should work diligently for, although it will not be achieved completely until the Prince of Peace is the Ruler). My prayer was that the war, started the night before, would be very brief and would result in a minimum of casualties, and that afterward we would have a long period of peace in the Middle East.

The ensuing days convinced me that the Almighty Lord of the nations had heard the heart cries not only of national leaders but also of stricken parents and spouses and children of loyal men and women in the armed forces who had mustered for duty.

Debates will go on about the Gulf War and its results for a long time, maybe for decades. The President never asked me for any of my thoughts about it, nor did I volunteer them at the time (or since). I was with him as a friend and pastor, not as a political adviser. Neither did he confide his innermost thoughts to me. He was a person who kept things to himself.

George Bush took the long view on many issues, particularly in international affairs. He was the U.S. envoy to China before full diplomatic relations were established, and he knew more about that country and about Oriental ways of thinking and acting than many of the academic and diplomatic experts. He also understood the enormous complexity of a country such as China, with its very different social and political system and its long history.

Barbara was an important part of his quiet self-confidence. A lot of Americans seemed to agree with Ruth's tongue in cheek comment that it was worth having George Bush in the White House if only because it made Barbara the First Lady.

She and Ruth were two of a kind in so many ways. No wonder they enjoyed being together. Both of them were totally devoted to their husbands and children. Both of them created a stylish but relaxed home atmosphere, where friends and strangers alike always felt welcome. (When George Bush was Vice President and the Bushes were living in a house on the grounds of the National Observatory, Ruth noticed lots of things Barbara did to transform that musty Victorian mansion into a home.) Both of them had a streak of good-humored impulsiveness that added a note of fun and spontaneity to almost any occasion. And both of them were quick with the quip, especially where their husbands were concerned. (When Ruth answered the phone at our house one day, the caller asked, "Is Billy handy?" "Not very," she retorted, "but he keeps trying!")

Ruth recalls with particular delight one visit we made to the Bushes at their summer home in Kennebunkport, Maine. Upon our arrival, Ruth was told to go to Barbara's bedroom, only to find that Barbara and the neighbors had pushed the bed against the wall, had piled the furniture on top of it to clear an open space, and were all on the floor vigorously exercising in time with a television workout program. Ruth's back problems forced her to sit on the sidelines, but she was sure she had more fun watching than they did exercising.

We first met George and Barbara Bush some years earlier, before he became prominent in national politics. I had met his father, Senator Prescott Bush, several times during my visits to Washington; I got to know him better after his retirement from the Senate, as a golfing partner at Hobe Sound, Florida. I also got acquainted with his wife, Dorothy Bush, a delightful and devout woman who was very supportive of our work across the years. The undisputed matriarch of their clan, she attended a Bible study group in Hobe Sound that had been started by some women following our Madison Square Garden Crusade in 1957.

In December 1988, I visited with the elder Mrs. Bush, and brought along my oldest daughter, Gigi. Of course, I had phoned ahead to see if it was all right to visit. By the time we got there, she had gathered 25 of her neighbors together.

"Billy," she said in her no-nonsense way, "I want you to teach the Bible. Tell us about Christ. Some of these people need to know."

I went there to have a pastoral prayer with a sick elderly lady, but here she was giving me an evangelistic platform. So I pulled the New Testament out of my pocket and went right to work, as ordered.

Another hilarious incident comes to my mind, which took place in 1979.

Both George and I were invited to address the Young Presidents' Organization at their annual meeting in Acapulco, Mexico. The Bushes, like us, were combining the speaking engagement with some vacation, and we ended up spending a great deal of time together. They were staying at the Princess Hotel, while we were staying with some friends who had a condominium several miles away.

One night Barbara showed slides of their time in Beijing, from which they had recently returned. Ruth especially enjoyed the glimpses of the land of her birth.

Another day a Mexican businessman invited the Bushes and us onto his yacht for a picnic on the beach a few miles away. Not having a pair of swimming trunks with me, I borrowed a pair of George's, which were white. Shortly after lunch, I got tired and wanted a nap. Instead of waiting for the rest of the group, I decided to walk back along the beach to the condominium.

As I turned a corner, I was stopped by an armed military guard. The beach where we'd had our picnic apparently was on the grounds of a Mexican naval base, and I was trespassing. To my horror, I realized I had no identification with me—I was still in George's swim trunks—nor did I even have a key to the condominium. To complicate matters, the guard didn't speak English, and I didn't speak

Spanish. He ordered me to sit on a bench until a superior officer could be summoned.

After much waiting and much explaining, the officer finally released me and allowed me to walk home, barefoot on the hot concrete. Only when I finally reached the condominium did I realize the bench had just been repainted and George's trunks had big smears of green paint across the rear! No amount of laundering could get them clean, but George said it was well worth sacrificing a pair of swim trunks just to enjoy a good laugh over my dilemma.

Times like those in Acapulco, I came to realize, were somewhat unusual for the Bushes. Usually, they did not spend vacation moments alone; mostly, they were surrounded by their family. No other presidential couple has impressed me so much with their family orientation. Family formed the center of their value system, along with their devout Episcopalian Christianity. The Bushes liked to surround themselves not only with family photos but also with the living—and lively—subjects of those pictures, the grandchildren. They did not give the children unlimited free run of the White House, certainly, but up at Kennebunkport the big old frame house shook and rattled constantly with scampering, shouting kids. One vivid memory was of watching their son, Jeb, round up his children and camp out on the lawn in a tent all night.

We stayed with the Bushes for a weekend during many of the summers of his vice presidency and presidency. In August 1990, just when the invasion of Kuwait by Iraq was occurring, we tried to get out of our scheduled weekend. We thought George would have far too much on his mind to tolerate us underfoot. But that was the very reason they insisted that we come. He wanted to talk with me, he said. We went.

Normally, at Kennebunkport everybody went to bed early, between nine and ten. And they got up early—always off and running, literally, from the first minute, contrary to my pattern of easing into the day. They played tennis like pros, set after set, all day long. And for keeps. Sometimes they played with pros such as Chris Evert.

If not on the court, the President was at the wheel of his speedboat, *Fidelity*. Their house was on a peninsula jutting out into the sea. The waves pounded the rocky coast relentlessly. To get to the boat, we had to climb down a wooden ladder. I always had trouble with that, but Ruth (with her perfect balance) had no problem. We put on white lifejackets and got into the boat. When George opened the throttle fully, I understood why we needed the jackets. He dodged in and out among the hundreds of different-colored lobster traps with the relaxed abandon of Lyndon Johnson careening around his ranch in a jeep. It must be congenital with Texans! He was a skillful navigator, but once in a while he nicked one of those lobster traps—and then paid reparation to the owner. If your heart could take the gravity pull, it was exhilarating. One of George's favorite spots for more moderate cruising was just off an island not far from his home—one covered with seals.

The Secret Service always had to keep up with him in their boat. There was also a larger boat keeping an eye on his place. When the war was on, security was increased; there were two or three boats out there then.

One summer years ago, George asked Ruth, "Would it be imposing on Billy if we asked him to speak to the young people tonight?"

"He'd be a whole lot more comfortable with a question-and-answer session," she responded.

That was the way I liked best to operate when I spoke to college students. So that was what we did at Kennebunkport. The young people sat around me—"wall-to-wall grandchildren and their friends," as Ruth described it—and asked me questions. Good ones about life and theology that challenged my thinking. And I tried to answer with what the Bible said. The next year, and the year after that, the children asked for another Q&A session. Those experiences helped form a personal bond between me and the four Bush sons and one daughter—a bond that has continued on an individual basis.

Always on Sundays at Kennebunkport, no matter what other activities might have been on the crammed vacation schedule, George and Barbara and Ruth and I would attend a church service (and sometimes two). Often he arranged for me to preach at the picturesque little St. Ann's Episcopal Church on the way into town.

One Sunday a new driver took us all to church. He drove rather quickly toward someone riding a bicycle. "You'd better watch that little old lady on a bike," said the President. "That happens to be my mother!"

On another Sunday—one when I was scheduled to preach at St. Ann's—I lost my sermon, which I had prepared especially for the occasion. I knew I had it with me when I stood up to sing; but when I sat down, I couldn't find it. I was still searching my pockets when it was time for me to take the pulpit. So I extemporized a sermon on an old faithful, the story of the Prodigal Son. It seemed to go well. And when I returned to my seat, there it was: the text of my sermon. I had been sitting on it. So much for my extended preparation!

The Bush family tempo was more subdued at the White House than at Kennebunkport when the younger children came around, but they were not overlooked by any means. After the State of the Union address in 1990, Ruth and I made for the second-floor Lincoln Bedroom to settle in for the night. The President loped down the hall as if headed for the Queen's Bedroom. But then he opened a hidden door in the wall and dashed up to the third floor, where the children always stayed when they came to visit. Instead of simply collapsing into bed after delivering a major speech to Congress and the nation, he wanted to say goodnight to those kids.

In 1986 some of the local North Carolina Republicans, knowing Ruth and I were friends with the Bushes, wanted to bring Vice President Bush out to our place when he flew into the state. They thought we might enjoy a get-together, but they also knew it might be politically useful to their cause. George knew that too, so he stayed away on purpose. Protective of my privacy and my nonpolitical stance, he wrote to explain that he did not want to expose me to the inevitable publicity his visit would bring. Ruth and I would have loved to see him relax in one of the rocking chairs on our porch. But we knew he was right, and we deferred to his good judgment.

The First Couple seemed to delight in showing the second floor of the White House—the family wing—to others. On the eve of the National Prayer Breakfast one year, when Ruth and I were again spending a night in the Lincoln Bedroom, the President called about twenty minutes before supper, while we were getting ready. "Hope you don't mind," he said apologetically, "but I've got about 60 members of the Senate and House coming up for a little tour of the living quarters. They've never seen it." Ruth grabbed her clothes and made a beeline for the bathroom.

When I stepped out of our room, I saw General Colin Powell, chairman of the joint chiefs of staff, and Defense Secretary Dick Cheney with a group that filled the upstairs hall. They had just finished a briefing with the President.

"Billy, you show them down at that end," the President said to me, "and I'll take them up at this end."

So I took about a third of them to the Queen's Bedroom and the Lincoln Bedroom—checking to make sure Ruth was concealed—and tried to give them a guided tour, telling them what little I knew from my several visits there.

At his inauguration in 1989, George Bush invited me to lead the various prayers during the public ceremony. I protested at first, pointing out that it was customary to have clergy from other traditions participate also (often a Jewish rabbi, a Catholic priest, and perhaps an Orthodox leader). He remained adamant, however, saying he felt more comfortable with me; besides, he added, he didn't want people to think he was just trying to play politics by having representatives of different faiths.

When the inauguration was over, we were invited to a luncheon in the Capitol Rotunda. Arriving there, we heard that the Bushes had gone to bid farewell to the Reagans, who were departing Washington. Since we had been friends with the Reagans for so many years, we wanted to see them off also. I took it upon myself to slip out. A Secret Service agent kindly took me to where they were embarking, but I got there just a little too late. I watched with mixed emotions as their helicopter lifted into the air, wishing I had thought ahead and arranged to say a final good-bye to a couple I admired so much.

After the luncheon, we were taken—to my surprise—to the President's box in the reviewing stand to watch the inaugural parade. During a break in the parade, the President motioned for me to come to him. "Billy, would you and Ruth mind going back to the White House and seeing my mother? She's up there watching the parade, and I know she'd just love to have you with her."

I said we would be delighted. Around ninety and in very frail health, Mrs. Bush had been flown in for the event in an ambulance plane with a doctor and a nurse. We found her in the Queen's Bedroom, propped up in bed, her eyes as blue as indigo and her face aglow. She looked like a queen herself, in spite of her fragility.

I sat there and held her hand for a few minutes, then asked if I could pray. She nodded with a smile, and I said a few sentences of thanksgiving to God that in His grace, George Bush was now President, and I asked the Lord to lead, guide, and protect George in the years ahead. When I was finished and looked back toward her, she had tears in her eyes and spoke in a whisper. "He'll need it."

Shortly afterward, I called him "Mr. President" for the first time, instead of "George." It was an awkward moment, and I stumbled a bit. He knew my dilemma, since many of his other friends felt the same way. He looked a bit wistful, and his gaze went to the far distance. No matter how much a president might wish it otherwise, there is a loneliness to that office that can never be completely overcome. That loneliness is one of the burdens of leadership.

The second White House state dinner during the Bush years was in honor of the Gorbachevs in 1990. I was seated next to Raisa Gorbachev, with President Bush at her other side. On my other side sat Jessica Tandy, who had won the Oscar that year for best film actress in *Driving Miss Daisy*. In anticipation of that seating arrangement, I asked Ambassador Dobrynin ahead of time what I could talk to Mrs. Gorbachev about. He said religion and philosophy were favorite topics of hers, and I found that to be true. We had an interesting conversation (through her interpreter). Though reported to be a staunch Communist, she admitted to me her belief that there had to be something higher than ourselves.

Since the Bushes left the White House in 1993, they have invited us to get together several times, in Houston or Kennebunkport, just to visit; whenever possible, we have done so. We have exchanged notes and talked on the telephone. "Thanks for checking in," he often says.

Our paths cross at other times also, and I will never forget how proud they were of their son George at his inauguration as governor of Texas in January 1995. I had been asked to lead the inaugural prayer, and as I did I was once again reminded not only of the Bushes' strong family ties but also of their strong commitment to public service—a commitment which they have passed on to the next generation.

33

The Pacific Giant

All our married life, Ruth has talked about China—and with good reason. China was the land of her birth, and the place where she spent the first seventeen years of her life. In 1916 her parents, Dr. and Mrs. L. Nelson Bell, went to China from their native Virginia as medical missionaries. In time Dr. Bell became the chief of surgery and superintendent of the largest Presbyterian mission hospital in the world, located in the town of Tsingkiangpu, North Kiangsu (now Jiangsu) Province, in east-central China, about 150 miles north of Shanghai. On June 10, 1920, Ruth was born there in a small Chinese house. The Bells already had a daughter, Rosa.

Growing up in China gave Ruth a love for the Chinese people and their culture that has never left her. China is the world's oldest continuous civilization. I read somewhere that the Chinese invented (or discovered) half the objects upon which the modern world rests. Sometimes I think Ruth eats, sleeps, and breathes China! She has taught me to love China too, including its food; at least once or twice a week she fixes us simple but authentic Chinese dishes. She has even succeeded in teaching me to use chopsticks with a fair degree of proficiency.

For many years, Ruth's greatest desire was to return to the land of her birth and to take me with her. She wanted to show me the places she loved and introduce me to some of the people she knew. She even prayed that it would be possible for me to preach in China. But if ever a dream seemed impossible, this was it!

Ruth left China in 1933 to attend high school at the Pyeng Yang Foreign School in Pyeng Yang (now Pyongyang), northern Korea. Trips back to China were sporadic—it was about a seven-day trip, both going and coming—but she made it back most Christmases. After high school in 1937, she came to the United States, where she enrolled at Wheaton College. In 1941 the Bells were finally forced to leave China because of the Japanese occupation; Ruth could return no more. The Chinese Communist victory under Mao Tse-tung in 1949 and the virulently antireligious policies of the Cultural Revolution in the 1960s and 1970s seemed to nail the door permanently shut.

The collapse of the Cultural Revolution after Chairman Mao's death in 1976 and the establishment of diplomatic relations between the United States and the People's Republic of China in 1979 marked the beginning of a new era. However, the guiding political philosophy in China continued to be a form of Communism that had been adapted to the Chinese situation. Atheism was still part of the official ideology, and religion was not encouraged.

By 1979 a few churches were being allowed to reopen, although they were subject to numerous restrictions. In 1980 Ruth and her two sisters, Rosa Bell Montgomery and Virginia Bell Somerville, and their brother, Clayton Bell, journeyed back to the country of their birth for a memorable visit. They found that much had changed in their old hometown of Tsingkiangpu. ("We felt like Rip van Winkle," Ruth said later.) At that time Tsingkiangpu was closed to foreigners, but special permission for their visit had been obtained through the good graces of former President Richard Nixon.

Much of the old hospital compound was still standing, including the Bells' home and the old Chinese house in which Ruth had been born. The larger home Ruth had grown up in was in sad disrepair—looking, as Ruth wrote, "like an old lady no longer loved or cared for." The women's hospital and other buildings were now being used for an industrial school. The little guest house where they were housed during their visit—each in a private room—had been freshly painted, and the bath had running water.

The hosts in Tsingkiangpu had frantically called the Friendship Association in Beijing to say they had no one who knew how to cook American food. They were greatly relieved to be told, "They want only Chinese food."

That first evening they had unexpected company: three members of one family—a brother and two sisters—all of whom had been delivered decades ago by Dr. Bell. The oldest, now living in Shanghai, had heard that Dr. Bell's children were coming home and traveled up-country to see them. "Most of the older Christians have died," she told them, "but the younger ones are carrying on."

The 1980 trip was unquestionably one of the highlights of Ruth's life. But it also increased Ruth's determination and prayers for the two of us to visit China together. Going as a tourist was no longer difficult, but securing permission for an extended preaching tour was quite another matter. Frankly, for several years I doubted if it would ever be possible.

I hoped and prayed right along with Ruth. My interest in China was motivated by much more than just a desire to visit her homeland, though. For one thing, China was now the world's largest nation, with a population of over 1 billion people; almost one out of every four people on the planet was Chinese.

More than that, almost every observer agreed that the twenty-first century could well become the "Century of the Pacific Rim." The future, they said, would belong to East Asia's burgeoning economies, with their teeming billions of people. My previous trips to Asia had convinced me they might well be right.

Furthermore, during China's history, Christianity had made very little impact on that society. It had always been perceived as an alien, exclusively European or "white man's" religion. Chinese authorities had failed to distinguish between those foreigners who went to China to exploit them and those who went to serve them. And the often-sordid history of Western colonialism in China only reinforced their belief that exploitation lay behind anything foreign. What a challenge to a Christian evangelist!

Because Ruth was so familiar with the Chinese situation, I asked her to coordinate the investigation and planning for a possible trip. She had already been talking informally with a small group of experts on China; at our request, they became an active working group to assist us.

That group included Sidney Rittenberg, an American who, because of his youthful idealism, had chosen to remain in China after World War II. For a period of time, he had been the only American member of the Chinese Communist Party; he had also been a close confidant of many of China's top leaders and was a superb English-Chinese interpreter. At two different times, he was accused of being an "imperialist spy" and imprisoned for a total of sixteen years, often in very harsh circumstances.

In spite of his years of suffering, I have never met a man with less bitterness toward his oppressors. At one stage of his life, he had memorized large sections of the New Testament. Now he and his Chinese wife, Yulin, were consultants for companies seeking to do business in China.

During a trip to Los Angeles in 1980, Sidney and Yulin saw us on television and immediately felt that this was a message China needed. Sidney's intimate knowledge of the Chinese bureaucracy and his sensitivity to China's long and impressive cultural history were invaluable to us.

Also assisting Ruth was Christian filmmaker Irvin S. Yeaworth. Called "Shorty" by everybody, he had accompanied Ruth and her sisters and brother on their visit to their old home in 1980 and had prepared an informal documentary film of that visit. He visited China several times on our behalf for advance discussions with officials about the invitation and our possible itinerary.

Dr. Carol Lee Hamrin, a Chinese affairs expert at the U.S. State Department and professor at The Johns Hopkins University, briefed us and helped us understand China's changing political and social currents.

David Aikman, *Time* magazine's former bureau chief in Beijing, brought to our discussions a firsthand knowledge of China's church situation.

Shortly before the trip, which was finally planned for 1988, I asked my associates Blair Carlson (who was born in Hong Kong of missionary parents) and John Akers to act as administrative coordinators. They worked closely with one of the co-sponsors of the visit, the Chinese People's Association for Friendship with Foreign Countries (usually called the Friendship Association), a semiofficial agency dedicated to better relations through nongovernment contacts.

In 1985 a preliminary invitation had arrived from Bishop K. H. Ting, head of the China Christian Council, whom Ruth had met during her 1980 trip. After a series of negotiations, a firm invitation arrived, asking us to preach in churches in several cities in September of 1987. I promised to give the invitation priority, pending further research into the details of the invitation.

"Please be assured that my association will do its best to comply with your requests," the president of the Friendship Association, Zhang Wenjin (who had been ambassador to the United States), wrote. "Even though it's your first visit, I believe you would not find [China] a strange land to you as it's the birthplace of your wife, and I am sure you'll make many friends during the visit."

The proposed 1987 date threw me into an immediate quandary. I was asked by Pope John Paul II to participate with him during that same time period in an unprecedented ecumenical service of worship during his visit to Columbia, South Carolina. It was not to be a Mass but a service of Scripture, prayer, and preaching. I was to speak on the subject of the family.

I was looking forward to that event, especially since the pope and I had a cordial relationship. Tex Reardon of my staff had been asked to advise the Catholics on some of the arrangements. (We had held a Crusade in the same stadium only a few months before.) John Akers, an ordained Presbyterian minister, was on the broad-based Protestant committee planning the service. I did not want the pope or the committee to think I was looking for an excuse to avoid the service.

By mutual agreement with our hosts in China, the official invitation was not to be made public until late July. But when I told our

Vatican contacts and the committee confidentially of the invitation to China, they were very understanding. In fact, our Roman Catholic contacts were especially supportive of our plans. They knew I had asked to meet with the leader of the officially recognized Catholic Church in China, which was not permitted to have formal relations with the Vatican.

I was, of course, excited about the possibilities in China. At the same time, both Ruth and I felt unprepared for the trip and even somewhat apprehensive. We yearned for more briefings on the situation as well as more time to prepare my messages. I realized too that I lacked a basic knowledge of Chinese protocol. For example, I kept forgetting that the family name came first in Chinese; I kept referring to China's paramount leader, Deng Xiaoping, as Mr. Ping.

The months prior to our planned visit were as busy as any others in our ministry. In June and July, we were involved in a number of Crusades throughout the Rocky Mountain and Northern Plains states. It was an unusual series of meetings, utilizing our associate evangelists as much as possible, but with me often preaching the closing meeting in each city. The series ended with a ten-day Crusade in Denver's Mile High Stadium. Toward the end of August, which was only a few weeks before we were scheduled to arrive in Beijing, we were in Helsinki, Finland, for another Crusade.

Ruth's own ambivalence about the trip was reflected in a postcard from Europe to our staff in Montreat. In it she said that her prayer was the same as the words of Moses quoted in Exodus 33:15: "If thy presence go not with me, carry us not up hence" (KJV).

Part of the problem was that we all knew China was a complex and difficult place. A great deal of care was needed to avoid mistakes or pitfalls that would bring embarrassment to our hosts or discredit to the Christian believers.

Our formal invitation, as I said, came from the China Christian Council, which was officially recognized by the government and also was affiliated with what was known as the "Three-Self Patriotic Movement." The term refers to China's churches' policy of being "self-supporting, self-governing, and self-propagating" and underlines the churches' independence from foreign influence and support. The movement had its roots in the thinking of nineteenth-century

American Presbyterian missionary John Livingston Nevius. His ideas were rejected by his co-workers in China but eventually adopted by missionaries in Korea, where the "Nevius Method" was credited with the rapid growth of the Korean church.

On the other hand, millions of Chinese Christians worshiped either as single family units or in so-called house churches, meeting as regularly as possible. These groups of believers were sometimes referred to as "meeting-point Christians." Many of the house churches were not affiliated with the officially sanctioned Three-Self Patriotic Movement. In many instances, they rejected the leadership of that body and its churches because of their ties to the government.

I did not want to offend either group, but I knew there would be pressure, especially from the Western press, to take sides or even to make some statement opposing the government's policies toward either group.

In addition, I knew China could be a political minefield. Although relations between the United States and China were more cordial than in the past, a number of thorny issues still remained, including human rights.

As had been the case in eastern Europe and the Soviet Union, I would need to weigh my statements very carefully to avoid misunderstanding. I had already sought advice from a wide variety of people knowledgeable about China, from former President Richard Nixon and former Secretary of State Henry Kissinger to the Archbishop of Canterbury, who had made a trip to China shortly before.

Immediately following the Helsinki Crusade, I flew to Tokyo for a few days of rest before continuing on to Beijing. By the time my longtime associate Henry Holley met me at the Tokyo airport, I was very tired and was suffering jet lag aggravated by vertigo and a bladder infection. One night I got out of bed, tripped over my briefcase in the dark, and ended up on the floor, with broken ribs and other internal injuries.

Henry took me to three different medical specialists in Tokyo; all agreed I must not undertake the trip to China. Indeed, the physical damage was so great that I had to be flown back to the United States for treatment at the Mayo Clinic. The aftereffects lingered for months, eventually involving surgical removal of one rib.

We worried about the impact of canceling the visit. Would our hosts understand the situation, or would they assume I had come up with a "diplomatic illness" and was really canceling for some obscure political reason? If they drew the latter conclusion, the trust we had so carefully built up with Chinese officials would be shattered. Almost certainly, in that case, we would never have an opportunity for a renewed invitation.

We took pains, therefore, to communicate my medical situation as fully as possible to them and to Ambassador Winston Lord at the American Embassy, both by telephone and through a letter that Shorty Yeaworth hand-delivered to our hosts.

Fortunately, they all understood and graciously accepted the situation. In the Lord's mercy, we were able to reschedule our itinerary and engagements for April 12 through 28, 1988. Following my release from the Mayo Clinic, I canceled everything that I could in the next few months and devoted as much time as possible to preparations for the trip.

Before our arrival in Beijing, several of our advance crew flew in from Hong Kong. On landing in Beijing, they experienced a fierce dust storm blowing in from the Gobi Desert, which ruined the film crew's plans to shoot scenes around the city before our heavy schedule began. On Tuesday, April 12, we arrived at the Beijing airport via a stopover in Hong Kong. Playing over the intercom of our CAAC (the Chinese airlines plane), Ruth noticed, was the song "Bridge over Troubled Waters." A bridge was exactly what we wanted to be! We even had the drawing of a bridge as the logo on our special luggage tags.

As we got off the plane, fine dust, almost like talcum powder, still hung in the air from the dust storm and caught in the throat, making speaking without coughing difficult. Ruth remembered such storms from her childhood.

We were given a red-carpet welcome at the airport by our two official hosts, Ambassador Zhang Wenjin and Bishop K. H. Ting, president of the China Christian Council. Ambassador Zhang, as I have noted, was president of the Chinese People's Association for Friendship with Foreign Countries, a title that did not begin to describe his courtesy and helpfulness. He was often described as "Mr.

Integrity," and was among those who had negotiated with Henry Kissinger in confidential talks some years before. The association's vice president, Liu Gengyin (whom Ruth had met in 1980), was also there.

In addition to Bishop Ting, the China Christian Council was represented by its vice president, Han Wenzao. American Ambassador Winston Lord was on hand too, to remind us that we were not out of touch with home.

The drive into the city from the airport took us past rows and rows of newly budding willows, flowering forsythia, and blooming fruit trees, a reminder that spring was at hand. Ruth was amazed at the traffic and the construction that had taken place in Beijing since her visit eight years before; skyscrapers were rising, and the old one-story dwellings that used to blanket the capital city were rapidly disappearing.

The next evening, we were given a welcome banquet in the Great Hall of the People. This building is a massive architectural marvel in the center of Beijing. Constructed in less than a year, it is the home of the National People's Congress.

Outside, the building looked more Russian than Chinese; but inside, each room was decorated with magnificent wall-hangings and furniture of a distinctively Chinese character. We were told it had a separate banquet hall named for each of China's twenty-seven provinces and numerous other assembly rooms.

I sat at a huge round table beside Ambassador Zhang amid other distinguished officials, including Bishop Ting, Zhao Puchu of China's Buddhist Association, and Ambassador Lord. In the introductory remarks, Ruth was called "a daughter of China" and I "a man of peace."

In response to their greetings, I stated my conviction that Jesus Christ was the only hope for lasting peace in the world, as well as peace with God through the Cross. That was the keynote of all my speeches, sermons, and remarks during the next two and a half weeks.

As the first course was served, Ambassador Zhang made an announcement through his interpreter, Mr. Su Guang: "We know that present here are many believers of Christianity. We also know

603

that they have this habit of praying before meals. We all respect this habit. So those of you who want to pray before meals, we respect you, and please go ahead." We prayed silently and gratefully. Never in all my previous travels in the Communist world had this happened.

During the dinner, Bishop Ting took a worn photograph from his wallet to show Ruth. It was of his mother, who had died recently. "She prayed for me every day," he said simply. "I miss her very much."

How quickly my notions about China and its people, in spite of my briefings, were shattered! In a span of seventeen days, covering two thousand miles and five major cities, we packed in more speaking and preaching engagements, interviews, social events, and even sight-seeing than I remembered from any other trip I'd taken (though not as much sight-seeing as I would have liked). Journalist Ed Plowman and photographer Russ Busby chronicled the entire odyssey, which evolved into a pictorial book published by the BGEA. We also took a television crew with us to document our trip. Both foreign and American press interviewed us at many stages, but their coverage hardly hinted at the impact all those experiences made on me. Several events remain as special highlights in my memory.

One was our visit with Premier Li Peng, who had been chosen as head of state just two days earlier by China's parliament, the National People's Congress. His main task was to administer the country's modernization policy. He invited us to visit him on Saturday afternoon, April 16, at a traditional Chinese-style building called the Pavilion of Lavender Light. It stood in a corner of the ancient walled compound known, in the days of the emperors, as the Forbidden City; this is the area in which high-level government officials live today. I was his second foreign visitor, the first having been President Corazon Aquino of the Philippines. I knew Premier Li was somewhat familiar with us, since our visit was preceded by personal notes of introduction from Nixon, Kissinger, and Bush.

"Although we have different faiths," the premier said on greeting me through his interpreter, "that doesn't matter and will not be any obstacle to our dialogue." I found it interesting that he seemed to be referring to Communism as a "faith." A slightly different wording of his statement appeared in the Chinese press: "We don't have the same 'God' but . . . it doesn't prevent us from having a good talk together."

In either version, whether he used the word *faith* or the word *God,* his was a striking statement. It suggested that in the heart of every human being lay an awareness of the need for something, or Someone, higher than ourselves to give meaning to life—even the heart of a Communist. Whatever his statement meant to him, it gave us a point of contact with each other, and we moved on to matters of mutual interest, including the need for morality and ethics in society.

We sat side by side (with Ruth next to me), facing the rest of the room. Three interpreters—including our friend Sidney Rittenberg—were just behind us. Premier Li and I chatted amiably for fifty minutes as we sipped hot tea.

He asked us if we'd had a nice trip, talked about the room's furnishings, and reviewed his plans for China's modernization. When it came my turn to speak—the guest was expected to take equal time and no more—I got carried away and took off on the Gospel. "You really do believe what you preach!" he said, when he could get a word in edgewise.

Although Premier Li frankly stated that he was an atheist, he and I also discussed the potential role for Christians in China's new environment of openness. Diplomacy would have prevented me from quoting his words if the Chinese press had not, the following day, reported them in some detail. "China can never be prosperous and strong only with material development," he said. "It also needs spiritual forces. . . . To become a strong country, material achievement alone is not enough. We need moral power too. There are four fundamental elements for building up moral strength, namely: ideals, discipline, morality, and culture. It is important to start from young people, to give them cultural education."

In fact, the present Chinese constitution, Premier Li told me, guaranteed freedom of religious belief. With amazing candor, he made a concession that was also reported in the Chinese press: "In the past we didn't practice it in full. We are trying to correct the past." Then he added, "But I must say that there are not too many believers in China."

Somewhere in the conversation, I commented that maybe fifty years from now, China could become a leading world power in the moral realm.

"I hope so too," he said almost wistfully. "But at the present time we have many problems. All sorts of criminal behavior happen among the young people. They refuse discipline."

Our visit with Premier Li had an unexpected side effect. By going public on television, on radio, and in the press about our private conversation, the premier created visibility and credibility for us that we could never have gotten otherwise and opened many doors for us. For example, later we were able to have frank question-and-answer sessions after my talks to professional groups, students, politicians, and church leaders. In addition, it gave an unusual degree of visibility to the Christians and churches of China I was visiting.

During the trip, we also met with a wide range of civic and political leaders, such as the mayor-elect of Shanghai, Zhu Rongji, who later became China's vice premier for economic development. Accompanied by the former mayor of that city, Wang Daohan, our group had a refreshing and informative cruise up and down the busy Huang Pu River, which at Shanghai reaches the China Sea and forms the harbor of this great commercial port. We also had dialogue with teachers and scholars in academic settings such as the Chinese Academy of Social Sciences in Beijing and the Institute of Chinese-American Studies in Nanjing, a joint effort between Nanjing University and The Johns Hopkins University.

Especially memorable was our meeting at Beijing University (also known as Beida University). It had been founded by missionaries, and its first president was Dr. John Leighton Stuart, a missionary who also was the last American ambassador to China before the Communist Revolution. We met in the splendid old Chinese-style residence in which Dr. Stuart had lived. The students and faculty who had been selected to attend asked numerous questions, including some dealing with the nature of the soul and the meaning of personal faith.

In addition, we met with members of the diplomatic and international community at a luncheon at Ambassador Lord's residence; several religious leaders were there also, including China's leading

Buddhist, Zhao Puchu, and countless fellow Christians whose fortitude and faith under past sufferings put me to shame. Ambassador Lord's wife, the well-known writer Bette Bao Lord, returned from the United States just in time to be hostess at the luncheon; she was a delightful and knowledgeable conversationalist.

In no place we visited was there any restriction on what I could say, and I took advantage of that to expound the Gospel to respectful and attentive audiences.

At Nanjing University, I noticed a contrast between the American exchange students and the Chinese students. The American students wanted to know about the political and economic situation at home; theirs were secular, materialistic concerns. The Chinese, on the other hand, asked mainly religious and philosophical questions. In America the role models for students are more often than not entertainment or sports stars, but in China they have traditionally been scholars and philosophers.

Wherever I met with Chinese scholars, I was impressed by their focus on moral topics. They were concerned that the modernization program be undergirded with moral values, as the premier had indicated.

The 200 seminarians I also addressed in Nanjing embodied the promise of a spiritual revival in China, and I was deeply impressed by their commitment and their ability.

In contrast to these academic settings was our brief sightseeing visit to the Great Wall. For all that I had read about it, it was spectacular beyond my imagination: fifteen hundred miles long—so extensive that our astronauts were able to see it from the moon—and in parts twenty-five centuries old.

At the wall, a group of delightful young schoolchildren gathered around to serenade us with patriotic songs. We sat down cross-legged on the pavement while our group reciprocated with some Sunday school choruses.

Then Chinese-born Dr. Charlotte Tan, a distinguished leukemia specialist from the Memorial Sloan-Kettering Cancer Center in New York City (who was traveling with us), taught them in their own Mandarin language to sing "Jesus Loves Me, This I Know, for the Bible Tells Me So." (Dr. Tan is known and respected throughout

China and was in great demand to give lectures at leading medical universities while with us. Her husband, Dr. Moses Hsu, also accompanied us; he is a noted scholar and Bible translator for the American Bible Society.) Ruth enjoyed the very thought of my singing to the children, since I can't carry a tune. Charlotte Tan and my son Franklin joined in to help drown me out.

Certainly, a major highlight was the opportunity to preach in a number of churches. Visiting with Christians who were part of the Three-Self Patriotic Movement, as well as those involved in the unregistered or house churches, I sensed a tremendous spiritual vitality. When I preached in historic Chongwenmen Church in Beijing, with Hong Kong seminary president Philip Teng as my interpreter, 1,500 people packed the 700-seat sanctuary.

As I entered, I noticed women kneeling at the altar and praying. Among the crowd at the service was a delegation of ethnic Chinese from Brazil. I urged my listeners to include in China's ambitious modernization program a moral and spiritual renewal as well—or a values system, as I explained to Charles Gibson when he interviewed me via satellite from Beijing on the *Good Morning America* program. Most of all, I urged them to open their hearts to Christ and His transforming power and love.

Congregations of thousands gathered also when I preached in the Muen Church and the Pure Heart Church in Shanghai. These and other churches in Shanghai—twenty-three Protestant and twenty Catholic—had been packed every Sunday since the government allowed churches to reopen beginning in 1979. In fact, I was told, some people got up before daylight to make sure they had a seat inside the church. In my limited experience, the Chinese congregations were always attentive, with many people taking notes as I spoke. In some churches, I saw people line up at book tables to buy Bibles and other Christian literature.

We experienced worship in less formal settings as well. In Guangzhou (formerly Canton), we veered off the main streets, going down dark winding alleyways. The Chinese coming toward us must have wondered just where these foreigners were going. Soon we could hear singing ahead and above us. We arrived, unannounced but not unexpected, at a three-story building that held an independent house church. People were crammed everywhere, including on the stairways; three-quarters of them appeared to be young. On the first two floors, they were watching color television sets that were monitoring the service on the third floor. One of the security people assigned to accompany us everywhere eventually cleared a way up the stairs to the top floor, where the pastor wanted me to speak. It seemed as though everyone had a Bible, and it was clear that they knew their way around the book.

I gave a "greeting" for about twenty minutes, hoping that my unplanned participation would not cause any trouble for them with the local authorities. It was so hot and crowded that for a moment I felt dizzy and thought I was going to faint.

"I felt I had been to the catacombs and back," Ruth wrote later in her diary, comparing this situation with that of the churches in Rome during their times of tribulation.

How many Christians were there in China by this time? The China Christian Council claimed four and a half million Protestants in their ranks. There was no way of getting an accurate count of independent house-church Christians, of course, but by some estimates there might have been 30 million or more. While still small when compared with China's huge population of 1.2 billion, all observers agreed the churches had grown greatly during the "hidden years" of the Cultural Revolution and afterward, often because of the silent witness of the Christians' love and integrity.

There were also an estimated 4 million Catholics, who were joined together in the officially recognized Catholic Patriotic Association. Technically, they were not *Roman* Catholics, since they were not permitted to have formal relations with the Vatican; but for all practical purposes, they were Catholics. The Catholic bishop in Shanghai was most cordial when I went to visit him; he asked me to convey some of his thoughts to the pope, which I promised to do. He showed me a copy of the four Gospels that he had translated into contemporary Chinese for distribution among the Catholics.

For me personally, the undisputed high spot of the trip was my chance to see Ruth's birthplace in Tsingkiangpu. It was now part of the larger community of Huaiyin, a metropolitan area made up of several former cities and towns in what is now called Jiangsu Province, with perhaps a quarter-million inhabitants. It straddled the Grand Canal, the longest man-made waterway in the world, originally completed in the thirteenth century and stretching a thousand miles from Yangzhou to Beijing. A little section of that metropolis, now called Qingjiang, was the old Presbyterian mission hospital compound; there Ruth was born and spent her childhood and early teen years.

The station had been founded in 1887 by Dr. and Mrs. Absalom Sydenstricker, parents of Pearl Buck; Ruth's parents, as I mentioned, went there in 1916. We discovered that Moses Chen, one of the hundreds of babies Dr. Bell delivered there, was currently the organist in the nearby church.

In order to get to Huaiyin, army pilots flew us in an old Russian propeller plane to the port city of Lianyungang. Making the final approach, the pilots saw large, black water buffalo grazing on the landing field, with one or two of them on the runway. The crew buzzed the field once to scare the herd off and then landed.

The port holds bittersweet memories for Ruth, for she and her family had been forced to flee China by ship from Lianyungang in 1937, after the Japanese bombed Shanghai and foreigners were ordered out. Now, half a century later, she was back. On the trip by car to Huaiyin from Lianyungang, we passed through miles and miles of what Ruth called "old China," with little villages, mud farmhouses with thatched roofs, ducks, a small pond, water buffalo, and a few chickens. "I felt at home," Ruth wrote in her diary. "I'm sure I have peasant blood in my veins!"

Halfway through the drive, we stopped for a break at a beautiful spot by a large lake. We sat in a dining room, sipped tea, and drank in the tranquil scene.

For the last half of the trip, Sidney Rittenberg sat beside me in the back of the car, giving me another helpful briefing on the situation in China. The whole trip took several hours, so there was plenty of time for me to ask him questions.

When we finally arrived in Huaiyin, we were an hour and a half late. The mayor, Madame Xu Yan, a lovely, highly educated lady, was waiting. She took us straight to the banquet hall, leaving us hardly enough time to wash our hands. Then we were served a magnificent feast.

Afterward the mayor showed us a film about the whole province—an area largely given over to agriculture. She did the narration herself. Then she led Ruth and me to a large, newly redecorated room in the government guest house where we were to spend the night.

At the welcome banquet, we learned that there were still people around town who remembered the Bell family. On the next day came the moment we had all been waiting for. Our drive through the city was almost like a parade. Crowds lined the streets, and people leaned out of the windows to watch us go by.

About the first thing Ruth spotted as we approached the former mission compound was the gray brick house the Bells had built, with her favorite room on the top floor. I had heard so much about this place for the forty-five years we had been married that I think I could have found my way around it blindfolded. As if we were in the Louvre in Paris or the National Gallery in Washington, Ruth pointed out to us the things so cherished in her memory: the mantelpieces, the rusty hooks that used to hold a porch swing, the creaking wood stairs to her private alcove under the eaves, where she slept, read, meditated, wrote, and enjoyed the glorious sunsets.

"Love and Mercy" they had called the mission hospital. We were happy to learn that the earsplitting construction noises nearby heralded the restoration of the complex to its original use as a hospital, though now it would be under government auspices. In a larger building to be added, Chinese acupuncture and herbal treatments would be combined with modern medical practices. The city officials showed us an old stone slab that had been dug up; its Chinese characters read "Love and Mercy Hospital."

Quite a crowd had gathered while we were touring the site. When we came out of one of the buildings, several made a dash for Ruth. They were old patients, nurses, and household staff from the Bell era. To Ruth, it was the highlight of this trip home. They clustered around me too as I led the group in a prayer of thanksgiving for the ministries by loved ones we remembered that day.

At one point, Ruth told them how someone had once asked her father in his latter years how many of his old patients in China were still alive. He thought a moment, then replied, "I would guess 90 percent are now dead." Then he added, "Which only shows that what we did for them spiritually is the most important." As Ruth spoke, a face in the crowd lit up with an understanding smile—undoubtedly one who remembered and still believed what the missionaries had taught.

Reminiscences between Ruth and old friends crowded the hours we spent there. I thought of her father and mother, and of Ken and Kay Gieser. The latter couple had befriended Ruth and me in our student days at Wheaton. An eye surgeon in China, he too had been forced to leave by the Japanese.

Various mementos were given Ruth, including, in a beautiful satin-lined, brocade-covered box, those rusty old swing hooks from the front porch. It was her sister Rosa who had spotted the hooks on their visit in 1980; afterward Ruth sent the gift box to her.

At the local church, seventy-four-year-old pastor Fei Su, who had been there since 1936, told us that as many as 800 attended Sunday services now in the old missionary house of Jim and Sophie Graham, spilling out into the yard. When Ruth saw the house in 1980, it was a wholesale grocery outlet, the former living room decorated by a picture of Chairman Mao. Now many of the partitions had been removed to provide room for the Christian worshipers. Pastor Fei estimated there were 130,000 Christians in that area of the province. One church member told us that the pastor had spent some years in prison during the Cultural Revolution.

Like Pastor Fei, a lot of Chinese clergy were getting old. It was remarkable that they had survived so long. But with growth both in the number of churches and in the attendance at services, new leaders were urgently needed. The twelve seminaries in China had only 600 students enrolled, I was told—hardly adequate for future staffing of the thousands of pulpits.

As the trip reached its halfway point, I was beginning to understand the insights Sidney had shared with me about the challenge to churches in China. He jotted down some of those thoughts while we were in Nanjing:

"The principal obstacle to the spread of Christianity in China has, from the first, been that Christ has been presented as a white Westerner and Christianity as a foreign importation. . . .

"The great challenge for Christianity in China is: (1) to become thoroughly Chinese, and thus to become truly, universally Christian; (2) to help fill the spiritual vacuum that has been created by the collapse of Chinese Communist ideology."

From Nanjing we traveled to Shanghai by train, a journey of several hours. Shanghai is one of the world's largest cities, with a population of over 12 million; and it has been the center of some of the nation's major economic reforms. Our hosts from the Friendship Association in Shanghai met us with a large, luxurious limousine, the kind reserved for the highest government leaders. They were honoring us with their very finest, but we felt awkward going to our appointments in such a pretentious automobile. We asked them to please get a smaller car, which they kindly did.

I preached in two churches in the city, and at a meeting of pastors. I was impressed with the number of youth who were in the services. We also met with a number of civic leaders at a reception in the same room where the historic Shanghai Communiqué had been signed by President Nixon and Premier Chou En-lai in 1972, which opened the door to closer contacts between the United States and China. (Incidentally, as Nixon was going to the Beijing airport to leave China, he called me on the telephone. I was staying at a Holiday Inn in Vero Beach, Florida, and had been following his visit on television. T.W. and I were just leaving for an appointment when the White House switchboard rang and connected us. He said he wanted to call because he knew how much China meant to Ruth and me, and to say that he felt there had been a real breakthrough in our relationship with China.)

Another highlight was the opportunity to meet with Pastor Wang Mingdao, one of China's best-known church leaders since the 1930s. He was well known even outside China for his steadfastness in the face of persecution. At one stage during the Cultural Revolution, he was given a life sentence; and he was still considered a nonperson by the authorities. None of the police officers or

613

government officials traveling with us would accompany us to his place, but they were waiting for us after the visit.

Pastor Wang and his wife lived in a humble third-floor apartment on an out-of-the-way street. Old and thin, he was sitting on a metal chair, asleep, when we arrived, his head on his folded arms resting on the simple kitchen table.

When he awoke, I asked if he had a word from the Lord for us. He was silent for some time. "Be faithful, even to the point of death," he finally said, "and I will give you the crown of life" (Revelation 2:10). Certainly, this godly leader exemplified that verse. We stayed at least half an hour, and our conversation was almost completely about the Bible and spiritual things.

Our two-and-a-half-week visit did not make us experts on such a complex cultural and sociopolitical system as contemporary China. However, we tried to learn as much as we could during our days there. Whenever possible, I watched and listened and asked questions. As I told a group in Hong Kong immediately after the trip, one of the greatest things I learned was how much I did not know about China. As Sidney said repeatedly, anyone who pretended to be an authority on China was only showing his ignorance.

Since that memorable trip in 1988, I have returned to China twice, in both instances stopping over for a few days in Beijing before going on to North Korea. Both times (1992, 1994) I have been staggered by China's explosive economic growth, with massive traffic jams and skyscrapers under construction. On each visit, my feeling about China's strategic place in the future has been reinforced. We continue to pray for China, that it may become a spiritual powerhouse in the future.

It gives Ruth and me special joy that our younger son, Ned, has become deeply committed to China. He now heads a small organization based in the Seattle area called East Gates Ministries International, devoted to assisting the Church in China through training, literature, and Bible distribution. As I write this, East Gates has been given official permission to print several million Bibles at the

Amity Printing Press in Nanjing, a joint project of the China Christian Council and the United Bible Societies. These are earmarked for legal distribution to house churches throughout China—groups that have had no reliable legal source of Bibles in the past.

God is still at work in the ancient land of China, and for that we rejoice.

34

Through Unexpected Doors

NORTH KOREA 1992 AND 1994

North Korea was the last place on earth we ever expected to go.

For one thing, the United States and North Korea were technically still at war. The Korean conflict had ended in 1953, but with only a cease-fire, not a peace treaty. That meant that the United States, as part of the United Nations contingent fighting on behalf of the Republic of Korea (South Korea), was still considered an enemy by North Korea, which also blamed the United States for dividing the Korean Peninsula after World War II.

It also meant that we had been in a state of war with North Korea longer than with any other nation in our history. The presence of American troops in South Korea only reinforced North Korea's vehement hostility toward the United States—a view constantly repeated in North Korean propaganda. But, in fact, the danger of armed conflict was still very real. At the beginning of 1992, a few months before we went to Pyongyang, former President Richard Nixon called the heavily armed Korean border potentially the most dangerous place on earth.

A further problem was North Korea's nonreligious ideology. Under its founder and leader, President Kim Il Sung, North Korea

616

had developed its own distinctive ideological approach to Communism, called "the Philosophy of the Juche Idea." The word *juche* means "self-reliance," and their ideology stressed national self-reliance following a strict model of thoroughgoing socialism. As part of this philosophy, North Korea at one time had banned all religious activity and proclaimed itself the first completely atheistic nation on earth. It was probably the most closed country in the world at that time, not only to all religion but to Western visitors.

In the 1930s, under Japanese colonial rule, the northern part of Korea was noted for its large population of Christians and its many churches. Indeed, Pyongyang—as the most Christian city in Asia—was sometimes called "the Jerusalem of the East." After the 1953 cease-fire, however, there were very few Christians left in North Korea. During the conflict, thousands of Christians lost their lives; many thousands more fled to the south. Of these refugees, a fair number became church leaders during South Korea's explosive growth in Christianity. Although North Korea's antireligious policies had eased in the intervening decades to the point that two small churches (one Catholic and one Protestant) had been built in Pyongyang with government permission in the late 1980s, we still had no reason to believe North Korea would ever welcome a Christian evangelist.

But still I remained interested in that small, isolated nation occupying the northern part of the Korean Peninsula. One reason was that it, like China, had played a major part in Ruth's younger years. In 1933 Dr. and Mrs. Bell sent Ruth to Korea for high school in Pyongyang (then known as Pyeng Yang). Ruth joined her older sister, Rosa, who had gone to Pyongyang a year earlier; their other sister, Virginia, would follow them later.

At that time, the Pyeng Yang Foreign School, established and run by American missionaries, was considered one of the finest boarding schools in Asia, with a reputation for sending more candidates on to earn medical degrees and doctorates than any other boarding school of its type in the world. But in 1937, when the Japanese invaded China, the Bells were forced to leave briefly for the port city of Tsingtao; that was when Ruth left for the United States and Wheaton College.

617

In subsequent years, after our marriage, the conversation would often turn to North Korea, especially when Sandy Yates Gartrell, Helen Bigger Lopez-Fresquet, or other friends from Ruth's high school days dropped by for a visit. A surprisingly large number of former missionaries to Korea and Americans born in Korea have settled in the Montreat area. In later years, Ruth also kept close ties with Korea through her sister and brother-in-law, Virginia and John Somerville, who served as Presbyterian missionaries in South Korea until their retirement. Their son Walter married a fine Christian girl whose father was originally from North Korea. Some of his relatives were still there. Tragically, he had not been able to have any contact with them because of the political situation.

Perhaps these connections explain why I could not get North Korea out of my mind or heart. It was far more than simply the personal challenge of going to a place where the Gospel was virtually unknown.

I had been to South Korea a number of times and had many friends there. In fact, some of our largest meetings have been there; in 1973 we drew around 500,000 a night, with more than 1 million in Yoido Plaza on the last day.

My Korean friends told me that millions of Koreans on both sides of the border were separated from their parents, brothers and sisters, even spouses; and on my visits to South Korea, I heard many such stories of separation. Unlike the East Germans and West Germans during the days of the Berlin Wall, these Koreans had been unable to have any contact at all with their relatives for decades. It was one of the most heartrending human tragedies on earth, although not well known by many Americans. Could a visit to the north do something to alleviate this problem, even in some small way? My approach had always been that of friendship rather than confrontation. It had worked in other parts of the world. Why not in North Korea?

All this was only in the back of my mind, with no specific plan, until Henry Holley and I were talking in Hong Kong a few days after the Crusade there in November 1990. He had worked for us in Asia for many years and had directed many of our Crusades there. He too felt a special closeness to Korea, partly from his time there as a master sergeant in the U.S. Marines. We were discussing a number of invitations we had in Asia.

"Where can we go next?" I asked Henry.

"You have been practically everywhere in the world, except one place," he said to me, sharing a burden he'd had for many years. "This place I have prayed for because of my love of the region."

I asked him where it was, and he said North Korea.

We talked about whether a visit to North Korea would be possible, and he said he believed we could find an opening. Ruth's having attended high school in what was now the capital city might just be the key, and this turned out to be the case.

We agreed that plans for a North Korean trip should be kept highly confidential, even within the BGEA. A few weeks later, Henry asked me if John Akers could work with him on the project. I agreed to that as long as John could continue his other work at Montreat.

For some months, they pursued a number of approaches to North Korea, all of which turned out to be dead ends. The problem was simple: we had never met anyone from North Korea, nor did we know how to make the necessary contacts. Furthermore, the United States had no diplomatic relationship with North Korea.

Henry's first effort was through Christian friends in South Korea; but in spite of their deep concern for their fellow Koreans across the border, the hostility between the two nations was such that they were unable to make any meaningful contacts.

He then discovered that a limited number of Korean Americans, including some clergy, had been to North Korea. At first that seemed like a hopeful channel. But North Korea clearly was suspicious of them as well, assuming (rightly or wrongly) that they would have ties with South Korea.

We also made an approach to some of our Christian friends in China, but they felt that they could not get involved.

John even made discreet contacts with the Vatican through our longtime friend Father Jerome Vereb, who had coordinated each of my visits with Pope John Paul II. One of the two churches recently opened in Pyongyang was Catholic, we knew, but we discovered through Father Vereb that it was not permitted to have any direct contact with the Vatican and did not have any ordained priests. The Vatican was as puzzled as we were about how to establish some kind of dialogue, since all their approaches in the past had been rebuffed.

Finally, a retired missionary to Korea who was now living in Montreat, Dr. Joseph Hopper, suggested to Ruth that Henry and John contact Stephen Linton, a scholar at Columbia University's Center for Korean Research. Dr. Linton turned out to be one of the people God would use to open the door to North Korea for us. For some years, Steve and his wife, Wonsook, an internationally known artist born in South Korea, had befriended several diplomats who were part of North Korea's mission to the United Nations. (At the time, North Korea—or the Democratic People's Republic of Korea, as it is officially known—had only observer status at the United Nations.) Steve was an able and knowledgeable scholar and a first-class linguist; he had grown up in South Korea in a third-generation Presbyterian missionary family and was deeply committed to what we were attempting to do.

With Steve's help, then, Henry Holley made an appointment with the North Korean ambassador to the United Nations, Ho Jong. Ambassador Ho smoothed the way for Henry and the others of our advance team to visit Pyongyang. At first their discussions seemed as though they would not lead anywhere. I was unknown by the North Korean officials, and they were suspicious of our motives.

After further discussions in both New York and Pyongyang over a period of a year, however, an official invitation finally arrived from the Korean Protestants Federation, representing the nation's several thousand Protestants, for us to go to Pyongyang. My only regret was that Ruth, on the advice of her doctors, was unable to join us. My son Ned, however, was able to go, and I was glad to have him, for he has a deep interest in Asia; as my son, he was treated as number two in protocol.

From the first, we knew that this would be unlike any other trip we had ever made, including those to eastern Europe, the Soviet Union, and China.

One reason was the highly sensitive political situation. Like it or not, the North Koreans would assume we were coming with the full approval of the American government. They were aware, for example, of my personal friendship with President George Bush. But no matter how much I stressed that I was not coming as a representative of the American government and that my primary concern was spiritual and not political, they found my motives very difficult to understand.

Another reason that it would be a different, and indeed a difficult, trip was the unique position of President Kim Il Sung. Called "the Great Leader" by every North Korean, he was the only president the country had ever had; the deep, almost mystical reverence in which he was held by its citizens far exceeded anything we had experienced in other countries. He truly was a father figure to his people. Almost every public building and every home prominently displayed a picture of him, often alongside a picture of his son and heir apparent, Kim Jong Il, known as "the Dear Leader."

We spent several days in Tokyo recovering from jet lag and getting adjusted to the time change from America. Then we went to Beijing to secure our visas at the North Korean Embassy there. While in the Chinese capital, on March 31, we were received by the recently appointed vice premier, Zhu Rongji, whose task was to oversee the economic development of the nation. We had met him during our trip to China in 1988.

I appreciated his taking the time to see us. His sense of humor and his knowledge of the West made him a delightful conversationalist. We spoke not only about the economic problems China faced but also about his society's need for moral and spiritual foundations. I stated my conviction that God had given us those foundations in the Bible. Then I told him briefly about Ned's work assisting the Amity Press in Nanjing to print Bibles for China's house churches. We then presented him with one of the Bibles, which he seemed glad to receive.

That afternoon Ned and I flew into Pyongyang with the others in our small Team on the North Korean national airline aboard a Russian-built TU–134, an older-model jet plane similar to the American DC–9. In accordance with their established protocol, I brought a gift to present to President Kim Il Sung, as well as one for his son, Kim Jong Il (although we never did meet the son).

The gift for the president was a large porcelain figurine of American waterfowl, which our friend Mrs. Helen Boehm had kindly helped us select. It had been carefully packed in a very large crate to prevent breakage. Our television crew had transported it with their equipment from the United States, but when they tried to load it onto the North Korean plane in Beijing, they discovered that it wouldn't go through the small cargo door of the TU–134. They frantically discarded the outer protective crate at the airport in order to get it in; fortunately, it arrived in one piece.

When we stepped off the plane in Pyongyang, we were met by several church and government officials, as well as by a pretty little girl dressed in a traditional red Korean dress. With a shy smile, she presented us with a bouquet of flowers. The North Korean press was well represented at our arrival. CNN's Beijing correspondent, Mike Chinoy, and his cameraman had been given special permission at our request to fly with us. He was one of the very few Western reporters to be granted a visa in some years and was told that footage could be shot only if we were in it.

A few minutes after our arrival, we were escorted into a reception room at the airport for a formal greeting from a delegation of Christians representing the Protestant and Catholic churches. After Chairman Kang Yong Sop of the Korean Protestants Federation read his welcoming statement, I replied from my prepared text: "I do not come as an emissary of my government or my nation, but as a citizen of the Kingdom of God. As Christ's ambassador, I have come first of all to visit the Christian community here—to have fellowship with my brothers and sisters in Christ, to pray and to worship with them, and to preach the Gospel of Jesus Christ in your churches."

Then I added that although my visit was nonpolitical, as a Christian and a follower of Jesus Christ, the Prince of Peace, I could not help but be concerned over the tensions that divided our two nations. "The D.P.R.K. and the United States are not natural enemies. It is past time that the suspicion and enmity which have characterized our relations for the last half-century were replaced with trust and friendship. I pray that this trip may be a positive step in that direction."

That apparently was the right note to strike, for excerpts of my arrival comments were carried by North Korean radio and television that night.

After the brief welcoming ceremony, we were taken in official cars to a beautiful Korean-style government guest house on the edge of Pyongyang overlooking the river.

Pyongyang itself was a surprise—one of the most beautiful large cities I have ever visited overseas. It had been virtually leveled by Allied bombers during the Korean War. Because the city had to be rebuilt from scratch, all the buildings were relatively new. Unlike many of the cities in other Communist countries we had visited, careful attention had been given to imaginative architecture, wide boulevards, and inviting public parks; and maintenance was clearly a priority.

I will never be able to think of North Korea without having a mental image of large numbers of people vigorously walking, both in the city and in the countryside. The capital city had efficient public transportation, including a deeply buried subway system with magnificent mosaics and chandeliers (somewhat like the older sections of the Moscow Metro). However, there were no automobiles in Pyongyang, except cars imported for government use; and, unlike in China, we saw only a few bicycles.

Several highlights of that first visit remain vivid in my memory. One, of course, was the opportunity to preach in the two churches that had opened only a few years before. Bongsu Church (Protestant) seated several hundred people; Changchung Church (Catholic) was somewhat smaller, although of similar design. Both had fine choirs; the Bongsu choir even gave a moving rendition of "How Great Thou Art" in English. The Korean Protestants Federation had been permitted to print several thousand Bibles and hymn books a few years before for the use of believers, and they still had a supply on hand. Steve Linton's uncle, Dr. Dwight Linton, a former missionary to South Korea, interpreted for me in the churches and also spoke in Korean to a gathering of pastors and church workers who had come to Pyongyang for the meetings.

Although these were the only church buildings in North Korea, we were told that several thousand Catholics and Protestants, out of a population of 23 million, met in small groups throughout the country—usually in homes—under the supervision of an approved pastor or church worker. These believers almost exclusively came from family backgrounds that were Christian, dating back as

623

far as the prewar days; evangelism of nonbelievers was still discouraged. Most believers, therefore, were older, although we saw a few younger men and women in the services.

Whenever possible, I commended the government officials I met with on their policy of allowing Christians to come together for worship. I pointed out to them, as I had done in other countries, that I believed Christians were among their best citizens—honest and hardworking—and that I hoped the day would come when their existence was encouraged and not merely tolerated.

Another memorable opportunity came at Kim Il Sung University, the country's leading educational institution and the training ground for many of its future leaders. Very few Americans had ever seen the university or met students there. To our surprise, the university invited me to deliver a lecture to 400 students in one of its main lecture halls. First, though, school officials had to be assured that I would be giving an academic lecture, not preaching. By mutual agreement, I lectured on "The Influence of Religion on American Society."

When we arrived at the campus, we were taken into a reception room where four or five faculty and a few others waited to meet us. After a cordial greeting, the vice chancellor turned to me for a response.

Assuming it was time for me to give my lecture—though the group was much smaller than I had been told to expect—I pulled my written text out of my pocket and prepared to launch into it. Someone gently informed me that the lecture was scheduled for later and that here I was expected to give only a brief, spontaneous greeting. Apparently, I hadn't understood Henry's briefing about arrangements, or perhaps we had been given the wrong information.

In the lecture itself (carefully written with the help of John and Steve), I acknowledged that I was probably not only the first American but the first Christian most of them had ever seen. I gave a profile of the American religious scene and the influence of the Judeo-Christian tradition on our legal and social systems. Explaining that I felt it was important for me to begin by defining my terms, I proceeded to give an extended summary of what Christians believe: "The Christian believes that we are not here by chance, but that the sovereign, all-powerful God of the universe created this world, and He created us for a purpose. . . . Down inside we sense that something is missing in our lives. There is an empty space and a loneliness in our hearts that we try to fill in all kinds of ways, but only God can fill it."

The students were extremely attentive and not at all hostile, though some admittedly had puzzled expressions. The lecture was far different from anything they had ever heard. Although copies of my lecture had been passed out in English and Korean, I saw many students taking careful notes; perhaps they were uncertain whether they would be permitted to retain the printed copies. The university's vice chancellor later told me that I was the first American ever to address their students.

Certainly the highlight of the trip, from one standpoint, was our meeting with President Kim Il Sung. It was not confirmed until just hours before it was to take place. On the morning of April 2, Ned and I, along with our small group, journeyed through the countryside about twenty or thirty miles to the compound where President Kim had a residence. It was a hilly, wooded area that reminded me of our part of North Carolina. President Kim greeted us very warmly as the cameras clicked. Then he had our entire party line up for an official photograph, which appeared in the North Korean newspapers the next day.

We then went into a smaller room with a long table down the center. The North Koreans sat on one side and we on the other as we exchanged greetings in the presence of our respective staffs. I was pleased to note that President Kim had included the leaders of the Korean Protestants Federation and the Korean Catholics Association in the meeting. The vice premier and foreign minister, Kim Yong Nam, was also present. We had met with him for almost two hours in his office the day before; in a very interesting conversation, he had reviewed his country's positions on foreign policy.

I found President Kim to be very alert, with a deep, gravelly voice and a strong, charismatic personality. He made a special point of welcoming me warmly to the Democratic People's Republic of Korea. Then, pointing outside at the early signs of spring, he expressed the hope that a new springtime was coming in D.P.R.K. /

U.S. relations. He apparently wanted those remarks made public, for he stated them while the press corps was still in the room. After a few minutes, the reporters were excused, and we resumed our conversations on a more detailed level.

I congratulated President Kim on his upcoming eightieth birthday on April 15; everywhere in Pyongyang we had seen preparations being made for huge public celebrations of the event. After thanking me, he asked if he might see me privately, with only our interpreters present.

I had been in contact with President Bush concerning our trip; and shortly before our departure, he had asked me to convey a brief verbal greeting to President Kim, which I was glad to do. We had already indicated to our hosts that we had been asked to do this. Although it was not a detailed message, the mere fact that an American President was extending a greeting to the head of a nation with which we were technically still at war was symbolically very significant to them. President Kim responded by asking me to convey a similar verbal message in return.

Pope John Paul II had also asked me to convey a message—a rather detailed one—to the North Korean leader. President Kim listened carefully but had no response. Our contacts later indicated that the pope had presented too comprehensive a proposal for the North Koreans to accept at that stage, given the lack of previous contact between the Vatican and the D.P.R.K.

Following our meeting, President Kim invited our whole Team to a magnificent luncheon of Korean specialties, held around a single massive circular table in a large room overlooking the wooded hills. Once again the area reminded me of home. The final course was Korean watermelon, apparently grown in a hothouse and very sweet. I casually remarked that it was the most delicious I had ever tasted. The next day a crate of watermelons arrived at our guest house for us to take home with us!

President Kim also sent over a splendid hand-embroidered tapestry depicting two colorful pheasants in a spectacular wooded setting. The tapestry was encased in a beautiful wooden frame inlaid with mother-of-pearl. His son, Kim Jong Il, gave us a gift of an ornamental chafing dish carved out of jade. Ned and the other members of our group were also given special gifts.

One other highlight of the trip was of a more personal nature—a visit to the site of the old Pyeng Yang Foreign School where Ruth and her two sisters had attended high school. All the buildings had been destroyed by bombs during the Korean War, but our hosts had researched the school's location and took us to the site. The original compound was quite extensive, for it had housed not only the Foreign School but also a number of mission houses and a school for Koreans. An uncle of President Kim Il Sung is reputed to have attended that school.

The location, now occupied by the Russian Embassy, is only a few blocks from the Mansudae Assembly Hall, where North Korea's Supreme People's Assembly meets. It is also near the Potong, one of two rivers that run through Pyongyang. We couldn't enter the embassy grounds themselves, although the section we saw appeared to be disused. (The Russian government had only a limited diplomatic presence in North Korea following the collapse of the Soviet Union.)

An older woman who was an active member of Bongsu Church and had ties with the missionaries in former times accompanied us, pointing out where the various buildings had been located. Afterward Ned and I stopped by the nearby Potong Gate, one of the main entrances into the old walled city.

"This will be the only thing Ruth might remember," one of our hosts told us. "Actually, even this is new, since the original gate was destroyed during the war. But the Great Leader, President Kim Il Sung, ordered it reconstructed to give our people a link to their heritage."

Ned and I then wandered over to the park along the nearby Taedong River. Ruth had told us many times about trying to learn to ice-skate on the hockey field, which the school had flooded in wintertime. But she never learned; her ankles were too weak. The "Back Hill," which she remembered as separating the school from the river, was actually the remains of an ancient city wall dating back possibly to the time of King David in the Old Testament.

During our meeting, President Kim made a point of inviting Ruth to come to Pyongyang in the future, and perhaps it will be possible someday. He also made it clear that he valued our interest in his people and hoped we would continue our friendship.

I agreed to do so because over the years I had developed a deep conviction that personal relationships sometimes do far more to overcome misunderstandings and tensions than formal diplomatic efforts do. It was largely for that reason that I later encouraged former President Jimmy Carter to make his trip to North Korea during a very tense time in June 1994. I had no interest in getting involved in the details of the political issues that divided our two nations, nor did President Kim seek to talk with me about them. However, I could not help but feel that in his heart he wanted peace with his adversaries before he died. I found him very responsive to friendship on a personal level.

Did the visit help the churches in some way? We had no firm way of knowing, of course, but we found it encouraging that the following January, President Kim included the two leaders of the Protestant and Catholic associations in the guest list for his annual New Year reception, the first time they had been given that kind of official recognition.

In 1993, a year after our first visit, Ned returned to Pyongyang at President Kim's invitation and was warmly welcomed by him. Ned showed him a brief video report of our visit, taken from one of our television programs, as well as a picture book of the trip that we had published. Both of these seemed to please President Kim; we had taken pains to be objective, neither overlooking nor emphasizing our differences. I couldn't help but be reminded of the words of Jesus in what has come to be called the Golden Rule: "In everything, do to others what you would have them do to you" (Matthew 7:12).

Ned's visit resulted in a further invitation for us to return to North Korea. President Kim even suggested to Ned that he (the president) and I might spend several days together and go fishing, which he said he enjoyed doing whenever he could. As a result, we made tentative plans to return in July or August of 1994, if our schedule permitted.

In the meantime, however, tensions between North Korea and the United States threatened to come to a boiling point over the issue of the international inspection of their nuclear facilities. The suspicion was that North Korea might be developing nuclear weapons. Some Western political leaders advocated a strict economic embargo if North Korea did not comply; others even talked in terms of selectively bombing the nuclear facilities.

These proposals alarmed me, because I was convinced that such actions would only stiffen the resolve of North Korea's leaders and could easily pave the way to another major war on the Korean Peninsula.

Once again I had no desire to get involved in the specific issues, but could our relationship with President Kim make some difference? He and I held diametrically opposite religious and philosophical beliefs, but for some reason he seemed to value our relationship. I knew that almost no one else from the West had been granted that kind of access.

Accordingly, we scrapped our plans for a visit during the summer of 1994 and instead accepted an invitation to return to Pyongyang for a few days following our January 1994 Crusade in Tokyo.

Before leaving the United States, I talked with President Clinton and gave him a report of my planned visit to North Korea. I also expressed a willingness to convey a message to President Kim, and he said he would consider it carefully. However, we had not heard from his office by the time we left.

Once again Ned accompanied me. After Tokyo we spent several days in Beijing, where I preached in two churches, including one house church, and met with several government leaders. The new American ambassador to China, Stapleton Roy, had us to lunch and briefed us on the North Korean situation from his perspective. We had first met him at Ambassador Lord's luncheon in Beijing in 1988; he told us then that he had just flown in from Tibet.

Ambassador Roy conveyed to me a message of greeting from President Clinton to President Kim and asked us to deliver it if we were received by him. As before, the announcement of our trip was withheld by mutual agreement until only a few days before the trip

629

was to take place, and we still were not sure what our exact schedule would be.

North Korea, which shared part of its northern border with Siberia, had a reputation for being very cold in the winter. But it was a clear and comparatively mild day when we stepped off the plane in Pyongyang on January 27, and the weather stayed that way the whole time we were there. "It looks like the God you believe in has made good weather," one of our government guides said to a Team member with a twinkle in his eyes.

Once again I was invited to give a lecture at Kim Il Sung University, this time in their largest lecture hall. I spoke on the major problems facing the world, comparing them to mountains that had to be crossed before our world could ever have peace. I pointed out that as a Christian, I was convinced that the root of all our problems came from the human heart, and that our greatest need was spiritual in nature. We need to be changed in our inner beings, I said. "When we come to know Christ by committing our lives to Him," I added, "God comes into our lives and begins to change us from within."

As before, they listened attentively; afterward several of them went to a microphone and asked a number of questions. While at the university, I also dropped by a class in English for some informal discussion and visited a museum devoted to the student days of President Kim's son, Kim Jong Il.

Early on Saturday, January 29, 1994, we got word that President Kim Il Sung would receive us that morning. We journeyed through the now-familiar countryside to the same residence where we had been received in 1992; and I found him just as alert and friendly as before. He embraced me and then, with the press corps still present, greeted me with words that deeply touched me, particularly given the differences in our points of view: "I consider it a great honor to have a friend like you in the United States. You have become like a member of our family."

After the journalists were dismissed, we discussed a number of topics of a general nature, including the possibility of a visit by Ruth. Then we adjourned for a private meeting, accompanied only by our interpreters. I conveyed to President Kim the message President Clinton had asked me to extend to him. In turn he asked me to convey a confidential message to my President.

Unlike the brief message he had asked me to give to President Bush during our previous visit, however, the one to President Clinton was fairly extensive. Several times Steve, who was interpreting for me, stopped to discuss the exact meaning of certain phrases with President Kim's interpreter to be sure there was no misunderstanding. The message included a specific proposal that President Kim felt would break the logjam in the difficult discussions over the nuclear issue.

I also took the opportunity to speak very directly about my own faith in Christ—a faith that, I reminded him, his own mother had professed. He acknowledged that she had taken him to church sometimes when he was a boy, although he admitted with a smile that he had always wanted to go fishing instead. He listened respectfully to what I said but made little comment.

This second visit to Pyongyang was filled with unexpected events and opportunities. One day we went to the central television studio for an unrehearsed interview by several Korean journalists. Having never done anything quite like that before, the people at the studio were intrigued by the suggestions that our television director, Roger Flessing, gave them to make the interview more spontaneous.

"Never before has a religious leader been given this much public attention," one of our hosts said later.

On Sunday morning, I preached in the recently opened Chilgol Church, the third church building to be constructed in Pyongyang. It was located at the edge of the city, beside the birthplace of President Kim's mother. Her birthplace was preserved as a national monument, and we visited it in the crisp morning air before the church service. We also visited President Kim's humble birthplace outside Pyongyang, a national shrine to which hundreds of thousands of North Koreans make a pilgrimage every year.

Sunday afternoon we had an unprecedented opportunity to speak to a large gathering of about 1,000 at the main lecture hall of the Great People's Study House, which was similar in function and prestige to America's Library of Congress. Never before had a foreigner been permitted to speak there. Furthermore, we were told, it was the first time in North Korea's history that a meeting with a religious emphasis had been held legally outside of a church building.

Steve and John knew from their discussions that the decision to grant us permission to speak in a public place was fiercely debated behind the scenes, but we had no idea why the way had opened up. Whatever the reason, I was grateful for the chance to present the Gospel to people who would have had very little, if any, contact with the Christian message in their lives.

I spoke on Jesus' words in Matthew 5:13—"You are the salt of the earth"—stressing the need for personal renewal through the power of Christ if we were to be the kind of people our world needs. Every seat in the auditorium was taken. The audience, which we understood was made up mainly of political and economic leaders, undoubtedly had been carefully selected, but that did not bother me in the least, for God could open the heart and mind of any person by His Holy Spirit as the truth of the Gospel was presented.

As soon as possible, I detailed President Kim Il Sung's message in a private letter to President Clinton, along with some of my own impressions. A few days later, at a press conference in Hong Kong, reporters repeatedly tried to get me to reveal at least something of the message's content. Of course, I refused. All I would say was that one of my staff had already taken the first available plane back to the United States to convey the letter to the White House. The unexpected death of President Kim six months later made his specific proposal obsolete, but in my view the general principles behind it could still serve as a basis for future contacts.

In late 1995, Ned was able to pay a further brief visit to North Korea. And he returned in 1996 to deliver eight hundred thousand pounds of American brown rice, provided jointly by his organization, East Gates Ministries International, and the World Emergency Fund of the BGEA. North Korea was experiencing a serious food shortage due to devastating floods the previous year. Vice Premier Kim Yong Nam expressed his nation's gratitude to Ned and repeated the invitation for Ruth and other members of our family, as well as friends from the Pyeng Yang Foreign School, to visit the country.

We continue to have contact with North Korea, asking God to give us wisdom as we seek to let the people of that nation know not only of our own friendship but also of the love of God in Jesus Christ.

35

New Days, New Directions

THE INTERNET

I had spoken innumerable times to live audiences in every conceivable type of place, from football stadiums and cricket grounds to bullfighting rings and aircraft carriers. I had also spoken countless times to invisible audiences over radio and television. But this was a first for me. America Online, in collaboration with *Time* magazine, had invited me to visit its interactive electronic service shortly after my seventy-fifth birthday in 1993.

I was in an electronic auditorium, participating by computer in an hour-long live interactive program, or "chat session." The first 300 people who signed in were the audience, typing questions on their computers. Seated at a table to my right were some personnel from America Online, including someone they hired to type my replies into their central computer.

As I felt my way into the process, it seemed like a cumbersome way to communicate. The setting was awkward and unfamiliar. The room was dimly lit, and in front of me questions flashed on a large screen. Next to me were my Bible and a stack of reference works, just in case I needed them.

634

I could answer only about a dozen questions during the hour, and 300 people didn't sound very impressive as an audience. But then someone informed me that additional thousands were standing "outside" the electronic auditorium, observing every question and answer.

"If there was only one person in today's world that you could bring to Christ," one participant asked, "who would it be, and why?"

"Every person is important to the Lord," I replied. "I don't think one person is more important than another person in God's sight."

Occasionally, accuracy got sacrificed as my answers were hurriedly typed in. "Prince of Peace" came out as "Prince of Peach"!

It was a fascinating experiment, and I thoroughly enjoyed it. A year or so later, *Christianity Today* established its own service on America Online, making live interactive sessions on Christian issues a daily occurrence. By 1996 the BGEA had its own Internet website, and counseling for our December 1996 Christmas television special was done completely over the Internet (since the space normally made available to us by churches for our telephone counseling centers was being put to other uses during the holiday season).

Fascinating though it was, the experiment with America Online was only an extension of what we had been doing throughout much of our ministry: seeking to use every means possible to extend the reach of the Gospel. The *message* of the Gospel never changes—and for good reason: God never changes, and neither does our basic spiritual need nor His answer to that need. But the *methods* of presenting that message do change—and in fact they must change if we are to keep pace with a changing world. If we fail to bridge the gap between us and those we hope to reach, our message will not be communicated, and our efforts will be in vain. During this century, God has given us new tools to do His work—electronic and visual tools, such as radio, films, television, telephones—and each of these has played an important role in the expansion of our ministry.

TELEVISION AND RADIO

My experience with the Internet brings to mind a number of similar situations. Most preachers and teachers would say, I think, that talking to a live audience stimulates the speaker. It still astonishes me, however, to realize that I can be all alone in front of a radio microphone or a television camera and still reach more people than I ever could in a lifetime of personal appearances. That is not only why we have put on our own radio and television programs but also why I have gone on a wide variety of commercial and secular programs as a guest.

Over the years, I have been invited to make special guest appearances on a variety of television shows—far too many to recount here. I have accepted as many of them as I could, everything from *The Tonight Show with Johnny Carson* to *Good Morning America*. My friend Larry King has had me on his nightly CNN interview program a number of times. One of Phil Donahue's earliest programs originated from the Ohio Reformatory for Women, with the governor and me as guests answering prisoners' questions. I've also been on shows starring the likes of Jack Benny and Joey Bishop, Bob Hope and Steve Allen. (On these programs I was usually cast in a skit.)

Some of the programs I've appeared on reach back almost to the beginnings of national television in the 1950s and 1960s. Dave Garroway had me on frequently, and Hugh Downs, the host of NBC's *Today* program for years, also interviewed me many times. Merv Griffin had me on his show a number of times and became one of my friends in the entertainment industry. One night during the program he asked me to take over as emcee, and, if I wanted, even to preach; I did end up giving a sermonette.

One of the ablest interviewers I have known is David Frost. We first met when he came to our 1954 meetings in London's Harringay Arena. (David's father was a Methodist preacher, and his mother spent a vacation with Ruth and me in our home.) Some of those I've met in the media have become good friends. Paul Harvey, the radio commentator, has probably been my best friend in the American media. He has always been very supportive of us and often keeps his many listeners informed about our work. We have been guests in his home many times, with his delightful wife, Angel.

Sometimes people have questioned whether a minister of the Gospel should be on entertainment shows. When it was announced that I was going to appear on *Laugh-In*—a television show that sometimes included sketches that were risqué or profane—we received so many letters from our supporters that I had to draft a special response just to answer their concerns.

"My sole purpose in accepting these invitations," I wrote, "is to witness for Christ in a totally secular environment. Very few Christians have this opportunity. [It is important] to keep contact with the millions of Americans that never darken the door of a church. . . . It seems to me that this was the method of our Lord. He went among publicans and sinners."

Did these television appearances make any spiritual impact on the lives of the individuals who were watching? That, of course, is difficult to measure. Only God knows the answer. Time after time, however, we have heard of people with no religious inclination whatsoever who came to a Crusade meeting or tuned in to one of our television specials just because they had first seen us on a secular program. In their eyes (and, perhaps more important, in the eyes of their peers), my having been on such programs took away the stigma of going to a religious meeting to hear me in person.

Once while in Florida, we were staying in a house on the beach. A man walked by, recognized me, and came back to say he had been converted to Christ after watching me on *The Jack Paar Show*.

Some years ago, a university student from Berkeley flew down to attend one of our meetings in Los Angeles. At Invitation time, he came forward to accept Christ. "I became convinced that you had something I wanted," he told us later, "when I saw you on Woody Allen's show."

SATELLITE TECHNOLOGY

With the advent of satellites that could take a signal from one country or one continent and broadcast it instantly to another, our television ministry took a significant leap.

In 1985 we used satellites for the first time, to simultaneously broadcast our meetings from Sheffield, England, all over Great Britain (which generally does not permit the purchase of time for religious programming on television and radio). We were building on the pattern first established three decades before with the landline relays during our London Crusade. Those 1985 telecasts went to all kinds of venues, from theaters and civic auditoriums to parish halls. In each location, a portable satellite dish received the signal, and the images were projected on a large screen.

From time to time, we had already used a similar pattern of sending a television signal to auditoriums and halls across a country if it was possible, using normal television relay methods such as cable and microwave. For example, during the Euro '70 Crusade (April 1970), our meetings in Dortmund, Germany, were relayed live to thirty-six cities across the continent. However, satellite technology now made it possible to relay images from a meeting to an almost *infinite* number of locations.

After the Sheffield meeting, our staff drew up an ambitious plan to extend our ministry across the world through simultaneous live satellite links. I struggled with that decision almost more than anything else in my ministry. On the one hand, the idea of preaching the Gospel instantly to hundreds of millions of people was very appealing. On the other hand, the projected cost was enormous. As I relate later, in 1987 our board decided to put it on hold. (God gave project director Bob Williams and his staff added grace to cope with the frustration of this period.) In retrospect, I believe we made the right decision.

In the next few years, satellite technology leapfrogged. In 1989 we extended the outreach from our Crusade meetings in London through satellites, reaching two hundred and fifty locations in England, Scotland, Wales, Northern Ireland, and the Republic of Ireland. Three of the services were relayed by satellite to almost three hundred locations in thirty countries in Africa—some by simultaneous transmission, some by delayed broadcast. As part of this effort, we inserted testimonies and musical segments that were indigenous to Africa, and my message was dubbed into eight languages.

Subsequent satellite outreaches from Hong Kong in 1990, Buenos Aires in 1991, and Essen, Germany, in 1993 covered thirty countries in Asia and the Pacific, almost all of Latin America, and the continent of Europe, respectively. The statistics were mind-boggling. The Hong Kong telecasts, for example, were translated into forty-eight languages and reached an estimated 100 million viewers each night. A spinoff was a separate program for India in 1991, using eleven thousand sets of videotapes interpreted into twenty-three languages and dialects that were circulated all over that nation. Yet all of these were setting the stage for an even greater outreach using satellite technology.

GLOBAL MISSION 1995

In March 1995, we went to San Juan, Puerto Rico, for a Crusade in Hiram Bithorn Stadium. Next door to the stadium, in a huge indoor arena, our staff oversaw the installation of a dazzling array of technical equipment to transmit the meetings via satellite to venues in one hundred and eighty five countries and territories. One network executive from a major international satellite corporation said that our project was a more complex undertaking than the broadcasts his organization had done of the Winter Olympics from Norway the previous year. It may have been the most extensive single evangelistic outreach in the history of the Church.

Skilled interpreters in booths at the arena translated the messages simultaneously into forty-eight languages. Musical portions and testimonies appropriate for various areas of the world were inserted into the regional programs. For example, the Mandarin language version featured Chinese Christian musical groups and a testimony by tennis star Michael Chang. Some broadcasts went out on a "silent channel"—that is, with silence during the time my message was being interpreted into Spanish in San Juan, so that local interpretation into other languages could be added.

Thousands of places around the world were set up to receive the telecasts through small, inexpensive satellite dishes or by means of videotape; the signals were then projected onto large screens. Settings ranged from theaters and sports palaces in the former Soviet Union to the refugee camps of Rwanda and the rain forests of French Guiana.

In one African country that had recently undergone serious political turmoil, the meetings took place in the main city square. One local church leader said, "Three years ago we would have been arrested for suggesting religious meetings like this."

639

In the capital of one eastern European country, the meetings were held in the building formerly used by the Communist Party for its annual conferences.

South Korea had one hundred and twenty locations. One large Presbyterian church there trained every one of its 17,000 members to be counselors in the effort.

An estimated 1 million attended the meetings in South Africa, with 50,000 commitment cards returned afterward.

A student at one of the satellite meetings in Kazakhstan told her counselor, "I've tried everything, and now I turn to God as the last hope. . . . Something happened for which I've waited all my life."

A prostitute in Mexico who had consistently abused her children came forward in one meeting to confess her sins and give her life to Christ in the presence of her children.

Later, videotapes of these Global Mission programs were rebroadcast over national television networks in many countries, extending the audience by additional tens of millions. In some countries with a strong non-Christian tradition, we did not advertise the programs in order to avoid problems for the local sponsors; but we still heard many stories of people who came to Christ in those places. We were particularly surprised that the door opened in India for a specially prepared program that made extensive use of music and drama before the message.

Subsequent efforts have added new dimensions to our outreach by satellite technology. In December 1996, for example, a Christmas television special, taped in advance and including my message on the meaning of Christmas, was beamed by satellite in thirty-three languages to thousands of locations in over two hundred countries and territories.

TELEPHONE COUNSELING

In recent years, our television ministry in the United States has extended its impact through another use of technology. In 1980 we introduced a telephone-counseling service for viewers, which was in operation when our telecasts were being aired. Victor Nelson and the Reverend Noble Scroggins, our director of spiritual counseling at the time, saw it as a way to extend our ministry to people who otherwise might never talk with someone seriously about their spiritual or personal concerns.

Whenever we plan to air a television broadcast, several telephone-counseling centers are set up across the country, usually in churches or colleges that offer us their facilities. Local volunteers are trained by our staff to handle calls from people who want to discuss a spiritual problem or to commit their lives to Christ. Each center might have as many as a hundred telephones. Calls often continue many hours after the telecast is over. The caller pays the cost of the telephone call if it's long-distance, a policy that has cut down on frivolous calls. At no point are the telephones used to solicit funds.

Terry Wilken, our present director of the telephone ministry, estimates that half a million people called in during the service's first ten years of operation. One-fourth of those indicated a desire to commit their lives to Jesus Christ. Some calls came from people who were lonely and simply wanted someone to talk to; others came from individuals with deep personal problems. Calls were relayed to a telephone counselor at random, but time after time God's sovereignty was seen in linking a caller to a telephone counselor who had a special ability to speak to that person's need.

In one recent series, a man called to receive Christ, then went on to share that he was an epileptic whose problems were made worse by his weakness for eating too many sweets. His counselor revealed that she too was an epileptic and had struggled with the same problem. She shared with the caller how she had found help with her self-discipline through Christ.

Another caller spoke of her spiritual quest, which had led her into a particular cult. Her telephone counselor had been involved in the same cult before coming to Christ and was able to lead the woman to a saving faith.

The potential of new technologies can hardly be overestimated. True, the best witness for Jesus Christ will always be the personal witness of one individual to another. But vast sections of the world today still have little or no indigenous Christian witness. God has given us new tools to reach this generation. For centuries the preacher's audience was limited by the distance his voice could travel—a distance measured at best in tens of yards. Now that distance has become limitless.

EVANGELISM TRAINING

Evangelism has always been the heartbeat of our ministry; it is what God has called us to do. But for many years, I have been concerned about training others to carry on the work of evangelism. No one person or organization can do everything that needs to be done, nor did God intend it to be that way.

As I noted in Chapter 31, this concern led to our Amsterdam conferences for itinerant evangelists in 1983 and 1986. But evangelism takes place in all kinds of ways, not just through itinerant evangelists. The training of counselors in our Crusades, for example, has equipped a host of men and women for more effective personal evangelism. Time after time we have been told that even if a Crusade never took place, the training that went on ahead of time would have been more than worth the effort.

But early on, we were confronted with another question. Did God want us to train people for evangelism in a more systematic way? We sensed that the answer was yes, and this led to several extensions of our ministry, especially in recent years.

Schools of Evangelism

In 1957 California businessman Lowell Berry attended one of our meetings in Madison Square Garden. Although he was already an active church member, his life was particularly touched by the New York City meetings. "All of a sudden, I realized that many ministers weren't making the Gospel clear to their congregations," he said.

During the 1958 San Francisco Crusade, he approached me with the idea of some type of training program for pastors. Teachers for such a program could very well be our own staff and any pastors who had skills in evangelism. I told him it sounded like a good idea, but we were involved in so many other things that I soon forgot about it.

Some time later he tackled me again on the subject.

"Lowell, that's a good idea," I responded again. "But this would cost a lot of money."

Lowell looked me straight in the eye. "Well, I have a lot of money," he replied.

After talking with others and praying about the matter, we became convinced that God was leading us to develop such a program. I asked Victor Nelson and Bob Ferm to begin planning. After a couple of limited efforts, we started our first full-scale program during the 1967 Kansas City Crusade. A thousand pastors and Christian workers enrolled.

For years the schools were held only in conjunction with our Crusades. A school during our 1967 Japan Crusade, for example, brought 3,000 pastors together for specialized training in that largely non-Christian nation. As we were finding in all of our Schools of Evangelism, those who attended not only benefited from the training but also were greatly encouraged by their fellowship with pastors whom they never would have met otherwise.

We eventually expanded our schools to places where Crusades were not being held, such as Africa, Nepal, Papua New Guinea, and Malaysia, as well as cities in the United States and Canada. Under Norm Mydske, our director for Latin America, dozens of schools were held throughout Central and South America.

Lowell was true to his word, generously underwriting the program during his lifetime and after his death providing for continued assistance through the Lowell Berry Foundation. To date, 100,000 pastors and Christian workers have attended a School of Evangelism under the leadership of John Dillon and, in recent years, Larry Backlund.

The Cove

Many years ago, Ruth and I came to the conviction that a large number of Christians, particularly laypeople, needed a greater understanding of the Bible. But relatively few of them had the opportunity to study the Bible in a systematic and practical way. Even those who had gone to church all their lives often had only a scattered, piecemeal view of the Bible and its parts. We were also concerned about men and women of high visibility who were coming to Christ. They had no place to go to learn the Bible and be discipled quietly and without interference. Most of these laypeople didn't have the time to get involved in an extended program of study, let alone to enroll in a Bible college or seminary.

As we prayed about this problem and discussed it with others, Ruth and I came to believe that a series of seminars and programs, lasting anywhere from a weekend to a month or more, should be taught by the finest Bible teachers in the world. Our stated goal became "training people in God's Word to win others to Christ." Thus was born the vision for The Billy Graham Training Center.

What came into focus was something between a conference center and a Bible school. We began to explore a number of properties throughout the United States. An extensive but bankrupt hotel complex in Wisconsin. A venerable but aging resort in Asheville. And so on.

One day my brother, Melvin, discovered a pristine piece of property right under our noses. It was less than a dozen miles from our home in Montreat. A beautiful cove surrounded by heavily forested mountains, it comprised some fifteen hundred acres, now complete with an exit ramp from the interstate highway. Ruth and I hiked as far as we could over the property. The only structure on it was a caretaker's cabin. Praying as we walked, we sensed that this was the place God had preserved for a Bible-training center.

When we inquired, we learned that the property was about to be snatched up by developers. We moved quickly, and in 1973 we were able to complete the purchase of the whole property at a fair price. But we could not move ahead immediately with such a large project; we already had made heavy commitments for the Lausanne and Amsterdam conferences.

When we were finally able to turn our attention to the property again, we decided to make it available to a Bible college we believed had the skills to put together a comprehensive, Bible-centered program for training laypeople. As time went on, though, it became clear that the financial commitment was beyond the college's capability, especially in light of their own institutional needs. Accordingly, in 1987 the BGEA board approved the development of the project under our own auspices.

The first director of The Billy Graham Training Center at The Cove (usually shortened to "The Cove") during its early stages was one of our senior Crusade directors, Larry Turner, with Tom Phillips as program director. They were followed by Jerry Miller, a dedicated Christian layman who had been a vice president with Texaco in Houston. He took early retirement from his position, at a considerable sacrifice in salary, to come with us. He brought in highly experienced land-use planners and specialized architects, and he oversaw construction. My son Franklin was asked by the BGEA board to be chairman of the committee that would monitor The Cove's development.

Parenthetically, our treasurer, George Bennett, very wisely suggested that for every $1 we put into building and construction, we put $1 into endowment. We have attempted to carry out that plan over the years.

The first new building to be completed was the chapel. Donated by the Chatlos Foundation of Miami, it is one of the most beautiful in the Carolinas. The stones for its walls were quarried on the property. The next structures were the training center building itself and two hotel-style inns, Shepherd's Inn and Pilgrim's Inn. Under The Cove's present director, Neil Sellers, other buildings are in the planning stages, although it is not our goal to become a large facility.

A youth camp on the property also serves hundreds of young people each year, challenging them to a commitment to Jesus Christ and giving them the practical tools to teach them how to live for Christ and build their lives on His Word.

The only textbook at The Cove is the Bible. Everyone has an opportunity not only to study one or more books of the Bible but also to be trained in personal evangelism.

The Wheaton Center

Some years ago, we were approached by a major eastern university, and then by the Library of Congress, asking what we planned to do with the archives—the old letters, files, and so on—of our organization. I had never given a thought to it and I was surprised that anyone would be interested in them, but the Library of Congress urged us to make definite plans (whether we involved the Library or not). As with The Cove, once we accepted the need for such a facility, we investigated a number of possible sites. The city of Charlotte urged us to house our archives there; a civic group offered to purchase a tract of land near the new campus of the University of North Carolina at Charlotte.

But Dr. Hudson Armerding, president of Wheaton College, and the chair of the board, Dr. Ken Gieser, strongly urged us to consider a site on their campus. An academic setting was best suited for the archives, they argued, and what better place than the college from which Ruth and I had graduated? Furthermore, Wheaton College was widely known for its high academic standards; in fact, it was often called the "Harvard" of the evangelical world. Not only did they promise a site, but Wheaton College agreed to raise the necessary funds.

Although some of our board members had questions, I supported the decision to place the project at Wheaton, and the BGEA board gave its approval. In time, plans were expanded to include within the same building not only the archives but a library and museum devoted to evangelism, seminar facilities, and space for the Wheaton College Graduate School. (I have always had a special interest in the graduate school; as a member of the college's board when it was considering a plan to close the graduate school, I was among those who spoke against it.) The name finally chosen—and approved by everyone but me—was the "Billy Graham Center."

While construction was still under way, Wheaton determined that it was unable to raise sufficient funds for the project and could not carry through on its commitment to us after all. This presented us with a dilemma, partly because several members of the BGEA board were also members of the Wheaton College board. We found ourselves pulled in two directions, therefore, but in the end the BGEA board agreed to make it a joint effort, with most of the resources for construction and maintenance raised by us. The building is owned by Wheaton College, and a BGEA liaison committee consults with the center as it develops programs in the history and theology of evangelism and evangelistic strategy. I am grateful that the college has seen the center as a positive contribution to its academic life, and that it has enabled the graduate school to have an expanded ministry.

Groundbreaking for the project took place in 1977; two years later, the cornerstone was laid. In September 1980, the five-story colonial-style building was completed. It was certainly larger than I had envisioned, but it allowed ample room for future program expansion.

The main speaker at the dedication was Ambassador Charles Malik, a Lebanese Christian who had been president of the United Nations General Assembly. In his address, he noted the almost total secularization of the great universities, many of which had been founded by Christians, and discussed the negative impact this secularization has had on Western civilization. He eloquently and forcefully challenged evangelicals to take seriously their calling to reclaim the intellectual initiative in our world.

"I must be frank with you," he said. "The greatest danger besetting American Evangelical Christianity is the danger of anti-intellectualism. . . . The result is that the arena of creative thinking is abdicated and vacated to the enemy. . . . At the heart [and mind] of the crisis in Western civilization lies the state of mind and the spirit in the universities.

"Christ being the light of the world, His light must be brought to bear on the problem of the formation of the mind. . . . Therefore, how can evangelism consider its task accomplished if it leaves the university unevangelized? This is the great task, the historic task, the most needed task, the task required loud and clear by the Holy Ghost Himself, to which the Billy Graham Center most humbly addresses itself."

Today a major part of the Billy Graham Center houses the Wheaton College Graduate School. The building also includes a state-of-the-art archival facility, which houses not only BGEA records but also the archives of a number of other evangelical missions, agencies, and leaders from the past.

A specialized library on evangelism is also located there; with two hundred thousand items, it is one of the largest collections of its type in the world.

A recently redesigned museum on the ground floor is devoted to the history of American evangelism—including our own ministry.

Of the tens of thousands of visitors it receives each year, many register a commitment to Jesus Christ as they are challenged by the Gospel message.

The heart of the center, however, is its series of programs aimed primarily at Christian leaders and heads of Christian organizations. These leaders help develop strategies for evangelism and missions through seminars, conferences, and specialized research projects.

JAMMIN' IN THE DOME

It was Saturday evening, October 29, 1994. On the stage of Atlanta's vast Georgia Dome, a high-energy rap musical group called dc-Talk was belting out a number at top volume, to the obvious delight of the 78,000 fans packing the stadium, almost all of whom were under the age of twenty-one. A high-tech light show flashed and pulsed from a sixty-foot-high truss overhead, part of nine trailerloads of equipment brought in especially for the production.

As I stepped onto the platform, I couldn't help but recall the rock concert I had attended in Miami twenty-five years before. But this was a musical event with a difference. All the artists were Christians. "Jammin' in the Dome," as it was called, was a special youth-night outreach we had planned as part of our Atlanta Crusade. Did some from the older generation wonder if I, or they, had any business being there? I suspect so.

Admittedly, it wasn't really my kind of music, nor was it what we have ordinarily featured in our meetings during most of our ministry. But times change. As long as the essential message of the Gospel is not obscured or compromised, we must use every legitimate method we can.

Just as Michael W. Smith and dc-Talk have captivated the audience in several of our special youth meetings in recent Crusades, so it was with the music in Atlanta. After the concert, the young musicians introduced me, gave me big bear hugs, then sat down behind me as I prepared to speak, and the crowd of young people grew quiet.

I opened my Bible to the familiar words of John 3:16: "For God so loved the world that he gave his one and only Son, that whoever believes in him shall not perish but have eternal life."

After reading that passage, I lifted my head and exclaimed, "Tonight Jesus Christ is alive!"

No sooner had I begun than the crowd interrupted me with a roaring cheer. When they quieted down, I continued to talk to them—not as a preacher but as an older man sharing what he had learned with a group of young people who wanted to listen. I told them the old and yet ever-new story of God's love for us in Jesus Christ.

At the Invitation, more than 5,000 came forward to make their commitment to Christ.

They represented a new generation, with a new outlook on life, and a new approach. As we had done so often in the past, once again we had explored new ways of bridging the gap, reaching out to a changing world with the unchanging message of Jesus Christ.

36

From Arkansas to Washington

PRESIDENT BILL CLINTON

When *Christianity Today* commemorated the fiftieth anniversary of my ministry with a special issue, dated November 13, 1995, President Bill Clinton sent the following letter for publication.

"The first time I saw Billy Graham was in Arkansas when I was about 11. He came right into the middle of our state's racial trouble to lead a Crusade and to spread a message of God's love and grace. When the citizen's council tried to get him to agree to segregate his meetings, he said, 'If I have to do that, I'm not coming.'

"I asked a Sunday school teacher in my church to drive me 50 miles to Little Rock so I could hear Dr. Graham preach because he was trying to live by what he said. For a good while thereafter, I tried to send a little bit of my allowance to his Crusades because of the impression he made on me then.

"I was elated when Billy came to Little Rock for another Crusade a few years ago when I was Governor. We had the chance to spend a good deal of time together, and I have treasured his friendship as well as his prayers and counsel ever since.

"I am grateful for the way his ministry and friendship have touched my life and, even more, for the unparalleled impact his Christian witness has had throughout the world.

"I am honored to be able to share this tribute with you and your readers on this special occasion."

His words touched me and reminded me also that none of us who preach can ever know who may be in the audience—even a future president.

I first met Bill Clinton while he was governor of Arkansas. I had been invited to speak at the 1985 National Governors' Conference in Boise, Idaho, and he sought me out to ask if we could spend some time together. We went out on the lawn and talked for a couple of hours. His quick mind and his warm personality impressed me immediately. We met again during our September 1989 Crusade in Little Rock.

Shortly before the Crusade, Mary Anne Stephens (who at the time was the wife of one of the wealthiest men in Arkansas, Jack Stephens) flew over in their corporate jet to pick me up and fly me to the Crusade. The plane was late arriving in North Carolina.

"We were waiting for Hillary," Mary Anne said with an apology, "but she never showed up; that's why we're so late."

The plane was filled with socialites; and Hillary, I soon learned, was the wife of the governor. She had been left behind because of an unforeseen engagement, but when we landed in Little Rock, she was there to greet me.

A day or two later, she asked me if we could have lunch and talk.

"I would be delighted to," I replied, "but I don't have private luncheons with beautiful ladies."

"We could sit in the middle of the dining room at the Capital Hotel where everybody would be able to see us," she said, "and still have a private conversation."

Which we did. We talked first about Park Ridge, Illinois, where she came from. She had attended a Methodist church there, and I had preached in the church several times. Herbert J. Taylor of Club Aluminum, who had been chairman of both of our Chicago-area Crusades (as well as active in other Christian causes), went to that church also.

I didn't know much about Mrs. Clinton before that meeting, except that she was a lawyer. She impressed me as a genuine intellectual as we talked. She moved knowledgeably from one subject to another—from some government project or political issue to a family or personal matter and back again. I left our luncheon greatly impressed by her.

Governor Clinton was honorary chair of that Little Rock Crusade. He and Hillary gave a luncheon for us, with a few of the Crusade's strongest supporters and leaders of the state invited too, including former governor Orval Faubus.

During that time Clinton asked me a favor. "My pastor is dying of cancer," he said. "He lives several miles from here. I'd like to drive you to his home, and we can read the Bible to him and pray with him and encourage him. He has meant a lot to me."

His pastor turned out to be one of the leading evangelical pastors in the Southern Baptist Convention, Dr. W. O. Vaught, who had played a pivotal part in getting us to come to Little Rock and was widely loved and respected.

The governor drove me out there, just the two of us. We were greeted by the pastor's wife and taken immediately into his bedroom. He was propped up with pillows and had his Bible open. He was down below a hundred pounds, and we all knew his time on earth was short.

"W. O.," I said in greeting. "We're certainly praying for you at this time, that if it is God's will you will be healed."

"I have something to say to you boys," said W. O. "Sit down."

And he started in with his Scofield Bible on the Second Coming of Christ and the hope of Heaven we have as believers in Christ. In spite of his frailty, he gave us a real Bible lesson that lasted thirty, perhaps forty minutes without stopping. Finally, he finished.

"Now let's have prayer," he said. "Let's each one of us pray. We'll pray for the Crusade."

So Governor Clinton and I got down on our knees by the bed. The governor prayed first, a wonderful prayer. Then I prayed. Then Pastor Vaught closed. I know both Bill Clinton and I felt that we had received far more encouragement from our visit than we ever could have given to his pastor.

After Clinton's election, some people criticized me for agreeing to pray at his inauguration. On certain issues, the new President had taken stands that disconcerted those who were morally more conservative, including some evangelical Christians. I felt it was important to keep my commitment to pray, however, even if I did not agree with everything he held. I also felt a warm personal affection for Mr. Clinton, whatever his viewpoints.

I also wanted to assure Mr. Clinton of my prayers, for no President stands outside the need for God's constant help and guidance. That is one reason I have always agreed to lead prayers on such occasions whenever asked. Furthermore, the Scripture commands us to pray "for kings and all those in authority, that we may live peaceful and quiet lives in all godliness and holiness. This is good, and pleases God our Savior" (1 Timothy 2:2–3). When the Apostle Paul wrote those words, a pagan emperor ruled the Roman Empire, but that did not nullify the command. I asked one person who tried to dissuade me, "Are you saying you don't think Mr. Clinton needs our prayers, or that we shouldn't pray for him?"

The night before the 1993 National Prayer Breakfast—Clinton's first as President—Ruth and I stayed at the White House. The Clintons had the governor of Hawaii there too. At dinner that evening, Hillary Clinton had me to her right and the governor to her left; they talked much of the time about health care, a deep concern of the First Lady's. Ruth sat at the other end of the table on the President's right. My sister Jean and her husband, Leighton Ford, were also dinner guests. It was a delightful and informal time, almost like a family gathering. The next morning, the President and I both got up early and had quite a talk while he was getting ready for his morning run.

Afterward we went together to the Washington Hilton for the National Prayer Breakfast. My good friend Doug Coe (who has done so much in his quiet way to work with leaders and to foster the Prayer-Breakfast movement in the United States and many other countries) escorted us to the platform. I found the sincere words of both Vice President Al Gore and President Clinton acknowledging their need of God's guidance very moving.

Two events from President Clinton's first term in office will always remain in my memory.

The first occurred in 1995, shortly after the tragic bombing of the federal office building in Oklahoma City. By any standard, that bombing—which resulted in the deaths of 168 men, women, and children, and injury to hundreds more—was a senseless, barbaric act. The whole nation was in a state of shock, but no one was touched so deeply as the citizens of Oklahoma City and the state of Oklahoma.

The day after the bombing, I received an invitation to participate in a special memorial service for the victims of the disaster from Governor Frank Keating and his wife, Cathy. Just a few weeks earlier she had been taken to our San Juan, Puerto Rico, Crusade by Laura Bush, wife of Governor George Bush of Texas. Mrs. Keating was coordinating the Oklahoma service. President and Mrs. Clinton came also, and in his simple but deeply moving words he extended his and his wife's sympathy to those who had suffered the loss of a loved one. By his presence and his speech, he also conveyed to everyone in Oklahoma the clear message that the whole nation was standing with them in their grief.

I spoke also to the assembled crowd—one of the most difficult things I have done in my life—telling them frankly that I did not understand why God allowed things like this to happen. Our knowledge is limited, I pointed out, and there are some things we will never understand this side of eternity. I reminded them, however, that even though we do not understand, God does not change. He is still the God of love and mercy; and in the midst of our sorrow and pain, we can turn to Him in faith and trust.

The service itself was unforgettable, but I will always especially remember joining President and Mrs. Clinton as we met privately with some of the families who had been affected by the bombing. There were no television cameras or reporters around, and Mr. Clinton had nothing to gain politically by taking the time to be with them. And yet seldom have I seen anyone express so movingly and sincerely a genuine sense of compassion and sympathy to those who were hurting. I felt that he, not I, was the real pastor that day. I couldn't help but wonder if his own years of hardship and pain as a child had given him an understanding of the heartache and pain of those who suffer, whatever the cause.

The second occasion took place on May 2, 1996, when Ruth and I were presented with the Congressional Gold Medal, the highest honor the Congress of the United States can bestow on a citizen. Our local congressional representative from western North Carolina, Charles Taylor, had first proposed the idea (without my knowledge) to the congressional leadership. Then (still without my knowledge), he had enlisted the support and help of my colleague T.W. Wilson.

The medal itself depicted Ruth and me on one side, with an image on the reverse of the new Ruth and Billy Graham Children's Health Center at Asheville's Memorial Mission Hospital. T.W. had worked with the hospital on the project, and funds from the sale of bronze copies of the medal went to help provide health care for poor children throughout Appalachia.

I felt totally unworthy of the honor, which was first given to George Washington in 1776; ours, we understood, was only the 114th such medal awarded in America's history. And I was delighted that Ruth was included in the honor, for without her partnership and encouragement over the years, my own work would have been impossible.

The ceremony itself was held in the Capitol Rotunda, with a number of officials from both parties participating, including Vice President Al Gore, Speaker of the House Newt Gingrich, Senate Majority Leader Bob Dole, Senate President Pro Tem Strom Thurmond, and our two senators from North Carolina, Jesse Helms and Lauch Faircloth.

Mr. Gore's comments were especially gratifying, for they pointed beyond Ruth and me to the sovereign purposes of God. "You have touched the hearts of the American family," he said. "In presenting this Gold Medal of Honor, . . . the United States of America makes a powerful statement about what is truly important in our national life. You have touched that part of the American spirit that knows Providence has a greater purpose for our nation."

(His comment about the American family reminded me of a delightful evening I had spent in the Gores' home some months before. The Vice President proudly introduced me to their children, and then he and I had a relaxing candlelight dinner in their dining room.)

655

I was especially pleased that many members of our families could be present in the Rotunda, including our five children and a number of grandchildren.

In his remarks, Bob Dole, who has a terrific sense of humor, quipped, "When the idea of awarding the Congressional Gold Medal [to the Grahams] was first raised, it received something rare in this building—unanimous approval."

On a more serious note, he kindly added that historians would soon be issuing their conclusions about the most influential people of the twentieth century, asserting that "any such list will be incomplete if it does not include the name of Billy Graham."

Statements like that always humble me. If there is any truth in what Mr. Dole said, it is only because many thousands of people have prayed for our ministry and given financially to make it possible. I replied that Ruth and I were accepting the medal on their behalf also, and that we both felt very unworthy of all the remarks that had been made and of the honor itself.

The previous day, President Clinton called and asked me to stop by the White House. We ended up spending much of the afternoon together, talking not only about the past and current events but also about the Bible and what it says about God's plan for our lives. It was a time of warm fellowship with a man who has not always won the approval of his fellow Christians but who has in his heart a desire to serve God and do His will.

After the award ceremony in the Capitol, Mr. Clinton showed up at the dinner hosted by Memorial Mission Hospital. "I hardly ever go to a place as President [that] Billy Graham hadn't been there before me preaching," he remarked to the crowd. Then he recalled again his boyhood experience of going to our Crusade in Little Rock at a time of great racial tension, and the impact it made on his life. He also spoke of our visits together across the years. After his remarks, he presented me with a framed copy of the legislative bill that authorized the Congressional Gold Medal for us, and the pen with which he had signed it. Afterward we went backstage, and he gave me a long hug before departing. It was a memorable conclusion to a memorable day.

As the 1996 election approached, I faced what by now was a familiar dilemma: two friends running against each other for the same office. Some people who were strongly in favor of one of the candidates particularly pressed me to come out in support of their candidate, but I steadfastly refused to do so. During the campaign, Elizabeth Dole (whom I had known for many years) attended our Charlotte Crusade one evening, and her presence was noted from the platform; some people took that as an implied endorsement of her husband. On the other hand, my appearances with the President from time to time undoubtedly made other people conclude that, by implication, I was endorsing him. My own prayer was that God's will would be done, and that He would grant wisdom, compassion, and integrity to whoever was elected to our highest office.

That was my prayer also as I stood on the podium on January 20, 1997, as President Clinton and Vice President Gore were inaugurated to their second term in office. It has been my prayer for every president I have known, whether casually or intimately. The burdens and responsibilities of that office are enormous, and no person can ever fulfill its demands with his own strength, but only with the grace and help of Almighty God. President Clinton knows the reality of that truth; and as America approaches the dawning of a new century, I pray that all who follow him in that office may know it as well.

Reflections

37

A Team Effort

Many decades ago, just as our work was beginning to expand, one of the wealthiest men in America wanted to meet me. He got in touch with me through my old mentor from Florida Bible Institute, W. T. Watson. Dr. Watson took me to Palm Beach to meet him.

"Well, Billy," the gentleman said, "you should be able to put all your time into the type of work you're doing—revival work and getting the Word out like you're doing. You ought not to be spending time trying to raise money."

Then he added, "I'll tell you what I'll do. I'm willing to underwrite your work so you won't have to worry about finances. Would you like me to?"

"I can't accept that," I replied immediately. "My work is spiritual work. We are getting about fifteen to twenty thousand letters a week. Most of those letters will have a little money in them, maybe $1, maybe $5. But every one of those letters is saying, 'We're praying for you.' If they know there's a rich man underwriting my work, they'll stop praying, and my work will take a nosedive. So I can't accept it."

The gentleman meant his offer sincerely, and I thanked him for it at the time. But I have never regretted refusing it.

I tell this story to underline an important point. As I reflect back over half a century, I realize more than ever that this ministry has been a team effort. Without the help of others—our supporters, our prayer partners, our Team and staff, and our board of directors—this ministry would not have been possible.

Lord Nelson, the British naval commander whose victories around the turn of the nineteenth century made him a national hero, once said (following Shakespeare) that it had been his happiness to command a band of brothers. He knew he had not gained his victories alone. That also has been one of our secrets—a band of brothers and sisters committed to Christ and to our ministry, whose support, advice, counsel, work, and prayers through the years have made it all possible. I could not have done it alone.

THE TEAM

Because the name of Billy Graham is usually so prominent in the media, many people cannot understand that our ministry has been a team effort. The dedicated men and women working with us have been willing to do anything and everything. More than once I have gone out to a stadium or arena and found Cliff Barrows, Grady Wilson, Charlie Riggs, or Walter Smyth putting chairs in place. Once I discovered one of our senior Crusade directors cleaning the toilet in the men's restroom shortly before a service.

The central core of our Team has been with us almost since the beginning. I will never be able to repay the debt I owe them for their friendship and their sacrifice over the years. Cliff Barrows, Grady Wilson, Walter Smyth, George Wilson, Bev Shea, Tedd Smith, Esther LaDow, Charlie Riggs, Russ Busby, T.W. Wilson—each has been with me for at least three decades. In the case of Grady—now gone to be with the Lord—and his brother T.W., the ties reach back to our youth. Many others in the BGEA have been with us almost as long; like Grady, some (such as Willis Haymaker) have gone on to Heaven.

In order to do whatever needed to be done, they have subordinated their personal privileges, reordered their priorities, accepted disappointments and endless changes in schedule, stretched their patience, absorbed criticism, and exhausted their energy. They were the Heaven-sent ones who propped me up when I was sagging and often protected me from buffetings that would have scared me or scarred me otherwise. They did not back away from correcting me when I needed it or counseling me with their wisdom when I faced decisions. I'm convinced that without them, burnout would have left me nothing but a charred cinder within five years of the 1949 Los Angeles Crusade.

Grady Wilson

As long as I live, I will miss having Grady Wilson at my side. From the beginning of our friendship, he was my God-given balance wheel. He left the pastorate to join Cliff and me in our original Team, helping us part of the time in our Los Angeles Crusade and coming with us permanently shortly thereafter.

I can see him now in his favorite garb, wearing his white ten-gallon Stetson hat, a western-style jacket, blue jeans, and a pair of fancy cowboy boots. I can still hear that North Carolina drawl of his, spinning a familiar tale that kept us all fascinated—often because of the embellishments he added every time he told it. His easygoing nature and his down-to-earth sense of humor saved the day for me many times. He refused to let any of us take ourselves too seriously, and his humor defused more than one strained meeting or tense situation.

He also took great delight in reminding us of our mistakes—such as the time at a Crusade in Memphis when I noted a sign on top of the city hall announcing how many days it was since the city had a traffic death. I intended to say, "I congratulate you on 157 days without a fatality." Instead, my twisted tongue said, "I congratulate you on 157 days without a fertility!"

Whether he was playing a practical joke on a Team member or reading the Scripture lesson on *The Hour of Decision* broadcast, Grady's accent carried not only the hint of his beloved South but also, it seemed to me, the joy of Heaven itself.

Through our decades together, Grady took the pulpit at times when I was sick or had laryngitis. His style was different from mine, but the Holy Spirit used him to point people to Christ.

Even when major heart attacks and diabetes began to lay him low, Grady never lost his sense of humor or the twinkle in his eyes. Hardly able to get about at the end, he insisted on coming to our Crusade in Columbia, South Carolina, in 1987. My next service with Grady was his funeral a few months later. I say "with" because I know that Grady was more alive on that day than ever, freed at last from his pain-racked body and rejoicing in the presence of the Lord he loved and served. The nurses and doctors in the hospital where he spent his final days spoke of his sense of humor, joyous attitude, and warm witness for Christ.

Cliff Barrows

From the moment I met Cliff Barrows, I knew he had a rare combination of strengths. He loves music, and he knows also the importance of music in touching the hearts of an audience. His uncanny ability to lead a Crusade choir of thousands of voices or an audience of a hundred thousand voices in a great hymn or Gospel chorus is absolutely unparalleled. When he leads the choir in singing "Just As I Am" when I begin the Invitation, he is just as much a part of what the Holy Spirit is doing in people's hearts as I could ever be. That well-known Gospel hymn has been used by God in Crusades all over the world to draw people to Himself, not only in English but also in other languages as well:

> Just as I am, without one plea,
> But that Thy blood was shed for me,
> And that Thou bidd'st me come to Thee,
> O Lamb of God, I come! I come!

Like Billy Sunday's famous song leader, Homer Rodeheaver, Cliff played a trombone with the best of them—a talent we often used in our earlier Crusades. Ruth remembers one lady—someone recently returned from a remote missionary post (where apparently the only musical instrument was the drum)—who wondered how he managed to slide that instrument up and down his throat so easily! Cliff's wide contacts with Christian musicians and other artists have brought to our Crusade platforms some of the most inspiring and gifted soloists, instrumentalists, and ensembles in the world.

No one can keep the complicated Crusade platform proceedings running more smoothly than he, whether it is adjusting the pulpit up or down to accommodate a speaker's or singer's height or cueing up a song that wasn't part of the advance plan for the service. He has a dramatic streak in him too—one that has made him a spellbinding storyteller in our children's meetings (something we incorporated regularly into our early Crusades and have reintroduced in recent years).

Cliff has also overseen with great ability other aspects of our work. Production of *The Hour of Decision* broadcasts, with the assistance of Johnny Lenning, has been almost entirely Cliff's responsibility. He also has directed the work of World Wide Pictures. At present he has oversight also of the production of our television ministry, working with our director of communications, television producer Roger Flessing.

But all of that talent is not the secret of Cliff's effectiveness. It is his humility and his willingness to be a servant, which spring from his devotional life and his daily walk with Christ. The love of Christ so monopolizes his heart and will that he never seeks his own advantage at the expense of others or puts another person down. I trust Cliff, and I love him like a brother. No one except Ruth (or perhaps Grady and T.W.) has held so many of my confidences. That does not mean he doesn't have strong convictions of his own, or that, like the other members of our Team, he doesn't express himself freely.

Cliff is a rugged man, equally at home horseback-riding in the Rockies or clearing the brush around his house. But he also has the gentleness and thoughtfulness of a loving father or brother. He is a reconciler; he has held our Team and Crusade workers together many times by enfolding them in his own warm Christian spirit.

When Cliff's hearing was threatened by a tumor a few years ago, and then when his talented and gracious wife, Billie, was diagnosed with incurable cancer, Ruth and I were stricken. We rejoiced with them when Cliff's problem was alleviated, and we wept and prayed as Billie's condition gradually worsened over a period of several years. Her funeral service was actually a celebration—a celebration not only of her life but of the hope we have of eternal life in Christ.

Billie and Cliff had five wonderful children whom Ruth and I love almost as though they are our own.

Cliff now makes his home in Georgia with his wife Ann whom God, in His grace, brought into Cliff's life.

By Cliff's side on every Crusade platform is a talented team of musicians on the organ and piano. For years Don Hustad played the organ; then he left to become professor of church music at Southern Baptist Seminary in Louisville, where he has trained a whole generation of church musicians. For the past thirty years, John Innes, originally from England, has brought his considerable talents to bear on the organ for us (as well as serving as organist for a large church in Atlanta).

But through the years, I have always known who would be sitting at the piano on my right in virtually every crusade: Tedd Smith. A native of Canada and a graduate of Toronto's Royal Conservatory of Music, Tedd first joined us in 1950. One music critic in New Zealand said of his musical skills, "He compels you to look, listen, and think" through his music and poetry. Not only is he an accomplished instrumentalist, but he's also a talented composer and arranger—and a poet too. Often he has worked with Cliff in arranging music and coordinating musical programs. In the last few years, Tedd has helped us develop our special youth-night programs, which make use of contemporary music to reach a new generation with the message of Christ.

George Beverly Shea

No discussion of our music team is complete without mentioning Bev Shea. Like Tedd Smith, Bev was born in Ontario, Canada, where his father was pastor of a Methodist church. I have already told how we began working together during my brief pastorate in Western Springs, Illinois.

Bev was the very first person I asked to join me in evangelism. He was well known in the Midwest, but at the same time he was humble; he couldn't say no, even to a Fuller Brush salesman! It was God who brought us together. Bev will always be remembered as "America's beloved Gospel singer," whose rich bass baritone voice has touched the hearts of millions in our Crusades and through his sixty-five recordings; one of them, "Songs of the Southland," was awarded a Grammy.

I have sometimes said that I would feel lost getting up to preach if Bev were not there to prepare the way through an appropriate song. But I will always be grateful not only for his musical contributions to our Crusades but also for his warm spirit and his personal friendship over the years. I don't believe I've ever heard him utter an unkind or critical word about anyone.

In 1976 his wife, Erma, died after an extended illness. They had a daughter, Elaine, and a son, Ron, who has become a valuable member of our Crusade-preparation staff. After repeated nudging by Team members, Bev began to date one of the receptionists in our Montreat office. Karlene and Bev were married in 1985 in a candlelight ceremony in our home and now live only a mile from us.

Walter Smyth

Before there was a BGEA, I preached for Walter Smyth. That was in Philadelphia with Youth for Christ. I had the privilege of performing the wedding for him and Ethel many decades ago. When we started Billy Graham Films, I asked Walter if he would head the distribution department, to see that the movies got the widest possible exposure. He agreed to come, and we opened an office on Connecticut Avenue in Washington, D.C.

Afterward, Walter was the overall director of all of our Crusades, then our international director. He organized a number of our Crusades himself and usually traveled with me when I went overseas. Since his retirement, he has been one of the people I have missed the most. I can't put into words all that he has meant to me both personally and in the ministry.

T.W. Wilson

Grady's older brother, T.W., has been so much a part of my life since youth that I feel as if he has been with our ministry forever. A gifted evangelist who held citywide meetings for years before joining our Team, T.W. often is a wise and practical counselor to people in trouble. His humor and his willingness to work long hours have been a source of great encouragement to all of us. I've leaned on him in practical ways perhaps more than on any other person in recent years. Blessed with good health, he also has another ability I don't have: he sleeps soundly every night.

Like many other members of our Team, T.W. has had other responsibilities, including the supervision of our office staff in Montreat and the oversight of our radio stations.

T.W. has often overseen another, less pleasant side of our work: security. Unfortunately, anyone in the public eye has to contend with threats from people who are mentally unstable or, in our case, violently opposed to what we do. In many Crusades, we have had threats against me or the Team, and there have been repeated threats against my family.

Some have had a humorous side to them.

Once, many years ago, when Ruth was pregnant, she answered a knock at the door.

"I'm Jesus Christ," the man said, trying to push his way into the house.

"Well," Ruth responded, "why did you have to knock? Why didn't you just come in through the closed door?"

He stopped and scratched his head, then got back into his car and drove down the mountain.

Other threats were really attempts to disrupt meetings. In 1980 I was invited to speak at the Oxford Union, Oxford University's famed debating society. Not a few future British prime ministers had honed their analytical skills while members, in part by learning to dissect the views of visiting speakers. Over the years, I was told, many distinguished men and women had refused to appear as guest speakers before the Union, fearing the merciless grilling they were certain to get in the question-and-answer period.

Nevertheless, I accepted the invitation and found the members very attentive. Their questions were thoughtful and, I felt, reflected a personal search for answers to life's basic questions. I had only one question I didn't know how to answer: "Why don't you pack up and go home?" Before I could think of a reply, his fellow students hissed loudly, and he sat down.

During that same visit to Oxford, I was speaking in the Town Hall. Some students from an anarchist group set off the fire alarm; others tried to shout me down. I just leaned into the microphone and kept on going, and the other students, ignoring the outbursts, listened all the more intently. Some of the anarchists climbed on the roof and cut the television cables through which we were transmitting to five other venues. After that meeting, Maurice Rowlandson, who represented us faithfully in Great Britain for many years as director of our London office, found his car surrounded by police, who were checking for a suspected bomb. It turned out to be a hoax.

But God was still at work. Canon Michael Green, who was active in coordinating those meetings, wrote me later that the student who did most of the shouting came to Christ later that night. Another student who made a commitment during the week said he did so mainly because of the emptiness he saw in the lives of those dissidents.

Still other threats were deadly in intent.

Once in Denver a man with a gun got into the stadium posing as one of the security officers; he had plans to assassinate me but was apprehended in time. In Cleveland one night, police arrested three men who were attempting to get on the platform at the Invitation—one with a knife, two with pistols. On still another occasion, police spotted a man with a rifle and telescopic sight in a tall building next to the stadium; he escaped but some weeks later was arrested on another charge.

In Oslo, Norway, a crowd of students blocked us wherever we went. When I met with King Olav, he told me they had done the same thing to him when he attended a church service. Shortly after our meeting began, the students broke out into shouts and screams. One man scaled the fence, cutting his hand on the barbed wire, and ran for the platform; he was determined to stop me. Team member Ralph Bell, who had been a star football player in his youth, tackled him just as he was about to reach the platform.

Not every threat has ended so happily. In Copenhagen, Denmark, a strong knock came at an arena door during the service, and a security guard opened it. Thinking the guard was me, someone threw acid in his face, and doctors had to fight to save his sight. I visited the guard in the hospital, thanking him for his faithfulness to his duties and lamenting the stiff price he had paid.

I am grateful for all those who have helped us with security over the years, although I can honestly say that I have never been nervous about such threats or been intimidated by them. My life is in God's hands, not those of someone who may oppose His work.

ORGANIZING THE CRUSADES

Every Crusade begins at the grassroots, usually with a group of concerned Christians who are burdened for their community and come together to seek God's will about reaching those around them for Christ. If they come to believe that a Crusade may be an effective way of accomplishing this, they contact our Minneapolis office.

For many years, Sterling Huston has been our director for North America. After a Crusade request comes in, Sterling visits the people who sent the request (if that seems indicated), and he meets with as broad a cross section of Christian and civic leaders as possible in the host city. Others who have broad experience with our Crusades, such as Larry Turner or Rick Marshall, also meet with local pastors and look at the practical problems, such as a suitable stadium, ease of access, and parking facilities. Those staff who work with our Crusades have sacrificed much, often being away from home for weeks at a time; and the debt I owe them is enormous.

Sterling was an engineer with a major industrial corporation before coming with us, and his analytical mind and careful attention to detail have been invaluable to me. He is a good example of a person who is gifted in ways I'm not and who has willingly used his gifts for the furtherance of our ministry. However, like everyone on our Team, he is also spiritually sensitive and is always concerned that we accept an invitation to a city only when God is clearly opening the door there. One of his key criteria is the level of prayer support in a city, for without that as a foundation, little will be accomplished spiritually.

Once a Crusade invitation is accepted, a Crusade director and a small support staff move to that city, often a year in advance. Their purpose is to assist the local committee in organizing every phase of the Crusade, from the recruitment of staff, ushers, and the choir to the construction of the platform and the raising of the budget. (The budget for each Crusade, by the way, is raised locally; afterward the finances are audited, and the audit is published in the local newspapers.) Every Crusade involves thousands of volunteers who have a deep burden for their community and come together using their various talents. Without them, an event of that size would be impossible. They are just as much a part of the Team as those of us who stand on the platform. And after each Crusade, it is our hope to leave behind people who have been trained or better equipped to use their gifts right there where they live.

ASSOCIATE EVANGELISTS

In an effort to reach as many parts of the world as possible, we have had several men with us over the years as associate evangelists. They have held hundreds of Crusades in almost every corner of the world, often in very difficult places. And during my Crusades, they have taken speaking engagements I have been unable to accept. Some, like Joe Blinco and Grady Wilson, have been called home to Heaven. Others, like Lane Adams and Leighton Ford, have gone into the pastorate or established their own ministries, and I rejoice in God's blessings on their work.

Grady was already with us when I asked young Leighton Ford to join us. He wanted to become an evangelist, but he was planning to go to the University of Toronto. I urged him and his parents to consider Wheaton College, which would train him for what he wanted to do. It was there that he met my sister Jean and married her, and he has been a wonderful brother-in-law ever since. After a career as a powerful associate evangelist with us, he felt led to fulfill his own vision of training small groups of evangelists.

Still others, like Roy Gustafson and Howard Jones, held Crusades from time to time, until their recent retirement. As our first black evangelist, Howard has had an impact not only in the American black community and in Africa but also in numerous city-wide Crusades. His son-in-law, Norman Sanders, has worked for us

671

for many years, both in the U.S. and in our international ministry. Roy knows the Middle East and the Holy Land as few others do; he has led hundreds of tours to the Holy Land that have made the Bible come alive for thousands.

Roy has also had a great impact on my son Franklin's spiritual growth and on his eventual decision to become an evangelist. He invited Franklin on several trips, helping him to become very knowledgeable on the Middle East, both religiously and politically. In the time since, Franklin has been a guest of the prime minister of Israel, the king of Jordan, and other leaders in that area.

Dr. Akbar Abdul-Haqq continues to hold Crusades in his native India (where they are called "Good News Festivals"), as well as in other countries. He has one master's degree in Oriental languages and another in philosophy. His doctoral degree from Northwestern University is in the history of religion, with a minor in systematic theology. For four years he was president of the Henry Martyn School of Islamic Studies. It is no wonder that he has been effective, especially among university students.

Another native Indian, Dr. Robert Cunville, keeps a busy schedule in his own country; he has held Crusades in many other places too, from Nepal to Wales. His humble spirit and his single-minded commitment to evangelism never cease to inspire me.

Until a stroke interrupted his ministry, Dr. John Wesley White held Crusades in countless towns and cities across America as well as his native Canada, and he hosted his own religious television program in Canada. With a D.Phil. from Oxford, John could have had a brilliant career in the academic world, but I have seldom met a man who had a deeper burden for evangelism. His unique brand of eloquent preaching is unforgettable. I have been especially grateful for the way John has been a mentor to Franklin, encouraging him and helping him develop his own skills as an effective evangelist. In addition to his other responsibilities, Franklin is now an associate evangelist with our Team. More than once I have said he is a better preacher now than I was at his age.

Another native of Canada, Ralph Bell, has substituted for me on occasion when illness has prevented me from preaching. A forceful and clear preacher of the Gospel, Ralph has not only held numerous citywide and church Crusades but has also had an especially fruitful ministry in prisons, one of the most difficult places to preach.

An able staff assists the associate evangelists in working with local churches and organizing their meetings. In addition, a fine group of gifted musicians have devoted their talents to the associate evangelists' Crusades. Franklin has experimented with new musical directions in his Crusades, utilizing a variety of groups and artists, from the Gaither Praise Band to singer Dennis Agajanian.

BOARD OF DIRECTORS

In 1957, during the New York Crusade, I took a brief break one day at insurance executive Roger Hull's home. On the way up the Connecticut turnpike, we talked about the organizational burden I was carrying.

"Billy, someday you're going to be embarrassed over this," he said to me. "You don't have a strong board. You've handled it well, but one of these days it's going to catch up with you. I think you ought to expand to a board of responsible businessmen who'll handle your finances."

We took Roger's advice, but in a way he hadn't expected. At the board meeting in November, we named him our first outside board member. In addition, we named a number of others, most of them businessmen: E. O. Spencer, Dr. V. Raymond Edman, J. Colgate Buckbee, Carloss Morris, Leighton Ford, Dr. Nelson Bell, and Dr. Roland Scherer. Cliff voiced the strong conviction, in which all the Team and board of directors concurred, that I should remain chairman of the board.

Over the next decade, I turned over all authority to the board. In time they appointed an executive committee. It meets frequently—usually every six weeks—to oversee the Association's business in detail. No paid employee of the BGEA—including myself—is a member of the executive committee of nine men and women, and an employee can attend an executive committee meeting only by invitation. The board also has a number of working subcommittees, such as the audit review committee and the personnel committee; and unlike most nonprofit religious organizations, we have an internal auditor.

Before anyone is officially invited to join the board, he or she is asked to affirm their commitment to the BGEA's principles, theology, and goals. Each person is also required to pledge that he or she will make the BGEA a priority and won't miss meetings, unless providentially hindered.

Most, if not all, have been busy men and women with many other responsibilities. They have been generous in their financial support, but we have never sought board members because of their ability to give. The most valuable assets they bring are their wise counsel and their practical experience. We have a separate board in Canada to oversee our work there. Our subsidiary organizations, such as World Wide Pictures and our two radio station units, likewise have separate boards.

I hesitate even to mention the names of some who have served on our BGEA board over the years (because for lack of space I have to omit many) whose contribution was invaluable at some stage. Nevertheless, a number of board members will always be uppermost in my memory. Allan Emery, Jr., became chairman of the executive committee and was later elected president of the BGEA. Financial adviser George Bennett has been a valuable member of the executive committee for many years; he was treasurer of Harvard University and also served on the boards of Ford Motor Company, Hewlett-Packard, and other major corporations.

Among the others were Houston title company executive Carloss Morris, Dallas baking company executive Bill Mead, Los Angeles pastor and black community leader Dr. E. V. Hill, department store executive Frank Coy, California automobile dealer Guy Martin, newspaper publisher and former ambassador to Spain Richard Capen, business entrepreneur Mary Crowley, corporation president Bill Pollard, Holiday Inns co-founder Bill Walton, seminary president Dr. Arthur Johnston, and Dr. Roger James, who has long been my local physician.

I miss those board members who have retired or gone ahead into the Lord's presence. Even if their names are not included here, I

674

am certain their mark on BGEA is lasting. I am sure I have not been worthy of the professional interest and prayerful involvement of the men and women—almost seventy at last count—who have served at one time or another on our board across the years. They have been personally loyal to me, but they have cared enough for the Lord's work to put the welfare of the BGEA above my agenda whenever that seemed wise.

Several of our Team continue on the board, such as Cliff and T.W.; their wide experience in evangelism is invaluable. Dr. John Corts, who is currently president and chief operating officer of the BGEA, also serves on the board. I have retained the position of chairman of the board.

My own son Franklin—who heads the Christian relief organizations Samaritan's Purse and World Medical Mission—joined the board in 1979. In 1995 the board unanimously elected Franklin as first vice chair, with the understanding that he would take over the leadership of the BGEA in the event of my incapacity or death. It was not an easy decision and our board studied the whole matter carefully, but I have been delighted at the way Franklin has matured in his new responsibilities and his ability to preach. I never dreamed he would become an evangelist in great demand in different parts of the world. Franklin's appointment not only ensures the continuity of our organization, but it also signals a renewed commitment by the board to the vision for world evangelism that gave birth to the BGEA. As one of our recent published annual reports stated, we're "grateful for our past, expectant for our future."

My work style—if it can be called that—has been to encourage free-wheeling discussion in board meetings and then to try to bring about a consensus. I cannot think of a major decision the board has ever made without coming to full agreement. If after extensive discussion a minority has still felt strongly opposed on any matter, that's been reason enough to question whether we really had the mind of the Lord in the matter. Every one of us in the BGEA takes seriously the admonition of Proverbs: "Plans fail for lack of counsel, but with many advisers they succeed" (Proverbs 15:22).

Several years ago, when our staff was excited about going on satellite television throughout the world, our executive committee turned it down. However, when we took the matter to the full board, they voted overwhelmingly to override the executive committee. That is the only serious division of vote I can ever remember us having in our history.

Inexperienced in board politics as Franklin may have been at the time, he urged the board to reconsider, suggesting that instead of trying to go worldwide, we should take one section of the world at a time and experiment to see whether it worked. After reconsideration, that's exactly what we did. As things turned out, it was the right decision.

FINANCES

Like it or not, money is an essential part of any ministry, and safeguards must be put in place to avoid abuses or misunderstandings and to handle all finances with integrity and openness. Most of our financial support comes from the thousands of people who send contributions to us every month. We have no large foundations behind us, and we are dependent on relatively small gifts to meet our expenses every year.

To maintain contact with those contributors, I write a monthly letter informing them of what we are doing and requesting their prayers for our work. At the end of each letter, I mention the financial picture and briefly invite them to share the challenge. We have always felt we should tell people straightforwardly what the financial situation is and then trust God's promise that He "will meet all your needs according to his glorious riches in Christ Jesus" (Philippians 4:19).

I write each letter; we have always avoided hiring professional fund-raising or public-relations organizations to help us with them. We could make large sums of money by selling or renting our mailing list to other organizations or commercial companies, but we have strictly refused to do so.

The other side of finances is expenses. Our executive committee oversees the budget, and all expenses are scrutinized carefully to be sure they are necessary. The board has also instituted policies about major expenses or the buying of equipment; approvals must be obtained before these are purchased.

Several years ago, we asked one of the largest and most distinguished law firms in America to assess our organization and its affiliates in every possible detail. After a two-year study, they reported that they had rarely found any organization, secular or religious, with higher standards or better financial controls. The Internal Revenue Service has audited us exhaustively and each time has commended us for our carefulness in financial matters. Our annual audited report (done by a major national accounting firm) is made public every year to anyone who desires it. Our able vice president for finance, Joel Aarsvold, has been with us for many years and constantly oversees our financial health and integrity.

When a few highly publicized financial scandals rocked some nonprofit organizations in America a few years back, we helped found the Evangelical Council for Financial Accountability, an independent agency to monitor the financial integrity of its member organizations. George Wilson was its first president.

MINNEAPOLIS AND MONTREAT

What goes on in the BGEA's main office? Almost every part of our ministry is supervised or coordinated from there. One department handles the incoming mail and makes sure letters are answered quickly and gifts are acknowledged with a receipt. Another section, our Christian Guidance Department, gives personal attention to letters from people seeking answers to personal problems—everything from a troubling Bible passage to a threatened suicide. Two hundred thousand letters a year are answered by the staff in this department; some are referred to people who can provide specialized counseling service in various parts of the country.

I can never say enough about the highly skilled and dedicated people God has given us; I only wish I could list them all, for they have been invaluable. When George Edstrom, one of our key people in Minneapolis, died some years ago, I honestly wondered whether the BGEA would survive, so dependent had we all become on his sound judgment and leadership with our staff.

Minneapolis is also the location of the staff of *Decision* magazine, which has one of the largest circulations of any Christian magazine in the world. Each issue is posted by our large mailing department, as are our monthly letters. World Wide Publications and World Wide Pictures are also headquartered in our Minneapolis offices.

Still another department deals with our associate evangelists and our Team, coordinating schedules and arrangements and assisting with the associate Crusades.

Our Schools of Evangelism, which train several thousand pastors a year, are also administered from Minneapolis.

On a much smaller scale is my personal office in Montreat, which includes T.W. as office manager, my secretary, and several other support staff. More than one businessman has told me that his own work would have been impossible without a good secretary, and that certainly has been true of me. My longtime secretaries Luverne Gustavson and Stephanie Wills each have brought their own personalities and gifts to their responsibilities, as did Wanda Ann Mercer and Martha Warkentin Bridges. I have marveled at their patience and their abilities, even under the pressures that often come with deadlines and unexpected events.

GEORGE WILSON

I can never think about our Minneapolis office without thinking of George and Helen Wilson. George helped build efficiency into our infant organization from the start. He never made a major move without proper authorization, keeping me fully informed of our activities, checking with me on every hiring development, even getting my approval for expenditures that I sometimes thought were trifling. As the Crusades increased in number and size, and as our radio and television ministries expanded and our mailing list grew, the Minneapolis office became indispensable. It also freed me from negotiations with local committees about Crusade accounting procedures and budgets; all of that, George took over.

In 1951—the BGEA's first full year of operation—we received 180,000 letters. By 1954 we were forced to hire about eighty employees to handle mail and take care of other administrative duties. Soon we purchased an aging office building in downtown Minneapolis, formerly used by the Standard Oil Company. In addition, we opened small offices in a number of foreign countries to handle film distribution, publications, foreign language editions of *Decision* magazine, and other evangelistic outreaches. At one time, we had offices in such diverse places as Hong Kong, Paris, London, Buenos Aires, Mexico City, Berlin, and Sydney. All of those were eventually closed as the need for them lessened. We had a thousand employees scattered among our various offices; now we are down to about five hundred full-time employees. We still maintain an office in Winnipeg for our many Canadian supporters and friends.

Admittedly, our first few years were rather informal organizationally. Often George and I would make major decisions just talking in the hallway for a few minutes whenever I was in town. We were flying by the seat of our pants, uncertain what the future held and not having any pattern to follow. No evangelist before us, for example, had ever faced the problem of getting organized to answer mail on such a scale. But we were constantly trying to keep pace with the opportunities God was opening up for us, and we were determined to maintain the strictest standards of integrity and accountability, in line with the commitments we had made several years before in Modesto.

George became a self-taught expert on office efficiency. Indeed, the *Wall Street Journal* once ran a story on the innovations he introduced to answer our mail and minimize our administrative expenses. At times he could be stubborn and determined. More than once I lost patience with him—and he with me, I suspect! But no one was more loyal or more committed to our ministry.

When George retired, Dr. John Corts was appointed by our board to replace him. John had been with BGEA for a number of years, involved in a wide range of responsibilities. After several years as president of a Christian college in Florida, he returned to oversee our Minneapolis office. His skills and ability to encourage those who work with him have been invaluable.

We have always refused, after holding a Crusade in a city, to allow our name to be used to perpetuate any local organizations or movements. Sometimes, for instance, ushers or counselors have wanted to form a permanent organization under the Graham name. That response is gratifying testimony to the fellowship they have discovered, and we're thankful for it, but we have consistently refused to allow any continuing organization to be formed using our name. Our complete support goes to the local churches that have invited us to come.

Much of my time over the years has actually been spent on organizational matters. Hardly a day passes that I'm not talking on the telephone or handling correspondence or meeting in conference about an administrative matter or a decision that can't be made by anyone else. Yes, at times I chafe under the load and yearn for the simpler days when our organization consisted of little more than a secretary or two. Because my heart is in the preaching, the ceaseless pressure of running a large organization can be oppressive.

The key has been our Team—a faithful and gifted staff that has carried the greatest part of the burden and relieved me of all but the most pressing administrative decisions and duties.

1996

With Grady Wilson and President Lyndon
Johnson, sharing a joke at the President's
Texas ranch.

Leading a prayer at the inauguration
of President Richard M. Nixon,
January 20, 1969.

With President Ronald Reagan at the Presidential Medal
of Freedom Ceremony at the White House, 1983.

Golfing with President
Gerald Ford, 1974.

Exchanging views with President Jimmy
Carter during a trip to Atlanta.

With President and Mrs. Bush the night the Persian Gulf War began, January
16, 1991. The inscription reads, "Billy—Thank you for being with us at this
critical moment in world history—Geo. Bush."

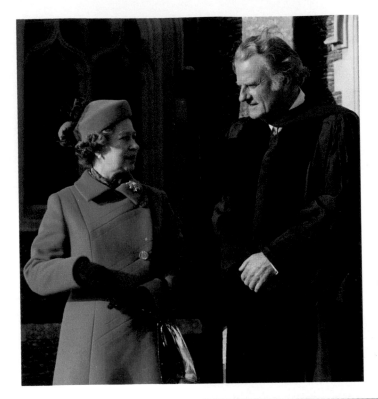

With Her
Majesty Queen
Elizabeth II,
following a
chapel service
at Sandringham,
1984.

George magazine editor-in-
chief, John F. Kennedy, Jr.,
interviews me in New York,
1996.

Famed boxing
champion
Muhammad Ali
visits us in our
Montreat home,
1979.

With Pope John
Paul II at the
Vatican, 1993.

Russian President
Boris Yeltsin
welcomes me to the
Kremlin following
the close of the 1991
Moscow School of
Evangelism.

In the Kremlin office
of President Mikhail
Gorbachev of the
Soviet Union, 1991.

On our fiftieth wedding anniversary, August 13, 1993, with children *(from left)* Ned, Gigi, Franklin, Ruth (Bunny), and Anne. Ruth is wearing her original wedding gown.

Speaking in the rotunda of the U.S. Capitol during the presentation of the Congressional Gold Medal to Ruth and me, May 2, 1996.

In the Oval Office with President Bill Clinton, 1996.

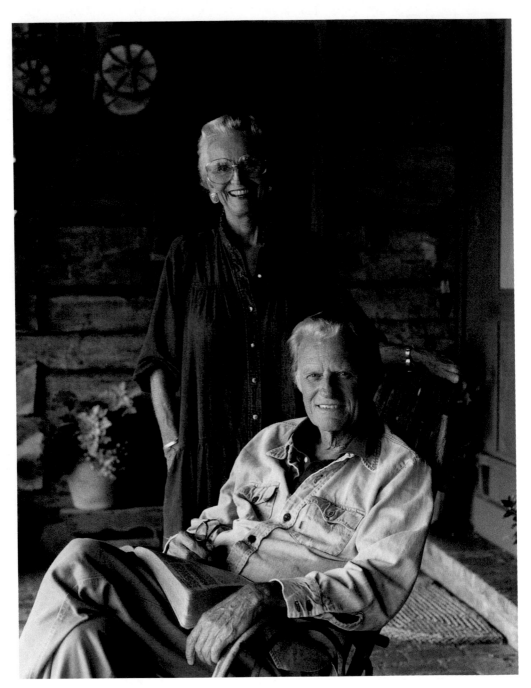

Relaxing at home, 1993.

38

A Half-Century of Friends

"Velma, you're going to beat us home. Tomorrow night you'll be in the arms of Jesus," I said to her on my home telephone just hours before her execution by lethal injection.

"Praise the Lord!" she replied with confidence in her voice.

Velma Barfield had become addicted to drugs and, by her own admission, had poisoned four people—including her mother—in cold blood. Now, after living on Death Row for six years while waiting for the legal system to exhaust all her appeals, she was about to become the first woman to be executed in the United States in twenty years.

We had never met in person, but she certainly was no stranger. For some time, Ruth had carried on a correspondence with her and talked with her over the telephone. Our daughter Anne visited her often in prison near Raleigh, North Carolina, praying with her and leading her in Bible studies. At Velma's request, Anne would witness her execution.

Velma turned in faith to Christ for forgiveness and became a vibrant, committed Christian shortly after her arrest. Her sins, she

681

firmly believed, were completely forgiven by God. All that was left for her to do was to pay society's ultimate price.

She did not take what she had done lightly; she had committed horrible crimes, and she knew it. Nor did she take God's forgiveness lightly, for it had cost Christ His life on the Cross. Yet through that death, she knew, God had demonstrated His love for sinners—even for a wretched sinner like herself.

"If I had the choice of living free on the outside [of prison] without my Lord, or living on Death Row with Him," she told Anne repeatedly, "I would choose Death Row."

Just a few months before her last day, Velma finished writing, at Ruth's urging, the story of her tragic life, a life filled with turmoil, drugs, anger, depression, violence, and—finally—the grace of God.

"I want my story told because I hope it will help people understand what God can do in the life of one loathsome and desperate human being," she wrote. "I understand what the Apostle [Paul] meant when he called himself the chief of sinners."

"God has turned your cell on Death Row into a most unusual pulpit," Ruth wrote her. "There are people who will listen to what you have to say because of where you are. As long as God has a ministry for you here, He will keep you here."

As I picked up my phone in Montreat to talk with her that last day of her life, I made sure my Bible was open before me on my desk. I knew she would want me to read some passages to her.

The next day she went peacefully to her death, her lips moving in silent prayer.

A month later, Anne and I slipped into the North Carolina Correctional Institute for Women for a special service. Virtually all the guards and inmates were present. I preached from John 3:16, pointing to the life of Velma Barfield as an example of what God can do in the life of a person who is committed to Christ. Prison, I told them, was one of the hardest places on earth to live as a Christian. A person's life is under constant scrutiny, and many inmates are cynical about supposed religious conversions. But Velma had demonstrated the reality of Christ through her life, and everyone present at that service knew it.

When I gave the Invitation, 200 responded, including several guards.

While there, I also went to the cell where Velma had been held in maximum security before her execution. "You know, since Velma's death, I just couldn't bring myself to come in here," the warden told me. "On the night of her execution, she was the happiest, the most radiant human being I ever met."

Why do I begin this chapter on a half-century of friends with the story of Velma Barfield?

One reason is that her life exemplified a central theme of the Christian faith: God's forgiveness in Christ is available to all, no matter who we are or what we have done.

Another reason is to emphasize that most of my ministry has not been spent with famous people, whether in the entertainment field or the financial or political arenas. Over the years, I have met so many of the rich and famous in many countries that it's impossible to mention—or even remember—them all. But presidents and royalty aren't typical of the people I've had contact with. Velma isn't typical either, to be sure. Still, 98 percent of my time has been spent with people who were never in the public eye.

Frankly, I'm reluctant to speak about the other 2 percent. I don't want to be accused of name-dropping. But I have crossed paths with a wide spectrum of leaders from all kinds of fields—politics, religion, business, education, entertainment, sports. Richard Nixon once told an interviewer that I knew more international leaders than he did.

I did not know whether that was accurate at the time, but it was probably inevitable that people came to that conclusion. Whenever I played golf with a president or visited with a prime minister or was seen with a leading entertainer or sports figure, the media paid attention. In reality, though, very little of my total time has been spent with such people. It may sound impressive to say that we have been with Her Majesty Queen Elizabeth II on a dozen different occasions—but those twelve occasions have been spread over forty years.

If I seem to concentrate on some of those friendships, it is only because I have come to know some of these leaders in a pastoral way and others simply as friends. Although people who are constantly in the public eye usually learn to shield their inner thoughts, they have the same personal problems and questions that we do. Sometimes such people have felt free to talk intimately with me, knowing that I would hold their remarks in confidence. Some of them have had serious character flaws; and when I have been aware of these, I have tried to do what I could, speaking to them privately and pastorally from the standpoint of the Bible's moral standards.

If some readers of these pages are disappointed that I have not titillated them with juicy tidbits of inside gossip, so be it. Even when the pressure has been great to reveal what went on in a private meeting, I have tried to answer only in the most general terms.

After leaving a session once with Cardinal Lustiger, the Archbishop of Paris, a reporter demanded to know what we had talked about. I replied that he could assume we had talked about religion. In spite of his insistence, that was all he could get out of me. The Bible is clear: "Do not betray another man's confidence" (Proverbs 25:9).

I never go to see important people—or anyone else—without having the deep realization that I am—first and foremost—an ambassador of the King of kings and Lord of lords. From the moment I enter the room, I am thinking about how I can get the conversation around to the Gospel. We may discuss a dozen peripheral things first, but I am always thinking of ways I can share Christ and His message of hope with them. I make every effort to be sensitive to their position and their viewpoint, but I rarely leave without attempting to explain the meaning of the Gospel unless God clearly indicates to me that it is not the right time for this person. No one has ever rebuffed me or refused to listen to me.

One time, fairly early in my ministry, I did not do that. The businessman I was visiting had great influence. Perhaps he intimidated me, or perhaps I was concerned that I would alienate him if I appeared to be too religious. At any rate, I said little or nothing about Jesus Christ. Afterward I was so disappointed in myself that I went back to my hotel room and fell on my knees, praying that God would forgive me. I begged Him for another chance, but I had absolutely no reason to expect that our paths would cross again.

Unexpectedly, a couple of weeks later, that businessman asked to see me. In the course of the conversation, I had a very natural opportunity to present a clear-cut Gospel witness. The whole incident made me resolve never again to be hesitant about sharing my faith in Christ with anyone.

What have I learned from my contacts with people who are leaders in their respective fields, from politics and entertainment to sports and business?

Five things come to mind.

First, leadership has its own set of special burdens and pressures. The life of a celebrated star or a powerful politician may seem glamorous and exciting, but in reality it seldom is.

From 1955 to 1960, I met with several dozen heads of state, from the prime minister of Japan to the prime minister of Israel. (In fact, in connection with our international ministry, I have continued to meet a wide spectrum of leaders over the years, including virtually every prime minister of Japan and chancellor of Germany.) Almost without exception, they were deeply pessimistic about the future of the world and heavily burdened by their political responsibilities.

Several years ago, I was talking to one prominent leader who, I suddenly discovered, was on the verge of suicide because he was so discouraged about the world and the circumstances he faced. I tried to comfort him and point him beyond his problems to God, and he seemed to find some hope in that message.

Second, leadership can be very lonely. Many years ago, I was at a White House dinner honoring the Shah of Iran. As I went through the receiving line, he greeted me warmly and asked me to visit him in Iran. Following our meetings in Nagaland, India, in 1972, we let him know that we would be stopping over in Tehran. He invited me to join him for dinner during that stopover. When I arrived, he was sitting all alone in a large room watching a videotape of the previous night's news from the United States. As he turned the TV off, I could see the loneliness and isolation etched in his face.

In the 1950s, when I was in New York City, I would occasionally slip by to visit Dag Hammarskjöld, secretary-general of the United Nations, and have prayer with him. He was a very thoughtful,

685

if lonely, man who was trying to make a difference for world peace, in large part because of his Christian convictions.

Third, people in positions of influence are often used by others for their own selfish ends. As a result, they learn to be on their guard. It happens all the time. But I have often deliberately gone out of my way to avoid giving the impression that I wanted to meet someone because of what he or she could do for me.

This has especially been true of the business leaders I have gotten to know. One night I was the houseguest of Ross Perot, the billionaire industrialist. He was a member of Highland Park Presbyterian Church in Dallas, which my brother-in-law, Clayton Bell, pastors. I found him to be one of the smartest men I had ever met.

"Ross," I said as we chatted, "I want to get something straight right now. I'll never ask you for one dime of money. I want our friendship just to be between you and me, and no money involved."

"You know," he replied, "I've never had anybody say that to me. They're all coming here wanting money!"

Another extremely wealthy Texan I came to know fairly well was oil billionaire H. L. Hunt. From time to time he made a point of offering to support any special projects we might have. But he had a different set of priorities from mine. When plans for our pavilion at the New York World's Fair were taking shape, I showed them to him.

"Mr. Hunt," I said, "this would be a good time for you to invest in the kingdom of God."

"Why don't you have something against Communism up there instead?" he asked. "I'd pay for that."

"No," I replied, "this is just going to be pro-Gospel. We're just going to preach the Gospel in this exhibit."

He was disappointed and never gave us anything toward the project.

Fourth, people in the public eye are often looked upon as role models, even when they do not want to be seen in that way.

Once a prominent media personality and I were at a hotel in West Virginia together. We had been friends for years, but at the time of this meeting he was, in his words, at a crossroads. As he recounted later, "I was on the edge of messing up my personal life." Part of his problem was that he was rebelling against the idea of being a leader and an example to others. "I don't *want* to be a leader," he exclaimed repeatedly.

"Well," I told him finally, "it doesn't make any difference whether you want to be a leader or not. You *are* a leader. Now all we're going to do between now and daybreak is decide whether you're going to be a good one or a bad one."

As we talked and prayed, he yielded his will to Christ in a fresh way.

A nationally known television talk-show host once approached me about making a regular appearance on his program. Shortly afterward, on his show, he asked me a direct question about sexual morality. I answered from the Bible as graciously but clearly as I could. Later I discovered that he was involved in an extramarital affair at the time. He never invited me back.

Sports and entertainment figures especially are seen as role models in our society. Athletes like tennis star Michael Chang, professional golfers Gary Player and Bernhard Langer, and football coach Tom Landry have taken a stand for Christ. They and many others have become friends of mine over the years, and they have been involved in our Crusades and our satellite television mission projects to various parts of the world.

When Muhammad Ali, the heavyweight boxing champion, came to visit us in Montreat, he couldn't get over the fact that we did not live in a mansion with liveried servants and a chauffeur. He was also surprised when I met him at the airport in my ten-year-old Oldsmobile.

I autographed a Bible for him. He accepted it graciously, but when he looked at my unreadable scrawl, he asked T.W., "What does that say?"

"It says *God Bless You*, and it's signed *Billy Graham*."

Ali handed the book back to me.

"How about printing *Billy Graham* under that. I want people to know it's you when I show it to them!"

I laughed and printed my name in big letters.

One entertainment personality whose friendship Ruth and I have particularly valued is country music singer Johnny Cash, along with his wife, June Carter Cash. Johnny has won just about every award in his field, and his distinctive voice is loved by millions around the world. Some years ago, Johnny and June began coming to our Crusades to sing, and their presence and witness to Christ have drawn countless people to meetings who might not otherwise have come.

We have laughed together and cried together as families, sharing each other's burdens during times of illness and heartache. We've been guests in each other's homes on many occasions and vacationed together from time to time. We have no better friends than Johnny and June.

British pop music star Cliff Richard has likewise appeared at a number of our Crusades to share his testimony of faith in Christ. I will never forget a small dinner in London to which I had invited a dozen people. One of the guests that evening was a former prime minister, Sir Alec Douglas-Home. Cliff Richard was also included, as well as a prominent member of the royal family and her husband. Most of the conversation that evening revolved around Christianity—especially the deity of Jesus Christ. One of the guests could not accept this; he had been reared in a sect on the fringes of Christianity that denied the full divinity of Jesus Christ. Cliff exhibited an astonishing knowledge of the Bible and of theology that evening as they vigorously discussed what the Bible taught. I ended up saying very little, grateful for Cliff's willingness to take a stand for Christ.

Fifth, many men and women who are leaders in secular fields have given relatively little thought to God. They tend to be preoccupied with this world instead of the next. Occasionally, however, I do meet a leader who is perceptive spiritually. One such, I recall, was President Figueres of Costa Rica, whom I met in 1958.

"The problem of the world is very simple to me," he stated. "I am a Catholic, but I agree with you that the problem of the world is here." He pointed to his heart. "Until we do something about the human heart, we cannot solve the problems of the world."

Even more memorable was German Chancellor Konrad Adenauer. One time when I was preaching in Germany, he invited me to his office. Coffee was served, but before my first sip, he started in.

"Young man, do you believe in the resurrection of Jesus Christ?"

"I most certainly do," I replied.

"So do I. If Jesus Christ is not risen from the dead, there is not one glimmer of hope for the human race. When I leave office, I'm going to spend the rest of my life studying and writing about the resurrection of Jesus Christ. It's the most important event in human history."

Since so much of our ministry has been spent in Great Britain, we have had more opportunities to meet a wide spectrum of people in leadership positions there, including almost all of the prime ministers since 1954.

Margaret Thatcher welcomed me to Number 10 Downing Street. Both her parents were dedicated Methodists, and she had great sympathy for our work.

Prime Minister Harold Wilson likewise was always very cordial toward me. At our first meeting, we talked about the fact that the British Labour movement had some of its roots in the evangelical revivals of Moody and others in Great Britain during the nineteenth century. (During our trips to Britain I have tried to meet with people who are involved in all kinds of political parties and social movements. I recall, for instance, a serious but very friendly discussion I had with Arthur Scargill, the head of the National Union of Mine Workers, during a time of serious labor unrest.)

No one in Britain has been more cordial toward us than Her Majesty Queen Elizabeth II. Almost every occasion I have been with her has been in a warm, informal setting, such as a luncheon or dinner, either alone or with a few family members or other close friends. Out of respect for her privacy and that of her family, I will say little more.

Her official position has prevented her from openly endorsing our Crusade meetings. But by welcoming us and having me preach on several occasions to the royal family at Windsor and Sandringham, she has gone out of her way to be quietly supportive of our mission. She is unquestionably one of the best-informed people on world affairs I have ever met. Part of that knowledge comes from the weekly in-depth briefings she is given by the prime minister, of course, but I have always found her highly intelligent and knowledgeable about a wide variety of issues, not just politics.

Once, when visiting the royal family at Sandringham in 1984, Ruth and I walked past a woman wearing an old raincoat, Wellingtons, and a scarf; she was bent over fixing some food for the dogs. We thought at first she was one of the housekeepers, but when she straightened up, we saw it was the Queen!

At the end of that visit, a doorman came up to the car just as we were departing. He had a box under his arm, which he handed to our friend Maurice Rowlandson, who had come to pick us up.

"A brace of pheasants from Her Majesty The Queen, for Mr. and Mrs. Graham," he said.

All the way back to London we debated what to do with them. Maurice suggested we take them to the hotel chef to be prepared and roasted. In the end, however, I decided that would be a waste. I asked Maurice to arrange for them to be stuffed by a taxidermist. Eventually, they arrived at our Montreat home in a glass case—truly pheasant under glass! Later Maurice admitted that shipping the case from England and getting it through U.S. customs had been one of the greater challenges of his life.

On one occasion when I was in Great Britain, the Queen was preparing her annual Christmas address to be broadcast on television around the world. To illustrate a point, she wanted to toss a stone into a pond to show how the ripples went out farther and farther. She asked me to come and listen to her practice the speech by the pond and give my impressions, which I did.

I always found her very interested in the Bible and its message. After preaching at Windsor one Sunday, I was sitting next to the Queen at lunch. I told her I had been undecided until the last minute about my choice of sermon and had almost preached on the healing of the crippled man in John 5. Her eyes sparkled and she bubbled over with enthusiasm, as she could do on occasion. "I wish you had!" she exclaimed. "That is my favorite story."

I believe one reason for the Queen's spiritual interest was the warm faith of her mother, Her Majesty Queen Elizabeth the Queen Mother. The first time we were with her was at Clarence House, her residence in London. She had invited Ruth and me for coffee, and when we arrived she greeted us warmly and introduced us to Princess Margaret. We were there about an hour, and within five minutes we felt relaxed because they both were so gracious.

The Queen Mother also impressed me with her sensitivity. I recall how nervous I was the first time I preached at Windsor, and afterward we went to the Queen Mother's lodge for a little reception. I was talking with her and Princess Margaret when we were offered drinks. The Queen Mother saw me hesitate slightly and immediately said, "I think I will have tomato juice." I said I would have the same. I believe she had sensed that I probably would not take any alcohol and had acted instantly to avoid any discomfort on my part.

But more than anything, the Queen Mother always impressed me with her quiet but firm faith. The last time I preached at Windsor, as I walked in I saw her sitting over to my right, with others in the royal family. She deliberately caught my eye and gestured slightly to let me know she was supporting me and praying for me.

One thing that has always impressed me about the British royal family has been their patronage of numerous charities and social agencies. In 1966 Ruth and I were invited by Princess Margaret to attend a celebration at the Tower of London honoring Dr. Barnardo's Homes, an organization founded to assist impoverished children and orphans. We came directly from a Crusade service at Earls Court (which Princess Alexandra had attended that night), and when we entered I suspected some people wondered why we had been invited. It was an elegant affair, and the guests were dancing to the music of a live orchestra; I found out later it was the first time a charity ball had been held at the Tower of London.

Then Princess Margaret and Lord Snowdon entered as everyone stood and the orchestra played a special piece. They came over and sat at our table, and a little later she leaned over to me and said, "Dr. Graham, would you mind speaking to this audience for a few minutes?" That was the first I knew I was to say anything, but I said I would be happy to. Thankfully, I had just read the life of Dr. Thomas Barnardo. Most people there, I realized, knew little about the background of the organization, so I told them about Barnardo's conversion to Christ and how it had motivated him to establish the homes. When I sat down, Princess Margaret kindly said, "That was exactly what we needed to hear."

It has also been my privilege to meet a number of the outstanding Christian leaders of our time, many of whom I have already mentioned in these pages. One whom I have yet to mention—and with whom I felt a special affinity—was the Roman Catholic preacher Bishop Fulton J. Sheen. Like me, he was something of an itinerant preacher. I vividly recall the first time we met. . . .

Being in a private sleeping compartment on a train usually gave the measure of quiet and rest I needed before an important engagement. In fact, in the early years, I often went from home by train, particularly if I was going to Washington or New York. It would stop at Black Mountain around four in the afternoon. By ten the next morning I would be in New York. Going home, I could leave New York at four in the afternoon and get to Black Mountain by ten or eleven the following morning. I got to know the conductors on the train, and I enjoyed those trips very much.

One night, on the train from Washington to New York, I was just drifting off to sleep when a knock came on the compartment door. I was too tired to answer it. It was, I thought, probably someone seeking an autograph or a photograph. In daytime I would have happily obliged, but this was the middle of the night.

The knocker persisted. I finally unlocked the compartment door and opened it a crack. There, greeting me, was one of the most familiar faces in America—not just to Roman Catholics but to everyone else. It was Bishop Sheen. We had never met, although I had watched his television program *Life Is Worth Living* from time to time and greatly admired his gifts as a preacher and communicator. So did many other Protestants. (Perhaps as many Protestants viewed his prime-time television program as did Catholics.)

"Billy, I know it's late," he said, "but may I come in for a chat and a prayer?"

I was in my pajamas, but I was delighted to see him and invited him in. We talked about our ministries and our common commit-

692

ment to evangelism, and I told him how grateful I was for his ministry and his focus on Christ.

As far as either of us knew, he was the first person ever to conduct a religious service on television. It had taken place on Long Island in 1940; at that time, there were only forty television sets within range.

That first broadcast was a Mass, with him as celebrant—but it was not the serene service he had anticipated. He had barely begun when he noticed that the candles were melting under the ferocious heat of the stage lights. The technicians kept tripping over the cables, and the audio began to screech. The whole disastrous affair, he said with a twinkle, was hardly an auspicious introduction of television as a medium through which to preach the Gospel!

We talked further and we prayed; and by the time he left, I felt as if I had known him all my life. Our paths crossed a number of times after that, and we became good friends. The last time we met was in January 1979, at the National Prayer Breakfast. By now Sheen was an archbishop, retired, enduring the severe problems of a failing heart. He had accepted the invitation against the advice of his cardiologist, who reluctantly agreed to accompany him. The organizers of the event had quietly asked me beforehand to be prepared to fill in at the last minute in case he could not carry on. Even as he made his halting way to the podium, I silently prayed that God would grant him the necessary physical and spiritual strength.

"Mr. President," he began, turning toward President and Mrs. Carter, "you are a sinner."

Instantly, he had everyone's undivided attention. Then, pointing to himself, he said, "I am a sinner."

"We are *all* sinners," he said as he looked around the huge ballroom at the sophisticated and influential audience, "and we all need to turn to God. . . ."

He then went on to preach one of the most challenging and eloquent sermons I have ever heard.

The following December he succumbed to the heart disease that had plagued him for years. I determined to go to New York to pay my respects at the funeral. I planned just to slip into St. Patrick's

Cathedral and sit at the back. Instead, I was escorted to the front of the church to sit near the casket with the prelates who had known him and worked with him.

I recall also one summer in Switzerland when I met Karl Barth, the great theologian, with his son Markus; they were also on vacation. He suggested we climb a mountain. I climbed with him for a while—as far as my shortness of breath allowed—and mentioned that I would be holding an outdoor meeting in Basel.

"Don't be disappointed if few people come," he said, trying to be kind.

I told him that people would indeed come, and that at the end I would give the Invitation.

He warned that nobody would respond.

When I did hold the meeting in Basel, Karl Barth showed up, in spite of the pouring rain. I recognized him huddled under an umbrella. As many as 15,000 others also showed up. I preached on the passage in the third chapter of John, "Ye must be born again." Hundreds streamed forward at the Invitation.

"I agreed largely with your sermon," he said afterward, "but I did not like that word *must*. I wish you could change that."

"It's a scriptural word, isn't it?"

He had to agree that it was. He felt, though, that one should not give an Invitation; one should just declare that God had already acted.

I heard him out and then said I would stick to Scripture.

In spite of our theological differences, we remained good friends.

When I was in Zurich with Emil Brunner, whose stature as a theologian was next to Barth's, he was warm, friendly, and supportive. He disagreed with Barth's views on this.

"Pay no attention to him," he said. "Always put that word *must* in. A man *must* be born again."

And he was in favor of the Invitation.

Another cleric I have not mentioned so far in these pages is Dr. Michael Ramsey, a giant of a man, a onetime Archbishop of Canterbury, and a delightful person. We were friends for many years. In 1961 we were sitting together on the steps of the Assembly Building in New Delhi, where we both were attending the World Council of Churches—he as a delegate, I as an observer.

"Now Billy G"—he always called me Billy G or Billy Baptist— "you know I don't agree with your methods. And I don't always agree with your theology. And in fact, Billy G, you've strengthened the evangelicals too much. That's the thing I'm afraid of."

"Yes," I replied, "I'm sure that may be one of the side effects, and I rather hope it is. But Dr. Ramsey, could we—you and I—be good personal friends? Do we have to part company because we disagree in methods and theology? Isn't that the purpose of the ecumenical movement, to bring together people of opposing views?"

A strong supporter of the ecumenical movement, he had to smile and agree with my logic.

One memorable occasion he and I shared was a dialogue held in Cambridge, England, in January 1981. (It was advertised everywhere as a *debate*.) It gave me the opportunity to organize in a more systematic way some thoughts I had been having on the place of evangelism in the modern church, and to focus my own thinking more intently on the Christian church's calling in the world.

Our hosts had booked us into the same hotel, and we arrived the day before the dialogue. As dinnertime approached, I called him on the house phone and asked if he would like to dine with me. We ordered from the menu, and as the dinner progressed, he revealed more and more of the points he planned to make against me. I have seldom been better prepared for a dialogue or a debate!

The following day, in Great St. Mary's, the university church— which was packed to overflowing—I fully acknowledged the importance of the Church's social witness, but at the same time I stressed the biblical priority and centrality of evangelism, a priority I felt was becoming lost in some ecclesiastical circles.

"God created His Church to extend to His kingdom . . . ," I stated. "The proclamation of the Gospel lies at the very heart of our mission to the world. That is why we must recover the biblical meaning of evangelism in its deepest sense and fullest scope. . . . Without proclamation, God's purpose will not come to pass, for without it, humanity will never come to Christ, and to acknowledge him as Lord."

Then I added my conviction: "Evangelism is not a calling reserved exclusively for the clergy. I believe one of the greatest priorities of the Church today is to mobilize the laity to do the work of evangelism."

Knowing a great number of people has its poignant side also, as I hear of the death of someone whose friendship I have valued and realize I will not see that person again. Sometimes their passing is tragic, and I feel it very sharply. I think, for example, of the death of Martin Luther King, Jr., in 1968. I was in Australia for a series of Crusades, and one day I was just finishing a round of golf when several journalists ran up.

"Dr. Martin Luther King has been shot," they said. "We would like your comments." I was confused at first because I did not know if it was the father (who had the same name) or the son, and they did not know either. Then I realized it must be Martin Jr., and I was almost in a state of shock. Not only was I losing a friend through a vicious and senseless killing, but America was losing a social leader and a prophet, and I felt his death would be one of the greatest tragedies in our history. There on the golf course I had all the journalists and the others gathered around, and we bowed in prayer for Dr. King's family, for the United States, and for the healing of the racial divisions of our world. I immediately looked into canceling my schedule and returning for the funeral, but it was impossible because of the great distance.

Yes, it has been a privilege to know some of the great men and women of the latter part of this century—people spanning the religious spectrum from Christianity to Buddhism to Judaism to Islam to atheism. Let me stress again, however, that most of my time has been spent with people who will never be in the public eye and yet who are just as important to God (and to us) as a queen or a president.

True greatness is not measured by the headlines a person commands or the wealth he or she accumulates. The inner character of a person—the undergirding moral and spiritual values and commitments—is the true measure of lasting greatness.

Some years ago now, Ruth and I had a vivid illustration of this on an island in the Caribbean. One of the wealthiest men in the world asked us to come to his lavish home for lunch. He was seventy-five years old, and throughout the entire meal he seemed close to tears.

"I am the most miserable man in the world," he said. "Out there is my yacht. I can go anywhere I want to. I have my private plane, my helicopters. I have everything I want to make me happy. And yet I'm miserable as hell."

We talked with him and had prayer with him, trying to point him to Christ, who alone gives lasting meaning to life.

Then we went down the hill to the small cottage where we were staying. That afternoon the pastor of the local Baptist church came to call. He was an Englishman, and he too was seventy-five. A widower, he spent most of his free time taking care of his two invalid sisters. He reminded me of a cricket—always jumping up and down, full of enthusiasm and love for Christ and for others.

"I don't have two pounds to my name," he said with a smile, "but I'm the happiest man on this island."

"Who do you think is the richer man?" I asked Ruth after he left.

We both knew the answer.

39

At Home

One day, Ruth noticed that little Bunny—I think she can only have been about three or four at the time—had more coins in her little red pocketbook than her weekly allowance allowed. She commented on this to Beatrice Long, who had begun helping her. Beatrice suggested that she watch the front yard the next time a car or bus stopped. Ruth did and was appalled to see Bunny walk up to the gate with her little red pocketbook over her arm. All she did was smile at the people. But with that smile and the little red pocketbook, the inevitable happened: the tourists slipped her some coins. Ruth quickly put a stop to that!

Bunny's harmless little exploit amused us, of course, but it also pointed out an increasingly troublesome issue for us: how to raise a family in the glare of constant public scrutiny.

In the early years of our marriage it was not a problem, of course. Two years after Ruth and I left Illinois to live in North Carolina (while I was traveling with Youth for Christ), we managed to buy a little house on the Presbyterian conference grounds of Montreat, two miles from the town of Black Mountain. Montreat was a small, close-knit community, mostly summer houses with a sprinkling of year-round residents, including a number of retired ministers and missionaries—a perfect place for us. The price of the house was $4,500, and it was located right across the street from Ruth's parents' home. It was really a summer house with a large lot and a stream; Ruth remodeled it, and it became our dream home.

It also was the home where most of our children spent their early childhood. As I have mentioned earlier, Gigi was born in 1945 while I was away. Having missed Gigi's birth, I was determined to be home during the births of our other children, and I will always be grateful that it was possible. Anne was born in 1948, and Ruth (always known to us as "Bunny") in December 1950. Every family should have a Gigi, Ruth often said—a child who is as heartstrong as she is headstrong. Gigi loved to manage things, especially her two younger sisters as they arrived. Gigi, actually timid inside, would think up mischief and then assign gentle Anne to carry it out. Bunny was the quiet one, whimsical, always well-behaved, the perfect third child. She had a wistful little face and a delightful sense of humor. When the boys were born—Franklin in 1952 and Ned in 1958—our family was complete. I was even in the delivery room for Ned's birth, an unforgettable experience. Each little personality gave Ruth and me a different joy, and a different challenge.

But as our ministry expanded and became well known, we began to experience serious problems with keeping our privacy. Several denominational conference centers were located in our area, and from time to time the attendees (and other tourists) would seek out our home. Occasionally, buses would even stop on the roadway, and curious people would pour into our yard. When this happened, we had to close the curtains hurriedly (or even crawl across the floor) to avoid prying eyes. Often they called out our names, asking us to come out and pose for photographs, and so on. Some pressed their faces against the windows to see inside. A few even took chips of wood from the rail fence or picked up pebbles as souvenirs. People meant no harm, I am sure, but it was disruptive, to say the least, and made a normal family life difficult.

It became evident that our family needed more privacy, especially with my being gone so much. Mike Wiley, business manager of the Montreat Conference Center, knew of a sizable piece of property up the mountain that had a couple of old cabins on it. Two families lived there, but Mike felt they would be willing to sell. He had a jeep, which was just about the only way up that rough road. On the ridge lay the giant remains of old chestnut trees that had perished because of the chestnut blight years before. The rest of the woods had been culled for salable timber and had been logged off. Now most of the mountain was covered with pine, oak, and poplar.

"You should have a place where you can get away," Mike said on the way up.

"I'd like to, Mike, but I don't know what in the world we'd do with it. Besides, we don't have that kind of money."

The property itself covered about one hundred and fifty acres. The cost was around $13.50 an acre, which sounded exorbitant to us.

We went back down the hill to pick up Ruth. As soon as she saw Little Piney Cove, as she named it, the wheels began to spin in her mind about what she could do with such a beautiful place.

As I was leaving for Los Angeles, I told Ruth I would leave the decision about the mountain property up to her. While I was away, she arranged with Mr. Hickey down at the Black Mountain Northwestern Bank, which already held the mortgage on our present house, to borrow the money.

As soon as the deal was closed, Ruth got to work on house plans, determined to create a homey Appalachian log-and-frame residence. She scoured the surrounding area to find deserted cabins whose logs and planks might be salvaged. (No one wanted old log cabins then.) Ruth also acquired some quality lumber for a very reasonable price from a Victorian mansion that was being demolished.

Exactly where to put the house became a subject of much debate; there were only a few possible spots. The one we finally selected had a magnificent view. There was a spring that never went dry, we were told, so we fed it into two reservoirs, which resulted in our having plenty of water.

"Before you build that house," recommended a friend, E. O. Spencer, a hotelier in Jackson, Mississippi, "I suggest you get an architect to at least look it over."

We thought that was a good idea, since much of the property was steep and the ground might not be stable.

"I have a man who works with me on my hotel-building projects," said E.O. "He has a lot of experience with land that shifts."

We agreed, and he sent his man, Joe Ware, an outstanding architect from Mississippi, to Montreat.

Ruth wanted to build on a level area below the ridge line; in fact, the builders had already cut into the hogback and made a ledge where they thought we could build.

"You can't do that," Joe told us in no uncertain terms, "unless you put pilings down to the bedrock."

We agreed, and after the pilings were sunk into the ground, a concrete slab was poured. Nine months later, we had a log-and-frame house that fitted the Appalachian mountain scenery, with smoke curling picturesquely out of the stone chimney. Ruth loved it and filled it with antiques she picked up at auctions, secondhand stores, and junk shops.

In the forty years since, the place has seen "a heap o' livin'" and has stood solid through all kinds of storms—internal as well as external. Ruth made it a safe and happy home for the children and a real refuge for me. She is satisfied just to be able to live within the embrace of those memory-mellowed walls, welcoming family and friends.

Our house on the mountain solved the problem of family privacy once and for all. Home was a refuge for me, a place I could truly relax. For that reason, we tended not to have guests when I came home from a long trip. Ruth knew that I needed rest and family time, as well as study time. But whenever I leave Montreat, privacy once again becomes a problem. I am recognized almost everywhere, and I am approached constantly. By nature I am a shy person, and I don't enjoy going out much.

But when I do go out—for example, to a restaurant—I am sometimes discovered, often (it seems) just when the meal has been served. Although hearing testimonies and meeting new people is an honor and an encouragement, it does have its drawbacks! A person comes over to shake my hand, and then another one to ask for an autograph, and then another one who wants to share a problem, and so on. Not a few times, after all the gracious conversation is done, I have found that my companions have finished their meals and mine has grown cold. This means that as a family, we can seldom enjoy a meal out together unless we request a private room. I remember being on vacation with our children once in Vero Beach, Florida. After we had been seated in the motel restaurant, a long line of people gathered to greet us, making it impossible for us to finish our meal.

We got used to the problem of dealing with intrusions, while being careful not to cut ourselves off or to keep ourselves from being open to people and their needs, even when it was inconvenient. More than once I have been on an airplane or sitting in a restaurant, returning from an exhausting trip or wanting to relax, and have had someone come up to share a personal problem or heartache with me. I always have tried to be gracious and to see it as another opportunity God was giving to help in whatever ways I could.

A more implacable problem for my family and me, however, was my constant travel. The only answer was to try to make our times together as normal as possible, and to concentrate on my family as much as possible during the times I was home. Nevertheless, as our children grew, the preaching Crusades occupied me, at times almost to the exclusion of family claims.

This is a difficult subject for me to write about, but over the years, the BGEA and the Team became my second family without my realizing it. Ruth says those of us who were off traveling missed the best part of our lives—enjoying the children as they grew. She is probably right. I was too busy preaching all over the world.

Only Ruth and the children can tell what those extended times of separation meant to them. For myself, as I look back, I now know that I came through those years much the poorer both psychologically and emotionally. I missed so much by not being home to see the children grow and develop. The children must carry scars of those separations too.

Recently, my children have told me that I have probably been too hard on myself. They remember vividly the times of fun we all had when I was at home. Gigi recalls how I used to invent games, especially one called "Spider," and how I played Rook with them, a card game learned from their grandparents, the Bells. Whenever I was home, I took them to school or met them when the schoolbus dropped them off in the afternoon, just so I could be with them as they went up the mountain toward home.

I now warn young evangelists not to make the mistakes I did. But Ruth reminds me that the situation is different today. There are many more evangelists and far more Christian programs on television and radio, so perhaps the need for constant travel is less necessary. When I started years ago, I was responding to an urgent need in the best way I knew how. And God has been faithful.

God's ideal for the home is to have both the father and the mother available to their children throughout their growing years. But sometimes separation can't be avoided. Military obligations, or employment transfers, or missionary assignments, or jury duty—even prison sentences—necessarily disrupt the ideal pattern. If the cause is as irreversible as incurable illness, divorce, or death, the pain is all the greater.

Given our own family situation, I have only respect and sympathy for the courageous and committed single parents who for a while (or for a lifetime) have to carry the burden alone. The secret of Ruth's survival was in her commitment—not only her marriage commitment before God of her love for me, but also her ministry commitment of the two of us to the Lord's purpose for our lives together. And Ruth will be the first to say that she loved her part—staying home with the children.

Our children could not possibly have missed their daddy nearly as much as I missed them and their mother when I was away. I wanted Ruth to be with me as often and as long as possible. I'm afraid I sometimes applied a lot of pressure, urging her to join me, which only added to her stress. Before she agreed to come across the Atlantic and join me for part of the All-Scotland Crusade in 1955, I wrote her impassioned, impatient reminders.

Ruth did come to Scotland, and she brought Gigi with her. She was nine years old then and could appreciate the visit to another country. The other children stayed with their grandparents.

Back at Montreat, whenever I had to leave, we gathered to say good-bye. We held hands and prayed. As I boarded the train, or later the plane, my heart would be heavy, and more than once I drove down the mountain with tears in my eyes.

Maybe it was a little easier for the girls; they experienced their mother's constancy and shared so many of her interests. And of course, Dr. and Mrs. Bell, Ruth's parents, were just across the street (and later down the hill). But the boys, with four women in the house, needed their father at home. Coming as the fourth child and my namesake, Franklin especially may have craved my companionship.

During the lengthy Madison Square Garden Crusade in 1957, Franklin was five. Back home, Ruth listened to his daily bedtime prayer before tucking him in. One night, after he thanked God for me and others of the Team in New York, he closed with, "And thank you for Mommy staying home."

It sounds angelic. But the girls' theme song around the house, day in and day out, was "Mama, get Franklin!" On Valentine's Day that year, she wrote the following item in her journal:

> Four full-blooded little Grahams. I feel this A.M. it's gotten quite beyond me. They fight, they yell, they answer back. Breakfast is dreadful. Franklin woke me at 4:15 thinking it was time to get up. . . . And when I did get up at 6:15, so did Anne and Franklin, and fought during the time I have with the Lord alone. Now they've gone off to school looking nice enough (for once) and with a good breakfast but with the scrappiest of family prayers. Only a longer blessing and their last two weeks' Bible verses yelled each above the other. Grumbling, interrupting, slurring one another, impudent to me. So now they're off, I'm in bed with my Bible thinking it through—or rather, trying to.

What I missed! And what Ruth missed by not having me to help her.

Whenever I did get home for a short stay between engagements, I would get a crash course in the agony and ecstasy of parenting. If Ruth had not been convinced that God had called her to fulfill that side of our partnership, and had not resorted constantly to God's Word for instruction and to His grace for strength, I don't see how she could have survived.

Another entry in her journal:

> Unlovingness and peevishness for any reason are inexcusable in a mother. Weary little hearts, eager for love and praise,

unsure of themselves, wanting desperately to look nice and be accepted, and receiving unending correction, nagging, tongue-lashing—how can any child flourish under it?

With this in mind, we did all we could to encourage the children and give them memories of life together as a family that would be warm and happy.

We have always been animal lovers, and we have had a succession of dogs who have been with us both as loving pets and loyal guards. A few of them have been real characters.

Years ago, when I was preaching in New England, I read a piece in a newspaper about the Great Pyrenees dogs; they are similar to St. Bernards, only white. I called the place that bred them and paid $75 for one we named Belshazzar. I had the dog shipped from Massachusetts to North Carolina, where the whole family fell in love with him. He was the biggest dog we'd had up to that point, loyal and loving, but he was a one-family dog and had little use for anyone else.

We had a Great Dane named Earl that I really liked, but he always seemed on the verge of a nervous breakdown. Maybe the fact that all five of our children had arrived by then, and that we had a couple of other dogs, contributed to Earl's problems. The veterinarian suggested we take him to a dog psychiatrist in New York City. We, his family, would be required to go with him. Apparently, only group therapy would help! We decided to let Earl work out his anxieties through exercise instead.

We also kept sheep when the children were small. Gigi and I were up the mountain one time, picking apples. When the ram set his sights on the same apples, I tried to shove him off, but he managed to knock me down. I tried to get up three times, but he knocked me down each time, and going down the embankment I must have hurt my leg. When Earl saw this, big coward though he was, he managed to drive the ram off.

I was scheduled to preach at the Polo Grounds in New York City two or three weeks later, with 80,000 expected. My orthopedist said I had a very deep fracture in my knee and must have a cast and walk with a cane.

I went to Hollywood not long after to speak at a charity dinner emceed by Frank Freeman, president of Paramount. On my way into the dinner, I ran into Jimmy Stewart and his wife, Gloria. She had just broken her leg skiing and had a cast and a crutch. So we limped in together—only to find that the dinner had been scheduled partly to get me on the live television program, Ralph Edwards's *This Is Your Life*.

The strongest and most controversial dog we ever had was Heidi, a short-haired St. Bernard from the St. Bernard Pass. We were staying in Switzerland at the time, and we picked her up when she was just a few weeks old. Once when she was on the upstairs porch, she fell off, breaking a leg. When Ruth tried to help her, she bit Ruth (as a wounded dog will). But from then on she was the most protective of all our dogs. She grew so big that when she leaned against a small Volkswagen, she put a dent in it. She also had a nasty habit: she liked to bite tires. Once she flattened three out of the four tires on a visiting telephone company truck.

My assistant Lee Fisher never could make friends with Heidi. And whenever Wanda Ann Mercer, my secretary at the time, came up to the house, Heidi went after her. Once Wanda Ann, whose voice was strong, just yelled back at her. The dog fell on the pavement in a dead faint, all four feet in the air.

In the early days, when I traveled by train frequently, Ruth and the children came down to the station in Black Mountain to welcome me home. I always got them some presents while away, and almost their first words were, "Daddy, did you bring us anything?" Ruth eventually broke them of that habit, telling them it wasn't polite. From then on, they would hold off until we got to the house and then engagingly ask, "Daddy, can we help you unpack your suitcase?"

Like most families, we had traditions we tried to keep on the holidays, and favorite games we liked to play. Once Ruth put the Thanksgiving turkey in front of me to carve, along with a stack of plates. I was preoccupied with the conversation, however, and after slicing one portion I put the knife down, resumed the conversation, and started eating from the top plate—much to the amusement of the children and everyone else at the table.

Sometimes we went fishing or played croquet in the yard or just tossed a ball around. When the children were younger, they enjoyed having me read to them or just roll around on the floor with them. I made a point of saying goodnight to each of them before they went to sleep.

During the 1957 New York Crusade, I met a wealthy Swiss-Armenian businessman and financier; he had read my book *Peace with God.* He invited our family to spend a summer as his guest in a house overlooking Lake Leman, as Lake Geneva is known in Switzerland. That sounded good to me. I was already committed to preach all over Europe the summer of 1960. With the family in Switzerland, I would be able to visit them frequently.

I left for Europe some weeks before Ruth and the children did. When the first break appeared in my schedule, T.W. and I drove from Germany to La Tour de Peilz, Switzerland. Eventually, we found the lovely house that had been loaned to us. As we drove into the yard, I saw a beautiful little child wandering out to greet us. Even after I got out of the car, it took some minutes before I realized that it was Ned. I hadn't seen him for many weeks.

It was during this visit that Gigi met this man's eldest son, Stephan. In 1963 she married Stephan Tchividjian in a picturesque old stone church, Le Temple de Montreux, above Montreux, Switzerland.

Franklin was almost six by the time Ned came along; he was named Nelson after Ruth's father and Edman after the president of Wheaton College, who was so beloved by both of us. Ruth had already used up her wedding veil in trimming the old bassinet four times, so this newcomer had to make do with a cradle.

With two boys in the household, my fathering was more urgently needed than ever. Still, sometimes I was away for months at a time. What I did when I was away apparently didn't impress the children much. One time, when the mountain house was being built, I was out in the yard shoveling some dirt from one spot to another. Franklin, watching intently, suddenly piped up and said, "Daddy, you *can* work!"

The traveling ministry was a costly investment of my time as far as my sons were concerned. Both of them, like many of their generation in the sixties and seventies, went through severe tests of their faith and standards. I tried to let all five of the children know that I loved them, no matter what they did; that I missed them when I was away; that I supported their mother's discipline of them; and that I wanted them to discover God's perfect plan for each of them.

Ruth and I were not perfect parents; and when I had to travel, Ruth sometimes felt like a single parent, with all the problems that that entailed. We tried to discipline the children fairly, but at the same time we tried not to lay down a lot of rules and regulations. When I objected to Franklin's long hair, Ruth reminded me that it wasn't a moral issue—and I kept my mouth shut on that subject thereafter. Actually, as Ruth pointed out with a twinkle in her eye, Franklin was in the tradition of the prophets and apostles.

Only once, I think, did I directly interfere with Franklin's plans. That was when Ruth called me from France, where she was visiting Gigi and her family. I was in Tokyo to address the Baptist World Alliance. Franklin was working in Nome, Alaska and, after she talked to him on the phone, Ruth begged me to call him and lay down the law. I was to tell him how strenuously we opposed his engagement; we were convinced they were too young and unsuited to each other. Ruth cut short her visit with Gigi and returned to Montreat, arriving when Franklin did. In two weeks' time their friendship was over, and we breathed more easily.

In a radio interview not many years ago, Franklin told about his rebel years of drinking, drugs, smoking, girls, and fast driving. These were things he said his mother and I knew nothing about—or so he thought. And he said he never forgot a conversation I had with him in Lausanne, Switzerland, in 1974. I assured him of our love, no matter what he did, where he went, or how he ended up. He knew that he could always phone us, collect, from anywhere in the world, and that whenever he wanted to come home, the door would always be open. He also knew we would never stop praying for him. It was actually during a trip to the Middle East, while in Jerusalem, that he made his firm decision to follow Christ.

Through it all, God did not let us lose hope. Ruth wrote beautifully about these struggles in one of her poems, titled "Sons."

When she wrote these words in 1978, she was thinking about the sons of our Team members and the families of other Christian workers whose fathers were forced to be away from home for extended periods of time.

> But
> what of the ones
> forsaken,
> Lord,
> even for You?
> These sons
> now grown
> who've never known
> fathers who
> had undertaken
> to leave all
> and follow You?
> Some sons,
> wounded beyond repair,
> bitter, confused, lost,
> these are the ones
> for whom
> mothers weep,
> bringing to You
> in prayer
> nights they cannot sleep—
> these, Lord,
> are what it cost.

Ned, as the youngest, may have gotten special privileges from us, along with special pestering from his older brother, whom he adored, and from his "mothering" sisters. He didn't seem as defensive as Franklin, though, and was more happy and outgoing. As with all of our children, Ned eventually went away to boarding school, but his school experience in England was not a happy one; we brought him back after only one year. His teen years too were troubled, with complications—including drugs—in high school and college. His many enthusiasms included photography, swimming, tennis, and skiing, but studying didn't make the list.

PKs, as "preacher's kids" are called, often have difficult, if not disastrous, periods in their lives. Maybe people expect too much of them because of their parentage. Or maybe they themselves expect too much, making unreasonably high demands on themselves in order to live up to others' expectations. And our kids were given a double burden: they were PKs with a well-known father. The girls would marry and change their last name, but the boys would be stuck with "Graham." While the PK issue was only a part of what we went through during the tumultuous years with the boys, it certainly played a role. I have known a lot of PKs who grew up resentful and rebellious, and not a few who brought disgrace on those who loved them most. In all fairness, though, it's worth noting that a lot more of them have distinguished themselves in adulthood and found their way into Who's Who listings instead of onto Wanted posters.

Certainly one of the great influences on our children was their grandparents. This was especially true of Dr. and Mrs. Bell. They lived nearby, and the children all felt a deep sense of loss when Dr. Bell died of a heart attack in his sleep in August 1973. Slightly over a year later, Mrs. Bell also slipped into the presence of the Lord.

My own parents were only a few hours away in Charlotte, and I was also thankful for their example of love and godliness. My father was the first to die, in August 1962, and that death made a deep impression on all of them—especially Ned, who was only four.

My mother continued to live in their home after his death, keeping active in her church and with her family. I visited her every time I could. When her health declined, we were fortunate enough to find a wonderful woman, Rose Adams, who lived with her and looked after her faithfully night and day. Rose said that every morning my mother would ask her to read Scripture and have a prayer with her. My sisters, Catherine and Jean, also spent much time with her.

Mother had asked the Lord that when it was time for her to die, she might not suffer needlessly. As the end approached, she slipped in and out of a coma. When I visited her for what turned out to be the last time, along with Melvin, we had a good talk with her, and she hugged and kissed us both. On August 14, 1981, she quietly left this earth in her sleep and entered Heaven. When word came, I wept and yet rejoiced at the same time. Of all the people I have ever known, she had the greatest influence on me. I am sure one reason that the Lord has directed and safeguarded me, as well as Ruth and the children, through the years was the prayers of my mother and father.

Ruth and I found out that for us, worrying and praying were not mutually exclusive. We trusted the Lord to bring the children through somehow in His own way in due time. On a day-to-day basis, however, we muddled through. But God was faithful. Today each one of them is filled with faith and fervor for the Lord's service.

Gigi, married to psychologist Dr. Stephan Tchividjian, has seven children, nine grandchildren, and counting. She has published several excellent books and enjoys life in their Florida community and church.

Anne, married to a Raleigh, North Carolina, dentist—Dr. Danny Lotz—is the mother of three. An excellent Bible teacher and author, she travels throughout the world speaking to church groups and conferences. She also helps us in our training programs for evangelism. She recently became a member of the BGEA board, bringing her vision and energy to that position.

Bunny (Ruth), now happily married to Richard McIntyre, suffered through the heartbreaking difficulties of divorce several years ago. She has three children and has written an excellent Bible storybook for children. Formerly an acquisitions editor for a major U.S. publisher, she is an effective speaker and teacher. She also works for Franklin's organization, Samaritan's Purse.

As for the boys, two memorable occasions symbolize for me the fulfillment of our prayers and the Lord's persistent pursuit of them.

One was January 10, 1982, in a church in Tempe, Arizona. After preaching the sermon, I joined several other ministers in laying my hands on the head of William Franklin Graham III to ordain him for the Gospel ministry. History was repeating itself some forty years after godly men had done the same for me in a Florida country church.

In the strange ways of providence, God led Franklin into a worldwide ministry to those who suffer from diseases and disasters, through his leadership of two relief organizations, Samaritan's Purse and World Medical Mission. The former was founded by Bob Pierce, who also founded World Vision. Franklin first became familiar with the work of Samaritan's Purse when Bob asked him to accompany him on some foreign trips. On Franklin's first big mission, with many harrowing adventures, he was involved in helping boat people who had escaped Vietnam.

He might have been inconsiderate of our feelings when he was struggling to find himself in the early years, but his sensitivity toward the needs of others now is his consuming passion. He is driven not only by humanitarian generosity and a real yearning to see people come to know Christ, but also by a trained and disciplined business sense for getting maximum benefits for people out of limited resources. A graduate of Montreat College, he has a degree in business administration from Appalachian State University. We rejoiced when God led him to his wife, Jane Austin. She reminds me of Ruth in her ability to juggle her responsibilities as a mother of four and wise counselor to her busy husband.

Franklin has explained to inquirers that the Lord called his daddy to the stadiums of the world and called him to the ditches. In recent years, he has been giving increasing leadership with the BGEA board, especially as chairman of its committee for developing our evangelism training center at The Cove in Asheville. In partnership with our associate evangelist Dr. John Wesley White, and more and more on his own, Franklin has preached evangelistic Crusades that have been greatly blessed of God. As I mentioned earlier, he was elected first vice chair of the BGEA board in 1995.

History repeated itself again several years later when Ned completed his seminary training and joined the pastoral staff of a Baptist church in Auburn, Washington. As in my case some fifty years before, Ned needed to satisfy the denominational requirement of baptism by immersion, since he came from a different church background, having grown up in the Montreat Presbyterian Church. He invited me out to do that. I prayed that as he came up out of the baptismal waters, he would feel the way I had back at

Silver Lake in Florida: that the power of God had come upon him in a fresh way.

Ruth wasn't able to make that trip with me, but she—ever the Presbyterian—did give me a letter for Ned. Under her signature, she scrawled the letters *PTL*. In many circles, that stands for "Praise the Lord." In this case, she explained, it meant "Presbyterians That Last." She admits that any stubborn streak in our children was inherited from her.

Ned met his future wife while he was at the Mayo Clinic, recovering from surgery after a bad fall. Carol was a nurse there, and clearly God led them together. A woman of great wisdom, she's a perfect helpmate for Ned. The younger of their two sons reminds me of Ned's grandfather, Nelson Bell.

In the mystery of divine leading, Ned later became president of East Gates Ministries International, whose ministry includes a strategic program to publish and distribute Bibles to house-church Christians in the People's Republic of China, his mother's birth place. Ned has also become a knowledgeable observer of China's culture and history. As I noted earlier, Ned's organization has been able to distribute almost two million copies of the Scriptures in China. What it will mean to have God's Word available throughout that enormous Communist country, only future historians will be able to record.

The five children, and the Christian spouses whom they married and whom Ruth and I have loved as if they were our own, have given us nineteen grandchildren. And the number of great-grandchildren keeps multiplying! When one family group or another arrives for their annual visit with us, we welcome them with open arms. By the time they leave, those same arms have grown weary from all the tugging and hugging, and our good-bye waves are weak—but enthusiastic! They understand.

One day one of our daughters, who was discovering how the little ripples of disagreement with her husband could swell into crashing waves of confrontation, said to Ruth, "Mother, I can't remember ever hearing you and Daddy argue."

Ruth probably chuckled inside as some of our "discussions" flashed across her memory. But her reply revealed a principle we had followed: "We made it a point never to argue in front of you children."

We thought that concealing our disagreements would spare them unnecessary pain and insecurity. Now I'm not so sure our approach was entirely correct. The girls have said that never seeing us argue left them wide open for surprise and disillusionment when the inevitable conflicts flared between them and their husbands. When the harmony of their households was disrupted, they assumed that their marriages weren't normal. Well, if the television soap operas and sitcoms set the current standard for marital bliss, I much prefer the route Ruth and I chose, in spite of its possible shortcomings.

Ruth and I don't have a perfect marriage, but we have a great one. How can I say two things that seem so contradictory? In a perfect marriage, everything is always the finest and best imaginable; like a Greek statue, the proportions are exact and the finish is unblemished. Who knows any human beings like that? For a married couple to expect perfection in each other is unrealistic. We learned that even before we were married.

Being human, not one of us will ever have a relationship with another person that doesn't have a wrinkle or a wart on it somewhere. The unblemished ideal exists only in "happily ever after" fairytales. I think that there is some merit to a description I once read of a married couple as "happily incompatible." Ruth likes to say, "If two people agree on everything, one of them is unnecessary." The sooner we accept that as a fact of life, the better we will be able to adjust to each other and enjoy togetherness. "Happily incompatible" is a good adjustment.

In many Crusades over the years, I have devoted at least one message to the subject of the family. In my Depression-era growing-up years, I suppose we Grahams on our North Carolina dairy farm bore some resemblance to the fictional Walton family on television. It's easy to feel nostalgic about simpler times, but they obviously were not *easier* times. Nor were they necessarily *happier* times.

What we did have back then was family solidarity. We really cared about each other, and we liked to do things together. Jesus' word picture of a hen gathering her brood under her wing fits my

mother. She saw to it that we gathered frequently and regularly—
and not just around the dinner table or in front of the radio for favorite broadcasts. She gathered us around herself and my father to
listen to Bible stories, to join in family prayers, and to share a sense
of the presence of God.

For many years, a Roman Catholic group sponsored an excellent radio dramatic series that had as its slogan, "The family that
prays together, stays together." Nothing can bring people closer to
each other than communal prayer. Even if worship in the home is
reluctantly endured by the children as simply a religious routine, it
builds a pattern that they themselves will often follow when they
have families of their own. There is no reason why family devotions
should be either dry or long. One verse wisely chosen will be remembered better than a whole chapter. Make it interesting, says
Ruth, and make it brief. That time together is a gathering, a family
reunion with Christ at the center. I believe such gatherings can help
strengthen families into the most durable bond of our society and
our civilization.

Except in emergencies, we never let a day go by but we had
Bible reading and prayer. As the children got older, we asked them
to participate. When I was home, I went up to tuck them in and to
pray with them. Sometimes Ruth would stay up till one or two o'-
clock if one of them wanted to talk. Some of the greatest conversations I've had with any of my children have been late at night.

At other times, I remember taking a child out into the woods
for some time alone. We would sit on a log or a rock and just talk.
Many Sundays when I was home, I would take Franklin up to a
special spot on top of the mountain, where we would spend time
together.

Today we have our prayer in the evening with whoever is in the
home. We also read a short passage of Scripture. Ruth wisely says
late at night is not the time for long readings.

None of our children live in Montreat now. Some live only a
couple of hours away, some thousands of miles away, but all seem to
enjoy coming back to the home place when they can. When Ruth
and I pray together each night for our daughters and sons and their

spouses, for our grandchildren, and for our great-grandchildren, our focus on God puts us right next to them anywhere in the world, praying for each other and for us.

Ruth and I thought that when the children were grown, we would be at the end of our parental responsibilities. We could just sit back and enjoy the grandchildren and great-grandchildren. But we've discovered that their concerns and burdens are also ours. Like their parents before them, they look to the older generation for advice, counsel, and help. The same principles and promises we applied to our children are still true for our grandchildren and great-grandchildren. We pray for each one each day and spend hours each week on the telephone with them.

Watching our children's children (and their children) growing up reawakens in Ruth and me both delightful memories of our own early years and concerns about how we raised the little ones God gave to us. Without question, the regrets are greatly outnumbered by the delights. The mistakes we did make were not fatal, and we both thank the Lord for that. And that bolsters our faith that He will do the same for the generations coming after us.

40

The Best Is Yet to Be

"I must be very honest with you," the neurosurgeon said. "Ruth's condition is life-threatening, and she might not survive. We need to do everything possible to save her."

Dr. Ralph Loomis sketched out the main problems: rampant infection, soaring fever, electrolytic imbalance, physical debilitation. Most of all, the almost-certain diagnosis of bacterial spinal meningitis, a dangerous infection of the membrane surrounding the spine— an infection that could easily invade the membrane around the brain, causing disability or death. A generation or two ago, the diagnosis of spinal meningitis was a virtual death sentence; now, with new and powerful antibiotics, there was at least some hope.

We were sitting in a small conference room in Asheville's Memorial Mission Hospital, an institution where Ruth's father had been a physician and leader on the staff. Two of our five children were born there; our oldest daughter, Gigi, commented that evening that her oldest son, Stephan-Nelson, had entered the world there exactly thirty-two years ago to the day. Not long before, the hospital had kindly designated its new state-of-the-art children's unit as the Ruth and Billy Graham Children's Health Center.

717

Was this also to be the place where Ruth would end her earthly pilgrimage?

"We'll do all we can," Dr. Loomis concluded, "but ultimately she is in the good Lord's hands."

Normally, Ruth was a person who dismissed questions about her health with a cheerful "I'm fine." But for years she had been battling chronic back pain, caused by a gradual but progressive degeneration of the spine. In recent months, the pain got worse. The medication was gradually increased in response, destroying her appetite and sending her weight plummeting below a hundred pounds.

In recent weeks she admitted that her pain was growing in intensity. Finally, in desperation, she submitted to an operation. An orthopedic surgeon who had been recommended by a friend implanted an anesthetic device capable of injecting small amounts of painkiller directly into her spinal area. Then infection set in. She was in agony and barely able to speak when we took her in to Memorial Mission. The only hope, Dr. Loomis stated, was emergency surgery to remove the source of the infection and counterattack the spinal meningitis.

As they wheeled her down the hall toward the operating room, I asked the attendants if we could pause and have a few moments together. I picked up a New Testament and turned to 1 Peter: "Blessed be the God and Father of our Lord Jesus Christ, which according to his abundant mercy hath begotten us again unto a lively hope by the resurrection of Jesus Christ from the dead, To an inheritance incorruptible, and undefiled, and that fadeth not away, reserved in heaven for you, Who are kept by the power of God through faith unto salvation ready to be revealed in the last time" (1 Peter 1:3–5, KJV).

Those words reminded us of the hope we have in Christ, assuring us that whether Ruth survived the operation or not, God would always keep her in His loving care. Then we held hands and had a brief prayer before the doors closed behind her.

As Gigi and a few of my friends waited with me in the hospital conference room, my mind turned back to all the experiences Ruth and I had shared together during our fifty-two years of marriage. How dependent I had become on her counsel and support and prayers! Our little group prayed together, humbly asking that God would guide the surgeon's hands and that His will would be done.

It seemed like an eternity before the doctor returned from the operating room.

"She's in critical but stable condition," he said, "and the next twenty-four to forty-eight hours will be crucial. It's encouraging she has made it this far."

"But she is so fragile," I said.

"Yes, Dr. Graham, I know how fragile she is. I personally carried her to the operating table. I held her in my arms, and I know she is fragile."

Shortly afterward, I slipped into the intensive-care unit to see her, grateful that she had come through the surgery and overjoyed at her weak but brave smile. Ruth remembers nothing that happened during the worst of those days.

Her sister Virginia Somerville (a registered nurse) and our daughter Gigi took turns sitting with her. The CAT scan the next day showed no sign that the meningitis was spreading to her brain. That was cause for great rejoicing. As news spread of her condition, people all over the country were praying, and we sensed their prayers upholding us both. Former President Bush called to express his concern shortly before leaving for a trip to the Middle East; Ruth's longtime friend June Carter Cash flew in to sit at the hospital and pray for several hours and was able to spend a few minutes with Ruth.

The day after the operation, Ruth's condition was still critical, but it had stabilized. To me, the most encouraging sign was that her sense of humor had returned. When she heard I was coming to visit her, she whispered to Gigi, "Please get my hairbrush and lipstick."

A day or two later, she asked for ice cream.

After a week, she was transferred out of the intensive-care unit and into a private room. Although her progress would be slow in the following weeks, we both knew that God had brought her through the crisis. One of the happiest days of my life was when she was finally released from the hospital a month later and came back to our home, which had seemed so empty without her.

This medical crisis, however, caused us both to pause and remember God's grace and mercy, not just in this crisis but during our whole lives. One reason God allows times of difficulty and suffering to come into our lives is so that we will not take Him for granted but will remember in a deeper way His faithfulness to us and our dependence on Him. Repeatedly during those hospital days, Ruth and I recalled the words of King David: "Bless the Lord, O my soul: and all that is within me, bless his holy name. Bless the Lord, O my soul, and forget not all his benefits" (Psalm 103:1–2, KJV).

Ruth's illness also reminded us forcefully that life is short and that every minute is a gift from God.

"What is the greatest surprise you have found about life?" a university student asked me several years ago.

"The brevity of it," I replied without hesitation.

As I have been working on this book, many of the things I have recounted seem as if they happened only yesterday. Time moves so quickly, and no matter who we are or what we have done, the time will come when our lives will be over. As Jesus said, "As long as it is day, we must do the work of him who sent me. Night is coming, when no one can work" (John 9:4).

In a similar vein, old age is a surprise to me.

"I've been taught as a Christian how to die," my longtime friend Allan Emery said to me recently, "but I'm discovering I haven't been taught how to deal with old age—with the time before we die."

Most of us, when we are young, think that we are never going to get old. I certainly admit feeling that way from time to time. In the 1950s, I recall telling reporters that I doubted if I would live too many more years; the pace I was keeping was sure to kill me, I said. As I approached my sixties, I felt the same way. I knew I was similar to my father physically as well as emotionally, and he had experienced the first of a series of strokes in his sixties.

And yet as I write this, God in His grace has granted me seventy-eight years of life, and I know my time on earth will not be over until He calls me home. I admit I don't like the burdens of old age—the slow decline in energy, the physical annoyances, the pain of losing loved ones, the sadness of seeing friends decline. But old age can be a special time of life, and God has lessons to teach us through it.

Certainly, one lesson is to remind us of our responsibility to be diligent in our service for God right now. I may not be able to do everything I once did (nor does God expect me to), but I am called to be faithful to what I can do.

Another lesson surely is to make us realize in a fuller way that this world is not our final home. If our hope truly is in Christ, we are pilgrims in this world, en route to our eternal home in Heaven. Old age should make us look forward with joyous anticipation to eternity. The Apostle Paul put it this way: "For our light and momentary troubles are achieving for us an eternal glory that far outweighs them all. So we fix our eyes not on what is seen, but on what is unseen. For what is seen is temporary, but what is unseen is eternal" (2 Corinthians 4:17–18).

A few years ago, the passing of time came home to me in a special way. For some years, I had sensed that something was wrong with me. I would tell Ruth about it in vague terms, but I was never able to put my finger on it. For example, one day in New York, T.W. and I were walking toward an intersection. As I approached the curb, my brain said *Stop!* but my legs kept going; I had to reach out and grab a light pole to keep from stumbling into the heavy traffic. I noticed also that my hands trembled at times and that my handwriting—admittedly, never very good—seemed to be getting worse.

Over the years, I've had a number of illnesses and surgeries, only a few of which I have recounted in these pages. Often they came just as we were about to embark on a Crusade or other project, and I could not help but wonder whether Satan was using them to attack our work in some way (and I suspect that was true). At the same time, though, God used them to teach me patience and to give me time that I might otherwise not have taken to read and contemplate.

Through those infirmities, God has also taught me to appreciate the great gift of modern medicine and doctors. Two in particular have been faithful friends and helpers. The first is Dr. Roger James in Asheville, who has acted as my personal physician, referring me to other local specialists when necessary and acting as liaison with my Mayo Clinic doctors; Roger is also a faithful member of the BGEA board. The other is Dr. E. Rolland Dickson at the Mayo Clinic. He and his wife, Rhea, have gone far beyond the call of duty, being good friends to Ruth and me as well as watching over my health. I have no doubt that their careful attention to my physical condition has given me added years of ministry.

At the conclusion of a visit to the Mayo Clinic several years ago, I got up to leave Dr. Dickson's office. Immediately, Rollie asked me to sit back down and get up again. "Something looks not quite right about the way you're getting up out of that chair," he said.

He made an appointment with one of the clinic's neurological specialists. After a battery of tests, the neurologist diagnosed a probable case of Parkinson's disease. No one in my family had ever had it, as far as I was aware, and I knew little about it.

The neurologist told me that Parkinson's, a progressive and incurable disease, slowly destroys the brain cells that deal with muscle control. At the same time, he outlined the new drugs that had been developed to slow its progress and control its symptoms. Thankfully, mine has been a type of Parkinson's that progresses slowly. The medications have undoubtedly given me additional years of ministry that I never could have expected a few decades ago.

At the same time, I know this will continue to cause me increasing difficulty. Someone asked me recently if I didn't think God was unfair, allowing me to have Parkinson's and other medical problems when I have tried to serve Him faithfully. I replied that I did not see it that way at all. Suffering is part of the human condition, and it comes to us all. The key is how we react to it, either turning away from God in anger and bitterness or growing closer to Him in trust and confidence.

Ironically, just at the time I find my own strength waning, God has provided new ways to extend our ministry through technology. As I have said elsewhere in these pages, until this century the extent of an evangelist's outreach was determined by the limits of his voice and the distribution of his writings. Now modern technologies have leapfrogged these barriers. Within the last few years, it has literally become possible to proclaim the Gospel to the entire world.

I am sure we would be staggered if we could see what will be possible a hundred, fifty, even ten years from now. If Jesus were here today, I have no doubt He would make use of every means possible to declare His message.

I have often said that the first thing I am going to do when I get to Heaven is to ask, "Why me, Lord? Why did You choose a farmboy from North Carolina to preach to so many people, to have such a wonderful team of associates, and to have a part in what You were doing in the latter half of the twentieth century?"

I have thought about that question a great deal, but I know also that only God knows the answer. "Now we see but a poor reflection; then we shall see face to face. Now I know in part; then I shall know fully, even as I am fully known" (1 Corinthians 13:12).

Every day a host of men and women serve Christ far more faithfully than I have done, often in hidden and difficult places, and I cannot help wondering why God entrusted such a highly visible ministry to us and not to them.

One of the joys of Heaven, I am convinced, will be discovering the hidden ways that God in His sovereignty acted in our lives on earth to protect us and guide us so as to bring glory to His name, in spite of our frailty.

As I look back over the years, however, I know that my deepest feeling is one of overwhelming gratitude. I cannot take credit for whatever God has chosen to accomplish through us and our ministry; only God deserves the glory, and we can never thank Him enough for the great things He has done.

Although I have much to be grateful for as I look back over my life, I also have many regrets. I have failed many times, and I would do many things differently.

For one thing, I would speak less and study more, and I would spend more time with my family. When I look back over the schedule I kept thirty or forty years ago, I am staggered by all the things we did and the engagements we kept. Sometimes we flitted from one part of the country to another, even from one continent to another, in the course of only a few days. Were all those engagements necessary? Was I as discerning as I might have been about which ones to take and which to turn down? I doubt it. Every day I was absent from my family is gone forever. Although much of that travel was necessary, some of it was not.

I would also spend more time in spiritual nurture, seeking to grow closer to God so I could become more like Christ. I would spend more time in prayer, not just for myself but for others. I would spend more time studying the Bible and meditating on its truth, not only for sermon preparation but to apply its message to my life. It is far too easy for someone in my position to read the Bible only with an eye on a future sermon, overlooking the message God has for me through its pages. And I would give more attention to fellowship with other Christians, who could teach me and encourage me (and even rebuke me when necessary).

If I had it to do over again, I would also avoid any semblance of involvement in partisan politics. On the whole, as I've already said, my primary concern in my contacts with political leaders has been as a pastor and spiritual counselor, not as a political adviser. When a president of the United States, for example, wept in my presence, or knelt with me to pray, or privately unburdened his concerns about his family, I was not thinking about his political philosophy or his personality but about his need for God's help.

And yet there have been times when I undoubtedly stepped over the line between politics and my calling as an evangelist. An evangelist is called to do one thing, and one thing only: to proclaim the Gospel. Becoming involved in strictly political issues or partisan politics inevitably dilutes the evangelist's impact and compromises his message. It is a lesson I wish I had learned earlier.

About one thing I have absolutely no regrets, however, and that is my commitment many years ago to accept God's calling to serve Him as an evangelist of the Gospel of Christ.

We live in a world of confusion. Competing and often contradictory intellectual and religious voices clamor for our attention and allegiance. In the midst of so many crosscurrents, how can we assert that *anything* is true? Is it not arrogance or narrow-mindedness to claim that there is only one way of salvation or that the way we follow is the right way?

I think not. After all, do we fault a pilot for being narrow-minded when he follows the instrument panel in landing in a rain-storm or at a fogbound airport? No, we *want* him to remain narrowly focused! And do we consider it arrogant or narrow-minded when a doctor points us to the one medicine that will cure us of a particular disease? The human race is infected with a spiritual disease—the disease of sin—and God has given us the remedy. Dare we do anything less than urge people to apply that remedy to their lives?

Since I first committed my life to Jesus Christ some sixty years ago, I have crossed paths with people who hold virtually every kind of religious and philosophical view imaginable. Often I am moved by the intensity of their spiritual searching and by the depth of their commitment. At the same time, as the years have gone by, I myself have become even more convinced of the uniqueness and truth of the Gospel of Christ.

Is that merely stubbornness on my part, or self-deception? No, it comes first of all from a deeper and growing understanding of who Jesus Christ was—and is. The Bible says that Jesus Christ was God in human flesh, that two thousand years ago God deliberately came down and took upon Himself human form in the person of Jesus Christ. Jesus was not just another great religious teacher, nor was He only another in a long line of individuals seeking after spiritual truth. He was, instead, truth itself. He was God incarnate. He alone could say, "I am the way and the truth and the life" (John 14:6).

The proof of that claim is that Christ broke the bonds of death through His resurrection from the dead, an event that was witnessed by hundreds. That sets Him apart from all other persons who have ever lived.

When I seek to point people to Christ, it is because I am convinced that He alone is God's answer to life's deepest problems. I have seen Him bring change in the lives of countless individuals who have turned to Him in true repentance and faith. One of the New Testament's most compelling images of spiritual conversion is found in the phrase *born again* or *new birth*. As I mentioned earlier, Jesus used it in His interview with the religious leader Nicodemus: "I tell you the truth, unless a man is born again, he cannot see the kingdom of God" (John 3:3). We each need what Jesus was teaching: a spiritual rebirth or renewal from within, by the power of God.

How is that possible?

Nicodemus asked the same question. Jesus replied that from one standpoint it is a mystery, for a spiritual rebirth is something only God can do. On the other hand, it takes place as we turn in faith to Christ and submit ourselves to Him. God Himself takes up residence in our lives through His Holy Spirit. He begins to change us from within and gives us a whole new reason for living. Whether it is a marriage that is restored, or an alcoholic who is released from his or her addiction, or a teenager who finds new direction and meaning, it all happens because God is at work.

As I noted earlier, on May 2, 1996, the United States Congress graciously presented Ruth and me with the Congressional Gold Medal.

In my remarks that day, I spoke of the coming third millennium of the Christian era and the moral and spiritual challenges it would present. No doubt we will continue to see staggering technological achievements in the twenty-first century, just as we have in the twentieth. And yet no century, despite our progress in technology, has been as bloody and as tragic as the twentieth has been. Why? Because our basic problems come from the human heart. And that's one reason the task of evangelism will always be essential.

No one knows the future, of course; only God knows the future, for it is in His hands.

What new opportunities await us in the new millennium, if God grants us more time before Christ comes again?

What new tyrannies will attempt to capture our world, and what new ideologies will deceive humans to take the wrong path in life?

Only God knows.

Certainly, some trends we see today may make evangelism more difficult. American Christians will face new challenges from living in a society that is increasingly pluralistic, not just religiously but in its lifestyles and its views about morality. Rampant, aggressive secularism may force Christians onto the defensive, or even reduce them to a despised minority. It has happened before. And the loss of our children to drugs or sensualism or the moral relativism propagated by mass entertainment does not bode well for our future.

Developments in technology mean that the various societies now influence each other in ways we never could have envisioned a few generations ago. The world is changing, and with it the methods of evangelism will change also. But the message will *not* change, for it is timeless, meant for every generation.

What is that message?

More than anything else, I yearn for people—including the readers of these pages—to understand the message of Christ and accept it as their own.

I recall an old Methodist preacher who came to Harringay Arena in London in 1954. "I have come here every night for ninety-three nights," he told us, "and I have heard only one message." He meant it as a compliment, for he knew as I did that there *is* only one Christian message.

The message is, first of all, a message about God. God created us in His image. He created us and loves us so that we may live in harmony and fellowship with Him. We are not here by chance. God put us here for a purpose, and our lives are never fulfilled and complete until His purpose becomes the foundation and center of our lives.

The message is also about the human race, and about each one of us. The Bible says that we have been separated and alienated from God because we have willfully turned our backs on Him and are determined to run our lives without Him. This is what the Bible means by *sin*—choosing our way instead of God's way, and not giving Him His rightful place in our lives. The evidence of this is all around us, in the moral chaos and heartache of our world. The headlines scream every day that we live in a broken, sin-ravaged world.

But in addition, the message declares that God still loves us. He yearns to forgive us and bring us back to Himself. He wants to fill our lives with meaning and purpose right now. Then He wants us to spend all eternity with Him in Heaven, free forever from the pain and sorrow and death of this world.

Moreover, God has done everything possible to reconcile us to Himself. He did this in a way that staggers our imagination. In God's plan, by His death on the Cross, Jesus Christ paid the penalty for our sins, taking the judgment of God that we deserve upon Himself when He died on the Cross. Now, by His resurrection from the dead, Christ has broken the bonds of death and opened the way to eternal life for us.

The resurrection also confirms for all time that Jesus was in fact who He said He was: the unique Son of God, sent from Heaven to save us from our sins. Now God freely offers us the gift of forgiveness and eternal life.

Finally, this message is about our response. Like any other gift, God's gift of salvation does not become ours until we accept it and make it our own. God has done everything possible to provide salvation. But we must reach out in faith and accept it.

How do we do this?

First, by confessing to God that we are sinners and in need of His forgiveness; then by repenting of our sins and, with God's help, turning from them.

Second, by committing our lives to Jesus Christ as Lord and Savior. The best-known verse in the New Testament states the Gospel concisely: "For God so loved the world that he gave his one and only Son, that whoever believes in him shall not perish but have eternal life. For God did not send his Son into the world to condemn the world, but to save the world through him" (John 3:16–17). God in His grace invites us to receive His Son into our lives today.

If you have never done so, I invite you to bow your head right now and by a simple prayer of faith open your heart to Jesus Christ. God receives us just as we are. No matter who we are or what we have done, we are saved only because of what Christ has done for us. I will not go to Heaven because I have preached to great crowds. I will go to Heaven for one reason: Jesus Christ died for me, and I am trusting Him alone for my salvation. Christ died for you also, and He freely offers you the gift of eternal life as you commit your life to Him.

When you do, you become a child of God, adopted into His family forever. He also comes to live within you and will begin to change you from within. No one who truly gives his or her life to Christ will ever be the same, for the promise of His Word is true: "Therefore, if anyone is in Christ, he is a new creation; the old has gone, the new has come! All this is from God, who reconciled us to himself through Christ and gave us the ministry of reconciliation" (2 Corinthians 5:17–18).

We have seen this happen countless times all over the world, and it can happen in your life as well. Open your life to Christ today.

The year World War II ended, I became a full-time evangelist. In the uncertainty of those times, many people were ready for a message that pointed them to stability and lasting values. In the providence of God, we were able to take advantage of the spiritual hunger and search for values that marked those years. Yet times changed, with everything from the sexual revolution to the disillusionment of the seventies sweeping our world, leading to new challenges and new opportunities for evangelism.

The same will be true in the future. Yet one thing will *not* change: God's love for humanity and His desire to see men and women yield their lives to Him and come to know Him in a personal way. The human spirit is never satisfied in a lasting way by anything less than God. We were made for Him, and anything less than Him leaves the vacuum of the human heart unfilled. The growing secularism and moral chaos of our age may actually make many people more open to the Gospel. As St. Augustine prayed to God many centuries ago, "You have made us for Yourself, and our heart is restless until it finds rest in You." It will be an exciting time to be alive.

No, I don't know the future, but I do know this: the best is yet to be! Heaven awaits us, and that will be far, far more glorious than anything we can ever imagine. As the Bible says, "Dear friends, now we are children of God, and what we will be has not yet been made known. But we know that when he appears, we shall be like him, for we shall see him as he is" (1 John 3:2). This is the hope of every believer. It is *my* hope, and I pray that it is your hope as well.

I know that soon my life will be over. I thank God for it, and for all He has given me in this life.

But I look forward to Heaven.

I look forward to the reunion with friends and loved ones who have gone on before.

I look forward to Heaven's freedom from sorrow and pain.

I also look forward to serving God in ways we can't begin to imagine, for the Bible makes it clear that Heaven is not a place of idleness.

And most of all, I look forward to seeing Christ and bowing before Him in praise and gratitude for all He has done for us, and for using me on this earth by His grace—just as I am.

Acknowledgments

Over three and a half centuries ago, John Donne penned the familiar words "No man is an island, entire of itself." Among other things, he was reminding us of our need for each other, and that we are dependent on others for anything we truly accomplish in life.

Certainly, that has been true of this book. As I stated in the Preface, I doubted that I would ever write an autobiography because I knew I did not have the ability or time to do it on my own. I knew I would need the help of others, and God has more than supplied that help through the gifted men and women who have assisted me with this project.

Back in the 1960s I had dictated a number of autobiographical notes and then set them aside, assuming I would never be able to complete an autobiography. Ten or eleven years ago I wrote to John Pollock, the noted British Anglican clergyman and author (who was considered a leading biographer in Britain of religious figures), and asked for his help and advice on starting my autobiography. He had written several biographies about me and was of great assistance in the early stages of planning for the book, and his memory-joggers and time-lines about our ministry were important in getting us started. It was soon clear that the task was greater and more complex than we had anticipated, however, and could not be finished as quickly as I had hoped.

As Ruth and I talked about the actual writing of the project, one of the first people who came to mind was Dr. Mel Lorentzen, professor of journalism at Wheaton College. I was delighted when he agreed to collaborate with us on the project. An able and experienced writer, Mel had the right blend of scholarship and personal understanding to tackle this task. I'll always remember the many delightful weeks we spent together while he interviewed Ruth and me and many of my associates. A serious heart attack limited the time he was able to give to the task, but without his diligence in helping me produce a first draft, this project might never have been possible.

Several years ago, I invited Jerry Jenkins, a well-known Christian author and writer for *Moody Monthly,* to work with us. He brought to the project his own fine gifts as a writer. He devoted considerable time to researching additional aspects of our ministry, checking the accuracy of details, and editing much of the first draft. He spent many hours asking me questions, and I recall with pleasure the times we were able to spend together (although it was a busy period in my ministry).

Over the years, Ruth has kept diaries, and she always wrote long letters home to her parents when she was traveling with me. These letters are a gold mine of stories and descriptions. In addition, I had kept diaries (more, actually, than I realized) on a number of our special trips and written letters and reports back to Ruth, with no thought that I would ever be using them in a book. There also were a number of films and other records documenting our ministry. All of these have refreshed my memory of events and people that had dimmed with the years. Team members and longtime friends have also contributed stories and helped refresh my memory. In shaping those stories into a narrative, I've consulted with other writers and solicited their help from time to time.

By the time the book began to take shape, I had clippings and writings all over my house and office, so I asked two of my associates who lived in Montreat to take charge of the project. I needed someone who could hold all the pieces together and keep the various people working, and I knew there was no one better qualified to do that than my personal secretary of many years, Stephanie Wills. Her meticulous attention to detail and her ability to keep track of countless sources have been invaluable. How she has kept up with this project in addition to all of her other responsibilities I do not know. But I am indeed grateful.

On the editorial side, I asked my friend and colleague Dr. John Akers if he would be responsible for helping me to fill in many of the gaps and to rewrite certain sections. I was delighted when he said yes.

During this time, two of my daughters, both with experience in writing and publishing, urged me to consult a friend of theirs in New Orleans, Bill Griffin, for the additional help we would need. Bill is a publishing professional with thirty-five years of experience as an editor with several major New York publishers and as religion editor of *Publishers Weekly* for a dozen years; he also has written a biography of C. S. Lewis. I was surprised when he indicated that he had been following our ministry for many years and would be more than delighted to help in editing what my staff and I were doing. He and John Akers became the project's editorial coordinators. They worked together as a team to bring the enormous amount of written material down to manageable size and to fill in the gaps that had not been covered.

Perhaps one of their greatest accomplishments was doing what I found it almost impossible to do: cut the manuscript down. Because my mind and heart kept overflowing with more memories of people and events, my tendency was to keep adding material rather than to take a red pencil to what we already had done. Several people (including Ruth) were even of the opinion that we needed at least three volumes—and that's certainly where we were headed— but I was afraid that if we did that we wouldn't finish the project in this lifetime!

Unfortunately, we had no choice but to leave out a number of people and events that were extremely important during our more than half-century of ministry. I apologize especially to those staff who have worked with us with such dedication in our various offices and ministries, and to all those who have been our close friends and supporters, whom we simply could not mention by name in these pages. I think especially of our directors and other staff who have labored tirelessly in setting up our Crusades, only a few of whom are mentioned here. The countless people who assisted in each city we visited—including the executive committees, the finance committees, the volunteer helpers, and so forth—likewise deserve a special word of appreciation. I hope they all will understand and will accept my deepest gratitude for all they have meant to me and to our work over the years.

Many others have helped in significant ways as well. Most of our archives are kept in the Billy Graham Center at Wheaton College, so a great deal of the material that we needed for this book was already available there. Bob Shuster and Paul Erickson have been a tremendous help to us in searching our archives and verifying or correcting facts.

Diane Holmquist and Nina Engen in our Minneapolis office, and Wanda Kiser and Elsie Brookshire in Montreat, not only have done an invaluable job in collecting and saving background material about our ministry, but have spent many long hours in researching our files to help us complete this manuscript.

I want to thank the staff in my personal office in Montreat, including Dr. David Bruce and Maury Scobee, for the many hours they have labored to help me on this book and for enduring the many changes I have made in my schedule and plans. That is one of my weaknesses, I know (and occasionally, perhaps, one of my strengths)!

I am indebted to Dr. John Corts, president and chief operating officer of our organization, for taking the responsibility as liaison with Clayton Carlson and others at HarperCollins; and to Russ Busby, who took most of the photographs you see in this book. Terri Leonard and her staff at Harper San Francisco have also gone far beyond the call of duty to ensure the accuracy of the final text.

I am especially grateful to all those unsung helpers who have labored behind the scenes for many years—those who have followed the ministry faithfully with daily prayers and frequent financial support. This effort to document our work is as much their ministry as it is ours.

Most of all, without my wife, Ruth, there would have been no autobiography to write, for she has been vital to my life and an integral part of our ministry.

I have read that Johann Sebastian Bach ended each composition with these words: *Soli Deo Gloria*—"To God alone be the glory." Those are my words as well, at the end of this project.

Billy Graham Crusades: 1947–1974

1947
Grand Rapids, Michigan
Charlotte, North Carolina

1948
Augusta, Georgia
Modesto, California

1949
Miami, Florida
Baltimore, Maryland
Altoona, Pennsylvania
Los Angeles, California

1950
Boston, Massachusetts
Columbia, South Carolina
Tour—New England States
Portland, Oregon
Minneapolis, Minnesota
Atlanta, Georgia

1951
Tour—Southern States
Fort Worth, Texas
Shreveport, Louisiana
Memphis, Tennessee
Seattle, Washington
Hollywood, California
Greensboro, North Carolina
Raleigh, North Carolina

1952
Washington, D.C.
Tour—American Cities
Houston, Texas
Jackson, Mississippi
Tour—American Cities
Pittsburgh, Pennsylvania
Albuquerque, New Mexico

1953
Tour—Florida Cities
Chattanooga, Tennessee
St. Louis, Missouri
Dallas, Texas
Tour—West Texas
Syracuse, New York
Detroit, Michigan
Asheville, North Carolina

1954
London, England
Europe Tour
Amsterdam
Berlin
Copenhagen
Düsseldorf
Frankfurt
Helsinki
Paris
Stockholm
Nashville, Tennessee
New Orleans, Louisiana
Tour—West Coast

1955
Glasgow, Scotland
Tour—Scotland Cities
London, England
Paris, France
Zurich, Switzerland
Geneva, Switzerland
Mannheim, West Germany
Stuttgart, West Germany
Nürnberg, West Germany
Dortmund, West Germany
Frankfurt, West Germany
U.S. Service Bases
Rotterdam, The Netherlands
Oslo, Norway
Gothenburg, Sweden
Aarhus, Denmark
Toronto, Ontario, Canada

1956
Tour—India and the Far East
Richmond, Virginia
Oklahoma City, Oklahoma
Louisville, Kentucky

1957
New York City, New York

1958
Caribbean Tour
San Francisco, California
Sacramento, California

Fresno, California
Santa Barbara, California
Los Angeles, California
San Diego, California
San Antonio, Texas
Charlotte, North Carolina

1959
Melbourne, Australia
Auckland, New Zealand
Sydney, Australia
Perth, Australia
Brisbane, Australia
Adelaide, Australia
Wellington, New Zealand
Christchurch, New Zealand
Canberra, Launceston, and
Hobart, Australia
Little Rock, Arkansas
Wheaton, Illinois
Indianapolis, Indiana

1960
Monrovia, Liberia
Accra, Ghana
Kumasi, Ghana
Lagos, Nigeria
Ibadan, Nigeria
Kaduna, Nigeria
Enugu, Nigeria
Jos, Nigeria
Bulawayo, South Rhodesia
Salisbury, Rhodesia
Kitwe, North Rhodesia
Moshi, Tanganyika
Kisumu, Kenya
Usumbura, Ruanda-Urundi
Nairobi, Kenya
Addis Ababa, Ethiopia
Cairo, Egypt
Tour—Middle East
Washington, D.C.
Rio de Janeiro, Brazil
Bern, Switzerland
Zurich, Switzerland
Basel, Switzerland
Lausanne, Switzerland
Essen, West Germany

Hamburg, West Germany
Berlin, West Germany
New York City (Spanish)

1961
Jacksonville, Florida
Orlando, Florida
Clearwater, Florida
St. Petersburg, Florida
Tampa, Florida
Bradenton-Sarasota, Florida
Tallahassee, Florida
Gainesville, Florida
Miami, Florida
Cape Canaveral, Florida
West Palm Beach, Florida
Vero Beach, Florida
Peace River Park, Florida
(Sunrise Service)
Boca Raton, Florida
Fort Lauderdale, Florida
Manchester, England
Glasgow, Scotland
Belfast, Ireland
Minneapolis, Minnesota
Philadelphia, Pennsylvania

1962
Tour—South America
Chicago, Illinois
Fresno, California
Redstone Arsenal, Alabama
Tour—South America
El Paso, Texas

1963
Paris, France
Lyon, France
Toulouse, France
Mulhouse, France
Nürnberg, West Germany
Stuttgart, West Germany
Los Angeles, California

1964
Birmingham, Alabama
Phoenix, Arizona
San Diego, California

Columbus, Ohio
Omaha, Nebraska
Boston, Massachusetts
Manchester, New Hampshire
Portland, Maine
Bangor, Maine
Providence, Rhode Island
Louisville, Kentucky

1965
Hawaiian Islands
Honolulu, Oahu
Kahului, Maui
Hilo, Hawaii
Lihue, Kauai
Dothan, Alabama
Tuscaloosa, Alabama
University of Alabama
Auburn, Alabama
Auburn University
Tuskegee Institute, Alabama
Montgomery, Alabama
Copenhagen, Denmark
Vancouver, British Columbia, Canada
Seattle, Washington
Denver, Colorado
Houston, Texas

1966
Greenville, South Carolina
London, England
Berlin, West Germany

1967
Ponce, Puerto Rico
San Juan, Puerto Rico
Winnipeg, Manitoba, Canada
Great Britain
Turin, Italy
Zagreb, Yugoslavia
Toronto, Ontario, Canada
Kansas City, Missouri
Tokyo, Japan

1968
Brisbane, Australia
Sydney, Australia

Portland, Oregon
San Antonio, Texas
Pittsburgh, Pennsylvania

1969
Auckland, New Zealand
Dunedin, New Zealand
Melbourne, Australia
New York City, New York
Anaheim, California

1970
Dortmund, West Germany
Knoxville, Tennessee
New York City, New York
Baton Rouge, Louisiana

1971
Lexington, Kentucky
Chicago, Illinois
Oakland, California
Dallas-Fort Worth, Texas

1972
Charlotte, North Carolina
Birmingham, Alabama
Cleveland, Ohio
Kohima, Nagaland, India

1973
Durban, South Africa
Johannesburg, South Africa
Seoul, Korea (South)
Atlanta, Georgia
Minneapolis St. Paul, Minnesota
Raleigh, North Carolina
St. Louis, Missouri

1974
Phoenix, Arizona
Los Angeles, California (25th Anniversary Celebration)
Rio de Janeiro, Brazil
Norfolk-Hampton, Virginia

Billy Graham Crusades: 1975–1996

1975
Albuquerque, New Mexico
Jackson, Mississippi
Brussels, Belgium
Lubbock, Texas
Taipei, Taiwan
Hong Kong

1976
Seattle, Washington
Williamsburg, Virginia
San Diego, California
Detroit, Michigan
Nairobi, Kenya

1977
Gothenburg, Sweden
Asheville, North Carolina
South Bend, Indiana
Tour—Hungary
Cincinnati, Ohio
Manila, Philippines
Good News Festivals in India

1978
Las Vegas, Nevada
Memphis, Tennessee
Toronto, Ontario, Canada
Kansas City, Missouri
Oslo, Norway
Stockholm, Sweden
Tour—Poland
Singapore

1979
São Paulo, Brazil
Tampa, Florida
Sydney, Australia
Nashville, Tennessee
Milwaukee, Wisconsin
Halifax, Nova Scotia, Canada

1980
Oxford, England
Cambridge, England
Indianapolis, Indiana
Edmonton, Alberta, Canada
Wheaton, Illinois
Okinawa, Japan
Osaka, Japan
Fukuoka, Japan
Tokyo, Japan
Reno, Nevada
Las Vegas, Nevada

1981
Mexico City, Mexico
Villahermosa, Mexico
Boca Raton, Florida
Baltimore, Maryland
Calgary, Alberta, Canada
San Jose, California
Houston, Texas

1982
Blackpool, England
Providence, Rhode Island
Burlington, Vermont
Portland, Maine
Springfield, Massachusetts
Manchester, New Hampshire
Hartford, Connecticut
New Haven, Connecticut

Summary of New England University and College Lecture Tour
Boston, Massachusetts
Northeastern University
Amherst, Massachusetts
University of Massachusetts
New Haven, Connecticut
Yale University
Cambridge, Massachusetts
Harvard University
Newton, Massachusetts
Boston College
Cambridge, Massachusetts
Massachusetts Institute of Technology
South Hamilton, Massachusetts
Gordon-Conwell Seminary
Hanover, New Hampshire
Dartmouth College
Boston, Massachusetts
Boise, Idaho
Spokane, Washington
Chapel Hill, North Carolina
German Democratic Republic
Wittenberg
Dresden (Saxony)
Görlitz
Stendal
Stralsund
Berlin
Czechoslovakia
Prague
Brno
Bratislava
Nassau, Bahamas

1983
Orlando, Florida
Tacoma, Washington
Sacramento, California
Oklahoma City, Oklahoma

1984
Anchorage, Alaska

Mission England
Bristol
Sunderland
Norwich
Birmingham
Liverpool
Ipswich
Seoul, Korea (South)
Union of Soviet Socialist Republics
Leningrad, Russia

Tallinn, Estonia
Novosibirsk, Siberia
Moscow, Russia
Vancouver, British Columbia,
Canada

1985
Fort Lauderdale, Florida
Hartford, Connecticut
Sheffield, England
Anaheim, California
Romania
Suceava
Cluj-Napoca
Oradea
Arad
Timisoara
Sibiu
Bucharest
Hungary
Pecs
Budapest

1986
Washington, D.C.
Paris, France
Tallahassee, Florida

1987
Columbia, South Carolina
Cheyenne, Wyoming
Fargo, North Dakota
Billings, Montana
Sioux Falls, South Dakota
Denver, Colorado
Helsinki, Finland

1988
People's Republic of China
Beijing
Huaiyin
Nanjing
Shanghai
Guangzhou

Union of Soviet Socialist
Republics
Zagorsk, Russia
Moscow, Russia
Kiev, Ukraine
Buffalo, New York
Rochester, New York
Hamilton, Ontario, Canada

1989
Syracuse, New York
London, England
Budapest, Hungary
Little Rock, Arkansas

1990
Berlin, West Germany
Albany, New York
Long Island, New York
Hong Kong

1991
Seattle and Tacoma,
Washington
Scotland
Edinburgh
Aberdeen
Glasgow
East Rutherford, New Jersey
New York, New York
(Central Park)
Buenos Aires, Argentina

1992
Pyongyang, Korea (North)
Philadelphia, Pennsylvania
Portland, Oregon
Moscow, Russia

1993
Essen, Germany
Pittsburgh, Pennsylvania
Columbus, Ohio

1994
Tokyo, Japan
Beijing, P.R.C.
Pyongyang, Korea (North)
Cleveland, Ohio
Atlanta, Georgia

1995
San Juan, Puerto Rico
Toronto, Ontario, Canada
Sacramento, California

1996
Minneapolis-St. Paul,
Minnesota
Charlotte, North Carolina

Books by Billy Graham

Calling Youth to Christ, Zondervan, 1947

America's Hour of Decision, Van Kampen Press, 1951

I Saw Your Sons at War, Billy Graham Evangelistic Association, 1953

Peace with God, 1st edition, Doubleday, 1953; revised and expanded, Word Books, 1984

Freedom from the Seven Deadly Sins, Zondervan, 1955

The Secret of Happiness, 1st edition, Doubleday, 1955; revised and expanded, Word Books, 1985

Billy Graham Talks to Teenagers, Zondervan, 1958

My Answer, Doubleday, 1960

Billy Graham Answers Your Questions, World Wide Publications, 1960

World Aflame, Doubleday, 1965

The Challenge, Doubleday, 1969

The Jesus Generation, Zondervan, 1971

Angels: God's Secret Agents, 1st edition, Doubleday, 1975; revised and
    expanded, Word Books, 1985

How to Be Born Again, Word Books, 1977

The Holy Spirit, Word Books, 1978

Till Armageddon, Word Books, 1981

Approaching Hoofbeats, Word Books, 1983

A Biblical Standard for Evangelists, World Wide Publications, 1984

Unto the Hills, Word Books, 1986

Facing Death and the Life After, Word Books, 1987

Answers to Life's Problems, Word Books, 1988

Hope for the Troubled Heart, Word Books, 1991

Storm Warning, Word Books, 1992

Index of Names and Places

This index is a compilation of names and places that are pertinent to the stories in this book.

Photographic Credits

Grateful acknowledgment is given to the following individuals and organizations for the photographs that appear in this book.

(Note: The Billy Graham Evangelistic Association is abbreviated as BGEA in this list of credits.)

SECTION I

Associated press: On the White House lawn, 1950.

BGEA, Russ Busby: With President Kim Il Sung; Graham family, 1962.

Author's collection: As an infant with mother; with father and sister, 1925; birthplace; in the goat cart; Sunday school graduation; Graham farm milking barn; Morrow and Frank Graham; Graham family in Florida, 1936; at Florida Bible Institute; with Ruth Bell; wedding day; young pastor and wife.

Billy Graham Archives: Preaching, 1939; Youth for Christ rally; planning trip to Europe; with T.W. Wilson.

SECTION 2

Author's collection: Picnicking near Montreat.

June Glenn, Jr.: Family photo, 1958.

Billy Graham Archives: Leaving on a trip; playing baseball; preaching in Harlem; leaving Number 10 Downing Street; the Team, 1953; radio broadcast from Atlanta, Georgia.

BGEA, Russ Busby: With sons Ned and Franklin; with associate evangelists; with Dr. L. Nelson Bell; at the Canadian National Exhibition.

Houston Press: With family and dog.

Dick Whittington: Los Angeles campaign.

New York Times: Times Square gathering.

London Daily Mirror: With columnist "Cassandra."

Ray Provost: Preparing to preach to American troops in Korea.

Seth Muse: With President and Mrs. Eisenhower.

Bruce Sifford Studio: Monitoring the broadcast.

SECTION 3

BGEA, Russ Busby: Final Chicago Crusade meeting; at the Kremlin with Boris Ponomarev; meeting with Prime Minister Margaret Thatcher; speaking in Auschwitz; at Harvard University; in Andhra Pradesh, India; in Belfast, Northern Ireland; in Oakland, California; evangelistic service in Hungary; crusade in Seoul, Korea; in Tallinn, Estonia; in Timisoara, Romania; with Premier Li Peng; welcome by Japanese Christians; visiting Ruth's childhood home in China; at the Great Wall of China.

Wide World Photos: With President John F. Kennedy; with Prime Minister Indira Gandhi; with Cardinal Richard J. Cushing.

Roy Gustafson: With Prime Minister Golda Meir.

Chicago Tribune: With Dr. Martin Luther King, Jr.

U.S. Air Force: Preaching to troops in Vietnam.

Tom McMahan: Preaching to Masai tribesmen.

Earl Davidson: Gathering in Central Park.

SECTION 4

BGEA, Russ Busby: Portrait of Billy Graham; inauguration of President Richard M. Nixon; with President Ronald Reagan; golfing with President Gerald Ford; with President Jimmy Carter; with Queen Elizabeth II; interviewed by John F. Kennedy, Jr.; with Muhammad Ali; welcomed by President Boris Yeltsin; visiting President Mikhail Gorbachev; fiftieth wedding anniversary; speaking at the U.S. Capitol; relaxing at home.

The White House: With Grady Wilson and President Lyndon Johnson; with President and Mrs. Bush; with President Bill Clinton.

L'OSSERVATORE ROMANO: With Pope John Paul II.